UNIVERSITY CASEBOOK SERIES®

BUSINESS ORGANIZATIONS

CASES AND MATERIALS

CONCISE TWELFTH EDITION

JAMES D. COX
Brainerd Currie Professor of Law
Duke University Law School

MELVIN ARON EISENBERG
Jesse H. Choper Professor of Law, Emeritus
University of California at Berkeley

FOUNDATION
PRESS

University Casebook Series is a trademark registered in the U.S. Patent and Trademark Office.

© 1940, 1950, 1951, 1958, 1959, 1970, 1980, 1988, 1995, 2000 FOUNDATION PRESS
© 2005, 2011 by THOMSON REUTERS/FOUNDATION PRESS
© 2014 LEG, Inc. d/b/a West Academic
© 2019 LEG, Inc. d/b/a West Academic
   444 Cedar Street, Suite 700
   St. Paul, MN 55101
   1-877-888-1330

Printed in the United States of America

ISBN: 978-1-68328-861-9

PREFACE

The Twelfth Concise Edition of this book builds on the firm foundation of the well-received prior editions, and contains a comprehensive and current body of leading cases and note materials on all significant forms of business organization. The book allows the adopting instructor to pick and choose from a rich array of material. Moreover, because the chapters and sections are modular, there is no fixed order in which the cases and note material must be addressed. The adopter has full control over the agenda; this book merely provides the stage and props.

Several important changes have been incorporated into this edition. Our coverage of LLCs has kept pace with the significant developments surrounding LLCs. Statutory developments and the caselaw continue to grow rapidly so that material devoted to LLCs has expanded with an emphasis on legal issues arising in the management of LLCs. Of importance is the explosion of cases that involve private ordering that is contemplated by LLP and LLC statutes; with this edition we add cases and note material focused on the limits of such private ordering and do so with close attention to the content of "good faith" and "fair dealing" in the LLP and LLC context.

This edition sets forth multiple developments in Delaware whose legislature and judiciary continue to innovate, especially in the areas of litigation and acquisitions. More generally, cases have been added throughout the casebook to reflect new developments and to present interesting applications of established doctrines. We include the many significant qualifications, and even retreats, by state courts from earlier adopted broad shareholder-protective positions. Materials also include the recent Supreme Court and circuit court decisions clarifying, expanding and constricting the scope of Rule 10b–5; the chapter devoted to the antifraud provision is substantially reorganized to reflect the contours of the contemporary content of the Rule 10b–5 cause of action. Throughout the Twelfth Edition there is rich note material synthesizing articles and studies that further examine contemporary developments.

Because of the importance of statutes in corporation law, students should refer to the Statutory Supplement whenever a cross-reference to that Supplement appears. When a cross-referenced statutory provision includes an Official Comment, the Comment should be read as well. Other cross-references to the Statutory Supplement (for example, references to excerpts from the Restatement (Second) of Agency) should be treated the same way.

In the preparation of this casebook, the following conventions have been used: Where a portion of the text of an original source (such as a case) has been omitted, the omission is indicated by ellipses. The omission of footnotes from original sources is not indicated, but the original footnote numbers are used for those footnotes that are retained.

The American Law Institute's Principles of Corporate Governance: Analysis and Recommendations (1994) is cited simply as ALI, Principles of Corporate Governance.

JAMES D. COX
MELVIN A. EISENBERG

April 2019

SUMMARY OF CONTENTS

TABLE OF CONTENTS

TABLE OF CASES

The principal cases are in bold type.

UNIVERSITY CASEBOOK SERIES®

BUSINESS ORGANIZATIONS

CASES AND MATERIALS

CONCISE TWELFTH EDITION

CHAPTER 1

AGENCY; THE SOLE PROPRIETORSHIP

1. THE SOLE PROPRIETORSHIP

The subject of this casebook is corporations and other business organizations. Business organizations take a variety of forms, some simple, some enormously complex. The most rudimentary form of business organization is the sole proprietorship, which is a firm that is owned by a single individual and is not cast in a legal form that can be utilized only by filing an organic document with the state under an authorizing statute.

The terminology *business organization* may seem to be an inappropriate characterization of a firm that has only a single individual owner and is not created pursuant to statute. However, there are two justifications for this characterization.

First, a firm that is wholly owned by an individual is nevertheless likely to have a degree of psychological and social identity separate from the individual. This separateness is often expressed by giving the firm its own name, like "Acme Shoe Company." Furthermore, a sole proprietor usually will consider only a certain portion of her property and cash as invested in the firm, and will keep a separate set of financial records for the firm, as if the firm's finances were separate from her own. Thus, if Alice Adams begins a new firm—say, Acme Shoe Company—she is likely to issue a balance sheet for Acme that does not show all of her assets and liabilities, but only those assets dedicated to, and those liabilities arising out, of the firm's operations. In short, as a psychological matter Adams and those who deal with her are likely to regard Acme as an enterprise that has a certain degree of separateness from Adams herself and a certain dedicated amount of capital. As a matter of law, however, a sole proprietorship has no separate identity from its owner. All of a sole proprietor's wealth is effectively committed to the firm, because an individual who owns a sole proprietorship has unlimited personal liability for obligations incurred in the conduct of the proprietorship's business.

The second justification for considering a sole proprietorship to be an organization is that typically a sole proprietor does not conduct the proprietorship's business by herself, but instead engages various people—managers, salespersons, technicians, and so forth—to act on her behalf, and subject to her control, in conducting the business. The employment by one person, *P*, of another, *A*, to act on *P*'s behalf, implicates the law of agency, which is an element of the law concerning all forms of business organization. In short, the sole proprietorship form, simple as it is, implicates many of the basic issues in the law of business organizations—the internal structure of the organization; the location of control over the organization; the liability of owners for transactions engaged in by their agents; potential conflicts of interest between an organization and its agents; and conflicts of interest between an organization and those with whom it deals, such as creditors.

Although sole proprietorships are the most rudimentary form of business organization, and taken as a class account for substantially less income than corporations and several other forms, sole proprietorships are the most numerous type of business organization in the United States. Based on tax returns, in 2015 (the latest year for which the figures were available) there were 25.2 million sole non-farm proprietorships in the United States, with total gross receipts of $1.44 trillion. United States Internal Revenue Service, 37 Statistics of Income Bulletin Fall 2017, Sole Proprietorship Returns at 2–3.

2. AGENCY

———

RESTATEMENT THIRD §§ 2.01–2.03, 2.05, 3.01, 3.03, 3.06, 4.01–4.02, 6.01–6.03, 6.10, 8.14

[See Statutory Supplement*]

———

A. THE AUTHORITY OF AN AGENT

An *agent* is a person who by mutual assent acts on behalf of another and subject to the other's control. The person for whom the agent acts is a *principal*. Agency law governs the relationship between agents and principals; the relationship between agents and persons with whom an agent deals, or purports to deal, on a principal's behalf; and the relationship between principals and such persons. (For ease of exposition, persons with whom an agent deals, or purports to deal, on a principal's behalf will be referred to as *third persons*). Principals are conventionally divided into three categories: disclosed, partially disclosed or unidentified, and undisclosed. A principal is *disclosed* if the third person is on notice both that the agent is acting on behalf of a principal and of the principal's identity. A principal is *partially disclosed* or *unidentified* if the third person is on notice that the agent is acting on behalf of a principal, but is not on notice of the principal's identity. A principal is

---

*   References in the Casebook to the *Statutory Supplement* are to *Corporations and Other Business Organizations—Statutes, Rules, Materials, and Forms* (M. Eisenberg ed., Foundation Press; revised annually).

undisclosed if the third person has no notice that the agent is acting on behalf of a principal rather than on his own behalf.

Agency is a consensual relationship. However, whether an agency relationship has been created does not turn on whether the parties either think of themselves as, or intend to be, principal and agent. Rather, "[a]gency is the fiduciary relationship that arises when one person (a 'principal') manifests assent to another person (an 'agent') that the agent shall act on the principal's behalf and subject to the principal's control, and the agent manifests assent or otherwise consents so to act." Restatement Third § 1.01. (In this Chapter the term *Restatement Second* refers to Restatement, Second, of Agency (1957), and the term *Restatement Third* refers to Restatement, Third, of Agency (2006).) "Whether a relationship is one of agency is a legal conclusion made after an assessment of the facts of the relationship and the application of the law of agency to those facts. Although agency is a consensual relationship, how the parties to any given relationship label it is not dispositive." Restatement Third § 1.02, Comment a.

———

Speed v. Muhanna
Court of Appeals of Georgia, 2005.
274 Ga. App. 899; 619 S.E.2d 324.

■ BLACKBURN, PRESIDING JUDGE.

... [O]n February 14, 1999, Speed injured his foot at a Sports Authority store. In November 1999, Speed retained Scott Zahler to represent him in pursuing any claims he might have "against Sports Authority, and any other Defendants later named or identified as a result of" the February 14 incident. . . .

Over a year later, Speed was hospitalized at Henry Medical Center from January 9, 2002, to January 20, 2002, during which time he was treated by Muhanna for deep venous thrombosis in his right leg. . . .

In June 2002, Zahler called Muhanna, told him that he was representing Speed in the premises liability case against Sports Authority, and asked Muhanna if he could depose him as Speed's treating physician in that case. When Muhanna wanted assurance that the action in which he was to be deposed was not a medical malpractice case, Zahler assured him that the case was against Sports Authority and not a medical malpractice case. Muhanna asked Zahler to put that assurance in writing.

On August 27, 2002, Zahler sent to Muhanna a letter, confirming. . . "that the subject matter of the deposition will be the care and treatment provided by you and Henry Medical Center in connection with Mr. Speed's medical condition. This is not a medical malpractice case *and neither now or in the future will you be subject to any type of malpractice claim.*" (Emphasis supplied.)

Thereafter, Muhanna met with Zahler and gave his deposition as scheduled on September 10, 2002. During the deposition, Muhanna was questioned about his care and treatment of Speed during his January 2002 hospitalization at Henry Medical Center, as well as about any causal connections between Speed's deep venous thrombosis and his prior foot injury at Sports Authority.

On January 8, 2004, using new counsel other than Zahler, Speed filed a medical malpractice suit against Muhanna alleging professional negligence in his care and treatment of Speed . . . . Muhanna filed an answer in which he asserted as a defense, among other things, that Speed had previously released any malpractice claim he might have against Muhanna and was thus barred from recovery in the action. On December 3, 2004, the trial court granted Muhanna's motion for summary judgment as to Speed's claim of medical malpractice on the ground that Zahler's August 27, 2002 letter to Muhanna was a release of that claim. This appeal followed.

Speed argues that Zahler had no authority to release his claim against Muhanna. Speed points out that he retained Zahler to represent him in his premises liability case against Sports Authority, but never hired Zahler to pursue a medical malpractice claim against Muhanna; thus, Zahler had no authority to release the medical malpractice claim against Muhanna. We disagree.

As an initial matter, it appears that Zahler had been given actual authority to release Speed's claims against Muhanna. In this case, Muhanna was contacted by Zahler, who represented Speed in his personal injury claims arising out of the incident which resulted in his injured foot. The only action pending at the time of contact was against Sports Authority. Zahler was authorized to investigate and pursue "*any and all* claims which [Speed] may have against Sports Authority, and *any other Defendants later named or identified,* as a result of" the incident at Sports Authority, and was making inquiries regarding Muhanna's care and treatment of Speed prior to a severe deterioration in his medical condition. As Speed's attorney, Zahler had authority to obtain Muhanna's deposition testimony in exchange for payment as an expert witness or some other bargained-for exchange, such as a covenant not to sue or a release. When Muhanna expressed his reluctance to be deposed, Zahler assured Muhanna that "neither now or in the future [would he] be subject to any type of malpractice claim." At no time did Zahler communicate to Muhanna any restrictions on his authority to act on Speed's behalf. Thus, Zahler had actual authority to negotiate with Muhanna on Speed's behalf.

Furthermore, even if he had not had actual authority to negotiate with Muhanna on Speed's behalf, Zahler had apparent authority to do so. . .

Under Georgia law an attorney of record has apparent authority to enter into an agreement on behalf of his client and the agreement is enforceable against the client by other settling parties. This authority is determined by the contract between the attorney and the client and by instructions given the attorney by the client, and in the absence of express restrictions the authority may be considered plenary by the court and opposing parties. The authority may be considered plenary unless it is limited by the client and that limitation is communicated to opposing parties. Therefore, from the perspective of the opposing party, in the absence of knowledge of express restrictions on an attorney's authority, the opposing party may deal with the attorney as if with the client, and the client will be bound by the acts of his attorney within the scope of his apparent authority. The client's remedy, where there have been restrictions not communicated to the opposing party, is against the attorney who overstepped the bounds of his agency, not against the third party.

Brumbelow v. Northern Propane Gas Co. 251 Ga. 674, 675, 308 SE2d 544 (1983). . . .

In this case, Zahler was representing Speed in the premises liability case against Sports Authority. Zahler's authority from Muhanna's perspective was plenary, and Zahler had apparent authority to elicit the cooperation and alliance of other potential defendants by giving assurances that no claim would be brought against them. Speed is bound by Zahler's acts within the scope of that apparent authority. . . .

Judgment affirmed.

———

NOTES ON SOURCES OF AGENT'S AUTHORITY

Under the law of agency, a principal is liable to a third person on a contract entered into by an agent on the principal's behalf if the agent had actual, apparent, or (traditionally) inherent authority to act on the principal's behalf in the way that he did, or the principal ratified the act or transaction. Although a principal's liability for an agent's tortious and contractual transactions both reflect the concept that a principal may be responsible for acts of an agent, the two types of liability involve different requirements. Broadly speaking, a principal's liability in tort requires a determination that the principal had the right to control the manner and means of the agent's performance or work and that the agent acted within the scope of his employment. In contrast, a principal's liability in contract requires a determination that the agent acted, or purported to act, on the principal's behalf and had actual, apparent, or inherent authority to do so, or the principal ratified the agent's act.[1] The various categories of authority will now be considered.

1.   Actual Authority. An agent has *actual authority* to transact with third persons in a given manner on a principal's behalf if the principal's words or conduct would lead a reasonable person in the agent's position to believe that the principal wishes the agent to so act. If an agent has actual authority to engage in a given type of transaction with a third person, and acts within the scope of that authority, the principal is bound to the third person.

> *Example I:* P goes to an office where, as he knows, several brokers have desks, and leaves upon the desk of A, thinking it to be the desk of X, a note signed by him, which states: "I authorize you to contract in my name for the purchase of 100 shares of GE stock at the market price." A comes in, finds the note and, not knowing of P's mistake, makes a contract with T, in P's name, for the purchase of the GE shares. A had actual authority to make the contract.[2]

If an agent has actual authority to transact with a third person in a given way, and did, the principal is bound even if the third person did not know that the agent had actual authority, and indeed even if the principal was undisclosed, so that the third person thought the agent was herself the principal. Accordingly, an undisclosed principal is bound by his agent's authorized transaction even though the agent purports to act strictly on her own behalf. One reason an undisclosed principal is bound is that she set the transaction in motion and stood to gain from it. A second reason is this: Even if the undisclosed principal was not directly liable to the third person, the agent would be. Therefore, the third person could sue the agent. If he did, the agent could then sue the principal for indemnification of the damages she had to pay the third person. (See Section 6 of this Note, infra.) Accordingly, allowing the third person to sue the undisclosed principal does not materially enlarge the principal's liability and collapses the two lawsuits into one.

Actual authority is contractual, in that it arises out of an agreement between the principal and the agent. By and large, therefore, the scope of an agent's actual authority is determined by the general principles of contract interpretation. There is, however, an important distinction between interpreting a conventional contract and interpreting an agency contact. Interpretation of a conventional contract usually focuses on the language of the contract and the surrounding circumstances when the contract was made. In contrast, interpretation of an agency contract is ambulatory, that is, it focuses on the reasonability of the agent's interpretation of his authority

---

[1]   In general, consensual but noncontractual transactions by an agent (for example, a filing) are treated the same as contractual transactions for agency-law purposes, and in any event do not often raise problems. Accordingly, what is said in this Note about contractual transactions normally applies to other consensual transactions as well.

[2]   All the Examples in this Note are literal or slightly modified versions of Illustrations in Restatement Second and Restatement Third. Examples written by the editors are labeled "Example," followed by a roman numeral. Examples that are taken verbatim from the Restatement of Agency are labeled "Illustration," followed by an Arabic numeral.

at the time he acts. As stated in Restatement Second § 33, Comments a and b:

> a.   *Authority an ambulatory power.* . . . [A]n agreement creating an agency relation has elements different from those of other contracts. . . . Whatever the original agreement or authority may have been, [an agent] is authorized at any given moment to do, and to do only, what he reasonably believes the principal desires him to do, in the light of what he knows or should know of the principal's purpose and the existing circumstances. [If the agent] knows facts which should lead him to believe that his authority is restricted or terminated, he has a duty to act only within the limits of the situation as it is currently known to him.

> **Illustrations.** . . .

> 2.   P, the owner of a factory running on half time for lack of orders, before leaving for his vacation, directs his purchasing agent to "put in our usual monthly coal supply of 1000 tons." The following day a large order comes in which will immediately put the factory on full running time. It may be found that A is authorized to purchase sufficient coal to keep the factory running, this depending upon whether or not P can easily be reached, the amount of discretion usually given to A, the condition of P's bank balance, and other factors.

> b.   *Authority distinct from contract of agency.* An agent is a fiduciary under a duty to obey the will of the principal as he knows it or should know it. This will may change, either with or without a change in events. Whatever it is at any given time, if the agent has reason to know it, his duty is not to act contrary to it. . . . Thus, whether or not the agent is authorized to do a particular act at a particular time depends, not only on what the principal told the agent, but upon a great variety of other factors, including changes in the situation after the instructions were given. The interpretation of authority, therefore, differs in this respect from the interpretation of a contract, even the contract of agency.

> The agent's authority may therefore be increased, diminished, become dormant or be destroyed, not only by further manifestations by the principal but also by the happening of events, dependent, in many situations, upon what the agent knows or should know as to the principal's purposes.

Restatement Third § 2.02, Comment c, makes essentially the same point: "[Q]uestions of interpretation that determine whether an agent acted with actual authority have a temporal focus that moves through time as the agent decides how to act, while questions of contractual interpretation focus on the parties' shared meaning as of the time of a promise or agreement." This point is exemplified by Illustrations 8 and 9:

> 8.   [The directors of P Corporation approve a plan to upgrade a plant that is suitable for the manufacture of one product line. P Corporation's Executive Vice President tells M, the plant manager,

to contract with an engineering firm for a redesign of the production process that must precede the upgrade work. After adopting the resolution, the directors abandon the upgrade plan and so notify the Executive Vice President. No one tells M, but] M reads in the newspaper that P Corporation's directors have discontinued the sole product line manufactured in the plant. M no longer has actual authority to make the contract with T.

9.   Same facts as [the bracketed language of Illustration 8], except that the upgrade plan depends on using a particular building technology. M is aware of this fact. After the directors adopt the resolution and M is directed to contract for the redesign work, M learns that regulatory restrictions will prevent P Corporation from using the particular technology on which the plan depends. M no longer has actual authority to make the contract with T.

2.   Actual Authority by Implication. Actual authority may be either express or implied. "It is possible for a principal to specify minutely what the agent is to do. To the extent that he does this, the agent may be said to have express authority. But most authority is created by implication. Thus, in the authorization to 'sell my automobile', the only fully expressed power is to transfer title in exchange for money or a promise to give money. In fact, under some circumstances . . . there may . . . be power to take or give possession of the automobile or to extend credit or to accept something in partial exchange. These powers are all implied or inferred from the words used, from customs and from the relations of the parties. They are described as 'implied authority.'" Restatement Second § 7, Comment c; *see also* Restatement Third § 2.02, Comment b.

A common type of implied actual authority is *incidental authority,* which is the authority to do incidental acts that are reasonably necessary to accomplish an actually authorized transaction or that usually accompany a transaction of that type. Here are two examples:

Example II: P directs A to sell goods by auction at a time and place at which, as P and A know, a statute forbids anyone but a licensed auctioneer to conduct sales by auction. Nothing to the contrary appearing, A has implied actual authority to employ a licensed auctioneer.

Example III: P authorizes A, a local broker, to sell land on P's behalf. It is the custom to make such sales by delivering a deed with certain covenants as to title. A has implied actual authority to execute and deliver proper deeds to purchasers and to insert in the deeds the usual covenants as to title.

3.   Apparent Authority. An agent has *apparent authority* to act in a given way on a principal's behalf in relation to a third person if manifestations of the principal to the third person (or manifestations by the agent to the third person that the principal authorized the agent to make) would lead a reasonable person in the third person's position to believe that the principal had authorized the agent to so act. If an agent has apparent authority and acts within the scope of that authority, the principal is bound. Here are four examples:

Example IV: P writes to A directing him to act as his agent for the sale of Blackacre. P sends a copy of this letter to T, a prospective purchaser. A has actual authority to sell Blackacre and, as to T, apparent authority.

Example V: Same facts as in Example IV, except that in the letter to A, P adds a postscript, not included in the copy to T, telling A to make no sale until after communication with P. A has no actual authority to sell Blackacre, but as to T, A has apparent authority.

Example VI: Same facts as in Example IV, except that after A and T have received the letters, P telegraphs a revocation to A. A has no actual authority to sell Blackacre, but as to T, A has apparent authority.

Example VII: P owns a granary and employs A to manage it. A's employment agreement with P states that A's authority to purchase grain is limited to transactions that do not exceed $5,000; larger purchases require P's express approval. This limit is unusual in the granary business. P directs A to tell T, a seller of grain, that A's authority to purchase grain is unlimited, because P believes this will induce T to give orders placed by A priority over orders placed by agents with limited authority. A represents to T that his authority to purchase grain is unlimited, and enters into a contract with T, on P's behalf, to buy $10,000 worth of grain. P is bound by the contract with T. A has actual authority to make the representation to T, and A has apparent authority to enter into the contract with T, because T reasonably believes A has authority to bind P to a contract to buy $10,000 worth of grain.

In most cases, actual and apparent authority go hand in hand, as Example IV suggests. For example, if P Bank appoints A as cashier, and nothing more is said, A will reasonably believe he has the authority that cashiers normally have (actual authority), and third persons who deal with A will reasonably believe the same thing (apparent authority). Apparent authority becomes salient in such a case if P Bank does not actually give A all the authority that cashiers usually have, and a customer deals with A, knowing that A is a cashier, but not knowing that P Bank has placed unusual limits on A's authority.

The apparent authority of A in the cashier hypothetical is a special type of apparent authority known as power of position. "[A]pparent authority can be created by appointing a person to a position, such as that of manager or treasurer, which carries with it generally recognized duties; to those who know of the appointment there is apparent authority to do the things ordinarily entrusted to one occupying such a position, regardless of unknown limitations which are imposed upon the particular agent." Restatement Second § 27, Comment a.

Example VIII: P bank appoints A as an information clerk, with authority only to answer depositors' questions. During alterations, however, the bank directs A to occupy the space normally occupied by one of the tellers, and puts up a sign that says "Information Window." The sign becomes displaced, and T, a depositor in the bank, makes a cash deposit with A, believing that A is a teller. P is bound by this transaction.

4. Agency by Estoppel. Another type of authority is known as "agency by estoppel." The core of agency by estoppel is described as follows in Restatement Third § 2.05:

> A person who has not made a manifestation that an actor has authority as an agent and who is not otherwise liable as a party to a transaction purportedly done by the actor on that person's account is liable to a third party who is induced to make a detrimental change in position because the transaction is believed to be on the person's account, if
>
> > (1) the person intentionally or carelessly caused such belief, or
> >
> > (2) having notice of such a belief and that it might induce others to change their positions, the person did not take reasonable steps to notify them of the facts.

Agency by estoppel is so close to apparent authority that for most practical purposes the former concept can be subsumed in the latter.

5. Inherent Authority. Under the doctrine of inherent authority, an agent may bind a principal in certain cases even when the agent had neither actual nor apparent authority. Restatement Second § 161 concerned the inherent authority of a general agent of a disclosed or partially disclosed principal. (Restatement Second § 3 defined a general agent as an agent who is authorized to conduct a series of transactions involving continuity of service. In contrast, a special agent was defined as an agent who is authorized to conduct only a single transaction, or only a series of transactions not involving continuity of service.)[3] This section provided that such a principal is liable for an act done on his behalf by a general agent even though the principal had forbidden the agent to do the act, if (i) the act usually accompanies or is incidental to transactions that the agent is authorized to conduct, and (ii) the third person reasonably believes the agent is authorized to do the act. Restatement Second § 194 concerned the inherent authority of agents of undisclosed principals. This Section provided that "A general agent for an undisclosed principal authorized to conduct transactions subjects his principal to liability for acts done on his account, if usual or necessary in such transactions, although forbidden by the principal to do them." Restatement Second § 194 did not require that the third person

---

[3]   Restatement Third § 2.01, Comment d states:

General and special agents. Courts have long distinguished between "general agents" and "special agents," a distinction that rests on both the objects of the discretion granted an agent and the mode of regulating the agent's exercise of discretion. The labels matter less than the underlying circumstances that warrant their application. The prototypical special agent is a real-estate broker who is authorized to conduct a single transaction. A special agent may also be authorized to conduct a series of transactions specified by the principal. The prototypical general agent is a manager of a business, who has authority to conduct a series of transactions and who serves the principal on an ongoing as opposed to an episodic basis. . . .

reasonably believed the agent was authorized to act. Indeed, such a requirement could not be imposed, because in the case of an undisclosed principal the third person will not know that he is dealing with an agent.

A major rationale of inherent authority, given in Restatement Second, is based on an analogy to the doctrine of respondeat superior:

> . . . It is inevitable that in doing their work, either through negligence or excess of zeal, agents will harm third persons or will deal with them in unauthorized ways. It would be unfair for an enterprise to have the benefit of the work of its agents without making it responsible to some extent for their excesses and failures to act carefully. The answer of the common law has been the creation of special agency powers or, to phrase it otherwise, the imposition of liability upon the principal because of unauthorized or negligent acts of his servants and other agents. . . .*

* * *

> . . . [The principal's liability under the doctrine of inherent authority] is based primarily upon the theory that, if one appoints an agent to conduct a series of transactions over a period of time, it is fair that he should bear losses which are incurred when such an agent, although without authority to do so, does something which is usually done in connection with the transactions he is employed to conduct. Such agents can properly be regarded as part of the principal's organization in much the same way as a servant is normally part of the master's business enterprise. . . . The basis of [inherent authority] is comparable to the liability of a master for the torts of his servant. . . . In the case of the master, it is thought fair that one who benefits from the enterprise and has a right to control the physical activities of those who make the enterprise profitable, should pay for the physical harm resulting from the errors and derelictions of the servants while doing the kind of thing which makes the enterprise successful. The rules imposing liability upon the principal for some of the contracts and conveyances of a general agent, whether or not a servant, which he is neither authorized nor apparently authorized to make, are based upon a similar public policy. Commercial convenience requires that the principal should not escape liability where there have been deviations from the usually granted authority by persons who are such essential parts of his business enterprise. In the long run it is of advantage to business, and hence to employers as a class, that third persons should not be required to scrutinize too carefully the mandates of permanent or semi-permanent agents who do no more than what is usually done by agents in similar positions.

Restatement Second § 8A, Comment a, § 161, Comment a.

---

*   Recall that the terms "master" and "servant" have technical meanings in agency law. (Footnote by ed.)

An alternative rationale for the doctrine of inherent authority is based on the principal's reasonable expectations. In a world with perfect information, faithful agents will follow all instructions impeccably. In the real world, however, agents acting in good faith will not infrequently deviate from their instructions, because agents, like everyone else, will make mistakes, which may take the form of misinterpreting their instructions or forgetting one of numerous instructions. Furthermore, an agent may reasonably believe that his principal's objective is best served by violating a particular instruction. A principal's instructions to her agent are necessarily given in the present to govern the future. The future, however, may develop in such a way that the agent reasonably believes that if the principal knew all the facts, she would not want the agent to follow a given instruction. Usually in such cases the agent could go back to the principal for further instructions. Sometimes, however, it is infeasible to take that course of action—for example, because a valuable opportunity must be taken immediately or not at all. These real-world facts are reflected in a passage in the Comment to Restatement Second § 8A: "It is inevitable that in doing their work, either through negligence or excess of zeal, agents will harm third persons or will deal with them in unauthorized ways. It would be unfair for an enterprise to have the benefit of the work of its agents without making it responsible to some extent for their excesses and failures to act carefully."

Given these realities, the doctrine of inherent authority is justified on the ground that it is or should be foreseeable to a principal, when he appoints an agent, that as a practical matter the agent, acting in good faith for the benefit of the principal, is likely to deviate occasionally from instructions. As between the principal—who appointed the agent, benefits from the agent's activities, and could or should have foreseen a certain range of deviations from his instructions to the agent—on the one hand, and the third person who contracts with the agent, on the other, a loss that results from a foreseeable deviation by the agent is better placed on the principal.

Restatement Third does not use the term "inherent agency power," on the ground that "[o]ther doctrines stated in this Restatement encompasses the justifications underpinning [the concept of inherent agency] including the importance of interpretation by the agent in the agent's relationship with the principle. . . ." *Id.* § 2.01 Comment b. The omission of the explicit term, inherent authority, from Restatement Third is unfortunate, but in various places the text and Comment of Restatement Third adopt positions that can best or only be explained by the concept of inherent authority. For example, Restatement Third § 2.02(2) defines the scope of actual authority in an expansive manner:

> An agent's interpretation of the principal's manifestations is reasonable if it reflects any meaning by the agent to be ascribed by the principal and, in the absence of any meaning known to the agent, as a reasonable person in the agent's position would interpret the manifestations in light of the context, including circumstances of which the agent has notice. . . .

Comment b to this section makes clear that in determining an agent's actual authority, a literal interpretation of the principal's manifestations does not always govern:

> An agent's understanding of the principal's interests and objectives is an element of the agent's reasonable interpretation of the principal's conduct. If a literal interpretation of a principal's communication to the agent would authorize an act inconsistent with the principal's interests or objectives known to the agent, it is open to question whether the agent's literal interpretation is reasonable.

Correspondingly, the Comment recognizes that an agent may properly act in a way that is knowingly at variance with the principal's original instructions if the agent believes that circumstances have changed since the initial instructions, if the principal were to reconsider the matter, different instructions would have been given, and it is impracticable to communicate with the principal for further clarification before action needs to be taken. For example, Restatement Third § 2.02, Illustration 22, provides:

> [Blackacre is to be sold at an auction. P retains A to bid at the auction on P's behalf, directing A to buy Blackacre but to offer no more than $250,000.] P owns and operates a golf course on land that almost entirely surrounds Blackacre. A has notice of P's long-term business plan to enhance the aesthetic and athletic qualities of the course and thereby make it more profitable. At the auction of Blackacre, A learns for the first time that there will be one other bidder, B. A also learns that B's plan for using Blackacre is to construct a cement factory on it. A is unable to contact P to relay this information and receive further instructions. A succeeds in purchasing Blackacre for P by bidding $260,000. A acted with actual authority.

Similarly § 2.02, Illustration 5, provides:

> P Corporation employs A as the Facilities Manager at an amusement park owned by P Corporation. A reports to B, P Corporation's Vice President for Leisure Activities. B directs A to arrange for the reseeding of the badly deteriorated lawn adjacent to the park's entrance. B also directs A to complete the reseeding by the end of the week. A purchases grass seed and directs groundskeepers to schedule time for reseeding. A then learns that the park location is in the path of a forecasted hurricane. A has actual authority to postpone the reseeding.

6.   Termination of Agent's Authority. As a general rule, a principal has the *power* to terminate an agent's authority at any time, even if doing so violates a contract between the principal and the agent, and even if it had been agreed that the agent's authority was irrevocable. This rule rests largely on the ground that contracts relating to personal services will not be specifically enforced. (There is an important but limited exception to this rule, which applies to a type of relationship known as an agency (or power) coupled with an interest. This exception will be discussed in Chapter 8, infra.) However, such a contract is effective to create liability for damages for wrongful termination. Here is an example:

> *Example XI:* In consideration of A's agreement to advertise and give his best energies to the sale of Blackacre, its owner, P, grants to A "a power of attorney, irrevocable for one year" to sell it. A advertises and spends time trying to sell Blackacre. At the end of three months P informs A that he revokes. A's authority is terminated, but A has a right to damages for breach of contract.

––––––––

What result if an agent forges the principal's name on an agreement with a third party while acting within the scope of the agent's apparent authority? Dreier represented Gardi in negotiating a settlement with JANA. While JANA had agreed to settle the dispute by paying Gardi $6.3 million, the parties disagreed whether the settlement should impose only unilateral or mutual obligations on the parties not to disparage the agreement. Gardi wanted the provision to be binding on both parties while JANA wished the provision to bind only Gardi. Dreier forged Gardi's signature on the version of the settlement agreeing only to unilateral non-disparagement. He then directed the settlement fund be issued to his trust account from which he embezzled the funds. When his skullduggery was discovered, Gardi sued JANA to reopen the dispute, arguing it was not bound by the settlement due to Dreier's forgery. The court reasoned:

> Dreier served as the conduit for all the communications between his clients and JANA; there is no evidence that Gardi dealt with JANA. JANA was justified in believing that the . . .[settlement] contained Gardi's signature. As a result of Dreier's fraud, JANA paid over $6.3 million, and should not be compelled to pay a second time. As between the Gardi Parties and JANA, the injury by Dreier's fraud must be allocated to the Gardi Parties, Dreier's principals.

Gardi v. Jana Partners, LLC, 450 B.R. 452, 459 (S.D.N.Y. 2011).

––––––––

Morris Oil Co. v. Rainbow Oilfield Trucking, Inc.
New Mexico Court of Appeals, 1987.
106 N.M. 237, 741 P.2d 840.

■ GARCIA, JUDGE. . . .

Defendant Dawn appeals from the judgment rendered against it in favor of Morris Oil Company, Inc. (Morris), based upon a determination that Rainbow Oilfield Trucking, Inc. (Rainbow) was Dawn's agent when it incurred indebtedness with Morris. We affirm the trial court.

FACTS

Appellant Dawn, the holder of a certificate of public convenience and necessity, is engaged in the oilfield trucking business in the Farmington area. Rainbow was a New Mexico corporation established for the purpose of operating an oilfield trucking business in the Hobbs area. Defendant corporations entered into several contracts whereby Rainbow would be permitted to use Dawn's certificate of public convenience and necessity in operating a trucking enterprise in Hobbs. Dawn reserved the right to full and complete control over the operations of Rainbow in New Mexico. Dawn was to collect all charges due and owing for transportation conducted by Rainbow and, after deducting a $1,000 per month "clerical fee" and a percentage of the gross receipts, was to remit the balance to Rainbow. Under a subcontract entered into by defendants, Rainbow was to be responsible for payment of operating expenses, including fuel; further, the subcontract provides that all operations utilizing fuel were to be under the direct control and supervision of Dawn. All billing for services rendered by Rainbow would be made under Dawn's name, with all monies to be collected by Dawn.

Defendants also entered into a terminal management agreement which provided that Dawn was to have complete control over Rainbow's Hobbs operation. The agreement further recited that Rainbow was not to become the agent of Dawn and was not empowered to incur or create any debt or liability of Dawn "other than in the ordinary course of business relative to terminal management." The agreement recited that Rainbow was to be an independent contractor and not an employee, and that liability on the part of Rainbow for creating charges in violation of the agreement would survive the termination of the agreement. Dawn was to notify Rainbow of any claim of such charges whereby Rainbow would assume the defense, compromise or payment of such claims.

Rainbow operated the oilfield trucking enterprise under these contractual documents, during which time Rainbow established a relationship with plaintiff Morris, whereby Morris installed a bulk dispenser at the Rainbow terminal and periodically delivered diesel fuel for use in the trucking operation. The enterprise proved unprofitable, however, and Rainbow ceased its operations and ultimately declared bankruptcy, owing Morris approximately $25,000 on an open account.

When Morris began its collection efforts against Rainbow, it determined that Rainbow had ceased its operations, everyone associated with Rainbow had moved back to Texas and it did not appear likely that the account would be paid. Morris was directed by Rainbow's representative in Texas to Dawn for payment of the account.

When Rainbow ceased its operations, Dawn was holding some $73,000 in receipts from the Hobbs operation. Dawn established an escrow account through its Roswell attorneys to settle claims arising from Rainbow's Hobbs operation. When Morris contacted Dawn with regard to the outstanding account, it was notified of the existence of the escrow account and was asked to forbear upon collection efforts, indicating that payment would be forthcoming from the escrow account. Dawn's representatives indicated that it was necessary to wait for authorization from Rainbow's parent Texas corporation before paying the account. At no time did Rainbow or Dawn question the amount or legitimacy of Morris' open account balance.

Dawn's principal [owner] further testified that the subcontract and terminal management agreement were cancelled by Dawn when he learned that Rainbow was incurring debts in Dawn's name. The charges owing to Morris, however, were incurred in the name of Rainbow and not Dawn.

Although some claims were paid from the attorneys' escrow account established by Dawn, there was no explanation at trial why the Morris claim was not paid. When Morris learned that the escrow funds had been disbursed without payment of its charges, it instituted this action and also sought to garnish the remaining $13,000 held by Dawn from the impounded funds. Rainbow did not defend, and the trial court entered a default judgment against Rainbow, from which it does not appeal.

DISCUSSION

The trial court found that Dawn retained the right to direct control and supervision of Rainbow's New Mexico operations, and that in the course of those operations, Rainbow incurred a balance of almost $25,000 on an open account with Morris for fuel used in the New Mexico operations. The trial court further found that when Rainbow defaulted on payments on Morris' account, Dawn made representations over a period of time concerning the existence of a fund held by Dawn to settle indebtedness created by Rainbow operating under the subcontract. The court determined that Morris delayed its collection efforts pending disbursement of the funds, and that Dawn was aware that Morris was relying upon Dawn's representations that payment would be made from the impounded fund. The trial court concluded that Rainbow was at all times in its dealings with Morris the agent of Dawn and, therefore, Dawn was responsible for the account balance.

Dawn urges one point of error on appeal; that the trial court erred in finding liability based on a principal-agent relationship between the defendants. Dawn relies upon the language in the terminal management agreement which states:

> 4.   Rainbow is not appointed and shall not become the agent of Dawn and is not empowered to incur or create any debt or liability of Dawn other than in the ordinary course of business relative to terminal management. Rainbow shall not enter into or cause Dawn to become a party to any agreement without the express written consent of Dawn.

> 5.   Rainbow shall be considered an independent contractor and not an employee of Dawn.

Dawn's reliance upon these paragraphs of the agreement is unpersuasive for two reasons. First, the agreement specifically states that Rainbow may create liabilities of Dawn in the ordinary course of business of operating the terminal. There is no question that the liability to Morris was incurred in the ordinary course of operating the trucking business. Second, the recitation of the parties in their contractual documents need not bind third parties who deal with one of them in ignorance of those instructions. *See* South Second Livestock Auction, Inc. v. Roberts, 69 N.M. 155, 364 P.2d 859 (1961); *see also* Great Northern R.R. Co. v. O'Connor, 232 U.S. 508, 34 S.Ct. 380, 58 L.Ed. 703 (1914).

While Dawn argues from cases discussing apparent authority, we view this as a case of undisclosed agency. Rainbow contracted in its own name and not in the name of Dawn Enterprises, Inc. Thus, this case involves concepts relating to undisclosed agency rather than to apparent authority, and is governed by principles of undisclosed principal-agent contracts. *See, e.g.,* 3 Am.Jur.2d Agency § 316 (1986).

It is well established that an agent for an undisclosed principal subjects the principal to liability for acts done on his account if they are usual or necessary in such transactions. Restatement Second § 194 (1958). This is true even if the principal has previously forbidden the agent to incur such debts so long as the transaction is in the usual course of business engaged in by the agent. *Id.*

The indebtedness in the instant case is squarely governed by well-established principles of agency where an undisclosed principal entrusts the agent with the management of his business. The undisclosed principal is subject to liability to third parties with whom the agent contracts where such transactions are usual in the business conducted by the agent, even if the contract is contrary to the express directions of the principal. Restatement Second § 195 (1958).

Dawn's reliance upon Bloodgood v. Woman's Ben. Ass'n, 13 P.2d 412 (N.M. 1932) is misplaced. Indeed, the case stands for the proposition that a principal may limit an agent's authority, and further, that the limitation will be binding upon a third party dealing with the agent if the third party has knowledge of the limitation of authority. Here there is no evidence that Morris had any actual knowledge of the existence of the Rainbow-Dawn agency, let alone any claimed limitations by Dawn on Rainbow's authority. It is undisputed that Morris thought it was dealing solely with Rainbow when it sold fuel.

Morris correctly observes that secret instructions or limitations placed upon the authority of an agent must be known to the party dealing with the agent, or the principal is bound as if the limitations had not been made. Chevron Oil Co. v. Sutton, 515 P.2d 1283 (N.M. 1973). . . .

Moreover, assuming arguendo that Dawn was not responsible for the indebtedness to Morris for the reasons urged on appeal, it is clear that Dawn ratified the open account after learning of its existence when

Morris contacted Dawn regarding payment. A principal may be held liable for the unauthorized acts of his agent if the principal ratifies the transaction after acquiring knowledge of the material facts concerning the transaction. Ulibarri Landscaping Material, Inc. v. Colony Materials, Inc., 639 P.2d 75 (Ct.App.1981).

It was undisputed that in several telephone conversations between the principals of Dawn and Morris, the material facts of the Morris open account were disclosed to Dawn. At no time did Dawn dispute the legitimacy or amount of the open account, and indeed assured Morris that payment would be forthcoming from the funds retained from Rainbow's revenues. Despite this, Dawn used the fund to pay itself a $1,000 per month clerical fee, to pay legal fees incurred as a result of its agency with Rainbow and to settle other claims arising from the Rainbow operations. Where the principal retains the benefits or proceeds of its business relations with an agent with knowledge of the material facts, the principal is deemed to have ratified the methods employed by the agent in generating the proceeds. *See id. See also* 3 Am.Jur.2d Agency § 194 (1986). The diesel fuel provided by Morris was used in Rainbow's trucking operation. Dawn collected the receipts due to Rainbow. Dawn seeks to retain the benefits of the agency with Rainbow, and yet at the same time disclaims responsibility for the business of the agent by which the benefits were generated. This it cannot do. Ulibarri Landscaping Material, Inc. v. Colony Materials, Inc.

In sum, for the foregoing reasons, we affirm.

IT IS SO ORDERED. . . .

■ BIVINS and MINZNER, JJ., concur.

NOTES ON LIABILITY OF AGENTS WHO ACTED FOR DISCLOSED, PARTIALLY DISCLOSED, OR UNDISCLOSED PRINCIPAL

1.   Disclosed Principal. If the principal was disclosed (that is, at the time of the transaction the third person had notice that the agent was acting on behalf of a principal, and also had notice of the principal's identity), and is bound by the agent's act because the agent had actual, apparent, or inherent authority or because the principal ratified the act, the general rule is that the agent is not bound to the third person. *See* Restatement Third § 6.01. The theory is that in such a case the third person did not expect the agent to be bound, he did expect the principal to be bound, and he should get just what he expected.

2.   Undisclosed Principal. If a principal was undisclosed (that is, if at the time of the transaction the agent purported to act on his own behalf), the general rule is that the agent is bound even though the principal is also bound. *See* Restatement Third § 6.03. The theory is that the third person must have expected the agent to be a party to the contract, because that is how the agent presented the transaction. However, there is a quirk in the law here. Under the traditional majority rule if the third person, after learning of an undisclosed principal's identity, obtains a judgment against the principal, the agent is discharged from liability even if the judgment is not satisfied. Similarly, if the third person obtains a judgment against the agent, the undisclosed principal is discharged from liability. Under the minority but better rule, neither the agent nor the principal is discharged if the third person obtains a judgment against the other, but instead is discharged only if the judgment is satisfied only by satisfaction of the judgment. This rule is adopted in Restatement Third § 6.09.

3. *Partially Disclosed Principal.* If the principal was partially disclosed (that is, if at the time of the transaction the third person had notice that the agent was acting on behalf of a principal, but did not have notice of the principal's identity), the general rule is that both the agent and the principal are bound to the third person. *See* Restatement Third § 6.02. The theory is that if the third person did not know the identity of the principal, and therefore could not investigate the principal's credit or reliability, he probably expected that the agent would be liable, either solely or alongside the principal.

———

NOTE ON RATIFICATION

Even if an agent has neither actual, apparent, nor inherent authority, the principal will be bound to the third person if the agent purported to act on the principal's behalf and the principal, with knowledge of the material facts, either (1) affirmed the agent's conduct by manifesting an intention to treat the agent's past conduct as authorized, or (2) engaged in conduct that is justifiable only if he has such an intention.

Manifesting an intention to treat an agent's conduct as authorized is sometimes known as *express ratification.* Here is an example:

> *Example IX:* A, who has no authority to bind P, purports to represent P in buying a horse from T. Later, P affirms the transaction. By that act, P becomes a party to the transaction.

Engaging in conduct that is justifiable only if the principal intends to treat the agent's conduct as authorized is sometimes known as *implied ratification.* The most common example occurs where as a result of the purported agent's transaction, the principal, with knowledge of the facts, receives or retains something to which he would otherwise not be entitled:

> *Example X:* P owns an advertising agency and employs A to service existing clients by purchasing space for the clients in advertising media. A does not have authority to set terms with clients. A executes an agreement with T that commits P to develop a new advertising campaign for T. P learns of the agreement and then retains an advance payment made by T for the new advertising campaign. By accepting and retaining the payment, P has ratified the unauthorized agreement made by A.

Ratification need not be communicated to the third person to be effective, although it must be objectively manifested by the principal. *See* Restatement Third § 4.01, Comment d. To be effective, however, a ratification must occur before either the third person has withdrawn or there has been a material change in circumstances that would make it inequitable to bind the third party unless the third party chooses to be bound. *See* Restatement Third § 4.05.

As Restatement Second § 82, Comment c pointed out, "The concept of ratification. . . . is unique. It does not conform to the rules of contracts, since it can be accomplished without consideration to or manifestation by the purported principal and without fresh consent by the other party." Restatement Third § 4.01, Comment b, provides the following rationale for the doctrine of ratification:

> Ratification often serves the function of clarifying situations of ambiguous or uncertain authority. A principal's ratification confirms or validates the agent's right to have acted as the agent did. That is, an agent's action may have been effective to bind the principal to the third party, and the third party to the principal, because the agent acted with apparent authority. *See* § 2.03. If the principal ratifies the agent's act, it is thereafter not necessary to establish that the agent acted with apparent authority. . . .

A related but different rationale for the doctrine was stated by Judge Posner in Goldstick v. ICM Realty, 788 F.2d 456, 460 (7th Cir.1986):

> . . . The best explanation [of the concept of ratification] may be that the principal would not have ratified the contract unless he had seen a commercial advantage in doing so, and that the advantage would be less if the ratification had no binding effect. Ordinarily a principal ratifies an agent's unauthorized transaction in order to protect the principal's relationship with the other party to the transaction, usually a customer or supplier: and for ratification to have this protective effect it has to be more than an idle gesture, signifying nothing because unenforceable.

A concept that is comparable to, but different from, ratification is authority by acquiescence. "[I]f the agent performs a series of acts of a similar nature, the failure of the principal to object to them is an indication that he consents to the performance of similar acts in the future under similar conditions." Restatement Second § 43, Comment b. *See also* Restatement Third § 2.02, Comment b. Suppose, for example, an agent engages in a series of comparable purchases on the principal's behalf. Prior to the first purchase, a reasonable person in the agent's position would not have thought he had authority to enter into such a transaction. Nevertheless, the principal did not object to that purchase or to later comparable purchases when she learned of them. At that point, a reasonable person in the agent's position would assume that the principal approved the agent's engaging in such purchases. Accordingly, the principal's acquiescence gives rise to actual authority and as to third persons who know of the acquiescence, the acquiescence also gives rise to apparent authority.

———

NOTES ON THIRD PERSON'S LIABILITY

The general rule is that if an agent enters into a contract with a third person on behalf of a principal and the agent's principal is liable to the third person under the contract, then the third person is liable to the principal. *See* Restatement Third §§ 6.01–6.03. The major exception is that the third person is not liable if the principal is undisclosed and the agent or the principal knew that the third person would not have knowingly dealt with the principal. *See* Restatement Third § 6.03, Comment d. Where an agent has entered into a contract with a third person on behalf of a principal, whether the agent will be liable to the third person depends in the first instance on whether the principal is bound to the third person. If the agent had actual, apparent, or inherent authority, or the principal ratified the agent's act, so that the principal is bound to the third person, the agent's liability to the third person largely depends on whether the principal was disclosed, undisclosed, as discussed earlier.

    1.   Where the Principal Is Not Bound. If the principal is not bound by the agent's act, because the agent did not have actual, apparent, or inherent authority, and the agent's act was not ratified, the general rule is that the agent is liable to the third person. The agent's liability in such cases is usually based on the theory that an agent makes an implied warranty of authority to the third person. However, a few authorities have adopted a theory that the agent can be held liable on the contract itself. In principle, the difference between the two theories might lead to a difference in the measure of damages: Under the liability-on-the-contract theory, the third person will recover against the agent the gains that the third person would have earned under the contract—essentially, expectation damages. In contrast, under the implied-warranty theory it might seem that the third person would recover only the losses he suffered by having entered into the transaction—essentially, reliance damages. However, both Restatement Second and Restatement Third, while adopting the implied-warranty theory, provide for an expectation measure of damages, just as if the liability-on-the-contract theory had been adopted. *See* Restatement Third § 6.10.

    2.   Liability of Agent to Principal. If an agent takes an action that he has no actual authority to perform, but the principal is nevertheless bound because the agent had apparent authority, the agent is liable to the principal for any resulting damages. *See* Restatement Third § 8.09, Comment b. Whether an agent is liable to the principal on the basis of an act that binds the principal by virtue of the agent's inherent but not actual authority is unsettled.

    3.   Liability of Principal to Agent. If an agent has acted within his actual authority, the principal is under a duty to indemnify the agent for payments the agent made that were made necessary in executing the principal's affairs. These include the following: (i) Authorized payments made by the agent on the principal's behalf. (ii) Payments made by the agent to a third person under a contract on which the agent was authorized to make himself liable (for example, where the agent acted on behalf of a partially disclosed or undisclosed principal). (iii) Payments of damages to third persons that the agent incurs because of an authorized act that constituted a breach of a contract with the third person for which the agent was liable to the third person. (iv) Expenses in defending actions brought against the agent by a third person because of the agent's authorized conduct. *See* Restatement Third § 8.14.

———

B. THE AGENT'S TORTIOUS CONDUCT

A central element of the law of agency is the liability, if any, of the principal to a third person with whom the agent interacts. This kind of liability falls into two broad classes: liability for contracts made or purported to be made by the agent on the principal's behalf, examined above, and liability for an agent's torts.

The liability of a principal for a tort committed by his agent is commonly referred to as either vicarious liability, respondeat superior ("let the master answer"), or enterprise liability. These three terms have slightly different connotations, but at bottom they express the same idea, which has been well-summarized by Professor Fishman:

> The adoption of enterprise liability under respondeat superior is justified on several policy grounds. First, the ability of the enterprise to spread the risk from losses is important. The enterprise is in a better position than . . . the injured third person to spread the risk of loss, either through insurance or the ability to factor the potential losses into the price for the goods produced. A second reason suggests that proper allocation of resources is promoted by requiring an enterprise to include in the price of its goods the costs of the accidents which are closely associated with the enterprise's operations. A third reason . . . is that the [principal] is in a position to control the employee and placing the risk of loss here could lead to greater safety. A fourth reason is that it is considered more equitable to place the liability on the [principal], because it provides greater assurance that the accident victim will be paid, or because there is a societal preference to make certain losses costs of doing business rather than losses to be borne by individual households.

Fishman, Inherent Agency Power—Should Enterprise Liability Apply to Agents' Unauthorized Contracts?, 19 Rutgers L.J. 1, 48–49 (1987).

In the context of vicarious liability for an agent's torts, traditionally a principal was referred to as a master and an agent was referred to as a servant. This approach was adopted in Restatement Second § 2, which defined a master as a principal who controls, or has the right to control, the physical conduct of an agent in the performance of the agent's services, and a servant as an agent whose physical conduct in the performance of services for the principal is controlled by or subject to the control of the principal. Restatement Second § 216 provided that a master was liable for the torts of his servants committed in while acting in the scope of their employment. Restatement Second § 228 defined the term scope of employment for this purpose as follows:

(1) Conduct of a servant is within the scope of employment if, but only if:

(a) it is of the kind he is employed to perform;

(b) it occurs substantially within the authorized time and space limits;

(c) it is actuated, at least in part, by a purpose to serve the master, and

(d) if force is intentionally used by the servant against another, the use of force is not unexpectable by the master.

(2) Conduct of a servant is not within the scope of employment if it is different in kind from that authorized, far beyond the authorized time or space limits, or too little actuated by a purpose to serve the master.

Restatement Third adopts a different terminology and a different test for vicarious liability. Rather than using the terms master and servant, Restatement Third uses the terms principal and employee. Under § 7.07(3), for the purpose of determining a principal's vicarious liability in tort, an "employee" is defined as an agent whose principal "controls or has the right to control the manner and means of the agent's performance of work. . . ." Restatement Third § 7.07 also adopts a revised definition of course of employment:

(1) An employer is subject to vicarious liability for a tort committed by its employee acting within the scope of employment.

(2) An employee acts within the scope of employment when performing work assigned by the employer or engaging in a course of conduct subject to the employer's control. An employee's act is not within the scope of employment when it occurs within an independent course of conduct not intended by the employee to serve any purpose of the employer.

————

Koutsogiannis v. BB&T

Supreme Court of South Carolina, 2005.
365 S.C. 145, 616 S.E.2d 425.

■ MOORE.

In July 1996, respondent financed the purchase of a car with a loan from . . . BB&T. In May 1999, respondent made a full cash payment for the month; however, the payment was improperly entered as a partial payment. BB&T claimed respondent owed the bank $ 23.76. Based on BB&T's own error, BB&T began collection efforts against respondent. Respondent continued to make regular payments, but then ceased payments in October 1999, due to BB&T's collection efforts and its inability to give him a correct pay-off figure.

BB&T referred the collection matter to an outside attorney. In negotiations with BB&T's attorney (Attorney), respondent's attorney attempted to establish a correct pay-off figure and sought to have BB&T correct the error on his credit report. When the attorneys could not reach a final agreement, BB&T commenced an action against respondent.

Meanwhile, respondent entered into a real estate contract to purchase a parcel of land with commercial potential. . . . Respondent lost the real estate deal due to BB&T's credit reporting error. After the real estate deal was lost, negotiations essentially ceased between the two attorneys and respondent filed counterclaims of libel, conversion, breach of contract accompanied by fraudulent intent, and gross negligence against BB&T. On behalf of BB&T, Attorney moved for summary judgment. The trial court granted summary judgment on both BB&T's claims and respondent's counterclaims in an order prepared by Attorney. The Court of Appeals reversed the court's order and stated respondent was never afforded an opportunity to argue the merits of his counterclaims. . . . Thereafter, respondent paid off the car loan and a jury trial was conducted on the counterclaims.

At trial, respondent sought to recover damages from BB&T based on BB&T's misconduct in handling the loan matter and vicarious liability for Attorney's misconduct in attempting to collect the debt and preparing the draft order for summary judgment. As to Attorney, respondent asserted Attorney engaged in dilatory tactics which intentionally prolonged the unsuccessful settlement negotiations. With respect to the preparation of the summary judgment order, respondent asserted Attorney intentionally sought to deceive the trial court and injure respondent.

BB&T requested a charge on the law of independent contractor.[1] BB&T's theory was that even if Attorney's conduct could be considered wrongful, he was, nonetheless, an independent contractor for whose misconduct BB&T was not vicariously liable. The request for the charge was denied; however, the trial court gave a detailed and extensive charge

---

[1]   The requested charge is as follows:

The principal's or master's liability is derived from his or her relationship to the agent, or servant. A master is one who has the right to control the manner and method of work performed. A servant is one whose work is subject to the supervision or control of the master. By contrast, an independent contractor is a person hired for a particular purpose or project, who is compensated on a project-by-project basis, and who exercises his own discretion over the manner and method of carrying out the work.

on the law of agency to the jury. The court further charged that the "acts of an attorney are directly attributable and binding upon the client."

At trial, Attorney testified he was paid by BB&T on a case-by-case basis and that BB&T did not supervise him or instruct him as to how he should handle the case. Sonja Allen, a BB&T employee who Attorney was required to report to regarding respondent's case, testified Attorney was a private lawyer who was sent cases by BB&T on a case-by-case basis. Allen stated she did not supervise Attorney in the sense that he was instructed on what methods to use to collect the debt. Allen stated Attorney kept her informed of significant events in the case. She stated she was aware there had been a summary judgment hearing and that Attorney had submitted documents for her approval before and after the hearing. She stated she would have reviewed the proposed summary judgment order prepared by Attorney.

The jury returned a verdict in favor of respondent on the counterclaim of gross negligence and awarded respondent $ 98,000.[2] The jury found in favor of BB&T on the other counterclaims.

DISCUSSION

BB&T argues that because a client may not be vicariously liable for the conduct of its attorney, the trial court erred by failing to charge the jury on the law of independent contractor. We disagree. . . .

The proper focus here is whether Attorney was acting within the scope of his representation when he committed the alleged acts of gross negligence. In the attorney-client relationship, clients are generally bound by their attorneys' acts or omissions during the course of the legal representation that fall within the apparent scope of their attorneys' authority. *See, e.g., Shelton v. Bressant, 312 S.C. 183, 312 S.C. 208, 439 S.E.2d 833 (1993)* (client bound by attorney's actions in settlement of a case; acts of attorney are directly attributable to and binding upon client). . . . As a result, BB&T can be held liable for its agent's, Attorney's, actions taken within his scope of representation, including possible torts committed by him. *See Rickborn v. Liberty Life Ins. Co., 321 S.C. 291, 468 S.E.2d 292 (1996)* (doctrine of apparent authority provides principal bound by agent's acts when principal has placed agent in such position that persons of ordinary prudence, reasonably knowledgeable with business usages and customs, are led to believe agent has certain authority and they in turn deal with agent based on that assumption). Therefore, the trial court did not err by failing to charge the law of independent contractor and charging only the law of agency. . . .

CONCLUSION

We find Attorney's engagement in settlement negotiations and in the preparation of the proposed summary judgment order is clearly within

---

[2] It cannot be determined from the jury verdict whether the jury found in favor of respondent on the counterclaim of gross negligence due to BB&T's own negligence or due to Attorney's negligence.

the scope of authority set out to him by BB&T. Any misconduct engaged in by Attorney during those actions is directly attributable to BB&T. . . .

AFFIRMED

———

Should a different conclusion be reached in *Koutsogiannis* if the attorney's tortious conduct was intentional? Compare the majority and dissenting opinions in *Horwitz v. Holabird*, 212 Ill.2d 816, 816 N.E.2d 272 (Ill. 2004).

———

C. THE AGENT'S DUTY OF LOYALTY

Jensen & Meckling, Theory of the Firm: Managerial Behavior, Agency Costs and Ownership Structure

3 J. Financial Economics 305, 308 (1976).

We define an agency relationship as a contract under which one or more persons (the principal(s)) engage another person (the agent) to perform some service on their behalf which involves delegating some decision making authority to the agent. If both parties to the relationship are utility maximizers there is good reason to believe that the agent will not always act in the best interests of the principal. The *principal* can limit divergences from his interest by establishing appropriate incentives for the agent and by incurring monitoring costs designed to limit the aberrant activities of the agent. In addition in some situations it will pay the *agent* to expend resources (bonding costs) to guarantee that he will not take certain actions which would harm the principal or to ensure that the principal will be compensated if he does take such actions. However, it is generally impossible for the principal or the agent at zero cost to ensure that the agent will make optimal decisions from the principal's viewpoint. In most agency relationships the principal and the agent will incur positive monitoring and bonding costs (non-pecuniary as well as pecuniary), and in addition there will be some divergence between the agent's decisions and those decisions which would maximize the welfare of the principal. The dollar equivalent of the reduction in welfare experienced by the principal due to this divergence is also a cost of the agency relationship, and we refer to this latter cost as the "residual loss". We define *agency costs* as the sum of:

(1) the monitoring expenditures by the principal,

(2) the bonding expenditures by the agent,

(3) the residual loss.

———

Tarnowski v. Resop

Supreme Court of Minnesota, 1952.
236 Minn. 33, 51 N.W.2d 801.

■ KNUTSON, JUSTICE.

Plaintiff desired to make a business investment. He engaged defendant as his agent to investigate and negotiate for the purchase of a route of coin-operated music machines. On June 2, 1947, relying upon the advice of defendant and the investigation he had made, plaintiff purchased such a business from Phillip Loechler and Lyle Mayer of Rochester, Minnesota, who will be referred to hereinafter as the sellers. The business was located at LaCrosse, Wisconsin, and throughout the surrounding territory. Plaintiff alleges that defendant represented to him that he had made a thorough investigation of the route; that it had 75 locations in operation; that one or more machines were at each location; that the equipment at each location was not more than six months old; and that the gross income from all locations amounted to more than $3,000 per month. As a matter of fact, defendant had made only a superficial investigation and had investigated only five of the locations. Other than that, he had adopted false representations of the sellers as to the other locations and had passed them on to plaintiff as his own. Plaintiff was to pay $30,620 for the business. He paid $11,000 down. About six weeks after the purchase, plaintiff discovered that the representations made to him by defendant were false, in that there were not more than 47 locations; that at some of the locations there were no machines and at others there were machines more than six months old, some of them being seven years old; and that the gross income was far less than $3,000 per month. Upon discovering the falsity of defendant's representations and those of the sellers, plaintiff rescinded the sale. He offered to return what he had received, and he demanded the return of his money. The sellers refused to comply, and he brought suit against them in the district court of Olmsted county. The action was tried, resulting in a verdict of $10,000 for plaintiff. Thereafter, the sellers paid plaintiff $9,500, after which the action was dismissed with prejudice pursuant to a stipulation of the parties.

In this action, brought in Hennepin County, plaintiff alleges that defendant, while acting as agent for him, collected a secret commission from the sellers for consummating the sale, which plaintiff seeks to recover under his first cause of action. In his second cause of action, he seeks to recover damages for [losses caused by defendant's wrong].

1.   With respect to plaintiff's first cause of action, the principle that all profits made by an agent in the course of an agency belonging to the principal, whether they are the fruits of performance or the violation of an agent's duty, is firmly established and universally recognized. Smitz v. Leopold, 53 N.W. 719 (Minn. 1892). . . .

It matters not that the principal has suffered no damage or even that the transaction has been profitable to him. *Raymond Farmers Elevator Co. v. American Surety Co.*, 290 N.W. 231 (Minn. 1940).

The rule and the basis therefore are well stated in *Lum v. Clark*, 57 N.W. 662 (Minn. 1894), where, speaking through Mr. Justice Mitchell, we said: "Actual injury is not the principle the law proceeds on, in holding such transactions void. Fidelity in the agent is what is aimed at, and, as a means of securing it, the law will not permit him to place himself in a position in which he may be tempted by his own private interests to disregard those of his principal. . . . It is not material that no actual injury to the company [principal] resulted, or that the policy recommended may have been for its best interest. Courts will not inquire into these matters. It is enough to know that the agent in fact placed himself in such relations that he might be tempted by his own interests to disregard those of his principal. The transaction was nothing more or less than the acceptance by the agent of a bribe to perform his duties in the manner desired by the person who gave the bribe. Such a contract is void. This doctrine rests on such plain principles of law, as well as common business honesty, that the citation of authorities is unnecessary."

The right to recover profits made by the agent in the course of the agency is not affected by the fact that the principal, upon discovering a fraud, has rescinded the contract and recovered that with which he parted. Restatement, Agency, § 407(2). Comment e on Subsection (2) reads: "If an agent has violated a duty of loyalty to the principal so that the principal is entitled to profits which the agent has thereby made, the fact that the principal has brought an action against a third person and has been made whole by such action does not prevent the principal from recovering from the agent the profits which the agent has made. Thus, if the other contracting party has given a bribe to the agent to make a contract with him on behalf of the principal, the principal can rescind the transaction, recovering from the other party anything received by him, or he can maintain an action for damages against him; in either event the principal may recover from the agent the amount of the bribe."

It follows that, insofar as the secret commission of $2,000 received by the agent is concerned, plaintiff had an absolute right thereto, irrespective of any recovery resulting from the action against the sellers for rescission.

2.   Plaintiff's second cause of action is brought to recover damages for (1) losses suffered in the operation of the business prior to rescission; (2) loss of time devoted to operation; (3) expenses in connection with rescission of the sale and investigation therewith; (4) nontaxable expenses in connection with the prosecution of the suit against the sellers; and (5) attorneys' fees in connection with the suit.

The case comes to us on a bill of exceptions. No part of the testimony of the witnesses is included, so we must assume that the evidence establishes the items of damage claimed by plaintiff. Our inquiry is limited to a consideration of the question whether a principal may recover of an agent who has breached his trust the items of damage mentioned after a successful prosecution of an action for rescission against the third parties with whom the agent dealt for his principal.

The general rule is stated in Restatement, Agency, § 407(1), as follows: "If an agent has received a benefit as a result of violating his duty of loyalty, the principal is entitled to recover from him what he has so received, its value, or its proceeds, and also the amount of damage thereby caused, except that if the violation consists of the wrongful disposal of the principal's property, the principal cannot recover its value and also what the agent received in exchange therefore."

In Comment a on Subsection (1) we find the following: ". . . In either event, whether or not the principal elects to get back the thing improperly dealt with or to recover from the agent its value or the amount of benefit which the agent has improperly received, he is, in addition, entitled to be indemnified by the agent for any loss which has been caused to his interest by the improper transaction. Thus, if the purchasing agent for a restaurant purchases with the principal's money defective food, receiving a bonus therefore, and the use of the food in the restaurant damages the business, the principal can recover from the agent the amount of money improperly expended by him, the bonus which the agent received, and the amount which will compensate for the injury to the business."

The general rule with respect to damages for a tortious act is that "The wrong-doer is answerable for all the injurious consequences of his tortious act, which according to the usual course of events and the general experience were likely to ensue, and which, therefore, when the act was committed, he may reasonably be supposed to have foreseen and anticipated." 1 Sutherland, Damages (4 ed.) § 45, quoted with approval in Sargent v. Mason, 112 N.W. 255, 257 (Minn. 1907). . . .

Bergquist v. Kreidler, 196 N.W. 964 (Minn. 1924), involved an action to recover attorneys' fees expended by plaintiffs in an action seeking to enforce and protect their right to the possession of real estate. Defendant, acting as the owner's agent, had falsely represented to plaintiffs that they could have possession on August 1, 1920. It developed after plaintiffs had purchased the premises that a tenant had a lease running to August 1, 1922, on a rental much lower than the actual value of the premises. Defendant (the agent) conceded that plaintiffs were entitled to recover the loss in rent, but contended that attorneys' fees and disbursements expended by plaintiffs in testing the validity of the tenant's lease were not recoverable. In affirming plaintiffs' right to recover we said, 196 N.W. 966 (Minn. 1924): ". . . the litigation in which plaintiffs became involved was the direct, legitimate, and a to be expected result of appellant's misrepresentation. The loss sustained by plaintiffs in conducting that litigation 'is plainly traceable' to appellant's wrong and he should make compensation accordingly."

So far as the right to recover attorneys' fees is concerned, the same may be said in this case. Plaintiff sought to return what had been received and demanded a return of his down payment. The sellers refused. He thereupon sued to accomplish this purpose, as he had a right to do, and was successful. His attorneys' fees and expenses of suit were directly traceable to the harm caused by defendant's wrongful act. As such, they are recoverable.

. . . The general rule applicable here is stated in 15 Am.Jur., Damages, § 144, as follows: "It is generally held that where the wrongful act of the defendant has involved the plaintiff in litigation with others or placed him in such relation with others as makes it necessary to incur expense to protect his interest, such costs and expenses, including attorneys' fees, should be treated as the legal consequences of the original wrongful act and may be recovered as damages."

The same is true of the other elements of damage involved. . . .

Affirmed.

————

Restatement Third § 8.05, Illustration 1

"P, who owns a stable of horses, employs A to take care of them. While P is absent for a month, and without P's consent, A rents the horses [for his own personal gain] to persons who ride them. Although being ridden is beneficial to the horses, A is subject to liability to P for the amount A receives for the rentals."

————

Reading v. Attorney-General

[1951] App.Cas. 507 (H.L.)

Reading was a sergeant in the Royal Army Medical Corps during World War II, stationed in Cairo. In 1943, an unidentified man asked Reading whether he would assist in selling cases of whisky and brandy in Cairo, for which he would be paid a few pounds. About a month later Reading was met by a man named Manole, who told Reading that a truck, which Reading was to board, would come at a specified time and place. Reading, dressed in uniform, boarded the truck and conducted it through Cairo. By arrangement he met Manole later on the same day, and received an envelope which contained £2,000. This process was repeated on a number of occasions. In all, Reading was paid around £20,000. The Crown (that is, the English Government) later seized these amounts, on the ground that they had been paid to Reading "for accompanying . . . a loaded lorry in and about Cairo whilst dressed in uniform and thereby falsely representing himself as acting in the course of his military duties . . . in order to avoid police inspection of the said lorry." Reading brought suit to recover the seized amount. Justice Denning, at trial, dismissed Reading's complaint:

> In my judgment, it is a principle of law that if a servant, in violation of his duty of honesty and good faith, takes advantage of his service to make a profit for himself, in this sense, that the assets of which he has control, or the facilities which he enjoys, or the position which he occupies, are the real cause of his obtaining the money, as distinct from being the mere opportunity for getting it, that is to say, if they play the predominant part in his obtaining the money, then he is accountable for it to the master. It matters not that the master has not lost any profit, nor suffered any damage. Nor does it matter that the master could not have done the act himself. It is a case where the servant has unjustly enriched himself by virtue of his service without his master's sanction. It is money which the servant ought not to be allowed to keep, and the law says it shall be taken from him and given to his master, because he got it solely by reason of the position which he occupied as a servant of his master. . . . [Reading] . . . was using his position as a sergeant in His Majesty's Army and the uniform to which his rank entitled him to obtain the money which he received. In my opinion any official position, whether marked by a uniform or not, which enables the holder to earn money by its use gives his master a right to receive the money so earned even though it was earned by a criminal act. "You have earned," the master can say, "money by the use of your position as my servant. It is not for you, who have gained this advantage, to set up your own wrong as a defence to my claim."

The House of Lords affirmed.

———

RESTATEMENT THIRD §§ 8.01–8.05

[See Statutory Supplement]

———

D. IMPUTATION OF AGENT'S KNOWLEDGE

As seen in the preceding material, agency law empowers principals to enter into enforceable contracts with third parties through the acts of the agent. By doing so, agency law not only is facilitative of contracting but also makes business enterprises possible. The next case illustrates a potential downside for the principal's engagement of an agent.

———

Carter v. Gugliuzzi

Supreme Court of Vermont, 1998.
168 Vt. 48, 716 A.2d 17.

■ JOHNSON, J.

Defendant Synergy Group, Inc., doing business as Smith Bell Real Estate, appeals from a superior court judgment in favor of plaintiff Diana Carter. Carter's suit alleged that Smith Bell, through its agents, had made a number of misrepresentations and omissions in connection with her purchase of a house. Smith Bell contends the court erred in ruling: . . . that the knowledge of its agent concerning wind conditions on the property could be imputed to Smith Bell. . . . We affirm the judgment imposing liability on Smith Bell . . . .

The material facts are largely undisputed: In 1990, Flavia Gugliuzzi and Ana Barreto (sellers) asked Ruth Bennett, a licensed real estate salesperson, to list their house for sale. . . . Bennett, who worked for Smith Bell . . . [and] worked under the supervision of David Crane, a licensed real estate broker and an officer, director, and shareholder of the company. In response to sellers' call, Bennett went to the house, located in the Pleasant Valley area of Underhill, to fill out a sales authorization, Multiple Listing Service (MLS) sheet, and a fact sheet highlighting special features of the house. . . .

The court . . . found that Crane knew, but did not disclose to Bennett or Carter, that the house was subject to frequent and severe winds, that one of the windows in the house had blown in years earlier, and that other houses in the area had suffered wind damage. Crane had lived in the Pleasant Valley area for seven years, had sold a number of nearby properties, and had been Underhill's zoning administrator. He was aware that Pleasant Valley occasionally experienced winds of over 80 miles-per-hour and often had winds in the 40 to 50 mile-per-hour range, and that many Valley residents, including Crane, had wind gauges on their homes to measure and compare wind speeds with their neighbors.

Diana Carter, a lawyer living in California, had been looking for a house to buy in Vermont since mid-1990. She contacted several realtors, including Liz Merrill, an agent from Lang Associates, who provided her with information on a number of houses, including the listing and fact sheets relating to the Underhill property. Carter was attracted by the size of the house, the acreage, and the fact that it was listed as being in "pristine" condition. Merrill, acting as a sub-agent for the seller, showed Carter the house twice. . . . Bennett assured Carter and Merrill that there had been full disclosure. Carter's offer of $ 200,000 for the house was accepted in August 1990.

. . . Several months later, a series of high winds toppled several trees on the property, blew in a number of windows, tore shingles off the house and garage, and blew gutters off the house.

Carter sued sellers and Smith Bell for fraud, negligent misrepresentation, and breach of contract . . . .

Following a court trial, the court ruled, inter alia, that Crane's knowledge of the presence of high winds was imputable to Smith Bell, and that the company, through its agents, was liable in tort for a number of misrepresentations and omissions, and for violations of the Act. The court found both Smith Bell and sellers liable for the wind damage, future replacement of windows, the cost of additional trees to create a wind break . . . . The total judgment was for $ 30,624 plus interest and costs. . . .

Smith Bell . . . contends the court erred in ruling that Crane's knowledge about the presence of high winds on the property could be imputed to the company. Crane, to recall, had supervised and consulted with the listing agent, Ms. Bennett, inspected the property, and conveyed certain information concerning the house to Carter. Hence, the trial court's threshold finding that Crane had operated as an agent of Smith Bell was thus amply supported by the evidence. . . .

A fundamental tenet of agency law holds that "the knowledge of an agent acting within the scope of his or her authority is chargeable to the principal, regardless of whether that knowledge is actually communicated." *Estate of Sawyer v. Crowell, 151 Vt. 287, 291, 559 A.2d 687, 690 (1989)*. Smith Bell argues that Crane's knowledge about the high winds should not have been imputed to the company because it was obtained outside the scope of his employment. Carter, in response, asserts that the general rule has been abrogated by decisions suggesting that information obtained outside the scope of employment may nevertheless be imputed to the principal, at least where it appears that the information "is actually in [the agent's] mind at the time he performs the act in question." *Simpson v. Central Vt. Ry., 95 Vt. 388, 395, 115 A. 299, 302 (1921)*.

The debate in this case is academic. For contrary to Smith Bell's claim, the trial court did not find that Crane's knowledge was obtained outside the scope of his employment. As noted earlier, the court found that Crane "had lived in the area, had listed and sold many nearby properties, and had been Underhill's zoning administrator. Mr. Crane was aware that Pleasant Valley . . . had winds of over 80 m.p.h." The court further noted that real estate licensees had a statutory duty to "fully disclose to a buyer all material facts within the licensee's knowledge concerning the property being sold." *26 V.S.A. § 2296(a)(10)*. Since the statute governing a real estate agent's duty to disclose made "no distinction as to the source of the knowledge," the court concluded that such knowledge was similarly imputable to the agent's principal regardless of the source.

The court's reasoning was sound. It is immaterial whether Crane's information was derived from his residence in the area, his listing and sale of other properties in the area, or his experience as the town's zoning officer. A broker's statutory duty is to fully disclose all material facts within his or her knowledge. . . . The rule reflects the reality that a broker's business consists precisely of acquiring and conveying information about the community, neighborhood conditions, comparable properties, and other local factors that may affect the value, marketing and sale of property. . . . Such information is always, in effect, acquired in the "scope of employment." It is thus meaningless to attempt to parse a broker's knowledge about a given property on the basis of the precise time, date, or circumstances in which it was obtained. Crane's knowledge concerning the presence of high winds on the property was properly imputed to Smith Bell.

    . . . [T]he judgment is affirmed.

———

CHAPTER 2

PARTNERSHIPS

INTRODUCTORY NOTE

Partnerships fall into several categories: general partnerships (Sections 1–9), limited partnerships (Section 10), limited liability partnerships, and limited liability limited partnerships (Section 11).

Although general partnerships had a rich history under the common law, they have long been governed by statute. Until recently, the relevant statute was the Uniform Partnership Act (the UPA), which was promulgated by the Uniform Law Commission (ULC), then known as the National Conference of Commissioners on Uniform State Laws, in 1914 and adopted in every state except Louisiana. In 1994, NCCUSL adopted the Revised Uniform Partnership Act (RUPA), which is intended to supersede the UPA. Under RUPA § 1006, RUPA applies to all partnerships formed after RUPA is adopted in any given state and, after a transition period, to partnerships formed even before RUPA was adopted. A large majority of the states have adopted RUPA, but a minority, including such important commercial states as Massachusetts, Michigan, and New York have not. In those states, partnerships are still governed by the UPA. Many of the cases in this Chapter were decided under the UPA. They are included here partly because the UPA is still in effect in a number of states, and partly because the case law under the UPA is much richer than that under the RUPA, and much of that case law is relevant under RUPA because RUPA continues many rules of the UPA. However, the Text Notes generally discuss both the UPA and RUPA, especially where RUPA makes a material change in the corresponding provision of the UPA.

———

As of 2015, there were 574,181 general partnerships in the United States, with an average of 4.3 partners each. Internal Revenue Service, Statistics of Income Bulletin, Spring 2018, Tbl. 8.

———

1. WHAT CONSTITUTES A GENERAL PARTNERSHIP?

Hilco Property Services, Inc. v. United States

929 F.Supp. 526 (D.N.H. 1996)

The conduct of the parties and the circumstances surrounding their relationship and transactions control the factual question of whether a partnership existed in cases where the parties have not documented their intentions in a written agreement. . . . Although there is no specific test to determine the existence of a partnership, the courts consult a variety of factors including whether the parties intended to proceed as partners, have shared profits and losses, [or] had the right to participate in the control of the enterprise. . . . [t]he question of intent is a crucial part of the calculus, 'the only necessary intent . . . is an intent to do those things which constitute a partnership.' *Id.* Thus, . . . [t]he key factor is not the subjective intent of the parties to form a partnership. . . . It is immaterial that the parties do not call their relationship, or believe it to be, a partnership, especially where the rights of third parties are concerned.

UNIFORM PARTNERSHIP ACT §§ 6, 7

[See Statutory Supplement]

REVISED UNIFORM PARTNERSHIP ACT §§ 102(11), 202

[See Statutory Supplement]

Martin v. Peyton

New York Court of Appeals, 1927.
246 N.Y. 213, 158 N.E. 77.

Appeal from Supreme Court, Appellate Division, First Department.

Action by Charles S. Martin against William C. Peyton and others. A judgment of the Special Term, entered on the report of a referee in favor of the defendants was affirmed by the Appellate Division (219 App.Div. 297, 220 N.Y.S. 29), and plaintiff appeals. Affirmed.

■ ANDREWS, J.

Much ancient learning as to partnership is obsolete. Today only those who are partners between themselves may be charged for partnership debts by others. (Partnership Law [Cons. Laws, ch. 39], sec. 11.) There is one exception. Now and then a recovery is allowed where in truth such relationship is absent. This is because the debtor may not deny the claim. (Sec. 27.)

Partnership results from contract, express or implied. If denied it may be proved by the production of some written instrument; by testimony as to some conversation; by circumstantial evidence. If nothing else appears the receipt by the defendant of a share of the profits of the business is enough. (Sec. 11.)

Assuming some written contract between the parties the question may arise whether it creates a partnership. If it be complete; if it expresses in good faith the full understanding and obligation of the parties, then it is for the court to say whether a partnership exists. It may, however, be a mere sham intended to hide the real relationship.

Then other results follow. In passing upon it effect is to be given to each provision. Mere words will not blind us to realities. Statements that no partnership is intended are not conclusive. If as a whole a contract contemplates an association of two or more persons to carry on as co-owners a business for profit a partnership there is. (Sec. 10.) On the other hand, if it be less than this no partnership exists. Passing on the contract as a whole, an arrangement for sharing profits is to be considered. It is to be given its due weight. But it is to be weighed in connection with all the rest. It is not decisive. It may be merely the method adopted to pay a debt or wages, as interest on a loan or for other reasons.

An existing contract may be modified later by subsequent agreement, oral or written. A partnership may be so created where there was none before. And again, that the original agreement has been so modified may be proved by circumstantial evidence—by showing the conduct of the parties.

In the case before us the claim that the defendants became partners in the firm of Knauth, Nachod & Kuhne, doing business as bankers and brokers, depends upon the interpretation of certain instruments. There is nothing in their subsequent acts determinative of or indeed material upon this question. And we are relieved of questions that sometimes arise. "The plaintiff's position is not," we are told, "that the agreements of June 4, 1921, were a false expression or incomplete expression of the intention of the parties. We say that they express defendants' intention and that that intention was to create a relationship which as a matter of law constitutes a partnership." Nor may the claim of the plaintiff be rested on any question of estoppel. "The plaintiff's claim," he stipulates, "is a claim of actual partnership, not of partnership by estoppel. . . ."

Remitted then, as we are, to the documents themselves, we refer to circumstances surrounding their execution only so far as is necessary to make them intelligible. And we are to remember that although the intention of the parties to avoid liability as partners is clear, although in language precise and definite they deny any design to then join the firm of K.N. & K.; although they say their interests in profits should be construed merely as a measure of compensation for loans, not an interest in profits as such; although they provide that they shall not be liable for any losses or treated as partners, the question still remains whether in fact they agree to so associate themselves with the firm as to "carry on as co-owners a business for profit."

In the spring of 1921 the firm of K.N. & K. found itself in financial difficulties. John R. Hall was one of the partners. He was a friend of Mr. Peyton. From him he obtained the loan of almost $500,000 of Liberty bonds, which K.N. & K. might use as collateral to secure bank advances. This, however, was not sufficient. The firm and its members had engaged in unwise speculations, and it was deeply involved. Mr. Hall was also intimately acquainted with George W. Perkins, Jr., and with Edward W. Freeman. He also knew Mrs. Peyton and Mrs. Perkins and Mrs.

Freeman. All were anxious to help him. He, therefore, representing K.N. & K., entered into negotiations with them. While they were pending a proposition was made that Mr. Peyton, Mr. Perkins and Mr. Freeman or some of them should become partners. It met a decided refusal. Finally an agreement was reached. It is expressed in three documents, executed on the same day, all a part of the one transaction. They were drawn with care and are unambiguous. We shall refer to them as "the agreement," "the indenture" and "the option."

We have no doubt as to their general purpose. The respondents were to loan K.N. & K. $2,500,000 worth of liquid securities, which were to be returned to them on or before April 15, 1923. The firm might hypothecate them to secure loans totaling $2,000,000, using the proceeds as its business necessities required. To insure respondents against loss K.N. & K. were to turn over to them a large number of their own securities which may have been valuable, but which were of so speculative a nature that they could not be used as collateral for bank loans. In compensation for the loan the respondents were to receive 40 per cent of the profits of the firm until the return was made, not exceeding, however, $500,000 and not less than $100,000. Merely because the transaction involved the transfer of securities and not of cash does not prevent its being a loan within the meaning of section 11. The respondents also were given an option to join the firm if they or any of them expressed a desire to do so before June 4, 1923.

Many other detailed agreements are contained in the papers. Are they such as may be properly inserted to protect the lenders? Or do they go further? Whatever their purpose, did they in truth associate the respondents with the firm so that they and it together thereafter carried on as co-owners a business for profit? The answer depends upon an analysis of these various provisions.

As representing the lenders, Mr. Peyton and Mr. Freeman are called "trustees." The loaned securities when used as collateral are not to be mingled with other securities of K.N. & K., and the trustees at all times are to be kept informed of all transactions affecting them. To them shall be paid all dividends and income accruing there from. They may also substitute for any of the securities loaned securities of equal value. With their consent the firm may sell any of its securities held by the respondents, the proceeds to go, however, to the trustees. In other similar ways the trustees may deal with these same securities, but the securities loaned shall always be sufficient in value to permit of their hypothecation for $2,000,000. If they rise in price the excess may be withdrawn by the defendants. If they fall they shall make good the deficiency.

So far there is no hint that the transaction is not a loan of securities with a provision for compensation. Later a somewhat closer connection with the firm appears. Until the securities are returned the directing management of the firm is to be in the hands of John R. Hall, and his life is to be insured for $1,000,000, and the policies are to be assigned as further collateral security to the trustees. These requirements are not unnatural. Hall was the one known and trusted by the defendants. Their acquaintance with the other members of the firm was of the slightest. These others had brought an old and established business to the verge of bankruptcy. As the respondents knew, they also had engaged in unsafe speculation. The respondents were about to loan $2,500,000 of good securities. As collateral they were to receive others of problematical value. What they required seems but ordinary caution. Nor does it imply an association in the business.

The trustees are to be kept advised as to the conduct of the business and consulted as to important matters. They may inspect the firm books and are entitled to any information they think important. Finally they may veto any business they think highly speculative or injurious. Again we hold this but a proper precaution to safeguard the loan. The trustees may not initiate any transaction as a partner may do. They may not bind the firm by any action of their own. Under the circumstances the safety of the loan depended upon the business success of K.N. & K. This success was likely to be compromised by the inclination of its members to engage in speculation. No longer, if the respondents were to be protected, should it be allowed. The trustees, therefore, might prohibit it, and that their prohibition might be effective, information was to be furnished them. Not dissimilar agreements have been held proper to guard the interests of the lender.

As further security each member of K.N. & K. is to assign to the trustees their interest in the firm. No loan by the firm to any member is permitted and the amount each may draw is fixed. No other distribution of profits is to be made. So that realized profits may be calculated the existing capital is stated to be $700,000, and profits are to be realized as promptly as good business practice will permit. In case the trustees think this is not done, the question is left to them and to Mr. Hall, and if they differ then to an arbitrator. There is no obligation that the firm shall continue the business. It may dissolve at any time. Again we conclude there is nothing here not properly adapted to secure the interest of the respondents as lenders. If their compensation is dependent on a percentage of the profits still provision must be made to define what these profits shall be.

The "indenture" is substantially a mortgage of the collateral delivered by K.N. & K. to the trustees to secure the performance of the "agreement." It certainly does not strengthen the claim that the respondents were partners.

Finally we have the "option." It permits the respondents or any of them or their assignees or nominees to enter the firm at a later date if they desire to do so by buying 50 per cent or less of the interests therein of all or any of the members at a stated price. Or a corporation may, if the respondents and the members agree, be formed in place of the firm. Meanwhile, apparently with the design of protecting the firm business against improper or ill-judged action which might render the option valueless, each member of the firm is to place his resignation in the hands of Mr. Hall. If at any time he and the trustees agree that such resignation should be accepted, that member shall then retire, receiving the value of his interest calculated as of the date of such retirement.

This last provision is somewhat unusual, yet it is not enough in itself to show that on June 4, 1921, a present partnership was created nor taking these various papers as a whole do we reach such a result. It is quite true that even if one or two or three like provisions contained in such a contract do not require this conclusion, yet it is also true that when taken together a point may come where stipulations immaterial separately cover so wide a field that we should hold a partnership exists. As in other branches of the law a question of degree is often the determining factor. Here that point has not been reached. . . .

The judgment appealed from should be affirmed, with costs.

■ CARDOZO, CH. J., POUND, CRANE, LEHMAN, KELLOGG AND O'BRIEN, JJ., concur.

Judgment affirmed, etc.

––––––

Lupien v. Malsbenden
Supreme Judicial Court of Maine, 1984.
477 A.2d 746.

■ McKUSICK, CHIEF JUSTICE.

Defendant Frederick Malsbenden appeals a judgment of the Superior Court (York County) holding him to partnership liability on a written contract entered into between plaintiff Robert Lupien and one Stephen Cragin doing business as York Motor Mart.[1] The sole issue asserted on appeal is whether the Superior Court erred in its finding that Malsbenden and Cragin were partners in the pertinent part of York Motor Mart's business. We affirm.

On March 5, 1980, plaintiff entered into a written agreement with Stephen Cragin, doing business in the town of York as York Motor Mart, for the construction of a Bradley automobile.[2] Plaintiff made a deposit of $500 towards the purchase price of $8,020 upon signing the contract, and made a further payment of $3,950 one week later on March 12. Both the purchase order of March 5, 1980, and a later bill of sale, though signed by Cragin, identified the seller as York Motor Mart. At the jury-waived trial, plaintiff testified that after he signed the contract he made visits to

––

[1]   Cragin "disappeared" several months before this action was commenced. Plaintiff Lupien originally named Cragin as a co-defendant. However, since Cragin was never served with process, the Superior Court at the behest of both Lupien and defendant Malsbenden dismissed the claim against Cragin.

[2]   A Bradley automobile is a "kit car" constructed on a Volkswagen chassis.

York Motor Mart on an average of once or twice a week to check on the progress being made on his car. During those visits plaintiff generally dealt with Malsbenden because Cragin was seldom present. On one such visit in April, Malsbenden told plaintiff that it was necessary for the latter to sign over ownership of his pickup truck, which would constitute the balance of the consideration under the contract, so that the proceeds from the sale of the truck could be used to complete construction of the Bradley. When plaintiff complied, Malsbenden provided plaintiff with a rental car, and later with a "demo" model of the Bradley, for his use pending the completion of the vehicle he had ordered. When it was discovered that the "demo" actually belonged to a third person who had entrusted it to York Motor Mart for resale, Malsbenden purchased the vehicle for plaintiff's use. Plaintiff never received the Bradley he had contracted to purchase.

In his trial testimony, defendant Malsbenden asserted that his interest in the Bradley operation of York Motor Mart was only that of a banker. He stated that he had loaned $85,000 to Cragin, without interest, to finance the Bradley portion of York Motor Mart's business.[3] The loan was to be repaid from the proceeds of each car sold. Malsbenden acknowledged that Bradley kits were purchased with his personal checks and that he had also purchased equipment for York Motor Mart. He also stated that after Cragin disappeared sometime late in May 1980, he had physical control of the premises of York Motor Mart and that he continued to dispose of assets there even to the time of trial in 1983.

The Uniform Partnership Act, adopted in Maine at 31 M.R.S.A. §§ 281–323 (1978 & Supp.1983–1984), defines a partnership as "an association of 2 or more persons . . . to carry on as co-owners[4] a business for profit." 31 M.R.S.A. § 286 (1978). Whether a partnership exists is an inference of law based on established facts. *See* Dalton v. Austin, 432 A.2d 774, 777 (Me.1981); Roux v. Lawand, 160 A. 756, 757 (Me. 1932); James Bailey Co. v. Darling, 111 A. 410, 411 (Me. 1920). A finding that the relationship between two persons constitutes a partnership may be based upon evidence of an agreement, either express or implied,

> to place their money, effects, labor, and skill, or some or all of them, in lawful commerce or business with the understanding that a community of profits will be shared. . . . No one factor is alone determinative of the existence of a partnership. . . .

Dalton v. Austin, 432 A.2d at 777; Cumberland County Power & Light Co. v. Gordon, 7 A.2d 619, 622 (Me. 1939). *See* James Bailey Co. v. Darling, 111 A. 410, 411 (Me. 1920). If the arrangement between the

---

[3]   Malsbenden's testimony indicated that Cragin carried on an automotive repair business at the York Motor Mart that was unrelated to the Bradley operation. Malsbenden testified, without contradiction, that he had no involvement with that other business.

[4]   As we made clear in Dalton v. Austin, 432 A.2d 774, 777 (Me.1981), the term "co-owners" as used in the statute does not necessarily mean joint title to all assets. On the contrary, "the right to participate in control of the business is the essence of co-ownership." *Id.*

parties otherwise qualifies as a partnership, it is of no matter that the parties did not expressly agree to form a partnership or did not even intend to form one:

> It is possible for parties to intend no partnership and yet to form one. If they agree upon an arrangement which is a partnership in fact, it is of no importance that they call it something else, or that they even expressly declare that they are not to be partners. The law must declare what is the legal import of their agreements, and names go for nothing when the substance of the arrangement shows them to be inapplicable.

James Bailey Co. v. Darling, 111 A. at 411 (Me. 1920) (quoting *Beecher v. Bush*, 7 N.W. 785, 785–86 (Mich. 1881)).

Here the trial justice concluded that, notwithstanding Malsbenden's assertion that he was only a "banker," his "total involvement" in the Bradley operation was that of a partner. The testimony at trial, both respecting Malsbenden's financial interest in the enterprise and his involvement in day-to-day business operations, amply supported the Superior Court's conclusion. Malsbenden had a financial interest of $85,000 in the Bradley portion of York Motor Mart's operations. Although Malsbenden termed the investment a loan, significantly he conceded that the "loan" carried no interest. His "loan" was not made in the form of a fixed payment or payments, but was made to the business, at least in substantial part, in the form of day-to-day purchases of Bradley kits, other parts and equipment, and in the payment of wages. Furthermore, the "loan" was not to be repaid in fixed amounts or at fixed times, but rather only upon the sale of Bradley automobiles.

The evidence also showed that, unlike a banker, Malsbenden had the right to participate in control of the business and in fact did so on a day-to-day basis.[5] According to Urbin Savaria, who worked at York Motor Mart from late April through June 1980, Malsbenden during that time opened the business establishment each morning, remained present through part of every day, had final say on the ordering of parts, paid for parts and equipment, and paid Savaria's salary. On plaintiff's frequent visits to York Motor Mart, he generally dealt with Malsbenden because Cragin was not present. It was Malsbenden who insisted that plaintiff trade in his truck prior to the completion of the Bradley because the proceeds from the sale of the truck were needed to complete the Bradley. When it was discovered that the "demo" Bradley given to plaintiff while he awaited completion of his car actually belonged to a third party, it was Malsbenden who bought the car for plaintiff's use. As of three years after the making of the contract now in litigation, Malsbenden was still doing business at York Motor Mart, "just disposing of property."

---

[5]   Thus its facts clearly distinguish the case at bar from *James Bailey Co. v. Darling*, 111 A. 410, 413 (Me. 1920), where although the defendant advanced money for the purchase of automobiles that was to be repaid upon the sale of individual automobiles, the defendant had no control over the business.

Malsbenden and Cragin may well have viewed their relationship to be that of creditor-borrower, rather than a partnership. At trial Malsbenden so asserts, and Cragin's departure from the scene in the spring of 1980 deprives us of the benefit of his view of his business arrangement with Malsbenden. In any event, whatever the intent of these two men as to their respective involvements in the business of making and selling Bradley cars, there is no clear error in the Superior Court's finding that the Bradley car operation represented a pooling of Malsbenden's capital and Cragin's automotive skills, with joint control over the business and intent to share the fruits of the enterprise. As a matter of law, that arrangement amounted to a partnership under 31 M.R.S.A. § 286.

The entry is:

■ JUDGMENT AFFIRMED.

———

NOTES ON THE FORMATION OF PARTNERSHIPS

1. Formalities. Certain types of business enterprises can only be organized—that is legally formed—by complying with statutory (and sometimes administrative) formalities and filing with the state. This is true, for example, of corporations, limited partnerships, limited liability partnerships, limited liability limited partnerships, and limited liability companies. However, some types of business enterprises, most notably sole proprietorships and general partnerships, can be formed without any formalities or filings.

The absence of a filing requirement reflects in part a conception that partnership status depends on the factual characteristics of a relationship between two or more persons, not on whether the persons think of themselves as having entered into a partnership. However, an important consequence of the absence of formalities or filing requirements to organize a partnership means that it is not always clear whether two or more persons who are associated in a business enterprise in some way are or are not partners.

Although no filings are required under either the UPA or RUPA, RUPA permits certain filings. *See, e.g.,* Note on the Authority of a Partner, Section 4, infra.

2. The Four-Element Test, Mutual Right of Control, and Loss-Sharing. It is sometimes said that where there is no express partnership agreement, a relationship will be considered a partnership only if four elements are present—an agreement to share profits, an agreement to share losses, a mutual right of control or management of the business, and a community of interest in the venture. *See, e.g.,* Weingart v. C & W Taylor Partnership, 809 P.2d 576 (Mont. 1991); Corpus Christi v. Bayfront Associates, Ltd., 814 S.W.2d 98 (Tex.App.1991). This four-element test departs from the statutory tests both UPA § 6(a) and RUPA § 202, which provide simply that with certain exceptions a partnership is "an association of two or more persons to carry on as co-owners a business for profit," and say nothing about control or loss-sharing.

Although the Comments to both UPA § 6(a) and RUPA § 202 also say that "to state that partners are co-owners of a business is to state that they each have the power of ultimate control," in fact even explicit partnership agreements frequently do not involve either ultimate control or loss-sharing for every partner. For example, many partnership agreements vest control in only one or more managing partners, or create elaborate allocations of voting power in which some partners do not have voting rights. Similarly, not every partnership agreement provides for loss-sharing by every partner. If explicit partnership agreements do not always include control and loss-sharing as elements of the partnership relation, why should courts require those elements as a condition to finding an implicit partnership?

A better approach is that the presence or absence of the four specified elements, including mutual control and loss-sharing, is evidence, but not a requirement, of a partnership. This approach was taken, for example, in Beckman v. Farmer, 579 A.2d 618, 627 (D.C.App.1990), where the court said that "[t]he customary attributes of partnership, such as loss sharing and joint control of decisionmaking are necessary guideposts of inquiry, but none is conclusive." Other cases have held that once profit-sharing has been shown, it is not essential to show that there was an agreement to share in losses. *See* Hansford v. Maplewood Station Business Park, 621 N.E.2d 347 (Ind.App.1993); Endsley v. Game-Show Placements, Ltd., 401 N.E.2d 768 (Ind.App.1980).

----

2. THE LEGAL NATURE OF A PARTNERSHIP

UNIFORM PARTNERSHIP ACT § 6

[See Statutory Supplement]

REVISED UNIFORM PARTNERSHIP ACT
§§ 102(11), 201 & 307(a)&(c)

[See Statutory Supplement]

NOTES ON THE LEGAL NATURE OF A PARTNERSHIP: ENTITY OR AGGREGATE STATUS

1. Entity vs. Aggregate—in General. Individuals may associate in a wide variety of forms. The issue often arises whether a given form of association has a legal status separate from that of its members or is simply an aggregate of its members. Frequently, this issue is stated in terms of whether a particular form of association is or is not a "separate legal entity" or a "legal person" (as opposed to a natural person, that is, an individual). A variety of issues may turn on the answer to this question—for example, whether the association can sue and be sued in its own name and whether it can hold property in its own right.

In the history of English and American law this issue arose in the context of many different kinds of associations, such as universities, charitable institutions, and even municipalities. In most cases the issue was eventually resolved in a straightforward way, but in the case of partnerships it continued to be vexing for a long time. The predominant although not exclusive view under the common law was that a partnership was not an entity but merely an aggregate of its members—or, as it was sometimes put, that a partnership was no more a legal entity than was a friendship.

2. *The UPA.* In 1902, the National Conference of Commissioners on Uniform State Laws determined to promulgate a Uniform Partnership Act. Dean James Barr Ames of the Harvard Law School was appointed to draft the Act. Subsequently, the Commissioners instructed Dean Ames, at his own urging, to draft the Act on the theory that a partnership is a legal entity. Accordingly, in the drafts submitted by Dean Ames a partnership was defined as "a legal person formed by the association of two or more individuals for the purpose of carrying on business with a view to profit", and various provisions of the drafts reflected the entity theory. However, Dean Ames died before the work was completed and his successor, Dean William Draper Lewis of the University of Pennsylvania Law School, was distinctly unfriendly to the entity view. Ultimately, Dean Lewis convinced the Commissioners to instruct him to draft the Act on the aggregate theory. UPA Section 6 therefore provides simply that "A partnership is an association of two or more persons to carry on as co-owners a business for profit." Although the language of this provision does not in itself render the entity-aggregate issue free from doubt (since an association can be either an aggregate or an entity), it is pretty clear that the Act was intended to adopt the aggregate rather than the entity theory of partnership.

However, that is not the end of the story. Having adopted the aggregate theory in principle, in practice the UPA deals with a number of specific issues (such as the ownership of partnership property) as if a partnership is an entity. For many purposes, this approach works pretty well. Generally speaking, however, the entity theory of partnership works much better than the aggregate theory. In cases where the UPA treats a partnership as if it is an entity, notwithstanding the aggregate theory, the results are good but the manner in which the statute reaches those results involves needlessly complex mechanics. In cases where the UPA does not treat the partnership as if it is an entity, the results tend to be bad.

3. *The Effect of Statutes Other than the UPA on UPA-Governed Partnerships.* The question often arises whether a partnership whose internal affairs are governed by a UPA state is to be treated as an aggregate or an entity for the purpose of statutes other than the UPA. This question is

a matter of legislative intent under the relevant statute. As in all such matters, the answer will depend on the language employed and the purposes manifested in the statute. The fact that the UPA adopts the aggregate theory will be relevant, but not dispositive, in answering the question. Even though a partnership is defined as an association under the UPA, a legislature may choose to treat a UPA-governed partnership as an entity for purposes of another statute, *See, e.g.*, United States v. A & P Trucking Co., 358 U.S. 121, 79 S.Ct. 203, 3 L.Ed.2d 165 (1958).

    4.   *RUPA.* In contrast to the UPA, RUPA confers entity status on partnerships. RUPA § 102(11), like UPA § 6, defines a partnership as "an association of two or more persons to carry on as co-owners a business for profit." However, RUPA § 201 then provides that "A partnership is an entity."

By conferring entity status on partnerships, RUPA was able to drastically simplify many partnership rules, such as those dealing with partnership property and partnership litigation. Nevertheless, entity status does not inherently resolve every issue to which it is relevant. Just as the drafters of the UPA, having denied entity status to partnerships, remained free to (and did) craft rules to reach entity-like results on certain issues, so the drafters of RUPA, having conferred entity status on partnerships, remained free to (and did) craft rules to reach aggregate-like results on certain issues.

To put this differently, no rule to govern any specific partnership-law issue can be derived or follows logically or by necessity from a partnership's legal-entity status under RUPA, any more than any rule on any specific issue can be derived, or follows "logically" or "by necessity" from the UPA's denial of that status. Having declared that a partnership is an entity, the drafters of RUPA still had to make policy choices on such issues as whether the partnership could hold property, could sue and be sued in its own name, and so forth. It is true that generally speaking the best rule in many of these areas is one that is consistent with entity status, but it is important not to forget that an independent policy choice must still be made on each issue. The adoption of legal-entity status for partnerships simplified the drafting of RUPA and gave a slight push toward certain entity rules. In some areas, however, RUPA reaches an aggregate-like result. For example, under RUPA, as under the UPA, a partner is individually liable for partnership debts. Under RUPA § 409(a), a partner has a duty of loyalty and care not only to the partnership but to the other partners. Under RUPA § 409(d), a partner's duty of good faith and fair dealing extends both to the partnership and to the other partners.

———

3. THE ONGOING OPERATION OF PARTNERSHIPS

A. MANAGEMENT

———

UNIFORM PARTNERSHIP ACT §§ 18(e), (g), (h), 19, 20

[See Statutory Supplement]

———

REVISED UNIFORM PARTNERSHIP ACT §§ 105, 401(h), (k), 402(b), 408(b)(c)

[See Statutory Supplement]

———

Summers v. Dooley

Supreme Court of Idaho, 1971.
94 Idaho 87, 481 P.2d 318.

■ DONALDSON, JUSTICE.

This lawsuit, tried in the district court, involves a claim by one partner against the other for $6,000. The complaining partner asserts that he has been required to pay out more than $11,000 in expenses without any reimbursement from either the partnership funds or his partner. The expenditure in question was incurred by the complaining partner (John Summers, plaintiff-appellant) for the purpose of hiring an additional employee. The trial court denied him any relief except for ordering that he be entitled to one half $966.72 which it found to be a legitimate partnership expense.

The pertinent facts leading to this lawsuit are as follows. Summers entered a partnership agreement with Dooley (defendant-respondent) in 1958 for the purpose of operating a trash collection business. The business was operated by the two men and when either was unable to work, the non-working partner provided a replacement at his own expense. In 1962, Dooley became unable to work and, at his own expense, hired an employee to take his place. In July, 1966, Summers approached his partner Dooley regarding the hiring of an additional employee but Dooley refused. Nevertheless, on his own initiative, Summers hired the man and paid him out of his own pocket. Dooley, upon discovering that Summers had hired an additional man, objected, stating that he did not feel additional labor was necessary and refused to pay for the new employee out of the partnership funds. Summers continued to operate the business using the third man and in October of 1967 instituted suit in the district court for $6,000 against his partner, the gravamen of the complaint being that Summers has been required to pay out more than

$11,000 in expenses, incurred in the hiring of the additional man, without any reimbursement from either the partnership funds or his partner. After trial before the court, sitting without a jury, Summers was granted only partial relief[1] and he has appealed. He urges in essence that the trial court erred by failing to conclude that he should be reimbursed for expenses and costs connected in the employment of extra help in the partnership business.

The principal thrust of appellant's contention is that in spite of the fact that one of the two partners refused to consent to the hiring of additional help, nonetheless, the non-consenting partner retained profits earned by the labors of the third man and therefore the non-consenting partner should be estopped from denying the need and value of the employee, and has by his behavior ratified the act of the other partner who hired the additional man.

The issue presented for decision by this appeal is whether an equal partner in a two man partnership has the authority to hire a new employee in disregard of the objection of the other partner and then attempt to charge the dissenting partner with the costs incurred as a result of his unilateral decision.

The State of Idaho has enacted specific statutes with respect to the legal concept known as "partnership." Therefore any solution of partnership problems should logically begin with an application of the relevant code provision.

In the instant case the record indicates that although Summers requested his partner Dooley to agree to the hiring of a third man, such requests were not honored. In fact Dooley made it clear that he was "voting no" with regard to the hiring of an additional employee.

An application of the relevant statutory provisions and pertinent case law to the factual situation presented by the instant case indicates that the trial court was correct in its disposal of the issue since a majority of the partners did not consent to the hiring of the third man. I.C. § 53–318(8) provides:

> "Any difference arising as to ordinary matters connected with the partnership business may be decided by a *majority of the partners. . . .*" (emphasis supplied). . . .

The intent of the legislature may be implied from the language used, or inferred on grounds of policy or reasonableness. . . . A careful reading of the statutory provision indicates that subsection 5 bestows *equal rights in the management and conduct of the partnership business* upon all of the partners. The concept of equality between partners with respect to management of business affairs is a central theme and recurs throughout the Uniform Partnership law, I.C. § 53–301 et seq., which has been enacted in this jurisdiction. Thus the only reasonable interpretation of

---

[1]   The trial court did award Summers one half of $966.72 which it found to be a legitimate partnership expense.

I.C. § 53–318(8) is that business differences must be decided by a majority of the partners provided no other agreement between the partners speaks to the issues. . . .

In the case at bar one of the partners continually voiced objection to the hiring of the third man. He did not sit idly by and acquiesce in the actions of his partner. Under these circumstances it is manifestly unjust to permit recovery of an expense which was incurred individually and not for the benefit of the partnership but rather for the benefit of one partner.

Judgment affirmed. Costs to respondent.

■ McQUADE, C.J., and McFADDEN, SHEPARD and SPEAR, JJ., concur.

———

Sanchez v. Saylor

129 N.M. 742, 13 P.3d 960 (2000)

Sanchez and Saylor were partners. A third party was considering lending money to the partnership to finance a proposed restructuring of the partnership's debt, but the potential lender required Sanchez to provide his personal financial statements as a condition to granting the loan, and Sanchez refused to furnish the statements. Saylor brought suit against Sanchez on the ground that Sanchez's refusal to provide his financial statements to the potential lender violated his fiduciary obligations. Held, for Sanchez:

> . . . We turn to Covalt v. High, 675 P.2d 999 (Ct.App.1983) . . . Covalt and High formed an oral partnership which owned and rented an office to a corporation, CSI, in which Covalt owned 25 percent of the corporate stock and High owned 75 percent. . . . After resigning from CSI, Covalt demanded that the partnership increase CSI's rent, but High took no action. *See id.* The increase in rent would benefit the partnership, but it was detrimental to High. The district court found that CSI could afford the rent increase and High had breached his fiduciary duty. *See id.*

In reversing, this Court stated that "all partners have equal rights in the management and conduct of the business of the partnership," that Covalt therefore "was legally invested with an equal voice in the management of the partnership affairs," and that "neither partner had the right to impose his will or decision concerning the operation of the partnership business upon the other." *Id.* at 703, 675 P.2d at 1002 (N.M.App. 1983). The fact that a proposal benefitted the partnership did not require High to agree. *See id.* As authority for its decision, *Covalt* cited UPA, Section 54–1–18(H), stating "any difference arising as to ordinary matters connected with the partnership business may be decided by a majority of the partners." Further, the Court relied on the interpretation of the UPA language by the Idaho Supreme Court in Summers v. Dooley, 481 P.2d 318 (Idaho 1971), that the language is mandatory rather than permissive in nature, and means that business differences must be decided by a majority, not by one of two equal partners when the other objects. *See* 481 P.2d at 320–21.

> Simply stated, *Covalt* says that, absent an enforceable agreement covering such circumstances of disagreement, when both partners in a two-partner partnership disagree on an advantageous prospective business transaction, it is dissolution, not an action for breach of fiduciary duty, that is the appropriate avenue of relief. . . .
>
> . . . Without [the *Covalt*] rule, virtually each instance in which one partner for personal reasons does not agree with a proposed transaction that will benefit the partnership can result in a claim for breach of his or her partnership or fiduciary duty. Absent an enforceable contractual duty to agree, if the two partners cannot agree and do not want to (or cannot) continue their partnership, under *Covalt* the remedy is dissolution. . . .

NOTES ON THE MANAGEMENT OF PARTNERSHIPS

1.   Voting.

a).   UPA. The cases and authorities are divided on the issue raised in Summers v. Dooley. In accord with *Summers* is Covalt v. High, 675 P.2d 999 (App.1983). But *see* National Biscuit Co. v. Stroud, 106 S.E.2d 692 (N.C. 1959).

The rule of UPA Section 18(h), that any difference arising as to ordinary matters connected with the partnership business may be decided by a majority of the partners, is subject to any agreement between the partners. Partnership agreements often contain provisions vesting management in a managing partner, a managing committee, senior partners, or some other group composed of less than all the partners, and such agreements override Section 18(h). The same result may be reached even without explicit agreement—for example on the basis of a course of conduct:

> [I]t is . . . well settled . . . that an agreement for exclusive control of the management of the business by one partner may be implied from the course of conduct of the parties. Here, it was fairly [inferable] from the course of conduct of Parks and Patterson that there was an implied agreement that Parks should be the managing partner.

Parks v. Riverside Ins. Co. of Am., 308 F.2d 175, 180 (10th Cir.1962). Such an implied agreement, if found, would pretty clearly block the nonmanaging partners from objecting to a decision of the managing partners relating to ordinary matters connected with the partnership business solely on the ground that the decision was not arrived at by a majority vote of all partners.

b).   RUPA. RUPA § 401(k) generally follows the voting rules of UPA § 18(h), although there are several differences between the sections. Under

UPA § 18(h), "Any difference arising as to ordinary matters connected with the partnership business may be decided by a majority of the partners; but no act in contravention of any agreement between the partners may be done rightfully without the consent of all the partners." Under RUPA § 401(k), "A difference arising as to a matter in the ordinary course of business of a partnership may be decided by a majority of the partners. An act outside the ordinary course of business of a partnership and an amendment to the partnership agreement may be undertaken only with the consent of all of the partners."

RUPA § 401(k) must be read in conjunction with RUPA § 102(12), which defines the term "partnership agreement" to mean "the agreement, written or oral, among the partners concerning the partnership." The Comment to this section observes:

> A partnership agreement is a contract, and therefore all statutory language pertaining to the partnership agreement must be understood in the context of the law of contracts.
>
> . . . [There is] a wide scope of authority for the partnership agreement . . . Those matters include not only all relations *inter se* the partners and the partnership but also "the business of the partnership and the conduct of that business." Section 105(a)(2). Moreover, the definition puts no limits on the form of the partnership agreement. To the contrary, the definition contains the phrase "whether oral, implied, in a record, or in any combination thereof."
>
> Unless the partnership agreement itself provides otherwise:
>
> A partnership agreement may comprise a number of separate documents (or records), however denominated; and
>
> Subject to 106(b) . . . a document, record, or understanding, etc. can be part of a partnership agreement only with the assent of all persons then partners.

2. *Participation.*

a). UPA. Since UPA Section 18(h) provides that partnership action requires a majority vote, what is added by UPA Section 18(e), which provides that all partners have equal rights in the management and conduct of the partnership business? Presumably, the effect of this Section is that absent contrary agreement, every partner must be consulted in partnership decisions.

> For a majority of partners to say; We do not care what one partner may say, we, being the majority, will do what we please, is, I apprehend, what this Court will not allow. So, again, with respect to making Mr. Robertson the treasurer, Mr. Const had a right to be consulted; his opinion might be overruled, and honestly overruled, but he ought to have had the question put to him and discussed: In all partnerships . . . the partners are bound to be true and faithful to each other: They are to act upon the joint opinion of all, and the

discretion and judgment of anyone cannot be excluded: What weight is to be given to it is another question. . . .

Const v. Harris, 37 Eng.Rep. 1191, 1202 (Ch.1824) (Lord Chancellor Eldon). Accordingly, absent contrary agreement, a majority of partners who make a decision without consulting a minority partner would violate § 18(e) even though the majority could have overridden the minority partner if he had been consulted.

b). RUPA. RUPA § 401(h) continues the rule of UPA § 18(e), by conferring on each partner the right to participate in management. The Comment to § 401(h) notes that UPA § 18(e) "has been interpreted broadly to mean that, absent contrary agreement, each partner has a continuing right to participate in the management of the partnership and to be informed about the partnership business, even if his assent . . . is not required."

B. INDEMNIFICATION AND CONTRIBUTION

UNIFORM PARTNERSHIP ACT §§ 18(a), (b), (c), (d), (f)

[See Statutory Supplement]

REVISED UNIFORM PARTNERSHIP ACT §§ 401(b)–(f), (j)

[See Statutory Supplement]

NOTE ON INDEMNIFICATION AND CONTRIBUTION

As discussed in Section 5, infra, partners are individually liable to partnership creditors for partnership obligations. As between the partners, however, each partner is liable only for his share of partnership obligations. Thus if one partner pays off a partnership obligation in full (or, for that matter, if he simply pays more than his share), he is entitled to indemnification from the partnership for the difference between his share of the obligation and the amount he paid.

Indemnification should be distinguished from contribution. In a proper case, a partner has a right to be indemnified by the partnership. In contrast, in a proper case the partnership has a right to require *contribution* from one or more partners. Thus the obligation to indemnify a partner is a partnership liability, while the obligation to make contribution is a liability of a partner. For example, partners may be required to make contribution to the partnership to fund a partnership obligation to indemnify another partner so that all partners share a burden that was initially placed on only one. Contribution may also be required for other purposes—in particular, paying off partnership creditors and equalizing capital losses.

"Indemnification resolves the apparent conflict between a partner's joint or joint and several liability, whereby a partner may be called upon to pay the entire amount of partnership debt to third parties under UPA § 15 and RUPA § 306 and the proportionate sharing of profits and losses among the partners under UPA § 18(a) and RUPA § 401(b). A partner who pays or incurs a personal liability to a third party on behalf of the partnership becomes a creditor of the partnership in the amount of the payment or liability, in effect subrogated to the rights of the creditor. . . . If a going partnership indemnifies the partner, all partners incur a detriment in proportion to their profit shares if the business is profitable, or otherwise according to their loss shares. If the partnership is unable to pay, all partners must contribute to make up the resulting deficit under UPA §§ 18(a) and 40(b)(II) and (d) and RUPA §§ 401(b) and 806(c) & (d) according to their loss shares. If the partners are unable to contribute or cannot be sued, the paying partner, rather than the third party, bears the loss." Christine Hurt, D. Gordon Smith, Alan R. Bromberg & Larry E. Ribstein, Bromberg & Ribstein on Partnership § 6.02(f) (2d ed. 2017).

————

4. THE AUTHORITY OF A PARTNER

————

UNIFORM PARTNERSHIP ACT §§ 3, 4(3), 9, 10, 11, 12, 13, 14

[See Statutory Supplement]

————

REVISED UNIFORM PARTNERSHIP ACT
§§ 301, 302, 303, 304, 305, 306

[See Statutory Supplement]

————

Northmon Investment Company v. Milford Plaza Associates

Supreme Court, Appellate Division, New York, 2001.
284 A.D.2d 250, 727 N.Y.S.2d 419.

■ SULLIVAN, P.J., ELLERIN, WALLACH, RUBIN and BUCKLEY, JJ.

Supreme Court, New York County . . . in a dispute between partners concerning appellants' [defendants'] authority to enter into a 99-year lease of real property constituting the partnership's only asset, found in respondents' favor that appellants lack such authority. . . . [The decision is] unanimously affirmed, with costs.

Appellants lack authority to enter into the contemplated 99-year lease even if such lease were to be deemed in the ordinary course of the partnership's business. A partner's authority to bind the partnership to transactions apparently in the ordinary course of the partnership's business (*see,* Partnership Law § 20[1]) does not affect the right of partners as between themselves to prevent contemplated transactions with third parties, or otherwise to assert their "equal rights in the management and conduct of the partnership business" (*see,* Partnership Law § 40[5]). Appellants cannot impose their decision to enter into this lease upon respondents (*see,* Riley v. Maran, 370 N.Y.S.2d 302 (N.Y. Sup. 1974); *see also,* Partnership Law § 40[8]), and, indeed, respondents' right to interfere with this or any other contract or prospective contract involving the partnership is "absolute" and "privileged, excusable and justified" (Braden v. Perkins, 22 N.Y.S.2d 144 (N.Y. Sup. 1940)). Nor do the newly discovered partnership agreements avail appellants. Assuming such agreements ... can be fairly construed to preclude respondents' interference with a contemplated or consummated long-term lease, it remains that the agreements, on their face, terminate the partnership in 2075, many years before the contemplated 99-year lease would expire. Since such a lease cannot be deemed ordinary, respondents would not be bound by it (*see,* Partnership Law § 40[2], [3][b], [c]). . . .

NOTES ON THE AUTHORITY OF A PARTNER

1.　UPA. The basic default rule governing a partner's *actual* authority under the UPA is that each partner is an agent of the partnership for the purpose of its business. However, the UPA's rule on a partner's *apparent* authority is somewhat ambiguous. Under the UPA, a partner has authority to bind the partnership by any act "for apparently carrying on in the usual way the business of the partnership of which he is a member." There is controversy whether this means the usual way *the partner's firm* carries on its business or the usual way *other firms* in the same locality engaged in the same general line of business carry on business. In Burns v. Gonzalez, 439 S.W.2d 128 (Tex.Civ.App.1969), the court adopted the latter view.

2.　RUPA. RUPA § 301(1) makes clear, as the UPA did not, that a partnership is bound by an act of the partner for apparently carrying on in the usual way (i) the partnership business or (ii) business *of the kind* carried on by the partnership. The Comment to § 301(1) states:

> Section 301(1). . . . clarifies that a partner's apparent authority includes acts for carrying on in the ordinary course "business of the kind carried on by the partnership," not just the business of the particular partnership in question. The UPA is ambiguous on this point, but there is some authority for an expanded construction. . . . *See, e.g.,* Burns v. Gonzalez, 439 S.W.2d 128, 131 (Tex.Civ.App.1969) (dictum). . . .

The treatment of authority under RUPA also differs from the UPA in certain other respects. For example, RUPA § 302 provides elaborate rules concerning when a transfer of partnership property is binding. In addition, as described below, RUPA addresses the important questions regarding the impact of knowledge or notice regarding authority as well as mechanisms for giving notice of an agent's authority.

3. *Notice.* RUPA § 301 makes subtle shifts in determining when the knowledge or notice of T, a third person, of a restriction on the authority of a partner, will prevent partnership liability from arising out of a transaction between T and a partner who purports to act on the partnership's behalf. "Under UPA section 9(1), the partnership was not bound by the unauthorized actions of a partner if the third party had '*knowledge*' of the partner's lack of authority. Under UPA section 9(1), a third party had knowledge when he or she had actual knowledge or '*when he has knowledge of such other facts as in the circumstances shows bad faith.*' This latter language creates an implied or inquiry notice, the exact parameters of which are ill-defined. Under RUPA, the third party will not be placed under a duty of inquiry or be deemed to have notice from the facts and circumstances. *Only actual knowledge or receipt of a notification of a partner's lack of authority will meet the standard.*" Merrill, Partnership Property and Partnership Authority Under the Revised Uniform Partnership Act, 49 Bus. Law. 83, 88–89 (1993) (emphasis added).

4. *Statement of Authority.* RUPA § 303 enables a partnership to file a "Statement of Partnership Authority." A *grant* of authority in such a Statement is normally conclusive in favor of third persons, even if they have no actual knowledge of the Statement, unless they have actual knowledge that the partner has no such authority. In contrast, a *limitation* on a partner's authority in such a Statement—other than a limitation on the partner's authority to transfer real property—will not be effective unless the third party *knows* of the limitation or the Statement has been delivered to him. In contrast, a limitation, in a Statement of Partnership Authority, of a partner's authority to transfer partnership *real property* is effective against all third persons if a certified copy of the Statement is filed in the real-property recording office.

Why would a partnership want to file a Statement that can *expand* a partner's authority simply because it is filed, but normally will not *limit* a partner's authority unless it is not only filed but also delivered? One answer is that persons who deal with a partnership may require such a Statement to ensure themselves that the partnership will be bound. Also, "[in] the process of searching for the grant of authority, the third party will acquire actual knowledge of any restriction on authority in a filed statement. [Furthermore,] the . . . partners may protect themselves by delivering the statement to all known creditors, actual or potential." Merrill, supra, at 89.

———

5. LIABILITY FOR PARTNERSHIP OBLIGATIONS

UNIFORM PARTNERSHIP ACT §§ 9, 13, 14, 15, 16, 17, 36

[See Statutory Supplement]

REVISED UNIFORM PARTNERSHIP ACT §§ 305, 306

[See Statutory Supplement]

NOTES ON LIABILITY FOR PARTNERSHIP OBLIGATIONS

1.   UPA. The provisions of the Uniform Partnership Act governing liability for partnership obligations reflect an amalgam of the entity and aggregate theories. On the one hand, UPA §§ 9, 13, and 14 make "the partnership" liable for defined acts of the partners. It might seem to follow that this liability could be enforced by a suit against the partnership. However, the UPA does not authorize such a suit, because it does not recognize a partnership as an entity, and unless authorized by statute, suit normally cannot be brought against an association that is not an entity. Suit against the individual partners on a partnership obligation is also difficult under the UPA. At common law, if an obligation is "joint and several," the obligors can be sued either jointly or separately. If, however, an obligation is only "joint," all the joint obligors must be joined in the suit, subject to a few exceptions where jurisdiction over all the obligors cannot be obtained. *See* C. Clark, Handbook of the Law of Code Pleading 373–74 (2d ed. 1947). Under UPA § 15(a), partners are jointly and severally liable for wrongful acts and omissions of the partnership such as torts, and breaches of trust. Under UPA § 15(b), however, partners are only jointly liable "for all other debts and obligations of the partnership," such as breaches of contract. Thus under the UPA, if, in an action based on a partnership's contractual obligation, the plaintiff does not join all the partners, the action normally can be dismissed on motion by the partners who were joined.

The inability of a UPA partnership contract creditor to sue a partnership in its own name is obviously undesirable, and many states have statutorily patched up the UPA rule. Some states achieved this objective by adopting a Common Name Statute, which explicitly allows a partnership to be sued in its own name. An example is N.Y.Civ.Prac.L. & R. § 1025: "Two or more persons conducting a business as a partnership may sue or be sued in the partnership name. . . . " Under such statutes, a judgment is binding on the partnership property and on the individual property of all partners who are served. Other states patched up the UPA by changing the rule that a contract creditor of a partnership needs to join all the partners in a suit to establish liability on the contract claim. Still other states adopted Joint

Debtor Statutes, which provide that a suit against joint obligors can proceed even if some of the obligors are not joined. *See, e.g.,* Cal.Civ.Proc.Code § 410.70. Under such statutes, a judgment is binding on both the joint (partnership) property and on the property of those partners who are served. And some states made all partnership liabilities joint and several, not just wrongful acts or omissions and breaches of trust.

 2. RUPA. Unlike the UPA, RUPA § 307(a) specifically provides that a partnership may both sue and be sued in its own name. Furthermore, RUPA § 306 provides that partners are jointly and severally liable for all obligations of the partnership. However, RUPA adds a new barrier to collecting against an individual partner. Under RUPA § 307, a judgment against a partner based on a claim against the partnership normally cannot be satisfied against the partner's individual assets unless and until a judgment on the same claim has been rendered against the partnership and a writ of execution on that judgment has been returned unsatisfied. To put this differently, RUPA § 307 adopts an exhaustion rule under which, in a suit against a partner based on a claim against the partnership, partnership assets must be exhausted before a partner's individual assets can be reached. (This exhaustion rule is made subject to certain exceptions, one of which is that the rule does not apply if the partnership is in bankruptcy.) In effect, RUPA takes an aggregate-like approach to a partner's liability, but an entity-like approach to collecting judgments based on that liability. RUPA § 307(c) also provides that, subject to certain exceptions, a judgment against a partnership is not by itself a judgment against a partner, and cannot be satisfied from a partner's assets unless there is also a judgment against the partner.

————

6. PARTNERSHIP INTERESTS AND PARTNERSHIP PROPERTY

————

UNIFORM PARTNERSHIP ACT §§ 8, 18(g), 24, 25, 26, 27, 28

————

REVISED UNIFORM PARTNERSHIP ACT
§§ 203, 204, 302(a), 501, 502, 503, 504, 505

[See Statutory Supplement]

————

NOTES ON PARTNERSHIP PROPERTY

1. UPA. Property that is used by a partnership may be either partnership property or property of a partner that is loaned by the partner to the partnership. The issue whether property used by the partnership is partnership property or the property of an individual partner may be important for several reasons. First, the issue may be important for purposes of determining who has the power to transfer the property. Property owned by the partnership can be transferred by the partnership. Property loaned to the partnership cannot be. Second, the issue may be important if creditors of the partnership are competing with creditors of an individual partner, and the question arises whether any given property is owned by the partnership or owned by the partner and loaned to the partnership. Third, the issue may be important if the partnership is dissolved: If property used by the partnership is partnership property, on dissolution the property must be sold or valued along with other partnership assets, and the proceeds of the sale or the value of the asset must be distributed among the partners. In contrast, if property used by the partnership is the individual property of a partner, on dissolution the property must normally be returned directly to that partner, rather than sold or valued for the account of all the partners.[1] This third issue may be especially important if the property is crucial to the partnership's business, so that as a practical matter whoever owns the property has the ability to continue the business.

If the aggregate theory of the UPA was strictly applied, a partnership could not own property. Rather, the property that the partners think of as partnership property would as a matter of law be held by the individual partners as joint tenants or tenants in common. Such a regime would be wholly impracticable. Accordingly, in the matter of partnership property, as in several other matters, the UPA lays down rules that effectively treat the partnership as if it were an entity. This objective is accomplished largely with smoke and mirrors. UPA § 8 recognizes the concept of "partnership property," and explicitly permits real property to be held in the partnership's name. UPA § 25(1) provides that "partnership property" is owned by the partners, under the ingenuous nomenclature tenancy in partnership. However, UPA § 25(2) then systematically strips from the individual partners every incident normally associated with ownership: (i) Under § 25(2)(a), a partner has no right to possess partnership property as an individual. (ii) Under § 25(2)(b), a partner cannot individually assign his rights in specific partnership property. (iii) Under § 25(2)(c), a partner's rights in specific partnership property cannot be subject to attachment or execution by a creditor of the partner in the latter's individual capacity. (iv) Under § 25(2)(d), when a partner dies his right in specific partnership property does not devolve on his heirs or legatees. (v) Under § 25(2)(e), widows, heirs, and next of kin cannot claim dower, curtesy, or allowances in a partner's right to specific partnership property. In short, under the UPA individual partners own the partnership property in theory, but in practice all the incidents of ownership are vested in the partnership, so that the "tenan[cy] in partnership" rule of the UPA has no real-world significance.

    2.   RUPA. RUPA, which confers entity status on partnerships, drops the elaborate tenancy-in-partnership apparatus of the UPA. Instead, RUPA § 203 provides that "Property acquired by a partnership is property of the

---

[1]   But *see* Pav-Saver Corp. v. Vasso Corp., 143 Ill.App.3d 1013, 97 Ill.Dec. 760, 493 N.E.2d 423 (1986) (wrongfully dissolving partner held not entitled to return of property).

partnership and not the partners individually." RUPA § 204 then sets out a series of rules and presumptions concerning whether any given property is partnership property or the separate property of a partner. These provisions are supplemented by § 501, which provides that "A partner is not a co-owner of partnership property and has no interest in partnership property which can be transferred, either voluntarily or involuntarily." The purpose of § 501 is to explicitly abolish the UPA concept of tenancy in partnership.

———————

NOTES ON PARTNERSHIP INTERESTS

1. *The Partner's Interest in the Partnership.* Although a partner does not own partnership property under the UPA except in a metaphysical sense, he does own his interest in the partnership, that is, his share of the partnership. The net result is a functional two-level ownership structure that is somewhat comparable to the two-level ownership structure in a corporation. In the case of a corporation, the corporation owns the corporate property and the shareholder owns shares in the corporation. In the case of a partnership, the partnership owns the partnership property—either in as a practical matter (under the UPA) or in full (under RUPA)—and the partner owns her interest in the partnership.

2. *Assignment.* As compared to ordinary property interests, a partnership interest is conditioned in one very important respect. Normally, the owner of a property interest can freely sell it, and a creditor can freely levy on it. In contrast, although a partnership interest is assignable, a partner cannot assign her partnership interest in a way that would substitute the transferee as a partner in the transferor's place, because it is a rule of partnership law that no person can become a partner without the consent of all the partners. Accordingly, when a partnership interest is assigned, for example to a creditor, the assignment normally is not a full transfer of the partner-assignor's interest. Instead, it is a transfer to secure a debt that the partner-assignor owes to the creditor-assignee. The creditor-assignee cannot levy on a partnership interest in such a way as to become a substituted partner, nor can the creditor recover his debt by selling the partnership interest to a third party who will be substituted as a partner. Accordingly, as pointed out in *Rapoport,* the assignee of a partnership interest does not become a partner (unless all the other partners consent), and has no right to get information about the partnership or to inspect the partnership books. As long as the partnership continues in existence, however, the assignee of a partnership interest does have a right to receive the distributions to which the assigning partner would otherwise be entitled, and on dissolution the assignee has a right to receive the assigning partner's financial interest. In practice, despite the limitations on the assignor's rights, partnership interests have a fairly high degree of assignability. *See* A. Bromberg, Enforcement of Partnership Obligations—Who is Sued for The Partnership?, 71 Neb. L. Rev. 143, 240 (1992).

A partner who has assigned her partnership interest remains a partner. However, RUPA § 601(4)(ii) explicitly permits the nonassigning partners to expel the assignor from the partnership, and UPA § 31(c) permits the nonassigning partners to dissolve the partnership as of right even if the partnership is not at will.

   3.   *Partnership Creditors Under UPA.* A partner's separate creditor (that is a creditor who has extended credit to a partner as an individual, rather than extending credit to the partnership) is in a position somewhat comparable to the assignee of a partnership interest. Under UPA § 28, if such a creditor obtains a judgment, he can get a *charging order* on the partner's partnership interest. Such an order effectively gives the creditor the right to be paid the partnership distributions to which the partner-debtor would be otherwise entitled. Moreover, the creditor can foreclose on the partnership interest, and thereby cause its sale. In that case, the buyer of the interest has the right to compel dissolution if the partnership is at will or the term of the partnership has expired. Alternatively, the creditor may put the individual partner into bankruptcy, which will result in dissolution of the partnership under UPA § 31(5).

   4.   *Partnership Creditors Under RUPA.* RUPA § 504 continues UPA § 28 largely unchanged in substance. RUPA § 504 does add some details that are not found in UPA § 28, but for the most part these details are consistent with the case law under § 28. Like the UPA, RUPA § 801(a) provides that a transferee of a partner's transferable interest is entitled to judicial dissolution of the partnership if the partnership is at will, or after the expiration of the partnership's term, or, in a partnership for a particular undertaking, after the completion of the undertaking.

   5.   *Priorities Under UPA.* A major problem in partnership law concerns the relative priorities of creditors of the partnership (partnership creditors) and creditors of a partner in the partner's individual capacity (separate creditors). UPA § 40(h) provides that as to partnership assets, partnership creditors have priority over separate creditors, and as to the partner's individual assets, separate creditors have priority over partnership creditors. *See* also UPA § 36(4). This rule, which was also in the Bankruptcy Act prior to 1978, is known as the *dual priorities* or *jingle* rule. The rule was widely criticized on the ground that it kept partnership creditors from getting the full benefit of the personal liability of the individual partners. The Bankruptcy Reform Act of 1978 responded to that criticism. Under Chapter 7 of the revised Bankruptcy Code, in a partnership bankruptcy, as to partnership assets the partnership creditors have priority over separate creditors. If debts to partnership creditors remain unpaid after the partnership assets are exhausted, partnership creditors are put on a parity with separate creditors in dividing up the partner's individual assets. 11 U.S.C. § 723(c). In the usual case the Bankruptcy Code preempts the UPA's jingle rule.

   6.   *Priorities Under RUPA.* To reflect the abolition of the jingle rule in the Bankruptcy Code RUPA drops the dual-properties rule of the UPA.

———

7. THE PARTNER'S DUTY OF LOYALTY

UNIFORM PARTNERSHIP ACT § 21

[See Statutory Supplement]

REVISED UNIFORM PARTNERSHIP ACT
§§ 105(c)(6)(8)(d), 409

[See Statutory Supplement]

Meinhard v. Salmon

New York Court of Appeals, 1928.
249 N.Y. 458, 164 N.E. 545.

Appeal from a judgment of the Appellate Division of the Supreme Court in the first judicial department, entered June 28, 1928, modifying and affirming as modified a judgment in favor of plaintiff entered upon the report of a referee.

■ CARDOZO, CH. J. On April 10, 1902, Louisa M. Gerry leased to the defendant Walter J. Salmon the premises known as the Hotel Bristol at the northwest corner of Forty-second street and Fifth avenue in the city of New York. The lease was for a term of twenty years, commencing May 1, 1902, and ending April 30, 1922. The lessee undertook to change the hotel building for use as shops and offices at a cost of $200,000. Alterations and additions were to be accretions to the land.

Salmon, while in course of treaty with the lessor as to the execution of the lease, was in course of treaty with Meinhard, the plaintiff, for the necessary funds. The result was a joint venture with terms embodied in a writing. Meinhard was to pay to Salmon half of the moneys requisite to reconstruct, alter, manage and operate the property. Salmon was to pay to Meinhard 40 per cent of the net profits for the first five years of the lease and 50 per cent for the years thereafter. If there were losses, each party was to bear them equally. Salmon, however, was to have sole power to "manage, lease, underlet and operate" the building. There were to be certain pre-emptive rights for each in the contingency of death.

The two were coadventurers, subject to fiduciary duties akin to those of partners (King v. Barnes, 109 N.Y. 267). As to this we are all agreed. The heavier weight of duty rested, however, upon Salmon. He was a coadventurer with Meinhard, but he was manager as well. During the early years of the enterprise, the building, reconstructed, was operated at a loss. If the relation had then ended, Meinhard as well as Salmon would have carried a heavy burden. Later the profits became large with the result that for each of the investors there came a rich return. For each, the venture had its phases of fair weather and of foul. The two were in it jointly, for better or for worse.

When the lease was near its end, Elbridge T. Gerry had become the owner of the reversion. He owned much other property in the neighborhood, one lot adjoining the Bristol Building on Fifth Avenue and four lots on Forty-Second Street. He had a plan to lease the entire tract for a long term to someone who would destroy the buildings then existing, and put up another in their place. In the latter part of 1921, he submitted such a project to several capitalists and dealers. He was unable to carry it through with any of them. Then, in January, 1922, with less than four months of the lease to run, he approached the defendant Salmon. The result was a new lease to the Midpoint Realty Company, which is owned and controlled by Salmon, a lease covering the whole tract, and involving a huge outlay. The term is to be twenty years, but successive covenants for renewal will extend it to a maximum of eighty years at the will of either party. The existing buildings may remain unchanged for seven years. They are then to be torn down, and a new building to cost $3,000,000 is to be placed upon the site. The rental, which under the Bristol lease was only $55,000, is to be from $350,000 to $475,000 for the properties so combined. Salmon personally guaranteed the performance by the lessee of the covenants of the new lease until such time as the new building had been completed and fully paid for.

The lease between Gerry and the Midpoint Realty Company was signed and delivered on January 25, 1922. Salmon had not told Meinhard anything about it. Whatever his motive may have been, he had kept the negotiations to himself. Meinhard was not informed even of the bare existence of a project. The first that he knew of it was in February when the lease was an accomplished fact. He then made demand on the defendants that the lease be held in trust as an asset of the venture, making offer upon the trial to share the personal obligations incidental to the guaranty. The demand was followed by refusal, and later by this suit. A referee gave judgment for the plaintiff, limiting the plaintiff's interest in the lease, however, to 25 per cent. The limitation was on the theory that the plaintiff's equity was to be restricted to one-half of so much of the value of the lease as was contributed or represented by the occupation of the Bristol site. Upon cross-appeals to the Appellate Division, the judgment was modified so as to enlarge the equitable interest to one-half of the whole lease. With this enlargement of plaintiff's interest, there went, of course, a corresponding enlargement of his attendant obligations. The case is now here on an appeal by the defendants.

Joint adventurers, like copartners, owe to one another, while the enterprise continues, the duty of the finest loyalty. Many forms of conduct permissible in a workaday world for those acting at arm's length, are forbidden to those bound by fiduciary ties. A trustee is held to something stricter than the morals of the market place. Not honesty alone, but the punctilio of an honor the most sensitive, is then the standard of behavior. As to this there has developed a tradition that is unbending and inveterate. Uncompromising rigidity has been the attitude of courts of equity when petitioned to undermine the rule of undivided loyalty by the "disintegrating erosion" of particular exceptions (Wendt v. Fischer, 243 N.Y. 439, 444). Only thus has the level of conduct for fiduciaries been kept at a level higher than that trodden by the crowd. It will not consciously be lowered by any judgment of this court.

The owner of the reversion, Mr. Gerry, had vainly striven to find a tenant who would favor his ambitious scheme of demolition and construction. Baffled in the search, he turned to the defendant Salmon in possession of the Bristol, the keystone of the project. He figured to himself beyond a doubt that the man in possession would prove a likely customer. To the eye of an observer, Salmon held the lease as owner in his own right, for himself and no one else. In fact he held it as a fiduciary, for himself and another, sharers in a common venture. If this fact had been proclaimed, if the lease by its terms had run in favor of a partnership, Mr. Gerry, we may fairly assume, would have laid before the partners, and not merely before one of them, his plan of reconstruction. The pre-emptive privilege, or, better, the pre-emptive opportunity, that was thus an incident of the enterprise, Salmon appropriated to himself in secrecy and silence. He might have warned Meinhard that the plan had been submitted, and that either would be free to compete for the award. If he had done this, we do not need to say whether he would have been under a duty, if successful in the competition, to hold the lease so acquired for the benefit of a venture then about to end, and thus prolong by indirection its responsibilities and duties. The trouble about his conduct is that he excluded his coadventurer from any chance to compete, from any chance to enjoy the opportunity for benefit that had come to him alone by virtue of his agency. This chance, if nothing more, he was under a duty to concede. The price of its denial is an extension of the trust at the option and for the benefit of the one whom he excluded.

No answer is it to say that the chance would have been of little value even if seasonably offered. Such a calculus of probabilities is beyond the science of the chancery. Salmon, the real estate operator, might have been preferred to Meinhard, the woolen merchant. On the other hand, Meinhard might have offered better terms, or reinforced his offer by alliance with the wealth of others. Perhaps he might even have persuaded the lessor to renew the Bristol lease alone, postponing for a time, in return for higher rentals, the improvement of adjoining lots. We know that even under the lease as made the time for the enlargement of the building was delayed for seven years. All these opportunities were cut away from him through another's intervention. He knew that Salmon was the manager. As the time drew near for the expiration of the lease, he would naturally assume from silence, if from nothing else, that the lessor was willing to extend it for a term of years, or at least to let it stand as a lease from year to year. Not impossibly the lessor would have done so, whatever his protestations of unwillingness, if Salmon had not given assent to a project more attractive. At all events, notice of termination, even if not necessary, might seem, not unreasonably, to be something to be looked for, if the business was over and another tenant was to enter. In the absence of such notice, the matter of an extension was one that would naturally be attended to by the manager of the enterprise, and not neglected altogether. At least, there was nothing in the situation to give warning to any one that while the lease was still in being, there had come to the manager an offer of extension which he had locked within his breast to be utilized by himself alone. The very fact that Salmon was in control with exclusive powers of direction charged him the more obviously with the duty of disclosure, since only through disclosure could opportunity be equalized. If he might cut off renewal by a purchase for his own benefit when four months were to pass before the lease would have an end, he might do so with equal right while there remained as many years (cf. Mitchell v. Reed, 61 N.Y. 123, 127). He might steal a march on his comrade under cover of the darkness, and then hold the captured ground. Loyalty and comradeship are not so easily abjured. . . .

We have no thought to hold that Salmon was guilty of a conscious purpose to defraud. Very likely he assumed in all good faith that with the approaching end of the venture he might ignore his coadventurer and take the extension for himself. He had given to the enterprise time and labor as well as money. He had made it a success. Meinhard, who had given money, but neither time nor labor, had already been richly paid. There might seem to be something grasping in his insistence upon more. Such recriminations are not unusual when coadventurers fall out. They are not without their force if conduct is to be judged by the common standards of competitors. That is not to say that they have pertinency here. Salmon had put himself in a position in which thought of self was to be renounced, however hard the abnegation. He was much more than a coadventurer. He was a managing coadventurer (Clegg v. Edmondson, 8 D.M. & G. 787, 807). For him and for those like him, the rule of undivided loyalty is relentless and supreme (Wendt v. Fischer, supra; Munson v. Syracuse, etc., R.R. Co., 103 N.Y. 58, 74). A different question would be here if there were lacking any nexus of relation between the business conducted by the manager and the opportunity brought to him as an incident of management (Dean v. MacDowell, 8 Ch.D. 345, 354; Aas v. Benham, 1891, 2 Ch. 244, 258; Latta v. Kilbourn, 150 U.S. 524). For this problem, as for most, there are distinctions of degree. If Salmon had received from Gerry a proposition to lease a building at a location far removed, he might have held for himself the privilege thus acquired, or so we shall assume. Here the subject-matter of the new lease was an extension and enlargement of the subject-matter of the old one. A managing coadventurer appropriating the benefit of such a lease without warning to his partner might fairly expect to be reproached with conduct that was underhand, or lacking, to say the least, in reasonable candor, if the partner were to surprise him in the act of signing the new instrument. Conduct subject to that reproach does not receive from equity a healing benediction.

A question remains as to the form and extent of the equitable interest to be allotted to the plaintiff. The trust as declared has been held to attach to the lease which was in the name of the defendant corporation. We think it ought to attach at the option of the defendant Salmon to the shares of stock which were owned by him or were under his control. The difference may be important if the lessee shall wish to execute an assignment of the lease, as it ought to be free to do with the consent of the lessor. On the other hand, an equal division of the shares might lead to other hardships. It might take away from Salmon the power of control and management which under the plan of the joint venture he was to have from first to last. The number of shares to be allotted to the plaintiff should, therefore, be reduced to such an extent as may be necessary to preserve to the defendant Salmon the expected measure of dominion. To that end an extra share should be added to his half.

Subject to this adjustment, we agree with the Appellate Division that the plaintiff's equitable interest is to be measured by the value of half of the entire lease, and not merely by half of some undivided part. A single building covers the whole area. Physical division is impracticable along the lines of the Bristol site, the keystone of the whole. Division of interests and burdens is equally impracticable. Salmon, as tenant under the new lease, or as guarantor of the performance of the tenant's obligations, might well protest if Meinhard, claiming an equitable interest, had offered to assume a liability not equal to Salmon's, but only half as great. He might justly insist that the lease must be accepted by his coadventurer in such form as it had been given, and not constructively divided into imaginary fragments. What must be yielded to the one may be demanded by the other. The lease as it has been executed is single and entire. If confusion has resulted from the union of adjoining parcels, the trustee who consented to the union must bear the inconvenience (Hart v. Ten Eyck, 2 Johns. Ch. 62). . . .

[Three judges dissented. Andrews, J., who wrote the dissenting opinion, agreed that "(w)ere this a general partnership I should have little doubt as to the correctness of this result assuming the new lease to be an offshoot of the old," but concluded that the parties' joint venture "had in view a very limited object and was to end at a limited time."]

———

Enea v. Superior Court

Court of Appeal of California, Sixth District, 2005.
34 Cal.Rptr.3d 513.

■ RUSHING, P.J.

Plaintiff Benny Enea brought this petition to set aside an order of respondent court summarily adjudicating [in defendant's favor] his cause of action against his former partners, defendants William Daniels and Claudia Daniels, for breaches of fiduciary duties consisting primarily of renting partnership property to themselves at less than its fair market value. . . .

BACKGROUND

For purposes of this analysis we largely accept the historical background recited in defendants' opposition to the petition. . . . Defendants state that in 1980, they and other family members formed a general partnership known as 3-D. The partnership's sole asset was a building that had been converted from a residence into offices. Some portion of the property—apparently the greater part—has been rented since 1981 on a month-to-month basis by a law practice of which William Daniels is apparently the sole member. From time to time the property was rented on similar arrangements to others, including defendant Claudia Daniels. Plaintiff's counsel stipulated in the court below that "the partnership agreement has as its principal purpose the ownership, leasing and sale of the only partnership assets, which is the building. . . . "

In 1993, plaintiff, a client of William Daniels, purchased a one-third interest in the partnership from the latter's brother, John P. Daniels. Plaintiff testified in deposition that he sought to profit from this investment either by sale at some point to a third party, or by defendants' "just buying [him] out." In 2001, however, plaintiff questioned William Daniels about the rents being paid for the property. According to the trial court's order granting summary adjudication, their relationship " 'began to unravel' and in 2003, Plaintiff was 'dissociated' from the partnership."

On August 6, 2003, plaintiff brought this action "to determine partner's buyout price and for damages." In his second cause of action, he alleged that . . . [he] was informed and believed they [defendants] had in fact been paying significantly less than fair rental value, "in breach of their fiduciary duty to plaintiff." . . .

Defendants moved to summarily adjudicate the second cause of action on the ground, among others, that they owed no fiduciary duty to plaintiff to pay fair market rent. As an "undisputed" fact in support of the motion, defendants asserted that they "did not have a fiduciary duty to pay fair market value rent for occupancy of" the building. The "supporting evidence" cited for this assertion was "Corporations Code Section 16404(b) and (c)." . . .

DISCUSSION . . .

. . . [This] case presents a very simple set of facts and issues. For present purposes it must be assumed that defendants in fact leased the property to themselves, or associated entities, at below-market rents. Defendants made no attempt to establish otherwise, let alone to establish the absence of triable issues of fact on the point. (See Code Civ. Proc., § 437c, subd. (c).) Therefore the sole question presented is whether defendants were categorically entitled to lease partnership property to themselves, or associated entities (or for that matter, to anyone) at less than it could yield in the open market. Remarkably, we have found no case squarely addressing this precise question. We are satisfied, however, that the answer is a resounding "No."

. . . "Partnership is a fiduciary relationship, and partners may not take advantages for themselves at the expense of the partnership." (*Jones v. Wells Fargo Bank* (2003) 112 Cal.App.4th 1527, 1540, 5 Cal.Rptr.3d 835; see *Jones v. H.F. Ahmanson & Co.* (1969) 1 Cal.3d 93, 108, 111, 81 Cal.Rptr. 592, 460 P.2d 464.)

Here the facts as assumed by the parties and the trial court plainly depict defendants taking advantages for themselves from partnership property *at the expense of the partnership*. The advantage consisted of occupying partnership property at below-market rates, i.e., less than they would be required to pay to an independent landlord for equivalent premises. The cost to the partnership was the additional rent thereby rendered unavailable for collection from an independent tenant willing to pay the property's value.

Defendants' objections to this reasoning ring hollow. Their main argument appears to be that their conduct was authorized by Corporations Code section 16404 (section 16404), which codifies the fiduciary duties of a partner under California law. The implication of such an argument is that section 16404 provides the *exclusive* statement of a partner's obligation to the partnership and to other partners. This premise would be correct if California had adopted, in its proposed form, the uniform law on which section 16404 is based. Section 404 of the Uniform Partnership Act (1997 rev.), also known as the Revised Uniform Partnership Act or RUPA, contains an explicitly exclusive enumeration of a partner's duties. After noting that a partner owes fiduciary duties of loyalty and care, the uniform Act declares that those duties are "limited to" obligations listed there. (RUPA § 404(b), (c).) While section 16404 retains this language with respect to the duty of care, it repudiates it with respect to the duty of loyalty, stating instead that ". . . [a] partner's duty of loyalty to the partnership and the other partners *includes* all of the following: . . . " (Italics added.)

The leading treatise on RUPA confirms that by altering the proposed language, the California Legislature rejected one of the "fundamental" changes the drafters sought to bring to partnership law, i.e., "an exclusive statutory treatment of partners' fiduciary duties." (Hillman et al., The Revised Uniform Partnership Act (2004 ed.), p. 202 (Hillman et al.).) The proposed uniform version "[b]y its terms . . . comprises an exclusive statement of the fiduciary duties of partners among themselves and to the partnership. The formulation is exclusive in two ways; the duties of loyalty and care are the only components of the partners' fiduciary duties, and the duties themselves are exclusively defined." (*Ibid.,* fns. omitted.) But several states, *most clearly California,* balked at the latter restriction, leaving the articulation of the duty of loyalty to traditional common law processes. . . .

Further, even if the statutory enumeration of duties were exclusive it would not entitle defendants to rent partnership property to themselves at below-market rates. The first duty listed in the statute is "[t]o account to the partnership and hold as trustee for it *any property, profit, or benefit* derived by the partner in the conduct . . . of the partnership business or *derived from a use by the partner of partnership property. . . .* " (Corp.Code, § 16404, subd. (b)(1); see *id.,* § 16401, subd. (g) ["A partner may use or possess partnership property only on behalf of the partnership"]; see RUPA, §. . . 401[(i)].)

Defendants persuaded the trial court that the conduct challenged by plaintiff was authorized by section 16404, subdivision (e), which states, "A partner does not violate a duty or obligation under this chapter or under the partnership agreement merely because the partner's conduct furthers the partner's own interest." The apparent purpose of this provision, which is drawn verbatim from RUPA section 404(e), is to excuse partners from accounting for incidental benefits obtained in the course of partnership activities *without detriment to the partnership.* It does not by its terms authorize the kind of conduct at issue here, which did not "merely" further defendants' own interests but did so by depriving the partnership of valuable assets, i.e., the space which would otherwise have been rented at market rates. Here, the statute entitled defendants to lease partnership property *at the same rent another tenant would have paid.* It did not empower them to occupy partnership property for their own exclusive benefit at partnership expense, in effect converting partnership assets to their own and appropriating the value it would otherwise have realized as distributable profits. Defendants' argument to the contrary seems conceptually indistinguishable from a claim that if a partnership's "primary purpose" is to purchase and hold investments, individual partners may freely pilfer its office supplies.

Defendants also persuaded the trial court that they had no duty to collect market rents in the absence of a contract expressly requiring them to do so. This argument turns partnership law on its head. Nowhere does the law declare that partners owe each other only those duties they explicitly assume by contract. On the contrary, the fiduciary duties at issue here are *imposed by law,* and their breach sounds in tort. . . . We have no occasion here to consider the extent to which partners might effectively limit or modify those delictual duties by an explicit agreement or whether the partnership agreement in fact required market rents by its terms. There is no suggestion that it purported to affirmatively *excuse* defendants from the delictual duty not to engage in self-dealing. Instead, their argument is predicated on the wholly untenable notion that they were entitled to do so unless the agreement explicitly declared otherwise.

Defendants also assert, and the trial court found, that the "primary purpose" of the partnership was to hold the building for appreciation and eventual sale. This premise hardly justified summary adjudication. If the partners had explicitly agreed *not* to derive market rents from the property, but to let it be used for the exclusive advantage of some of them indefinitely, there would be some basis to contend that defendants were entitled to conduct themselves as they did—or at least that plaintiff was estopped to complain. But the mere anticipation of eventual capital gains as the main economic benefit to be derived from the venture has no tendency whatsoever to entitle individual partners to divert to their own advantage benefits that would otherwise flow to the partnership.

While this observation is sufficient to dispose of the point, we cannot help but note indications in the record that the falling-out between plaintiff and defendants apparently arose not only because William Daniels insisted on paying rents lower than plaintiff thought were proper, but also because he refused to sell the property until he was ready to retire from his law practice. Proof of such a dispute would highlight a direct conflict arising quite foreseeably from defendants' self-dealing. As emphasized by defendants, plaintiff testified in deposition that "he was 'looking to make a profit on the deal' either upon the sale of the Property at some point in time *or by [defendants] 'just buying [him] out.'* " (Italics added.) It is difficult to see why defendants would be in any hurry to buy plaintiff out so long as they could enjoy the property at a discounted rent. Presumably, they profited from the property every day this situation persisted, while plaintiff was deprived of any benefit whatsoever until it suited defendants to sell. By then, of course, they would have received months or years of direct financial advantage for which, according to them, they had no obligation to account to plaintiff or the partnership. This situation put them in direct conflict with both the partnership and plaintiff *even in terms of the "primary purpose"* they so emphatically claim for the partnership. . . .

DISPOSITION

Let a peremptory writ of mandate issue directing respondent court to vacate its order granting defendants' motion for summary adjudication of plaintiff's second cause of action, and to enter a new order denying said motion. . . .

■ MIHARA AND MCADAMS, JJ., concur.

———

Robert W. Hillman, Donald J. Weidner & Allan G. Donn, The Revised Uniform Partnership Act § 404, at 381–386

2017–2018 ed.

Approval of Partner Self-Interest. The first statutory clarification . . . [of a partner's fiduciary obligation under RUPA] is potentially one of the most powerful changes in partnership law under R.U.P.A. It is embodied in Section 404(e): 'A partner does not violate a duty or obligation under this [Act] or under the partnership agreement merely because the partner's conduct furthers the partner's own interest.' The provision is new, it has no parallel in the U.P.A.

What does Section 404(e) mean? There are two different interpretations of the new section, one that is narrow and the other broad.

Under the narrow interpretation, Section 404(e) is essentially an evidentiary rule that could be paraphrased as 'the fact that a partner directly personally benefits from the partner's conduct in the partnership context does not, without more, establish a violation of the partner's duties or obligations under RUPA or the partnership agreement.'

Under the broad interpretation, Section 404(e) means that partners are free to pursue their short-term, individual self-interest without notice to or the consent of the partnership, subject only to the specific restrictions contained in the Section 404(b) duty of loyalty—in effect that the pursuit of self-interest cannot be a violation of the non-fiduciary obligation of good faith and fair dealing.

According to Official Comments 5a, a partner as such is not a trustee and is not held to the same standards as a trustee and subsection (e) makes clear that a partner's conduct is not deemed to be improper merely because it serves the partner's own individual interest. The Comment further states that the subsection "underscores the partner's rights as an owner and principal in the enterprise, which must always be balanced against his duties and obligations as an agent and fiduciary."

According to the RUPA Reporter, "The drafters of RUPA wanted statutory statement of the pursuit of self-interest that is legitimate under current case law." The principle reflects the policy judgment that overly broad statements of fiduciary duty tend to invite costly and wasteful litigation and threats of litigation.[176]

Careful examination of the development of the language that eventually became Section 404(e), and consideration of the academic literature from which the drafters took direction, seem to favor the broader reading.

---

[176] Weidner, Cadwalader, RUPA and Fiduciary Duty, 54 Wash.&Lee L. Rev. 877, 905–06 (1997).

―――――

NOTES ON SUITS BY A PARTNER AGAINST A PARTNERSHIP

1. *UPA and Intramural Litigation.* One method by which a partner can vindicate her rights against other partners is by a suit for an accounting. UPA § 22 provides a right to an accounting when a partner is wrongfully excluded from the business (§ 22(a)), or when the right to an accounting is granted under the partnership agreement (§ 22(b)), or in a suit to account for appropriation of an unauthorized benefit in violation of § 21 (§ 22(c)), or whenever other circumstances render it just and reasonable (§ 22(d)). However, "cases involving such actions are rare. An action for an accounting usually indicates that an atmosphere of mistrust exists in the partnership. In this situation, the easy dissolution permitted under the UPA will often be the appropriate course to follow, particularly if there is no uncompleted term or undertaking." Christine Hurt, A. Gordon Smith, Alan R. Bromberg & Larry E. Ribstein, Bromberg & Ribstein on Partnership § 6.08(b) (2d ed. 2018).

What about simply suing for the damages resulting from the alleged wrong, rather than suing for an accounting? UPA § 13 provides that "[w]here, by any wrongful conduct or omission of any partner acting in the ordinary course of business of the partnership or with the authority of his co-partners, loss or injury is caused to any person, *not being a partner in the partnership* . . . the partnership is liable therefor. . . . " (Emphasis added.) By reason of the italicized phrase, this section is commonly interpreted not to authorize a suit by a partner against a partnership. As a result, the courts have often limited a partner's remedies against the partnership to suits for either dissolution or an accounting. *See* Beckman v. Farmer, 579 A.2d 618, 649 (D.C.App.1990); Hubbard, Alternative Remedies in Minority Partners' Suits on Partnership Causes of Action, 39 Sw. L. J. 1022 (1986). In *Beckman,* the court justified the rule on the ground that "practical difficulties commend the settlement of accounts before an action at law between partners can be maintained. The value of partners' respective interests cannot be determined while accounts are in flux, but only after partnership liabilities are satisfied, all assets are marshalled, the partners' capital accounts adjusted, and the amount of any surplus ascertained." *Id.* at 649–50. This justification is unconvincing. It may be true that the complete settlement of partnership accounts is easier at the termination of the partnership, but a partner who wants to make a claim against the partnership is not asking for a complete settlement of accounts. Given the weak or nonexistent justification of the traditional rule, it is not surprising that the rule is subject to several exceptions. "[For example, an accounting in] equity may not be necessary when breach of the partnership agreement, wrongful dissolution, fraudulent breach of trust, or misappropriation of money clearly belonging to another partner is charged. . . . " *Beckman* at 650.

2. *RUPA.* RUPA § 305, which is the counterpart of UPA § 13, drops the phrase "not being a partner in the partnership." The Comment states that this change "is intended to permit a partner to sue the partnership on a

tort or other theory during the term of the partnership, rather than being limited to the remedies of dissolution and accounting."

---

8. DISSOLUTION (I): DISSOLUTION BY RIGHTFUL ELECTION

UNIFORM PARTNERSHIP ACT §§ 29, 30, 31(1), 38(1), 40

[See Statutory Supplement]

REVISED UNIFORM PARTNERSHIP ACT §§ 601, 602, 603, 701, 801, 802, 804, 807

[See Statutory Supplement]

Girard Bank v. Haley

460 Pa. 237, 332 A.2d 443 (1975)

Mrs. Reid, a partner in an at-will UPA partnership, had sent the following letter to the other three partners: "I am terminating the partnership which the four of us entered into on the 28th day of September, 1958." The issue was whether this letter caused a dissolution of the partnership. The chancellor, at trial, held that it did not, because neither in the letter nor at trial did Mrs. Reid offer evidence to justify a termination of the partnership. Reversed.

In supposing that justification was necessary the learned court below fell into error. Dissolution of a partnership is caused, under § 31 of the [UPA], "by the express will of any partner." The expression of that will need not be supported by any justification. If no "definite term or particular undertaking [is] specified in the partnership agreement," such an at-will dissolution does not violate the agreement between the partners; indeed, an expression of a will to dissolve is effective as a dissolution even if in contravention of the agreement. Ibid. We have recognized the generality of a dissolution at will. If the dissolution results in breach of contract, the aggrieved partners may recover damages for the breach and, if they meet certain conditions, may continue the firm business for the duration of the agreed term or until the particular undertaking is completed. *See* § 38 of the Act. . . .

The remaining question is whether or not the unilateral dissolution made by Mrs. Reid violated the partnership agreement. The agreement contains no provision fixing a definite term, and the sole "undertaking" to which it refers is that of maintaining and leasing real property. This statement is merely one of general purpose, however, and cannot be said to set forth a "particular undertaking" within the meaning of that phrase as it is used in the Act. A "particular undertaking" under the statute must be capable of accomplishment at some time, although the exact time may be unknown and unascertainable at the date of the agreement. Leasing property, like many other trades or businesses, involves entering into a business relationship which may continue indefinitely; there is nothing "particular" about it. We thus conclude, on the record before us, that the dissolution of the partnership was not in contravention of the agreement.

———

Disotell v. Stiltner

100 P.3d 890 (Alaska 2004)

This case, decided under UPA, raised essentially the same issue as *Creel*, and the court came out the same way:

> In Dreifuerst v. Dreifuerst, cited by Disotell on appeal, the Wisconsin Court of Appeals, construing a statute identical to Alaska's, held that lawful dissolution gives each partner the right to force liquidation. [Dreifuerst v. Dreifuerst, 280 N.W.2d 335, 338 (App.1979).] Other courts have recognized that the winding up that follows partnership dissolution generally involves liquidation of the partnership assets. Indeed, the drafters' official comment on the uniform statute explains:

> The right given to each partner [by the statute], where no agreement has been made, to have his share of the surplus paid to him in cash makes certain an existing uncertainty. At present it is not certain whether a partner may or may not insist on a physical partition of the property remaining after third persons have been paid.

> Although the language of the Act and the general rule would seem to favor liquidation and cash distribution absent agreement to do otherwise, some courts construing statutes identical to section .330 have refused to compel liquidation. [Citing *Creel*, among other cases.]

> We decline to follow the line of cases holding that the statute requires liquidation. We hold that the superior court did not err in reading subsection .330(a) to allow it to permit Stiltner to buy out Disotell's partnership interest. Careful reading of the text of [Alaska Statutes] 32.05.330(a) does not convince us that this subsection absolutely compels liquidation

and forbids a buyout. Under appropriate, although perhaps limited, circumstances, a buyout seems a justifiable way of winding up a partnership. The superior court reasoned that a buyout would reduce economic waste by avoiding the cost of appointing a receiver and conducting a sale. Even though there was no ongoing business, the superior court noted that the expense of a sale could total as much as twelve percent of the property's value. This was a valid reason and potentially benefitted both partners. The potential savings were significant. The court's effort to avoid further loss to both partners justifies its decision to offer Stiltner the buyout option. Further, properly conducted, a buyout guaranteed Disotell a fair value for his partnership interest. Liquidation exposed Disotell to the risk that no buyer would offer to pay fair market value for the property. A liquidation sale in which no other buyers participated might have given Stiltner an opportunity to buy the property for less than fair market value, to Disotell's disadvantage.

———

McCormick v. Brevig

Supreme Court of Montana, 2004.
322 Mont. 112, 96 P.3d 697.

■ JIM RICE, JUSTICE

. . . [Joan McCormick and Clark Brevig, brother and sister, were equal partners in a ranching partnership.]

Disagreements concerning management of the ranch, and particularly, management of the debt load on the ranch, caused Clark and Joan's relationship to deteriorate. By the early 1990s, cooperation between Clark and Joan regarding the operation of the ranch and securing of loans necessary to fund the ranch had essentially ceased, and they began looking for ways to dissolve the Partnership.

In 1995, Joan brought suit against Clark and the Partnership, alleging that Clark had converted Partnership assets to his own personal use, and sought an accounting of the Partnership's affairs. She also requested a determination that Clark had engaged in conduct warranting a decree of expulsion. Alternatively, Joan sought an order dissolving and winding up the Partnership. . . .

. . . . On April 3, 2000, the District Court issued findings of fact and conclusions of law, finding that neither Clark nor Joan had dissociated from the Partnership, [and] that Joan was a 50 percent partner. . . . The court further concluded that the Partnership should be dissolved and its business wound up, and reasoned that appointment of a special master was appropriate in order to determine the amount of the parties' respective capital contributions and Partnership assets.

On February 7, 2001, following the appointment and discharge of the two previous masters, Larry Blakely, CPA ("Blakely") was appointed special master. . . .

On December 12, 2002, Blakely filed his final report with the court, . . . valuing Joan's interest in the Partnership at $795,629. Joan objected to Blakely's findings and a hearing followed. On January 29, 2003, the District Court entered findings of fact and conclusions of law, accepting Blakely's findings and valuing Joan's interest in the Partnership at $1,107,672. Clark thereafter tendered this amount to Joan for the purchase of her interest, which Joan rejected. This appeal followed. . . .

DISCUSSION

After ordering dissolution of the Partnership, did the District Court err by failing to order liquidation of the Partnership assets, and instead granting Clark the right to purchase Joan's Partnership interest at a price determined by the court?

Joan contends that when a partnership is dissolved by judicial decree, Montana's Revised Uniform Partnership Act, § 35–10–101 et seq., MCA (2001), requires liquidation by sale of partnership assets and distribution in cash of any surplus to the partners. In response, Clark asserts that there are other judicially acceptable methods of distributing partnership assets upon dissolution besides liquidating assets through a forced sale. For the reasons set forth below, we conclude that the Revised Uniform Partnership Act requires liquidation of partnership assets and distribution of the net surplus in cash to the partners upon dissolution entered by judicial decree when it is no longer reasonably practicable to carry on the business of the partnership. . . .

Partnership law in Montana and throughout the United States has been primarily derived from the Uniform Partnership Act ("UPA"), which was originally promulgated by the Uniform Law Commissioners in 1914. Under the UPA, the law of partnership breakups was couched in terms of dissolution. A partnership was dissolved and its assets liquidated upon the happening of specific events, the most significant of which was the death of a partner or any partner expressing a will to leave the partnership. Montana adopted the UPA in 1947.

In 1993, our legislature significantly amended the UPA by adopting the Revised Uniform Partnership Act, or RUPA.[1] Unlike the UPA, RUPA now provides two separate tracks for the exiting partner. The first track applies to the dissociating partner, and does not result in a dissolution, but in a buy-out of the dissociating partner's interest in the partnership. *See* § 35–10–616, MCA. The term "dissociation" is new to the act, and

---

[1]   Although the 1993 Legislature did not amend the title of the UPA, it adopted the changes embodied within the Revised Uniform Partnership Act ("RUPA") and, therefore, we shall refer to the act throughout this opinion as "RUPA."

occurs upon the happening of any one of ten events specified in § 35–10–616, MCA. Examples of events leading to dissociation include bankruptcy of a partner and death, *see* § 35–10–616(6)(a) and (7)(a), MCA, but does not include a judicially ordered dissolution of the partnership.

The second track for the exiting partner does involve dissolution and winding up of the partnership's affairs. Section 35–10–624, MCA, sets forth the events causing dissolution and winding up of a partnership, and includes the following:

> *Events causing dissolution and winding up of partnership business. . . .*
>
> (5)   a judicial decree, issued upon application by a partner, that:
>
> (a)   the economic purpose of the partnership is likely to be unreasonably frustrated;
>
> (b)   another partner has engaged in conduct relating to the partnership business that makes it not reasonably practicable to carry on the business in partnership with that partner; or
>
> (c)   it is not otherwise reasonably practicable to carry on the partnership business in conformity with the partnership agreement[.]

In this case, the District Court dissolved the Partnership pursuant to § 35–10–624(5), MCA. In so doing, it recognized that, in the absence of a partnership agreement to the contrary, the only possible result under RUPA was for the partnership assets to be liquidated and the proceeds distributed between the partners proportionately. The court reasoned, however, that the term "liquidate" had a variety of possible meanings, one of which was "to assemble and mobilize the assets, settle with the creditors and debtors and apportion the remaining assets, if any, among the stockholders or owners." Applying this definition, which the court had obtained from *Black's Law Dictionary*, the court concluded that a judicially ordered buy-out of Joan's interest in the Partnership by Clark was an acceptable alternative to liquidation of the partnership assets through a compelled sale. . . .

It is true that this Court has previously utilized dictionaries when seeking to define the common use and meaning of terms. *See* Ravalli County v. Erickson, 2004 MT 35, 13, 320 Mont. 31, 13, 85 P.3d 772, 13. However, in this case, we conclude that it was not necessary for the District Court to resort to such devices. Section 35–10–629(1), MCA, clearly provides that "[i]n winding up a partnership's business, the assets of the partnership must be applied to discharge its obligations to creditors, including partners who are creditors. Any surplus must be applied to pay *in cash* the net amount distributable to partners in accordance with their right to distributions pursuant to subsection (2)." (Emphasis added.) Furthermore, subsection (2) of the statute provides:

Each partner is entitled to a settlement of all partnership accounts upon winding up the partnership business. In settling accounts among the partners, the profits and losses that result from the *liquidation of the partnership assets* must be credited and charged to the partners' accounts. The partnership shall make a distribution to a partner in an amount equal to that partner's positive account balance.

(Emphasis added.) Thus, the common purpose and plain meaning of the term "liquidation," as it is used in § 35–10–629(2), MCA, is to reduce the partnership assets to cash, pay creditors, and distribute to partners the value of their respective interest. *See also* 59A Am.Jur.2d *Partnership* § 1100 (2003). This is all part of the process of "winding up" the business of a partnership and terminating its affairs.

Clark invites this Court to take a liberal reading of § 35–10–629, MCA, and cites Creel v. Lilly (1999), 729 A.2d 385 (1999), in support of the proposition that judicially acceptable alternatives exist to compelled liquidation in a dissolution situation. At issue in *Creel* was whether the surviving partners of a partnership had a duty to liquidate all partnership assets because there was no provision in the partnership agreement providing for the continuation of the partnership upon a partner's death, and the estate had not consented to the continuation of business. *Creel*, 729 A.2d at 387. After examining cases in which other courts had elected to order an in-kind distribution rather than a compelled liquidation, or had allowed the remaining partners to purchase the withdrawing partner's interest in the partnership, the court concluded that the UPA did not mandate a forced sale of all partnership assets in order to ascertain the true value of the business, and that "winding up" was not always synonymous with liquidation. *Creel*, 729 A.2d at 403. The court further noted that it would have reached the same conclusion regardless of whether the UPA or RUPA governed since, under RUPA, the remaining partners could have elected to continue business following the death of one of the partners. *Creel*, 729 A.2d at 397.

However, of critical distinction between the facts in *Creel* and the case *sub judice* is the manner in which the partners exited the entity. In *Creel* one of the partners had died. Here, Joan sought a court ordered dissolution of the Partnership. Under RUPA, the death of a partner triggers the provisions of § 35–10–619, MCA, which allows for the purchase of the dissociated partner's interest in the partnership, much like what was ordered in *Creel*. Conversely, a court ordered dissolution pursuant to § 35–10–624(5), MCA, as in this case, results in the dissolution and winding up of the partnership. Thus, *Creel* is both legally and factually distinguishable.

Furthermore, the cases relied upon by the court in *Creel* in reaching its conclusion that liquidation of assets was not always mandated upon dissolution, Nicholes v. Hunt (1975), 541 P.2d 820 (Or. 1975), Logoluso v.

Logoluso (1965), 233 Cal.App.2d 523, 43 Cal.Rptr. 678, Gregg v. Bernards (1968), 443 P.2d 166, Goergen v. Nebrich (1958), 174 N.Y.S.2d 366 (Misc. 2d 1958), and Fortugno v. Hudson Manure Co. (1958), 144 A.2d 207 (N.J. Super. 1958), are likewise pre-RUPA holdings, which are inapposite to the facts at issue in this case.

Accordingly, we conclude that when a partnership's dissolution is court ordered pursuant to § 35–10–624(5), MCA, the partnership assets necessarily must be reduced to cash in order to satisfy the obligations of the partnership and distribute any net surplus in cash to the remaining partners in accordance with their respective interests. By adopting a judicially created alternative to this statutorily mandated requirement, the District Court erred. . . .

Affirmed in part, reversed in part, and remanded for further proceedings consistent with this opinion.

————

NOTES ON DISTRIBUTIONS IN DISSOLUTION AND "SERVICES PARTNERS"

1. UPA. UPA § 40(b) sets out the rules for the distribution of assets after a partnership is dissolved. The priorities for distribution, in order, are as follows: (1) Paying off creditors other than partners. (2) Paying off partners for obligations to the partners other than obligations for capital or profits (for example, a loan that a partner made to the partnership). (3) Paying off partners in respect of capital. (4) Paying off partners in respect of profits. All these priorities, even those in respect of partnership capital and profits, are defined as "liabilities"—an unusual meaning of that term, which normally refers to debts, not to ownership or equity claims.

Under UPA § 40(d), the partners must contribute the amount necessary to satisfy liabilities as provided in § 18(a). Section 18(a), in turn, provides that each partner shall contribute toward the losses sustained by the partnership, according to his share in the profits. "Losses" in § 18(a) is defined, like "liabilities" in § 40(b), to include losses to capital.

2. RUPA. RUPA § 401(j) continues the rule of UPA § 18. The Comment supporting the predecessor of the 2013 RUPA made clear that the rule is intended to apply in the capital-loss context, and provides the following justification for applying the rule to the detriment of services partners:

> The default rules [of § 401(h)] apply, as does UPA Section 18(a), where one or more of the partners contribute no capital, although there is case law to the contrary. *See, e.g.,* Kovacik v. Reed, 315 P.2d 314 (Cal.2d 1957); Becker v. Killarney, 532 N.E.2d 931 (Ill.App.3d 1988). It may seem unfair that the contributor of services, who contributes little or no capital, should be obligated to contribute toward the capital loss of the large contributor who contributed no services. In entering a partnership with such a

capital structure, the partners should foresee that application of the default rule may bring about unusual results and take advantage of their power to vary by agreement the allocation of capital losses.

Comment to § 401(h) RUPA (1997).

This attempt at justification does more to show why RUPA § 401(j) is wrong than why it is right. The Comment begins by frankly recognizing that the result "may seem unfair." It then states that even if the rule is unfair the partners can contract around it. Of course, any rule of partnership law, no matter how unsound, could be "justified" by the argument that it can be contracted around. The point of partnership law, however, should be to make rules that the partners probably would have agreed to if they had addressed the issue, not to make bad rules that the partners can contract around. Furthermore, many partners don't know partnership law, and therefore won't realize they need to contract around any given rule. Indeed, because persons can be partners without having an intention to form a partnership, many partners don't even realize that they are partners, let alone realize that they should consider contracting around any given rule of partnership law.

––––––––

NOTE ON JOINT VENTURES

As pointed out in the previous Note, some courts have held that a services partner need not contribute toward a capital loss where the enterprise is a "joint venture" rather than a partnership. The line between a joint venture and a partnership is exceedingly thin. "[M]ost courts have [distinguished] between isolated transactions and continuing enterprises by classifying the former as joint ventures." 1 Alan R. Bromberg & Larry Ribstein, Bromberg & Ribstein on Partnership § 2.06(a) (2011).

Some commentators take the position that joint ventures are generally governed by partnership law. *See, e.g., id.* at 192 ("Whether a [joint venture] is considered a partnership or merely analogized to one, the venturers are governed by the rules applicable to partners"); Comment, The Joint Venture: Problem Child of Partnership, 38 Calif. L. Rev. 860 (1950). In contrast, other commentators argue that joint ventures are a separate form and therefore not entirely subject to partnership rules. *See, e.g.,* Jaeger, Partnership or Joint Venture?, 37 Notre Dame L. Rev. 138 (1961). The same split is found in the cases. Some cases suggest that it makes no legal difference whether an enterprise is characterized as a partnership or a joint venture, while others suggest that special rules apply to joint ventures.

As a realistic matter, what seems to be involved is this: Some rules of the UPA, such as Section 18(a), produce unsatisfactory results in certain kinds of cases. Courts that want to avoid these results will sometimes do so, if they plausibly can, by holding that a "special rule" applies to joint ventures, and that the enterprise in the case at hand is a joint venture and therefore falls within the special rule. In many or most such cases, the desired result could probably be reached, without applying special rules to joint ventures, by finding that the parties had an implied agreement that overrides the relevant rule of the UPA.

Joint venture participants frequently are corporations that pool their resources toward a common project. Sarah Sanga, A Theory of Corporate Joint Ventures, 106 Cal. L. Rev. 1437, 1457 (2018), points out that such arrangements contain an inherent contradiction with respect to duties and obligations. Partnership law applies to joint ventures and in doing so carries forward the obligations of its members not to compete with the partnership. *See e.g.*, RUPA § 404(b)(3). On the other hand, as developed later in Section 15 of Chapter 3, corporations have obligations to their respective set of shareholders so that their manager's duty of loyalty calls for them to seek wealth increasing business opportunities that may be within the joint venture's sphere of interest. Professor Sanga points out that carefully crafted covenants not the compete (CNC) are the key feature to addressing the inherent conflicts joint venturers can otherwise face in meeting these differently focused duties of loyalty:

> CNCs organize the venture's opportunities by swapping the default loyalty standard for a bright-line loyalty rule. The result is that co-venturers can more readily distinguish partnership opportunities from those which are "fair game" for either co-venturer to seize. For any given opportunity, both sides can more confidently don the "partner's hat" or the "competitor's hat."

Page v. Page

Supreme Court of California, 1961.
55 Cal.2d 192, 10 Cal.Rptr. 643, 359 P.2d 41.

■ TRAYNOR, J.

Plaintiff and defendant are partners in a linen supply business in Santa Maria, California. Plaintiff appeals from a judgment declaring the partnership to be for a term rather than at will.

The partners entered into an oral partnership agreement in 1949. Within the first two years each partner contributed approximately $43,000 for the purchase of land, machinery, and linen needed to begin the business. From 1949 to 1957 the enterprise was unprofitable, losing approximately $62,000. The partnership's major creditor is a corporation, wholly owned by plaintiff, that supplies the linen and machinery necessary for the day-to-day operation of the business. This corporation holds a $47,000 demand note of the partnership. The partnership operations began to improve in 1958. The partnership earned $3,824.41 in that year and $2,282.30 in the first three months of 1959. Despite this improvement plaintiff wishes to terminate the partnership.

The Uniform Partnership Act provides that a partnership may be dissolved "By the express will of any partner when no definite term or particular undertaking is specified." (Corp.Code, § 15031, subd. (1)(b).) The trial court found that the partnership is for a term, namely, "such reasonable time as is necessary to enable said partnership to repay from partnership profits, indebtedness incurred for the purchase of land, buildings, laundry and delivery equipment and linen for the operation of such business. . . . " Plaintiff correctly contends that this finding is without support in the evidence.

Defendant testified that the terms of the partnership were to be similar to former partnerships of plaintiff and defendant, and that the understanding of these partnerships was that "we went into partnership to start the business and let the business operation pay for itself,—put in so much money, and let the business pay itself out." There was also testimony that one of the former partnership agreements provided in writing that the profits were to be retained until all obligations were paid. . . .

Viewing this evidence most [favorably] for defendant, it proves only that the partners expected to meet current expenses from current income and to recoup their investment if the business were successful.

Defendant contends that such an expectation is sufficient to create a partnership for a term under the rule of Owen v. Cohen, 19 Cal.2d 147, 150 [119 P.2d 713]. In that case. . . . the partners borrowed substantial amounts of money to launch the enterprise and there was an understanding that the loans would be repaid from partnership profits. . . . [T]he court properly held that the partners impliedly promised to continue the partnership for a term reasonably required to allow the partnership to earn sufficient money to accomplish the understood objective. . . .

In the instant case, however, defendant failed to prove any facts from which an agreement to continue the partnership for a term may be implied. The understanding to which defendant testified was no more than a common hope that the partnership earnings would pay for all the necessary expenses. Such a hope does not establish even by implication a "definite term or particular undertaking" as required by section 15031, subdivision (1)(b), of the Corporations Code.

All partnerships are ordinarily entered into with the hope that they will be profitable, but that alone does not make them all partnerships for a term and obligate the partners to continue in the partnerships until all of the losses over a period of many years have been recovered.

Defendant contends that plaintiff is acting in bad faith and is attempting to use his superior financial position to appropriate the now profitable business of the partnership. Defendant has invested $43,000 in the firm, and owing to the long period of losses his interest in the partnership assets is very small. The fact that plaintiff's wholly owned corporation holds a $47,000 demand note of the partnership may make it difficult to sell the business as a going concern. Defendant fears that upon dissolution he will receive very little and that plaintiff, who is the managing partner and knows how to conduct the operations of the partnership, will receive a business that has become very profitable because of the establishment of Vandenberg Air Force Base in its vicinity. Defendant charges that plaintiff has been content to share the losses but now that the business has become profitable he wishes to keep all the gains.

There is no showing in the record of bad faith or that the improved profit situation is more than temporary. In any event these contentions are irrelevant to the issue whether the partnership is for a term or at will. Since, however, this action is for a declaratory judgment and will be the basis for future action by the parties, it is appropriate to point out that defendant is amply protected by the fiduciary duties of copartners.

Even though the Uniform Partnership Act provides that a partnership at will may be dissolved by the express will of any partner (Corp.Code, § 15031, subd. (1)(b)), this power, like any other power held by a fiduciary, must be exercised in good faith.

We have often stated that "Partners are trustees for each other, and in all proceedings connected with the conduct of the partnership every partner is bound to act in the highest good faith to his copartner and may not obtain any advantage over him in the partnership affairs by the slightest misrepresentation, concealment, threat or adverse pressure of any kind." (Llewelyn v. Levi, 157 Cal. 31, 37 [106 P. 219]; Richards v. Fraser, 122 Cal. 456, 460 [55 P. 246]; Yeomans v. Lysfjord, 162 Cal.App.2d 357, 361–362 [327 P.2d 957]; cf. MacIsaac v. Pozzo, 26 Cal.2d 809, 813 [161 P.2d 449]; Corp.Code, § 15021.). . . .

A partner at will is not bound to remain in a partnership, regardless of whether the business is profitable or unprofitable. A partner may not, however, by use of adverse pressure "freeze out" a copartner and appropriate the business to his own use. A partner may not dissolve a partnership to gain the benefits of the business for himself, unless he fully compensates his copartner for his share of the prospective business opportunity. In this regard his fiduciary duties are at least as great as those of a shareholder of a corporation.

In the case of In re Security Finance Co., 49 Cal.2d 370, 376–377 [317 P.2d 1], we stated that although shareholders representing 50 per cent of the voting power have a right under Corporations Code, section 4600, to dissolve a corporation, they may not exercise such right in order "to defraud the other shareholders [citation], to 'freeze out' minority shareholders [citation], or to sell the assets of the dissolved corporation at an inadequate price. [Citation.]"

Likewise in the instant case, plaintiff has the power to dissolve the partnership by express notice to defendant. If, however, it is proved that plaintiff acted in bad faith and violated his fiduciary duties by attempting to appropriate to his own use the new prosperity of the partnership without adequate compensation to his copartner, the dissolution would be wrongful and the plaintiff would be liable as provided by subdivision (2)(a) of Corporations Code, section 15038 (rights of partners upon wrongful dissolution) for violation of the implied agreement not to exclude defendant wrongfully from the partnership business opportunity.*

The judgment is reversed.

————

NOTES ON PARTNERSHIP BREAKUP UNDER THE UPA

1.   Setting the Stage. One of the most difficult problems in partnership law is how to treat the issues that arise where a partnership breakup occurs because a person's status as a partner is terminated, because the partnership is terminated as a going concern, or both. (The difficulty of these issues is illustrated by the fact that the rules concerning these issues occupy about a third of the text and comment of RUPA.) The UPA and RUPA adopt different strategies toward both the underlying substantive issues and the relevant nomenclature. This Note will focus on partnership breakup under the UPA. A Note below will concern partnership breakup under RUPA.

Before getting directly into the legal issues, it is useful to outline the business economics involved.

Assume that a partnership is to be terminated as a going concern. Typically, the termination process will fall into three phases.

a).   The first phase consists of an event—which may be a decision by one or more partners or by a court—that sets the termination in motion. Under the UPA, this phase is referred to as *dissolution.*" The principal draftsman of the UPA explained the manner in which that statute uses the term "dissolution" as follows:

> [The term "dissolution" is used in the UPA to designate] a change in the relation of the partners caused by any partner ceasing to be associated in the carrying on of the business. As thus used "dissolution" does not terminate the partnership, it merely ends the carrying on of the business in that partnership. The partnership continues until the winding up of partnership affairs is completed.

Lewis, The Uniform Partnership Act, 24 Yale L.J. 617, 626–27 (1915).

b).   The second phase consists of the process of actually terminating the partnership's business. Inevitably, some period of time must elapse between the moment at which the event that sets in motion the termination of the business occurs and the moment at which the termination of the business is completed. For example, if a partnership is in the manufacturing business, to terminate the business the partnership will need to pay off its debts, settle

---

*   The consequences of wrongful dissolution are considered in Section 9, infra. [Footnote by ed.]

its contracts with employees and suppliers, find a purchaser for its factory, and so forth. Under the UPA this phrase is referred to as "winding up."

   c).   The final phase consists of the completion of the second phase and an end to the partnership as a going concern. Under the UPA this phase is referred to as "termination."

   To put all of this somewhat differently, the term "dissolution" is used in the UPA to describe a change in the *legal status* of the partners and the partnership. The term "winding-up" is used to describe the *economic* event of liquidation that follows dissolution.

   Under the UPA, any termination of a person's status as a partner effects a dissolution of the partnership, because UPA § 29 defines dissolution as "the change in the relation of partners caused by any partner ceasing to be associated in the carrying on" of the partnership's business. It's not easy to see why this should be so when, as often happens, the remaining partners rightfully carry on the partnership's business after one partner has departed. Basically, the UPA's treatment of this issue seems to have been driven by conceptualism. The UPA treats a partnership as an aggregate of persons to carry on business for profit as co-owners, rather than as an entity. Because the UPA treats a partnership as an aggregate, the drafters seemed to have believed that it followed logically that any change in the identity of the partners necessarily worked a dissolution of the partnership. If a partnership is conceptualized as an aggregate of the partners, and if the partners in Partnership P are A, B, C, and D, then it may have seemed to the drafters of the UPA that if D ceases to be a partner, Partnership P must be dissolved, because there is no longer an aggregate of A, B, C, and D. The law, however, should not be built on deductive logic, but on policy, morality, and experience. We make legal rules because they are desirable, not because they are deducible. If a person ceases to be a partner, the law can treat the partnership as either dissolved or not dissolved. Which course the law takes should depend on which treatment best protects the reasonable expectations of partners. This, in turn, depends on what consequences the law attaches to dissolution.

   Broadly speaking, dissolution may carry consequences among the partners; between the partners as a group and third persons such as individuals or firms with whom the partnership has contracted; and for tax purposes. The remainder of this Note will consider each of these areas.

   2.   Consequences Among the Partners. UPA § 38(2)(b) provides if a partner, *W*, wrongfully causes dissolution, although the partnership is dissolved, the remaining partners can continue the partnership's business. To do so, the remaining partners must either pay *W* the value of her partnership interest (but not including the value of the partnership's good will) minus any damages caused by the dissolution, or put up a bond to secure such a payment and indemnify *W* against present and future partnership liabilities.

   UPA § 38(1) provides that "[w]hen dissolution is [rightfully] caused . . . each partner . . . unless otherwise agreed, may have the partnership property applied to discharge its liabilities, and the surplus applied to pay in cash the net amount owing to the respective partners." It is well accepted that under the "unless" clause, the partnership agreement can provide that after the termination of a person's status as a partner (and therefore, under the UPA, after dissolution of the partnership) the remaining partners can continue the partnership *business*, even if the partnership has been dissolved and the dissolution is rightfully caused. *See, e.g.*, Meehan v. Shaughnessy, 535 N.E.2d 1255 (Mass. 1989); Adams v. Jarvis, 127 N.W.2d 400 (Wis.2d 1964). Agreements that enable remaining partners to continue the partnership's business after dissolution are common, especially in large partnerships. Such agreements are usually known as business-continuation agreements or, more simply, continuation agreements. Typically, continuation agreements include not only the right of the remaining partners to continue the partnership's business, but also the terms on which the partner who causes dissolution (or his estate) will be compensated for his partnership interest.

   3.   *Effect of Dissolution on the Relationship Between the Partnership and Third Parties.* As among the partners, it frequently won't matter very much whether the withdrawal of a partner does or does not cause dissolution, because as among the partners a continuation agreement can generally override the effects that dissolution would otherwise have. However, dissolution may affect the relationship of the partnership to third persons. For example, suppose that a partnership consisting of partners A, B, C, and D is dissolved by the withdrawal of D, but the business of the partnership is continued by A, B, and C under a continuation agreement. Under the UPA, because the partnership has been dissolved, the partnership of A, B, and C may be deemed a new partnership for legal purposes, so that the partnership's assets and agreements, such as leases, licenses, or franchises, must be transferred to the new partnership. *See* Report of the ABA Subcommittee on the Revision of the U.P.A., 43 Bus. Law. 121, 160–62 (1987). In a much remarked-on case, *Fairway Development Co. v. Title Insurance Co.*, 621 F.Supp. 120 (N.D.Ohio 1985), Fairway, a partnership, sued Title Insurance Co. under a title guarantee policy. The policy had been issued at a time when the partners in Fairway were B, S, and W. Subsequently, B and S transferred their partnership interests to W and a third party, X. W and X continued Fairway's business under the Fairway name. The court nevertheless held that Title Insurance Co. was not bound under its policy, because the partnership to which it had issued the policy had been legally dissolved.

   A debated point under the UPA is whether a partnership agreement can provide not only that the partnership business may be continued after dissolution, but also that the withdrawal of a partner will not cause dissolution, so that the partnership's relation with third parties will not be affected by a partner's withdrawal, as happened in the *Fairway* case. The prevailing (but not unanimous) answer is no, on the ground that UPA § 31 expressly states that "[d]issolution is caused" by the withdrawal of a partner.

———

NOTES ON PARTNERSHIP BREAKUP UNDER RUPA

RUPA's provisions on partnership breakup are even more complex than those of the UPA.

1. Nomenclature. To begin with nomenclature, RUPA continues to use the terms "dissolution," "winding up," and "termination." However, RUPA adds a new term, *dissociation,* to describe the termination of a person's status as a partner.

2. Events of Dissociation. Although the term "dissociation" is new, the concept is not. Even under the UPA, a variety of events result in the termination of a person's status as a partner, and there is a very substantial overlap between the UPA and RUPA concerning the description of those events. For example, RUPA § 602(a) continues the rule of the UPA that every partner has the right to withdraw (dissociate) from the partnership at any time, rightfully or wrongfully, by express will. RUPA § 602(c) provides that a partner who wrongfully dissociates is liable to the partnership and to the other partners for damages caused by the dissociation. Furthermore, if a partner wrongfully dissociates, the partnership can continue without him.

3. Rightful and Wrongful Dissociation. RUPA § 602 distinguishes between events of dissociation that involve rightful conduct by the dissociated partner and events of dissociation that involve wrongful conduct. An event of dissociation is rightful unless it is specified as wrongful in § 602(b). The major types of wrongful dissociation are: (i) A dissociation that is in breach of an express provision of the partnership agreement. (ii) A withdrawal of a partner by the partner's express will before the expiration of the partnership term or the completion of an undertaking for which the partnership was formed. (iii) A partner has engaged in wrongful conduct that adversely and materially affected the partnership business. (iv) A partner has willfully or persistently committed a material breach of the partnership agreement, or of a duty of care, loyalty, good faith, and fair dealing owed to the partnership or the other partners under § 404.

The Comment to RUPA § 602 states:

> [Under 602(a)] . . . a partner has the power to dissociate at any time by expressing a will to withdraw, even in contravention of the partnership agreement. The phrase "rightfully or wrongfully" reflects the distinction between a partner's *power* to withdraw in contravention of the partnership agreement and a partner's *right* to do so. . . . [Thus,] although a partner can not be enjoined from exercising the power to dissociate, the dissociation may be wrongful under subsection (b). . . .

> Subsection (b) . . . lists exhaustively ("only if") the dissociations that are "wrongful." The label has three consequences:

> Under Subsection (c) liability for resulting damages . . .

> Under Section 701(h) postponement of payment of the buyout price until the term expires or the undertaking is completed; and

Under Section 804, exclusion from the winding up process, if the dissociations results in dissolution of the partnership.

This subsection states a default rule. The partnership agreement can expand the list. . . . In theory, the partnership agreement can provide for liquidated damages (subject to the requirements of contract law) and, in theory, can also shrink or even eliminate the list of wrongful dissociations. . . .

4. *Consequences of Dissociation.* The partnership-breakup provisions of RUPA are driven by functional considerations, rather than by the "nature" of a partnership (although the Comments occasionally lapse into conceptual justifications based on the entity theory). Along these lines, RUPA, unlike the UPA, does not provide that every termination of a person's status as a partner—every dissociation—causes dissolution. Instead, the key issue is whether dissociation has occurred, and what are the consequences of the kind of dissociation that occurred.

There is an important distinction here between the partnership and the partnership's business. Under the UPA, if the partnership status of one or more partners is terminated the partnership is dissolved, but the remaining partners may continue the business, albeit as a new partnership. (For example, the remaining partners might agree on a buyout price with the departing partners, or might buy the partnership business at an auction pursuant to winding up, or might continue the business under a continuation agreement.) Under RUPA, however, the dissociation of a partner does not necessarily cause dissolution. For example, upon a wrongful dissociation or a dissociation by death the partnership is not dissolved—and therefore the partnership's business continues—unless within ninety days a majority of the remaining partners dissociate or agree to wind up. Rather than necessarily causing dissolution, under RUPA dissociation leads to two forks in the statutory road: winding up under Article 8, or a mandatory buyout under Article 7. Which fork must be taken under RUPA depends on the nature of the event of dissociation.

a). *First Fork: Required Winding Up.* RUPA § 801 describes the events of dissociation that require the partnership to be wound up. These events include notice of a partner's express will to withdraw in a partnership at will, the expiration of the partnership's term in a partnership for a term, and an uncured event that makes it unlawful for all or substantially all of the partnership's business to be continued. The Official Comment adds:

. . . Under RUPA, not every partner dissociation causes a dissolution of the partnership. Only certain departures trigger a dissolution. The basic rule is that a partnership is dissolved, and its business must be wound up, only upon the occurrence of one of the events listed in Section 801. All other dissociations result in a buyout of the partner's interest under Article 7 and a continuation of the partnership entity and business by the remaining partners.

Section 801 continues two basic rules from the UPA. First, it continues the rule that any member of an *at-will* partnership has the right to force a liquidation. Second, by negative implication, it continues the rule that the partners who wish to continue the business of a *term* partnership can not be forced to liquidate the business by a partner who withdraws prematurely in violation of the partnership agreement.

b). Second Fork: Required Buyout. If upon the dissociation of a partner, winding up is not required under § 801, then RUPA § 701 requires a mandatory buyout of the dissociated partner's interest by the partnership. However, if the dissociation was wrongfully caused by the dissociated partner, § 701(c) provides that the buyout price under § 701(b) is to be reduced by damages for the wrongful dissociation. Furthermore, under § 701(h) a partner who wrongfully dissociates before the expiration of a definite partnership term or the completion of a particular undertaking, is not entitled to payment of any portion of the buyout price until the expiration of the term or completion of the undertaking, unless the partner establishes to the satisfaction of the court that earlier payment will not cause undue hardship to the business of the partnership. A deferred payment must be adequately secured and bear interest. Under § 701(b) the buyout price of a dissociated partner's interest is the amount that would have been distributable to the dissociating partner if the partnership was wound up as of the date of dissociation, and the assets of the partnership were then sold at a price equal to or greater of the liquidation value or the value based on a sale of the entire business as a going concern without the dissociated partner.

———

Corrales v. Corrales

198 Cal. App.4th 221, 129 Cal. Rptr.3d 428 (2011)

Corrales illustrates the important difference posed by the two-forks—windup vs. buyout—under RUPA. Rudy and Richard, two brothers, formed a partnership at will to repair, refurbish and sell computer tape drives. Richard mailed a "notice of dissociation" to Rudy when he learned that his brother had started a competing business. Soon thereafter Rudy and Richard each filed suits against the other and much of the ensuing trial was devoted to determining the value of the partnership for buyout purposes, each invoking the California version of RUPA section 701. Both parties sought review of the ultimate value placed on the business by the trial judge. The appellate court remanded the case, admonishing all parties and the lower court, that the brothers' dispute was not guided by section 701, but rather section 801 et. seq., since the partnership was at will. Under section 801, there is no procedure in the statute for a buyout. Instead, section 807 commands that the partnership must be wound up, with creditors being paid with such adjustments to the individual partner's accounts as necessary after paying the creditor.

———

9. DISSOLUTION (II): DISSOLUTION BY JUDICIAL DECREE AND WRONGFUL DISSOLUTION

———

UNIFORM PARTNERSHIP ACT §§ 31(2), 32, 38(2)

[See Statutory Supplement]

———

REVISED UNIFORM PARTNERSHIP ACT §§ 601, 602, 603, 701, 801, 802, 804, 807

[See Statutory Supplement]

———

Congel v. Malfitano

Court of Appeals of New York, 2018.
31 N.Y.3d 272, 101 N.E.3d 341, 76 N.Y.S.3d 873.

■ FAHEY, J.

A partnership is a voluntary, contractual association in which persons carry on a business for profit as co-owners. In the agreement establishing a partnership, the partners can chart their own course. New York's Partnership Law creates default provisions that fill gaps in partnership agreements, but where the agreement clearly states the means by which a partnership will dissolve, or other aspects of partnership dissolution, it is the agreement that governs the change in relations between partners and the future of the business. . . .

I.

In 1985, defendant and seven others entered into a written agreement (the Agreement) to form a general partnership known as "Poughkeepsie Galleria Company" (the Partnership), for the ownership, operation, and management of a shopping mall. . . . Defendant initially had a 2.25% ownership interest . . . which increased to 3.08% by the mid-2000s. In addition to the minority partners, the Partnership had a majority owner, Moselle Associates, which controlled a little over 56% of the Partnership.

The Agreement provided that the Partnership "shall continue until it is terminated as hereinafter provided." In a subsequent provision, the Agreement stated that the Partnership would dissolve upon "[t]he election by the Partners to dissolve the Partnership" or "[t]he happening of any event which makes it unlawful for the business of the Partnership to be carried on or for the Partners to carry it on in Partnership."

The Agreement further stated that "[a]ll decisions to be made by the Partners shall be made by the casting of votes at a meeting of such

Partners" and that "[t]he affirmative vote of no less than fifty-one percent (51%)" of the partners "shall be required to approve any matter presented for decision." Day-to-day control of the Partnership was vested in a three-member Executive Committee . . . .

In the mid-2000s, defendant decided to withdraw from the Partnership. Defendant asserts that certain conduct by plaintiffs related to the Partnership troubled him, and that when he challenged plaintiffs, they did not address his concerns. He explored the option of a buyout of his interest, but negotiations failed.

On November 24, 2006, defendant wrote to his partners:

"[I]n accordance with Section 62 (1) (b) of the Partnership Law, and as a general partner of the Partnership I hereby elect to dissolve the Partnership and by this notice the Partnership is hereby dissolved."

Partnership Law § 62 (1)(b) states that a partner may unilaterally dissolve a partnership, without violating the partnership agreement, if "no definite term or particular undertaking is specified" in the agreement and the partnership is therefore "at will." Defendant insisted that his partners were compelled to liquidate. . . . .

The partners took the position that defendant had wrongfully dissolved the Partnership,[1] and they continued the business, in the same name as before, pursuant to Partnership Law § 69 (2)(b). That provision states, with certain conditions, that when dissolution is caused in violation of a partnership agreement, "[t]he partners who have not caused the dissolution wrongfully, if they all desire to continue the business in the same name . . . may do so, during the agreed term for the partnership and for that purpose may possess the partnership property."

In January 2007, plaintiffs, as the Partnership's Executive Committee and on behalf of the Partnership, commenced this breach of contract action, seeking a declaratory ruling that defendant had wrongfully dissolved the Partnership, as well as damages. . . .

Supreme Court granted summary judgment to plaintiffs, holding that the Partnership was not an "at-will" partnership, because it specified a "particular undertaking" within the meaning of Partnership Law § 62 (1) (b), and that defendant's dissolution of the Partnership breached the Agreement. . . .

[T]he Appellate Division upheld Supreme Court's ruling on the wrongfulness of the dissolution, albeit on different grounds, finding that the Agreement specified a "definite term" or temporal limit under Partnership Law § 62(1)(b) (61 AD3d 807, 808–809, 877 N.Y.S.2d 443 [2d

---

[1]   Plaintiffs did not take the position that defendant's action had no legal effect and failed to dissolve the Partnership. On appeal, plaintiffs concede that the Partnership dissolved by operation of law. The dispute concerns whether the dissolution violated the Agreement. Consequently, we have no occasion to consider whether plaintiffs would prevail if they had argued that under the Agreement a purported unilateral dissolution is no dissolution at all.

Dept 2009]). In a separate order issued on the same date, the Appellate Division affirmed Supreme Court's order granting summary judgment to plaintiffs . . . . The Appellate Division remitted for further proceedings on, among other things, the issue of damages for breach of contract (*id.*).

On remittal in Supreme Court . . . plaintiffs contended that they were entitled to fees on any actions they were compelled to take so as to avoid liquidation. They sought $2,717,314.50 in attorneys' fees and $79,705.50 in experts' fees.

Supreme Court ruled that plaintiffs were entitled to attorneys' fees and experts' fees, as part of their damages, reasoning that those costs "are not incidental to the litigation" but instead are "damages caused by the defendant's breach" of the Agreement. . . .

Partnership Law § 69(2)(c)(II) states that when a partner dissolves a partnership in contravention of the partnership agreement, and the remaining partners continue the business in the same name, the dissolving partner has "the right as against his copartners . . . to have the value of his interest in the partnership, less any damages caused to his copartners by the dissolution, ascertained and paid to him in cash, or [have] the payment secured by bond approved by the court, and to be released from all existing liabilities of the partnership; but in ascertaining the value of the partner's interest the value of the good-will of the business shall not be considered."

Consequently, in November 2011, Supreme Court conducted a bench trial to establish the value of defendant's interest in the Partnership, taking into account the value of goodwill, and the amount of damages, if any, that defendant owed to plaintiffs. At the outset of trial, the parties stipulated that the value of defendant's interest in the Partnership as of November 24, 2006 was $4,850,000.00. . . .

Supreme Court ruled that the stipulated value of $4,850,000.00 would be reduced by 15% or $727,500.00 to represent the value of the Partnership's goodwill. The trial court reasoned "that the partnership does indeed possess goodwill of its own," because the mall "and its tenants attract regular, loyal shoppers, which point towards the existence of some goodwill." The trial court explained that "a potential purchaser of the Poughkeepsie Galleria would more than likely pay more for an established going concern that already has tenant retail stores that attract a loyal customer base," and in this manner "would pay extra for the acquisition of goodwill." . . .

[T]he Appellate Division held that the evidence at trial supported Supreme Court's determination that the Partnership "had goodwill in connection with the operation of the shopping mall that it owned" (141 AD3d at 75). . . . On the subject of attorneys' fees, the Appellate Division held that "the reasonable amount of certain legal expenses incurred by the plaintiffs" constituted "recoverable expenditures directly occasioned and made necessary by the defendant's breach of the partnership agreement, and were thus properly included as damages" (*id*.). . . .

We granted defendant leave to appeal . . . .

II.

The first issue, as framed by the parties, is whether defendant's unilateral dissolution of the Partnership violated the Agreement. The trial court and the Appellate Division both ruled that the dissolution was wrongful, but focused on whether the Agreement specified a "definite term" or "particular undertaking" under Partnership Law § 62 (1) (b). Defendant contends that the Partnership was "at will" because the Agreement did not contain a "definite term" or "particular undertaking" under the statute. Plaintiffs urge us to affirm on an alternative ground, namely that because the Agreement sets out the methods of dissolving the Partnership in accordance with the Agreement, the wrongfulness of defendant's dissolution can be decided without recourse to the statute. We agree with plaintiffs on this issue.

The governing law of partnerships in New York is the Partnership Law of 1919, which enacted into law the original Uniform Partnership Act (UPA). It is well established, however, that "[t]he Partnership Law's provisions are, for the most part, default requirements that come into play in the absence of an agreement" (*Ederer v Gursky*, 9 NY3d 514, 526, 881 N.E.2d 204, 851 N.Y.S.2d 108 [2007]). The statutory scheme "applies only when there is either no partnership agreement governing the partnership's affairs, the agreement is silent on a particular point, or the agreement contains provisions contrary to law. Where an agreement addresses a particular issue, the terms of the agreement control, and the rights and obligations of the parties are determined by reference to principles of contract law. Thus, an agreement specifying the circumstances under which a partnership may be dissolved is not at will." (*BPR Group Ltd. Partnership v Bendetson*, 453 Mass 853, 863–864, 906 N.E.2d 956 [2009] [internal quotation marks and citations omitted]; *accord e.g. Matter of Popkin & Stern*, 340 F3d 709, 714 [8th Cir 2003]). . . .

[P]arties to a partnership agreement generally have the right to contract around a provision of the Partnership Law, provided of course they do so in language that is "clear, unequivocal and unambiguous" (*Springsteen v Samson*, 32 NY 703, 706 [1865] . . . . No particular magic words need be recited, provided that the parties' intent is clear. With these principles in mind, we now summarize the Partnership Law provisions relied on by the lower courts, in order to assess whether they come into play or whether the Agreement controls. . . .

Here, the Agreement stated that the Partnership "shall continue until it is terminated as hereinafter provided," and, in a subsequent provision, stated that the Partnership would dissolve upon "[t]he election by the Partners to dissolve the Partnership" or "[t]he happening of any event which makes it unlawful for the business of the Partnership to be carried on or for the Partners to carry it on in Partnership." The partners clearly intended that the methods provided in the Agreement for dissolution were the only methods whereby the partnership would dissolve *in accordance with the Agreement*, and by implication that unilateral dissolution would breach the Agreement. In other words, the Agreement contemplated dissolution only in two instances, leaving no room for other means of dissolution that would be in accordance with its terms.[6]

It follows that Partnership Law § 62(1)(b) has no application here, because the parties to the Agreement clearly specified under what terms it could be properly dissolved, i.e., what would constitute a dissolution under the Agreement and what would constitute a dissolution in contravention of it. Accordingly, this was plainly not intended to be an "at-will" partnership. . . .

Although the lower courts erred in applying Partnership Law § 62(1)(b) to decide whether defendant violated the Agreement, the conclusion they reached, i.e., that defendant's dissolution was wrongful, is correct. . . .

IV.

With respect to the reduction for goodwill, Partnership Law § 69(2)(c)(II) gives a partner who dissolves a partnership in contravention of the partnership agreement the right "to have the value of his interest in the partnership, less any damages caused to his copartners by the dissolution, ascertained and paid to him in cash, . . . but in ascertaining the value of the partner's interest the value of the good-will of the business shall not be considered." In other words, any goodwill component in the value of the partner's interest must be deducted. Defendant argues that he should not have been assessed a goodwill deduction.

Goodwill is an intangible asset of a business, corresponding in this context to what a buyer would pay for the business, over and above its value as a mere sum of tangible assets, because of the patronage and support of regular customers. Goodwill consists in "every positive advantage, that has been acquired by a proprietor in carrying on [a] business, whether connected with the premises in which the business is conducted, or with the name under which it is managed, or with any other matter carrying with it the benefit of the business" (*Spaulding v Benenati*, 57 NY2d 418, 424, 442 N.E.2d 1244, 456 N.Y.S.2d 733 n 3 [1982] [internal quotation marks and citation omitted]). It is, in Judge Cardozo's words, what people "will pay for any privilege that gives a reasonable expectancy of preference in the race of competition. . . .

---

[6] As we have noted (*see* footnote 1), plaintiffs do not argue that defendant's action had no legal effect and failed to dissolve the Partnership. Consequently, we have no occasion to consider whether the Agreement left no room for *any* other means of dissolution, whether proper or wrongful.

Defendant argues that the Partnership lacked goodwill as a matter of law. He contends that goodwill does not exist in a real estate holding, citing *Cohen v Cohen* (279 AD2d 599, 719 N.Y.S.2d 700 [2d Dept 2001]) and *Matter of Cinque v Largo Enters. of Suffolk County* (212 AD2d 608, 622 N.Y.S.2d 735 [2d Dept 1995]) for the proposition that when holdings consist solely of real property and cash, no part of the value of the business is attributable to goodwill. Defendant misreads these cases. They do not hold that real estate holdings can never have goodwill value as a matter of law, but merely assert in each case that the subject real estate holding did not have a goodwill component as a matter of fact . . . .

In short, the goodwill question is a factual one. In a case such as this, with affirmed findings of fact, our scope of review is narrow. . . . Here, the trial court found, based on the expert testimony and other evidence, that the shopping mall and the mall's tenants attract regular, loyal shoppers, and there is record support for the affirmed finding that the value of the Partnership included, in addition to its real property and cash, a goodwill component.[9] . . . For these reasons, Supreme Court properly determined the value of defendant's interest in the Partnership. . . .

*   *   *

The New York Court of Appeals rejected the plaintiffs' request that their attorney fees (the fees were in excess of $2 million) should be treated as "damages" arising from the defendant's wrongful dissolution. The court also upheld the Appellate Division's holding that the value of the defendant's interest should be reduced by a "minority discount" (the discount applied was 66 percent); it believed such a discount would surely be applied in an arms-length sale of a minority interest of a partner, at least when there is a majority holder as there was in the case. The Court of Appeals held that a minority discount was implicit in the statute: "the statute does not contemplate a valuation of the entire business as if it were being sold on the open market, but rather a determination of the fair market value of the wrongfully dissolving partner's interest as if that interest were being sold piecemeal and the rest of the business continuing as going concern." Did the defendant pay a steep a price for his wrongful withdrawal?

————

NOTE ON WRONGFUL DISSOLUTION

Congel v. Malfitano illustrates the drastic consequences that can befall a wrongfully dissolving partner under the UPA—damages against the partner, a valuation of this partner's interest that does not reflect the real value of

---

[9]   Defendant observes that the Partnership did not manage the mall, solicit tenants, negotiate leases, or have employees; that was the job of its agent, Pyramid Companies. Nevertheless, even though the Partnership was not directly responsible for day-to-day operations, it owned a shopping mall, with local reputational advantages, from which the Partnership derived goodwill value, just as Pyramid might have goodwill for responsible management of malls.

the interest because goodwill is not taken into account, and a continuation of the business without the partner. These consequences may have a special impact in a partnership without an expressly specified term. Suppose one of the partners, *A*, elects to dissolve such a partnership on the theory that the partnership is at will. If the court finds that despite the absence of a specified term, the partnership is for a term as a matter of implication, *A* will have dissolved the partnership in contravention of the partnership agreement. The penalties for guessing wrong on whether the court will make such a finding "may act as significant disincentives to dissolution [and may therefore] tend to stabilize the partnership." Hillman, The Dissatisfied Participant in the Solvent Business Venture: A Consideration of the Relative Permanence of Partnerships and Close Corporations, 67 Minn. L. Rev. 1, 34 (1982). For comparable reasons a partner who believes that other partners have engaged in wrongful conduct is taking a risk if she tries to dissolve a partnership through a self-help election, as opposed to going to court for a decree under UPA Section 32. The other side of the coin is that judicial proceedings entail delay.

———

NOTE ON THE EXPULSION OF A PARTNER

The expulsion of a partner without good cause prior to the end of the partnership term is ordinarily a wrongful violation of the partnership agreement, and a wrongfully expelled partner ordinarily has a right to have the partnership dissolved and liquidated. *See* UPA §§ 31(1)(d); 32(1)(d); 38(1). In contrast, under UPA § 38(1) "if dissolution is caused by the expulsion of a partner, bona fide under the partnership agreement and if the expelled partner is discharged from all partnership liabilities, either by payment or agreement . . . , he shall receive in cash only the net amount due him from the partnership." Under this section, a partnership agreement may lawfully provide that a partner can be expelled without cause upon a designated vote of the remaining partners. *See* Lawlis v. Kightlinger & Gray, 562 N.E.2d 435 (Ind.App.1990); Miller v. Foulston, Siefkin, Powers & Eberhardt, 790 P.2d 404 (Kan. 1990).

To fall within UPA § 31(1)(d), an expulsion must be "bona fide." In *Lawlis*, supra, the court stated that "if the power to involuntarily expel partners granted by a partnership agreement is exercised in bad faith or for a 'predatory purpose,' . . . the partnership agreement is violated, giving rise to an action for damages the affected partner has suffered as a result of his expulsion." *Id.* at 440. What does "bona fide" or "good faith" mean in this context? It cannot mean that a partner may be expelled only for cause: under such an interpretation, the power to expel a partner under an expulsion provision of a partnership agreement would be no greater than the power to expel a partner even in the absence of an expulsion provision. In *Lawlis* the court said, "the expelling partners act in 'good faith' regardless of motivation if [the expulsion] does not cause a wrongful withholding of money or property legally due the expelled partner at the time he is expelled." *Id.* at 443. This seems too restrictive. In *Winston & Strawn v. Nosal*, 664 N.E.2d 239

(Ill.App.3d 1996), Nosal was expelled from a law firm, Winston & Strawn. The expulsion followed (1) Nosal's request for partnership information concerning actions of the partnership's executive committee—in particular, concerning actions of Fairchild, the managing partner—in increasing the compensation and ownership interests of the committee members, and (2) Nosal's threat to sue if his request for information was not granted. Winston & Strawn then brought an action for a declaratory judgment that the expulsion was valid under the partnership agreement. The trial court granted summary judgment for Winston & Strawn. Reversed:

> It is well-established that a fiduciary relationship exists between partners and that each partner is bound to exercise the utmost good faith and honesty in all matters relating to the partnership business. . . .

> In this case, there is no dispute that the partnership agreement places no restriction upon the expulsion of a partner other than approval by the requisite majority. However, the agreement also grants all partners unrestricted access "to the books and records of the partnership." Access to partnership books is also guaranteed under section 19 of the Act. . . .

> Nosal claims that the documents he sought would have revealed the executive committee's plan to retain much of the firm's wealth and management power in the hands of its members. Specifically, the documents would have proven that upon assuming control, and without generally notifying the remaining capital partners, the executive committee dramatically increased the total number of partnership "points," or portions of ownership interest in the firm, and then awarded themselves large increases.

> Indeed, the record substantiates that in 1990, the executive committee voted its members considerable increases in individual points which were not given to the remaining capital partners. Nosal's evidence indicates that other capital partners were never notified about this action, and that when Nosal . . . sought to learn about it, [he was] repeatedly denied documents expressly guaranteed [to him] under the partnership agreement. . . .

> Nosal also alleges that Fairchild intentionally kept such data from him because Nosal could have uncovered evidence of Fairchild's ongoing fraudulent billing scheme subsequently discovered by the firm.

> . . . We note that among the documents sought by Nosal was a firm auditor's internal control report, which arguably could have disclosed questionable billing practices by Fairchild. It cannot be ignored that Nosal's [expulsion] immediately succeeded his ongoing requests for sensitive firm information, and came just days after he presented Fairchild with a draft complaint threatening to sue the firm to enforce his right to examine books and records. The evidence further indicates that it was Fairchild, in his discretion, who was largely instrument in the sudden decision to outplace Nosal despite

the fact that just a week before, Nosal was given a favorable review, a compensation increase, and assurances . . . that he was not among those to be outplaced.

Fairchild's steadfast refusal of Nosal's access to records, his role in the outplacement, and the fact that it occurred just after Nosal's threatened lawsuit, raise an inference that Nosal was expelled solely because he persisted in invoking rights belonging to him under the partnership agreement and that the reasons advanced by the firm were pretextual. Regardless of the discretion conferred upon partners under a partnership agreement, this does not abrogate their high duty to exercise good faith and fair dealing in the execution of such discretion. Labovitz, 545 N.E.2d 304 (Ill.App.3d 1989). Nosal has sufficiently raised a triable issue that his expulsion occurred in breach of this duty.

————

10. LIMITED PARTNERSHIPS

A. THE UNIFORM LIMITED PARTNERSHIP ACTS

The limited partnership is an historical form of business organization. Unlike general partnerships, limited partnerships are basically creatures of statute, although they have nonstatutory historical antecedents. The Revised Uniform Limited Partnership Act (RULPA) § 101 defines a limited partnership as "a partnership formed by two or more persons under the laws of this State and having one or more general partners and one or more limited partners." RULPA § 201 provides that in order to form a limited partnership a certificate of limited partnership must be filed in the office of the Secretary of State. The certificate must state the name of the limited partnership, the name and business address of each general partner, the latest date upon which the limited partnership is to dissolve, and the name and address of the agent for service of process. Sections 102 and 201 of the 2001 Act are comparable.

As of 2015, there were 414,388 limited partnerships in the United States, with an average of 30 partners in each partnership. Statistics of Income Bulletin, Spring 2018, Tbl. 8.

Over the course of time, the Commissioners on Uniform State Laws have promulgated several uniform limited partnership acts.

In 1916, the Commissioners promulgated the original Uniform Limited Partnership Act. It was adopted in every state except Louisiana. In 1976, the Commissioners promulgated a replacement for the Uniform Limited Partnership Act, called the Revised Uniform Partnership Act. The new Act modernized the prior Act, and reflected the influence of the corporate model. It has been widely but not universally adopted.

In 1985, the Commissioners amended the Revised Uniform Limited Partnership Act in a number of important respects. The states are still in the process of adopting (or not adopting) these amendments.

In 2001, the Commissioners adopted the Uniform Limited Partnership Act (2001). As of the time this casebook is written, that Act has been adopted in 21 states.

In the balance of this Section, the original Uniform Limited Partnership Act will sometimes be referred to as the ULPA; the Revised Uniform Partnership Act, as amended in 1985, will sometimes be referred to as RULPA; and the Uniform Limited Partnership Act (2001) will sometimes be referred to as the 2001 Act.

———

B. FORMATION OF LIMITED PARTNERSHIPS

———

REVISED UNIFORM LIMITED PARTNERSHIP ACT §§ 101, 201

[See Statutory Supplement]

———

UNIFORM LIMITED PARTNERSHIP ACT (2001) §§ 102, 201

[See Statutory Supplement]

———

C. LIABILITY OF LIMITED PARTNERS

———

REVISED UNIFORM LIMITED PARTNERSHIP ACT § 303

[See Statutory Supplement]

———

UNIFORM LIMITED PARTNERSHIP ACT (2001) § [303]

[See Statutory Supplement]

———

Gateway Potato Sales v. G.B. Investment Co.

Court of Appeals of Arizona, 1991.
170 Ariz. 137, 822 P.2d 490.

■ TAYLOR, JUDGE.

Gateway Potato Sales (Gateway), a creditor of Sunworth Packing Limited Partnership (Sunworth Packing), brought suit to recover payment for goods it had supplied to the limited partnership. Gateway sought recovery from Sunworth Packing, from Sunworth Corporation as general partner, and from G.B. Investment Company (G.B. Investment) as a limited partner, pursuant to Arizona Revised Statutes Annotated (A.R.S.) § 29–319. Under § 29–319, a limited partner may become liable for the obligations of the limited partnership under certain circumstances in which the limited partner has taken part in the control of the business. . . .

FACTS

Sunworth Corporation and G.B. Investment formed Sunworth Packing in November 1985 for the purpose of engaging in potato farming in Arizona. The limited partnership certificate and agreement of Sunworth Packing, filed with the office of the Arizona Secretary of State, specified Sunworth Corporation as the general partner and G.B. Investment Company as the limited partner. The agreement recited that the limited partner would not participate in the control of the business. The agreement further stated that the limited partner would not become liable to the creditors of the partnership, except to the extent of its initial contribution and any liability it may incur with an Arizona bank as a signatory party or guarantor of a loan and/or line of credit.

In late 1985, Robert C. Ellsworth, the president of Sunworth Corporation, called Robert Pribula, the owner of Gateway, located in Minnesota, to see if Gateway would supply Sunworth Packing with seed potatoes. Pribula hesitated to supply the seed potatoes without receiving assurance of payment because Pribula was aware that Ellsworth had previously undergone bankruptcy. Pribula, however, decided to sell the seed potatoes to Sunworth Packing after being assured by Ellsworth that he was in partnership with a large financial institution, G.B. Investment Company, and that G.B. Investment was providing the financing, was actively involved in the operation of the business, and had approved the purchase of the seed potatoes. Thereafter, from February 1986 through April 1986, Gateway sold substantial quantities of seed potatoes to Sunworth Packing.

While supplying the seed potatoes, Pribula believed that he was doing business with a general partnership (i.e., Sunworth Packing Company, formed by Sunworth Corporation and G.B. Investment Company). The sales documents used by the parties specified "Sunworth Packing Company" as the name of the partnership. Pribula was neither aware of the true name of the partnership nor that it was a limited partnership.

All of Gateway's dealings were with Ellsworth. Pribula neither contacted G.B. Investment prior to selling the seed potatoes to the limited partnership nor did he otherwise attempt to verify any of the statements Ellsworth had made about G.B. Investment's involvement. The only direct contact between G.B. Investment and Gateway occurred some time after the sale of the seed potatoes. It is, however, disputed whether G.B. Investment ever provided any assurance of payment to Gateway.

G.B. Investment's vice-president, Darl Anderson, testified in his affidavit that G.B. Investment had exerted no control over the daily management and operation of the limited partnership, Sunworth Packing. This testimony was contradicted, however, by the affidavit testimony of Ellsworth which was presented by Gateway in opposing G.B. Investment's motion for summary judgment. According to Ellsworth, G.B. Investment's employees, Darl Anderson and Thomas McHolm, controlled the day-to-day affairs of the limited partnership and made Ellsworth account to them for nearly everything he did. This day-to-day contact included but was not limited to approval of most of the significant operational decisions and expenditures and the use and management of partnership funds without Ellsworth's involvement.[1]

---

[1]   Ellsworth described with some specificity the ways in which G.B. Investment's control was exerted:

a. During the early months of the Partnership, Thomas McHolm and/or Darl Anderson were at the Partnership's offices on a daily basis directing the operation of the Partnership, and thereafter, they were at the Partnership's offices at least 2–3 times per week reviewing the operations of the business, directing changes in operations, and instructing me to make certain changes in operating the Partnership's affairs;

b. G.B. Investment Company was solely responsible for obtaining a $150,000.00 line-of-credit loan for the Partnership with Valley National Bank of Arizona, and it also signed documents guaranteeing the repayment of the loan;

c. As the President of the general partner, I was not permitted to make any significant independent business decisions concerning the operations of the Partnership, but was directed to have all business decisions approved with Darl Anderson and/or Thomas McHolm, or was directed to carry out decisions made by Darl Anderson and/or Thomas McHolm. For example, instead of using Partnership funds to pay certain creditors and suppliers, I was directed by Darl Anderson and/or Thomas McHolm to use the Partnership funds to purchase additional machinery and equipment; . . .

f. During a great portion of the duration of the Partnership, Thomas McHolm and/or Darl Anderson oversaw the daily operations of the Partnership because I had to have all expenditures approved by Thomas McHolm and/or Darl Anderson and Darl Anderson had to approve and sign checks issued by the Partnership, including without limitation payroll checks and invoices for telephone charges, utilities, publications, interest payments, bank card charges, supplies, etc. Copies of a sampling of the invoices and the corresponding checks are attached hereto as Exhibit 2; . . .

i. At least on two separate occasions, approximately in August, 1986 and again in November, 1986, Darl Anderson caused sums of monies (approximately $8,000 and $7,000 respectively) to be withdrawn from the Partnership account (No. 2270–8018) with Valley National Bank without the prior knowledge or consent of myself, as the President of the general partner of the Partnership. These monies were paid directly to G.B. Investment, and the withdrawals caused other checks of the Partnership to be dishonored due to insufficient funds and left the Partnership without sufficient funds to meet its payroll obligations;

Ellsworth testified further that he had described G.B. Investment's control of the business operation to Pribula. Pribula confirmed that Ellsworth had informed him that G.B. Investment's employees, McHolm and Anderson, were at the partnership's office on a frequent basis, that Ellsworth reported directly to them, that daily operations of the partnership were reviewed by representatives of G.B. Investment, and that Ellsworth had to get their approval before making certain business decisions.

DISCUSSION . . .

Subsection (a) of A.R.S. § 29–319 sets forth the general rule that a limited partner who is not also a general partner is not liable for the obligations of the limited partnership.

> [A] limited partner is not liable for the obligations of a limited partnership unless he is also a general partner or, in addition to the exercise of his rights and powers as a limited partner, he takes part in the control of the business. However, if the limited partner's participation in the control of the business is not substantially the same as the exercise of the powers of a general partner, he is liable only to persons who transact business with the limited partnership with actual knowledge of his participation in control. . . .

In A.R.S. § 29–319(a), the legislature stopped short of expressly stating that if the limited partner's participation in the control of the business is substantially the same as the exercise of the powers of a general partner, he is liable to persons who transact business with a limited partnership even though they have no knowledge of his participation and control. It has made this statement by implication, though, by stating to the opposite effect that "if the limited partner's participation in the control of the business is not substantially the same as the exercise of the powers of a general partner, he is liable only to persons who transact business with the limited partnership with actual knowledge of his participation in control." A.R.S. § 29–319(a).

We believe this interpretation is strengthened by an examination of the legislative history of Arizona's limited partnership statute. It is further strengthened by the legislature's refusal to modify this statute to correspond to the Revised Uniform Limited Partnership Act, as amended in 1985. Prior to 1982, Arizona's limited partnership statute was

---

j. Darl Anderson and/or Thomas McHolm caused certain expenses of the Partnership to be paid directly by G.B. Investment Company, to-wit: refrigeration equipment; and

k. After the Partnership defaulted on its loan payments to Valley National Bank, a loan which had been guaranteed by G.B. Investment Company, Darl Anderson, without my knowledge or consent, instructed the Valley National Bank to proceed with declaring the loan to be in default and to pursue its remedies under its Security Agreement with the Partnership, to-wit: to sell the equipment and machinery that it held as collateral at a foreclosure auction. At the foreclosure auction held on March 3, 1987, by Valley National Bank, Darl Anderson, on behalf of G.B. Investment Company, bought the equipment and machinery previously owned by Sunworth Corporation.

patterned after the Uniform Limited Partnership Act (ULPA), which was drafted in 1916. Section 7 of the ULPA provided that "[a] limited partner shall not become liable as a general partner unless, in addition to the exercise of his rights and powers as a limited partner, he takes part in the control of the business." Uniform Limited Partnership Act § 7, 6 U.L.A. 559 (1969).[3]

The Revised Uniform Limited Partnership Act (RULPA) was drafted in 1976. . . . In 1982, the Arizona legislature adopted the RULPA after repealing its enactment of the ULPA. . . . Presently, A.R.S § 29 319(a) dealing with a limited partner's liability to third parties is very similar to the 1976 version of section 303(a) of the RULPA which stated:

> Except as provided in subsection (d), a limited partner is not liable for the obligations of a limited partnership unless he is also a general partner or, and in addition to the exercise of his rights and powers as a limited partner, he takes part in the control of the business. However, if the limited partner's participation in the control of the business is not substantially the same as the exercise of the powers of a general partner, he is liable only to persons who transact business with the limited partnership with actual knowledge of his participation in control.

. . . The drafters' comment to section 303 explained that limited partners exercising all of the powers of a general partner would not escape liability by avoiding direct dealings with third parties. The comment stated:

> Section 303 makes several important changes in Section 7 of the prior uniform law. The first sentence of Section 303(a) carries over the basic test from former Section 7 whether the limited partner "takes part in the control of the business" in order to ensure that judicial decisions under the prior uniform law remain applicable to the extent not expressly changed. The second sentence of Section 303(a) reflects a wholly new concept. Because of the difficulty of determining when the "control" line has been overstepped, it was thought it unfair to impose general partner's liability on a limited partner except to the extent that a third party had knowledge of his participation in control of the business. On the other hand, in order to avoid permitting a limited partner to exercise all of the powers of a general partner while avoiding any direct dealings with third parties, the "is not substantially the same as" test was introduced. . . .

Id. at 326 cmt.

In 1985, the drafters of the RULPA backtracked from the position taken in section 303(a) of the 1976 Act. The new amendments reflect a

---

[3] The language of Arizona's then § 29–307 was taken verbatim from section 7 of the ULPA. . . .

reluctance to hold a limited partner liable if the limited partner had no direct contact with the creditor. The 1985 revised RULPA section 303(a) was amended to provide as follows:

> Except as provided in Subsection (d), a limited partner is not liable for the obligations of a limited partnership unless he is also a general partner or, in addition to the exercise of his rights and powers as a limited partner, he participates in the control of the business. However, if the limited partner participates in the control of the business, he is liable only to persons who transact business with the limited partnership reasonably believing, based upon the limited partner's conduct, that the limited partner is a general partner.

Id. at 325 (emphasis added). The comment to section 303 was also revised to explain the reason for the amendment. The revised comment states:

> Section 303 makes several important changes in Section 7 of the 1916 Act. The first sentence of Section 303(a) differs from the text of Section 7 of the 1916 Act in that it speaks of participating (rather than taking part) in the control of the business; this was done for the sake of consistency with the second sentence of Section 303(a), not to change the meaning of the text. It is intended that judicial decisions interpreting the phrase "takes part in the control of the business" under the prior uniform law will remain applicable to the extent that a different result is not called for by other provisions of Section 303 and other provisions of the Act. The second sentence of Section 303(a) reflects a wholly new concept in the 1976 Act that has been further modified in the 1985 Act. It was adopted partly because of the difficulty of determining when the "control" line has been overstepped, but also (and more importantly) because of a determination that it is not sound public policy to hold a limited partner who is not also a general partner liable for the obligations of the partnership except to persons who have done business with the limited partnership reasonably believing, based on the limited partner's conduct, that he is a general partner. . . .

Id. at 326 cmt. (emphasis added).

The Arizona legislature, however, has not revised A.R.S. § 29–319(a) to correspond to the section 303 amendments. The Arizona statute continues to impose liability on a limited partner whenever the "substantially the same as" test is met, even though the creditor has no knowledge of the limited partner's control. It follows then that no contact between the creditor and the limited partner is required to impose liability.

Moreover, whereas section 303 of the RULPA states that the creditor's reasonable belief must be "based upon the limited partner's conduct," under A.R.S. § 29–319 the only requirement is that the creditor has had "actual knowledge of [the limited partner's] participation in control." The statute does not state that this knowledge must be based upon the limited partner's conduct. The comments to the original version of section 303 of the RULPA, from which Arizona's statute is taken, make it clear that only when the "substantially the same as" test is met is direct contact not a requirement. Conversely, if the "substantially the same as" test is not met, direct contact is required. Under the facts presented in this case, Gateway had no direct contact with G.B. Investment until after the sales were concluded. We conclude, therefore, that G.B. Investment would be liable only if the "substantially the same as" test was met.

Whether a limited partner has exercised the degree of control that will make him liable to a creditor has always been a factual question. This is so regardless of whether the particular statute involved is patterned after section 7 of the ULPA or after section 303 of the RULPA. E.g., Alzado v. Blinder, Robinson & Co., 752 P.2d 544 (Colo.1988); Gast v. Petsinger, 228 Pa.Super. 394, 323 A.2d 371 (1974); Holzman v. DeEscamilla, 86 Cal.App.2d 858, 195 P.2d 833 (1948). Our current Arizona statute lists activities that a limited partner may undertake without participating in controlling the business. It also states that other activities may be excluded from the definition of such control. Where activities do not fall within the "safe harbor" of A.R.S. § 29–319(b), it is necessary for a trier-of-fact to determine whether such activities amount to "control." In the absence of actual knowledge of the limited partner's participation in the control of the partnership business, there must be evidence from which a trier-of-fact might find not only control, but control that is "substantially the same as the exercise of powers of a general partner."

We conclude that the evidence Gateway presented in this case should have allowed it to withstand summary judgment. The affidavit testimony of Ellsworth raises the issue whether he was merely a puppet for the limited partner, G.B. Investment. While a few of the activities Ellsworth listed may have fallen within the protected areas listed in A.R.S. § 29–319(b), others did not. Ellsworth's detailed statement raises substantial issues of material facts.

Viewing the facts in the light most favorable to Gateway, we cannot say as a matter of law that G.B. Investment was entitled to summary judgment. We conclude that Gateway is entitled to a determination by trial of the extent of control exercised by G.B. Investment over Sunworth Packing.

For the foregoing reasons, we reverse the judgment of the trial court and remand for further proceedings.

■ EHRLICH, P.J., and CLABORNE, J., concur.

D. CORPORATE GENERAL PARTNERS

NOTE ON CORPORATE GENERAL PARTNERS

It seems likely that the plaintiff in *Gateway* sued the limited partner, rather than the general partner, because the sole general partner was a corporation with limited assets. Ordinarily, shareholders are not liable for their corporation's debts. Therefore, if both the limited partnership and the corporate general partner had insufficient assets to pay the debt to the plaintiff, the plaintiff would have been unable to collect on the limited partnership's debt unless the limited partner was liable.

Section 303(b)(1) of RULPA and Section 601(4)(C) of the 2001 Act explicitly recognize that a corporation can be a general partner in a limited partnership. Although a director or officer of a corporate general partner is not liable for the debts of a limited partnership merely because he participates in the control of the partnership's business in his capacity as director or officer of the general partner, he may become liable if the corporate directors and officers fail to maintain their corporate identity in conducting partnership affairs through the corporation, or if corporate assets are intermingled with partnership assets, or if the corporation is not sufficiently capitalized, *see* Mursor Builders, Inc. v. Crown Mountain Apartment Associates, 467 F.Supp. 1316 (D.V.I. 1978); Western Camps, Inc. v. Riverway Ranch Enterprises, 70 Cal.App.3d 714, 138 Cal.Rptr. 918 (1977), or under the principle of the following case.

———————

In re USACafes, L.P. Litigation

Court of Chancery of Delaware, 1991.
600 A.2d 43.

■ ALLEN, CHANCELLOR.

These consolidated actions arise out of the October 1989 purchase by Metsa Acquisition Corp. of substantially all of the assets of USACafes, L.P., a Delaware limited partnership (the "Partnership") at a cash price of $72.6 million or $10.25 per unit. Plaintiffs are holders of limited partnership units. They bring these cases as class actions on behalf of all limited partnership unitholders except defendants. The relief sought includes, inter alia, the imposition of constructive trusts on certain funds received by defendants in connection with the Metsa sale and an award of damages to the class resulting from the sale.

The Partnership was formed in the 1986 reorganization of the business of USACafes, Inc., a Nevada corporation. Also formed as part of that reorganization was USACafes General Partner, Inc. (the "General Partner"), a Delaware corporation that acts as the general partner of the Partnership. Both the Partnership and the General Partner are named as defendants in this action. A second category of defendants is composed of Sam and Charles Wyly, brothers who together own all of the stock of the General Partner, sit on its board, and who also personally, directly or indirectly, own 47% of the limited partnership units of the Partnership. Sam Wyly chairs the Board of the General Partner.

The third category of defendants are four other individuals who sit on the board of directors of the General Partner. All of these persons are alleged to have received substantial cash payments, loan forgiveness, or other substantial personal benefits in connection with the 1989 Metsa purchase.

The last of the defendants is Metsa, the buyer of the Partnership's assets. Metsa is not alleged to be related in any way to the Wylys or any other defendant except as a buyer in the transaction under review.

The . . . Amended Complaint

The amended complaint's . . . central theory involves an alleged breach of the duty of loyalty. In essence, it claims that the sale of the Partnership's assets was at a low price, favorable to Metsa, because the directors of the General Partner all received substantial side payments that induced them to authorize the sale of the Partnership assets for less than the price that a fair process would have yielded. Specifically, it is alleged that, in connection with the sale, (1) the Wylys received from Metsa more than $11 million in payments (or promises to pay in the future) which were disguised as consideration for personal covenants not to compete; (2) the General Partner (which the Wylys wholly own) received a $1.5 million payment right in consideration of the release of a claim that plaintiffs assert was non-existent; (3) defendant Rogers, a director of the General Partner and President of the Partnership was forgiven the payment of a $956,169 loan from the Partnership and was given an employment agreement with the Partnership that contemplated a one million dollar cash payment in the event, then imminent, of a "change in control"; (4) defendant Tuley, also a director of the General Partner, was forgiven repayment of a $229,701 loan; and (5) the other directors were given employment agreements providing for a $60,000 payment in the event of a change in control. In sum, it is alleged that between $15 and $17 million was or will be paid to the directors and officers of the General Partner by or with the approval of Metsa; those payments are alleged to constitute financial inducements to the directors of the General Partner to refrain from searching for a higher offer to the Partnerships. Plaintiffs add that, even assuming that Metsa was the buyer willing to pay the best price, some part at least of these "side payments" should have gone to the Partnership. . . .

The Pending Motions . . .

[The gist of] the director defendants' motion to dismiss for failure to state a claim with respect to the sale of the Partnership's assets . . . is the assertion that the directors of the General Partner owed the limited partners no duty of loyalty or care. In their view their only duty of loyalty was to the General Partner itself and to its shareholders (i.e., the Wyly brothers). . . .

In my opinion the assertion by the directors that the independent existence of the corporate General Partner is inconsistent with their owing fiduciary duties directly to limited partners is incorrect. Moreover, even were it correct, their position on this motion would have to be rejected in any event because the amended complaint expressly alleges that they personally participated in the alleged breach by the General Partner itself, which admittedly did owe loyalty to the limited partners.

The first basis of this holding is the more significant. While I find no corporation law precedents directly addressing the question whether directors of a corporate general partner owe fiduciary duties to the partnership and its limited partners, the answer to it seems to be clearly indicated by general principles and by analogy to trust law. I understand the principle of fiduciary duty, stated most generally, to be that one who controls property of another may not, without implied or express agreement, intentionally use that property in a way that benefits the holder of the control to the detriment of the property or its beneficial owner. . . . [T]he central aspect of the relationship is, undoubtedly, fidelity in the control of property for the benefit of another. See generally Robert Flannigan, The Fiduciary Obligation, 9 Oxford J. Legal St. 285 (1989).

The law of trusts represents the earliest and fullest expression of this principle in our law, but courts of equity have extended it appropriately to achieve substantial justice in a wide array of situations. Thus, corporate directors, even though not strictly trustees, were early on regarded as fiduciaries for corporate stockholders. E.g., Koehler v. Black River Falls Iron Co., 67 U.S. (2 Black) 715, 17 L.Ed. 339 (1862); Wardell v. Union Pac. R.R. Co., 103 U.S. 651, 26 L.Ed. 509 (1880). When control over corporate property was recognized to be in the hands of shareholders who controlled the enterprise, the fiduciary obligation was found to extend to such persons as well. Allied Chemical & Dye Corp. v. Steel & Tube Co., 14 Del.Ch. 1, 120 A. 486, 491 (1923).

. . . [A] large number of trust cases do stand for a principle that would extend a fiduciary duty to such persons in certain circumstances. The problem comes up in trust law because modernly corporations may serve as trustees of express trusts. Thus, the question has arisen whether directors of a corporate trustee may personally owe duties of loyalty to cestui que trusts of the corporation. A leading authority states the accepted answer:

> The directors and officers of [a corporate trustee] are certainly under a duty to the beneficiaries not to convert to their own use property of the trust administered by the corporation. . . . Furthermore, the directors and officers are under a duty to the beneficiaries of trusts administered by the corporation not to cause the corporation to misappropriate the

property. . . . The breach of trust need not, however, be a misappropriation. . . . Any officer [director cases are cited in support here] who knowingly causes the corporation to commit a breach of trust causing loss . . . is personally liable to the beneficiary of the trust. . . .

Moreover, a director or officer of a trust institution who improperly acquires an interest in the property of a trust administered by the institution is subject to personal liability. He is accountable for any profit. . . . Even where the trustee [itself] is not liable, however, because it had no knowledge that the director was making the purchase . . . , the director . . . is liable to the beneficiaries. . . . The directors and officers are in a fiduciary relation not merely to the [corporation] . . . but to the beneficiaries of the trust administered by the [corporation].

4 A. Scott & W. Fratcher, The Law of Trusts § 326.3, at 304–306 (4th ed. 1989) (citing cases) ["Scott on Trusts"].

The theory underlying fiduciary duties is consistent with recognition that a director of a corporate general partner bears such a duty towards the limited partnership. That duty, of course, extends only to dealings with the partnership's property or affecting its business, but, so limited, its existence seems apparent in any number of circumstances. Consider, for example, a classic self-dealing transaction: assume that a majority of the board of the corporate general partner formed a new entity and then caused the general partner to sell partnership assets to the new entity at an unfairly small price, injuring the partnership and its limited partners. Can it be imagined that such persons have not breached a duty to the partnership itself? And does it not make perfect sense to say that the gist of the offense is a breach of the equitable duty of loyalty that is placed upon a fiduciary? . . . [I]n some instances, for example the use by a director of confidential information concerning the partnership's business not yet known by the board of the general partner, there may be no breach of loyalty or care by the general partner itself to abet, yet there may be director liability to the partnership by the director. Cf. cases cited at 4 Scott on Trusts § 326.3, at n. 7.

Two courts have, in fact, held a sole shareholder/director of a corporate general partner personally liable for breach of fiduciary duty to limited partners, although without much discussion of the issue here considered. See Tobias v. First City National Bank and Trust Co., 709 F.Supp. 1266, 1277–78 (S.D.N.Y.1989); Remenchik v. Whittington, Tex.Ct.App., 757 S.W.2d 836 (1988). . . .

While these authorities extend the fiduciary duty of the general partner to a controlling shareholder, they support as well, the recognition of such duty in directors of the General Partner who, more directly than a controlling shareholder, are in control of the partnership's property. It is not necessary here to attempt to delineate the full scope of that duty. It may well not be so broad as the duty of the director of a corporate trustee. But it surely entails the duty not to use control over the partnership's property to advantage the corporate director at the expense of the partnership. That is what is alleged here.

The amended complaint contains the following allegations:

16. The General Partner and its directors, the named individual defendants, are in a fiduciary relationship with the plaintiffs and the other Unitholders of USACafes. . . .

17. . . . Through their unit ownership and executive positions [the director defendants] have dominated and controlled the affairs of USACafes. Among other things, they have . . . failed to adequately solicit or consider alternative proposals for USACafes, have failed to negotiate in good faith to enhance Unitholders' values and, instead, have agreed to sell all of its assets to Metsa, which will result in the minority limited partners receiving the grossly inadequate price of $10.25 per Unit. As inducement to the individual defendants to agree to the Metsa proposal, Metsa offered to pay and the individual defendants agreed to accept, certain additional payments (approximately $17 million) that were not offered to the classes. . . .

19. The individual defendants and the General Partner participated in the wrongdoing complained of in order to divert the valuable assets of USACafes for their own benefit by entering into highly favorable compensation arrangements with Metsa as part of the liquidation of USACafes.

I therefore conclude that the amended complaint does allege facts which if true establish that the director defendants have breached fiduciary obligations imposed upon them as directors of a Delaware corporation or have participated in a breach of such duties by the General Partner. . . .

The motions of the individual defendants, the General Partner, and the Partnership to dismiss the claims arising out of the sale of the Partnership's assets is denied. . . .

————

E. THE TAXATION OF UNINCORPORATED BUSINESS ORGANIZATIONS

Taxation is a major issue in the choice of business form. There are two basic patterns of business taxation under the Internal Revenue Code, which may be called firm taxation and flow-through taxation.

Under *firm taxation*, a business firm is taxable on its income. Accordingly, if the firm has income or expenses, or gains or losses, those items go into the firm's taxable income, not into the taxable income of the firm's owners. If the firm then makes distributions to its owners out of after-tax income, the owners ordinarily pay taxes on those distributions. This is sometimes referred to as "double taxation."

Under *flow-through* taxation, a firm is not subject to taxation. Instead, all of the firm's income and expenses, and gains and losses, are taxable directly to the firm's owners. Distributions are not taxed. There is no "double taxation" effect. If the firm has losses, the owners can utilize the losses to offset their income from other sources.

Whether firm taxation or flow-through taxation is preferable for the owners of an enterprise depends in any given case on corporate and individual tax rates, the owners' circumstances, and other variables. Generally speaking, under present tax rates the owners of a firm will ordinarily regard flow-through taxation as preferable to firm taxation.

Historically, a firm-taxation pattern applied more or less automatically to corporations, and a flow-through taxation pattern applied more or less automatically to partnerships. Until recently, however, it was often less clear which type of taxation would be applied to forms of business organization that are intermediate between general partnerships and corporations—forms such as the limited partnership. This issue has now been resolved by the IRS's "check-the-box" Regulations. Under these Regulations, any domestic unincorporated business that constitutes an "eligible entity" can elect either flow-through taxation or firm (corporate) taxation. If an eligible entity has only one owner, the entity will be disregarded for tax purposes—that is, all of the entity's income and expenses and gains and losses will be attributed to the owner.

Generally speaking, an eligible entity is any business entity other than (i) a corporation or (ii) a business entity that is specifically made taxable as corporation under the Internal Revenue Code. The most important entity in the second category is the *master limited partnership*. Essentially, a master limited partnership is a limited partnership whose limited-partnership interests are publicly traded—that is, traded on an established securities market, or readily tradeable on a secondary market. With certain exceptions, under the Internal Revenue Code publicly traded limited partnerships are taxed as corporations, and cannot elect flow-through (partnership) taxation.

There is another important respect in which the tax comparison of the traditional forms has been blurred. Just as publicly traded limited partnerships are now normally taxed like corporations, so the Internal Revenue Code provides a route through which partnership-tax treatment can be achieved by certain corporate enterprises. Subchapter S of the Code (I.R.C. §§ 1361–1379) permits the owners of qualifying corporations to elect a special tax status under which the corporation and its shareholders receive flow-through taxation that is comparable (although not identical) to partnership taxation. The taxable income of an S corporation is computed essentially as if the corporation were an individual. With some exceptions, items of income, loss, deduction, and credit, are passed through to the shareholders on a pro rata basis, and added to or subtracted from each shareholder's gross income.

Among the conditions for making and maintaining a Subchapter S election are the following: (1) The corporation may not have more than one hundred shareholders. (2) The corporation may not have more than one class of stock. (3) All the shareholders must be individuals or qualified estates or trusts. (4) No shareholder may be a nonresident alien. The amount of the corporation's assets and income is immaterial under Subchapter S. Do shareholders of a corporation electing Subchapter S treatment have a duty not to transfer their shares in a way that renders that renders the company ineligible for Subchapter S? See Merner v. Merner, 129 Fed. Appx. 342 (9th Cir. 2005) (concluding that California would not likely impose a fiduciary obligation so as to bar a transfer of shares causing a corporation to lose its Subchapter S tax status).

The 2017 omnibus tax act reduced tax rates for corporations and individuals. The maximum rate for corporations is now 21 percent. One feature of the legislation provides that a taxpayer (other than a corporation) who receives flow-through income such as from a sole proprietorship, partnership, LLC, or Subchapter S corporation is entitled to a deduction equal to 20 percent of the taxpayer's "qualified business income" (this refers to income from a trade or business but excludes service business such as income from a law firm or medical practice).

As of 2010, there were 6,342,218 corporations in the United States; (about 70 percent are Subchapter S corporations). Internal Revenue Service, 2013 Statistics of Income: Corporation Tax Returns, Fig. E.

———

F. FIDUCIARY OBLIGATIONS OF LIMITED PARTNERS AND THE OBLIGATION OF GOOD FAITH

Dieckman v. Regency GP LP

Supreme Court of the State of Delaware, 2017.
155 A. 3d 358.

■ SEITZ, JUSTICE . . .

The plaintiff is a limited partner/unitholder in the publicly-traded master limited partnership ("MLP"). The general partner proposed that the partnership be acquired through merger with another limited partnership in the MLP family. The seller and buyer were indirectly owned by the same entity, creating a conflict of interest. Because conflicts of interest often arise in MLP transactions, those who create and market MLPs have devised special ways to try to address them. The general partner in this case sought refuge in two of the safe harbor conflict resolution provisions of the partnership agreement—"Special Approval" of the transaction by an independent Conflicts Committee, and "Unaffiliated Unitholder Approval."

In the MLP context, Special Approval typically means that a Conflicts Committee composed of members independent of the sponsor and its affiliates reviewed the transaction and made a recommendation to the partnership board whether to approve the transaction. Unaffiliated Unitholder Approval is typically just that—a majority of unitholders unaffiliated with the general partner and its affiliates approve the transaction. Under the partnership agreement, if either safe harbor is satisfied, the transaction is deemed not to be a breach of the agreement.

The partnership agreement required that the Conflicts Committee be independent, meaning that its members could not be serving on affiliate boards and were independent under the audit committee independence rules of the New York Stock Exchange. The plaintiff alleged in the complaint that the general partner failed to satisfy the Special Approval safe harbor because the Conflicts Committee was itself conflicted. According to the plaintiff, one of the Committee's two members began evaluating the transaction while still a member of an affiliate's board, and then resigned from the affiliate's board four days after he began his review to then become a member of the Conflicts Committee. On the same day the transaction closed, the committee member was reappointed to the seat left vacant for him on the affiliate's board.

The plaintiff also alleged that the general partner failed to satisfy the Unaffiliated Unitholder Approval safe harbor because the general partner made false and misleading statements in the proxy statement to secure that approval. In the 165-page proxy statement sent to the unitholders, the general partner failed to disclose the conflicts within the Conflicts Committee. Instead, the proxy statement stated that Special Approval had been obtained by an independent Conflicts Committee.

The general partner moved to dismiss the complaint and claimed that, in the absence of express contractual obligations not to mislead investors or to unfairly manipulate the Conflicts Committee process, the general partner need only satisfy what the partnership agreement expressly required—to obtain the safe harbor approvals and follow the minimal disclosure requirements. In other words, whatever the general partner said in the proxy statement, and whomever the general partner appointed to the Conflicts Committee, was irrelevant because only the express requirements of the partnership agreement controlled and displaced any implied obligations not to undermine the protections afforded unitholders by the safe harbors. . . .

I. . . .

D.

After plaintiff filed his complaint challenging the fairness of the merger transaction, the defendants moved to dismiss under Court of Chancery Rule 12(b)(6), invoking the protections of Special Approval and Unaffiliated Unitholder Approval under the LP Agreement. The Chancellor reached only the Unaffiliated Unitholder Vote safe harbor. After finding that all fiduciary duties were displaced by contractual terms, the court noted that the LP Agreement contained "just a single disclosure requirement" and thus the LP Agreement terms "unambiguously extinguish the duty of disclosure and replace it with a single disclosure requirement." According to the court, given the express disclosure obligation, the implied covenant of good faith and fair dealing "has no work to do" because "the express waiver of fiduciary duties and the clearly defined disclosure requirement . . . prevent the implied covenant from adding any additional disclosure obligations to the agreement." Once the Unaffiliated Unitholder Vote safe harbor applied, the court dismissed the case because "the Merger is deemed approved by all the limited partners, including plaintiff, and is immune to challenge for contractual breach."

II.

The appeal comes to us from the Court of Chancery's decision granting the defendants' motion to dismiss. Our review is de novo.

A.

We start with the settled principles of law governing Delaware limited partnerships. The Delaware Revised Uniform Limited Partnership Act ("DRUPLA") gives "maximum effect to the principle of freedom of contract." One freedom often exercised in the MLP context is eliminating any fiduciary duties a partner owes to others in the partnership structure. The act allows drafters of Delaware limited partnerships to modify or eliminate fiduciary-based principles of governance, and displace them with contractual terms.

With the contractual freedom accorded partnership agreement drafters, and the typical lack of competitive negotiations over agreement terms, come corresponding responsibilities on the part of investors to read carefully and understand their investment. Investors must appreciate that "with the benefits of investing in alternative entities often comes the limitation of looking to the contract as the exclusive source of protective rights." In other words, investors can no longer hold the general partner to fiduciary standards of conduct, but instead must rely on the express language of the partnership agreement to sort out the rights and obligations among the general partner, the partnership, and the limited partner investors.

Even though the express terms of the agreement govern the relationship when fiduciary duties are waived, investors are not without some protections. For instance . . . [t]he DRUPLA provides for the implied covenant of good faith and fair dealing, which cannot be eliminated by contract.

The implied covenant is inherent in all contracts and is used to infer contract terms "to handle developments or contractual gaps that the asserting party pleads neither party anticipated." It applies "when the party asserting the implied covenant proves that the other party has acted arbitrarily or unreasonably, thereby frustrating the fruits of the bargain that the asserting party reasonably expected." The reasonable expectations of the contracting parties are assessed at the time of contracting. In a situation like this, involving a publicly traded MLP, the pleading-stage inquiry focuses on whether, based on a reading of the terms of the partnership agreement and consideration of the relationship it creates between the MLP's investors and managers, the express terms of the agreement can be reasonably read to imply certain other conditions, or leave a gap, that would prescribe certain conduct, because it is necessary to vindicate the apparent intentions and reasonable expectations of the parties.

B.

The Court of Chancery decided that the implied covenant could not be used to remedy what the plaintiff alleged were faulty safe harbor approvals because the LP Agreement waived fiduciary-based standards of conduct and contained an express contractual term addressing what disclosures were required in merger transactions. According to the court, the implied covenant had "no work to do" because the express disclosure requirement displaced the implied covenant.

The Court of Chancery erred by focusing too narrowly on whether the express disclosure provision displaced the implied covenant. Instead, it should have focused on the language of the safe harbor approval process, and what its terms reasonably mean. . . .

We find that implied in the language of the LP Agreement's conflict resolution provision is a requirement that the General Partner not act to undermine the protections afforded unitholders in the safe harbor process. Partnership agreement drafters, whether drafting on their own, or sitting across the table in a competitive negotiation, do not include obvious and provocative conditions in an agreement like "the General Partner will not mislead unitholders when seeking Unaffiliated Unitholder Approval" or "the General Partner will not subvert the Special Approval process by appointing conflicted members to the Conflicts Committee." But the terms are easily implied because "the parties must have intended them and have only failed to express them because they are too obvious to need expression." Stated another way, "some aspects of the deal are so obvious to the participants that they never think, or see no need, to address them."

Our use of the implied covenant is based on the words of the contract and not the disclaimed fiduciary duties. Under the LP Agreement, the General Partner did not have the full range of disclosure obligations that a corporate fiduciary would have had. Yet once it went beyond the minimal disclosure requirements of the LP Agreement, and issued a 165-page proxy statement to induce the unaffiliated unitholders not only to approve the merger transaction, but also to secure the Unaffiliated Unitholder Approval safe harbor, implied in the language of the LP Agreement's conflict resolution provision was an obligation not to mislead unitholders.

Further, the General Partner was required to form a Conflicts Committee comprised of members who:

> [A]re not (a) security holders, officers or employees of the General Partner, (b) officers, directors or employees of any Affiliate of the General Partner or (c) holders of any ownership interest in the Partnership Group other than Common Units and who also meet the independence standards required of directors who serve on an audit committee of a board of directors established by the Securities Exchange Act of 1934, as amended, and the rules and regulations of the Commission thereunder and by the National Securities Exchange on which the Common units are listed or admitted to trading.

As with the contract language regarding Unaffiliated Unitholder Approval, this language is reasonably read by unitholders to imply a condition that a Committee has been established whose members genuinely qualified as unaffiliated with the General Partner and independent at all relevant times. Implicit in the express terms is that the Special Committee membership be genuinely comprised of qualified members and that deceptive conduct not be used to create the false appearance of an unaffiliated, independent Special Committee.

C.

. . . [W]e find that the plaintiff has pled sufficient facts to support his claims that those safe harbors were unavailable to the General Partner. Instead of staffing the Conflicts Committee with independent members, the plaintiff alleges that the chair of the two-person Committee started reviewing the transaction while *still* a member of an Affiliate board. Just a few days before the General Partner created the Conflicts Committee, the same director resigned from the Affiliate board and became a member of the General Partner's board, and then a Conflicts Committee member.

Further, after conducting the negotiations with ETE over the merger terms and recommending the merger transaction to the General Partner, the two members of the Conflicts Committee joined an Affiliate's board the day the transaction closed. The plaintiff also alleges that the Conflicts Committee members failed to satisfy the audit committee independence rules of the New York Stock Exchange, as required by the LP Agreement.

In the proxy statement used to solicit Unaffiliated Unitholder Approval of the merger transaction, the plaintiff alleges that the General Partner materially misled the unitholders about the independence of the Conflicts Committee members. In deciding to approve the merger, a reasonable unitholder would have assumed based on the disclosures that the transaction was negotiated and approved by a Conflicts Committee composed of persons who were not "affiliates" of the general partner and who had the independent status dictated by the LP Agreement. This assurance was one a reasonable investor may have considered a material fact weighing in favor of the transaction's fairness.

The plaintiff has therefore pled facts raising sufficient doubt about the General Partner's ability to use the safe harbors to shield the merger transaction from judicial review. Thus, we reverse the judgment of the Court of Chancery . . . .

Brinckerhoff v. Enbridge Energy Co.

Supreme Court of the State of Delaware, 2017.
159 A.3d 242.

■ SEITZ, JUSTICE.

The plaintiffs, Peter Brinckerhoff and his trust, are long-term investors in Enbridge Energy Partners, L.P. ("EEP"), a Delaware master limited partnership ("MLP"). . . .As followers of this investment space know, MLPs are set up in the petroleum transportation business to allow sponsors and public investors to take advantage of favorable tax laws. Another benefit under Delaware law is the ability to eliminate common law duties in favor of contractual ones, thereby restricting disputes to the four corners of the limited partnership agreement ("LPA").

MLPs are typically families of entities that often engage in internal business transactions, referred to as dropdowns, rollups, insider financings, incentive distribution rights, and equity investments. Because the entities proposing transactions often have representatives seated at both sides of the negotiating table, the LPAs typically attempt to address conflicts using various contractual tools. Even so, disputes still arise over whether the conflicted parties have complied with the letter and spirit of the LPA. . . .

. . . In 2014, [Enbridge, Inc. (Enbridge), the ultimate parent entity that controlled EEP's general partner, EEP GP] proposed that EEP repurchase Enbridge's interest in the Alberta Clipper project ("Alberta Clipper Interest") . . . . As part of the billion dollar transaction, EEP would . . . issue to Enbridge $694 million of a new class of EEP partnership securities designated Class E Units, repay $306 million in outstanding loans made by EEP GP to EEP, and, central to the current dispute, amend the LPA to effect a "Special Tax Allocation" whereby the public investors would be allocated items of gross income that would otherwise be allocated to EEP GP.

The allocation of gross income for tax purposes has important consequences to the public investors. According to Brinckerhoff, the Special Tax Allocation unfairly benefited Enbridge by reducing its tax obligations by hundreds of millions of dollars while increasing the taxes of the public investors, thereby undermining the investor's long-term tax advantages in their MLP investment.

Brinckerhoff filed suit and alleged that the defendants breached the LPA . . . by

> (a) agreeing to repurchase the same asset—the Alberta Clipper Interest—EEP sold to Enbridge six years earlier, on terms Brinckerhoff claims were not "fair and reasonable" as required by Section 6.6(e) of the LPA . . . .

EEP GP and its Affiliates moved to dismiss, claiming that, regardless of any breach of the LPA's specific affirmative requirements, before Brinckerhoff could pursue his claims, he first had to plead facts leading to an inference that the defendants acted in bad faith. In other words, EEP GP and its affiliates were free to breach *any* of the LPA's specific requirements, so long as they did so in good faith. The defendants also argued that to allege bad faith, Brinckerhoff had to plead facts that ruled out all legitimate explanations for the defendants' actions except for bad faith—a pleading hurdle borrowed from one of the most demanding corporate law standards, that of "waste."

The Court of Chancery . . . ended up dismissing the complaint. Though the court believed that in the corporate context Brinckerhoff's allegations would have stated a claim, it concluded that so long as EEP GP acted in good faith, it was free to breach any of the LPA's specific requirements. Once that standard applied, the court found that Brinckerhoff had failed to allege bad faith conduct by EEP GP, which required dismissal of the complaint.

On appeal, Brinckerhoff has challenged the reasonableness of the Court of Chancery's interpretation of the LPA. . . .

We agree with . . . the defendants that the Special Tax Allocation did not breach Sections 5.2(c) and 15.3(b) governing new unit issuance and tax allocations. But, we find that the Court of Chancery erred when it held that other "good faith" provisions of the LPA "modified" Section 6.6(e)'s specific requirement that the Alberta Clipper transaction be "fair and reasonable to the Partnership." . . .

The Court of Chancery cannot be faulted for faithfully applying our earlier decision in *Brinckerhoff III*, and its rigorous pleading standard for bad faith. But we now change course from our earlier decision and adhere to the more traditional definition of bad faith utilized in Delaware entity law. We hold that bad faith is sufficiently alleged under the Enbridge LPA if the plaintiff pleads facts supporting an inference that EEP GP did not reasonably believe it was acting in the best interest of the partnership. Accepting the facts as pled, as we must on an appeal from a motion to dismiss, Brinckerhoff has met this standard. . . .

The Court of Chancery did its best to attempt to reconcile complex contractual provisions and confusing precedent. . . In this appeal, we change course from the earlier pleading standard announced in *Brinckerhoff III* to which the Court of Chancery was bound, and apply the definition of bad faith that is commonly used in our entity law and incorporated into the Enbridge LPA. . . .

The DRULPA [Delaware Revised Uniform Limited Partnership Act] permits the LPA drafter to disclaim fiduciary duties, and replace them with contractual duties. The drafter cannot, however, disclaim the implied covenant of good faith and fair dealing. If fiduciary duties have been validly disclaimed, the limited partners cannot rely on traditional fiduciary principles to regulate the general partner's conduct. Instead, they must look exclusively to the LPA's complex provisions to understand their rights and remedies. . . .

Turning to the provisions of the Enbridge LPA, Section 6.10(d) of the LPA modifies, waives or limits common law duties in favor of contractual duties:

> Any standard of care and duty imposed by this Agreement or under the Delaware Act of any applicable law, rule or regulation shall be modified, waived or limited as required to permit the General Partner to act under this Agreement or any other agreement contemplated by this Agreement and to make any decision pursuant to the authority prescribed in this Agreement, so long as such action is reasonably believed by the General Partner to be in the best interests of the Partnership.

In *Norton v. K-Sea Transp. Partners, L.P.*, we interpreted language nearly identical to Section 6.10(d), and held that it unconditionally eliminated all common law standards of care and fiduciary duties, and substituted a contractual good faith standard of care—that the General Partner "reasonably believe that its action is in the best interest of, or not inconsistent with, the best interests of the Partnership." Although the accuracy of this interpretation is the subject of legitimate debate,[31]

---

[31]   The Court of Chancery has questioned this Court's interpretation of Section 6.10(d). Instead of an unconditional waiver of extra-contractual duties, one could interpret the Section to impose "a condition precedent to the effectiveness of the provisions of the LP Agreement that purport to modify, waive, or limit standards of care or duties otherwise imposed by law." *In re Kinder Morgan, Inc. Corp. Reorganization Litig.*, 2015 Del. Ch. LEXIS 221, 2015 WL 4975270, at *5, n. 1 (Del. Ch. Aug. 20, 2015), *aff'd sub nom. The Haynes Family Trust v. Kinder Morgan G.P., Inc.*, 135 A.3d 76, 2016 Del. LEXIS 136, 2016 WL 912184 (Del. 2016) (TABLE). This is because the language modifying, waiving, or limiting standards of review and duties is effective "so long as" the General Partner "reasonably believed" its decision was in "the best interest of the Partnership." 2015 Del. Ch. LEXIS 221, [WL] at *5. If the general partner failed to act in the best interest of the Partnership, a condition precedent to the modification of fiduciary duties failed to occur, and arguably common law fiduciary duties would then apply to the general partner.

we choose in this case not to upset *Norton*'s settled interpretation of Section 6.10(d). Thus, we will not reinterpret Section 6.10(d), and instead will replace any standard of care and duty "imposed by this Agreement or under the Delaware Act or any applicable law, rule or regulation" with a contractual good faith standard. . . .

The Alberta Clipper transaction is a contract with an Affiliate (Enbridge) to sell property (Alberta Clipper Interest) back to the Partnership (EEP). Section 6.6, entitled "Contracts with Affiliates," and in particular Section 6.6(e), directly addresses the affirmative obligation EEP GP must satisfy for such transactions: "[n]either the General Partner nor any of its Affiliates shall sell, transfer or convey any property to, or purchase any property from, the Partnership, directly or indirectly, except pursuant to transactions that are fair and reasonable to the Partnership."

Even though Section 6.6(e) imposes an affirmative obligation on EEP GP, the Court of Chancery held that Section 6.10(d)'s contractual good faith standard "modifies" Section 6.6(e), and requires Brinckerhoff to first show that EEP GP lacked good faith in approving the transaction. We are at a loss to understand how it does. Section 6.6(e) imposes an affirmative obligation on EEP GP when contracting with Affiliates. Section 6.10(d), on the other hand, is a general standard of care that operates in the spaces of the LPA without express standards. Although EEP GP must act in good faith under the LPA, and is not subject to fiduciary standards of care, it still must comply with the specific requirements of the LPA. The Court of Chancery confused the general standard of care under Section 6.10(d) with the LPA's more specific requirements. It also violated settled rules of contract interpretation, requiring that the court prefer specific provisions over more general ones. . . .

Section 6.8(a) exculpates EEP GP and other Indemnitees from monetary damages for actions taken in good faith. But, Section 6.8(a) does not grant EEP GP absolute immunity from suit for any actions taken in good faith. Instead, it only immunizes EEP GP and other Indemnitees from monetary damages. Equitable remedies are still available. The availability of equitable remedies no doubt motivated our Court to issue the remand order in *Brinckerhoff II*, asking the Court of Chancery to consider the availability of reformation and rescission as remedies for breach of Section 6.6(e) of the LPA. And, as will be discussed later, Brinckerhoff has pled viable claims that the defendants acted in bad faith when undertaking the Alberta Clipper transaction.

Our interpretation of the Enbridge LPA—Section 6.6(e) is a specific affirmative obligation of EEP GP which is not displaced by other general provisions—is the only one consistent with the overall framework of the LPA. It is also consistent with settled contract interpretation principles. The defendants' interpretation would render many of the LPA's specific requirements a nullity. . . .

Brinckerhoff alleged that the Alberta Clipper transaction breached three specific provisions of the LPA—Sections 6.6(e) (the Alberta Clipper transaction must be "fair and reasonable" to the Partnership); 5.2(c) (tax conventions, allocations, and amendments cannot have a "material adverse effect on the Partners"); and 15.3(b) (LPA amendments cannot "enlarge the obligations" of any investor without their consent). Although the Court of Chancery did not fully consider the viability of these claims, they were presented to the court and "in the interest of justice and for the sake of judicial economy, we decide those issues *de novo*."

A.

Under Section 6.6(e), "[n]either the General Partner nor any of its Affiliates shall sell, transfer or convey any property to, or purchase any property from, the Partnership, directly or indirectly, except pursuant to transactions that are fair and reasonable to the Partnership." The requirements of 6.6(e) are deemed satisfied, however, "as to any transaction the terms of which are no less favorable to the Partnership than those generally being provided to or available from unrelated third parties." In other words, the fairness and reasonableness of the transaction can be assessed by comparing it to arms-length transactions. Further, the fairness and reasonableness "shall be considered in the context of all similar or related transactions." The fair and reasonable standard is "something similar, if not equivalent to entire fairness review."

We find that Brinckerhoff has pled sufficient facts leading to an inference that the Alberta Clipper transaction was not "fair and reasonable to the Partnership" because EEP repurchased assets from Enbridge "less favorable to the Partnership than those generally being provided to or available from unrelated third parties." According to Brinckerhoff, EEP paid $200 million more to repurchase the same assets it sold in 2009, despite declining EBITDA, slumping oil prices, and the absence of the expansion rights sold in 2009. He also alleged that, through the Special Tax Allocation, EEP GP added hundreds of millions of dollars more in benefits for Enbridge to the detriment of the public unitholders. These allegations are sufficient to state a claim for breach of the requirements of Section 6.6(e).

. . . We find that Brinckerhoff has pled facts supporting an inference that EEP GP acted in bad faith in approving the Alberta Clipper transaction. . . .

The LPA does not define good faith. In *Brinckerhoff III*, we . . . held that "[t]o state a claim based on bad faith," EEP GP's decision to enter into the Joint Venture Transaction "must be 'so far beyond the bounds of reasonable judgment that it seems essentially inexplicable on any ground other than bad faith.'"

On the same day we decided *Brinckerhoff III*, we also decided *Norton*, and took a different approach to define bad faith. Using essentially the same language of Section 6.10(d) of the Enbridge LPA, the *Norton* LPA modified any standard of care or duty to permit the general partner to act under the LPA "so long as such action is reasonably believed by [the general partner] to be in, or not inconsistent with, the best interests of the Partnership."

In *Norton*, we found that this expression of the standard of care . . . also supplied the definition of good faith for the stand-alone good faith requirement in the exculpatory provision . . .

We believe the approach taken in *Norton* . . . is more faithful to the specific language of the Enbridge LPA, and does not rely on extra-contractual notions of waste and a heightened pleading burden to plead bad faith. . . . [C]onsistent with contract interpretation rules, we believe good faith was intended to be used consistently throughout the LPA. Thus, we depart from our earlier decision in *Brinckerhoff III*, and hold that to plead a claim that EEP GP did not act in good faith, Brinckerhoff must plead facts supporting an inference that EEP GP did not reasonably believe that the Alberta Clipper transaction was in the best interests of the Partnership. As our prior cases have established, the use of qualifier "reasonably" imposes an objective standard of good faith.

Here, Brinckerhoff has pled facts supporting an inference that EEP GP did not reasonably believe in good faith that the Alberta Clipper transaction was fair and reasonable to the Partnership. . . .

Because we have determined that Brinckerhoff has pled a viable claim for breach of the express terms of the LPA, we reverse the Court of Chancery's April 29, 2016 decision and remand the matter for further proceedings consistent with this Opinion. . . .

———

11. LIMITED LIABILITY PARTNERSHIPS

———

REVISED UNIFORM PARTNERSHIP ACT
§§ 102(9), 306(c), 901

[See Statutory Supplement]

———

NOTE ON LIMITED LIABILITY PARTNERSHIPS

Another important new form of business organization is the limited liability partnership ("LLP"). Essentially, LLPs are general partnerships, with one core difference and one ancillary difference. The core difference is that, as the name indicates, the liability of general partners of a limited liability partnership is less extensive than the liability of a general partner as discussed in the excerpt from Bromberg & Ribstein that follows. The ancillary difference is that LLPs must be registered with the appropriate state office. Every state has now adopted LLP statutes.

A variant on the LLP is the limited liability limited partnership, LLLP, in which the liability of the general partners in a limited partnership is limited.

————

Bromberg & Ribstein, Limited Liability Partnerships, The Revised Uniform Partnership Act, and the Uniform Limited Partnership Act

§ 3.02–3.04 (2005 ed.).

§ 3.02   LIMITED "TORT" LIABILITY IN LLPs

. . . [One] common form of LLP statute . . . limits liability for particular categories of conduct—that is, for negligence or other misconduct by a co-partner or other agent or employee of the firm [as opposed to breach of contract]. The model for these provisions is a prior version of the Delaware statute, which provides that a partner "is not liable for debts and obligations of or chargeable to the partnership arising from negligence, wrongful acts, or misconduct, whether characterized as tort, contract or otherwise, committed while the partnership is a registered limited liability partnership and in the course of the partnership business by another partner or an employee, agent, or representative of the partnership." . . .

Statutes that limit partners' liability only for misconduct-based claims raise some questions about the types of vicarious liability that are limited. The language clearly applies to any form of negligence or misconduct. . . . Professional malpractice liability arising out of partners' negligence is certainly included in the exception to vicarious liability despite the fact that this liability probably could be characterized as rising out of the contractual relationship between the professional and the client. . . . Thus, it is significant that the original partial-shield Delaware statute was amended in 1994 to provide that it limits vicarious liability for conduct "whether characterized as tort, contract or otherwise." . . .

§ 3.03   LIMITED LIABILITY FOR ALL TYPES OF CLAIMS

. . . [Most LLP] statutes provide that liability is limited for all partnership debts and obligations. For example, the Revised Uniform Partnership Act provides:

> An obligation of partnership incurred while the partnership is a limited liability partnership, whether arising in contract, tort, or otherwise, is solely the obligation of the partnership. A partner is not personally liable, directly or indirectly, including

by way of contribution or otherwise, for such a partnership obligation solely by reason of being or so acting as a partner. . . .

LLP statutes that eliminate partners' *vicarious* liability for all types of claims . . . nevertheless preserve partners' liability for their own misconduct, including faulty supervision of other partners, discussed below in Section 3.04. . . . Also, it is important to keep in mind that the *partnership* retains vicarious liability for its' partners' acts. Partners therefore remain liable at least up to their investment in the firm, and perhaps beyond this if they have agreed with their co-partners to contribute toward partnership losses.

§ 3.04   PARTNERS' DIRECT LIABILITY

Nothing in the LLP statutes or in statutes . . . relieves owners from liability for their own misconduct. "Limited liability" means only that owners are not, solely as owners, vicariously liable for the firm's debts. . . .

The statutes both preserve whatever liability partners may have had under the common law and, perhaps, provide for an additional statutory category of liability for misconduct. . . . An important model is the original version of the Delaware statute, which provides that the liability limitation "shall not affect the liability of a partner in a registered limited liability partnership for his own negligence, wrongful acts, or misconduct, or that of any person under his direct supervision and control." . . .

It is uncertain under the supervision-type of provision whether the partner must be negligent or at fault in order to be held liable. Stating that the LLP provisions "shall not affect" the partner's liability suggests that the statute only continues any liability partners may have had for their own misconduct or for negligently failing to monitor or supervise others. But it is not clear to what pre-existing supervisory liability the statute might be referring other than partners' *vicarious* liability under traditional partnership law, which is supposedly eliminated by LLP registration.

. . . [N]ot all LLP statutes include potentially confusing language on supervisory or other indirect liability. Some provide for liability only for the partner's own wrongs or omit any extra language on liability of individual members and provide in varying terms that a partner in an LLP is not individually liable merely because of her partnership status. This preserves partners' common law liability for their own misconduct without risking creating new categories of statutory liability.

———

NOTE ON LIABILITY FOR INVOLVEMENT

An issue that can arise in a professional LLP, when more than one partner was involved in a decision in some way, is what level of involvement will subject a partner to liability for his own conduct if the decision is later attacked. In Megadyne Information Systems v. Rosner, Owens & Nunziato, L.L.P., 2002 WL 31112563 (Cal. App. 2002), an unreported opinion, the court stated "All three partners offered declarations averring Owens was 'the sole attorney' who handled the Megadyne matter and that neither of the other two had 'any involvement' in the case. To contradict that showing, Megadyne [the plaintiff] offered Owens's testimony that 'there might have been discussions' with his two partners that Megadyne had a viable legal malpractice claim against Irell & Manella. This is sufficient to create a triable issue of fact as to whether the partners were personally involved in the firm's breach of fiduciary duties. If the partners had *discussions* that Megadyne could sue Irell & Manella for malpractice, it is reasonable to infer that they knew Megadyne's claim against OCTA was time-barred and that they participated in the decision to not disclose this fact to Megadyne while the firm continued to represent it."

CHAPTER 3

THE FOUNDATIONS OF A CORPORATION

1. THE CHARACTERISTICS OF A CORPORATION

A corporation is a legal person or legal entity. As such, a corporation has an existence separate from its owners, that is, its shareholders. A corporation is formed by filing an instrument, known variously as a certificate of incorporation, articles of incorporation, or a charter[1] in an appropriate state office—usually the office of the Secretary of State. A certificate of incorporation is often, although not always, a relatively simple document; a sample form can be found in the Statutory Supplement.

The central characteristics of a corporation are as follows:

1. *Limited Liability.* Normally, shareholders are not personally liable for corporate obligations. This legal rule is conventionally expressed by the statement that shareholders have limited liability. The managers of a corporation are also normally not personally liable for corporate obligations: as long as corporate managers act on the corporation's behalf and within their authority, they are treated like agents, not principals, for liability purposes. In contrast, in a simple general partnership each partner is liable for the partnership's obligations. See Chapter 2, Section 5.

2. *Free Transferability of Ownership Interests.* At least in publicly held corporations, ownership (or *equity*) interests, represented by shares of stock, are usually freely transferrable. In contrast, a partnership interest in a general partnership, other than a purely economic interest, cannot be transferred without the consent of all the partners unless otherwise agreed. See Chapter 2, Section 6.

3. *Continuity of Existence.* The legal existence of a corporation is usually perpetual, unless a shorter term is specified in the certificate of incorporation. This makes a corporation relatively secure against early termination, and has a beneficial impact on long-term planning. *See* Rock & Wachter, Waiting for the Omelet to Set, 24 J. Corp. L. 913 (1999). In contrast, partnerships usually have limited terms, and in any event are easily dissolved. See Chapter 2, Sections 8, 9.

4. *Centralized Management.* In publicly held corporations, the power to manage the business of the corporation is legally vested in the board of directors, although in practice much of that power is normally

Page v. Page.

305

---

[1] For ease of exposition, the term *certificate of incorporation* will be employed to denote either a certificate of incorporation, articles of incorporation, or a charter.

exercised by the corporation's executives. Shareholders, as such, have no right to participate in management. In contrast, in a general partnership, unless otherwise agreed, all partners have a right to participate in the conduct of the business. See Chapter 2, Section 3.

5.   *Entity Status.* Because a corporation is a legal person or entity, it can exercise powers and have rights in its own name. For example, a corporation can sue or be sued, and can own real and personal property. In contrast, in states where the governing law is the Uniform Partnership Act, general partnerships are not deemed to have entity status, although they do have entity status in states where the Revised Uniform Partnership Act is the governing law. See Chapter 2, Section 2.

These central attributes make the corporation a highly desirable form for an enterprise that is to be publicly held, because the owners of such an enterprise will normally put a very high premium on limited liability and free transferability and will also value centralized management and continuity of interest. In the case of an enterprise that is not to be publicly held, and in particular an enterprise that is to be held by a relatively small number of shareholders, most or all of whom are managers, the choice of form is more complex, because the owners may value certain partnership attributes, such as participation by all owners in management and limited transferability of interests. Accordingly, such an enterprise may take the form of either a corporation, a limited liability company (LLC), a general partnership, a limited liability partnership, a limited partnership, or a limited liability partnership. The partnership forms have been considered in Chapter 2. The LLC form will be considered in Chapter 8.

———

2.   THE ARCHITECTURE OF CORPORATE LAW

Corporation law is often conceived of as state law, but this conception is much too narrow. Corporate law serves various functions. It enables corporations to be organized. It provides corporations with certain endowments—most prominently, entity status, limited liability, perpetual existence, the right to own property and to make contracts, and the power to sue and be sued. It sets the level of care required of directors and officers. It provides a special remedial structure to resolve claims by shareholders against directors and officers. It facilitates various transactions and conduct in which a corporation may choose to engage. It addresses various kinds of conflict of interest. (These may be either *traditional conflicts*, which typically involve self-interested transactions between managers and their corporations, or *positional conflicts*, which involve actions by managers to maintain and enhance their positions.) Any body of rules that addresses one or more of these functions is part of corporate law.

Viewed from this perspective, corporate law consists of four major modules: state statutory law; state judge-made law; federal law, such as the Securities Acts and Sarbanes-Oxley; and private ordering, or "soft law," such as stock-exchange rules for listed companies. Each of these modules serves a distinct function. State statutory law enables corporations to be organized, provides corporations with various endowments, and facilitates corporate transactions. State judge-made law sets the level of care required of officers and directors, regulates traditional conflicts of interest, and gives content to remedial structures to protect shareholder rights and resolve shareholder claims. Federal law regulates certain traditional conflicts directly, through rules on insider training, and regulates positional conflicts of interest indirectly, through rules that govern the proxy voting system and through regulation of the flow of information concerning management's performance. The rules of the major stock exchanges regulate positional conflicts directly, by requiring an independent board and committees to monitor the corporation's executives. Accordingly, this book will concern state corporate law and those aspects of federal law that regulate the ongoing conduct of the corporation, and will also include the New York Stock Exchange's governance rules for listed companies.[2]

3. WHICH STATE'S LAW GOVERNS A CORPORATION'S INTERNAL AFFAIRS?

One element that will often figure in the decision where to incorporate an enterprise is which state's law the decision makers want to govern the corporation's internal affairs. Although, as shown in the preceding Note, a corporation's internal affairs may be governed by four different legal modules, often state law will often be paramount. The law permits an enterprise to incorporate in any state it chooses—even a state in which the enterprise will do little or no business. If an enterprise incorporates in such a state, the question may arise, whose law governs the corporation's internal affairs—the state of incorporation, or a state, if there is one, where the corporation does most of its business? The normal rule is that the law of the state of incorporation will govern the corporation's internal affairs. However, some states, including California and New York, have adopted provisions in their corporate statutes under which designated sections of the statutes are applicable to the internal affairs of certain corporations incorporated in another state. The following two cases address such statutes.

---

[2] The New York Stock Exchange has combined with Euronext, and the formal title of the Exchange, or at least the holding company for the Exchange and Euronext, is NYSE Euronext. However, the Exchange is still conventionally referred to as the New York Stock Exchange, or sometimes the NYSE, and that convention will be followed in this Book.

VantagePoint Venture Partners 1996
v. Examen, Inc.

Supreme Court of Delaware, 2005.
871 A.2d 1108.

■ HOLLAND, JUSTICE:

This is an expedited appeal from the Court of Chancery following the entry of a final judgment on the pleadings. We have concluded that the judgment must be affirmed.

Delaware Action

On March 3, 2005, the plaintiff-appellee, Examen, Inc. ("Examen"), filed a Complaint in the Court of Chancery against VantagePoint Venture Partners, Inc. ("VantagePoint"), a Delaware Limited Partnership and an Examen Series A Preferred shareholder, seeking a judicial declaration that pursuant to the controlling Delaware law and under the Company's Certificate of Designations of Series A Preferred Stock ("Certificate of Designations"), VantagePoint was not entitled to a class vote of the Series A Preferred Stock on the proposed merger between Examen and a Delaware subsidiary of Reed Elsevier Inc.

California Action

On March 8, 2005, VantagePoint filed an action in the California Superior Court seeking: (1) a declaration that Examen was required to identify whether it was a "quasi-California corporation" under section 2115 of the California Corporations Code[1]; (2) a declaration that Examen was a quasi-California corporation pursuant to California Corporations Code section 2115 and therefore subject to California Corporations Code section 1201(a), and that, as a Series A Preferred shareholder, VantagePoint was entitled to vote its shares as a separate class in connection with the proposed merger; (3) injunctive relief; and (4) damages incurred as the result of alleged violations of California Corporations Code sections 2111(f) and 1201.

---

[1]   Section 2115 of the California Corporations Code purportedly applies to corporations that have contacts with the State of California, but are incorporated in other states. *See* Cal. Corp.Code §§ 171 (defining "foreign corporation"); and Cal. Corp.Code §§ 2115(a), (b). Section 2115 of the California Corporations Code provides that, irrespective of the state of incorporation, foreign corporations' articles of incorporation are deemed amended to comply with California law and are subject to the laws of California if certain criteria are met. *See* Cal. Corp.Code § 2115 (emphasis added). To qualify under the statute: (1) the average of the property factor, the payroll factor and the sales factor as defined in the California Revenue and Taxation Code must be more than 50 percent during its last full income year; and (2) more than one-half of its outstanding voting securities must be held by persons having addresses in California. *Id.* If a corporation qualifies under this provision, California corporate laws apply "to the exclusion of the law of the jurisdiction where [the company] is incorporated." *Id.* Included among the California corporate law provisions that would govern is California Corporations Code section 1201, which states that the principal terms of a reorganization shall be approved by the outstanding shares of each class of each corporation the approval of whose board is required. *See* Cal. Corp.Code §§ 2115, 1201.

Delaware Action Decided

On March 10, 2005, the Court of Chancery granted Examen's request for an expedited hearing on its motion for judgment on the pleadings. On March 21, 2005, the California Superior Court stayed its action pending the ruling of the Court of Chancery. On March 29, 2005, the Court of Chancery ruled that the case was governed by the internal affairs doctrine as explicated by this Court in *McDermott v. Lewis*.[2] In applying that doctrine, the Court of Chancery held that Delaware law governed the vote that was required to approve a merger between two Delaware corporate entities.

. . . [VantagePoint appealed and the Supreme Court] granted its request for an expedited appeal. . . .

Facts

Examen was a Delaware corporation engaged in the business of providing web-based legal expense management solutions to a growing list of Fortune 1000 customers throughout the United States. Following consummation of the merger on April 5, 2005, LexisNexis Examen, also a Delaware corporation, became the surviving entity. VantagePoint is a Delaware Limited Partnership organized and existing under the laws of Delaware. VantagePoint, a major venture capital firm that purchased Examen Series A Preferred Stock in a negotiated transaction, owned eighty-three percent of Examen's outstanding Series A Preferred Stock (909,091 shares) and no shares of Common Stock.

On February 17, 2005, Examen and Reed Elsevier executed the Merger Agreement, which was set to expire on April 15, 2005, if the merger had not closed by that date. Under the Delaware General Corporation Law and Examen's Certificate of Incorporation, including the Certificate of Designations for the Series A Preferred Stock, adoption of the Merger Agreement required the affirmative vote of the holders of a majority of the issued and outstanding shares of the Common Stock and Series A Preferred Stock, *voting together as a single class*. Holders of Series A Preferred Stock had the number of votes equal to the number of shares of Common Stock they would have held if their Preferred Stock was converted. Thus, VantagePoint, which owned 909,091 shares of Series A Preferred Stock and no shares of Common Stock, was entitled to vote based on a converted number of 1,392,727 shares of stock.

There were 9,717,415 total outstanding shares of the Company's capital stock (8,626,826 shares of Common Stock and 1,090,589 shares of Series A Preferred Stock), representing 10,297,608 votes on an as-converted basis. An affirmative vote of at least 5,148,805 shares, constituting a majority of the outstanding voting power on an as-converted basis, was required to approve the merger. If the stockholders were to vote by class, VantagePoint would have controlled 83.4 percent of the Series A Preferred Stock, which would have permitted

---

[2]   McDermott Inc. v. Lewis, 531 A.2d 206 (Del. 1987).

VantagePoint to block the merger. VantagePoint acknowledges that, if Delaware law applied, it would not have a class vote.

Chancery Court Decision

The Court of Chancery determined that the question of whether VantagePoint, as a holder of Examen's Series A Preferred Stock, was entitled to a separate class vote on the merger with a Delaware subsidiary of Reed Elsevier, was governed by the internal affairs doctrine because the issue implicated "the relationship between a corporation and its stockholders."

. . . [T]he Court of Chancery determined that section 2115's requirement that stockholders vote as a separate class conflicts with Delaware law, which, together with Examen's Certificate of Incorporation, mandates that the merger be authorized by a majority of all Examen stockholders voting together as a single class. The Court of Chancery concluded that it could not enforce both Delaware and California law. Consequently, the Court of Chancery decided that the issue presented was solely one of choice-of-law, and that it need not determine the constitutionality of section 2115.

VantagePoint's Argument

According to VantagePoint, "the issue presented by this case is not a choice of law question, but rather the constitutional issue of whether California may promulgate a narrowly-tailored exception to the internal affairs doctrine that is designed to protect important state interests." VantagePoint submits that "Section 2115 was designed to provide an additional layer of investor protection by mandating that California's heightened voting requirements apply to those few foreign corporations that have chosen to conduct a majority of their business in California and meet the other factual prerequisite of Section 2115." Therefore, VantagePoint argues that "Delaware either must apply the statute if California can validly enact it, or hold the statute unconstitutional if California cannot." . . .

Internal Affairs Doctrine

In *CTS Corp. v. Dynamics Corp. of Am.*, the United States Supreme Court stated that it is "an accepted part of the business landscape in this country for States to create corporations, to prescribe their powers, and to define the rights that are acquired by purchasing their shares."[6] In *CTS*, it was also recognized that "[a] State has an interest in promoting stable relationships among parties involved in the corporations it charters, as well as in ensuring that investors in such corporations have an effective voice in corporate affairs."[7] The internal affairs doctrine is a long-standing choice of law principle which recognizes that only one state

---

[6]   CTS Corp. v. Dynamics Corp. of Am., 481 U.S. 69, 91, 107 S.Ct. 1637, 95 L.Ed.2d 67 (1987).

[7]   *Id.*

should have the authority to regulate a corporation's internal affairs—the state of incorporation.[8]

The internal affairs doctrine developed on the premise that, in order to prevent corporations from being subjected to inconsistent legal standards, the authority to regulate a corporation's internal affairs should not rest with multiple jurisdictions.[9] It is now well established that only the law of the state of incorporation governs and determines issues relating to a corporation's internal affairs. By providing certainty and predictability, the internal affairs doctrine protects the justified expectations of the parties with interests in the corporation.

The internal affairs doctrine applies to those matters that pertain to the relationships among or between the corporation and its officers, directors, and shareholders. The Restatement (Second) of Conflict of Laws § 301 provides: "application of the local law of the state of incorporation will usually be supported by those choice-of-law factors favoring the need of the interstate and international systems, certainty, predictability and uniformity of result, protection of the justified expectations of the parties and ease in the application of the law to be applied." Accordingly, the conflicts practice of both state and federal courts has consistently been to apply the law of the state of incorporation to "the entire gamut of internal corporate affairs."[14]

The internal affairs doctrine is not, however, only a conflicts of law principle. Pursuant to the Fourteenth Amendment Due Process Clause, directors and officers of corporations "have a significant right . . . to know what law will be applied to their actions"[15] and "[s]tockholders . . . have a right to know by what standards of accountability they may hold those managing the corporation's business and affairs."[16] Under the Commerce Clause, a state "has no interest in regulating the internal affairs of foreign corporations."[17] Therefore, this Court has held that an "application of the internal affairs doctrine is mandated by constitutional principles, except in the 'rarest situations,' "[18] e.g., when "the law of the

---

[8]   McDermott Inc. v. Lewis, 531 A.2d 206 (Del.1987). Accord State Farm Mut. Auto. Ins. Co. v. Superior Court, 114 Cal.App.4th 434, 442, 8 Cal.Rptr.3d 56 (2d Dist.2003), citing Edgar v. MITE Corp., 457 U.S. 624, 645, 102 S.Ct. 2629, 73 L.Ed.2d 269 (1982).

[9]   *See* Edgar v. MITE Corp., 457 U.S. at 645.

[14]   McDermott Inc. v. Lewis, 531 A.2d at 216 (quoting John Kozyris, *Corporate Wars and Choice of Law*, 1985 Duke L.J. 1, 98 (1985)). The internal affairs doctrine does not apply where the rights of third parties external to the corporation are at issue, *e.g.*, contracts and torts. *Id. See* also Rogers v. Guaranty Trust Co. of N.Y., 288 U.S. 123, 130–31, 53 S.Ct. 295, 77 L.Ed. 652 (1933).

[15]   McDermott Inc. v. Lewis, 531 A.2d at 216.

[16]   *Id.* at 217.

[17]   *Id.* (quoting Edgar v. MITE Corp. 457 U.S. 624, 645–46, 102 S.Ct. 2629, 73 L.Ed.2d 269 (1982)).

[18]   *Id.* (quoting CTS Corp. v. Dynamics Corp. of Am., 481 U.S. 69, 90, 107 S.Ct. 1637, 95 L.Ed.2d 67 (1987)).

state of incorporation is inconsistent with a national policy on foreign or interstate commerce."[19]

California Section 2115

VantagePoint contends that section 2115 of the California Corporations Code is a limited exception to the internal affairs doctrine. Section 2115 is characterized as an outreach statute because it requires certain foreign corporations to conform to a broad range of internal affairs provisions. Section 2115 defines the foreign corporations for which the California statute has an outreach effect as those foreign corporations, half of whose voting securities are held of record by persons with California addresses, that also conduct half of their business in California as measured by a formula weighing assets, sales and payroll factors. . . .

In her comprehensive analysis of the internal affairs doctrine, Professor Deborah A. DeMott examined section 2115. As she astutely points out:

> In contrast to the certainty with which the state of incorporation may be determined, the criteria upon which the applicability of section 2115 hinges are not constants. For example, whether half of a corporation's business is derived from California and whether half of its voting securities have record holders with California addresses may well vary from year to year (and indeed throughout any given year). Thus, a corporation might be subject to section 2115 one year but not the next, depending on its situation at the time of filing the annual statement required by section 2108.[23]

Internal Affairs Require Uniformity

In *McDermott v. Lewis*, this Court noted that application of local internal affairs law (here California's section 2115) to a foreign corporation (here Delaware) is "apt to produce inequalities, intolerable confusion, and uncertainty, and intrude into the domain of other states that have a superior claim to regulate the same subject matter. . . ."[24] Professor DeMott's review of the differences and conflicts between the Delaware and California corporate statutes with regard to internal affairs, illustrates why it is imperative that only the law of the state of incorporation regulate the relationships among a corporation and its officers, directors, and shareholders. To require a factual determination to decide which of two conflicting state laws governs the internal affairs of a corporation at any point in time, completely contravenes the importance of stability within inter-corporate [sic *intra*-corporate?]

---

[19] *Id.*

[23] Deborah A. DeMott, *Perspectives on Choice of Law for Corporate Internal Affairs*, 48 Law & Contemp. Probs. 161, 166 (1985).

[24] McDermott Inc. v. Lewis, 531 A.2d 206, 216 (Del.1987) (quoting Kozyris at 98).

relationships that the United States Supreme Court recognized in *CTS.* . . .

State Law of Incorporation Governs Internal Affairs

In *McDermott*, this Court held that the "internal affairs doctrine is a major tenet of Delaware corporation law having important federal constitutional underpinnings."[32]

. . . Examen is a Delaware corporation. The legal issue in this case—whether a preferred shareholder of a Delaware corporation had the right, under the corporation's Certificate of Designations, to a Series A Preferred Stock class vote on a merger—clearly involves the relationship among a corporation and its shareholders. As the United States Supreme Court held in *CTS*, "[n]o principle of corporation law and practice is more firmly established than a *State's authority* to regulate domestic corporations, including the authority to *define the voting rights of shareholders*."[34]

In *CTS*, the Supreme Court held that the Commerce Clause "prohibits States from regulating subjects that 'are in their nature national, or admit only of one uniform system, or plan of regulation,' "[35] and acknowledged that the internal affairs of a corporation are subjects that require one uniform system of regulation. In *CTS*, the Supreme Court concluded that "[s]o long as each State regulates voting rights *only in the corporations it has created*, each corporation will be subject to the law of only one State."[37] Accordingly, we hold Delaware's well-established choice of law rules and the federal constitution mandated that Examen's internal affairs, and in particular, VantagePoint's voting rights, be adjudicated exclusively in accordance with the law of its state of incorporation, in this case, the law of Delaware.

Any Forum—Internal Affairs—Same Law

VantagePoint acknowledges that the courts of Delaware, as the forum state, may apply Delaware's own substantive choice of law rules. VantagePoint argues, however, that Delaware's "choice" to apply the law of the state of incorporation to internal affairs issues—notwithstanding California's enactment of section 2115—will result in future forum shopping races to the courthouse. VantagePoint submits that, if the California action in these proceedings had been decided first, the California Superior Court would have enjoined the merger until it was factually determined whether section 2115 is applicable. If the statutory prerequisites were found to be factually satisfied, VantagePoint submits

---

[32]   McDermott Inc. v. Lewis, 531 A.2d 206, 209 (Del.1987).

[34]   CTS Corp. v. Dynamics Corp. of Am., 481 U.S. 69, 89, 107 S.Ct. 1637, 95 L.Ed.2d 67 (1987) (emphasis added). *See* Restatement (Second) of Conflict of Laws § 304 (1971) (concluding that the law of the incorporating State generally should "determine the right of a shareholder to participate in the administration of the affairs of the corporation").

[35]   CTS Corp. v. Dynamics Corp. of Am., 481 U.S. at 89, 107 S.Ct. 1637 (quoting Cooley v. Bd. of Wardens, 53 U.S. 299, 319, 12 How. 299, 13 L.Ed. 996 (1851)).

[37]   *Id.* (emphasis added).

that the California Superior Court would have applied the internal affairs law reflected in section 2115, "to the exclusion" of the law of Delaware—the state where Examen is incorporated.

In support of those assertions, VantagePoint relies primarily upon a 1982 decision by the California Court of Appeals in Wilson v. Louisiana-Pacific Resources, Inc.[41] In *Wilson v. Louisiana-Pacific Resources, Inc.*, a panel of the California Court of Appeals held that section 2115 did not violate the federal constitution by applying the California Code's mandatory cumulative voting provision to a Utah corporation that had not provided for cumulative voting but instead had elected the straight voting structure set forth in the Utah corporation statute. The court in *Wilson* did not address the implications of the differences between the Utah and California corporate statutes upon the expectations of parties who chose to incorporate in Utah rather than California. As Professor DeMott points out, "[a]lthough it is possible under the Utah statute for the corporation's charter to be amended by the shareholders and the directors, that mechanical fact does not establish California's right to coerce such an amendment" whenever the factual prerequisites of section 2115 exist.[44]

Wilson was decided before the United States Supreme Court's decision in *CTS* and before this Court's decision in *McDermott*. Ten years after *Wilson*, the California Supreme Court cited with approval this Court's analysis of the internal affairs doctrine in *McDermott*, in particular, our holding that corporate voting rights disputes are governed by the law of the state of incorporation.[45] Two years ago, in *State Farm v. Superior Court*, a different panel of the California Court of Appeals questioned the validity of the holding in *Wilson* following the broad acceptance of the internal affairs doctrine over the two decades after *Wilson* was decided.[46] In *State Farm*, the court cited with approval the United States Supreme Court decision in *CTS Corp. v. Dynamics* and our decision in *McDermott*. In *State Farm*, the court also quoted at length that portion of our decision in *McDermott* relating to the constitutional imperatives of the internal affairs doctrine.

Since *Wilson* was decided, the United States Supreme Court has recognized the constitutional imperatives of the internal affairs doctrine.[50] In *Draper v. Gardner*, this Court acknowledged the *Wilson*

---

[41]   Wilson v. La.-Pac. Res., Inc., 138 Cal.App.3d 216, 187 Cal.Rptr. 852 (1982).

[44]   Deborah A. DeMott, *Perspectives on Choice of Law for Corporate Internal Affairs*, 48 Law & Contemp. Probs. 161, 187–88 (1985).

[45]   *See* Nedlloyd Lines B.V. v. Superior Court, 3 Cal.4th 459, 11 Cal.Rptr.2d 330, 834 P.2d 1148, 1155 (1992), *citing McDermott Inc. v. Lewis*, 531 A.2d 206 (Del.1987).

[46]   State Farm Mut. Auto. Ins. Co. v. Superior Court, 114 Cal.App.4th 434, 8 Cal.Rptr.3d 56 (2d Dist.2003).

[50]   *E.g.,* Edgar v. MITE Corp. 457 U.S. 624, 102 S.Ct. 2629, 73 L.Ed.2d 269 (1982); CTS Corp. v. Dynamics Corp. of Am., 481 U.S. 69, 107 S.Ct. 1637, 95 L.Ed.2d 67 (1987). *See also* Kamen v. Kemper Fin. Serv., 500 U.S. 90, 111 S.Ct. 1711, 114 L.Ed.2d 152 (1991).

opinion in a footnote[51] and nevertheless permitted the dismissal of a Delaware action in favor of a California action in which a California court would be called upon to decide the internal affairs "demand" issue involving a Delaware corporation. As stated in *Draper*, we had no doubt that after the *Kamen* and *CTS* holdings by the United States Supreme Court, the California courts would "apply Delaware [demand] law [to the internal affairs of a Delaware corporation], given the vitality and constitutional underpinnings of the internal affairs doctrine."[52] We adhere to that view in this case.

Conclusion

The judgment of the Court of Chancery is affirmed. The Clerk of this Court is directed to issue the mandate immediately.*

———

NEW YORK BUSINESS CORPORATION LAW
§§ 1317, 1318, 1319, 1320

[See Statutory Supplement]

———

4. SELECTING A STATE OF INCORPORATION

The choice of governing state law is one, but only one element in a decision where to incorporate. A corporation that will have only a few owners will usually be incorporated locally, that is, in the state in which the corporation will have its principal place of business. Partly this is for tax reasons. If a corporation does business in a state, the state will impose a doing-business tax on the corporation on a basis that reflects the amount of that business. If a corporation is incorporated in a state, the state may impose a franchise tax on the corporation for the privilege of incorporation, even if the corporation does little or no business in the state. Elements of the doing-business tax and franchise tax may overlap, so that if a corporation does business mainly in one state, and that state imposes a franchise tax, its total tax bill usually will be lower if it is incorporated in that state. Furthermore, a local attorney, familiar with local corporate law, may be hesitant about rendering formal opinions on the law of another state, and is therefore likely to recommend local incorporation so that he can confidently give legal advice to the corporation after it is organized. The prior paragraph presents the conventional view and has a good deal of intuitive appeal for the reasons set forth above. *See e.g.*, Jens Dammann & Mathias Schundeln, The Incorporation Choices of Privately Held Corporations, 27 J. L. Econ. &

---

[51] Draper v. Gardner, 625 A.2d 859, 867 n. 10 (Del.1993).

[52] *Id.* at 867.

* *See also* In re the Topps Company Shareholders Litigation, 924 A.2d 951 (Del. Ch. 2007). (Footnote by eds.)

Org. 79, 81–82, 110 (2011). However, the table below, from a recent study of thousands of companies filing materials with the SEC—such filings occurring because funds were being privately or publicly raised—challenges this conventional view. As seen below, a much larger percentage of private companies are formed in Delaware and not the state of their headquartered state:

TABLE 1. State of Incorporation by Public or Private Status

	Not Incorporated in Headquarters State			Incorporated in Headquarters State
	Delaware Incorporation	Nevada Incorporation	Other State Incorporation	
Private Corporations	64.0%	2.5%	3.1%	30.3%
Public Corporations	48.7%	22.3%	8.1%	20.9%

Robert Anderson IV, The Delaware Trap: An Empirical Analysis of Incorporation Decisions, 91 So. Cal. L. Rev. 657, 675 (2018). What might cause a local lawyer to prefer Delaware over local law as the body of law to govern a local private client firm?

Public

In the case of a publicly held corporation, a different calculus prevails. For such a corporation the franchise tax is likely to be inconsequential in comparison with the corporation's total revenues, so that tax consequences are unlikely to figure heavily in the choice of the state of incorporation. Furthermore, although franchise-tax revenues are likely to be inconsequential to large states, they may represent an enormous source of revenue to a state with a small fiscal base. The legislature of a small state therefore has a great economic incentive to design a corporate statute that will attract incorporation or reincorporation from other states—particularly by large publicly held corporations, who will pay larger franchise taxes. Even a large state has an incentive to design a statute that will attract incorporation, because the revenues of its corporate bar may depend in part on the extent of local incorporation.

why Delaware

One very small state, Delaware, is by far the most successful state in attracting incorporation, and especially reincorporation from other states, by publicly held corporations. The reason why Delaware is so successful in attracting initial incorporations and reincorporations by publicly held corporations is hotly contested. One position, known as the race to the bottom, is most closely associated with William Cary's seminal article, Federalism and Corporate Law: Reflections Upon Delaware, 83 YALE L.J. 663 (1974). This position is as follows. State corporate law is a product that states sell on a market that has come to be known as the market for corporate charters. Although shareholder approval is required for determining a corporation's state of incorporation, as a practical matter in publicly held corporations the decision is made by managers and rubber-stamped by the shareholders. Institutional shareholders have become increasingly active in the last ten to twenty years, and might well be able to block reincorporation to a state with a statute that is either quirky, *extremely* management-friendly, or both. However, it's unlikely that institutional shareholders would try to block reincorporation in Delaware, whose corporate statute is now pretty much middle-of-the-road, and which offers various advantages, described below.

Now suppose a principal is represented by an agent whom the principal cannot closely monitor. A third party who wishes to sell Product X to the principal through the agent will have an incentive to give the agent a side payment—a bribe—to induce the agent to purchase Product X on the principal's behalf. In the market for corporate law, the shareholders are in the position of the principal, managers are in the position of the agent, and the legislature is in the position of the third party. Under basic agency-cost theory, a state legislature has an incentive to give managers side payments to induce them to cause their corporations to incorporate or reincorporate in the legislature's state. For a variety of reasons, the side payments cannot take the form of money. Instead, the side payments take the form of a suboptimal statutory approach to regulating managers' traditional and positional conflicts of interest.

A counter position, known as race-to-the-top, was formulated by Ralph Winter and others. *See* Winter, State Law, Shareholder Protection, and the Theory of the Corporation, 6 J. Leg. Stud. 271 (1977). Winter argued that if Delaware law unduly favored managers, shareholders in Delaware corporations would earn lower-than-normal returns, and Delaware corporations therefore would have a higher cost of capital. This would either bankrupt Delaware corporations in the product markets or cause the ouster of management through the market in corporate control, which operates through takeover bids. Therefore, managers would avoid incorporating in Delaware if its law unduly favored managers. Since Delaware is by far the most popular state of incorporation for large publicly held corporations, the race-to-the-bottom analysis, Winter said, must be wrong. Indeed, Winter argued, the incentive for states to sell corporate charters must lead Delaware (and other states) to produce an optimal statutory corporate law regime, because a state that offers the optimal, value-maximizing statutory regime will attract the most incorporations. This argument has only limited power, both because it runs counter to agency-cost theory and because it depends on a drastic overstatement of the power of the product market, the capital market, and the takeover market for these purposes.

Begin with the product market. The costs to the corporation of suboptimal state legislative rules are likely to be relatively small when compared to the corporation's income. Small costs will seldom if ever bankrupt corporations in imperfectly competitive product markets, because corporations operating in such markets usually have the capacity to absorb huge losses and still stay solvent.

The cost of raising equity capital is also unlikely to have a significant effect on the choice of the state of incorporation. First, largely publicly held corporations typically don't raise much money by issuing new equity in the capital market, as opposed to reinvesting earnings or borrowing. Second, even if a corporation does raise capital by issuing new equity, the impact of a suboptimal legal regime will fall on shareholders, not managers. For example, suppose that C Corporation is incorporated in a state, S, which has a suboptimal corporate statute. C Corporation wants to raise $500,000 by selling stock into the capital market. If not for the adverse impact of S's suboptimal legal regime, C could raise $500,000 by issuing 10,000 shares at $50 per share. Given the adverse impact of S's legal regime, to raise $500,000 C must sell 11,111 shares at $45 per share. This dilutes the value of C's stock, and that dilution is a cost. However, that cost will be borne by C's shareholders, rather than by its managers. If the managers own stock or stock options, they will suffer some loss in the value of the stock or options. However, this loss will normally be small compared to the gain the managers can reap from engaging in conflict-of-interest transactions that S's suboptimal legal regime fails to properly regulate.

The market for corporate control—or more accurately, the hostile-takeover market—also has only limited impact in this context. A hostile takeover bid cannot succeed unless it includes a premium that is significantly above the market price of the target's stock. Partly this is because most existing shareholders of the target will value their stock at a price higher than the market price, or they would already have sold. Partly it is because the target's managers can create formidable obstacles to a takeover that often result in bidding contests and that normally can be overcome, if at all, only by paying shareholders a substantial premium over the pre-tender market price. Furthermore, shares of stock held by the public are by definition minority holdings, and traditionally the price of minority stock is discounted from full value—so that, for example, negotiated or "friendly" acquisitions frequently are effected at a price well above the capitalization of the corporation, that is, the number of shares outstanding times the market price of the shares. Accordingly, to complete a successful hostile takeover, a bidder normally must pay a premium of 20–30%, more or less, above the market price of the target's stock. In addition, a hostile bidder must also pay very large fees to investment bankers, lawyers, and other professionals. Since the suboptimality of a state's statutory-law regime is highly unlikely to reduce the value of a corporation by more than a few percentage points, these huge premiums and fees will almost never be economically justified if the bidder's only strategy is to replace a suboptimal legal regime with an optimal legal regime.

Several commentators have attempted to resolve differences between the race-to-the-bottom and race-to-the-top arguments through the generation and analysis of data, but the studies are inconclusive. For example, in an article published in 2001, Rob Daines calculated that based on stock-market valuations, Delaware firms were worth 5% more, on average than non-Delaware firms in twelve out of the sixteen years during the period 1981–1996. Daines, Does Delaware Law improve Firm Value?, 62 J. Financial Econ. 559–71. In a later article, however, Guhan Subrahmanian recalculated the value of Delaware firms during the period 1991–1996, and extended the analysis to the period 1997–2001. Subrahmanian concluded that Delaware firms were worth approximately 3% more than non-Delaware firms during the period 1991–1993, and approximately 2% more than non-Delaware firms during the period 1994–1996. Furthermore, after 1996 the value of Delaware firms did not differ in a statistically different way from the value of non-Delaware firms. Subrahmanian, The Disappearing Delaware Effect, 20 J. Law., Econ. & Org. 32 (2004).

The inconclusive nature of the stock-market data on the race-to-the-bottom, race-to-the-top debate is not surprising. There are a number of reasons why it is difficult if not impossible to assess the optimality of the Delaware statute by analyzing stock-market valuations.

Delaware law consists of judge-made law as well as legislative law. Delaware's judge-made law is vastly richer than the judge-made law of any other state, and Delaware judges are skilled in corporation law. Therefore, even if Delaware's statutory law is suboptimal, that defect might be more than offset by the advantages of Delaware's judge-made law.

If a corporation is incorporated in a given state, it is often necessary to get legal opinions from counsel in that state, as opposed to a corporation's regular counsel, on a legal issue affecting a proposed corporate transaction or course of conduct. Delaware has a high-quality bar that is skilled in corporate law, to whom regular corporate counsel located in other states, can turn with confidence. Most large states also have high-quality corporate bars, but few if any small states can offer a corporate bar that matches Delaware's. Furthermore, the Delaware corporate bar puts in a lot of effort to make sure that the Delaware statute is technically up to speed. Even if the Delaware statute is suboptimal, therefore, its cost could be offset by these advantages.

As Michael Klausner has pointed out, because so many publicly held corporations are incorporated in Delaware, incorporation there brings in its train a benefit known as network externality. When a product implicates network externality, the value of the product to each user increases as more people use it. For example, if fifty million people have telephones, each telephone has more value to its user than if fifty thousand people have telephones. As a result of the network externality effect, a product that attracts a large following can be more valuable to each user than a better product that has only a small following. For example, due to network externality, it may be more efficient to use Microsoft Word even if there are better word-processing programs, because so many other people use Word and are familiar with it. Similarly, it may be more efficient to incorporate in Delaware, whether or not Delaware statutory law is better than other state statutory law, just because so many corporations use and are familiar with Delaware law. *See* Klausner, Corporations, Corporate Law, and Network of Contract, 81 VA. L. REV. 757 (1995). Furthermore, because so many corporations have incorporated in Delaware, it has become a good address, like Park Avenue in New York City, or Park Place in Monopoly. In short, even if the Delaware statute was suboptimal, the cost of that suboptimality could be offset by the network-externality and good-address benefits that Delaware incorporation brings.

Related to network effects is a *linqua franca* theory, which views Delaware law as something of a second language that transaction lawyers share that is particularly valued by their clients when investing in a firm whose principal place of business is in another state. Brian Broughman, Jesse M. Fried & Darian Ibrahim, Delaware Law as Linqua Franca: Theory and Evidence, 57 J. Law & Econ. 865 (2014), in a study of 1,850 startup firms financed by venture capitalists, find that as the number of out-of-state investors increased from zero to two the percentage of Delaware incorporations increased from 68 to 82 percent; thereafter, the addition of a single out-of-state investor increased the likelihood of Delaware incorporation by 4–6 percent. An implication of *linqua franca* is "[f]or [another] state to be successful, enough lawyers would need to learn a second or third 'language' " . . . so that this "raises the barrier to competition. . . ." *Id.* at 870.

Today, there isn't that much significant difference between the Delaware statute and most other state statutes. That's not surprising. If all states are competing for management favor, their statutes are likely to converge. But if the state statutes converge, then even if the state statutes as a group are suboptimal, the Delaware statute might not be more suboptimal than other statutes. As Kahan and Kamar have put it, the race is over and Delaware has won. Kahan and Kamar, The Myth of State Competition in Corporate Law, 55 STAN. L. REV. 679 (2002). Now that Delaware has won the race, and holds a kind of monopoly position, the Delaware legislature has a special incentive *not* to lead in the adoption of innovative suboptimal rules. This special incentive is to avoid massive federal intervention in corporate law.[3] Unlike the states, the federal government has an interest in the efficiency of national securities markets and, partly because its revenues depend heavily on corporate income, on the efficiency of the corporate system. For various reasons, the federal government does not intervene to correct every suboptimal

[3]   *See* Melvin A. Eisenberg, The Structure of Corporation Law, 89 COLUM. L. REV. 461 (1989).

state law rule. However, as state statutory corporate law becomes highly suboptimal, the risk of federal intervention increases. If comprehensive national corporate-law rules were established for publicly held corporations, over time Delaware could lose its leading position, because there would be less incentive to incorporate in one state rather than the other. Therefore, precisely because of its historical success in the charter market, Delaware is more threatened by the possibility of comprehensive federal intervention than any other state. Furthermore, because of Delaware's massive market share, innovative suboptimal rules in Delaware are more likely to provoke federal intervention than innovative suboptimal rules any other state. Accordingly, having achieved a monopoly position in significant part because of its past leadership in offering suboptimal rules, Delaware now has an incentive not to lead in the adoption of innovative suboptimal rules. *See also*, Brian R. Cheffins, Steven A. Bank & Harwell Wells, Shareholder Protection Across Time, 68 Fl. L. Rev. 691 (2017) (using an index that tracked changes in Delaware, Illinois and MBCA statutes the authors find that shareholder protection has declined modestly since 1900 but the protections lost under state corporate statutes were more than offset by changes introduced by federal securities laws and stock exchange listing requirements).

Finally, a comparison between the Delaware statute and other state statutes has limited significance not only because the difference between state statutes tends to be small, but also because of the limited significance of state statutory corporation law. Much of the real action in corporation law is not in state statutory law, but in the other three modules of corporation law described in the Note on the Architecture of Corporate Law—state judge-made law, federal law, and private ordering or soft law. The effect of small differences between state statutes tend to be swamped by the overriding significance of the law in those other modules. Of course, it is the general social interest that state statutory law be optimal, but suboptimal state statutory law can be and is compensated for in many respects by the law in the other three modules.

Because the law of the state of incorporation normally (although not invariably) governs a corporation's internal corporate affairs, and because Delaware is the preeminent state for publicly held corporations, Delaware law constitutes one major axis of this book. Another major axis of this book is the Model Business Corporation Act, which was originally promulgated, and is regularly revised, by the Committee on Corporate Laws of the American Bar Association's Business Law Section. Although the Model Act has no official status, it serves as the template for the statutes of a great many states. Recurring reference will also be made in this book to the California and New York corporate statutes, because as a result of their size and commercial significance, those states account for a significant portion of all corporations.

―――――

5. ORGANIZING A CORPORATION

DEL. GEN. CORP. LAW §§ 101, 102, 103, 106, 107, 108, 109

[See Statutory Supplement]

MODEL BUS. CORP. ACT §§ 2.01, 2.02, 2.03, 2.05, 2.06

[See Statutory Supplement]

After the state of incorporation has been selected, the corporation must be organized (created) in that state by the incorporators, who may be either the prospective owners of the corporation or their agent.[4] The first, and basic, legal step in organizing a corporation is to file a certificate of incorporation in a designated office in the state in which the organizers have chosen to corporate. Once the certificate of incorporation has been filed, the corporation must issue stock to get its business up and running. However, the power to issue stock is normally vested in the board; the board, in turn, is normally elected by the shareholders; and until stock is issued, there are no shareholders.

There are two alternative mechanisms for solving this problem. Under the law of some states, such as New York, the corporation's incorporators have the powers of directors until directors are elected and the powers of shareholders until stock is issued. N.Y.Bus.Corp.Law §§ 404(a), 615(c). Under this approach, the incorporators will typically adopt by-laws, and elect initial directors to serve until the first annual meeting of shareholders. Under the law of other states, such as Delaware, the initial directors can be named in the corporation's certificate of incorporation. *See* Del.Gen.Corp.Law §§ 107, 108. If the initial directors are named in the certificate of incorporation, the functions of the incorporators pass to the directors when the certificate is filed and recorded, and the directors, rather than the incorporators, adopt by laws. Del.Gen.Corp.Law §§ 107, 108(a). After the initial directors are named, either by the incorporators or in the certificate of incorporation, they will hold an organization meeting. A typical agenda for such a meeting is reflected in the Form of Minutes of Organization Meeting that follows this Note.

In connection with the issuance of stock, there is a crucial distinction between authorized stock and issued stock. An important function of a certificate of incorporation is to designate the classes of stock, and the

---

[4]   It is usually unnecessary to have more than one incorporator. For ease of exposition, however, in this Chapter the term *incorporators* will be used to mean either a single incorporator or several incorporators.

number of shares of each class, that the corporation is authorized to issue. Only stock that has been authorized in the certificate of incorporation can be issued. If the corporation's authorized stock consists of one class of common stock, the certificate need only designate the number of authorized shares. If there is to be more than one class of stock, and particularly if there are to be one or more classes of preferred stock (that is, stock that carries a preference over common stock as to dividends, on liquidation, or both) the certificate of incorporation must either designate the terms of each class, or empower the board to issue portions of an authorized class of stock in series from time to time, and to designate the terms of each series as it is issued. Authorized stock that has not yet been issued is known as authorized but unissued stock. Authorized stock that has been issued is known as issued stock or outstanding stock. Sometimes a corporation repurchases stock that it has previously issued. Such stock may be referred to as treasury stock or as authorized and issued but not outstanding stock.

The power to issue authorized but unissued stock, and the price at which the stock will be issued, is vested in the board, subject only to very limited constraints. One constraint is that the board cannot issue more stock than is authorized in the certificate of incorporation. At common law, another constraint was that existing shareholders had the right to subscribe a proportionate part of a new issue. This is known as the preemptive right. The right was riddled with exceptions—for example, it did not apply to stock that was issued for property rather than cash. Modern statutes provide that shareholders have no preemptive rights unless the certificate of incorporation so provides. Few do. However, even where shareholders do not have a preemptive right the board may not issue stock on a non-pro-rata basis for the purpose of reallocating or perpetuating control. *See, e.g.,* Note on Condec v. Lunkenheimer, Chapter 4, section 1, infra; Schwartz v. Marien, 335 N.E.2d 334 (N.Y. 1975). The shareholders' right to prohibit a non-pro-rata stock issuance for an improper purpose is sometimes referred to as a quasi-preemptive right.

Normally, stock is issued by a corporation in a simultaneous exchange for cash, property, or services. In some cases, however, a would-be shareholder enters into a subscription agreement under which he agrees to purchase a corporation's stock when it is issued to him at a future date. Typically in such cases the corporation has not yet been formed, and the agreement is made on the would-be corporation's behalf by its incorporators. Agreements of this type are called preincorporation subscriptions.

There is a good deal of old law on various aspects of such agreements. The old rule was that a preincorporation subscription was only a continuing offer by the subscriber, and that a subscriber therefore was not bound if he timely revoked. Under that rule a subscriber could revoke his agreement until the moment of incorporation or, in the alternative, until the corporation, once formed, issued stock to the subscriber. There was an exception where the mutual promises of subscribers were expressed as consideration for each other. In that case, a contract was deemed to be formed immediately. In addition, subscription agreements entered into after the corporation was formed were treated as ordinary contracts, and raised no special problems of enforceability.

Modern corporate statutes have changed the treatment of preincorporation subscriptions. Most statutes now provide that preincorporation subscriptions are irrevocable for a specified period of time unless all the subscribers consent to a revocation or the agreement otherwise provides. *See, e.g.,* Del.Gen.Corp.Law § 165 (preincorporation subscription agreements irrevocable for six months except with the consent of all other subscribers); Model Act § 6.20(a) (same). Accordingly, under modern statutes the old law relating to subscriptions is of greatly diminished importance, and current cases on the subject are rare.

———

FORM OF MINUTES OF ORGANIZATION MEETING

[See Statutory Supplement]

———

FORM OF BY-LAWS

[See Statutory Supplement]

———

FORM OF STOCK CERTIFICATE

[See Statutory Supplement]

———

DEL. GEN. CORP. LAW § 109

[See Statutory Supplement]

———

MODEL BUS. CORP. ACT §§ 2.06, 10.20–10.21

[See Statutory Supplement]

———

6. THE BASIC TYPES OF FINANCIAL SECURITIES

As will be seen, in the partnership form of doing business, the economic rights of owners are set forth in the partnership agreement (and in the absence of such an agreement default rules are provided by the state partnership law). In the corporate setting as well as the limited liability company the owners' rights are set forth in the company's articles of incorporation and articles of organization, respectively. In the corporation the owners are commonly referred to as stockholders or shareholders and in the limited liability company as members. An initial question for a corporation is how to finance its business. The three major modes of corporate finance are common stock, preferred stock and debt. The following describes the basic features of typical equity financing instruments used in the corporation. The features common to debt are discussed in the next section.

    1.   *Common Stock.* A cornerstone of corporate law is that all shares have the same rights, privileges and preferences as other shares, unless the articles of incorporation otherwise provide. The most basic form of ownership is represented by common shares. Traditionally, shares of common stock are conceived as ownership or *equity* interests in the corporation, so that the body of common shareholders are the corporation's owners. Normally, but not invariably, common stock carries the right to vote in the election of directors and certain other matters. Typically, or at least often, dividends are paid on common stock, but many corporations do not pay dividends, and in any event whether dividends are paid, and if so in what amount, is generally in the discretion of the board. As a result, common stock has no fixed claim on the corporation. Partly for this reason, modern financial theory often conceives of common stock as ultimate or *residual* ownership. "Common shareholders are often thought of as the owners of the firm or as the holders of the *equity* interest in the firm. . . . The equity interest is sometimes usefully thought of as the *residual* interest—the claim to what is left after all senior claimants have been satisfied." W. Klein & J. Coffee, Business Organization and Finance 286 (11th ed. 2010) (emphasis added). The "senior claimants" to which Coffee & Klein refer are debt and preferred stock.

    2.   *Preferred Stock.* Preferred stock is a hybrid that combines the ownership element of common stock and the senior nature of debt. The basic elements of preferred stock are described as follows in Hunt, Williams & Donaldson, Basic Business Finance 358–61 (5th ed. 1974):

> From the purely legal point of view . . . preferred stock is a type of ownership and thus takes a classification similar to that of the common stock. . . . Unlike [a] bond, . . . preferred stock does not contain any promise of repayment of the original investment; and as far as the shareholders are concerned, this must be considered as a permanent investment for the life of the company. Further, there is no legal obligation to pay a fixed rate of return on the investment.
>
> The special character of the preferred stock lies in its relationship to the common stock. When a preferred stock is used as a part of the corporate capital structure, the rights and

responsibilities of the owners as the residual claimants to the asset values and earning power of the business no longer apply equally to all shareholders. Two types of owners emerge, representing a voluntary subdivision of the overall ownership privileges. Specifically, the common shareholders agree that the preferred shareholder shall have "preference" or first claim in the event that the directors are able and willing to pay a dividend. In the case of what is termed a nonparticipating or *straight preferred stock*, which is the most frequent type, the extent of this priority is a fixed percentage of the par value of the stock or a fixed number of dollars per share in the case of stock without a nominal or par value. . . .

In most cases the prior position of preferred stock also extends to the disposition of assets in the event of liquidation of the business. Again, the priority is only with reference to the common stock and does not affect the senior position of creditors in any way. . . .[*]

Typically, preferred stock carries a dividend that is payable periodically—often, quarterly—in the board's discretion. Thus the most obvious difference between debt and preferred stock is that debtholders have a fixed claim on the corporation for interest and principal, while preferred shareholders normally have no fixed claims for distributions. Instead, the claims of preferred stock for distributions are only contingent: *If* the corporation proposes to pay a dividend on common, *then* it must first pay a designated dividend to the preferred. *If* the corporation liquidates, *then* before it distributes anything to the common it must satisfy the preferred's liquidation preference.

Often, the preferred's dividend preference is "cumulative"—that is, no dividend can be paid on common unless all prior dividends on the preferred have been paid. (If a preferred is noncumulative, a dividend can be paid on common as long as the current dividend on the preferred is paid.) Often too, preferred is given the right to vote on the election of directors if, but only if, preferred dividends are in default for a designated number of periods.

3.   *Convertibles, Classified Stock, and Derivatives.* In the modern world, the basic elements of common stock, preferred stock, and debt are often disaggregated, and their fragments are combined to design more exotic corporate securities. For example, preferred stock is often issued in several classes, and common stock may be issued in several classes as well (*classified common*). In such cases, each class enjoys somewhat different rights than the others in respect of voting, dividend, or liquidation rights, or all three. Many preferred stocks, and some bonds, are made convertible into common stock at the option of the holder, on

---

[*]   As quoted in V. Brudney & W. Bratton, Corporate Finance—Cases and Material 335–36 (4th ed. 1993).

specified terms. Furthermore, new types of securities may be "derived" from common stock, in the sense that although the securities are not themselves common stock, their value largely depends on the value of a corporation's common stock and on the terms of their relationship to the common stock. The simplest example is a "right" or "warrant," which is a security issued by the corporation that gives the holder a right or option to purchase common stock on specified terms.

INTRODUCTION TO TYPES OF DEBT AND DEBT COVENANTS

Debt is a fixed claim against the corporation for principal and interest. The major types of corporate debt are *trade debt, bank debt, bonds, debentures*, and *notes.*

(a) *Trade debt.* When a business purchases goods or services, payment is typically not due for thirty, sixty, or ninety days. Trade debt consists principally of amounts that a corporation owes for such goods and services at any point in time. Trade debt appears on a corporation's balance sheet as Accounts Payable.

(b) *Bank debt.* A business will often be financed in significant part by commercial-bank loans. Bank loans appear on a corporation's balance sheet under captions such as Loans Payable.

(c) *Bonds and debentures.* Another method of financing a corporation is to issue bonds or debentures. Essentially, bonds and debentures are promises, embodied in an instrument, to repay amounts that the firm has borrowed on a long-term basis, typically by selling the bonds on the general market or on some special market. Bonds appear on a corporation's balance sheet under captions such as Bonds Payable, or under a caption that describes specific bond issues, such as 7.5% Senior Debentures. Unlike bank loans, bonds and debentures normally represent money borrowed from the public, or at least from a significant group of lenders or investors. "As a matter of historical practice, bonds and debentures are long term obligations issued under indentures, bonds generally being secured obligations and debentures being unsecured obligations." W. Bratton, Corporate Finance—Cases and Materials 240 (6th ed. 2008).

> A bond [or] debenture . . . is simply a promise by the borrower to pay a specified amount on a specified date, together with interest at specified times, on the terms and subject to the conditions spelled out in a governing indenture. . . . Bonds [and] debentures . . . are, then . . . promissory notes issued pursuant to and governed by longer contracts [known as indentures]. Some of the governing terms and conditions will be set out on the face of the [bond or debenture]. Most terms, however, will be in the [indenture] that governs the instrument and will be merely referred to on its face. The note incorporates the contract by reference. . . .

It is the practice in both financial and legal writing to use "bond" as a generic term for all long term debt securities. . . .

Id. at 240. Bratton describes an *indenture* as follows:

> An indenture is a contract entered into between the borrowing corporation and a trustee. The trustee administers the payments of interest and principal, and monitors and enforces compliance with other obligations on behalf of the bondholders as a group. The indenture defines the assorted obligations of the borrower, the rights and remedies of the holders of the bonds, and the role of the trustee.
>
> The borrower contracts with a trustee rather than directly with the holders of the bonds so as to permit the bonds to be sold in small denominations to large numbers of scattered investors. Given widespread ownership in small amounts, unilateral monitoring and enforcement by each holder is not cost effective. The device of the trust solves this problem. . . .
>
> The "bonds" and the "indenture" need to be conceptually distinguished. The bonds set out a promise to pay that runs to the holders of the bonds. The indenture is a bundle of additional promises (including a backup promise to pay) that run to the trustee. The bondholders are third party beneficiaries of the promises in the indenture. Even though the promises in the bonds run directly to the holders, the bonds are subject to the indenture and therefore may be enforced directly by the holders only to the extent that the indenture allows. Indentures generally constrain the unilateral enforcement rights of small holders, channeling enforcement through the central agency of the trustee. The device of the trust indenture, then, not only facilitates enforcement by the widely scattered holders, but also restrains such enforcement. It facilitates borrowing in small amounts from large numbers of widely scattered lenders not only by constraining the issuer as against the holders, but by protecting the issuer from the holders.

Id. at 241–242.

(d) *Notes.* There is no legally recognized distinction between bonds and debentures, on the one hand, and notes, on the other. However, "Under the historical practice, notes may be long term or short term obligations, but in either case are not issued pursuant to an indenture. Recent practice has changed this. Today, 'notes' often are issued pursuant to indentures as unsecured long term obligations. But they tend to be intermediate term securities, coming due in ten years or less, where 'debentures' tend to mature in ten years or more." Id. at 240.

7. THE SEDUCTIVE QUALITIES OF DEBT

A question that first arises when the corporation is formed and recurs throughout the life of the corporation is whether the corporation and its owners are well advised to include debt within its capital structure. As will be seen in the material that follows, debt has many virtues; but like good food, too much of it can lead to serious adverse consequences.

John D. Ayer, Guide to Finance for Lawyers, 295–297
(2001).

Introduction

Skeeter, your old college roommate, has just started work in the Investor Relations Office at WidgetCo. Although he cheerfully admits he does not know much of anything about finance, he has a pleasant manner that soothes customers on the telephone. Meanwhile, he figures the new job will give him a chance to play catch-up with some of his classmates and their sparkling new MBAs. So, you are not surprised by his enthusiasm when he comes charging through your door, eager to tell you about his latest insight.

"It's amazing," he says, "I cannot understand how everyone overlooked this so far."

You raise an eyebrow, which is all the encouragement he needs to continue.

"Last year, we had earnings of $100. We are a highly stable company, so we pay it all out to shareholders. We have 10 shares, each selling for $100, which implies a market capitalization of $1,000. Shareholders, then, get $10 a share, which translates into a rate of return of 10 percent."

Skeeter pauses to let you admire these marvels.

"But," he begins again, "we can *borrow* money at eight percent."

He pauses for dramatic effect. The barest flicker on your forehead is enough to set him off again.

"Don't you see?" He continues. "We should *borrow* $500 in perpetuity. Then we will use the $500 to buy back five shares. We will have to pay $40 a year in debt service. That leaves us $60 a year to distribute among our five shares of stock. At 10 percent, that means that we have increased the value of a share from $100 to $120, and the total market capitalization from $500 to $600—a 20 percent gain. It is like magic! I have asked for an appointment with the CEO so I can tell him all about it first thing in the morning!"

But even as he spoke, Skeeter's expression turned forlorn.

"There is only one puzzle," he said sadly.

Again, an eyebrow is enough.

"I mean," he continued, "if it works for five shares, why shouldn't we go the whole way? Why not retire 10 shares and borrow $1,000? We will pay $80 a year in interest. That leaves us $20 a year in return on"—and here he looked genuinely baffled"—well, on no investment at all."

Skeeter sounds like a good kid, and the chances are he will figure out before making a fool of himself in front of the CEO that $20/0 = an infinite return, which is too good to be true even in the widget business. To start with his last, absurd, example: if WidgetCo is financed with *all* debt and *no* equity, then the debt *is* the *equity*, and will demand a corresponding return—in this case, 10 percent. There can be no triumph of form over substance here; equity is the one who bears the equity risk, no matter what the name.

As to the less extreme case, if Skeeter is in error, he has the excuse of good company. Many investors, older and wiser than he, have believed that you could increase firm value by increasing leverage (at least up to a point). Old-time financial analysts, including the Securities Exchange Commission, expended valuable resources trying to identify the "optimal" debt-equity ratio—i.e., the mix of debt and equity that would maximize firm value.

Enter the great revolutionaries of modern finance theory, Franco Modigliani and Merton Miller (MM). . . . MM argued that, under clean-test-tube assumptions, . . . the value of the firm is the value of the assets, and you cannot change the value of the "liability/net-worth" side of the balance sheet by monkeying around with the . . . [ratio of debt to equity].[2]

MM understood, of course, that a change in leverage may change the *gross* returns payable to shareholders. Thus, in Skeeter's first example above, Skeeter showed how to increase the payout from $10 a share to $12, but what Skeeter overlooked (as MM argue) is that we have also changed the *risk* of the equity investment.

Recall the first rule of leverage: equity comes behind debt. Equity of a leveraged company is always more risky than equity of an unleveraged company, because debt gets paid first, leaving equity to get paid if (and only if) there is enough to trickle down. Equity investors, faced with a higher risk, will demand a higher rate of return, and a higher rate of return translates into a lower share price. For example, suppose the rate on WidgetCo equity rose from 10 percent (unleveraged) to 12 percent (leveraged). Then the value of a (leveraged) WidgetCo share would be $12/(0.12) = $10, just as before. . . .

---

[2]   Franco Modigliani and Merton H. Miller, *The Cost of Capital, Corporate Finance and the Theory of Investment*, 38 AMER. ECON. REV. 261 (1958).

An Arbitrage Proof of MM

There are many ways to demonstrate the MM argument. One is to consider the possibility of *arbitrage*. We have often seen that if two identical assets bear different prices, then there is a profit for an instant, no-risk (arbitrage) profit, and that such profits do not exist except in fleeting moments of transition.

We can apply arbitrage analysis to the MM insight. Take the case of Imogen, an investor, who is thinking about a flutter on Skeeter's WidgetCo. As a benchmark, suppose she can buy *the whole company*—which is to say, all of the equity, and (if there is any), all of the debt. In that case, surely, her only concern will be the asset return, and that she will accept an aggregate rate of 10 percent. If WidgetCo earns $100 a year (as above), and if it is all equity financed, she will be willing to pay $1,000 for all the equity.

But, supposing WidgetCo is financed with $500 of debt at eight percent, she can get $40 of the cash flow for $500 by purchasing debt. To get the other $60, she must buy all the equity. But it cannot be that she will be willing to pay more than $500 for the equity; otherwise, she would be paying different prices for the same cash flows, violating the arbitrage rule. . . .

———

NOTE ON THE TAX SHIELD OF DEBT

In their path breaking articles supporting the irrelevance of the firm's capital structure and dividend policies on the value of the firm, Modigliani and Miller make several assumptions. Among their assumptions is there are no taxes. Ah, heaven! What is the impact of taxes on how managers and investors approach the choice between debt and equity in the financing choices facing the firm?

Corporations are taxpayers and, when they distribute their earnings and profits, the receiving shareholders are taxed on the amount distributed to them. We therefore see that a downside of the corporate form is double taxation; the corporation pays a tax on its profits and shareholders pay a tax on dividends distributed from those profits. There are some notable qualifications to the statement that business entities face double taxation of their profits. First, many shareholders are not taxable entities because they are charitable institutions, pension funds and the like. Second, as later material will show, the tax laws allow small business entities to enjoy pass-through treatment so that the business itself is only a reporting entity but is not a tax payer. For example, a partnership files only an information return with the Internal Revenue Service but is not taxed on its income; instead, its profits are attributed to each of its partners who are taxed on the amount attributed to the partner regardless of whether any of the profits was distributed to the partner. The discussion that follows focuses heavily on the tax laws treatment of debt which is the same for all taxable business entities. In considering the preference of debt over equity, the key factor is that under the Internal Revenue Code interest is a deductible expense whereas dividends are not. As will be seen, this distinction dramatically tilts the choice of financing toward debt and substantially qualifies the insights of Modigliani and Miller. To illustrate this point, assume that Alpha Corporation and Beta Corporation are identical except that Alpha has no debt and capital of $100,000 (10,000 shares) whereas Beta has issued $50,000 in bonds (interest rate of 8%) and $50,000 in stock (5,000 shares), that each company earned $20,000 before interest and taxes, and that the applicable corporate tax rate is 50 percent. Assume each pursues a dividend policy of distributing all profits to owners. Under these assumptions, the following are the income statements for the two firms:

	Alpha	Beta
Income before Taxes and Interest	$20,000	$20,000
Less: Interest		4,000
Taxable Income	20,000	16,000
Taxes	10,000	8,000
Net Income	10,000	8,000

First observe that Alpha's taxes are $2000 higher than those of Beta. What explains this? Second, pursuant to M & M irrelevance theorem the total cost of capital should be the same for both Alpha and Beta. If we assume that Alpha's cost of capital is 10 percent then the weighted average cost of capital for Beta would be 12 percent as well. Since bonds bear a market rate of 8 percent this means that the equity would carry a discount rate of 16 percent. So viewed, the total value of Alpha is $10,000 ÷ 12% = $83, 333. In comparison, the value of Beta is the value of the bonds, $50,000, plus the value of the equity, $8,000 ÷ 16% = $50,000, for a total firm value of $100,000.

> Looking at the figures from another perspective, we can say that the effect of the corporation income tax is to make the government a 50 percent partner in the equity claims, but not in the debt claims, in the corporation. Thus, the government's claim in Corporation A[lpha] is to half of $100,000, or $50,000, while its claim in B[eta] is to half of only $50,000, or $25,000. The True complexities of the corporation income tax . . . would require some modifications and qualifications if one sought complete precision in this analysis, but those would be minor quibbles. They would not affect the basic point of this analysis, which is that the securities of the corporation using debt are significantly more valuable than those of the corporation using (less or) no debt and the difference is attributable solely to the apparent tax advantages of debt. This is the essence of the view—reflected in the "capital structure puzzle" phrase—that American corporations should be more highly leveraged than they are.

William A. Klein, John C. Coffee, Jr. & Frank Partnoy, Business Organization and Finance Legal and Economic Principles 367 (11th ed. 2010).

The tax shield provided by debt is no longer without limit. The multifaceted tax act passed in 2017 limits the amount a corporation is entitled to deduct as business interest in any taxable year beginning after December 31, 2017. The business interest deducted generally shall not exceed the sum of (i) the business interest income of the corporation for such taxable year plus (ii) 30% of the "adjusted taxable income" of the corporation for such taxable year. Until 2022, adjusted taxable income means the earnings of the corporation *before* deduction of interest, taxes, depreciation or amortization (EBITDA). In 2022, the deductible amount is more constrained as adjustable taxable income for this purpose is then calculated after earnings are reduced by any charges for depreciation and amortization charges (EBIT). The limitation does not apply to a corporation for a taxable year if the corporation's average annual gross receipts for the prior three taxable years does not exceed $25 million.

————

NOTE ON LEVERAGE AND THE RISK OF FINANCIAL DISTRESS

The preceding note demonstrates that in a world with taxation of corporate earnings in which interest is a deductible business expense and dividends are not deductible, the value of the firm is increased by the introduction of debt to its capital structure. But can too much of a good thing be harmful?

If there is a possibility of bankruptcy, and if administrative and other costs associated with bankruptcy are significant, the leveraged firm may be less attractive to investors than the unlevered one. With perfect capital markets, zero bankruptcy costs are assumed. If the firm goes bankrupt, assets presumably can be sold at their economic values with no liquidating or legal costs involved. Proceeds from the sale are distributed according to the priority of claims on assets . . . If capital markets are less than perfect, however, there may be administrative costs, and assets may have to be liquidated at less than their economic values. These administrative costs and the "shortfall" in liquidating values from economic value represent a drain on the system from the viewpoint of the debt and equity holders. . . .

In the event of bankruptcy, security holders as a whole receive less than they would have in the absence of bankruptcy costs. To the extent that the levered firm has a greater possibility in bankruptcy than the unlevered one, it would be a less attractive investment, all other things being the same. The possibility of bankruptcy is not a linear function of the debt-to-equity ratio but rather increases at an increasing rate beyond some threshold. As a result, the expected cost of bankruptcy also increases in this accelerating manner and would be expected to have a corresponding negative effect on the value of the firm.

Put another way, investors are likely to penalize the price of the stock as leverage increases. . . . As debt is added, the required rate of return rises, and this increment represents a financial-risk premium. In the absence of bankruptcy costs, the required rate of return would rise in a linear manner according to M & M ... However, allowing for bankruptcy costs and an increasing probability of bankruptcy with increasing financial leverage, the required rate of return on equity would be expected to rise at an increasing rate beyond some point. At first there might be a negligible probability of bankruptcy, so there would be little or no penalty. As financial leverage increases, so too does the penalty. For extreme leverage, the penalty becomes very substantial indeed.

James C. Van Horne & John M. Wachowicz, Jr., Fundamentals of Financial Management 459–60 (13th Ed. 2008). Professors Van Horne and Wachowicz also point out that monitoring costs for debt holders increases with the amount of debt; these costs rise at an increasing rate as the amount of leverage increases.

––––––––

8.   EQUITABLE SUBORDINATION OF SHAREHOLDER CLAIMS

––––––––

UNIFORM FRAUDULENT TRANSFER ACT § 4(a)

[See Statutory Supplement]

––––––––

BANKRUPTCY CODE § 548

[See Statutory Supplement]

––––––––

NOTE ON EQUITABLE SUBORDINATION OF SHAREHOLDER CLAIMS

Under the doctrine of equitable subordination, when a corporation is in bankruptcy, debt claims that a controlling shareholder has against the corporation may be subordinated to the claims of other persons, including the claims of preferred shareholders, on various equitable grounds. The doctrine of equitable subordination is often referred to as the "Deep Rock" doctrine, named after the corporation—a subsidiary—in the seminal case of Taylor v. Standard Gas & Electric Co., 306 U.S. 307, 59 S.Ct. 543, 83 L.Ed. 669 (1939). The Court in that case subordinated the parent's claim, as a creditor of the subsidiary, to the claims of other creditors and preferred stockholders of the subsidiary, because of the parent's improper management of the subsidiary for the parent's benefit, and because the subsidiary had been inadequately capitalized. See also Pepper v. Litton, 308 U.S. 295, 310, 60 S.Ct. 238, 246, 84 L.Ed. 281 (1939); Hackney & Benson, Shareholder Liability for Inadequate Capital, 43 U.Pitt.L.Rev. 837 (1982).

[T]hree conditions must be satisfied before exercise of the power of equitable subordination is appropriate. (i) The claimant [who may be an owner, director, or officer of the bankrupt corporation] must have engaged in some type of inequitable conduct. . . . (ii) The misconduct must have resulted in injury to the creditors of the bankrupt or conferred an unfair advantage on the claimant. . . . (iii) Equitable subordination of the claim must not be inconsistent with the provisions of the Bankruptcy Act. . . .

In determining whether these three conditions are satisfied three principles must be kept in mind. The first is that inequitable conduct directed against the bankrupt or its creditors may be sufficient to warrant subordination of a claim irrespective of whether it was related to the acquisition or assertion of that claim. . . .

The second principle is that a claim or claims should be subordinated only to the extent necessary to offset the harm which the bankrupt and its creditors suffered on account of the inequitable conduct. For example, if a claimant guilty of misconduct asserts two claims, each worth $10,000, and the injury he inflicted on the bankrupt or its creditors amounted to $10,000, only one of his claims should be subordinated. Since the exercise of the subordination power is governed by equitable principles, . . . subordination of the other claim would be improper.

The third guiding principle relates to allocation of the burden of proof. . . .

To constitute the type of challenge contemplated by the Court, an objection resting on equitable grounds cannot be merely formal, but rather must contain some substantial factual basis to support its allegation of impropriety. . . . The proper rule is that

> the claimant's verified proof of claim obliges the objecting trustee to come forward with enough substantiations to overcome the claimant's *prima facie* case and thus compel [the claimant] to actually prove the validity and honesty of his claim.

Benjamin v. Diamond, 563 F.2d 692, 699–702 (5th Cir.1977) (citing 3A J. Moore & L. King, Collier on Bankruptcy, § 63.06, at 1785 (14th ed. 1976)).

————

Gannett Co. v. Larry

221 F.2d 269 (2d Cir.1955)

Gannett Company was in the newspaper-publishing business. Berwin Paper was also in the business of publishing a newspaper. To ensure a supply of newsprint in view of a threatened shortage, Gannett purchased all the stock of Berwin Paper, and converted Berwin from a publisher to a newsprint supplier. Gannett lent substantial sums to Berwin for that purpose. The threatened newsprint shortage never materialized. As a result, by 1952 the newsprint market had changed completely, and Berwin was operating at a loss. In 1953, Berwin became insolvent, and a trustee in bankruptcy was appointed. The court subordinated Gannett's claim for the sums it had loaned to Berwin to the claims of other creditors. "[T]he losses suffered by Berwin were suffered, not in an attempt by Gannett primarily to make the subsidiary a financially profitable proposition, but to turn it into a source of newsprint, of no interest to the other creditors—unless financially profitable—but of distinct interest to Gannett, whether or not financially profitable, because of Gannett's newsprint shortage. Because of this factor. . . . 'It would be unfair to allow the claim of Gannett on a parity with other creditors who lacked the interest which Gannett had in Berwin's disastrous experiment in the newsprint field.' In such circumstances, proof of fraud or illegality is not necessary."

NOTE ON EQUITABLE SUBORDINATION VS. PIERCING THE VEIL

Hackney & Benson comment that "As compared with denying to a shareholder his privilege of limited liability, the equitable remedy of subordination is much less drastic: it simply takes an investment already made, and denies it the status of a creditor's claim on a parity with outside creditors, whereas imposing liability for corporate debts undermines the essential premise of limited liability—that a shareholder's risk is limited to the amount of his investment. . . . It is logical, therefore, for the courts to have found it fair to subordinate a controlling person's claim based upon a lesser evidence of misuse of the corporate form than what is required to impose affirmative personal liability for all corporate obligations. Furthermore, if actual shareholder capital were so small as to result in treating a shareholder loan as equity, then the equity as supplemented by the subordinated loan may be deemed an adequate cushion to support limited liability. Accordingly, inadequate capitalization may result in subordination when it does not necessarily require imposition of affirmative liability." Hackney & Benson, supra, at 882.

NOTE ON CHARACTERIZATION OF PROMOTER'S ADVANCES

Undercapitalization plays an important role in equitable subordination, as it does in piercing the corporate veil. It also can play a role in characterizing the advance as debt or equity. *See* Michael R. Tucker, Debt Recharacterization During an Economic Trough: Trashing Historical Tests to Avoid Discouraging Insider Lending, 71 Ohio. St. L. J. 187 (2010).

In Arnold v. Phillips, 117 F.2d 497 (5th Cir.1941), cert. denied 313 U.S. 583, 61 S.Ct. 1102, 85 L.Ed. 1539 (1941), Arnold formed a brewery company with capital stock of $50,000, paid for in cash. He then lent the brewery $75,000, so that it would have enough to start operations. The business was profitable for about two years and was able to pay Arnold salary, periodic interest on the debt, and even repaid some of the debt's principal. Then the business began to lose heavily, and Arnold advanced almost $50,000. Eventually, the brewery went into bankruptcy liquidation. In the bankruptcy proceedings, a mortgage held by Arnold to secure his loans was held invalid on the ground of inadequate capitalization insofar as the mortgage represented money Arnold loaned the brewery to build and equip its plant, but valid as to subsequent advances made after the brewery became a going concern. The court said:

> The two series of advances differ materially as respects their nature and purpose. Those made before the enterprise was launched were, as the district court found, really capital. Although the charter provided for no more capital than $50,000, what it took to build the plant and equip it was a permanent investment, in its nature capital. . . . There can be little doubt that what he contributed to the plant was actually intended to be capital, notwithstanding the charter was not amended and demand notes were taken. . . .

> After two years of prosperity, with the original capital thus enlarged demonstrated to be sufficient, with a book surplus of nearly $100,000 after payment of large salaries and dividends in the form of interest, there arose a situation very different from that in the beginning. Adversity then occurring raised a problem not different from that which commonly faces a corporation having losses. It may borrow to meet its needs. Had this corporation borrowed of a bank upon the security of the plant, the debt would no doubt be valid. What would render it invalid when Arnold furnished the money? . . .

> It would be hard to say in this case that $50,000 was not a substantial capital, and impossible so to say after holding that the real capital was $125,500, though some was irregularly paid in [as a purported loan].

Compare Fairchild Dornier GMBH v. Official Comm. of Unsecured Creditors, 453 F.3d 225, 234 (4th Cir. 2006) ('In many cases, an insider will be the only party willing to make a loan to a struggling business, and recharacterization should not be used to discourage good-faith loans.") *with* Estes v. N & D Properties, Inc., 799 F.2d 726, 733 (11th Cir. 1986) ("Shareholder loans may be deemed capital contributions . . . where the trustee proves that the loans were made when no other disinterested lender would have extended credit.").

Whether an advance to the firm by an insider is debt or equity assumes particular importance when the company is in bankruptcy. The debt-equity distinction, in addition to guiding the priority to payment that insiders receive from the bankrupt company, is critical to determining whether payments received in connection with the instrument during the period leading up to a firm's bankruptcy can be retained by the insider. Under section 548 of the Bankruptcy Act, a transfer is constructively fraudulent, and therefore can be set aside and recovered by the bankruptcy trustee, when the debtor, within two years before the bankruptcy filing, makes a transfer of assets either while either insolvent or with an unreasonably small capital and receives "less than a reasonably equivalent value in exchange" for the transfer. Payments of interest on debt or toward debt principal are deemed "reasonably equivalent value." On the other hand, payments to purchase stock or pay dividends are not. Thus, if while insolvent the company paid $500,000 on a promissory note held by its controlling stockholder, the payments could be avoided under section 548 if the debt was in fact deemed to be disguised equity. *See* In re Fitness Holdings, Int'l, 714 F.3d 1141 (9th Cir. 2013).

———

9. REQUISITES FOR VALID ACTION BY THE BOARD

———

DEL. GEN. CORP. LAW §§ 141(b), (f), (i), 229

[See Statutory Supplement]

———

MODEL BUS. CORP. ACT §§ 8.20, 8.21, 8.22, 8.23, 8.24

[See Statutory Supplement]

———

Fogel v. U.S. Energy Systems, Inc.
Court of Chancery of Delaware, 2007.
2007 WL 4438978.

■ CHANDLER, CHANCELLOR

. . .

I.   FACTUAL FINDINGS . . .

[Fogel was chairman and CEO of U.S. Energy, a publicly traded Delaware corporation. The other directors were Feinstein, Strauss and Schneider. In 2007 the company was experiencing significant problems with its operations in the United Kingdom. The board resolved at its June 14, 2007, meeting to meet again on June 29, 2007, for the purpose of interviewing potential candidates to advise the company with respect to the challenges it was facing. The meeting was duly noticed to occur at the New York offices of Hunton & Williams at 10 a.m. June 29th for the purpose of interviewing and hiring an advisor.

Prior to the morning of June 29th, Feinstein, Strauss and Schneider talked among themselves regarding Fogel's performance. They formed a consensus that he should be terminated. On the morning of June 29th, the three directors gathered in the firm's counsel's office and resolutely decided to fire Fogel. They then proceeded to a conference room where the meeting was to occur. There, Feinstein asked Fogel to resign; he also stated that if Fogel did not resign Fogel would be fired. Strauss and Schneider were in attendance, but remained quiet (both later testified that they were in full agreement with everything Feinstein said to Fogel). Fogel left the meeting; Feinstein, Strauss and Schneider remained to conduct the scheduled interviews. That night Schneider called Fogel and asked for his resignation; Fogel declined. Thereupon Schneider informed him that he was therefore terminated.

On July 1, pursuant to authority conferred by the bylaws to the CEO/Chairman, Fogel called a special meeting of the stockholders for the purpose of voting to remove the three non-officer directors and electing their replacements. Later that day, at a regularly scheduled board meeting, the board formally passed a resolution regarding Fogel's termination. Thereafter the board ignored Fogel's call of a special meeting.]

At issue here is whether or not Fogel was still the CEO and Chairman when he called for a special meeting of shareholders. If the decision of the independent directors on June 29 constituted formal action by the Company's board of directors, Mr. Fogel was terminated before July 1 and, therefore, had no authority to call for a special meeting. If, however, that decision was not valid, Fogel was not properly terminated until the formal resolution on July 1, which was passed after he called for the special meeting.

II. ANALYSIS

. . .

A. It is unclear that a meeting actually occurred when the independent directors purported to terminate Mr. Fogel.

Although the Corporation Law does not prescribe in detail formal requirements for board meetings, the meetings do have to take place. The evidence presented at trial leaves many doubts about whether the confrontation between the independent directors and Mr. Fogel on the morning of June 29 constitutes a meeting. The mere fact that directors are gathered together does not a meeting make. There was no formal call to the meeting, and there was no vote whatsoever. The independent directors caucused on their own in what they admit was not a meeting and informally decided among themselves how they would proceed. Simply "polling board members does not constitute a valid meeting or effective corporate action."[10]

In fact, Mr. Strauss admitted on cross examination that it was his understanding that the independent directors would ask Mr. Fogel to resign *prior to* the scheduled board meeting. When the three independent

---

[10] Liberis v. Europa Cruises Corp., C.A. No. 13103, 1996 Del. Ch. LEXIS 11, 1996 WL 73567, at *6 (Del. Ch. Feb. 8, 1996).

directors arrived in the conference room, Mr. Strauss and Mr. Schneider stood in silence as Mr. Feinstein relayed the decision to Mr. Fogel, who was given no opportunity to respond or defend himself. There was no discussion of the issue and no vote of the board members. Such a hasty, unhelpful gathering cannot satisfy *section 141*'s conception of a meeting, the primary vehicle that drives corporate action. Meetings represent more than a mere technicality; they are a substantive protection. A proper meeting should be informative and should encourage the free exchange of ideas so that a corporation's directors—through their active, meaningful participation—may keep themselves fully informed and in compliance with their fiduciary duty of care. The exchange on the morning of June 29 was unidirectional and was insufficient to constitute a meeting under Delaware law.

B.   *If a meeting did occur, it is void because the independent directors obtained Mr. Fogel 's attendance by deception.*

. . . Before a corporation may hold a special meeting of its board of directors, each director must receive notice as prescribed by the bylaws; to the extent such a meeting is held without notice, the meeting and "all acts done at such a meeting are void." Although there is no "hard and fast legal rule that directors be given advance notice of all matters to be considered at a meeting," there must be notice sufficient to allow directors "an adequate opportunity to protect [their] interests." Where a director is tricked or deceived about the true purpose of a board meeting, and where that director subsequently does not participate in that meeting, any action purportedly taken there is invalid and void.

Here, the evidence at trial indicated that the independent directors had begun planning to terminate Mr. Fogel soon after the June 14 meeting. Indeed, the defendants spent a great deal of time at trial belaboring their argument that Mr. Fogel was doing a poor job as CEO, trying to indicate that he should have seen his termination coming after the disastrous meeting on June 14. Even if, however, Mr. Fogel had some reason to suspect that the others were thinking about firing him, I . . . cannot help but conclude that the independent directors' failure to inform Fogel about their plan was intentional. At trial, the independent directors argued passionately that they believed terminating Mr. Fogel was in the best interests of the Company and that their decision to do so was undertaken in good faith. That may be so, but deceiving Mr. Fogel about their intentions by omission is not appropriate.

Mr. Fogel was deceived into attending this meeting because the other directors decided to keep secret their plan to terminate his employment with the Company. It is, of course, true that Mr. Fogel lacked the votes necessary to protect his employment, but had he known beforehand, he could have exercised his right under the bylaws to call for a special meeting *before* the board met. The deception renders the meeting and any action taken there void.

C.   Because the meeting either did not occur or was void, the purported June 29 termination could not have been ratified by the July 1 resolution.

Defendants argued that even if the June 29 meeting and termination were technically deficient, any problems were cured when the board formally ratified the actions taken on the 29th during its July 1 meeting. That is not a tenable position under Delaware law. When a corporate action is void, it is invalid *ab initio* and cannot be ratified later. The action taken at the July 1 meeting may have resulted in Mr. Fogel's termination, but that termination was only effective as of *that* vote. By the time the board cast that vote, however, Mr. Fogel had already issued his call for a special meeting of the shareholders of the Company.

. . .

III. CONCLUSION

The mere congregation of a corporation's directors in the same room does not necessarily result in a board meeting, and the mere fact that three out of four directors determined how they wished to proceed does not obviate the need for adherence to bylaws and the General Corporation Law. U.S. Energy's independent directors polled one another and informally decided that they should fire the Company's CEO. They communicated this predetermined conclusion to Mr. Fogel by ambush on June 29. Either because there was no proper meeting of the U.S. Energy board or because Mr. Fogel's attendance at the meeting was procured by deceit, the board's action is void *ab initio*. Therefore, Mr. Fogel was still employed and was still authorized to call for a special election of stockholders on July 1. U.S. Energy and its board are hereby ordered to hold such a meeting. . . .

————

Compare: *Klaassen v. Allegro Dev. Corp.*, 106 A.3d 1035 (Del. 2014), reached a different result than *Fogel*. Allegro Development Corporation had a board of five directors, one of which was Klaassen; in several phone calls the four outside directors discussed their rising unhappiness with Klaassen and plotted to terminate him at the upcoming regularly scheduled November board meeting. In preparation for this meeting, Hood, one of the outside directors, spoke with Klaassen to make sure that he would have Allegro's general counsel in attendance at the November meeting explaining that the board may need legal guidance should it decide to exercise its redemption option on some outstanding shares. This was a false statement as the real reason for the outside directors wanting counsel to be there was to handle details of Klaassen's termination. At the November board meeting, the four outside directors fired Klaassen and appointed Hood to be the new CEO. Klaassen initially was cooperative; he worked with Hood and others on the transition in the executive suite and negotiated an agreement for him to be an "Executive Consultant" to Allegro. Time, however, did not heal all wounds. Seven months after being fired, Klaassen sued, alleging that his termination was invalid because he did not receive any pre-meeting notice that his termination would be considered and that he had been deceived as to the purpose of the meeting by Hood's failure to state the real purpose of wishing counsel to attend the November meeting was to handle legal issues related to his termination. The Delaware Supreme Court held that because Klaassen's termination occurred at a regular board meeting no advance notice of the matter was required. With respect to Klaassen's claim he had been deceived, the court concluded the claim was equitable in nature and, contrary to language in *Fogel*, deception gives rise to a voidable, not a void, claim. The Supreme Court affirmed the Court of Chancery's holding that Klaassen's claim was barred because Klaassen's cooperation following his termination established the equitable defense of acquiescence.

See also, Certified Security Systems, Inc. v. Yuspeh, 713 So.2d 558, 564 (La. App. 1998), where Hansen, David and Charles were the company's directors. Acting without a board meeting, Hansen and David terminated Charles as the firm's CEO. Charles' challenge to their action was unsuccessful: "[R]equiring the Board to call a formal meeting to be held for the purpose . . .would indeed have been a vain and useless act."

————

NOTES ON REQUISITES FOR VALID ACTION BY THE BOARD

A single director normally has no power to either act for the corporation or to cause the corporation to act. Instead, directors normally can only act as a body. The validity of an action by the board of directors depends on the requirements for meetings, notice, quorum, and voting. These rules can be considered at two levels. At the first level are rules that set out the formalities for board action. At the second level are rules concerning the consequence of noncompliance with the first-level rules.

Level 1: The Governing Rules. (Unless otherwise indicated, the following account is based on predominant statutory patterns.)

a). Meetings. Usually, directors must act at a duly convened meeting at which a quorum is present. Most statutes provide that a meeting of the board can be conducted by conference phone or by any other means of communication through which all participating directors can simultaneously hear each other. In addition, most statutes permit the board to act by unanimous written consent without a meeting.

b). Notice. Formal notice is not required for a regularly scheduled board meeting, because if the meeting is a regularly scheduled one, the directors are already on notice of its date, time, and place. In the case of a special meeting, notice of date, time, and place must be given to every director. The notice need not state the purpose of a meeting, unless the certificate of incorporation or the bylaws otherwise provide. The statutes usually provide that notice must be given a stated period in advance of the meeting, but then add that the stated period may be made shorter or longer by the certificate of incorporation or by-laws. Most statutes provide that notice can be waived in writing before or after a meeting and that attendance at a meeting constitutes a waiver unless the director attends merely to protest against holding the meeting.

c).   Quorum. A quorum of the board consists of a majority of the full board, that is, a majority of the authorized number of directors—not simply a majority of the directors who attend the meeting or a majority of the directors then in office (which may be less than the authorized number of directors because of board vacancies). Most statutes permit the certificate of incorporation or bylaws to require a greater number for a quorum than a majority of the full board. A substantial minority of the statutes, including the Delaware statute and the Model Act, permit the certificate or bylaws to set a lower number, but usually no less than one-third of the full board.

d).   Voting. Assuming that a quorum is present when a vote is taken, the affirmative vote of a majority of those present, not simply a majority of those voting, is required for action. Most statutes provide that the articles or bylaws can require a super-majority vote for board action.

Level 2: Consequences of Noncompliance. The consequences of noncompliance with the requisites for board action are not always clear. In publicly held corporations, where bureaucratic order usually prevails, an uncured defect of notice, the lack of a quorum, or the lack of the requisite affirmative vote will usually render board action ineffective. However, in close corporations, where formalities are seldom followed, the results of a failure to observe proper formalities are less clear-cut. Unless otherwise indicated, the balance of this Note concerns cases involving close corporations.

a).   Unanimous Explicit Although Informal Approval. Some older cases held that informal approval by directors—that is, an approval that is given without the requisite formalities—is ineffective even if the approval is explicit and unanimous. *See, e.g.,* Baldwin v. Canfield, 1 N.W. 261, 270 (Minn. 1879). These cases are of doubtful validity today. More characteristic is Gerard v. Empire Square Realty Co., 187 N.Y.S. 306 (N.Y. App. Div. 1921). Plaintiff brought an action against several related corporations to recover damages for breach of an employment contract. The corporations' shares were owned by five persons, all of whom were directors. Because of dissension, no shareholders' or directors' meetings were held, but there was evidence that each director had separately agreed to the hiring of the plaintiff. The court held that on these facts the corporations were bound:

> I think that under the circumstances of the case we are considering, where the directors own all the capital stock of the corporations, where they are members of the same family but so at variance that directors' and stockholders' meetings are not held, their action, concurred in by all, although separately and not as a body, binds the corporation. We must recognize the fact that [the business of a corporation is], perhaps the majority of instances, conducted by officers and directors little informed in the law of corporations, who often act informally, sometimes without meetings or even by-laws. To hold that in all instances technical

conformity to the requirements of the law of corporations is a condition to a valid action by the directors, would be to lay down a rule of law which could be used as a trap for the unwary who deal with corporations, and to permit corporations sometimes to escape liability to which an individual in the same circumstances would be subjected.

The results in this area are too disparate to be captured by a single clear rule. However, most modern courts probably would hold that unanimous explicit but informal approval by all the directors is effective where a person who has contracted with a corporate officer has been led to regard his transaction with the corporation as valid, and all the shareholders are directors or have acquiesced either in the transaction or in a past practice of informal board action. *See* Anderson v. K.G. Moore, Inc., 376 N.E.2d 1238 (Mass.App.1978), cert. denied, 439 U.S. 1116, 99 S.Ct. 1020, 59 L.Ed.2d 74 (1979).

b).   Explicit Approval by a Majority of the Directors Coupled with Acquiescence by Remaining Directors. Suppose that a majority of the directors, acting without a formal board meeting, explicitly approved a transaction, while the remaining directors knew of the transaction and took no action to disavow it, so that they may be said to have acquiesced. The difference between this case and the case in which all the directors explicitly but informally approve a transaction is not very significant. Accordingly, the courts will normally treat the two cases alike. *See, e.g.,* Winchell v. Plywood Corp., 85 N.E.2d 313 (Mass. 1949). The same result will normally follow even if there is no explicit approval by a majority of the directors, but all the directors acquiesce. *See e.g.,* Juergens v. Venture Capital Corp., 295 N.E.2d 398 (Mass. App. 1973); Pierce v. Astoria Fish Factors, Inc., 640 P.2d 40 (Wash.App. 1982).

c).   Majority Approval or Acquiescence. Suppose that a majority of the directors of a corporation approve a transaction, explicitly or by acquiescence, but the remaining directors lack knowledge of the transaction. Some courts have refused to hold the corporation liable under these circumstances. *See, e.g.,* Hurley v. Ornsteen, 42 N.E.2d 273 (Mass. 1942). Other courts have held the corporation liable if the shareholders acquiesced in the transaction, or if the shareholders or the remaining directors acquiesced in a practice of informal action by the directors. One theory is that if the shareholders have tolerated informal action by the directors over a period of time, they have by acquiescence authorized the directors to act in that manner. *See, e.g.,* Holy Cross Gold Mining & Milling Co. v. Goodwin, 223 P. 58 (Colo. 1924).

d).   Unanimous Written Consent. Finally, modern statutory rules provide that the board can act by written consent even without a meeting.[5]

---

[5]   In Village of Brown Deer v. City of Milwaukee, 114 N.W.2d 493 (Wis. 1962), cert. denied 371 U.S. 902, 83 S.Ct. 205, 9 L.Ed.2d 164 (1962), the court stated that, "The legislature has said that the corporation could act informally, without a meeting, by obtaining the consent in writing of all of the directors. In our opinion, this pronouncement has preempted the field and prohibits corporations from acting informally without complying with the statute." However, in *Brown Deer* apparently only a majority of the directors knew of the transaction in question, so there

NOTE ON BOARD COMMITTEES

Boards of publicly held corporations often delegate significant authority to committees. The notice, quorum, and voting rules applicable to committees mirror those applicable to the board itself. At one time, the most prominent board committee was the executive committee, which typically was given most of the powers of the board between board meetings, subject to stated limits. Executive committees, while undoubtedly still important, have fallen in prominence. The Conference Board, 34th Annual Board of Directors Survey 18 (2010) reported that as of 2007, only 42% of surveyed corporations had executive committees. Today, the most important committees are the oversight committees—in particular, the audit committee, the compensation committee, the nominating committee, and the corporate-governance committee. These committees will be discussed in detail in Chapter 4.

10. THE NORMAL REQUISITES FOR VALID SHAREHOLDER ACTION

DEL. GEN. CORP. LAW §§ 211, 213, 214, 216, 222, 228

[See Statutory Supplement]

MODEL BUS. CORP. ACT
§§ 7.01, 7.02, 7.03–7.07, 7.21, 7.25–7.28

[See Statutory Supplement]

Gwyn R. Hartman Revocable Living Trust v. S. Mich. Bancorp, Inc.

United States Court of Appeals for the Sixth Circuit, 2015.
780 F.3d 724.

■ SUTTON, CIRCUIT JUDGE. . . .

Whenever a Michigan corporation holds a shareholder meeting, it must disclose any proposals on the agenda that a shareholder wishes to submit for shareholder action. In 2012, one of Southern Michigan

---

was no unanimous approval, formal or informal. Other cases decided in states that have unanimous-written-consent statutes have held that the corporation was bound by unanimous informal consent. See Note, Corporations: When Informal Action by Corporate Directors Will Be Permitted to Bind the Corporation, 53 B.U.L.Rev. 101, 120 (1973).

Bancorp's shareholders asked the company to circulate a proposal before the company's 2013 annual meeting. In its proxy statement discussing the agenda for the meeting, Bancorp neither distributed the proposal nor described it. After the proposal was voted down at the meeting, the shareholder sued Bancorp and the chairman of its board of directors for violating their statutory and common law disclosure obligations. A federal district court dismissed the complaint . . . .

Bancorp's bylaws do not permit the corporation to claw back fees paid to directors found liable for breaching their fiduciary duties. In 2012, the Gwyn R. Hartman Revocable Living Trust, a Bancorp shareholder, drafted a one-paragraph resolution exhorting Bancorp's board to fill that gap. It asked the board to include the resolution in Bancorp's proxy statement for the upcoming annual meeting along with a two-paragraph "supporting statement" invoking the need for more "director accountability." . . .

The board refused. Its March 2013 proxy statement told shareholders merely that a shareholder planned to propose a resolution urging the board to amend the company's bylaws. If that resolution materialized, the statement continued, the directors would use their "discretionary authority" to vote it down by treating all submitted proxies as no-votes absent instructions to the contrary. The statement said nothing else about the proposal or its substance.

When the annual meeting convened a month or so later, the trust's representative objected to the sufficiency of the disclosure, and objected again when the proposal came up for a vote. The vote did not go the trust's way. Just 150,000 shares favored the proposal, and more than 1.7 million shares opposed it.

The trust sued Bancorp and John H. Castle, the company's chairman and CEO, for "intentional[ly] withholding" its proposal from the proxy statement and for "denying" the trust "any meaningful opportunity to solicit votes." . . . The district court dismissed the complaint for failing to state a claim on which relief could be granted.

. . .

The relevant Michigan statute requires companies to give shareholders "written notice of the time, place if any, and purposes" of any upcoming meeting. Mich. Comp. Laws § 450.1404. "[N]otice of the purposes of a meeting," the statute continues, "shall include notice of shareholder proposals" that a shareholder intends to submit for a vote. *Id.* We are hard-pressed to understand how mere acknowledgement of the existence of a proposal—without describing even its subject matter—amounts to "notice" under the statute. . . .

[T]he Michigan courts have not looked kindly on bare-bones disclosures of this ilk. In *Bourne v. Sanford*, 327 Mich. 175, 41 N.W.2d 515 (Mich. 1950), the directors tried to convene a board meeting to dissolve a company without letting its only shareholder know. That was impermissible, the Court held: "We can hardly conceive of an occasion when it is more vital to have a meeting at which there could be a general discussion, interchange of views and consultation of the directors." *Id.* at 521–22. Had the shareholder been properly notified, he could have prepared for the meeting, made his case, and perhaps changed the outcome. *Id.* at 522. A state appellate court . . . concluded that Michigan's "purpose-notice" requirement is designed to help shareholders "study [a] proposal, arrive at a position, and either oppose it or support it" before the meeting itself. *Id.* at 546.

Bancorp's notice did not satisfy these requirements. Its proxy statement said merely that a shareholder intended to submit a resolution calling upon the board to amend the company's bylaws. But it never specified *which* bylaw or *what* topic the bylaw covered. With such skeletal "disclosure" in hand, a shareholder would never know whether the resolution sought to change the bylaws' record-date procedure or their compensation-committee guidelines or their indemnification rules or their amendment restrictions or their discussion of director liability. . . .

Other States have endorsed the principles set forth in *Bourne* . . . . These endorsements make clear that, at a minimum, a meeting notice "should sufficiently apprise [shareholders] of matters to be considered at the meeting, give them information upon which they may exercise intelligent judgment with reference to the proposed questions, and open up avenues for obtaining additional information." 5 Fletcher Cyclopedia of the Law of Corporations § 2008 (2014). . . .

For these reasons, we reverse the district court's judgment and remand for further proceedings.

―――――

NOTES ON THE NORMAL REQUISITES FOR VALID SHAREHOLDER ACTION

1.   Notice of Meeting. Shareholders normally take action at an annual or special meeting (although if certain conditions are met shareholders can act by written consent, see below). Notice of place, time, and date is required for the annual meeting of shareholders and for any special meeting. The notice of a special meeting must also describe the purpose for which the meeting is called. Under most state statutes, the notice of an annual meeting must describe the matters to be acted upon only in certain cases—for example, when it is proposed to amend the certificate of incorporation, sell substantially all of the corporation's assets, engage in a merger, or dissolve. Some state statutes, and the federal Proxy Rules, also require a description of purpose in the notice of an annual meeting. However, the Proxy Rules do not apply to all corporations. See Chapter 5.

Because the identity of the shareholders of a publicly held corporation constantly changes, normally notice of a meeting is given to those persons who are shareholders of record on a designated date prior to the meeting—

the *record date*—not to those persons who are record or beneficial owners on the actual date of the meeting. A record date is normally fixed in the by-laws or by the board, within prescribed statutory limits. If a record date is not fixed in this manner, the statutes usually provide that the record date will be the day of, or the business day preceding, the day on which the notice of meeting is sent. Under an older alternative procedure that is still sanctioned in some statutes, but is generally regarded as archaic, the corporation can close its stock-transfer books as of a given date, and give notice of a shareholders' meeting only to those persons who were record holders on the date the books were closed.

Section 213 of the Delaware General Corporation Law and Section 7.07 of the Model Act now provide that the board can set two separate record dates—one record date that determines which shareholders are entitled notice of a meeting, and another later record date that determines which shareholders can vote at the meeting. (These revisions to the Delaware statute and the Model Act are intended to deal with the problem of empty voting, discussed in Chapter 4, Section 2.

2.   *Quorum.* Under most of the statutes, a majority of the shares entitled to vote is necessary for a quorum unless the certificate of incorporation sets a higher or lower figure. A substantial majority of the statutes provide that the certificate cannot set a quorum lower than one-third of the shares entitled to vote. Most of the remaining statutes set no minimum.

3.   *Voting.*

a).   *Ordinary Matters.* Under many statutes, the affirmative vote of a majority of the shares present (in person or by proxy) at a meeting is required for shareholder action on ordinary matters. Under some statutes, however, only the affirmative vote of a majority of those voting is required. If a statute requires the affirmative vote of a majority of those present, an abstention effectively counts as a negative vote. Virtually all the statutes permit the certificate of incorporation to set a higher vote than would otherwise be required. Under some of the statutes, a certificate amendment that adds a provision requiring a higher-than-normal vote may be adopted only by the same vote as that required under the amendment.

b).   *Fundamental Changes.* A group of actions known as fundamental changes—amendment of the certificate of incorporation, merger, sale of substantially all assets, and dissolution—often require approval by a majority or sometimes two-thirds of the outstanding voting shares, rather than a majority of those present or voting at the meeting. However, the Model Act requires approval or fundamental changes by only a majority of the shares voting, provided a majority of the outstanding shares are present at the meeting.

c).   *Written Consent.* Most statutes provide that the shareholders can act by written consent, without a meeting, if certain conditions are satisfied. These conditions vary from state to state. Under Section 228(a) of the Delaware statute, an action that is required or permitted to be taken at a shareholders' meeting may be taken without a meeting by the written consent of all the shareholders entitled to vote on the action. Similarly, under Section 704(b) of the Model Act, the articles of incorporation may provide that the shareholders can act without a meeting by the written consent of shareholders who have the minimum number of votes required to take the action at a meeting. Model Act Section 7.04 is comparable to Delaware Section 704.

4. *Meeting in a Digital Age.* More than half the states now have provisions that permit "remote participation" (sometimes referred to as "virtual meetings") by shareholders at meetings. States are divided over whether exercise of this power occurs only with the approval of the board of directors or whether remote participation can be authorized in either the articles of incorporation or bylaws. Delaware's approach is typical in requiring steps to verify that each person participating remotely is a stockholder or proxyholder; the corporation is to implement measures to facilitate one participating remotely to read; hear, and vote at the meeting; and the corporation must have the ability to record the vote or action by one participating remotely. Del. Gen. Corp. L. § 211(a)(2)(B). A large group of states only require that shareholders be able to hear one another. *See e.g.,* Ind. Code § 23–1–29–1(d). In 2017, five percent of the S&P Companies held their annual meeting totally online and another 16 percent combined in-person meetings with an audio or video component. BNA 49 Sec. Reg. & L. Rept. 1101 (July 10, 2017).

————

Espinoza v. Zuckerberg

Court of Chancery of Delaware, 2015.
124 A.3d 47.

■ BOUCHARD, CHANCELLOR

[After Facebooks' board of directors approved substantial stock options for its non-executive directors, a shareholder sued alleging the awards were wasteful, self-dealing and a breach of the directors' fiduciary duties. The defendants moved for summary judgment, alleging the directors' decision regarding their compensation was entitled to the highly deferential business judgment rule presumption. The plaintiff's argued the compensation constituted self dealing so that under Delaware law defendants had the burden to prove entire fairness of compensation awards. Defendants replied that Mark Zuckerberg, who had 61.6 percent of the voting power for Facebook had ratified the directors' self-awarded compensation so that under Delaware law the highly protective business judgment rule applied. Zuckerberg's ratification was alleged to have occurred in paragraph 11 of the following affidavit that was filed with the motion for summary judgment.]

11. Although I was never presented with an opportunity to approve formally the 2013 equity awards to Facebook's Non-Executive Directors or the Annual Compensation Program in

my capacity as a Facebook stockholder, had an opportunity presented itself, I would have done so. If put to a vote, I would vote in favor of the 2013 equity awards to Facebook's Non-Executive Directors, as well as the Annual Compensation Program, and if presented with a stockholder written consent approving them, I would sign it.

On February 18, 2015, plaintiff deposed Zuckerberg. During his deposition, Zuckerberg testified as follows regarding Facebook's board of directors:

These are the people who I want and—and who I think will serve the company best, and I think that the compensation plan that we have is doing its job of attracting and retaining them over the long term.

Zuckerberg never executed a written consent under 8 *Del. C.* § 228, which would have triggered an obligation to notify non-consenting stockholders of the action taken. . . .

The DGCL provides two methods for stockholders to express assent on a matter concerning the affairs of the corporation: (1) by voting in person or by proxy at a meeting of stockholders, or (2) by written consent. In both cases, the statute contains a number of formal requirements that, with the reinforcement of this Court's precedents, ensure precision in stockholder voting and transparency to all stockholders.

Significantly, . . . "[p]rompt notice of the taking of the corporate action" by written consent must be provided to the non-consenting stockholders. Thus, Section 228 ensures some level of transparency for non-consenting stockholders. Indeed, this Court has refused to make a written consent effective under Section 228 when the consenting stockholders failed to provide the required prompt notice to the non-consenting stockholders, until the failure to provide notice was remedied. . . .

In sum, the provisions of the DGCL governing the ability of stockholders to take action, whether by voting at a meeting or by written consent, demonstrate the importance of ensuring precision, both in defining the exact nature of the corporate action to be authorized, and in verifying that the requirements for taking such an action are met, including that the transaction received enough votes to be effective. They also demonstrate the importance of providing transparency to stockholders, whose rights are affected by the actions of the majority. . . .

In my opinion, the policies underlying the DGCL provisions governing the taking of stockholder action further support the conclusion that stockholders—including controlling stockholders like Zuckerberg—must observe statutory formalities when seeking to ratify director action. Doing so will avoid ambiguity and misinterpretation by ensuring that actions taken by stockholders are defined with precision and—where a single controlling stockholder is not present—that the requisite level of approval was obtained, and will promote transparency for the benefit of all stockholders. As the Delaware Supreme Court recently stated, "[c]ertainty and efficiency are critical values when determining how stockholder voting rights have been exercised."

———

11. THE ELECTION OF DIRECTORS

Special voting rules may apply in the election of directors: These rules involve staggered boards, cumulative voting, and plurality voting.

———

A. STAGGERED BOARDS

A staggered (or "classified") board of directors is a board that is divided into two or more classes, each of which is elected separately for staggered terms. So, for example, if a staggered board has three classes of directors, with three directors in each class, then all nine directors would serve three-year terms, but each year only three directorships would be up for election. The rationale for staggered boards is said to be that they ensure continuity. This rationale is weak, because where continuity is desirable the shareholders will continue directors in office in any event. Although staggered boards preceded the rise of hostile takeovers, after that phenomenon occurred, a staggered board came to be seen as a defense against a takeover, because a multi-year process was required to oust an incumbent majority of directors. For example, if a board is unclassified and the year is 2019, a majority of the shareholders could elect an entirely new board at the corporation's 2019 annual meeting. If, however, a board has three classes, a majority of the shareholders could not elect a majority of the board until 2020; and if a board has four classes, a majority of the shareholders could not elect a majority of the board until 2021. In the interim, the dissident majority would have their investment in the corporation tied up without acquiring control of the corporation. That is a very unappetizing prospect, especially for a takeover bidder, and will often deter prospective bidders from making a takeover bid.

A staggered board, particularly in conjunction with the ubiquitous poison pill, is a potent and controversial defense against a corporate takeover. As illustrated earlier, replacing a majority of a board of directors on a staggered board takes two consecutive annual shareholders meetings. Commentators and activists have argued that the staggered board and poison pill combination entrenches managers and should be disallowed by courts. Indeed, a staggered board "is the most powerful takeover defense available." Michael Klausner, The Empirical Revolution in Law: Fact and Fiction in Corporate Law and Governance, 65 Stan. L. Rev. 1325, 1352–53 (2013).

Because altering the procedures for electing directors requires an amendment to the article of incorporation, the status quo was thought to be that boards of companies without staggered boards wanted to adopt them, but could not without shareholder approval, while shareholders of companies with staggered boards wanted to eliminate them, but could not without board approval. Illustrating this situation, 44% of S&P 100 Companies had a staggered board in 2003. This paradigm has ended as more and more corporations, particularly the largest ones, declassify (de-stagger) their boards. Indeed, the move to a declassified board has happened quickly among large companies. Thus, in 2009 only 16% of S&P 100 Companies had a staggered board, whereas in 2003 44% of them had staggered boards. Marcel Kahan & Edward Rock, Embattled CEOS, 88 Tex. L. Rev. 987, 1007–09 (2010). As the table below reflects, among the largest companies a classified board is the exception and not the rule.

Board elections	S&P 500	S&P MidCap 400	S&P SmallCap 600	S&P 1500	Russell 3000
Annual elections	90%	64%	55%	69%	59%
Majority voting in director elections	89%	62%	43%	64%	47%

Ernst & Young Global Limited, EY Center for Board Matters: Corporate Governance By The Numbers, Board Elections (Mark Manoff & Stephen W. Klemash, eds., 2017) (current as of Mar. 31 2017) *available at* http://www.ey.com/us/en/issues/governance-and-reporting/ey-corporate-governance-by-the-numbers#boardelections.

As the above table shows, 90% of S&P 500 Companies now hold annual elections for the full board of directors. While staggered boards remain more prevalent among smaller firms, they have followed the largest companies' lead and begun de-staggering. Incidence of staggered boards in S&P MidCap 400 companies decreased from 67% in 2003 to 36% in 2017. Among S&P SmallCap 600 companies incidence decreased from 61% in 2003 to 45% in 2017. What explains why classified boards become more common as firm size declines?

———

B. CUMULATIVE VOTING

1. In General. Under the traditional system of voting for directors—sometimes referred to as *straight voting*—a shareholder can cast, for each open directorship, a number of votes equal to the number of her shares. For example, assume that the board of Blue Corporation consists of seven directors; Blue has 300 outstanding shares; Shareholder S owns 100 shares; shareholder T owns 200 shares; and all seven directorships are up for election. Under straight voting, S can cast a total of 700 votes, but cannot cast more than 100 votes for any nominee. More generally, under straight voting, minority shareholders can never elect even a single director over the opposition of the majority. For example, in the Blue Corporation hypothetical, since under straight voting S can cast no more than 100 votes for any of her seven nominees, and T can cast 200 votes for each of his seven nominees, T can elect all the directors.

In contrast, under the system of *cumulative voting*, a shareholder can distribute among her nominees, in any way she pleases, a number of votes equal to the number of her shares times the number of directors to be elected. (In a relatively small number of states, cumulative voting is made mandatory by constitution or by statute. More typically, however, the statutes permit rather than require cumulative voting.) So, for example, suppose that S, who has 700 votes, casts 350 votes each for two of her nominees, A and B. If T casts 200 votes for each of his seven nominees, S will elect two directors, because each of her nominees will receive more votes (350) than any of T's nominees (200). T, in turn, will elect five directors, because each of his nominees will receive 200 votes and S has used up all of her votes on A and B. Suppose that T casts 351 votes for each of two of his candidates. In that case, T can cast only 698 votes for his other five nominees. Accordingly, some of T's candidates will receive less than 350 votes, and S will still elect two of her nominees to the board.

2.   *Mathematics.* Aranow & Einhorn, Proxy Contests for Corporate Control 10.04[B] (3d ed. 1998) discusses the mathematics of cumulative voting, as follows:

The mathematics of cumulative voting can become a very involved subject which we will not undertake to discuss in all its aspects. There are two basic formulas, both of which are relatively simple. The first formula is used to determine the minimum number of shares needed to elect a particular number of directors:

$$X = \frac{(S \times N)}{D + 1} + 1$$

X = minimum number of shares needed
S = total number of shares that will be voted at meeting
N = number of directors desired to elect
D = total number of directors to be elected

For example, assume there exists a corporation with 1,000 shares outstanding and seven directors to be elected. A minority stockholders' group wishes to elect two directors. It is estimated that 800 shares will be voted at the meeting. Applying these figures to the formula, the resulting calculation is:

$$\frac{(800 \times 2)}{7 + 1} + 1 = 201$$

The stockholders' group knows that it must have ownership or control of at least 201 shares in order to elect two directors.

The second formula can be used to determine how many directors can be elected by a group controlling a particular number of shares:

$$N = \frac{(X) \times (D + 1)}{S}$$

N = number of directors that can be elected

X = number of shares controlled

D = total number of directors to be elected

S = total number of shares that will be voted at meeting

In the example above, assume that the stockholders' group knows it will control 201 shares. Applying the figures to this formula, the resulting calculation is:

$$\frac{201 \times 8}{800} = 2.01$$

Thus, cumulation will result in the election of two directors. There are several other formulas that can be applied to more complicated questions.*

3. *Cumulative Voting and Staggered Boards.* An issue raised by cumulative voting is whether, when cumulative voting is required either

---

*   Jesse Fried points out that:

The standard formula for determining the minimum number of shares necessary to elect a particular number of directors yields an easily interpretable result only when the expression $(S \times N)/(D + 1)$ is a whole number.

Suppose, as in the Aranow and Einhorn example, that there is a corporation with seven directors to be elected and a minority group wishes to elect two directors. However, 803 shares (rather than the 800 shares used in their example) will be voted at the meeting. The standard formula indicates that the number of shares needed to elect two directors is now:

$[(803 \times 2)/(7 + 1)] + 1 = 201.75$

If there are only whole shares, does this mean that the minority group needs 201 to elect two directors, or 202 shares? The answer is, surprisingly, 201—if the standard formula does not yield a whole number you must round down to determine the number of whole shares needed.

If there are fractional shares, then the standard formula yields the wrong result.

A more useful formula for determining the minimum number of shares needed (X), is $X > (S \times N)/(D+1)$

If there are fractional shares, then any fraction greater than the righthandside expression will allow you to elect N directors. If there are whole shares, then you round up to the next whole number. [Footnote by ed.]

by state law or by a corporation's certificate of incorporation, a corporation can have a staggered board. The percentage of stock that minority shareholders must hold to elect at least one director under cumulative voting varies inversely with the number of directors to be elected. Accordingly, a 12% minority (for example) can elect one director if nine directors are to be elected, but cannot elect any directors if three directors are to be elected. Putting this more generally, if a board is classified, a minority must hold more stock to elect a single director than if a board of the same size is unclassified, because the number of directors to be elected each year is only a fraction of the full board, and the fewer directors that are to be elected, the more votes the minority must have to elect their candidates. In *Wolfson v. Avery*, 126 N.E.2d 701 (Ill. 1955), the Illinois court held that, for this reason, an Illinois Constitutional requirement of cumulative voting prohibited staggered boards. (The Illinois Constitution was later amended to eliminate this requirement.) In *Bohannan v. Corporation Commission*, 313 P.2d 379 (Ariz.1957), the Arizona court held to the contrary. Subsequently, the Arizona legislature enacted a statutory provision that permitted classification if a board had nine or more directors.

The Delaware Chancery Court addressed this issue in 2010 in *eBay Domestic Holdings, Inc. v. Newmark*, 16 A.3d 1(Del. Ch. 2010). Craig Newmark founded craigslist in 1995. In time, craigslist became the most popular classifieds website in the United States. At an early point, craigslist had three shareholders: Craig Newmark (Craig) and Jim Buckmeister (Jim), who together held 72% of craigslist's stock, and Phillip Knowlton (Phillip), who held the remainder. The craigslist certificate of incorporation provided for a three-member board to be elected under cumulative voting. The board of craigslist then consisted of Craig, Jim, and Phillip. Later, Phillip sold his craigslist shares to eBay, then primarily an auction website, and an eBay representative was designated as the third craigslist director in Phillip's place. Subsequently, eBay launched its own online classifieds website; this aroused Craig and Jim who caused the amendment of craigslist's certificate of incorporation to provide for a staggered board whereby only one director would be elected each year to serve a three-year term. Whereas the mechanics of cumulative voting with all three directors were elected annually enabled eBay with its 28% stake in craigslist to elect one director, as a practical matter the staggered-board amendments cut off eBay's ability to place a director on the craigslist board. Nevertheless, the court held that the amendments were valid:

> Delaware law does not require that minority stockholders such as eBay have board representation. Delaware corporations do not have to adopt cumulative voting for the benefit of minority stockholders, and Delaware corporations have the express power to implement staggered boards. If a corporation implements a staggered board, and this renders the

corporation's cumulative voting system ineffective, minority stockholders have not been deprived of anything they are entitled to under the common law or the DGCL, because minority stockholders are not entitled to a cumulative voting system in the first instance. It is true that by approving the staggered board amendments, Jim and Craig implemented a corporate governance structure that had a disparate and, from eBay's point of view, unfavorable impact on eBay. This is not the sort of disparate treatment, however, that can be classified as self-dealing because the law expressly allows a majority stockholders to elect the entire board. Thus, the staggered board amendments cannot be subjected to entire fairness review on the grounds that eliminating eBay's ability to elect a director was a form of self-dealing.

C. PLURALITY VOTING

Another special voting rule that applies to the election of directors is plurality voting. Under the general rule applicable to shareholder voting, shareholders can act only by a majority vote. In the election of directors, however, traditionally a plurality vote sufficed, that is, the nominees who received the most votes were elected even if none of them has a majority. However, this rule has come under heavy pressure in the last few years, and is rapidly changing, as described in the following material.

Bryn R. Vaaler, Majority Election of Directors: Where Are We Today?
(Dorsey & Whitney, November 2007).*

Shareholder activists have maintained that plurality voting does not adequately permit shareholders to express disapproval. They argue that votes withheld have no real effect. In an uncontested election, each nominee in the board's slate will still be elected so long as he or she receives at least one affirmative vote, even if a majority of votes are withheld. If directors must receive an affirmative majority of votes cast to be elected, then withheld or negative votes will have real meaning. . . .

In 2005, shareholder activists, led by the Council of Institutional Investors and labor union pension funds, began flooding larger public companies with letters and formal shareholder proposals requesting

---

*   © Dorsey & Whitney LLP. This article originally appeared in Dorsey's Corporate Update, and included the following disclaimer: "This article is intended for general information purposes only and should not be construed as legal advice or legal opinions on any specific facts or circumstances. An attorney-client relationship is not created or continued by reading this article. . . . " (Footnote by ed.)

boards to initiate amendments to their charters necessary to implement a majority-voting regime for directors. . . .

. . . [In January 2006, Intel announced] that it had adopted a new bylaw provision requiring election of directors by a majority of votes cast, except in contested elections. Under the Intel bylaw (as amended), a new director nominee, in an uncontested election, who fails to receive a majority of votes cast in his or her favor is not elected. An incumbent nominee who fails to get the required vote remains in place under the so-called "holdover" rule (i.e., directors remain in place until their successor is elected and qualified) contained in the DGCL and all other corporate statutes, but must tender his or her resignation. Intel's board governance committee must decide whether to accept or reject the resignation within 90 days.

The Intel bylaw rapidly became the gold standard for shareholder activists promoting the cause of majority election. This is because it actually adopts a majority-vote standard (instead of just a resignation policy) and because it is part of the company's charter documents and may be made less easy to change or eliminate without shareholder consent than a mere board-adopted governance principle.

A Delaware corporation, like Intel, may adopt a majority-election standard by bylaw amendment, which may be approved by either the board or the shareholders. Most other state corporate statutes . . . currently require that a change to the default plurality-voting rule be made in the articles of incorporation, not the bylaws. So, adoption of an Intel-type bylaw is not an option, and corporations incorporated in those states would have to amend their articles (usually requiring *both* board and shareholder approval) to adopt a true majority-voting requirement or instead adopt a Pfizer-type governance policy. . . .

Activists have also called for states to change the default rule in their corporate statutes from plurality to majority and make other changes to accommodate majority-voting bylaws and policies.

[In 2006, the Model Act was amended to] . . . permit either the shareholders or the board to amend the bylaws to provide that, in uncontested elections, a director nominee receiving more votes withheld than in favor would generally serve no more than a 90-day transitional term. If adopted by shareholders, such a bylaw amendment may not be rescinded or modified by the board. The Model Act amendments also . . . permit opting out of the "holdover" rule by amendment to the articles of incorporation. . . .

[Also in 2006,] . . . the Delaware legislature amended the DGCL to provide that a shareholder-adopted bylaw requiring a greater vote for election of directors could not be rescinded or modified by the board and to affirm the validity of conditional director resignations.

———

NOTE ON TREND IN PLURALITY VS. MAJORITY VOTING

Between 2003 and 2009, majority voting went from the outlier within the S&P 100 (10%) to the dominant majority (90%). The rapid adoption of majority voting led "experienced observers like Martin Lipton [to opine] that '... majority voting will become universal.'" Marcel Kahan & Edward Rock, Embattled CEOS, 88 Tex. L. Rev. 987, 1010–11 (2010). Though majority voting has not been adopted as widely by smaller companies, there has been a substantial increase in the rate of majority voting in companies outside of the S&P 500 as well. Ernst & Young Global Limited, *supra.* In 2009, only 17% of companies outside the S&P 500 had adopted majority voting. *Id.* As the table shows, 62% of S&P MidCap 400 companies, 43% of S&P SmallCap 600 companies, and 43% of Russell 3000 companies now use majority voting in director elections.

———

DEL. GEN. CORP. LAW § 141(c)

[See Statutory Supplement]

———

MODEL BUS. CORP. ACT § 8.25

[See Statutory Supplement]

———

D. PROXY ACCESS

Proxy access refers to a procedures, generally set forth in the corporation's bylaws, whereby shareholders can nominate individuals to stand for election to the board of directors without incurring the expense of undertaking a proxy solicitation. Absent such a provision, nominations are the domain of the board of directors. The same forces that fed the movement toward majority vote provisions—the growing presence of institutional investors and the rise of activist investors—underlie the growing prevalence of proxy access provisions. The typical provision provides very limited access, because the pattern is to limit nominations to no greater than twenty percent of total board seats and condition the right on the proponent owning 3 percent of the voting stock for three years. At the end of 2017, about five hundred public companies (sixty-five percent of S&P 500 companies) provided proxy access provisions of one type or another.

———

E. SHORT SLATES

In recent years, dissident shareholders have increasingly run a short slate of directors for election—that is, a slate of candidates for less than all, and usually less than a majority, of the directors to be elected. This approach has several advantages. Proxy advisory firms, such as ISS, and large institutional investors are often more supportive of short slates than of efforts to replace all or a majority of the board. Moreover, change-in-control provisions are pervasive, and trigger a variety of outcomes that may adversely affect the shareholders, such as additional compensation to executives or immediate vesting of future rights. Running a short slate avoids triggering a change-in-control provision. A short slate also avoids triggering "poison puts," that is, provisions in a company's debt instruments that require the company to repurchase outstanding debt obligations upon the occurrence of certain defined events, which sometimes include incumbent directors ceasing to constitute a majority of the board.

———

12. REMOVAL OF DIRECTORS

In theory, under certain conditions directors may be removed by the shareholders, the board, or a court, depending on state law, as described in the following Note. In practice, however, removal of directors under state law is unusual (although the federal law allows the removal of directors for certain violations of the securities laws).

———

DEL. GEN. CORP. LAW § 141(k)

[See Statutory Supplement]

———

In re VAALCO Energy Shareholder Litig.

Court of Chancery of Delaware, 2015.
CA No. 11775-VCL.
Transcript 62–66.

[For many years, VAALCO Energy, Inc. had a classified board so that its directors served three-year terms with only one-third of the board elected annually. Both its charter and bylaws provided that the directors could only be removed for cause. In 2009, VAALCO declassified its board, but did not change its charter provision that continued to provide that shareholders could only remove a director for cause. Following a near 80 percent decline in its stock price in 2014, relations between its management and shareholders deteriorated. A shareholder group ("the Group 42") owning about 11 percent of the company filed Schedule 13D announcing they could seek changes in VAALCO's board and senior management. The filing prompted management to adopt a poison pill and several other defensive measures. Thereafter Group 42 announced it would seek to remove and replace the VAALCO directors at a special stockholders' meeting. The announcement explained that Group 42 believed directors could be removed under Delaware Section 141(k) with or without cause, since the board was neither classified nor elected via cumulative voting. VAALCO asserted its charter was controlling so that removal could only occur for cause. Litigation ensued. Days before the special shareholder meeting, the vice-chancellor, ruling from the bench, granted Group 42's motion for summary judgment on the issue:]

I do believe that [VAALCO's] Article V, Section 3 of the charter and Article III, Section 2 of the bylaws, which provide for only for-cause removal in the context of a nonclassified board, conflict with Section 141(k) of the Delaware General Corporation Law and are, therefore, invalid. This analysis is driven by the plain language of 141(k). 141(k) states affirmatively "Any director or the entire board of directors may be removed, with or without cause, by the holders of a majority of the shares then entitled to vote at an election of directors . . . ." That is the rule. It then continues. So technically it's a comma and identifies two exceptions: "except as follows:" One exception is " . . . a corporation whose board is classified as provided in subsection (d) . . . ." Another exception is subsection 2, "In the case of a board of directors having cumulative voting . . . ." For better or for worse, those are the two statutory exceptions. . . .

What I think is the defendants' strongest argument against the plain language of 141(k) and this reading is the language in 141(d), which, for better or for worse, says that "The directors of any corporation organized under this chapter may, by the certificate of incorporation or by an initial bylaw, or by a bylaw adopted by a vote of the stockholder, be divided into 1, 2 or 3 classes . . . ." This creates, at least on its face, the somewhat oxymoronic concept of a single-class classified board. As the defendants see that, that single-class board would be classified and, hence, the directors only would be subject to removal for cause. That, I think, is a pretty novel reading of 141(d). I don't think anybody out there has ever touted the idea of single-class classified boards triggering removal for cause. . . .

Here, what we have is a declassified straight board. We have a declassified straight board that does not try to get into 141(k)(1) that way but, rather, admits that it is a straight board. . . .

NOTES ON THE REMOVAL OF DIRECTORS

1.   Removal by the Shareholders. Shareholders can remove a director for cause even in the absence of a statute that so provides. *See, e.g.,* Auer v. Dressel, 118 N.E.2d 590 (N.Y. 1954); Campbell v. Loew's, Inc., 134 A.2d 852 (Del.Ch. 1957). However, shareholders cannot remove a director without cause in the absence of specific authority to do so under the statute, the certificate of incorporation, or the by-laws. *See, e.g.,* Frank v. Anthony, 107 So.2d 136 (Fla.App.1958). For statutes that permit the shareholders to remove a director without cause, *see, e.g.*, Cal.Corp.Code § 303(a); Model Bus.Corp.Act § 8.08. A certificate or by-law provision may not authorize the removal without cause of directors elected after the provision has been adopted. *See, e.g.*, Crown EMAK Partners, LLC v. Kurz, 992 A.2d 377 (Del. Supr. 2010); Everett v. Transnation Dev. Corp., 267 A.2d 627 (Del.Ch.1970).

2. *Removal by the Board.* In the absence of statute, the board cannot remove a director either with or without cause. *See, e.g.*, Bruch v. National Guarantee Credit Corp., 116 A. 738 (Del.Ch. 1922). It is uncertain whether the certificate of incorporation can change this rule. *See* Dillon v. Berg, 326 F.Supp. 1214 (D.Del.1971), aff'd 453 F.2d 876 (3d Cir.); Bruch v. National Guarantee Credit Corp., supra. Other statutes permit removal of a director for specified reasons, such as conviction of a felony, *see, e.g.*, Calif.Corp.Code § 302. A few statutes permit the board to remove a director for cause or for specified reasons if the certificate of incorporation so provides. *See, e.g.*, N.J.Stat.Ann. § 14A:6–6.

3. *Removal by a Court.* The cases are divided on whether a court can remove directors for cause in the absence of statute. Compare Webber v. Webber Oil Co., 495 A.2d 1215 (Me.1985) (courts do not have power to remove directors) with Ross v. 311 N. Cent. Ave. Bldg. Corp., 264 N.E.2d 406 (Ill. App. 1970) (courts have power to remove directors, at least for fraud or the like). Some statutes permit the courts to remove a director for specified reasons, such as fraudulent or dishonest acts. These statutes usually provide that a petition to the court requesting such removal can be brought only by a designated percentage of the shareholders (most commonly 10%), by the attorney general, or in some cases, by either. *See, e.g.*, Calif.Corp.Code § 304; N.Y.Bus.Corp.Law § 706(d).

---

13. THE CLASSICAL ULTRA VIRES DOCTRINE

Two long-standing and related issues in corporate law are what if any limits are corporations subject to in the conduct of their business and what should be in the objective of a for-profit corporation. This section and the next concern those issues.

INTRODUCTORY NOTE

1. *The Classical Ultra Vires Doctrine.* Under the classical theory of corporate existence, the corporation is regarded as a fictitious person, endowed with life and capacity only insofar as provided in its charter. Early corporate charters tended to narrowly circumscribe the sphere of activities in which a corporation could engage. Transactions outside that sphere were characterized by the courts as ultra vires (beyond the corporation's power) and unenforceable—unenforceable against the corporation because beyond the corporation's powers, and unenforceable by the corporation on the ground of lack of mutuality. A leading example is Ashbury Railway Carriage & Iron

Co. v. Riche, 7 L.R. Eng. & Ir.App. 653 (1875). Ashbury was authorized by its charter "to make and sell, or lend on hire, railway-carriages and wagons, and all kinds of railway plant, fittings, machinery, and rolling-stock; to carry on the business of mechanical engineers and general contractors; to purchase and sell, as merchants, timber, coal, metals, or other materials; and to buy and sell any such materials on commission, or as agents." *Id.* at 654. Ashbury purchased the right to construct and operate a railway line in Belgium, and Riche contracted to do the construction. After Riche had done some of the work, Ashbury repudiated the contract. Riche brought suit. The House of Lords held for Ashbury on the ground that it lacked the power under its charter to build a railroad, and therefore lacked the power to contract for that purpose.

The original purpose of the ultra vires doctrine seems to have been to protect the public or the state from unsanctioned corporate activity. Accordingly, under classical English law even unanimous shareholder ratification was not a bar to an ultra vires defense if the transaction was outside the sphere of activities stated in its charter. *See Ashbury*, supra; Frommel, Reform of the Ultra Vires Rule: A Personal View, 8 The Company Lawyer 11 (1987).

2.   Powers and Purposes. In theory, the classical ultra vires doctrine was applicable to two somewhat different questions. The first question was whether a corporation had acted beyond its purposes, that is, had engaged in a type of business activity not permitted under its certificate. The second question was whether the corporation had exercised a power not specified in its certificate. In practice, the two questions tended to merge. For example, certificates of incorporation commonly contained clauses that described each of the corporation's purposes and powers as both purposes and powers.

3.   Limitations on the Ultra Vires Doctrine. Ultra vires was always regarded by the commentators as an unsound doctrine, and the history of the doctrine is one of steady erosion, which proceeded along several fronts:

a).   It was established even in early cases that corporate powers could be implied as well as explicit. *See* Sutton's Hospital Case, 77 Eng. Rep. 960 (1613). The courts eventually became very liberal in finding implied powers, including implied powers to enter into business activities not specified in the certificate. For example, in Jacksonville, Mayport, Pablo Ry. & Navigation Co. v. Hooper, 160 U.S. 514, 526, 16 S.Ct. 379, 40 L.Ed. 515 (1896), the Supreme Court held that a Florida company whose purpose, under its charter, was to run a railroad, could also engage in leasing and running a resort hotel located at the railroad's seaside terminus, because the resort could increase the railroad's business.

b).   Generally speaking, ultra vires was not a defense to corporate tort or criminal liability. Furthermore, even in areas where ultra vires was a defense, it could not be used to reverse completed transactions. Accordingly, the major impact of the doctrine was confined to executory contracts.

c).   Even as applied to executory contracts, the scope of the ultra vires doctrine was limited. The major problem in such cases occurred where one party had performed under the contract; that party sued for the contract price of its performance; and the nonperforming party raised the defense of ultra vires. Under the majority view, the nonperforming party, having received a benefit under the contract, was estopped from asserting an ultra vires defense. *See, e.g.,* Joseph Schlitz Brewing Co. v. Missouri Poultry & Game Co., 229 S.W. 813 (Mo. 1921). Under the minority view, known as the federal rule, part performance did not have an estoppel effect, on the theory that an ultra vires contract was prohibited by law and therefore void. Even the cases taking this view, however, usually permitted the performing party to recover in restitution for the value of any benefit conferred. *See, e.g.,* Central Trans. Co. v. Pullman's Palace Car Co., 139 U.S. 24, 11 S.Ct. 478, 35 L.Ed. 55 (1891).

d). Under American law, unanimous shareholder approval barred the ultra vires defense unless creditors would be injured. *See* Note, 83 U.Pa.L.Rev. 479, 488–92 (1935).

e). Drafters of certificate-of-incorporation provisions began writing endless and crushingly boring certificate provisions that enumerated every business purpose and power imaginable. Eventually, most statutes made this kind of drafting unnecessary by providing that the certificate could provide simply that the corporation could engage in any lawful business, and by setting out a laundry list of powers that are conferred on every corporation even without enumeration in the certificate.

f). Finally, modern statutes have adopted provisions that almost (but not quite) abolish the ultra vires doctrine. The Delaware and Model Act provisions in the following cross-references are examples. Similar statutes have been adopted in all but a few states. *See* Schaeftler, Ultra Vires-Ultra Useless: The Myth of State Interest in Ultra Vires Acts of Business Corporations, 9 J.Corp.Law 81, 81–83 & n. 6 (1983).

———

DEL. GEN. CORP. LAW §§ 101(b), 102(a)(3), 121, 122, 124

[See Statutory Supplement]

———

MODEL BUS. CORP. ACT §§ 3.01(A), 3.02, 3.04

[See Statutory Supplement]

———

14. THE OBJECTIVE AND CONDUCT OF THE CORPORATION

This Section concerns the question, to what extent may a corporation act in a manner that is not intended to maximize corporate profits? Although this question is sometimes put in terms of whether a given act would be ultra vires, the question penetrates much more deeply into the nature of the corporate institution, and its place in society, than does the classical ultra vires doctrine.

———

A. THE MAXIMIZATION OF SHAREHOLDER WEALTH

Henry Hu, New Financial Products, The Modern Process of Financial Innovation, and the Puzzle of Shareholder Welfare
69 Tex.L.Rev. 1273, 1278–1283 (1991).

The most basic principle of corporate law is that a corporation is to be primarily run for the pecuniary benefit of its shareholders. Apart from the impact of nonstockholder constituency statutes and notions of social responsibility generally, few would disagree with this principle as a general matter.

But what does this principle mean in the usual day-to-day operation of publicly held corporations? . . .

The traditional conception of the basic pecuniary goals of a corporation is based on the simple premise that what is good for the corporation is good for the shareholder. If corporate welfare is furthered, as through the maximization of earnings or earnings per share, shareholder welfare is presumed to be furthered as well. . . .

The traditional conception is based on two related assumptions. First, accounting-based measures such as earnings or earnings per share are appropriate indicators of corporate performance. Second, the welfare of a shareholder is largely coincident with the welfare of the corporation.

Unfortunately, both of these classic assumptions are of limited validity. Financial theorists have long argued—and corporate managers are starting to realize—that maximization of total corporate earnings or even earnings per share does not necessarily maximize shareholder wealth. Earnings growth as a sole measure of corporate performance fails to measure the risk characteristics of corporate investments, the extent of investments in working and fixed capital needed to sustain the firm, dividend policy, and the time value of money. . . .

The second assumption underlying the traditional conception, that the welfare of the corporation is coincident with the welfare of its shareholder, is also fundamentally flawed. For example, there may be a conflict of interest concerning risk between the corporation and its shareholders. . . . [M]odern financial theory suggests that corporations concerned about the well-being of shareholders will generally take more risks than corporations concerned about the entity's own well-being; shareholders can, by holding a portfolio of stocks, diversify away much of the risk that a corporation might itself find daunting. Similarly, there may be a conflict of interest as to time. For example, from the point of view of shareholders, the best thing to do with the typical company in a dying industry may be to liquidate the company immediately, pay the net proceeds to shareholders, and allow shareholders to put the money to better use. From the point of view of the company itself—and its managers and employees—long-term decline may be preferable.

[A second, competing] conception of the pecuniary goals of a corporation is directly focused on the welfare of the shareholder. Under this view, shareholder wealth maximization is sought directly, rather than as a by-product of corporate welfare. Managers should seek to take those actions that maximize the wealth of shareholders through a combination of maximizing the actual short-or long-term trading price of each share of common stock and the dividends they actually receive. There is no focus on measures of corporate performance like accounting earnings and no concern for the corporation independent of the welfare of its shareholders.

The shift to this second conception has been gradual but discernible. Most academics now believe that shareholder wealth maximization is the basic pecuniary objective of the modern publicly held corporation. Judges have typically subscribed to this standard only in the most limited of circumstances, typically in the context of a sale of the entire company.

———

B. INTERESTS OTHER THAN MAXIMIZATION OF SHAREHOLDERS' WEALTH

NOTE ON DODGE V. FORD MOTOR CO.

One of the most famous cases in corporation law is Dodge v. Ford Motor Co., 204 Mich. 459, 170 N.W. 668 (Mich. 1919). The case is unusual in its early consideration of the issue (or at least one aspect of the issue) that is now known as corporate social responsibility.

Ford Motor Co. had been incorporated in 1903. Henry Ford owned 58% of Ford Motor's stock and controlled the board. Two Dodge brothers owned 10%, and five other shareholders owned the balance. From 1908 on, Ford Motor had paid a regular annual dividend of $1.2 million, and between December 1911 and October 1915, it paid special dividends totaling $41 million. In 1916, Henry Ford declared it to be the settled policy of the company not to pay in the future any special dividends, but to put back into the business for the future all of the earnings of the company, other than the regular dividend of $1.2 million. "My ambition," declared Mr. Ford, "is to employ still more men; to spread the benefits of this industrial system to the greatest possible number, to help them build up their lives and their homes. To do this, we are putting the greatest share of our profits back into the business." At the time of the announcement, Ford Motor had a surplus of $112 million, including $52.5 million in cash.

The Dodge brothers then brought a suit whose objects included compelling a dividend equal to 75% of the accumulated cash surplus. The trial court ordered Ford Motor to declare a dividend of $19.3 million—equal to half of its cash surplus as of July 31, 1916 minus special dividends paid between the time the complaint was filed and July 31, 1917.[6] The Michigan Supreme Court affirmed this portion of the trial court's decree:

> When plaintiffs made their complaint and demand for further dividends the Ford Motor Company had concluded its most prosperous year of business. The demand for its cars at the price of the preceding year continued. . . . [I]t reasonably might have expected a profit for the year [beginning August 1, 1916], of upwards of $60,000,000. . . . Considering only these facts, a refusal to declare and pay further dividends appears to be not an exercise of discretion on the part of the directors, but an arbitrary refusal to do what the circumstances required to be done. These facts and others call upon the directors to justify their action, or failure or refusal to act. In justification, the defendants have offered testimony [proving that: Ford Motor had a general policy to reduce the price of its cars every year while maintaining or improving quality. It could have produced 600,000 cars in the year beginning August 1, 1916, and sold them for $440 each. However, the policy of reducing prices called for the cars to be sold at $360 each, a difference of $48 million.]
>
> The plan, as affecting the profits of the business for the year beginning August 1, 1916, and thereafter, calls for a reduction in the selling price of the cars. . . . In short, the plan does not call for and is not intended to produce immediately a more profitable business but a less profitable one; not only less profitable than formerly but less profitable than it is admitted it might be made. The apparent immediate effect will be to diminish the value of shares and the returns to shareholders.

---

[6]   Henry Ford had earlier given an interview to the Detroit News, in which he said:

I do not believe that we should make such an awful profit on our cars. A reasonable profit is right, but not too much. So it has been my policy to force the price of the car down as fast as production would permit, and give the benefits to users and laborers. . . .

The cross-examination of Henry Ford in Dodge v. Ford built on that interview:

Counsel: Do you still think those profits were awful profits?

Ford: Well, I guess I do, yes.

Counsel: And for that reason you were not satisfied to continue to make such awful profits?

Ford: We don't seem to be able to keep the profits down.

Counsel: Are you trying to keep them down? What is the Ford Motor Company organized for except profits, will you tell me, Mr. Ford?

Ford: Organized to do as much good as we can, everywhere for everybody concerned. And incidentally to make money.

Counsel: Incidentally to make money?

Ford: Yes, sir.

The interview and the colloquy are reported in M. Todd Henderson, The Story of Dodge v. Ford: Everything Else is New Again, in Corporate Law Stories 37, 61–62 (J. Mark Ramseyer, ed. 2009). Henderson's essay also extensively chronicles the background to Dodge v. Ford.

It is the contention of plaintiffs that the apparent effect of the plan is intended . . . to continue the corporation henceforth as a semi-eleemosynary institution and not as a business institution. In support of this contention they point to the attitude and to the expressions of Mr. Henry Ford. . . .

. . . [Mr. Ford's] testimony creates the impression, also, that he thinks the Ford Motor Company has made too much money, has had too large profits, and that although large profits might be still earned, a sharing of them with the public, by reducing the price of the output of the company, ought to be undertaken. We have no doubt that certain sentiments, philanthropic and altruistic, creditable to Mr. Ford, had large influence in determining the policy to be pursued by the Ford Motor Company—the policy which has been herein referred to.

It is said by his counsel that—

"Although a manufacturing corporation cannot engage in humanitarian works as its principal business, the fact that it is organized for profit does not prevent the existence of implied powers to carry on with humanitarian motives such charitable works as are incidental to the main business of the corporation." . . .

The difference between an incidental humanitarian expenditure of corporate funds for the benefit of the employees, like the building of a hospital for their use and the employment of agencies for the betterment of their condition, and a general purpose and plan to benefit mankind at the expense of others, is obvious. There should be no confusion (of which there is evidence) of the duties which Mr. Ford conceives that he and the stockholders owe to the general public and the duties which in law he and his codirectors owe to protesting, minority stockholders. A business corporation is organized and carried on primarily for the profit of the stockholders. The powers of the directors are to be employed for that end. The discretion of directors is to be exercised in the choice of means to attain that end and does not extend to a change in the end itself, to the reduction of profits or to the nondistribution of profits among stockholders in order to devote them to other purposes.

. . . As we have pointed out, and the proposition does not require argument to sustain it, it is not within the lawful powers of a board of directors to shape and conduct the affairs of a corporation for the merely incidental benefit of shareholders and for the primary purpose of benefitting others, and no one will contend that if the avowed purpose of the defendant directors was to sacrifice the interests of shareholders it would not be the duty of the courts to interfere.

———

NOTE ON MAXIMIZING FOR THE LONG-TERM VS. THE SHORT-TERM

As developed later in Chapter 4, activist investors increasingly launch campaigns seeking to introduce a variety of changes in the operations of targeted public companies. This has sparked cries, mostly from pro-management commentators, that such investors are myopic, being concerned only with improving the firm's "short-term" financial performance and not its long-term performance. However, a manager's obeisance to the latter appears well supported in the case law:

> The fiduciary obligation to maximize the value of the corporation for the benefit of its stockholders does not mean that directors must sacrifice greater value that can be achieved over the long term in pursuit of short-term strategies, and it certainly does not mean that directors must attempt to maximize the public company's stock price on a daily or quarterly basis. The fiduciary relationship requires that the directors act prudently, loyally, and in good faith to maximize the corporation's value over the *long-term* for its stockholders' benefit.

Virtus Capital L.P. v. Eastman Chem. Co., 2015 WL 580553, at 16 n. 5 (Del. Ch. Feb. 11, 2015) (emphasis added). The impressive amount of judicial authority for company directors having discretion to pursue long-term gains over more immediate gains reflects the fact that short-term gains that are smaller than long-term gains would not necessarily be preferred by shareholders. *See* Mark J. Roe, Corporate Short-Termism—In the Boardroom and in the Courtroom, 68 Bus. Law. 977 (2013). If the risk-adjusted long-term gains have a greater present worth than the risk-adjusted short-term strategy, why would it be optimal for shareholders to prefer a short-term strategy?

Consider the following simple example. A Delaware corporation exists for two periods, today and tomorrow. We can think of today as the "short term" and tomorrow as the "long term." We assume that the interest rate is zero and that shareholders are risk neutral. Assuming the interest rate is zero means that we do not have to discount future cash flows; assuming that investors are risk neutral means that we can value future cash flows as their expected values without making adjustments for risk aversion or risk-seeking behavior.

The corporation has a single asset today, $100 in cash. The corporation can liquidate and return that $100 to shareholders today, or the corporation can invest the $100 in a project. Tomorrow, the project will return $110 with a 60 percent probability and $80 with a 40 percent probability. Shareholders do not like this project. It has a negative net present value because it requires investment of $100 for an expected value of $98 (($110 × 60%) + ($80 × 40%)). If the corporation announces a policy (believed by the market) to liquidate instead of invest, then the current stock value will be $100, reflecting the impending payment of the $100 in cash. If the corporation announces a policy (believed by the market) to invest in the project, then the current stock value will be $98, the expected value of the project. All of the risk-neutral shareholders will prefer liquidation, since $100 is more than the expected value of the project of $98.

What does Delaware law require of the directors of this simple Delaware corporation? In particular, does the law require the directors to liquidate the corporation and deliver $100 to the shareholders—a rule amounting to the maximization of current stock price, and the outcome that these posited risk-neutral shareholders would prefer? Or does the law require the directors to pursue the project, since there is a good chance (60 percent, more likely than not) that doing so will deliver to the shareholder a return that is higher than the current stock price, even though none of the existing risk-neutral shareholders would choose it? Or does the law allow the directors to make either decision, without fear of second guessing by the courts?

Note that it does not matter whether a shareholder wants out today or tomorrow. If the corporation is committed to the investment, then a shareholder who wants out today can sell his claim to another risk-neutral investor for his share percentage of $98, the expected value of the project. That share percentage of $98 is exactly the expected value faced by the shareholder who intends to hold his claim until tomorrow. Nor is a "short-term" shareholder leaving money on the table if he wants liquidation today. While it is true that the long-term investment may pay off at $110, it is also true that it may pay off at $80. A rational valuation (i.e., the expected value in this example) makes short-termism the value-maximizing strategy.

While this is a simple example, my judgment is that current law would allow the Delaware directors to choose either strategy. They could choose the liquidation strategy on the rationale that it is, after all, the value-maximizing strategy and the strategy that shareholders would prefer. They also could choose the long-term investment strategy on the rationale that, while it does not maximize current share value, it does deliver a better-than-even chance of a 10 percent increase in value (remember, by assumption true interest rates are 0 percent) and a remaining—less than even—chance of a loss of only 25 percent.

See J.B. Heaton, The "Long Term" in Corporate Law, 72 Bus. Law. 353, 357–359 (2017). Building on the above example, Heaton raises the question whether the numerous cases supporting manager's broad discretion within the long-term versus short-term debate is actually an embrace of an objective of corporate sustainability and not wealth maximization. On this objective, consider the following, written by the Chief Justice Strine of the Delaware Supreme Court:

Why can't we, people ask, have corporations focus on the creation of sustainable wealth, by engaging in fundamentally sound and sustainable business investment and operations? And by doing that, create jobs that investors, their children, and grandchildren can have to live well. By that means, end-user investors will have the main thing they really need, which is a good job. And they will also have a solid investment portfolio to provide for themselves in retirement and to pay for their kids' education. Wouldn't we all be a winner, they ask, with this sort of alignment.

Leo E. Strine, Jr., Securing Our Nation's Economic Future: A Sensible, Nonpartisan Agenda to Increase Long-Term Investment and Job Creation in the United States, 71 Bus. Law. 1081, 1082–83 (2016).

———

The shareholder primacy model illustrated in *Dodge v. Ford Motor Co.* is questioned by commentators. Professors Blair and Stout see the directors' role as that of mediating among the interests of multiple constituencies within the corporation. Margaret M. Blair & Lynn A. Stout, A Team Production Theory of Corporate Law, 85 Va. L. Rev. 247 (1999). In contrast, Professor Bainbridge champions a very different model—that of "director primacy." Under this view, it is the board of directors that hires the multiple factors of production, so that the board is not to be regarded as an agent or extension of aspirations of the shareholders. Stephen M. Bainbridge, 88 Iowa L. Rev. 1 (2002). *See* Lynn Stout, The Shareholder Value Myth (2012) (exploring among other problems the effects on the firm of conflicting tugs toward maximizing value by short-term investors versus long-term investors).

———

NOTE ON OTHER CONSTITUENCIES UNDER DELAWARE LAW

The Delaware courts have made several pronouncements—not all of which seem to be consistent—on this issue. Most or all of these pronouncements have occurred in takeover cases, and have addressed the board's power to take an action, in favor of other constituencies, whose effect is to block a takeover. The seminal Delaware case on that issue is *Unocal Corp. v. Mesa Petroleum Co.*, 493 A.2d 946, 955 (Del. 1985). (This case is set out in Chapter 14, Section 2.) There the court said:

> In [determining] the board's exercise of corporate power to forestall a takeover bid our analysis begins with the basic principle that corporate directors have a fiduciary duty to act in the best interests of the corporation's stockholders. . . .

> * * *

> An aspect of review [of a board action to block a tender offer] is the element of balance. [A] defensive measure must be reasonable in relation to the threat posed. This entails an analysis by the directors of the nature of the takeover bid and its effect on the corporate enterprise. Examples of [such concerns] may include: inadequacy of the price offered, nature and timing of the offer,

questions of illegality, the impact on the "constituencies" other than shareholders (i.e., creditors, customers, employees, and perhaps even the community generally), the risk of nonconsummation, and the quality of securities being offered in the exchange. . . .

These two passages seem to pull in opposite directions: the first passage focuses only on interests of the shareholders, while the second passage refers to the interests of other constituencies as well. However, in a later case, *Revlon, Inc. v. MacAndrews & Forbes Holdings, Inc.*, 506 A.2d 173, 176 (Del. 1986), the Delaware Court put an important limit on the second passage in *Unocal:*

> . . . [W]hile concern for various corporate constituencies is proper when addressing a takeover threat, that principle is limited by the requirement that there be some rationally related benefit accruing to the stockholders.

* * *

The Revlon board argued that it acted in good faith in protecting the noteholders because *Unocal* permits consideration of other corporate constituencies. Although such considerations may be permissible, there are fundamental limitations upon that prerogative. A board may have regard of various constituencies in discharging its responsibilities, provided there are rationally related benefits accruing to the stockholders.

The Delaware cases also suggest that a board can act against threats to "corporate policy." Some passages in *Paramount Communications, Inc. v. Time Inc.*, 571 A.2d 1140 (Del. 1989), seem to suggest this possibility. For example, in that case the court mentioned, with apparent approval, that the board was motivated by a desire to see "to the preservation of Time's 'culture,' i.e., its perceived editorial integrity in journalism. . . ." Other language in the case, however, seems to focus on a threat to the shareholder's interests. Unanswered is whether reliance on "corporate policy" can be independent of considering whether that policy advances the shareholder interests.

This issue was revisited in *eBay Domestic Holdings, Inc. v. Newmark*, 16 A.3d 1 (Del. Ch. 2010), discussed earlier in connection with how a classified board can reduce the influence of a minority stockholder. Craig and Jim, two of craiglist's three shareholders, wanted to prevent eBay, the third shareholder, from being able to name one of craiglist's directors or purchase more craiglist stock. To this end, Craig and Jim adopted several defensive measures, including a staggered board and a poison pill that would prevent eBay from purchasing more craigslist stock by diluting the value of any shares that eBay purchased. eBay filed an action challenging these measures. Under Unocal v. Mesa Petroleum Co., supra, a corporation could adopt this kind of defensive measure if it was a reasonable response to a threat to the corporation's policy and effectiveness.

Although craigslist was a for-profit corporation, it operated its business largely as a community service. Nearly all classified advertisements on craigslist were placed free of charge, and craigslist did not sell advertising space. Its revenue stream consisted solely of fees for online job postings in certain cities and for apartment listings in New York City. These fees were more than enough to meet craigslist's operating and capital needs. The craigslist management team, consisting principally of Craig and Jim, were committed to this community-service approach to doing business, so that for most of its history craigslist had not focused on monetizing its site. Craig and Jim sought to bring the defensive measures within *Unocal* and *Paramount* by arguing that they properly perceived that eBay posed a threat to craigslist's policy and effectiveness, including departure from craigslist's public-service culture in favor of increased monetization. The court rejected this defense:

> It is true that on the unique facts of a particular case— *Paramount Communications, Inc. v. Time, Inc.*[7]—this Court and the Delaware Supreme Court accepted defensive action by the directors of a Delaware corporation as a good faith effort to protect a specific corporate culture. It was a muted embrace. Chancellor Allen wrote only that that he was "not persuaded that there may not be instances in which the law might recognize as valid a perceived threat to a 'corporate culture' that is shown to be palpable (for lack of a better word), distinctive and advantageous."[8] This conditional, limited, and double-negative-laden comment was offered in a case that involved the journalistic independence of an iconic American institution. Even in that fact-specific context, the acceptance of the amorphous purpose of "cultural protection" as a justification for defensive action did not escape criticism.
>
> More importantly, *Time* did not hold that corporate culture, standing alone, is worthy of protection as an end in itself. Promoting, protecting, or pursuing non-stockholder considerations must lead at some point to value for stockholders. When director decisions are reviewed under the business judgment rule, this Court will not question rational judgments about how promoting non-stockholder interests—be it through making a charitable contribution, paying employees higher salaries and benefits, or more general norms like promoting a particular corporate culture— ultimately promote stockholder value. Under the *Unocal* standard, however, the directors must act within the range of reasonableness.
>
> Ultimately, defendants failed to prove that craigslist possesses a palpable, distinctive, and advantageous culture that sufficiently promotes stockholder value to support the indefinite implementation of a poison pill. Jim and Craig did not make any serious attempt to prove that the craigslist culture, which rejects any attempt to further monetize its services, translates into increased profitability for stockholders. I am sure that part of the reason craigslist is so popular is because it offers a free service that is also extremely useful. It may be that offering free classifieds is

---

[7]   571 A.2d 1140 (Del. 1990).

[8]   Paramount Communications, Inc. v. Time, Inc., 1989 WL 79880, at *4 (Del. Ch. July 14, 1989), *aff'd*, 571 A.2d 1140 (Del. 1990).

an essential component of a successful online classifieds venture. After all, by offering free classifieds, craigslist is able to attract such a large community of users that real estate brokers in New York City gladly pay fees to list apartment rentals in order to access the vast community of craigslist users. Likewise, employers in select cities happily pay fees to advertise job openings to craigslist users. . . .

Giving away services to attract business is a sales tactic, however, not a corporate culture. . . . The existence of a distinctive craigslist "culture" was not proven at trial. It is a fiction, invoked almost talismanically for purposes of this trial in order to find deference under *Time*'s dicta.

. . . As an abstract matter, there is nothing inappropriate about an organization seeking to aid local, national, and global communities by providing a website for online classifieds that is largely devoid of monetized elements. . . . The corporate form in which craigslist operates, however, is not an appropriate vehicle for purely philanthropic ends, at least not when there are other stockholders interested in realizing a return on their investment. Jim and Craig opted to form craigslist, Inc. as a *for-profit Delaware corporation* and voluntarily accepted millions of dollars from eBay as part of a transaction whereby eBay became a stockholder. Having chosen a for-profit corporate form, the craigslist directors are bound by the fiduciary duties and standards that accompany that form. Those standards include acting to promote the value of the corporation for the benefit of its stockholders. The "Inc." after the company name has to mean at least that. Thus, I cannot accept as valid for the purposes of implementing the Rights Plan a corporate policy that specifically, clearly, and admittedly seeks *not* to maximize the economic value of a for-profit Delaware corporation for the benefit of its stockholders—no matter whether those stockholders are individuals of modest means or a corporate titan of online commerce. If Jim and Craig were the only stockholders affected by their decisions, then there would be no one to object. eBay, however, holds a significant stake in craigslist, and Jim and Craig's actions affect others besides themselves. . .

16 A.3d at 32–34.

————

OTHER CONSTITUENCY STATUTES

Thirty-three states (but not Delaware and not the Model Act) have "other constituency" statutes. The Illinois statute is illustrative of the orientation of such statutes:

In discharging the duties of their respective positions, the board of directors, committees of the board, individual directors and individual officers may, in considering the best long term and short term interests of the corporation, consider the effects of any action (including without limitation, action which may involve or relate to a change or potential change in control of the corporation) upon employees, suppliers and customers of the corporation or its subsidiaries, communities in which offices or other establishments of the corporation or its subsidiaries are located, and all other pertinent factors.

805 Ill. Comp. Stat. Ann. 5/8.85 (West 1989).

There appears four distinct variations among the statutes: 1) whether the authority to consider constituencies other than shareholders is limited to the takeover context, 2) whether consideration of other constituencies is discretionary or mandatory, 3) whether all constituencies are to be considered in equal weight, and 4) whether the authority is set forth in the corporate statute and hence available to all incorporate firms or is permitted to be included in the articles of incorporation if the corporation so chooses. *See generally* Kathleen Hale, Corporate Law and Stakeholders: Moving Beyond Stakeholder Statutes, 45 Ariz. L. Rev. 823 (2003).

———

Milton Friedman, The Social Responsibility of Business **Is to Increase its Profits**

The New York Times Magazine, September 13, 1970. . . .

. . .

In a free-enterprise, private-property system, a corporate executive is an employee of the owners of the business. He has direct responsibility to his employers. That responsibility is to conduct the business in accordance with their desires, which generally will be to make as much money as possible while conforming to the basic rules of the society, both those embodied in law and those embodied in ethical custom. Of course, in some cases his employers may have a different objective. A group of persons might establish a corporation for an eleemosynary purpose—for example, a hospital or a school. The manager of such a corporation will not have money profit as his objective but the rendering of certain services.

In either case, the key point is that, in his capacity as a corporate executive, the manager is the agent of the individuals who own the corporation or establish the eleemosynary institution, and his primary responsibility is to them. . . .

That is why, in my book *Capitalism and Freedom*, I . . . have said that in such a society, "there is one and only one social responsibility of business—to use it resources and engage in activities designed to increase its profits so long as it stays within the rules of the game, which is to say, engages in open and free competition without deception or fraud."

———

Oliver Hart & Luigi Zingales, Companies Should Maximize Shareholder Welfare Not Market Value

2 J. Law, Finance and Accounting 247 (2017).

Friedman's article has been enormously influential and his general position, that companies should maximize profit or market value, commands wide acceptance among both economists and lawyers today. . . .

In this article we take issue with one part of Friedman's argument. We follow him in supposing that, for many public companies, shareholder welfare is an appropriate objective. However, we argue that it is too narrow to identify shareholder welfare with market value. The ultimate shareholders of a company (in the case of institutional investors, those who invest in the institutions) are ordinary people who in their daily lives are concerned about money, but not just about money. They have ethical and social concerns. . . . Not only do shareholders give to charity, . . . but they also internalize externalities to some extent. For example, someone might buy an electric car rather than a gas guzzler because he or she is concerned about pollution or global warming; she might use less water in her house or garden than is privately optimal because water is a scarce good; she might buy fair trade coffee even though it is more expensive and no better than regular coffee; she might buy chicken from a free range farm rather than from a factory farm; etc. As another example, many owners of privately-held firms appear to care about the welfare of their workers beyond what profit maximization would require.

However, if consumers and owners of private companies take social factors into account and internalize externalities in their own behavior, why would they not want the public companies they invest in to do the same? To put it another way, if a consumer is willing to spend $100 to reduce pollution by $120, why would that consumer not want a company he or she holds shares in to do this too?

A response that Milton Friedman or his followers might make is: we should separate money-making activities from ethical activities. Let companies make money and let individuals and governments deal with externalities. In some settings (like charity, which is Friedman's leading example), this is a powerful argument, but as a general matter we disagree with it because we believe that money-making and ethical activities are often inseparable. Consider the case of Walmart selling high-capacity magazines of the sort used in mass killings. If shareholders are concerned about mass killings, transferring profit to shareholders to spend on gun control might not be as efficient as banning the sales of high-capacity magazines in the first place.

More generally, Friedman's separability assumption requires consumers to have a (scalable) project that is the reverse of the project implemented by the corporation. But is there any reason to think that the reverse of an oil digging project, say, always exists? In many cases this would seem to defy belief.

In this paper we will be particularly interested in non-separable activities, where profit and damage are inextricably connected for technological reasons. The company has the technology to create both, and individuals do not have the technology (costlessly) to undo this. In this case we will argue that Friedman's conclusions do not hold: shareholder welfare is not equivalent to market value. In contrast, in the case where the externality is separable from money-making, such as with charitable giving by companies, Friedman's argument is correct.

———

NOTE ON BENEFIT AND FLEXIBLE PURPOSE CORPORATIONS

Pursuant to very recent legislative developments, a new corporate form, the "benefit corporations," is authorized. A benefit corporation's articles of incorporation, while not strictly nonprofit, nonetheless commits the corporation to provide benefits to the general public or the environment. The formation of such an entity reflects the desire of their founders and owners to pursue certain social, philanthropic objectives within an entity that also seeks profits for its shareholders. To some extent, benefit corporations are something of a hybrid between the typical for-profit corporation and the totally non-profit corporation. In 2010, Maryland became the first state to adopt a benefit corporation statute and has been quickly joined by a score of states including California, Delaware, New Jersey, New York, Pennsylvania and Virginia. The typical benefit corporation statute provides that the benefit corporation "shall have the purpose of creating a general public benefit" and "may have a specific public benefit as set forth in its charter." *See* Model Benefit Corporation Legislation § 201. The enabling statute further defines "general public benefit" as the "material, positive impact on society and the environment." Moreover, most of the statutes expressly provide that such general or specific benefits "are in the best interests of the corporation."

Statues commonly provide that "specific public benefit includes . . .

i. Providing low-income or underserved individuals or communities with beneficial products or services;

ii. Promoting economic opportunity for individuals or communities beyond the creation of jobs in the ordinary course of business;

iii. Preserving the environment;

iv. Improving human health

v. Promoting the arts, sciences, or advancement of knowledge;

    vi.   Increasing the flow of capital to entities with a public benefit purpose;

    vii. The accomplishment of any other particular benefit for society or the environment.

See e.g., Cal. Corp. Code § 14601(e) (West 2011); N.J. Stat. Ann. § 14A:18–1 (West 2011).

The text of benefit corporation statutes clearly mandate that the directors consider the social constituency; in contrast, other constituency statutes only *permit* non-shareholder interests to be considered and those statutes sometimes even restrict this discretion to instances in which control of the corporation is at issue. For example, the California statute, which is mirrored in other state benefit corporation statutes, provides: "In discharging their duties and considering the best interests of the corporation, the directors shall consider the impact of any proposed action" upon "shareholders," "employees," "customers," "the local and global environment," and "the ability of the benefit corporation to accomplish its general, and any specific, public benefit corporation." *See e.g.,* Cal. Corp. Code § 14620(b) (West 2011); N.Y. Bus. Corp. Law § 1707(a)(1) (McKinney 2011). Many of the benefit corporation statutes expressly provide that the directors have no obligation "to give priority" to any person, group or objective. *See e.g.,* Cal. Corp. Code § 14620(d) (West 2011); N.Y. Bus. Corp. Law § 1707(a)(3) (McKinney 2011). Furthermore, all states require benefit corporations to provide annual benefit reports to shareholders and the public via posting on the firm's website. *See e.g.,* Cal. Corp. Code § 14630; Md. Code Ann. Corps. & Ass/ns § 5–6C–08(c) (West 2011); N.Y. Bus. Corp. Law § 1708(c) (McKinney 2011).

———

A.P. Smith Mfg. Co. v. Barlow

Supreme Court of New Jersey, 1953.
98 A.2d 581, appeal dismissed, 346 U.S. 861, 74 S.Ct. 107, 98 L.Ed. 373 (1953).

■ JACOBS, J. The Chancery Division, in a well-reasoned opinion by Judge Stein, determined that a donation by the plaintiff The A.P. Smith Manufacturing Company to Princeton University was *intra vires.* Because of the public importance of the issues presented, the appeal duly taken to the Appellate Division has been certified directly to this court under Rule 1:5–1(*a*).

The company was incorporated in 1896 and is engaged in the manufacture and sale of valves, fire hydrants and special equipment, mainly for water and gas industries. Its plant is located in East Orange and Bloomfield and it has approximately 300 employees. Over the years the company has contributed regularly to the local community chest and on occasions to Upsala College in East Orange and Newark University, now part of Rutgers, the State University. On July 24, 1951 the board of directors adopted a resolution which set forth that it was in the corporation's best interests to join with others in the 1951 Annual Giving to Princeton University, and appropriated the sum of $1,500 to be transferred by the corporation's treasurer to the university as a contribution towards its maintenance. When this action was questioned by stockholders the corporation instituted a declaratory judgment action in the Chancery Division and trial was had in due course.

Mr. Hubert F. O'Brien, the president of the company, testified that he considered the contribution to be a sound investment, that the public expects corporations to aid philanthropic and benevolent institutions, that they obtain good will in the community by so doing, and that their charitable donations create favorable environment for their business operations. In addition, he expressed the thought that in contributing to liberal arts institutions, corporations were furthering their self-interest in assuring the free flow of properly trained personnel for administrative and other corporate employment. Mr. Frank W. Abrams, chairman of the board of the Standard Oil Company of New Jersey, testified that corporations are expected to acknowledge their public responsibilities in support of the essential elements of our free enterprise system. He indicated that it was not "good business" to disappoint "this reasonable and justified public expectation," nor was it good business for corporations "to take substantial benefits from their membership in the economic community while avoiding the normally accepted obligations of citizenship in the social community." Mr. Irving S. Olds, former chairman of the board of the United States Steel Corporation, pointed out that corporations have a self-interest in the maintenance of liberal education as the bulwark of good government. He stated that "Capitalism and free enterprise owe their survival in no small degree to the existence of our private, independent universities" and that if American business does not aid in their maintenance it is not "properly protecting the long-range interest of its stockholders, its employees and its customers." Similarly, Dr. Harold W. Dodds, President of Princeton University, suggested that if private institutions of higher learning were replaced by governmental institutions our society would be vastly different and private enterprise in other fields would fade out rather promptly. Further on he stated that "democratic society will not long endure if it does not nourish within itself strong centers of non-governmental fountains of knowledge, opinions of all sorts not governmentally or politically originated. If the time comes when all these centers are absorbed into government, then freedom as we know it, I submit, is at an end."

The objecting stockholders have not disputed any of the foregoing testimony nor the showing of great need by Princeton and other private institutions of higher learning and the important public service being rendered by them for democratic government and industry alike. Similarly, they have acknowledged that for over two decades there has been state legislation on our books which expresses a strong public policy in favor of corporate contributions such as that being questioned by them.

Nevertheless, they have taken the position that (1) the plaintiff's certificate of incorporation does not expressly authorize the contribution and under common-law principles the company does not possess any implied or incidental power to make it, and (2) the New Jersey statutes which expressly authorize the contribution may not constitutionally be applied to the plaintiff, a corporation created long before their enactment. *See* R.S. 14:3–13; R.S. 14:3–13.1 et seq.

In his discussion of the early history of business corporations Professor Williston refers to a 1702 publication where the author stated flatly that "The general intent and end of all civil incorporations is for better government." And he points out that the early corporate charters, particularly their recitals, furnish additional support for the notion that the corporate object was the public one of managing and ordering the trade as well as the private one of profit for the members. *See* 3 Select Essays on Anglo-American Legal History 201 (1909); 1 Fletcher, Corporations 6 (rev. ed. 1931). . . . However, with later economic and social developments and the free availability of the corporate device for all trades, the end of private profit became generally accepted as the controlling one in all businesses other than those classed broadly as public utilities. Cf. Dodd, For Whom Are Corporate Managers Trustees?, 45 Harv. L. Rev. 1145, 1148 (1932). As a concomitant the common-law rule developed that those who managed the corporation could not disburse any corporate funds for philanthropic or other worthy public cause unless the expenditure would benefit the corporation. Hutton v. West Cork Railway Company, 23 Ch.D. 654 (1883); Dodge v. Ford Motor Co., 170 N.W. 668 (Mich. 1919). . . . During the 19th Century when corporations were relatively few and small and did not dominate the country's wealth, the common-law rule did not significantly interfere with the public interest. But the 20th Century has presented a different climate. Berle and Means, The Modern Corporation and Private Property (1948). Control of economic wealth has passed largely from individual entrepreneurs to dominating corporations, and calls upon the corporations for reasonable philanthropic donations have come to be made with increased public support. In many instances such contributions have been sustained by the courts within the common-law doctrine upon liberal findings that the donations tended reasonably to promote the corporate objectives. . . .

When the wealth of the nation was primarily in the hands of individuals they discharged their responsibilities as citizens by donating freely for charitable purposes. With the transfer of most of the wealth to corporate hands and the imposition of heavy burdens of individual taxation, they have been unable to keep pace with increased philanthropic needs. They have therefore, with justification, turned to corporations to assume the modern obligations of good citizenship in the same manner as humans do. Congress and state legislatures have enacted laws which encourage corporate contributions, and much has recently been written to indicate the crying need and adequate legal basis therefor. . . . In actual practice corporate giving has correspondingly increased. . . . During the first world war corporations loaned their personnel and contributed substantial corporate funds in order to insure survival; during the depression of the '30s they made contributions to alleviate the desperate hardships of the millions of unemployed; and during the second world war they again contributed to insure survival. They now recognize that we are faced with other, though nonetheless vicious, threats from abroad which must be withstood without impairing the vigor of our democratic institutions at home and that otherwise victory will be pyrrhic indeed. More and more they have come to recognize that their salvation rests upon sound economic and social environment which in turn rests in no insignificant part upon free and vigorous nongovernmental institutions of learning. It seems to us that just as the conditions prevailing when corporations were originally created required that they serve public as well as private interests, modern conditions require that corporations acknowledge and discharge social as well as private responsibilities as members of the communities within which they operate. Within this broad concept there is no difficulty in sustaining, as incidental to their proper objects and in aid of the public welfare, the power of corporations to contribute corporate funds within reasonable limits in support of academic institutions. But even if we confine ourselves to the terms of the common-law rule in its application to current conditions, such expenditures may likewise readily be justified as being for the benefit of the corporation; indeed, if need be the matter may be viewed strictly in terms of actual survival of the corporation in a free enterprise system. . . .

In 1930 a statute was enacted in our State which expressly provided that any corporation could cooperate with other corporations and natural persons in the creation and maintenance of community funds and charitable, philanthropic or benevolent instrumentalities conducive to public welfare, and could for such purposes expend such corporate sums as the directors "deem expedient and as in their judgment will contribute to the protection of the corporate interests." . . .

In 1950 a more comprehensive statute was enacted. L. 1950, c. 220; N.J.S.A. 14:3–13.1 et seq. In this enactment the Legislature declared that it shall be the public policy of our State and in furtherance of the public interest and welfare that encouragement be given to the creation and maintenance of institutions engaged in community fund, hospital, charitable, philanthropic, educational, scientific or benevolent activities or patriotic or civic activities conducive to the betterment of social and economic conditions; and it expressly empowered corporations acting singly or with others to contribute reasonable sums to such institutions, provided, however, that the contribution shall not be permissible if the donee institution owns more than 10% of the voting stock of the donor and provided, further, that the contribution shall not exceed 1% of capital and surplus unless the excess is authorized by the stockholders at a regular or special meeting. To insure that the grant of express power in the 1950 statute would not displace preexisting power at common law or otherwise, the Legislature provided that the "act shall not be construed as directly or indirectly minimizing or interpreting the rights and powers of corporations, as heretofore existing, with reference to appropriations, expenditures or contributions of the nature above specified." N.J.S.A. 14:3–13.3. . . .

The appellants contend that the foregoing New Jersey statutes may not be applied to corporations created before their passage. Fifty years before the incorporation of The A.P. Smith Manufacturing Company our Legislature provided that every corporate charter thereafter granted "shall be subject to alteration, suspension and repeal, in the discretion of the legislature." L.1846, p. 16; R.S. 14:2–9. A similar reserved power was placed into our State Constitution in 1875 (Art. IV, Sec. VII, par. 11), and is found in our present Constitution. . . .

. . . We are entirely satisfied that within the orbit of above authorities the legislative enactments found in R.S. 14:3–13 and N.J.S.A. 14:3–13.1 et seq. and applied to pre-existing corporations do not violate any constitutional guarantees afforded to their stockholders.

. . . And since in our view the corporate power to make reasonable charitable contributions exists under modern conditions, even apart from express statutory provision, its enactments simply constitute helpful and confirmatory declarations of such power, accompanied by limiting safeguards.

In the light of all of the foregoing we have no hesitancy in sustaining the validity of the donation by the plaintiff. There is no suggestion that it was made indiscriminately or to a pet charity of the corporate directors in furtherance of personal rather than corporate ends. On the contrary, it was made to a preeminent institution of higher learning, was modest in amount and well within the limitations imposed by the statutory enactments, and was voluntarily made in the reasonable belief that it would aid the public welfare and advance the interests of the plaintiff as a private corporation and as part of the community in which it operates. We find that it was a lawful exercise of the corporation's implied and incidental powers under common-law principles and that it came within the express authority of the pertinent state legislation. As has been indicated, there is now widespread belief throughout the nation that free and vigorous non-governmental institutions of learning are vital to our democracy and the system of free enterprise and that withdrawal of corporate authority to make such contributions within reasonable limits would seriously threaten their continuance. Corporations have come to recognize this and with their enlightenment have sought in varying measures, as has the plaintiff by its contribution, to insure and strengthen the society which gives them existence and the means of aiding themselves and their fellow citizens. Clearly then, the appellants, as individual stockholders whose private interests rest entirely upon the well-being of the plaintiff corporation, ought not be permitted to close their eyes to present-day realities and thwart the long-visioned corporate action in recognizing and voluntarily discharging its high obligations as a constituent of our modern social structure.

The judgment entered in the Chancery Division is in all respects Affirmed.

―――――

DEL. GEN. CORP. LAW § 122(9), (12)

[See Statutory Supplement]

―――――

MODEL BUS. CORP. ACT § 3.02(12)–(14)

[See Statutory Supplement]

―――――

NOTES ON THE CONDUCT OF THE CORPORATION

1.   Statutory Provisions. Virtually all states have now adopted statutory provisions relating to corporate contributions that are comparable to Del.Gen.Corp.Law § 122(9) and Model Bus.Corp.Act § 3.02(13). Although typically these provisions do not explicitly incorporate a limit of reasonableness, the commentators generally agree that such a limit is to be implied. Of particular significance is the commentary of Ray Garrett, a principal figure in the drafting history of the Model Act:

> Donations should be reasonable in amount in the light of the corporation's financial condition, bear some reasonable relation to the corporation's interest, and not be so "remote and fanciful" as to excite the opposition of shareholders whose property is being used. Direct corporate benefit is no longer necessary, but corporate interest remains as a motive.

Garrett, Corporate Donations, 22 BUS. LAW. 297, 301 (1967).

2.   Boundaries of Discretion. There is very little direct authority on the permissibility of taking ethical considerations into account in framing corporate action where doing so might not enhance profits. However, statutory provisions like Model Bus.Corp.Act § 3.02(13) provide indirect support for doing so, since it would be anomalous to permit the corporation to donate money it has already earned for public welfare or charitable purposes, while prohibiting the corporation from forgoing a limited amount of profits in the service of generally recognized ethical principles. On the question on the inherent discretion of directors within the business judgment rule to sacrifice profits in the public interest, *see* Einer Elhauge, Sacrificing Corporate Profits in the Public Interest, 80 N.Y.U. L. Rev. 733 (business judgment rule necessarily accords discretion to boards to tradeoff profits for the public interest).

The Conference Board conducts an annual survey of corporate giving. The Board's 2013 Corporate Contributions Report is based on giving in 2012 by 240 participants. The median contribution was 1 percent of pretax income. The study included sixty of the largest companies in the Fortune 100 whose median giving was nearly $61 million (the median giving by all other companies in the study was $13.54 million).

————

AMERICAN LAW INSTITUTE, PRINCIPLES OF CORPORATE GOVERNANCE §§ 2.01, 6.02

[See Statutory Supplement]

————

CONN. GEN. STATS. ANN. §§ 33–756

[See Statutory Supplement]

————

IND. CODE ANN. § 23–1–35–1

[See Statutory Supplement]

————

N.Y. BUS. CORP. LAW § 717

[See Statutory Supplement]

————

PENNSYLVANIA CONSOL. STATS. ANN. TITLE 15, §§ 1711, 1715, 1716, 1717, 2502

[See Statutory Supplement]

————

NOTE ON POLITICAL CONTRIBUTIONS BY CORPORATIONS

Corporate involvement in political elections has been a much debated topic for over a century. The Tillman Act of 1907 barred corporations directly contributing to political campaigns or elections. More recently, the Bipartisan Campaign Reform Act of 2002 imposed many more restrictions on corporate campaign contributions and practices. However, *Citizens United v. Federal Election Commission*, 558 U.S. 310 (2010), held that the corporation enjoys certain freedoms under the First Amendment. As a result of *Citizens United*, corporations enjoy the same First Amendment right as individuals to engage in unlimited spending on political issues and campaigns, provided the corporation acts independently of any campaign or candidate.

A host of corporate governance questions flow from *Citizens United*. The focus of the debate is who decides what cause or candidate to support and how much to contribute as well as what level of transparency should surround the decision. Currently, corporate decisions regarding such expenditures are treated as ordinary business decisions so that executives, most importantly the CEO, enjoy broad discretion over whose cause or campaign will be supported and what level of support will be provided. There is some evidence that corporate practices are evolving toward modest involvement of independent directors in such decisions. For example, Professor Bebchuk and Jackson report that whereas only 2 of 120 surveyed public corporations in 2007 required board-level approval of political contributions, by 2009 a study of the 100 largest public corporations found that 34 required board-level approval of political contributions. *See* Lucian A. Bebchuk & Robert J. Jackson, Corporate Political Speech: Who Decides?, 124 Harv. L. Rev. 83, 87–88 (2010). Another evolving practice is disclosure of political contributions. For example, by 2012, approximately half of the corporations comprising the S&P 100 Index disclosed their political spending. Many contributions, of course, are to various political action committees or industry organizations that direct the collected sums to more specific causes and candidates.

From a corporate governance perspective (rather than the broader political view), should the approach to who decides, and what level of transparency should surround the decision, be different for political contributions than for charitable contributions? Do charitable and political contributions each present the same potential problem? What might that problem be?

CHAPTER 4

THE LEGAL STRUCTURE OF PUBLICLY HELD CORPORATIONS

Melvin A. Eisenberg,
The Structure of the Corporation 1
(1976).

Corporate law is constitutional law; that is, its dominant function is to regulate the manner in which the corporate institution is constituted, to define the relative rights and duties of those participating in the institution, and to delimit the powers of the institution vis-à-vis the external world.

—————

INTRODUCTORY NOTE

This Chapter concerns the power and roles of a corporation's three major organs—the board, the shareholders, and the executives (particularly the chief executive officer, or CEO)—in the governance of publicly held corporations.[*]

Publicly held corporations, taken as a group, are the driving force of the American economy, and also play very important roles in American political and social life. Accordingly, the governance of publicly held corporations is a matter of critical concern. Corporate governance involves a number of issues, such as ensuring a reliable flow of information to the board and to the shareholders, and ensuring that the corporation's conduct conforms to law. However, since publicly held corporations are primarily, although not exclusively, economic institutions, probably the most important objective of corporate governance is to provide mechanisms that will increase the likelihood that such corporations will be efficiently managed. Because the dominant figure in American publicly held corporations is the CEO, a core problem of corporate governance is the design of mechanisms that will monitor CEOs and, where necessary, remove inefficient CEOs.

Some of this work can be done by market forces, but these forces are insufficiently strong to reliably accomplish that objective. For example, the

---

[*] There is no settled definition of a publicly held corporation. ALI, Principles of Corporate Governance § 1.31 defines a publicly held corporation as one that has 500 or more holders of its equity securities and $5 million or more of total assets. ALI Section 1.24 defines a large publicly held corporation as one that has 2,000 or more holders of its equity securities and $100 million or more of total assets. In this Chapter, the terms *corporation* and *publicly held corporation* will be used interchangeably.

market for corporate control, which operates through takeovers, provides only very loose discipline of managers. A hostile takeover bidder must incur substantial out-of-pocket expenditures for legal fees, printing, and advertising to make a bid; must incur additional out-of-pocket expenses of if the incumbent management resists the bid, as it usually does; and typically must offer a price at least 30% or so above the market price of the corporation's if the bid is to be successful. As a result, a hostile bidder can make a profit by replacing the incumbent management only if the management is so inefficient that a successful bidder can raise the price of the stock in excess of the premium and the out-of-pocket costs for making and pressing the bid. Similarly, the so-called market for managers has completely broken down, as evidenced by the huge salaries and bonuses paid to commercial and investment bank executives whose incompetence was one substantial cause of the recession that began in 2008, and of Enron and other corporate debacles before that. This is not to say that markets don't work at all in disciplining inefficient managers, but only that they are very far from perfect instruments in achieving that objective. Therefore, it is important to shape the role of the board and the shareholders to help accomplish the objective. Like markets, neither the board nor the shareholders can be counted on to reliably accomplish that objective. However, because all institutions to accomplish that objective are imperfect, it is important to have multiple such institutions in place.

————

The role and power of the major corporate organs can best be understood by considering the distribution of power among these organs in law and in practice. Section 1 considers the legal distribution of power between the board and the shareholders. Section 2 considers the ways in which corporate practice affects that distribution. Section 3 considers the distribution of power between the board and the executives.

————

1. THE LEGAL DISTRIBUTION OF POWER BETWEEN THE BOARD AND THE SHAREHOLDERS, AND EQUITABLE LIMITS ON THE BOARD'S LEGAL POWER

A. THE LEGAL DISTRIBUTION OF POWER BETWEEN THE BOARD AND THE SHAREHOLDERS

————

DEL. GEN. CORP. LAW § 141(a)

[See Statutory Supplement]

————

MODEL BUS. CORP. ACT § 8.01(b)

[See Statutory Supplement]

———

Charlestown Boot & Shoe Co. v. Dunsmore

New Hampshire Supreme Court, 1880.
60 N.H. 85.

Case. Demurrer to the declaration in which the following facts were alleged:—The plaintiffs are a manufacturing corporation having for its object a dividend of profits, and commenced business in 1871. Dunsmore was elected director in 1871 and Willard in 1873, and entered upon the discharge of their duties, and have continued so to act by virtue of successive elections until the present time. December 10, 1874, the corporation* voted to choose a committee to act with the directors to close up its affairs, and chose one Osgood for such committee. Osgood tendered his services, but the defendants refused to act with him, and contracted new debts to a larger extent than allowed by law. By their negligence, debts due to the corporation to the amount of $2,161.23 have been wholly lost. By their negligence in disposing of the goods of the corporation, a loss has accrued of $3,300.40. By their neglect to sell the buildings and machinery of the corporation when they might and ought, and were urged by Osgood to sell, the same depreciated in value to the extent of $20,000.

Also for that the plaintiffs owned and possessed a certain shop of the value of $10,000, and a large amount of machinery and fixtures of the value of $10,000; "and whereas it was the duty of said defendants, directors as aforesaid, to procure sufficient and proper insurance against fire to be made on said property, and keep the same so sufficiently insured, of all which the said defendants had notice, yet they did not and would not keep the said property so insured, and afterwards, to wit, on the 28th day of April, 1878, while the said property was so remaining without insurance, the same was wholly consumed by fire and wholly lost to the plaintiff, whereby the plaintiff suffered great loss and damage, to wit, $20,000."

■ SMITH, J. The provision of the statute is, that the business of a dividend paying corporation shall be managed by the directors. The statute reads, "The business of every such corporation shall be managed by the directors thereof, subject to the by-laws and votes of the corporation, and under their direction by such officers and agents as shall be duly appointed by the directors or by the corporation." G.L., c. 148, s. 3; Gen.Stats., c. 134, s. 3. The only limitation upon the judgment or discretion of the directors is such as the corporation by its by-laws and votes shall impose. It may define its business, its nature and extent,

---

* By "the corporation," as that term used in this opinion, the court seems to mean the body of shareholders. (Footnote by ed.)

prescribe rules and regulations for the government of its officers and members, and determine whether its business shall be wound up or continued; but when it has thus acted, the business as thus defined and limited is to be managed by its directors, and by such officers and agents under their direction as the directors or the corporation shall appoint. The statute does not authorize a corporation to join another officer with the directors, nor compel the directors to act with one who is not a director. They are bound to use ordinary care and diligence in the care and management of the business of the corporation, and are answerable for ordinary negligence. March v. Railroad, 43 N.H. 516, 529; Scott v. Depeyster, 1 Edw. Ch. 513, 543; Ang. & Ames Corp., § 314. There is no difference in this respect between the agents of corporations and those of natural persons, unless expressly made by the charter or by-laws. *Id.*, § 315. It would be unreasonable to hold them responsible for the management of the affairs of the corporation if compelled to act with one who to a greater or less extent could control their acts. The statute not only entrusts the management of the business of the corporation to the directors, but places its other officers and agents under their direction. When a statute provides that powers granted to a corporation shall be exercised by any set of officers or any particular agents, such powers can be exercised only by such officers or agents, although they are required to be chosen by the whole corporation; and if the whole corporation attempts to exercise powers which by the charter are lodged elsewhere, its action upon the subject is void. Insurance Co. v. Keyser, 32 N.H. 313, 315. The vote choosing Osgood a committee to act with the directors in closing up the affairs of the plaintiff corporation was inoperative and void.

The declaration also alleges that it was the duty of the defendants, as directors, to keep the property of the corporation insured. There is no statute that makes it the duty of the directors of a corporation to keep its property insured, and there are no facts alleged from which we can say, as matter of law, that it was the duty of the defendants to insure the property of the corporation.

Demurrer sustained.

■ STANLEY, J., did not sit: the others concurred.

———

Franchise Services of North America v. United States

891 F.3d 198, 208–09 (5th Cir. 2018)

In its acquisition of Advantage Rent-A-Car, FSNA incurred substantial fees to its investment bank, Macquarie Capital, for advisory work on the transaction. To facilitate the acquisition, Macquarie arranged for its wholly owned subsidiary to purchase $15 million of newly authorized FSNA convertible preferred stock. As part of that transaction, FSNA amended its articles of incorporation to include a "golden share" provision whereby FSNA was barred from entering voluntary bankruptcy without the approval of the preferred stock issued to the subsidiary. In contrast, a decision by a corporation to enter voluntary bankruptcy is normally made solely by its board of directors. The acquisition went badly, FSNA filed for bankruptcy, and the subsidiary and Macquarie sued, claiming the voluntary bankruptcy petition was not duly authorized. The court accepted the validity of the golden share provision under Delaware law. "It is one thing to look past corporate governance documents and the structure of a corporation when a creditor has negotiated authority to veto a debtor's decision to file a bankruptcy petition; it is quite another to ignore those documents when the owners retain for themselves the decision whether to file bankruptcy." Furthermore, the court did not believe it relevant that the preferred holder was a wholly owned subsidiary of a creditor to FSNA.

———

DEL. GEN. CORP. LAW § 141(k)

[See Statutory Supplement]

———

CAL. CORP. CODE §§ 303, 304

[See Statutory Supplement]

———

N.Y. BUS. CORP. LAW § 706

[See Statutory Supplement]

———

B. EQUITABLE LIMITS ON THE BOARD'S LEGAL POWERS

Schnell v. Chris-Craft Industries, Inc.

Supreme Court of State of Delaware, 1971.
285 A.2d 437.

■ HERRMANN, JUSTICE (for the majority of the court):

This is an appeal from the denial by the Court of Chancery of the petition of dissident stockholders for injunctive relief to prevent management* from advancing the date of the annual stockholders' meeting from January 11, 1972, as previously set by the by-laws, to December 8, 1971. . . .

It will be seen that the Chancery Court considered all of the reasons stated by management as business reasons for changing the date of the

---

*   We use this word as meaning "managing directors".

meeting; but that those reasons were rejected by the Court below in making the following findings:

"I am satisfied, however, in a situation in which present management has disingenuously resisted the production of a list of its stockholders to plaintiffs or their confederates and has otherwise turned a deaf ear to plaintiffs' demands about a change in management designed to lift defendant from its present business doldrums, management has seized on a relatively new section of the Delaware Corporation Law for the purpose of cutting down on the amount of time which would otherwise have been available to plaintiffs and others for the waging of a proxy battle. Management thus enlarged the scope of its scheduled October 18 directors' meeting to include the by-law amendment in controversy after the stockholders committee had filed with the S.E.C. its intention to wage a proxy fight on October 16.

"Thus plaintiffs reasonably contend that because of the tactics employed by management (which involve the hiring of two established proxy solicitors as well as a refusal to produce a list of its stockholders, coupled with its use of an amendment to the Delaware Corporation Law to limit the time for contest), they are given little chance, because of the exigencies of time, including that required to clear material at the S.E.C., to wage a successful proxy fight between now and December 8. . . . "

In our view, those conclusions amount to a finding that management has attempted to utilize the corporate machinery and the Delaware Law for the purpose of perpetuating itself in office; and, to that end, for the purpose of obstructing the legitimate efforts of dissident stockholders in the exercise of their rights to undertake a proxy contest against management. These are inequitable purposes, contrary to established principles of corporate democracy. The advancement by directors of the by-law date of a stockholders' meeting, for such purposes, may not be permitted to stand. Compare Condec Corp. v. Lunkenheimer Co., 230 A.2d 769 (Del.Ch.1967).

When the by-laws of a corporation designate the date of the annual meeting of stockholders, it is to be expected that those who intend to contest the reelection of incumbent management will gear their campaign to the by-law date. It is not to be expected that management will attempt to advance that date in order to obtain an inequitable advantage in the contest.

Management contends that it has complied strictly with the provisions of the new Delaware Corporation Law in changing the by-law date. The answer to that contention, of course, is that inequitable action does not become permissible simply because it is legally possible. . . .

We are unable to agree with the conclusion of the Chancery Court that the stockholders' application for injunctive relief here was tardy and came too late. . . .

Accordingly, the judgment below must be reversed and the cause remanded, with instructions to nullify the December 8 date as a meeting date for stockholders; to reinstate January 11, 1972 as the sole date of the next annual meeting of the stockholders of the corporation; and to take such other proceedings and action as may be consistent herewith regarding the stock record closing date and any other related matters.

[The dissenting opinion of Chief Justice Wolcott is omitted.]

———

A.A. Berle & G. Means, The Modern Corporation and Private Property

220 (rev. ed. 1967)

"[A]n underlying thesis in corporation law . . . could be applied to each and every power in the whole corporate galaxy. Succinctly stated, the thesis appears to be that all powers granted to a corporation or to the management of a corporation, or to any group within the corporation, whether derived from statute or charter or both, are necessarily and at all times exercisable only for the ratable benefit of all the shareholders as their interest appears. That, in consequence, the *use* of the power is subject to equitable limitation when the power has been exercised to the detriment of their interest, however absolute the grant of power may be in terms, and however correct the technical exercise of it may have been."

———

Blasius Industries, Inc. v. Atlas Corp.
Court of Chancery of Delaware, 1988.
564 A.2d 651.

■ Opinion by ALLEN, CHANCELLOR. . . .

[Blasius Industries] challenges the validity of board action taken at a telephone meeting of December 31, 1987 that added two new members to Atlas' seven member board. That action was taken as an immediate response to the delivery to Atlas by Blasius the previous day of a form of stockholder consent that, if joined in by holders of a majority of Atlas' stock, would have increased the board of Atlas from seven to fifteen members and would have elected eight new members nominated by Blasius. . . .

I conclude that, even though defendants here acted on their view of the corporation's interest and not selfishly, their December 31 action constituted an offense to the relationship between corporate directors and shareholders that has traditionally been protected in courts of equity. As a consequence, I conclude that the board action taken on December 31 was invalid and must be voided. . . .

I.

Blasius Acquires a 9% Stake in Atlas.

Blasius is a new stockholder of Atlas. It began to accumulate Atlas shares for the first time in July, 1987. On October 29, it filed a Schedule 13D with the Securities Exchange Commission disclosing that, with affiliates, it then owned 9.1% of Atlas' common stock. It stated in that filing that it intended to encourage management of Atlas to consider a restructuring of the Company or other transaction to enhance shareholder values. It also disclosed that Blasius was exploring the feasibility of obtaining control of Atlas, including instituting a tender offer or seeking "appropriate" representation on the Atlas board of directors.

Blasius has recently come under the control of two individuals, Michael Lubin and Warren Delano, who after experience in the commercial banking industry, had, for a short time, run a venture capital operation for a small investment banking firm. Now on their own, they apparently came to control Blasius with the assistance of Drexel Burnham's well noted junk bond mechanism. Since then, they have made several attempts to effect leveraged buyouts, but without success. . . .

The prospect of Messrs. Lubin and Delano involving themselves in Atlas' affairs, was not a development welcomed by Atlas' management. Atlas had a new CEO, defendant Weaver, who had, over the course of the past year or so, overseen a business restructuring of a sort. Atlas had sold three of its five divisions. It had just announced (September 1, 1987) that it would close its once important domestic uranium operation. The goal was to focus the Company on its gold mining business. By October, 1987, the structural changes to do this had been largely accomplished. Mr. Weaver was perhaps thinking that the restructuring that had occurred should be given a chance to produce benefit before another restructuring (such as Blasius had alluded to in its Schedule 13D filing) was attempted, when he wrote in his diary on October 30, 1987:

13D by Delano & Lubin came in today. Had long conversation w/MAH & Mark Golden [of Goldman Sachs] on issue. All agree we must dilute these people down by the acquisition of another Co. w/stock, or merger or something else.

The Blasius Proposal of A Leverage Recapitalization or Sale

Immediately after filing its 13D on October 29, Blasius' representatives sought a meeting with the Atlas management. Atlas dragged its feet. A meeting was arranged for December 2, 1987 following the regular meeting of the Atlas board. Attending that meeting were Messrs. Lubin and Delano for Blasius, and, for Atlas, Messrs. Weaver, Devaney (Atlas' CFO), Masinter (legal counsel and director) and Czajkowski (a representative of Atlas' investment banker, Goldman Sachs).

At that meeting, Messrs. Lubin and Delano suggested that Atlas engage in a leveraged restructuring and distribute cash to shareholders. In such a transaction, which is by this date a commonplace form of transaction, a corporation typically raises cash by sale of assets and significant borrowings and makes a large one-time cash distribution to shareholders. The shareholders are typically left with cash and an equity interest in a smaller, more highly leveraged enterprise. Lubin and Delano gave the outline of a leveraged recapitalization for Atlas as they saw it.

Immediately following the meeting, the Atlas representatives expressed among themselves an initial reaction that the proposal was infeasible. On December 7, Mr. Lubin sent a letter detailing the proposal. In general, it proposed the following: (1) an initial special cash dividend to Atlas' stockholders in an aggregate amount equal to (a) $35 million, (b) the aggregate proceeds to Atlas from the exercise of option warrants and stock options, and (c) the proceeds from the sale or disposal of all of Atlas' operations that are not related to its continuing minerals operations; and (2) a special non-cash dividend to Atlas' stockholders of an aggregate $125 million principal amount of 7% Secured Subordinated Gold-Indexed Debentures. The funds necessary to pay the initial cash dividend were to principally come from (i) a "gold loan" in the amount of $35,625,000, repayable over a three to five year period and secured by 75,000 ounces of gold at a price of $475 per ounce, (ii) the proceeds from the sale of the discontinued Brockton Sole and Plastics and Ready-Mix Concrete businesses, and (iii) a then expected January, 1988 sale of uranium to the Public Service Electric & Gas Company. . . .

The proposal met with a cool reception from management. . . .

On December 30, 1987, Blasius caused Cede & Co. (the registered owner of its Atlas stock) to deliver to Atlas a signed written consent (1) adopting a precatory resolution recommending that the board develop and implement a restructuring proposal, (2) amending the Atlas bylaws to, among other things, expand the size of the board from seven to fifteen members—the maximum number under Atlas' charter, and (3) electing eight named persons to fill the new directorships. . . .

The reaction was immediate. Mr. Weaver conferred with Mr. Masinter, the Company's outside counsel and a director, who viewed the consent as an attempt to take control of the Company. They decided to call an emergency meeting of the board, even though a regularly scheduled meeting was to occur only one week hence, on January 6, 1988. The point of the emergency meeting was to act on their conclusion (or to seek to have the board act on their conclusion) "that we should add at least one and probably two directors to the board. . . . " (Tr. 85, Vol. II). A quorum of directors, however, could not be arranged for a telephone meeting that day. A telephone meeting was held the next day. At that meeting, the board voted to amend the bylaws to increase the size of the board from seven to nine and appointed John M. Devaney and Harry J.

Winters, Jr. to fill those newly created positions. Atlas' Certificate of Incorporation creates staggered terms for directors; the terms to which Messrs. Devaney and Winters were appointed would expire in 1988 and 1990, respectively.

The Motivation of the Incumbent Board In Expanding the Board and Appointing New Members.

In increasing the size of Atlas' board by two and filling the newly created positions, the members of the board realized that they were thereby precluding the holders of a majority of the Company's shares from placing a majority of new directors on the board through Blasius' consent solicitation, should they want to do so. Indeed the evidence establishes that that was the principal motivation in so acting.

The conclusion that, in creating two new board positions on December 31 and electing Messrs. Devaney and Winters to fill those positions the board was principally motivated to prevent or delay the shareholders from possibly placing a majority of new members on the board, is critical to my analysis of the central issue posed by the first filed of the two pending cases. If the board in fact was not so motivated, but rather had taken action completely independently of the consent solicitation, which merely had an incidental impact upon the possible effectuation of any action authorized by the shareholders, it is very unlikely that such action would be subject to judicial nullification. *See, e.g.,* Frantz Mg. Co. v. EAC Indus., 501 A.2d 401, 407 (Del. 1985); Moran v. Household Int'l, Inc., 490 A.2d 1059, 1080 (Del.Ch. 1985), aff'd, 500 A.2d 1346 (Del. 1985). The board, as a general matter, is under no fiduciary obligation to suspend its active management of the firm while the consent solicitation process goes forward. . . .

In this setting I conclude that, while the addition of these qualified men would, under other circumstances, be clearly appropriate as an independent step, such a step was in fact taken in order to impede or preclude a majority of the shareholders from effectively adopting the course proposed by Blasius. . . .

II.

Plaintiff attacks the December 31 board action as a selfishly motivated effort to protect the incumbent board from a perceived threat to its control of Atlas. Their conduct is said to constitute a violation of the principle, applied in such cases as Schnell v. Chris-Craft Industries, 285 A.2d 437 (Del. 1971), that directors hold legal powers [subject] to a supervening duty to exercise such powers in good faith pursuit of what they reasonably believe to be in the corporation's interest. . . . Defendants . . . Aronson v. Lewis, 473 A.2d 805 (Del. 1984) . . .

[Defendants] say that, in creating two new board positions and filling them on December 31, they acted without a conflicting interest (since the Blasius proposal did not, in any event, challenge *their* places on the board) . . . and they acted in good faith (since they were motivated, they say, to protect the shareholders from the threat of having an impractical, indeed a dangerous, recapitalization program foisted upon them). . . .

III . . .

On balance, I cannot conclude that the board was acting out of a self-interested motive in any important respect on December 31. I conclude rather that the board saw the "threat" of the Blasius recapitalization proposal as posing vital policy differences between itself and Blasius. It acted, I conclude, in a good faith effort to protect its incumbency, not selfishly, but in order to thwart implementation of the recapitalization that it feared, reasonably, would cause great injury to the Company.

The real question the case presents, to my mind, is whether, in these circumstances, the board, even if it *is* acting with subjective good faith (which will typically, if not always, be a contestable or debatable judicial conclusion), may validly act for the principal purpose of preventing the shareholders from electing a majority of new directors [emphasis in original]. The question thus posed is not one of intentional wrong (or even negligence), but one of authority *as between the fiduciary and the beneficiary* (not simply legal authority, *i.e.,* as between the fiduciary and the world at large).

IV.

It is established in our law that a board may take certain steps— such as the purchase by the corporation of its own stock—that have the effect of defeating a threatened change in corporate control, when those steps are taken advisedly, in good faith pursuit of a corporate interest, and are reasonable in relation to a threat to legitimate corporate interests posed by the proposed change in control. *See* Unocal Corp. v. Mesa Petroleum Co., 493 A.2d 946 (Del. 1985) . . . Does this rule—that the reasonable exercise of good faith and due care generally validates, in equity, the exercise of legal authority even if the act has an entrenchment effect—apply to action designed for the primary purpose of interfering with the effectiveness of a stockholder vote? Our authorities, as well as sound principles, suggest that the central importance of the franchise to the scheme of corporate governance, requires that, in this setting, that rule not be applied and that closer scrutiny be accorded to such [a] transaction.

1.   *Why the deferential business judgment rule does not apply to board acts taken for the primary purpose of interfering with a stockholder's vote, even if taken advisedly and in good faith.*

A.   *The question of legitimacy.*

The shareholder franchise is the ideological underpinning upon which the legitimacy of directorial power rests. Generally, shareholders have only two protections against perceived inadequate business performance. They may sell their stock (which, if done in sufficient numbers, may so affect security prices as to create an incentive for altered managerial performance), or they may vote to replace incumbent board members.

It has, for a long time, been conventional to dismiss the stockholder vote as a vestige or ritual of little practical importance. It may be that we are now witnessing the emergence of new institutional voices and arrangements that will make the stockholder vote a less predictable affair than it has been. Be that as it may, however, whether the vote is seen functionally as an unimportant formalism, or as an important tool of discipline, it is clear that it is critical to the theory that legitimates the exercise of power by some (directors and officers) over vast aggregations of property that they do not own. Thus, when viewed from a broad, institutional perspective, it can be seen that matters involving the integrity of the shareholder voting process involve [considerations] not present in any other context in which directors exercise delegated power.

B.   *Questions of this type raise issues of the allocation of authority as between the board and the shareholders.*

The distinctive nature of the shareholder franchise context also appears when the matter is viewed from a less generalized, doctrinal point of view. From this point of view, as well, it appears that the ordinary considerations to which the business judgment rule originally responded are simply not present in the shareholder voting context. That is, a decision by the board to act for the primary purpose of preventing the effectiveness of a shareholder vote inevitably involves the question who, as between the principal and the agent, has authority with respect to a matter of internal corporate governance. That, of course, is true in a very specific way in this case which deals with the question who should constitute the board of directors of the corporation, but it will be true in every instance in which an incumbent board seeks to thwart a shareholder majority. A board's decision to act to prevent the shareholders from creating a majority of new board positions and filling them does not involve the exercise of *the corporation's power* over its property, or with respect to *its* rights or obligations; rather, it involves allocation, between shareholders as a class and the board, of effective power with respect to governance of the corporation. This need not be the case with respect to other forms of corporate action that may have an entrenchment effect—such as the stock buybacks present in *Unocal, Cheff* or *Kors v. Carey,* Action designed principally to interfere with the effectiveness of a vote inevitably involves a conflict between the board and a shareholder majority. Judicial review of such action involves a determination of the legal and equitable obligations of an agent towards his principal. This is not, in my opinion, a question that a court may leave to the agent finally to decide so long as he does so honestly and competently; that is, it may not be left to the agent's business judgment.

> 2. *What rule does apply: per se invalidity of corporate acts intended primarily to thwart effective exercise of the franchise or is there an intermediate standard?*

Plaintiff argues for a rule of *per se* invalidity once a plaintiff has established that a board has acted for the primary purpose of thwarting the exercise of a shareholder vote. Our opinions in Canada Southern Oils, Ltd. v. Manabi Exploration Co., 96 A.2d 810 (Del. Ch. 1953) and Condec Corp. v. Lunkenheimer Co., 230 A.2d 769 (Del. Ch. 1967) could be read as support for such a rule of *per se* invalidity. . . .

. . . A *per se* rule that would strike down, in equity, any board action taken for the primary purpose of interfering with the effectiveness of a corporate vote would have the advantage of relative clarity and predictability.[4] It also has the advantage of most vigorously enforcing the concept of corporate democracy. The disadvantage it brings along is, of course, the disadvantage a *per se* rule always has: it may sweep too broadly. In two recent cases dealing with shareholder votes, this court struck down board acts done for the primary purpose of impeding the exercise of stockholder voting power. In doing so, a *per se* rule was not applied. Rather, it was said that, in such a case, the board bears the heavy burden of demonstrating a compelling justification for such action. . . .

In my view, our inability to foresee now all of the future settings in which a board might, in good faith, paternalistically seek to thwart a shareholder vote, counsels against the adoption of a *per se* rule invalidating, in equity, every board action taken for the sole or primary purpose of thwarting a shareholder vote, even though I recognize the transcending significance of the franchise to the claims to legitimacy of our scheme of corporate governance. It may be that some set of facts would justify such extreme action. This, however, is not such a case.

> 3. *Defendants have demonstrated no sufficient justification for the action of December 31 which was intended to prevent an unaffiliated majority of shareholders from effectively exercising their right to elect eight new directors.*

The board was not faced with a coercive action taken by a powerful shareholder against the interests of a distinct shareholder constituency (such as a public minority). It was presented with a consent solicitation by a 9% shareholder. Moreover, here it had time (and understood that it had time) to inform the shareholders of its views on the merits of the proposal subject to stockholder vote. The only justification that can, in such a situation, be offered for the action taken is that the board knows better than do the shareholders what is in the corporation's best interest. While that premise is no doubt true for any number of matters, it is

---

[4] While it must be admitted that any rule that requires for its invocation the finding of a subjective mental state (*i.e.,* a primary purpose) necessarily will lead to controversy concerning whether it applies or not, nevertheless, once it is determined to apply, this *per se* rule would be clearer than the alternative discussed below.

irrelevant (except insofar as the shareholders wish to be guided by the board's recommendation) when the question is who should comprise the board of directors. The theory of our corporation law confers power upon directors as the agents of the shareholders; it does not create Platonic masters. It may be that the Blasius restructuring proposal was or is unrealistic and would lead to injury to the corporation and its shareholders if pursued. Having heard the evidence, I am inclined to think it was not a sound proposal. The board certainly viewed it that way, and that view, held in good faith, entitled the board to take certain steps to evade the risk it perceived. It could, for example, expend corporate funds to inform shareholders and seek to bring them to a similar point of view. *See, e.g.* Hall v. Trans-Lux Daylight Picture Screen Corp., 171 A. 226, 227 (Del.Ch.1934); Hibbert v. Hollywood Park, Inc., 457 A.2d 339 (Del.1983). But there is a vast difference between expending corporate funds to inform the electorate and exercising power for the primary purpose of foreclosing effective shareholder action. A majority of the shareholders, who were not dominated in any respect, could view the matter differently than did the board. If they do, or did, they are entitled to employ the mechanisms provided by the corporation law and the Atlas certificate of incorporation to advance that view.* They are also entitled, in my opinion, to restrain their agents, the board, from acting for the principal purpose of thwarting that action.

I therefore conclude that, even finding the action was taken in good faith, it constituted an unintended violation of the duty of loyalty that the board owed to the shareholders. I note parenthetically that the concept of an unintended breach of the duty of loyalty is unusual but not novel. That action will, therefore, be set aside by order of this court. . . .

————

NOTE ON FURTHER PROCEEDINGS IN BLASIUS

During the pendency of Blasius's attack on the action of the directors in adding two members to the board, Blasius presented Atlas with shareholder consents purporting to show that a majority of Atlas's shareholders had adopted Blasius's proposals to enlarge the board from seven to fifteen, elect eight new directors nominated by Blasius, and take certain other actions. Atlas appointed Manufacturers Hanover Trust Company to act as judge of the shareholders' "vote." Manufacturers reported that the vote had been extremely close, but that none of Blasius's proposals had succeeded. Blasius then brought a second case, in which it challenged certain of Manufacturers' determinations. That case was consolidated with Blasius's attack on the action of the directors in adding two members to the board. The court upheld most of Manufacturers' determinations, including its conclusion that Blasius had lost the vote, and rendered judgment in the second case for the defendants.

————

*   *Id.* at 663.

NOTE ON THE BUSINESS JUDGMENT RULE

Corporate law employs a number of different standards of judicial review of the conduct of directors and officers, depending on the type of conduct involved. The most lenient standard—the standard that is easiest for directors and officers to satisfy—is the business judgment rule, referred to in *Blasius*. The meaning and application of this rule is considered in depth in Chapter 9. At this point suffice to say that under the business judgment rule, if certain conditions are satisfied, a disinterested director or officer will not be liable for the adverse consequences of a bad decision unless the decision was irrational. In *Blasius*, Chancellor Allen in effect concluded that conduct that interferes with shareholder voting is not reviewed under the business judgment rule. Instead, a much more stringent standard of review—the standard of compelling justification—should be applied.

C. THE ROLE OF BYLAWS IN THE ALLOCATION OF POWER BETWEEN THE BOARD AND THE SHAREHOLDERS

A corporation normally has two foundational instruments: its certificate of incorporation and its bylaws. Together with state, federal, and soft law (such as governance rules of a stock exchange on which the corporation's shares are listed), these foundational instruments set out the rules that govern the roles and powers of corporate organs and officers and other important matters. If there is a conflict between the certificate and the bylaws, the certificate controls.

Corporate bylaws address a variety of matters. Customarily they set forth the time, place and manner of giving notice for stockholders meeting. As seen earlier, corporate statutes generally permit the bylaws to provide higher or lower quorum or voting requirements than the default rules set forth in the statute. Bylaws frequently set forth the express powers of company officers. Importantly, corporate statutes permit both the board of directors and the shareholders to adopt, amend or repeal bylaws. Not surprisingly, during the past few years bylaw provisions have been something of a battleground between incumbent management and activists shareholders.

One defensive use of bylaws by management has been the "advance notice bylaw." Generally, stockholders are not required to give advance notice in order to introduce business or nominate directors at an annual meeting, unless the corporation has explicitly imposed such a requirement via an advance notice bylaw. An advance notice bylaw requires as a predicate to any shareholder proposing a matter for shareholder action at an upcoming meeting that the proposing shareholder must give advance notice of such intention a specified number of days before the meeting. In the case of director nominations, such bylaws often also require that shareholders provide specified information about the nominees.

Advance notice bylaws have two purposes: to ensure the orderly functioning of shareholder meetings and to be used as a defensive strategy against activist shareholders. The former is achieved by ensuring that shareholders can prepare and inform themselves prior to a vote. The latter is achieved by allowing the incumbent board time to mount a defensive strategy against insurgents. Arguable *Blasius* should dominate discussion in this areas because advance notice bylaws directly impact shareholder voting. However, *Blasius* is glaringly absent in the judicial consideration of the ever-expanding area of advance notice bylaws. Advance notice bylaws have now become a standard fixture within U.S. companies. They are frequently upheld by both Delaware courts and courts of other jurisdictions, and have been for many years.

In an era where the prevalent theme within corporate law is private ordering, in which the bylaws are the medium for fulfilling that objective, Delaware courts have, when addressing challenges to an advance notice bylaw, employed interpretative tools from contract law as well as a blend of equity and fiduciary obligation considerations. But, as yet, *Blasius* has not been a focal point. For example, in *Mentor Graphics Corp. v. Quickturn Design Sys., Inc.*, 728 A.2d 25 (Del. Ch.), *aff'd on other grounds sub nom. Quickturn Design Sys., Inc. v. Shapiro*, 721 A.2d 1281 (Del. 1998), the court upheld a ninety day advance notice bylaw that had been adopted unilaterally by the target's board of directors in response to Mentor Graphics' tender offer; before the amendment, Quickturn's bylaws, while authorizing holders of ten percent of the company's shares to convene a special stockholders' meeting, were unclear regarding who would set the meeting date and how quickly such a meeting would be convened. Mentor Graphics challenged the board-adopted bylaw under *Blasius* as well as *Unocal* (a doctrine that governs defensive maneuvers generally that is examined in Chapter 14, *infra*). The challenge was rebuffed on the ground the bylaw was a reasonable step to avoid having a special shareholders meeting convened with insufficient time for the shareholders to adequately inform themselves regarding the action proposed to be taken at the meeting.

Frequently, courts narrowly construe the scope of a challenged advance notice bylaw so as not to unnecessarily erode the shareholders' voting rights. Thus, in *JANA Master Fund, Ltd. v. CNET Networks, Inc.*, 954 A.2d 335, 337 (Del. Ch.), the plaintiff ("JANA") informed the board of defendant CNET Networks, Inc. ("CNET") that it wished to solicit proxies for its director nominees and various proposals. CNET's bylaws required a shareholder seeking to nominate directors, or to propose other business at the annual meeting, to have beneficially owned $1,000 of common stock for not less than one year. Because JANA had only acquired its shares eight months prior to the expected date of the meeting, CNET contended that JANA's planned proxy solicitation was in violation of the bylaws. The advance notice bylaw also stated that notice must "comply with the federal securities laws governing shareholder proposals a corporation must include in its own proxy materials." The court held that this language clearly indicated that the bylaw only applied to proposals and nominations that are to be included in the company's proxy materials. Since JANA intended to finance the proxy mailings itself, the court concluded that the bylaw was inapplicable.

————

CA, Inc. v. AFSCME Employees Pension Plan

Supreme Court of State of Delaware, 2008.
953 A.2d 227.

■ JACOBS, JUSTICE: . . .

I.   *FACTS*

CA is a Delaware corporation whose board of directors consists of twelve persons, all of whom sit for reelection each year. CA's annual meeting of stockholders is scheduled to be held on September 9, 2008. CA intends to file its definitive proxy materials with the SEC on or about July 24, 2008 in connection with that meeting.

AFSCME, a CA stockholder, is associated with the American Federation of State, County and Municipal Employees. On March 13, 2008, AFSCME submitted a proposed stockholder bylaw (the "Bylaw" or "proposed Bylaw") for inclusion in the Company's proxy materials for its 2008 annual meeting of stockholders. The Bylaw, if adopted by CA stockholders, would amend the Company's bylaws to provide as follows:

> RESOLVED, that pursuant to *section 109 of the Delaware General Corporation Law* and Article IX of the bylaws of CA, Inc., stockholders of CA hereby amend the bylaws to add the following Section 14 to Article II:

> The board of directors shall cause the corporation to reimburse a stockholder or group of stockholders (together, the "Nominator") for reasonable expenses ("Expenses") incurred in connection with nominating one or more candidates in a contested election of directors to the corporation's board of directors, including, without limitation, printing, mailing, legal, solicitation, travel, advertising and public relations expenses, so long as (a) the election of fewer than 50% of the directors to be elected is contested in the election, (b) one or more candidates nominated by the Nominator are elected to the corporation's board of directors, (c) stockholders are not permitted to cumulate their votes for directors, and (d) the election occurred, and the Expenses were incurred, after this bylaw's adoption. The amount paid to a Nominator under this bylaw in respect of

a contested election shall not exceed the amount expended by the corporation in connection with such election.

CA's current bylaws and Certificate of Incorporation have no provision that specifically addresses the reimbursement of proxy expenses. Of more general relevance, however, is Article SEVENTH, Section (1) of CA's Certificate of Incorporation, which tracks the language of *8 Del. C. § 141(a)* and provides that:

> The management of the business and the conduct of the affairs of the corporation shall be vested in [CA's] Board of Directors.

It is undisputed that the decision whether to reimburse election expenses is presently vested in the discretion of CA's board of directors, subject to their fiduciary duties and applicable Delaware law.

On April 18, 2008, CA notified the SEC's Division of Corporation Finance (the "Division") of its intention to exclude the proposed Bylaw from its 2008 proxy materials. The Company requested from the Division a "no-action letter" stating that the Division would not recommend any enforcement action to the SEC if CA excluded the AFSCME proposal.[2] CA's request for a no-action letter was accompanied by an opinion from its Delaware counsel . . . [that] concluded that the proposed Bylaw is not a proper subject for stockholder action, and that if implemented, the Bylaw would violate the Delaware General Corporation Law ("DGCL").

On May 21, 2008, AFSCME responded to CA's no-action request with a letter taking the opposite legal position. The AFSCME letter was accompanied by an opinion from AFSCME's Delaware counsel . . . [that] concluded that the proposed Bylaw is a proper subject for shareholder action and that if adopted, would be permitted under Delaware law.

The Division was thus confronted with two conflicting legal opinions on Delaware law. . . . To obtain guidance, the SEC, at the Division's request, certified two questions of Delaware law to this Court. . . .

II. *THE CERTIFIED QUESTIONS*

The two questions certified to us by the SEC are as follows:

1.   Is the AFSCME Proposal a proper subject for action by shareholders as a matter of Delaware law?

2.   Would the AFSCME Proposal, if adopted, cause CA to violate any Delaware law to which it is subject? . . .

---

[2]   Under Sections (i)(1) and (i)(2) of SEC Rule 14a–8, a company may exclude a stockholder proposal from its proxy statement if the proposal "is not a proper subject for action by the shareholders under the laws of the jurisdiction of the company's organization," or where the proposal, if implemented, "would cause the company to violate any state law to which it is subject." *See 17 C.F.R. § 240.14a–8.*

III. *THE FIRST QUESTION*

A. *Preliminary Comments . . .*

[T]he DGCL empowers both the board of directors and the shareholders of a Delaware corporation to adopt, amend or repeal the corporation's bylaws. *8 Del. C. § 109(a)* relevantly provides that:

> After a corporation has received any payment for any of its stock, the power to adopt, amend or repeal bylaws shall be in the stockholders entitled to vote . . . ; provided, however, any corporation may, in its certificate of incorporation, confer the power to adopt, amend or repeal bylaws upon the directors. . . . The fact that such power has been so conferred upon the directors . . . shall not divest the stockholders . . . , of the power, nor limit their power to adopt, amend or repeal bylaws. . . .

[B]y its terms *Section 109(a)* vests in the shareholders a power to adopt, amend or repeal bylaws that is legally sacrosanct, *i.e.,* the power cannot be non-consensually eliminated or limited by anyone other than the legislature itself. If viewed in isolation, *Section 109(a)* could be read to make the board's and the shareholders' power to adopt, amend or repeal bylaws identical and coextensive, but *Section 109(a)* does not exist in a vacuum. It must be read together with *8 Del. C. § 141(a)*, which pertinently provides that:

> The business and affairs of every corporation organized under this chapter shall be managed by or under the direction of a board of directors, except as may be otherwise provided in this chapter or in its certificate of incorporation.

No such broad management power is statutorily allocated to the shareholders. Indeed, it is well-established that stockholders of a corporation subject to the DGCL may not directly manage the business and affairs of the corporation, at least without specific authorization in either the statute or the certificate of incorporation. Therefore, the shareholders' statutory power to adopt, amend or repeal bylaws is not coextensive with the board's concurrent power and is limited by the board's management prerogatives under *Section 141(a)*.[7]

> [I]t follows that, to decide whether the Bylaw proposed by AFSCME is a proper subject for shareholder action under Delaware law, we must first determine: (1) the scope or reach of the shareholders' power to adopt, alter or repeal the bylaws of a Delaware corporation, and then (2) whether the Bylaw at issue here falls within that permissible scope. . . .

---

7   Because the board's managerial authority under *Section 141(a)* is a cardinal precept of the DGCL, we do not construe *Section 109* as an "except[ion] . . . otherwise specified in th[e] [DGCL]" to *Section 141(a)*. Rather, the shareholders' statutory power to adopt, amend or repeal bylaws under *Section 109* cannot be "inconsistent with law," including *Section 141(a)*.

B. *Analysis*

1.

Two other provisions of the DGCL, *8 Del. C. §§ 109(b)* and *102(b)(1)*, bear importantly on the first question and form the basis of contentions advanced by each side. *Section 109(b)*, which deals generally with bylaws and what they must or may contain, provides that:

> The bylaws may contain any provision, not inconsistent with law or with the certificate of incorporation, relating to the business of the corporation, the conduct of its affairs, and its rights or powers or the rights or powers of its stockholders, directors, officers or employees.

And *Section 102(b)(1)*, which is part of a broader provision that addresses what the certificate of incorporation must or may contain, relevantly states that:

> (b) In addition to the matters required to be set forth in the certificate of incorporation by subsection (a) of this section, the certificate of incorporation may also contain any or all of the following matters:
>
> (1) Any provision for the management of the business and for the conduct of the affairs of the corporation, and any provision creating, defining, limiting and regulating the powers of the corporation, the directors and the stockholders, or any class of the stockholders. . . . ; if such provisions are not contrary to the laws of this State. Any provision which is required or permitted by any section of this chapter to be stated in the bylaws may instead be stated in the certificate of incorporation.

AFSCME relies heavily upon the language of *Section 109(b)*, which permits the bylaws of a corporation to contain "any provision . . . relating to the . . . rights or powers of its stockholders [and] directors. . . . " The Bylaw, AFSCME argues, "relates to" the right of the stockholders meaningfully to participate in the process of electing directors, a right that necessarily "includes the right to nominate an opposing slate."

CA argues, in response, that *Section 109(b)* is not dispositive, because it cannot be read in isolation from, and without regard to, *Section 102(b)(1)*. CA's argument runs as follows: the Bylaw would limit the substantive decision-making authority of CA's board to decide whether or not to expend corporate funds for a particular purpose, here, reimbursing director election expenses. *Section 102(b)(1)* contemplates that any provision that limits the broad statutory power of the directors must be contained in the certificate of incorporation. Therefore, the proposed Bylaw can only be in CA's Certificate of Incorporation, as distinguished from its bylaws. Accordingly, the proposed bylaw falls outside the universe of permissible bylaws authorized by *Section 109(b)*.

Implicit in CA's argument is the premise that *any* bylaw that in *any* respect might be viewed as limiting or restricting the power of the board of directors automatically falls outside the scope of permissible bylaws. That simply cannot be. That reasoning, taken to its logical extreme, would result in eliminating altogether the shareholders' statutory right to adopt, amend or repeal bylaws. Bylaws, by their very nature, set down rules and procedures that bind a corporation's board and its shareholders. In that sense, most, if not all, bylaws could be said to limit the otherwise unlimited discretionary power of the board. Yet *Section 109(a)* carves out an area of shareholder power to adopt, amend or repeal bylaws that is expressly inviolate. Therefore, to argue that the Bylaw at issue here limits the board's power to manage the business and affairs of the Company only begins, but cannot end, the analysis needed to decide whether the Bylaw is a proper subject for shareholder action. The question left unanswered is what is the scope of shareholder action that *Section 109(b)* permits yet does not improperly intrude upon the directors' power to manage corporation's business and affairs under *Section 141(a)*. . . .

2.

It is well-established Delaware law that a proper function of bylaws is not to mandate how the board should decide specific substantive business decisions, but rather, to define the process and procedures by which those decisions are made. As the Court of Chancery has noted:

> Traditionally, the bylaws have been the corporate instrument used to set forth the rules by which the corporate board conducts its business. To this end, the DGCL is replete with specific provisions authorizing the bylaws to establish the procedures through which board and committee action is taken. . . . [T]here is a general consensus that bylaws that regulate the process by which the board acts are statutorily authorized[15]. . . .

Examples of the procedural, process-oriented nature of bylaws are found in both the DGCL and the case law. For example, *8 Del. C. § 141(b)* authorizes bylaws that fix the number of directors on the board, the number of directors required for a quorum (with certain limitations), and the vote requirements for board action. *8 Del. C. § 141(f)* authorizes bylaws that preclude board action without a meeting.[17] . . . Such purely

---

[15]   *Hollinger Intern., Inc. v. Black, 844 A.2d 1022, 1078–79 (Del. Ch. 2004)* (internal footnotes omitted), *aff'd, 872 A.2d 559 (Del. 2005)*. . . .

[17]   *See also, e.g., 8 Del. C. § 211(a) & (b)* (bylaws may establish the date and the place of the annual meeting of the stockholders); *§ 211(d)* (bylaws may specify the conditions for the calling of special meetings of stockholders); *§ 216* (bylaws may establish quorum and vote requirements for meetings of stockholders and "[a] bylaw amendment adopted by stockholders which specifies the votes that shall be necessary for the election of directors shall not be further amended or repealed by the board of directors."); *§ 222* (bylaws may regulate certain notice requirements regarding adjourned meetings of stockholders).

procedural bylaws do not improperly encroach upon the board's managerial authority under *Section 141(a)*.

The process-creating function of bylaws provides a starting point to address the Bylaw at issue. It enables us to frame the issue in terms of whether the Bylaw is one that establishes or regulates a process for substantive director decision-making, or one that mandates the decision itself. . . . We conclude that the Bylaw, even though infelicitously couched as a substantive-sounding mandate to expend corporate funds, has both the intent and the effect of regulating the process for electing directors of CA. Therefore, we determine that the Bylaw is a proper subject for shareholder action, and set forth our reasoning below.

Although CA concedes that "restrictive procedural bylaws (such as those requiring the presence of all directors and unanimous board consent to take action) are acceptable," it points out that even facially procedural bylaws can unduly intrude upon board authority. The Bylaw being proposed here is unduly intrusive, CA claims, because, by mandating reimbursement of a stockholder's proxy expenses, it limits the board's broad discretionary authority to decide whether to grant reimbursement at all. CA further claims that because (in defined circumstances) the Bylaw mandates the expenditure of corporate funds, its subject matter is necessarily substantive, not process-oriented, and, therefore falls outside the scope of what *Section 109(b)* permits.[19]

Because the Bylaw is couched as a command to reimburse ("The board of directors shall cause the corporation to reimburse a stockholder"), it lends itself to CA's criticism. But the Bylaw's wording, although relevant, is not dispositive of whether or not it is process-related. The Bylaw could easily have been worded differently, to emphasize its process, as distinguished from its mandatory payment, component.[20] By saying this we do not mean to suggest that this Bylaw's reimbursement component can be ignored. What we do suggest is that a bylaw that requires the expenditure of corporate funds does not, for that

---

[19] CA actually conflates two separate arguments that, although facially similar, are analytically distinct. The first argument is that the Bylaw impermissibly intrudes upon board authority because it mandates the expenditure of corporate funds. The second is that the Bylaw impermissibly leaves no role for board discretion and would require reimbursement of the costs of a subset of CA's stockholders, even in circumstances where the board's fiduciary duties would counsel otherwise. Analytically, the first argument is relevant to the issue of whether the Bylaw is a proper subject for unilateral stockholder action, whereas the second argument more properly goes to the separate question of whether the Bylaw, if enacted, would violate Delaware law.

[20] For example, the Bylaw could have been phrased more benignly, to provide that "[a] stockholder or group of stockholders (together, the 'Nominator') shall be entitled to reimbursement from the corporation for reasonable expenses ('Expenses') incurred in connection with nominating one or more candidates in a contested election of directors to the corporation's board of directors in the following circumstances. . . ." Although the substance of the Bylaw would be no different, the emphasis would be upon the shareholders' entitlement to reimbursement, rather than upon the directors' obligation to reimburse. As discussed in Part IV, *infra*, of this Opinion, in order for the Bylaw not to be "not inconsistent with law" as *Section 109(b)* mandates, it would also need to contain a provision that reserves the directors' full power to discharge their fiduciary duties.

reason alone, become automatically deprived of its process-related character. A hypothetical example illustrates the point. Suppose that the directors of a corporation live in different states and at a considerable distance from the corporation's headquarters. Suppose also that the shareholders enact a bylaw that requires all meetings of directors to take place in person at the corporation's headquarters. Such a bylaw would be clearly process-related, yet it cannot be supposed that the shareholders would lack the power to adopt the bylaw because it would require the corporation to expend its funds to reimburse the directors' travel expenses. Whether or not a bylaw is process-related must necessarily be determined in light of its context and purpose.

The context of the Bylaw at issue here is the process for electing directors—a subject in which shareholders of Delaware corporations have a legitimate and protected interest. The purpose of the Bylaw is to promote the integrity of that electoral process by facilitating the nomination of director candidates by stockholders or groups of stockholders. Generally, and under the current framework for electing directors in contested elections, only board-sponsored nominees for election are reimbursed for their election expenses. Dissident candidates are not, unless they succeed in replacing at least a majority of the entire board. The Bylaw would encourage the nomination of non-management board candidates by promising reimbursement of the nominating stockholders' proxy expenses if one or more of its candidates are elected. In that the shareholders also have a legitimate interest, because the Bylaw would facilitate the exercise of their right to participate in selecting the contestants. . . .

The shareholders of a Delaware corporation have the right "to participate in selecting the contestants" for election to the board. The shareholders are entitled to facilitate the exercise of that right by proposing a bylaw that would encourage candidates other than board-sponsored nominees to stand for election. The Bylaw would accomplish that by committing the corporation to reimburse the election expenses of shareholders whose candidates are successfully elected. That the implementation of that proposal would require the expenditure of corporate funds will not, in and of itself, make such a bylaw an improper subject matter for shareholder action. Accordingly, we answer the first question certified to us in the affirmative.

That, however, concludes only part of the analysis. The DGCL also requires that the Bylaw be "not inconsistent with law." Accordingly, we turn to the second certified question, which is whether the proposed Bylaw, if adopted, would cause CA to violate any Delaware law to which it is subject.

IV. *THE SECOND QUESTION*

In answering the first question, we have already determined that the Bylaw does not facially violate any provision of the DGCL or of CA's Certificate of Incorporation. The question thus becomes whether the

Bylaw would violate any common law rule or precept. Were this issue being presented in the course of litigation involving the application of the Bylaw to a specific set of facts, we would start with the presumption that the Bylaw is valid and, if possible, construe it in a manner consistent with the law.... The certified questions, however, request a determination of the validity of the Bylaw in the abstract. Therefore, in response to the second question, we must necessarily consider any possible circumstance under which a board of directors might be required to act. Under at least one such hypothetical, the board of directors would breach their fiduciary duties if they complied with the Bylaw. Accordingly, we conclude that the Bylaw, as drafted, would violate the prohibition, which our decisions have derived from *Section 141(a)*, against contractual arrangements that commit the board of directors to a course of action that would preclude them from fully discharging their fiduciary duties to the corporation and its shareholders.

This Court has previously invalidated contracts that would require a board to act or not act in such a fashion that would limit the exercise of their fiduciary duties. In *Paramount Communications, Inc. v. QVC Network, Inc.,* we invalidated a "no shop" provision of a merger agreement with a favored bidder (Viacom) that prevented the directors of the target company (Paramount) from communicating with a competing bidder (QVC) the terms of its competing bid in an effort to obtain the highest available value for shareholders....

AFSCME argues that it is unfair to claim that the Bylaw prevents the CA board from discharging its fiduciary duty where the effect of the Bylaw is to relieve the board entirely of those duties in this specific area.

That response, in our view, is more semantical than substantive. No matter how artfully it may be phrased, the argument concedes the very proposition that renders the Bylaw, as written, invalid: the Bylaw mandates reimbursement of election expenses in circumstances that a proper application of fiduciary principles could preclude. That such circumstances could arise is not farfetched. Under Delaware law, a board may expend corporate funds to reimburse proxy expenses "[w]here the controversy is concerned with a question of policy as distinguished from personnel o[r] management." But in a situation where the proxy contest is motivated by personal or petty concerns, or to promote interests that do not further, or are adverse to, those of the corporation, the board's fiduciary duty could compel that reimbursement be denied altogether.

It is in this respect that the proposed Bylaw, as written, would violate Delaware law if enacted by CA's shareholders. As presently drafted, the Bylaw would afford CA's directors full discretion to determine what *amount* of reimbursement is appropriate, because the directors would be obligated to grant only the "reasonable" expenses of a successful short slate. Unfortunately, that does not go far enough, because the Bylaw contains no language or provision that would reserve to CA's directors their full power to exercise their fiduciary duty to decide whether or not it would be appropriate, in a specific case, to award reimbursement at all.

In arriving at this conclusion, we express no view on whether the Bylaw as currently drafted, would create a better governance scheme from a policy standpoint. We decide only what is, and is not, legally permitted under the DGCL. That statute, as currently drafted, is the expression of policy as decreed by the Delaware legislature. Those who believe that CA's shareholders should be permitted to make the proposed Bylaw as drafted part of CA's governance scheme, have two alternatives. They may seek to amend the Certificate of Incorporation to include the substance of the Bylaw; *or* they may seek recourse from the Delaware General Assembly.

Accordingly, we answer the second question certified to us in the affirmative.

————

SEC PROXY RULE 14a–8

————

DEL. GEN. CORP. LAW §§ 112, 113

————

2. CORPORATE GOVERNANCE AND THE RISE OF INSTITUTIONAL SHAREHOLDERS

A. SHAREHOLDER VOTING

NOTE ON WEIGHTED VOTING IN PUBLICLY HELD CORPORATIONS

In most publicly held corporations, only common shareholders have voting rights, and each share of common stock each carries one vote. However, voting rights can also be conferred on preferred stock or even on bonds. Furthermore, a corporation may have two or more classes of common stock, each with different voting rights. In such cases, often one class has voting power out of all proportion to its equity interest in the corporation. Stock structures like these are sometimes referred to as dual-class common, super-voting stock, or weighted voting. Although not new, the incidence of such structures increased during the 1980s, when they were often installed as an anti-takeover defense. In theory, the creation of such a structure affects only the relative rights of different shareholders, not the allocation of power between managers and shareholders. In practice, however, these structures usually involve the issuance of super-voting stock to members of a control group for the purpose of allowing the group to maintain control, and defend against takeovers, with only a minimum investment in the corporation.

In *Stroh v. Blackhawk Holding Corp.,* 272 N.E.2d 1 (Ill. 1971), Blackhawk's certificate of incorporation authorized a Class A and a Class B Common stock. The Class B stock voted share-for-share with Class A stock, but was entitled neither to dividends nor to participate in the proceeds of a liquidation. After Blackhawk's formation, its promoters purchased 500,000 shares of Class B at a quarter of a cent per share, and 87,868 shares of Class A at $3.40 per share, and thereafter sold Class A stock to the public at $4 per share. As of June 1968, Blackhawk had outstanding 1,237,681 Class A shares and 500,000 Class B shares, the latter representing an investment of $1250 but carrying 28.78% of the total vote. The court upheld the validity of the B stock:

> . . . Section 14 of the Business Corporation Act . . . provides that shares of stock in an Illinois corporation may be divided into classes,

>> "with such designations, preferences, qualifications, limitations, restrictions and such special or relative rights as shall be stated in the articles of incorporation. The articles of incorporation shall not limit or deny the voting power of the shares of any class. . . . "

> Section 14 . . . clearly expresses the intent of the legislature to be that parties to a corporate entity may create whatever restrictions and limitations they may want with regard to their corporate stock by expressing such restrictions and limitations in the articles of incorporation. . . .

> . . . It has long been the common practice in Illinois to classify shares of stock such that one may invest less than another in a corporation, and yet have control. One of two shareholders may purchase ten shares of a class of stock issued at its par value of $1,000 per share, and his business partner may purchase 100 shares of another class of the corporate stock issued at its par value of $10 per share. The parties, for varying reasons, may be very willing that the party investing the $1,000 have control of the management of the corporation, as opposed to the party having the investment of $10,000. . . .

> In this case the parties went one step further than is customary. The stock which could be bought cheaper, and yet carry the same voting power per share, was not permitted to share at all in the dividends or assets of the corporation. This additional step did not invalidate the stock.

In *Providence & Worcester Co. v. Baker,* 378 A.2d 121 (Del.1977), P & W's certificate provided that each holder of common stock had one vote per share for his first 50 shares, but only one vote per 20 shares for all shares over 50. The validity of these limitations was challenged by the trustees in bankruptcy of Penn Central Transportation Co., who held 28% of P & W's stock but were effectively restricted to 3% of the total voting power. The court upheld the restrictions under Del. § 212(a), which states that "[u]nless otherwise provided in the certificate of incorporation . . . each stockholder shall be entitled to 1 vote for each share of capital stock held by such stockholder." *Id.* at 122, quoting 8 Del. Code Ann. § 213. The court concluded that "if the General Assembly intended to bar the type of restriction on stockholders' voting rights here under review, such prohibition would appear in § 212. . . . Under § 212(a), voting rights of stockholders may be varied from the 'one share-one vote' standard by the certificate of incorporation. . . . " *See also* Lacos Land Co. v. Arden Group, Inc., 517 A.2d 271 (Del.Ch.1986).

Delaware upheld a plan to establish "tenure voting" in *Williams v. Geier*, 671 A.2d 1368 (Del. 1996), whereby the company's shareholders approved a recapitalization in which each share would initially have ten votes; however, upon a change in ownership, a share would revert to having one vote until it was held for three years (shares held in street name were presumed to have short-term owners and relegated to one vote per share).

Because there is evidence that the holding period of many institutional investors is measured in weeks, and not months, there is rising concern that institutions seek only short-term gains so that their short-termism inhibits company managers from pursuing long-terms strategies that are better for the firm. *See* David J. Berger, Steven Davidoff Solomon & Aaron J. Benjamin, Tenure Voting and the U.S. Public Company, 72 Bus. Law. 295 (2017); Lynne L. Dallas & Jordan M. Barry, Long-Term Shareholders and Time-Phased Voting, 40 Del. J. Corp. L. 541 (2016) (a 1980 investment in 12 companies that maintained tenure voting through 2013 yielded a return six time greater than the S&P 500). To those who believe short-termism is harmful, tenure voting is seen as one of the antidotes.

Another approach is dual-class shares whereby the class of common shares issued to insiders has super-voting rights whereas shares issued to the public carry one vote per share. It is not unusual that IPOs firms have such a dual class structure. Indeed, when Snap, Inc. (a/k/a Snap Chat) went public only non-voting common shares were sold the public; a handful of its managers held all the voting shares. Earlier, the SEC attempted to prohibit the exchanges from listing dual-class shares, but the court held the SEC lacked authority to enter this area. Business Roundtable v. SEC, 905 F.2d 406 (D.C. Cir. 1990). Nonetheless, the exchanges were pressured by the SEC with the end result they adopted voting rights policies that restrict dual-class and tenure voting structures unless they are in place when the company went public, such as what occurred with Snap, Inc. *See* NYSE Rule 313.00(A); Nasdaq Rule 5640.

Super-voting shares, particularly those issued initially to the firm's founders, raise concerns whether, at least over time, the arrangement exacerbates agency costs by the twin effects of insider voting power being disproportionate to their equity in the firm and that the super voting power entrenching existing management. *See e.g.,* Ronald Masulis, Cong Wang & Fei Xie, Agency Problems at Dual-Class Companies, 64 J. Fin. 1697 (2009) (finding that the greater that the insider's percentage of total voting power exceeds equity ownership the greater the evidence of high compensation, value-destroying acquisitions, and lower returns on capital-investment decisions). Lucian A. Bebchuk & Kobi Kastiel, The Untenable Case for Perpetual Dual-Class Stock, 103 Va. L. Rev. 585, 590 (2017)("as time passes, the potential costs of a dual-class structure tend to increase while the potential benefits tend to erode" so that debate should focus on barring such voting structures or mandating that they end after a fixed period of time).

Very large firms must consider one potential consequence of super-voting shares, possible exclusion from leading stock indices. In 2017 many of the world's largest stock indexes, such as those maintained by S&P (e.g., S&P 500), exclude from their index companies with dual-class shares. This can impact the demand for the shares; for example, about $7 trillion of managed securities are benchmarked to the S&P Index. These changes were introduced in 2017. As a result, certain well-known companies that were already public, such as Alphabet, with dual-class structures were grandfathered into the index.

In several situations, Congress has acted to prevent abuses in this area. For example, the Investment Company Act Section 18 forbids the issuance of nonvoting stock by companies subject to that act. And as seen, the rules of the major stock exchanges also set limits on weighted voting in listed companies.

NEW YORK STOCK EXCHANGE, LISTED COMPANY MANUAL § 313.00

[See Statutory Supplement]

NOTE ON EMPTY VOTING AND RECORD DATE(S)

In an influential article, The New Vote Buying: Empty Voting and Hidden (Morphable) Ownership, 79 So. Cal. L. Rev. 811 (2006), Henry Hu and Bernard Black developed the concept of empty voting, that is, arrangements under which a person holds more votes than shares, so that his votes have been emptied of an accompanying economic stake. Hu and Black begin by pointing out the severe tension between empty voting and the predicates of the corporate system.

> The vote is the core source of shareholder power. The standard contractarian theory of the corporation supports assigning voting rights to common shareholders in proportion to share ownership. Doing so places the power to oversee company managers in the hands of residual owners, who have an incentive to exercise that power to increase firm value; the more shares owned, the greater the incentive and thus the greater the number of votes. Linking shares to votes also facilitates the operation of the market for corporate control. Empirical evidence supports the concern with a disparity between insiders' voting power and economic interest by showing that such a disparity predicts reduced firm value. Beyond this instrumental role of voting, shareholder voting is a core ideological basis for managerial authority, legitimating managers' exercise of authority over property the managers do not own.

Yet the derivatives revolution in finance ... and related growth in the share lending market, are making it easier and cheaper to decouple economic ownership from voting power. Hedge funds and company insiders are taking advantage of this new opportunity. Sometimes, they hold more votes than shares—a pattern we call "empty voting" because the votes have been emptied of an accompanying economic stake. In extreme cases, an investor can vote despite having negative economic ownership, which gives the investor an incentive to vote in ways that reduce the company's share price. . . .

A recent public instance of empty voting illustrates the potential risks from empty voting. Perry Corp., a hedge fund, owned 7 million shares of King Pharmaceuticals. In late 2004, Mylan Laboratories agreed to buy King in a stock-for-stock merger at a substantial premium, but Mylan's shares dropped sharply when the deal was announced. To help Mylan obtain shareholder approval for the merger, Perry bought 9.9% of Mylan, becoming Mylan's largest shareholder. But Perry fully hedged the market risk associated with its Mylan shares. Perry thus had **9.9%** *voting ownership* and **zero** *economic ownership*. Including its position in King, Perry's overall economic interest in Mylan was **negative**. The more Mylan (over) paid for King, the more Perry stood to profit.*

Hu and Black develop and discuss various techniques by which empty voting can be achieved. They call one of these techniques "record data capture."

Before a shareholder meeting, a company's board of directors establishes a voting record date. Shareholders who hold shares at the close of business on the record date have the right to vote at the meeting, which is typically a month or so after the record date. One way to hold votes without economic ownership ... is record date capture—borrowing shares in the share lending market for a limited period around the record date.

So far as the company is concerned, the borrower owns the shares (and the associated votes). In a typical loan, the borrower contracts with the share lender to (1) return the shares to the lender at any time at the election of either side, and (2) pay to the lender an amount equal to any dividends or other distributions the borrower receives on the shares. [The loan contract] leaves the borrower holding votes without economic ownership, while the lender has economic ownership without votes. . . .

In early 2006, a ... questionable use of record date capture appears to have occurred in Hong Kong. Henderson Land offered to buy the 25% minority interest in Henderson Investment, a publicly held affiliate. Most minority shareholders favored the buyout, and Henderson Investment's share price increased substantially.

---

* Emphasis in original.

Under Hong Kong law, however, the buyout could be blocked by a negative vote of 10% of the "free floating" shares—in this case about 2.5% of the outstanding shares. To everybody's surprise, 2.7% of the shares were voted against the buyout. Henderson Investments shares fell 17% the day after the voting outcome was announced.

What happened? It appears that one or more hedge funds borrowed Henderson Investment shares before the record date, voted against the buyout, and then sold those shares short, thus profiting from its private knowledge that the buyout would be defeated. One hedge fund alone may have held enough shares to defeat the buyout.

. . . [Here], hedge funds used record date capture to obtain votes. . . . [O]ne or more hedge funds held a negative overall economic interest—or more precisely, would have negative economic ownership by the time the voting outcome was known. These hedge fund shareholders apparently blocked a deal that would benefit other shareholders.

Consider next a variant record date capture. If shares cannot be borrowed, an alternative vote capture technique is available that promises nearly empty voting. An investor can buy shares just before the record date and sell them soon thereafter. The investor incurs round-trip transaction costs, but has economic ownership for only a short period of time. The investor can hedge this limited risk fully buy buying put options on the shares. . . .

Short-term ownership plus such a hedge entails fully or substantially empty voting. The timing of this limited ownership further attenuates the link between economic ownership and voting rights. The record date is well before the date at which votes are cast. There is no reason to expect company-specific news on the record date. By the time the voting outcome is known, the investor will have shed any economic exposure, and will suffer no ill effects from voting in ways that reduce firm value; indeed, as in Henderson Investments, the investor could even gain from doing so.

Id. at 814–015, 832–33, 834–35

As will be examined more closely in the next chapter, the persons who are listed as shareholders on the corporation's records are known as *record owners*. For a variety of reasons, the persons who actually own shares—the *beneficial* owners—often differ from the record owners. For example, the stock of individual and even institutional shareholders is often held in "street name," that is, in the name of a broker or a bank. Brokers, banks, and others, in turn, often deposit the stock they hold in regional stock depositories (described below), which place the stock under still another name.

To promote certainty, in various contexts corporation law confers rights on record owners, rather than beneficial owners. One of these contexts is voting: normally, only record owners have the right to notice of a meeting and the right to vote.

When a corporation proposes to hold a meeting at which a shareholder vote will be taken, it must give notice of the meeting. To comply with the disclosure requirements of federal law, the notice frequently must be given a month or so before the meeting will take place. Because shares in publicly held corporations are constantly changing hands, the group of persons who are record owners on the date notice is given will differ from the persons who are record owners on the meeting date. Accordingly, if the shareholders entitled to vote at the meeting were the record holders as of the meeting date, then some shareholders entitled to vote would not have received notice of the meeting (because they purchased their shares after the notice was given), and the vote would be invalid.

To resolve this dilemma, the law permits corporations to set a *record date*—which is typically on or around the date that notice of the relevant meeting is given—for determining the shareholders who will be entitled to vote at the meeting. As a result, those persons, and only those persons, who are record shareholders on the record date are entitled to vote. However, this response creates a different problem. For example, assume the record date is February 14th and the meeting date is March 15th and that Alice transferred her shares to Bob on February 28th. A statutory regime that focuses only on a single date of record enables Alice to vote the shares despite her subsequent sale of those shares; this leads to what is commonly referred to as "empty voting" whereby voting rights are in a person with no economic interest in the shares. To address this, some state statutes permit the company bylaws to set a date for notice of the stockholder meeting and a *separate* date for determining the shares entitled to vote at the meeting. The latter date is much closer to the meeting date than the date of notice of the meeting. *See* Del. Gen. Code §§ 212(a) & 219(a); MBCA § 7.07(e). Under an older, more draconian, procedure, which is now little used, in lieu of setting a record date the corporation could close its transfer books, that is, could refuse to record transfers of stock between the time of the close of the books and the time of the meeting. As a result, all persons who were record holders when the transfer books were closed would still be record holders on the meeting date.

B. FINANCIAL INSTITUTIONS AND THEIR ADVISORS

NOTES ON THE ROLE OF SHAREHOLDERS UNDER MODERN CORPORATE PRACTICE

1. Introduction. Notwithstanding the board's extensive legal power to determine most corporate matters, shareholders do have some the legal power. To begin with, shareholders have the right to elect directors. Next, a group of important corporate changes must be approved by both the board and the shareholders. These changes, commonly referred to as *fundamental changes*, include amendments of the corporation's certificate of incorporation, sales of substantially all of the corporation's assets, dissolution of the corporation, and economically significant mergers.

Further, shareholders normally can amend the corporation's bylaws without the board's concurrence if the content of the amendment is proper (see the *CA* case, supra). Finally, shareholders have power to determine a grab-bag of other matters, most of them inconsequential. However, corporate law and practice puts constraints on the exercise of these powers. Historically, these constraints were very strong. In the last ten to twenty years, the constraints, while still very significant, have been weakening.

2. *Background.* At one time, corporation law reflected an inverted-pyramid model of corporate governance. Under this model, at the top of the inverted pyramid were the shareholders, who own the corporation, who elect the board of directors, and whose approval is required for fundamental corporate changes. At the next level down was the board, which manages the corporation's business, makes business policy, and selects the officers. At the bottom of the inverted pyramid were the officers, who under this model act as agents of the board and execute its policies and decisions.

This traditional model was called into drastic question in 1932, with the publication of Berle & Means's classic work, *The Modern Corporation and Private Property*. One of the authors' principal conclusions, revolutionary at the time, was that in publicly held corporations *control* had come to be divorced from *ownership*, because the ownership of publicly held corporations was often highly dispersed, that is, was characterized by a pattern of shareholdings in which no individual, firm, or compact group owned more than a miniscule fraction of a corporation's stock. Where shareholdership is highly dispersed the corporation will be controlled not by the shareholders, but by management—that is, by the board and the executives. This is what Berle & Means meant by the separation of ownership, which still lay with the shareholders, and control, which had shifted to management.

There are two major reasons why management rather than shareholders are likely to have full control of corporations with highly dispersed shareholdership.

First, it will not be rational for a shareholder who owns only a miniscule percentage of the share to invest time in reviewing the corporation's affairs in depth. As a result, the shareholders of a corporation with highly dispersed shareholdership will be rationally apathetic concerning those affairs. Apathy among retail investors continues to be a significant concern. Among S&P 500 companies, 21.7 percent of the shares were not voted in 2015. Evidence that a good portion of this non-voting was by retail investors is that substantial increases in the number of non-voted shares followed regulatory changes in 2009 and 2011 that removed the authority brokers once enjoyed to vote the shares they held in street name when not instructed by their beneficial owners how their shares were to be voted. *See* Kobi Kastiel & Yaron Nili, In Search of the "Absent" Shareholders: A New Solution to Retail Investors' Apathy, 41 Del. J. Corp. L. 55, 61–62 (2016).

Second, when shareholdership is highly dispersed, shareholders face a collective-action problem, that is, a problem of coordinating their decisions and actions. The collective-action problem might not be too important if the interests of managers were perfectly aligned with the interests of shareholders. However, although the two sets of interests are aligned in many respects, they radically diverge in others. For example, inefficient CEOs want to stay in office, while shareholders want inefficient CEOs to be removed. The bottom line is that until twenty to thirty years ago, the role of shareholders in publicly held corporations was largely one of extreme passivity. This passivity was reflected in the so-called Wall Street Rule—"If you don't like management, sell your stock"—and a corollary, "If you don't sell, vote with management."

3. *The Rise of Institutional Shareholders.* Approximately thirty years ago, the extreme passivity embodied in the Wall Street Rule began to be replaced by shareholder activism of varying intensity. This shift from relatively complete shareholder passivity to varying degrees of shareholder activism was precipitated by a dramatic increase in the percentage of stock held by institutional, as opposed to individual shareholders, from 6% in 1950 to around 50% in recent years, and even more in the largest corporations. The institutionalization of stock ownership has led to the prevalence of blockholders—those who own at least five percent of a firm's common stock. Based on a large sample drawn from NYSE, Amex and Nasdaq listed companies, Professor Holderness reports that blockholders on average own 39 percent of the common stock of the listed companies. Holderness finds that such ownership decreases with firm size so that blockholders account for only 16 percent of the largest firms in the sample, those included in the S&P 500. Clifford G. Holderness, The Myth of Diffuse Ownership in the United States, 22 Rev. of Financial Studies 1377 (2009).

4. *Mediums for Activism in the Public Company.* The increase in shareholder activism takes various forms. The simplest form involves taking an active posture in voting on management and shareholder proposals, that is, considering such proposals on their merits, rather than automatically voting with management. A more aggressive form of activism is to originate shareholder proposals. In theory, another possible form of activism could involve nominating directorial candidates. For the most part, however, institutional investors have not followed that path, perhaps out of concern that an investor who has a representative on a corporation's board and trades in the corporation's stock might be liable for insider trading. However, institutions sometimes join movements begun by others to oust incumbent directors and replace them with new directors. In such cases, the new directors would not be representatives of, or even selected by, a given institutional investor, so that the insider-trading problem is less salient.

Still another form of activism relating to director elections involves withholding votes in favor of incumbent directors who are up for reelection.

The intellectual origin of shareholders withholding their vote lies in a 1990 presentation to large institutional investors by former SEC Commissioner and then Stanford Law Professor Joe Grundfest. Grundfest proposed that shareholders "just vote no" in director elections. Though under the plurality voting system that prevailed at the time, withhold votes would have no legal effect no matter how many were cast, he argued that the symbolic impact of withhold votes, especially when coupled with shareholder communications with management, could act as an annual referendum on managerial performance, and "be a catalyst for improved oversight that would benefit all corporate constituencies, as well as the economy at large." . . .

Although there was some early enthusiasm for the initiative, it took several more years before Grundfest's proposal caught on. The turning point probably lies in the 2004 Disney board election, when 45% of the shares were withheld from Disney CEO Michael Eisner. This campaign was highly publicized for a variety of reasons: it involved a large entertainment company; it pitted Eisner against Roy Disney, the nephew of the legendary founder of the company; and because Roy Disney spent more than $2 million in campaigning for shareholders to vote "no." Even though Eisner received a majority of the votes cast, the board of Disney immediately stripped him of his position as chairman and Eisner resigned as CEO the following year. The Disney withhold campaign showed shareholders that, in the right circumstances, a high withhold vote is both achievable and effective in inducing governance changes. . . .

. . . According to Georgeson's survey of S & P 1500 companies, there were 79 directors in 2009 who received a majority withhold votes and 469 directors who received a withhold vote in excess of 30% of the votes cast. . . . [M]any boards care about the number of withhold votes even if it does not affect the outcome of an election and significant withhold votes often induce governance changes. Withhold votes thus represent an important form of shareholder activism. . . .

Marcel Kahan & Edward B. Rock, The Insignificance of Proxy Access, New York University Law and Economics Working Papers, Paper 240, at 12–13, 26 (2010).

There is an intimate connection between withhold voting and plurality voting. Withhold voting allows shareholders who oppose a candidate to forcefully express that opposition, even if they can't vote against the candidate. In contrast, under a regime of straight voting, it is possible to vote no in director elections, and withhold voting is therefore unnecessary.

Another very important form of activism consists of direct discussion between institutional investors and management. Such discussion may concern either specific issues, such as a proposed merger, or general corporate policies. As a practical matter, institutional investors probably get more done through direct discussion than through voting. However, there is an important relation between discussion and voting, because the actual or implied threat that an institutional investor will vote in a certain way is an important incentive for managers to take seriously the concern expressed by institutional investors.

5.   *Types of Institutional Investors.* The various forms of institutional-investor activism raise the question, what is the competence of institutional

investors in their shareholder capacity? Institutional investors are not equipped to make, or even meaningfully assess, ordinary-course business decisions. There are, however, several areas in which institutional investors have substantial competence. For example, institutional investors can meaningfully assess a corporation's governance rules. Managers are self-interested in these rules, because the rules bear on the preservation and enhancement of managerial positions. Institutional investors normally have no direct conflict of interest concerning their portfolio corporations' governance rules, and may have special competence in this area, because they can review governance rules across corporations as a class.

Institutional investors can also meaningfully assess proposed structural changes, such as mergers. Managers are often also self-interested in structural changes, which will normally either enhance or threaten to reduce their positions. Furthermore, institutional investors may have special competence to evaluate the financial desirability of proposed structural changes, because while corporate managers are expert in making operational business decisions, institutional investors are expert in making the kinds of financial decisions often involved in structural changes. Moreover, often the market will react to a proposed structural change, and institutional investors can use the market's reaction as strong evidence of the proposal's merit. Institutional investors also can frequently play a meaningful role in evaluating the success of a corporation's business strategies and the competence of its CEO, again with the help of market signals.

Institutional investors fall into a number of categories:

a). Private Pension Plans. Private pension plans are established by private employers to provide retirement income to their employees. The most important provisions of these plans concern the location of power over the selection of the plan's assets (portfolio decisions) and over how to vote shares in the plan's portfolio (voting decisions). Private pension plans often delegate portfolio decisions, voting decisions, or both, to other fiduciaries, usually banks, who administer the plans.

b). Public Pension Plans. Public pension plans are established by public employers, such as states and cities, to provide retirement income for their employees. As in the case of private pension plans, decision making powers may be either vested in managers or other employees of the public entity or delegated to independent fiduciaries. Often portfolio decisions are delegated while voting decisions are retained.

c). Independent Non-Profit Pension Funds. A not-for-profit organization may also run pension plans for designated classes of individuals. In particular, Teachers Insurance and Annuity Association—College Retirement Equity Funds (TIAA-CREF, or Teachers) has created huge nonprofit pension plans to cover individuals in specified employee groups; in the case of Teachers, professors and employees of research, medical, cultural, and nonprofit organizations. Teachers' portfolio is massive; as of 2011 it was number 86 in the list of the Fortune 500 largest corporations.

d). Banks. The trust departments of banks often manage private pension plans, and serve as trustees for individuals and estates.

e). Investment Companies. An investment company manages money on behalf of individuals—or, less commonly, other entities—who buy shares in the investment company, which in turn invests the money in other companies or other types of assets. In open-ended investment companies, which primarily are mutual funds, an investor has the right to withdraw her investment at any time in exchange for the value of her prorated portion of the investment company's assets at the time of withdrawal. In closed-end investment companies, an investor does not have the right to withdraw her investment, but she can sell her shares in the investment company on the open market.

f). Insurance Companies. Insurance companies accumulate huge amounts of cash from the premiums paid by their insureds, which the companies hold until insured-against events occur. This cash is invested by the insurance companies in portfolios that typically include corporate stock.

g). Foundations. Foundations, such as universities and religious institutions, typically have endowments which they invest under the direction of internal or external portfolio managers.

h). Unions. Some large unions have pension plans for their members, and these plans often own significant amounts of stock. Unions may also hold stock to take advantage of federal proxy rules that allow shareholders to make proposals in the corporate proxy materials (see Chapter 5).

i). Hedge Funds. The most recent form of financial institution, the hedge fund, owes its existence to the various regulatory restraints that the Investment Company Act of 1940 imposes on mutual funds. For example, because of the Act, mutual funds cannot borrow money to thereby increase their returns via leverage. Hedge funds are similar to mutual funds in that they pool investments and are formed by professional investment managers; however, because their investors are wealthy individuals or financial institutions they fall within one of the exemptions to the Investment Company Act. An important difference flows from the redemption rights of investors. Most mutual fund investors enjoy a right to have their shares redeemed on short notice; this right has the effect of causing mutual funds to invest in readily marketable securities so that they can easily meet redemption requests. In contrast, hedge fund investors have very limited withdrawal rights and even this right is conditioned on the withdrawal not being harmful to other fund investors. Thus, hedge funds can invest in illiquid assets, including startups (i.e. venture capital) or total ownership of once public companies (private equity). The typical hedge fund advisor charges a base fee equal to 1–2 percent of the assets under management and also garners a significant incentive fee, usually 20 percent on gains, usually each is paid periodically. Because hedge funds market themselves to wealthy individuals and financial institutions, they suffer from fewer conflicts of interest than do other institutional investors. *See* Marcel Kahan & Edward B. Rock, Hedge Funds in Corporate Governance and Corporate Control, 155 U. Penn. L. Rev. 1021, 1062–1068 (2007). In 2013, 2,300 investment advisors managing over $7 trillion in fund assets filed reports with the SEC identifying 6,700 hedge funds. SEC, Annual Staff Report on the Use of Data Collected from Private Fund Systemic Risk Reports (July 25, 2013).

j).   Private Equity is an asset class consisting of equity securities in operating companies that are not publicly traded on a stock exchange. A private equity firm is a company that makes investments in private equity through a variety of investment strategies, including leveraged buyouts, venture capital, and growth capital. Typically, a private equity firm raises money to create separate private equity funds that are invested in accordance with specific investment strategies. Private equity firms generally receive a return on their investments through one of the following avenues:

- *Management Fees*—A share in the profits earned from each private equity fund that the firm manages.

- *Initial Public Offerings* (IPOs)—If shares of the operating company are offered to the public, the offering will provide an immediate realization to the private equity firm, and a public market into which the firm can later sell additional shares.

- *A Merger or Acquisition*—The operating company may be sold for either cash or shares in another company.

- *A Recapitalization*—Cash may be distributed by the operating company to the private equity firm, either from cash flow generated by the operating company or through issuing debt or other securities to fund a distribution.

Private equity firms often demand long holding periods by their shareholders, to allow for an IPO, a turnaround of an operating company, or a sale of the company. As a result, private-equity-firm shareholders usually are large investors who can commit large sums of money for long periods of time.

6.   Conflicting Interest Faced by Many Financial Institutions. The reason why the composition of institutional investors, and more especially the changes in that composition over time, matters a good deal, is that some institutional investors have economic ties to the managers of portfolio companies, or to managers as a class, that tends to inhibit them from voting against management, and even more strongly from taking the lead against management. Take, for example, banks. If the trust department of Bank B holds Corporation C stock as a trustee, and Corporation C is also a client of Bank B's commercial department, a trust officer of Bank B will think long and hard before voting against a proposal made by C's management or voting for a shareholder proposal that C's management opposes. Insurance companies, like banks, often have extensive commercial contracts with corporations whose stock they hold in their investment portfolios. Mutual funds may want to stay on management's good side to keep open their lines of access to information about a portfolio company's business corporation's business. An external manager of a corporate pension fund may fear that if he votes against management positions, the corporate sponsor will switch to another external manager.

In contrast, several classes of institutional investors, such as public pension funds and hedge funds, seldom have economic ties to the management of portfolio corporations that would render them economically self-interested in voting decisions. These two types of institutional investors have become leaders in shareholder activism.* Furthermore, once economically non-conflicted institutional investors take a position on an issue, it is not easy for other institutional investors to duck the issue. Kahan & Rock report as follows on the roles of hedge funds:

> [A]ctivist hedge funds have emerged as critical new players in both corporate governance and corporate control. Hedge funds have created headaches for CEOs and corporate boards by pushing for changes in management and changes in business strategy, including opposing acquisitions favored by management both as shareholders of the acquirer and as shareholders of the target, and by making unsolicited bids. The list of companies that have been subjected to campaigns by hedge funds and other activist investors includes McDonald's, Time Warner, H.J. Heinz Company, [and many others]. According to Wachtell Lipton partner Patricia Vlahakis, hedge funds conducted 137 activist campaigns just in the fourth quarter of 2007. In many of these instances, hedge funds have been able to win outright or at least to wrest substantial concessions from the management of the companies they target. . . .

> This new activism by hedge funds has become a prime irritant for CEOs. Martin Lipton, the renowned advisor to corporate boards, recently listed attacks by activist hedge funds as key issues for directors. Alan Murray from the *Wall Street Journal* calls hedge funds the new leader on the "list of bogeymen haunting the corporate boardroom," and his colleague Jesse Eisinger notes that these days hedge funds are the "shareholder activists with the most clout.

Kahan & Rock, Embattled CEOs, 88 Tex. L. Rev. 987, 998–1000 (2010).

7. *Developments Prompting the Conflicted to Join the Movement.* The growth of institutional-investor activism has also been facilitated by changes in the law. For example, at one time the SEC's Proxy Rules made it very difficult for institutional investors to communicate with each other to determine whether it was in their mutual interests to combine forces in voting on a management or shareholder proposal or in initiating a proposal of their own. However, in 1992 the SEC revised the Proxy Rules to remove most of the constraints on communication among institutional investors. The

---

* Some institutional investors who don't have economic conflicts of interest may have conflicts of a different kind. Jill Fisch reports that a number of public pension funds have been criticized for focusing on social investing at the possible expense of maximizing profits. Comparable concerns have been raised with respect to university endowments, which may face pressure from members of the university community to engage in socially responsible investing. Similarly, sovereign wealth funds have been described as pursuing objectives such as the promotion of environmentally friendly strategies or the support of national champions. See Jill E. Fisch, Securities Intermediaries and the Separation Of Ownership, 33 Seattle U. L. Rev. 877, at 882 (2010). However, these types of conflict differ in kind, frequency, and intensity from conflicts that result from economic ties to management.

SEC has also made it easier to make shareholder proposals; to propose short (that is, partial) slates of directorial candidates, which are often more palatable to institutional investors than slates that would replace all of the incumbents; and to gain access to the corporation's proxy statement in the nomination of candidates for the board. See Chapter 5. Another federal agency, the U.S. Department of Labor ("DOL"), was also an agent or change in this area. One of the DOL's responsibilities is to administer of the Employee Retirement Income Security Act (ERISA). Under ERISA, a person who exercises discretion over pension-plan assets must manage those assets "solely in the interest of the participants and beneficiaries and for the exclusive purpose of providing benefits to participants and their beneficiaries." This is known as the "exclusive benefit rule." In 1988, the DOL issued a well-publicized letter which stated that the fiduciary duties of pension-plan managers included voting decisions. The SEC also acted to require heightened transparency among mutual funds with respect to votes they cast when voting shares of companies in their portfolio.

Finally institutional-investor activism has been affected by the development of proxy advisory services that make recommendations, principally to institutional investors, on how to vote on issues that are coming before a corporation's shareholders. The most important of these services is Institutional Shareholders Services, or ISS (now owned by RiskMetrics), which has the largest client base. The second most important, with the second-largest client base, is Glass, Lewis. In effect, the clients of these services form research coalitions by pooling their funds through the subscription prices they pay for the services' bulletins.

There is much debate regarding how much influence the recommendations of these services have in terms of how many votes the recommendations will swing, but among those who believe they exercise a good deal of influence the debate is whether they are themselves sufficiently accountable for their recommendations. It is generally recognized that the recommendations, particularly those of ISS, are influential, although commentators disagree about how influential. Different commentators have concluded that ISS alone influences institutional shareholder votes by 6–10%, 14 to 21%, 19%, 30%, and a third or more. See, e.g., Stephen Choi, Jill Fisch & Marcel Kahan, The Power of Proxy Advisors: Myth or Reality?, 59 Emory L.J. 869 (2010). Choi et al. conclude that "ISS's power is partially due to the fact that ISS (to a greater extent than other advisors) bases its recommendations on factors that shareholders consider important. . . ." Thus, ISS is not so much a Pied Piper followed blindly by institutional investors as it is an information agent and guide, helping investors to identify voting decisions that are consistent with their existing preferences. *See generally* M. Denes, J.M. Karpoff & V. Williams, Thirty Years of Shareholder Activism: A Survey of Empirical Research, 44 J. Corp. Fin. 405 (2017).

8. *The Special Case of Mutual Funds.* The last decade has witnessed a sea change in how mutual funds vote the shares of their portfolio companies which has accelerated as investors have increasingly deserted actively management mutual funds for index funds. Today, mutual funds

support activist in nearly half of the campaigns that are launched with the consequential effects of increasing the campaigns' success and reducing the holdings that an activist believes needed to achieve credibility in launching its effort. *See e.g.* David Benoit & Kirsten Grind, Activists' Secret Ally: Big Mutual Funds, Wall St. J. at A-1 (Aug. 10, 2015).

An important component of this area of financial products are passive index funds, mainly index mutual funds and exchange traded funds (ETFs); each share a fundamental characteristic of seeking to replicate stock indices, e.g., S&P 500; they differ primarily in that trading in an index mutual fund occur once a day after the market has closed whereas ETFs are bought and sold continuously during trading hours. Passive index funds have grown rapidly in recent years, and now own more than 12 percent of the shares of S&P 500 firms.

> [T]he passive index fund industry remains highly concentrated. The market is dominated by Blackrock, Vanguard and State Street (the "Big Three") which, overall, manage over 90 percent of all assets under management in passive equity funds. Such a high concentration of the passive index fund industry has contributed to the re-concentration of listed company ownership in the U.S. For example, Blackrock has a 5% stake in at least two thousand (out of about 3,900) listed companies in the U.S.; similarly Vanguard has about 1,900 5% blockholdings. The 5% blockholdings of Blackrock and Vanguard are much more numerous than those of the world's largest actively managed fund group (Fidelity Investments), which holds about 700 5% holdings in the U.S. Considering the size of their equity interests, the Big Three taken together are the largest shareholder in most U.S. listed companies. In particular, they are largest owner of nearly 90% of public companies in the S&P 500 and of at least the 40% of all U.S. listed companies.

Giovanni Strampelli, Are Passive Index Funds Active Owners? Corporate Governance Consequences of Passive Investing 55 U. San Diego L. Rev. 803, 810–11 (2018).

The popular view is that passive index funds are not impactful in shaping corporate governance. *See e.g.,* Dorothy S. Lund, The Case Against Passive Shareholders Voting, 43 J. Corp. L. 493 (2018). This view does not match up with findings from a study of the relative size of mutual fund holdings in thousands of public companies and changes in corporate governance that are associated with those holdings. Ian Appel, Donald Keim, & Todd Gormley, Passive Investors, Not Passive Owners, 121 J. Fin. Econ. 111 (2016), finds that ownership by passive investors is associated with more independent directors on the board, more poison pill removals, the elimination of restrictions on the ability of shareholders to call special meetings, and fewer dual class share structures. The authors believe these findings reflect the influence of the institution's large voting block.

What are the incentives of passive index funds to incur non-trivial costs to monitor their portfolio companies and engage their managers so as to improve performance? Consider the 2018 letter Larry Fink, the CEO of

Blackrock sent to CEOs of the largest companies in its index funds, observing that, in managing Blackrock's index funds, "BlackRock cannot express its disapproval by selling the company's securities as long as that company remains in the relevant index. As a result, our responsibility to engage and vote is more important than ever. In this sense, index investors are the ultimate long-term investors—providing patient capital for companies to grow and prosper." Nonetheless, the business model of passive index funds calls for low administrative budgets so that even giants such as Black Rock have very small staffs dedicated to governance issues related to their thousands of portfolio companies. Analysis of the voting records of passive index funds document that with few exceptions they support the position recommended by management.

9.   *Activist Hedge Funds.* The mode of operation of activist hedge funds, who sometimes are characterized by their older name, "corporate raiders," acquire a distinctly minority stake in target companies and then demand changes in the firm under threat of engaging in a hostile proxy contest. Regular hedge funds operate mainly automated systems and profit from rapid arbitrage; activist hedge funds earn positive returns by engaging targeted corporations who are believed to be performing poorly so as to cause changes in their practices that will increase the value of the targeted firm.

Activist hedge funds' tactics generally fall into seven categories (parenthetical indicates percentage of occasions within the large study sample):

(1)   Communicating with the board/management on a regular basis with the goal of enhancing shareholder value (51.2%);

(2)   Seeking board representation without a proxy contest or confrontation with the existing board/management (11.9%);

(3)   Formal shareholder proposals, or public criticism of the company and demanding changes (35.1%);

(4)   Threats to wage a proxy contest in order to gain board representation, or to sue the company for breaching its fiduciary duty (7.3%);

(5)   Proxy contest to replace the board (13.1%);

(6)   Suing the company (4.7%); and

(7)   Taking control of the company with a takeover bid (4.6%.).

A. Brav, Wei Jiang & H. Kim, Hedge Fund Activism: A Review, 4 Foundations and Trends in Finance 185, 199 (2009).

Hedge funds have been particularly active in transactions involving potential changes in corporate control. This activism broadly falls into three categories. First, as shareholders of the potential acquirer, hedge funds have tried to prevent the consummation of the transaction. Second, as shareholders of the potential target, hedge funds have tried to block the deal or improve the terms for target shareholders. Third, hedge funds have themselves—sometimes on their own, sometimes as part of a group—tried to acquire companies.

. . . . [H]edge funds differ markedly from mutual funds and public pension funds. Mutual fund and public pension fund activism, if it occurs, tends to be incidental and ex post: when fund management notes that portfolio companies are underperforming, or that their governance regime is deficient, they will sometimes become active. In contrast, hedge fund activism is strategic and ex ante: hedge fund managers first determine whether a company would benefit from activism, then take a position and become active. Hedge fund activism represents a blurring of the line between risk arbitrage and battles over corporate strategy and control.

Kahan & Rock, Hedge Funds in Corporate Governance and Corporate Control, 155 U. Pa. L. Rev. 1021, 1034 & 1069 (2007).

Studies consistently report that a 6–7 percent stock price increase is associated with the filing of Schedule 13D by an activist fund. *See e.g.,* L. Bebchuk, A. Brav, & W. Jiang, The Long-term Effects of Hedge Fund Activism, 115 Colum. L. Rev. 1085, 1122 (2015). However, studies generally do not find this rise is thereafter followed by long-term gains in the target firm's operating performance or stock price returns. *See e.g.,* Marco Becht, *et. al.,* The Returns to Hedge Fund Activism: An International Study, 30 Rev. Fin. Stud. 2933 (2017); M. Cremers, E. Giambana, S.M. Sepe & Y. Wang, Hedge Fund Activism, Firm Valuation and Stock Return, 2018 Working Paper, available at http://ssrn.com/abstract=2693231. Disquieting is evidence that research and development expenditures are reduced in the wake of hedge fund activism and that cash payments to shareholders, usually through share repurchases increase. *See e.g.,* A. Brav, W. Jiang, S. Ma & X. Tian, How Does Hedge Fund Activism Reshape Corporate Innovation?, 130 J. Fin. Econ. 237 (2018).

———

Ronald J. Gilson & Jeffrey N. Gordon, The Agency Costs of Agency Capitalism: Activist Investors and the Revaluation of Governance Rights

113 Colum. L. Rev. 863, 867 (2013).

[T]he activist shareholders are governance intermediaries: They function to monitor company performance and then to present to companies and institutional shareholders concrete proposals for business strategy through mechanisms less drastic than takeovers. These activists gain their power not because of their equity stakes, which are not controlling, but because of their capacity to present convincing plans to institutional shareholders, who ultimately will decide whether the activists' proposed plan should be followed. . . . [I]nstitutional shareholders are not "rationally apathetic" as were the dispersed owners on whose behalf the institutions now hold shares, but instead are "rationally reticent": Intermediary institutional holders will respond to proposals but are unlikely themselves to create them. The role for activist shareholders is to potentiate voice; specialists in monitoring combine through the capital markets with specialist in low-cost diversification to provide a form of market-based stewardship.

The governance problem that arises from the "separation of ownership from control" is the undervaluation of the vote as a mechanism to impose change. The reconcentration of ownership through institutions adds only marginally to the value of the vote, much less than otherwise would be expected, because of the agency problems of capitalism. The role of the new entrant into the governance story, the activist shareholder, is to increase the value of the vote held by the institutions by teeing up the intervention choices at low cost to the institutional owners. If the intervention is successful, the activist's equity position will increase in value, as will that of the institutions. The expectation of the increase gives the activist the incentive to proceed, which in turn mitigates a problem of agency capitalism.

———

Gilson and Gordon reference Nickolay Gantchev, The Costs of Shareholder Activism: Evidence from a Sequential Decision Model, 107 J. Fin. Econ. 610 (2013), observing there were 1,164 activist campaigns between 2000 and 2007 with a 29% success rate.

———

Brav, Jiang, Partnoy & Thomas, Hedge Fund Activism, Corporate Governance, and Firm Performance
63 J. Fin. 1729 (2008).

We find that hedge funds increasingly engage in a new form of shareholder activism and monitoring that differs fundamentally from previous activist efforts by other institutional investors. . . . Unlike mutual funds and pension funds, hedge funds are able to influence corporate boards and managements due to key differences arising from their different organizational form and the incentives that they face. Hedge funds employ highly incentivized managers who manage large unregulated pools of capital. Because they are not subject to regulation that governs mutual funds and pension funds, they can hold highly concentrated positions in small numbers of companies, and use leverage and derivatives to extend their reach. Hedge fund managers also suffer few conflicts of interest because they are not beholden to the management of the firms whose shares they hold. In sum, hedge funds are better positioned to act as informed monitors than other institutional investors.

Hedge fund activists tend to target companies that are typically "value" firms, with low market value relative to book value, although they are profitable with sound operating cash flows and return on assets. Payout at these companies before intervention is lower than that of matched firms. Target companies also have more takeover defenses and pay their CEOs considerably more than comparable companies. Relatively few targeted companies are large-cap firms, which is not surprising given the comparatively high cost of amassing a meaningful stake in such a target. Targets exhibit significantly higher institutional ownership and trading liquidity. These characteristics make it easier for activists to acquire a significant stake quickly. . . .

We find that the market reacts favorably to activism, consistent with the view that it creates value. The filing of a Schedule 13D revealing an activist fund's investment in a target firm results in large positive average abnormal returns, in the range of 7% to 8%, during the (−20,+20) announcement window. . . . We find that the positive returns at announcement are not reversed over time, as there is no evidence of a negative abnormal drift during the 1-year period subsequent to the announcement. . . . Moreover, target prices decline upon the exit of a hedge fund only after it has been unsuccessful, which indicates that the information reflected in the positive announcement returns conveys the market's expectation for the success of activism. . . .

Activism that targets the sale of the company or changes in business strategy, such as refocusing and spinning-off noncore assets, is associated with the largest positive abnormal partial effects, at 8.54% and 5.95%, respectively (the latter figure is lower than the overall sample average because most events target multiple issues). This evidence suggests that hedge funds are able to create value when they see large allocative inefficiencies. In contrast, we find that the market response to capital structure-related activism—including debt restructuring, recapitalization, dividends, and share repurchases—is positive yet insignificant. We find a similar lack of statistically meaningful reaction for governance-related activism—including attempts to rescind takeover defenses, to oust CEOs, to enhance board independence, and to curtail CEO compensation. Hedge funds with a track record of successful activism generate higher returns, as do hedge funds that initiate activism with hostile tactics.

The positive market reaction is also consistent with ex post evidence of overall improved performance at target firms. On average, from the year before to the year after an announcement, total payout increases by 0.3 to 0.5 percentage points (as a percentage of the market value of equity, relative to an all-sample mean of 2.2 percentage points), and book value leverage increases by 1.3 to 1.4 percentage points (relative to an all-sample mean of 33.5 percentage points). Both changes are consistent with a reduction of agency problems associated with free cash flow and subject managers to increased market discipline. We also find improvement in return on assets and operating profit margins, but this takes longer to manifest. The post-event year sees little change compared to the year prior to intervention. However, EBITDA/Assets (EBITDA/Sales) at target firms increases by 0.9 to 1.5 (4.7 to 5.8) percentage points two years after intervention. . . .

Hedge fund activists are not short-term in focus, as some critics have claimed. The median holding period for completed deals is about one year, calculated as from the date a hedge fund files a Schedule 13D to the date when the fund no longer holds a significant stake in a target company. The calculation substantially understates the actual median holding period, because it necessarily excludes a significant number of events for which no exit information is available by March 2007 [when the authors ceased collecting data]. Analysis of portfolio turnover rates of the funds in our sample suggests holding periods of closer to 20 months.

Since shareholders are by no means the only party affected by hedge fund activism we also ask whether other stakeholders are impacted. In particular, we consider the possibility that the positive stock market reaction to activism might reflect wealth redistribution from creditors and executives. We find that hedge fund activism does not shift value from creditors to shareholders. Indeed, the 174 targets with no long-term debt have slightly *higher* announcement returns than the rest of the sample. On the other hand, we do see evidence that hedge fund activism shifts value away from senior managers. In particular, hedge fund activism is not kind to CEOs of target firms. During the year after the announcement of activism, average CEO pay declines by about $1 million dollars, and the CEO turnover rate increases by almost 10 percentage points, controlling for the normal turnover rates in the same industry, and for firms of similar size and stock valuation. . . .

Although some commentators have characterized hedge fund activism as fundamentally hostile to managers, we find that hedge fund activists are openly hostile in less than 30% of cases (hostility includes a threatened or actual proxy contest, takeover, lawsuit, or public campaign that is openly confrontational). More commonly, hedge fund activists cooperate with managers, at least at the initial stages of their intervention, and achieve all or most of their stated goals in about two-thirds of all cases. Managerial opposition to hedge fund activism may stem from its negative impact on CEO pay and turnover even if it ultimately creates value for shareholders.

Our findings have important implications for the policy debate about hedge fund activism. Although some prominent legal commentators, including leading corporate lawyers and European regulators, have called for restrictions on hedge fund activism because of its supposedly short-term orientation, our results suggest that activist hedge funds are not short-term holders. Activists also appear to generate substantial value for target firm shareholders. Indeed, our evidence of the market's positive response to hedge fund activism, and the subsequent success of activists, challenges the premises of proposals requiring increased hedge fund regulation.

For policy makers, our paper shows important distinctions between the role of hedge funds and other private institutional investors such as private equity firms. Despite their frequently aggressive behavior, activist hedge funds do not typically seek control in target companies. The median maximum ownership stake for the entire sample is about 9.1%. Even at the 95th percentile in the full sample, the stake is 31.5%— far short of the level for majority control. Activists rely on cooperation from management or, in its absence, support from fellow shareholders to implement their value-improving agendas. This explains why hedge fund activists tend to target companies with higher institutional holdings and analyst coverage, both of which suggest a more sophisticated shareholder base. It is also common for multiple hedge funds to coordinate by cofiling Schedule 13Ds (about 22% of the sample) or acting in tandem without being a formal block. Although some regulators have criticized such informal block behavior as anticompetitive, coordination among hedge funds can benefit shareholders overall by facilitating activism at relatively low individual ownership stakes.

The new evidence presented in this paper suggests that activist hedge funds occupy an important middle ground between internal monitoring by large shareholders and external monitoring by corporate raiders. Activist hedge funds are more flexible, incentivized, and independent than internal monitors, and they can generate multiple gains from targeting several companies on similar issues. Conversely, activist hedge funds have advantages over external corporate raiders, because they take smaller stakes, often benefit from cooperation with management, and have support from other shareholders. This hybrid internal-external role puts activist hedge funds in a potentially unique position to reduce the agency costs associated with the separation of ownership and control. . . .

———

Further investigation of the effects of hedge funds activism in 2008–14 finds that activist funds producing the most positive results achieve success not solely by the targets they select but because of their reputation that has been earned through prior successful engagements. This cohort of top performing hedge funds engage in fewer campaigns, but target much larger and more profitable firms than the poorer performing hedge funds.

> The Top Investor Hedge Funds . . . had greater financial clout; they had existed for longer than other activists and had significantly larger assets under management. They also had greater expertise; they had a greater ability to force board changes at the firms they target. Top Investor Hedge Funds

specifically stated an intent to replace directors, were more involved in proxy fights and lawsuits, and won three times as many proxy fights and lawsuits as other activists. They also target more entrenched firms indicating higher agency costs, but, nevertheless, were more successful in gaining board seats, and implementing changes after intervening, improving operating performance.

C.N.V. Krishnan, Frank Partnoy & Randall S. Thomas, The Second Wave of Hedge Fund Activism: The Importance of Reputation, Clout, and Expertise, J. Corp. Fin. 296, 314 (2016).

By and large, activist shareholders pursue goals they believe are in the best interests of the corporation and are not subject to the equitable restraint of a regulating fiduciary duty. The latter reflects the general view that absent a control position there is no over-arching fiduciary obligation that shareholders in a public company owe the corporation or one another. Should this axiom be reexamined where the shareholder's activism is guided by personal rather than the corporation's interests?

> The high profile proxy battle to remove Steven Burd as Chairman and CEO of Safeway, Inc., provides another thought-provoking example of the many ways activist investors can use their shareholder status to push for favorable treatment in their other dealings with the firm. Burd was taking a hard-line stance in labor negotiations with the United Food & Commercial Workers Union, which represents grocery workers. He argued that Safeway needed to lower its labor costs to compete with non-unionized chains like WalMart. The California Public Employees' Retirement System (CalPERS), a large pension fund representing California employees, organized a proxy campaign to remove Burd from the corner office. It was soon revealed that the CalPERS' President, Sean Harrigan, who was also a career labor organizer and an official of the United Food & Commercial Workers' Union. Burd survived the attempt to oust him after it was widely reported that the grocery workers' union was using CalPERS as a stand-in in its battle with Safeway over pay and benefits. . . .

Iman Anabtawi & Lynn Stout, Fiduciary Duties for Activist Shareholders, 60 Stan. L. Rev. 1255, 1285–1286 (2008) (arguing in favor of a latent fiduciary duty to the firm and its shareholders that arises when the shareholder has a material, personal economic interest).

————

NOTE ON THE PROBLEM OF FREE-RIDING

In theory, institutional-investor activism might be dampened by a free-rider problem, because any expenses for activism that an investor incurs may benefit other shareholders more than it benefits the investor. For example, suppose that Institution S holds 1% of Corporation C's stock. Corporation C has a governance rule, such as an anti-takeover rule, that diminishes the value of C's stock. If the only benefit to S from incurring expenses to repeal the rule would be the increased value of S's stock in C, then 1% of S's expenses would benefit S, and the remaining 99% would benefit C's other shareholders, who will free-ride on S's expenses.

However, for a number of reasons the free-rider problem is easy to exaggerate:

(1)   If the expected gain from activism will exceed the expected costs, a rational shareholder will engage in activism even when other shareholders will free-ride,

(2)   The cost of activism may be little more than the cost of performing the fiduciary duty to exercise care in voting.

(3)   Often the same issue will recur in a number of portfolio corporations—for example, how to vote on proposals to deal with certain kinds of anti-takeover provisions. In that case, the investor need only make a one-time expenditure to determine its position on the issue, and can then amortize the expenditure over a number of voting decisions.

(4)   A vote on a recurring issue may send a message to all portfolio corporations, and therefore may have an economic benefit to the investor beyond its impact on the value of the investor's stock in a given portfolio corporation.

———

3. VOTE BUYING

Portnoy v. Cryo-Cell International, Inc.

Court of Chancery of Delaware, 2008.
940 A.2d 43.

■ STRINE, VICE CHANCELLOR.

This case involves a challenge to the results of a contested corporate election. Cryo-Cell International, Inc. ("Cryo-Cell" or the "Company") is a small public company that has struggled to succeed. By early 2007, several of its large stockholders were considering mounting a proxy contest to replace the board.

One of those stockholders, Andrew Filipowski, used management's fear of replacement to strike a deal for himself to be included in the management slate for the 2007 annual meeting. Another stockholder, plaintiff David Portnoy, filed a dissident slate (the "Portnoy Slate").

Going into the week of the annual meeting, Cryo-Cell's chief executive officer, defendant Mercedes Walton, was desperate because, in her words, "the current board and management [were] losing by huge margins." Aside from actually asking the FBI to intervene in the proxy contest on the side of management, Walton ginned up a plan with

Filipowski to win the proxy contest. That plan involved Walton acting as a "matchmaker" by finding stockholders willing to sell their shares to Filipowski. In exchange for this alliance, Walton promised Filipowski that if their "Management Slate" prevailed, Cryo-Cell's board would, using their power as corporate directors, expand the board to add another seat that Filipowski's designee would fill. That designee was a subordinate who had within the recent past resolved an SEC insider trading investigation by agreeing to disgorge trading profits and to be jointly liable for trading profits made by his tippees. This plan was not disclosed to the Cryo-Cell stockholders, who did not realize that if they voted for management, they would in fact be electing a seven, not six member board, with two, not one, Filipowski representatives.

In an effort to secure another key bloc of votes, Walton used a combination of threats (the ending of cooperation on key projects) and inducements (the long-sought but never before granted removal of a restrictive legend) to secure the vote of Saneron CCEL Therapeutics Inc. That leverage was enhanced by the fact that Cryo-Cell owned 38% of Saneron's shares and that Saneron depended on Cryo-Cell's laboratory space to conduct many of its own operations. Notwithstanding that, Saneron had gone into the week before the meeting undecided about how to vote. Walton "locked up" Saneron only after employing these persuasive strategies involving the threatened withholding and actual granting of concessions on the part of Cryo-Cell as a corporation.

Even after employing these methods, Walton and her board went into the day of the annual meeting fearing defeat. They had rented the meeting room from the 11 a.m. start time only until 1 p.m. But Walton did not want to close the polls and count the vote when the scheduled presentations at the meeting were over. So she had members of her management team make long, unscheduled presentations to give her side more time to gather votes and ensure that they had locked in two key blocs. She overruled motions to close the polls.

Even after the filibusters, Walton still harbored doubt that the Management Slate would prevail if the vote was counted and the meeting was concluded. So, at around 2 p.m., Walton declared a very late lunch break, supposedly in response to a request made much earlier.

In fact, Walton desired the break so that she would have more time to seek votes and so that she could confirm that the major blockholders had switched their votes to favor the Management Slate. Only after confirming the switches did Walton resume the meeting at approximately 4:45 p.m., declare the polls closed, and have the vote counted.

The post-meeting vote count resulted in the Management Slate squeaking out a victory by an extremely small margin. . . .

In this opinion, I decline Portnoy's request to declare his side the victor in the election process. . . . Rather than seating a board for the

Cryo-Cell stockholders, I believe the more appropriate remedy to be a requirement that Cryo-Cell have another election at a special meeting to be held promptly. Because the stockholders should not be required to bear extra expense because of management's misconduct, the Management Slate will be required to fund their own re-election campaign and to pay any costs incurred by the Company to hold the special meeting, including the cost of a special master to preside over the meeting. . . .

II.   The Merits Of Portnoy's Claims . . .

A.   The Addition Of Filipowski To The Management Slate . . .

Portnoy contends that the deal struck between Walton and the other incumbents, on the one hand, and Filipowski, on the other, to add Filipowski to the Management Slate in exchange for his support in the proxy fight constituted an illegal vote-buying arrangement.

On this claim, which has some color, I find in favor of the defendants. My conclusion rests on several grounds. Initially, I note that an arrangement of this kind fits comfortably, as a linguistic matter, within the traditional definition of so-called "vote buying" used in our jurisprudence. As defined by Vice Chancellor Hartnett in his important decision in *Schreiber v. Carney,* "[v]ote-buying . . . is simply a voting agreement supported by consideration personal to the stockholder, whereby the stockholder divorces his discretionary voting power and votes as directed by the offeror." *447 A.2d 17, 23 (Del. Ch. 1982).* In this case, I have no doubt that the voting agreement between the Filipowski Group and the incumbents was only assented to by Filipowski after he was offered a candidacy on the Management Slate. What I am more doubtful about is whether an arrangement of this kind—where the incumbents offer a potential insurgent a seat on the management slate in exchange for the potential insurgent's voting support—should trigger the sort of heightened scrutiny rightly given to more questionable arrangements. . . .

To deal with these complexities, *Schreiber* declined to find that vote buying was, in the first instance, per se improper. Rather, *Schreiber* articulated a two-pronged analysis. In the first instance, if the plaintiff can show that the "object or purpose [of the vote buying was] to defraud or in some way disenfranchise the other stockholders," the arrangement would be "illegal per se." Putting this in terms that I think are truer to the way our corporate law works, what I take from this is that if the plaintiff proved that the arrangement under challenge was improperly motivated, then the arrangement would be set aside in equity, irrespective of its technical compliance with the DGCL. . . .

Subjecting an agreement to add a potential insurgent to a management slate to the *Schreiber* intrinsic fairness test would, in my view, be an inadvisable and counterproductive precedent. . . . [Vice-Chancellor Strine reasoned that if the intrinsic fairness were to be so available, this would create litigatable issues regarding a large number of useful compromises of a type nearly impossible to resolve without trial.]

In being chary about extending *Schreiber's* reach to this context, I do not underestimate the value of being included in the management slate. An offer to be on the management slate will often promise a near certainty of eventual election. At the very least, it will relieve the insurgent of having to pay for his own candidacy and to run a contested election against corporate insiders who do not have to pay their own solicitation costs. Instead, the insurgent would be on the inside track, so to speak.

But being on the inside track is different than being on the board, and that difference suggests that employing an entire fairness standard to such arrangements is overkill. If the only arrangement at issue is a promise to add a potential insurgent to the management slate in exchange for the insurgent's voting support, then the arrangement is subject to stockholder policing in an obvious, but nonetheless, potent form. That policing occurs at the ballot box itself.

Here, to be specific, the Cryo-Cell stockholders went to the polls knowing that Filipowski had been added to the Management Slate. Those stockholders also knew that Filipowski had contracted to vote the Filipowski Group's shares for the Management Slate. Although it was not publicly disclosed that Filipowski's agreement to vote for the Management Slate had been conditioned on his addition to that Slate, and that the incumbents had added Filipowski to the Management Slate in exchange for his support, that inference was, I think, unmistakable to any rational stockholder. . . . Given that the electorate's own opportunity to decide for itself whether Filipowski should serve, I think it unwise, as a matter of our common law, to apply the intrinsic fairness test to this situation. . . . The notion that judges should chew over the complicated calculus made by incumbent boards considering whether to add to the management slate candidates proposed by a large blockholder whose velvety suggestions were cloaking an unmistakably clenched fist seems to run against many of the sound reasons for the business judgment rule. . . . When stockholders can decide for themselves whether to seat a candidate who obtained a place on a management slate by way of such bargaining, it seems unwise to formulate a standard that involves the potential for excessive and imprecise judicial involvement.

In my view, a mere offer of a position on a management slate should not be considered a vote-buying arrangement subject to a test of entire fairness, and for that reason, I see no reason to condemn the addition of Filipowski to the Management Slate. . . .

For all these reasons, I conclude that Portnoy's attack on this aspect of the incumbents' dealings with Filipowski fails.

B.   The Promise Of A Second Board Seat For The Filipowski Group

I reach a different conclusion, however, about the later arrangement that was reached with Filipowski shortly before the annual meeting. As I found previously, Walton (acting at the very least with the apparent authority of her board colleagues, who were extremely deferential to her leadership) promised Filipowski that if the Management Slate won, the incumbent board majority would use its powers under the Company's bylaws to expand the Cryo-Cell board from six members to seven and to fill the new seat with Filipowski's designee, Roszak. That promise was made in response to Roszak's request—as Filipowski's negotiator—and made in exchange for Filipowski's promise to go out and buy more shares (and therefore votes). . . .

I believe that this arrangement differed in materially important respects from the prior agreement to place Filipowski on the Management Slate. For starters, Walton did not merely promise someone a shot at getting elected by the stockholders by running in the advantaged posture of being a member of a management slate. She promised that she and her incumbent colleagues would use their powers as directors of Cryo-Cell to increase the size of the board and seat Roszak. This was therefore a promise that would not be, for the duration of the term, subject to prior approval by the electorate. . . .

I am chary about addressing the promise of a second board seat that was made to Filipowski on broader grounds than is necessary. For me, there is a very clear and important, but narrow, reason why this later arrangement with Filipowski was improper and inequitably tainted the election process: it was a very material event that was not disclosed to the Cryo-Cell stockholders.

"[D]irectors of Delaware corporations are under a fiduciary duty to disclose fully and fairly all material information within the board's control when it seeks shareholder action." *Arnold v. Soc'y for Savings Bancorp., Inc., 650 A.2d 1270, 1277 (Del. 1994)* (quoting *Stroud v. Grace, 606 A.2d 75, 84 (Del. 1992)*). That disclosure "obligation attaches to proxy statements and any other disclosures in contemplation of stockholder action."

On the day they voted, the Cryo-Cell stockholders knew that a vote for the Management Slate would seat six directors, including Filipowski. They had to know that Filipowski's support for the Management Slate was in large measure motivated by his own inclusion.

What the Cryo-Cell stockholders did not know was that Walton had promised that the board would use its fiduciary powers to expand the board to seven members and seat another person designated by Filipowski. Problematically, the Cryo-Cell stockholders did not know that Filipowski clearly intended to designate Roszak, a person whose recent past would have weighed heavily on the mind of a rational stockholder considering whether to seat him as a fiduciary. . . .

For many of the reasons that supported my earlier decision regarding Filipowski's inclusion on the Management Slate, an agreement of this kind that was made and disclosed in advance of an election is subject to the important fairness check of the stockholder vote itself. By contrast, the disinterested Cryo-Cell electorate voted in ignorance of the actual board that would govern them in the event the Management Slate won.

C.   Management's Influence Over Saneron's Vote . . .

I begin with my conclusion that Walton breached her fiduciary duties by intentionally using corporate assets to coerce Saneron in the exercise of its voting rights. As I have found, Walton both threatened Saneron (with the loss or at least cooling of a strategic partnership vital to it) and granted it an inducement (the lifting of a restrictive legend on its shares) in order to extract a commitment from Saneron to vote for the Management Slate.

There is no doubt that threatening Saneron was improper conduct by Walton, whereby she used her power as a fiduciary to control assets of Cryo-Cell for the purpose of entrenching herself in office. . . .

Given that Walton clearly used company resources to coerce Saneron in the voting process and thereby breached her duty of loyalty, it was the defendants' burden to show that Saneron's vote was not influenced by her misbehavior. They have not convinced me of that at all. Rather, the circumstances surrounding Saneron's decision to vote for the Management Slate are more consistent with a bargained-for exchange, in which Saneron got a removal of the restrictive legend and the hope of future cooperation from Cryo-Cell in exchange for casting an early and important vote for the Management Slate. Walton's own words regarding the effect of her tactics said it best: those tactics "locked up" Saneron's vote. . . .

Although a change in the voting of the Saneron bloc alone would not have turned the election, Walton's improper conduct and its non-disclosure contributes to my overall sense that the election was tainted by misbehavior by insiders who could not win an election simply using the traditionally powerful advantages afforded incumbents. Our law has no tolerance for unfair election tactics of this kind.

D.   The Annual Meeting

I now come to Portnoy's last complaint. That is about how Walton conducted the meeting. . . .

What, however, is more uncertain is that Walton acted inequitably in her conduct of the meeting. The reality is that she did not take a "lupper" break of nearly three hours at 2 p.m. so that the attendees at the meeting could eat. Because Walton undertook action that affected the conduct of an election of directors in a potentially important way, the defendants bear the burden to show that Walton's actions were "motivated by a good faith concern for the stockholders' best interests, and not by a desire to entrench [herself.]" They have failed to prove that Walton's tactics were undertaken in selfless good faith.

Walton's behavior during the day was analogous to a corrupted soccer referee, intent on adding extra time so that the game would end only when her favored team had a sure lead. . . . When Walton was asked to count the vote, she replied with the jejune response that the request was out of order. At trial, she could not explain what that response was supposed to mean. It sounds to the court like something out of Robert's Rules of Order that Walton had heard invoked by someone trying to fake their way through a local town council meeting or had seen when watching a congressional debate on C-Span.

This is not to say that Walton had no discretion to keep the polls open. But what she did was to stall without being honest about why she was acting.

If she were being candid, she would have admitted that she was waiting for confirmation that two large blockholders' votes had been switched before having the vote counted. Indeed, if she were being perfectly candid, she would have admitted that she was keeping the polls open so that the Management Slate could continue its efforts to secure more votes by purchase because she was concerned that it would lose even with their votes. Even with less candor, she could have straightforwardly said that she was keeping the polls open to a time certain so that the parties could continue their contest for votes.

Instead, she first tried to pull off a filibuster, subjecting the stockholders to unscheduled bloviation from her management subordinates. Particularly disturbing is Walton's choice to have presentations made on laboratory research and sales when she might have instead released the company's 10-Q, which was already prepared, and had the CFO, who was at the meeting, explain Cryo-Cell's disappointing financial results. But providing the stockholders with information such as actual up-to-date financial results that might have been material to how they chose to vote their shares was not Walton's concern. Stalling was. During the filibuster, Walton rejected another request to hold the vote. Again, she ruled that request "out of order" for no articulated reason.

It was then that she used the pretense that everyone needed lunch to delay the vote. That move gave her side time, which they used, to ensure that they had the votes to prevail. And lest anyone be moved by the attendees' need for sustenance, by any measure they would have dined earlier—at the traditional time of lunch, in fact—had Walton closed the polls when the events scheduled to precede the vote had concluded. . . .

[I]t is impossible to ignore the unfairness of Walton's behavior . . . . If an electoral contestant assumes the role of presiding over the meeting, she has an obligation to do so fairly. Walton did not do so. She stalled so that her side could win the game, knowing that if the game ended when it was scheduled to end, her side would lose. Then she was dishonest about the reasons for delay.

For all these reasons, I find that Portnoy has proven that serious breaches of fiduciary duty tainted the election. . . .

The parties shall collaborate on the appropriate date and location for a prompt special meeting and present a conforming order, in advance of seeking a conference this week with the court at which the order will be finalized and a special master appointed.

————

4. FUNDING PROXY CONTESTS

What are the public policy implications of the following: Who should be able to have access to the corporation's resources in contested elections? Incumbents? Insurgents? What kind of proxy contest expenses should be reimbursed? Should reimbursement be conditioned on whether the party seeking reimbursement was successful in securing a majority of the seats on the board? Elected to the board? Should reimbursement of expenses incurred to oppose successfully an initiative supported by management? *See generally* Lucian Ayre Bebchuk & Marcel Kahan, A Framework for Analyzing Legal Policy Towards Proxy Contests, 78 Cal. L. Rev. 1073 (1990); Melvin A. Eisenberg Access to the Corporate Proxy Machinery, 83 Harv. L. Rev. 1489 (1970).

————

Rosenfeld v. Fairchild Engine and Airplane Corp.

Court of Appeals of New York, 1955.
309 N.Y. 168, 128 N.E.2d 291.

■ FROSSEL, JUDGE. In a stockholder's derivative action brought by plaintiff, an attorney, who owns 25 out of the company's over 2,300,000 shares, he seeks to compel the return of $261,522, paid out of the corporate treasury to reimburse both sides in a proxy contest for their expenses. The Appellate Division, 284 App.Div. 201, 132 N.Y.S.2d 273, has unanimously affirmed a judgment of an Official Referee, Sup., 116 N.Y.S.2d 840, dismissing plaintiff's complaint on the merits, and we agree. . . .

Of the amount in controversy $106,000 was spent out of corporate funds by the old board of directors while still in office in defense of their position in said contest; $28,000 [was] paid to the old board by the new board after the change of management following the proxy contest, to compensate the former directors for such of the remaining expenses of their unsuccessful defense as the new board found was fair and reasonable; payment of $127,000, representing reimbursement of expenses to members of the prevailing group, was expressly ratified by a 16 to 1 majority vote of the stockholders.

The essential facts are not in dispute. . . . The Appellate Division found that the difference between plaintiff's group and the old board "went deep into the policies of the company", and that among these Ward's contract was one of the "main points of contention". The Official Referee found that the controversy "was based on an understandable difference in policy between the two groups, at the very bottom of which was the Ward employment contract".

By way of contrast with the findings here, in Lawyers' Advertising Co. v. Consolidated Ry., Lighting & Refrigerating Co., 187 N.Y. 395, at page 399, 80 N.E. 199, at page 200, which was an action to recover for the cost of publishing newspaper notices not authorized by the board of directors, it was expressly found that the proxy contest there involved was "by one faction in its contest with another for the control of the corporation . . . a contest for the perpetuation of their offices and control." We there said by way of *dicta* that under *such* circumstances the publication of certain notices on behalf of the management faction was not a corporate expenditure which the directors had the power to authorize.

Other jurisdictions and our own lower courts have held that management may look to the corporate treasury for the reasonable expenses of soliciting proxies to defend its position in a bona fide policy contest. . . .

It should be noted that plaintiff does not argue that the aforementioned sums were fraudulently extracted from the corporation; indeed, his counsel conceded that "the charges were fair and reasonable", but denied "they were legal charges which may be reimbursed for". This is therefore not a case where a stockholder challenges specific items, which, on examination, the trial court may find unwarranted, excessive or otherwise improper. . . .

If directors of a corporation may not in good faith incur reasonable and proper expenses in soliciting proxies in these days of giant corporations with vast numbers of stockholders, the corporate business might be seriously interfered with because of stockholder indifference and the difficulty of procuring a quorum, where there is no contest. In the event of a proxy contest, if the directors may not freely answer the challenges of outside groups and in good faith defend their actions with respect to corporate policy for the information of the stockholders, they and the corporation may be at the mercy of persons seeking to wrest control for their own purposes, so long as such persons have ample funds to conduct a proxy contest. The test is clear. When the directors act in good faith in a contest over policy, they have the right to incur reasonable and proper expenses for solicitation of proxies and in defense of their corporate policies, and are not obliged to sit idly by. The courts are entirely competent to pass upon their *bona fides* in any given case, as well as the nature of their expenditures when duly challenged.

It is also our view that the members of the so-called new group could be reimbursed by the corporation for their expenditures in this contest by affirmative vote of the stockholders. With regard to these ultimately successful contestants, as the Appellate Division below has noted, there was, of course, "no duty . . . to set forth the facts, with corresponding obligation of the corporation to pay for such expense". However, where a majority of the stockholders chose—in this case by a vote of 16 to 1—to reimburse the successful contestants for achieving the very end sought and voted for by them as owners of the corporation, we see no reason to deny the effect of their ratification nor to hold the corporate body powerless to determine how its own moneys shall be spent.

The rule then which we adopt is simply this: In a contest over policy, as compared to a purely personal power contest, corporate directors have the right to make reasonable and proper expenditures, subject to the scrutiny of the courts when duly challenged, from the corporate treasury for the purpose of persuading the stockholders of the correctness of their position and soliciting their support for policies which the directors believe, in all good faith, are in the best interests of the corporation. The stockholders, moreover, have the right to reimburse successful contestants for the reasonable and bona fide expenses incurred by them in any such policy contest, subject to like court scrutiny. That is not to say, however, that corporate directors can, under any circumstances, disport themselves in a proxy contest with the corporation's moneys to an unlimited extent. Where it is established that such moneys have been spent for personal power, individual gain or private advantage, and not in the belief that such expenditures are in the best interests of the stockholders and the corporation, or where the fairness and reasonableness of the amounts allegedly expended are duly and successfully challenged, the courts will not hesitate to disallow them.

The judgment of the Appellate Division should be affirmed, without costs.

■ DESMOND, JUDGE (concurring). We granted leave to appeal in an effort to pass, and in the expectation of passing, on this question, highly important in modern-day corporation law: is it lawful for a corporation, on consent of a majority of its stockholders, to pay, out of its funds, the expenses of a "proxy fight", incurred by competing candidates for election as directors? Now that the appeal has been argued, I doubt that the question is presented by this record. . . .

. . . The reason why that important question is, perhaps, not directly before us in this lawsuit is because, as the Appellate Division properly held, [284 App.Div. 201, 132 N.Y.S.2d 273] plaintiff failed "to urge liability as to specific expenditures". The cost of giving routinely necessary notice is, of course, chargeable to the corporation. It is just as clear, we think, that payment by a corporation of the expense of "proceedings by one faction in its contest with another for the control of the corporation" is *ultra vires,* and unlawful. Lawyers' Advertising Co. v. Consolidated Ry., Lighting & Refrigerating Co., 187 N.Y. 395, 399, 80 N.E. 199, 200. Approval by directors or by a majority stock vote could not validate such gratuitous expenditures. Continental Securities Co. v. Belmont, 206 N.Y. 7, 99 N.E. 138, 51 L.R.A., N.S., 112. Some of the payments attacked in this suit were, on their face, for lawful purposes and apparently reasonable in amount but, as to others, the record simply does not contain evidentiary bases for a determination as to either lawfulness or reasonableness. Surely, the burden was on plaintiff to go forward to some extent with such particularization and proof. It failed to do so, and so failed to make out a prima facie case.

We are, therefore, reaching the same result as did the Appellate Division but on one only of the grounds listed by that court, that is, failure of proof. We think it not inappropriate, however, to state our general views on the question of law principally argued by the parties, that is, as to the validity of corporate payments for proxy solicitations and similar activities in addition to giving notice of the meeting, and of the questions to be voted on. For an answer to that problem we could not do better than quote from this court's opinion in the Lawyers' Advertising Co. case, 187 N.Y. 395, 399, 80 N.E. 199, 200, supra: "The remaining notices were not legally authorized and were not legitimately incidental to the meeting or necessary for the protection of the stockholders. They rather were proceedings by one faction in its contest with another for the control of the corporation, and the expense thereof, as such, is not properly chargeable to the latter.... [I]t would be altogether too dangerous a rule to permit directors in control of a corporation and engaged in a contest for the perpetuation of their offices and control, to impose upon the corporation the unusual expense of publishing advertisements or, by analogy, of dispatching special messengers for the purpose of procuring proxies in their behalf." ...

The judgment should be affirmed, without costs.

■ VAN VOORHIS, JUDGE (dissenting). ...

No resolution was passed by the stockholders approving payment to the management group. It has been recognized that not all of the $133,966 in obligations paid or incurred by the management group was designed merely for information of stockholders. This outlay included payment for all of the activities of a strenuous campaign to persuade and cajole in a hard-fought contest for control of this corporation. It included, for example, expenses for entertainment, chartered airplanes and limousines, public relations counsel and proxy solicitors. However legitimate such measures may be on behalf of stockholders themselves in such a controversy, most of them do not pertain to a corporate function but are part of the familiar apparatus of aggressive factions in corporate contests. ...

The Appellate Division acknowledged in the instant case that "It is obvious that the management group here incurred a substantial amount of needless expense which was charged to the corporation," but this conclusion should have led to a direction that those defendants who were incumbent directors should be required to come forward with an explanation of their expenditures under the familiar rule that where it has been established that directors have expended corporate money for their own purposes, the burden of going forward with evidence of the propriety and reasonableness of specific items rests upon the directors. . . . The complaint should not have been dismissed as against incumbent directors due to failure of plaintiff to segregate the specific expenditures which are *ultra vires,* but, once plaintiff had proved facts from which an inference of impropriety might be drawn, the duty of making an explanation was laid upon the directors to explain and justify their conduct. . . .

There is no doubt that the management was entitled and under a duty to take reasonable steps to acquaint the stockholders with essential facts concerning the management of the corporation, and it may well be that the existence of a contest warranted them in circularizing the stockholders with more than ordinarily detailed information. . . .

What expenses of the incumbent group should be allowed and what should be disallowed should be remitted to the trial court to ascertain, after taking evidence, in accordance with the rule that the incumbent directors were required to assume the burden of going forward in the first instance with evidence explaining and justifying their expenditures. Only such as were reasonably related to informing the stockholders fully and fairly concerning the corporate affairs should be allowed. The concession by plaintiff that such expenditures as were made were reasonable in amount does not decide this question. By way of illustration, the costs of entertainment for stockholders may have been, and it is stipulated that they were, at the going rates for providing similar entertainment. That does not signify that entertaining stockholders is reasonably related to the purposes of the corporation. The Appellate Division, as above stated, found that the management group incurred a substantial amount of needless expense. That fact being established, it became the duty of the incumbent directors to unravel and explain these payments.

Regarding the $127,556 paid by the new management to the insurgent group for their campaign expenditures, the question immediately arises whether that was for a corporate purpose. . . .

. . . The case most frequently cited and principally relied upon from among [the] Delaware decisions is Hall v. Trans-Lux Daylight Picture Screen Corp. [20 Del.Ch. 78]. There the English case was followed of Peel v. London & North Western Ry. Co. . . . which distinguished between expenses merely for the purpose of maintaining control, and contests over policy questions of the corporation. In the Hall case the issues concerned a proposed merger, and a proposed sale of stock of a subsidiary corporation. These were held to be policy questions, and payment of the management campaign expenses was upheld.

In our view, the impracticability [of distinguishing between expenses incurred merely for the purpose of maintaining control, and expenses in contests over policy questions] is illustrated by the statement in the Hall case, supra, 20 Del.Ch. at page 85, 171 A. at page 229, that "It is impossible in many cases of intracorporate contests over directors, to sever questions of policy from those of persons". This circumstance is stressed in Judge Rifkind's opinion in [Steinberg v. Adams, 90 F.Supp. 604] at page 608: "The simple fact, of course, is that generally policy and personnel do not exist in separate compartments. A change in personnel is sometimes indispensable to a change of policy. A new board may be the symbol of the shift in policy as well as the means of obtaining it."

. . . [I]nasmuch as it is generally impossible to distinguish whether "policy" or "personnel" is the dominant factor, any averments must be accepted at their face value that questions of policy are dominant. Nowhere do these opinions mention that the converse is equally true and more pervasive, that neither the "ins" nor the "outs" ever say that they have no program to offer to the shareholders, but just want to acquire or to retain control, as the case may be. In common experience, this distinction is unreal. . . .

The main question of "policy" in the instant corporate election, as is stated in the opinions below and frankly admitted, concerns the long-term contract with pension rights of a former officer and director, Mr. J. Carlton Ward, Jr. The insurgents' chief claim of benefit to the corporation from their victory consists in the termination of that agreement, resulting in an alleged actuarial saving of $350,000 to $825,000 to the corporation, and the reduction of other salaries and rent by more than $300,000 per year. The insurgents had contended in the proxy contest that these payments should be substantially reduced so that members of the incumbent group would not continue to profit personally at the expense of the corporation. If these charges were true, which appear to have been believed by a majority of the shareholders, then the disbursements by the management group in the proxy contest fall under the condemnation of the English and the Delaware rule.

These circumstances are mentioned primarily to illustrate how impossible it is to distinguish between "policy" and "personnel", . . . but they also indicate that personal factors are deeply rooted in this contest. That is certainly true insofar as the former management group is concerned. . . .

Some expenditures may concededly be made by a corporation represented by its management so as to inform the stockholders, but there is a clear distinction between such expenditures by management and by mere groups of stockholders. The latter are under no legal obligation to assume duties of managing the corporation. They may endeavor to supersede the management for any reason, regardless of whether it be advantageous or detrimental to the corporation but, if they succeed, that is not a determination that the company was previously mismanaged or that it may not be mismanaged in the future. A change in control is in no sense analogous to an adjudication that the former directors have been guilty of misconduct. The analogy of allowing expenses of suit to minority stockholders who have been successful in a derivative action based on misconduct of officers or directors, is entirely without foundation.

Insofar as a management group is concerned, it may charge the corporation with any expenses within reasonable limits incurred in giving widespread notice to stockholders of questions affecting the welfare of the corporation. . . . Expenditures in excess of these limits are *ultra vires*. The corporation lacks power to defray them. The corporation lacks power to defray the expenses of the insurgents in their entirety. The insurgents were not charged with responsibility for operating the company. No appellate court case is cited from any jurisdiction holding otherwise. No contention is made that such disbursements could be made, in any event, without stockholder ratification; they could not be ratified except by unanimous vote if they were *ultra vires*. The insurgents, in this instance, repeatedly announced to the stockholders in their campaign literature that their proxy contest was being waged at their own personal expense. If reimbursement of such items were permitted upon majority stockholder ratification, no court or other tribunal could pass upon which types of expenditures were "needless", to employ the characterization of the Appellate Division in this case. Whether the insurgents should be paid would be made to depend upon whether they win the stockholders election and obtain control of the corporation. It would be entirely irrelevant whether the corporation is "benefitted" by their efforts or by the outcome of such an election. The courts could not indulge in a speculative inquiry into that issue. That would truly be a matter of business judgment. In some instances corporations are better governed by the existing management and in others by some other group which supersedes the existing management. Courts of law have no jurisdiction to decide such questions, and successful insurgent stockholders may confidently be relied upon to reimburse themselves whatever may be the real merits of the controversy. The losers in a proxy fight may understand the interests of the corporation more accurately than their successful adversaries, and agitation of this character may ultimately result in corporate advantage even if there be no change in management. Nevertheless, under the judgment which is appealed from, success in a proxy contest is the indispensable condition upon which reimbursement of the insurgents depends. Adventurers are not infrequent who are ready to take advantage of economic recessions, reduction of dividends or failure to increase them, or other sources of stockholder discontent to wage contests in order to obtain control of well-managed corporations, so as to divert their funds through legal channels into other corporations in which they may be interested, or to discharge former officers and employees to make room for favored newcomers according to the fashion of political patronage, or for other objectives that are unrelated to the sound prosperity of the enterprise. The way is open and will be kept open for stockholders and groups of stockholders to contest corporate elections, but if the promoters of such movements choose to employ the costly modern media of mass persuasion, they should look for reimbursement to themselves and to the stockholders who are aligned with them. If the law be that they can be recompensed by the corporation in case of success, and only in that event, it will operate as a powerful incentive to persons accustomed to taking calculated risks to increase this form of high-powered salesmanship to such a degree that, action provoking reaction, stockholders' meetings will be very costly. To the financial advantages promised by control of a prosperous corporation, would be added the knowledge that the winner takes all insofar as the campaign expenses are concerned. To the victor, indeed, would belong the spoils. . . .

■ CONWAY, C.J., and BURKE, J., concur with FROESSEL, J.; DESMOND, J., concurs in part in a separate opinion; VAN VOORHIS, J., dissents in an opinion in which DYE and FULD, JJ., concur.

Judgment affirmed.

———

Professor Harris observes: "[T]he vast majority of corporate elections are ho-hum affairs. The incumbent directors of the firm spend freely from the corporate treasury to put on lavish campaigns for their own reelection. And, similar to a politician who amasses a large war chest meant to scare off potential rivals, the current board members are mostly reelected without opposition. . . . Election outcomes are predictable." Lee Harris, Shareholder Campaign Funds: A Campaign Subsidy Scheme for Corporate Elections, 58 U.C.L.A. L. Rev. 167, 168–69 (2010) [hereinafter Campaign Funds]. Consider the chart below, which relies on data from companies that have actually experienced a contested corporate election in recent years, 2006–2008. . . . [A]pproximately 133 firms received an election challenge, on average 44 contested corporate elections per year. . . .

Summary Statistics for Contested Corporate
Election Spending (2006–2008)

	Median	Mean	Min	Max	Total
Challenges Per Year	46	44	31	56	133
Incumbent Expenses	$200,000	$1.2 mill.	$6,000	$22 mill.	$138 mill.
Challenger Expenses	$225,000	$652,130	$350	$9 mill.	$84 mill.
Outstanding Shares	26.4 mill.	99.6 mill.	11,000	2.386 bill.	12.948 bill.

Id. at 210. In an expanded study of 190 contested elections in 2006–2009, multivariate analysis found the following variables to the statistically correlated with election outcomes: percentage of shares owned by the incumbents, firm size (challengers success rate declines as firm size increases), and the identity of the challenger (institutions enjoy greater success than individuals). Lee Harris, The Politics of Shareholder Voting, 86 N.Y. U. Law Rev. 1761, 1797–1800 (2011).

———

Heineman v. Datapoint Corp.

611 A.2d 950 (Del.1992)

"The complaint alleges a successful contest for corporate control, with the victors in that contest using their newly acquired positions to cause the corporation to reimburse the costs of waging that contest. Proof of these facts at trial would represent a *prima facie* case of director self-dealing."

———

5. THE ALLOCATION OF POWER BETWEEN THE BOARD AND THE CEO

———

AMERICAN LAW INSTITUTE, PRINCIPLES OF CORPORATE GOVERNANCE §§ 3.01, 3.02, 3.05, 3A.01–3A.05

[See Statutory Supplement]

———

NEW YORK STOCK EXCHANGE LISTED COMPANY MANUAL ¶ 303A

[See Statutory Supplement]

———

SARBANES-OXLEY ACT OF 2002

[See Statutory Supplement]

———

NOTES ON THE MANAGEMENT OF PUBLICLY HELD CORPORATIONS

1. The Managing Model of the Board. In the traditional model of corporate structure, the board managed the business of the corporation (the *managing model* of the board).* This model was reflected in the traditional corporate statutes, which provided that the business of the corporation shall be managed by the board. In the case of closely held corporations, which operate very informally, the model was probably never accurate, and if the model was ever accurate of publicly held corporations, it no longer is. Although the board still plays a central role in the corporation, today it is widely understood that under modern practice in publicly held corporations, the management function is ordinarily located in the executives, and the central figure in the corporation is not the board but the chief executive officer (CEO).

The limited role of the board in publicly held corporations is the result of two critical constraints.

The first constraint concerns time. A recent survey of a number of directors by Korn/Ferry International found reported that the respondents spent an average of 16 hours a month on board matters, including travel. Korn/Ferry International, 34th Annual Board of Directors Study 10 (2010). If travel is put aside, the average time directors spend on board matters is probably no more than 145 hours a year. The businesses of large publicly held corporations are far too complex to be managed by directors who are essentially part-time in that capacity. The number of board meetings is also very limited. More than half the respondents reported that their board meet six times a year or less. Id. at 33. A complex nationwide or global business cannot be managed through occasional meetings.

The second constraint on the role of the board concerns information. The distribution of information in the corporation is highly asymmetrical: the executives have enormously more information than the board, and generally control the flow of information to the board. By controlling the information that the board receives, the executives can often, and indeed usually, shape the decisions that the board makes.

2. The Monitoring Model of the Board. Because of the unrealistic nature of the managing model, in the last thirty years there has been a shift from a managing model to a monitoring model. Under the monitoring model, the primary, although not exclusive, functions of the board of a publicly held

———

*   For ease of exposition, unless the context indicates otherwise, in the balance of this Chapter the terms *directors, boards,* and *shareholders* will refer to directors, boards, or shareholders of publicly held corporations.

corporation are to select, regularly evaluate, fix the compensation of, and, where appropriate, replace the senior executives; monitor the conduct of the corporation's business to evaluate whether the business is being properly managed; and review and, where appropriate, approve, major corporate plans and policies formulated by the corporation's executives.

This functional component of the monitoring model is complemented by a structural component. If the board has the function of monitoring the senior executives, it must be structured to effectuate that function. This in turn requires that the board consist of at least a majority of directors who are independent of the senior executives. The composition of boards is strongly moving in that direction. A survey of the 100 largest American corporations found that in 81 of the corporations, independent directors comprised 75% or more of the boards. The rules of the New York Stock Exchange and NASDAQ now require listed corporations to have a majority of independent directors. These rules also require the boards of such corporations to have audit, nominating, and compensation committees, all composed exclusively of independent directors, to aid in implementing the monitoring function. The Korn/Ferry study found that all of the corporations represented in its survey had audit and compensation committees, 96% had nominating committees, and all these committees were composed exclusively of independent directors. *Id.* at 13.

Another structural feature that has emerged recently to reinforce the independence of directors is the designation of a lead independent director in corporations where the CEO is also Chairman of the Board. The Korn/Ferry study reported, "Once considered controversial and divisive, a lead director is now seen as integral in fostering a positive working relationship with the CEO, maintaining independence of the board from management, and stimulating open discourse among outside directors by serving as an impartial sounding board. Four of five (80 percent) of the . . . respondents have an elected or appointed lead director who presides at executive sessions and evaluates the CEO. This practice has been integrated with astounding speed: only 32 percent of respondents' boards had formalized the lead director role in 2002." *Id.* at 27.

Today, the monitoring model of the board of publicly held corporations is widely accepted, and has been adopted in most or all large publicly held corporations. Ultimately, the utility of this model rests on its economic advantage in providing an additional system to monitor the efficiency of management—in particular, the CEO. The monitoring board, taken alone, is an imperfect mechanism to achieve that end, but because all systems to monitor the efficiency of management are imperfect, it is important to construct a matrix of overlapping monitoring systems. The monitoring board is an important element of that matrix.

Marcel Kahan & Edward Rock, Embattled CEOs
88 Tex. L. Rev. 987, 1025–26 (2010).

As Jeff Gordon has recently shown, the nominal independence of board members has increased dramatically since the 1950s. Gordon estimates that the percentage of inside directors has steadily decreased from 50% in 1950 to around 10% in 2005 and that the percentage of independent directors has correspondingly increased from around 20% to around 80%. . . .

[T]he Investor Responsibility Research Center (IRRC) . . . categorizes each director as an employee of the company, a linked director (a former employee, family member of an employee, or a director who provides, or whose employer provides, services to the company, or is a significant customer), or an independent director. We collected information of these categorizations for the years 2000 and 2007 for companies in the S & P 500 Index, for the Midcap (S & P 400) Index, and for the SmallCap (S & P 600) Index. The IRRC data shows a decline of average total board size for S & P 500 companies (but not for companies in the other indices), as well as a decline in the number of employee directors from about 2.1 to 1.5. Depending on the index, the average percentage of employee directors declined from 17% to 24% in 2000 to 14% and 18% in 2007. Linked directors experience a steeper decline, from around 1.3 to 1.6 in 2000 to 0.6 in 2007, while the number of directors categorized as independent increased. For all companies combined, the percentage of linked directors declined from 14,5% to 6.4% over this seven-year period.

* * *

. . . There are several useful metrics for determining what boards spend their time on. One important measure is whether a board has established a committee devoted to certain tasks and how frequently that committee meets. Virtually all larger companies have had audit and compensation committees for a significant period of time. But the number of companies with nominating and corporate-governance committees has increased significantly. According to Korn/Ferry, the percentage of companies with nominating committees hovered in the low-to mid-seventies until 2002, increased to 87% in 2003, and further increased to over 95% from 2004 on. The percentage of companies with corporate-governance committees (which are not regulated by NASDAQ standards) gradually increased from 39% in 1997 to 48% in 2001, and then increased at a more rapid rate to 96% in 2007. The changed NYSE and NASDAQ listing requirements presumably account for at least a portion of this increase. Many companies, however, had added these committees before they were required to do so. The trend in corporate-governance committees, not required by Sarbanes-Oxley or NASDAQ listing standards, showing an increase even in the pre-Sarbanes-Oxley period, suggests that a significant portion of the increase may be unrelated to the changed [regulatory and listing] standards. . . .

"The number of meetings of committees with monitoring functions—the audit, compensation, nominating, corporate-governance, and succession committees—has generally increased.

Table 6: Committee Meetings per Year

	1997	2001	2007
Audit	3	4	9
Compensation	4	5	6
Nominating	2	3	4
Corporate Governance	3	3	4
Succession	5	5	6
Executive	4	4	4

. . ."

———

Jill E. Fisch, Book Review of Macey, The Overstated Promise of Corporate Governance

77 U. Chi. L. Rev. 923, 930–31 (2010).

. . . [A]s Jeff Gordon suggests, the evolution of the monitoring board appears to be more a product of market forces than regulatory intervention. To be sure, the Delaware courts have encouraged the use of independent directors in the context of specific decisions, such as evaluating tender offers or responding to derivative litigation, but these decisions neither require a majority independent board nor limit the board's role to monitoring. Sarbanes-Oxley and the self-regulating organization (SRO) rules mandate increased board independence, but these requirements are of relatively recent origin and largely reflect preexisting corporate norms. Indeed, probably the most substantial factor in the move to independent monitoring boards has been the market pressure imposed by institutional investors.

Whether those pressures were misguided remains an open question. Several empirical studies have shown that independent boards function more effectively in specific situations. James Cotter, Anil Shivdasani, and Marc Zenner find that independent boards enhance target shareholder gains from takeovers. Michael Weisbach shows that independent boards are more likely to respond to poor performance by replacing the CEO. John Byrd and Kent Hickman report that firms with a majority of outside directors make better acquisitions. More recent analysis suggests that the regulatory mandates for independence may themselves provide independent value. For example, Vidhi Chhaochharia and Yaniv Grinstein find that the imposition of SRO board independence rules upon companies reduced CEO compensation.

More generally, increased board independence may have been a factor in modernizing corporations away from the overdiversified and inefficient conglomerates of the 1970s. One contributing factor is the ability of outside directors to respond to the information provided by the capital markets through stock prices. As Jeff Gordon observes, 'the increasing informativeness and value of stock market signals' gave the outside directors an easy tool to use in their effort to enhance shareholder value. Transparent and efficient stock prices enable directors to use 'stock price maximization as the measure of managerial success.' This in turn simplifies the board's role as monitor.

_____

NOTE ON THE ROLE OF TAKEOVERS IN THE STRUCTURE OF THE CORPORATION

Until around the [mid-1960s,] it was extremely difficult for insurgents to oust the incumbent management of a publicly held corporation by voting new directors into office. In principle, such an ouster could be achieved through a proxy fight. However, for a variety of reasons, especially costs, proxy fights were not often launched, and when launched were only intermittently successful. It was also difficult to *acquire* a corporation over the opposition of its managers, because the principal forms of acquisition, such as mergers and the purchase of substantially all of a corporation's assets, require approval by the board of the corporation that is to be acquired.

Beginning in the [mid-1960s], however, hostile takeovers developed as an important way to oust incumbent managements and effect acquisitions. In a hostile takeover, A, the *bidder* makes a *bid* or *tender offer* to purchase stock in B, the *target*, up to a stated amount and subject to certain conditions. The bid is made to the target's shareholders over the head of the target's management, who are resisting an acquisition by the bidder.* The tender-offer price is almost invariably well above the prevailing market price for the target's stock.

Because a tender offer is made to the target's shareholders, rather than to the target corporation, the approval of the target's board is not required. However, target managements almost invariably resist hostile takeover bids by causing the corporation to take defensive actions to block the bid. These defensive actions often involve a restructuring of the allocation of power between management and shareholders. If the allocation of power between management and shareholders is thought of as a dashboard fuel gauge, with

_____

* Some takeovers are "friendly," that is, they are acquisitions of stock in the target made with the support of the target's board. These transactions are not really takeovers, because that term connotes a combination that is effected over the head, and against the wishes of the target's board. Accordingly, for ease of exposition in this Note the term *takeover* will be used interchangeably with the term *hostile takeover*.

shareholder power at one end and management power at the other, these defensive actions are intended to, and invariably do, move the needle closer to the management-power end of the gauge.

Sometimes defensive actions are taken in the middle of a hostile takeover fight. Often, however, the corporation's governance rules are restructured by a defensive action taken before a hostile tender offer emerges, with the idea of precluding or at least dampening the prospect of such an offer. Much of modern corporate governance—and in particular, the modern allocation of power between shareholders and management—is shaped either by managerial responses to actual takeover bids or by managerial actions to forestall possible takeover bids.

The central legal issue concerning takeovers is what standard of review the courts should apply in reviewing the defensive actions by management. This subject is examined closely later in the book. In *Unitrin, Inc. v. American General Corp.*, 651 A.2d 1361 (Del. 1995), the Delaware Supreme Court embraced a standard of enhanced judicial scrutiny of such defensive maneuvers, but provided an important gloss by cautioning that its scrutiny is carefully balanced:

> This Court has recognized "the prerogative of a board of directors to resist a third party's unsolicited acquisition proposal or offer." *Paramount Communications, Inc. v. QVC Network, Inc.*, Del.Supr., 637 A.2d 34, 43 n. 13 (1994). The Unitrin Board did not have unlimited discretion to defeat the threat it perceived from the American General Offer by any draconian means available. . . . [The board must prove it acted reasonably whereby] the nature of the threat associated with a particular hostile offer sets the parameters for the range of permissible defensive tactics. Accordingly, the purpose of enhanced judicial scrutiny is to determine whether the Board acted reasonably in "relation . . . to the threat which a particular bid allegedly poses to stockholder interests." *Mills Acquisition Co. v. Macmillan, Inc.*, Del.Supr., 559 A.2d 1261, 1288 (1989).

———

CHAPTER 5

SHAREHOLDER INFORMATIONAL RIGHTS & PROXY VOTING

1. SHAREHOLDER INFORMATION RIGHTS UNDER STATE AND FEDERAL LAW

A. INSPECTION OF BOOKS AND RECORDS

DEL. GEN. CORP. LAW §§ 219, 220

[See Statutory Supplement]

REV. MODEL BUS. CORP. ACT §§ 7.20, 16.01–16.04

[See Statutory Supplement]

CAL. CORP. CODE §§ 1600, 1601

[See Statutory Supplement]

N.Y. BUS. CORP. LAW § 624

[See Statutory Supplement]

Saito v. McKesson HBOC, Inc.

Supreme Court of State of Delaware, 2002.
806 A.2d 113.

■ BERGER, JUSTICE.

In this appeal, we consider the limitations on a stockholder's statutory right to inspect corporate books and records. The statute, 8 Del.C. § 220, enables stockholders to investigate matters "reasonably related to [their] interest as [stockholders]" including, among other things, possible corporate wrongdoing. It does not open the door to the wide ranging discovery that would be available in support of litigation. For this statutory tool to be meaningful, however, it cannot be read narrowly to deprive a stockholder of necessary documents solely because the documents were prepared by third parties or because the documents predate the stockholder's first investment in the corporation. A stockholder who demands inspection for a proper purpose should be given access to all of the documents in the corporation's possession, custody or control, that are necessary to satisfy that proper purpose. Thus, where a § 220 claim is based on alleged corporate wrongdoing, and assuming the allegation is meritorious, the stockholder should be given enough information to effectively address the problem, either through derivative litigation or through direct contact with the corporation's directors and/or stockholders.

Factual and Procedural Background

On October 17, 1998, McKesson Corporation entered into a stock-for-stock merger agreement with HBO & Company ("HBOC"). On October 20, 1998, appellant, Noel Saito, purchased McKesson stock. The merger was consummated in January 1999 and the combined company was renamed McKesson HBOC, Incorporated. HBOC continued its separate corporate existence as a wholly-owned subsidiary of McKesson HBOC.

Starting in April and continuing through July 1999, McKesson HBOC announced a series of financial restatements triggered by its year-end audit process. During that four month period, McKesson HBOC reduced its revenues by $327.4 million for the three prior fiscal years. The restatements all were attributed to HBOC accounting irregularities. The first announcement precipitated several lawsuits, including a derivative action pending in the Court of Chancery, captioned *Ash v. McCall*, Civil Action No. 17132. Saito was one of four plaintiffs in the *Ash* complaint, which alleged that: (i) McKesson's directors breached their duty of care by failing to discover the HBOC accounting irregularities before the merger; (ii) McKesson's directors committed corporate waste by entering into the merger with HBOC; (iii) HBOC's directors breached their fiduciary duties by failing to monitor the company's compliance with financial reporting requirements prior to the merger; and (iv) McKesson HBOC's directors failed in the same respect during the three months following the merger. Although the Court of Chancery granted defendants' motion to dismiss the complaint, the dismissal was without prejudice as to the pre-merger and post-merger oversight claims.

In its decision on the motion to dismiss, the Court of Chancery specifically suggested that Saito and the other plaintiffs "use the 'tools at hand,' most prominently § 220 books and records actions, to obtain information necessary to sue derivatively."[2] Saito was the only Ash plaintiff to follow that advice. The stated purpose of Saito's demand was:

---

[2]   Ash v. McCall, 2000 WL 1370341, *15 (Del.Ch.).

(1) to further investigate breaches of fiduciary duties by the boards of directors of HBO & Co., Inc., McKesson, Inc., and/or McKesson HBOC, Inc. related to their oversight of their respective company's accounting procedures and financial reporting; (2) to investigate potential claims against advisors engaged by McKesson, Inc. and HBO & Co., Inc. to the acquisition of HBO & Co., Inc. by McKesson, Inc.; and (3) to gather information relating to the above in order to supplement the complaint in *Ash v. McCall*, et al., . . . in accordance with the September 15, 2000 Opinion of the Court of Chancery.

Saito demanded access to eleven categories of documents, including those relating to Arthur Andersen's pre-merger review and verification of HBOC's financial condition; communications between or among HBOC, McKesson, and their investment bankers and accountants concerning HBOC's accounting practices; and discussions among members of the Boards of Directors of HBOC, McKesson, and/or McKesson HBOC concerning reports published in April 1997 and thereafter about HBOC's accounting practices or financial condition. . . .

DISCUSSION

Stockholders of Delaware corporations enjoy a qualified common law and statutory right to inspect the corporation's books and records.[3] Inspection rights were recognized at common law because, "[a]s a matter of self-protection, the stockholder was entitled to know how his agents were conducting the affairs of the corporation of which he or she was a part owner."[4] The common law right is codified in 8 Del.C. § 220, which provides in relevant part:

(b) Any stockholder . . . shall, upon written demand under oath stating the purpose thereof, have the right . . . to inspect for any proper purpose the corporation's stock ledger, a list of its stockholders, and its other books and records, and to make copies or extracts therefrom. A proper purpose shall mean a purpose reasonably related to such person's interest as a stockholder.

Once a stockholder establishes a proper purpose under § 220, the right to relief will not be defeated by the fact that the stockholder may have secondary purposes that are improper. The scope of a stockholder's inspection, however, is limited to those books and records that are necessary and essential to accomplish the stated, proper purpose.

After trial, the Court of Chancery found "credible evidence of possible wrongdoing," which satisfied Saito's burden of establishing a proper purpose for the inspection of corporate books and records. But the Court of Chancery limited Saito's access to relevant documents in three respects. First, it held that, since Saito would not have standing to bring

---

[3]   Shaw v. Agri-Mark, Inc., 663 A.2d 464 (Del.1995).
[4]   Id. at 467.

an action challenging actions that occurred before he purchased McKesson stock, Saito could not obtain documents created before October 20, 1998. Second, the court concluded that Saito was not entitled to documents relating to possible wrongdoing by the financial advisors to the merging companies. Third, the court denied Saito access to any HBOC documents, since Saito never was a stockholder of HBOC. We will consider each of these rulings in turn.

A.   *The Standing Limitation*

By statute [8 Del. C. § 327], stockholders who bring derivative suits must allege that they were stockholders of the corporation "at the time of the transaction of which such stockholder complains. . . . " The Court of Chancery decided that this limitation on Saito's ability to maintain a derivative suit controlled the scope of his inspection rights. As a result, the court held that Saito was "effectively limited to examining conduct of McKesson and McKesson HBOC's boards following the negotiation and public announcement of the merger agreement."

Although we recognize that there may be some interplay between the two statutes, we do not read § 327 as defining the temporal scope of a stockholder's inspection rights under § 220. The books and records statute requires that a stockholder's purpose be one that is "reasonably related" to his or her interest as a stockholder. The standing statute, § 327, bars a stockholder from bringing a derivative action unless the stockholder owned the corporation's stock at the time of the alleged wrong. If a stockholder wanted to investigate alleged wrongdoing that substantially predated his or her stock ownership, there could be a question as to whether the stockholder's purpose was reasonably related to his or her interest as a stockholder, especially if the stockholder's only purpose was to institute derivative litigation. But stockholders may use information about corporate mismanagement in other ways, as well. They may seek an audience with the board to discuss proposed reforms or, failing in that, they may prepare a stockholder resolution for the next annual meeting, or mount a proxy fight to elect new directors. None of those activities would be prohibited by § 327.

Even where a stockholder's only purpose is to gather information for a derivative suit, the date of his or her stock purchase should not be used as an automatic "cut-off" date in a § 220 action. First, the potential derivative claim may involve a continuing wrong that both predates and postdates the stockholder's purchase date. In such a case, books and records from the inception of the alleged wrongdoing could be necessary and essential to the stockholder's purpose. Second, the alleged post-purchase date wrongs may have their foundation in events that transpired earlier. In this case, for example, Saito wants to investigate McKesson's apparent failure to learn of HBOC's accounting irregularities until months after the merger was consummated. Due diligence documents generated before the merger agreement was signed may be essential to that investigation. In sum, the date on which a stockholder first acquired the corporation's stock does not control the scope of records available under § 220. If activities that occurred before the purchase date are "reasonably related" to the stockholder's interest as a stockholder, then the stockholder should be given access to records necessary to an understanding of those activities.[10]

B. *The Financial Advisors' Documents*

The Court of Chancery denied Saito access to documents in McKesson-HBOC's possession that the corporation obtained from financial and accounting advisors, on the ground that Saito could not use § 220 to develop potential claims against third parties. On appeal, Saito argues that he is seeking third party documents for the same reason he is seeking McKesson HBOC documents—to investigate possible wrongdoing by McKesson and McKesson HBOC. Since the trial court found that to be a proper purpose, Saito argues that he should not be precluded from seeing documents that are necessary to his purpose, and in McKesson HBOC's possession, simply because the documents were prepared by third party advisors.

We agree that, generally, the source of the documents in a corporation's possession should not control a stockholder's right to inspection under § 220. It is not entirely clear, however, that the trial court restricted Saito's access on that basis. The Court of Chancery decided that Saito's interest in pursuing claims against McKesson HBOC's advisors was not a proper purpose. It recognized that a secondary improper purpose usually is irrelevant if the stockholder establishes his need for the same documents to support a proper purpose. But the court apparently concluded that the categories of third party documents that Saito demanded did not support the proper purpose of investigating possible wrongdoing by McKesson and McKesson HBOC.

We cannot determine from the present record whether the Court of Chancery intended to exclude all third party documents, but such a blanket exclusion would be improper. The source of the documents and the manner in which they were obtained by the corporation have little or no bearing on a stockholder's inspection rights. The issue is whether the documents are necessary and essential to satisfy the stockholder's proper purpose. In this case, Saito wants to investigate possible wrongdoing relating to McKesson and McKesson HBOC's failure to discover HBOC's accounting irregularities. Since McKesson and McKesson HBOC relied on financial and accounting advisors to evaluate HBOC's financial condition and reporting, those advisors' reports and correspondence would be critical to Saito's investigation.

---

[10] As noted . . . above, a Section 220 proceeding does not open the door to wide ranging discovery. See *Brehm v. Eisner*, 746 A.2d 244, 266–67 (Del.2000) (Plaintiffs "bear the burden of showing a proper purpose and [must] make specific and discrete identification, with rifled precision . . . [to] establish that each category of books and records is essential to the accomplishment of their articulated purpose . . . "); *Security First Corp. v. U.S. Die Casting and Dev. Co.*, 687 A.2d 563, 568, 570 (Del.1997) ("mere curiosity or desire for a fishing expedition" is insufficient.).

C. *HBOC Documents*

Finally, the Court of Chancery held that Saito was not entitled to any HBOC documents because he was not a stockholder of HBOC before or after the merger. Although Saito is a stockholder of HBOC's parent, McKesson HBOC, stockholders of a parent corporation are not entitled to inspect a subsidiary's books and records, "[a]bsent a showing of a fraud or that a subsidiary is in fact the mere alter ego of the parent. . . . "[11] The Court of Chancery found no basis to disregard HBOC's separate existence and, therefore, denied access to its records.

We reaffirm this settled principle, which applies to those HBOC books and records that were never provided to McKesson or McKesson HBOC. But it does not apply to relevant documents that HBOC gave to McKesson before the merger, or to McKesson HBOC after the merger. We assume that HBOC provided financial and accounting information to its proposed merger partner and, later, to its parent company. As with the third party advisors' documents, Saito would need access to relevant HBOC documents in order to understand what his company's directors knew and why they failed to recognize HBOC's accounting irregularities.

Conclusion

Based on the foregoing, the decision of the Court of Chancery is AFFIRMED in part and REVERSED in part, and this matter is REMANDED for further action in accordance with this decision. Jurisdiction is not retained.

———

NOTES ON SHAREHOLDERS' INSPECTION RIGHTS

1. "No Fishing:" The Credible Basis Requirement. As a general proposition investigating for wrongdoing or mismanagement is a proper purpose for shareholder access; courts nonetheless condition access on the requesting stockholder showing by a preponderance of the evidence a "credible basis" from which the court can infer there is possible mismanagement or wrongdoing such that further investigation is in order. *See e.g., Seinfeld v. Verizon Comm. Inc.,* 909 A.2d 117 (Del. 2006) (the credible basis "threshold may be satisfied by a credible showing, through documents, logic, testimony or otherwise, that there are legitimate issues of wrongdoing"); *Ihrig v. Frontier Equity Exchange Assoc.,* 128 P.3d 993 (Kan. Ct. App. 2006). One development that has stimulated shareholder resort to the state-based rights to inspect corporate records is Congress' passage of the Private Securities Litigation Reform Act of 1995 (PSLRA), studied later in Chapter 11. A central feature of the PSLRA is that discovery against defendants alleged to have committed securities fraud is barred until all pretrial motions have been resolved. A key pretrial motion is the motion to dismiss; under the PSLRA's heightened pleading requirement the investor's complaint must set forth with particularity facts that establish a "strong inference" that the

---

[11]   *Skouras v. Admiralty Enterprises, Inc.,* 386 A.2d 674, 681 (Del.Ch.1978).

defendants have either knowingly or recklessly committed a material misrepresentation. Hence, to satisfy this pleading standard as well as the state law requirements to plead fiduciary breaches with "particularity" plaintiffs frequently invoke their shareholder inspection rights to obtain information to flesh out the allegations for the securities fraud complaint. *See* Randall S. Thomas & Kenneth J. Martin, Using State Inspection Statutes for Discovery in General Securities Fraud Actions, 77 B.U.L. Rev. 69 (1997).

Delaware Section 220(b)(1) broadly provides shareholder access to "books and records," whereas Section 16.02(b) of the Model Act identifies specific types of documents, e.g., "accounting records," "minutes" and "financial statements." This difference caused the Massachusetts Supreme Court to adopt a less demanding standard than Delaware applies when a shareholder sought access to minutes of director meetings. *Chitwood v. Vertex Pharm. Inc.*, 476 Mass. 667, 678, 71 N.E.3d 492, 501 (Mass. 2017) (access granted when shareholder alleges particular facts that permit reasonable inference the records could reveal wrongdoing or mismanagement). Nonetheless, under the MBCA inspection is limited to the types of documents set forth in MBCA § 16.02(b). The court observed: "The inverse of the Biblical adage that to whom much is given, much is expected is that to whom less is given, less is expected. See Luke 12:48 (Revised Standard Version)" *Id.*

2.   *Common Law; Interpretation of the Statutes.* At common law, a shareholder "acting in good faith for the purpose of advancing the interests of the corporation and protecting his own interest as a stockholder" has a right to examine the corporate books and records at reasonable times. *Albee v. Lamson & Hubbard Corp.*, 320 Mass. 421, 424, 69 N.E.2d 811, 813 (1946). The general rule is that the shareholder has the burden of alleging and proving good faith and proper purpose. *Id. But see Bennett v. Mack's Supermarkets, Inc.*, 602 S.W.2d 143 (Ky.1979).

Many or most legislatures have now enacted statutes governing the right of inspection. Many of these statutes are more limited in their coverage than the common law rule. For example, a statute may apply only to certain kinds of shareholders (such as those who are record holders of at least 5% of the corporation's stock or who have been record holders for at least six months) or only to certain kinds of books and records. A common problem of interpretation is whether the statutes: (i) Preserve the common law rule that the shareholder must prove a proper purpose; (ii) Discard the proper-purpose test; or (iii) Preserve the proper-purpose test, but place on the corporation the burden of proving that the shareholder's purpose is improper. Generally, the last interpretation is followed, at least if the language is ambiguous. *See, e.g., Crane Co. v. Anaconda Co.*, 39 N.Y.2d 14, 382 N.Y.S.2d 707, 346 N.E.2d 507 (1976). A second common problem of interpretation is whether the statutes replace or supplement the common law. The general answer is that the statutes supplement the common law, so that a suit for inspection that does not fall within the relevant statute can still be brought under the common law. See, e.g., Bank of Heflin v. Miles, 294 Ala. 462, 318 So.2d 697 (1975).

To illustrate, New York courts have long interpreted the state shareholder inspection statute as supplementing and not replacing the common law. *See Rockwell v. SCM Corp.*, 496 F. Supp. 1123, 1126 (S.D.N.Y. 1980) ("A review of New York law leads to the inescapable conclusion that the common law right of inspection survived enactment of [section] 624 of the Business Corporation Law."); *Ret. Plan for Gen. Employees of the City of North Miami Beach v. McGraw-Hill Companies, Inc*, 120 A.D.3d 1052, 992 N.Y.S.2d 220, 223 (1st Dep't 2014) ("[t]he statutory right supplemented, but did not replace, the common-law right"). The common law right is broader than the statutory right; it can cover all relevant books and records. *See Gimpel v. Bolstein*, 125 Misc. 2d 45, 477 N.Y.S.2d 1014, 1023 (Sup. Ct. 1984) (allowing shareholder "full access to all corporate financial, shareholder, and account books"). However, the common law right is not an absolute right: the shareholder's request must be in good faith and with a proper purpose. Further, the scope of inspection is limited to those documents that are "relevant and necessary" to the shareholder's proper purpose. *See Tatko v. Tatko Bros. Slate Co., Inc.*, 173 A.D.2d 917, 569 N.Y.S.2d 783, 785 (3d Dep't 1991).

3.   *"Proper Purpose."* Among the purposes the courts have recognized as "proper," are to determine the financial condition of the corporation, to ascertain the value of the petitioner's shares, and to obtain a mailing list for the solicitation of proxies from shareholders. A purpose is proper even though it yields no benefit to the corporation. Not surprisingly, it is an improper purpose to seek access to gain information that will be used in a competing enterprise. Query, what reasoning would deny Mr. Saito's request to obtain documents that bear on whether HBOC-McKesson had claims against its third party advisors?

4.   *Mixed Purposes.* Suppose the shareholder has mixed purposes, one proper and one not. In *Helmsman Management Services, Inc. v. A & S Consultants, Inc.*, 525 A.2d 160, 164, 166 (Del.Ch.1987), the court held that "Once it is determined that a shareholder has a proper purpose that is primary, any secondary purpose or ulterior motive that the stockholder might have is irrelevant." Accordingly, "even if [the shareholder] does have an ulterior (*i.e.*, a non-shareholder-related) purpose, it would still not be barred from relief under [Del.Gen.Corp.Law] § 220, unless the ulterior purpose is also its primary purpose."

5.   *The Pillsbury Case.* In *State ex rel. Pillsbury v. Honeywell, Inc.*, 291 Minn. 322, 191 N.W.2d 406 (1971), Pillsbury was a shareholder of Honeywell, Inc. Pillsbury opposed the Vietnam war, and asked Honeywell to produce its shareholder ledger and all corporate records dealing with weapons and munitions manufacture. Pillsbury admitted that his sole motive in purchasing Honeywell stock was to persuade Honeywell to cease producing munitions, but argued that the desire to communicate with fellow shareholders was per se a proper purpose. Honeywell argued that a proper purpose contemplates a concern with investment return. The Minnesota court held for Honeywell:

> Several courts agree with petitioner's contention that a mere desire to communicate with other shareholders is, per se, a proper

purpose. . . . This would seem to confer an almost absolute right to inspection. We believe that a better rule would allow inspections only if the shareholder has a proper purpose for such communication. . . .

Petitioner had utterly no interest in the affairs of Honeywell before he learned of Honeywell's production of fragmentation bombs. Immediately after obtaining this knowledge, he purchased stock in Honeywell for the sole purpose of asserting ownership privileges in an effort to force Honeywell to cease such production. . . . Such a motivation can hardly be deemed a proper purpose germane to his economic interest as a shareholder.

Honeywell was a Delaware corporation, and the Minnesota Court apparently assumed for purposes of the case that Delaware law applied, or in any event was no different than Minnesota law insofar as relevant. In *Credit Bureau Reports, Inc. v. Credit Bureau of St. Paul, Inc.,* 290 A.2d 691 (Del.1972), however, the Delaware Supreme Court repudiated the *Pillsbury* case insofar as it applied to requests for stockholder lists:

[In] General Time Corporation v. Talley Industries, Inc., Del.Supr., 240 A.2d 755 (1968). . . . we stated that, under [Del.Gen.Corp.Law] § 220, "the desire to solicit proxies for a slate of directors in opposition to management is a purpose reasonably related to the stockholder's interest as a stockholder"; and we held that "any further or secondary purpose in seeking the list is irrelevant." Those rulings are dispositive. . . . The defendant corporation . . . relies upon Pillsbury v. Honeywell, Inc., Minn., 191 N.W.2d 406 (1971). Insofar as the *Pillsbury* case is inconsistent herewith, it is inconsistent with [§ 220] as properly applied.

See also The Conservative Caucus Research, Analysis & Education Foundation, Inc. v. Chevron Corp., 525 A.2d 569 (Del.Ch.1987) (granting access to the list of stockholders to solicit their support for a proposal to discourage the corporation from continuing to do business in Angola).

6. Stockholder Lists. As a practical matter, the courts are understandably more willing to grant access to stockholder lists and the like than to grant access to otherwise-confidential financial and business information, such as internal data and contracts. In the case of business and financial information, the shareholder will normally have to show the court a specific and plausible reason why the information is needed. In contrast, in the case of stockholder lists a statement by a shareholder that he wants the list to communicate with other shareholders will usually, although not always, suffice. This distinction is understandable. Requiring the production of a stockholder list is almost invariably a necessary step for shareholders to exercise their role in corporate governance, imposes only a minimum burden on the corporation, and usually cannot injure the business of the corporation. In contrast, other kinds of information may be costly to produce, may have the potential to injure the corporation's business if misused, and (depending on the information) may not be necessary for the normal exercise of the shareholder's role.

In some cases, the statutes themselves distinguish between different types of corporate books and records. See, e.g., Del.Gen.Corp.Law § 220; see also Model Act §§ 7.20(b), 16.02.

B. THE STOCKHOLDER LIST IN A DEMATERIALIZED WORLD

Concept Release on the U.S. Proxy System
SEC, Exchange Act Rel. No. 62495 (July 14, 2010).

II. The Current Proxy Distribution and Voting Process

A fundamental tenet of state corporation law is that shareholders have the right to vote their shares to elect directors and to approve or reject major corporate transactions at shareholder meetings. Under state law, shareholders can appoint a proxy to vote their shares on their behalf at shareholder meetings, and the major national securities exchanges generally require their listed companies to solicit proxies for all meetings of shareholders. Because most shareholders do not attend public company shareholder meetings in person, voting occurs almost entirely by the use of proxies that are solicited before the shareholder meeting, thereby resulting in the corporate proxy becoming "the forum for shareholder suffrage." Issuers with a class of securities registered under Section 12 of the Securities Exchange Act of 1934 ("Exchange Act") . . . are required to comply with the federal proxy rules . . . when soliciting proxies from shareholders.

A. Types of Share Ownership and Voting Rights

The proxy solicitation process starts with the determination of who has the right to receive proxy materials and vote on matters presented to shareholders for a vote at shareholder meetings. The method for making this determination depends on the way the shares are owned. There are two types of security holders in the U.S.—registered owners and beneficial owners.

1. Registered Owners

Registered owners (also known as "record holders") have a direct relationship with the issuer because their ownership of shares is listed on records maintained by the issuer or its transfer agent. State corporation law generally vests the right to vote and the other rights of share ownership in registered owners.[25] Because registered owners have the right to vote, they also have the authority to appoint a proxy to act on their behalf at shareholder meetings.

---

[25] See, e.g., *Del. Code Ann. tit. 8, § 219(c)*; Model Bus. Corp. Act § 1.40(21); but see Model Bus. Corp. Act § 7.23 (permitting corporations to establish procedures by which beneficial owners become entitled to exercise rights, including voting rights, otherwise exercisable by shareholders of record).

Registered owners can hold their securities either in certificated form or in electronic (or "book-entry") form through a direct registration system ("DRS"), which enables an investor to have his or her ownership of securities recorded on the books of the issuer without having a physical securities certificate issued. Under DRS, an investor can electronically transfer his or her securities to a broker-dealer to effect a transaction without the risk, expense, or delay associated with the use of securities certificates. . . .

2. Beneficial Owners

The vast majority of investors in shares issued by U.S. companies today are beneficial owners, which means that they hold their securities in book-entry form through a securities intermediary, such as a broker-dealer or bank. This is often referred to as owning in "street name." A beneficial owner does not own the securities directly. Instead, as a customer of the securities intermediary, the beneficial owner has an entitlement to the rights associated with ownership of the securities.[31]

B. The Process of Soliciting Proxies . . .

1. Distributing Proxy Materials to Registered Owners

It is a relatively simple process for an issuer to send proxy materials to registered owners because their names and addresses are listed in the issuer's records, which are usually maintained by a transfer agent. . . . Registered owners execute the proxy card and return it to the issuer's transfer agent or vote tabulator for tabulation.

2. Distributing Proxy Materials to Beneficial Owners . . .

a. The Depository Trust Company

In most cases, the chain of ownership for beneficially owned securities of U.S. companies begins with the Depository Trust Company ("DTC"), a registered clearing agency acting as a securities depository.[33] Most large U.S. broker-dealers and banks are DTC participants, meaning that they deposit securities with, and hold those securities through, DTC. DTC's nominee, Cede & Co., appears in an issuer's stock records as the sole registered owner of securities deposited at DTC. DTC holds the deposited securities in "fungible bulk," meaning that there are no specifically identifiable shares directly owned by DTC participants. Rather, each participant owns a pro rata interest in the aggregate number of shares of a particular issuer held at DTC. Correspondingly,

---

[31]   . . . Under the UCC, beneficial owners have a "securities entitlement" to the fungible bulk of securities held by the broker-dealer or bank. . . . A securities intermediary is obligated to provide the entitlement holder with all of the economic and governance rights that comprise the financial asset and that the entitlement holder can look only to that intermediary for performance of the obligations. See generally *UCC 8–501* et seq. (1994).

[33]   DTC provides custody and book-entry transfer services of securities transactions in the U.S. market involving equities, corporate and municipal debt, money market instruments, American depositary receipts, and exchange-traded funds. In accordance with its rules, DTC accepts deposits of securities from its participants (i.e., broker-dealers and banks), credits those securities to the depositing participants' accounts, and effects book-entry movements of those securities. . . .

each customer of a DTC participant-such as an individual investor-owns a pro rata interest in the shares in which the DTC participant has an interest.

Once an issuer establishes a date for the shareholder meeting and a record date for shareholders entitled to vote on matters presented at the meeting, it sends a formal announcement of these dates to DTC, which DTC forwards to all of its participants. The issuer then requests from DTC a "securities position listing" as of the record date, which identifies the participants having a position in the issuer's securities and the number of securities held by each participant. . . . The record date securities position listing establishes the number of shares that a participant is entitled to vote through its DTC proxy.

For each shareholder meeting, DTC executes an "omnibus proxy" transferring its right to vote the shares held on deposit to its participants.[42] In this manner, broker-dealer and bank participants in DTC obtain the right to vote directly the shares that they hold through DTC.

b.   Securities Intermediaries: Broker-Dealers and Banks

Once the issuer identifies the DTC participants holding positions in its securities, it is required to send a search card[43] to each of those participants, as well as other securities intermediaries that are registered owners, to determine whether they are holding shares for beneficial owners and, if so, the number of sets of proxy packages needed to be forwarded to those beneficial owners. . . .

Commission rules require broker-dealers to respond to the issuer . . . [and broker].

Once the search card process is complete, the issuer should know the approximate number of beneficial owners owning shares through each securities intermediary. The issuer must then provide the securities intermediary, or its third-party proxy service provider, with copies of its proxy materials (including, if applicable, a Notice of Internet Availability of Proxy Materials) for forwarding to those beneficial owners. The securities intermediary must forward these proxy materials to beneficial owners no later than five business days after receiving such materials.[47]

---

[42]   As noted in recent litigation, the execution by DTC of an omnibus proxy is neither automatic nor legally required, but occurs as a matter of common practice. *Kurz v. Holbrook*, 989 A.2d 140, 170 (Del. Ch. 2010), *rev'd on other grounds, Crown EMAK Partners, LLC v. Kurz*, 992 A.2d 377 (Del. 2010) ("There does not appear to be any authority governing when a DTC omnibus proxy is issued, who should ask for it, or what event triggers it. The parties tell me that DTC has no written policies or procedures on the matter.").

[43]   The search card must request: (1) the number of beneficial owners; (2) the number of proxy soliciting materials and annual reports needed for forwarding by the intermediaries to their beneficial owner customers; and (3) the name and address of any agent appointed by the bank or broker-dealer to process a request for a list of beneficial owners. . . .

[47]   *17 CFR 240.14b–1(b)(2)* and *17 CFR 240.14b–2(b)(3)*. The exchanges have rules that regulate the process and procedures by which member firms must transmit proxy materials to beneficial owners, collect voting instructions from beneficial owners, and vote shares held in the member firm's name. See, e.g., NYSE Rules 450 through 460 and FINRA Rule 2251.

Securities intermediaries are entitled to reasonable reimbursement for their costs in forwarding these materials.

Instead of receiving and executing a proxy card (as registered owners receive and do), the beneficial owner receives a "voting instruction form" or "VIF" from the securities intermediary, which permits the beneficial owner to instruct the securities intermediary how to vote the beneficially owned shares. . . .

C. Proxy Voting Process

Once the proxy materials have been distributed to the registered owners and beneficial owners of the securities, the means by which shareholders vote their shares differs. . . . [R]egistered owners execute the proxy card and return it to the vote tabulator, either by mail, by phone, or through the Internet. Beneficial owners, on the other hand, indicate their voting instructions on the VIF and return it to the securities intermediary or its proxy service provider, either by mail, by phone, or through the Internet. The securities intermediary, or its proxy service provider, tallies the voting instructions that it receives from its customers. . . . [T]he securities intermediary, or its proxy service provider, then executes and submits to the vote tabulator a proxy card for all securities held by the securities intermediary's customers.

In certain situations, a broker-dealer may use its discretion to vote shares if it does not receive instructions from the beneficial owner of the shares. Historically, broker-dealers were generally permitted to vote shares on uncontested matters, including uncontested director elections, without instructions from the beneficial owner. The NYSE recently revised this rule to prohibit broker-dealers from voting uninstructed shares with regard to any election of directors.[52]

D. The Roles of Third Parties in the Proxy Process

Issuers, securities intermediaries, and shareholders often retain third parties to perform a number of proxy-related functions, including forwarding proxy materials, collecting voting instructions, voting shares, soliciting proxies, tabulating proxies, and analyzing proxy issues,.

1. Transfer Agents

Issuers are required to maintain a record of security holders for state law purposes[53] and often hire a transfer agent to maintain that record. Transfer agents, as agents of the issuer, are obliged to confirm to a vote tabulator (if the transfer agent does not itself perform the tabulation function) matters such as the amount of shares outstanding, as well as the identity and holdings of registered owners entitled to vote. . . .

---

[52]   NYSE Rule 452 and NYSE Listed Issuer Manual § 402.08(B). . . .

[53]   E.g., *Del. Code Ann. tit. 8, § 219(a)*; Model Bus. Corp. Act § 16.01(c).

2. Proxy Service Providers

To facilitate the proxy material distribution and voting process for beneficial owners, securities intermediaries typically retain a proxy service provider to perform a number of processing functions, including forwarding the proxy materials by mail or electronically and collecting voting instructions.[57] To enable the proxy service provider to perform these functions, the securities intermediary gives the service provider an electronic data feed of a list of beneficial owners and the number of shares held by each beneficial owner on the record date. The proxy service provider, on behalf of the intermediary, then requests the appropriate number of proxy material sets from the issuer for delivery to the beneficial owners. Upon receipt of the packages, the proxy service provider, on behalf of the intermediary, mails either the proxy materials with a VIF, or a Notice of Internet Availability of Proxy Materials, to beneficial owners. . . .

3. Proxy Solicitors

Issuers sometimes hire third-party proxy solicitors to identify beneficial owners holding large amounts of the issuers' securities and to telephone shareholders to encourage them to vote their proxies consistent with the recommendations of management. This often occurs when there is a contested election of directors, and issuer's management and other persons are competing for proxy authority to vote securities in the election (commonly referred to as a "proxy contest"). In addition, an issuer may hire a proxy solicitor in uncontested situations when voting returns are expected to be insufficient to meet state quorum requirements or when an important matter is being considered. . . .

4. Vote Tabulators

Under many state statutes, an issuer must appoint a vote tabulator (sometimes called "inspectors of elections" or "proxy tabulators") to collect and tabulate the proxy votes as well as votes submitted by shareholders in person at a meeting.[60] We understand that often the issuer's transfer agent will act as the vote tabulator. . . . However, sometimes the issuer will hire an independent third party to perform this function, often to certify important votes. The vote tabulator is ultimately responsible for determining that the correct number of votes has been submitted by each registered owner. . . .

5. Proxy Advisory Firms

Institutional investors typically own securities positions in a large number of issuers. . . . Some institutional investors may retain an investment adviser to manage their investments, and may also delegate proxy voting authority to that adviser. To assist them in their voting

---

[57] A single proxy service provider, Broadridge Financial Services, Inc. ("Broadridge"), states that it currently handles over 98% of the U.S. market for such proxy vote processing services. . . .

[60] See, e.g., *Del. Code Ann. tit. 8, § 231*; Model Bus. Corp. Act § 7.29.

decisions, . . . [they] frequently hire proxy advisory firms to provide analysis and voting recommendations on matters appearing on the proxy. . . . Some proxy advisory firms also provide consulting services to issuers on corporate governance or executive compensation matters, such as helping to develop an executive compensation proposal to be submitted for shareholder approval. Some proxy advisory firms may also qualitatively rate or score issuers, based on judgments about the issuer's governance structure, policies, and practices. . . .

A. Issuer Communications with Shareholders

1. Background

The first area of concern that we address arises out of the practice of holding securities in street name—that is, interposing securities intermediaries between issuers and the beneficial owners of their securities. This practice developed in order to facilitate the prompt and accurate processing of an increasingly large volume of securities transactions. . . .

[T]he enormous volume of transactions cleared and settled in the U.S., which currently involve transactions valued at over $1.48 quadrillion annually, requires a centralized netting facility (i.e., NSCC) and a depository (i.e., DTC) that facilitates book-entry settlement of securities transactions. . . .

In light of recent developments in corporate governance, including the elimination of the broker discretionary vote on uncontested elections of directors, commentators have claimed a greater need for issuers to be able to communicate with their shareholders. These commentators have argued that the number of contested issues in shareholder meetings has increased, that voting outcomes are under more pressure, and that, as a result, certain changes should be made to our rules in order to facilitate communications by issuers with their beneficial owners. More broadly, commentators have questioned whether the current system of share ownership and the Commission's communications and proxy rules adequately serve the needs of investors and issuers. . . .

To promote direct communication between issuers and their beneficial owners, we adopted rules in 1983 . . . to require broker-dealers and banks to provide issuers, at their request, with lists of the names and addresses of beneficial owners who did not object to having such information provided to issuers. These owners are often referred to as "non-objecting beneficial owners" or "NOBOs." When a beneficial owner objects to disclosure of its name and address to the issuer—often referred to as "objecting beneficial owners" or "OBOs"—the beneficial owner may be contacted only by the securities intermediary (or the intermediary's agent) with the customer relationship with the beneficial owner. According to one estimate, 70% to 80% of all public issuers' shares are held in street name, and 75% of those shares, or 52% to 60% of all shares, are held by OBOs. It is our understanding that some types of large institutional investors, such as mutual funds and retirement plans, often choose OBO status.[153] . . .

Issuers have indicated to the staff that the majority of their street name securities are held by OBOs through securities intermediaries, making it very difficult to determine the identity and holdings of their investors. Issuers believe that the recent changes in corporate governance, including the move to majority voting of directors, the elimination of broker discretionary voting in uncontested director elections, and a possible drop in retail voting percentages, call for more direct communication between issuers and their shareholders. These communications may include using a proxy solicitor to contact shareholders by telephone. However, an issuer cannot make these direct appeals for shareholders to participate in the issuer's corporate governance if it does not know the identity of those shareholders.

Issuers also have indicated to the staff that they face considerable expense in communicating with beneficial owners, either OBOs or NOBOs, indirectly through securities intermediaries or their agents. Issuers are required to reimburse securities intermediaries for expenses incurred in forwarding communications to beneficial owners. These expenses include reimbursement for postage, envelopes and communication expenses as well as fees to proxy service providers.

Some issuers have claimed that the expense of obtaining the list of NOBOs from the securities intermediary or its proxy service provider deters some issuers, particularly widely-held issuers, from using the NOBO list to communicate with beneficial owners. We have also received expressions of concern from broker-dealers about the difficulty of maintaining an accurate NOBO list when a class of securities is actively traded. . . .

———

NOTE ON BROKER'S DISCRETION TO VOTE CUSTOMER SHARES.

New York Stock Exchange rules regulate brokers in firms that are members of that exchange. Among the rules the NYSE applies to its members are those that regulate the voting of proxies (these rules apply even when the proxy is for a company that is not listed on the NYSE). The rules generally allow a broker to exercise discretionary voting authority on behalf of customers on all "routine" proxy proposals, provided the broker has not received specific voting instructions from the customer. In January 2012, the NYSE amended its Rule 452 to provide that the election of directors is not routine, i.e., the broker does not have discretionary authority to vote on a client's behalf in the election of directors. Also deemed not routine are various governance resolutions such as declassifying the board of directors,

---

[153] One recent report states that while "73% of retail shareholders are NOBOs, . . . [m]ost institutional shareholders—about 71%—are OBOs, accounting for about 91% of all institutionally held shares." SIFMA Report . . . [on the Shareholder Communication Process with Street Name Holders, and the NOBO-OBO Mechanism (June 10, 2010)] at 7.

majority voting, supermajority voting, and providing rights to call special stockholder meetings. Furthermore, the Dodd-Frank Wall Street Reform and Consumer Protection Act prohibits brokers exercising their discretion to vote on matters involving executive compensation, including say-on-pay-votes. These steps are widely seen as increasing the power of shareholders, particularly strengthening the position of institutional holders, who regularly vote, as contrasted with the too frequently slumbering retail investors whose shares could be voted by their brokers; the broker typically vote in favor of positions advocated by a firm's board.

Consider one adverse and unintended consequence of the changes to NYSE Rule 452. In the typical election, retail investor participation averages less than 30 percent whereas institutional participation averages slightly above 90 percent. Such passivity by retail investors has caused some companies not being able to undertake changes when their internal procedures require a super-majority vote. *See* Scott Hirst, Frozen Charters, 34 Yale J. on Reg. 91 (2017) (in the three years after the broker-voting change took effect, 54 of the 63 companies charter amendments failed despite receiving overwhelming shareholder support would have had their amendments pass had the 2012 broker-voting change not been implemented); Kobi Kastiel & Yaron Nili, In Search of the "Absent" Shareholders: A New Solution to Retail Investors' Apathy, 41 Del. J. Corp. L. 55, 62 (2016) (finding a dramatic increase in non-voted shares among S&P 500 firms following changes to NYSE Rule 452). A possible antidote is to permit a retail investor to give the broker a suite of standing voting instructions (SVIs) whereby brokers could vote a customer's shares pursuit to generic guidelines provided by the customer. Currently institutional investors can do this but retail customers cannot. What are the pros and cons of permitting SVIs for retail investors? *See generally,* Jill E. Fisch, Standing Voting Instructions: Empowering the Excluded Retail Investor, 102 Minn. L. Rev. 11 (2017).

———

NOTE ON CONSENTS AND WHO'S A RECORD HOLDER

The medium for shareholder voting is frequently the execution of written consents and not via the proxy or voting at the stockholders' meeting. Section 228(a) of the Delaware General Corporation Law expressly authorizes action by consent, unless the articles of incorporation provide otherwise. The action is deemed approved "if a consent or consents in writing setting forth the action so taken, shall be signed by the *holders* of outstanding stock having not less than the minimum number of votes that would be necessary to authorize or take such action at a meeting at which all shares entitled to vote thereon were present and voted" (emphasis added). Section 228(c) also provides that the consent must bear the signature of "each stockholder." See also MBCA § 7.04(b) (authorizing action without a meeting through consents executed by "*holders* of outstanding shares having not less than the minimum number of votes that would be required to authorize or take action at a meeting at which all shares entitled to vote on the action were present and voted") (emphasis added).

————

F. Balotti & J. Finkelstein, The Delaware Law of Corporations and Business Associations § 7.45

(3d ed. 2005 Supp.).

A 'stocklist' for most public corporations consists of far more than simply a list of stockholders with their addresses and numbers of shares. A stockholder with a proper purpose has a right to obtain subsidiary information available to the corporation including magnetic tape compilations, breakdowns of stockholdings by depository nominees, and (where appropriate) lists of beneficial owners of stock available to the issuer pursuant to [SEC] Rule 14b–1(c) (the 'NOBO list'). Similarly, a shareholder is ordinarily entitled to transfer sheets from the date of the list provided to him to the meeting date, expiration of the tender offer, or other relevant date.

However, the corporation is not required to manufacture such items for the convenience of the stockholder if the corporation does not already have access to them. In *R.B. Associates of New Jersey, L.P. v. The Gilette Co.,* [C.A. No. 9711 (Del.Ch. Mar.22, 1988)], a stockholder sought to require a corporation to obtain a NOBO list which it did not already have in its possession in order to produce it to the stockholder seeking inspection. The Court of Chancery held:

> Neither broad concepts of fairness, nor the words of Section 220, in my opinion, require that a corporation be forced, in each instance, to exercise the option created by the applicable SEC rules at the behest of a shareholder. What fairness does require, and what our opinions repeatedly return to, is the principle that relief in a Section 220 case should afford to a shareholder the same information as the corporation has in its books, records, and other papers.

————

C. REPORTING UNDER STATE LAW

———

MODEL BUS. CORP. ACT §§ 16.20

[See Statutory Supplement]

———

CAL. CORP. CODE § 1501

[See Statutory Supplement]

———

N.Y. BUS. CORP. LAW § 624(e)

[See Statutory Supplement]

———

An important aspect of ownership in any form of business is being informed regarding the company's financial performance and position. This information is collected in financial statements that are internally prepared periodically for the company's management to enable them to assess the firm's operations. Since this information is already in the firm's management's possession, arguably a company could without too much additional effort distribute the information, at least periodically, to shareholders. Hence, approximately half the states follow the Model Business Corporation Act § 16.20 and require that every corporation must furnish to its shareholders *annual* financial statements, including a balance sheet and an income statement. The statements must be prepared on the basis of generally accepted accounting principles (GAAP) if the corporation prepares its financial statements on that basis. About twenty states are less demanding. For example, N.J.Stat.Ann. § 14A:5–28, simply provides that a corporation must furnish "its balance sheet as at the end of the preceding fiscal year, and its profit and loss and surplus statements for such fiscal year" upon a shareholder's written request. Delaware is alone in having no provision mandating corporations to furnish financial statements to shareholders even on written request.

In considering the importance of requiring corporations periodically to disclose basic financial information to their shareholders, consider the plight of Jay Biederman, who was the former manager of Domo, Inc. a Delaware incorporated startup whose estimated market value in 2016 was about $2 billion. In January 2015 Biederman invoked his right under Section 220 of the Delaware statute to inspect financial statements for the purpose of determining the value of his shares. Delaware law has long held this is a proper purpose for accessing the financial records. After spending nearly $100,000 in legal fees litigating his right, Biederman did ultimately gain access to the desired records, albeit not until two years had lapsed since making his initial request. Rolfe Winkler, *Former Worker Wins Access Suit*, Wall St. J. at B5 (Jan. 27, 2017).

———

D. AN OVERVIEW OF THE SEC AND THE SECURITIES EXCHANGE ACT

SEC, The Investor's Advocate: How the SEC Protects Investors, Maintains Market Integrity, and Facilitates Capital Formation
(2010).

Introduction

The mission of the U.S. Securities and Exchange Commission is to protect investors, maintain fair, orderly, and efficient markets, and facilitate capital formation. . . .

The laws and rules that govern the securities industry in the United States derive from a simple and straightforward concept: all investors, whether large institutions or private individuals, should have access to certain basic facts about an investment prior to buying it, and so long as they hold it. To achieve this, the SEC requires public companies to disclose meaningful financial and other information to the public. This provides a common pool of knowledge for all investors to use to judge for themselves whether to buy, sell, or hold a particular security. Only through the steady flow of timely, comprehensive, and accurate information can people make sound investment decisions. . . .

The SEC oversees the key participants in the securities world, including securities exchanges, securities brokers and dealers, investment advisors, and mutual funds. Here the SEC is concerned primarily with promoting the disclosure of important market-related information, maintaining fair dealing, and protecting against fraud. . . .

Creation of the SEC

The SEC's foundation was laid in an era that was ripe for reform. Before the Great Crash of 1929, there was little support for federal regulation of the securities markets. . . .

When the stock market crashed in October 1929, public confidence in the markets plummeted. Investors large and small, as well as the banks who had loaned to them, lost great sums of money in the ensuing Great Depression. There was a consensus that for the economy to recover, the public's faith in the capital markets needed to be restored. Congress held hearings to identify the problems and search for solutions.

Based on the findings in these hearings, Congress—during the peak year of the Depression—passed the Securities Act of 1933. This law, together with the Securities Exchange Act of 1934, which created the SEC, was designed to restore investor confidence in our capital markets by providing investors and the markets with more reliable information and clear rules of honest dealing. . . .

Securities Exchange Act of 1934

With this Act, Congress created the Securities and Exchange Commission. The Act empowers the SEC with broad authority over all aspects of the securities industry. This includes the power to register, regulate, and oversee brokerage firms, transfer agents, and clearing agencies as well as the nation's securities self regulatory organizations (SROs). The various stock exchanges, such as the New York Stock Exchange, and American Stock Exchange are SROs. The Financial Industry Regulatory Authority . . . is also an SRO.

The Act also identifies and prohibits certain types of conduct in the markets and provides the Commission with disciplinary powers over regulated entities and persons associated with them.

The Act also empowers the SEC to require periodic reporting of information by companies with publicly traded securities.

Corporate Reporting

In contrast to the narrow to non-existent state disclosure requirements, a cornerstone of the Securities Exchange Act is the requirement for companies to file with the SEC, quarterly (Form 10-Q) and annually (Form 10-K), a broad range of financial and non-financial information (e.g., officer and director background, material conflict of interest transactions, and material developments). Certain events can also trigger the company to report the matter on Form 8-K. These requirement applies to companies listed on a national securities exchange or with more than $10 million in assets whose securities are held by 2000 or more record holders. These reports are available to the public through the SEC's EDGAR database. www.sec.gov.

Proxy Solicitations

The Securities Exchange Act also governs the disclosure in materials used to solicit shareholders' votes in annual or special meetings held for the election of directors and the approval of other corporate action. This information, contained in proxy materials, must be filed with the Commission in advance of any solicitation to ensure compliance with the disclosure rules. Solicitations, whether by management or shareholder groups, must disclose all important facts concerning the issues on which holders are asked to vote. . . .

———

SECURITIES EXCHANGE ACT § 12(a), (b), (g)

[See Statutory Supplement]

SECURITIES EXCHANGE ACT RULE 12g–1

[See Statutory Supplement]

E. PERIODIC DISCLOSURE UNDER THE SECURITIES EXCHANGE ACT

SECURITIES EXCHANGE ACT § 13(a)

[See Statutory Supplement]

SECURITIES EXCHANGE ACT RULES 13a–1, 13a–11, 13a–13

SECURITIES EXCHANGE ACT FORMS 8-K, 10-K, 10-Q

[See Statutory Supplement]

NOTE IN PERIODIC REPORTING BY REGISTERED CORPORATIONS

The Securities Exchange Act addresses the informational deficiencies in state law by imposing periodic-reporting requirements on corporations with a security registered under section 12. Section 13 of the Act, and the rules promulgated thereunder, require such corporations to file a Form 10-K annually, a Form 10-Q quarterly, and a Form 8-K generally within four business days after the occurrence of certain specified events. Among the matters that trigger an 8-K Report are a change in control of the corporation, the acquisition or disposition of a significant amount of assets, a change of accountants, the termination of a material definitive agreement, the departure of a director or principal officer (CEO, president, chief operating officer, chief financial officer, chief accounting officer, or any person performing similar functions), amendments to the articles or bylaws, amendments to the corporation's code of ethics, and waivers of a provision of the corporation's code of ethics. The Form 10-K must include audited financial statements; management's discussion of the corporation's financial condition and results of operations; and disclosure concerning legal proceedings, developments in the corporation's business, executive compensation, conflict-of-interest transactions, and other specified issues. The Form 10-Q must include quarterly financial data prepared in accordance with generally accepted accounting principles; a management report; and disclosures concerning legal proceedings, defaults on senior securities, and other specified issues. Periodic reporting is also required under the Proxy Rules in connection with the corporation's annual meeting.

The Exchange Act's reporting requirements are triggered if one of the following occurs: 1) per section 12(a) when the firm has a security that is listed on a national securities exchange such as the New York Stock Exchange or Nasdaq; or 2) per section 12(g) when the firm on the last day of its fiscal year has 2000 or more holders of record of a class of its security, has assets in excess of $10 million (this standard is set by rule 12g–1 and episodically adjusted), *and* is engaged in interstate commerce; or 3) per section 15(d) the firm has registered securities pursuant to a public offering of its securities and there are not less than 300 holders of that class of security.

In 2012, Congress enacted the Jumpstart Our Business Startups Act (JOBS Act) that among other provisions amended section 12(g) to increase from 500 to 2000 the holders of record criterion for an over-the-counter traded security to become a reporting company. A curious provision of the JOBS Act imposes reporting company status, even though the company has fewer than 2000 holders, if it has at least 500 holders who are non-accredited investors. SEC Rule 501(a) defines accredited investors and includes individuals with a net worth of $1 million (excluding personal residence) or whose annual income in the prior two years exceeded $200,000. In light of the material studied earlier in this section describing how shareholder records are maintained in an era when most shares are held in street name, how is a company whose shares are traded over-the-counter to determine whether it must register with the SEC? The disclosure required by the Securities Exchange Act's periodic reporting requirements is sometimes called *structured* disclosure, because what must be disclosed and how it must be disclosed is structured by the relevant SEC rules. Another example of structured disclosure is the disclosure required under the Securities Act when a corporation makes a public offering of its securities.

Of course, a corporation may make voluntary timely disclosure of material corporate developments even if not required to do so by law. Furthermore, the rules of the major stock exchanges often require listed corporations to make timely disclosure of material developments.

———

F. DISCLOSURE UNDER STOCK EXCHANGE RULES

———

NEW YORK STOCK EXCHANGE, LISTED COMPANY MANUAL §§ 202.01, 202.03, 202.05, 202.06

[See Statutory Supplement]

———

2. THE PROXY RULES: AN INTRODUCTION

This and the next two Sections concern the Proxy Rules, which are promulgated by the SEC. The following terms are important in considering these Rules:

Proxy holder. A person authorized to vote shares on a shareholder's behalf.

Proxy, form of proxy, or *proxy form.* The written instrument in which such an authorization is embodied. (The term proxy is also sometimes used to mean a proxy holder, but for purposes of clarity that usage will be avoided in this Chapter.)

Proxy solicitation. The process by which shareholders are asked to give their proxies.

Proxy statement. A written statement sent to shareholders as a means of proxy solicitation.

Proxy materials. The proxy statement and form of proxy.

————

SECURITIES EXCHANGE ACT § 14(a) & (c)

————

SECURITIES EXCHANGE ACT RULES 14a–1–14a–6, 14c–2, 14c–3, SCHEDULE 14A, SCHEDULE 14C

[See Statutory Supplement]

————

FORM OF PROXY

[See Statutory Supplement]

————

NOTES—AN OVERVIEW OF THE PROXY RULES

1. Background. Proxy voting is the dominant mode of shareholder decisionmaking in publicly held corporations. There are two basic reasons for this. First, shareholders in such corporations are often geographically dispersed, so that a given shareholder may not live near the site of the meeting. Second, a given shareholding will normally represent only a small fraction of a shareholder's total wealth. Accordingly, physical attendance at a shareholders' meeting is normally an uneconomical use of a shareholder's time when he can vote by proxy.

A natural outgrowth of the preference for proxy voting is proxy solicitation—the process of systematically contacting shareholders, and urging them to execute and return proxy forms that authorize named proxyholders to cast the shareholder's votes, either in a manner designated in the proxy form or according to the proxyholder's discretion.

Despite this state of affairs, as of the 1930's state law hardly regulated proxy voting, except in the extreme case in which proxies had been fraudulently solicited. Abuses were notorious and widespread. Accordingly, Congress entered the field in 1934 through Section 14(a) of the Securities Exchange Act. In itself, Section 14(a) has no effect on private conduct: its only effect was to authorize the SEC to promulgate rules that govern private conduct. Pursuant to Section 14(a), the SEC has promulgated a set of Proxy Rules that serve a variety of purposes.

2. *Format Requirements.* One purpose of the Proxy Rules is to regulate the form or presentation the ballot (proxy) itself. The proxy's format is addressed in Rules 14a–4 and 14a–5, calling for, among other requirements, that the proxy be clearly (in bold-face type no less) identified as a proxy, that there be a box for the proxy giver to express approval, disapproval or abstention with respect to *each* matter to be voted upon, that the proxy pertaining to the election of directors must provide a means for the proxy giver to withhold approval for voting for a nominee, that any request for discretionary authority to vote may be sought only with respect to matters the solicitor did not have notice of at least 45 days before the date the proxy materials were sent in the prior year's annual meeting, and that all written materials be at least 10-point roman type.

3. *Short-Slate Proxy.* Rule 14a–4(d), the so-called short-slate provision, facilitates efforts to oppose management's dominance of the election of directors. To understand this provision, assume management nominates a slate of five directors, A, B, C. D. and E and that a group of holders wish to support the efforts of Insurgent to place two individuals, X and Y, on the board. Assume further that Insurgent believes A and B should not serve on the board but has no objection to the election of C, D and E. Rule 14a–4(d) permits Insurgent's proxy materials to request proxies for X and Y as well as C, D and E. Such a solicitation by Insurgent is likely to be more attractive to shareholders than the pre-Rule 14a–4(d) SEC interpretation whereby the short-slate solicitor was permitted to request proxies only for his candidates, X and Y; under the former regulatory approach, shareholders legitimately believed that to be able to vote for X and Y they had to forsake voting to fill all five vacant seats. Moreover, if the shareholder returned both Insurgent's ballot and management's ballot by, for example, voting for X, Y, C, D and E, under applicable state law the later executed proxy prevails over the earlier granted proxy. Rule 14a–4(d) thus introduces a reasonable approach by which shareholders can "split" their votes.

4. *The "Universal Proxy."* In 2016, the SEC proposed the use of a "universal proxy" as a means to accommodate activist shareholders who advance a short slate of nominees. Absent a universal proxy only shareholders who attend the meeting can as a practical matter vote for nominees on both management and the dissident proxies. As a practical matter, a shareholder who does not attend the stockholder meeting is unable to vote for some management's nominees and vote for the nominees of the dissidents on the dissident's proxy. This is because under corporate law, if a

shareholder submits two different proxies, the most recently executed proxy is counted on the theory it revokes the earlier proxy. The dissident can try to overcome this feature by including on its proxy not only its nominees but also some of management's nominees so that solicited shareholders have a sense they are voting for the exact number of nominees as there are seats up for election. But the management nominees the dissident chooses to include may well not be the nominees the shareholder would have preferred among the larger set of management nominees. The universal proxy overcomes this problem. As proposed by the SEC, when there is a contested board election, the proxy used by management and the insurgent must include the names of *all* the nominees, those of management and those of the insurgent, so that shareholders can thereby choose among all the candidates rather than being forced into an all-or-nothing choice. Contestants, however, will have to direct shareholders to each other's proxy statements for information regarding the background of their respective candidates. In the face of strong opposition from company CEOs, who argued the universal proxy would prove disruptive, the SEC has not further pursued this topic.

5.   *Anti-Bundling.* One clever method to obtain approval of a matter likely not to be popular with shareholders (e.g., an antitakeover amendment provision) is to include within that proposal a provision that would be popular with stockholders (e.g., an enriching restructuring). The proxy rules go part way toward addressing the distorted choice that the bundling of unrelated resolutions can pose to shareholders. Rule 14a–4(b) requires separate voting on matters that are not "related." Management can, however, continue to condition separately voted-on proposals so that neither becomes effective without the approval of the other.

In its spring 2013 proxy statement, Apple included the following in a single proposal submitted to its shareholders:

> To amend the Apple articles of incorporation to (1) eliminate certain language relating to the terms of office of directors so as to facilitate the adoption of majority voting for the election of directors; (2) eliminate the board of directors authority without shareholder approval to issue preferred stock having superior rights over common; (3) establish a minimum par value for Apple's common shares; and (4) eliminate certain obsolete provisions in Apple's articles related to preferred shares.

Greenlight, a hedgefund, opposed the second item as it believed Apple should issue to its shareholders a new class of preferred stock with substantial dividend rights as a means for compelling Apple to significantly increase its overall dividends. It therefore sued to compel each of the four items to be separately presented to the stockholders. Among Apple's defenses was that shareholders were being asked to vote on a single issue-whether to amend its articles. This and other arguments raised by Apple were quickly dispensed with by the court and it granted a preliminary injunction of any shares on the bundled items. The district court concluded "the present bundling of items forces shareholders . . .to approve or disapprove a package of items and approve or disapprove matters they would not if presented separately." Even though the proposals in the whole can be seen as shareholder friendly, the court reasoned that the absence of coercion was not the only objective of the anti-bundling provision. The court observed that SEC has sought to allow shareholders to communicate their views to the board, which bundling of such disconnected items would frustrate. *Greenlight Capital, L.P. v. Apple, Inc.,* 2013 U.S. Dist. LEXIS 24716 *19–20 (S.D.N.Y. Feb. 22, 2013). *See also* Koppel v. 4987 Corp., 167 F.3d 125 (2d Cir. 1999) (question of fact whether single resolution seeking stockholder approval to waive a default in a lease of property to one of the firm's promoters, sell the leased property, and distribute the proceeds to shareholders were related matters).

Despite the anti-bundling rule and court decisions enforcing the rule, bundling continues to vex investors. *See* James D. Cox, Fabrizio Ferri, Colleen Honigsberg & Randall S. Thomas, Quieting the Shareholders' Voice: Empirical Evidence of Pervasive Bundling in Proxy Solicitations, 89 S. Cal. L. Rev 1175 (2016) (study of 1300 management proposal for amendments to articles or bylaws finding 28.8 percent were coupled with unrelated matters with 6.2 percent coupling a material negative value proposal with a material positive value proposal).

6.   *Mandated Disclosure.* One purpose of the Proxy Rules is to require full disclosure in connection with transactions that shareholders are being asked to approve, such as mergers, certificate amendments, or election of directors. This purpose is accomplished in the first instance by Rule 14a–3 and Schedule 14A. Rule 14a–3 provides that no solicitation of proxies that is subject to the Proxy Rules shall be made unless the person being solicited "is concurrently furnished or has previously been furnished with a written proxy statement containing the information specified in Schedule 14A." Schedule 14A details the information that must be furnished when specified types of transactions are to be acted upon by the shareholders. Rule 14a–3 and Schedule 14A are backed up by Rule 14a–9, examined later in this chapter, which provides that no solicitation subject to the Proxy Rules shall contain any statement that is false or misleading with respect to any material fact or omits a material fact.

When proxies for the election of directors are solicited on behalf of a corporation that is subject to the Proxy Rules, the corporation must send an Annual Report to its shareholders, either in advance of or concurrently with the proxy statement. The Annual Report compelled by Rule 14a–3 is not the same as the annual report on Form 10-K that reporting companies must file with the SEC, but nonetheless embodies the core information requirements found in Form 10-K *and* Rule 14a–3 requires companies when soliciting proxies to offer to provide the full Form 10-K. Disclosure has, however, moved into the digital age, thus saving many a tree from the pulp mill. Rule 14a–16 permits issuers to satisfy the proxy statement delivery requirement by providing shareholders with the website where the materials are available, at no cost; the rule also requires companies to provide via first-class mail paper copies of the materials if requested by a shareholder.

As seen above, the contents of the Annual Report to shareholders are governed by Rule 14a–3. The Report must include, among other things, the corporation's financial statements, selected financial data, and management's discussion and analysis (commonly referred to as the "MD & A") of the corporation's financial condition and results of operations. Either the Annual Report or the Proxy Statement must prominently feature an undertaking to furnish a copy of the Form 10-K to any shareholder, without charge, upon written request.

To encourage informality and directness in the Annual Report to shareholders, Rule 14a–3(c) provides that the Report is not to be deemed either soliciting material within the Proxy Rules or a "filing" under Securities Exchange Act § 18 (which expressly provides civil liability for misrepresentations appearing in reports "filed" with the SEC). Any material misrepresentations in proxy materials can, however, be addressed under Rule 14a–9, or even Rule 10b–5, discussed later.

Consider for a moment the relevance to shareholders of some of the items that Rule 14a–3 requires to be disclosed in the annual report. Much of this disclosure is only very loosely related to any specific action the shareholders are asked to vote upon. For example, Rule 14a–3 provides that the proxy statement for an annual meeting at which directors are to be elected must be accompanied by an annual report that includes audited balance sheets for each of the corporation's two most recent fiscal years, audited income statements for its three most recent fiscal years, and certain other information. Under Items 7 and 8 of Schedule 14A, the proxy statement for an annual meeting at which directors are being elected must disclose the compensation of the five most highly paid executives and the executive officers as a group (including not only salary, but bonuses, deferred compensation, stock options, and the like), and disclosure of significant conflict-of-interest transactions during the corporation's last fiscal year involving, among others, directors, executive officers, and five percent beneficial owners. Under Item 7, the proxy statement for such a meeting must also disclose a good deal of information regarding the corporation's audit, nominating, and compensation committees such as the number of meetings each committee held during the last fiscal year and the functions it performs.

Finally, if a corporation's stock is registered under section 12, and the corporation proposes to take an action that requires shareholder approval, or to hold an annual meeting at which directors are to be elected, then even if the corporation is not soliciting proxies it must distribute essentially the same information that would be required if it was soliciting proxies. See § 14(c), Regulation 14C, and Schedule 14C. This set of rules has its principal bite where the corporation has a controlling shareholder who can take actions at the shareholder level without soliciting proxies.

7.   *Filing with SEC.* Rule 14a–6 governs the filing of proxy materials with the SEC. In broad overview, the preliminary proxy statement and the ballot ("form of proxy") must be filed with the SEC 10 days before the definitive copies of these materials are expected to be sent or given to shareholders. The prefiling provides the SEC with time to review the materials should it wish. The filed materials become immediately available and can be used in solicitations, although the actual circulation of the ballot must await the filing of the definitive proxy statement. Thus, the proxy

solicitation customarily begins with the preliminary filing followed later by the circulation of the ballot when the definitive proxy statement is filed with the SEC. There are two broad notable dispensations to the above filing requirements. First, per Rule 14a–12, the prefiling requirement pertains to the proxy statement and ballot; thus, oral and *other* written communications, regardless of the subject matter of the solicitation, are permitted, provided the written solicitation materials are filed with the SEC, the solicitors are identified, the communication bears a legend advising that the proxy statement should be read when it is available (and disclosing that the statement can be obtained when available for free from the SEC's website), and a proxy statement is sent to solicited security holder when it is available. Second, no *preliminary* filing is required for solicitations in connection with a meeting if the *only* action to be taken is the election of directors, approval of the auditor, voting on a shareholder proposal pursuant to Rule 14a–8, *infra*, or ratification of certain executive compensation proposals; in these instances it is sufficient that the proxy statement and form of proxy are filed at least contemporaneous with their use. *See e.g.*, Shoen v. AMERCO, 885 F.Supp. 1332, 1346 (D. Nev. 1994) (management's communication to stockholders in opposition to a shareholder proposal made under Rule 14a–8 was not exempt since the shareholder-proponent intended to introduce at the meeting other matters that were not circulated to the shareholders pursuant to Rule 14a–8).

    8.   *The Scope of "Proxy Solicitation."* Rule 14a–2 provides that the Proxy Rules "apply to every solicitation of a proxy with respect to securities registered pursuant to section 12 of the Act," subject to certain exceptions described below. The definitions of "proxy" and "solicitation" are extremely broad. Under Rule 14a–1(f), the term "proxy" means "every proxy, consent, or authorization within the meaning of section 14(a) of the Act. The consent or authorization may take the form of failure to object or to dissent." Under Rule 14a–1(*l*)(1), the term "solicitation" includes "(i) [a]ny request for a proxy . . . ; (ii) [a]ny request to execute or not to execute, or to revoke, a proxy; or (iii) [t]he furnishing of a form of proxy or other communication to security holders under circumstances reasonably calculated to result in the procurement, withholding or revocation of a proxy."

    This language has been given a very expansive interpretation. For example, in *Studebaker Corp. v. Gittlin*, 360 F.2d 692 (2d Cir.1966), Gittlin, a shareholder in Studebaker, had solicited authorizations from other Studebaker shareholders to inspect Studebaker's stockholder list for the purpose of meeting the five percent test under the relevant New York inspection statute. Judge Friendly stated:

        . . . The assistant general counsel of the SEC . . . stated at the argument that the Commission believes § 14(a) should be construed, in all its literal breadth, to include authorizations to inspect stockholders lists, even in cases where obtaining the authorizations was not a step in a planned solicitation of proxies.

        We need not go that far to uphold the order of the district court. In SEC v. Okin, 132 F.2d 784 (2d Cir.1943), this court ruled that a letter which did not request the giving of any authorization was subject to the Proxy Rules if it was part of "a continuous plan" intended to end in solicitation and to prepare the way for success. This was the avowed purpose of Gittlin's demand for inspection of the stockholders list. . . .

Id. at 695–96.

The full breadth of the above *Gitlin-Okin* formulation was captured in *Long Island Lighting Co. v. Barbash*, 779 F.2d 793 (2d Cir. 1985), where the court ruled that despite the First Amendment the proxy rules could reach a newspaper advertisement placed by individuals who were unrelated to one of the proxy contest combatants. The advertisement chastised the current LILCO management and called for converting the Long Island utility to public ownership. Management successfully sought to enjoin the advertisement for violating various proxy rule requirements, pointing to the fact LILCO was then engaged in a proxy contest with a local politician who had raised similar issues as those raised in the advertisement although there was no connection between the ad's sponsor and no mention whatever in the ad of the on-going proxy contest. Communications supportive of a position of one side that occur during or close proximity of a proxy solicitation are more easily drawn into the regulatory purview of proxy rules. *See* Shoen v. AMERCO, 885 F.Supp. 1332 (D. Nev. 1994) (newsletter and flyer supportive of company's management that was distributed to holders of ESOP by the plan's trustees three weeks before management began its proxy solicitation deemed a proxy solicitation); Capital Real Estate Investors Tax Exempt Fund Ltd. Partnership v. Schwartzberg, 929 F.Supp. 105, 113 (S.D.N.Y. 1996) (management press releases extolling benefits of merger would not be proxy solicitation if they were "purely factual" description of the transaction; however, the challenged release was viewed as preconditioning shareholders toward a favorable view of the transaction and accordingly deemed a proxy).

There are notable exemptions. Perhaps the most significant exemption is Rule 14a–1(*l*)(2) that lists several acts that are excluded, most significantly, (iv) authorizes instances in which it does not constitute a solicitation for *the security holder* to announce his intent to vote in a certain manner. This provision greatly facilitates "just say no" campaigns institutions have waged from time-to-time to express disapproval of incumbent management's policies; relying on this rule, activist financial institutions can publicize their decisions to withhold their votes for some or all the directors standing for election in the expectation the announcement will influence others. *See* Joseph A. Grundfest, Just Vote No: A Minimalist Strategy for Dealing with Barbarians Inside the Gages, 45 Stan. L. Rev. 857 (1993) (withholding votes for some directors is a low cost, and one of the few effective, means by which institutional holders can effectively manifest displeasure with the long-term strategies they believe are deficient); Diane Del Guercio, Laura Seery & Tracie Woidtke, Do Boards Pay Attention When Institutional Investor Activists "Just Vote No"?, 90 J. Fin. Econ. 84 (2008) (finding significant correlation between such campaigns and CEO turnover accompanied by subsequent operating and stock price improvements).

Another useful exemption is provided in Rule 14a–2(b)(2) which excludes from most (but not the anti-misrepresentation rule in Rule 14a–9) proxy requirements a security holder's communication directed to ten or fewer persons.

Rule 14a–2(b)(1) exempts from the filing and delivery requirements a communication by any person "who does not, at any time during such solicitation, seek directly or indirectly, . . . the power to act as proxy for a security holder and does not furnish or otherwise request" a form of proxy. For example, financial institutions may confer among themselves and with their third-party advisor how they can individually vote their shares. The exemption is not available to ten categories of persons, such as the company, its management, or a group whose ownership exceeds five percent and has not professed a lack of interest in control of the company. *See e.g.,* MONY Group v. Highfields Capital, 368 F.3d 138 (2d Cir. 2004) (institutional investor outside the exemption when, in opposition to management's solicitation, it sent a blank duplicate of management's ballot with its letter opposing the matter). The breadth of Rule 14a–2(b)(1) has always been a matter of some doubt. In adopting the provision, the SEC observed it feared that without this exemption "every expression of opinion concerning a publicly-traded corporation . . . would [due to the breadth of "proxy" and "solicitation" as defined in its rules] raise serious questions under the [F]ree [S]peech [C]lause of the First Amendment."

Rule 14a–2(b)(1) clearly reaches recommendations that proxy advisors provide their clients. But, as illustrated by *Gas Natural, Inc. v. Osborne*, 2015 U.S. App. LEXIS 15277 (Sixth Cir. Aug. 27, 2015), it is a good deal broader than that. Osborne had been terminated as Gas Natural's CEO, and removed from its slate of nominees for the upcoming annual board election. Three weeks before the stockholder meeting, Osborne wrote to the shareholders criticizing Gas Natural's management and "ask[ed] for [the shareholders'] help in running these greedy individuals out of our company." In subsequent communications he referred to the directors and officers as Nazis, claimed the company was broke, and criticized the decision to rehire its former chief operating officer. Contemporaneous with his initial letter, he requested a list of the stockholders as well as the NOBO list, stating he wished the lists "so I can solicit their support to be reinstated to the Board." He later testified he wanted "to put forward a slate of [directors] who would be supportive of his views." However, he never put forth such a slate and did not directly or indirectly seek the power to act as proxy for any shareholder. The district court, on the strength of *Okin*, granted a permanent injunction against Osborne for not complying with the filing and delivery requirements of the proxy rules. The Sixth Circuit reversed, holding the communication fell within Rule 14a–(2)(b)(1); the panel believed Osborne did request "shareholders to withhold or revoke proxies for the" upcoming meeting. However, Osborne did not request authority to act as a proxy. As such, the communications fell squarely within the scope of the exemption which excludes communications that does not request the shareholders to execute proxies, does not request authority to act as proxy for any shareholder, and that does not include a proxy form. Furthermore, the Sixth Circuit found that none of the enumerated exceptions to the exemption applied.

9. Chat Rooms. Through Rule 14a–17 the SEC encourages companies and others to establish Internet-based shareholder forums where shareholders can communicate among themselves and with management on matters related to the company. However, a communication made through such a forum whose substantive content is a solicitation must comply with the proxy filing and disclosure requirements if the communication is within 60 days of the shareholder meeting date.

3. THE PROXY RULES: SHAREHOLDER ACCESS

A. THE DISSIDENT'S ACCESS PROVISION: RULE 14a–7

SECURITIES EXCHANGE ACT RULE 14a–7

[See Statutory Supplement]

The proxy rules from time-to-time address more than disclosure. One such instance is Rule 14a–7 which provides a means for a shareholder who wishes to solicit proxies to gain access to her fellow stockholders. This provision requires that the company shall in response to a request by a record or beneficial holder either provide a list of stockholders or circulate the requesting holder's materials. Rule 14a–7 only applies if the company has or intends itself to engage in a proxy solicitation and the company (except in the narrow instance involving so-called roll-up transactions) has the option of either providing the list or mailing the requesting security holder's materials. If the latter option is chosen by the company, the requesting security holder must provide the required postage and sufficient copies of the materials to be forwarded. Which option do you believe the company will prefer?

B. SHAREHOLDER PROPOSALS UNDER RULE 14a–8

Rule 14a–8 permits a shareholder initiated proposal to be included on management's proxy statement, provided the proposing shareholder has been a beneficial owner[1] of one percent or $2,000 of the company's voting shares for at least one year. Rule 14a–8(i) sets forth several grounds upon

---

[1] SEC Staff Legal Bulletin No. 14(F) (Oct. 18, 2011) addresses what is required to establish that a proponent is the beneficial owner. As seen earlier, most shares are held in street name so that the beneficial owner's name does not appear among the list of owners on DTC's records. When this occurs a shareholder seeking to prove eligibility must submit a statement of ownership from the broker or bank in whose name the shares are registered on DTC's records. The SEC also addresses the rare situation where the customer's dealings have been through a broker who is not a participant in DTC.

which the company is permitted to exclude a proposal from its proxy statement, such as that the proposal is not a proper subject for shareholder action under state law or deals with a matter relating to the company's ordinary business.

––––––

SECURITIES EXCHANGE ACT RULE 14a–8

[See Statutory Supplement]

––––––

NOTE ON NO-ACTION LETTERS INTERPRETING RULE 14a-8

Rule 14a–8 provides that if management believes a shareholder proposal may properly be excluded from the corporation's proxy statement under Rule 14a–8, it must submit to the SEC staff a statement of the reasons why it deems omission of the proposal to be proper. If the staff agrees with management's statement, it sends management a "no-action letter"—that is, a letter stating that if the shareholder proposal is omitted, no action will be taken by the SEC. If the staff disagrees with management's statement, its letter briefly states its disagreement with the issuer's opinion that the proposal can be omitted. Such letters are referred to as no-action letters, although in the case where the SEC disagrees with management's conclusion that the proposal can be omitted no-action is a misnomer; the SEC's staff's disagreement is a clear statement that if the company omits the proposal this could lead to an SEC enforcement action. In such cases management may still omit the shareholder proposal, and run the risk of legal proceedings by the SEC, but this option is seldom pursued. It is important to understand that no-action letters are opinions of the staff of the SEC, and not the commissioners. As such, no-action letters are not reviewable "orders" of an agency under the Administrative Procedure Act. Board of Trade of the City of Chicago v. SEC, 883 F.2d 525 (7th Cir. 1989).

––––––

SEC Staff Legal Bulletin 14H addresses how to interpret Rule 14a–8(i)(9), which provides a proposal is excludable if it directly conflicts with one of the company's own proposals to be submitted to the shareholders at the same meeting. Under the test set forth in the Bulletin a conflict exists if the reasonable shareholder could not logically vote in favor of both proposals. How should the SEC rule if the shareholder proposes that the CEO cannot also be the board chair and the board is proposing the board chair should be the CEO? What if the shareholder proposal is that a holder or holders of 3 percent of the voting stock can nominate up to 3 members of the board of directors in opposition of management's bylaw proposal that limits any shareholder nomination of directors to a holder or holders of 5 percent of the company's voting shares?

––––––

On the overall efficacy of the shareholder proposal rule, consider the following:

Gibson Dunn, Shareholder Proposal Developments

During the 2018 Proxy Season (July 12, 2018).

A. Overview of Shareholder Proposals Submitted

Shareholders submitted 788 proposals during the 2018 proxy season, down 5% from 827 in 2017 and down 14% from 916 in 2016.

Across four broad categories[3] of shareholder proposals in 2018— social and environmental, governance, corporate civic engagement, and executive compensation—social and environmental proposals continued to be the most frequently submitted proposals (representing 43% of all proposals submitted), followed by governance proposals (36%), corporate civic engagement proposals (12%), executive compensation proposals (7%), and other proposals (2%). Key year-over-year trends in these categories include:

Social and environmental proposals

- **Social proposals.** The number of social proposals submitted during the 2018 proxy season increased slightly to 202 (compared to 201 in 2017). The largest sub-category, representing 34% of these proposals, continued to be anti-discrimination and diversity-related proposals, with 68 submitted in 2018 (down from 69 in 2017).

---

[3] Categorizing shareholder proposals can, at times, be a subjective endeavor. We categorize shareholder proposals based on subject matter as follows:

Social proposals cover a wide range of issues and include proposals relating to: (i) discrimination and other diversity-related issues (including board diversity); (ii) the gender/ethnicity pay gap; (iii) board committees on human rights; (iv) social and environmental qualifications for director nominees; (v) reporting on societal concerns, such as dissemination of misinformation ("fake news") and gun safety; and (vi) reporting on drug pricing increases.

Environmental proposals include proposals addressing: (i) climate change (including climate change reporting, greenhouse gas emissions goals, climate change risks, and public policy advocacy on climate change); (ii) recycling; (iii) renewable energy; (iv) hydraulic fracturing; and (v) sustainability reporting.

Governance proposals include proposals addressing: (i) shareholder special meeting rights; (ii) proxy access; (iii) majority voting for director elections; (iv) independent board chairman; (v) declassifying the board of directors; (vi) shareholder written consent; (vii) eliminate/reduce supermajority voting; (viii) director term limits; and (ix) stock ownership guidelines.

Corporate civic engagement proposals include proposals addressing: (i) political contributions disclosure; (ii) lobbying policies and practices disclosure; and (iii) support for charitable organizations.

Executive compensation proposals include proposals addressing: (i) compensation clawback policies; (ii) performance metrics; (iii) severance and change of control payments; (iv) equity award vesting; (v) executive compensation disclosure; and (vi) limitations on executive compensation.

- **Environmental proposals.** Environmental proposals remained popular during the 2018 proxy season, with 139 proposals submitted (down from 144 in 2017). The largest sub-category, representing 52% of these proposals, continued to be climate change proposals, with 72 submitted in 2018 (up from 69 in 2017).

- **Governance proposals.** The number of governance proposals submitted during the 2018 proxy season declined slightly to 281 (compared to 288 in 2017). The largest sub-category, representing 27% of these proposals, was shareholder special meeting rights proposals, with 75 submitted (up significantly from 26 in 2017). This reflects a shift in focus from 2017, when proxy access was the largest sub-category of these proposals.

- **Corporate civic engagement proposals.** The number of corporate civic engagement proposals submitted during the 2018 proxy season decreased to 92 (compared to 111 in 2017). The largest sub-category, representing 92% of these proposals, continued to be political contributions and lobbying expenditures, with 85 submitted in 2018 (compared to 87 in 2017).

- **Executive compensation proposals.** The number of executive compensation proposals submitted during the 2018 proxy season increased slightly to 55 (compared to 48 in 2017). The largest sub-category, representing 36% of these proposals, was proposals seeking to include social or environmental-focused performance measures (including, among other things, diversity, cybersecurity, data privacy and risks arising from drug pricing) in executive compensation, with 20 submitted in 2018 (compared to 10 in 2017). . . .

In terms of who submitted proposals, there were 224 different proponents this year, up from 187 proponents last year. Combined with the fact that fewer proposals were submitted this year versus last, this means that, on average, individual proponents submitted fewer proposals. . . . Proponents that have submitted (or co-filed) at least 20 proposals this year include:

Top Proponents by Number Submitted		
Proponent	**#**	**Primary focus areas**
John Chevedden & associates	187	Governance & executive compensation
New York State Common Retirement Fund	48	Political, diversity & environmental

Trillium Asset Management	35	Environmental
Zevin Asset Management	29	Political, diversity & environmental
As You Sow Foundation	28	Environmental
Walden Asset Management	26	Political & diversity
Mercy Investment Services	23	Political, diversity & environmental

B. Overview of Shareholder Proposal Outcomes

The table below shows the outcomes of the 788 shareholder proposals submitted during the 2018 proxy season (as compared to the 827 proposals submitted in 2017). One of the big trends this year was the significant increase in the number of proposals that were withdrawn, which now almost equals the number of proposals that were excluded.

Shareholder Proposal Outcomes

	2018	2017
Excluded pursuant to a no-action request	16% (125)	23% (189)
Withdrawn by the proponent	15% (116)	9% (77)
Went to a vote	41% (325)	40% (331)
Pending a vote	19% (153)	28% (234)

Shareholder proposals voted on during the 2018 proxy season averaged support of 32.7%, up from 29.0% in 2017. The proposals that received the highest support, including two categories of proposals that averaged majority support, were:

Top Proposals by Voting Results

Proposal	2018	2017
Eliminate/reduce supermajority voting	74.7% (8)	64.3% (7)
Majority voting in director elections	59.9% (2)	62.3% (7)
Shareholder action by written consent	41.8% (33)	45.6% (12)
Shareholder special meeting rights	41.2% (51)	42.9% (15)
Climate change	32.8% (20)	32.6% (28)
Political contributions & lobbying	29.5% (45)	27.8% (20)

Overall, 10.2% of shareholder proposals voted on during the 2018 proxy season received majority support, compared to 10.9% of proposals the prior year. . . .

III. SHAREHOLDER PROPOSAL NO-ACTION REQUESTS

A. Overview of No-Action Requests

During the 2018 proxy season, companies submitted 256 no-action requests to the Staff, down 11% from 288 in 2017. This year, the Staff granted 64% of no-action requests, a substantial decrease from 78% in 2017 and the lowest level since 2015. At the same time, the number of withdrawn no-action requests increased by 25% to 52, the highest level since 2015. The table below summarizes the Staff's no-action request responses during the 2018 and 2017 proxy seasons.

No-Action Request Statistics		
	2018	**2017**
Total no-action requests submitted	256	288
No-action requests withdrawn	52	41
Pending no-action requests	10	5
Staff responses	194	242
Exclusions granted	125 (64%)	189 (78%)
Exclusions denied	69 (36%)	53 (22%)

The most common grounds for the Staff to grant no-action requests in 2018 were ordinary business and substantial implementation, each representing 33% of successful requests, and procedural grounds, representing 15% of successful requests.

———

NOTE ON "SETTLEMENTS" OF SHAREHOLDER PROPOSALS

Over the past few decades there has been not only a rise in the number of social and environmental proposals but a significant increase in the number of those proposals ultimately are withdrawn because of a settlement reached between the proponent and the company. Bauer, et. al., Who Withdraws Shareholder Proposals and Does it Matter? An Analysis of Sponsor identity and Pay Practices, 23 Corp. Governance 472, 477 tbl. 1 (2015). Such settlements typically take the form of a memorandum of understanding that sets forth what the company has agreed to do in exchange for the proposal's withdrawal; the settlements are private, not public documents, being neither published by the company nor circulated among its stockholders.

> Settlement agreements on corporate campaign finance disclosure have become commonplace at large, publicly held U.S. companies. The CPA [Center of Political Accountability, a nonprofit that has taken a leading role in coordinating shareholder activism on campaign finance disclosures] has reported the existence of 141 agreements that set political spending and campaign finance disclosure practices at a major U.S. company; ISS reported that at

least eleven proposals on political spending disclosure were withdrawn at U.S. companies in 2014. That year was the most successful year yet for political spending proposals that reached a shareholder vote. . . . Perhaps in reaction to this success, in 2015, at least twenty public companies were reported to settle proposals on campaign finance disclosure. Thus, in the two years from 2014 to 2015, at least thirty-one proposal settlements set campaign finance disclosure standards at U.S. public companies.

Sarah C. Haan, Shareholder Proposal Settlements and the Private Ordering of Private Elections, 126 Yale L. J. 262, 284–85 (2016). Are such settlements a win-win situation for the proponent and the company?

————

C. SHAREHOLDER ACCESS TO THE NOMINATING PROCESS

Directors customarily are nominated by the board of directors, usually through a nominating committee. The nominees thereafter appear on the company's proxy statement circulated among the stockholders. A shareholders who wishes to effect change in the board' composition may advance his own nominees and undertake a proxy contest to win votes for the insurgent slate, This would entail a substantial expenditure by the disgruntled shareholders to prepare and circulate their own proxies; waiting until the stockholders meeting to advance one's own nominees is too late since by that time the company will have obtained proxies supporting its slate and most likely there will be too few shareholders at the meeting to change the tide that management has created with its earlier proxy solicitations. Thus, activist shareholders have long sought some means to gain even limited access to the nomination process, believing this would be the most direct and effective method of empowering shareholders who seek to influence the direction of the firm Not surprisingly, much of the business community and their attorneys oppose shareholder access to the nominating process. They believe that shareholder access has the potential to turn every election into a contest, that such contests would prove expensive and would discourage qualified candidates from agreeing to be on the company's slate. They also fear that boards could become "Balkanized" with directors nominated by shareholders tending to represent "special interests" and overall weaken the cohesiveness of the board.

In the past few years there have been several developments that have moved toward empowering shareholders with limited access to the process of nominating directors:

Delaware and the Model Act now authorize bylaw provisions that authorized procedures for stockholders to nominate directors as well as bylaws authorizing reimbursement of insurgent proxy expenses. See Del. Code Ann. tit. 8 § 112; MBCA § 2.06.

The SEC has amended Rule 14a–8(i)(8) to expressly allow shareholders to make proposals to broaden (but not narrow) proxy access as provided in Rule 14a–11.

In July 2010, Congress passed the sweeping financial reform legislation, The Dodd-Frank Wall Street Reform and Consumer Protection Act amended section 14(a) of the Exchange Act to expressly authorize the SEC to adopt rules providing for shareholders to nominate directors to the boards of reporting companies.

Swiftly following the enactment of Dodd-Frank, the SEC adopted Rule 14a–11. However, *Business Roundtable v. Securities and Exchange Commission*, 647 F.3d 1144 (D.C. Cir. 2011), invalidated Rule 14a–11, holding that the SEC acted arbitrarily and capriciously in adopting it. The D.C. Circuit reasoned the SEC failed to fulfill the statutory review standard when considering the impact of Rule 14a–11 on efficiency, competition, and capital formation, *Business Roundtable* summarized the SEC's faults as follows:

Here the Commission inconsistently and opportunistically framed the costs and benefits of the rule; failed adequately to quantify the certain costs or to explain why those costs could not be quantified; neglected to support its predictive judgments; contradicted itself; and failed to respond to substantial problems raised by commenters.

647 F.3d at 1148–49.

———

4. MATERIALLY MISLEADING PROXIES AND RULE 14a–9

———

SECURITIES EXCHANGE ACT RULE 14a–9

[See Statutory Supplement]

———

NOTE ON J.I. CASE CO. V. BORAK

In *J.I. Case Co. v. Borak,* 377 U.S. 426, 84 S.Ct. 1555, 12 L.Ed.2d 423 (1964), the Supreme Court held that a shareholder could bring a private action for violation of the Proxy Rules, although neither the 1934 Act nor the Proxy Rules themselves explicitly provide for such an action. The rationale in *Borak* was as follows:

... Private enforcement of the proxy rules provides a necessary supplement to Commission action. As in antitrust treble damage litigation, the possibility of civil damages or injunctive relief serves as a most effective weapon in the enforcement of the proxy requirements. The Commission advises that it examines over 2,000 proxy statements annually and each of them must necessarily be expedited. Time does not permit an independent examination of the facts set out in the proxy material and this results in the Commission's acceptance of the representations contained therein at their face value, unless contrary to other material on file with it. Indeed, on the allegations of respondent's complaint, the proxy material failed to disclose alleged unlawful market manipulation of the stock of ATC, and this unlawful manipulation would not have been apparent to the Commission until after the merger.

We, therefore, believe that under the circumstances here it is the duty of the courts to be alert to provide such remedies as are necessary to make effective the congressional purpose.

Id. at 432–33, 84 S.Ct. at 1560.

———

Cort v. Ash

422 U.S. 66, 95 S.Ct. 2080, 45 L.Ed.2d 26 (1975)

"In determining whether a private remedy is implicit in a statute not expressly providing one, several factors are relevant. First, is the plaintiff 'one of the class for whose *especial* benefit the statute was enacted,' Texas & Pacific R. Co. v. Rigsby, 241 U.S. 33, 39, 36 S.Ct. 482, 484, 60 L.Ed. 874 (1916) (emphasis supplied)—that is, does the statute create a federal right in favor of the plaintiff? Second, is there any indication of legislative intent, explicit or implicit, either to create such a remedy or to deny one? . . . Third, is it consistent with the underlying purposes of the legislative scheme to imply such a remedy for the plaintiff? . . . And finally, is the cause of action one traditionally relegated to state law, in an area basically the concern of the States, so that it would be inappropriate to infer a cause of action based solely on federal law?"

———

Mills v. Electric Auto-Lite Co.

Supreme Court of the United States, 1970.
396 U.S. 375, 90 S.Ct. 616, 24 L.Ed.2d 593.

■ MR. JUSTICE HARLAN delivered the opinion of the Court.

This case requires us to consider a basic aspect of the implied private right of action for violation of § 14(a) of the Securities Exchange Act of 1934,[1] recognized by this Court in J.I. Case Co. v. Borak, 377 U.S. 426, 84 S.Ct. 1555, 12 L.Ed.2d 423 (1964). As in *Borak* the asserted wrong is that a corporate merger was accomplished through the use of a proxy statement that was materially false or misleading. The question with

---

[1]   48 Stat. 895, as amended, 15 U.S.C. § 78n(a).

which we deal is what causal relationship must be shown between such a statement and the merger to establish a cause of action based on the violation of the Act.

I

Petitioners were shareholders of the Electric Auto-Lite Company until 1963, when it was merged into Mergenthaler Linotype Company. They brought suit on the day before the shareholders' meeting at which the vote was to take place on the merger, against Auto-Lite, Mergenthaler, and a third company, American Manufacturing Company, Inc. The complaint sought an injunction against the voting by Auto-Lite's management of all proxies obtained by means of an allegedly misleading proxy solicitation; however, it did not seek a temporary restraining order, and the voting went ahead as scheduled the following day. Several months later petitioners filed an amended complaint, seeking to have the merger set aside and to obtain such other relief as might be proper.

In Count II of the amended complaint, which is the only count before us,[5] petitioners predicated jurisdiction on § 27 of the 1934 Act, 15 U.S.C. § 78aa. They alleged that the proxy statement sent out by the Auto-Lite management to solicit shareholders' votes in favor of the merger was misleading, in violation of § 14(a) of the Act and SEC Rule 14a–9 thereunder. (17 CFR § 240.14a–9.) Petitioners recited that before the merger Mergenthaler owned over 50% of the outstanding shares of Auto-Lite common stock, and had been in control of Auto-Lite for two years. American Manufacturing in turn owned about one-third of the outstanding shares of Mergenthaler, and for two years had been in voting control of Mergenthaler and, through it, of Auto-Lite. Petitioners charged that in light of these circumstances the proxy statement was misleading in that it told Auto-Lite shareholders that their board of directors recommended approval of the merger without also informing them that all 11 of Auto-Lite's directors were nominees of Mergenthaler and were under the "control and domination of Mergenthaler." Petitioners asserted the right to complain of this alleged violation both derivatively on behalf of Auto-Lite and as representatives of the class of all its minority shareholders.

On petitioners' motion for summary judgment with respect to Count II, the District Court for the Northern District of Illinois ruled as a matter of law that the claimed defect in the proxy statement was, in light of the circumstances in which the statement was made, a material omission. The District Court concluded, from its reading of the *Borak* opinion, that it had to hold a hearing on the issue whether there was "a causal connection between the finding that there has been a violation of the disclosure requirements of § 14(a) and the alleged injury to the plaintiffs"

---

[5]   In the other two counts, petitioners alleged common-law fraud and that the merger was *ultra vires* under Ohio law.

before it could consider what remedies would be appropriate. (Unreported opinion dated February 14, 1966.)

After holding such a hearing, the court found that under the terms of the merger agreement, an affirmative vote of two-thirds of the Auto-Lite shares was required for approval of the merger, and that the respondent companies owned and controlled about 54% of the outstanding shares. Therefore, to obtain authorization of the merger, respondents had to secure the approval of a substantial number of the minority shareholders. At the stockholders' meeting, approximately 950,000 shares, out of 1,160,000 shares outstanding, were voted in favor of the merger. This included 317,000 votes obtained by proxy from the minority shareholders, votes that were "necessary and indispensable to the approval of the merger." The District Court concluded that a causal relationship had thus been shown, and it granted an interlocutory judgment in favor of petitioners on the issue of liability, referring the case to a master for consideration of appropriate relief. (Unreported findings and conclusions dated Sept. 26, 1967; opinion reported at 281 F.Supp. 826 (1967)).

The District Court made the certification required by 28 U.S.C. § 1292(b), and respondents took an interlocutory appeal to the Court of Appeals for the Seventh Circuit. That court affirmed the District Court's conclusion that the proxy statement was materially deficient, but reversed on the question of causation. The court acknowledged that, if an injunction had been sought a sufficient time before the stockholders' meeting, "corrective measures would have been appropriate." 403 F.2d 429, 435 (1968). However, since this suit was brought too late for preventive action, the courts had to determine "whether the misleading statement and omission caused the submission of sufficient proxies," as a prerequisite to a determination of liability under the Act. If the respondents could show, "by a preponderance of probabilities, that the merger would have received a sufficient vote even if the proxy statement had not been misleading in the respect found," petitioners would be entitled to no relief of any kind. *Id.,* at 436.

The Court of Appeals acknowledged that this test corresponds to the common-law fraud test of whether the injured party relied on the misrepresentation. However, rightly concluding that "[r]eliance by thousands of individuals, as here, can scarcely be inquired into" (*id.,* at 436 n. 10), the court ruled that the issue was to be determined by proof of the fairness of the terms of the merger. If respondents could show that the merger had merit and was fair to the minority shareholders, the trial court would be justified in concluding that a sufficient number of shareholders would have approved the merger had there been no deficiency in the proxy statement. In that case respondents would be entitled to a judgment in their favor.

Claiming that the Court of Appeals has construed this Court's decision in *Borak* in a manner that frustrates the statute's policy of enforcement through private litigation, the petitioners then sought review in this Court. We granted certiorari, 394 U.S. 971, 89 S.Ct. 1470, 22 L.Ed.2d 752 (1969), believing that resolution of this basic issue should be made at this stage of the litigation and not postponed until after a trial under the Court of Appeals' decision.

II

As we stressed in *Borak,* § 14(a) stemmed from a congressional belief that "[f]air corporate suffrage is an important right that should attach to every equity security bought on a public exchange." H.R.Rep. No. 1383, 73d Cong., 2d Sess., 13. The provision was intended to promote "the free exercise of the voting rights of stockholders" by ensuring that proxies would be solicited with "explanation to the stockholder of the real nature of the questions for which authority to cast his vote is sought." *Id.,* at 14; S.Rep. No. 792, 73d Cong., 2d Sess., 12; see 377 U.S., at 431, 377 U.S. 426, 84 S.Ct. 1555, 1559, 12 L.Ed.2d 423. The decision below, by permitting all liability to be foreclosed on the basis of a finding that the merger was fair, would allow the stockholders to be bypassed, at least where the only legal challenge to the merger is a suit for retrospective relief after the meeting has been held. A judicial appraisal of the merger's merits could be substituted for the actual and informed vote of the stockholders.

The result would be to insulate from private redress an entire category of proxy violations—those relating to matters other than the terms of the merger. Even outrageous misrepresentations in a proxy solicitation, if they did not relate to the terms of the transaction, would give rise to no cause of action under § 14(a). Particularly if carried over to enforcement actions by the Securities and Exchange Commission itself, such a result would subvert the congressional purpose of ensuring full and fair disclosure to shareholders.

Further, recognition of the fairness of the merger as a complete defense would confront small shareholders with an additional obstacle to making a successful challenge to a proposal recommended through a defective proxy statement. The risk that they would be unable to rebut the corporation's evidence of the fairness of the proposal, and thus to establish their cause of action, would be bound to discourage such shareholders from the private enforcement of the proxy rules that "provides a necessary supplement to Commission action." J.I. Case Co. v. Borak, 377 U.S., at 432, 84 S.Ct. at 1560.[9]

---

[9] The Court of Appeals' ruling that "causation" may be negated by proof of the fairness of the merger also rests on a dubious behavioral assumption. There is no justification for presuming that the shareholders of every corporation are willing to accept any and every fair merger offer put before them; yet such a presumption is implicit in the opinion of the Court of Appeals. That court gave no indication of what evidence petitioners might adduce, once respondents had established that the merger proposal was equitable, in order to show that the shareholders would nevertheless have rejected it if the solicitation had not been misleading. Proof of actual reliance by thousands of individuals would, as the court acknowledged, not be feasible, see R. Jennings & H. Marsh, Securities Regulation, Cases and Materials 1001 (2d ed. 1968); and reliance on the *nondisclosure* of a fact is a particularly difficult matter to define or

Such a frustration of the congressional policy is not required by anything in the wording of the statute or in our opinion in the *Borak* case. Section 14(a) declares it "unlawful" to solicit proxies in contravention of Commission rules, and SEC Rule 14a–9 prohibits solicitations "containing any statement which . . . is false or misleading with respect to any material fact, or which omits to state any material fact necessary in order to make the statements therein not false or misleading. . . . " Use of a solicitation that is materially misleading is itself a violation of law, as the Court of Appeals recognized in stating that injunctive relief would be available to remedy such a defect if sought prior to the stockholders' meeting. In *Borak,* which came to this Court on a dismissal of the complaint, the Court limited its inquiry to whether a violation of § 14(a) gives rise to "a federal cause of action for rescission or damages," 377 U.S., at 428, 84 S.Ct. at 1558. Referring to the argument made by petitioners there "that the merger can be dissolved only if it was fraudulent or non-beneficial, issues upon which the proxy material would not bear," the Court stated: "But the causal relationship of the proxy material and the merger are questions of fact to be resolved at trial, not here. We therefore do not discuss this point further." *Id.,* at 431, 84 S.Ct. at 1559. In the present case there has been a hearing specifically directed to the causation problem. The question before the Court is whether the facts found on the basis of that hearing are sufficient in law to establish petitioners' cause of action, and we conclude that they are.

Where the misstatement or omission in a proxy statement has been shown to be "material," as it was found to be here, that determination itself indubitably embodies a conclusion that the defect was of such a character that it might have been considered important by a reasonable shareholder who was in the process of deciding how to vote.[10] This requirement that the defect have a significant *propensity* to affect the voting process is found in the express terms of Rule 14a–9, and it adequately serves the purpose of ensuring that a cause of action cannot be established by proof of a defect so trivial, or so unrelated to the

---

prove, see 3 L. Loss, Securities Regulation, 1766 (2d ed. 1961). In practice, therefore, the objective fairness of the proposal would seemingly be determinative of liability. But, in view of the many other factors that might lead shareholders to prefer their current position to that of owners of a larger, combined enterprise, it is pure conjecture to assume that the fairness of the proposal will always be determinative of their vote. Cf. Wirtz v. Hotel, Motel & Club Employees Union, 391 U.S. 492, 508, 88 S.Ct. 1743, 1752, 20 L.Ed.2d 763 (1968).

[10]   . . . In this case, where the misleading aspect of the solicitation involved failure to reveal a serious conflict of interest on the part of the directors, the Court of Appeals concluded that the crucial question in determining materiality was "whether the minority shareholders were sufficiently alerted to the board's relationship to their adversary to be on their guard." 403 F.2d at 434. An adequate disclosure of this relationship would have warned the stockholders to give more careful scrutiny to the terms of the merger than they might to one recommended by an entirely disinterested board. Thus, the failure to make such a disclosure was found to be a material defect "as a matter of law," thwarting the informed decision at which the statute aims, regardless of whether the terms of the merger were such that a reasonable stockholder would have approved the transaction after more careful analysis. See also Swanson v. American Consumer Industries, Inc., 415 F.2d 1326 (C.A.7th Cir.1969).

transaction for which approval is sought, that correction of the defect or imposition of liability would not further the interests protected by § 14(a).

There is no need to supplement this requirement, as did the Court of Appeals, with a requirement of proof of whether the defect actually had a decisive effect on the voting. Where there has been a finding of materiality, a shareholder has made a sufficient showing of causal relationship between the violation and the injury for which he seeks redress if, as here, he proves that the proxy solicitation itself, rather than the particular defect in the solicitation materials, was an essential link in the accomplishment of the transaction. This objective test will avoid the impracticalities of determining how many votes were affected, and, by resolving doubts in favor of those the statute is designed to protect, will effectuate the congressional policy of ensuring that the shareholders are able to make an informed choice when they are consulted on corporate transactions. . . .

III

Our conclusion that petitioners have established their case by showing that proxies necessary to approval of the merger were obtained by means of a materially misleading solicitation implies nothing about the form of relief to which they may be entitled. We held in *Borak* that upon finding a violation the courts were "to be alert to provide such remedies as are necessary to make effective the congressional purpose," noting specifically that such remedies are not to be limited to prospective relief. 377 U.S., at 433, 434, 84 S.Ct. at 1560. In devising retrospective relief for violation of the proxy rules, the federal courts should consider the same factors that would govern the relief granted for any similar illegality or fraud. One important factor may be the fairness of the terms of the merger. Possible forms of relief will include setting aside the merger or granting other equitable relief, but, as the Court of Appeals below noted, nothing in the statutory policy "requires the court to unscramble a corporate transaction merely because a violation occurred." 403 F.2d at 436. In selecting a remedy the lower courts should exercise " 'the sound discretion which guides the determinations of courts of equity,' " keeping in mind the role of equity as "the instrument for nice adjustment and reconciliation between the public interest and private needs as well as between competing private claims." Hecht Co. v. Bowles, 321 U.S. 321, 329–330, 64 S.Ct. 587, 591–592, 88 L.Ed. 754 (1944), quoting from Meredith v. Winter Haven, 320 U.S. 228, 235, 64 S.Ct. 7, 11, 88 L.Ed. 9 (1943). . . .

. . . [A] determination of what relief should be granted in Auto-Lite's name must hinge on whether setting aside the merger would be in the best interests of the shareholders as a whole. In short, in the context of a suit such as this one, § 29(b) leaves the matter of relief where it would be under *Borak* without specific statutory language—the merger should be set aside only if a court of equity concludes, from all the circumstances, that it would be equitable to do so. Cf. SEC v. National Securities, Inc., 393 U.S. 453, 456, 463–464, 89 S.Ct. 564, 566, 570, 21 L.Ed.2d 668 (1969).

Monetary relief will, of course, also be a possibility. Where the defect in the proxy solicitation relates to the specific terms of the merger, the district court might appropriately order an accounting to ensure that the shareholders receive the value that was represented as coming to them. On the other hand, where, as here, the misleading aspect of the solicitation did not relate to terms of the merger, monetary relief might be afforded to the shareholders only if the merger resulted in a reduction of the earnings or earnings potential of their holdings. In short, damages should be recoverable only to the extent that they can be shown. If commingling of the assets and operations of the merged companies makes it impossible to establish direct injury from the merger, relief might be predicated on a determination of the fairness of the terms of the merger at the time it was approved. These questions, of course, are for decision in the first instance by the District Court on remand, and our singling out of some of the possibilities is not intended to exclude others. . . .

For the foregoing reasons we conclude that the judgment of the Court of Appeals should be vacated and the case remanded to that court for further proceedings consistent with this opinion.

It is so ordered.

[The opinion of Justice Black, concurring in part and dissenting in part, is omitted.]

———

NOTE ON FURTHER PROCEEDINGS IN MILLS V. ELECTRIC AUTO-LITE

On remand, the District Court held the exchange to be unfair and awarded damages of $1,233,918.35, as well as approximately $740,000 in pre-judgment interest. The Seventh Circuit reversed, concluding that the merger terms were fair and the plaintiff was therefore not entitled to damages. 552 F.2d 1239 (7th Cir.1977), cert. denied, 434 U.S. 922, 98 S.Ct. 398, 54 L.Ed.2d 279.

———

TSC Industries, Inc. v. Northway, Inc.

Supreme Court of the United States, 1970.
426 U.S. 438, 96 S.Ct. 2126, 48 L.Ed.2d 757.

[In a case involving alleged disclosure violations in the approval of a merger, the Supreme Court addressed the issue of how materiality was to be defined, as follows:]

... [I]n *Mills,* ... we held that there was no need to demonstrate that the alleged defect in the proxy statement actually had a decisive effect on the voting. So long as the misstatement or omission was material, the causal relation between violation and injury is sufficiently established, we concluded, if "the proxy solicitation itself ... was an essential link in the accomplishment of the transaction." 396 U.S., at 385, 90 S.Ct., at 622. After *Mills,* then, the content given to the notion of materiality assumes heightened significance. . . .

The question of materiality, it is universally agreed, is an objective one, involving the significance of an omitted or misrepresented fact to a reasonable investor. Variations in the formulation of a general test of materiality occur in the articulation of just how significant a fact must be or, put another way, how certain it must be that the fact would affect a reasonable investor's judgment. . . .

The Court of Appeals in this case concluded that material facts include "all facts which a reasonable shareholder *might* consider important." 512 F.2d, at 330 (emphasis added). This formulation of the test of materiality has been explicitly rejected by at least two courts as setting too low a threshold for the imposition of liability under Rule 14a–9. Gerstle v. Gamble-Skogmo, Inc., 478 F.2d 1281, 1301–1302 (C.A.2 1973); Smallwood v. Pearl Brewing Co., 489 F.2d 579, 603–604 (C.A.5 1974). . . .

... [T]he disclosure policy embodied in the proxy regulations is not without limit. See id., at 384, 90 S.Ct., at 621. Some information is of such dubious significance that insistence on its disclosure may accomplish more harm than good. The potential liability for a Rule 14a–9 violation can be great indeed, and if the standard of materiality is unnecessarily low, not only may the corporation and its management be subjected to liability for insignificant omissions or misstatements, but also management's fear of exposing itself to substantial liability may cause it simply to bury the shareholder in an avalanche of trivial information—a result that is hardly conducive to informed decisionmaking. Precisely these dangers are presented, we think, by the definition of a material fact adopted by the Court of Appeals in this case—a fact which a reasonable shareholder *might* consider important. We agree with Judge Friendly, speaking for the Court of Appeals in *Gerstle,* that the "might" formulation is "too suggestive of mere possibility, however unlikely." 478 F.2d, at 1302.

The general standard of materiality that we think best comports with the policies of Rule 14a–9 is as follows: an omitted fact is material if there is a substantial likelihood that a reasonable shareholder would consider it important in deciding how to vote. This standard is fully consistent with *Mills* general description of materiality as a requirement that "the defect have a significant *propensity* to affect the voting process." It does not require proof of a substantial likelihood that disclosure of the omitted fact would have caused the reasonable investor to change his vote. What the standard does contemplate is a showing of a substantial likelihood that, under all the circumstances, the omitted fact would have assumed actual significance in the deliberations of the reasonable shareholder. Put another way, there must be a substantial likelihood that the disclosure of the omitted fact would have been viewed by the reasonable investor as having significantly altered the "total mix" of information made available.

————

What are the characteristics of the reasonable shareholder by which a materiality determinations is made? Should this be an expansive or restricted interpretation of the probable information needs of the reasonable shareholder?

Speculators and chartists of Wall and Bay Streets are also "reasonable" investors entitled to the same legal protection afforded conservative traders. Thus, material facts include not only information disclosing the earnings and distributions of a company but also those facts which affect the probable future of the company and those which affect the desire of investors to buy, sell or hold the company securities.

SEC v. Texas Gulf Sulphur Co., 401 F.2d 833, 849 (2d Cir. 1968), *cert. denied*, 394 U.S. 976 (1969).

————

Virginia Bankshares, Inc. v. Sandberg

Supreme Court of the United States, 1991.
501 U.S. 1083, 111 S.Ct. 2749, 115 L.Ed.2d 929.

■ JUSTICE SOUTER delivered the opinion of the Court.

Section 14(a) of the Securities Exchange Act of 1934, 48 Stat. 895, 15 U.S.C. § 78n(a), authorizes the Securities and Exchange Commission to adopt rules for the solicitation of proxies, and prohibits their violation. In J.I. Case Co. v. Borak, 377 U.S. 426, 84 S.Ct. 1555, 12 L.Ed.2d 423 (1964), we first recognized an implied private right of action for the breach of § 14(a) as implemented by SEC Rule 14a–9, which prohibits the solicitation of proxies by means of materially false or misleading statements.[2]

---

2   . . .

The questions before us are whether a statement couched in conclusory or qualitative terms purporting to explain directors' reasons for recommending certain corporate action can be materially misleading within the meaning of Rule 14a–9, and whether causation of damages compensable under § 14(a) can be shown by a member of a class of minority shareholders whose votes are not required by law or corporate bylaw to authorize the corporate action subject to the proxy solicitation. We hold that knowingly false statements of reasons may be actionable even though conclusory in form, but that respondents have failed to demonstrate the equitable basis required to extend the § 14(a) private action to such shareholders when any indication of congressional intent to do so is lacking.

I

In December 1986, First American Bankshares, Inc. (FABI), a bank holding company, began a "freeze-out" merger, in which the First American Bank of Virginia (Bank) eventually merged into Virginia Bankshares, Inc. (VBI), a wholly owned subsidiary of FABI. VBI owned 85% of the Bank's shares, the remaining 15% being in the hands of some 2,000 minority shareholders. FABI hired the investment banking firm of Keefe, Bruyette & Woods (KBW) to give an opinion on the appropriate price for shares of the minority holders, who would lose their interests in the Bank as a result of the merger. Based on market quotations and unverified information from FABI, KBW gave the Bank's executive committee an opinion that $42 a share would be a fair price for the minority stock. The executive committee approved the merger proposal at that price, and the full board followed suit.

Although Virginia law required only that such a merger proposal be submitted to a vote at a shareholders' meeting, and that the meeting be preceded by circulation of a statement of information to the shareholders, the directors nevertheless solicited proxies for voting on the proposal at the annual meeting set for April 21, 1987.[3] In their solicitation, the directors urged the proposal's adoption and stated they had approved the plan because of its opportunity for the minority shareholders to achieve a "high" value, which they elsewhere described as a "fair" price, for their stock.

Although most minority shareholders gave the proxies requested, respondent Sandberg did not, and after approval of the merger she sought damages in the United States District Court for the Eastern District of Virginia from VBI, FABI, and the directors of the Bank. She

---

The Federal Deposit Insurance Corporation (FDIC) administers and enforces the securities laws with respect to the activities of federally insured and regulated banks. See Section 12(i) of the Exchange Act, 15 U.S.C. § 78*l*(i). An FDIC rule also prohibits materially misleading statements in the solicitation of proxies, 12 CFR § 335.206 (1991), and is essentially identical to Rule 14a–9. See generally Brief for SEC et al. as Amici Curiae 4, n. 5.

[3]   Had the directors chosen to issue a statement instead of a proxy solicitation, they would have been subject to an SEC antifraud provision analogous to Rule 14a–9. See 17 CFR 240.14c–6 (1990). See also 15 U.S.C. § 78n(c).

pleaded two counts, one for soliciting proxies in violation of § 14(a) and Rule 14a–9, and the other for breaching fiduciary duties owed to the minority shareholders under state law. Under the first count, Sandberg alleged, among other things, that the directors had not believed that the price offered was high or that the terms of the merger were fair, but had recommended the merger only because they believed they had no alternative if they wished to remain on the board. At trial, Sandberg invoked language from this Court's opinion in Mills v. Electric Auto-Lite Co., 396 U.S. 375, 385, 90 S.Ct. 616, 622, 24 L.Ed.2d 593 (1970), to obtain an instruction that the jury could find for her without a showing of her own reliance on the alleged misstatements, so long as they were material and the proxy solicitation was an "essential link" in the merger process.

The jury's verdicts were for Sandberg on both counts, after finding violations of Rule 14a–9 by all defendants and a breach of fiduciary duties by the Bank's directors. The jury awarded Sandberg $18 a share, having found that she would have received $60 if her stock had been valued adequately. . . .

On appeal, the United States Court of Appeals for the Fourth Circuit affirmed . . . , holding that certain statements in the proxy solicitation were materially misleading for purposes of the Rule, and that respondents could maintain their action even though their votes had not been needed to effectuate the merger. 891 F.2d 1112 (1989).[4] We granted certiorari because of the importance of the issues presented. 495 U.S. 903, 110 S.Ct. 1921, 109 L.Ed.2d 285 (1990).

II

The Court of Appeals affirmed petitioners' liability for two statements found to have been materially misleading in violation of § 14(a) of the Act, one of which was that "The Plan of Merger has been approved by the Board of Directors because it provides an opportunity for the Bank's public shareholders to achieve a high value for their shares." App. to Pet. for Cert. 53a. Petitioners argue that statements of opinion or belief incorporating indefinite and unverifiable expressions cannot be actionable as misstatements of material fact within the meaning of Rule 14a–9, and that such a declaration of opinion or belief should never be actionable when placed in a proxy solicitation incorporating statements of fact sufficient to enable readers to draw their own, independent conclusions.

A

We consider first the actionability per se of statements of reasons, opinion or belief. Because such a statement by definition purports to express what is consciously on the speaker's mind, we interpret the jury

---

4   The Court of Appeals reversed the District Court, however, on its refusal to certify a class of all minority shareholders in Sandberg's action. Consequently, it ruled that petitioners were liable to all of the Bank's former minority shareholders for $18 per share. 891 F.2d, at 1119.

verdict as finding that the directors' statements of belief and opinion were made with knowledge that the directors did not hold the beliefs or opinions expressed, and we confine our discussion to statements so made.[5] That such statements may be materially significant raises no serious question. The meaning of the materiality requirement for liability under § 14(a) was discussed at some length in TSC Industries, Inc. v. Northway, Inc., 426 U.S. 438, 96 S.Ct. 2126, 48 L.Ed.2d 757 (1976), where we held a fact to be material "if there is a substantial likelihood that a reasonable shareholder would consider it important in deciding how to vote." Id., at 449, 96 S.Ct., at 2132. We think there is no room to deny that a statement of belief by corporate directors about a recommended course of action, or an explanation of their reasons for recommending it, can take on just that importance. Shareholders know that directors usually have knowledge and expertness far exceeding the normal investor's resources, and the directors' perceived superiority is magnified even further by the common knowledge that state law customarily obliges them to exercise their judgment in the shareholders' interest. Cf. Day v. Avery, 179 U.S.App.D.C. 63, 71, 548 F.2d 1018, 1026 (1976) (action for misrepresentation). Naturally, then, the share owner faced with a proxy request will think it important to know the directors' beliefs about the course they recommend, and their specific reasons for urging the stockholders to embrace it.

B

1

But, assuming materiality, the question remains whether statements of reasons, opinions, or beliefs are statements "with respect to . . . material fact[s]" so as to fall within the strictures of the Rule. Petitioners argue that we would invite wasteful litigation of amorphous issues outside the readily provable realm of fact if we were to recognize liability here on proof that the directors did not recommend the merger for the stated reason. . . .

Attacks on the truth of directors' statements of reasons or belief, however, need carry no such threats. Such statements are factual in two senses: as statements that the directors do act for the reasons given or hold the belief stated and as statements about the subject matter of the reason or belief expressed. In neither sense does the proof or disproof of such statements implicate the concerns expressed in Blue Chip Stamps [v. Manor Drug Stores, 421 U.S. 723, 95 S.Ct. 1917, 44 L.Ed.2d 539 (1975)]. The root of those concerns was a plaintiff's capacity to manufacture claims of hypothetical action, unconstrained by independent evidence. Reasons for directors' recommendations or statements of belief are, in contrast, characteristically matters of corporate record subject to documentation, to be supported or attacked

---

[5]   In TSC Industries, Inc. v. Northway, Inc., 426 U.S. 438, 444, n. 7, 96 S.Ct. 2126, 2130, n. 7, 48 L.Ed.2d 757 (1976), we reserved the question whether scienter was necessary for liability generally under § 14(a). We reserve it still.

by evidence of historical fact outside a plaintiff's control. Such evidence would include not only corporate minutes and other statements of the directors themselves, but circumstantial evidence bearing on the facts that would reasonably underlie the reasons claimed and the honesty of any statement that those reasons are the basis for a recommendation or other action, a point that becomes especially clear when the reasons or beliefs go to valuations in dollars and cents.

It is no answer to argue, as petitioners do, that the quoted statement on which liability was predicated did not express a reason in dollars and cents, but focused instead on the "indefinite and unverifiable" term, "high" value, much like the similar claim that the merger's terms were "fair" to shareholders. The objection ignores the fact that such conclusory terms in a commercial context are reasonably understood to rest on a factual basis that justifies them as accurate, the absence of which renders them misleading. Provable facts either furnish good reasons to make a conclusory commercial judgment, or they count against it, and expressions of such judgments can be uttered with knowledge of truth or falsity just like more definite statements, and defended or attacked through the orthodox evidentiary process that either substantiates their underlying justifications or tends to disprove their existence. . . . In this case, whether $42 was "high," and the proposal "fair" to the minority shareholders depended on whether provable facts about the Bank's assets, and about actual and potential levels of operation, substantiated a value that was above, below, or more or less at the $42 figure, when assessed in accordance with recognized methods of valuation.

Respondents adduced evidence for just such facts in proving that the statement was misleading about its subject matter and a false expression of the directors' reasons. Whereas the proxy statement described the $42 price as offering a premium above both book value and market price, the evidence indicated that a calculation of the book figure based on the appreciated value of the Bank's real estate holdings eliminated any such premium. The evidence on the significance of market price showed that KBW had conceded that the market was closed, thin and dominated by FABI, facts omitted from the statement. There was, indeed, evidence of a "going concern" value for the Bank in excess of $60 per share of common stock, another fact never disclosed. However conclusory the directors' statement may have been, then, it was open to attack by garden-variety evidence, subject neither to a plaintiff's control nor ready manufacture, and there was no undue risk of open-ended liability or uncontrollable litigation in allowing respondents the opportunity for recovery on the allegation that it was misleading to call $42 "high." . . .

2

Under § 14(a), then, a plaintiff is permitted to prove a specific statement of reason knowingly false or misleadingly incomplete, even when stated in conclusory terms. In reaching this conclusion we have considered statements of reasons of the sort exemplified here, which misstate the speaker's reasons and also mislead about the stated subject matter (e.g., the value of the shares). A statement of belief may be open to objection only in the former respect, however, solely as a misstatement of the psychological fact of the speaker's belief in what he says. In this case, for example, the Court of Appeals alluded to just such limited falsity in observing that "the jury was certainly justified in believing that the directors did not believe a merger at $42 per share was in the minority stockholders' interest but, rather, that they voted as they did for other reasons, e.g., retaining their seats on the board." 891 F.2d, at 1121.

The question arises, then, whether disbelief, or undisclosed belief or motivation, standing alone, should be a sufficient basis to sustain an action under § 14(a), absent proof by the sort of objective evidence described above that the statement also expressly or impliedly asserted something false or misleading about its subject matter. We think that proof of mere disbelief or belief undisclosed should not suffice for liability under § 14(a), and if nothing more had been required or proven in this case we would reverse for that reason.

On the one hand, it would be rare to find a case with evidence solely of disbelief or undisclosed motivation without further proof that the statement was defective as to its subject matter. While we certainly would not hold a director's naked admission of disbelief incompetent evidence of a proxy statement's false or misleading character, such an unusual admission will not very often stand alone, and we do not substantially narrow the cause of action by requiring a plaintiff to demonstrate something false or misleading in what the statement expressly or impliedly declared about its subject.

On the other hand, to recognize liability on mere disbelief or undisclosed motive without any demonstration that the proxy statement was false or misleading about its subject would authorize § 14(a) litigation confined solely to what one skeptical court spoke of as the "impurities" of a director's "unclean heart." Stedman v. Storer, 308 F.Supp. 881, 887 (S.D.N.Y.1969) (dealing with § 10(b)). This, we think, would cross the line that *Blue Chip Stamps* sought to draw. While it is true that the liability, if recognized, would rest on an actual, not hypothetical, psychological fact, the temptation to rest an otherwise nonexistent § 14(a) action on psychological enquiry alone would threaten just the sort of strike suits and attrition by discovery that *Blue Chip Stamps* sought to discourage. We therefore hold disbelief or undisclosed motivation, standing alone, insufficient to satisfy the element of fact that must be established under § 14(a). . . .

III

The second issue before us, left open in Mills v. Electric Auto-Lite Co., 396 U.S., at 385, n. 7, 90 S.Ct., at 622, n. 7, is whether causation of damages compensable through the implied private right of action under § 14(a) can be demonstrated by a member of a class of minority shareholders whose votes are not required by law or corporate bylaw to authorize the transaction giving rise to the claim.

[The Court held that the answer to this question was, no. The plaintiffs argued that such a claim could be supported by two theories: that the proxy statement was an essential link between the director's proposal and the merger (1) because VBI and FABI would have been unwilling to proceed with the merger unless the minority approved, and (2) because the vote of the minority was the means to satisfy a state statutory requirement of minority shareholder approval as a condition for saving the merger from voidability resulting from a conflict of interest. The court rejected the first theory on the ground that acceptance of the concept would give rise to speculative claims. As to the second theory, the court said:]

This case does not . . . require us to decide whether § 14(a) provides a cause of action for lost state remedies, since there is no indication in the law or facts before us that the proxy solicitation resulted in any such loss. The contrary appears to be the case. Assuming the soundness of respondents' characterization of the proxy statement as materially misleading, the very terms of the Virginia statute indicate that a favorable minority vote induced by the solicitation would not suffice to render the merger invulnerable to later attack on the ground of the conflict. The statute bars a shareholder from seeking to avoid a transaction tainted by a director's conflict if, inter alia, the minority shareholders ratified the transaction following disclosure of the material facts of the transaction and the conflict. Va.Code § 13.1–691(A)(2) (1989). Assuming that the material facts about the merger and Beddow's interests were not accurately disclosed, the minority votes were inadequate to ratify the merger under state law, and there was no loss of state remedy to connect the proxy solicitation with harm to minority shareholders irredressable under state law. Nor is there a claim here that the statement misled respondents into entertaining a false belief that they had no chance to upset the merger, until the time for bringing suit had run out.[14]

IV

The judgment of the Court of Appeals is reversed.

It is so ordered.

[The opinion of Justice Scalia, concurring in Parts I and III and, concurring in result, and the opinions of Justices Blackmun, Kennedy, Marshall and Stevens, concurring in Part I and II and dissenting from Part III, are omitted.]

---

[14]   Respondents do not claim that any other application of a theory of lost state remedies would avail them here. It is clear, for example, that no state appraisal remedy was lost through a § 14(a) violation in this case. . . .

Wilson v. Great American Industries, Inc.

979 F.2d 924 (2d Cir.1992)

Chenango engaged in a merger with Great American. Plaintiffs, who had been minority shareholders in Chenango, alleged that material misstatements in the Proxy Statement caused them to exchange their shares of Chenango common stock for new preferred stock in Great American. At the time of the merger, the defendants (Great American, Chenango, and various officers, directors, and attorneys connected with those two corporations) owned 73 percent of Chenango's stock, which was well over the two-thirds necessary under New York law to approve a merger. New York law required that Chenango have a shareholders' meeting to approve the merger, but the only informational requirement under the New York statute was that each shareholder be given notice of the meeting accompanied by a "copy of the plan of merger." Chenango, despite its overwhelming share ownership, sought approval of the merger by Chenango's minority shareholders. Unlike *Virginia Bankshares,* state law accorded stockholders who voted against the merger with a means to receive the fair value for their shares, i.e., an appraisal remedy. The Second Circuit held that *Virginia Bankshares* did not bar the plaintiffs' action if, as a result of false statements in the Proxy Statement, the plaintiffs had lost their appraisal right or some other state remedy by being duped into voting for the transaction. See also Howing Co. v. Nationwide Corp., 972 F.2d 700, 709–710 (6th Cir.1992), *cert. denied* 507 U.S. 1004, 113 S.Ct. 1645, 123 L.Ed.2d 266 (1993); cf. Scattergood v. Perelman, 945 F.2d 618 (3d Cir.1991).

NOTE ON THE STANDARD OF FAULT IN PRIVATE ACTIONS UNDER THE PROXY RULES

Under *Borak* and *Mills,* shareholders have standing to bring an action under Rule 14a–9, which prohibits false or misleading proxy statements. Does a plaintiff-shareholder prevail in such an action if he shows that a proxy statement was false or misleading by virtue of a material misstatement or omission, or must he also show that the misstatement or omission was committed with either knowledge of the falsity or reckless disregard of the truth? If the plaintiff must show fault, does negligence suffice?

In the leading case of *Gerstle v. Gamble-Skogmo, Inc.,* 478 F.2d 1281 (2d Cir.1973), the Second Circuit, in an opinion written by Judge Friendly, held that negligence sufficed to establish liability under Rule 14a–9:

> We thus hold that in a case like this, where the plaintiffs represent the very class who were asked to approve a merger on the basis of a misleading proxy statement and are seeking compensation from the beneficiary who is responsible for the preparation of the statement, they are not required to establish any evil motive or even reckless disregard of the facts. Whether in

situations other than that here presented "the liability of the corporation issuing a materially false or misleading proxy statement is virtually absolute, as under Section 11 of the 1933 Act with respect to a registration statement," Jennings & Marsh, Securities Regulation: Cases and Materials 1358 (3d ed. 1972), we leave to another day. 478 F.2d at 1298–1301. Accord: Herskowitz v. Nutri/System, Inc., 857 F.2d 179 (3d Cir.1988), cert. denied 489 U.S. 1054, 109 S.Ct. 1315, 103 L.Ed.2d 584 (1989); Gould v. American-Hawaiian Steamship Co., 535 F.2d 761 (3d Cir.1976).

Nonetheless, Judge Friendly reasoned that strict liability would be too blunt a tool to ferret out the kind of deceptive practices congress sought to address. *See also Shidler v. All American Life & Financial Corp.,* 775 F.2d 917, 927 (8th Cir.1985) (rejecting liability without fault); *Adams v. Standard Knitting Mills, Inc.,* 623 F.2d 422 (6th Cir.1980), cert. denied 449 U.S. 1067, 101 S.Ct. 795, 66 L.Ed.2d 611. ("scienter should be an element of liability in private suits under the proxy provisions as they apply to outside accountants").

The Supreme Court has several times explicitly taken note of the position taken in *Gerstle* and other cases that scienter is not an element of liability under § 14(a), and has each time declined to address the issue. *See Ernst & Ernst v. Hochfelder,* 425 U.S. 185, 209 n. 28, 96 S.Ct. 1375, 1388 n. 28, 47 L.Ed.2d 668 (1976); *TSC Indus., Inc. v. Northway,* 426 U.S. 438, 444 n. 7, 96 S.Ct. 2126, 2130 n. 7, 48 L.Ed.2d 757 (1976); *Virginia Bankshares,* supra, at note 5.

———

NOTE ON STATE LAW

Perhaps as a result of experience under the Proxy Rules, the standards applied by state courts today, in reviewing the adequacy of disclosure to shareholders under state law in connection with a matter proposed for a shareholder vote, is quite similar to the standards under the Proxy Rules. See Chapter 10, Section 5, infra.

———

CHAPTER 6

PERSONAL LIABILITY IN A CORPORATE CONTEXT

Although limited liability is a central attribute of the corporate form, there are several contexts in which personal liability may be imposed upon a shareholder or upon a person associated with a proposed or defectively formed corporation. Three of these contexts will be discussed in this Chapter: the liability of a promoter for preincorporation transactions he engages in on behalf of a proposed corporation; the liability of a person who is a would-be shareholder in a defectively formed corporation; and the liability of a shareholder for corporate obligations. Each of these contexts also implicates issues other than personal liability, and these issues will also be discussed in this Chapter.

---

1. PREINCORPORATION TRANSACTIONS BY PROMOTERS

A promoter is a person who transforms an idea into an enterprise by bringing together persons and assets, and overseeing the steps required to bring the enterprise into existence. Often, a promoter of a proposed corporation enters into preincorporation contracts for the benefit of a corporation that has not yet been formed. If, as is usually the case, the corporation is subsequently formed, issues may arise regarding who is liable under the preincorporation contract.

(a) *Liability of the promoter.* The general rule is that when a promoter makes a contract for the benefit of a proposed corporation, the promoter is personally liable on the contract, and remains liable even after the corporation is formed. There is an exception if the party who contracted with the promoter knew that the corporation was not in existence at the time of the contract and nevertheless agreed to look solely to the corporation for performance. In such cases the promoter is not deemed a party to the contract. An agreement of this type may be express or implied. As a practical matter, it is often difficult to predict whether, in the absence of an express agreement of this type, a court will find an implied agreement.

For example, in *Goodman v. Darden, Doman & Stafford Assocs.*, 670 P.2d 648 (Wash. 1983), Goodman had proposed to renovate an apartment building owned by Darden, Doman & Stafford Associates (DDS). During the course of negotiations, Goodman informed DDS that he would be forming a corporation to limit his personal liability. In August 1979, a contract was made between DDS and "BUILDING DESIGN AND DEVELOPMENT INC. (In Formation) John A. Goodman, President."

DDS knew that the Building Design corporation was not yet in existence. On November 1, Goodman filed articles of incorporation. Between August and December 1979, DDS made five progress payments on the contract. The first check was made out to "Building Design and Development Inc.—John Goodman." Goodman struck out his name as payee, endorsed the check "Bldg. Design & Dev. Inc., John A. Goodman, Pres," and instructed DDS to make further payments only to the corporation. DDS did so. The court held that Goodman was liable on the contract with DDS:

> . . . The fact that a contracting party knows that the corporation is nonexistent does not indicate any agreement to release the promoter. To the contrary, such knowledge alone would seem to indicate that the members of DDS intended to make Goodman a party to the contract. They could not hold the corporation, a nonexistent entity, responsible and of course they would expect to have recourse against someone (Goodman) if default occurred. . . .
>
> The only other evidence of the parties' intent to make the corporation the sole party to the contract is that the progress payments were made payable to the corporation. However, they were so written only at the instruction of Goodman and in fact the first check written by DDS after the signing of the contract was written to the corporation *and* Goodman as an individual. This evidence does not show by reasonable certainty that DDS intended to contract only with the corporation. . . .

Id. at 652–53.

In contrast, in *Company Stores Development Corp. v. Pottery Warehouse, Inc.*, 733 S.W.2d 886 (Tenn. App. 1987), Company Stores leased a store to Pottery Warehouse, Inc., for five years. Pottery Warehouse was not incorporated at the time of the lease. The lease recited that the corporation was to be organized, and was signed by the promoter as follows:

THE POTTERY WAREHOUSE, INC., a corporation to be formed under the laws of the State of Tennessee

BY Jane M. Vosseller

Its President. . . .

The court held that the promoter was not liable:

> In the instant case, the stipulations of fact establish the plaintiff intended to look solely to Pottery Warehouse, Inc., for satisfaction of the obligation arising under the lease at the time of execution. At the time the lease was signed, plaintiff was aware of the nonexistence of the corporate entity and did not require Vosseller to sign the agreement in an individual capacity but as a president of a future corporate entity. The

lease imputes no intention on the part of Vosseller to be bound personally.

Id. at 888.

(b) *Liability of the Corporation.* A corporation that is formed after a promoter has entered into a contract on its behalf is not bound by the contract, without more. The reason is that the corporation was not in existence when the contract was made, and therefore did not authorize— and indeed could not have authorized—the promoter to enter into the contract on its behalf. However, after the corporation has been formed it may become bound in one of several ways. "The usual grounds that have been suggested are ratification, adoption, novation, and that the proposition made to the promoters is a continuing offer to be accepted or rejected by the corporation when it comes into being, and upon acceptance becomes an original contract on its part; and the liability has also been sustained on the ground that the corporation, by accepting the benefits of a contract, takes it cum onere, and is estopped to deny its liability on the contract." Clifton v. Tomb, 21 F.2d 893 (4th Cir.1927). In *Illinois Controls, Inc. v. Langham*, 70 Ohio St.3d 512, 524, 639 N.E.2d 771, 781 (1994), the court held that if a promoter is liable on a contract under the law of promoter's liability, the fact that the corporation also becomes liable on the contract by adopting it does not relieve the promoter of liability. Instead, in such a case the promoter and the corporation are jointly and severally liable.

———

RESTATEMENT (THIRD) OF AGENCY § 6.04

[See Statutory Supplement]

———

RESTATEMENT (SECOND) OF CONTRACTS § 326

[See Statutory Supplement]

———

2. CONSEQUENCES OF DEFECTIVE INCORPORATION

———

MODEL BUS. CORP. ACT §§ 2.03, 2.04

[See Statutory Supplement]

———

DEL. GEN. CORP. LAW §§ 106, 329

[See Statutory Supplement]

NOTES ON DEFECTIVE INCORPORATION

Sometimes there is a defect in the process of forming a corporation. For example, the certificate of incorporation may fail to include a required provision in proper form, or may be improperly filed. The issue then arises, what is the effect of the defect on the corporation's status. This issue is usually put in terms of whether a corporation exists de jure, de facto, by estoppel, or not at all. The issue most commonly arises when a third party seeks to hold the would-be shareholders personally liable on the ground that corporate status was not attained, and therefore neither was limited liability. The issue may also arise in a quo warranto proceeding brought by the state to test the validity of corporate statutes. This form of proceeding derives from an ancient prerogative writ issued on behalf of the King against one who falsely claimed an office or franchise. Most states provide by statute for such proceedings, often without using the term quo warranto. See, e.g., N.Y. Bus. Corp. Law § 109; Cal. Corp. Code § 180(a).

1.   De Jure Corporation. A corporation that is organized in compliance with the requirements of the relevant statute is a *de jure corporation.* A de jure corporation's status cannot be attacked either by private parties or by the state in a quo warranto proceeding. People v. Ford, 128 N.E. 479 (Ill. 1920). Most courts hold that perfect compliance with the statutory requirements for incorporation is not required to attain de jure status. Instead, substantial compliance will suffice. Therefore, an enterprise that fails to meet all the requirements for incorporation may nevertheless be a de jure corporation if the noncompliance is insubstantial. What constitutes substantial compliance is determined on a case-by-case basis, according to the nature of the unsatisfied requirement and the extent to which compliance has been attempted. For example, if the certificate of incorporation was properly filed except that the address for the corporation's principal place of business stated the wrong street number, there undoubtedly would be substantial compliance.

Some courts hold that for a corporation to attain de jure status there must be exact compliance with all "mandatory" statutory requirements but the failure to comply with requirements that are only "directory" will not will not preclude de jure status. *See, e.g., J.W. Butler Paper Co. v. Cleveland,* 77 N.E. 99 (Ill. 1906). Whether a particular requirement is mandatory or directory for this purpose is a matter of statutory interpretation. For example, in *People v. Ford, supra,* the Illinois attorney general filed a proceeding, in the nature of quo warranto, against three incorporators who had failed to comply with a statutory requirement that the certificate of incorporation be sealed. The incorporators had used incorporation forms provided by the office of the Illinois Secretary of State, and these forms neither contained nor mentioned a seal. The court concluded that the corporation had de jure status. The provision for a seal was only directory, the court said, because the purpose of the statute was to make a public record and a seal did not further that purpose.

2. *De Facto Corporation.* A *de facto* corporation is said to exist when the steps taken to incorporate the enterprise were insufficient to result in a de jure corporation with respect to a challenge by the state in a quo warranto proceeding, but were sufficient to treat the enterprise as a corporation with respect to third parties. In such cases, the enterprise's corporate status can be invalidated by the state through quo warranto proceedings, but cannot be invalidated by third parties. To qualify as a de facto corporation, there must have been a colorable attempt to incorporate and some exercise of corporate privileges. For example, in *Cantor v. Sunshine Greenery, Inc.,* 398 A.2d 571 (N.J. 1979), on November 21, B reserved the corporate name "Sunshine Greenery, Inc." with the Secretary of State. On December 3, B and C executed a certificate of incorporation and sent it by mail to the Secretary of State together with the filing fee. On December 16, Sunshine Greenery entered into a lease. For some unexplained reason, the certificate of incorporation was not officially filed by the Secretary of State until December 18, two days after the lease was executed. The court held that Sunshine Greenery was a de facto corporation prior to December 18, and therefore B and C were not personally liable on the lease.

3. *Estoppel.* In many cases in which neither a de jure nor a de facto corporation has been formed, the courts have held that a third party who has dealt with an enterprise on the basis that it is a corporation is estopped from denying the enterprise's corporate status, as are the corporation and its shareholders. Neither the precise contours of the estoppel theory nor its relationship to the de facto theory has ever been entirely clear. It is sometimes said that the estoppel theory differs from the de facto theory in that estoppel is effective for only a specific transaction. However, the de facto theory also may be effective only for a specific transaction, because a decision in one law suit that a corporation has de facto status will normally not be given res judicata effect in a law suit brought by an unrelated plaintiff on an unrelated transaction. As a practical matter, however, there is likely to be a difference between the *precedential* effects of decisions based on the estoppel theory and decisions based on the de facto theory. Because a decision based on the estoppel theory will normally turn heavily on the *plaintiff's* conduct, it may have only a limited precedential effect on future cases brought by other plaintiffs based on other transactions. In contrast, a decision based on the de facto theory will normally turn on the *defendant's* conduct in attempting to organize a corporation. Because that conduct will also be the focus of any future de facto case involving those defendants, a decision that a de facto corporation was or was not formed by the conduct may have a significant precedential effect on other parties even though it does not have a res judicata effect.

The most important category of estoppel cases occur when a third party who has dealt with an enterprise on the basis that it is a corporation seeks to impose personal liability on the would-be shareholders, who in turn defend on the ground that the third person, having dealt with the enterprise as a corporation, is estopped to deny that the enterprise has corporate status. Here the issue is whether, as a matter of equity, the claimant, having dealt with the enterprise as if it were a corporation, should be prevented—

estopped—from treating it as anything else. A leading case in this category is *Cranson v. International Bus. Mach. Corp.*, 200 A.2d 33 (Md. 1964). I.B.M. had sold typewriters to the Real Estate Service Bureau on credit. I.B.M. dealt with the Bureau as if the Bureau was a corporation. In fact, it wasn't, because without the knowledge of its would-be shareholders, their attorney had negligently failed to file the certificate of incorporation before the transaction with I.B.M. The court held that although the organizational defects in the case might have prevented the Bureau from being a de facto corporation, "I.B.M. having dealt with the Bureau as if it were a corporation and relied on its credit rather than that of [the would-be shareholders], is estopped to assert that the Bureau was not incorporated at the time the typewriters were purchased."

4. *Who May Be Held Liable.* If a would-be corporation is neither a de jure corporation, a de facto corporation, or a corporation by estoppel, the courts have divided on which would-be shareholders may be held personally liable for debts incurred in the corporation's name. Older decisions imposed personal liability on all of the would-be shareholders, on the theory that if the enterprise is not a corporation, it is a partnership, and therefore the would-be shareholders are general partners. *See, e.g., Harrill v. Davis,* 168 F. 187 (8th Cir. 1909). The modern trend, however, imposes personal liability only against those owners who actively participated in the management of the business. Those owners who actively participated are held personally liable as if they were partners, but passive investors are not. Model Business Corporation Act § 2.04 takes a different approach. Under that provision, only persons acting as or on behalf of a corporation who knew there was no incorporation are jointly and severally liable for the would-be corporation's liabilities. This provision protects would-be shareholders of defectively formed corporations in cases where the would-be shareholders honestly and reasonably, although erroneously, believed that a corporation had been properly formed. Model Act § 2.04 eliminates much but not necessarily all of the need for estoppel doctrine.

———

Fred McChesney, Doctrinal Analysis and Statistical Modeling in Law: The Case of Defective Incorporation

71 Wash. U.L.Q. 493, 498–99 (1993)

Three requirements are typically cited for application of the de facto corporation doctrine. There must have been: (1) a statute in existence by which incorporation was legally possible; (2) a 'colorable' attempt to comply with the statute; and (3) some actual use or exercise of corporate privileges. Because every state has a corporation statute and defendants ordinarily have been acting under the aegis of a supposed corporation, the three factors typically dissolve into one: whether defendants' attempts to incorporate had gone far enough to be deemed 'colorable compliance.' For example, an attempt to file the articles of incorporation, albeit unsuccessful, has frequently sufficed as the necessary attempt at statutory compliance. 'In addition, some cases and commentators have added good faith of corporation or associates as a fourth element. [The good faith requirement] is often omitted, however, because a colorable compliance with the incorporation statute usually encompasses a good faith attempt to incorporate.'

_____

3. VEIL PIERCING

_____

DEL. GEN. CORP. LAW § 102(b)(6)

[See Statutory Supplement]

_____

MODEL BUS. CORP. ACT § 6.22(b)

[See Statutory Supplement]

_____

INTRODUCTORY NOTE ON LIMITED LIABILITY

It is commonly said that shareholders have limited liability for corporate obligations. Actually, however, shareholders ordinarily have *no* liability for corporate obligations. Under modern statutes, a shareholder's risk is ordinarily limited to her *investment*; that is, the most a shareholder stands to lose, even if the corporation fails, is the amount that she paid for her shares. Nevertheless, the term *limited liability* is universally used to refer to the no-liability rule, and therefore will be used in this book as well.

It is also sometimes said that shareholders are not liable for corporate obligations because corporations are separate legal entities. In fact, however, the entity status of corporations has almost nothing to do with shareholder limited liability. For example, English law conferred entity status on corporations long before shareholders were afforded limited liability. Similarly, the Revised Uniform Partnership Act (RUPA) confers entity status on partnerships, but also provides that the partners are individually liable for all partnership obligations once the partnership's assets are exhausted. Accordingly, although cases in which liability is imposed on shareholders, despite the ordinary rules, are commonly said to involve "disregard of the corporate entity" or "piercing the corporate veil," really these cases involve only a conclusion that under given kinds of circumstances there are good reasons why the normal statutory rule of limited liability should not be applied.

It should also be borne in mind that corporate managers, as well as corporate shareholders, are ordinarily not liable for corporate obligations. Shareholders are not liable for corporate obligations by statute. In contrast, managers are not liable for corporate obligations on straightforward agency principles: In the case of a contract that is made by an agent within his authority, the agent is not liable as long as she purported to act in that capacity and the identity of her principal was disclosed. Similarly, in the case of a tort by a subordinate employee, a manager normally will not be vicariously liable to the injured party even if the employee was the manager's subordinate. However, a corporate manager may be liable to a third party if he personally commits or directs the commission of the tortious action. The liability of corporate managers to third parties is considered in more detail in the Note on Civil Liabilities of Directors and Officers in Chapter 9, Section 1(C).

Walkovszky v. Carlton

Court of Appeals of New York, 1966.
18 N.Y.2d 414, 276 N.Y.S.2d 585, 223 N.E.2d 6.

■ FULD, JUDGE. This case involves what appears to be a rather common practice in the taxicab industry of vesting the ownership of a taxi fleet in many corporations, each owning only one or two cabs.

The complaint alleges that the plaintiff was severely injured four years ago in New York City when he was run down by a taxicab owned by the defendant Seon Cab Corporation and negligently operated at the time by the defendant Marchese. The individual defendant, Carlton, is claimed to be a stockholder of 10 corporations, including Seon, each of which has but two cabs registered in its name, and it is implied that only the minimum automobile liability insurance required by law (in the amount of $10,000) is carried on any one cab. Although seemingly independent of one another, these corporations are alleged to be "operated . . . as a single entity, unit and enterprise" with regard to financing, supplies, repairs, employees and garaging, and all are named as defendants.[1] The plaintiff asserts that he is also entitled to hold their stockholders personally liable for the damages sought because the multiple corporate structure constitutes an unlawful attempt "to defraud members of the general public" who might be injured by the cabs.

The defendant Carlton has moved, pursuant to CPLR 3211(a)7, to dismiss the complaint on the ground that as to him it "fails to state a cause of action". The court at Special Term granted the motion but the Appellate Division, by a divided vote, reversed, holding that a valid cause of action was sufficiently stated. The defendant Carlton appeals to us, from the nonfinal order, by leave of the Appellate Division on a certified question.

The law permits the incorporation of a business for the very purpose of enabling its proprietors to escape personal liability (see, e.g., Bartle v. Home Owners Co-op., 309 N.Y. 103, 106, 127 N.E.2d 832, 833) but, manifestly, the privilege is not without its limits. Broadly speaking, the courts will disregard the corporate form, or, to use accepted terminology,

---

[1]   The corporate owner of a garage is also included as a defendant.

"pierce the corporate veil", whenever necessary "to prevent fraud or to achieve equity". (International Aircraft Trading Co. v. Manufacturers Trust Co., 297 N.Y. 285, 292, 79 N.E.2d 249, 252.) In determining whether liability should be extended to reach assets beyond those belonging to the corporation, we are guided, as Judge Cardozo noted, by "general rules of agency". (Berkey v. Third Ave. Ry. Co., 244 N.Y. 84, 95, 155 N.E. 58, 61, 50 A.L.R. 599.) In other words, whenever anyone uses control of the corporation to further his own rather than the corporation's business, he will be liable for the corporation's acts "upon the principle of *respondeat superior* applicable even where the agent is a natural person". . . . Such liability, moreover, extends not only to the corporation's commercial dealings . . . but to its negligent acts as well. . . .

In [Mangan v. Terminal Transp. System, 247 App.Div. 853, 286 N.Y.S. 666, mot. for lv. to app. den. 272 N.Y. 676, 286 N.Y.S. 666,] the plaintiff was injured as a result of the negligent operation of a cab owned and operated by one of four corporations affiliated with the defendant Terminal. Although the defendant was not a stockholder of any of the operating companies, both the defendant and the operating companies were owned, for the most part, by the same parties. The defendant's name (Terminal) was conspicuously displayed on the sides of all of the taxis used in the enterprise and, in point of fact, the defendant actually serviced, inspected, repaired and dispatched them. These facts were deemed to provide sufficient cause for piercing the corporate veil of the operating company—the nominal owner of the cab which injured the plaintiff—and holding the defendant liable. The operating companies were simply instrumentalities for carrying on the business of the defendant without imposing upon it financial and other liabilities incident to the actual ownership and operation of the cabs. . . .

In the case before us, the plaintiff has explicitly alleged that none of the corporations "had a separate existence of their own" and, as indicated above, all are named as defendants. However, it is one thing to assert that a corporation is a fragment of a larger corporate combine which actually conducts the business. (See Berle, The Theory of Enterprise Entity, 47 Col.L.Rev. 343, 348–350.) It is quite another to claim that the corporation is a "dummy" for its individual stockholders who are in reality carrying on the business in their personal capacities for purely personal rather than corporate ends. (See African Metals Corp. v. Bullowa, 288 N.Y. 78, 85, 41 N.E.2d 466, 469.) Either circumstance would justify treating the corporation as an agent and piercing the corporate veil to reach the principal but a different result would follow in each case. In the first, only a larger *corporate* entity would be held financially responsible . . . while, in the other, the stockholder would be personally liable. . . . Either the stockholder is conducting the business in his individual capacity or he is not. If he is, he will be liable; if he is not, then it does not matter—insofar as his personal liability is concerned—that the enterprise is actually being carried on by a larger "enterprise entity". (See Berle, The Theory of Enterprise Entity, 47 Col.L.Rev. 343.)

At this stage in the present litigation, we are concerned only with the pleadings and, since CPLR 3014 permits causes of action to be stated "alternatively or hypothetically", it is possible for the plaintiff to allege both theories as the basis for his demand for judgment. In ascertaining whether he has done so, we must consider the entire pleading, educing therefrom " 'whatever can be imputed from its statements by fair and reasonable intendment.' " (Condon v. Associated Hosp. Serv., 287 N.Y. 411, 414, 40 N.E.2d 230, 231. . . .) Reading the complaint in this case most favorably and liberally, we do not believe that there can be gathered from its averments the allegations required to spell out a valid cause of action against the defendant Carlton.

The individual defendant is charged with having "organized, managed, dominated and controlled" a fragmented corporate entity but there are no allegations that he was conducting business in his individual capacity. Had the taxicab fleet been owned by a single corporation, it would be readily apparent that the plaintiff would face formidable barriers in attempting to establish personal liability on the part of the corporation's stockholders. The fact that the fleet ownership has been deliberately split up among many corporations does not ease the plaintiff's burden in that respect. The corporate form may not be disregarded merely because the assets of the corporation, together with the mandatory insurance coverage of the vehicle which struck the plaintiff, are insufficient to assure him the recovery sought. If Carlton were to be held individually liable on those facts alone, the decision would apply equally to the thousands of cabs which are owned by their individual drivers who conduct their businesses through corporations organized pursuant to section 401 of the Business Corporation Law, Consol.Laws, c. 4 and carry the minimum insurance required by subdivision 1 (par. [a]) of section 370 of the Vehicle and Traffic Law, Consol.Laws, c. 71. These taxi owner-operators are entitled to form such corporations (cf. Elenkrieg v. Siebrecht, 238 N.Y. 254, 144 N.E. 519, 34 A.L.R. 592), and we agree with the court at Special Term that, if the insurance coverage required by statute "is inadequate for the protection of the public, the remedy lies not with the courts but with the Legislature." It may very well be sound policy to require that certain corporations must take out liability insurance which will afford adequate compensation to their potential tort victims. However, the responsibility for imposing conditions on the privilege of incorporation has been committed by the Constitution to the Legislature (N.Y. Const., art. X, 1) and it may not be fairly implied, from any statute, that the Legislature intended, without the slightest discussion or debate, to require of taxi corporations that they carry automobile liability insurance over and above that mandated by the Vehicle and Traffic Law.

This is not to say that it is impossible for the plaintiff to state a valid cause of action against the defendant Carlton. However, the simple fact is that the plaintiff has just not done so here. While the complaint alleges that the separate corporations were undercapitalized and that their assets have been intermingled, it is barren of any "sufficiently particular[ized] statements" (CPLR 3013; see 3 Weinstein-Korn-Miller, N.Y.Civ.Prac., par. 3013.01 et seq., pp. 30–142 et seq.) that the defendant Carlton and his associates are actually doing business in their individual capacities, shuttling their personal funds in and out of the corporations "without regard to formality and to suit their immediate convenience." (Weisser v. Mursam Shoe Corp., 2 Cir., 127 F.2d 344, 345, 145 A.L.R. 467, supra.) Such a "perversion of the privilege to do business in a corporate form" (Berkey v. Third Ave. Ry. Co., 244 N.Y. 84, 95, 155 N.E. 58, 61, 50 A.L.R. 599, supra) would justify imposing personal liability on the individual stockholders. (See African Metals Corp. v. Bullowa, 288 N.Y. 78, 41 N.E.2d 466, supra.) Nothing of the sort has in fact been charged, and it cannot reasonably or logically be inferred from the happenstance that the business of Seon Cab Corporation may actually be carried on by a larger corporate entity composed of many corporations which, under general principles of agency, would be liable to each other's creditors in contract and in tort.[3]

In point of fact, the principle relied upon in the complaint to sustain the imposition of personal liability is not agency but fraud. Such a cause of action cannot withstand analysis. If it is not fraudulent for the owner-operator of a single cab corporation to take out only the minimum required liability insurance, the enterprise does not become either illicit or fraudulent merely because it consists of many such corporations. The plaintiff's injuries are the same regardless of whether the cab which strikes him is owned by a single corporation or part of a fleet with ownership fragmented among many corporations. Whatever rights he may be able to assert against parties other than the registered owner of the vehicle come into being not because he has been defrauded but because, under the principle of *respondeat superior,* he is entitled to hold the whole enterprise responsible for the acts of its agents.

In sum, then, the complaint falls short of adequately stating a cause of action against the defendant Carlton in his individual capacity.

The order of the Appellate Division should be reversed, with costs in this court and in the Appellate Division, the certified question answered in the negative and the order of the Supreme Court, Richmond County, reinstated, with leave to serve an amended complaint.

---

[3] In his affidavit in opposition to the motion to dismiss, the plaintiff's counsel claimed that corporate assets had been "milked out" of, and "siphoned off" from the enterprise. Quite apart from the fact that these allegations are far too vague and conclusory, the charge is premature. If the plaintiff succeeds in his action and becomes a judgment creditor of the corporation, he may then sue and attempt to hold the individual defendants accountable for any dividends and property that were wrongfully distributed (Business Corporation Law, §§ 510, 719, 720).

■ KEATING, JUDGE (dissenting).

The defendant Carlton, the shareholder here sought to be held for the negligence of the driver of a taxicab, was a principal shareholder and organizer of the defendant corporation which owned the taxicab. The corporation was one of 10 organized by the defendant, each containing two cabs and each cab having the "minimum liability" insurance coverage mandated by section 370 of the Vehicle and Traffic Law. The sole assets of these operating corporations are the vehicles themselves and they are apparently subject to mortgages.[1]

From their inception these corporations were intentionally undercapitalized for the purpose of avoiding responsibility for acts which were bound to arise as a result of the operation of a large taxi fleet having cars out on the street 24 hours a day and engaged in public transportation. And during the course of the corporations' existence all income was continually drained out of the corporations for the same purpose.

The issue presented by this action is whether the policy of this State, which affords those desiring to engage in a business enterprise the privilege of limited liability through the use of the corporate devise, is so strong that it will permit that privilege to continue no matter how much it is abused, no matter how irresponsibly the corporation is operated, no matter what the cost to the public. I do not believe that it is.

Under the circumstances of this case the shareholders should all be held individually liable to this plaintiff for the injuries he suffered. (See Mull v. Colt Co., D.C., 31 F.R.D. 154, 156; Teller v. Clear Service Co., 9 Misc.2d 495, 173 N.Y.S.2d 183.) At least, the matter should not be disposed of on the pleadings by a dismissal of the complaint. "If a corporation is organized and carries on business without substantial capital in such a way that the corporation is likely to have no sufficient assets available to meet its debts, it is inequitable that shareholders should set up such a flimsy organization to escape personal liability. The attempt to do corporate business without providing any sufficient basis of financial responsibility to creditors is an abuse of the separate entity and will be ineffectual to exempt the shareholders from corporate debts. It is coming to be recognized as the policy of law that shareholders should in good faith put at the risk of the business unencumbered capital reasonably adequate for its prospective liabilities. If capital is illusory or trifling compared with the business to be done and the risks of loss, this is a ground for denying the separate entity privilege." (Ballantine, Corporations [rev. ed., 1946], § 129, pp. 302–303.) . . .

■ DESMOND, C.J., and VAN VOORHIS, BURKE and SCILEPPI, JJ., concur with FULD, J.

---

[1]   It appears that the medallions, which are of considerable value, are judgment proof. (Administrative Code of City of New York, § 436–2.0.) [Footnote by the court.]

■ KEATING, J., dissents and votes to affirm in an opinion in which BERGAN, J., concurs.

Order reversed, etc.

––––––––

NOTE ON FURTHER PROCEEDINGS IN WALKOVSZKY V. CARLTON

Following the decision in *Walkovszky,* the plaintiff amended his complaint. The Appellate Division held that "the amended complaint sufficiently alleges a cause of action against appellant, i.e., that he and the other individual defendants were conducting the business of the taxicab fleet in their individual capacities." Walkovszky v. Carlton, 29 A.D.2d 763, 287 N.Y.S.2d 546 (1968). That decision was affirmed by the Court of Appeals, 23 N.Y.2d 714, 296 N.Y.S.2d 362, 244 N.E.2d 55 (1968), noting that the amended complaint "now meets the pleading requirements set forth in [our prior] opinion and states a valid cause of action." Neither opinion stated the particulars in which the amended complaint differed from the original.

––––––––

Minton v. Cavaney

Supreme Court of California, 1961.
56 Cal.2d 576, 15 Cal.Rptr. 641, 364 P.2d 473.

■ TRAYNOR, JUSTICE. The Seminole Hot Springs Corporation, hereinafter referred to as Seminole, was duly incorporated in California on March 8, 1954. It conducted a public swimming pool that it leased from its owner. On June 24, 1954 plaintiffs' daughter drowned in the pool, and plaintiffs recovered a judgment for $10,000 against Seminole for her wrongful death. The judgment remains unsatisfied.

On January 30, 1957, plaintiffs brought the present action to hold defendant Cavaney personally liable for the judgment against Seminole. Cavaney died on May 28, 1958 and his widow, the executrix of his estate, was substituted as defendant. The trial court entered judgment for plaintiffs for $10,000. Defendant appeals.

Plaintiffs introduced evidence that Cavaney was a director and secretary and treasurer of Seminole and that on November 15, 1954, about five months after the drowning, Cavaney as secretary of Seminole and Edwin A. Kraft as president of Seminole applied for permission to issue three shares of Seminole stock, one share to be issued to Kraft, another to F.J. Wettrick and the third to Cavaney. The commissioner of corporations refused permission to issue these shares unless additional information was furnished. The application was then abandoned and no shares were ever issued. There was also evidence that for a time Seminole used Cavaney's office to keep records and to receive mail. Before his death Cavaney answered certain interrogatories. He was asked if Seminole "ever had any assets?" He stated that "insofar as my own personal knowledge and belief is concerned said corporation did not have any assets." Cavaney also stated in the return to an attempted execution that "[I]nsofar as I know, this corporation had no assets of any kind or character. The corporation was duly organized but never functioned as a corporation."

Defendant introduced evidence that Cavaney was an attorney at law, that he was approached by Kraft and Wettrick to form Seminole, and that he was the attorney for Seminole. Plaintiffs introduced Cavaney's answer to several interrogatories that he held the post of secretary and treasurer and director in a temporary capacity and as an accommodation to his client.

Defendant contends that the evidence does not support the court's determination that Cavaney is personally liable for Seminole's debts and that the "alter ego" doctrine is inapplicable because plaintiffs failed to show that there was " '(1) . . . such unity of interest and ownership that the separate personalities of the corporation and the individual no longer exist and (2) that, if the acts are treated as those of the corporation alone, an inequitable result will follow.' " Riddle v. Leuschner, 51 Cal.2d 574, 580, 335 P.2d 107, 110; Automotriz Del Golfo De California S.A. De C.V. v. Resnick, 47 Cal.2d 792, 796, 306 P.2d 1, 63 A.L.R.2d 1042; Minifie v. Rowley, 187 Cal. 481, 487, 202 P. 673.

The figurative terminology "alter ego" and "disregard of the corporate entity" is generally used to refer to the various situations that are an abuse of the corporate privilege. . . . The equitable owners of a corporation, for example, are personally liable when they treat the assets of the corporation as their own and add or withdraw capital from the corporation at will . . . ; when they hold themselves out as being personally liable for the debts of the corporation . . . ; or when they provide inadequate capitalization and actively participate in the conduct of corporate affairs. . . .

In the instant case the evidence is undisputed that there was no attempt to provide adequate capitalization. Seminole never had any substantial assets. It leased the pool that it operated, and the lease was forfeited for failure to pay the rent. Its capital was " 'trifling compared with the business to be done and the risks of loss . . .' " Automotriz Del Golfo De California S.A. De C.V. v. Resnick, supra, 47 Cal.2d 792, 797, 306 P.2d 1, 4. The evidence is also undisputed that Cavaney was not only the secretary and treasurer of the corporation but was also a director. The evidence that Cavaney was to receive one-third of the shares to be issued supports an inference that he was an equitable owner (see Riddle v. Leuschner, supra, 51 Cal.2d 574, 580, 335 P.2d 107), and the evidence that for a time the records of the corporation were kept in Cavaney's office supports an inference that he actively participated in the conduct of the business. The trial court was not required to believe his statement that he was only a "temporary" director and officer "for accommodation." In any event it merely raised a conflict in the evidence that was resolved adversely to defendant. Moreover, section 800 of the Corporations Code provides that ". . . the business and affairs of every corporation shall be controlled by a board of not less than three directors." Defendant does not claim that Cavaney was a director with specialized duties (see 5 U.Chi.L.Rev. 668). It is immaterial whether or not he accepted the office of director as an "accommodation" with the understanding that he would not exercise any of the duties of a director. A person may not in this manner divorce the responsibilities of a director from the statutory duties and powers of that office. . . .

In this action to hold defendant personally liable upon the judgment against Seminole plaintiffs did not allege or present any evidence on the issue of Seminole's negligence or on the amount of damages sustained by plaintiffs. They relied solely on the judgment against Seminole. Defendant correctly contends that Cavaney or his estate cannot be held liable for the debts of Seminole without an opportunity to relitigate these issues. . . . Cavaney was not a party to the action against the corporation, and the judgment in that action is therefore not binding upon him unless he controlled the litigation leading to the judgment. . . .

The judgment is reversed.

■ GIBSON, C.J., and PETERS, WHITE and DOOLING, JJ., concur.

■ [The opinion of JUSTICE SCHAUER, concurring and dissenting, is omitted. JUSTICE MCCOMB concurred without opinion.]

———

Arnold v. Browne

27 Cal.App.3d 386, 396, 103 Cal.Rptr. 775, 783 (1972)

Evidence of inadequate capitalization is, at best, merely a factor to be considered by the trial court in deciding whether or not to pierce the corporate veil (Harris v. Curtis, 8 Cal.App.3d 837, 841, 87 Cal.Rptr. 614). To be sure, it is an important factor, but no case has been cited, nor have any been found, where it has been held that this factor alone *requires* invoking the equitable doctrine prayed for in the instant case.

———

Slottow Fidelity Federal Bank v. American Casualty Co.

10 F.3d 1355 (9th Cir. 1993)

[T]he plaintiffs . . . had an excellent argument under an alter ego theory for piercing the corporate veil. To begin with, [the] initial capitalization of $500,000 was woefully inadequate for a corporation that handled trust agreements of the magnitude involved here. The investors claimed damages [against the corporation] in the range of $10,000,000; the case settled for nearly half that. Under California law, inadequate capitalization of a subsidiary may alone be a basis for holding the parent corporation liable for acts of the subsidiary. See, e.g., Nilsson, Robbins,

Dalgarn, Berliner, Carson & Wurst v. Louisiana Hydrolec, 854 F.2d 1538, 1544 (9th Cir.1988). . . .

———

Truckweld Equipment Co., Inc. v. Olson

26 Wash.App. 638, 645, 618 P.2d 1017, 1022 (1980)

Although there may be situations in which a corporation is so thinly capitalized that it manifests a fraudulent intent, we do not find such to be true in the case at bar. . . . Olson acquired Aztec when it was financially troubled; he was not the original incorporator and he sought only to improve Aztec's profit picture. Despite gross sales of over $800,000 it appears a combination of unfortunate timing and persistent working capital problems sounded Aztec's death knell. We know of no rule of law requiring a corporate stockholder to commit additional private funds to an already faltering corporation.

———

Radaszewski v. Telecom Corp.

981 F.2d 305 (8th Cir.1992)

In order to pierce the corporate veil, a plaintiff must show, among other things, that the defendant's control of a subsidiary has

> been used by the defendant to commit fraud or wrong, to perpetrate the violation of a statutory or other positive legal duty, or dishonest and unjust act in contravention of plaintiff's legal rights. . . . "

[Collet v. American National Stores, Inc., 708 S.W.2d 273, 284 Mo.App. 1986]. To satisfy this . . . element, plaintiff cites no direct evidence of improper motivation or violation of law on Telecom's part. He argues, instead, that Contrux was undercapitalized.

... [T]he creation of an undercapitalized subsidiary justifies an inference that the parent is either deliberately or recklessly creating a business that will not be able to pay its bills or satisfy judgments against it. . . .

Here, the District Court held, and we assume, that Contrux [the subsidiary] was undercapitalized in the accounting sense. Most of the money contributed to its operation by Telecom [the parent] was in the form of loans, not equity, and, when Contrux first went into business, Telecom did not pay for all of the stock that was issued to it. . . . Telecom in effect concedes that Contrux's balance sheet was anemic, and that, from the point of view of generally accepted accounting principles, Contrux was inadequately capitalized. Telecom says, however, that this doesn't matter, because Contrux had $11,000,000 worth of liability insurance available to pay judgments like the one that Radaszewski hopes to obtain. No one can say, therefore, the argument runs, that Telecom was improperly motivated in setting up Contrux, in the sense of either knowingly or recklessly establishing it without the ability to pay tort judgments.

In fact, Contrux did have $1,000,000 in basic liability coverage, plus $10,000,000 in excess coverage. This coverage was bound on March 1, 1984, about five and one-half months before the accident involving Radaszewski. Unhappily, Contrux's insurance carrier became insolvent two years after the accident and is now in receivership. . . .

The District Court rejected this argument. Undercapitalization is undercapitalization, it reasoned, regardless of insurance. The Court said:

> The federal regulation does not speak to what constitutes a properly capitalized motor carrier company. Rather, the regulation speaks to what constitutes an appropriate level of *financial responsibility*.

. . . This distinction escapes us. The whole purpose of asking whether a subsidiary is 'properly capitalized,' is precisely to determine its 'financial responsibility.' If the subsidiary is financially responsible, whether by means of insurance or otherwise, the policy behind . . . the *Collet* test is met. Insurance meets this policy just as well, perhaps even better, than a healthy balance sheet."

————

Sea-Land Services, Inc. v. Pepper Source

United States Court of Appeals, Seventh Circuit, 1993.
993 F.2d 1309.

■ TIMBERS, SENIOR CIRCUIT JUDGE.

Appellants appeal from a judgment entered after a bench trial in the Northern District of Illinois, James F. Holderman, *District Judge,* piercing the corporate veil and awarding appellee $118,132.61 in damages. . . .

[Appellee Sea-Land Services, Inc. ("Sea-Land"), an ocean carrier, shipped peppers on behalf of The Pepper Source ("PS"), one of the appellants here. PS then stiffed Sea-Land on the freight bill, which was rather substantial. Sea-Land filed a federal diversity action for the money it was owed. On December 2, 1987, the district court entered a default judgment in favor of Sea-Land and against PS in the amount of $86,767.70. But PS was nowhere to be found; it had been "dissolved" in mid-1987 for failure to pay the annual state franchise tax. Worse yet for Sea-Land, even had it not been dissolved, PS apparently had no assets. With the well empty, Sea-Land could not recover its judgment against PS. Hence the instant lawsuit.

[In June 1988, Sea-Land brought this action against Gerald J. Marchese and five business entities he owns: PS, Caribe Crown, Inc., Jamar Corp., Salescaster Distributors, Inc., and Marchese Fegan

Associates. Marchese also was named individually. Sea-Land sought by this suit to pierce PS's corporate veil and render Marchese personally liable for the judgment owed to Sea-Land, and then "reverse pierce" Marchese's other corporations so that they, too, would be on the hook for the $87,000. Thus, Sea-Land alleged in its complaint that all of these corporations "are alter egos of each other and hide behind the veils of alleged separate corporate existence for the purpose of defrauding plaintiff and other creditors." Count I, § 11. Not only are the corporations alter egos of each other, alleged Sea-Land, but also they are alter egos of Marchese, who should be held individually liable for the judgment because he created and manipulated these corporations and their assets for his own personal uses. Count III, §§ 9–10. (Hot on the heels of the filing of Sea-Land's complaint, PS took the necessary steps to be reinstated as a corporation in Illinois.)

[In an order dated June 22, 1990, the trial court discussed and applied the test for corporate veil-piercing explicated in *Van Dorn Co. v. Future Chemical and Oil Corp.,* 753 F.2d 565 (7th Cir.1985). Analyzing Illinois law, we held in *Van Dorn* that

> a corporate entity will be disregarded and the veil of limited liability pierced when two requirements are met:
>
>> [F]irst, there must be such unity of interest and ownership that the separate personalities of the corporation and the individual [or other corporation] no longer exist; and second, circumstances must be such that adherence to the fiction of separate corporate existence would sanction a fraud or promote injustice.

753 F.2d at 569–70. As for determining whether a corporation is so controlled by another to justify disregarding their separate identities, the Illinois cases, as we summarized them in *Van Dorn,* focus on four factors: "(1) the failure to maintain adequate corporate records or to comply with corporate formalities, (2) the commingling of funds or assets, (3) undercapitalization, and (4) one corporation treating the assets of another corporation as its own."

[The first and most striking feature that emerges from our examination of the record is that these corporate defendants are, indeed, little but Marchese's playthings. Marchese is the sole shareholder of PS, Caribe Crown, Jamar, and Salescaster. None of the corporations ever held a single corporate meeting. During his deposition, Marchese did not remember any of these corporations ever passing articles of incorporation, bylaws, or other agreements. As for physical facilities, Marchese runs all of these corporations out of the same, single office, with the same phone line, the same expense accounts, and the like. And how he does "run" the expense accounts! When he fancies to, Marchese "borrows" substantial sums of money from these corporations—interest free, of course. The corporations also "borrow" money from each other when need be, which left at least PS completely out of capital when the

Sea-Land bills came due. What's more, Marchese has used the bank accounts of these corporations to pay all kinds of personal expenses, including alimony and child support payments to his ex-wife, education expenses for his children, maintenance of his personal automobiles, health care for his pet—the list goes on and on. Marchese did not even have a personal bank account!]* In sum, there can be no doubt that the "shared control/unity of interest and ownership" part of the *Van Dorn* test is not met in this case.

. . . The issues raised by the second prong of *Van Dorn* were tried on July 6 and 7, 1992. On July 9, 1992, the [district] court entered judgment for Sea-Land, awarding it $118,132.61 in damages. The court concluded that Sea-Land satisfied the second prong of *Van Dorn* by establishing wrongs beyond its inability to collect on its judgment.

On the instant appeal, appellants contend that the evidence presented by Sea-Land at trial was insufficient to satisfy the second prong of *Van Dorn*. They also assert that the court misapplied Illinois law in reaching its decision. . . .

. . . Sea-Land adduced sufficient evidence at trial to establish additional wrongs to justify piercing the corporate veil. First, Sea-Land demonstrated that Marchese and his corporations were unjustly enriched. We have defined "unjust enrichment" as the receipt of money or its equivalent under circumstances that, in equity and good conscience, suggest that it ought not to be retained because it belongs to someone else. *Midcoast Aviation, Inc. v. General Elec. Credit Corp.,* 907 F.2d 732, 737 (7th Cir.1990). At trial, Sea-Land demonstrated that Marchese obtained countless benefits at the expense of not only Sea-Land, but the Internal Revenue Service (IRS) and other creditors as well. Indeed, Marchese used PS funds to pay his personal expenses as well as expenses incurred by his other corporations. As a result, PS was left without sufficient funds to satisfy Sea-Land or PS's other creditors. *American Trade Partners v. A-1 Int'l Importing Enter.,* 770 F.Supp. 273, 278 (E.D.Pa.1991) (corporate veil pierced on basis of unjust enrichment where managing shareholder, with knowledge of debt to creditor, used corporation's funds to pay personal expenses). Since Marchese was enriched unjustly by his intentional manipulation and diversion of funds from his corporate entities, to allow him to use these same entities to avoid liability "would be to sanction an injustice." *Gromer, Wittenstrom & Meyer, P.C. v. Strom,* 140 Ill.App.3d 349, 354, 489 N.E.2d 370, 374 (1986).

Sea-Land also satisfied the second prong of *Van Dorn* by demonstrating at trial that Marchese used his corporate entities as "playthings" to avoid his responsibilities to creditors. An accountant testified that Marchese's payment of personal expenses with corporate

---

* The bracketed paragraphs are adapted from a prior appeal in this case, 941 F.2d 519 (7th Cir. 1991).

funds enabled those corporations to avoid their monetary obligations to vendors, creditors, and federal and state tax authorities. One example was Marchese's withdrawal of $19,000 as salary from Jamar Corporation. This withdrawal rendered Jamar insolvent and thus unable to satisfy liabilities in excess of $450,000. Marchese also frequently took "shareholder loans" from the corporations to pay personal expenses, leaving the corporations with insufficient funds to satisfy liabilities as they became due. Further, a tax accountant testified that Marchese's business practices were replete with illegal transactions. Indeed, as we previously recognized, "for years Marchese flagrantly has disregarded the tax code concerning the treatment of corporate funds." *Sea-Land, supra,* 941 F.2d at 522 n. 2.

Marchese's practice of avoiding liability to Sea-Land and other creditors by insuring that his corporations had insufficient funds with which to pay their debts, is ground for piercing the corporate veil. *Van Dorn, supra,* 753 F.2d at 572–73 (piercing of corporate veil allowed where subsidiary was stripped by parent corporation of its assets and rendered insolvent to the prejudice of creditor). Further, as the district court here properly recognized, Marchese was the "dominant force" behind all of the corporations and was responsible for the manipulation and diversion of corporate funds without regard for creditors or the law. *B. Kreisman & Co. v. First Arlington Nat'l Bank,* 91 Ill.App.3d 847, 415 N.E.2d 1070 (1980) (piercing corporate veil proper where defendant was the dominant force behind corporation). On the basis of the facts adduced at trial, the court properly concluded that Sea-Land satisfied the second-prong of *Van Dorn* and therefore was entitled to pierce the corporate veil. . . .

Appellants further assert that Sea-Land fails to satisfy the requirement that a nexus exist between its injuries and the fraud or injustice committed by appellants. *South Side Bank v. T.S.B. Corp.,* 94 Ill.App.3d 1006, 419 N.E.2d 477 (1981). This claim fails, however, in view of the fact that Marchese assured Sea-Land in 1987 that it would receive payment from PS as long as there were sufficient funds. The court's findings that Marchese knew at that time that he would manipulate the funds of PS so as to insure that Sea-Land would not be paid, and that he eventually did manipulate those funds, were not clearly erroneous. Since Marchese's intentional and improper financial maneuvering caused Sea-Land's inability to collect on its default judgment, the required nexus existed here. . . .

Affirmed.

———

Berkey v. Third Ave. Ry. Co.

244 N.Y. 84, 94–95 155 N.E. 58, 61 (1926) (Cardozo, J.)

The whole problem of the relation between parent and subsidiary corporations is one that is still enveloped in the mists of metaphor. Metaphors in law are to be narrowly watched, for starting as devices to

liberate thought, they end often by enslaving it. We say at times that the
corporate entity will be ignored when the parent corporation operates a
business through a subsidiary which is characterized as an 'alias' or a
'dummy.' All this is well enough if the picturesqueness of the epithets
does not lead us to forget that the essential term to be defined is the act
of operation. Dominion may be so complete, interference so obtrusive that
by the general rules of agency the parent will be a principal and the
subsidiary an agent. Where control is less than this, we are remitted to
the tests of honesty and justice. Ballentine, Parent and Subsidiary
Corporations, 14 Cal.Law Review, 12, 18, 19, 20. The logical consistency
of a juridical conception will indeed be sacrificed at times, when the
sacrifice is essential to the end that some accepted public policy may be
defended or upheld. This is so, for illustration, though agency in any
proper sense is lacking, where the attempted separation between parent
and subsidiary will work a fraud upon the law. . . . At such times unity is
ascribed to parts which, at least for many purposes, retain an
independent life, for the reason that only thus can we overcome a
perversion of the privilege to do business in a corporate form.

––––––––––

NOTE ON AN EMPIRICAL ANALYSIS OF PIERCING CASES

In his classic study, Piercing The Corporate Veil: An Empirical Study, 76
Cornell L.Rev. 1036 (1991), Professor Robert Thompson reported the results
of an empirical analysis of 2,000 piercing cases, most decided between the
mid-1950s and the mid-1980s. Courts pierced the corporate veil in
approximately 40% of the cases, although there were often noticeable
differences in the rate of plaintiffs' success according to the category of case
and the state in which the case was decided. The corporate veil was pierced
more often in contract cases (42%) than in tort cases (31%). In no case was
the corporate veil of a publicly held corporation pierced to impose liability on
public shareholders, although many cases apparently involved piercing the
veil of a subsidiary of a publicly held corporation to make the publicly held
parent liable. Others have also empirically studied veil-piercing decisions.
One study found that courts pierce twice as often to hold individuals liable
as they do to hold entities liable where a parent-subsidiary relationship
exists, that veil piercing arguments are more successful in contract cases
than tort cases (whereas, with regression analysis, the type of claim—tort
vs. contract—does not bear a statistical relationship to explain why the veil
was pierced in the context of other factors before a court), that appellate
courts are far more likely to pierce the veil than trial courts in cases in which
the dominant stockholder is an individual (but no difference was observed in
the parent-subsidiary context), and that over time there does not appear to
be any statistically significant change in the percentage of cases in which the
veil-piercing argument succeeds. John H. Matheson, Why Courts Pierce: An
Empirical Study of Piercing the Corporate Veil, 7 Berkeley Bus. L. J. 1
(2010). But see Peter B. Oh, Veil Piercing, 89 Tex. L. Rev. 81 (2010) (finding
higher percentage of success in tort than contract claims, but documenting

that success in either category rises with allegations that fraudulent misrepresentations were committed against the claimant, that assets were siphoned away by the dominant stockholder, or that the firm was undercapitalized); Christina L. Boyd & David A. Hoffman, Disputing Limited Liability, 104 Nw. U. L. Rev. 853 (2010) (voluntary creditor is 17 percent more likely to succeed in veil piercing claim than involuntary, e.g., tort, claimant and the overall success rate in piercing the veil is inversely related to the number of employees of the entity to be pierced). All studies conclude that doctrine in this area is not clear so that results are difficult to predict, but overall success rates are such that veil piercing remains a most attractive option for those seeking payment of their claims.

---

4. THE CORPORATE ENTITY AND THE INTERPRETATION OF STATUTES AND CONTRACTS

Brotherhood of Locomotive Eng'rs v. Springfield Terminal Ry. Co.

United States Court of Appeals for the First Circuit, 2000.
210 F.3d 18.

[Two unions sued under the Railway Labor Act alleging the defendants, Springfield Terminal Railway Co. and Aroostook and Bangor Resources, Inc. (ABR) were violating a collective bargaining agreement. The unions and Springfield were involved in labor negotiations that failed. Springfield then had (ABR), a wood products company, perform railroad switching work for Springfield's customers; this work had been historically performed by the unions. The two appellant companies, though in different industries, shared several of the same directors. Although nominally an independent corporation, ABR was not totally unconnected to Springfield. Springfield was a wholly owned subsidiary of Guilford Transportation Industries, Inc. ("Guilford"), a holding company that owned several railroads in New England. Guilford, in turn, was closely held (at the time of the dispute) by four individuals who also served as its directors: David Andrew Fink, David Armstrong Fink, Richard Kelso and Timothy Mellon. Both of the Finks and Mellon were also the sole owners of ABR. The three companies shared the same four directors at the time the dispute arose: the three ABR owners plus Richard Kelso. While David Andrew Fink served as President of Springfield, his son, David Armstrong Fink, served as President of ABR. The trial court held that the evidence indicated Springfield controlled ABR and granted an injunction based on its finding that Springfield was using ABR to violate the collective bargaining provisions and frustrate the Act's intent. Appellant companies appealed. The Circuit Court of Appeals framed the issue before it as follows:

Unless the district court properly treated ABR as the alter ego
of Springfield, and properly disregarded the separateness of the
two corporations by piercing the corporate veil of ABR, it could
not attribute ABR's conduct to Springfield and enjoin ABR from
switching Springfield customers. We must therefore assess
whether veil piercing was appropriate.

The Court of Appeals affirmed and held that since mediation was still
occurring, Springfield could not use ABR as it non-union switching arm
to pressure appellees to accept wage concessions Springfield sought.]

A. Federal Common Law of Veil Piercing

We must determine whether state law or federal common law
governs the veil-piercing inquiry. In federal question cases, such as this
one, we look to federal choice of law principles. See *Texas Indus., Inc. v.
Radcliff Materials, Inc.*, 451 U.S. 630, 642, 68 L. Ed. 2d 500, 101 S. Ct.
2061 (1981) . . . If the federal statute in question demands national
uniformity, federal common law provides the determinative rules of
decision. See *United States v. Kimbell Foods, Inc.*, 440 U.S. 715, 728, 59
L. Ed. 2d 711, 99 S. Ct. 1448 (1979).

National uniformity is essential in the interpretation of labor law.
Federal courts have fashioned a body of federal common law to govern
labor disputes, recognizing that harmonious labor relations are essential
to interstate commerce. . . .

To say that federal common law applies in this case does not fully
resolve the matter. . . . Federal courts are not bound by "the strict
standards of the common law alter ego doctrine which would apply in a
tort or contract action." *Capital Tel. Co. v. FCC*, 162 U.S. App. D.C. 192,
498 F.2d 734, 738 (D.C. Cir. 1974). . . . Instead, the rule in federal cases
is founded only on the broad principle that "a corporate entity may be
disregarded in the interests of public convenience, fairness and equity."
Town of Brookline v. Gorsuch, 667 F.2d 215, 221 (1st. Cir. 1981). In
Gorsuch we recognized that this principle must be applied with sensitivity
to the demands of the federal statute at issue:

> In applying this rule, federal courts will look closely to the
> purpose of the federal statute to determine whether the statute
> places importance on the corporate form, an inquiry that usually
> gives less respect to the corporate form than does the strict
> common law alter ego doctrine.

Id.

B. The Railway Labor Act and Veil Piercing

The major purpose of Congress in passing the Railway Labor Act was
to "provide a machinery to prevent strikes." *Texas & N.O.R. Co. v.
Brotherhood of Ry. & S.S. Clerks*, 281 U.S. 548, 565, 74 L. Ed. 1034, 50
S. Ct. 427 (1930) . . . . The risk of strikes was considered to be
"particularly acute in the area of 'major disputes,' those disputes

involving the formation of collective agreements and efforts to change them." *Shore Line* 396 U.S. at 148. For these disputes, the railroad and union representatives who drafted the Act favored non-binding mediation. See *id.* at 148–49. To prevent strikes from breaking out while mediation was underway, the Act required that both parties maintain the pre-dispute status quo. See *id.* at 149. As the Court noted in Shore-Line, the Act's status quo provision was "central to its design":

> Its immediate effect is to prevent the union from striking and management from doing anything that would justify a strike. In the long run, delaying the time when the parties can resort to self-help provides time for tempers to cool, helps create an atmosphere in which rational bargaining can occur, and permits the forces of public opinion to be mobilized in favor of a settlement without a strike or lockout. Moreover, since disputes usually arise when one party wants to change the status quo without undue delay, the power which the Act gives the other party to preserve the status quo for a prolonged period will frequently make it worthwhile for the moving party to compromise with the interests of the other side and thus reach agreement without interruption to commerce.

Id. at 150. The Act fashioned a fundamental compromise: during the RLA mediation procedures, the union must refrain from striking and the carrier must refrain from implementing the contested policy. . . .

In several cases, courts have engaged in veil piercing when the carrier used an affiliate to escape its collective bargaining agreement and violate the status quo requirements of the RLA. . . .

Common ownership by itself is insufficient to pierce the veil. See *United States v. Best-foods*, 524 U.S. 51, 118 S. Ct. 1876, 1884, 141 L. Ed. 2d 43 (1998) ("[A] parent corporation . . . is not liable for the acts of its subsidiaries."). The record must include evidence that the carrier used the related corporation for the purpose of evading the collective bargaining agreement and the status quo requirements of the RLA. In making this determination, no single factor is dispositive. . . .

We emphasize, however, that the record need not portray the related corporation as a "sham" business, expressly created or operated primarily to defeat the RLA. . . . It must be remembered that veil piercing in the RLA context serves a different function than it does in the ordinary state law veil piercing cases. In a typical tort or contract case, the primary purpose of the veil-piercing analysis is exposure of the assets of one corporation for payment of the debts or obligations of a related corporation. In the RLA major dispute proceedings, veil piercing operates only to block the related corporation from assisting the carrier in altering the collective bargaining agreement before mediation procedures are exhausted. . . .

In this way, RLA veil piercing is similar to the well-established practice of extending the scope of an injunction to include non-parties acting in concert with parties to defeat the injunction's purpose. See Fed. R. Civ. P. 65(d) (injunctions can block activities of non-parties who act "in active concert or participation" with enjoined parties). . . .

With these principles in mind, we turn to the findings of the district court.

C. The District Court's Findings . . .

While the evidence supporting the district court's finding that Springfield used ABR to circumvent its collective bargaining agreement with the Unions was circumstantial, there was, contrary to the insistence of the dissent, sufficient evidence to support that conclusion. First, the district court properly noted that the overlap in ownership between Springfield and ABR was almost total. Three of the four individuals who owned Springfield (through the Guilford holding company) were the sole owners of ABR. At the time the dispute arose, the three corporations (Guilford, Springfield and ABR) had the same four directors: specifically, the three owners of ABR, plus Richard Kelso.

Although the "close family relationship" between ABR and Springfield is not dispositive of the veil-piercing inquiry, the district court also properly relied upon a chronology of events which supports an inference that Springfield was using ABR to violate its collective bargaining agreement and defeat the RLA status quo requirements. Notably, Springfield only invited ABR to start performing switching for its customers after Springfield was unable to convince the Unions to accept wage concessions. Also, the Springfield vice-president who approached ABR, Sydney Culliford, was described by one union leader as the key player in the failed labor negotiations. Likewise, the ABR executive who decided that the wood products shop should start switching for Springfield customers was David Armstrong Fink, who in addition to being President of ABR was also an owner of Guilford and director of Springfield (and several months later, Springfield's executive vice-president). It was not unreasonable for the district court to conclude that the work was shifted to ABR after the first round of failed negotiations as a way of pressuring the Unions to accept wage concessions, and [of] circumventing the RLA strictures that bar these unilateral changes. The dissent argues that this reading of the evidence must be rejected because ABR only performed switching for Springfield customers Lincoln and Champion after they had already (and independently) decided to stop using Springfield for switching. However, the only evidence that Lincoln and Champion had chosen to end their switching agreement with Springfield before ABR was presented as an alternative comes from assertions by Springfield managers and officers. The district court did not credit this version of events in its opinion, and nothing compelled it to do so. Springfield and ABR officials participated together in discussions with Lincoln and Champion over who should perform the switching. . . . Other evidence indicates that even after ABR took over the day-to-day switching work, Lincoln saw ABR as simply the non-union switching arm of Springfield. On one occasion when Lincoln needed to change its switching schedule, it wrote a letter to Springfield, not ABR, informing it of its needs. . . .

Taken together, this evidence amply supports the conclusions that ABR was not acting as an independent company in providing switching services, that Springfield was attempting to convert two of ABR's thirty-four employees into its non-union switching arm, and that Springfield was using ABR as a lever against the Unions, pressuring them to accept lower pay by changing the status quo in the middle of negotiations. Given that a central purpose of the RLA is to block such tactics, see *Shore Line*, 396 U.S. at 148, the district court did not err in enjoining ABR from switching Springfield consignees while Springfield and the Unions completed the RLA mediation procedures.

IV.

For all of the above reasons, the judgment below is affirmed.

■ STAHL, CIRCUIT JUDGE, DISSENTING.

I believe the majority. . . misapprehends the federal law on piercing the corporate veil. . . .

While the majority is correct that in ERISA cases, we have crafted "a 'less rigorous' veilpiercing standard," ante at 13, we have not crafted one that is standardless. Contrary to the majority, which contends that veil piercing typically is appropriate to effectuate legislation, this court always has engaged in a more searching inquiry. . . . Instead,

> [a] court using the federal standard should consider (1) whether the parent and the subsidiary ignored the independence of their separate operations, (2) whether some fraudulent intent existed on the principals' part, and (3) whether a substantial injustice would be visited on the proponents of the veil pierce should the court validate the corporate shield.

United Elec., Radio & Mach. Workers v. 163 Pleasant St. Corp., 960 F.2d at 1092–93. As the *163 Pleasant* court noted, "fraudulent intent is the sine qua non to the remedy's availability." Id. at 1093; see also id. at 1095 ("Veil piercing cannot occur without some degree of moral culpability on the parent corporation's part."); *American Bell*, 736 F.2d at 886–87 (finding piercing appropriate only when "the corporations simply acted interchangeably and in disregard of their corporate separateness" (internal quotation marks and citations omitted)). . . .

This case presents no evidence of fraudulent intent nor any evidence of a lack of corporate independence. ABR was formed to operate a sawmill and a wood products plant. . . . It is not a shill. It began its operations not after, or as a result of, the railroad's failed negotiations with the Unions, but in 1994, which was two years before the labor contract even began. It began switching to satisfy its own production needs. It shares with Springfield neither books, funds, nor offices. It shares with Springfield no corporate officers and with the exception of David Armstrong Fink, who is the president of ABR and a vice-president of Springfield, no common employees. Indeed, all it does share with Springfield is some ownership congruence, but the record is silent on the degree of that overlap because it fails to indicate what percentages of each company the Finks and Mellon own. . . .

To justify disregarding the corporate form in a case with mere ownership overlap, the majority relies entirely on cases that involve wholly owned subsidiaries. . . .

Finally, the import of the court's decision today has much significance for ABR. . . . The majority's conclusion . . . does not allow ABR, a nonrailroad and a legitimate business, the right to expand its switching operations to other entities that also desire timely and flexible switching, nor does it regain for Springfield the switching business it already has lost.

I respectfully dissent.

————

NOTES ON INTERPRETATION

The following three issues often arise:

(1) Does a statute or contract that applies to a corporation also apply, by implication, to the corporation's shareholders? For example, if Corporation A agrees with X not to compete with X, may A's sole shareholder compete with X?

(2) Does a statute or contract that applies to an individual also apply, by implication, to a corporation that the individual owns? For example, if a statute prohibits non-citizens from owning ships that ply the U.S. coastal trade, does the statute also prohibit a corporation from owning ships if all of the corporation's stock is held by noncitizens? These issues do not concern whether liability should be imposed on the corporation's shareholders despite the general rule of limited liability. Rather, they are questions of interpretation. In making such interpretations, it must be borne in mind that on the one hand, the law normally treats a corporation and its shareholders as distinct, but on the other hand, the legislature or the contracting parties may not intend to treat a corporation and its shareholders as distinct for all purposes.

Two of the leading cases in this area are *United States v. Milwaukee Refrigerator Transit Co.*, 142 Fed. 247, 255 (E.D.Wis.1905), and *Anderson v. Abbott*, 321 U.S. 349, 64 S.Ct. 531, 88 L.Ed. 793 (1944). In *Milwaukee*, a statute prohibited railroads from giving rebates to shippers. The statute was held applicable to a corporation that was not itself a shipper, but had been formed by a shipper's officers and principal shareholders for the purpose of obtaining what were in substance rebates. "[A] corporation will be looked upon as a legal entity as a general rule, and until sufficient reason to the contrary appears; but, when the notion of legal entity is used to defeat public convenience . . . the law will regard the corporation as an association of persons." In *Anderson*, a statute made a shareholder in a national bank liable for the debts of the bank "to the amount of his stock therein, at the par value thereof in addition to the amount invested in such stock." The question was whether this statute applied to shareholders of a parent corporation with a national bank subsidiary, even though technically only the parent was a shareholder in the bank. The Supreme Court concluded that the parent's shareholders would be deemed shareholders of the bank for the purpose of the statute, on the ground that to hold otherwise would permit that purpose to be undercut:

> It has often been held that the interposition of a corporation will not be allowed to defeat a legislative policy, whether that was the aim or only the result of the arrangement. . . .

> To allow this holding company device to succeed would be to put the policy of double liability at the mercy of corporation finance.

321 U.S. at 362–63, 64 S.Ct. at 537–38.

(3) A related question is whether a judicial order that enjoins a corporation from engaging in certain proscribed practices can be circumvented by carrying out those practices through a wholly owned subsidiary? In *United States Public Interest Res. Group v. Atlantic Salmon of Maine*, 261 F. Supp. 2d 17 (D. Me. 2003), the veil was pierced to hold parent in contempt because its subsidiary's conduct violated an earlier order enjoining the parent from releasing pollutants into the river. After the order was granted, the defendant transferred the polluting operations to a wholly owned subsidiary. The following was emphasized by the court: there was identical membership on two boards, approval by the parent was required for any increase in the compensation of the subsidiary's manager, regulatory compliance was assumed by the parent, and the subsidiary's dealings with parent were only at cost.

———

NOTE ON THE CORPORATION'S FAITH

The Religious Freedom Restoration Act (RFRA) prohibits the "Government [from] substantially burden[ing] a person's exercise of religion" unless the Government "demonstrates that application of the burden to the person (1) is in furtherance of a compelling governmental interest; and (2) is the least restrictive means of furthering that compelling governmental interest." *Burwell v. Hobby Lobby Stores, Inc.*, 573 U.S. 682, 134 S. Ct. 2751, 134 L. Ed.2d 675 (2014), held that Hobby Lobby Stores, Inc.'s rights under the RFRA were violated by provisions of the Patient Protection and Affordable Care Act (ACA) that required employers with 50 or more full-time employees to provide health care that included providing a menu of contraceptive coverage. Hobby Lobby had about 500 stores and 13,000 employees. It was owned by five members of the Green family. Each family member had signed a pledge to run the business in accordance with the family's religious beliefs as well as to use family assets to support Christian ministries. The Greens believe that life begins at conception and that it violated their religion to facilitate access to certain contraceptive drugs or devices that operate after that point. They specifically objected to four methods of contraception mandated by the ACA.

The majority opinion held that "person" as used in the RFRA includes corporations. This point was to some extent conceded by the Department of Health and Human Services which had earlier decided to provide faith-based exemptions to non-profit corporations on a case-by-case basis. The majority supported its conclusion by the fact that the Act included corporations among those deemed a "person." From this foundation it was, for the majority, axiomatic that because the RFRA accorded protection to a "person's" faith that a corporation, even one for profit, could have a faith protected by the RFRA. In reaching this conclusion, the majority emphasized that Hobby Lobby was a close corporation "owned and controlled by members of a single family, and no one has disputed the sincerity of their religious beliefs." The majority further found that the RFRA's other provisions, set forth above, were also met so that the ACA could not be applied to require Hobby Lobby to provide the contraceptive coverages it objected.

———

CHAPTER 7

THE SPECIAL PROBLEMS OF SHAREHOLDERS IN CLOSE CORPORATIONS

1. INTRODUCTION

Corporations can be divided into three classes: (1) *Publicly held corporations*, which typically have a large number of shareholders, and whose shares are publicly traded. (2) *Private corporations*, whose shares are not publicly traded, although they may have more than a small number of shareholders. (3) *Close corporations*, a subset of private corporations. Close corporations have only a small number of shareholders, and are typically characterized by owner-management. In important respects, close corporations resemble partnerships, and indeed close corporations are sometimes colloquially referred to as "incorporated partnerships." Traditionally, however, courts imposed upon close corporations norms that were designed with an eye to publicly held corporations, rather than the norms of partnership law, or norms designed with close corporations in mind. There have been three types of responses to this problem. First, many legislatures have given special treatment to close corporations. Second, shareholders in close corporations often attempt to contract around traditional corporation-law norms. Third, modern courts have come to understand that close corporations often need special treatment. The first kind of response is discussed in the Note that follows. The second and third responses are illustrated by the materials in the balance of this Chapter.

———

NOTES ON LEGISLATIVE STRATEGIES TOWARD THE CLOSE CORPORATION

The principal strategies to be examined are those exemplified by Delaware, New York, and the Model Act. Almost all other close-corporation legislation either derives from or closely parallels one of these statutes.

    1. Unified Strategies. One legislative strategy is to make no special provision for close corporations as such, but to modify traditional statutory norms so that they will meet the needs of close corporations although applicable to publicly held corporations as well.

    2. The New York and the Model Act Strategies. A second legislative strategy is to follow the unified approach up to a point, but to add one or two important provisions that are applicable only to those corporations that satisfy certain criteria. Thus N.Y.Bus.Corp.Law § 620(c) authorizes certain kinds of certificate provisions "so long as no shares of the corporation are listed on a national securities exchange or regularly quoted in an over-the-counter market by one or more members of a national or affiliated securities association." Similarly, Model Act § 7.32 authorizes certain kinds of shareholder agreements in corporations that are not listed on a national securities exchange or traded in a market maintained by one or more members of a national securities association.

3.   *Statutory Close Corporations.*

a).   Selective References. A third legislative strategy follows the unified approach up to a point, but adds an integrated set of provisions that are explicitly made applicable *only* to corporations that both satisfy certain criteria, for, and formally elect, statutory close-corporation status (for example, Subchapter XIV of the Delaware General Corporation Law). In effect therefore, the statute contemplates a special subclass of close corporations, which may be called *statutory close corporations.* Under Del. Gen. Corp. Law § 342, a corporation can qualify for statutory close-corporation status if its certificate provides that:

(1)   All of the corporation's issued stock of all classes . . . shall be represented by certificates and shall be held of record by not more than a specified number of persons, not exceeding 30; and

(2)   All of the issued stock of all classes shall be subject to one or more of the restrictions on transfer permitted by § 202 of this title; and

(3)   The corporation shall make no offering of any of its stock of any class which would constitute a "public offering" within the meaning of the United States Securities Act of 1933. . . .

Under § 343, a corporation that qualifies for statutory close-corporation status can elect such status by adopting a heading in its certificate that states the name of the corporation and the fact that it is a close corporation.

Most of the substantive provisions of Del.Gen.Corp.Law Subchapter XIV are enabling—that is, most of the provisions do not regulate the conduct of the shareholders or managers of such corporations, but simply authorize shareholders in statutory close corporations to enter into arrangements that might otherwise be unenforceable or of doubtful validity. Subchapter XIV provides enormous flexibility—so much so, that for a well-advised corporation that elects to qualify under this Subchapter, many or most governance issues will turn on the lawyer's drafting, rather than on corporate law. On the other hand, the remaining provisions of the Delaware General Corporation Law are sufficiently flexible so that much the same is true even for close corporations that are not statutory close corporations under Subchapter XIV.

b).   Significance of Statutory Close Corporations. The data shows that only a tiny fraction of newly formed corporations elect to become statutory close corporations. 1 O'Neal and Thompson's Close Corporations and LLCs § 1.20 (rev. 3d ed. 2018). The result is that for practical purposes, statutory close corporation provisions are much ado about very little. For example, O'Neal & Thompson found that as of the late Twentieth Century, Wisconsin reported 5,101 statutory close corporations out of 98,602 total incorporations. Alabama reported 5,324 statutory close corporations out of 155,198 total corporations. Pennsylvania reported approximately 24,000 statutory close corporations out of approximately 580,000 total corporations. The Kansas Secretary of State's office reported less than 5 percent statutory close corporations and "probably a lot less," adding that observations of attorneys and experienced people indicate that the number has been declining. Delaware reported 16,684 statutory close corporations in 1985. Four other states enacting statutory close-corporation supplements reported even smaller numbers—863 statutory close corporations out of 82,694 total corporations in Missouri; 828 statutory close corporations out of 97,009 total corporations in Montana; 742 statutory close corporations out of 63,172 in Nevada; and 753 statutory close corporations out of 12,422 total corporations in Wyoming. In Texas, about 6% of filing corporations elected close corporation status.

"The greatest use of statutory close corporation status appears to be in California. A 1978 survey of 300 articles of incorporation filed in California showed 28 percent filed as statutory close corporations. A 1985 survey of 200 California incorporations found 19 percent to be statutory close corporations. The attorney who conducted the California surveys suggests, however, that the number is 'entirely misleading' because many corporations electing to become statutory close corporations are organized by nonlawyers using printed forms who do not understand the reasons they are electing statutory close corporation status. He states further that many lawyers mistakenly believe they have to elect close corporation status to be eligible to elect the tax status provided by Subchapter S of the Internal Revenue Code or believe they have to elect such status to come within the 'short form' exemption of the California securities law. After excluding corporations formed by nonlawyers, those formed by lawyers under erroneous beliefs, and one-person corporations seeking to avoid corporate formalities while retaining corporate limited liability, the attorney conducting the surveys concluded that the number of 'real' situations for the use of the statutory close corporation would be extremely small but also undeterminable." Id.

———

NOTE ON NON-ELECTING CORPORATIONS

Where a statute defines a class of statutory close corporations, and provides that only those corporations that explicitly opt in to the statutory provisions are covered by those provisions, a difficult issue arises concerning the effect of the statute on close corporations that do not opt in to become statutory close corporations. This issue is especially important because so few close corporations elect statutory close-corporation status. In *Ramos v. Estrada,* 8 Cal.App.4th 1070, 10 Cal.Rptr.2d 833 (1992), Broadcast Corp. was owned by two groups. Under an agreement, each group was required to vote for the directors upon whom a majority of the group had agreed. The Estradas, who were members of one group, wanted to vote in a different way from the majority of their group. The issue was whether the voting agreement was enforceable. Section 706 of the California Corporation Code provided as follows:

> (a) Notwithstanding any other provision of this division, an agreement between two or more shareholders of a close corporation [defined under section 158(a) as "a corporation whose articles contain . . . a provision that all of the corporation's issued shares of all classes shall be held of record by not more than a specified number of persons, not exceeding 35, and a statement 'This corporation is a close corporation.'], if in writing and signed by the parties thereto, may provide that in exercising any voting rights the shares held by them shall be voted as provided by the agreement, or as the parties may agree or as determined in accordance with a procedure agreed upon by them. . . .

> (d) This section shall not invalidate any voting or other agreement among shareholders . . . which agreement . . . is not otherwise illegal."

Although Broadcast Corp. was not a statutory close corporation, the court held that the voting agreement was enforceable:

> Even though this corporation does not qualify as a close corporation, this agreement is valid and binding on the Estradas. . . .

> The Legislative Committee comment regarding section 706, subdivision (d) states that "[t]his subdivision is intended to preserve any agreements which would be upheld under court decisions even though they do not comply with one or more of the requirements of this section, including voting agreements of corporations other than close corporations." . . .

> The instant agreement is valid, enforceable and supported by consideration.

A much different position was taken by the Delaware court in *Nixon v. Blackwell,* 626 A.2d 1366 (Del.1993):

> We wish to address . . . [w]hether there should be any special, judicially-created rules to "protect" minority stockholders of closely-held Delaware corporations.

> The case at bar points up the basic dilemma of minority stockholders in receiving fair value for their stock as to which there is no market and no market valuation. It is not difficult to be sympathetic, in the abstract, to a stockholder who finds himself or herself in that position. A stockholder who bargains for stock in a closely-held corporation and who pays for those shares . . . can make a business judgment whether to buy into such a minority position, and if so on what terms. One could bargain for definitive provisions of self-ordering permitted to a Delaware corporation through the certificate of incorporation or by-laws by reason of the provisions in 8 Del.C. §§ 102, 109, and 141(a). Moreover, in addition to such mechanisms, a stockholder intending to buy into a minority

position in a Delaware corporation may enter into definitive stockholder agreements, and such agreements may provide for elaborate earnings tests, buy-out provisions, voting trusts, or other voting agreements. See, e.g., 8 Del.C. § 218; Sonitrol Holding Co. v. Marceau Investissements, Del.Supr., 607 A.2d 1177 (1992).

The tools of good corporate practice are designed to give a purchasing minority stockholder the opportunity to bargain for protection before parting with consideration. It would do violence to normal corporate practice and our corporation law to fashion [a] ruling which would result in a court-imposed stockholder buy-out for which the parties had not contracted.

In 1967, when the Delaware General Corporation Law was significantly revised, a new Subchapter XIV entitled "Close Corporations; Special Provisions," became a part of that law for the first time. . . . [S]ubchapter XIV applies only to "close corporations," as defined in section 342. "Unless a corporation elects to become a close corporation under this subchapter in the manner prescribed in this subchapter, it shall be subject in all respects to this chapter, except this subchapter." 8 Del.C. § 341. The corporation before the Court in this matter, is not a "close corporation." Therefore it is not governed by the provisions of Subchapter XIV.

One cannot read into the situation presented in the case at bar any special relief for the minority stockholders in this closely-held, but not statutory "close corporation" because the provisions of Subchapter XIV relating to close corporations and other statutory schemes preempt the field in their respective areas. It would run counter to the spirit of the doctrine of independent legal significance, and would be inappropriate judicial legislation for this Court to fashion a special judicially-created rule for minority investors when the entity does not fall within those statutes, or when there are no negotiated special provisions in the certificate of incorporation, by-laws, or stockholder agreements. The entire fairness test, correctly applied and articulated, is the proper judicial approach. . . .

See also *Sundberg v. Lampert Lumber Co.,* 390 N.W.2d 352 (Minn.App.1986); *Hunt v. Data Management Resources, Inc.,* 26 Kan.App.2d 405, 985 P.2d 730 (1999).

———

2. VOTING ARRANGEMENTS AT THE SHAREHOLDER LEVEL

A. SHAREHOLDER VOTING AGREEMENTS

———

DEL. GEN. CORP. LAW §§ 212(e), 218(c)

[See Statutory Supplement]

———

MODEL BUS. CORP. ACT §§ 7.22(d), 7.31

[See Statutory Supplement]

———

CAL. CORP. CODE §§ 158(a), 705(e), 706

[See Statutory Supplement]

———

N.Y. BUS. CORP. LAW §§ 609(f), 620

[See Statutory Supplement]

———

Ringling Bros.-Barnum & Bailey Combined Shows v. Ringling

Supreme Court of Delaware, 1947.
29 Del.Ch. 610, 53 A.2d 441.

Suit by Edith Conway Ringling against Ringling Brothers-Barnum & Bailey Circus Combined Shows, Inc., and others to determine the right of individual defendants to hold office as directors or officers of the corporation and to determine the validity of election of directors at the 1946 annual stockholders' meeting. From a decree for complainant entered in conformity with opinion of the Vice Chancellor, 49 A.2d 603, the defendants appeal. . . .

■ PEARSON, JUDGE.

The Court of Chancery was called upon to review an attempted election of directors at the 1946 annual stockholders meeting of the corporate defendant. The pivotal questions concern an agreement between two of the three present stockholders, and particularly the effect of this agreement with relation to the exercise of voting rights by these two stockholders. At the time of the meeting, the corporation had outstanding 1000 shares of capital stock held as follows: 315 by petitioner Edith Conway Ringling; 315 by defendant Aubrey B. Ringling Haley (individually or as executrix and legatee of a deceased husband); and 370 by defendant John Ringling North. The purpose of the meeting was to elect the entire board of seven directors. The shares could be voted cumulatively. Mrs. Ringling asserts that by virtue of the operation of an agreement between her and Mrs. Haley, the latter was bound to vote her shares for an adjournment of the meeting, or in the alternative, for a certain slate of directors. Mrs. Haley contends that she was not so bound for reason that the agreement was invalid, or at least revocable.

The two ladies entered into the agreement in 1941. It makes like provisions concerning stock of the corporate defendant and of another corporation, but in this case, we are concerned solely with the agreement as it affects the voting of stock of the corporate defendant. The agreement recites that each party was the owner "subject only to possible claims of creditors of the estates of Charles Ringling and Richard Ringling, respectively" (deceased husbands of the parties), of 300 shares of the capital stock of the defendant corporation; that in 1938 these shares had been deposited under a voting trust agreement which would terminate in 1947, or earlier, upon the elimination of certain liability of the corporation; that each party also owned 15 shares individually; that the parties had "entered into an agreement in April 1934 providing for joint action by them in matters affecting their ownership of stock and interest in" the corporate defendant; that the parties desired "to continue to act jointly in all matters relating to their stock ownership or interest in" the corporate defendant (and the other corporation). The agreement then provides as follows:

"Now, Therefore, in consideration of the mutual covenants and agreements hereinafter contained the parties hereto agree as follows:

"1. Neither party will sell any shares of stock or any voting trust certificates in either of said corporations to any other person whosoever, without first making a written offer to the other party hereto of all of the shares or voting trust certificates proposed to be sold, for the same price and upon the same terms and conditions as in such proposed sale, and allowing such other party a time of not less than 180 days from the date of such written offer within which to accept same.

"2. In exercising any voting rights to which either party may be entitled by virtue of ownership of stock or voting trust certificates held by them in either of said corporation, each party will consult and confer with the other and the parties will act jointly in exercising such voting rights in accordance with such agreement as they may reach with respect to any matter calling for the exercise of such voting rights.

"3. In the event the parties fail to agree with respect to any matter covered by paragraph 2 above, the question in disagreement shall be submitted for arbitration to Karl D. Loos, of Washington, D.C. as arbitrator and his decision thereon shall be binding upon the parties hereto. Such arbitration shall be exercised to the end of assuring for the respective corporations good management and such participation therein by the members of the Ringling family as the experience, capacity and ability of each may warrant. The parties may at any time by written agreement designate any other individual to act as arbitrator in lieu of said Loos.

"4. Each of the parties hereto will enter into and execute such voting trust agreement or agreements and such other instruments as, from time to time they may deem advisable and as they may be advised by counsel are appropriate to effectuate the purposes and objects of this agreement.

"5. This agreement shall be in effect from the date hereof and shall continue in effect for a period of ten years unless sooner terminated by mutual agreement in writing by the parties hereto.

"6. The agreement of April 1934 is hereby terminated.

"7. This agreement shall be binding upon and inure to the benefit of the heirs, executors, administrators and assigns of the parties hereto respectively."

The Mr. Loos mentioned in the agreement is an attorney and has represented both parties since 1937, and, before and after the voting trust was terminated in late 1942, advised them with respect to the exercise of their voting rights. At the annual meetings in 1943 and the two following years, the parties voted their shares in accordance with mutual understandings arrived at as a result of discussions. In each of these years, they elected five of the seven directors. Mrs. Ringling and Mrs. Haley each had sufficient votes, independently of the other, to elect two of the seven directors. By both voting for an additional candidate, they could be sure of his election regardless of how Mr. North, the remaining stockholder, might vote.[1]

Some weeks before the 1946 meeting, they discussed with Mr. Loos the matter of voting for directors. They were in accord that Mrs. Ringling should cast sufficient votes to elect herself and her son; and that Mrs. Haley should elect herself and her husband; but they did not agree upon a fifth director. The day before the meeting, the discussions were continued, Mrs. Haley being represented by her husband since she could not be present because of illness. In a conversation with Mr. Loos, Mr. Haley indicated that he would make a motion for an adjournment of the meeting for sixty days, in order to give the ladies additional time to come

---

[1]   Each lady was entitled to cast 2205 votes (since each had the cumulative voting rights of 315 shares, and there were 7 vacancies in the directorate). The sum of the votes of both is 4410, which is sufficient to allow 882 votes for each of 5 persons. Mr. North, holding 370 shares, was entitled to cast 2590 votes, which obviously cannot be divided so as to give to more than two candidates as many as 882 votes each. It will be observed that in order for Mrs. Ringling and Mrs. Haley to be sure to elect five directors (regardless of how Mr. North might vote) they must act together in the sense that their combined votes must be divided among five different candidates and at least one of the five must be voted for by both Mrs. Ringling and Mrs. Haley.

to an agreement about their voting. On the morning of the meeting, however, he stated that because of something Mrs. Ringling had done, he would not consent to a postponement. Mrs. Ringling then made a demand upon Mr. Loos to act under the third paragraph of the agreement "to arbitrate the disagreement" between her and Mrs. Haley in connection with the manner in which the stock of the two ladies should be voted. At the opening of the meeting, Mr. Loos read the written demand and stated that he determined and directed that the stock of both ladies be voted for an adjournment of sixty days. Mrs. Ringling then made a motion for adjournment and voted for it. Mr. Haley, as proxy for his wife, and Mr. North voted against the motion. Mrs. Ringling (herself or through her attorney, it is immaterial which), objected to the voting of Mrs. Haley's stock in any manner other than in accordance with Mr. Loos' direction. The chairman ruled that the stock could not be voted contrary to such direction, and declared the motion for adjournment had carried. Nevertheless, the meeting proceeded to the election of directors. Mrs. Ringling stated that she would continue in the meeting "but without prejudice to her position with respect to the voting of the stock and the fact that adjournment had not been taken." Mr. Loos directed Mrs. Ringling to cast her votes 882 for Mrs. Ringling, 882 for her son, Robert, and 441 for a Mr. Dunn, who had been a member of the board for several years. She complied. Mr. Loos directed that Mrs. Haley's votes be cast 882 for Mrs. Haley, 882 for Mr. Haley, and 441 for Mr. Dunn. Instead of complying, Mr. Haley attempted to vote his wife's shares 1103 for Mrs. Haley, and 1102 for Mr. Haley. Mr. North voted his shares 864 for a Mr. Woods, 863 for a Mr. Griffin, and 863 for Mr. North. The chairman ruled that the five candidates proposed by Mr. Loos, together with Messrs. Woods and North, were elected. The Haley-North group disputed this ruling insofar as it declared the election of Mr. Dunn; and insisted that Mr. Griffin, instead, had been elected. A directors' meeting followed in which Mrs. Ringling participated after stating that she would do so "without prejudice to her position that the stockholders' meeting had been adjourned and that the directors' meeting was not properly held." Mr. Dunn and Mr. Griffin, although each was challenged by an opposing faction, attempted to join in voting as directors for different slates of officers. Soon after the meeting, Mrs. Ringling instituted this proceeding.

The Vice Chancellor determined that the agreement to vote in accordance with the direction of Mr. Loos was valid as a "stock pooling agreement" with lawful objects and purposes, and that it was not in violation of any public policy of this state. He held that where the arbitrator acts under the agreement and one party refuses to comply with his direction, "the Agreement constitutes the willing party . . . an implied agent possessing the irrevocable proxy of the recalcitrant party for the purpose of casting the particular vote." It was ordered that a new election be held before a master, with the direction that the master should recognize and give effect to the agreement if its terms were properly invoked. [In reaching this result, Vice Chancellor Seitz stated, "Here an implied agency based on an irrevocable proxy is fully justified to implement the Agreement without doing violence to its terms. Moreover, the provisions of the Agreement make it clear that the proxy may be treated as one coupled with an interest so as to render it irrevocable under the circumstances. . . . Obviously, to deny specific performance here would be tantamount to declaring the Agreement invalid. Since petitioner's rights in this respect were properly preserved at the stockholders' meeting, the meeting was a nullity to the extent that it failed to give effect to the provisions of the Agreement here involved. However, I believe it preferable to hold a new election rather than attempt to reconstruct the contested meeting. In this way the parties will be acting with explicit knowledge of their rights."]

Before taking up defendants' objections to the agreement, let us analyze particularly what it attempts to provide with respect to voting, including what functions and powers it attempts to repose in Mr. Loos, the "arbitrator". The agreement recites that the parties desired "to continue to act jointly in all matters relating to their stock ownership or interest in" the corporation. The parties agreed to consult and confer with each other in exercising their voting rights and to act jointly—that is, concertedly; unitedly; towards unified courses of action—in accordance with such agreement as they might reach. Thus, so long as the parties agree for whom or for what their shares shall be voted, the agreement provides no function for the arbitrator. His role is limited to situations where the parties fail to agree upon a course of action. In such cases, the agreement directs that "the question in disagreement shall be submitted for arbitration" to Mr. Loos "as arbitrator and his decision thereon shall be binding upon the parties". These provisions are designed to operate in aid of what appears to be a primary purpose of the parties, "to act jointly" in exercising their voting rights, by providing a means for fixing a course of action whenever they themselves might reach a stalemate.

Should the agreement be interpreted as attempting to empower the arbitrator to carry his directions into effect? Certainly there is no express delegation or grant of power to do so, either by authorizing him to vote the shares or to compel either party to vote them in accordance with his directions. The agreement expresses no other function of the arbitrator than that of deciding questions in disagreement which prevent the effectuation of the purpose "to act jointly". The power to enforce a decision does not seem a necessary or usual incident of such a function. Mr. Loos is not a party to the agreement. It does not contemplate the transfer of any shares or interest in shares to him, or that he should undertake any duties which the parties might compel him to perform. They provided that they might designate any other individual to act instead of Mr. Loos. The agreement does not attempt to make the arbitrator a trustee of an express trust. What the arbitrator is to do is for the benefit of the parties, not for his own benefit. Whether the parties accept or reject his decision is no concern of his, so far as the agreement or the surrounding circumstances reveal. We think the parties sought to bind each other, but to be bound only to each other, and not to empower the arbitrator to enforce decisions he might make.

From this conclusion, it follows necessarily that no decision of the arbitrator could ever be enforced if both parties to the agreement were unwilling that it be enforced, for the obvious reason that there would be no one to enforce it. Under the agreement, something more is required after the arbitrator has given his decision in order that it should become compulsory: at least one of the parties must determine that such decision shall be carried into effect. Thus, any "control" of the voting of the shares, which is reposed in the arbitrator, is substantially limited in action under the agreement in that it is subject to the overriding power of the parties themselves.

The agreement does not describe the undertaking of each party with respect to a decision of the arbitrator other than to provide that it "shall be binding upon the parties". It seems to us that this language, considered with relation to its context and the situations to which it is applicable, means that each party promised the other to exercise her own voting rights in accordance with the arbitrator's decision. The agreement is silent about any exercise of the voting rights of one party by the other. The language with reference to situations where the parties arrive at an understanding as to voting plainly suggests "action" by each, and "exercising" voting rights by each, rather than by one for the other. There is no intimation that this method should be different where the arbitrator's decision is to be carried into effect.

Assuming that a power in each party to exercise the voting rights of the other might be a relatively more effective or convenient means of enforcing a decision of the arbitrator than would be available without the power, this would not justify implying a delegation of the power in the absence of some indication that the parties bargained for that means. The method of voting actually employed by the parties tends to show that they did not construe the agreement as creating powers to vote each other's shares; for at meetings prior to 1946 each party apparently exercised her own voting rights, and at the 1946 meeting, Mrs. Ringling, who wished to enforce the agreement, did not attempt to cast a ballot in exercise of any voting rights of Mrs. Haley. We do not find enough in the agreement or in the circumstances to justify a construction that either party was empowered to exercise voting rights of the other.

Having examined what the parties sought to provide by the agreement, we come now to defendants' contention that the voting provisions are illegal and revocable. They say that the courts of this state have definitely established the doctrine "that there can be no agreement, or any device whatsoever, by which the voting power of stock of a Delaware corporation may be irrevocably separated from the ownership of the stock, except by an agreement which complies with Section 18 of the Corporation Law [concerning voting trusts] and except by a proxy coupled with an interest. . . . "

[Section 18] authorizes, among other things, the deposit or transfer of stock in trust for a specified purpose, namely, "vesting" in the transferee "the right to vote thereon" for a limited period; and prescribes numerous requirements in this connection. Accordingly, it seems reasonable to infer that to establish the relationship and accomplish the purpose which the statute authorizes, its requirements must be complied with.

But the statute does not purport to deal with agreements whereby shareholders attempt to bind each other as to how they shall vote their shares. Various forms of such pooling agreements, as they are sometimes called, have been held valid and have been distinguished from voting trusts. . . . We think the particular agreement before us does not violate Section 18 or constitute an attempted evasion of its requirements, and is not illegal for any other reason.

Generally speaking, a shareholder may exercise wide liberality of judgment in the matter of voting, and it is not objectionable that his motives may be for personal profit, or determined by whims or caprice, so long as he violates no duty owed his fellow shareholders. Heil v. Standard G. & E. Co., 17 Del.Ch. 214, 151 A. 303. The ownership of voting stock imposes no legal duty to vote at all. A group of shareholders may, without impropriety, vote their respective shares so as to obtain advantages of concerted action. They may lawfully contract with each other to vote in the future in such way as they, or a majority of their group, from time to time determine.

Reasonable provisions for cases of failure of the group to reach a determination because of an even division in their ranks seem unobjectionable. The provision here for submission to the arbitrator is plainly designed as a deadlock-breaking measure, and the arbitrator's decision cannot be enforced unless at least one of the parties (entitled to cast one-half of their combined votes) is willing that it be enforced. We find the provision reasonable. It does not appear that the agreement enables the parties to take any unlawful advantage of the outside shareholder, or of any other person. It offends no rule of law or public policy of this state of which we are aware.

Legal consideration for the promises of each party is supplied by the mutual promises of the other party. The undertaking to vote in accordance with the arbitrator's decision is a valid contract. The good faith of the arbitrator's action has not been challenged and, indeed, the record indicates that no such challenge could be supported.

Accordingly, the failure of Mrs. Haley to exercise her voting rights in accordance with his decision was a breach of her contract. . . .

. . . The Court of Chancery may, in a review of an election, reject votes of a registered shareholder where his voting of them is found to be in violation of rights of another person. Compare: In re Giant Portland Cement Co., 26 Del.Ch. 32, 21 A.2d 697; In re Canal Construction Co., 21 Del.Ch. 155, 182 A. 545. It seems to us that upon the application of Mrs. Ringling, the injured party, the votes representing Mrs. Haley's shares should not be counted. Since no infirmity in Mr. North's voting has been demonstrated, his right to recognition of what he did at the meeting should be considered in granting any relief to Mrs. Ringling; for her rights arose under a contract to which Mr. North was not a party.

With this in mind, we have concluded that the election should not be declared invalid, but that effect should be given to a rejection of the votes representing Mrs. Haley's shares. No other relief seems appropriate in this proceeding. Mr. North's vote against the motion for adjournment was sufficient to defeat it. With respect to the election of directors, the return of the inspectors should be corrected to show a rejection of Mrs. Haley's votes, and to declare the election of the six persons for whom Mr. North and Mrs. Ringling voted.

This leaves one vacancy in the directorate. The question of what to do about such a vacancy was not considered by the court below and has not been argued here. For this reason, and because an election of directors at the 1947 annual meeting (which presumably will be held in the near future) may make a determination of the question unimportant, we shall not decide it on this appeal. If a decision of the point appears important to the parties, any of them may apply to raise it in the Court of Chancery, after the mandate of this court is received there.

An order should be entered directing a modification of the order of the Court of Chancery in accordance with this opinion.

————

NOTES ON SHAREHOLDER VOTING AGREEMENTS AND IRREVOCABLE PROXIES

Contracts among shareholders concerning the manner in which their shares will be voted—usually known as voting or pooling agreements—are of two general types. In one type, the parties agree in advance on the exact way in which they will vote their shares during the term of the contract: for example, they may agree to vote for each other as directors. In a second type, the parties do not agree in advance on the exact way in which they will vote their shares, but instead agree that during the term of the contract they will vote their shares as a unit, in a way to be decided by agreement, ballot, or other means.

1. Seeking an Appropriate Remedy. Suppose a voting agreement is breached. Money damages are normally an inadequate remedy for breach of a voting agreement. Nevertheless, in the past, courts that upheld such agreements divided on whether they will be specifically enforced. Although the modern trend is strongly in favor of granting that remedy, because the courts are sometimes reluctant to specifically enforce voting agreements, the parties to such an agreement may expressly or impliedly substitute a self-executing remedy, such as giving each other proxies to vote each other's stock. In *Smith v. San Francisco & N.P. Ry. Co.,* 47 P. 582 (Cal. 1897) three shareholders agreed to vote their shares together as determined by ballot. The court held that the agreement impliedly gave the two shareholders in the majority on any ballot an irrevocable proxy to vote the shares of the third. In *Ringling,* the Chancellor similarly held that the arbitrator had an implied proxy to vote the parties' shares as he determined, but the Delaware Supreme Court reversed on this issue.[1]

2.   *Proxy Coupled with an Interest.* A proxy has been treated as an agency relationship, in which the shareholder is the principal and the proxyholder is the agent. It is a rule of agency law, however, that a principal can terminate an agent's authority at will, even if the termination is in breach of contract (although in such cases the principal may be liable to the agent in damages). See Restatement, Second, of Agency § 118. There is an exception to this rule in cases where the agent holds a "power coupled with an interest," or, as the Restatements of Agency call it, a "power given as security." See Restatement (Second) of Agency §§ 138, 139; Restatement (Third) of Agency §§ 3.12, 3.13. Generally speaking, this exception is applicable to arrangements in which it is understood that the "agent" or power-holder has an interest in the subject-matter to which the power relates, and is therefore not expected to execute the power solely on the power-giver's behalf—the crux of the normal agency relationship—but on his own behalf as well. Accordingly, the safest way to insure that a proxy will be irrevocable is to confer it upon a proxyholder who has an "interest" in the shares to which the proxy relates. Relatively clear examples are cases where the proxyholder is a pledgee of the shares or has agreed to purchase the shares. See N.Y.Bus.Corp.Law § 609(f)(1) & (2). Del. Gen. Corp. Law § 212(e) provide that "A proxy may be made irrevocable regardless of whether the interest with which it is coupled is an interest in the stock itself or an interest in the corporation generally."

———

Haft v. Haft
Court of Chancery of Delaware, 1995.
671 A.2d 413.

■ ALLEN, CHANCELLOR

[Herbert Haft, the founder and CEO of Dart Group Corporation, transferred 172,730 shares of Dart Class B common stock to his son, Ronald Haft. Class B was Dart's sole class of voting stock. The transferred shares constituted 57% of the outstanding Class B, and

---

[1]   Compare Me. Bus.Corp.Law § 617(2):

When [a written voting] agreement specifies how the shares shall be voted, or provides a clear formula for ascertaining how the shares shall be voted, in case of a breach or anticipatory breach thereof by one or more parties thereto, the agreement shall, unless it specifically provides otherwise, be deemed to constitute an irrevocable proxy to the parties not in breach to vote all shares subject to the agreement in accordance with the terms of the agreement.

therefore carried the power to elect the Dart board. In exchange for the stock, Roland gave Herbert a promissory note and granted Herbert a lifetime irrevocable proxy to vote the transferred shares. Subsequently, Ronald sought to revoke the proxy. The court held that Herbert Haft's interest in Dart by virtue of his CEO position was sufficient to render specifically enforceable Ronald's undertaking not to revoke the proxy.]

Under the Delaware corporation law (§ 212(e)) an interest sufficient to support an irrevocable proxy must be either "an interest in the stock itself or an interest in the corporation generally." 8 Del.Ch. § 212(e) (1991). Do Herbert Haft's interests, other than as a secured creditor, qualify under the statute? As I now explain, in my opinion they do. . . .

The predecessor of Section 212 was amended as part of the general revision of the Delaware General Corporation Law in 1967. The language in question ("an interest in the corporation generally") was introduced into our statute at that time. The apparent purpose for doing so was to erase the implication arising from dicta in a 1933 Master's Report, which had been confirmed by this court. The report was in the case of In re *Chilson*, Del.Ch., 168 A. 82 (1933). The *Chilson* dicta was to the effect that in order to support irrevocability of a proxy, the holder had to have an interest in the stock itself. . . .

. . . [I]it is appropriate to acknowledge that the corporate law has tended to distrust and discourage the separation of the shareholder claim as equity investor (i.e., the right to enjoy distributions on stock if, as, and when declared) from the right to vote stock. . . . A powerful argument can be advanced that generally the congruence of the right to vote and the residual rights of ownership will tend towards efficient wealth production.

A proxy is, of course, a means temporarily to split the power to vote from the residual ownership claim of the stockholder. In the vast number of instances in which proxies to vote stock are used, however, this split occasions no significant divergence between the interests of the proxy holder and the holder of the residual corporate interest because the proxy is of relatively short duration and in all events is revocable unilaterally. Thus, in effect, the grant of the proxy represented a judgment (which may be enforced through revocation) that the holder of the proxy will exercise it in the economic interest of the residual owner. A potentially inefficient split between the interests of the voter and the interests of the residual owners may, however, develop when the proxy is irrevocable. Such a holder is free from the unilateral control of the grantor and may be expected to be inclined to exercise voting rights in a way that benefits himself. There is of course, as a general matter, nothing legally suspect in contracting parties exercising contracted for rights in a self-interested manner. Yet the exercise of voting control over corporations by persons whose interest in them is not chiefly or solely as a residual owner will create circumstances in which the corporation will be less than optimally efficient in the selection of risky investment projects. (A simple, if gross, example: the holder of an irrevocable proxy with voting control might simply refuse to elect a board that will accept the best investment projects (those with the highest risk adjusted rate of return) unless some side payment to him is arranged). The special additional costs associated with such a divorce between ownership and voting (the costs being expressed either as an otherwise unnecessary expense or as the selection of non-optimizing investment projects) will of course tend to diminish as the voter's interest becomes aligned with the residual owners interest. . . .

. . . I confess to the view that a corporation law rule allowing for the specific enforceability of an irrevocable proxy that is coupled only with the holder's interest in maintaining a salaried office seems mischievous in terms of its possible efficiency effects. But in light of the 1967 amendment to the Delaware statutory law . . . and the absence of contrary precedent, I am required to express the opinion that such an interest—the interest that Herbert Haft had and retains as the senior executive officer of Dart—is sufficient under our law to render specifically enforceable the express contract for an irrevocable proxy. . . .

B. VOTING TRUSTS

DEL. GEN. CORP. LAW § 218

[See Statutory Supplement]

MODEL BUS. CORP. ACT § 7.30

[See Statutory Supplement]

CAL. CORP. CODE § 706

[See Statutory Supplement]

NOTES ON VOTING TRUSTS

1.   Background. A voting trust is a device by which shareholders separate the voting rights in, and the legal title to, their shares from the beneficial ownership of the shares. This is accomplished by conferring the voting rights and legal title on one or more voting trustees, while retaining the ultimate right to distributions and appreciation. Usually, two or more shareholders are involved, so that the voting trust is a type of pooling agreement. Sometimes, however, only one shareholder is involved—for example, where a sole shareholder creates a voting trust to satisfy creditors or to vest control of his business in managers. The creation of a voting trust normally requires the execution of a written trust agreement between participating shareholders and the voting trustees, and a transfer to the trustee, for a specified period, of the shareholders' stock certificates and the legal title to their stock. The voting trustee then registers the transfer on the corporation's books, so that during the term of the trust the trustee is the record owner of the shares, entitled to vote in the election of directors and often on other matters as well. Dividends are paid by the corporation to the trustee, but are almost invariably then paid over by the trustee to the beneficial owners. Several statutes require the trustee to issue certificates of beneficial interest to participating shareholders, and frequently such certificates are issued, even where not statutorily required, to facilitate trading in the beneficial interests.

Voting trusts are an effective and a moderately simple way to separate control and beneficial ownership for a limited period of time. The separation is self-executing, because the trustee is the legal owner and is registered as such on the corporation's books. The separation survives transfers by the beneficial owners, since they can transfer only their retained equitable interests (essentially, most ownership rights except the right to vote during the term of the trust). Upon termination of the voting trust, the beneficial owners receive stock certificates which reinstate them as complete owners, registered as such on the corporation's books.

2.   Validity. The early attitude of some courts toward voting trusts was highly unfavorable. *See, e.g., Warren v. Pim,* 59 A. 773, 789 (N.J. Eq. 1904) ("[a]ny arrangement that permanently separates the voting power from stock ownership nullifies, to the extent of the stock involved, the annual submission of the question of the management of the company to the stockholders"). The majority of courts, however, have either declared voting trusts to be valid or held that the plaintiff was not in a position to attack them. *See, e.g., Massa v. Stone,* 190 N.E.2d 217 (Mass. 1963).

Today, statutes both explicitly validate voting trusts and regulate their creation and their content. Among the most common forms of regulation are a maximum time period (usually ten years), and a requirement that the voting trust agreement be filed with the corporation and open to inspection. Such statutes are normally deemed to preempt the common law rules governing the validity of voting trusts. The cases are not entirely uniform in dealing with the consequences of failure to comply with the statutory requirements. Some cases have held that such a failure invalidates the voting trust. See, e.g., Abercrombie v. Davies, discussed below. *Smith v. Biggs Boiler Works Co.,* 32 Del.Ch. 147, 82 A.2d 372 (1951) (voting trust held to be invalid where no provision was made for deposit of stock with trustees); *Christopher v. Richardson,* 394 Pa. 425, 147 A.2d 375 (1959) (voting trust held to be invalid where under its terms the trust might have exceeded statutory ten-year period). Other cases have been considerably more tolerant. For example, in *De Marco v. Paramount Ice Corp.,* 30 Misc.2d 158, 102 N.Y.S.2d 692 (1950), a voting trust was attacked on the ground that a copy of the trust agreement had not been filed in the office of the corporation, as required by the statute. The answer stated that the agreement had been filed after the plaintiff's suit was brought. The court held that "the failure to file merely means that the trust agreement is not invalid but merely inoperative to permit the trustees to exercise the voting rights granted thereby until it is so filed."

3.   *Overlap of Voting Trusts and Shareholders' Voting Agreements.* In the context of close corporations, voting trusts may sometimes be used, like voting agreements, to allocate voting control in other than a pro rata manner, or to preserve the solidarity of a faction consisting of less than all the shareholders. Because voting trusts and voting agreements may have substantially overlapping purposes, the substantive legal rules applicable to one of these two legal forms have sometimes been applied to an arrangement that was nominally cast in the other form. Thus in *Abercrombie v. Davies,* 130 A.2d 338 (Del. 1957), the Delaware Supreme Court held that an "Agent's Agreement" that in form was a voting agreement was in substance was a voting trust was unenforceable because the statutory provisions governing voting trusts had not been complied with. Conversely, in *Oceanic Exploration Co. v. Grynberg,* 428 A.2d 1 (Del.1981), the Delaware Supreme Court held that an agreement that was denominated a voting trust was not a voting trust in substance and therefore was enforceable despite a failure to comply with the voting trust statute.

———

C. CLASSIFIED STOCK

———

DEL. GEN. CORP. LAW §§ 102(a)(6), 212(a)

[See Statutory Supplement]

———

MODEL BUS. CORP. ACT §§ 6.01, 7.21, 8.04

[See Statutory Supplement]

———

NOTE ON CLASSIFIED STOCK

"One of the simplest and most effective ways of assuring that all the participants or that particular minority shareholders will have representation on the board of directors is to set up two or more classes of stock, provide that each class is to vote for and elect a specified number or a stated percentage of the directors, and then issue each class or a majority of shares in each class to a different shareholder or faction of shareholders. . . . Class A common stock might be given power, for instance, to elect three directors and Class B common stock power to elect two." 1 F.H. O'Neal & R. Thompson, O'Neal's Close Corporations § 3.19 (rev. 3d ed.2010). A few statutes validate this technique explicitly, *see, e.g.,* N.Y.Bus.Corp.Law § 703, and most of the remaining statutes validate it implicitly by providing that a corporation may have one or more classes of stock with such voting powers as shall be stated in the certificate, *see e.g.,* Del.Gen.Corp.Law § 151(a). In its simplest version, the use of classified common does not necessarily involve voting power for any class that is disproportionate to the investment made by that class. Often, however, separate classes carry voting power whose weight differs considerably from the relative investment made by their holders. At the extreme, a class of stock may have proprietary rights but no voting power, or voting power but no proprietary rights.

In *Lehrman v. Cohen,* 43 Del.Ch. 222, 222 A.2d 800 (1966), Giant Food, Inc. had two classes of common stock designated Class AC and Class AL, respectively. Each class was entitled to elect two members of Giant Food's four-member board. The Cohen and Lehrman families each owned one of the two classes. Over the years, there were differences of opinion between the two families concerning Giant Food's operating policies. To obviate the risk of deadlock, eventually an arrangement was made to establish a fifth directorship. Under the arrangement, Giant Food's certificate of incorporation was amended to create a third class of common stock, designated Class AD, which consisted of one share of $10 per value stock. The Class AD stock had the right to elect one director, but essentially had no right to distributions and could be called—that is, redeemed—for $10 by a vote of the other four directors. The Class AD share was issued to Giant Food's long-time counsel, Joseph Danzansky, who by prearrangement voted the share for himself as the fifth director.

Subsequently, the plaintiff, a member of the Lehrman family who at that point owned all the AL stock, claimed that the Class AD stock was illegal on the ground that in substance it was a voting trust and did not comply with the voting trust statute. The court rejected this argument:

> The criteria of a voting trust under our decisions have been summarized by this Court in *Abercrombie v. Davies,* 36 Del.Ch. 371, 130 A.2d 338 (1957). The tests there set forth, accepted by both sides of this cause as being applicable, are as follows: (1) the voting rights of the stock are separated from the other attributes of ownership; (2) the voting rights granted are intended to be irrevocable for a definite period of time; and (3) the principal

purpose of the grant of voting rights is to acquire voting control of the corporation. . . .

. . . The AD arrangement did not separate the voting rights of the AC or the AL stock from the other attributes of ownership of those classes of stock. Each AC and AL stockholder retains complete control over the voting of his stock; each can vote his stock directly; no AL or AC stockholder is divested of his right to vote his stock as he sees fit; no AL or AC stock can be voted against the shareholder's wishes; and the AL and AC stock continue to elect two directors each.

The court also held that it was not illegal to create a class of stock having voting rights but no proprietary rights.

3. AGREEMENTS CONTROLLING DECISIONS THAT ARE WITHIN THE BOARD'S DISCRETION

Voting arrangements of the kind discussed in Section 2 control only those matters that are decided on a shareholder level. Typically, however, the issues that are most important to shareholders in a close corporation are determined on a board level—for example, managerial positions, managerial compensation, and dividends. If the shareholders attempt to also control these matters by agreement, the problem arises whether, or under what conditions, such an agreement is valid in the face of the normal statutory provision that the business of the corporation shall be managed by or under the direction of the board. That question is addressed by the materials in this section.

McQuade v. Stoneham
Court of Appeals of New York, 1934.
263 N.Y. 323, 189 N.E. 234.

Appeal, by permission of Court of Appeals, from judgment of Appellate Division, First Department, unanimously affirming judgment for plaintiff for $42,827.38 and other relief.

■ POUND, CH. J.

The action is brought to compel specific performance of an agreement between the parties, entered into to secure the control of National Exhibition Company, also called the baseball club (New York Nationals or "Giants"). This was one of Stoneham's enterprises which used the New York Polo Grounds for its home games. McGraw was manager of the Giants. McQuade was, at the time the contract was entered into, a city magistrate. . . .

Defendant Stoneham became the owner of 1,306 shares, or a majority of the stock of National Exhibition Company (there being then 2,500 shares outstanding). Plaintiff and defendant McGraw each purchased seventy shares of his stock. Plaintiff paid Stoneham $50,338.10 for the stock he purchased. As a part of the transaction the agreement in question was entered into. It was dated May 21, 1919. Some of its pertinent provisions are:

"VIII. The parties hereto will use their best endeavors for the purpose of continuing as directors of said company and as officers thereof the following:

"Directors: Charles A. Stoneham, John J. McGraw, Francis X. McQuade, with right to the party of the first part (Stoneham) to name all additional directors as he sees fit.

"Officers: Charles A. Stoneham, president; John J. McGraw, vice-president; Francis X. McQuade, treasurer.

"IX. No salaries are to be paid to any of the above officers or directors, except as follows: President, $45,000; vice-president, $7,500; treasurer, $7,500.

"X. There shall be no change in said salaries, no change in the amount of capital, or the number of shares, no change or amendment of the by-laws of the corporation or any matters regarding the policy of the business of the corporation or any matters which may in anywise affect, endanger or interfere with the rights of minority stockholders, excepting upon the mutual and unanimous consent of all . . . of the parties hereto.

"XIV. This agreement shall continue and remain in force so long as the parties or any of them or the representative of any own the stock referred to in this agreement, to wit, the party of the first part, 1,166 shares, the party of the second part 70 shares and the party of the third part 70 shares, except as may otherwise appear by this agreement. . . . "

In pursuance of this contract Stoneham became president and McGraw vice-president of the corporation. McQuade became treasurer. In June, 1925, [McQuade's] salary was increased to $10,000 a year. He continued to act until May 2, 1928, when Leo J. Bondy was elected to succeed him. The board of directors consisted of seven men. The four outside of the parties hereto were selected by Stoneham and he had complete control over them. At the meeting of May 2, 1928, Stoneham and McGraw refrained from voting, McQuade voted for himself and the other four voted for Bondy. Defendants did not keep their agreement with McQuade to use their best efforts to continue him as treasurer. On the contrary, he was dropped with their entire acquiescence. At the next stockholders' meeting he was dropped as a director, although they might have elected him.

The courts below have refused to order the reinstatement of McQuade, but have given him damages for wrongful discharge, with a right to sue for future damages.

The cause for dropping McQuade was due to the falling out of friends. McQuade and Stoneham had disagreed. The trial court has found in substance that their numerous quarrels and disputes did not affect the orderly and efficient administration of the business of the corporation; that plaintiff was removed because he had antagonized the dominant Stoneham by persisting in challenging his power over the corporate treasury and for no misconduct on his part. The court also finds that plaintiff was removed by Stoneham for protecting the corporation and its minority stockholders. We will assume that Stoneham put him out when he might have retained him, merely in order to get rid of him.

Defendants say that the contract in suit was void because the directors held their office charged with the duty to act for the corporation according to their best judgment and that any contract which compels a director to vote to keep any particular person in office and at a stated salary is illegal. Directors are the exclusive executive representatives of the corporation, charged with administration of its internal affairs and the management and use of its assets. They manage the business of the corporation (Gen.Corp.Law, Cons.Laws, c. 23, sec. 27). "An agreement to continue a man as president is dependent upon his continued loyalty to the interests of the corporation" (Fells v. Katz, 256 N.Y. 67, 72, 175 N.E. 516, 517). So much is undisputed.

Plaintiff contends that the converse of this proposition is true and that an agreement among directors to continue a man as an officer of a corporation is not to be broken so long as such officer is loyal to the interests of the corporation and that, as plaintiff has been found loyal to the corporation, the agreement of defendants is enforceable.

Although it has been held that an agreement among stockholders whereby it is attempted to divest the directors of their power to discharge an unfaithful employee of the corporation is illegal as against public policy (Fells v. Katz, supra), it must be equally true that the stockholders may not, by agreement among themselves, control the directors in the exercise of the judgment vested in them by virtue of their office to elect officers and fix salaries. Their motives may not be questioned so long as their acts are legal. The bad faith or the improper motives of the parties does not change this rule (Manson v. Curtis, 223 N.Y. 313, 324, 119 N.E. 559). Directors may not by agreements entered into by stockholders abrogate their independent judgment (Creed v. Copps, 103 Vt. 164, 71 A.L.R.Ann. 1287).

Stockholders may, of course, combine to elect directors. That rule is well settled. As Holmes, Ch. J., pointedly said (Brightman v. Bates, 175 Mass. 105, 110, 55 N.E. 809, 811): "If stockholders want to make their power felt, they must unite. There is no reason why a majority should not agree to keep together." The power to unite is, however, limited to the election of directors and is not extended to contracts whereby limitations are placed on the power of directors to manage the business of the corporation by the selection of agents at defined salaries.

The minority shareholders whose interests McQuade says he has been punished for protecting, are not, aside from himself, complaining about his discharge. He is not acting for the corporation or for them in this action. It is impossible to see how the corporation has been injured by the substitution of Bondy as treasurer in place of McQuade. As McQuade represents himself in this action and seeks redress for his own wrongs, "we prefer to listen to [the corporation and the minority stockholders] before any decision as to their wrongs" (Faulds v. Yates, 57 Ill. 416).

It is urged that we should pay heed to the morals and manners of the market place to sustain this agreement, and that we should hold that its violation gives rise to a cause of action for damages, rather than base our decision on any outworn notions of public policy. Public policy is a dangerous guide in determining the validity of a contract, and courts should not interfere lightly with the freedom of competent parties to make their own contracts. We do not close our eyes to the fact that such agreements, tacitly or openly arrived at, are not uncommon, especially in close corporations where the stockholders are doing business for convenience under a corporate organization. . . .

We are constrained by authority to hold that a contract is illegal and void so far as it precludes the board of directors, at the risk of incurring legal liability, from changing officers, salaries or policies or retaining individuals in office, except by consent of the contracting parties. On the whole, such a holding is probably preferable to one which would open the courts to pass on the motives of directors in the lawful exercise of their trust. . . .

The judgment of the Appellate Division and that of the Trial Term should be reversed and the complaint dismissed, with costs in all courts.

[The court also held that the agreement violated the Inferior Criminal Courts Act, which provided that "[n]o city magistrate shall engage in any other business or profession . . . , but each of said justices and magistrates shall devote his whole time and capacity, so far as the public interest demands, to the duties of his office. . . . " At the date of the agreement McQuade was a city magistrate, and he did not resign his position until after commencement of the action.]

■ [The opinion of LEHMAN, J., concurring in the result, is omitted.]

NOTE ON CLARK V. DODGE

In *Clark v. Dodge,* 269 N.Y. 410, 199 N.E. 641 (1936), two corporations manufactured medicinal preparations under secret formulas. Clark owned

25%, and Dodge owned 75%, of the stock of each corporation. Clark and Dodge entered into an agreement which provided that (1) Dodge would vote for Clark as a director. (2) Dodge, acting in his directorial capacity, would continue Clark as general manager as long as Clark proved faithful, efficient, and competent. (3) Clark would always receive as salary or dividends one-fourth of the corporation's net income. (4) No salaries to other officers would be unreasonable in amount or incommensurate with the services rendered by those officers. The court held that the agreement was valid:

> Except for the broad dicta in the *McQuade* opinion, we think there can be no doubt that the agreement here in question was legal and that the complaint states a cause of action. There was no attempt to sterilize the board of directors as in [*McQuade*]. . . .

> If there was any invasion of the powers of the directorate under that agreement it is so slight as to be negligible; and certainly there is no damage suffered by or threatened to anybody. The broad statements in the *McQuade* opinion, applicable to the facts there, should be confined to those facts.

Galler v. Galler

Supreme Court of Illinois, 1964, reh. denied 1964.
32 Ill.2d 16, 203 N.E.2d 577.

■ UNDERWOOD, JUSTICE. . . .

[Two brothers, Benjamin and Isadore Galler incorporated Galler Drug Company in 1924, having earlier operated the business as equal partners. In combination they each owned 47 ½ percent of the company; the remaining shares were owned by an employee, Rosenberg, who is not involved in the litigation. In July 1962 suit was commenced by Emma Galler, Benjamin's widow, and while it was pending Isadore and his spouse, Rose, agreed to purchase Rosenberg's shares. Emma opposed the transaction, arguing that pursuant to the agreement, summarized below, she had a right to acquire half of the shares Rosenberg proposed to sell. The parties thereupon stipulated that until the dispute underlying the suit is resolved, the Rosernberg shares would not be voted or transferred. The following facts are background to the suit.]

In March, 1954, Benjamin and Isadore, on the advice of their accountant, decided to enter into an agreement for the financial protection of their immediate families and to assure their families, after the death of either brother, equal control of the corporation. [The agreement was executed in July 1955, after Benjamin had fallen ill. In September 1956, Emma agreed to permit Isadore's son Aaron to become president for one year and agreed that she would not interfere with the business during that year. In December 1957, Benjamin died.] The evidence is undisputed that defendants had decided prior to Benjamin's death they would not honor the agreement, but never disclosed their intention to plaintiff or her husband. . . .

Shortly after Benjamin's death, Emma went to the office and demanded the terms of the 1955 agreement be carried out. Isadore told her that anything she had to say could be said to Aaron, who then told her that his father would not abide by the agreement. He offered a modification of the agreement by proposing the salary continuation payment but without her becoming a director. When Emma refused to modify the agreement and sought enforcement of its terms, defendants refused and this suit followed.

During the last few years of Benjamin's life both brothers drew an annual salary of $42,000. Aaron, whose salary was $15,000 as manager of the warehouse prior to September, 1956, has since the time that Emma agreed to his acting as president drawn an annual salary of $20,000. In 1957, 1958, and 1959 a $40,000 annual dividend was paid. Plaintiff has received her proportionate share of the dividend.

The July, 1955, agreement in question here, entered into between Benjamin, Emma, Isadore and Rose, recites that Benjamin and Isadore each own 47½% of the issued and outstanding shares of the Galler Drug Company, an Illinois corporation, and that Benjamin and Isadore desired to provide income for the support and maintenance of their immediate families. No reference is made to the shares then being purchased by Rosenberg. The essential features of the contested portions of the agreement are substantially as set forth in the opinion of the Appellate Court: (2) that the bylaws of the corporation will be amended to provide for a board of four directors; that the necessary quorum shall be three directors; and that no directors' meeting shall be held without giving ten days notice to all directors. (3) The shareholders will cast their votes for the above named persons (Isadore, Rose, Benjamin and Emma) as directors at said special meeting and at any other meeting held for the purpose of electing directors. (4, 5) In the event of the death of either brother his wife shall have the right to nominate a director in place of the decedent. (6) Certain annual dividends will be declared by the corporation. The dividend shall be $50,000 payable out of the accumulated earned surplus in excess of $500,000. If 50% of the annual net profits after taxes exceeds the minimum $50,000 then the directors shall have discretion to declare a dividend up to 50% of the annual net profits. If the net profits are less than $50,000 nevertheless the minimum $50,000 annual dividend shall be declared, providing the $500,000 surplus is maintained. Earned surplus is defined. (9) The certificates evidencing the said shares of Benjamin Galler and Isadore Galler shall bear a legend that the shares are subject to the terms of this agreement. (10) A salary continuation agreement shall be entered into by the corporation which shall authorize the corporation upon the death of Benjamin Galler or Isadore Galler, or both, to pay a sum equal to twice the salary of such officer, payable monthly over a five-year period. Said sum shall be paid to the widow during her widowhood, but should be paid to such widow's children if the widow remarries within the five-year period. (11, 12) The parties to this agreement further agree and hereby grant to the corporation the authority to purchase, in the event of the death of either Benjamin or Isadore, so much of the stock of Galler Drug Company held by the estate as is necessary to provide sufficient funds to pay the federal estate tax, the Illinois inheritance tax and other administrative expenses of the estate. If as a result of such purchase from the estate of the decedent the amount of dividends to be received by the heirs is reduced, the parties shall nevertheless vote for directors so as to give the estate and heirs the same representation as before (2 directors out of 4, even though they own less stock), and also that the corporation pay an additional benefit payment equal to the diminution of the dividends. In the event either Benjamin or Isadore decides to sell his shares he is required to offer them first to the remaining shareholders and then to the corporation at book value, according each six months to accept the offer.

The Appellate Court found the 1955 agreement void because "the undue duration, stated purpose and substantial disregard of the provisions of the Corporation Act outweigh any considerations which might call for divisibility" and held that "the public policy of this state demands voiding this entire agreement". . . .

At this juncture it should be emphasized that we deal here with a so-called close corporation. . . . For our purposes, a close corporation is one in which the stock is held in a few hands, or in a few families, and wherein it is not at all, or only rarely, dealt in by buying or selling. (Brooks v. Willcuts, 8th Cir.1935, 78 F.2d 270, 273.) Moreover, it should be recognized that shareholder agreements similar to that in question here are often, as a practical consideration, quite necessary for the protection of those financially interested in the close corporation. While the shareholder of a public-issue corporation may readily sell his shares on the open market should management fail to use, in his opinion, sound business judgment, his counterpart of the close corporation often has a large total of his entire capital invested in the business and has no ready market for his shares should he desire to sell. He feels, understandably, that he is more than a mere investor and that his voice should be heard concerning all corporate activity. Without a shareholder agreement, specifically enforceable by the courts, insuring him a modicum of control, a large minority shareholder might find himself at the mercy of an oppressive or unknowledgeable majority. Moreover, as in the case at bar, the shareholders of a close corporation are often also the directors and officers thereof. With substantial shareholding interests abiding in each member of the board of directors, it is often quite impossible to secure, as in the large public-issue corporation, independent board judgment free from personal motivations concerning corporate policy. For these and other reasons too voluminous to enumerate here, often the only sound basis for protection is afforded by a lengthy, detailed shareholder agreement securing the rights and obligations of all concerned. For a discussion of these and other considerations, see Note, "A Plea for Separate Statutory Treatment of the Close Corporation", 33 N.Y.U.L.Rev. 700 (1958). . . .

This court has recognized, albeit *sub silentio,* the significant conceptual differences between the close corporation and its public-issue counterpart in, among other cases, Kantzler v. Benzinger, 214 Ill. 589, 73 N.E. 874, where an agreement quite similar to the one under attack here was upheld. Where, as in *Kantzler* and here, no complaining minority interest appears, no fraud or apparent injury to the public or creditors is present, and no clearly prohibitory statutory language is violated, we can see no valid reason for precluding the parties from reaching any arrangements concerning the management of the corporation which are agreeable to all. . . .

Since the question as to the duration of the agreement is a principal source of controversy, we shall consider it first. The parties provided no specific termination date, and while the agreement concludes with a paragraph that its terms "shall be binding upon and shall inure to the benefits of" the legal representatives, heirs and assigns of the parties, this clause is, we believe, intended to be operative only as long as one of the parties is living. It further provides that it shall be so construed as to carry out its purposes, and we believe these must be determined from a consideration of the agreement as a whole. Thus viewed, a fair construction is that its purposes were accomplished at the death of the survivor of the parties. While these life spans are not precisely ascertainable, and the Appellate Court noted Emma Galler's life expectancy at her husband's death was 26.9 years, we are aware of no statutory or public policy provision against stockholders' agreements which would invalidate this agreement on that ground. . . . While defendants argue that the public policy evinced by the legislative restrictions upon the duration of voting trust agreements (Ill.Rev.Stat.1963, chap. 32, par. 157.30a) should be applied here, this agreement is not a voting trust, but as pointed out by the dissenting justice in the Appellate Court, is a straight contractual voting control agreement which does not divorce voting rights from stock ownership. . . . While limiting voting trusts in 1947 to a maximum duration of 10 years, the legislature has indicated no similar policy regarding straight voting agreements although these have been common since prior to 1870. In view of the history of decisions of this court generally upholding, in the absence of fraud or prejudice to minority interests or public policy, the right of stockholders to agree among themselves as to the manner in which their stock will be voted, we do not regard the period of time within which this agreement may remain effective as rendering the agreement unenforceable.

The clause that provides for the election of certain persons to specified offices for a period of years likewise does not require invalidation. In Kantzler v. Benzinger, 214 Ill. 589, 73 N.E. 874, this court upheld an agreement entered into by all the stockholders providing that certain parties would be elected to the offices of the corporation for a fixed period. In Faulds v. Yates, 57 Ill. 416, we upheld a similar agreement among the majority stockholders of a corporation, notwithstanding the existence of a minority which was not before the court complaining thereof. See also Hornstein, "Judicial Tolerance of the Incorporated Partnership," 18 Law and Contemporary Problems 435 at page 444.

We turn next to a consideration of the effect of the stated purpose of the agreement upon its validity. The pertinent provision is: "The said Benjamin A. Galler and Isadore A. Galler desire to provide income for the support and maintenance of their immediate families." Obviously, there is no evil inherent in a contract entered into for the reason that the persons originating the terms desired to so arrange their property as to provide post-death support for those dependent upon them. Nor does the fact that the subject property is corporate stock alter the situation so long as there exists no detriment to minority stock interests, creditors or other public injury. It is, however, contended by defendants that the methods provided by the agreement for implementation of the stated purpose are, as a whole, violative of the Business Corporation Act (Ill.Rev.Stat.1963, chap. 32, pars. 157.28, 157.30a, 157.33, 157.34, 157.41) to such an extent as to render it void *in toto*.

The terms of the dividend agreement require a minimum annual dividend of $50,000, but this duty is limited by the subsequent provision that it shall be operative only so long as an earned surplus of $500,000 is maintained. It may be noted that in 1958, the year prior to commencement of this litigation, the corporation's net earnings after taxes amounted to $202,759 while its earned surplus was $1,543,270, and this was increased in 1958 to $1,680,079 while earnings were $172,964. The minimum earned surplus requirement is designed for the protection of the corporation and its creditors, and we take no exception to the contractual dividend requirements as thus restricted. Kantzler v. Benzinger, 214 Ill. 589, 73 N.E. 874.

The salary continuation agreement is a common feature, in one form or another, of corporate executive employment. It requires that the widow should receive a total benefit, payable monthly over a five-year period, aggregating twice the amount paid her deceased husband in one year. This requirement was likewise limited for the protection of the corporation by being contingent upon the payments being income tax-deductible by the corporation. The charge made in those cases which have considered the validity of payments to the widow of an officer and shareholder in a corporation is that a gift of its property by a noncharitable corporation is in violation of the rights of its shareholders and *ultra vires*. Since there are no shareholders here other than the parties to the contract, this objection is not here applicable, and its effect, as limited, upon the corporation is not so prejudicial as to require its invalidation.

Having concluded that the agreement, under the circumstances here present, is not vulnerable to the attack made on it, we must consider the accounting feature of this action. . . .

We hold defendants must account for all monies received by them from the corporation since September 25, 1956, in excess of that theretofore authorized. . . .

Affirmed in part and reversed in part, and remanded with directions.

NOTE ON FURTHER PROCEEDINGS IN GALLER V. GALLER

The decree in *Galler* ordered Isadore and Rose to "account for all monies received by them from the company since September 25, 1956 [up to the time of the decree], in excess of that theretofore authorized," but provided that Isadore and Aaron be allowed "fair compensation . . . for services rendered by them to the corporation during said period." On remand, defendants argued that the salaries of Aaron and Isadore during the relevant period represented the fair market value of their services, and in any event since Isadore's $42,000 salary after Benjamin's death was a continuation of his salary under the agreement, it had been "theretofore authorized" within the meaning of the decree. The appellate court rejected both arguments. As to the former issue, the court adopted the findings of a master who valued Isadore's services at $10,000/year and Aaron's at $15,000/year. As to whether continuation of Isadore's $42,000 salary was authorized by the agreement, the court said

> . . . Isadore's continued receipt of the same salary upon the death of Benjamin without the *quid pro quo* for his brother's family, is an alteration of the past arrangement, and was without authorization.

> Furthermore, the clear import of the 1955 shareholders' agreement is that the partnership-like arrangement was intended to remain after the death of either Benjamin or Isadore. While not specifically addressing itself to salaries, the agreement provides that upon the death of either Benjamin or Isadore, four directors are to be elected; two from Isadore's family and two from Benjamin's family. The officers and their salaries are voted upon by the directors. Dividends are required to be paid provided $500,000 earned surplus is maintained. It may be inferred that this agreement sought to replace a deceased brother's position as an officer with members of his family, thereby permitting them to share equally in the company's earnings, including salaries, a significant means of distributing the corporate profits. This inference is not negated by the fact that no provision in the 1955

agreement requires equality of salaries between the family branches.

For more disputes among the Gallers after the Supreme Court's decree, *see Galler v. Galler*, 217 N.E.2d 111 (Ill.App.1966); *Galler v. Galler*, 238 N.E.2d 274 (Ill.App.1968).

————

DEL. GEN. CORP. LAW §§ 102(b)(1), 141(a), 142(b), 350, 351, 354

[See Statutory Supplement]

————

MODEL BUS. CORP. ACT §§ 2.02(b), 2.06, 7.32, 8.01(b)

[See Statutory Supplement]

————

N.Y. BUS. CORP. LAW § 620

[See Statutory Supplement]

————

CAL. CORP. CODE §§ 158, 186, 300, 312

[See Statutory Supplement]

————

Adler v. Svingos

80 A.D.2d 764, 436 N.Y.S.2d 719 (1981)

Adler, Shaw, and Svingos each owned 33⅓% of the shares of 891 First Ave. Corp., a New York corporation that operated a restaurant. The corporation's certificate of incorporation was filed in November 1978. In December 1978, Adler, Shaw, and Svingos executed a Stockholders' Agreement. Paragraph 8 of the Agreement provided that all corporate operations, including changes in corporate structure, would require unanimous consent of the three signatories. Subsequently, when Adler and Shaw sought to sell the business, Svingos objected, relying upon the Stockholders' Agreement. Adler and Shaw then brought an action seeking to strike paragraph 8 of the Agreement as void under New York B.C.L. § 620(b), on the ground that under section 620(b) a provision that restricts the board in the management of the business of the corporation must be located in the certificate of incorporation. Svingos counterclaimed, and asked for reformation of the certificate of incorporation to reflect Paragraph 8 of the Stockholders' Agreement. The trial court granted summary judgment against Svingos. Reversed.

In *Zion v. Kurtz* (50 N.Y.2d 92), the Court of Appeals interpreted analogous provisions of the Delaware General Corporation Law and held enforceable, as between the parties to it, a provision of a shareholders' agreement between all the shareholders, proscribing corporate action without the consent of a minority shareholder, even though the disputed provision was not incorporated in the corporate charter as required by Delaware's statute. Speaking for the majority, Judge Meyer stated . . . "Since there are no intervening rights of third persons, the agreement requires nothing that is not permitted by statute, and all of the stockholders of the corporation assented to it, the certificate of incorporation may be ordered reformed, by requiring Kurtz [whose position was analogous to that of plaintiffs Adler and Shaw] to file the appropriate amendments, or more directly he may be held estopped to rely upon the absence of those amendments from the corporate charter".

The principles set forth in *Zion* are controlling here. We conclude that it was error to grant partial summary judgment to plaintiffs and to dismiss defendant's first counterclaim. Indeed, the record warrants granting the defendant's motion for partial summary judgment reforming the certificate to reflect the unanimity of the stockholders' agreement.

———

4. SUPERMAJORITY VOTING AND QUORUM REQUIREMENTS AT THE SHAREHOLDER AND BOARD LEVELS

Sutton v. Sutton

Court of Appeals of New York, 1994.
84 N.Y.2d 37, 637 N.E.2d 260, 614 N.Y.S.2d 369.

■ SIMONS, JUDGE.

In this . . . proceeding, petitioners seek (1) a declaration that an amendment to the certificate of incorporation of Bag Bazaar, Ltd. is valid and (2) to compel respondent David S. Sutton, as a director of the corporation, to sign and deliver a certificate of amendment to petitioners for filing. Respondent has refused to execute the certificate, contending it is not valid because the amendment had the support of only 70% of the shareholders when the certificate of incorporation required unanimous approval. The appeal requires an interpretation of section 616(b) of the Business Corporation Law which states that supermajority provisions in a certificate of incorporation may be amended by a two-thirds vote unless the certificate "specifically" provides otherwise. . . .

In 1963, the certificate of incorporation of Bag Bazaar, Ltd. was amended to provide that "[t]he unanimous vote or consent of the holders of all the issued and outstanding shares of Common Stock of the corporation shall be necessary for the transaction of any business * * * of the corporation, including amendment to the certificate of incorporation". At that time the business was run by Abraham Sutton and none of the parties to this litigation was a shareholder. In 1971 Abraham's brother, respondent David S. Sutton, purchased 30 shares. Two years later Abraham's son, petitioner Solomon A. Sutton, joined the business and subsequently acquired 30 shares. On Abraham's death, in 1987, his widow, petitioner Yvette Sutton, inherited Abraham's remaining 40 shares. Thus, petitioners now own 70% of the outstanding shares of the corporation and respondent and his wife own 30 shares. Petitioner Solomon A. Sutton serves as one of the two directors of the company and respondent David S. Sutton as the other.

The corporation was run without incident for nearly 30 years under Abraham's leadership. After he relinquished control of the company, however, disputes arose between Solomon and David Sutton concerning the management of the corporation. These disputes culminated in an April 1992 shareholders' meeting, where petitioners voted their 70% of the shares in favor of a resolution to strike the unanimity provision, while respondent's 30% of the shares voted against the resolution.

Respondent, as a director of the corporation, refused to sign a certificate of amendment reflecting the deletion of the unanimity provision, thereby preventing the amendment from taking effect. Accordingly, petitioners commenced this proceeding and moved for judgment declaring the resolution valid and enforceable and compelling respondent to sign the certificate of amendment. . . . Supreme Court granted the petition and . . . [t]he Appellate Division reversed . . . .

To support their position on this appeal, petitioners contend that the Legislature added the word "specifically" to section 616(b) because it recognized that a unanimity provision gives minority shareholders the ability to deadlock any and all corporate action. The amendment was intended to minimize deadlocks by permitting a two-thirds majority of the shareholders to alter or delete the unanimity requirement unless the certificate of incorporation explicitly stated otherwise. Respondent maintains that "specifically" was added to the statute to clarify that if more than a two-thirds vote was required to amend a unanimity provision, the certificate should state exactly what greater percentage is needed. They maintain that this certificate satisfied that requirement by declaring that a unanimous vote was required for any amendment.

The history of Business Corporation Law § 616(b) begins with Benintendi v. Kenton Hotel, 294 N.Y. 112, 60 N.E.2d 829, where this Court invalidated a unanimity provision adopted by unanimous shareholder vote. We reasoned that such a provision was antithetical to the basic concept of corporate governance by majority rule and contrary to public policy (id., at 118–119, 60 N.E.2d 829). In 1948, the Legislature abrogated *Benintendi* by enacting section 9 of the Stock Corporation Law, which authorized unanimity provisions when approved by a unanimous vote (see, L.1948, ch. 862). The effect of section 9 was to require unanimous shareholder consent to either add or amend a unanimity provision (see, 3 White, New York Corporations § 616.02, at 6–378 [13th ed.]). In 1951, this section was amended to allow adoption or change of a supermajority provision by a two-thirds or greater vote. A unanimous vote was still required, however, where the certificate called for a unanimous vote; where the unanimity provision itself required such a vote; or where the unanimity provision was adopted prior to the effective date of the 1951 amendment (see, L. 1951, ch. 717).

In 1961, the Business Corporation Law was adopted to replace the Stock Corporation Law, and section 9 was substantially reenacted as Business Corporation Law § 616(b) and § 709(b). However, in 1962, prior to the 1963 effective date of the Business Corporation Law, a series of changes were made, including the addition of the word "specifically" in section 616(b). As finally enacted, section 616(b) provides that "[a]n amendment of the certificate of incorporation which changes or strikes out a [supermajority] provision * * * shall be authorized at a meeting of shareholders by vote of the holders of two-thirds of all outstanding shares entitled to vote thereon, or of such greater proportion of shares * * * as may be provided specifically in the certificate of incorporation" (emphasis added). According to the Legislative Study Committee the word "specifically" was one of a number of "technical" amendments added to the chapter to clarify existing language and avoid minor inconsistencies. It was not intended to effect a substantive change in the law (Mem. of Joint Legis.Comm. To Study Revision of Corp. Laws, Bill Jacket, L.1962, ch. 834, at 86).

Thus, nothing in the legislative history or the statute itself suggests the necessity for a discrete paragraph addressed solely to the supermajority provision and explicitly declaring the vote required for its amendment. The history reveals that Stock Corporation Law § 9 stated that a provision in the certificate of incorporation requiring unanimous consent could only be amended by unanimous consent and this provision was substantially reenacted in the Business Corporation Law.* Inasmuch as the Legislature did not intend the "technical" revisions added before the effective date of the Business Corporation Law to change the existing law substantively, the present statute should be construed as section 9 of the Stock Corporation Law was. Unanimity was required under the prior law to amend a unanimity provision, such as this one, and the addition of the word "specifically" merely provides that a two-thirds

---

    * While the 1951 amendments to that section allowed a unanimity provision to be amended by a two-thirds vote in certain instances, petitioners acknowledge that the provision at issue here would have required unanimous shareholder consent to amend, despite the 1951 amendment. (Footnote by the court.)

majority may now amend a unanimity provision unless the certificate requires a greater percentage.

The provision in Bag Bazaar's certificate is unambiguous: it requires unanimous shareholder consent for the transaction of "any business * * * including amendment to the certificate of incorporation." To read section 616(b) as requiring more to address amendment of the super-majority provision would be unnecessarily restrictive in light of the legislative history. The certificate need only clearly state what vote, if greater than two thirds, is required to amend a unanimity provision. The certificate of Bag Bazaar, Ltd. does so. . . .

Finally, petitioners note that unless section 616(b) is read as requiring an explicit certificate provision governing the amendment of unanimity provisions, majority shareholders will be unable to conduct the business of a corporation in the face of opposition from the minority. But as respondent notes, there is nothing inherently unfair or improper about a voluntary organization's consensual decision to assure protection for minority shareholders, and shareholders are not without remedies where deadlocks do arise (see generally, Business Corporation Law § 1104).

Accordingly, the order of the Appellate Division should be affirmed, with costs.

■ KAYE, C.J., and TITONE, BELLACOSA, SMITH, LEVINE and CIPARICK, JJ., concur.

Order affirmed, with costs.

———

N.Y. BUS. CORP. LAW §§ 616, 709

[See Statutory Supplement]

———

DEL. GEN. CORP. LAW §§ 102(b)(4), 141(b), 216

[See Statutory Supplement]

———

CAL. CORP. CODE §§ 204, 602

[See Statutory Supplement]

———

MODEL BUS. CORP. ACT §§ 7.27, 7.32, 8.24

[See Statutory Supplement]

———

5. FIDUCIARY OBLIGATIONS OF SHAREHOLDERS IN CLOSE CORPORATIONS

Donahue v. Rodd Electrotype Co.

Supreme Judicial Court of Massachusetts, 1975.
367 Mass. 578, 328 N.E.2d 505.

■ TAURO, CHIEF JUSTICE.

The plaintiff, Euphemia Donahue, a minority stockholder in the Rodd Electrotype Company of New England, Inc. (Rodd Electrotype), a Massachusetts corporation, brings this suit against the directors of Rodd Electrotype, Charles H. Rodd, Frederick I. Rodd and Mr. Harold E. Magnuson, against Harry C. Rodd, a former director, officer, and controlling stockholder of Rodd Electrotype and against Rodd Electrotype (hereinafter called defendants). The plaintiff seeks to rescind Rodd Electrotype's purchase of Harry Rodd's shares in Rodd Electrotype and to compel Harry Rodd "to repay to the corporation the purchase price of said shares, $36,000, together with interest from the date of purchase." The plaintiff alleges that the defendants caused the corporation to purchase the shares in violation of their fiduciary duty to her, a minority stockholder of Rodd Electrotype.[4]

The trial judge, after hearing oral testimony, dismissed the plaintiff's bill on the merits. He found that the purchase was without prejudice to the plaintiff and implicitly found that the transaction had been carried out in good faith and with inherent fairness. The Appeals Court affirmed with costs. Donahue v. Rodd Electrotype Co. of New England, Inc., 1 Mass.App. 876, 307 N.E.2d 8 (1974). The case is before us on the plaintiff's application for further appellate review. . . .

[Briefly, the facts were as follows: In the mid-1930s Harry Rodd and Joseph Donahue had become employees of Royal Electrotype (the predecessor of Rodd Electrotype). Donahue's duties were confined to operational matters within the plants, and he never participated in the management aspect of the business. In contrast, Rodd's advancement within the company was rapid, and in 1946 he became general manager and treasurer. Subsequently Rodd acquired 200 of the corporation's 1000 shares and Donahue (at Rodd's suggestion) acquired 50 shares. In 1955 Rodd became president and general manager, and later that year Royal itself purchased the remaining 750 shares, so that Rodd and Donahue became Royal's sole shareholders, owning 80% and 20% of its stock, respectively. In 1960 the corporation was renamed Rodd Electrotype, and

---

[4]   In form, the plaintiff's bill of complaint presents, at least in part, a derivative action, brought on behalf of the corporation, and, in the words of the bill, "on behalf of . . . [the] stockholders" of Rodd Electrotype. Yet . . . the plaintiff's bill, in substance, was one seeking redress because of alleged breaches of the fiduciary duty owed *to her,* a minority stockholder, by the controlling stockholders.

We treat the bill of complaint (as have the parties) as presenting a proper cause of suit in the personal right of the plaintiff. . . .

in the early 60's Harry Rodd's two sons, Charles and Frederick, took important positions with the company. In 1965 Charles succeeded his father as president and general manager.

In 1970 Harry Rodd was seventy-seven years old and not in good health, and his sons wished him to retire. Prior to 1967 Harry had distributed 117 of his 200 shares equally among his sons and his daughter, and had returned 2 shares to the corporate treasury. Harry insisted that as a condition to his retirement some financial arrangement be made with respect to his remaining 81 shares. Accordingly, Charles, acting on the corporation's behalf, negotiated for the purchase of 45 of Harry's shares for $800/share—a price which, Charles testified, reflected book and liquidating value. At a special board meeting in July 1970, the corporation's board (then consisting of Charles and Frederick Rodd and a lawyer) voted to have the corporation make the purchase at this price. Subsequently Harry Rodd sold 2 shares to each of his three children at $800/share, and gave each child 10 shares as a gift.[7] Meanwhile Donahue had died and his 50 shares had passed to his wife and son. When the Donahues learned that the corporation had purchased Harry Rodd's shares, they offered their shares to the corporation on the terms given to Harry but the offer was rejected.[10] This suit followed.]

In her argument before this court, the plaintiff has characterized the corporate purchase of Harry Rodd's shares as an unlawful distribution of corporate assets to controlling stockholders. She urges that the distribution constitutes a breach of the fiduciary duty owed by the Rodds, as controlling stockholders, to her, a minority stockholder in the enterprise, because the Rodds failed to accord her an equal opportunity to sell her shares to the corporation. The defendants reply that the stock purchase was within the powers of the corporation and met the requirements of good faith and inherent fairness imposed on a fiduciary in his dealings with the corporation. They assert that there is no right to equal opportunity in corporate stock purchases for the corporate treasury. For the reasons hereinafter noted, we agree with the plaintiff and reverse the decree of the Superior Court. However, we limit the applicability of our holding to "close corporations," as hereinafter defined. Whether the holding should apply to other corporations is left for decision in another case, on a proper record.

A.   *Close Corporations.* In previous opinions, we have alluded to the distinctive nature of the close corporation . . . but have never defined precisely what is meant by a close corporation. There is no single, generally accepted definition. Some commentators emphasize an "integration of ownership and management" (Note, Statutory Assistance for Closely Held Corporations, 71 Harv.L.Rev. 1498 [1958]), in which the

---

[7]   An inference is permissible that the "gift" of these shares was a part of the "deal" for the stock purchase.

[10]   Between 1965 and 1969, the company offered to purchase the Donahue shares for amounts between $2,000 and $10,000 ($40 to $200 a share). The Donahues rejected these offers.

stockholders occupy most management positions. . . . Others focus on the number of stockholders and the nature of the market for the stock. In this view, close corporations have few stockholders; there is little market for corporate stock. The Supreme Court of Illinois adopted this latter view in Galler v. Galler, 32 Ill.2d 16, 203 N.E.2d 577 (1964). . . . We accept aspects of both definitions. We deem a close corporation to be typified by: (1) a small number of stockholders; (2) no ready market for the corporate stock; and (3) substantial majority stockholder participation in the management, direction and operations of the corporation.

As thus defined, the close corporation bears striking resemblance to a partnership. . . . Just as in a partnership, the relationship among the stockholders must be one of trust, confidence and absolute loyalty if the enterprise is to succeed. . . .

In Helms v. Duckworth, 101 U.S.App.D.C. 390, 249 F.2d 482 (1957) . . . Judge Burger, now Chief Justice Burger, writing for the court, emphasized the resemblance of the two-man close corporation to a partnership: "In an intimate business venture such as this, stockholders of a close corporation occupy a position similar to that of joint adventurers and partners. While courts have sometimes declared stockholders 'do not bear toward each other that same relation of trust and confidence which prevails in partnerships,' this view ignores the practical realities of the organization and functioning of a small 'two-man' corporation organized to carry on a small business enterprise in which the stockholders, directors, and managers are the same persons" (footnotes omitted). Id. at 486.

Although the corporate form provides . . . advantages for the stockholders (limited liability, perpetuity, and so forth), it also supplies an opportunity for the majority stockholders to oppress or disadvantage minority stockholders. The minority is vulnerable to a variety of oppressive devices, termed "freeze-outs," which the majority may employ. . . . An authoritative study of such "freeze-outs" enumerates some of the possibilities: "The squeezers . . . may refuse to declare dividends; they may drain off the corporation's earnings in the form of exorbitant salaries and bonuses to the majority shareholder-officers and perhaps to their relatives, or in the form of high rent by the corporation for property leased from majority shareholders . . . ; they may deprive minority shareholders of corporate offices and of employment by the company. . . ."

The minority can, of course, initiate suit against the majority and their directors. Self-serving conduct by directors is proscribed by the director's fiduciary obligation to the corporation. . . . However, in practice, the plaintiff will find difficulty in challenging dividend or employment policies. Such policies are considered to be within the judgment of the directors . . . [G]enerally, plaintiffs who seek judicial assistance against corporate dividend or employment policies do not prevail. . . .

Thus, when these types of "freeze-outs" are attempted by the majority stockholders, the minority stockholders, cut off from all corporation-related revenues, must either suffer their losses or seek a buyer for their shares. Many minority stockholders will be unwilling or unable to wait for an alteration in majority policy. Typically, the minority stockholder in a close corporation has a substantial percentage of his personal assets invested in the corporation. The stockholder may have anticipated that his salary from his position with the corporation would be his livelihood. Thus, he cannot afford to wait passively. He must liquidate his investment in the close corporation in order to reinvest the funds in income-producing enterprises.

At this point, the true plight of the minority stockholder in a close corporation becomes manifest. He cannot easily reclaim his capital. In a large public corporation, the oppressed or dissident minority stockholder could sell his stock in order to extricate some of his invested capital. By definition, this market is not available for shares in the close corporation. In a partnership, a partner who feels abused by his fellow partners may cause dissolution by his "express will . . . at any time" . . . and recover his share of partnership assets and accumulated profits. . . . By contrast, the stockholder in the close corporation or "incorporated partnership" may achieve dissolution and recovery of his share of the enterprise assets only by compliance with the rigorous terms of the applicable chapter of the General Laws. . . .

Thus, in a close corporation, the minority stockholders may be trapped in a disadvantageous situation. No outsider would knowingly assume the position of the disadvantaged minority. The outsider would have the same difficulties. To cut losses, the minority stockholder may be compelled to deal with the majority. This is the capstone of the majority plan. Majority "freeze-out" schemes which withhold dividends are designed to compel the minority to relinquish stock at inadequate prices. . . . When the minority stockholder agrees to sell out at less than fair value, the majority has won.

Because of the fundamental resemblance of the close corporation to the partnership, the trust and confidence which are essential to this scale and manner of enterprise, and the inherent danger to minority interests in the close corporation, we hold that stockholders[17] in the close corporation owe one another substantially the same fiduciary duty in the operation of the enterprise[18] that partners owe to one another. In our

---

[17] We do not limit our holding to majority stockholders. In the close corporation, the minority may do equal damage through unscrupulous and improper "sharp dealings" with an unsuspecting majority. See Helms v. Duckworth, 101 U.S.App.D.C. 390, 249 F.2d 482 (1957).

[18] We stress that the strict fiduciary duty which we apply to stockholders in a close corporation in this opinion governs *only* their actions relative to the operations of the enterprise and the effects of that operation on the rights and investments of other stockholders. We express no opinion as to the standard of duty applicable to transactions in the shares of the close

previous decisions, we have defined the standard of duty owed by partners to one another as the "utmost good faith and loyalty." Cardullo v. Landau, 329 Mass. 5, 8, 105 N.E.2d 843 (1952); DeCotis v. D'Antona, 350 Mass. 165, 168, 214 N.E.2d 21 (1966). Stockholders in close corporations must discharge their management and stockholder responsibilities in conformity with this strict good faith standard. They may not act out of avarice, expediency or self-interest in derogation of their duty of loyalty to the other stockholders and to the corporation.

We contrast this strict good faith standard with the somewhat less stringent standard of fiduciary duty to which directors and stockholders of all corporations must adhere in the discharge of their corporate responsibilities. Corporate directors are held to a good faith and inherent fairness standard of conduct (Winchell v. Plywood Corp., 324 Mass. 171, 177, 85 N.E.2d 313 [1949]) and are not "permitted to serve two masters whose interests are antagonistic." Spiegel v. Beacon Participations, 297 Mass. 398, 411, 8 N.E.2d 895, 904 (1937). "Their paramount duty is to the corporation, and their personal pecuniary interests are subordinate to that duty." Durfee v. Durfee & Canning, Inc., 323 Mass. 187, 196, 80 N.E.2d 522, 527 (1948).

The more rigorous duty of partners and participants in a joint adventure, here extended to stockholders in a close corporation, was described by then Chief Judge Cardozo of the New York Court of Appeals in Meinhard v. Salmon, 249 N.Y. 458, 164 N.E. 545 (1928): "Joint adventurers, like co-partners, owe to one another, while the enterprise continues, the duty of the finest loyalty. Many forms of conduct permissible in a workaday world for those acting at arm's length, are forbidden to those bound by fiduciary ties. . . . Not honesty alone, but the punctilio of an honor the most sensitive, is then the standard of behavior." Id. at 463–464, 164 N.E. at 546 . . .

B. *Equal Opportunity in a Close Corporation.* Under settled Massachusetts law, a domestic corporation, unless forbidden by statute, has the power to purchase its own shares. . . . An agreement to reacquire stock "[is] enforceable, subject, at least, to the limitations that the purchase must be made in good faith and without prejudice to creditors and stockholders." . . . When the corporation reacquiring its own stock is a close corporation, the purchase is subject to the additional requirement, in the light of our holding in this opinion, that the stockholders, who, as directors or controlling stockholders, caused the corporation to enter into the stock purchase agreement, must have acted with the utmost good faith and loyalty to the other stockholders.

To meet this test, if the stockholder whose shares were purchased was a member of the controlling group, the controlling stockholders must

---

corporation when the corporation is not a party to the transaction. Cf. Andrews, The Stockholder's Right to Equal Opportunity in the Sale of Shares, 78 Harv.L.Rev. 505 (1965). Compare Perlman v. Feldmann, 219 F.2d 173 (2d Cir.), cert. den. 349 U.S. 952, 75 S.Ct. 880, 99 L.Ed. 1277 (1955) with Zahn v. Transamerica Corp., 162 F.2d 36 (3d Cir.1947).

cause the corporation to offer each stockholder an equal opportunity to sell a ratable number of his shares to the corporation at an identical price. Purchase by the corporation confers substantial benefits on the members of the controlling group whose shares were purchased. These benefits are not available to the minority stockholders if the corporation does not also offer them an opportunity to sell their shares. The controlling group may not, consistent with its strict duty to the minority, utilize its control of the corporation to obtain special advantages and disproportionate benefit from its share ownership. See Jones v. H.F. Ahmanson & Co., 1 Cal.3d 93, 108, 81 Cal.Rptr. 592, 460 P.2d 464 (1969); Note, 83 Harv.L.Rev. 1904, 1908 (1970). Cf. Brudney and Chirelstein, Fair Shares in Corporate Mergers and Takeovers, 88 Harv.L.Rev. 297, 334 (1974).

The benefits conferred by the purchase are twofold: (1) provision of a market for shares; (2) access to corporate assets for personal use. By definition, there is no ready market for shares of a close corporation. The purchase creates a market for shares which previously had been unmarketable. It transforms a previously illiquid investment into a liquid one. If the close corporation purchases shares only from a member of the controlling group, the controlling stockholder can convert his shares into cash at a time when none of the other stockholders can. Consistent with its strict fiduciary duty, the controlling group may not utilize its control of the corporation to establish an exclusive market in previously unmarketable shares from which the minority stockholders are excluded. See Jones v. H.F. Ahmanson & Co. . . .

The purchase also distributes corporate assets to the stockholder whose shares were purchased. Unless an equal opportunity is given to all stockholders, the purchase of shares from a member of the controlling group operates as a *preferential* distribution of assets. In exchange for his shares, he receives a percentage of the contributed capital and accumulated profits of the enterprise. The funds he so receives are available for his personal use. The other stockholders benefit from no such access to corporate property and cannot withdraw their shares of the corporate profits and capital in this manner unless the controlling group acquiesces. Although the purchase price for the controlling stockholder's shares may seem fair to the corporation and other stockholders under the tests established in the prior case law (see Spiegel v. Beacon Participations, 297 Mass. 398, 429, 8 N.E.2d 895 [1937]; Winchell v. Plywood Corp., 324 Mass. 171, 178, 85 N.E.2d 313 [1949]), the controlling stockholder whose stock has been purchased has still received a relative advantage over his fellow stockholders, inconsistent with his strict fiduciary duty—an opportunity to turn corporate funds to personal use.

The rule of equal opportunity in stock purchases by close corporations provides equal access to these benefits for all stockholders. We hold that, in any case in which the controlling stockholders have exercised their power over the corporation to deny the minority such equal opportunity, the minority shall be entitled to appropriate relief. To the extent that language in Spiegel v. Beacon Participations, 297 Mass. 398, 431, 8 N.E.2d 895 (1937), and other cases suggests that there is no requirement of equal opportunity for minority stockholders when a close corporation purchases shares from a controlling stockholder, it is not to be followed.

C. *Application of the Law to this Case.* We turn now to the application of the learning set forth above to the facts of the instant case.

The strict standard of duty is plainly applicable to the stockholders in Rodd Electrotype. Rodd Electrotype is a close corporation [under the test set out above]. . . .

. . . In testing the stock purchase from Harry Rodd against the applicable strict fiduciary standard, we treat the Rodd family as a single controlling group. . . . From the evidence, it is clear that the Rodd family was a close-knit one with strong community of interest. . . .

Moreover, a strong motive of interest requires that the Rodds be considered a controlling group. When Charles Rodd and Frederick Rodd were called on to represent the corporation in its dealings with their father, they must have known that further advancement within the corporation and benefits would follow their father's retirement and the purchase of his stock. . . .

On its face, then, the purchase of Harry Rodd's shares by the corporation is a breach of the duty which the controlling stockholders, the Rodds, owed to the minority stockholders, the plaintiff and her son. The purchaser distributed a portion of the corporate assets to Harry Rodd, a member of the controlling group, in exchange for his shares. The plaintiff and her son were not offered an equal opportunity to sell their shares to the corporation. In fact, their efforts to obtain an equal opportunity were rebuffed by the corporate representative. As the trial judge found, they did not, in any manner, ratify the transaction with Harry Rodd.

Because of the foregoing, we hold that the plaintiff is entitled to relief. Two forms of suitable relief are set out hereinafter. The judge below is to enter an appropriate judgment. The judgment may require Harry Rodd to remit $36,000 with interest at the legal rate from July 15, 1970, to Rodd Electrotype in exchange for forty-five shares of Rodd Electrotype treasury stock. This, in substance, is the specific relief requested in the plaintiff's bill of complaint. Interest is manifestly appropriate. A stockholder, who, in violation of his fiduciary duty to the other stockholders, has obtained assets from his corporation and has had those assets available for his own use, must pay for that use. See Silversmith v. Sydeman, 305 Mass. 65, 74, 25 N.E.2d 215 (1940). Cf. Spiegel v. Beacon Participations, 297 Mass. 398, 420, 8 N.E.2d 895 (1937). In the alternative, the judgment may require Rodd Electrotype to purchase all of the plaintiff's shares for $36,000 without interest. In the circumstances of this case, we view this as the equal opportunity which the plaintiff should have received. Harry Rodd's retention of thirty-six shares, which were to be sold and given to his children within a year of the Rodd Electrotype purchase, cannot disguise the fact that the corporation acquired one hundred per cent of that portion of his holdings (forty-five shares) which he did not intend his children to own. The plaintiff is entitled to have one hundred per cent of her forty-five shares similarly purchased.[30]

The final decree, in so far as it dismissed the bill as to Harry C. Rodd, Frederick I. Rodd, Charles H. Rodd, Mr. Harold E. Magnuson and Rodd Electrotype Company of New England, Inc., and awarded costs, is reversed. The case is remanded to the Superior Court for entry of judgment in conformity with this opinion.

So ordered.[*]

■ WILKINS, JUSTICE (concurring).

I agree with much of what the Chief Justice says in support of granting relief to the plaintiff. However, I do not join in any implication (see, e.g., footnote 18 and the associated text) that the rule concerning a close corporation's purchase of a controlling stockholder's shares applies to all operations of the corporation as they affect minority stockholders. That broader issue, which is apt to arise in connection with salaries and dividend policy, is not involved in this case. The analogy to partnerships may not be a complete one.

———

NOTE ON NIXON V. BLACKWELL

In *Nixon v. Blackwell*, 626 A.2d 1366 (Del.Supr.1993), E.C. Barton & Co. had two classes of stock outstanding: Class A Voting Common Stock and Class B Nonvoting Common Stock. All the Class A stock and most of the Class B stock was held by or for the benefit of corporate employees. The plaintiffs, who were not employees, owned 25% of the Class B.

There was no public market for, or trading in, either class of the corporation's stock. This created a liquidity problem for the shareholders—that is, the shareholders could not readily convert the stock into cash by selling it. Over the years, the corporation addressed the liquidity problem in several ways:

---

[30]   If there has been a significant change in corporate circumstances since this case was argued, this is a matter which can be brought to the attention of the court below and may be considered by the judge in granting appropriate relief in the form of a judgment.

[*]   See also Comolli v. Comolli, 241 Ga. 471, 246 S.E.2d 278 (1978); cf. Schwartz v. Marien, 37 N.Y.2d 487, 335 N.E.2d 334, 373 N.Y.S.2d 122 (1975). For additional cases and materials on the fiduciary obligations of shareholders in close corporations, see Section 7(a), infra. (Footnote by ed.)

(i)   The Corporation established an Employee Stock Ownership Plan (ESOP) designed to hold Class B stock for the benefit of eligible employees of the Corporation. Under the plan, terminating and retiring employees were entitled to receive their interest in the ESOP by taking either Class B stock or cash in lieu of stock. Most terminating employees and retirees elected to receive cash in lieu of stock. Thus, the ESOP provided employee-shareholders with a substantial measure of liquidity that was not available to non-employee shareholders.

(ii)   The corporation also purchased "key man" life-insurance policies on certain employees, with death benefits payable to the corporation. The corporation, in turn, agreed to use a portion of these benefits to repurchase its stock from the employee-shareholders' estates.

(iii)   Occasionally, the corporation offered to purchase the Class B stock of the non-employee stockholders through self-tender offers.

There was a suggestion, at least, that the programs for providing liquidity to employee-shareholders reflected the plan of the founder of the corporation, from whom the plaintiffs had inherited their stock.

The plaintiffs, who were non-employee shareholders, argued that the corporation's directors, all of whom were employees, were improperly pursuing a discriminatory liquidity policy that favored employee-shareholders over non-employee shareholders through the ESOP and the key-man life-insurance policies. At trial, the Vice Chancellor found for the plaintiffs on the ground that the defendants breached their fiduciary duty as directors, and treated the plaintiffs unfairly, by providing no means through which non-employee shareholders could liquidate their stock at fair value, while providing liquidity for terminating and retiring employees. The Delaware Supreme Court reversed:

> The trial court in this case . . . appears to have adopted the novel legal principle that Class B stockholders had a right to "liquidity" equal to that which the court found to be available to the defendants. It is well established in [Delaware] jurisprudence that stockholders need not always be treated equally for all purposes. . . . To hold that fairness necessarily requires precise equality is to beg the question. . . .

> . . . [The] holding of the trial court overlooks the significant facts that the minority stockholders were not: (a) employees of the Corporation; (b) entitled to share in an ESOP; (c) qualified for key man insurance; or (d) protected by specific provisions in the certificate of incorporation, by-laws, or a stockholders' agreement.

> There is support in this record for the fact that the ESOP is a corporate benefit and was established, at least in part, to benefit the Corporation. Generally speaking, the creation of ESOPs is a normal corporate practice and is generally thought to benefit the corporation. The same is true generally with respect to key man insurance programs. . . .

> Accordingly, we hold that the Vice Chancellor erred as a matter of law in concluding that the liquidity afforded to the

employee stockholders by the ESOP and the key man insurance required substantially equal treatment for the non-employee stockholders. Moreover, the Vice Chancellor failed to evaluate and articulate, for example, whether or not and to what extent (a) corporate benefits flowed from the ESOP and the key man insurance; (b) the ESOP and key man insurance plans are novel, extraordinary, or relatively routine business practices; (c) [the founder's] plan for employee management and benefits should be honored; and (d) the self-tenders showed defendants' willingness to provide an exit opportunity for the plaintiffs. . . .

We hold on this record that defendants have met their burden of establishing the entire fairness of their dealings with the non-employee Class B stockholders, and are entitled to judgment. The record is sufficient to conclude that plaintiffs' claim that the defendant directors have maintained a discriminatory policy of favoring Class A employee stockholders over Class B non-employee stockholders is without merit. The directors have followed a consistent policy originally established by . . . the founder of the Corporation. . . .

———

Rosenthal v. Rosenthal

543 A.2d 348 (Me.1988)

In this case, the trial court judge set out the following four specific fiduciary duties owed by the business associates in a close corporation to each other:

(1) To act with that degree of diligence, care and skill which ordinarily prudent persons would exercise under similar circumstances in like positions;

(2) To discharge the duties affecting their relationship in good faith with a view to furthering the interests of one another as to the matters within the scope of the relationship;

(3) To disclose and not withhold from one another relevant information affecting the status and affairs of the relationship;

(4) To not use their position, influence or knowledge respecting the affairs and organization that are subject to the relationship to gain any special privilege or advantage over the other person or persons involved in the relationship. . . .

On appeal, the Maine Supreme Court affirmed. "For the first time on appeal defendants object to the [trial judge's] definition of the scope of the [shareholders'] duties as including 'furthering the interests of one another,' rather than being restricted to furthering the interests of the business enterprise. We can find no clear error in that instruction, however, given the special nature of the [shareholders'] family business, which most closely resembles a single complex family partnership doing business through numerous entities of varied legal forms. . . . The duties owed in the circumstances here presented necessarily flowed to the other business associates, as well as to the [shareholders'] enterprise as a whole and the component entitles." (Emphasis by the court.)

———

Wilkes v. Springside Nursing Home, Inc.

Supreme Judicial Court of Massachusetts, 1976.
370 Mass. 842, 353 N.E.2d 657.

■ HENNESSEY, CHIEF JUSTICE.

[The plaintiff (Wilkes) filed a bill in equity for declaratory judgment, naming as defendants T. Edward Quinn,[3] Leon L. Riche, the executors of Lawrence R. Connor, and the Springside Nursing Home, Inc. Wilkes sought, among other forms of relief, damages in the amount of the salary he would have received had he continued as a director and officer of Springside subsequent to March, 1967. The court referred the suit to a master. The master's report was confirmed, a judgment was entered dismissing Wilkes's action on the merits, and the Massachusetts Supreme Court granted direct appellate review.] . . .

. . . [W]e reverse so much of the judgment as dismisses Wilkes's complaint and order the entry of a judgment substantially granting the relief sought by Wilkes under the second alternative set forth above.

A summary of the pertinent facts as found by the master is set out in the following pages. . . .

In 1951 Wilkes acquired an option to purchase a building and lot located on the corner of Springside Avenue and North Street in Pittsfield, Massachusetts, the building having previously housed the Hillcrest Hospital. Though Wilkes was principally engaged in the roofing and siding business, he had gained a reputation locally for profitable dealings in real estate. Riche, an acquaintance of Wilkes, learned of the option, and interested Quinn (who was known to Wilkes through membership on the draft board in Pittsfield) and Pipkin (an acquaintance of both Wilkes and Riche) in joining Wilkes in his investment. The four men met and decided to participate jointly in the purchase of the building and lot as a real estate investment which, they believed, had good profit potential on resale or rental.

The parties later determined that the property would have its greatest potential for profit if it were operated by them as a nursing home. Wilkes consulted his attorney, who advised him that if the four men were to operate the contemplated nursing home as planned, they would be partners and would be liable for any debts incurred by the partnership and by each other. On the attorney's suggestion, and after

---

[3] T. Edward Quinn died while this action was sub judice. The executrix of his estate has been substituted as a party-defendant. . . .

consultation among themselves, ownership of the property was vested in Springside, a corporation organized under Massachusetts law.

Each of the four men invested $1,000 and subscribed to ten shares of $100 par value stock in Springside.[6] At the time of incorporation it was understood by all of the parties that each would be a director of Springside and each would participate actively in the management and decision making involved in operating the corporation.[7] It was, further, the understanding and intention of all the parties that, corporate resources permitting, each would receive money from the corporation in equal amounts as long as each assumed an active and ongoing responsibility for carrying a portion of the burdens necessary to operate the business.

The work involved in establishing and operating a nursing home was roughly apportioned, and each of the four men undertook his respective tasks.[8] Initially, Riche was elected president of Springside, Wilkes was elected treasurer, and Quinn was elected clerk.[9] Each of the four was listed in the articles of organization as a director of the corporation.

At some time in 1952, it became apparent that the operational income and cash flow from the business were sufficient to permit the four stockholders to draw money from the corporation on a regular basis. Each of the four original parties initially received $35 a week from the corporation. As time went on the weekly return to each was increased until, in 1955, it totalled $100.

In 1959, after a long illness, Pipkin sold his shares in the corporation to Connor, who was known to Wilkes, Riche and Quinn through past transactions with Springside in his capacity as president of the First Agricultural National Bank of Berkshire County. Connor received a weekly stipend from the corporation equal to that received by Wilkes, Riche and Quinn. He was elected a director of the corporation but never held any other office. He was assigned no specific area of responsibility in the operation of the nursing home but did participate in business

---

[6]   On May 2, 1955, and again on December 23, 1958, each of the four original investors paid for and was issued additional shares of $100 par value stock, eventually bringing the total number of shares owned by each to 115.

[7]   Wilkes testified before the master that, when the corporate officers were elected, all four men "were . . . guaranteed directorships." Riche's understanding of the parties' intentions was that they all wanted to play a part in the management of the corporation and wanted to have some "say" in the risks involved; that, to this end, they all would be directors; and that "unless you [were] a director and officer you could not participate in the decisions of [the] enterprise."

[8]   Wilkes took charge of the repair, upkeep and maintenance of the physical plant and grounds; Riche assumed supervision over the kitchen facilities and dietary and food aspects of the home; Pipkin was to make himself available if and when medical problems arose; and Quinn dealt with the personnel and administrative aspects of the nursing home, serving informally as a managing director. Quinn further coordinated the activities of the other parties and served as a communication link among them when matters had to be discussed and decisions had to be made without a formal meeting.

[9]   Riche held the office of president from 1951 to 1963; Quinn served as president from 1963 on, as clerk from 1951 to 1967, and as treasurer from 1967 on; Wilkes was treasurer from 1951 to 1967.

discussions and decisions as a director and served additionally as financial adviser to the corporation.

In 1965 the stockholders decided to sell a portion of the corporate property to Quinn who, in addition to being a stockholder in Springside, possessed an interest in another corporation which desired to operate a rest home on the property. Wilkes was successful in prevailing on the other stockholders of Springside to procure a higher sale price for the property than Quinn apparently anticipated paying or desired to pay. After the sale was consummated, the relationship between Quinn and Wilkes began to deteriorate.

The bad blood between Quinn and Wilkes affected the attitudes of both Riche and Connor. As a consequence of the strained relations among the parties, Wilkes, in January of 1967, gave notice of his intention to sell his shares for an amount based on an appraisal of their value. In February of 1967 a directors' meeting was held and the board exercised its right to establish the salaries of its officers and employees.[10] A schedule of payments was established whereby Quinn was to receive a substantial weekly increase and Riche and Connor were to continue receiving $100 a week. Wilkes, however, was left off the list of those to whom a salary was to be paid. The directors also set the annual meeting of the stockholders for March, 1967.

At the annual meeting in March,[11] Wilkes was not reelected as a director, nor was he reelected as an officer of the corporation. He was further informed that neither his services nor his presence at the nursing home was wanted by his associates.

The meetings of the directors and stockholders in early 1967, the master found, were used as a vehicle to force Wilkes out of active participation in the management and operation of the corporation and to cut off all corporate payments to him. Though the board of directors had the power to dismiss any officers or employees for misconduct or neglect of duties, there was no indication in the minutes of the board of directors' meeting in February, 1967, that the failure to establish a salary for Wilkes was based on either ground. The severance of Wilkes from the payroll resulted not from misconduct or neglect of duties, but because of the personal desire of Quinn, Riche and Connor to prevent him from continuing to receive money from the corporation. Despite a continuing deterioration in his personal relationship with his associates, Wilkes had consistently endeavored to carry on his responsibilities to the corporation in the same satisfactory manner and with the same degree of competence

---

[10]   The by-laws of the corporation provided that the directors, subject to the approval of the stockholders, had the power to fix the salaries of all officers and employees. This power, however, up until February, 1967, had not been exercised formally; all payments made to the four participants in the venture had resulted from the informal but unanimous approval of all the parties concerned.

[11]   Wilkes was unable to attend the meeting of the board of directors in February or the annual meeting of the stockholders in March, 1967. He was represented, however, at the annual meeting by his attorney, who held his proxy.

he had previously shown. Wilkes was at all times willing to carry on his responsibilities and participation if permitted so to do and provided that he receive his weekly stipend.

1.   We turn to Wilkes's claim for damages based on a breach of the fiduciary duty owed to him by the other participants in this venture. In light of the theory underlying this claim, we do not consider it vital to our approach to this case whether the claim is governed by partnership law or the law applicable to business corporations. This is so because, as all the parties agree, Springside was at all times relevant to this action, a close corporation as we have recently defined such an entity in Donahue v. Rodd Electrotype Co. of New England, Inc. . . . [where] we held that "stockholders in the close corporation owe one another substantially the same fiduciary duty in the operation of the enterprise that partners owe to one another." . . .

In the *Donahue* case we recognized that one peculiar aspect of close corporations was the opportunity afforded to majority stockholders to oppress, disadvantage or "freeze out" minority stockholders. . . .

. . . One . . . device which has proved to be particularly effective in accomplishing the purpose of the majority is to deprive minority stockholders of corporate offices and of employment with the corporation . . . This "freeze-out" technique has been successful because courts fairly consistently have been disinclined to interfere in those facets of internal corporate operations, such as the selection and retention or dismissal of officers, directors and employees, which essentially involve management decisions subject to the principle of majority control . . .

The denial of employment to the minority at the hands of the majority is especially pernicious in some instances. A guaranty of employment with the corporation may have been one of the "basic reason[s] why a minority owner has invested capital in the firm." . . . The minority stockholder typically depends on his salary as the principal return on his investment, since the "earnings of a close corporation . . . are distributed in major part in salaries, bonuses, and retirement benefits." 1 F.H. O'Neal, Close Corporations § 1.07 (1971).[13] Other noneconomic interests of the minority stockholder are likewise injuriously affected by barring him from corporate office. See F.H. O'Neal, "Squeeze-Outs" of Minority Shareholders 79 (1975). Such action severely restricts his participation in the management of the enterprise, and he is relegated to enjoying those benefits incident to his status as a stockholder. See Symposium—The Close Corporation, 52 Nw.U.L.Rev. 345, 386 (1957). In sum, by terminating a minority stockholder's employment or by severing him from a position as an officer or director, the majority effectively frustrate the minority stockholder's purposes in

---

[13]   We note here that the master found that Springside never declared or paid a dividend to its stockholders.

entering on the corporate venture and also deny him an equal return on his investment.

The *Donahue* decision acknowledged, as a "natural outgrowth" of the case law of this Commonwealth, a strict obligation on the part of majority stockholders in a close corporation to deal with the minority with the utmost good faith and loyalty. On its face, this strict standard is applicable in the instant case. The distinction between the majority action in *Donahue* and the majority action in this case is more one of form than of substance. Nevertheless, we are concerned that untempered application of the strict good faith standard enunciated in Donahue to cases such as the one before us will result in the imposition of limitations on legitimate action by the controlling group in a close corporation which will unduly hamper its effectiveness in managing the corporation in the best interests of all concerned. The majority, concededly, have certain rights to what has been termed "selfish ownership" in the corporation which should be balanced against the concept of their fiduciary obligation to the minority. See Hill, The Sale of Controlling Shares, 70 Harv.L.Rev. 986, 1013–1015 (1957); Note, 44 Iowa L.Rev. 734, 740–741 (1959); Symposium—The Close Corporation, 52 Nw.U.L.Rev. 345, 395–396 (1957).

Therefore, when minority stockholders in a close corporation bring suit against the majority alleging a breach of the strict good faith duty owed to them by the majority, we must carefully analyze the action taken by the controlling stockholders in the individual case. It must be asked whether the controlling group can demonstrate a legitimate business purpose for its action. See Bryan v. Brock & Blevins Co., 343 F.Supp. 1062, 1068 (N.D.Ga.1972), aff'd, 490 F.2d 563, 570–571 (5th Cir.1974); Schwartz v. Marien, 37 N.Y.2d 487, 492, 373 N.Y.S.2d 122, 335 N.E.2d 334 (1975). . . . In asking this question, we acknowledge the fact that the controlling group in a close corporation must have some room to maneuver in establishing the business policy of the corporation. It must have a large measure of discretion, for example, in declaring or withholding dividends, deciding whether to merge or consolidate, establishing the salaries of corporate officers, dismissing directors with or without cause, and hiring and firing corporate employees.

When an asserted business purpose for their action is advanced by the majority, however, we think it is open to minority stockholders to demonstrate that the same legitimate objective could have been achieved through an alternative course of action less harmful to the minority's interest. See Schwartz v. Marien, supra. . . . If called on to settle a dispute, our courts must weigh the legitimate business purpose, if any, against the practicability of a less harmful alternative.

Applying this approach to the instant case it is apparent that the majority stockholders in Springside have not shown a legitimate business purpose for severing Wilkes from the payroll of the corporation or for refusing to reelect him as a salaried officer and director. . . .

It is an inescapable conclusion from all the evidence that the action of the majority stockholders here was a designed "freeze out" for which no legitimate business purpose has been suggested. Furthermore, we may infer that a design to pressure Wilkes into selling his shares to the corporation at a price below their value well may have been at the heart of the majority's plan.[14]

In the context of this case, several factors bear directly on the duty owed to Wilkes by his associates. At a minimum, the duty of utmost good faith and loyalty would demand that the majority consider that their action was in disregard of a long-standing policy of the stockholders that each would be a director of the corporation and that employment with the corporation would go hand in hand with stock ownership; that Wilkes was one of the four originators of the nursing home venture; and that Wilkes, like the others, had invested his capital and time for more than fifteen years with the expectation that he would continue to participate in corporate decisions. Most important is the plain fact that the cutting off of Wilkes's salary, together with the fact that the corporation never declared a dividend (see note 13 supra), assured that Wilkes would receive no return at all from the corporation.

2. . . . Therefore our order is as follows: So much of the judgment as dismisses Wilkes's complaint and awards costs to the defendants is reversed.[16] The case is remanded . . . for further proceedings concerning the issue of damages. Thereafter a judgment shall be entered declaring that Quinn, Riche and Connor breached their fiduciary duty to Wilkes as a minority stockholder in Springside, and awarding money damages therefor. Wilkes shall be allowed to recover from Riche, the estate of T. Edward Quinn and the estate of Lawrence R. Connor, ratably, according to the inequitable enrichment of each, the salary he would have received had he remained an officer and director of Springside. In considering the issue of damages the judge on remand shall take into account the extent to which any remaining corporate funds of Springside may be diverted to satisfy Wilkes's claim.

———————

Zimmerman v. Bogoff

402 Mass. 650, 524 N.E.2d 849 (1988)

"[T]he Donahue remedy is not intended to place a strait jacket on legitimate corporate activity. Where the alleged wrongdoer can demonstrate a legitimate business purpose for his action, no liability will result unless the wronged shareholder succeeds in showing that the

———————

[14] This inference arises from the fact that Connor, acting on behalf of the three controlling stockholders, offered to purchase Wilkes's shares for a price Connor admittedly would not have accepted for his own shares.

[16] We do not disturb the judgment in so far as it dismissed a counterclaim by Springside against Wilkes arising from the payment of money by Quinn to Wilkes after the sale in 1965 of certain property of Springside to a corporation owned at that time by Quinn and his wife. . . .

proffered legitimate objective could have been achieved through a less harmful, reasonably practicable, alternative mode of action. . . . "

———

Merola v. Exergen Corp.

Supreme Judicial Court of Massachusetts, 1996.
423 Mass. 461, 668 N.E.2d 351.

■ LYNCH, JUSTICE.

The plaintiff, a former vice president of Exergen Corporation (Exergen) and a former minority stockholder of that corporation, brought suit in the Superior Court against Exergen and the president and majority stockholder, Francesco Pompei, because of his termination as an officer and employee of Exergen . . . [The complaint] alleged that the corporation was a "close corporation," and that Pompei, as the majority stockholder, violated his fiduciary obligations to the plaintiff as a minority stockholder by terminating his employment without cause. . . .

. . . [T]he judge found that the corporation was a "close corporation" and that Pompei had breached his fiduciary obligations to the plaintiff by failing to give him an opportunity to become a major stockholder and by terminating his employment. She adopted the jury's advisory conclusion that he had been damaged only by the termination of employment to the extent of $50,000. . . .

We summarize the facts found by the judge. Exergen was formed in May, 1980, as a corporation in the business of developing and selling infrared heat detection devices. From Exergen's inception to the date of trial, Pompei, the founder, was the majority shareholder in the corporation, as well as its president, owning over sixty per cent of the shares issued. At all relevant times, Pompei actively participated in and controlled the management of Exergen and, as the majority shareholder, had power to elect and change Exergen's board of directors.

The plaintiff began working for Exergen on a part-time basis in late 1980 while he was also employed full-time by Analogic Corporation. In the course of conversations with Pompei in late 1981, and early 1982, the plaintiff was offered full-time employment with Exergen, and he understood that, if he came to work there and invested in Exergen stock, he would have the opportunity to become a major shareholder of Exergen and for continuing employment with Exergen.

As of March 1, 1982, the plaintiff resigned from Analogic and began working full time for Exergen. He also then began purchasing shares in Exergen when the company made periodic offerings to its employees. From March, 1982, through June, 1982, the plaintiff purchased 4,100 shares at $2.25 per share, for a total of $9,225. Exergen announced at the Exergen shareholders meeting in September, 1982, another option program to purchase shares at $5 per share within one year. By late

1983, the plaintiff had exercised his option to purchase an additional 1,200 shares. The plaintiff was not offered additional stock options after late 1983. . . .

Principles of employment law permit the termination of employees at will, with or without cause excepting situations within a narrow public policy exception. King v. Driscoll, 418 Mass. 576, 581–582, 638 N.E.2d 488 (1994), and cases cited. However, the termination of a minority shareholder's employment may present a situation where the majority interest has breached its fiduciary duty to the minority interest. Id. at 586, 638 N.E.2d 488. Wilkes v. Springside Nursing Home, Inc., supra at 852–853, 353 N.E.2d 657. There the court concluded that the majority stockholders had attempted unfairly to "freeze out" a minority stockholder by terminating his employment, in part because their policy and practice was to divide the available resources of the corporation equally by way of salaries to the shareholders who all participated in the operation of the enterprise. Id. at 846, 353 N.E.2d 657. . . . Given those facts, this court concluded that the other shareholders did not show a legitimate business purpose for terminating the minority stockholder and that the other parties acted "in disregard of a longstanding policy of the stockholders that each would be a director of the corporation and that employment with the corporation would go hand in hand with stock ownership." Id. at 853, 353 N.E.2d 657.

Here, although the plaintiff invested in the stock of Exergen with the reasonable expectation of continued employment, there was no general policy regarding stock ownership and employment, and there was no evidence that any other stockholders had expectations of continuing employment because they purchased stock. The investment in the stock was an investment in the equity of the corporation which was not tied to employment in any formal way. The plaintiff acknowledged that he could have purchased 5,000 shares of stock while he was working part time before resigning from his position at Analogic Corporation and accepting full-time employment at Exergen. He testified that he was induced to work for Exergen with the promise that he could become a major stockholder. There was no testimony that he was ever required to buy stock as a condition of employment.

Unlike the *Wilkes* case, there was no evidence that the corporation distributed all profits to shareholders in the form of salaries. On the contrary, the perceived value of the stock increased during the time that the plaintiff was employed. The plaintiff first purchased his stock at $2.25 per share and, one year later, he purchased more for $5 per share. This indicated that there was some increase in value to the investment independent of the employment expectation. Neither was the plaintiff a founder of the business, his stock purchases were made after the business was established, and there was no suggestion that he had to purchase stock to keep his job.

The plaintiff testified that, when he sold his stock back to the corporation in 1991, he was paid $17 per share. This was a price that had been paid to other shareholders who sold their shares to the corporation at a previous date, and it is a price which, after consulting with his attorney, he concluded was a fair price. With this payment, the plaintiff realized a significant return on his capital investment independent of the salary he received as an employee.

We conclude that this is not a situation where the majority shareholder breached his fiduciary duty to a minority shareholder. "[T]he controlling group in a close corporation must have some room to maneuver in establishing the business policy of the corporation." Wilkes v. Springside Nursing Home, Inc., supra at 851, 353 N.E.2d 657. Although there was no legitimate business purpose for the termination of the plaintiff, neither was the termination for the financial gain of Pompei or contrary to established public policy. Not every discharge of an at-will employee of a close corporation who happens to own stock in the corporation gives rise to a successful breach of fiduciary duty claim. The plaintiff was terminated in accordance with his employment contract and fairly compensated for his stock. He failed to establish a sufficient basis for a breach of fiduciary duty claim under the principles of Donahue v. Rodd Electrotype Co., supra. . . .

Judgment reversed.

———

6. RESTRICTIONS ON THE TRANSFERABILITY OF SHARES, AND MANDATORY-SALE PROVISIONS

INTRODUCTORY NOTE

This Section concerns the extent to which restrictions on transferability can be imposed on the stock of close corporations. One of the traditional norms of corporate law was that ownership interests in corporations—that is, shares of stock—were freely transferable, as were the rights that accompanied these interests, such as the right to vote on various matters. In contrast, a basic norm of partnership law was that a partner could not transfer all of his rights in a partnership without the unanimous consent of all of his partners. The partnership norm is a much better fit for small enterprises, including close corporations, than the traditional corporate norm, because where an enterprise is owned by a small number of persons, the identity of each co-owner is of vital importance to the remaining co-owners. Accordingly, shareholder agreements in close corporations commonly either limit the transferability of shares; require the shareholder or his estate to sell his shares back to the corporation or to the other shareholders on the occurrence of certain events, such as an offer from a third party or death; or both. At first, the courts had difficulty with restrictions on the transferability of close corporation stock, partly because the restrictions seemed to violate traditional corporate norms, and partly because corporate stock was viewed as property and property was viewed as freely alienable. Eventually, however, the courts began to approach restrictions on transferability on a functional rather than a doctrinal basis. When restrictions are approached on a functional basis, two intertwined issues must be addressed. First, is the relevant type of restriction fair? Second, where the restriction involves a compulsory sale of the shareholder's stock at a fixed or formula price, is the price fair? The materials in this section develop these issues.

F.B.I. Farms, Inc. v. Moore

Supreme Court of Indiana, 2003.
798 N.E.2d 440.

We hold that as a general proposition, restrictions on corporate share transfers may require approval of the transfer by the corporation's Board of Directors, at least in a family-owned corporation. Although generally valid against purchasers with notice of them, such restrictions may not prevent a creditor from foreclosing a lien on the shares, but a purchaser who buys at a foreclosure sale with notice of the restrictions acquires the shares subject to the restrictions. We also hold that if shares are subject to a right of first refusal, and the holder of the right has notice of the foreclosure, the holder cannot exercise the right against a purchaser at a foreclosure sale after the purchaser has taken title to the shares without objection from the holder of the rights.

Factual and Procedural Background

F.B.I. Farms, Inc., was formed in 1976 by Ivan and Thelma Burger, their children, Linda and Freddy, and the children's spouses. Each of the three couples transferred a farm and related machinery to the corporation in exchange for common stock in the corporation. At the time, Birchell Moore was married to Linda. Linda and Moore deeded a jointly-owned 180-acre farm to F.B.I., and 2,507 shares were issued to Moore and one to Linda. These 2,508 shares represented approximately fourteen percent of the capitalization of F.B.I.

In 1977, the Board of Directors of F.B.I. consisted of Moore, Ivan, Freddy and Linda. The minutes of a 1977 meeting of the Board recite that the following restrictions on the transfer of shares were "adopted":

1)   No stock of said corporation shall be transferred, assigned and/or exchanged or divided, unless or until approved by the Directors thereof;

2)   That if any stock be offered for sale, assigned and/or transferred, the corporation should have the first opportunity of purchasing the same at no more than the book value thereof;

3)   Should said corporation be not interested, and could not economically offer to purchase said stock, any stockholder of

record should be given the next opportunity to purchase said
stock, at a price not to exceed the book value thereof;

4)   That if the corporation was not interested in the stock,
and any stockholders were not interested therein, then the same
could be sold to any blood member of the family. Should they be
desirous of purchasing the same, then at not more than the book
value thereof.

Linda's marriage to Moore was dissolved in 1982. As part of the
dissolution proceedings, Linda was awarded all of the F.B.I. shares and
Moore was awarded a monetary judgment in the amount of $155,889.80,
secured by a lien on Linda's shares.

F.B.I. filed for bankruptcy protection in 1989 and emerged from
Chapter 11 Bankruptcy in 1991. Moore's judgment against Linda
remained unsatisfied, and in April 1998 he sought a writ of execution of
his lien. The corporation, through its counsel, responded with a letter to
Moore's counsel demanding payment of the $250,700 subscription price
for the 2,507 shares that were initially issued to Moore but had since
been transferred to Linda. Moore obtained the writ of execution in June
1999. . . . A sheriff's sale went forward and in February 2000 Moore
purchased all 2,924 shares owned by Linda at the time for $290,450.67.

In December 2000 Moore instituted this suit against F.B.I., its
shareholders, and Linda seeking a declaratory judgment that the
attempted cancellation of the shares by the defendants was invalid, that
Moore properly retained ownership of the shares, and that the shares
were unencumbered by restrictions and were freely transferable. . . .

I.   Transfer Restrictions

A.   General Principles

Most of the issues in this case are resolved by the Indiana statute
governing share transfer restrictions. Indiana Code section 23–1–26–8
essentially mirrors Model Business Corporation Act § 6.27, which
authorizes restrictions on the transfer of shares. The Indiana statute
reads as follows: . . .

(c)   A restriction on the transfer or registration of transfer
of shares is authorized:

(1)   to maintain the corporation's status when it is
dependent on the number or identity of its shareholders;

(2)   to preserve exemptions under federal or state
securities law; or

(3)   for any other reasonable purpose.

(d)   A restriction on the transfer or registration of transfer
of shares may, among other things:

(1)   obligate the shareholder first to offer the
corporation or other persons (separately, consecutively, or

simultaneously) an opportunity to acquire the restricted shares;

(2) obligate the corporation or other persons (separately, consecutively, or simultaneously) to acquire the restricted shares;

(3) require the corporation, the holders of any class of its shares, or another person to approve the transfer of the restricted shares, if the requirement is not manifestly unreasonable; or

(4) prohibit the transfer of the restricted shares to designated persons or classes of persons, if the prohibition is not manifestly unreasonable. . . .

Corporate shares are personal property. At common law, any restriction on the power to alienate personal property was impermissible. *Doss v. Yingling,* 95 Ind. App. 494, 500, 172 N.E. 801, 803 (1930). Despite this doctrine, Indiana, like virtually all jurisdictions, allows corporations and their shareholders to impose restrictions on transfers of shares. The basic theory of these statutes is to permit owners of a corporation to control its ownership and management and prevent outsiders from inserting themselves into the operations of the corporation. *Id.* at 502–03, 172 N.E. 801; 12 William Meade Fletcher et al, Fletcher Cyclopedia of the Law of Private Corporations, § 5454 (1996). Chief Justice Holmes stated the matter succinctly a century ago: "Stock in a corporation is not merely property. It also creates a personal relation analogous otherwise than technically to a partnership. . . . [T]here seems to be no greater objection to retaining the right of choosing one's associates in a corporation than in a firm." Barrett v. King, 181 Mass. 476, 63 N.E. 934, 935 (1902). As applied to a family-owned corporation, this remains valid today.

Transfer restrictions are treated as contracts either between shareholders or between shareholders and the corporation.[35] *Doss,* 95 Ind.App. at 502, 172 N.E. at 803; Butner v. United States, 440 U.S. 48, 55 . . . (1979) (the validity and enforcement of restrictions are governed by state law just like any other contract); Boston Safe Deposit & Trust Co., et al. v. North Attleborough Chapter of the Am. Red Cross, et al., 330 Mass. 114, 111 N.E.2d 447, 449 (Mass. 1953) (restrictions in the articles of organization are binding on a shareholder by reason of the contract

---

[35] The Indiana statute provides that restrictions are valid if included in the articles, the bylaws, an agreement among shareholders or an agreement between the corporation and shareholders. I.C. § 23–1–26–8(a) (1998). None of these was done here. However, no one challenges the restrictions as defective in their initial adoption. At least as to Moore, who approved them as a director and had actual knowledge of them, under these circumstances, the restrictions constitute a contract as to all of those shareholders who approved the adoption of the restrictions. *Shortridge v. Platis,* 458 N.E.2d 301, 304 (Ind.Ct.App.1984) (a buy-sell restriction is analyzed by the court as a contract); 18A Am.Jur.2d *Corporations* § 687 (1985) (courts sustain a restriction whether valid as a bylaw or not, on the ground that it constitutes a valid agreement between the stockholders and the corporation, particularly as applied to stockholders who assent to, or participate in, the adoption of the bylaw).

made with the corporation when she accepted the certificates of stock containing the printed restrictions). Apart from any statutory requirements, restrictions on transfer are to be read, like any other contract, to further the manifest intention of the parties. Because they are restrictions on alienation and therefore disfavored, the terms in the restrictions are not to be expanded beyond their plain and ordinary meaning. 12 Fletcher § 5455 (1996).

For a party to be bound by share transfer restrictions, that party must have notice of the restrictions. I.C. § 23–1–26–8(b) (1998). Here, the restrictions on transfer of F.B.I. shares were neither "noted conspicuously" on the certificates nor contained in the information statement referred to in Indiana Code 23–1–26–8(b), but there is no doubt that Moore, the buyer at the sheriff's sale, had notice of the restrictions. He was therefore bound by them. State ex rel. Hudelson v. Clarks Hill Tel. Co., 139 Ind. App. 507, 510, 218 N.E.2d 154, 156 (1966).

Finally, a closely held corporation is a "corporation in which all of the outstanding stock is held by just a few individuals, or by a small group of persons belonging to a single family." J.R. Kemper, Validity of "Consent Restraint" on Transfer of Shares of Close Corporation, 69 A.L.R.3d 1327, 1328 (1976). In 1977, F.B.I. plainly fell within that description; it was owned by six individuals, all members of a single family. Closely held corporations have a viable interest in remaining the organization they envision at incorporation and transfer restrictions are an appropriate means of maintaining the status quo.

B.   Rights of First Refusal

Paragraphs (2) and (3) of the restrictions created rights of first refusal in F.B.I. and its shareholders. A transfer in violation of restrictions is voidable at the insistence of the corporation. Groves v. Prickett, 420 F.2d 1119, 1122 (9th Cir.1970). F.B.I. and its shareholders argue that Moore should have been obliged to offer the shares to the corporation or a shareholder pursuant to those provisions. Moore responds, and the Court of Appeals agreed, that he was not a shareholder until he purchased the shares at the sheriff's sale. He contends he therefore had no power to offer the shares. This misses the point that before Linda could transfer her shares, she was obliged to offer them to F.B.I. and the other shareholders. Moore was on notice of that requirement. Moore, as the buyer, had the right to demand that Linda initiate the process to exercise or waive the right to first refusal.

Thus, if the corporation had insisted on its right of first refusal, Linda would have been obliged to sell to F.B.I. (or its shareholders). And Moore, as a buyer on notice of the restrictions, had the right to insist that that process go forward. But the corporation and its shareholders were aware of the sheriff's sale and did nothing to assert the right of first refusal. They cannot sit back and let the sale go forward, await future events, then claim a right to purchase on the same terms as Moore. McCroden v. Case, 602 N.W.2d 736, 743–44 (S.D.1999) (transfer restriction is waived by stockholder's failure to exercise "first option" preemptive rights); Calton v. Calton, 118 N.C.App. 439, 456 S.E.2d 520, 523 (1995) (no justiciable controversy existed where no shareholder exercised the right to purchase stock, intended to exercise the right, or was even financially able to do so at the time the action was filed; shareholders waived any right to object to the transfers where they had knowledge of both the testator's death and the restrictions contained on the stock certificates, no shareholder asked to purchase any of the stock, and shareholders waited eighteen months to file an action); Puro v. Puro, 40 A.D.2d 784, 337 N.Y.S.2d 586, 587 (N.Y.App.Div.1972) (transfer restrictions are not self-executing). In sum, F.B.I. and its shareholders had rights of first refusal, but failed to exercise them. As a result, the sale to Moore proceeded as if the shares had been offered and the corporation refused the opportunity. To hold otherwise would be to give F.B.I. and its shareholders a perpetual option to purchase but no obligation to do so. Having failed to demand their right to buy at the time of the sale, the rights of first refusal gave them no ability to upset the sale conducted by the sheriff.

C. Restrictions on Transfer with Board Approval

The restrictions "adopted" in paragraphs (1) and (4) are more problematic. Indiana's statute, reflecting the common law, requires that restrictions on share transfers be reasonable. I.C. § 23–1–26–8(c)(3), (d)(3), and (d)(4). The general common law doctrine surrounding evaluation of the reasonableness of restrictions is well established. A restriction is reasonable if it is designed to serve a legitimate purpose of the party imposing the restraint and the restraint is not an absolute restriction on the recipient's right of alienability. Bernard F. Cataldo, *Stock Transfer Restrictions and the Closed Corporation,* 37 Va. L.Rev. 229, 232–33 (1951). The Indiana statute is somewhat more generous in allowing restrictions on classes of buyers unless "manifestly unreasonable." I.C. 23–1–26–8(d)(4). Several factors are relevant in determining the reasonableness of any transfer restriction, including the size of the corporation, the degree of restraint upon alienation; the time the restriction was to continue in effect, the method to be used in determining the transfer price of shares, the likelihood of the restriction's contributing to the attainment of corporate objectives, the possibility that a hostile stockholder might injure the corporation, and the probability of the restriction's promoting the best interests of the corporation. 18A Am.Jur.2d *Corporations* § 683 (1985). At one extreme, a restriction that merely prescribes procedures that must be observed before stock may be transferred is not unreasonable. State ex rel. Howland v. Olympia Veneer Co., 138 Wash. 144, 244 P. 261 (1926). At the other end of the spectrum, restrictions that are fraudulent, oppressive, unconscionable, Tourtelott v. Chestnuts Salon, No. 00–5496 2001 R.I.Super. LEXIS 19 at * 6 (R.I. Sup.Ct. Jan. 17, 2001), 2001 WL 91393, or the result of a breach of the fiduciary duty that shareholders in a close corporation owe to one

another, will not be upheld. Cressy v. Shannon Cont'l Corp., 177 Ind.App.
224, 378 N.E.2d 941, 945 (1978); 12 Fletcher § 5455 (1996). The
restrictions on F.B.I.'s shares, like most, are somewhere in the middle.
They impose substantive limitations on transfer, but are not alleged to
be the result of fraud or breach of fiduciary duty.

The trial court, in its order granting partial summary judgment,
concluded that the restriction precluding transfer without Board
approval was reasonable at the time that it was adopted, but the lengthy
and difficult history between the parties had rendered the restriction
unreasonable. Under basic contract law principles, the reasonableness of
a term of a contract is evaluated at the time of its adoption. First Fed.
Sav. Bank v. Key Mkts., 559 N.E.2d 600, 603 (Ind.1990). The same is true
of share transfer restrictions. As a result, evaluating the reasonableness
of the restrictions in light of subsequent developments is inappropriate.
For that reason, we do not agree that the restriction requiring director
approval became unreasonable based upon events and disputes within
the family that occurred after the restrictions had been adopted. To be
sure, the parties find themselves in a difficult dispute as is sometimes
the case in a family business following a dissolution. But when F.B.I. was
formed and the family farms were effectively pooled, the shareholders
agreed that the Board would be permitted to restrict access to the shares.
To the extent that restriction devalues the shares in the hands of any
individual shareholder by reason of lack of transferability, it is the result
of the bargain they struck. The policy behind enforcement of these
restrictions is to encourage entering into formal partnerships by
permitting all parties to have confidence they will not involuntarily end
up with an undesired co-venturer. Presumably for that reason, the
statute permits a restriction that requires a transferee to be approved by
the Board of Directors, and to that extent may severely limit
transferability.

A "consent restriction" such as this has been considered
unreasonable by some courts. 2 Cox, Hazen, O'Neal *Corporations* § 14.10
(2002); Harry G. Henn & John R. Alexander, *Laws of Corporations,* § 281
(1983). However, the General Assembly has allowed precisely this type
of restriction in Indiana Code section 23–1–26–8(d)(3). That section
provides that transfer restrictions may require the approval of "the
corporation, the holders of any class of its shares, or another person"
before the shares may be transferred. Board approval is one permissible
way of implementing approval by "the Corporation" under this section.
See also Wright v. Iredell Telephone Co., 182 N.C. 308, 108 S.E. 744, 747
(1921) (upholding a restriction requiring the approval of the corporation's
directors).

D. Restrictions on Transfer Except to "Blood Members of the Family"

We also find the "blood-member" restriction to be enforceable as
protecting a viable interest. Mathews v. United States, 226 F.Supp. 1003,

1009 (E.D.N.Y.1964) (recognized "intact family ownership" as an interest worth protecting by a restriction). These are family farmers in corporate form. It is apparent from the nature of the corporation that the Burger family had an interest in maintaining ownership and operation of F.B.I. in the hands of family members. Although one may quibble with the terminology, and there may be some individuals where status as blood members is debatable, we think it plain enough that all parties to this dispute either are or are not blood members of the Burger family. All are either direct descendants of Ivan or spouses of Ivan or of one of his children. . . .

III. Restrictions as Applied to Involuntary Transfers

The Court of Appeals held that the restrictions on Linda's shares did not apply by their terms to the sheriff's sale and, as a result, did not bar the sheriff's sale to Moore. We agree that Moore acquired the shares at the sheriff's sale, but not because the restrictions were inapplicable by their terms.

The Court of Appeals relied on cases stating that involuntary transfers fall within the terms of a restriction only if the language of the restrictions specifically identifies them. F.B.I. Farms, 769 N.E.2d at 692. This doctrine has been developed largely in cases involving intestate transfers by a decedent, Stern v. Stern, 146 F.2d 870, 870 (D.C.Cir.1945), and in marriage dissolution proceedings where a transfer is made to a spouse. Castonguay v. Castonguay, 306 N.W.2d 143, 146 (Minn.1981).

The sheriff's sale where Moore purchased Linda's shares was an involuntary transfer. Transfers ordered incident to marriage dissolutions and transfers under intestate law may also be deemed involuntary. We think the governing principle is not the same for all forms of "involuntary" transfers. The language of the restrictions in this case does not specifically refer to involuntary transfers of any kind. Rather, it seems to contemplate restricting all transfers, voluntary and involuntary, by providing that no stock of the corporation should be "transferred, assigned, exchanged, divided, or sold" without complying with the restrictions. The intent of the parties is thus rather plain: to restrict ownership to the designated group, and to preclude transfer by any means. The question is whether that intent should be permitted to prevail in the face of countervailing policies.

Transfer by intestacy is in some sense involuntary, but it may also be viewed as a voluntary act of the decedent who had the option to leave a will. If a transfer could not be made by gift during lifetime, for example, to an offspring regarded by other shareholders as an undesirable partner, we see no reason to permit it at death by the decedent's choice to die intestate. There are, however, forms of involuntary transfers that a private agreement may not prevent because the agreement would unreasonably interfere with the rights of third parties. In a dissolution, the interests of the spouse require permitting transfer over the stated intent of the parties. Similarly, creditors of the shareholder cannot be stymied by a private agreement that renders foreclosure of a lien impossible. For that reason, we agree with the trial court that the sheriff's sale transferred the shares to Moore despite the restrictions. Transfer restrictions cannot preclude transfer in a foreclosure sale and thereby leave creditors without recourse. This does not turn on a doctrine of construction. Rather we hold that requiring an explicit bar specifically naming transfer by intestacy or by testamentary disposition should not be necessary. If the language purports to bar all transfers, and by its terms would apply to intestacy, devise or any other means of transfer, it should be given effect unless the restriction violates some policy.

Although we agree with Moore that he could purchase the shares at the sale, it is also the case that he purchased the shares with knowledge of the restrictions. We conclude that he could not acquire more property rights than were possessed by Linda as his seller. U.C.C. § 8–302 (1994) (the purchaser of an investment security acquires the rights in the security his transferor had or had actual authority to convey). The shares in Linda's hands were valued with restrictions in place, and therefore it is not unfair to her creditors that a purchaser at a foreclosure sale acquire the disputed shares subject to the same restrictions, and with whatever lessened value that produces. To be sure, the effect of such a restriction may be to make the shares unmarketable to any buyer. But the creditor retains the option to bid at the sale and, if successful, succeed to the shareholders' interest. The creditor then gets the assets the debtor used to secure the underlying obligation. If the creditor wants collateral free of restrictions, the creditor must negotiate for that at the outset of the arrangement.

Conclusion

We . . . uphold the trial court's finding that the transfer restrictions did not prevent the sheriff's sale, and that the transfer restrictions remain applicable to the shares in Moore's hands. We reverse the trial court's ruling that the two disputed transfer restrictions are unreasonable and therefore unenforceable, and find that the director-approval and blood-member restrictions are reasonable and enforceable. The case is remanded for further proceedings consistent with this opinion.

■ SHEPARD, C.J., and DICKSON and SULLIVAN, JJ., concur.

■ RUCKER, J., concurs in result without opinion.

———

Evangelista v. Holland

27 Mass.App.Ct. 244, 537 N.E.2d 589 (1989)

A shareholders' agreement allowed the corporation to buy out, for $75,000, the estate of any deceased shareholder. The corporation brought suit against the estate of a deceased shareholder to enforce the agreement. There was strong evidence that the decedent's stock was worth at least $191,000. Held, for the corporation:

> The executors suggest that to require them to part with their interest in the business for so much less than the [value of the stock] violates the duty of good faith and loyalty owed one another by stockholders in a closely held corporation. . . . Questions of good faith and loyalty do not arise when all the stockholders in advance enter into an agreement for the purchase of stock of a withdrawing or deceased stockholder. . . . That the price established by a stockholders' agreement may be less than the appraised or market value is unremarkable. Such agreements may have as their purpose: the payment of a price for a decedent's stock which will benefit the corporation or surviving stockholders by not unduly burdening them; the payment of a price tied to life insurance; or fixing a price which assures the beneficiaries of the deceased stockholder of a predetermined price for stock which might have little market value. . . . When the agreement was entered into in 1984, the order and time of death of stockholders was an unknown. There was a "mutuality of risk."

DEL. GEN. CORP. LAW §§ 202, 342, 347, 349

[See Statutory Supplement]

CAL. CORP. CODE §§ 204(a)(3), (b), 418

[See Statutory Supplement]

MODEL BUS. CORP. ACT § 6.27

[See Statutory Supplement]

NOTES ON RESTRICTIONS ON TRANSFERABILITY AND MANDATORY SALES OF STOCK

1. *Restrictions on Transferability.* Although some of the earlier cases held that any restriction on the transferability of shares constituted an illegal restraint on alienation, the modern cases hold that "reasonable" restrictions are valid and enforceable. Three basic types of restrictions are commonly used in close corporations: (1) *First refusals.* These prohibit a sale of shares to a third party unless the shares have first been offered to the corporation, the other shareholders, or both, on the same terms as those offered by the

third party. (2) *First options.* These prohibit a transfer of shares to a third party unless the shares have first been offered to the corporation, the other shareholders, or both, at a price fixed under the terms of the option. (3) *Consent restraints.* These prohibit a transfer of shares to a third party without the permission of the corporation's board or shareholders.

Of these three types, first refusals are the least restrictive and are widely upheld. *See, e.g., Groves v. Prickett,* 420 F.2d 1119 (9th Cir.1970). The restrictiveness of a first option depends largely on the relationship between the option price and a fair price at the time the option is triggered. The courts have been giving increasing latitude to this type of provision. *See, e.g., In re Mather's Estate,* 189 A.2d 586 (Pa. 1963) where an agreement that set an option price of $1 per share was enforced although the actual value of the stock was $1,060 per share. A consent restraint is normally the most restrictive of the three basic types, and at one time such a restraint was almost certain to be deemed invalid. However, some recent statutes specifically contemplate the validity of consent restraints (*see, e.g.,* Del. § 202), and as *F.B.I.* suggests, the courts have also begun to be more tolerant of these restrictions.

In spite of the increasingly tolerant climate, the validity of consent restraints remains uncertain in the absence of statute or authoritative precedent. In *Rafe v. Hindin,* 29 A.D.2d 481, 288 N.Y.S.2d 662 (1968), Plaintiff and Defendant each owned 50% of the stock of Bil Cy Realty, which they had organized in 1963. A legend on each stock certificate made the stock nontransferable except to the other shareholder, and written permission from the other shareholder was required to record a transfer of the stock on Bil Cy's books. Plaintiff brought an action for a declaratory judgment that the legend on the certificate was void, and that the stock was transferable without Defendant's consent. The court so held:

> In New York certificates of stock are regarded as personal property and are subject to the rule that there be no unreasonable restraint on alienation. . . .

> The legend on the stock certificate at bar contains no provision that the individual defendant's consent may not be unreasonably withheld. Since the individual defendant is thus given the arbitrary power to forbid a transfer of the shares of stock by the plaintiff, the restriction amounts to annihilation of property. The restriction is not only not reasonable, but it is against public policy and, therefore, illegal. It is an unwarrantable and unlawful restraint on the sale of personal property, the sale and interchange of which the law favors, and in restraint of trade.

2.   *Mandatory Sales.* The three basic types of restraints discussed above limit the shareholders' power of transfer. Other types of arrangements go further, and give the corporation or the remaining shareholders an option to purchase a shareholder's stock upon the occurrence of one or more designated contingencies even if the shareholder wants to retain the stock. A common example is an arrangement under the corporation is given an option to repurchase any stock that it has issued to an employee who is

terminated. The courts have tended to enforce such arrangements, even when the option price is quite low in relation to the value of the stock at the time the repurchase right is triggered. *See, e.g., St. Louis Union Trust Co. v. Merrill Lynch, Pierce, Fenner & Smith Inc.,* 562 F.2d 1040 (8th Cir.1977), cert. denied, 435 U.S. 925, 98 S.Ct. 1490, 55 L.Ed.2d 519 (1978).

Another common example of a mandatory-sale provision is a buy-sell or survivor-purchase agreement. This kind of agreement provides that (i) on the death of a close corporation shareholder his estate has an obligation to sell its shares to the corporation, or the remaining shareholders, at a price fixed under the agreement; and (ii) the corporation or the remaining shareholders have an obligation (rather than an option) to purchase the shares. A major purpose of these agreements is to provide liquidity to the decedent's estate. If a corporation is closely held, the market for its shares is usually negligible. In the absence of such an agreement, therefore, the estate might be in a bad position if liquid assets are needed to meet estate's tax liabilities. A buy-sell or survivor-purchase agreement provides the estate with funds satisfy its tax liabilities, and also enables the corporation to control the identity of its shareholders. The corporation's obligation is often funded in whole or in part by insurance on the shareholders' lives.

3.   Problems of Interpretation. Restrictions on transfer give rise to recurring problems of interpretation—in particular, whether a given type of disposition is within the scope of the restriction. The courts often give restrictions on transfer a strict interpretation. For example, some courts have held that unless explicitly otherwise provided, restrictions on transfer are inapplicable to testamentary transfers, *see, e.g., Avrett and Ledbetter Roofing and Heating Co. v. Phillips,* 354 S.E.2d 321 (N.C.App. 1987), and to transfers by operation of law, such as by a divorce decree, *see, e.g., Castonguay v. Castonguay,* 306 N.W.2d 143 (Minn.1981). Restrictions on transfer are also often interpreted to be inapplicable to transfers between existing shareholders. *See, e.g., Remillong v. Schneider,* 185 N.W.2d 493 (N.D.1971). That rule of interpretation may result in an uncontemplated shift of control where a transfer between shareholders involves swing shares, that is, shares which, when added to an existing holding, will swing the balance of power to a shareholder who previously did not have that power. *Cf.* Lank v. Steiner, 43 Del.Ch. 262, 224 A.2d 242 (1966).

4.   The UCC. Uniform Commercial Code Article 8 deals with investment securities. Section 8–204 provides that "A restriction on transfer of a security imposed by the issuer, even if otherwise lawful, is ineffective against a person without knowledge of the restriction unless: (1) the security is certificated and the restriction is noted conspicuously on the security certificate; or (2) the security is uncertificated and the registered owner has been notified of the restriction."

———

Nemec v. Shrader

991 A.2d 1120 (Del. 2010)

[Joseph Nemec was a long-time director and senior officer of Booz Allen, a national consulting firm. He retired in March 2006. Gerd Wittkemper was in a comparable position. At the time of their retirements, Nemec owned 76,000 Booz Allen shares, or about 2.6% of the outstanding shares, and Wittkemper owned 28,000 shares, or about 1% of the outstanding shares.

Booz Allen shares held by retired employees were subject to redemption (call) by Booz Allen, starting two years after the employee's retirement, at a price equal to the shares' book value. Accordingly, Nemec's and Wittkemper's shares became subject to redemption in March 2008. In October 2007, Booz Allen had begun negotiating the sale of one of its two business units to The Carlyle Group at a very favorable price. If the Carlyle transaction was consummated, it would add a very large amount to the book value of Booz Allen's shares. News of the reported transaction began circulating in January 2008. Thereafter, Booz Allen's CEO assured Nemec that allowing him to retain his shares until after the Carlyle deal closed was an "easy moral decision."

Morals apparently did not carry the day, because Booz Allen redeemed Nemec's and Wittkemper's shares in April 2008, when the Carlyle transaction had not been completed but was virtually assured of being completed. (It was completed three months later, at a price of $2.54 billion.) The book value of Booz Allen shares at the time of the redemption was about $162.46 per share. By excluding Nemec and Wittkemper from the fruits of the Carlyle transaction, nearly $60 million, or about $700 per share, was added to the proceeds received by Booz Allen's remaining shareholders.

Nemec and Wittkemper brought suit against Booz Allen and members of its board on the ground that the redemption was a breach of the implied covenant of good faith and fair dealing. The Delaware Supreme Court held for Booz Allen, three-to-two. The majority said:]

The implied covenant of good faith and fair dealing involves a "cautious enterprise," inferring contractual terms to handle developments or contractual gaps that the asserting party pleads neither party anticipated. "[O]ne generally cannot base a claim for breach of the implied covenant on conduct authorized by the agreement." [Dunlap v. State Farm & Cas. Co., 878 A.2d 434, 441 (Del. 2005)]. We will only imply contract terms when the party asserting the implied covenant proves that the other party has acted arbitrarily or unreasonably, thereby frustrating the fruits of the bargain that the asserting party reasonably expected. When conducting this analysis, we must assess the parties' reasonable expectations at the time of contracting and not rewrite the contract to appease a party who later wishes to rewrite a contract he now believes to have been a bad deal. Parties have a right to enter into good and bad contracts, the law enforces both. . . .

The Chancellor found no cognizable claim for a breach of the implied covenant because the Stock Plan explicitly authorized the redemption's price and timing, and Booz Allen, Nemec, and Wittkemper received exactly what they bargained for under the Stock Plan. The Chancellor wrote "[c]ontractually negotiated put and call rights are intended by both parties to be exercised at the time that is most advantageous to the party invoking the option."

No facts gleaned from the complaint suggest that anyone negotiating for the working stockholders would have made such a concession—nor does the complaint point to any reason they should have. Nothing except the absence of specific language contemplating a private equity, post retirement buyout supports a view that it can be inferred that had the parties to the Stock Plan specifically addressed the issue *at the time of contract,* they would have agreed to preclude the Company from exercising its redemption right before the Carlyle transaction closed. The implied covenant will not infer language that contradicts a clear exercise of an express contractual right. Our colleagues' thoughtful dissent suggests that we neglect to note that the challenged conduct (redeeming the retired stockholders shares) must "further *a legitimate interest of the party relying on the contract*" [emphasis supplied by the dissent]. The Company's directors, at the time of the decision to redeem owed fiduciary duties to the corporation and its stockholders. The redemption would not affect the Company directly. However, a failure to redeem the now retired stockholders' shares consistent with the Company's right under the stock plan would directly reduce the working stockholders' distribution by $60 million. If the Company's directors had not exercised the Company's absolute contractual right to redeem the retired stockholders shares, the working stockholders had a potential claim against the directors for favoring the retired stockholders to the detriment of the working stockholders.

The dissent stated:

A party does not act in bad faith (the majority argues) by relying on contract provisions for which that party bargained, even if the result is to eliminate advantages the counterparty would otherwise receive. That is a correct, but incomplete, statement of the law. To avoid running afoul of the implied covenant, the challenged conduct must also further a legitimate interest of the party acting in reliance on the contract. Stated differently, under Delaware case law, a contracting party, even where expressly empowered to act, can breach the implied covenant if it exercises that contractual power arbitrarily or unreasonably. Here, the complaint adequately alleges that the Company's redemption of the plaintiffs' shares prejudiced the plaintiffs while serving no legitimate interest of the Company. In those circumstances, therefore, the redemption would have been arbitrary and unreasonable, for which reason the complaint stated a cognizable claim for breach of the implied covenant. . . .

It is now settled Delaware law that a contracting party's exercise of a power in reliance on an explicit contractual provision may be deemed "arbitrary" or "unreasonable" where the other contracting party is thereby disadvantaged and no legitimate interest of the party exercising the right is furthered by doing so. *Dunlap v. State Farm Fire & Cas. Co.,* a case where this Court most recently addressed the implied covenant, stands squarely for that proposition.

In *Dunlap*, the plaintiff requested its excess liability insurer to approve a proposed agreement to settle with a primary insurer for an amount less than the underlying primary insurer's coverage limits. The excess insurer refused, relying on a contractual and statutory "exhaustion of primary insurance" requirement. Although the insurer had no improper motive for refusing to consent, this Court found it inferable from the complaint that the insurer's refusal to waive the exhaustion requirement was arbitrary and in breach of the implied covenant. The reasons were that the plaintiff's damages indisputably exceeded all available insurance benefits and a waiver would not have prejudiced the insurer. Here, Booz Allen—like the excess insurer in *Dunalp*—had an express contractual right. Here, as in *Dunlap*, the Company would have incurred no prejudice by forbearing to exercise that right until after the Carlyle closing. In these circumstances, Booz Allen's exercise of that right before closing, which resulted in material prejudice to the plaintiffs, invokes—and pleads a cognizable claim for breach of—the implied covenant. . . .

Because the majority concludes otherwise, we respectfully dissent.

———

7. DISSOLUTION AND ASSOCIATED REMEDIES

A. DISSOLUTION FOR DEADLOCK

DEL. GEN. CORP. LAW §§ 273, 355

[See Statutory Supplement]

MODEL BUS. CORP. ACT §§ 14.30, 14.34

[See Statutory Supplement]

N.Y. BUS. CORP. LAW §§ 1002, 1104, 1111

[See Statutory Supplement]

Wollman v. Littman

New York Supreme Court, Appellate Div., First Dept., 1970.
35 A.D.2d 935, 316 N.Y.S.2d 526.

■ PER CURIAM . . .

The stock of the corporation is held, fifty percent each, by two distinct groups, one of which, the Nierenberg sisters, are plaintiffs, and the other, the Littmans, defendants, each group having equal representation on the board of directors. The corporation's business is the selling of artificial fur fabrics to garment manufacturers. Defendants, the Littmans, allegedly had the idea for the business and developed a market for the fabrics among its manufacturing customers. Plaintiffs are the daughters of Louis Nierenberg, the main stockholder of Louis Nierenberg, Inc., who procures the fabrics and sells them to the corporation. The Littmans, in a separate action in which they are plaintiffs, charge the plaintiffs here (the Nierenberg sisters) and Louis Nierenberg Corporation with seeking to lure away the corporation's customers for Louis Nierenberg Corporation and with doing various acts to affect the corporation's business adversely. The Nierenberg faction countered with this suit, claiming that the bringing of the other action indicates that the corporate management is at such odds among themselves that effective management is impossible. Special Term agreed, but we do not. Irreconcilable differences even among an evenly divided board of directors do not in all cases mandate dissolution. . . . Here, two factors would require further exploration. The first is that the functions of the two disputing interests are distinct, one selling and the other procuring, and each can pursue its own without need for collaboration. The second is that a dissolution which will render nugatory the relief sought in the representative action would actually accomplish the wrongful purpose that defendants (Nierenberg) are charged with in that action. It would not only squeeze the Littmans out of the business but would require the receiver to dispose of the inventory with the Nierenbergs the only interested purchaser financially strong enough to take advantage of the situation. Such a result, if supported by the facts, would be intolerable to a court of equity. A trial of the issues is necessitated. On that trial it has been agreed by both counsel it would be advantageous to have the representative action and the action for dissolution tried together, though not consolidated (for a discussion of the distinction, see the comprehensive opinion in Padilla v. Greyhound Lines, 29 A.D.2d 495, 288 N.Y.S.2d 641), and it is so directed.

We affirm the appointment of a receiver. His function, however, should be limited to the necessities indicated, namely, to the orderly functioning of the regular course of business of the corporation until the further order of the court.

NOTES ON DISSOLUTION FOR DEADLOCK

1. Deadlock Provisions. A number of statutes provide for involuntary dissolution on a showing of deadlock. A few of the statutes define deadlock in terms of an equally divided board or body of shareholders, but most are phrased broadly enough to include deadlock brought about by supermajority or veto arrangements.

2. Discretion. The deadlock statutes are generally interpreted to make dissolution discretionary even when deadlock is shown to exist, and especially in the past, the courts have often been reluctant to order dissolution of a profitable corporation on the ground of deadlock. However, profitability is not a bar to dissolution for deadlock. In *Weiss v. Gordon,* 32 A.D.2d 279, 301 N.Y.S.2d 839 (1969), the court stated, "The earlier thinking stressed the distinction between the corporation as an entity and the shareholders, and as long as the former could continue to function profitably the relationship between the shareholders was of no moment (*cf. Matter of Radom & Neidorff, Inc.,* 307 N.Y. 1, 119 N.E.2d 563 (1954). It is being increasingly realized that the relationship between the stockholders in a close corporation vis-a-vis each other in practice closely approximates the relationship between partners (*see Mtr. of Surchin v. Approved Bus. Mach.,* 55 Misc.2d 888, 890, 286 N.Y.S.2d 580, 583 (1967). As a consequence, when a point is reached where the shareholders who are actively conducting the business of the corporation cannot agree, it becomes in the best interests of those shareholders to order a dissolution. . . . "

B. DISSOLUTION FOR OPPRESSION AND MANDATORY BUY-OUT

MODEL BUS. CORP. ACT § 14.30, 14.34

[See Statutory Supplement]

CAL. CORP. CODE §§ 1800, 1804, 2000

[See Statutory Supplement]

N.Y. BUS. CORP. LAW §§ 1104–a, 1111, 1118

[See Statutory Supplement]

NOTE ON HETHERINGTON AND DOOLEY

At one time, courts were extremely reluctant to order the involuntary dissolution of a profitable business, on the ground that it was bad social policy to break up such a business. In 1977, John Hetherington and Michael Dooley published a celebrated article on this problem, Illiquidity and Exploitation: A Proposed Statutory Solution to the Remaining Close Corporation Problem, 63 Va.L.Rev. 1 (1977). In this article, the authors pointed out that a judicial order to dissolve a corporation was unlikely to lead to the breakup of a profitable business. The reason is that if it is advantageous to continue a business, then after dissolution is ordered, normally either one or more of the shareholders or a third party would purchase and continue the business. Hetherington & Dooley backed up this point with empirical data by analyzing the fifty-four reported involuntary dissolution cases decided between 1960 and 1976. In half of the fifty-four cases, the plaintiff had been successful; in the other half, unsuccessful. Of the twenty-seven cases in which the plaintiff had been successful, the corporation's business was actually liquidated in only six. In seventeen cases, one party bought out the other. In three cases, the business was sold to an outsider. In one case, there was no buyout or other change. Of the twenty-seven cases in which plaintiff was unsuccessful, in fourteen cases one party bought out the other; in six cases there was no change in ownership; in two cases the business was sold to a third party; in three cases, the business was liquidated; and in two cases, the result was unknown.

Furthermore, Hetherington & Dooley pointed out, dissolution, or something like it, was a central remedy for disaffected shareholders in close corporations because given the limits of reasonable foreseeability, shareholders who organized such corporations could not possibly plan in advance to deal with all the interpersonal problems that might occur between them. Therefore, Hetherington & Dooley concluded, in the case of a close corporation a remedy comparable to, but stronger than, dissolution—specifically, free exit through a mandatory buyout of the minority's interest on the minority's demand—should be available.

> The emphasis on contractual arrangements [in close corporations] reveals a fundamental misunderstanding of the nature of close corporations. Whether the parties adopt special contractual arrangements is much less important than their ability to sustain a close, harmonious relationship over time. The continuance of such a relationship is crucial because it reflects what is perhaps the fundamental assumption made by those who decide to invest in a close corporation: they expect that during the life of the firm the shareholders will be in substantial agreement as to its operation.

> Time and human nature may cause a divergence of interests and a breakdown in consensus, however. . . .

> Our thesis is that the problem of exploitation is uniquely related to liquidity and, for that reason, it is resistant to solution by ex ante contractual arrangements or by ex post judicial relief for breach of fiduciary duty. Accordingly, we [propose that the law should require] the majority to repurchase the minority's interest at the request of the latter and subject to appropriate safeguards.

The insights and empirical data in the Hetherington & Dooley article form a backdrop to the materials in this section.

Matter of Kemp & Beatley, Inc.

Court of Appeals of New York, 1984.
64 N.Y.2d 63, 484 N.Y.S.2d 799, 473 N.E.2d 1173.

■ COOKE, CHIEF JUDGE. . . .

I

The business concern of Kemp & Beatley, incorporated under the laws of New York, designs and manufactures table linens and sundry tabletop items. The company's stock consists of 1,500 outstanding shares held by eight shareholders. Petitioner Dissin had been employed by the company for 42 years when, in June 1979, he resigned. Prior to resignation, Dissin served as vice-president and a director of Kemp & Beatley. Over the course of his employment, Dissin had acquired stock in the company and currently owns 200 shares.

Petitioner Gardstein, like Dissin, had been a long-time employee of the company. Hired in 1944, Gardstein was for the next 35 years involved in various aspects of the business including material procurement, product design, and plant management. His employment was terminated by the company in December 1980. He currently owns 105 shares of Kemp & Beatley stock.

Apparent unhappiness surrounded petitioners' leaving the employ of the company. Of particular concern was that they no longer received any distribution of the company's earnings. Petitioners considered themselves to be "frozen out" of the company; whereas it had been their experience when with the company to receive a distribution of the company's earnings according to their stockholdings, in the form of either dividends or extra compensation, that distribution was no longer forthcoming.

Gardstein and Dissin, together holding 20.33% of the company's outstanding stock, commenced the instant proceeding in June 1981, seeking dissolution of Kemp & Beatley pursuant to section 1104–a of the Business Corporation Law. Their petition alleged "fraudulent and oppressive" conduct by the company's board of directors such as to render petitioners' stock "a virtually worthless asset." Supreme Court referred the matter for a hearing, which was held in March 1982.

Upon considering the testimony of petitioners and the principals of Kemp & Beatley, the referee concluded that "the corporate management has by its policies effectively rendered petitioners' shares worthless, and . . . the only way petitioners can expect any return is by dissolution". Petitioners were found to have invested capital in the company expecting, among other things, to receive dividends or "bonuses" based upon their stock holdings. Also found was the company's "established buyout policy" by which it would purchase the stock of employee shareholders upon their leaving its employ.

The involuntary-dissolution statute (Business Corporation Law, § 1104–a) permits dissolution when a corporation's controlling faction is found guilty of "oppressive action" toward the complaining shareholders. The referee considered oppression to arise when "those in control" of the corporation "have acted in such a manner as to defeat those expectations of the minority stockholders which formed the basis of [their] participation in the venture." The expectations of petitioners that they would not be arbitrarily excluded from gaining a return on their investment and that their stock would be purchased by the corporation upon termination of employment, were deemed defeated by prevailing corporate policies. Dissolution was recommended in the referee's report, subject to giving respondent corporation an opportunity to purchase petitioners' stock.

Supreme Court confirmed the referee's report. It, too, concluded that due to the corporation's new dividend policy petitioners had been prevented from receiving any return on their investments. Liquidation of the corporate assets was found the only means by which petitioners would receive a fair return. The court considered judicial dissolution of a corporation to be "a serious and severe remedy." Consequently, the order of dissolution was conditioned upon the corporation's being permitted to purchase petitioners' stock. The Appellate Division affirmed, without opinion. 99 A.D.2d 445, 471 N.Y.S.2d 245.

At issue in this appeal is the scope of section 1104–a of the Business Corporation Law. Specifically, this court must determine whether the provision for involuntary dissolution when the "directors or those in control of the corporation have been guilty of . . . oppressive actions toward the complaining shareholders" was properly applied in the circumstances of this case. We hold that it was, and therefore affirm.

II

Judicially ordered dissolution of a corporation at the behest of minority interests is a remedy of relatively recent vintage in New York. Historically, this State's courts were considered divested of equity jurisdiction to order dissolution, as statutory prescriptions were deemed exclusive (see Hitch v. Hawley, 132 N.Y. 212, 217, 30 N.E. 401). . . .

. . . [T]he Legislature has shown a special solicitude toward the rights of minority shareholders of closely held corporations by enacting section 1104–a of the Business Corporation Law. That statute provides a mechanism for the holders of at least 20% of the outstanding shares of a corporation whose stock is not traded on a securities market to petition for its dissolution "under special circumstances" (see Business Corporation Law, § 1104–a, subd. [a]). The circumstances that give rise to dissolution fall into two general classifications: mistreatment of complaining shareholders (subd. [a], par. [1]), or misappropriation of corporate assets (subd. [a], par. [2]) by controlling shareholders, directors or officers.

Section 1104–a (subd. [a], par. [1]) describes three types of proscribed activity: "illegal", "fraudulent", and "oppressive" conduct. The first two terms are familiar words that are commonly understood at law. The last, however, does not enjoy the same certainty gained through long usage. As no definition is provided by the statute, it falls upon the courts to provide guidance (see Goncalves v. Regent Int. Hotels, 58 N.Y.2d 206, 218, 460 N.Y.S.2d 750, 447 N.E.2d 693).

The statutory concept of "oppressive actions" can, perhaps, best be understood by examining the characteristics of close corporations and the Legislature's general purpose in creating this involuntary-dissolution statute. It is widely understood that, in addition to supplying capital to a contemplated or ongoing enterprise and expecting a fair and equal return, parties comprising the ownership of a close corporation may expect to be actively involved in its management and operation. . . . The small ownership cluster seeks to "contribute their capital, skills, experience and labor" toward the corporate enterprise. . . .

As a leading commentator in the field has observed: "Unlike the typical shareholder in a publicly held corporation, who may be simply an investor or a speculator and cares nothing for the responsibilities of management, the shareholder in a close corporation is a co-owner of the business and wants the privileges and powers that go with ownership. His participation in that particular corporation is often his principal or sole source of income. As a matter of fact, providing employment for himself may have been the principal reason why he participated in organizing the corporation. He may or may not anticipate an ultimate profit from the sale of his interest, but he normally draws very little from the corporation as dividends. In his capacity as an officer or employee of the corporation, he looks to his salary for the principal return on his capital investment, because earnings of a close corporation, as is well known, are distributed in major part in salaries, bonuses and retirement benefits." (O'Neal, Close Corporations [2d ed.], § 1.07, at pp. 21–22 [n. omitted].)

Shareholders enjoy flexibility in memorializing these expectations through agreements setting forth each party's rights and obligations in corporate governance (see, generally, Kessler, Shareholder-Managed Close Corporation Under the New York Business Corporation Law, 43 Fordham L.Rev. 197; Davidian, op. cit., 56 St. John's L.Rev. 24, 29–30, and nn. 21–22). In the absence of such an agreement, however, ultimate decision-making power respecting corporate policy will be reposed in the holders of a majority interest in the corporation (see, e.g., Business Corporation Law, §§ 614, 708). A wielding of this power by any group controlling a corporation may serve to destroy a stockholder's vital interests and expectations.

As the stock of closely held corporations generally is not readily salable, a minority shareholder at odds with management policies may be without either a voice in protecting his or her interests or any reasonable means of withdrawing his or her investment. This predicament may fairly be considered the legislative concern underlying the provision at issue in this case; inclusion of the criteria that the corporation's stock not be traded on securities markets and that the complaining shareholder be subject to oppressive actions supports this conclusion.

Defining oppressive conduct as distinct from illegality in the present context has been considered in other forums. The question has been resolved by considering oppressive actions to refer to conduct that substantially defeats the "reasonable expectations" held by minority shareholders in committing their capital to the particular enterprise (see, e.g., Mardikos v. Arger, 116 Misc.2d 1028, 457 N.Y.S.2d 371; Matter of Barry One Hour Photo Process, 111 Misc.2d 559, 444 N.Y.S.2d 540. . . .) This concept is consistent with the apparent purpose underlying the provision under review. A shareholder who reasonably expected that ownership in the corporation would entitle him or her to a job, a share of corporate earnings, a place in corporate management, or some other form of security, would be oppressed in a very real sense when others in the corporation seek to defeat those expectations and there exists no effective means of salvaging the investment.

Given the nature of close corporations and the remedial purpose of the statute, this court holds that utilizing a complaining shareholder's "reasonable expectations" as a means of identifying and measuring conduct alleged to be oppressive is appropriate. A court considering a petition alleging oppressive conduct must investigate what the majority shareholders knew, or should have known, to be the petitioner's expectations in entering the particular enterprise. Majority conduct should not be deemed oppressive simply because the petitioner's subjective hopes and desires in joining the venture are not fulfilled. Disappointment alone should not necessarily be equated with oppression.

Rather, oppression should be deemed to arise only when the majority conduct substantially defeats expectations that, objectively viewed, were both reasonable under the circumstances and were central to the petitioner's decision to join the venture. It would be inappropriate, however, for us in this case to delineate the contours of the courts' consideration in determining whether directors have been guilty of oppressive conduct. As in other areas of the law, much will depend on the circumstances in the individual case.

The appropriateness of an order of dissolution is in every case vested in the sound discretion of the court considering the application (see Business Corporation Law, § 1111, subd. [a]). Under the terms of this statute, courts are instructed to consider both whether "liquidation of the corporation is the only feasible means" to protect the complaining shareholder's expectation of a fair return on his or her investment and whether dissolution "is reasonably necessary" to protect "the rights or interests of any substantial number of shareholders" not limited to those complaining (Business Corporation Law, § 1104–a, subd. [b], pars. [1], [2]). Implicit in this direction is that once oppressive conduct is found, consideration must be given to the totality of circumstances surrounding the current state of corporate affairs and relations to determine whether some remedy short of or other than dissolution, constitutes a feasible means of satisfying both the petitioner's expectations and the rights and interests of any other substantial group of shareholders (see, also, Business Corporation Law, § 1111, subd. [b], par. [1]).

By invoking the statute, a petitioner has manifested his or her belief that dissolution may be the only appropriate remedy. Assuming the petitioner has set forth a prima facie case of oppressive conduct, it should be incumbent upon the parties seeking to forestall dissolution to demonstrate to the court the existence of an adequate, alternative remedy (cf. Baker v. Commercial Body Bldrs., 264 Or. 614, 507 P.2d 387, supra; White v. Perkins, 213 Va. 129, 189 S.E.2d 315). A court has broad latitude in fashioning alternative relief, but when fulfillment of the oppressed petitioner's expectations by these means is doubtful, such as when there has been a complete deterioration of relations between the parties, a court should not hesitate to order dissolution. Every order of dissolution, however, must be conditioned upon permitting any shareholder of the corporation to elect to purchase the complaining shareholder's stock at fair value (see Business Corporation Law, § 1118).

One further observation is in order. The purpose of this involuntary dissolution statute is to provide protection to the minority shareholder whose reasonable expectations in undertaking the venture have been frustrated and who has no adequate means of recovering his or her investment. It would be contrary to this remedial purpose to permit its use by minority shareholders as merely a coercive tool (see Davidian, op. cit., 56 St. John's L.Rev. 24, 59–60, and nn. 159–160). Therefore, the minority shareholder whose own acts, made in bad faith and undertaken with a view toward forcing an involuntary dissolution, give rise to the complained-of oppression should be given no quarter in the statutory protection (cf. Mardikos v. Arger, 116 Misc.2d 1028, 1032, 457 N.Y.S.2d 371, supra).

III

There was sufficient evidence presented at the hearing to support the conclusion that Kemp & Beatley had a long-standing policy of awarding *de facto* dividends based on stock ownership in the form of "extra compensation bonuses." Petitioners, both of whom had extensive experience in the management of the company, testified to this effect. Moreover, both related that receipt of this compensation, whether as true dividends or disguised as "extra compensation", was a known incident to ownership of the company's stock understood by all of the company's principals. Finally, there was uncontroverted proof that this policy was changed either shortly before or shortly after petitioners' employment ended. Extra compensation was still awarded by the company. The only difference was that stock ownership was no longer a basis for the payments; it was asserted that the basis became services rendered to the corporation. It was not unreasonable for the fact finder to have determined that this change in policy amounted to nothing less than an attempt to exclude petitioners from gaining any return on their investment through the mere recharacterization of distributions of corporate income. Under the circumstances of this case, there was no error in determining that this conduct constituted oppressive action within the meaning of section 1104–a of the Business Corporation Law.

Nor may it be said that Supreme Court abused its discretion in ordering Kemp & Beatley's dissolution, subject to an opportunity for a buy-out of petitioners' shares. After the referee had found that the controlling faction of the company was, in effect, attempting to "squeeze-out" petitioners by offering them no return on their investment and increasing other executive compensation, respondents, in opposing the report's confirmation, attempted only to controvert the factual basis of the report. They suggested no feasible, alternative remedy to the forced dissolution. In light of an apparent deterioration in relations between petitioners and the governing shareholders of Kemp & Beatley, it was not unreasonable for the court to have determined that a forced buy-out of petitioners' shares or liquidation of the corporation's assets was the only means by which petitioners could be guaranteed a fair return on their investments.

Accordingly, the order of the Appellate Division should be modified, with costs to petitioners-respondents, by affirming the substantive determination of that court but extending the time for exercising the option to purchase petitioners-respondents' shares to 30 days following this court's determination.

■ JASEN, JONES, WACHTLER, MEYER and SIMONS, JJ., concur.

■ KAYE, J., taking no part.

Order modified, with costs to petitioners-respondents, in accordance with the opinion herein and, as so modified, affirmed.

———

Meiselman v. Meiselman

309 N.C. 279, 307 S.E.2d 551 (1983)

"Professor O'Neal, perhaps the foremost authority on close corporations, points out that many close corporations are companies based on personal relationships that give rise to certain 'reasonable expectations' on the part of those acquiring an interest in the close corporation. Those 'reasonable expectations' include, for example, the parties' expectation that they will participate in the management of the business or be employed by the company. O'Neal, *Close Corporations: Existing Legislation and Recommended Reform,* 33 Bus.Law 873, 885 (1978). . . .

"Thus, when personal relations among the participants in a close corporation break down, the 'reasonable expectations' the participants had, for example, an expectation that their employment would be secure, or that they would enjoy meaningful participation in the management of the business—become difficult if not impossible to fulfill. In other words, when the personal relationships among the participants break down, the majority shareholder, because of his greater voting power, is in a position to terminate the minority shareholder's employment and to exclude him from participation in management decisions.

"Some may argue that the minority shareholder should have bargained for greater protection before agreeing to accept his minority shareholder position in a close corporation. However, the practical realities of this particular business situation oftentimes do not allow for such negotiations. . . .

"Apparently in response to these commentators' uniform calls for reform in this area of corporate law, many state legislatures have enacted statutes giving the tribunals in their states the power to grant relief to minority shareholders under more liberal circumstances. . . .

"In helping to establish this growing trend toward enactment of more liberal grounds under which dissolution will be granted to a complaining shareholder, the legislature in this State enacted in 1955 N.C.G.S. § 55–125(a)(4), the statute granting superior court judges the 'power to liquidate the assets and business of a corporation in an action by a shareholder when it is established' that '[l]iquidation is reasonably necessary for the protection of the rights or interests of the complaining shareholder.' . . .

"[B]efore it can be determined whether, in any given case, it has been 'established' that liquidation is 'reasonably necessary' to protect the complaining shareholder's 'rights or interest,' the particular 'rights or interests' of the complaining shareholder must be articulated. This is so because N.C.G.S. § 55–125(a)(4) refers to the 'rights or interests' of *the complaining shareholder';* the statute does not refer to the 'rights or interests' of shareholders generally. . . . [W]e hold that a complaining shareholder's 'rights or interests' in a close corporation include the 'reasonable expectations' the complaining shareholder has in the corporation. These 'reasonable expectations' are to be ascertained by examining the entire history of the participants' relationship. That history will include the 'reasonable expectations' created at the inception of the participants' relationship; those 'reasonable expectations' as altered over time; and the 'reasonable expectations' which develop as the participants engage in a course of dealing in conducting the affairs of the corporation. The interests and views of the other participants must be considered in determining 'reasonable expectations.' The key is *'reasonable.'* In order for plaintiff's expectations to be reasonable, they must be known to or assumed by the other shareholders and concurred in by them. Privately held expectations which are not made known to the other participants are not 'reasonable.' Only expectations embodied in understandings, express or implied, among the participants should be recognized by the court. . . .

"Defendants argue, however, that . . . [a shareholder] is only entitled to relief if his traditional shareholder rights have been infringed. They contend that those traditional shareholder rights include the right to notice of stockholders' meetings, the right to vote cumulatively, the right of access to the corporate offices and to corporate financial information, and the right to compel the payment of dividends. . . .

"While it may be true that a shareholder in, for example, a publicly held corporation may have 'rights or interests' defined as defendants argue, a shareholder's rights in a closely held corporation may not necessarily be so narrowly defined. . . . "

———

Thompson, The Shareholder's Cause of Action for Oppression

48 Bus.Law. 699, 709–12, 715–716 (1993)

"Oppression as a ground for dissolution was included in the Illinois and Pennsylvania corporations acts in 1933, in the first Model Business Corporation Act in 1946, and in the English Companies Act of 1948.

Thirty-seven American states now include oppression or a similar term in their corporations statutes. . . . "

———

McCann v. McCann

Supreme Court of Idaho, 2012.
152 Idaho 809, 275 P.3d 824.

[Ron and Bill each inherited 36.7 percent of the shares of McCann Ranch & Livestock Co., Inc.; the remaining shares, also inherited, were owned by their mother, Gertrude. Bill's salary increased from $48,000 to $144,000 following the death of his father, Gertrude began receiving a consulting fee, and Ron was removed from the board of directors and was not employed by the company. Moreover, because Gertrude was in need of money, the corporation purchased her home. Over a few years installment payments on the home purchase and consulting fees totaled about 75 percent of the company's net income. Ron sued, seeking dissolution of the firm under Idaho Code Section 30–1–1430(2)(b) and such equitable relief as appropriate.]

Regardless of his ownership interest, Ron is not entitled to a seat on the board of directors. Nor is he entitled to corporate employment. Nor is there evidence he is entitled to a dividend. By themselves, any payments from the Corporation do not harm Ron any more than they harm the other shareholders. However, they may be used as facts to support a squeeze-out. Each of these actions may fall under the business judgment rule, but those are issues of fact. Even if the business judgment rule applies, it is possible for courts to find such actions harmful if the end result could have been achieved with less injury to the minority shareholder. *See Wilkes v. Springside Nursing Home, Inc.*, 370 Mass. 842, 353 N.E.2d 657, 663 (Mass. 1976) ("If called on to settle a dispute, our courts must weigh the legitimate business purpose, if any, against the practicability of a less harmful alternative."). Also, the ownership structure of the Corporation requires an additional level of analysis that places these actions beyond the scope of the business judgment rule.

Here, the Corporation used corporate funds to make payments to Gertrude. Since the payments were going directly to pay Gertrude's expenses, she did not experience any harm from the transactions.

In this light, the actions of the Corporation and its directors have an effect on Ron above and beyond the effect of every other shareholder. Each of these transactions hurts Ron specifically. . . .

The Corporation went to great lengths to provide Gertrude with the money she needed. However, because the Corporation did not use an alternate and less harmful means of providing for Gertrude, it may be argued that the transactions were not made in good faith. The Corporation could have issued a dividend that would benefit all shareholders. Instead, Ron lost his voice in corporate decisions, his corporate employment, and received no meaningful benefit from his ownership stake. The transactions with Gertrude, coupled with the other aforementioned corporate actions, appear to be an attempt to marginalize and squeeze-out Ron. . . .

Ron makes two prayers for equitable relief . . . . First, he requests a court-ordered buyout of his shares in the corporation for market value. In the alternative, he requests the creation of a spin-off, subsidiary corporation that consists of his 36.68% share in the current corporation.

In its Memorandum and Order Concerning Various Motions, the district court found that equitable forms of relief are "appropriate as somewhat less onerous methods of remedying corporate oppression."

> Nevertheless, as a condition of obtaining any type of equitable relief [Ron] must prove both the statutory requirements contained in I.C. Section 30–1–1430(2)(b). There must be proof that both elements of I.C. Section 30–1–1430(2)(b) were violated; only then is the court authorized to fashion relief, whether the relief is authorized by statute or by equitable principles.

These findings bring into question whether I.C. § 30–1–1430 abrogated any common law that would otherwise apply here. . . .

Idaho Code section 30–1–1430 is part of the statutory framework of the Idaho Business Corporation Act, and dissolution is only one possible remedy under the act. I.C. §§ 30–1–101 to 30–1–1704. For example, where dissolution is sought, a court may issue injunctions, appoint a receiver or custodian *pendente lite*, or take other action to preserve corporate assets until a full hearing can he held. I.C. § 30–1–1431. Additionally, the act gives corporations or other shareholders the option to purchase the shares of a petitioning shareholder in lieu of dissolution. I.C. § 30–1–1434. . . .

Idaho Code § 30–1–1430 does not contain any explicit language on whether it preserves or abrogates any common law. . . .

It is well established in Idaho that equitable claims will not be considered when an adequate legal remedy is available. . . .

Dissolution of a corporation is a drastic remedy that should be invoked with extreme caution and only when justice requires it . . . . In some circumstances, dissolution may be a disproportionate and inadequate remedy. If a district court finds a breach of fiduciary duty, and I.C. § 30–1–1430(2)(b) is not an adequate remedy, any alternative remedy . . . not found in the above referenced statutory framework can be utilized. . . .

Idaho Code § 30–1–1430 states . . .:

The Idaho district court . . . may dissolve a corporation:

. . .

(2) In a proceeding by a shareholder if it is established that:

. . .

(b) The directors or those in control of the corporation have acted or are acting in a manner that is illegal, oppressive or fraudulent, and irreparable injury to the corporation is threatened or being suffered by reason thereof . . . .

In their motion for summary judgment, Respondents focused on the second element, irreparable injury. They argued that the lack of irreparable injury is dispositive, but noted that the oppression element may present issues of fact. For purposes of summary judgment, the district court treated all of the alleged corporate actions as if they were illegal, oppressive or fraudulent. Generally, oppressive conduct includes actions that defeat the reasonable expectations held by minority shareholders. . . .

a. Definition of "Irreparable Injury"

The district court defined irreparable injury as "that injury which cannot be adequately compensated monetarily." This is similar to Black's Law Dictionary's definition, which defines irreparable injury as "an injury that cannot be adequately measured or compensated by money and is therefore often considered remediable by injunction." Black's Law Dictionary 856 (9th Ed. 2009). . . .

By eliminating monetary injury from the definition for irreparable injury, the definition used by the district court becomes unreasonable in the context of the entire statute. Monetary loss can constitute irreparable injury to a corporation if the money cannot be recovered. We find that the plain, usual, and ordinary interpretation of irreparable in I.C. § 30–1–1430(2) is any injury that is impossible to remedy or repair. *See Webster's Third New International Dictionary, Unabridged Edition* 1196 (1971).

b. Definition of "Threatened"

This Court must also determine when irreparable injury is being threatened. To define when irreparable injury is threatened, the district court looked to case law. In other contexts, threatened injury must be "real" and "imminent." *See Miller v. Ririe Joint Sch. Dist. No. 252*, 132 Idaho 385, 388, 973 P.2d 156, 159 (1999). Additionally, speculative injury does not constitute irreparable injury; a mere possibility is not enough. *Caribbean Marine Serv. Co. v. Baldridge*, 844 F.2d 668, 674 (9th Cir. 1988) . . . . We agree with the trial court that "threatened," as it is used in I.C. § 30–1–1430(2), means a real and non-remote, non-speculative threat of injury.

Putting the elements together under the statute, irreparable injury is any impossible to repair injury that results from illegality, oppression, or fraud to the corporation and which is neither remote nor speculative, or it is being suffered.

3. Ron's alleged facts establish that irreparable injury to the corporation is being threatened.

. . . Whether the claims constitute irreparable injury can be determined by applying the above mentioned definitions to Ron's factual assertions.

. . . [A]ny corporate resources that were transferred to Gertrude and cannot be recovered would constitute an injury to the Corporation. It is reasonable to believe that the roughly $600,000 in payments to Gertrude will not be recoverable because the payments were made to cover Gertrude's needs. If true, the allegations before this Court show that the money is not recoverable and would constitute irreparable injury.

The potential tax penalties and liability stemming from the Corporation's transactions represent a prospective harm to the corporation. As alleged in the expert testimony, the potential tax penalties are neither speculative nor remote, even though no pending audit or notification from a taxing authority has been made. Assuming the allegations are true, tax penalties are a foreseeable consequence of the corporate transactions. Because these alleged transactions are in furtherance of illegality and oppression to the corporation, they satisfy the statutory elements of I.C. § 30–1–1430(2)(b).

Ron's removal from the board of directors and the Corporation's unwillingness to employ Ron or declare larger dividends constitute harm to Ron individually. Since harm to the corporation is required, these claims do not satisfy the statute.

We hold that the loss of corporate value and the potential tax penalties alleged by Ron satisfies the statutory elements of I.C. § 30–1–1430(2)(b), and we vacate the district court's dismissal of Count II, the corporate dissolution claim. . . .

———

Haynsworth, The Effectiveness of Involuntary Dissolution Suits as a
    Remedy for Close Corporation Dissension

35 Clev.St. L.Rev. 25 (1987)

In recent years courts have increasingly focused on developing the concept of oppression, and proof of oppressive conduct is rapidly becoming the most likely avenue for minority shareholder relief in close corporations. Three definitions of oppression have been used in the cases.

The first, drawn from English case law is:

burdensome, harsh and wrongful conduct . . . a lack of probity and fair dealing in the affairs of a company to the prejudice of some portion of its members; or a visual departure from the standards of fair dealing, and a violation of fair play on which every shareholder who entrusts his money to a company is entitled to rely.

Under this definition, oppression is basically a breach of the general fiduciary duty of good faith and fair dealing that majority shareholders in a corporation owe to the minority shareholders.

The second definition, first enunciated in the now famous case of *Donahue v. Rodd Electrotype Company of New England, Inc.,* is conduct that constitutes a violation of the strict fiduciary duty of 'utmost good faith and loyalty' owed by partners *inter se.* This standard, which is based on the analogy of close corporation shareholders who are active in management to general partners in a partnership, is theoretically higher than the 'good faith and inherent fairness' standard normally applicable in a corporation.

The third definition of oppression, initially derived from English case law, and long advocated by Dean F. Hodge O'Neal as well as other leading close corporation experts, is conduct which frustrates the reasonable expectations of the investors. The reasonable expectations doctrine has been gaining wide acceptance in the past few years. Decisions in at least eight states have explicitly adopted this concept, and decisions in at least nine additional states have implicitly recognized it. The approval of the reasonable expectations doctrine by the New York Court of Appeals in the 1984 case of *In re Kemp & Beatley, Inc.* is quite significant and will undoubtedly influence other courts.

———

MICH. COMP. LAWS § 450.1489

[See Statutory Supplement]

———

MINN. STAT. ANN. § 302A.751

[See Statutory Supplement]

———

McCallum v. Rosen's Diversified, Inc.

United States Court of Appeals, Eighth Circuit, 1998.
153 F.3d 701.

■ BEAM, CIRCUIT JUDGE.

William B. McCallum, a minority shareholder in Rosen's Diversified, Inc. (RDI), appeals from two adverse grants of summary judgment. McCallum seeks to have his shares in RDI redeemed for fair value pursuant to a court ordered buy-out. The district court held that McCallum failed to present evidence showing that RDI acted unfairly prejudicial toward him. We reverse and remand for a determination of the fair value of McCallum's shares.

I. BACKGROUND

This case involves a contentious dispute between the minority and controlling shareholders of a closely held Minnesota corporation. Two brothers, Elmer and Ludwig Rosen, founded RDI as a livestock trading business in the late 1940's. Today, RDI has grown into a thriving company, primarily engaged in meat packing and other agricultural businesses. In 1992, RDI had more than $400 million in sales. Members of the Rosen family own a majority of RDI's outstanding capital stock.

In January 1984, RDI hired McCallum, who had previously provided legal services to the company, as Executive Vice President and Chief Executive Officer (CEO). He was named a director in 1986. RDI performed well under McCallum's command. Accordingly, RDI rewarded McCallum—and three other key employees—with a bonus of $186,815 in cash and 12,000 shares of common stock in the company.[2] According to RDI, these payments were made because the key employees were almost entirely responsible for the financial success of the corporation, because the compensation package of the employees had been artificially low, and in order to maintain the unswerving loyalty of these employees. The parties did not enter into a shareholder's agreement or provide any mechanism for the transfer of those shares if circumstances changed.

By 1991, the amiable relationship between McCallum and RDI deteriorated, ultimately resulting in McCallum's termination and removal from the board. Subsequently, McCallum proposed that RDI redeem his shares for $5 million. RDI responded with an offer to redeem the shares for $600,000, which was at a small premium over the value determined by the annual valuation for RDI's Employee Stock Ownership Program (ESOP). The parties could not agree on a price and extensive litigation has followed. . . . The present case involves McCallum's 12,000 shares of RDI common stock which is not contained in the ESOP.

McCallum alleges that RDI's controlling shareholders have acted unfairly prejudicial toward him because they: (1) undermined his authority as CEO; (2) excluded him from important company decisions; (3) engaged in conduct directed at minimizing the value of the company; (4) terminated his employment; (5) offered to redeem his shares at an artificially low price; (6) denied him access to company books, records, and financial information; (7) engaged in self-dealing, usurped company opportunities, and commingled personal ventures with the affairs of the company.

The district court dismissed many of McCallum's allegations as improperly pleaded derivative claims. The district court dismissed

---

[2]   During the course of his employment, McCallum also received approximately 3,300 shares of common stock in RDI through an Employee Stock Ownership Program (ESOP). McCallum's total ownership represented nearly 3% of the company's capital stock.

McCallum's request for a buyout of his stock on a subsequent motion for summary judgment. McCallum appeals.

II. DISCUSSION . . .

Concerned with the vulnerable position of minority shareholders in closely held corporations, the Minnesota legislature has provided the courts with broad equitable authority to protect the interests of minority shareholders. See Minn.Stat. § 302A.751 (amended 1994) (hereinafter "Section 751"). Section 751 provides for the buy-out of a minority shareholder's interest when "the directors or those in control of the corporation have acted in a manner unfairly prejudicial toward one or more shareholders in their capacities as shareholders or directors . . . or as officers or employees of a closely held corporation."

The phrase "unfairly prejudicial" is to be interpreted liberally. See *Pedro v. Pedro*, 463 N.W.2d 285, 288–89 (Minn.Ct.App.1990). One commentator, who helped draft certain revisions to the Minnesota Business Corporation Act and Section 751, stated that:

> The section is remedial in nature and should be liberally construed as an addition to the rights afforded non-controlling shareholders by law and the corporation's governing documents. The broad scope of Section 751 reflects the Legislature's trust in the ability of the judiciary to achieve equitable results on the facts appearing in individual cases.

See Joseph Edward Olson, Statutory Changes Improve Position of Minority Shareholders in Closely Held Corporations, *The Hennepin Lawyer*, Sept.–Oct.1983, at 11. In deciding whether to order a buy-out, the courts should consider "the reasonable expectations of the shareholders" with respect to each other and the corporation. See Minn.Stat. § 302A.751, subd. 3a (amended 1994). Oftentimes, a shareholder's reasonable expectations include a significant voice in management and an opportunity to work. See Olson at 23.

We find that the uncontested facts demonstrate that McCallum's reasonable expectations were defeated. RDI terminated McCallum's employment as CEO and subsequently offered to purchase his RDI shares at a small premium over the value determined by an annual valuation for RDI's ESOP. McCallum had received these shares as compensation for his outstanding service and as an inducement to remain at RDI, in order to foster its continued growth. Although the employment relationship later deteriorated, our focus is on McCallum's reasonable expectations at the inception of the relationship. See Minn.Stat. § 302A.751, subd. 3a.

On his termination, McCallum was divested of his primary expectations as a minority shareholder in RDI—an active role in the "management of the corporation and input as an employee." Pedro, 463 N.W.2d at 289. This expectation was particularly reasonable since McCallum was CEO of RDI. We need not extend our holding as far as the

Minnesota Court of Appeals, which held that controlling shareholders that terminate the employment of a minority shareholder must make a good-faith effort to buy out the shareholder at a fair price. See *Sawyer v. Curt & Co.*, 1991 WL 65320, at *2 (Minn.Ct.App. Feb.12, 1991) (publication order vacated). We simply hold that terminating the CEO—as opposed to an employee that did not have a significant role in management—and then offering to redeem his stock, which was issued partially to lure him to remain at the company, constituted conduct toward McCallum as a shareholder sufficient to invoke the requirements of the Minnesota Act. Accordingly, we remand the matter for a determination of the fair value of his stock.

On remand, the district court shall determine the fair value of McCallum's shares in accordance with Minn.Stat. § 302A.751, subd. 2 (amended 1994) and put an end to this pugnacious litigation. We express no opinion on the fair value of McCallum's shares or whether the ESOP valuation represents fair value.

III. CONCLUSION

For the foregoing reasons, we reverse the judgment of the district court and remand for further proceedings consistent with this opinion.

———

Muellenberg v. Bikon Corp.

143 N.J. 168, 669 A.2d 1382 (1996)

Bikon Corporation was owned by Muellenberg, Passerini, and Burg. Muellenberg and Passerini were the majority shareholders. Burg, the minority shareholder, was Bikon's general manager. Burg sued Muellenberg and Passerini on the ground of oppression. The court held that Burg had been oppressed and gave him the right to buy out the majority shareholders:

> The statute . . . plainly allows the minority to seek a court order for the sale of the stock of "any other shareholder." In most situations, oppressed minority shareholders will lack the resources to buy out the interests of controlling shareholders. As a result, claims of oppression are typically remedied by arranging for the corporation or the majority shareholders to buy out the interests of the minority shareholder. In this case, the record contained the following evidence in support of Burg: Burg was willing and able to purchase the shares of Muellenberg and Passerini; Burg, who owns the land on which BNJ's offices are located, was most active in operating the company since its inception; Burg is the only shareholder who works full-time for BNJ and the company has been his only source of income for over ten years; Burg was primarily responsible for developing the company's contacts in the United States and Canada and is best situated to maintain the existing

operation; and finally, it was Burg who sought to preserve the corporation at a time when Muellenberg and Passerini attempted to dissolve it. . . .

Thus, while a minority buy-out of the majority is an uncommon remedy, it was the appropriate one here. . . . This remedy is authorized by N.J.S.A. 14A:12–7(8) and is consistent with decisions holding that courts are not limited to statutory remedies, but have a wide variety of equitable remedies also available to them. *Brenner*, . . . 134 N.J. at 516. . . .

———

Brodie v. Jordan

447 Mass. 866, 857 N.E.2d 1076 (Mass. 2006)

[Walter Brodie, Robert Jordan and David Barbuto founded Malden Centerless Grinding Co. in 1979. Each was an equal owner. Walter ceased being active in Malden Centerless in 1992 and upon his death in 1997 his one-third ownership passed to his wife, Mary Brodie. At the 1997 annual meeting, Brodie nominated herself to serve as a director but Jordan and Barbuto voted against her. For several years the corporation has paid no dividends and held no shareholders' meetings. Barbuto has his own business and is the lessor of the building occupied by Malden Centerless. Jordan works full time at Malden Centerless for which he receives a salary. The defendants did not respond to Brodie's repeated request for various information about the company and refused her request for a financial evaluation of the company so she might find a buyer for her shares. Brodie brought suit in 1998. The trial court found that Jordan and Barbuto had breached their fiduciary obligations to Brodie and ordered the defendants to purchase her shares. A divided Appeals Court affirmed, with the majority upholding both the finding of breach of fiduciary duty and the remedy. The Supreme Court reversed with respect to the remedy.]

We have previously analyzed freeze-outs in terms of shareholders' "reasonable expectations" both explicitly and implicitly. . . . A number of other jurisdictions, either by judicial decision or by statute, also look to shareholders' "reasonable expectations" in determining whether to grant relief to an aggrieved minority shareholder in a close corporation. . . . As discussed *infra*, we believe that this mode of analysis is useful at both the liability and the remedy stages of freeze-out litigation.

In the present case, the Superior Court judge properly analyzed the defendants' liability in terms of the plaintiff's reasonable expectations of benefit. The judge found that the defendants had interfered with the plaintiff's reasonable expectations by excluding her from corporate decision-making, denying her access to company information, and hindering her ability to sell her shares in the open market. In addition, the judge's findings reflect a state of affairs in which the defendants were the only ones receiving any financial benefit from the corporation. The

Appeals Court determined that the findings were warranted, and the defendants have not sought further appellate review with respect to liability. Thus, the only question before us is whether, on this record, the plaintiff was entitled to the remedy of a forced buyout of her shares by the majority. We conclude that she was not so entitled. . . .

The remedy should neither grant the minority a windfall nor excessively penalize the majority. Rather, it should attempt to reset the proper balance between the majority's "concede[d] . . . rights to what has been termed 'selfish ownership,' " *Wilkes v. Springside Nursing Home, Inc., supra* at 850–851, and the minority's reasonable expectations of benefit from its shares. . . .

Here, the Superior Court judge ordered the defendants to buy out the plaintiff at the price of an expert's estimate of her share of the corporation, a remedy that no Massachusetts appellate court has previously authorized. The problem with this remedy is that it placed the plaintiff in a significantly *better* position than she would have enjoyed absent the wrongdoing, and well exceeded her reasonable expectations of benefit from her shares.

Haynsworth, The Effectiveness of Involuntary Dissolution Suits as a Remedy for Close Corporation Dissension

35 Cleve.St.L.Rev. 25 (1987).

What results actually occur in close corporation involuntary dissolution suits? One way to answer this question is to examine existing published opinions. For the purposes of this article, the opinions published in 1984 and 1985 in which involuntary dissolution was one of the major causes of action were analyzed. . . .

. . . [A] total of forty-seven cases . . . qualified for the sample [but ten of the cases involved technical legal issues in which no decision on the type of relief, if any, had been made at the time the opinion was issued].

Of the remaining thirty-seven cases, a buy-out was the most frequent relief ordered by the court or elected by the defendants. This result occurred in twenty of the decisions (fifty-four percent). Dissolution was ordered in ten of the cases (twenty-seven percent). In four of the cases (eleven percent), no substantial relief was granted to the plaintiff on the merits. Finally, in the three other cases (eight percent) relief other than either dissolution or a buy-out was the exclusive remedy ordered. . . .

What is somewhat surprising is the number of cases in which a court-supervised buy-out is the result of the involuntary dissolution suit. In a previous study of the fifty-four involuntary dissolution opinions decided between 1960–1976 conducted by [Hetherington and Dooley], a court-ordered or court supervised buy-out was involved in only three of the cases, whereas dissolution was ordered in sixteen of the twenty-seven cases in which some affirmative relief was granted [in the present sample]. . . .

_____

8. CUSTODIANS AND PROVISIONAL DIRECTORS

Two other possible remedies for deadlock are the appointment of either a custodian or a provisional director. The following materials address those remedies.

_____

DEL. GEN. CORP. LAW §§ 226, 352, 353

[See Statutory Supplement]

_____

CAL. CORP. CODE §§ 308, 1802

[See Statutory Supplement]

_____

Shawe v. Elting

Supreme Court of Delaware, 2017.
157 A. 3d 142.

■ SEITZ, JUSTICE, for the Majority:

Philip Shawe and his mother, Shirley Shawe, have filed an interlocutory appeal from the Court of Chancery's August 13, 2015 opinion and July 18, 2016 order, and related orders, appointing a custodian under 8 *Del. C.* § 226 to sell TransPerfect Global, Inc., a Delaware corporation. . . .

On appeal, the Shawes do not challenge the Court of Chancery's many factual findings of serious dysfunction and deadlock. Instead, Philip Shawe claims for the first time on appeal that the court exceeded its statutory authority when it ordered the custodian to sell a solvent company. Alternatively, Shawe contends that less drastic measures were available to address the deadlock. . . .

We disagree with the Shawes and affirm the Court of Chancery's judgment. . . .

I.

TransPerfect Global, Inc. ("TPG") is a Delaware corporation that acts as a holding company for the main operating company, TransPerfect Translations International, Inc. ("TPI"), a New York corporation. Both entities will be referred to as the "Company." The Company provides translation, website localization, and litigation support services from 92 offices in 86 worldwide cities. It has over 3,500 full-time employees and maintains a network of over 10,000 translators, editors, and proofreaders in about 170 different languages. Elting and Shawe co-founded the Company and are co-chief executive officers and board members.

TPG has 100 shares of common stock issued and outstanding, divided fifty shares to Elting, forty-nine shares to Shawe, and one share to Shirley Shawe. In this Opinion, we refer to Philip Shawe as "Shawe," and Shirley Shawe by her full name. The one share allocated to Shirley Shawe allowed TPG to claim the benefits of being a majority women-owned business. We credit the Court of Chancery's finding, based on evidence introduced at trial, that Shawe "has treated his mother's share as his own property and himself as a 50% co-owner of the Company."

After a corporate reorganization in 2007, TPG's bylaws provided for a three member board of directors, or a different number fixed by the stockholders. Elting and Shawe have been the only directors since the Company's reorganization in 2007.

To fully appreciate the personal nature of the long-running discord . . . , we go back to the Company's founding and the troubled romantic relationship between the founders. Elting and Shawe co-founded the business in 1992 while living together in a dormitory room attending New York University's business school. They were engaged in 1996, but Elting called the marriage off in 1997. As the Court of Chancery found, "Shawe did not take the break-up well, and would 'terrorize' her and say 'horrendous things' about her husband, Michael Burlant, whom she married in 1999." On two separate occasions, Shawe responded to the rejection by crawling under Elting's bed and refusing to leave.[3]

As the Company grew, the founders were not satisfied with their financial success, and brought their simmering personal discontent into the Company's business affairs. The Court of Chancery catalogued the serious clashes over the years between Shawe and Elting and their surrogates before, and remarkably, during the litigation:

- Shawe engaged in a secret campaign to spy on Elting and invade her privacy by intercepting her mail, monitoring her phone calls, accessing her emails (including thousands of privileged communications with her counsel), and entering her locked office without permission on numerous occasions as well as sending his so-called "paralegal" there at 4:47 a.m. on another occasion.

---

[3]   When Elting ended their engagement, Shawe refused to leave the apartment and crawled under her bed and stayed there for at least half an hour. App. to Opening Br. at 2393 (Trial Tr.). On another occasion, Elting was traveling alone in Buenos Aires looking for space to open a new office. She arrived at her hotel room to find that Shawe had showed up unannounced. When she asked him to leave, he crawled under her hotel bed and stayed there for about half an hour. *Id.*

- Shawe co-opted the services of Company advisors (*e.g.*, Gerber and Kasowitz) to assist him in advancing his personal agenda against Elting.

- Shawe unilaterally hired numerous employees to perform Shared Services functions (Accounting and Finance) and even to work in divisions Elting managed . . . without her knowledge or consent by creating "off book" arrangements and fabricating documents.

- Shawe sought to have Elting criminally prosecuted by referring to her as his ex-fiancée seventeen years after the fact when filing a "Domestic Incident Report" as a result of a seemingly minor altercation in her office.

- Shawe disparaged Elting and tried to marginalize her within the Company by gratuitously disseminating a memorandum . . . to employees in her own division accusing her of collusion and financial improprieties.

- Shawe disparaged Elting publicly by unilaterally issuing a press release in the Company's name containing false and misleading statements.

These were just some of the highlights of the facts found by the Court of Chancery after a lengthy trial. The court also made detailed findings about continuous acrimonious disputes over personal and business expenses, weekly if not daily temper tantrums, and "mutual hostaging" between the founders over proposed acquisitions, stockholder distributions, employee hiring, pay and bonuses, and office locations. The court also found that Shawe bullied Elting and those aligned with her, expressing his desire to "create constant pain" for Elting until she agreed with Shawe's plans. It was common for senior officers to be drawn into their disputes, who were then abused by threatened firings, substantial fines, inappropriate emails, and by withholding compensation and promotions.

Specific to the Company's operations, the Court of Chancery heard days of testimony leading to findings that:

- Elting refused to pay litigation counsel to defend significant ongoing patent infringement litigation.

- Shawe fired real estate professionals, public relations professionals, refused to execute leases, and interfered with the Company's payroll processes.

- Shawe refused to engage in an annual expense true up, and interfered with the annual review of the Company's financials and its audit process.

- Shawe falsified corporate records to avoid review by Elting. . . .

II.

. . .

The conflict eventually distilled down to Elting's petition under 8 *Del. C.* § 226 to declare a deadlock and appoint a custodian to sell TPG.

The court dedicated enormous resources to the dispute. It held twelve hearings, decided sixteen motions, and conducted a six-day trial. Before its final decision, the Court of Chancery took the measured step of appointing a custodian to serve as a mediator to assist Shawe and Elting to try and settle their disputes. The court also delayed its post-trial decision for two months to await the parties' ongoing efforts to resolve the controversy. After the many attempts at settlement failed, the Court of Chancery issued its 104-page decision finding that "the evidence presented at trial warrants the appointment of a custodian to sell the Company to resolve the deadlocks between Shawe and Elting."

First, the Court of Chancery found that Elting had satisfied the requirements of § 226(a)(1) to appoint a custodian for stockholder deadlock because the parties stipulated that they were divided and unable to elect successor directors. Next, the court held that Elting satisfied the three requirements of § 226(a)(2) for appointment of a custodian due to director deadlock. As to the first requirement, the existence of deadlocks, the court reviewed in painstaking detail its many factual findings, now undisputed on appeal, supporting its conclusion that the distrust Shawe and Elting have for each other "strikes at the heart of the palpable dysfunction that exists in the governance of the Company."

The Court of Chancery also held that the second requirement, the stockholders' inability to break the director deadlock, was satisfied by the parties' stipulation of deadlock.

Turning to the final requirement, harm to the business, the Court of Chancery considered the profitability of the Company, but also made the commonsense observation that the statute contemplates appointment of custodians for profitable corporations which, like distressed companies, can suffer or be threatened with irreparable injury. The court then catalogued some of the many examples of actual and threatened irreparable injury to the Company. . . [it received testimony of many of the company's senior officers who labeled the fewu "the biggest business issue" facing the company, that the disputes were harming employee morale and well-being, that the dispute and resulting stressful environment prompted the "mass exodus in Accounting and Finance" and employees felt they were caught in the crossfire between Shawe and Elting.] Shawe himself acknowledged "the potential for grievously harming" the Company by his continued feuding with Elting.

The Court of Chancery also found that major clients who are free to use competitive services have expressed concerns about the dispute. Shawe and Elting have also been unable to agree on acquisitions which generally accounted for between 16.5–20% of the Company's annual revenue and 8–14% of its annual net profit. The Company has made no acquisitions since 2013. As the Court of Chancery held:

> [A]lthough it is true that the Company is and has been a profitable enterprise to date, its governance structure is irretrievably dysfunctional. The Company already has suffered from this dysfunction and, in my view, is threatened with much more grievous harm to its long-term prospects if the dysfunction is not addressed.

When it came to the scope of the custodian's authority, the Court of Chancery considered three alternatives. First, the court could do nothing and "leave the parties to their own devices." The court rejected this option because the "management of the Company is one of complete and utter dysfunction that is causing the business to suffer and threatens it with irreparable harm notwithstanding its profitability to date." . . . The court thus decided against the "do nothing" option because "equity will not suffer a wrong without a remedy."

Second, the court considered whether to appoint a custodian to serve as a third director or act in some capacity to break the ties between the two factions. He rejected this option . . . .

This left the Court of Chancery with a final option—"appoint a custodian to sell the Company so that Shawe and Elting can be separated and the enterprise can be protected from their dysfunctional relationship." The court recognized that the remedy was "unusual," and "should be implemented only as a last resort and with extreme caution." . . .

III. . . .

A. . . .

Shawe does not contest the Court of Chancery's ruling that a custodian may be appointed under § 226(a)(1) due to the stockholder deadlock between Shawe and Elting, and their inability to elect successor directors. Nor could he. Shawe and Elting stipulated to the stockholder deadlock required by the statute.

Shawe does challenge the Court of Chancery's appointment of a custodian under § 226(a)(2), claiming that the court misapplied the requirement that the court find irreparable injury to the business of the corporation. According to Shawe, the court improperly relied on case law defining irreparable injury in the temporary injunction context, instead of applying a supposedly more rigorous "imminent corporate paralysis" standard under § 226. Shawe argues that applying the wrong standard "trivializes and undermines Section 226" because judicial intervention is only permitted in "extreme circumstances."

First, the argument is academic because Shawe agreed that the Court of Chancery was authorized to appoint a custodian under

§ 226(a)(1). Elting need not show irreparable injury under the first part of the statute. Further, the Court of Chancery did not misapply the threatened or actual irreparable injury requirement. As the court observed, "irreparable injury" is "a familiar equitable principle" which takes into account factors like "harm to a corporation's reputation, goodwill, customer relationships, and employee morale." . . .

Far from trivializing the irreparable injury requirement, the Court of Chancery accepted the fact that the Company was profitable, but also recognized the extremely dysfunctional relationship between the founders and its effect on all of the Company's operations. If allowed to persist, the Company was likely to continue on the path of plummeting employee morale, key employee departures, customer uncertainty, damage to the Company's public reputation and goodwill, and a fundamental inability to grow the Company through acquisitions.

We will not disturb these factual findings on appeal. The trial record amply supports the Court of Chancery's finding that the deadlock and dysfunction between the founders is causing threatened and actual irreparable injury to the Company.

B.

Having decided that the Court of Chancery properly exercised its discretion under § 226 to appoint a custodian of the Company, we turn to Shawe's primary argument raised for the first time on appeal—that the custodian statute does not authorize the court to order the custodian to sell the Company over the stockholders' objection. Shawe also argues that instructing the custodian to sell the Company is an extreme remedy, and should not have been imposed without first attempting less-drastic remedies, such as using the custodian as a third director to break the ongoing deadlocks between the founders. . . .

Section 226(b) of the statute provides that:

> A custodian appointed under this section shall have all the powers and title of a receiver appointed under § 291 of this title, but the authority of the custodian is to continue the business of the corporation, and not to liquidate its affairs and distribute its assets, except when the Court shall otherwise order, and except in cases arising under paragraph (a)(3) of this section or § 352(a)(2) of this title.[34]

. . . Under the express language of the custodian statute, the Court of Chancery has the authority to "otherwise order" the custodian to "liquidate [the Company's] affairs and distribute its assets" rather than "continue the business of the corporation." . . .

Under a plain reading of § 226(b), the custodian has the powers of a receiver under § 291, and his duties are to continue the business unless the Court otherwise orders, and except under the special circumstances

---

[34]   8 *Del. C.* § 226(b).

of abandoned businesses and close corporations. Rules of interpretation should not be invoked to contort the plain language of a statute in a manner inconsistent with its plain meaning. . . .

[The dissent, questioned the authority of the Chancellor to order the sale of the parties' shares in TPG instead of ordering the custodian to dispose of the operating assets of TPI. The dissent based its argument on DGCL § 273 that expressly calls for asset sales as a remedy when two equal owners in a corporate joint venture are deadlocked. . . . Nonetheless, the majority upheld the order to sell the owners' stock in TPG, reasoning to do otherwise would elevate form over substance and that it would be inefficient to allow the parties to retain their TPG shares for the purpose of then receiving a liquidating distribution when the operating assets of TPI were sold.]

Shawe also faults the Court of Chancery for ordering a sale instead of experimenting with less-intrusive measures. We agree with Shawe that a sale is a remedy to be employed reluctantly and cautiously, after a consideration of other options. The Court of Chancery should always consider less drastic alternatives before authorizing the custodian to sell a solvent company. But the remedy to address the deadlock is ultimately within the Court of Chancery's discretion.

The court did not abuse its discretion in this case. First, the court attempted other less intrusive measures by appointing a custodian immediately after trial ended to serve "as a mediator to assist Elting and Shawe in negotiating a resolution of their disputes." Almost three months later, after the first attempt at mediation failed, the court gave the parties another month before issuing its post-trial opinion "to afford them additional time to seek to resolve their disputes through the auspices of the mediator." The Court of Chancery was also aware of repeated efforts to resolve the dispute in New York, including settlement discussions, a mediation, and multiple sessions with a court-appointed Special Master. The Court of Chancery gave the parties every opportunity to resolve their acrimonious dispute outside the courthouse.

Further, the court considered whether to appoint a custodian "to serve as a third director or some form of tie-breaking mechanism in the governance of the Company." But the court rejected this option because:

> [I]t would enmesh an outsider, and, by extension, the Court into matters of internal corporate governance for an extensive period of time. Shawe and Elting are both relatively young. Absent a separation, their tenure as directors and co-CEOs of the Company could continue for decades. It is not sensible for the Court to exercise essentially perpetual oversight over the internal affairs of the Company.

And, although Shawe characterizes the Chancellor's remedy as extremely intrusive, the appointment of a custodian to act as a constant monitor and tie-breaker—which is what would be required given the abundant record that Shawe and Elting cannot work together constructively—would itself be expensive, cumbersome, and very intrusive. Moreover, that approach would not facilitate, as the Chancellor's ruling does, the ability of the Company to capitalize on its business model in the efficient, flexible way that commerce demands. By preserving the Company as a whole in his remedy and allowing it to be owned and managed in the manner required to take advantage of evolving opportunities and to meet challenges effectively, the Chancellor's remedy also was well designed to protect the other constituencies of the Company—notably its employees—by positioning the company to succeed and thus to secure the jobs of its workforce.

The Chancellor was in the best position to assess the viability of options short of sale. Aware of the "extreme caution" that must be exercised before ordering a sale, he nonetheless determined that "the painfully obvious conclusion is that Shawe and Elting need to be separated from each other in the management of the Company. Their dysfunction must be excised to safeguard the Company."

We will not second-guess that first-hand judgment on appeal. . . .

V. . . .

Dissent by: VALIHURA [omitted]

———

NOTES ON CUSTODIANS AND PROVISIONAL DIRECTORS

1. Provisional Director. The appointment of a provisional director may enable one faction to make changes in the control structure of the corporation whose effects will persist even after the provisional director has left the scene. For example, in *In re Jamison Steel Corp.*, 158 Cal.App.2d 27, 322 P.2d 246 (1958), one faction controlled 240 shares of stock and the other faction controlled the remaining 160 shares. Under the corporation's articles, the board consisted of four directors, and under cumulative voting, each faction could elect two of the four. Board meetings in December 1955 and December 1956 resulted in tie votes on several issues, including elections to certain offices and the size of the dividend. After the 1955 meeting, the majority faction petitioned the court for the appointment of a provisional director on the ground of deadlock. The lower court appointed a provisional director with authority to vote for an amendment to the articles of incorporation. The California Supreme Court affirmed, although recognizing that the provisional director might vote with the majority's two directors to increase the board to five, and thereby permanently alter the balance of power.

Hetherington & Dooley argue that the provisional-director remedy is unsound:

No state or public interest appears to justify [appointing a provisional director and thereby] depriving the resisting party of the right to veto corporate decisions. The power to veto is an important property right, to which the resisting party is entitled by virtue of his shareholdings. It is the best protection against exploitation and oppression that a shareholder in a close corporation can have, short of the power to impose his will on the other party. . . . The faction that has the support of the provisional director has little or no incentive to seek to settle its differences with the minority faction.

Hetherington & Dooley, Illiquidity and Exploitation: A Proposed Statutory Solution to the Remaining Close. Corporation Problem, 63 Va.L.Rev. 1, 21–22 (1977).

2. Custodian vs. Dissolution. The distinctive aspect of the custodian remedy is that unlike dissolution, if a custodian is appointed the business continues, and unlike a provisional director, a custodian normally has complete authority over the business.

————

9. ARBITRATION

————

RINGLING v. RINGLING BROS. BARNUM & BAILEY CIRCUS

[Section 2, supra]

————

Lane v. Abel-Bey

70 A.D.2d 838, 418 N.Y.S.2d 25 (1979), aff'd, 50 N.Y.2d 864 (1980)

A shareholders' agreement provided that "[a]ll disputes arising in connection with this agreement shall be finally settled by arbitration." One of the shareholders claimed that the corporation had failed to enter into an employment contract with him, as the agreement required; had paid excessive compensation; and had made improper payments to other shareholders. Held, the claims were subject to arbitration. "We do not agree with petitioner's argument that, because the second and third claims are in the nature of derivative suits, public policy precludes arbitration of such claims. . . . We are not concerned here with claims relating to the business conduct of a publicly held corporation, but rather with such claims addressed to the business conduct of a close corporation. Arbitration of claims of a derivative nature are not against public policy in a close corporation . . . "

————

Shell, Arbitration and Corporate Governance

67 N.C.L.Rev. 517 (1989)

[Section 2 of the Federal Arbitration Act] makes enforceable any 'written provision in any ... contract evidencing a transaction involving commerce to settle by arbitration' any existing or future dispute ...

[A]fter nearly seventy years of legal evolution, arbitration is now utilized in New York as a close corporation remedy for virtually every kind of corporate dispute. Indeed, detailed case administration statistics compiled by the American Arbitration Association reveal that between 1984 and August 1988 the AAA received over one thousand claims and counterclaims worth over $118,000,000 under its case administration category dealing with close corporation disputes. These claims include disputes regarding stock valuation and appraisal, allegations of breach of contract, mismanagement, misrepresentation, wrongful discharge, and breach of fiduciary duty.

... [T]he Supreme Court has ... [interpreted Federal Arbitration Act] as preempting attempts by the states to preclude access to the arbitral forum. When parties can convince a court that their close corporation dispute involves interstate commerce, they may be able to bypass even express statutory restrictions on arbitration, such as [a] ... requirement that an arbitration clause appear in the charter. Id. at 524, 533.

———

CHAPTER 8

LIMITED LIABILITY COMPANIES

DELAWARE LIMITED LIABILITY COMPANY ACT
§§ 18–101, 18–107, 18–201, 18–206, 18–301,
18–303, 18–401, 18–402, 18–504

[See Statutory Supplement]

———

Meyer v. Oklahoma Alcoholic Beverage Laws Enforcement Commission

Oklahoma Court of Appeals, 1995.
890 P.2d 1361.

The issue is one of first impression—whether an LLC, created pursuant to the . . . [Oklahoma] LLC Act, is eligible for issuance of a retail package store liquor license. . . . Indeed, the issue could only have arisen after the 1992 legislative creation of the new form of business entity. LLCs were not a recognized business entity in this state at the time of adoption of our Constitution . . . . We conclude that the constitutional directives do prohibit the holding of a license by an LLC and, thus, the lower court did err in its conclusion.

The pertinent constitutional provisions are *Okla. Const. art. 28, §§ 4 and 10*. Section 4, in pertinent part, provides:

Not more than one retail package license shall be issued to any person or general or limited partnership. . . .

Meyer argues that an LLC is essentially a partnership. . . .

Meyer claims that its expert witness, the only witness in all the proceedings, testified that an LLC was a partnership. However, contrary to Meyer's contention, the witness's testimony was not so unequivocal. The totality of the testimony was that an LLC is a hybrid that has attributes of both corporations and partnerships. The witness indicated an LLC is more like a partnership, but noted the primary difference is that all owners/members have limited liability in an LLC—something not found in partnerships. We conclude that the limitation of liability of all LLC members is a substantial difference especially relevant to the provisions of our liquor laws.

Our examination of the pertinent constitutional provisions leads us to conclude that their evident purpose was the assignment of personal responsibility for compliance with the liquor laws. Thus, business forms that did not insure such personal responsibility were excluded from eligibility for licensing.

───────

1. INTRODUCTION: FORMATION AND MANAGEMENT OF LLCs

Limited liability companies (LLCs) are noncorporate entities that are created under statutes that combine elements of corporation and partnership law. As under corporation law, the owners ("members") of LLCs have limited liability. As under partnership law, an LLC has great freedom to structure its internal governance by agreement. Like a corporation, an LLC is an entity, so that it can, for example, hold property and sue and be sued in its own name. LLCs come in two flavors: member-managed LLCs, which are managed by their members, and manager-managed LLCs, which are managed by managers who may or may not be members.

As of 2010, there were 2.1 million LLCs in existence, compared to 590,000 partnerships, 375,000 limited partnerships, and 142,000 limited liability partnerships. LLCs are growing faster in absolute numbers than other non-corporate forms, which have steadily declined or remained static since 2001. U.S. Internal Revenue Service, Statistics of Income Bulletins, Fall 2012, at 84–86.

Like privately held corporations, small LLCs tend to be formed in the state where their business was located. An extensive study of where LLCs are formed found that overall 92 percent are formed in the state of their principal place of business; the number that incorporate outside the principal place of business decreases to 83 percent for LLC for firms with 100–999 employees and 38 percent for LLCs with 5000 or more employees. Delaware attracts 54 percent of the LLCs that form outside their principal place of business. *See* Jens Dammann & Matthias Schundeln, Where Are Limited Liability Companies Formed? An Empirical Analysis, 55 J. Law & Econ. 741 (2012).

The LLC is a relatively new form, and the LLC statutes are highly variable. Because the LLC is of such recent origin, iterations of the Uniform Limited Liability Company Act[1] have not enjoyed anywhere near the impact on state statutes as has the Model Business Corporation Act. Thus, there is a good deal of variation across the states in their respective LLC acts. Nonetheless, LLC statutes have certain core features in common. Owners are referred to as *members* who frequently, but not always, are the *managers* of the day-to-day operations of the

───────

[1]   The National Conference of Commissioners on Uniform State Laws promulgated the first Uniform Limited Liability Company Act in 1996. That version contained many more partnership-like provisions than can be found in most state LLC statutes. This characteristic somewhat explains its limited acceptance by the states. In 2006 the Conference substantially revised its earlier provision with the Revised Uniform Limited Liability Company Act.

company. The document filed with the state that creates the LLC is the *articles of organization*; however, the fullest treatment of, the members' and managers' rights and even duties are set forth in an *operating agreement.*

Central to the attractiveness of the LLC is the provision in every LLC statute that the members and managers of an LLC are not liable for the LLC's debts, obligations, and other liabilities. For example, section 304(a) of the Uniform Limited Liability Company Act provides:

The debts, obligations, or other liabilities of the limited liability company, whether in contract, tort or otherwise:

(1) are solely the debts, obligations, or other liabilities of the company; and

(2) do not become the debts, obligations, or other liabilities of a member or manager *solely by reason* of the member acting as a member or manager acting as a manager. (emphasis added)

In *Pepsi-Cola Bottling Co. v. Handy*, 2000 WL 364199 (Del. Ch.2000), Pepsi alleged that the defendants had committed a series of misrepresentations in the sale of land on the eve of their forming an LLC and their becoming its sole members. Defendants invoked Del. L.L.C. A. § 18–303(a) which also provided that members are not liable solely by reason of being a member. Does this provision shield the member from personal liability to Pepsi-Cola?

Racing Investment Fund 2000, LLC v. Clay Ward Agency, Inc.

Supreme Court of Kentucky, 2010.
320 S.W. 654.

[Racing Investment Fund was formed as an LLC to purchase, train and race thoroughbred horses. Section 4.3(a) of the operating agreement provided "The Investor Members . . . shall be obligated to contribute to the capital of the Company, on a pro-rata basis in accordance with their respective Percentage Interests, such amounts as may be reasonably deemed advisable by the Manager from time to time in order to pay operating, administrative, or other business expenses of the Company which have occurred, or which the Manager reasonably anticipates. . . ." Section 275.150 of the Kentucky LLC statute provided "(1) no member . . . of a limited liability company . . . shall be personally liable by reason of being a member" but further provided "(2) Notwithstanding the provisions in subsection (1) . . . under a written operating agreement . . . a member or manager may agree to be obligated personally for any of the debts, obligations, and liabilities of the limited liability company."

Racing defaulted on insurance premiums owed the Clay Ward Agency. Clay Ward sued, obtained a default judgment against Racing, and the trial court ordered Racing to make a capital call on its members pursuant to the terms of the operating agreement. Reversed.]

. . . [A]n operating agreement providing for future capital contributions by the LLC's members is neither "unique" as suggested by Clay Ward nor "atypical" as described by the Court of Appeals. Many businesses choosing the limited liability company form have circumstances that require periodic capital infusion. *See* Alberty at § 4.02(b) ("Often, an LLC will need financing in stages, and staggered contributions by members will be anticipated at the time the LLC is organized. . . . Both anticipated and unanticipated later capital contributions should be addressed in an LLC's organizational documents.") Section 4.3(a) is a provision designed to assure members will contribute additional capital, as deemed necessary by the Manager, to advance Racing Investment's thoroughbred racing venture. While Clay Ward's insurance premiums were indeed a legitimate business expense for which the Manager could have made a capital call, that premise alone does not lead *a fortiori* to the relief ordered by the trial court. Simply put, Section 4.3(a) is a not-uncommon, on-going capital infusion provision, not a debt-collection mechanism by which a court can order a capital call and, by doing so, impose personal liability on the LLC's members for the entity's outstanding debt. Clay Ward insists that its quest to be paid is not about individual member liability, but there is no other way to construe what occurs when a court orders a capital call be made to pay for a particular LLC debt. From any viewpoint, the shield of limited liability has been lifted and the LLC's members have been held individually liable for its debt.

KRS 275.150 emphatically rejects personal liability for an LLC's debt unless the member or members, as the case may be, have agreed through the operating agreement or another written agreement to assume personal liability. Any such assumption of personal liability, which is contrary to the very business advantage reflected in the name "limited liability company", must be stated clearly in unequivocal language which leaves no room for doubt about the parties' intent. Section 4.3(a) of Racing Investment's Operating Agreement does not begin to meet this standard. A provision designed to provide on-going capital infusion as necessary, at the Manager's discretion, for the conduct of the entity's business affairs is simply not an agreement "to be obligated personally for any of the debts, obligations and liabilities of the limited liability company." *KRS 275.150(2)*. To reiterate, assumption of personal liability by a member of an LLC is so antithetical to the purpose of a limited liability company that any such assumption must be stated in unequivocal terms leaving no doubt that the member or members intended to forego a principal advantage of this form of business entity. On this score, Section 4.3(a) simply does not qualify. . . .

NOTES ON ORGANIZATIONAL CONSIDERATIONS IN FORMING LLC

1.　Articles of Organization; Powers. An LLC is formed by filing articles of organization in a designated state office—usually, the office of the Secretary of State. The statutes all allow LLCs to be formed by a single person. Most LLC statutes call for very little to be set forth in the articles. The articles must include the name of the LLC, the address of its principal place of business or registered office in the State, and the name and address of its agent for service of process. Many statutes also require the articles to state: (1) The purpose of the LLC. (2) If the LLC is to be manager-managed, the names of the initial managers, and if the LLC is to be member-managed, the names of its initial members. (3) The duration of the LLC or the latest date on which it is to dissolve. Some statutes also require the articles to include various kinds of additional information, the nature of which varies considerably.

Most statutes either provide that LLCs have all the powers necessary to effectuate their purposes or contain an exhaustive laundry list of an LLC's powers. *See e.g.,* Del. Limited Liability Company Act § 18–1–6(b) (company has the "powers . . . necessary or convenient to the conduct, promotion or attainment of the business purposes or activities" of the company); Uniform Limited Liability Company Act § 105 ("A limited liability company has the capacity to sue and be sued in its own name and the power to do all things necessary or convenient to carry on its activities.")

2.　Operating Agreement. An LLC's articles of organization are usually very sketchy. In most LLCs, the critical foundational instrument is the *operating agreement* (sometimes called by another name, such as "limited liability company agreement"), which is an agreement among the LLC's members concerning the conduct of its affairs. The operating agreement typically provides for the governance of the LLC, its capitalization, the admission and withdrawal of members, and distributions. Because most LLC statutes provide few rules for the governance of the company, the operating agreement is the central organizational document because it customarily sets for the rules for governance. The paucity of statutory prescriptions reflects a key feature of LLCs; they are essentially contractual so that private ordering is expected, if not demanded by the fact that the LLC act rarely provides default rules as we find in corporate statutes. Delaware is explicit with respect to the role of private ordering. *See* Delaware Limited Liability Company Act § 18–1101(b) "It is the policy of this chapter to give the maximum effect to the principle of freedom of contract and to the enforceability of limited liability company agreements."

Most states provide that the articles are paramount if they conflict with a provision in the operating agreement . *See* N.Y. Ltd. Liab. Co. Law § 417(a); The Uniform Act divides the baby: the operating agreement controls over the articles with respect to "managers, members and members' transferees" and the articles control with respect to others "who reasonably rely on the articles to their detriment." ULLCA § 112(d),

3.　Management by Whom? Most of the statutes provide, as a default rule which prevails unless otherwise agreed, that an LLC is to be managed by its members. A few statutes provide that unless otherwise agreed, an LLC is to be managed by managers, who may but need not be members. The most common statutory provision is that the statutory default rule concerning management can be varied only by a provision in the LLC's articles of organization, but many statutes provide that the default rule can be varied in the operating agreement. One way to vary the statutory default rule is to completely reverse it—either by providing for manager management in a state where the default rule is member management, or by providing for member management in a state where the default rule is manager management. Another way to vary the statutory default rule is to distribute management functions between members and managers.

4.   *Authority to Act for the LLC*

a). Member-Managed LLCs. In a member-managed LLC, each member has power to bind the LLC for any act that is for apparently carrying on the business of the LLC in the usual way or ordinary course. Even if an action is not in the usual or ordinary course, the remaining members may confer on a member actual authority to bind the LLC to an action or a given type of action. Conversely, the members as a group may withdraw the actual authority of one or more members to take a certain kind of action that is in the ordinary or usual course. In that case, if a member takes such an action the LLC will be bound by virtue of the member's apparent authority, but the member will be obliged to indemnify the LLC for any loss that results from her contravention of the other members' decision.

b). Manager-Managed LLCs. In manager-managed firms, typically only the managers have apparent authority to bind the firm. Members of a manager-managed LLC have no apparent authority to bind the LLC. Most of the statutes provide that a manager in a manager-managed LLC has the same authority as a member in a member-managed firm.

c). Co-Extensive Authority. In a few states, the default rule confers authority on both members and managers. For example, Section 18–402 of the Delaware Limited Liability Company Act provides "Unless otherwise provided in a limited liability company agreement, each member and manager has the authority to bind the limited liability company."

5.   *Series LLC.* The most sophisticated form of business entity is the series LLC. Series LLCs are authorized in about one-third of the states. A series LLC consists of a "master" LLC within which there are one or more series of members, managers, interests or assets. Although each of the "cells" can have distinct powers, liabilities, and objectives with respect to specific property within the cell, each of multiple cells is within a single LLC. The profits, losses, and liabilities of each cell are legally separate from the other cells in the series. The cells may have common, some overlap or totally different members whose rights can be common or quite distinct. The distinctions among cells and members are set forth in the master LLC's operating agreement.

Estate of Collins v. Geist

Supreme Court of Idaho, 2007.
143 Idaho 821, 153 P.3d 1167.

■ EISMANN, JUSTICE.

This is an appeal from summary judgments dismissing the Respondents from an action seeking to void various conveyances of real property made to them. In seeking to void the conveyances, the Appellants asserted that the person executing the deeds to the Respondents did not have authority to do so . . . . We affirm . . . .

I.   FACTS AND PROCEDURAL HISTORY

On October 22, 1999, Michael Collins and Russell D. Purcell (Purcell) formed a limited liability company named CBS of Idaho, L.L.C. (CBS of Idaho). They did so at the request of E. A. Collins, Michael's father. The articles of organization of the limited liability company stated that management of the company would be vested in managers, and it named Michael and Purcell as the initial managers. E. A. Collins owned a business in Nevada named Collins Building Systems that built steel and Styrofoam houses. CBS of Idaho was formed to market steel and Styrofoam houses in Idaho.

On September 21, 2000, Michael Collins filed articles of amendment to the articles of organization of CBS of Idaho. The articles of amendment changed its name to Kanaka Rapids Ranch, L.L.C. (Kanaka Rapids), removed Purcell as a manager, and added E.A. Collins as a manager.

On September 26, 2000, Collins Brothers Corporation, a Nevada Corporation, deeded to Kanaka Rapids various parcels of real property located in Twin Falls County, Idaho. The corporation was owned by E. A. Collins and his brother, and the transfer was done in consideration for the corporation redeeming all of the stock owned by E. A. Collins. The real property deeded to Kanaka Rapids consisted of various improved and unimproved building lots and a model home. The sole purpose of Kanaka Rapids was to develop and sell that property.

During the period from November 2, 2000 through September 10, 2001, Michael Collins executed deeds on behalf of Kanaka Rapids conveying various lots. The Respondents are persons and entities who were purchasers or subsequent purchasers of the lots.

On January 11, 2001, E. A. Collins died. His estate is being probated in Nevada. It has assets valued at approximately $ 2.5 million and debts totaling almost $ 35 million. On March 29, 2004, the Estate of E. A. Collins (Estate) commenced this action on its own behalf and on behalf of Kanaka Rapids seeking to set aside the deeds of the Respondents in order to recover that property for the Estate. The Estate contended that Michael Collins was not a manager of Kanaka Rapids and therefore did not have authority to act on its behalf. It also contended that the deeds were void because Michael Collins did not have written authorization from Kanaka Rapids to sign the deeds on its behalf. . . .

The district court granted the Respondents' motions for summary judgment and entered judgments dismissing this action as to them. It determined that Michael Collins had the apparent authority to act on behalf of Kanaka Rapids. . . . The Plaintiffs then appealed.

II. ISSUES ON APPEAL

1. Is there a genuine issue of material fact as to whether Michael Collins was a manager of Kanaka Rapids?

2. Does a manager of a limited liability company need written authorization to convey real property of the company? . . .

III. ANALYSIS

A. Is There a Genuine Issue of Material Fact as to Whether Michael Collins Was a Manager of Kanaka Rapids? . . .

Appellants argue that Michael Collins could not have been a manager of Kanaka Rapids because there was no operating agreement.

Idaho Code § 53–601(9) states, " 'Manager' means, with respect to a limited liability company that has set forth in its articles of organization that it is to be managed by managers, the person or persons designated in accordance with *section 53–621, Idaho Code." Section 53–621(1)* provides, "Unless an operating agreement vests management of the limited liability company in a manager or managers, management of the business affairs of the limited liability company shall be vested in the members." Thus, there must be an operating agreement vesting management of the limited liability company in a manager or managers for them to manage the business affairs of the company.

An "operating agreement" is "any agreement, written or oral, among all of the members as to the conduct of the business and affairs of a limited liability company." *I.C. § 53–601(11)*. Because an operating agreement must have been agreed to by all the members, the first issue is to identify who were the members of Kanaka Rapids?

The Appellants argue that Michael Collins could not be a member of Kanaka Rapids because he did not provide any capital in exchange for his membership. In their arguments, the Appellants focus upon contributions of capital made after September 21, 2000. The articles of amendment filed on that date did not create Kanaka Rapids. It merely changed the name of CBS of Idaho to Kanaka Rapids Ranch, L.L.C.. If Michael Collins was a member of CBS of Idaho, he was also a member of Kanaka Rapids.

Idaho Code § 53–626 provides:

A limited liability company interest may be issued in exchange for cash, property, services rendered, guarantee of an obligation of the limited liability company, a promissory note or other obligation to contribute cash or property or to perform services, or other valuable consideration.

During his deposition, Michael Collins was asked whether he provided capital to form CBS of Idaho, and he answered that he did not. Capital is "[m]oney or assets invested, or available for investment, in a business." *Black's Law Dictionary* 200 (Bryan A. Garner ed., 7th ed., West 1999). *Idaho Code § 53–626* does not require that a person exchange money or assets for his or her membership in a limited liability company. Michael Collins testified that he used his credit to obtain the construction loans for the two homes that CBS of Idaho constructed. His testimony in this regard is uncontradicted. The use of his credit to obtain the construction loans suffices as valuable consideration under *Idaho Code § 53–626*.

Relying upon *Idaho Code § 53–640(1)(a)*,[1] the Appellants argue that Michael Collins could not become a member without either a written operating agreement or the written consent of all members. Michael Collins and Purcell were the only persons involved in the formation of CBS of Idaho. Although they formed the limited liability company at the request of E. A. Collins, Michael Collins testified that his father had no role in the company prior to the filing of the articles of amendment on September 21, 2000. His testimony in that regard is uncontradicted. Purcell did not provide any valuable consideration to the company. His involvement was limited to signing his name on the articles of organization. He testified, "My involvement ended the day after—the same day I signed this [the articles of organization] and walked out." When asked if he was a member, Purcell answered, "Nothing more than forming the piece of paper." The evidence in the record shows that Michael Collins was the only person who could be a member of CBS of Idaho. Where there is only one person involved in a limited liability company, that person is not prevented from becoming a member because he or she did not give written consent.

An operating agreement is "any agreement, written or oral, among all of the members as to the conduct of the business and affairs of a limited liability company." *I.C. § 53–601(11)*. Since Michael Collins was the only member of CBS of Idaho, there would be an operating agreement if he was in agreement regarding the conduct of the business and affairs of the company. It is undisputed that he was because he ran the company by himself. Because Michael Collins, the sole member, obviously agreed that he would conduct the business and affairs of CBS of Idaho, there

---

[1] That statute provides:

(1) Subject to subsection (2) of this section [specifying the effective time of admission], a person may become a member in a limited liability company:

(a) In the case of a person acquiring a limited liability company interest directly from the limited liability company, upon compliance with an operating agreement or, if an operating agreement does not so provide in writing, upon the written consent of all members.

was an operating agreement for CBS of Idaho, and Michael Collins qualified as being a manager.

On September 21, 2000, Michael Collins filed articles of amendment changing the name of the limited liability company to Kanaka Rapids Ranch, L.L.C. (Kanaka Rapids), removing Purcell as a manager, and adding E. A. Collins as a manager. Purcell had no objection to being removed as a manager.[2] It is unclear whether E. A. Collins was added as both a manager and a member of Kanaka Rapids. In his affidavit filed on August 16, 2004, Michael Collins stated that his father was added as a member. At his deposition taken about one month later, Michael Collins testified that he did not know if his father was a member. His father could become a member by complying with a written operating agreement or upon the written consent of all members. *I.C. § 53–640(1)(a)*. Kanaka Rapids did not have a written operating agreement, and there was no written consent of all members unless the Articles of Amendment would so qualify since they were signed by the only other member, Michael Collins. That document, however, does not indicate on its face that E. A. Collins is being added as a member. The form has a preprinted line stating, "The information on managers/members shall be amended as follows:" and then states that Purcell is being deleted and E. A. Collins is being added. It does not state whether he is being added as a manager, a member, or both. Since he replaced Purcell who was listed as a manager in the Articles of Organization, it would seem that E. A. Collins was added as a manager. Consistent with the standard of summary judgment, however, we will assume that E.A. Collins became a member on September 21, 2000, when the articles of amendment were filed.

Appellants argue that Michael could not be a manager without an operating agreement for Kanaka Rapids and that in his deposition he testified that the company had no operating agreement. Implicit in their argument is once a new member is added, there must be a new operating agreement.

In his affidavit filed on August 16, 2004, Michael stated that he and his father agreed that he would manage Kanaka Rapids. . . .

The Appellants rely solely upon Michael Collins's statement in his deposition to argue that there was no operating agreement, or at least to argue that there was a genuine issue of material fact as to whether there was an operating agreement. Michael Collins gave a plausible explanation for the statement he made in his deposition, and the other evidence in the record clearly shows that there was an operating agreement. An operating agreement can be "any agreement, written or oral, among all of the members as to the conduct of the business and

---

[2]   Purcell was listed as a manager in the articles of organization. Unless required in the operating agreement, a manager does not have to be a member of the limited liability company. *I.C. § 53–621(2)(b)*. After being given a copy of the articles of amendment deleting him as a manager, Purcell testified, "I got a phone call from Michael telling me they were going to take me off of CBS and Al [Michael's father] was going to be put on CBS. My answer was great and that was it, but I never saw the document."

affairs of a limited liability company," *I.C. § 53–601(11).* The uncontradicted evidence is that E. A. Collins was living in Las Vegas, Michael Collins was living in Idaho, and E. A. Collins left the management of Kanaka Rapids to his son Michael. Appellants have not pointed to any evidence indicating that E. A. Collins was in any way involved in conducting the business and affairs of Kanaka Rapids. . . . There is no genuine issue of material fact on this issue. The conduct of Michael and E. A. Collins clearly showed that they had agreed that Michael would conduct the business and affairs of Kanaka Rapids. Thus, Michael Collins qualified as a manager of Kanaka Rapids.

Appellants argue that there is no evidence that Michael Collins contributed any capital or valuable consideration to Kanaka Rapids. There was no requirement that he do so. Kanaka Rapids was a continuation of CBS of Idaho. Neither the name change nor the investment made by E.A. Collins required an additional investment by Michael Collins in order for him to remain a member.

B. Does a Manager of a Limited Liability Company Need Written Authorization to Convey Real Property of the Company?

The Appellants contend that the conveyances of the lots to the Respondents were void because Michael Collins did not have written authorization from Kanaka Rapids to sign the documents on its behalf. In making this argument, Appellants rely upon *Idaho Code § 55–601*, which provides, "A conveyance of an estate in real property may be made by an instrument in writing, subscribed by the party disposing of the same, or by his agent thereunto authorized by writing." They also rely upon the similar requirement in *Idaho Code § 9–503.*[3]

Idaho Code § 53–616(2)(b) provides:

Every manager is an agent of the limited liability company for the purpose of its business or affairs, and the act of any manager, including but not limited to, the execution in the name of the limited liability company of any instrument, for apparently carrying on in the usual way the business or affairs of the limited liability company of which he is a manager binds the limited liability company, unless the manager so acting has, in fact, no authority to act for the limited liability company in the particular matter, and the person with whom the manager is dealing has knowledge of the fact that the manager has no such authority.

As a manager, Michael Collins had the apparent authority to bind Kanaka Rapids when he executed in its name an instrument "for

---

[3]   That statute provides:

No estate or interest in real property, other than for leases for a term not exceeding one (1) year, . . . can be created, granted . . . otherwise than by . . . a conveyance or other instrument in writing, subscribed by the party . . . or by his lawful agent thereunto authorized by writing.

apparently carrying on in the usual way [its] business or affairs." The usual business of Kanaka Rapids was to develop and sell the real estate lots. The Appellants have not pointed to any evidence showing that Michael Collins lacked the actual authority to convey the lots and that any of the Respondents had knowledge of any such lack of actual authority.

Idaho Code § 53–634(5)(a) provides, "Title to property of the limited liability company that is held in the name of the limited liability company may be transferred by an instrument of transfer executed by any manager in the name of the limited liability company." A limited liability company, not being a living being, can only act through its agents. As a manager, Michael Collins was an agent of Kanaka Rapids, and *Idaho Code § 53–634(5)(a)* granted him statutory authority to execute instruments transferring the lots to the Respondents. "It is well established that '[a] specific statute . . . controls over a more general statute when there is any conflict between the two." *Tuttle v. Wayment Farms, Inc., 131 Idaho 105, 108, 952 P.2d 1241, 1244 (1998)* (quoting *Ausman v. State, 124 Idaho 839, 842, 864 P.2d 1126, 1129 (1993)*). Thus, *Idaho Code §§ 55–601* and *9–503* do not apply insofar as they required written authorization for Michael Collins to sign the conveyances on behalf of Kanaka Rapids. . . .

IV. Conclusion

The judgment of the district court is affirmed. . . .

———

NOTES ON MEMBERS' RIGHTS

1.   Voting by Members. Just over half the statutes provide that unless otherwise agreed, members vote per capita, that is, one vote per member. The remaining statutes provide that unless otherwise agreed, members vote pro rata, that is, by financial interest. Normally, members act by a majority vote, per capita or pro rata as the case may be. However, some of the statutes require a unanimous vote for certain actions, such as an amendment of the articles or the operating agreement.

2.   Inspection of Books and Records. The statutes generally provide that members are entitled to access to the LLC's books and records or to specified books and records. Many of the statutes include an explicit provision that the inspection must be for a proper purpose. Like many other features of LLC statutes, LLC statutes authorize considerable private ordering with respect to member inspection rights. *See e.g.,* Del. Limited Liability Company Act § 18–305(a) (operating agreement or other document can set forth "reasonable standards (including standards governing information and documents") to obtain information "reasonably related to the member's interest as a member"). Kasten v. Doral Dental USA, LLC., 301 Wis. 2d 598, 733 N.W. 2d 300 (Wis. 2007) (recognizing that Wisconsin's LLC statute accords broad inspection rights to members subject to limitation by the operating agreement and holding that operating agreement's reference to "Company documents" and "records" even extended inspection to certain company emails).

    3.   Distributions. Most LLC statutes that address the issue of distributions provide that unless otherwise agreed, distributions to members are to be made pro rata according to the members' contributions. However, a number of statutes provide that in the absence of an agreement to the contrary, distributions are to be made on a per capita basis. Importantly, most LLC statutes prohibit distributions that will render the company unable to pay its bills as they mature or that will reduce its assets below its liabilities. *See e.g.,* Uniform Limited Liability Company Act § 405(a).

    4.   Members' Interests. A member of an LLC has financial rights and may also have governance rights as a member—that is, apart from any governance rights that she may have as a manager in a manager-managed LLC. A member's *financial* rights include her right to receive distributions. A member's *governance* rights include her right, if any, to participate in management, to vote on certain issues, and to be supplied with information. Most statutes define a member's interest in an LLC to consist of the member's financial rights, but some define a member's interest to include her governance rights.

    Generally speaking, a member of an LLC can freely transfer her financial rights by transferring her interest in the LLC. However, a majority of the statutes provide that a member can transfer her governance rights only with the unanimous consent of all the other members. Some statutes provide that a member can transfer her governance rights with the approval of a majority of the other members, or a majority of other members' financial interests, depending on the statute. Most statutes permit consent requirements for transfers of management interests to be varied in the articles of incorporation or operating agreement.

    It is clear that a member who assigns her interest (that is, her financial rights) normally cannot include an assignment of her governance rights unless otherwise agreed or approved by the other members, but it is not always clear whether a member who assigns her financial rights retains her governance rights. A number of statutes provide that a member who assigns her membership interest loses her membership status. Some statutes don't speak to the issue. A few provide that a member who assigns her membership interest loses her membership status if and when the assignee becomes a member. A few statutes provide that if a member assigns her membership interest, the remaining members can remove her as a member.

    If a member of an LLC assigns her interest in the LLC as a pledge to secure a debt, rather than in an outright sale, and if the creditor gets a judgment against the member based on the debt, the creditor can get a charging order against the member's interest. A charging order gives the creditor the right to the member's share of any distributions.

    More recently enacted LLC statutes permit the LLC to issue classes of ownership interests (or groups of members) so that different rights, privileges and preferences can vary across classes. *See* Delaware Limited Liability Company Act § 18–302(a).

Ott v. Monroe

Virginia Supreme Court, 2011.
282 Va. 403, 719 S.E.2d 309 (Va. 2011).

In 2003, Dewey and Lou Ann Monroe formed a Virginia LLC in which Lou Ann was the manager although having only a 20 percent membership interest (Dewey owned the remaining 80 percent). Their membership agreement provided that '[except] as provided herein, no Member shall transfer his membership or ownership, or any portion or interest thereof, to any non-Member person, without the written consent of all other Members, except by death, intestacy, devise, or otherwise by operation of law." Another provision provided "any Member . . . may transfer all or any portion of the Member's Interest at any time . . . [to] other Members [or] [t]he spouse, children or other descendants of any Member."

Dewey died in 2004. His will (executed before the LLC was formed) bequeathed his entire estate to his daughter, Janet. Janet promptly acted quickly to remove Lou Ann as manager and elected herself as the LLC's manager. Held: Va. L.L.C. Act § 13–1–1040.1(7)(a) provides that a member is disassociated from the company upon the member's death. Consequently, upon Dewey's death, only the right to share in profits and losses and to receive distributions survived and could be passed to Janet through the will. Janet was therefore a mere assignee by operation of law under Va. L.L.C. Act § 13–1–1040.2. The court held this outcome could not be changed by the operating agreement.

* * *

Ott illustrates significant surprises that can arise under early LLC statutes enacted before the IRS adopted the "check the box" approach for non-corporate entities. In that earlier era numerous restrictions were included in LLC statutes so as to clearly distinguish features of the LLC from those of a corporation. As *Ott* reflects, these features continue in less modern LLC statutes. Consider how *Ott* would be decided under the Uniform Limited Liability Company Act. *See* ULLCA §§ 602(7)(A), 603(a)(1)&(3), & 105(b)&(c). For Delaware's response, *see* Del. L.L.C. A. §§ 18–702, 18–705 & 18–1101(b).

----

2. LLCS AND THE DISTINCT ENTITY CONCEPT

A. THE ENTITY FEATURE AND ITS DISREGARD

3519–3513 Realty, LLC v. Law

Superior Court of New Jersey, Appellate Division, 2009.
406 N. J. Super. 423, 967 A.2d 954.

3519–3513 Realty, LLC ("Realty") . . . is the owner of the three-unit building located at 3513 Hudson Avenue in Union City. Isaac Rosenberg, the sole member of Realty, acquired title to the building in August 2002. In 2007, Rosenberg formed Realty and transferred title to the building to Realty. Defendants are month-to-month tenants who occupy one of the units in the building. They received a Notice to Quit terminating their tenancy as of March . . . . The ground asserted in the Notice was that Rosenberg wished to occupy the apartment himself. Defendants resisted, asserting that Realty could not invoke that section of the statute. . . .

N.J.S.A. 2A:18–61.1 limits the grounds upon which a landlord may seek to remove a tenant. *Subsection (l)(3)* of the statute permits a landlord to remove a tenant if "[t]he owner of a building of three residential units or less seeks to personally occupy a unit . . . ." Realty argues that Rosenberg, as its sole member, is entitled to invoke this subsection because he wished to live in the particular unit. . . . Defendants, on the other hand, argue that Rosenberg is not the owner of the building and that Realty, as a limited liability company, cannot personally occupy the apartment.

A court that is called upon to construe a statute should do so in light of the statute's overall purpose and policy. . . .

Here, the clear purpose of this statute is to protect residential tenants from the effects of what the Legislature has recognized to be a severe shortage of rental housing in this state. . . . Its overall purpose is to prevent the eviction of blameless tenants by limiting the permissible bases for their removal. . . .

We reject appellant's argument that the construction adopted by the trial court leads to an absurd result. Rather, were we to adopt the appellant's approach, and overlook the distinction between Realty and its member Rosenberg, we would be construing the statute in a manner at odds with its purpose because we would be expanding the universe of parties entitled to dispossess blameless tenants from their residence.

Appellant contends that the statute will be satisfied because the unit will continue to be used for residential purposes. That, however, is not dispositive. We cannot so easily disregard the fact that Rosenberg is not the owner of the building; his limited liability company is the owner. . . .

Finally, appellant contends that adopting the trial court's construction unreasonably requires expenditure of money and time to transfer the property back to Rosenberg's name, individually, with the accompanying risk of incurring personal liability. While not unsympathetic to the dilemma posed, we are not free to relieve Rosenberg of the consequences which flow from the considered choices he earlier made.

Affirmed.

————

GreenHunter Energy, Inc. v. W. Ecosystems Tech., Inc.

Supreme Court of Wyoming, 2014.
2014 WY 144; 337 P.3d 454.

■ DAVIS, JUSTICE.

Appellant GreenHunter Energy, Inc. is the sole member of a limited liability company, GreenHunter Wind Energy, LLC (LLC). It appeals from a district court decision piercing the LLC's veil to hold it liable for the LLC's contractual obligations to Appellee Western Echosystems Technology, Inc. (Western). . . .

In 2009, Appellee Western and the LLC entered into a contract whereby Western undertook to provide the LLC consulting services related to the potential development of a wind turbine farm in Platte County, Wyoming. While Western performed under the contract, the LLC paid nothing for Western's services. Western consequently brought a breach of contract action against the LLC and obtained a judgment in the amount of $43,646.10. . . . The judgments cannot be satisfied because the LLC has no assets upon which Western can execute.

. . . Western brought this action against Appellant, the sole member of the LLC, seeking to pierce the LLC's veil and hold Appellant liable for the LLC's contractual obligations. . . .

At trial, Western argued that Appellant was the LLC's alter ego and presented evidence, much of it uncontroverted, that it felt proved as much. Western was able to demonstrate that the LLC is a wholly-owned subsidiary of Appellant, the latter being the sole member and manager of the former. The LLC consistently carried an operating capital balance which was insufficient to cover its debts, and on numerous occasions its account had a balance of zero. Western showed that Appellant decided when and how much money to advance to the LLC to allow it to pay its accounts payable. Therefore Appellant, as the sole source of operating funds for the LLC, decided which of its creditors would be paid. Although Appellant advanced funds to permit the LLC to pay some creditors, it did not transfer any funds to allow the LLC to pay Western.

Western was also able to show that the LLC did not have employees of its own, but that employees of Appellant performed services for and on behalf of the LLC, including negotiation of wind farm leases and other agreements. The LLC's chairman and general counsel held the same positions with Appellant.

Western also established that Appellant and the LLC have the same business address. All bookkeeping and financial management of the LLC were performed by employees of Appellant . . .

For its part, Appellant presented evidence . . such as certain LLC filings with Wyoming's Secretary of State and the LLC's general ledger from 2007 through 2011. These documents tended to demonstrate that the two entities were detached, and that they maintained separate accounts.

The district court . . . pierced the LLC's veil and awarded a judgment of $45,807.94 against Appellant for the amount the LLC had not paid under its contract with Western . . . .

In order to determine how to approach piercing in this case involving a limited liability company, we begin by studying the development of the law governing business organizations. . . .

Because of the formalities required of corporations, and the tax treatment of their earnings, new types of business entities were conceived. In 1977, Wyoming enacted a statute that allowed the creation of limited liability companies. . . . [In 2010, Wyoming amended the act].

The new Act provides limited liability companies with even more flexibility. For example, it eliminated prior provisions dealing with a one-member "flexible limited liability company," and it allowed any limited liability company to simply be formed with a single member. Wyo. Stat. Ann. § 17–29–401. The single member is allowed to manage the company by statutory design. *See* Wyo. Stat. Ann. § 17–29–102(a)(x), (xi), (xiii); § 17–29–407. The 2010 Act . . . [provides]:

> (b) The failure of a limited liability company to observe any particular formalities relating to the exercise of its powers or management of its activities is not a ground for imposing liability on the members or managers for the debts, obligations or other liabilities of the company.

Wyo. Stat. Ann. § 17–29–304.

The language of § 17–29–304 is clear. . . . Failure of a limited liability company to adhere to the formalities required of a corporation is not a basis for disregarding the company in an action seeking to pierce its veil. By passing the 2010 Act, the legislature determined that even greater flexibility and informality are acceptable features of a limited liability company. . . . Additional provisions of the 2010 Act confirm that there are relatively few statutorily mandated formalities in order to allow significant freedom and flexibility in the management structure and operation of the company. . . .

 . . . We must now determine what test should be applied under the 2010 Act, and what factors may be considered in determining whether to pierce the veil of a limited liability company, which "is an entity distinct from its members." Wyo. Stat. Ann. § 17–29–104(a).

After a solicitous study of this Court's precedent, the legislative developments, and authority outside our borders, we conclude that . . . [t]he veil of a limited liability company may be pierced under exceptional circumstances when: (1) the limited liability company is not only owned, influenced and governed by its members, but the required separateness has ceased to exist due to misuse of the limited liability company; and (2) the facts are such that an adherence to the fiction of its separate existence would, under the particular circumstances, lead to injustice, fundamental unfairness, or inequity. . . .

This test is fact-driven and flexible, and it focuses on whether the limited liability company has been operated as a separate entity as contemplated by statute, or whether the member has instead misused the entity in an inequitable manner to injure the plaintiff. . . .

Undercapitalization

. . . The district court did not rely solely on undercapitalization to determine that piercing the veil was warranted. Rather, undercapitalization was one of several factors it considered in the totality of the circumstances of this case . . . [T]he evidence supports the district court's findings that:

> In early 2009, LLC and [Western] entered into a Professional Services Contract, wherein [Western] contracted to provide consulting services to LLC relating to a wind energy project in Platte County, Wyoming . . . . On June 8, 2009 [Western] submitted Invoice # 28355 to LLC in the amount of $5,022.85. As of June 9, 2009, LLC did not have any funds within its operating account. [Western] submitted subsequent invoices to LLC, which went unpaid. During the periods when these invoices were submitted to LLC, LLC often had $0.00 balances in its operating account and received periodic money transfers from [Appellant]. [Appellant] has at all times maintained the sole discretion to decide when funds would be transferred to LLC, to decide the amount of money that would be transferred to LLC, and to decide which bills of LLC would be paid with transferred monies. When [Appellant] stopped providing money transfers to LLC, LLC became insolvent and was unable to pay creditors, including [Western].

Our review of the record confirms the accuracy of the district court's finding that during the periods when Western's invoices were submitted to the LLC, it often had no money in its operating account, and that it received periodic money transfers from Appellant, which decided how much money would be transferred to the LLC to pay specific bills it decided to pay, and when. . . .

Based upon these facts, and other evidence introduced at trial, the district court correctly concluded that Appellant "failed to adequately capitalize LLC, that LLC was undercapitalized at all times relevant to this suit, and that LLC lacks corporate assets."

Appellant correctly points out that start-up companies, new business ventures, and early stage companies sometimes may not have initial capital or income sufficient to cover their expenses, and that they do in fact require periodic capital infusions from members to meet their financial obligations. However, in this case, the evidence supports the district court's finding that the LLC had inadequate capital due to manipulation by its member, a publicly traded corporation, and that Appellant used its position to control "the amount of money that would be transferred to LLC, and to decide which bills of LLC would be paid with transferred monies." Put another way, the LLC was continually undercapitalized by choice, not by external forces . . . .

Intermingling of business and finances

Appellant also asserts that the district court misunderstood the factor of intermingling business and finances between it and the LLC, and the court therefore misapplied the law to the evidence. It contends the district court should have focused solely on "whether or not Appellant and the LLC maintained separate accounting, bank accounts, accounts payable, accounts receivable, and could clearly demonstrate such distinction."

Appellant and the LLC did maintain separate bank accounts and business records. If the analysis could end there, Appellant would have a convincing case. However, Appellant's argument ignores other facets of this factor which must be considered . . . . [T]he district court found the following with respect to intermingling:

- The overlap between the LLC's and Appellant's ownership, membership and management was considerable and to an extent such that, when considered with other factors, piercing was appropriate. Appellant and the LLC utilized Appellant's accounting department, and in fact the same accountants managed the finances of both entities. They had the same business address and creditors of the LLC mailed their invoice to Appellant's address for processing. The LLC's tax returns were consolidated with the tax returns of Appellant.

- The LLC did not have any employees who were independent of Appellant; rather, all of the LLC's functions were carried out by employees of Appellant. Employees of Appellant negotiated and entered into contracts on behalf of the LLC, and these same individuals decided which of the LLC's creditors to pay through contributions from Appellant.

- Appellant assigned its own employees to perform work of the LLC, and although Appellant "charged" the LLC for the labor performed by Appellant's personnel, Appellant directly paid its employees for that work.

- The LLC had no revenue separate from Appellant. Funds were commingled in the sense that the LLC's bills that Appellant wanted paid were settled with Appellant's funds which were "passed through" the LLC by periodic transfers. A particular bill was paid only if and when when Appellant decided to transfer funds to pay it.

- The LLC entered into an agreement with Western to procure services for the purpose of supporting and benefitting Appellant's business. . . .

- Appellant manipulated the assets and liabilities in a manner such that Appellant improperly reaped all of the rewards and benefits of the LLC's activities, while simultaneously saddling the LLC with all of its losses and liabilities, including the unpaid bills for services rendered by Western. . . .

Based upon this, and other evidence in the record, the LLC was not only owned, influenced and governed by Appellant, but the entities had ceased to be separate due to Appellant's misuse of the LLC. Furthermore, the facts are such that adherence to the fiction of the LLC's separate existence would, under these particular circumstances, lead to an unjust and inequitable result. We conclude that the district court's findings of fact were not clearly erroneous and did not otherwise err in applying those findings to the law. . . .

Fraud

We have made it clear that a showing of fraud or an intent to defraud is not necessary to disregard the legal fiction of a separate entity. . . . Our analysis could therefore stop here. However, the district court also found that Appellant's "course of conduct, which was executed in the name of the LLC, wherein it engaged and contracted with [Western] for valuable services knowing that it could not or would not pay [Western's] bill when received, constitutes a fraud that should not enjoy protection" behind the veil of limited liability. . . .

While not a prerequisite for piercing a limited liability company's veil, fraud can be a powerful reason to do so. . . .

Appellant argues, *inter alia*, that Western failed to present any evidence of fraud, or the intention by Appellant to commit any fraud, and the district court erred by inferring fraud from the facts of the case. We agree with Appellant on this point.

The elements of fraud have been clearly set forth by this Court, and we have explained that the facts supporting those elements must be alleged clearly and distinctly, and proven by clear and convincing evidence.

The elements of a claim for relief for fraud are a false representation made by the defendant which is relied upon by the plaintiff to his damage, the asserted false representation must be made to induce action, and the plaintiff must reasonably believe the representation to be true. A plaintiff who alleges fraud must do so clearly and distinctly, and fraud will not be imputed to any party when the facts and circumstances out of which it is alleged to arise are consistent with honesty and purity of intention. Fraud must be established by clear, unequivocal and convincing evidence, and will never be presumed.

White v. Shane Edeburn Constr., 285 P.3d 949, 957 (quotation marks omitted).

There is no evidence that Appellant made false statements that Western relied upon in entering into the contract with the LLC or in continuing to perform services thereunder. . . . The parties simply entered into an agreement that Western trusted would be performed by the LLC, and it was not.

However, we believe the district court instinctively applied the test we have set forth above, although it used the term "fraud." It found that Appellant misused the LLC in order to improperly manipulate the situation to avoid paying for services which benefitted it, that it failed to maintain adequate separation, and that to allow it to do so would be unjust and inequitable. Thus, even though there was no fraud in the classic and technical sense, the district court's decision to pierce the LLC's veil . . . was legally correct . . . .

———

The Uniform Limited Liability Act § 304(b) includes the following provision that is common in most states:

> The failure of a limited liability company to observe any particular formalities relating to the exercise of its powers or management of its activities is not a ground for imposing liability on the members or managers for the debts, obligations, or other liabilities of the company.

How much comfort does the above provision provide dominant members of an LLC in their conduct of the company's affairs? *See e.g.,* Kubican v. Tavern, 232 W.Va. 268, 752 S.E.2d 299 (2013).

———

B. SUITS ON BEHALF OF THE LLC

Most of the statutes explicitly permit members of LLCs to bring derivative actions on the LLC's behalf, based on a breach of fiduciary duties. *See e.g.,* Del. L. L. C. Act § 18–1001; U.L.L.C. Act § 902. *Tzolis v. Wolff,* 10 N.Y. 3d 100, 855 N.Y.S.2d 6, 884 N.E.2d 1005 (N.Y. 2008), recognized that members have a right to initiate a derivative suit on behalf of the LLC, despite the statute not expressly providing for such a suit, reasoning:

> In addressing the question, we continue to heed the realization that influenced Chancellor Walworth in 1832, and Lord Hardwicke 90 years earlier: When fiduciaries are faithless to their trust, the victims must not be left wholly without a remedy. As Lord Hardwicke put it, to "determine that frauds of this kind are out of the reach of courts of law or equity" would lead to "an intolerable grievance" (*Charitable Corp. v. Sutton*, 2 Atk at 406).

> To hold that there is no remedy when corporate fiduciaries use corporate assets to enrich themselves was unacceptable in 1742 and in 1832, and it is still unacceptable today. Derivative suits are not the only possible remedy, but they are the one that has been recognized for most of two centuries, and to abolish them in the LLC context would be a radical step.

> . . . Several courts have held that there is no derivative remedy for LLC members. . . . But since the Legislature obviously did not intend to give corporate fiduciaries a license to steal, a substitute remedy must be devised. Perhaps responding to this need, some courts have held that members of an LLC have their own, direct claims against fiduciaries for conduct that injured the LLC—blurring, if not erasing, the traditional line between direct and derivative claims. . . . Similarly, Supreme Court's decision in this case upheld several of plaintiffs' claims that are not in issue here, characterizing the claims as direct, though they might well be derivative under traditional analysis (*see generally*, Kleinberger, *Direct Versus Derivative and The Law of Limited Liability Companies*, 58 Baylor L Rev 63 [2006]).

> Substituting direct remedies of LLC members for the old-fashioned derivative suit—a substitution not suggested by anything in the language of the Limited Liability Company Law—raises unanswered questions. Suppose, for example, a corporate fiduciary steals a hundred dollars from the treasury of an LLC. Unquestionably he or she is liable to the LLC for a hundred dollars, a liability which could be enforced in a suit by the LLC itself. Is the same fiduciary also liable to each injured LLC member in a direct suit for the member's share of the same money? What, if anything, is to be done to prevent double liability? No doubt, if the Legislature had indeed abolished the derivative suit as far as LLCs are concerned, we could and would answer these questions and others like them. But we will not readily conclude that the Legislature intended to set us on this uncharted path. . . .

[C]ourts have repeatedly recognized derivative suits in the absence of express statutory authorization (*Robinson v. Smith*, 3 Paige Ch 222 [1832]; *Klebanow v. New York Produce Exch.*, 344 F2d 294 [2d Cir 1965]; *Riviera Congress Assoc. v. Yassky*, 18 NY2d 540 [1966]). In light of this, it could hardly be argued that the mere absence of authorizing language in the Limited Liability Company Law bars the courts from entertaining derivative suits by LLC members. . . .

The LLC poses difficult jurisdictional issues when suits are brought in the federal court on the basis of diversity of citizenship. In determining the citizenship of an LLC, it is the citizenship of its members and not the state in which the LLC is formed or has its principal place of business (as it is with a corporation); and, if one of the LLC's members is itself an LLC, the citizenship of that LLC is determined by the citizenship of its own members. *See* D.B. Zwirn Special Opportunities Fund, L.P. v. Mehrotra, 661 F.3d 124, 126–27 (1st Cir. 2011).

Elf Atochem North America, Inc. v. Jaffari
Supreme Court of Delaware, 1999.
727 A.2d 286, 293–295.

[The members of Malek LLC agreed in writing that any action against a member brought by a member must be submitted to arbitration in San Francisco, California. Elf initiated direct and derivative suits in Delaware against fellow member Jafari, alleging he had misappropriated funds and business opportunities of the LLC. Jafari moved to dismiss the suit on the ground that their agreement required disputes by a member to be submitted to an arbitrator in California. Elf replied that the agreement only referred to suits by a member. He further argued that since the derivative suit was on behalf of the LLC, and because the LLC was not itself a party to the members' agreement, the derivative suit was outside the choice of forum and agreement to arbitrate.]

Notwithstanding Malek LLC's failure to sign the Agreement, Elf's claims are subject to the arbitration and forum selection clauses of the Agreement. The Act is a statute designed to permit members maximum flexibility in entering into an agreement to govern their relationship. It is the members who are the real parties in interest. The LLC is simply their joint business vehicle. This is the contemplation of the statute in prescribing the outlines of a limited liability company agreement.

Classification by Elf of its Claims as Derivative is Irrelevant

Elf argues that the Court of Chancery erred in failing to classify its claims against Malek LLC as derivative. Elf contends that, had the court properly characterized its claims as derivative instead of direct, the arbitration and forum selection clauses would not have applied to bar adjudication in Delaware. . . .

Although Elf correctly points out that Delaware law allows for derivative suits against management of an LLC, Elf contracted away its right to bring such an action in Delaware and agreed instead to dispute resolution in California. That is, Section 13.8 of the Agreement specifically provides that the parties *(i.e.,* Elf) agree to institute "no action at law or in equity based upon *any* claim arising out of or related to this Agreement" except an action to compel arbitration or to enforce an arbitration award.[42] Furthermore, under Section 13.7 of the Agreement, each member *(i.e.,* Elf) "consented to the exclusive jurisdiction of the state and federal courts sitting in California in *any* action on a claim arising out of, under or in connection with this Agreement or the transactions contemplated by this Agreement."

. . . [T]he Agreement . . . [does] not distinguish between direct and derivative claims. They simply state that the members may not initiate *any* claims outside of California. Elf initiated this action in the Court of Chancery in contravention of its own contractual agreement. As a result, the Court of Chancery correctly held that all claims, whether derivative or direct, arose under, out of or in connection with the Agreement, and thus are covered by the arbitration and forum selection clauses.

This prohibition is so broad that it is dispositive of Elf's claims . . .

The Court of Chancery was correct in holding that Elf's claims bear directly on Jaffari's duties and obligations under the Agreement. Thus, we decline to disturb its holding.

———

3. FIDUCIARY DUTIES

The fiduciary duties of managers and members of LLCs are largely unspecified by the LLC statutes. Presumably, in deciding LLC cases involving fiduciary duties the courts will borrow from the corporate and partnership case-law.

Despite the lack of extensive specification, the LLC statutes, like the corporate and partnership statutes, do include important provisions concerning particular issues of fiduciary duty. For example, most although not all of the statutes specify the elements of the duty of care. Some statutes provide that a manager will be liable only for gross negligence, bad faith, recklessness, or equivalent conduct. Others require a manager to act as would a prudent person in similar circumstances.

About two-thirds of the LLC statutes provide a mechanism for the authorization of self-interested transactions by disinterested managers or members. Of particular importance is that many of the LLC statutes permit the operating agreement to limit or define the scope of certain fiduciary duties. *See e.g.,* Delaware Limited Liability Company Act § 18–1101(e); Uniform Limited Liability Company Act § 110(b)&(d). Although most statues generally prohibit a waiver of the duty of good faith, they do authorize the operating agreement to prescribe standards for assessing whether performance is in good faith and constitutes fair dealing. Uniform Limited Liability Company Act § 110(d)(5).

Salm v. Feldstein
Supreme Court, Appellate Division, New York, 2005.
20 A.D.3d 469, 799 N.Y.S.2d 104.

In an action to recover damages for breach of fiduciary duty and fraud, the plaintiff appeals from a judgment of the Supreme Court . . . granting the defendant's motion for summary judgment. . . .

ORDERED that the judgment is reversed, on the law, with costs. . . .

The plaintiff and the defendant were the members of World Wide Automotive, LLC (hereinafter the company), a limited liability company that owned an automobile dealership (hereinafter the dealership), each having an equal financial interest in the company. The defendant was the managing member of the company. On June 2, 2003, the defendant purchased the plaintiff's membership interest in the company under a redemption and settlement agreement (hereinafter the contract) providing for a payment to the plaintiff in the sum of $3,750,000, and a consulting contract with the plaintiff which would pay him a five-year aggregate sum of $1,350,000. On June 4, 2003, the defendant sold the dealership to a nonparty for the sum of $16 million.

The plaintiff commenced this action against the defendant to recover damages for breach of fiduciary duty and fraud. The plaintiff alleged that the defendant misrepresented the value of the dealership as being between $5 and $6 million and failed to disclose that the nonparty purchaser had made a firm offer to purchase the dealership for the sum of $16 million before May 31, 2003. The defendant moved for summary judgment dismissing the complaint and the plaintiff cross-moved to compel discovery. The Supreme Court granted the motion and denied the cross motion. We reverse.

As the managing member of the company and as a co-member with the plaintiff, the defendant owed the plaintiff a fiduciary duty to make full disclosure of all material facts (*see Birnbaum v. Birnbaum,* 73 N.Y.2d

461, 465, 541 N.Y.S.2d 746, 539 N.E.2d 574, *citing Meinhard v. Salmon,* 249 N.Y. 458, 468, 164 N.E. 545; *Blue Chip Emerald v. Allied Partners,* 299 A.D.2d 278, 750 N.Y.S.2d 291). Moreover, because the defendant had a fiduciary relationship with the plaintiff, the disclaimers contained in the contract, upon which the defendant relies, did not relieve him of the obligation of full disclosure (*see Blue Chip Emerald v. Allied Partners, supra*). Although the defendant denies the plaintiff's allegation that he failed to keep the plaintiff informed of all communications with the nonparty purchaser, the alacrity with which the dealership was sold after the plaintiff conveyed his interest in the company to the defendant was sufficient to establish "that facts essential to justify opposition may exist but cannot then be stated" (CPLR 3212[f]). The defendant's motion for summary judgment should, therefore, have been denied. . . .

———

Compare. Pappas v. Tzolis, 20 N.Y.3d 228, 233, 958 N.Y.S.2d 656, 660, 982 N.E.2d 576, 579 (N.Y. 2012). Pappas, Ifantopulos and Tzolis formed Vrahos LLC for the purpose of operating a long-term lease on a building in Manhattan. They agreed that Vrahos would sublease the property, its sole asset, to Tzolis. A few months later, Tzolis suggested that Pappas and Ifantopoulos sell their interest to Tzolis, explaining that he preferred to take over the prime lease and thereby avoid making further rental payments. Negotiations ensued, resulting in a buyout whereby Tzolis paid $1.5 million for their interests in the LLC. The sale agreement provided that "each of the undersigned Sellers . . . has performed their [sic] own due diligence in connection with such assignments. Each of the undersigned Sellers has engaged its own legal counsel, and is not relying on any representation by Steve Tzolis or any of his agents or representatives. . . ." Six months after the assignment, Tzolis assigned the lease to Extell Development Company for $17.5 million. Pappas and Ifantopoulos brought suit, alleging that Tzolis had breached his fiduciary duty to them; through their post-sale efforts they learned that Tzolis had begun negotiating with Extell before their sale to Tzolis had closed.

The Superior Court dismissed the case and the Appellate Division reversed, holding Tzolis had breached his fiduciary duty to keep them informed of any and all opportunities he was pursuing. With respect to the non-reliance clause in their agreement, the court held that Tzolis had an overriding duty to disclose his dealings with Extell before they signed the agreement. On appeal, the New York Court of Appeals reversed and dismissed the complaint:

> Here, plaintiffs were sophisticated businessmen represented by counsel. Moreover, plaintiffs' own allegations make it clear that at the time of the buyout, the relationship between the parties was not one of trust, and reliance on Tzolis's representations as a fiduciary would not have been reasonable. According to plaintiffs, there had been numerous business disputes, between Tzolis and them, concerning the sublease.

Both the complaint and Pappas's affidavit opposing the motion to dismiss portray Tzolis as uncooperative and intransigent in the face of plaintiffs' preferences concerning the sublease. The relationship between plaintiffs and Tzolis had become antagonistic, to the extent that plaintiffs could no longer reasonably regard Tzolis as trustworthy. Therefore, crediting plaintiffs' allegations, the release contained in the Certificate is valid, and plaintiffs cannot prevail on their cause of action alleging breach of fiduciary duty.

Practically speaking, it is clear that plaintiffs were in a position to make a reasoned judgment about whether to agree to the sale of their interests to Tzolis. The need to use care to reach an independent assessment of the value of the lease should have been obvious to plaintiffs, given that Tzolis offered to buy their interests for 20 times what they had paid for them just a year earlier.

VGS, Inc. v. Castiel

Court of Chancery of Delaware.
2000 WL 1277372.

■ STEELE, VICE CHANCELLOR. . . .

I. Facts

David Castiel formed Virtual Geosatellite LLC (the "LLC") on January 6, 1999 in order to pursue a Federal Communications Commission ("FCC") license to build and operate a satellite system which its proponents claim could dramatically increase the "real estate" in outer space capable of transmitting high speed internet traffic and other communications. When originally formed, it had only one Member— Virtual Geosatellite Holdings, Inc. ("Holdings"). On January 8, 1999, Ellipso, Inc. ("Ellipso") joined the LLC as its second Member. Several weeks later, on January 29, 1999, Sahagen Satellite Technology Group LLC ("Sahagen Satellite") became the third Member of the LLC.

David Castiel controls both Holdings and Ellipso. Peter Sahagen, an aggressive and apparently successful venture capitalist, controls Sahagen Satellite.

Pursuant to the LLC Agreement, Holdings received 660 units (representing 63.46% of the total equity in the LLC), Sahagen Satellite received 260 units (representing 25%), and Ellipso received 120 units (representing 11.54%). The founders vested management of the LLC in a Board of Managers. As the majority unitholder, Castiel had the power to appoint, remove, and replace two of the three members of the Board of Managers. Castiel, therefore, had the power to prevent any Board decision with which he disagreed. Castiel named himself and Tom Quinn to the Board of Managers. Sahagen named himself as the third member of the Board.

Not long after the formation of the LLC, Castiel and Sahagen were at odds. . . .

Sahagen ultimately convinced Quinn that Castiel must be ousted from leadership in order for the LLC to prosper. As a result, Quinn (Castiel's nominee) covertly "defected" to Sahagen's camp, and he and Sahagen decided to wrest control of the LLC from Castiel. . . .

On April 14, 2000, without notice to Castiel, Quinn and Sahagen acted by written consent to merge the LLC under Delaware law into VGS, Inc. ("VGS"), a Delaware corporation. Accordingly, the LLC ceased to exist, its assets and liabilities passed to VGS, and VGS became the LLC's legal successor-in-interest. VGS's Board of Directors is comprised of Sahagen, Quinn, and Neel Howard. Of course, the incorporators did not name Castiel to VGS's Board.

On the day of the merger, Sahagen executed a promissory note to VGS in the amount of $10 million plus interest. In return, he received two million shares of VGS Series A Preferred Stock. VGS also issued 1,269,200 shares of common stock to Holdings, 230,800 shares of common stock to Ellipso, and 500,000 shares of common stock to Sahagen Satellite. Once one does the math, it is apparent that Holdings and Ellipso went from having a 75% controlling combined ownership interest in the LLC to having only a 37.5% interest in VGS. On the other hand, Sahagen and Sahagen Satellite went from owning 25% of the LLC to owning 62.5% of VGS.

There can be no doubt why Sahagen and Quinn, acting as a majority of the LLC's board of managers did not notify Castiel of the merger plan. Notice to Castiel would have immediately resulted in Quinn's removal from the board and a newly constituted majority which would thwart the effort to strip Castiel of control. Had he known in advance, Castiel surely would have attempted to replace Quinn with someone loyal to Castiel who would agree with his views. Clandestine machinations were, therefore, essential to the success of Quinn and Sahagen's plan.

II. Analysis . . .

. . . Section 18–404(d) of the LLC Act states in pertinent part:

> Unless otherwise provided in a limited liability company agreement, on any matter that is to be voted on by managers, the managers may take such action without a meeting, without prior notice and without a vote if a consent or consents in writing, setting forth the action so taken, shall be signed by the managers having not less than the minimum number of votes that would be necessary to authorize such action at a meeting (emphasis added).

Therefore, the LLC Act, read literally, does not require notice to Castiel before Sahagen and Quinn could act by written consent. The LLC Agreement does not purport to modify the statute in this regard. . . .

Section 18–404(d) has yet to be interpreted by this Court or the Supreme Court. Nonetheless, it seems clear that the purpose of permitting action by written consent without notice is to enable LLC managers to take quick, efficient action in situations where a minority of managers could not block or adversely affect the course set by the majority even if they were notified of the proposed action and objected to it. The General Assembly never intended, I am quite confident, to enable two managers to deprive, clandestinely and surreptitiously, a third manager representing the majority interest in the LLC of an opportunity to protect that interest by taking an action that the third manager's member would surely have opposed if he had knowledge of it. My reading of Section 18–404(d) is grounded in a classic maxim of equity—"Equity looks to the intent rather than to the form." In this hopefully unique situation, this application of the maxim requires construction of the statute to allow action without notice only by a constant or fixed majority. It can not apply to an illusory, will-of-the wisp majority which would implode should notice be given. Nothing in the statute suggests that this court of equity should blind its eyes to a shallow, too clever by half, manipulative attempt to restructure an enterprise through an action taken by a "majority" that existed only so long as it could act in secrecy.

Sahagen and Quinn each owed a duty of loyalty to the LLC, its investors and Castiel, their fellow manager. Castiel or his entities owned a majority interest in the LLC and he sat as a member of the board representing entities and interests empowered by the Agreement to control the majority membership of the board. The majority investor protected his equity interest in the LLC through the mechanism of appointment to the board rather than by the statutorily sanctioned mechanism of approval by members owning a majority of the LLC's equity interests. It may seem somewhat incongruous, but this Agreement allows the action to merge, dissolve or change to corporate status to be taken by a simple majority vote of the board of managers rather than rely upon the default position of the statute which requires a majority vote of the equity interest. Instead the drafters made the critical assumption, known to all the players here, that the holder of the majority equity interest has the right to appoint and remove two managers, ostensibly guaranteeing control over a three member board. When Sahagen and Quinn, fully recognizing that this was Castiel's protection against actions adverse to his majority interest, acted in secret, without notice, they failed to discharge their duty of loyalty to him in good faith. They owed Castiel a duty to give him prior notice even if he would have interfered with a plan that they conscientiously believed to be in the best interest of the LLC. Instead, they launched a preemptive strike that furtively converted Castiel's controlling interest in the LLC to a minority interest in VGS without affording Castiel a level playing field on which to defend his interest. "[Another] traditional maxim of equity holds that equity regards and treats that as done which in good conscience ought to be done." In good conscience, under these circumstances, Sahagen and Quinn should have given Castiel prior notice.

Many hours were spent at trial focusing on contentions that Castiel has proved to be an ineffective leader in whom employees and investors have lost confidence. . . . But the issue of who is best suited to run the LLC should not be resolved here but in board meetings where all managers are present and all members appropriately represented, and/or in future litigation, if it unfortunately becomes necessary. . . .

III. Conclusion

For the reasons stated above, I find that a majority vote of the LLC's Board of Managers could properly effect a merger. But, I also find that Sahagen and Quinn failed to discharge their duty of loyalty to Castiel in good faith by failing to give him advance notice of their merger plans under the unique circumstances of this case and the structure of this LLC Agreement. Accordingly, I declare that the acts taken to merge the LLC into VGS, Inc. to be invalid and the merger is ordered rescinded. An order consistent with this opinion, resolving the current claims of the parties is attached . . .

———

Solar Cells, Inc. v. True North Partners, LLC

Court of Chancery of Delaware.
2002 WL 749163.

■ CHANDLER, J.

This action concerns the proposed merger of defendant First Solar, LLC ("First Solar" or the "Company") with and into First Solar Operating, LLC ("FSO"), the wholly-owned operating subsidiary of First Solar Ventures, LLC ("FSV"). The plaintiff, Solar Cells, Inc. ("Solar Cells"), alleges that the individual defendant managers of First Solar,[1] acting at the direction of defendant True North Partners, LLC ("True North" and, collectively, "the defendants"), acted in bad faith in approving the proposed merger and that the defendants will be unable to prove the entire fairness of that merger.

On March 13, 2002, Solar Cells filed a motion for a temporary restraining order requesting that this Court enjoin the proposed merger. . . .

---

[1]   The individual defendants are First Solar Managers elected by True North: Michael J. Ahearn ("Ahearn"), Michael L. Pierce ("Pierce"), and Michael Gallagher ("Gallagher").

I. BACKGROUND FACTS

Solar Cells, an Ohio corporation, was founded in 1987 by Harold A. McMaster ("McMaster") to develop, design, and manufacture products and processes for photovoltaic electricity generation-technology commonly referred to as "solar power." . . .

McMaster designed technologies and processes for manufacturing photovoltaic cells making use of heretofore-unknown techniques that were predicted to revolutionize the solar power industry. . . . True North, an Arizona limited liability company, was brought in to provide needed financing. Solar Cells and True North formed First Solar as a Delaware limited liability company in February 1999 to commercialize McMaster's solar technology.

First Solar is managed pursuant to the Operating Agreement of First Solar, LLC ("Operating Agreement"). The Operating Agreement required Solar Cells to contribute patented and proprietary technology— valued in the Operating Agreement at $35 million—to First Solar. True North was to contribute $35 million in capital to First Solar and, also pursuant to the Operating Agreement, was required to, and did, loan First Solar an additional $8 million. In return for their contributions, Solar Cells and [True North] each received 4,500 of First Solar's Class A membership units. Solar Cells also received 100% of First Solar's Class B membership units.[4] The business and affairs of First Solar is conducted by five Managers. The Operating Agreement permits True North to elect three of those Managers (the "True North Managers") and Solar Cells to elect the remaining two Managers (the "Solar Cells Managers"). It is undisputed that, since its inception, First Solar has been managed by True North.

First Solar's continuing development and manufacturing expenditures, as well as its inability to produce a marketable product, eventually depleted the Company's initial funding. By early 2001 it became apparent that continued operations would require additional funding. To this end, in March 2001, First Solar retained investment banker Adams, Harkness & Hill, Inc. ("AHH") to find a strategic investor for the Company. In order for the Company to continue operating while AHH searched for a strategic investor, True North agreed to make an additional $15 million loan to First Solar.

The Loan Agreement between First Solar and True North bundled True North's original $8 million loan and the new $15 million loan and represented a funding commitment by True North of up to a total of $23 million through December 31, 2001. Upon either the receipt of outside investment or at the end of its funding commitment, the Loan Agreement gave True North the option of converting some or all of the loan amount

---

[4]   According to the Operating Agreement, Class A Units had voting rights, and Class B Units had no voting rights.

into Class A Units of First Solar[5] or to retain the investment as a loan with liquidation preferences. . . .

From December 2001 through March 2002, the parties engaged in unsuccessful negotiations regarding different alternatives for financing and restructuring First Solar. On March 5, 2002, True North purported to convert $250,000 of its outstanding loans to First Solar into Class A Units at a conversion ratio based on a January 8, 2002 AHH valuation of First Solar at $32,000,000. On March 7, 2002, the True North Managers executed a written consent approving the challenged merger of First Solar into FSO, a Delaware limited liability company wholly owned by True North. On March 11, 2002, Solar Cells received notice of the proposed merger, which was scheduled to close on March 15, 2002, and the terms of that merger. In connection with the merger, True North would convert its remaining outstanding loans into equity at the same ratio as the March 5, 2002 conversion. The merger would occur based on a total valuation of First Solar at $32 million with First Solar ownership units being exchanged for ownership units of the surviving company. The end result of the merger-related transactions would be that Solar Cells would go from owning 50% of the Class A Units of First Solar to owning 5% of the membership units of the surviving company. On March 13, 2002, Solar Cells filed a complaint and request for temporary restraining order enjoining consummation of the proposed merger. True North agreed not to cause its Managers to close the merger before this Court's decision on Solar Cells' motion for a preliminary injunction filed in response to that agreement. . . .

IV. ANALYSIS

A. Likelihood of Success on the Merits

The defendants argue that all of the actions taken in connection with the proposed merger were clearly authorized by the Operating Agreement. They further argue that the Operating Agreement limited any fiduciary duties owed by True North Managers. Section 4.18(a) of the Operating Agreement provides, in relevant part:

> Solar Cells and [First Solar] acknowledge that the True North Managers have fiduciary obligations to both [First Solar] and to True North, which fiduciary obligations may, because of the ability of the True North Managers to control [First Solar] and its business, create a conflict of interest or a potential conflict of interest for the true North Managers. Both [First Solar] and Solar Cells hereby waive any such conflict of interest or potential conflict of interest and agree that neither True North nor any True North Manager shall have any liability to [First Solar] or to Solar Cells with respect to any such conflict of interest or potential conflict of interest, provided that the True

---

[5] The loan was convertible either at the same value as AHH proposed to outside investors or at a "conversion ratio" specified in the Loan Agreement.

North managers have acted in a manner which they believe in good faith to be in the best interest of [First Solar].

I note that this clause purports to limit *liability* stemming from any conflict of interest. Solar Cells has not requested that this Court impose liability on the individual defendants. It is currently only seeking to *enjoin* the proposed merger. Therefore, exculpation for personal liability has no bearing on the likelihood that Solar Cells would be successful on the merits of its contention that the proposed merger is inequitable and should be enjoined. Even if waiver of liability for engaging in conflicting interest transactions is contracted for, that does not mean that there is a waiver of all fiduciary duties to Solar Cells. Indeed, § 4.18(a) expressly states that the True North Managers must act in "good faith." It is undisputed that First Solar was, and is, in financial distress. Months of unsuccessful negotiations have been ongoing in an attempt to come to an agreement as to how to remedy that situation. On March 6, 2002, the full Board of Managers met and the True North Managers made no mention of the planned merger. The *very next day,* March 7, 2002, the three True North Managers met and by written consent approved the proposed merger. No effort was made to inform the Solar Cells Managers that this action was contemplated, or imminent, when those facts were surely known at the time of the March 6 meeting.[8] At the earliest, Solar Cells was given notice of the fact, and terms, of the proposed merger (which were presented as a *fait accompli*) via facsimile on March 8, 2002—a week before consummation of a merger that will apparently reduce Solar Cells' interest from 50% to 5%. These actions do not appear to be those of fiduciaries acting in good faith. As the Supreme Court and this Court have made clear, it is not an unassailable defense to say that what was done was in technical compliance with the law.[9] The facts before me make it likely, in my opinion, that the defendants would be required to show the entire fairness of the proposed merger.

The party with the burden of establishing entire fairness must establish that the challenged transaction was the result of fair dealing and offered a fair price. Fair dealing pertains to the process by which the transaction was approved and looks at the terms, structure, and timing of the transaction. Fair price includes all relevant factors "relat[ing] to the economic and financial considerations of the proposed merger."[10]

The defendants argue that there is nothing inherently unfair about the structure of the merger—a holding company with a wholly-owned operating subsidiary. Solar Cells points out, however, that there was no independent bargaining mechanism set up to protect its interests. In fact, there was no negotiation at all. All of the decisions regarding the terms of the merger and its approval were made unilaterally by True North

---

[8]   The plaintiff contends that documents produced during discovery reveal that the defendants had been planning the proposed merger since at least February 27, 2002.

[9]   *See Schnell v. Chris-Craft Indus.,* 285 A.2d 437 (Del.1971).

[10]   *See Weinberger v. UOP, Inc.,* 457 A.2d 701, 711 (Del.1983).

through its representative Managers. No advance notice of this merger was given to Solar Cells. The fact that the Operating Agreement permits action by written consent of a majority of the Managers and permits interested transactions free from personal liability does not give a fiduciary free reign to approve any transaction he sees fit regardless of the impact on those to whom he owes a fiduciary duty. . . .

I am unconvinced by defendants' argument that the merger was fair to Solar Cells because Solar Cells retains voting rights in the surviving company. On matters where the unit-holders can vote, Solar Cells is diluted from an equal (50%) voice, to only 5%. . . . In my opinion, the facts before me establish a reasonable likelihood that defendants will not be able to establish that the proposed merger was the result of fair dealing.

Application of the entire fairness standard requires a demonstration of both fair dealing and fair price. Having considered the fair dealing component of the standard, I turn now to the fair price analysis. . . .

For purposes of the present motion only, I am satisfied that there is a reasonable probability that the Court will not find the January 2002 valuation to be entirely fair. First, the author of AHH's January 2002 valuation materials described those materials as a "quick and dirty" analysis of First Solar's value on that date. This contrasts with the earlier valuations in August and November of 2001, valuations that were based on multiple methodologies to arrive at a value for First Solar that ranged from $103 million in August 2001 to $72 million in November 2001, or almost two to three times the January 2002 valuation. Second, AHH's January 2002 valuation employed only a discounted cash flow analysis. Although the lower valuation in January 2002 was the basis upon which True North would acquire a 95% interest in First Solar and Solar Cells would fall to a 5% interest, the significantly lower valuation failed to employ any other method of valuation as a "crosscheck" to the discounted cash flow analysis. Because earlier valuations relied on multiple valuation methodologies, it is a reasonable inference that AHH's "quick and dirty" analysis is less reliable and authoritative. Third, the January 2002 formula used a much lower exit multiple (a 6.9 x free cash flow terminal year multiple) than did earlier valuation formulas (which used an 11 x free cash flow terminal year multiple), with no apparent rationale for that lower multiple. Fourth, AHH's lower valuation resulted from the use of a much higher discount rate (35%) than the valuations it performed only five months earlier (30%), even though the outlook for the solar cell industry was improving in that period and even though interest rates were generally falling.[11]

---

[11]   Even True North's litigation expert, Mr. Brian DiLucente, arrived at a much higher value for First Solar ($51.9 million). DiLucente was able to reduce his $51.9 million valuation to $31.1 million, but to do so, he was forced to apply a 40% "marketability" discount. The courts of this State, however, have repeatedly rejected the applicability of such discounts. . . . Furthermore, after putting to one side DiLucente's apparent improper application of a marketability discount, his $51.9 million valuation for First Solar likely was improperly depressed by other aspects of his discounted cash flow analysis. For example, DiLucente applied

... I conclude that it is reasonably likely this Court will find the January 2002 $32 million valuation of First Solar not to be a fair price because it is irreconcilable with the earlier valuations only a few months before True North decided to go forward with the proposed merger. Because Solar Cells has demonstrated a reasonable likelihood of success on the merits of its entire fairness claim, I turn next to the irreparable harm and balance of the equities component of the preliminary injunction standard.

B. *Irreparable Harm*

In order to show irreparable harm, the injury must be one for which money damages will not be an adequate remedy. Additionally, the threatened harm must be "imminent, unspeculative, and genuine."

Solar Cells argues that it will be harmed irreparably by the dilution of its equity position and voting power as unit-holders. It also alleges that the loss of its bargained-for participation in company management is an irreparable harm. . . .

The defendants . . . argue that since True North had the right to nominate a majority of First Solar's Managers, True North could control the business and affairs of the Company. That reality is unaltered with the surviving company. The defendants reason, therefore, that Solar Cells has suffered no harm by losing its right to appoint managers. That argument carries no weight whatsoever. To accept that assertion would be to believe that every time the ability to elect a manager or director of a corporation is negotiated, there is no benefit derived therefrom if there is not a right to elect a majority of the managers or directors. Such a notion would certainly come as a surprise to all those who have given valuable consideration in negotiating such valueless rights. The right to participate in a management group is a valuable right whether or not that participation includes control of the group. In this case, it is undisputed that Solar Cells will lose that right if the proposed merger closes, thereby suffering an irreparable harm. . . .

V. CONCLUSION

For the reasons stated, I grant plaintiff's motion for preliminary injunction. . . .

———

Private ordering is a central feature of the law of LLCs as it is with partnerships. Thus, similar to the RUPA, most LLC statutes permit the parties to modify in significant ways their fiduciary obligations. For

---

a discount rate as high as 45%, based on his subjective view of First Solar's Company specific risk. But Dilucente admitted in his deposition testimony that he had no expertise in the solar cell industry and limited knowledge of the specific company, First Solar, that his analysis purported to value. This Court has been, understandably in my view, suspicious of expert valuations offered at trial that incorporate subjective measures of company specific risk premia, as subjective measures may easily be employed as a means to smuggle improper risk assumptions into the discount rate so as to affect dramatically the expert's ultimate opinion on value. . . .

example, Section 110 of the Uniform Limited Liability Company Act permits the operating agreement to restrict or eliminate fiduciary obligations that otherwise apply in self-dealing transactions or even competing with the firm provided the departure is not "manifestly unfair." The parties can prescribe procedures whereby an act that otherwise would violate the duty of loyalty can be authorized or ratified. The "manifestly unfair" governor does not apply to the Uniform Act's authorization for the operating agreement to set forth specific types or categories of activities that will be beyond the duty of loyalty, to modify the duty of care (but it may not authorize intentional misconduct or knowing violations of the law), to alter any other duty, and to prescribe standards by which to measure the contractual obligation of good faith and fair dealing.

Section 18–1101(e) Delaware's Limited Liability Company Act broadly authorizes the operating agreement to limit or even eliminate fiduciary duties of members, managers or other persons to the company, member or manager; the only exception is that the operating agreement "may not limit or eliminate liability for any act or omission that constitutes a bad faith violation of the implied contractual covenant of good faith or fair dealing."

———

Gatz Props., LLC v. Auriga Capital Corp.

Supreme Court of State of Delaware, 2012.
59 A.3d 1206.

PER CURIAM: . . .

I.   *FACTUAL AND PROCEDURAL HISTORY*

[Peconic Bay, LLC, a Delaware limited liability company was formed to hold a long-term lease from Gatz Properties LLC for the purpose of developing a golf course on Long Island. Its manager was Gatz Properties, which itself was managed and controlled by William Gatz. The LLC operating agreement for Peconic Bay conditioned certain major decisions on obtaining the approval of 66 2/3s percent of the Class A membership interests and 51 percent of the Class B membership interests. The Gatz family controlled 85 percent of Peconic's Class A membership interests and 52 percent of the Class B membership interests.

A $6 million dollar loan, secured by the property, was obtained to construct the golf course and American Golf Corp. was retained to manage the course pursuant a long-term management contract that American Golf could exercise its right in 2010 and terminate the management contract. In 2007, it was apparent to Gatz that American Golf would terminate the contract; the golf course was never profitable and American Golf was a "demoralized operator" who had neglected maintenance to such an extent that the course's poor physical condition adversely affected revenues. Seeing that a change was imminent, in 2007 Gatz commissioned an appraisal that reported that the land with golf course improvements would have a value of $10.1 million, but the value would be 50 percent higher if the land were commercially developed.

Over the course of the second half of 2007, Matthew Galvin, acting on behalf of RDC Golf Group, Inc., made two successive offers ($3.75 million and $4.15 million) to purchase the remainder of Peconic's long-term lease (about 30 years). Gatz refused to provide Galvin an opportunity to conduct due diligence in connection with the offers and even criticized Galvin's revenue projections of $4 million as being overly-optimistic (those estimates implied a value of $6–8 million). Nonetheless, Gatz did present Galvin's first two offers to the membership which unanimously rejected the offers. Thereafter, Gatz told Galvin, "no further discussions would be fruitful unless RDC is willing to discuss a price well north of $6 million." Galvin responded that RDC "may have an interest north of $6 million" and asked Gatz to suggest a target range. Gatz refused to offer arrange. Galvin then asked Gatz to sit down with him and negotiate. Gatz did not respond.   Gatz informed the members that negotiations with RDC had broken off with their best offer of $4.15 million and he offered to purchase their interests based on a cash sales price of $5.6 million. All but one of the minority members rejected Gatz's offer. Thereupon, Gatz retained Laurence Hirsch to appraise the property. He never informed Hirsch of Galvin's $4.15 million offer or Galvin's revenue projections. Hirsch therefore depended heavily on American Golf's historical performance and estimated the course's value being $2.8–3.9 million.

In December 2008, Gatz proposed to auction Peconic Bay. This was approved by the voting power of the Gatz controlled interests. Gatz then hired Maltz Auctions to conduct the auction, even though Maltz had no experience with the sale of golf courses. Moreover, Maltz's marketing was limited to small-print classified advertisements in general newspapers and magazines, online advertisements on websites, and direct mailings. There was no evidence that Maltz made any effort to target golf course brokers, managers or operators. The auction occurred on August 18, 2009 and had a single bidder for Peconic Bay—Gatz. He purchased Peconic Bay for $50,000 cash and assuming its outstanding debt of $5.4 million. Among Peconic Bay's assets was approximately $1.6 million cash held in reserves.

Section 15 of Peconic Bay's operating agreement prohibited the manager or any member entering into agreements with the firm or its members "on terms and conditions which are less favorable to the Company than the terms and conditions of similar agreements which could then be entered into with arms-length third parties, without the consent of a majority of the non-affiliated Members (such majority to be deemed to be the holders of 66 2/3s of the Interests which are not held by affiliates of the person or entity that would be a party to the proposed agreement)."]

In 2010, Auriga and the remaining LLC minority members brought this Court of Chancery action for money damages. After a trial, the court ruled in favor of Auriga, holding that Gatz had breached "both his contractual and fiduciary duties" to Peconic Bay's minority members. The court awarded damages of $776,515. . . . This appeal by Gatz followed. . . .

III. ANALYSIS

A. Did Gatz Owe Fiduciary Duties To The Other Members Of Peconic Bay?

The pivotal legal issue presented on this appeal is whether Gatz owed contractually-agreed-to fiduciary duties to Peconic Bay and its minority investors. Resolving that issue requires us to interpret Section 15 of the LLC Agreement, which both sides agree is controlling. . . .

The Court of Chancery determined that Section 15 imposed fiduciary duties in transactions between the LLC and affiliated persons. We agree. To impose fiduciary standards of conduct as a contractual matter, there is no requirement in Delaware that an LLC agreement use magic words, such as "entire fairness" or "fiduciary duties." Indeed, Section 15 nowhere expressly uses either of those terms. Even so, we construe its operative language[18] as an explicit contractual assumption by the contracting parties of an obligation subjecting the manager and other members to obtain a fair price for the LLC in transactions between the LLC and affiliated persons. Viewed functionally, the quoted language is the contractual equivalent of the entire fairness equitable standard of conduct and judicial review.[19]

We conclude that Section 15 of the LLC Agreement, by its plain language, contractually adopts the fiduciary duty standard of entire fairness, and the "fair price" obligation which inheres in that standard. Section 15 imposes that standard in cases where an LLC manager causes the LLC to engage in a conflicted transaction with an affiliate without the approval of a majority of the minority members. There having been

---

[18] The operative language of Section 15 is "on terms and conditions which are less favorable to the Company than the terms and conditions of similar agreements which could then be entered into with arms-length third parties, without the consent of a majority of the non-affiliated Members".

[19] We previously have reached a similar result in the partnership context. See Gotham Partners, supra, 817 A.2d at 171. In Gotham, we affirmed the Court of Chancery's finding, which the parties did not contest, that the Partnership Agreement imposed entire fairness obligations. Section 7.05 of that Agreement permitted self-dealing transactions, provided that the terms of any such transaction are substantially equivalent to terms obtainable by the Partnership from a comparable unaffiliated third party, "reflecting the fair price prong. Section 7.10, which required an independent audit committee to review and approve the self-dealing transactions, reflected the fair dealing prong." Id. The LLC Agreement language employed in this case is substantially identical. Section 15 explicitly mandates a fair price analysis, but offers as a safe harbor a majority-of-the-minority vote. We interpret that contractual obligation here, as we did in Gotham, as the contracted-for functional equivalent.

no majority-of-the-minority approving vote in this case, the burden of establishing the fairness of the transaction fell upon Gatz. That burden Gatz could easily have avoided. If (counterfactually) Gatz had conditioned the transaction upon the approval of an informed majority of the nonaffiliated members, the sale of Peconic Bay would not have been subject to, or reviewed under, the contracted-for entire fairness standard.[20]

We therefore uphold the Court of Chancery's determination that Gatz breached his contractually adopted fiduciary duties to the minority members of Peconic Bay. . . .

Entire fairness review normally encompasses two prongs, fair dealing and fair price.[27] "However, the test for fairness is not a bifurcated one as between fair dealing and price. All aspects of the issue must be examined as a whole since the question is one of entire fairness." In this case, given the language of Section 15 which speaks only in terms of fair price, the Court of Chancery formally applied only the fair price prong. But, in doing so that court also properly considered the "fairness" of how Gatz dealt with the minority "because the extent to which the process leading to the self-dealing either replicated or deviated from the behavior one would expect in an arms-length deal bears importantly on the price determination." The court further held that "in order to take cover under the contractual safe harbor of Section 15, Gatz bears the burden to show that he paid a fair price to acquire Peconic Bay." We agree.

The trial judge found facts, solidly grounded in the record, that firmly support his conclusion that Gatz breached his contracted-for duty to the LLC's minority members. Regarding price, the court found that "Peconic Bay was worth more than what Gatz paid." Gatz argued, but failed to convince the court, that "the Property had no positive value." The court did not regard the absence of competing bids at the auction as persuasive evidence that the price Gatz paid to cash out the minority members was fair. As the court found, "even as of the date of the Auction, the fundamentals of Peconic Bay were such as to make [the court] conclude that an offer above the debt would have been economically justifiable." The Court of Chancery also properly relied on Auriga's expert witness's discounted cash flow analysis, which valued Peconic Bay at approximately $8.9 million.

The court also found as fact that had "Gatz dealt with Galvin with integrity in 2007, it seems probable that Peconic Bay could have been

---

[20]   That result contrasts with the outcome that it would obtain in the traditional corporate law setting, where an informed majority-of-the-minority shareholder vote operates to shift the burden of proof on the issue of fairness. *Kahn v. Lynch Commc'n Sys., Inc.*, 638 A.2d 1110, 1117 (Del. 1994).

[27]   *Weinberger v. UOP, Inc.*, 457 A.2d 701, 711 (Del. 1983). HN5 Fair dealing "embraces questions of when the transaction was timed, how it was initiated, structured, negotiated, disclosed to the directors, and how the approvals of the directors and the stock-holders were obtained." Id. Fair price "relates to the economic and financial considerations of the proposed" transaction. Id.

sold in a way that generated to the Minority Members a full return of their invested capital ($725,000) plus a 10% aggregate return ($72,500)." In reaching that result, the court relied on the fact that Gatz had rebuffed Galvin's interest in discussing a deal "well north of $6 million." The court also found persuasive Galvin's explanation of why, under the circumstances, an over $6 million price was justifiable.

As for fair dealing, the Court of Chancery did not "view the Auction process as generating a price indicative of what Peconic Bay would fetch in a true arms-length negotiation." Indeed, the court found, the Auction was a "sham," "the culmination of Gatz's bad faith efforts to squeeze out the Minority Members." The court concluded that "[b]y failing for years to cause Peconic Bay to explore its market alternatives, Gatz manufactured a situation of distress to allow himself to purchase Peconic Bay at a fire sale price at a distress sale."

These conclusions flow persuasively from the evidence of record. Gatz's decision to auction off Peconic Bay as a distressed property—as opposed to engaging a broker experienced in the golf course industry to sell the company or its prime assets in an orderly way—was wholly unnecessary. Peconic Bay's cash reserves would have afforded Gatz ample time to structure a sale of the property consistent with his contracted-for fiduciary obligation. The court found that "even in the context of an auction approach, the indifference and unprofessionalism of the marketing effort [was] patent." That finding rested on, among other things: (i) the absence of any direct outreach to industry players, (ii) the fact that Gatz failed to inform Maltz of RDC's expressions of interest, (iii) the rushed time frame of the marketing, and (iv) the auction terms themselves. The Court of Chancery properly concluded "that the Auction was not a process that anyone acting with minimal competency and in good faith would have used to obtain fair value for Peconic Bay."

We are satisfied that Gatz failed to carry his burden of proving that he discharged his contracted for entire fairness obligation. Accordingly, we affirm that court's determination of liability solely on contractual grounds. . . .

C.   Unnecessary Construction Of LLC Statute To Provide Default Fiduciary Duties

At this point, we pause to comment on one issue that the trial court should not have reached or decided. We refer to the court's pronouncement that the Delaware Limited Liability Company Act imposes "default" fiduciary duties upon LLC managers and controllers unless the parties to the LLC Agreement contract that such duties shall not apply. Where, as here, the dispute over whether fiduciary standards apply could be decided solely by reference to the LLC Agreement, it was improvident and unnecessary for the trial court to reach out and decide, sua sponte, the default fiduciary duty issue as a matter of statutory construction. The trial court did so despite expressly acknowledging that the existence of fiduciary duties under the LLC Agreement was "no longer contested by the parties."[61] For the reasons next discussed, that court's statutory pronouncements must be regarded as dictum without any precedential value.[62]

. . . In these circumstances we decline to express any view regarding whether default fiduciary duties apply as a matter of statutory construction. The Court of Chancery likewise should have so refrained. . . .

[T]he merits of the issue whether the LLC statute does—or does not—impose default fiduciary duties is one about which reasonable minds could differ. Indeed, reasonable minds arguably could conclude that the statute—which begins with the phrase, "[t]o the extent that, at law or in equity, a member or manager or other person has duties (including fiduciary duties)"—is consciously ambiguous. That possibility suggests that the "organs of the Bar" (to use the trial court's phrase) may be well advised to consider urging the General Assembly to resolve any statutory ambiguity on this issue . . .

D. Damages

Having found that the defendants had breached a contracted-for fiduciary duty arising from equity, and that the LLC Agreement did not dictate otherwise, the Court of Chancery awarded equitable damages as a remedy.[74] . . .

The trial court determined that if Gatz had engaged with Galvin in 2007, as Gatz's contracted for entire fairness duty required, Peconic Bay could probably have been sold at a price that returned to the minority investors both their initial capital ($725,000) plus a 10% aggregate return ($72,500).[83] The court found Galvin's testimony sufficiently credible to support a "fair price" above $6 million. Auriga's damages expert's report also supports that finding. As the trial court aptly noted, although Gatz "had no duty to sell his interests," he did not have "a free license to mismanage Peconic Bay so as to deliver it to himself for an unfair price."[84]

The Court of Chancery arrived at a damage award of $776,515, which represented a full return of the minority members' capital

---

[74] This case echoes our ruling in Gotham Partners, L.P. v. Hallwood Realty Partners, L.P.: The Partnership Agreement provides for contractual fiduciary duties of entire fairness. Although the contract could have limited the damage remedy for breach of these duties to contract damages, it did not do so. The Court of Chancery is not precluded from awarding equitable relief as provided by the entire fairness standard where, as here, the general partner breached its contractually created fiduciary duty to meet the entire fairness standard and the partnership agreement is silent regarding damages. The Court of Chancery in this case may award equitable relief as provided by the entire fairness standard and is not limited to contract damages for two reasons: (1) this case involves a breach of the duty of loyalty and such a breach permits broad, discretionary, and equitable remedies; and (2) courts will not construe a contract as taking away other forms of appropriate relief, including equitable relief, un-less the contract explicitly provides for an exclusive remedy.

[84] Peconic Bay's debt exceeded $5.4 million. Even accounting for the cash reserves, an offer of $3.75 million would leave Peconic Bay insolvent

contributions plus a 10% aggregate return, less the $20,985 the minority members received at the Auction. That award is slightly less than the amount a sale in 2007 for $6.5 million would have yielded. The court noted that its damages award was modest and that "the record could support a higher one." The damages award was based on conscience and reason, and we uphold it. . . .

IV. CONCLUSION

For the foregoing reasons, the judgment of the Court of Chancery is AFFIRMED.

————

NOTE ON IMPLIED COVENANT OF GOOD FAITH AND FAIR DEALING

Many states provide that even though the operating agreement of LLCs or a limited partnership agreement can restrict or even eliminate fiduciary obligations, the implied covenant of good faith and fair dealing cannot be qualified through such private ordering. *See e.g.,* Del. L.L.C. Act § 18–1101(c)(e); U.L.L.C. Act § 105(d)(6). The law of contracts is the source of the implied covenant so that an understanding of the protection the covenant provides logically begins there. In August 2013, the Delaware legislature added section 18–1104 to its LLC Act to clarify that default fiduciary duties exist unless the operating agreement provides otherwise.

The Restatement (Second) of Contracts § 205 sweepingly pronounces that "[e]very contract imposes upon each party a duty of good faith and fair dealing in its performance and enforcement." The ultimate question, therefore, is what does the implied covenant require of the parties to a contract? The Restatement leaves this question to the comments, defining good faith as a context-dependent moving target guided by the parties' expectations and community standards of decency:

> The phrase "good faith" is used in a variety of contexts, and its meaning varies somewhat with the context. Good faith performance or enforcement of a contract emphasizes faithfulness to an agreed common purpose and consistency with the justified expectations of the other party; it excludes a variety of types of conduct characterized as involving "bad faith" because they violate community standards of decency, fairness or reasonableness.

Restatement (Second) of Contracts § 205, cmt. A.

Courts seeking to give meaning to the term "good faith" often look to the Uniform Commercial Code § 2–101(20) for guidance; that provision states "'[g]ood faith,' . . . means honesty in fact and observance of reasonable commercial standards of fair dealing." The merchant-specific definition § 2–103(1)(b) similarly provides that "'[g]ood faith' in the case of a merchant means honesty in fact and the observance of reasonable commercial standards of fair dealing in the trade." Both definitions, and many courts, emphasize that good faith consists of honesty and context-specific reasonableness.

In the contract context, courts have largely ratified the Restatement position by holding that what constitutes good faith in a particular case is dependent on the reasonable expectations of the parties at the time of agreement. The implied duty prohibits a party from "doing anything that will destroy or injure the other party's right to receive the benefit of the fruits of the agreement." 17A C.J.S. *Contracts* § 437 (2016). In other words, the duty of good faith and fair dealing prevents one party from taking advantage of another party in a way that could not have been contemplated at the time of the agreement, or which nominally complies with the express terms of the contract, but which clearly violates the spirit of the agreement. *See e.g., Dunlap v. State Farm Fire & Cas. Co.,* 878 A.2d 434, 444 (Del. 2005).Thus, the implied covenant is a mechanism for excluding certain conduct as inconsistent with the spirit of the contract, rather than one used to require certain affirmative conduct. Stated as an affirmative obligation, "[i]n the absence of an express provision, the law will imply an agreement by the parties to a contract to perform those things that according to reason and justice they should do in order to carry out the purpose for which the contract was made . . . ." *Daniel B. Van Campen Corp. v. Building and Const. Trades Council of Philadelphia and Vicinity,* 195 A.2d 134, 136 (Pa. Super. Ct. 1963)

  1. *Common Applications.*

  a). Discretion. Perhaps the most common situation that the implied covenant is applied arises when one party to a contract has a level of discretion in the performance of a particular term. Unless explicitly provided, that party's discretion is not absolute. Rather, it must exercise its discretion in good faith. *See e.g., Travellers Int'l, A.G. v. Trans World Airlines, Inc.,* 41 F.3d 1570, 1575 (2d Cir. 1994).

  b). Term So Fundamental, It Was Not Reduced to Writing. The implied covenant is also used to incorporate a term that is so basic or fundamental to the parties' agreement it was simply assumed (by both parties) at the time of formation. The covenant becomes a mechanism for recognizing and giving legal effect to the fact that "parties occasionally have understandings or expectations that were so fundamental that they did not need to negotiate about those expectations." *Allen v. El Paso Pipeline GP Co., LLC,* 113 A.3d 167, 184 (Del. Ch. 2014).

  c). To Account for Unforeseen Contingencies While Furthering the Parties Agreement. The implied covenant is also used to incorporate a term that is in furtherance of the parties' agreement when the parties' agreement, due to the limitations of human knowledge and the costs of negotiation, does not address a particular occurrence. The covenant becomes a mechanism for adapting a contract, consistent with its terms, to the reality that "[e]ven the most skilled and sophisticated parties will necessarily 'fail to address a future state of the world . . . because contracting is costly and human knowledge imperfect.'" *Lonergan v. EPE Holdings, LLC,* 5 A.3d 1008, 1018 (Del. Ch. 2010).

  2. *Limitations.*

  a). No New Independent Rights or Duties. The implied covenant does not impose new or independent rights or duties on either party. Rather, it is a mechanism for enforcing the spirit of the rights and duties expressly agreed to in the contract. In other words, the implied covenant attaches to the express terms of the agreement and requires that those specific terms be performed and enforced fairly and in good faith.

While every implied covenant expands the terms of the contract to some extent, "[t]he implied obligation must arise from the language used or it must be indispensable to effectuate the intentions of the parties." In this sense, the implied covenant of good faith, despite its theoretical ubiquity, is like any other implied covenant. *See, e.g., Avidity Partners, LLC v. State*, 165 Cal. Rptr. 3d 299, 323 (Cal. Ct. App. 2013) ("Before an implied covenant may be imposed: the implication must arise from the language used or be necessary to effectuate the intention of the parties . . . .")

b). Cautious Application. Courts, particularly those in Delaware, use the implied covenant only with great caution and reluctance. Not only is the covenant used cautiously, but, out of respect for the principle of freedom of contract, courts are also hesitant to apply the implied covenant. Use of the implied covenant is "rare" and is only an "occasional necessity," not the rule. The implied covenant is not a means to rebalance economic interests or to protect a party who should have protected themselves.

c). Must Relate to an Express Term. The implied covenant is a duty that attaches to the performance of the express terms; it does not impose a general duty of good faith and fair dealing on the parties, but rather a duty to perform and enforce the *particular* terms of the contract in good faith. *See e.g., Rekhter v. State*, 323 P.3d 1036, 1041 (Wash. 2014). It is an obligation to carry out the terms of the contract. Accordingly, to state a claim for breach of the implied covenant, a plaintiff must allege that the defendant failed to abide by a particular contractual term in good faith.

————

Gerber v. Enter. Prods. Holdings, LLC

Delaware Supreme Court, 2013.
67 A.3d 400.

■ JACOBS, JUSTICE

[Joel Gerber initiated suits on behalf of former public holders of Delaware limited partnership units in Enterprise GP Holdings, L.P. (EPE) alleging unfairness in the 2009 sale by EPE of its subsidiary, Teppco GP, to a second limited partnership, Enterprise Products Partner, LP (Enterprise Products LP). This is referred to as the 2009 Sale. On that same date, Teppco LP was sold to Enterprise Products in a separate but related transaction (the Teppco LP sale). The facts indicate that EPE had acquired Teppco in 2007 for $1.1 billion but that the 2009 sale resulted in only $100 being paid to EPE. Duncan was a controlling person in EPE as well as Enterprise Products L.P. Gerber also challenged the fairness of the merger of EPE into Enterprise Products LP. The Court of Chancery found that the primary purpose of the 2010 merger was to eliminate the claims related to the disposition of Teppco.

In connection with these sales, the Audit, Conflict, and Governance Committee (ACGC), of Enterprise Products GP sought a fairness opinion from Morgan Stanley as to EPE and the public limited partnership (LP) unit holders. Morgan Stanley opined that *combined*, the consideration to be paid for Teppco GP and Teppco LP by Enterprise Products LP was fair to EPE. Morgan Stanley specifically expressed no opinion on the fairness of how the consideration was divided between Teppco GP and Teppco LP. Relying on this opinion, the ACGC recommended, and the board approved, the sales.

Morgan Stanley also provided a fairness opinion for the 2010 transaction. The record reflects that transactions began with Enterprise Products LP initiating negotiations with the board of directors of Enterprise Products GP to merge EPE into Enterprise Products LP (a reverse merger). After considering the LP unit holder's current and possible legal claims against Enterprise Products GP, for example, those related to the Teppco sale, the ACGC agreed on an exchange whereby "each LP unit of EPE would be converted into a right to 1.5 LP units of Enterprise Products LP." Morgan Stanley opined that this exchange ratio was fair to the LP unit holders of EPE. Morgan Stanley did not, however, take into consideration the value of the LP unit holders' potential legal claims when offering its opinion. This deficiency was not disclosed to the EPE LP unit holders in the proxy materials. As Duncan and his affiliates controlled 76% of the LP units, the merger was approved.

Gerber, on behalf of the public unit holders, brought suit under several theories of liability, including breach of the implied covenant of good faith and fair dealing, with regard to the 2009 sale of Teppco GP and the 2010 merger of EPE into Enterprise Products LP. The defendants argued that there was no breach by anyone as the transactions complied with the provisions of the partnership agreement and thereby precluded Gerber's claims. Specifically, the defendants relied on two provisions of the limited partnership agreement (LPA), sections 7.9(a)(i) and 7.10(b).

Section 7.9(a)(i) provided:

> Unless otherwise expressly provided in this Agreement, whenever a potential conflict of interest exists or arises between the General Partner or any of its Affiliates, on the one hand, and the Partnership or any Partner, on the other hand, any resolution or course of action by the General Partner or its Affiliates in respect of such conflict of interest shall be permitted and deemed approved by all Partners, and shall not constitute a breach of this Agreement . . . , or of any duty stated or implied by law or equity, if the resolution or course of action in respect of such conflict of interest is:
>
> (i)   Approved by Special Approval; . . .

Special approval is defined as "approval by a majority of the members of the [ACGC]."

Section 7.10(b) provided:

> The General Partner may consult with . . . [experts or] investment bankers . . . and any act taken or omitted to be taken in reliance upon the opinion of such Persons as to matters that the General Partner reasonably believes to be within such Person's professional or expert competence shall be conclusively presumed to have been done or omitted in good faith and in accordance with such opinion.

Granting the defendants' motion to dismiss, the Court of Chancery held that the breach of contractual fiduciary duty claims failed because the sale and merger had each been granted "special approval" satisfying the fiduciary requirements of the partnership agreement. The implied covenant claims failed because, while the special approval process was constrained by the implied covenant of good faith, the ACGC relied on the opinions offered by Morgan Stanley when granting special approval, thus entitling their actions to a conclusive presumption of good faith under section 7.10(b) Gerber appealed.]

We begin our analysis by addressing LPA Section 7.10(b)'s conclusive presumption of good faith. We start there because the foundational premise of the Court of Chancery's analysis is that Section 7.10(b) bars any claim under the implied covenant. With respect to the 2009 Sale, the Vice Chancellor explicitly held that:

> The Complaint can fairly be read to allege that Enterprise Products GP acted in bad faith when it chose to use the [Section 7.9(a)] Special Approval Process. . . . According to the Complaint, the 2009 Sale was a grossly unfair transaction that involved EPE selling an asset for $100 million that two years previously it had purchased for $1.1 billion. . . . [Consequently,] if Enterprise Products GP was going to be able to get EPE to undertake the 2009 Sale free from challenge, Enterprise Products GP would have to obtain Special Approval of the 2009 Sale. According to the Complaint, Enterprise Products GP . . . exercised, in bad faith, the discretion it had to use the Special Approval process to take advantage of the LPA's duty limitations.

The Court of Chancery . . . concluded that "[a]lthough the well-pled facts of the Complaint may suggest that Enterprise Products GP breached the implied covenant, that claim is precluded by Section 7.10(b) of the LPA [limited partnership agreement]." . . .

We conclude . . . that the foundational premise of the court's reasoning is flawed. Specifically, insofar as Section 7.10(b) creates a conclusive presumption of good faith, that provision does not bar a claim under the implied covenant.

The flaw in the court's reasoning stems from a decision by the LPA's drafters to define a contractual fiduciary duty in terms of "good faith"— a term that is also and separately a component of the "implied covenant of *good faith* and fair dealing." Although that term is common, the LPA's contractual fiduciary duty describes a concept of "good faith" very different from the good faith concept addressed by the implied covenant. In *ASB Allegiance Real Estate Fund v. Scion Breckenridge Managing Member, LLC*, the Court of Chancery articulated the important differences between the implied covenant and the fiduciary duty concepts of good faith.[46] We adopt this well-reasoned analysis as a correct statement of our law:

> The implied covenant seeks to enforce the parties' contractual bargain by implying only those terms that the parties would have agreed to during their original negotiations if they had thought to address them. Under Delaware law, a court confronting an implied covenant claim asks whether it is clear from what was expressly agreed upon that the parties who negotiated the express terms of the contract would have agreed to proscribe the act later complained of as a breach of the implied covenant of good faith—had they thought to negotiate with respect to that matter. While this test requires resort to a counterfactual world—what if—it is nevertheless appropriately restrictive and commonsensical.
>
> The temporal focus is critical. Under a fiduciary duty or tort analysis, a court examines the parties as situated at the time of the wrong. The court determines whether the defendant owed the plaintiff a duty, considers the defendant's obligations (if any) in light of that duty, and then evaluates whether the duty was breached. Temporally, each inquiry turns on the parties' relationship as it existed at the time of the wrong. . . .
>
> An implied covenant claim, by contrast, looks to the past. It is not a free-floating duty unattached to the underlying legal documents. It does not ask what duty the law should impose on the parties given their relationship at the time of the wrong, but rather what the parties would have agreed to themselves had they considered the issue in their original bargaining positions at the time of contracting. . . .
>
> The retrospective focus applies equally to a party's discretionary rights. The implied covenant requires that a party refrain from arbitrary or unreasonable conduct which has the effect of preventing the other party to the contract from receiving the fruits of its bargain. *When exercising a discretionary right, a party to the contract must exercise its*

---

[46] 50 A.3d 434, 440–42 (Del. Ch. 2012), *aff'd in part, rev'd in part on other grounds*, 68 A.3d 665, 2013 Del. LEXIS 235, 2013 WL 1914714 (Del. May 9, 2013) (emphasis added).

discretion reasonably.... [W]hat is "arbitrary" or "unreasonable"—or conversely "reasonable"—depends on the parties' original contractual expectations, not a "free-floating" duty applied at the time of the wrong.

... Like a common law fiduciary duty, Section 7.9(b)'s contractual fiduciary duty analysis looks to the parties as situated at the time of the wrong, and inquires whether Enterprise Products GP or its Affiliates "believe[d] that the determination or other action [was] in the best interests of the Partnership." That is different from the standard that is embedded in the implied covenant.

LPA Section 7.10(b)'s conclusive presumption must be read together with Section 7.9(b). Section 7.9(b) imposes a contractual fiduciary duty to act in "good faith," and defines "good faith" for the "purposes of this [a]greement." Under Section 7.10(b), Enterprise Products GP and its Affiliates are conclusively presumed to have met this standard if they rely upon the opinion of a qualified expert advisor. Nothing in Section 7.10(b) pertains to or addresses the implied covenant.

Section 7.10(b) is a contractual provision that establishes a procedure the general partner may use to conclusively establish that it met its contractual fiduciary duty. But, the implied covenant attaches to Section 7.10(b), as it attaches to the rest of the LPA. Therefore, Enterprise Products GP's attempt to take advantage of Section 7.10(b) may itself be subject to a claim that it was arbitrary and unreasonable and in violation of the implied covenant. The conclusive presumption of "good faith" applies only to the contractual fiduciary duty. It cannot operate retroactively to alter the parties' reasonable expectations at the time of contracting, and it cannot be used to fill every gap in the LPA.

... Examples readily come to mind of cases where a general partner's actions in obtaining a fairness opinion from a qualified financial advisor themselves would be arbitrary or unreasonable, and "thereby frustrat[e] the fruits of the bargain that the asserting party reasonably expected." To suggest one hypothetical example, a qualified financial advisor may be willing to opine that a transaction is fair even though (unbeknownst to the advisor) the controller has intentionally concealed material information that, if disclosed, would require the advisor to opine that the transaction price is in fact not fair. More extreme would be a case where the controller outright bribes the financial advisor to opine (falsely) that the transaction is fair. In a third example, the financial advisor, eager for future business from the controller, compromises its professional valuation standards to achieve the controller's unfair objective.

Having so determined, we next analyze whether Gerber has pled facts that, if true, would establish that Enterprise Products GP breached the implied covenant. Applying the implied covenant is a "cautious enterprise" and we will only infer "contractual terms to handle developments or contractual gaps that the asserting party pleads neither party anticipated." Gerber must show that Enterprise Products GP "acted arbitrarily or unreasonably, thereby frustrating the fruits of the bargain that [Gerber] reasonably expected." "When conducting this analysis, we must assess the parties' reasonable expectations at the time of contracting;" and will not imply terms to "rebalanc[e] economic interests after events that could have been anticipated, but were not, that later adversely affected one party to a contract."

According to the Complaint, the 2009 Sale was a grossly unfair transaction wherein the Defendants caused EPE to sell Teppco GP to Enterprise Products LP for only 9% of EPE's original purchase price. . . . The Complaint pleads that the Morgan Stanley 2009 opinion did not address whether holders of EPE's LP units received fair consideration for their Teppco GP interest. Instead, Morgan Stanley addressed only the total consideration paid in both the Teppco LP Sale (which did not include any consideration for EPE's LP unitholders) and the 2009 Sale, and explicitly disclaimed to opine as to the fairness of any specific component of the total consideration.

. . . [E]ven though Gerber forewent the protections available under common law fiduciary principles, he still retained a reasonable contractual expectation that the Defendants would properly follow the LPA's substitute standards. That requires us to decide whether an implied covenant claim is stated where the defendant allegedly has attempted to satisfy its contractual obligations by relying on a fairness opinion that did not value the consideration that the LP unitholders actually received.

We answer that question in the affirmative. When Gerber purchased EPE LP units, he agreed to be bound by the LPA's provisions, which conclusively deemed Enterprise Products GP's contractual fiduciary duty to be satisfied, if Enterprise Products GP relied upon the opinion of a qualified expert. At the time of contracting, however, Gerber could hardly have anticipated that Enterprise Products GP would rely upon a fairness opinion that did not fulfill its basic function—evaluating the consideration the LP unitholders received for purposes of opining whether the transaction was financially fair. Although Section 7.10(b) does not prescribe specific standards for fairness opinions, we may confidently conclude that, had the parties addressed the issue at the time of contracting, they would have agreed that any fairness opinion must address whether the consideration received for Teppco GP in 2009 was fair, in order to satisfy Section 7.9(b)'s contractual fiduciary duty. Gerber has pled that Enterprise Products GP engaged in a manifestly unfair transaction, and then relied on an unresponsive fairness opinion, to ensure that its contractual fiduciary duty would be conclusively presumed to have been discharged. That is the type of arbitrary, unreasonable conduct that the implied covenant prohibits.

A similar analysis applies equally to the 2010 Merger challenges. The Vice Chancellor held that the Complaint pled that a principal purpose of the 2010 Merger was to terminate the 2007 and 2009 Claims. Despite that purpose, Morgan Stanley did not independently value the 2007 and 2009 Claims in assessing the 2010 Merger's fairness in that firm's 2010 opinion, nor did Enterprise Products GP obtain another valuation. Although the Morgan Stanley 2010 opinion stated that the 2010 Merger consideration was fair without considering the 2007 and 2009 Claims; it did not "address whether the consideration was fair *with* the [2007 and 2009 Claims]." Gerber could not fairly be charged with having anticipated that Enterprise Products GP would merge EPE for the purpose of eliminating EPE's derivative claims, but then rely on a fairness opinion that did not even consider those claims' value. Although Section 7.10(b) does not explicitly so require, we conclude that the parties would certainly have agreed, at the time of contracting, that any fairness opinion contemplated by that provision would address the value of derivative claims where (as here) terminating those claims was a *principal purpose* of a merger. Therefore, Gerber has sufficiently pled that Enterprise Products GP breached the implied covenant in the course of taking advantage of Section 7.10(b)'s conclusive presumption.

Although Gerber has pled that Enterprise Products GP breached the implied covenant, that does not end the analysis. If Enterprise Products GP independently satisfied the contractual Special Approval safe harbor in Section 7.9(a), then by Section 7.9(a)'s plain language, the general partner did not breach the LPA. Therefore the Court must address this second layer of contractual insulation, and determine whether the Complaint cognizably alleges that Enterprise Products GP violated the implied covenant in its effort to comply with Section 7.9(a). . . .

[The Supreme Court Supreme Court held that the complaint sufficiently alleged facts to support a claim that the Special Approval process contemplated by the parties had not been met and therefore violated the implied covenant. Cognizable contractual claims therefore existed with respect to all the challenged transactions.]

---

4. DISASSOCIATION AND DISSOLUTION

Lieberman v. Wyoming.com LLC
Supreme Court of Wyoming, 2004.
82 P. 3d 274.

■ GOLDEN, JUSTICE.

Wyoming.com LLC (hereinafter "Wyoming.com") is a Wyoming limited liability company of which E. Michael Lieberman was a member. In 1998, Lieberman filed a notice of withdrawal of member with Wyoming.com, and the remaining members of Wyoming.com accepted Lieberman's withdrawal as tendered. The parties subsequently could not agree on the financial consequences of Lieberman's withdrawal and filed a petition for declaratory judgment on the issue. Ultimately, the district court, by way of summary judgment, ordered liquidation of Lieberman's equity interest at its capital account value as of the date of his withdrawal as a member. Lieberman appeals.

The Wyoming LLC Act contains no provision relating to the fate of a member's equity interest upon the member's dissociation. Thus, it was entirely up to the members of Wyoming.com to contractually provide for terms of dissociation. Upon careful review of all the agreements entered into by the parties regarding Wyoming.com, we determine that the agreements contain no provision regarding the equity interest of a dissociating member. Since we can find no provision mandating a different result, Lieberman retains his equity interest. Lieberman is under no obligation to sell his equity interest, and Wyoming.com is under no obligation to buy Lieberman's equity interest. . . . The decision of the district court liquidating Lieberman's equity interest is reversed, and we remand to the district court for a declaration of the parties' rights consistent with this opinion. . . .

[Steven and Sandra Mosssbrook, along with Liberman founded the firm in late 1994. Lieberman's initial capital contribution was $20,000, consisting of services rendered and to be rendered. On February 27, 1998, Lieberman was terminated as vice-president of Wyoming.com and was required to leave the premises. He subsequently gave written notice in a document titled, "Notice of Withdrawal of Member Upon Expulsion: Demand for Return of Contributions to Capital." He then demanded the return of "his share of the current value of the company," which he estimated to be $400,000. The members accepted his withdrawal, elected to continue the business rather than dissolve the business, and approved the return of Lieberman's $20,000 capital contribution. Lieberman refused the $20,000.]

[Because the Wyoming statutes do not address the rights of a member who has disassociated], this Court must look to the agreements entered into by the members of Wyoming.com to determine the rights and obligations of the members with regards to a member who has dissociated. The rights and obligations of the members of Wyoming.com are determined pursuant to the operating agreements of Wyoming.com. The record reveals that the parties entered into "Articles of Organization of Wyoming.com LLC" (the "Articles") and an "Operating Agreement of Wyoming.com LLC" (the "Operating Agreement"). These agreements establish Wyoming.com, provide for Wyoming.com's operation, and set forth the mutual obligations between each of Wyoming.com's members. At all times the members have been free to contract any provision they desired, so long as the provision did not conflict with the limited requirements of the Wyoming LLC Act. Determining the fate of Lieberman's equity interest requires this Court to construe these agreements.

A contract may consist of several documents . . . which this Court reviews as a whole with the goal of determining the intention of the contracting parties as expressed by their own words. . . .

The operating agreements of Wyoming.com vest Lieberman with an ownership interest. Lieberman can only be divested of this ownership interest if the members of Wyoming.com contracted for such divestment. Wyoming.com argues that Lieberman's withdrawal as a member mandates his withdrawal as an equity owner, thus triggering a liquidation of his equity interest. In . . . [*Lieberman v. Wyoming.com,* 11 P.3d 353 (Wyo. 2000)] this Court clarified that "under the Wyoming LLC act, a member's interest in an LLC consists of economic and non-economic interests." *Id. at 357.* These interests are distinct. It is clear from Lieberman's notice of withdrawal that he had no intention of forfeiting his economic, or equity, interest in the company. Lieberman's withdrawal regarded his non-economic membership interest only.

The operating agreements clearly anticipate a situation where a person could be an equity owner in Wyoming.com but not a member. Provision 4.3 of the Operating Agreement, . . . provides that, if a transferee of an ownership interest is not unanimously approved by the remaining members, the transferee maintains the rights of equity ownership but will not be a member.[3] Logically, given the absence of any contractual provision to the contrary, there is no reason to treat a withdrawing member any differently from someone who buys into Wyoming.com without becoming a member. Thus, Lieberman is not a member of Wyoming.com, but he maintains his equity interest and all rights and obligations attendant thereto.

The parties essentially admit this in their respective briefs. Lieberman argues that there is nothing in the agreements allowing Wyoming.com to acquire his ownership interest at less than fair market value, while Wyoming.com argues that there is nothing in the agreements requiring Wyoming.com to pay fair market value for Lieberman's ownership interest. Both arguments are correct. There simply is no contractual agreement that any party must buy or sell an ownership interest for any amount.

Having failed to contractually provide for mandatory liquidation or a buyout, the parties are left in status quo. We have long held that it is the duty of this Court to construe contracts made between parties, not to make a contract for them. . . . We will enforce the contract as written and accepted by the parties. Lieberman maintains his equity interest in Wyoming.com. . . .

---

[3]   *Wyo. Stat. Ann. § 17–15–122* contains a similar provision regarding the transferability of interest. The transferee does not become a member without unanimous approval of all members.

CONCLUSION

Lieberman has withdrawn as a member of Wyoming.com and all remaining members unanimously accepted his withdrawal as a member. Lieberman thus is no longer a member of Wyoming.com. Lieberman does, however, maintain his equity interest in Wyoming.com. There is no contractual provision for a buy-out of his equity interest. Therefore Lieberman cannot force Wyoming.com to buy his interest, and Wyoming.com cannot force Lieberman to sell his interest. Because the members of Wyoming.com failed to contractually provide for a buy-out, Lieberman remains an equity holder in Wyoming.com. There are no further rights or obligations of the parties for this court to construe with regards to this situation. The grant of summary judgment is reversed and the matter remanded to the district court for a declaration of the parties' rights consistent with this opinion.

■ LEHMAN, JUSTICE, dissenting, with whom KITE, JUSTICE, joins.

I respectfully dissent. . . .

As the majority noted . . . , we must review the contract of the parties as a whole with the goal of determining the intent of the contracting parties. The right of a member to withdraw from membership in the LLC is evidenced in the provisions of the operating agreement. Also clearly expressed is the right of the remaining members to continue the business after such a withdrawal. The provision addressing this right states:

> 9. Continuity. The remaining members of the LLC, providing they are two or more in number, will have the right to continue the business on the death, retirement, resignation, expulsion, bankruptcy or dissolution of a member or occurrence of any other event which terminates the continued membership of a member in this LLC, in accordance with the voting provisions of the Operating Agreement of the Company.

This provision allows any member to terminate his membership in Wyoming.com by taking any of the listed actions and provides the remaining members the right to continue the business. This provision evidences the parties' intent to allow a member to completely terminate his membership in the LLC without also terminating the LLC. Hand in hand with these rights is the implication that should the remaining members elect to continue, they will have to compensate the withdrawing member for his interest in some manner. It seems intuitive that if the parties allowed for withdrawal and continuation, they must have had some intent to deal with those events. Because the provision mentions nothing of forfeiting the interest or simply becoming a non-member equity owner, the agreement to continue thus implies that there must be some sort of buyout.

Furthermore, the LLC statutory scheme implies that, absent other agreement, a member has a right to terminate his continued membership in the LLC and be compensated for this interest. . . . [A]n LLC is a hybrid organization including characteristics of both a partnership and a corporation. At the time the legislature enacted the original LLC statutes, an important consideration was the tax ramifications of the newly created entity. At that time, in order to obtain taxation as a partnership, an LLC could have no more than two of four corporate characteristics: limited liability, central management, free transferability of interests, and continuity of life. . . . The LLC entity provided for limited liability and central management. Therefore, to avoid corporate taxation, the typical LLC statutes choose to utilize partnership principles, rather than corporate principles, for exiting members in order to avoid the LLC having continuity of life.

Partnership exit rules ordinarily allow for any partner to dissolve the firm at any time and demand liquidation and accordingly be paid for his equity interest. . . . The legislature clearly recognized this as the normal partnership rule and impliedly endorsed such a rule by providing for an exception to this rule if the members agreed otherwise in their operating agreement. *Wyo. Stat. Ann. § 17–15–123.* In a sense, carrying on the business following a terminating event became the exception to the general rule that the business would cease when a member left for any reason. Thus, the resulting implication is a member may terminate his membership in an LLC and must be paid for this interest unless otherwise provided.

Therefore, I reach the conclusion that under the terms of the LLC as provided by the Articles of Organization and Operating Agreement, and under the statute, Lieberman could withdraw as a member of Wyoming.com resulting in a forced buyout of his entire interest. The majority concludes, "Lieberman's withdrawal regarded his non-economic membership interest only." . . . I cannot agree with this conclusion. While a member's interest does in fact consist of an economic and non-economic interest, a withdrawing member does not envision that his withdrawal will result in this split in his interest. . . .

In fact, the majority's resolution has created a situation where the remaining members are in a position of power to dictate the terms of any negotiations for a buyout. The remaining members are now conceivably in a position to retain earnings and avoid distributions, but as an equity owner Lieberman would still be required to pay taxes on those earnings. Additionally, Lieberman is no longer a member. He will not be drawing the salary of the member or controlling his equity interest in any manner. While it could be said that this situation arose because of Lieberman's withdrawal, it should be noted that under the majority's analysis the result would apply equally to an expelled member. In such an instance, some of the members could expel a member and then refuse to negotiate for a buyout. Such a result begs for the oppression of one party. While I agree with the majority that it is not our duty to write contract provisions for parties that have failed to do so, I believe it would be much worse to fail to provide a remedy. . .

Therefore, absent a provision in the operating agreement, a member's equity interest should be valued at what he would have received had the business been dissolved on the day he terminated his membership in the LLC. I recognize that, because the business is not actually dissolving, this valuation may be difficult and will have to be based to some extent on estimates and appraisals. However, a similar valuation method is used upon the dissociation of a partner from a partnership when the partnership agreement has failed to provide for a valuation method. *See Wyo. Stat. Ann. §§ 17–21–603(a), 17–21–701(a), (b)*. Presumably, then, such estimates and appraisals are attainable. . . .

Lastly, in instances where a departing member's share is to be valued as detailed above, the remaining members have elected to continue the company. Therefore, some consideration must be given to the duties and hardship the company may encounter as a result of paying the departing member's equity interest. . . . These observations lead me to conclude that the payment of the departing member's equity interest may take place over a reasonable period of time to avoid the liquidation of essential assets and the possible undercapitalization of the LLC. To be entitled to prolong the payment over a reasonable time, the LLC must show that immediate payment in full would jeopardize the company's ability to carry on its ordinary business and provide for its creditors. Should payment over time be required, such payment should be secured by a promissory note that provides for reasonable interest. Furthermore, until the member is paid in full, that member should still receive any distributions to which his interest is entitled much like a transferee without the right to participate in the management of the business would under *Wyo. Stat. Ann. § 17–15–122*. . . .

———

Was the result reached by the majority more consistent with what would have occurred if the parties had formed a partnership? Corporation? Which of the two positions advocated in the opinions is more likely to stimulate capital formation? The Delaware LLC act does not directly address the rights of disassociating members. *Cf.* Del. L. L.C.A. § 18–306 (A limited liability company agreement may provide that: (1) A member who fails to perform in accordance with, or to comply with the terms and conditions of, the limited liability company agreement shall be subject to specified penalties or specified consequences . . . "). In contrast, Section 602 of the Uniform Limited Liability Company Act has a lengthy list of events constituting disassociation that not surprisingly includes voluntary withdrawal. The consequences of dissociation are set forth in section 603 and include termination of the disassociating member's right to participate in management and thus transforming that person's status to that of a transferee. Section 701 narrowly defines the instances in which disassociation will dictate that the firm dissolve and wind up its affairs:

(4)   on application by a member, the entry by[appropriate court] of an order dissolving the company on the grounds that:

> (A) the conduct of all or substantially all of the company's activities and affairs is unlawful; or
>
> (B) it is not reasonably practicable to carry on the company's activities and affairs in conformity with the certificate of organization and the operating agreement; or
>
> (C) the managers or those members in control of the company:
>
> > (i)   have acted, are acting, or will act in a manner that is illegal or fraudulent; or
> >
> > (ii) have acted or are acting in a manner that is oppressive and was, is, or will be directly harmful to the applicant.

Would a different result have been reached in *Lieberman* under either the Delaware or Uniform Act? About twenty states follow the ULLCA § 701(4)(C(ii) in providing that oppression is a grounds for dissolution and oppression in the LLC context is defined similarly to that studied earlier in Chapter 7.

The LLC statutes differ considerably in their treatment of dissolution, that is, the termination of a member's interest in an LLC other than by the member's voluntary transfer of her interest. Ribstein and Keatinge describe the dissolution provisions of the LLC statutes as follows:

> LLC statutes vary on members' power to voluntarily withdraw and receive the value of their interests. Some provide for withdrawal at any time subject to a notice requirement. This is justified by the need . . . to provide some liquidity for otherwise locked-in interests. Some statutes eliminate any default right to withdraw or permit voluntary termination of membership status, but deny a default right to be paid on resignation. These statutes are based in part on the disruption a buyout right may cause a firm, and in part on the need to reduce the tax valuation of the departing partner's interest in familiar firms. . . .
>
> Most LLC statutes provide that a withdrawing member is entitled to some payment on withdrawal. The statutes use different formulations. Some are based on a return of contributions, while others provide for payment of fair market value in addition to, or instead other distributions to which the member is entitled (apparently including regular payouts that the member was entitled to receive before withdrawal). The statutes also provide for adjustment of the payment to exclude goodwill in the event of wrongful withdrawal. . . .

Consistent with [the] potential costs of dissolution at will, LLC statutes increasingly provide that dissociation does not dissolve or trigger liquidation of the firm. . . .

LLC statutes generally allow dissolution by judicial decree. Some allow judicial dissolution when it is "not reasonably practicable to carry on the business in conformity with the parties' agreement." Where the statute provides only for dissolution, it is not clear whether the court can order other relief, including buyout.

L. Ribstein & R. Keatinge, Limited Liability Companies 11–3—11–19 (2nd ed. 2009).

Reese v. Newman

District of Columbia Court of Appeals, 2016.
131 A.3d 880.

■ KING, SENIOR JUDGE:

Appellant, C. Allison Defoe Reese, and appellee, Nicole Newman, were co-owners of ANR Construction Management, LLC ("ANR"). Following disputes over management of the company, Newman notified Reese in writing that she intended to withdraw from, dissolve, and wind-up the LLC. Reese did not want to dissolve the LLC but preferred that Newman simply be dissociated so that Reese could continue the business herself. Newman filed an action for judicial dissolution in the Superior Court along with a number of other claims. Reese filed a counterclaim for Newman's dissociation in addition to other claims. Following a jury trial, the jury awarded Newman $19,000 on her conversion claim, and found grounds for both judicial dissolution and forced dissociation of Newman; the court, thereafter, ordered judicial dissolution of the LLC. All other claims by the parties were rejected. Reese appeals from a judgment entered on the jury verdicts, and the trial court's order of dissolution. We affirm.

. . .

Reese argues that the trial court erred when it purported to use discretion in choosing between dissolution of the LLC, as proposed by Newman, and forcing dissociation of Newman from the LLC, as proposed by Reese. Reese argues that the statute does not allow for any discretion by the court, and that, in fact, the statute mandates that the court order dissociation of Newman based on the jury's findings. We disagree.

. . . Our analysis starts with the plain language of the statute . . . .

Reese argues that the court was required to dissociate Newman from the LLC under D.C. Code § 29–806.02 (5) which reads:

A person *shall* be dissociated as a member from a limited liability company when:

. . .

(5) On application by the company, the person is expelled as a member by judicial order because the person has:

(A) Engaged, or is engaging, in wrongful conduct that has adversely and materially affected, or will adversely and materially affect, the company's activities and affairs;

(B) Willfully or persistently committed, or is willfully and persistently committing, a material breach of the operating agreement or the person's duties or obligations under § 29–804.09; or

(C) Engaged in, or is engaging, in conduct relating to the company's activities which makes it not reasonably practicable to carry on the activities with the person as a member. . . .

(emphasis added).

. . . While the introductory language of § 29–806.02 does use the word "shall"—that command is in no way directed at the trial judge. It reads, "[a] person shall be dissociated . . . when," and then goes on to recite fifteen separate circumstances describing different occasions *when a person shall be dissociated from an LLC*. That is to say, when one of the events described in subparagraphs (1) through (15) occurs, the member shall be dissociated. Subparagraph (5), however, is merely one instance for which a person *shall be dissociated*; that is, when and if a judge has ordered a member expelled because she finds that any conditions under (5)(A)–(C) have been established. In other words, the command in the introductory language is not directed at the trial judge, it is directed at all the circumstances set forth in subparagraphs (1) through (15) each of which identifies a different basis for which a member of an LLC shall be dissociated. There is nothing in the language of § 29–806.02 (5) that strips a judge of her discretion because it does not require the judge to expel the member if any of the enumerated conditions are established. In short, § 29–806.02 (5) means: when a judge has used her discretion to expel a member of an LLC by judicial order, under any of the enumerated circumstances in (5)(A)–(C), that member *shall* be dissociated.

. . .

Not only does the plain language necessitate an interpretation contrary to Reese's interpretation but additional authority persuades us as well. The District's law adopts language almost identical to the Revised Uniform Limited Liability Company Act (2013) ("RULLCA").[8] Section 602 (6) of the RULLCA is substantially mirrored in § 29–806.02 (5) of the D.C. Code. The comments to § 602 provide solid guidance:

---

[8] *Compare* D.C. Code § 29–806.02 *with* Revised Unif. Ltd. Liab. Co. Act § 602.

"[w]here grounds exist for both dissociation and dissolution, a court has the discretion to choose between the alternatives." RULLCA § 602 cmt. P 6 (citing *Robertson v. Jacobs Cattle Co.*, 285 Neb. 859, 830 N.W.2d 191, 201–02 (Neb. 2013)). The notion that a judge has discretion to choose between alternatives (dissociation or dissolution) when grounds for both exist bolsters our view that the language in § 29–806.02 (5) is not compulsory. Otherwise, when grounds for both dissolution and dissociation were present, dissolution would never be mandated by a court because dissociation of a member would always necessarily trump it.

In sum, we hold that § 29–806.02 (5) can only be interpreted to mean: when a judge finds that any of the events in (5)(A)–(C) have taken place, she may (*i.e.*, has discretion to) expel by judicial order a member of an LLC, and when a judge has done so the member *shall* be dissociated. Moreover, when both grounds for dissociation of a member and dissolution of the LLC exist, the trial judge has discretion to choose either alternative.

Here, the jury was asked to respond to specific interrogatories on the grounds for both dissociation and dissolution. The jury found that grounds were present for either outcome. The trial judge acknowledged that both options were on the table and then exercised her discretion in ordering that dissolution take place. We find no reason to disturb that order.

Haley v. Talcott

Court of Chancery of Delaware, 2004.
864 A.2d 86.

■ STRINE, VICE CHANCELLOR . . .

[In 2001, Matthew Haley and Gregory Talcott created a restaurant called the Redfin Seafood Grill. Haley operated the Grill. Talcott borrowed the money to start up the Grill, and owned it. However, a series of agreements made clear that the parties would treat the Grill as a joint venture. For example, an Employment Agreement provided that after Talcott's start-up loan was paid off, Haley would receive half the Grill's profits and would be awarded half the proceeds from any sale of the Grill. Furthermore, when the Grill was opened, Talcott obtained an option to purchase the property on which the Grill was located (the Property), and Talcott gave Haley the right to participate in any exercise of the option by paying 50% of the purchase price. If Haley did so, then he would be either a 50% owner of the Property or a 50% of the entity, if any, formed to hold the property.

[The Grill was very successful: by the second year of its existence, the start-up money had been repaid to Talcott, both parties were drawing salaries, and the parties each received approximately $150,000 in profit sharing. In 2003, the parties formed Matt & Greg Real Estate, LLC, to take advantage of the option to purchase the Property. Section 18 of the LLC Agreement provided that upon one member's written notice of an election to quit the LLC, the remaining member could elect to purchase the departing member's interest for fair market value. If the remaining member so elected, the parties could either agree on the fair value or have the fair value determined by arbitration. If the remaining member failed to so elect, the LLC would be liquidated.

[The option price to purchase the Property was $720,000. The LLC took out a mortgage loan for that amount, exercised the option, and obtained the Property. To secure the loan, Haley and Talcott individually signed personal guaranties for the entire amount of the mortgage. The Grill continued to operate at the site, paying the LLC $6,000 per month in rent, which was sufficient to cover the LLC's monthly obligation to the mortgagee. Thus by Fall 2003, the parties appeared poised to reap the fruits of their labors.

[At that point, however, Haley and Talcott suffered a serious falling out. In October 2003, Talcott effectively discharged Haley as a manager of the Redfin Grill. In November, Haley rejected a new lease that Talcott proposed for the Grill, and voted to terminate the Grill's lease and sell the Property, which was appraised at $18 million in June 2004. As a 50% member, Haley could not force the LLC to take action on these proposals, because Talcott opposed them. By virtue of the stalemate, the status quo continued—a result that Talcott favored. The Grill's lease expired, but the Grill continued to pay $6,000 per month to the LLC in a month-to-month arrangement. This amount exceeded the LLC's required monthly mortgage payment by $800, so the situation remained stable.

[With only a 50% ownership interest in the LLC, Haley could not force the termination of the Grill's lease and evict the Grill as a tenant, nor could he force the sale of the Property. Haley then brought an action under § 18–802 of the Delaware Limited Liability Company Act, which permits a court to decree dissolution of an LLC "whenever it is not reasonably practicable to carry on the business in conformity with a limited liability company agreement."]

III. Legal Analysis . . .

Haley alleges that pursuant to 6 Del. C. § 18–802 the court should exercise its discretion and dissolve the LLC because it is not reasonably practicable for it to continue the business of the company in conformity with the LLC Agreement. . . .

Haley argues that dissolution is required because the two 50% managers cannot agree how to best utilize the sole asset of the LLC, the Property, because no provision exists for breaking a tie in the voting interests, and because the LLC cannot take any actions, such as entering contracts, borrowing or lending money, or buying or selling property, absent a majority vote of its members. Because this circumstance resembles corporate deadlock, Haley urges that 8 Del. C. § 273 provides a relevant parallel for analysis. . . . [Delaware Gen. Corp. Law 273(a) provides, in relevant part:

> If the stockholders of a corporation of this state, having only 2 stockholders each of whom own 50% of the stock therein, shall be engaged in a joint venture and if such stockholders shall be unable to agree upon the desirability of discontinuing such joint venture and disposing of the assets used in such venture, either stock holder may, unless otherwise provided in the certificate of incorporation of the corporation or in a written agreement between stockholders, file with the Court of Chancery a petition stating that it desires to discontinue such joint venture and to dispose of the assets used in such venture in accordance with a plan to be agreed on by both stockholders or that, if no such plan shall be agreed upon by both stockholders, the corporation be dissolved.]

Here, the key facts about the parties' ability to work together are not rationally disputable. Therefore, my decision on the motion largely turns on two legal issues: 1) if the doctrine of corporate deadlock is an appropriate analogy for the analysis of a § 18–802 claim on these facts; and 2) if so, and if action to break the stalemate is necessary to permit the LLC to function, [or] whether, because of the contract-law foundations of the Delaware LLC Act, Haley should be relegated to the contractual exit mechanism provided in the LLC Agreement. . . .

Section 18–802 of the Delaware LLC Act is a relatively recent addition to our law, and, as a result, there have been few decisions interpreting it. Nevertheless, § 18–802 has the obvious purpose of providing an avenue of relief when an LLC cannot continue to function in accordance with its chartering agreement. Thus § 18–802 plays a role for LLCs similar to the role that § 273 of the DGCL plays for joint venture corporations with only two stockholders. . . .

. . . Section 273 essentially sets forth three pre-requisites for a judicial order of dissolution: 1) the corporation must have two 50% stockholders, 2) those stockholders must be engaged in a joint venture, and 3) they must be unable to agree upon whether to discontinue the business or how to dispose of its assets. Here, by analogy, each of the three provisions is indisputably met.

First, there is no dispute that the parties are 50% members of the LLC. . . .

Second, there is no rational doubt that the parties intended to be and are engaged in a joint venture. . . . The relationship between Haley and Talcott indicates active involvement by both parties in creating a restaurant for their mutual benefit and profit, and the Employment Contract shows that Haley was to be the "Operations Director" of the Redfin Grill, a position that, according to [a] Letter Agreement, would only be terminated if the restaurant was sold. Haley was also entitled to a 50% share of the Redfin Grill's profits. In short, Haley and Talcott were in it together for as long as they owned the restaurant, equally sharing the profits as provided in the Employment Contract. . . .

Finally, the evidence clearly supports a finding of deadlock between the parties about the business strategy and future of the LLC. [Haley expressed] his desire to end the lease of the Redfin Grill and sell the Property at fair market value. The very fact that dissolution has not occurred, combined with Talcott's opposition in this lawsuit, leads inevitably to the conclusion that Talcott opposes such a disposition of the assets. Neither is Talcott's opposition surprising given his economic interest in the continued success of the Redfin Grill, success that one must assume relies, in part, on a continuing favorable lease arrangement with the LLC. . . .

. . . Clearly, Talcott understands that the end of Haley's managerial role from the Redfin Grill profoundly altered their relationship as co-members of the LLC. After all, it has left Haley on the outside, looking in, with no power. Of course, Talcott insists that the LLC can and does continue to function for its intended purpose and in conformity with the agreement, receiving payments from the Redfin Grill and writing checks to meet its obligations under the mortgage on Talcott's authority. But that reality does not mean that the LLC is operating in accordance with the LLC Agreement. Although the LLC is technically functioning at this point, this operation is purely a residual, inertial status quo that just happens to exclusively benefit one of the 50% members, Talcott, as illustrated by the hands-tied continuation of the expired lease with the Redfin Grill. With strident disagreement between the parties regarding the appropriate deployment of the asset of the LLC, and open hostility as evidenced by the related suit in this matter, it is not credible that the LLC could, if necessary, take any important action that required a vote of the members. Abundant, uncontradicted documents in the record demonstrate the inability of the parties to function together.

For all these reasons, if the LLC were a corporation, there would be no question that Haley's request to dissolve the entity would be granted. But this case regards an LLC, not a corporation, and more importantly, an LLC with a detailed exit provision. That distinguishing factor must and is considered next. . . .

The Delaware LLC Act is grounded on principles of freedom of contract. For that reason, the presence of a reasonable exit mechanism bears on the propriety of ordering dissolution under 6 Del. C. § 18–802. When the agreement itself provides a fair opportunity for the dissenting member who disfavors the inertial status quo to exit and receive the fair market value of her interest, it is at least arguable that the limited liability company may still proceed to operate practicably under its contractual charter because the charter itself provides an equitable way to break the impasse. . . .

. . . [However,] forcing Haley to exercise the contractual exit mechanism would not permit the LLC to proceed in a practicable way that accords with the LLC Agreement, but would instead permit Talcott to penalize Haley without express contractual authorization.[35]

Why? Because the parties agree that exit mechanism in the LLC Agreement would not relieve Haley of his obligation under the personal guaranty that he signed to secure the mortgage from County Bank. If Haley is forced to use the exit mechanism, Talcott and he both believe that Haley would still be left holding the bag on the guaranty. It is therefore not equitable to force Haley to use the exit mechanism in this circumstance. While the exit mechanism may be workable in a friendly departure when both parties cooperate to reach an adequate alternative agreement with the bank, the bank cannot be compelled to accept the removal of Haley as a personal guarantor. Thus, the exit mechanism fails as an adequate remedy for Haley because it does not equitably effect the separation of the parties. Rather, it would leave Haley with no upside potential, and no protection over the considerable downside risk that he would have to make good on any future default by the LLC (over whose operations he would have no control) to its mortgage lender. Thus here . . . the parties do not, in fact, "have at their disposal a far less drastic means to resolve their personal disagreement." . . .

For the reasons discussed above, I find that it is not reasonably practicable for the LLC to continue to carry on business in conformity with the LLC Agreement. The parties shall confer and, within four weeks, submit a plan for the dissolution of the LLC. The plan shall include a procedure to sell the Property owned by the LLC within a commercially reasonable time frame. Either party may, of course, bid on the Property.

IT IS SO ORDERED.

---

[35] Stated plainly and putting aside Haley's proposal to sell the Property, it is an interesting question whether the 50% member of an LLC that operates an on-going business, and who does not favor inertial policy, must exit rather than force dissolution, particularly when the cost of the exit procedure would, as here, be borne solely by him. Arguably, it is economically more efficient—absent an explicit requirement that the party disfavoring inertia exit if he is dissatisfied—to order dissolution, and allow both parties to bid as purchasers, with the assets going to the highest bidder (inside or outside) who presumably will deploy the asset to its most valuable use. It is also concomitantly arguable that if parties wish to force the co-equal member disfavoring inertia to exit rather than seek dissolution, then they should explicitly contract upfront in the LLC agreement that exit (or the triggering of a buy-sell procedure, giving incentives for the business to be retained by the member willing to pay the highest value) is the required method of breaking any later-arising stalemate.

CHAPTER 9

THE DUTY TO ACT WITH CARE, IN GOOD FAITH, AND LAWFULLY

1. THE DUTY OF CARE

A. THE BASIC STANDARD OF CARE

Francis v. United Jersey Bank

Supreme Court of New Jersey, 1981.
87 N.J. 15, 432 A.2d 814.

■ POLLOCK, J.

The primary issue on this appeal is whether a corporate director is personally liable in negligence for the failure to prevent the misappropriation of trust funds by other directors who were also officers and shareholders of the corporation.

Plaintiffs are trustees in bankruptcy of Pritchard & Baird Intermediaries Corp. (Pritchard & Baird), a reinsurance broker or intermediary. Defendant Lillian P. Overcash is the daughter of Lillian G. Pritchard and the executrix of her estate. At the time of her death, Mrs. Pritchard was a director and the largest single shareholder of Pritchard & Baird. Because Mrs. Pritchard died after the institution of suit but before trial, her executrix was substituted as a defendant. United Jersey Bank is joined as the administrator of the estate of Charles Pritchard, Sr., who had been president, director and majority shareholder of Pritchard & Baird.

This litigation focuses on payments made by Pritchard & Baird to Charles Pritchard, Jr. and William Pritchard, who were sons of Mr. and Mrs. Charles Pritchard, Sr., as well as officers, directors and shareholders of the corporation. Claims against Charles, Jr. and William are being pursued in bankruptcy proceedings against them.

The trial court, sitting without a jury, characterized the payments as fraudulent conveyances within N.J.S.A. 25:2–10 and entered judgment of $10,355,736.91 plus interest against the estate of Mrs. Pritchard. 392 A.2d 1233 (Law Div.1978). The judgment includes damages from her negligence in permitting payments from the corporation of $4,391,133.21 to Charles, Jr. and $5,483,799.02 to William. The trial court also entered judgment for payments of other sums plus interest: (1) against the estate of Lillian Pritchard for $33,000 accepted by her during her lifetime; (2) against the estate of Charles Pritchard, Sr. for $189,194.17 paid to him during his lifetime and $168,454 for payment of taxes on his estate; and (3) against Lillian Overcash individually for $123,156.51 for payments to her.

The Appellate Division affirmed, but found that the payments were a conversion of trust funds, rather than fraudulent conveyances of the assets of the corporation. 407 A.2d 1253 (N.J.Super. 1979). We granted certification limited to the issue of the liability of Lillian Pritchard as a director. 412 A.2d 791 (N.J. 1980).

Although we accept the characterization of the payments as a conversion of trust funds, the critical question is not whether the misconduct of Charles, Jr. and William should be characterized as fraudulent conveyances or acts of conversion. Rather, the initial question is whether Mrs. Pritchard was negligent in not noticing and trying to prevent the misappropriation of funds held by the corporation in an implied trust. A further question is whether her negligence was the proximate cause of the plaintiffs' losses. Both lower courts found that she was liable in negligence for the losses caused by the wrongdoing of Charles, Jr. and William. We affirm.

I

The matrix for our decision is the customs and practices of the reinsurance industry and the role of Pritchard & Baird as a reinsurance broker. Reinsurance involves a contract under which one insurer agrees to indemnify another for loss sustained under the latter's policy of insurance. Insurance companies that insure against losses arising out of fire or other casualty seek at times to minimize their exposure by sharing risks with other insurance companies. Thus, when the face amount of a policy is comparatively large, the company may enlist one or more insurers to participate in that risk. Similarly, an insurance company's loss potential and overall exposure may be reduced by reinsuring a part of an entire class of policies (e.g., 25% of all of its fire insurance policies). The selling insurance company is known as a ceding company. The entity that assumes the obligation is designated as the reinsurer.

The reinsurance broker arranges the contract between the ceding company and the reinsurer. In accordance with industry custom before the Pritchard & Baird bankruptcy, the reinsurance contract or treaty did not specify the rights and duties of the broker. Typically, the ceding company communicates to the broker the details concerning the risk. The broker negotiates the sale of portions of the risk to the reinsurers. In most instances, the ceding company and the reinsurer do not communicate with each other, but rely upon the reinsurance broker. The ceding company pays premiums due a reinsurer to the broker, who deducts his commission and transmits the balance to the appropriate reinsurer. When a loss occurs, a reinsurer pays money due a ceding company to the broker, who then transmits it to the ceding company.

The reinsurance business was described by an expert at trial as having "a magic aura around it of dignity and quality and integrity." A telephone call which might be confirmed by a handwritten memorandum is sufficient to create a reinsurance obligation. Though separate bank accounts are not maintained for each treaty, the industry practice is to segregate the insurance funds from the broker's general accounts. Thus, the insurance fund accounts would contain the identifiable amounts for transmittal to either the reinsurer or the ceder. The expert stated that in general three kinds of checks may be drawn on this account: checks payable to reinsurers as premiums, checks payable to ceders as loss payments and checks payable to the brokers as commissions.

. . . [Charles Pritchard Sr. and George Baird founded the company in 1959. Since 1964, when Pritchard bought Baird's interest, the company has been owned by Mr. and Mrs. Pritchard and their two sons. After Charles, Sr. died, Lillian owned 48 percent of the company.]

The corporate minute books reflect only perfunctory activities by the directors, related almost exclusively to the election of officers and adoption of banking resolutions and a retirement plan. None of the minutes for any of the meetings contain a discussion of the loans to Charles, Jr. and William or of the financial condition of the corporation. Moreover, upon instructions of Charles, Jr. that financial statements were not to be circulated to anyone else, the company's statements for the fiscal years beginning February 1, 1970, were delivered only to him.

Charles Pritchard, Sr. was the chief executive and controlled the business in the years following Baird's withdrawal. Beginning in 1966, he gradually relinquished control over the operations of the corporation. In 1968, Charles, Jr. became president and William became executive vice president. Charles, Sr. apparently became ill in 1971 and during the last year and a half of his life was not involved in the affairs of the business. He continued, however, to serve as a director until his death on December 10, 1973. Notwithstanding the presence of Charles, Sr. on the board until his death in 1973, Charles, Jr. dominated the management of the corporation and the board from 1968 until the bankruptcy in 1975.

Contrary to the industry custom of segregating funds, Pritchard & Baird commingled the funds of reinsurers and ceding companies with its own funds. All monies (including commissions, premiums and loss monies) were deposited in a single account. Charles, Sr. began the practice of withdrawing funds from the commingled account in transactions identified on the corporate books as "loans." As long as Charles, Sr. controlled the corporation, the "loans" correlated with corporate profits and were repaid at the end of each year. Starting in 1970, however, Charles, Jr. and William begin to siphon ever-increasing sums from the corporation under the guise of loans. As of January 31, 1970, the "loans" to Charles, Jr. were $230,932 and to William were $207,329. At least by January 31, 1973, the annual increase in the loans exceeded annual corporate revenues. By October 1975, the year of bankruptcy, the "shareholders' loans" had metastasized to a total of $12,333,514.47.

The trial court rejected the characterization of the payments as "loans." 392 A.2d 1233 (N.J.Super. 1978) No corporate resolution authorized the "loans," and no note or other instrument evidenced the debt. Charles, Jr. and William paid no interest on the amounts received. The "loans" were not repaid or reduced from one year to the next; rather, they increased annually.

The designation of "shareholders' loans" on the balance sheet was an entry to account for the distribution of the premium and loss money to Charles, Sr., Charles, Jr. and William. As the trial court found, the entry was part of a "woefully inadequate and highly dangerous bookkeeping system." 392 A.2d 1233 (N.J.Super. 1978).

The "loans" to Charles, Jr. and William far exceeded their salaries and financial resources. If the payments to Charles, Jr. and William had been treated as dividends or compensation, then the balance sheets would have shown an excess of liabilities over assets. If the "loans" had been eliminated, the balance sheets would have depicted a corporation not only with a working capital deficit, but also with assets having a fair market value less than its liabilities. The balance sheets for 1970–1975, however, showed an excess of assets over liabilities. This result was achieved by designating the misappropriated funds as "shareholders' loans" and listing them as assets offsetting the deficits. Although the withdrawal of the funds resulted in an obligation of repayment to Pritchard & Baird, the more significant consideration is that the "loans" represented a massive misappropriation of money belonging to the clients of the corporation.

The "loans" were reflected on financial statements that were prepared annually as of January 31, the end of the corporate fiscal year. Although an outside certified public accountant prepared the 1970 financial statement, the corporation prepared only internal financial statements from 1971–1975. In all instances, the statements were simple documents, consisting of three or four 8½ § 11 inch sheets.

The statements of financial condition from 1970 forward demonstrated:

	Working Capital Deficit	Shareholders' Loans	Net Brokerage Income
1970	$ 389,022	$ 509,941	$ 807,229
1971	not available	not available	not available
1972	$ 1,684,289	$ 1,825,911	$1,546,263
1973	$ 3,506,460	$ 3,700,542	$1,736,349

	Working Capital Deficit	Shareholders' Loans	Net Brokerage Income
1974	$ 6,939,007	$ 7,080,629	$ 876,182
1975	$10,176,419	$10,298,039	$ 551,598

Those financial statements showed working capital deficits increasing annually in tandem with the amounts that Charles, Jr. and William withdrew as "shareholders' loans." In the last complete year of business (January 31, 1974, to January 31, 1975), "shareholders' loans" and the correlative working capital deficit increased by approximately $3,200,000.

The funding of the "loans" left the corporation with insufficient money to operate. Pritchard & Baird could defer payment on accounts payable because its clients allowed a grace period, generally 30 to 90 days, before the payment was due. During this period, Pritchard & Baird used the funds entrusted to it as a "float" to pay current accounts payable. By recourse to the funds of its clients, Pritchard & Baird not only paid its trade debts, but also funded the payments to Charles, Jr. and William. Thus, Pritchard & Baird was able to meet its obligations as they came due only through the use of clients' funds.

The pattern that emerges from these figures is the substantial increase in the monies appropriated by Charles Pritchard, Jr. and William Pritchard after their father's withdrawal from the business and the sharp decline in the profitability of the operation after his death. This led ultimately to the filing in December, 1975, of an involuntary petition in bankruptcy and the appointments of the plaintiffs as trustees in bankruptcy of Pritchard & Baird.

Mrs. Pritchard was not active in the business of Pritchard & Baird and knew virtually nothing of its corporate affairs. She briefly visited the corporate offices in Morristown on only one occasion, and she never read or obtained the annual financial statements. She was unfamiliar with the rudiments of reinsurance and made no effort to assure that the policies and practices of the corporation, particularly pertaining to the withdrawal of funds, complied with industry custom or relevant law. Although her husband had warned her that Charles, Jr. would "take the shirt off my back," Mrs. Pritchard did not pay any attention to her duties as a director or to the affairs of the corporation. 392 A.2d 1233 (N.J.Super.L. 1978).

After her husband died in December 1973, Mrs. Pritchard became incapacitated and was bedridden for a six-month period. She became listless at this time and started to drink rather heavily. Her physical condition deteriorated, and in 1978 she died. The trial court rejected testimony seeking to exonerate her because she "was old, was grief-stricken at the loss of her husband, sometimes consumed too much alcohol and was psychologically overborne by her sons." 162 N.J.Super.

at 371, 392 A.2d 1233. That court found that she was competent to act and that the reason Mrs. Pritchard never knew what her sons "were doing was because she never made the slightest effort to discharge any of her responsibilities as a director of Pritchard & Baird." 392 A.2d 1233 (N.J.Super.L. 1978).

II

A preliminary matter is the determination of whether New Jersey law should apply to this case. Although Pritchard & Baird was incorporated in New York, the trial court found that New Jersey had more significant relationships to the parties and the transactions than New York. The shareholder, officers and directors were New Jersey residents. The estates of Mr. and Mrs. Pritchard are being administered in New Jersey, and the bankruptcy proceedings involving Charles, Jr., William and Pritchard & Baird are pending in New Jersey. Virtually all transactions took place in New Jersey. Although many of the creditors are located outside the state, all had contacts with Pritchard & Baird in New Jersey. Consequently, the trial court applied New Jersey law. 392 A.2d 1233 (N.J.Super.L. 1978). The parties agree that New Jersey law should apply. We are in accord.

III

Individual liability of a corporate director for acts of the corporation is a prickly problem. Generally directors are accorded broad immunity and are not insurers of corporate activities. The problem is particularly nettlesome when a third party asserts that a director, because of nonfeasance, is liable for losses caused by acts of insiders, who in this case were officers, directors and shareholders. Determination of the liability of Mrs. Pritchard requires findings that she had a duty to the clients of Pritchard & Baird, that she breached that duty and that her breach was a proximate cause of their losses.

The New Jersey Business Corporation Act, which took effect on January 1, 1969, was a comprehensive revision of the statutes relating to business corporations. One section, N.J.S.A. 14A:6–14, concerning a director's general obligation had no counterpart in the old Act. That section makes it incumbent upon directors to discharge their duties in good faith and with that degree of diligence, care and skill which ordinarily prudent men would exercise under similar circumstances in like positions. [N.J.S.A. 14A:6–14]. . . .

. . . [The principle underlying] N.J.S.A. 14A:6–14 is . . . that directors must discharge their duties in good faith and act as ordinarily prudent persons would under similar circumstances in like positions. Although specific duties in a given case can be determined only after consideration of all of the circumstances, the standard of ordinary care is the wellspring from which those more specific duties flow.

As a general rule, a director should acquire at least a rudimentary understanding of the business of the corporation. Accordingly, a director should become familiar with the fundamentals of the business in which the corporation is engaged. [Campbell v. Watson, 62 N.J.Eq. 396, 50 A. 120 (Ch.1901)]. Because directors are bound to exercise ordinary care, they cannot set up as a defense lack of the knowledge needed to exercise the requisite degree of care. If one "feels that he has not had sufficient business experience to qualify him to perform the duties of a director, he should either acquire the knowledge by inquiry, or refuse to act." *Ibid.*

Directors are under a continuing obligation to keep informed about the activities of the corporation. Otherwise, they may not be able to participate in the overall management of corporate affairs. Barnes v. Andrews, 298 F. 614 (S.D.N.Y.1924). . . . Directors may not shut their eyes to corporate misconduct, and then claim that because they did not see the misconduct, they did not have a duty to look. The sentinel asleep at his post contributes nothing to the enterprise he is charged to protect. Wilkinson v. Dodd, 42 N.J.Eq. 234, 245, 7 A. 327 (Ch.1886), aff'd 42 N.J.Eq. 647, 9 A. 685 (E. & A.1887).

Directorial management does not require a detailed inspection of day-to-day activities, but rather a general monitoring of corporate affairs and policies. Williams v. McKay, [46 N.J.Eq. 25, 36, 18 A. 824 (Ch.1889)]. Accordingly, a director is well advised to attend board meetings regularly. Indeed, a director who is absent from a board meeting is presumed to concur in action taken on a corporate matter, unless he files a "dissent with the secretary of the corporation within a reasonable time after learning of such action." N.J.S.A. 14A:6–13 (Supp.1981–1982). Regular attendance does not mean that directors must attend every meeting, but that directors should attend meetings as a matter of practice. A director of a publicly held corporation might be expected to attend regular monthly meetings, but a director of a small, family corporation might be asked to attend only an annual meeting. The point is that one of the responsibilities of a director is to attend meetings of the board of which he or she is a member. That burden is lightened by N.J.S.A. 14A:6–7(2) (Supp.1981–1982), which permits board action without a meeting if all members of the board consent in writing.

While directors are not required to audit corporate books, they should maintain familiarity with the financial status of the corporation by a regular review of financial statements. *Campbell,* supra, 62 N.J.Eq. at 415, 50 A. 120; *Williams,* supra, 46 N.J.Eq. at 38–39, 18 A. 824; *see* Section of Corporation, Banking and Business Law, American Bar Association, "Corporate Director's Guidebook," 33 Bus. Law. 1595, 1608 (1978) (Guidebook). . . . In some circumstances, directors may be charged with assuring that bookkeeping methods conform to industry custom and usage. Lippitt v. Ashley, 89 Conn. 451, 464, 94 A. 995, 1000 (Sup.Ct.1915). The extent of review, as well as the nature and frequency of financial statements, depends not only on the customs of the industry, but also on the nature of the corporation and the business in which it is engaged. Financial statements of some small corporations may be prepared internally and only on an annual basis; in a large publicly held corporation, the statements may be produced monthly or at some other regular interval. Adequate financial review normally would be more informal in a private corporation than in a publicly held corporation.

Of some relevance in this case is the circumstance that the financial records disclose the "shareholders' loans". Generally directors are immune from liability if, in good faith,

> they rely upon the opinion of counsel for the corporation or upon written reports setting forth financial data concerning the corporation and prepared by an independent public accountant or certified public accountant or firm of such accountants or upon financial statements, books of account or reports of the corporation represented to them to be correct by the president, the officer of the corporation having charge of its books of account, or the person presiding at a meeting of the board. [N.J.S.A. 14A:6–14]

The review of financial statements, however, may give rise to a duty to inquire further into matters revealed by those statements. Corsicana Nat'l Bank v. Johnson, 251 U.S. 68, 71, 40 S.Ct. 82, 84, 64 L.Ed. 141 (1919). . . . Upon discovery of an illegal course of action, a director has a duty to object and, if the corporation does not correct the conduct, to resign. *See* Dodd v. Wilkinson, 42 N.J.Eq. 647, 651, 9 A. 685 (E. & A.1887); Williams v. Riley, 34 N.J.Eq. 398, 401 (Ch.1881).

In certain circumstances, the fulfillment of the duty of a director may call for more than mere objection and resignation. Sometimes a director may be required to seek the advice of counsel. *Guidebook,* supra, at 1631. One New Jersey case recognized the duty of a bank director to seek counsel where doubt existed about the meaning of the bank charter. Williams v. McKay, supra, 46 N.J.Eq. at 60, 18 A. 824. The duty to seek the assistance of counsel can extend to areas other than the interpretation of corporation instruments. Modern corporate practice recognizes that on occasion a director should seek outside advice. A director may require legal advice concerning the propriety of his or her own conduct, the conduct of other officers and directors or the conduct of the corporation. In appropriate circumstances, a director would be "well advised to consult with regular corporate counsel (or his own legal adviser) at any time in which he is doubtful regarding proposed action. . . . " *Guidebook,* supra, at 1618. Sometimes the duty of a director may require more than consulting with outside counsel. A director may have a duty to take reasonable means to prevent illegal conduct by co-directors; in an appropriate case, this may include threat of suit. *See* Selheimer v. Manganese Corp., 423 Pa. 563, 572, 584, 224 A.2d 634, 640, 646 (Sup.Ct.1966) (director exonerated when he objected, resigned, organized shareholder action group, and threatened suit).

A director is not an ornament, but an essential component of corporate governance. Consequently, a director cannot protect himself behind a paper shield bearing the motto, "dummy director."... Thus, all directors are responsible for managing the business and affairs of the corporation. N.J.S.A. 14A:6–1 (Supp.1981–1982); 1 G. Hornstein, Corporation Law and Practice § 431 at 525 (1959).

The factors that impel expanded responsibility in the large, publicly held corporation may not be present in a small, close corporation. Nonetheless, a close corporation may, because of the nature of its business, be affected with a public interest. For example, the stock of a bank may be closely held, but because of the nature of banking the directors would be subject to greater liability than those of another close corporation. Even in a small corporation, a director is held to the standard of that degree of care that an ordinarily prudent director would use under the circumstances. M. Mace, The Board of Directors of Small Corporations 83 (1948).

A director's duty of care does not exist in the abstract, but must be considered in relation to specific obligees. In general, the relationship of a corporate director to the corporation and its stockholders is that of a fiduciary. Whitfield v. Kern, 122 N.J.Eq. 332, 341, 192 A. 48 (E. & A.1937). Shareholders have a right to expect that directors will exercise reasonable supervision and control over the policies and practices of a corporation. The institutional integrity of a corporation depends upon the proper discharge by directors of those duties.

While directors may owe a fiduciary duty to creditors also, that obligation generally has not been recognized in the absence of insolvency. *Whitfield,* supra, 122 N.J.Eq. at 342, 345, 192 A. 48. With certain corporations, however, directors are [deemed] to owe a duty to creditors and other third parties even when the corporation is solvent. Although depositors of a bank are considered in some respects to be creditors, courts have recognized that directors may owe them a fiduciary duty. *See Campbell,* supra, 62 N.J.Eq. at 406–407, 50 A. 120. Directors of nonbanking corporations may owe a similar duty when the corporation holds funds of others in trust. *Cf.* McGlynn v. Schultz, 90 N.J.Super. 505, 218 A.2d 408 (Ch.Div.1966), aff'd 95 N.J.Super. 412, 231 A.2d 386 (App.Div.), certif. den. 50 N.J. 409, 235 A.2d 901 (1967) (directors who did not insist on segregating trust funds held by corporation liable to the *cestuis que trust*).

Courts in other states have imposed liability on directors of nonbanking corporations for the conversion of trust funds, even though those directors did not participate in or know of the conversion.... The distinguishing circumstances in regard to banks and other corporations holding trust funds is that the depositor or beneficiary can reasonably expect the director to act with ordinary prudence concerning the funds held in a fiduciary capacity. Thus, recognition of a duty of a director to those for whom a corporation holds funds in trust may be viewed as another application of the general rule that a director's duty is that of an ordinary prudent person under the circumstances.

The most striking circumstances affecting Mrs. Pritchard's duty as a director are the character of the reinsurance industry, the nature of the misappropriated funds and the financial condition of Pritchard & Baird. The hallmark of the reinsurance industry has been the unqualified trust and confidence reposed by ceding companies and reinsurers in reinsurance brokers. Those companies entrust money to reinsurance intermediaries with the justifiable expectation that the funds will be transmitted to the appropriate parties. Consequently, the companies could have assumed rightfully that Mrs. Pritchard, as a director of a reinsurance brokerage corporation, would not sanction the commingling and the conversion of loss and premium funds for the personal use of the principals of Pritchard & Baird.

As a reinsurance broker, Pritchard & Baird received annually as a fiduciary millions of dollars of clients' money which it was under a duty to segregate.[6] To this extent, it resembled a bank rather than a small family business. Accordingly, Mrs. Pritchard's relationship to the clientele of Pritchard & Baird was akin to that of a director of a bank to its depositors. All parties agree that Pritchard & Baird held the misappropriated funds in an implied trust. That trust relationship gave rise to a fiduciary duty to guard the funds with fidelity and good faith. Ellsworth Dobbs, Inc. v. Johnson, 50 N.J. 528, 553, 236 A.2d 843 (1967); General Films, Inc. v. Sanco Gen. Mfg. Corp., supra, 153 N.J.Super. at 372–373, 379 A.2d 1042.

As a director of a substantial reinsurance brokerage corporation, she should have known that it received annually millions of dollars of loss and premium funds which it held in trust for ceding and reinsurance companies. Mrs. Pritchard should have obtained and read the annual statements of financial condition of Pritchard & Baird. Although she had a right to rely upon financial statements prepared in accordance with N.J.S.A. 14A:6–14, such reliance would not excuse her conduct. The reason is that those statements disclosed on their face the misappropriation of trust funds.

From those statements, she should have realized that, as of January 31, 1970, her sons were withdrawing substantial trust funds under the guise of "Shareholders' Loans." The financial statements for each fiscal year commencing with that of January 31, 1970, disclosed that the working capital deficits and the "loans" were escalating in tandem. Detecting a misappropriation of funds would not have required special expertise or extraordinary diligence; a cursory reading of the financial statements would have revealed the pillage. Thus, if Mrs. Pritchard had read the financial statements, she would have known that her sons were converting trust funds. When financial statements demonstrate that

---

[6]   Following the Pritchard & Baird bankruptcy, New York, a reinsurance center, adopted legislation regulating reinsurance intermediaries. One statute codified the industry standard by prohibiting reinsurance intermediaries from commingling their funds with funds of their principals. N.Y.Ins.Law § 122–a(9) (McKinney Supp.1980–1981).

insiders are bleeding a corporation to death, a director should notice and try to stanch the flow of blood.

In summary, Mrs. Pritchard was charged with the obligation of basic knowledge and supervision of the business of Pritchard & Baird. Under the circumstances, this obligation included reading and understanding financial statements, and making reasonable attempts at detection and prevention of the illegal conduct of other officers and directors. She had a duty to protect the clients of Pritchard & Baird against policies and practices that would result in the misappropriation of money they had entrusted to the corporation. She breached that duty.

IV

Nonetheless, the negligence of Mrs. Pritchard does not result in liability unless it is a proximate cause of the loss. . . .

Cases involving nonfeasance present a much more difficult causation question than those in which the director has committed an affirmative act of negligence leading to the loss. Analysis in cases of negligent omissions calls for determination of the reasonable steps a director should have taken and whether that course of action would have averted the loss.

Usually a director can absolve himself from liability by informing the other directors of the impropriety and voting for a proper course of action. Dyson, "The Director's Liability for Negligence," 40 Ind.L.J. 341, 365 (1965). . . .

Even accepting the hypothesis that Mrs. Pritchard might not be liable if she had objected and resigned, there are two significant reasons for holding her liable. First, she did not resign until just before the bankruptcy. Consequently, there is no factual basis for the speculation that the losses would have occurred even if she had objected and resigned. Indeed, the trial court reached the opposite conclusion: "The actions of the sons were so blatantly wrongful that it is hard to see how they could have resisted any moderately firm objection to what they were doing." 162 N.J.Super. at 372, 392 A.2d 1233. Second, the nature of the reinsurance business distinguishes it from most other commercial activities in that reinsurance brokers are encumbered by fiduciary duties owed to third parties. In other corporations, a director's duty normally does not extend beyond the shareholders to third parties.

In this case, the scope of Mrs. Pritchard's duties was determined by the precarious financial condition of Pritchard & Baird, its fiduciary relationship to its clients and the implied trust in which it held their funds. Thus viewed, the scope of her duties encompassed all reasonable action to stop the continuing conversion. Her duties extended beyond mere objection and resignation to reasonable attempts to prevent the misappropriation of the trust funds. *Campbell,* supra, 62 N.J.Eq. at 427, 50 A. 120. . . .

In assessing whether Mrs. Pritchard's conduct was a legal or proximate cause of the conversion, "[l]egal responsibility must be limited to those causes which are so closely connected with the result and of such significance that the law is justified in imposing liability." Prosser, supra, § 41 at 237. Such a judicial determination involves not only considerations of causation-in-fact and matters of policy, but also common sense and logic. Caputzal v. The Lindsay Co., 48 N.J. 69, 77–78 (1966). The act or the failure to act must be a substantial factor in producing the harm. Prosser, supra, § 41 at 240; Restatement (Second) of Torts, §§ 431, 432 (1965).

Within Pritchard & Baird, several factors contributed to the loss of the funds: comingling of corporate and client monies, conversion of funds by Charles, Jr. and William and dereliction of her duties by Mrs. Pritchard. The wrongdoing of her sons, although the immediate cause of the loss, should not excuse Mrs. Pritchard from her negligence which also was a substantial factor contributing to the loss. Restatement (Second) of Torts, supra, § 442B, comment b. Her sons knew that she, the only other director, was not reviewing their conduct; they spawned their fraud in the backwater of her neglect. Her neglect of duty contributed to the climate of corruption; her failure to act contributed to the continuation of that corruption. Consequently, her conduct was a substantial factor contributing to the loss.

Analysis of proximate cause is especially difficult in a corporate context where the allegation is that nonfeasance of a director is a proximate cause of damage to a third party. Where a case involves nonfeasance, no one can say "with absolute certainty what would have occurred if the defendant had acted otherwise." Prosser, supra, § 41 at 242. Nonetheless, where it is reasonable to conclude that the failure to act would produce a particular result and that result has followed, causation may be inferred. *Ibid.* We conclude that even if Mrs. Pritchard's mere objection had not stopped the depredations of her sons, her consultation with an attorney and the threat of suit would have deterred them. That conclusion flows as a matter of common sense and logic from the record. Whether in other situations a director has a duty to do more than protest and resign is best left to case-by-case determinations. In this case, we are satisfied that there was a duty to do more than object and resign. Consequently, we find that Mrs. Pritchard's negligence was a proximate cause of the misappropriations.

To conclude, by virtue of her office, Mrs. Pritchard had the power to prevent the losses sustained by the clients of Pritchard & Baird. With power comes responsibility. She had a duty to deter the depredation of the other insiders, her sons. She breached that duty and caused plaintiffs to sustain damages.

The judgment of the Appellate Division is affirmed.

■ For affirmance JUSTICES SULLIVAN, PASHMAN, CLIFFORD, SCHREIBER, HANDLER and POLLOCK—6.

For reversal—none.*

———

MODEL BUS. CORP. ACT §§ 8.30, 8.31

[See Statutory Supplement]

———

CAL. CORP. CODE § 309

[See Statutory Supplement]

———

NEW YORK BUS. CORP. LAW § 717

[See Statutory Supplement]

———

ALI, PRINCIPLES OF CORPORATE GOVERNANCE §§ 4.01(a), (b), 4.02, 4.03

[See Statutory Supplement]

———

NOTE ON CAUSATION

Cases in the duty-of-care area sometimes raise difficult causation issues. Two of these issues often arise together: (1) If the violation of the duty of care consists of an omission by a director, would the loss have occurred even if the director had not violated his duty? (2) If the whole board, or a substantial majority of the directors, violates the duty of care, can an individual director be excused on the ground that the result would have been the same even if she had acted differently?

These issues were addressed in the well-known case of *Barnes v. Andrews,* 298 Fed. 614 (S.D.N.Y.1924), decided by Judge Learned Hand, sitting as a trial judge. Liberty Starters Corporation was organized in 1918 to manufacture starters for Ford motors and airplanes. Andrews became a

---

* Some earlier cases involving the liability of inactive spouse- or figurehead-directors went the other way. In Berman v. LeBeauInter-America, Inc., 509 F.Supp. 156, 161 (S.D.N.Y.), aff'd mem. 697 F.2d 872 (2d Cir. 1981), a director was held not liable on the ground that he was a "virtual figurehead." In Allied Freightways, Inc. v. Cholfin, 325 Mass. 630, 633, 91 N.E.2d 765, 768 (1950), the court rested nonliability on causation grounds, concluding that it was doubtful whether, if the spouse, Mrs. Cholfin, had taken steps to familiarize herself with the conduct of the business by her husband she could have changed the situation. "Upon a careful reading of the evidence, we do not think that it can quite be said that the neglect of her official duties as a director was a contributing cause of the loss sustained by the corporation by the wrongful withdrawals of its funds, save only the amounts used for her personal benefits."

director in October 1919, and served until he resigned in June 1920. During Andrews's incumbency there had been only two board meetings, one of which he could not attend. Andrews was the largest shareholder and a friend of Liberty's president, Maynard, who had induced him to become a director. Andrews's only attention to Liberty's affairs consisted of talks with Maynard as they met from time to time. In 1921, Liberty went into receivership as a result of mismanagement. Andrews was sued for violating the duty of care by not paying sufficient attention to the corporation's affairs.

Judge Hand began by holding that Andrews had violated his duty of care:

> . . . It is not enough to content oneself with general answers that the business looks promising and that all seems prosperous. Andrews was bound, certainly as the months wore on, to inform himself of what was going on with some particularity, and, if he had done so, he would have learned that there were delays in getting into production which were putting the enterprise in most serious peril. . . . Having accepted a post of confidence, he was charged with an active duty to learn whether the company was moving to production, and why it was not, and to consider, as best he might, what could be done to avoid the conflicts among the personnel, or their incompetence, which was slowly bleeding it to death.

Id. at 615–16.

Hand went on to hold, however, that the plaintiff also had to prove that Liberty's losses would not have occurred if Andrews had properly performed his duties, and that no such showing had been made:

> . . . This cause of action rests upon a tort, as much though it be a tort of omission as though it had rested upon a positive act. The plaintiff must accept the burden of showing that the performance of the defendant's duties would have avoided loss, and what loss it would have avoided. . . .

> When the corporate funds have been illegally lent, it is a fair inference that a protest would have stopped the loan, and that the director's neglect caused the loss. But when a business fails from general mismanagement, business incapacity, or bad judgment, how is it possible to say that a single director could have made the company successful, or how much in dollars he could have saved? Before this cause can go to a master, the plaintiff must show that, had Andrews done his full duty, he could have made the company prosper, or at least could have broken its fall. He must show what sum he could have saved the company. Neither of these has he made any effort to do.

> The defendant is not subject to the burden of proving that the loss would have happened, whether he had done his duty or not. If he were, it would come to this: That, if a director were once shown slack in his duties, he would stand charged prima facie with the difference between the corporate treasury as it was, and as it would

be, judged by a hypothetical standard of success. How could such a standard be determined? How could anyone guess how far a director's skill and judgment would have prevailed upon his fellows, and what would have been the ultimate fate of the business, if they had? How is it possible to set any measure of liability, or to tell what he would have contributed to the event? Men's fortunes may not be subjected to such uncertain and speculative conjectures. It is hard to see how there can be any remedy, except one can put one's finger on a definite loss and say with reasonable assurance that protest would have deterred, or counsel persuaded, the managers who caused it. No men of sense would take the office, if the law imposed upon them a guaranty of the general success of their companies as a penalty for any negligence.

Id. at 616–18.

Some passages in *Barnes v. Andrews* may be read to suggest that an inattentive director will not be liable for a loss that would have been prevented by an attentive board unless it is shown that if the director had been attentive, his colleagues would have followed his lead. Such a suggestion would be out of keeping with general legal rules on the responsibility of joint actors, and hard to accept as a matter of either fairness or policy. However, *Barnes v. Andrews* can also be read to stand for the more modest proposition that an inattentive director will not be liable for a corporate loss if full attentiveness by *all* the directors would not have saved the situation, because in that case the inattentiveness of any single director will not have been a cause-in-fact of the loss. That is the position taken in § 7.18(b) of the ALI's Principles of Corporate Governance. Under this section, if the board as a whole has violated its duty of care, by either commission or omission, each director will be liable for any loss of which the board's failure is the cause-in-fact and the legal (or proximate) cause:

> (b)   A violation of [a standard of conduct] is the legal cause of loss if the plaintiff proves that (i) satisfaction of the applicable standard would have been a substantial factor in averting the loss, and (ii) the likelihood of injury would have been foreseeable to an ordinarily prudent person in a like position to that of the defendant and under similar circumstances. It is not a defense to liability in such cases that damage to the corporation would not have resulted but for the acts or omissions of other individuals.

The Comment to § 7.18 elaborates this position as follows:

> When multiple corporate officials fail to perform a duty whose omission is a legal cause of the loss, a problem of concurrent causation arises. Potentially, each defendant might claim that his or her conduct was less causally significant than that of others. To prevent each member of the collective body from evading liability by pointing to the concurrent omissions of others, the last sentence of § 7.18(b) specifies that "[i]t is not a defense to liability in such cases that damage to the corporation would not have resulted but

for the acts or omissions of other individuals." This statement is consistent with the general approach of the law of torts to problems of concurrent causation, but § 7.18 takes no position on whether liability in such a case should be joint and several or should be apportioned in terms of culpability among those responsible.

In *Cede & Co. v. Technicolor, Inc.,* 634 A.2d 345 (Del. 1993), modified, 636 A.2d (Del. 1994) (followed by extensive remands and appeals), the trial court rendered judgment for defendants on the ground that the plaintiff had the burden of proving injury and had not done so. The Delaware Supreme Court reversed. The Court concluded that based on the record, the directors had breached the duty of care. Given that conclusion, it held, the Chancellor's determination that the plaintiff had the burden of proving injury was erroneous. Bearing in mind that Delaware treats the business judgment rule as a presumption, the court held that if a plaintiff shows there was a breach of the duty of care, that showing overcomes the presumption of the rule and establishes a prima facie case of liability, even without a showing of injury. The burden then shifts to the defendants to show that the transaction was entirely fair. In the course of its opinion, the court explicitly rejected the reasoning of *Barnes v. Andrews.*

———

B. THE BUSINESS JUDGMENT RULE

Kamin v. American Express Co.

Supreme Court, Special Term, N.Y. County, Part 1, 1976.
86 Misc.2d 809, 383 N.Y.S.2d 807, aff'd on opinion below 54 A.D.2d 654,
387 N.Y.S.2d 993 (1st Dept.1976).

■ EDWARD J. GREENFIELD, JUSTICE:

In this stockholders' derivative action, the individual defendants, who are the directors of the American Express Company, move for an order dismissing the complaint for failure to state a cause of action pursuant to CPLR 3211(a)(7), and alternatively, for summary judgment pursuant to CPLR 3211(c).

The complaint is brought derivatively by two minority stockholders of the American Express Company, asking for a declaration that a certain dividend in kind is a waste of corporate assets, directing the defendants not to proceed with the distribution, or, in the alternative, for monetary damages. The motion to dismiss the complaint requires the Court to presuppose the truth of the allegations. It is the defendants' contention that, conceding everything in the complaint, no viable cause of action is made out.

After establishing the identity of the parties, the complaint alleges that in 1972 American Express acquired for investment 1,954,418 shares of common stock of Donaldson, Lufken and Jenrette, Inc. (hereafter DLJ), a publicly traded corporation, at a cost of $29.9 million. It is further alleged that the current market value of those shares is approximately $4.0 million. On July 28, 1975, it is alleged, the Board of Directors of American Express declared a special dividend to all stockholders of record pursuant to which the shares of DLJ would be distributed in kind. Plaintiffs contend further that if American Express were to sell the DLJ shares on the market, it would sustain a capital loss of $25 million, which could be offset against taxable capital gains on other investments. Such a sale, they allege, would result in tax savings to the company of approximately $8 million, which would not be available in the case of the distribution of DLJ shares to stockholders. It is alleged that on October 8, 1975 and October 16, 1975, plaintiffs demanded that the directors rescind the previously declared dividend in DLJ shares and take steps to preserve the capital loss which would result from selling the shares. This demand was rejected by the Board of Directors on October 17, 1975.

It is apparent that all the previously-mentioned allegations of the complaint go to the question of the exercise by the Board of Directors of business judgment in deciding how to deal with the DLJ shares. The crucial allegation which must be scrutinized to determine the legal sufficiency of the complaint is paragraph 19, which alleges:

> "19. All of the defendant Directors engaged in or acquiesced in or negligently permitted the declaration and payment of the Dividend in violation of the fiduciary duty owed by them to Amex to care for and preserve Amex's assets in the same manner as a man of average prudence would care for his own property."

Plaintiffs never moved for temporary injunctive relief, and did nothing to bar the actual distribution of the DLJ shares. The dividend was in fact paid on October 31, 1975. Accordingly, that portion of the complaint seeking a direction not to distribute the shares is deemed to be moot, and the Court will deal only with the request for declaratory judgment or for damages.

Examination of the complaint reveals that there is no claim of fraud or self-dealing, and no contention that there was any bad faith or oppressive conduct. The law is quite clear as to what is necessary to ground a claim for actionable wrongdoing.

> "In actions by stockholders, which assail the acts of their directors or trustees, courts will not interfere unless the powers have been illegally or unconscientiously executed; or unless it be made to appear that the acts were fraudulent or collusive, and destructive of the rights of the stockholders. Mere errors of judgment are not sufficient as grounds for equity interference, for the powers of those entrusted with corporate management are largely discretionary." Leslie v. Lorillard, 110 N.Y. 519, 532, 18 N.E. 363, 365. . . .

More specifically, the question of whether or not a dividend is to be declared or a distribution of some kind should be made is exclusively a matter of business judgment for the Board of Directors.

> ". . . Courts will not interfere with such discretion unless it be first made to appear that the directors have acted or are about to act in bad faith and for a dishonest purpose. It is for the directors to say, acting in good faith of course, when and to what extent dividends shall be declared . . . The statute confers upon the directors this power, and the minority stockholders are not in a position to question this right, so long as the directors are acting in good faith . . . "

Thus, a complaint must be dismissed if all that is presented is a decision to pay dividends rather than pursuing some other course of conduct. Weinberger v. Quinn, 264 App.Div. 405, 35 N.Y.S.2d 567, affd. 290 N.Y. 635, 49 N.E.2d 131. A complaint which alleges merely that some course of action other than that pursued by the Board of Directors would have been more advantageous gives rise to no cognizable cause of action. Courts have more than enough to do in adjudicating legal rights and devising remedies for wrongs. The directors' room rather than the courtroom is the appropriate forum for thrashing out purely business questions which will have an impact on profits, market prices, competitive situations, or tax advantages. As stated by Cardozo, J., when sitting at Special Term, the substitution of someone else's business judgment for that of the directors "is no business for any court to follow." Holmes v. St. Joseph Lead Co., 84 Misc. 278, 283, 147 N.Y.S. 104, 107, quoting from Gamble v. Queens County Water Co., 123 N.Y. 91, 99, 25 N.E. 201, [202].

It is not enough to allege, as plaintiffs do here, that the directors made an imprudent decision, which did not capitalize on the possibility of using a potential capital loss to offset capital gains. More than imprudence or mistaken judgment must be shown.

> "Questions of policy of management, expediency of contracts or action, adequacy of consideration, lawful appropriation of corporate funds to advance corporate interests, are left solely to their honest and unselfish decision, for their powers therein are without limitation and free from restraint, and the exercise of them for the common and general interests of the corporation may not be questioned, although the results show that what they did was unwise or inexpedient." Pollitz v. Wabash Railroad Co., 207 N.Y. 113, 124, 100 N.E. 721, 724.

Section 720 of the Business Corporation Law permits an action against directors for "the neglect of, or failure to perform, or other violations of his duties in the management and disposition of corporate assets committed to his charge." This does not mean that a director is chargeable with ordinary negligence for having made an improper decision, or having acted imprudently. The "neglect" referred to in the statute is neglect of duties (i.e., malfeasance or nonfeasance) and not misjudgment. To allege that a director "negligently permitted the declaration and payment" of a dividend without alleging fraud, dishonesty or nonfeasance, is to state merely that a decision was taken with which one disagrees.

Nor does this appear to be a case in which a potentially valid cause of action is inartfully stated. . . . The affidavits of the defendants and the exhibits annexed thereto demonstrate that the objections raised by the plaintiffs to the proposed dividend action were carefully considered and unanimously rejected by the Board at a special meeting called precisely for that purpose at the plaintiffs' request. The minutes of the special meeting indicate that the defendants were fully aware that a sale rather than a distribution of the DLJ shares might result in the realization of a substantial income tax saving. Nevertheless, they concluded that there were countervailing considerations primarily with respect to the adverse effect such a sale, realizing a loss of $25 million, would have on the net income figures in the American Express financial statement. Such a reduction of net income would have a serious effect on the market value of the publicly traded American Express stock. This was not a situation in which the defendant directors totally overlooked facts called to their attention. They gave them consideration, and attempted to view the total picture in arriving at their decision. While plaintiffs contend that according to their accounting consultants the loss on the DLJ stock would still have to be charged against current earnings even if the stock were distributed, the defendants' accounting experts assert that the loss would be a charge against earnings only in the event of a sale, whereas in the event of distribution of the stock as a dividend, the proper accounting treatment would be to charge the loss only against surplus. While the chief accountant for the SEC raised some question as to the appropriate accounting treatment of this transaction, there was no basis for any action to be taken by the SEC with respect to the American Express financial statement.

The only hint of self-interest which is raised, not in the complaint but in the papers on the motion, is that four of the twenty directors were officers and employees of American Express and members of its Executive Incentive Compensation Plan. Hence, it is suggested, by virtue of the action taken earnings may have been overstated and their compensation affected thereby. Such a claim is highly speculative and standing alone can hardly be regarded as sufficient to support an inference of self-dealing. There is no claim or showing that the four company directors dominated and controlled the sixteen outside members of the Board. Certainly, every action taken by the Board has some impact on earnings and may therefore affect the compensation of those whose earnings are keyed to profits. That does not disqualify the inside directors, nor does it put every policy adopted by the Board in question. All directors have an obligation, using sound business judgment, to maximize income for the benefit of all persons having a stake in the welfare of the corporate entity. *See*, Amdur v. Meyer, 15 A.D.2d 425, 224 N.Y.S.2d 440, appeal dismissed 14 N.Y.2d 541, 248 N.Y.S.2d 639, 198 N.E.2d 30. What we have here as revealed both by the complaint and by the affidavits and exhibits, is that a disagreement exists between two minority stockholders and a unanimous Board of Directors as to the best way to handle a loss already incurred on an investment. The directors are entitled to exercise their honest business judgment on the information before them, and to act within their corporate powers. That they may be mistaken, that other courses of action might have differing consequences, or that their action might benefit some shareholders more than others presents no basis for the superimposition of judicial judgment, so long as it appears that the directors have been acting in good faith. The question of to what extent a dividend shall be declared and the manner in which it shall be paid is ordinarily subject only to the qualification that the dividend be paid out of surplus (Business Corporation Law Section 510, subd. b). The Court will not interfere unless a clear case is made out of fraud, oppression, arbitrary action, or breach of trust.

Courts should not shrink from the responsibility of dismissing complaints or granting summary judgment when no legal wrongdoing is set forth. . . .

In this case it clearly appears that the plaintiffs have failed as a matter of law to make out an actionable claim. Accordingly, the motion by the defendants for summary judgment and dismissal of the complaint is granted.

———

ALI, PRINCIPLES OF CORPORATE GOVERNANCE § 4.01(c)

[See Statutory Supplement]

———

NOTES ON DIVERGENCE WITHIN THE BUSINESS JUDGMENT RULE

1. Standard of Conduct vs. Standard of Review. A *standard of conduct* states how an actor should conduct a given activity or play a given role. A *standard of review* states the test a court should apply when it reviews an actor's conduct to determine whether to impose liability or grant injunctive relief. In many or most areas of law, standards of conduct and standards of review are identical. For example, the standard of conduct that governs an automobile driver is that he should drive carefully. Correspondingly, the standard of review in a liability claim against a driver is whether he drove carefully. The standard of conduct that governs an agent who engages in a transaction with his principal that involves the subject matter of the agency is that the agent must deal fairly. Correspondingly, the standard of review in a liability claim by the principal against an agent based on such a transaction is whether the agent dealt fairly.

An identity between standards of conduct and standards of review is so common that it is easy to overlook the fact that the two kinds of standards may diverge in any given area—that is, the standard of conduct that states how an actor should conduct himself may differ from the standard of review by which courts determine whether to impose liability on the basis of the actor's conduct. A divergence of standards of conduct and standards of review is particularly common in corporation law.

The duty of care is a leading example of this divergence. The traditional *standard of conduct* applicable to directors and officers in the performance of their functions, in relation to matters in which they are not self-interested, varies somewhat in its formulation, but the basic standard is set forth in Section 4.01(a) of the ALI's *Principles of Corporate Governance.* "A director or officer has a duty to the corporation to perform the director's or officer's functions in good faith, in a manner that he or she reasonably believes to be in the best interests of the corporation, and with the care that an ordinarily prudent person would reasonably be expected to exercise in a like position and under similar circumstances." The application of this standard of conduct to the functions of directors results in several distinct duties—in particular, the duty to monitor, the duty of inquiry, the duty to make prudent or reasonable decisions on matters that the board is obliged or chooses to act upon, and the duty to employ a reasonable process to make decisions.

Officers have comparable duties, although for most officers decisionmaking is likely to be more important than monitoring.

On their face, the duties of directors are fairly demanding, insofar as they are measured by reasonability. In practice, however, the standards of review applied to the performance of these duties are less stringent than the standards of conduct on which the duties are based. *Compare* Model Act Section 8.30 *with* Section 8.31. This is especially true when the quality of a decision, as opposed to the quality of the decisionmaking process, is called into question. In such cases a much less demanding standard of review may apply under the business judgment rule.

The business judgment rule consists of four conditions and, if the four conditions are satisfied, a special standard of review applicable to claims that are based on the quality of a decision.

The four conditions are as follows:

First, the director must have made a decision. So, for example, a director's failure to make due inquiry, or any other simple failure to take action (as opposed to a deliberate decision not to act), does not qualify for protection under the business judgment rule.

Second, the director must have informed himself with respect to the business judgment to the extent he reasonably believes appropriate under the circumstances—that is, he must have employed a reasonable decisionmaking process.

Third, the decision must have been made in good faith—a condition that is not satisfied if, among other things, the director knows that the decision violates the law.

Fourth, the director may not have a financial interest in the subject matter of the decision. For example, the business judgment rule is inapplicable to a director's decision to approve the corporation's purchase of his property.

If the conditions of the business judgment rule are not satisfied, then the standard by which the quality of a decision is reviewed is comparable to the standard of conduct for making the decision—that is, the standard of review is based on entire fairness or reasonability. This is nicely illustrated by the Delaware Supreme Court's 1993 decision in *Cede & Co. v. Technicolor, Inc.*, 634 A.2d 345, followed by extensive remands and appeals.

In that case, Perelman, the CEO of MacAndrews & Forbes, Inc. ("MAF"), entered into negotiations with Kamerman, the CEO of Technicolor, with a view to an acquisition of Technicolor by MAF. On the basis of limited information, Goldman Sachs, an investment banker, told Kamerman that a price of $20–22 per share was worth pursuing, that a $25 price might be feasible, and that Kamerman should consider other possible purchasers. Six days later, Kamerman and Perelman agreed on a price of $23. That evening, Kamerman called a special meeting of Technicolor's Board, to be held two days later. At the meeting, the board approved an agreement to transfer Technicolor to MAF at the $23 price, and recommended that Technicolor's shareholders accept that price.

At the trial, the Chancellor found that it was a matter of grave doubt whether Technicolor's board had exercised due care in making its decision, for the following reasons, among others: (1) The agreement was not preceded by a prudent search of alternatives. (2) Given the terms of the merger and the circumstances, the directors had no reasonable basis to assume that a better offer from a third party could be expected once the agreement was signed. (3) Most of the directors had little or no knowledge of an impending sale of the company until they arrived at the meeting, and only a few of them had any knowledge of the terms of the sale.

On the basis of these reasons, the Delaware Supreme Court held that Technicolor's board failed to reach an informed decision when it made its decision, so the business judgment rule did not apply. As a result, the directors had the burden of showing that the transaction was entirely fair. If the $23 price was not entirely fair, the directors would be liable for damages. And, the court added, because the business judgment rule did not apply, the directors had the burden of proving that the price was entirely fair.

2. Being Reasonable vs. Being Rational. If the four conditions of the business judgment rule *are* satisfied, the quality of a director's decision will be reviewed, not to determine whether the decision was *reasonable*, but only under a much more limited standard. There is some difference of opinion as to how that limited standard should be formulated. A few courts have stated that the standard is whether the director acted in good faith. *See, e.g., In re RJR Nabisco, Inc. Shareholders Litig.*, [1988–89 Transfer Binder] Fed. Sec.

L. Rep. (CCH) ¶ 94194, at 91,710 n.13 (Del. Ch. Jan. 31, 1989). However, if the four conditions of the business judgment rule are satisfied, the prevalent formulation of the standard of review under the rule is that the decision must merely be *rational*, or must have a *rational basis*, or the like. *See* ALI, Principles of Corporate Governance § 4.01(c)(3). This standard of review may be referred to as the business-judgment standard.

An example of a decision that fails to satisfy the rationality standard is a decision that cannot be coherently explained. For example, in *Selheimer v. Manganese Corp. of America*, 224 A.2d 634 (Pa.1966), a corporation's managers poured almost all of the corporation's funds into the development of a single plant, even though they knew that the plant could not be operated profitably for a number of reasons, including lack of a railroad siding and proper storage areas. The court imposed liability because the managers' conduct "defie[d] explanation; in fact, the defendants have failed to give any satisfactory explanation or advance any justification for [the] expenditures." (In contrast, a decision may be unreasonable, but not irrational, if there are good reasons for and against the decision, but under the circumstances a person of sound judgment, giving appropriate weight to the reasons for and against, would not have made the decision. Accordingly, a decision may be unreasonable even though it was supported by some affirmative reasons and was therefore explicable, although on balance undesirable.)

3.   *The Action for Waste.* An allegation of "waste" in the corporate setting refers to a claim that a transaction is so one-sided that no rational business person would believe the transaction represented a fair exchange. A similar definition is found in the ALI's Principles of Corporate Governance:

> A transaction constitutes a "waste of corporate assets" if it involves an expenditure of corporate funds or a disposition of corporate assets for which no consideration is received in exchange and for which there is no rational business purpose, or if consideration is received in exchange, the consideration the corporation receives is so inadequate in value that no person of ordinary sound business judgment would deem it worth that which the corporation has paid.

Id. § 1.42. As so stated, an assessment whether waste has occurred would appear to be exclusively an objective inquiry. As such, allegations of waste have in modern times enabled challenges to executive compensation to survive the defendants' procedural challenges, but not to liability based purely on objective assessments whether the compensation was excessive. *See* Randall S. Thomas & Kenneth J. Martin, Litigating Challenges to Executive Pay: An Exercise in Futility?, 79 Wash. U. L. Q. 569, 573–85 (2001). Consider whether penetrating judicial inquiry into the benefits/ burdens of a transaction would draw courts into the very terrain that the presumptions underlying the business judgment rule warns courts not to enter? This concern underlies not only the absence in modern times of successful waste actions but how the action has mutated into an action focused on bad faith where an extreme imbalance in the values exchanges are treated as indicative of the fiduciary failing to act in good faith. *See e.g., In re Walt Disney Co. Derivative Litig.*, 907 A.2s 693, 749 (Del. Ch. 2005) ("waste is an act of bad faith"). In this way, at least in Delaware, waste is treated as a subset of good faith under the umbrella duty of loyalty. Is this a sensible development? A welcome development?

> Whatever objections one might raise to merging waste into good faith, there are also arguments to be made in favor of that move. For one, waste claims have often hinted at fiduciary violations; it has always been difficult to imagine cases of waste where someone did not violate his or her fiduciary duties. A transaction so irrational as to be wasteful, in other words, is also one so irrational as to suggest that directors demonstrated "a conscious disregard for [their] duties" in approving it. From their inception, indeed, waste claims have often appeared to have a fictive quality, with allegations of "irrationality" cloaking an implication that the transaction benefitted the decision-maker. If waste claims have always carried with them a whiff of fiduciary violations, then it may not be a radical leap to treat a waste claim as really asserting a fiduciary breach.

Hartwell Wells, The Life (and Death?) of Corporate Waste, 74 Wash. & Lee L. Rev. 1239, 1290 (2017).

———

Smith v. Van Gorkom

Supreme Court of State of Delaware, 1985.
488 A.2d 858.

■ Before HERMANN, C.J., and MCNEILLY, HORSEY, MOORE and CHRISTIE, JJ., constituting the Court en banc.

■ HORSEY, JUSTICE (FOR THE MAJORITY):

This appeal from the Court of Chancery involves a class action brought by shareholders of the defendant Trans Union Corporation ("Trans Union" or "the Company"), originally seeking rescission of a cash-out merger of Trans Union into the defendant New T Company ("New T"), a wholly-owned subsidiary of the defendant, Marmon Group, Inc. ("Marmon"). Alternate relief in the form of damages is sought against the defendant members of the Board of Directors of Trans Union, New T, and Jay A. Pritzker and Robert A. Pritzker, owners of Marmon.[1]

---

[1]   The plaintiff, Alden Smith, originally sought to enjoin the merger; but, following extensive discovery, the Trial Court denied the plaintiff's motion for preliminary injunction by unreported letter opinion dated February 3, 1981. On February 10, 1981, the proposed merger was approved by Trans Union's stockholders at a special meeting and the merger became effective on that date. Thereafter, John W. Gosselin was permitted to intervene as an additional plaintiff; and Smith and Gosselin were certified as representing a class consisting of all persons, other than defendants, who held shares of Trans Union common stock on all relevant dates. At the time of the merger, Smith owned 54,000 shares of Trans Union stock, Gosselin owned 23,600 shares, and members of Gosselin's family owned 20,000 shares.

Following trial, the former Chancellor granted judgment for the defendant directors by unreported letter opinion dated July 6, 1982.[2] Judgment was based on two findings: (1) that the Board of Directors had acted in an informed manner so as to be entitled to protection of the business judgment rule in approving the cash-out merger; and (2) that the shareholder vote approving the merger should not be set aside because the stockholders had been "fairly informed" by the Board of Directors before voting thereon. The plaintiffs appeal.

Speaking for the majority of the Court, we conclude that both rulings of the Court of Chancery are clearly erroneous. Therefore, we reverse and direct that judgment be entered in favor of the plaintiffs and against the defendant directors for the fair value of the plaintiffs' stockholdings in Trans Union. . . .

I.

The nature of this case requires a detailed factual statement. The following facts are essentially uncontradicted. . . .

Trans Union was a publicly-traded, diversified holding company, the principal earnings of which were generated by its railcar leasing business. During the period here involved, the Company had a cash flow of hundreds of millions of dollars annually. However, the Company had difficulty in generating sufficient taxable income to offset increasingly large investment tax credits (ITCs). . . .

B.

[Jerome Van Gorkom, Trans Union's Chairman and Chief Executive Officer, met with senior management on August 27, 1980, to discuss Trans Union's difficulty in producing sufficient taxable income to offset its increasing investment-tax credits and accelerated-depreciation deductions.] Donald Romans, Chief Financial Officer of Trans Union, stated that his department had done a "very brief bit of work on the possibility of a leveraged buy-out." . . . The work consisted of a "preliminary study" of the cash which could be generated by the Company if it participated in a leveraged buy-out. As Romans stated, this analysis "was very first and rough cut at seeing whether a cash flow would support what might be considered a high price for this type of transaction."

On September 5, at another Senior Management meeting which Van Gorkom attended, Romans again brought up the idea of a leveraged buy-out as a "possible strategic alternative" to the Company's acquisition program. Romans and Bruce S. Chelberg, President and Chief Operating Officer of Trans Union, had been working on the matter in preparation for the meeting. According to Romans: They did not "come up" with a price for the Company. They merely "ran the numbers" at $50 a share

---

2   Following trial, and before decision by the Trial Court, the parties stipulated to the dismissal, with prejudice, of the Messrs. Pritzker as parties defendant. However, all references to defendants hereinafter are to the defendant directors of Trans Union, unless otherwise noted.

and at $60 a share with the "rough form" of their cash figures at the time. Their "figures indicated that $50 would be very easy to do but $60 would be very difficult to do under those figures." This work did not purport to establish a fair price for either the Company or 100% of the stock. It was intended to determine the cash flow needed to service the debt that would "probably" be incurred in a leveraged buy-out, based on "rough calculations" without "any benefit of experts to identify what the limits were to that, and so forth." These computations were not considered extensive and no conclusion was reached.

At this meeting, Van Gorkom stated that he would be willing to take $55 per share for his own 75,000 shares. He vetoed the suggestion of a leveraged buy-out by Management, however, as involving a potential conflict of interest for Management. Van Gorkom, a certified public accountant and lawyer, had been an officer of Trans Union for 24 years, its Chief Executive Officer for more than 17 years, and Chairman of its Board for 2 years. It is noteworthy in this connection that he was then approaching 65 years of age and mandatory retirement.

For several days following the September 5 meeting, Van Gorkom pondered the idea of a sale. . . .

Van Gorkom decided to meet with Jay A. Pritzker, a well-known corporate takeover specialist and a social acquaintance. However, rather than approaching Pritzker simply to determine his interest in acquiring Trans Union, Van Gorkom assembled a proposed per share price for sale of the Company and a financing structure by which to accomplish the sale. Van Gorkom did so without consulting either his Board or any members of Senior Management except one: Carl Peterson, Trans Union's Controller. Telling Peterson that he wanted no other person on his staff to know what he was doing, but without telling him why, Van Gorkom directed Peterson to calculate the feasibility of a leveraged buy-out at an assumed price per share of $55. Apart from the Company's historic stock market price,[5] and Van Gorkom's long association with Trans Union, the record is devoid of any competent evidence that $55 represented the per share intrinsic value of the Company. . . .

Van Gorkom arranged a meeting with Pritzker at the latter's home on Saturday, September 13, 1980. Van Gorkom prefaced his presentation by stating to Pritzker: "Now as far as you are concerned, I can, I think, show how you can pay a substantial premium over the present stock price and pay off most of the loan in the first five years. . . . If you could pay $55 for this Company, here is a way in which I think it can be financed."

Van Gorkom then reviewed with Pritzker his calculations based upon his proposed price of $55 per share. Although Pritzker mentioned $50 as a more attractive figure, no other price was mentioned. However,

---

[5]   The common stock of Trans Union was traded on the New York Stock Exchange. Over the five year period from 1975 through 1979, Trans Union's stock had traded within a range of a high of $39½ and a low of $24¼. Its high and low range for 1980 through September 19 (the last trading day before announcement of the merger) was $38¼–$29½.

Van Gorkom stated that to be sure that $55 was the best price obtainable, Trans Union should be free to accept any better offer. Pritzker demurred, stating that his organization would serve as a "stalking horse" for an "auction contest" only if Trans Union would permit Pritzker to buy 1,750,000 shares of Trans Union stock at market price which Pritzker could then sell to any higher bidder. After further discussion on this point, Pritzker told Van Gorkom that he would give him a more definite reaction soon.

On Monday, September 15, Pritzker advised Van Gorkom that he was interested in the $55 cash-out merger proposal and requested more information on Trans Union. . . .

On Thursday, September 18, Van Gorkom met again with Pritzker. At that time, Van Gorkom knew that Pritzker intended to make a cash-out merger offer at Van Gorkom's proposed $55 per share. Pritzker instructed his attorney, a merger and acquisition specialist, to begin drafting merger documents. There was no further discussion of the $55 price. However, the number of shares of Trans Union's treasury stock to be offered to Pritzker was negotiated down to one million shares; the price was set at $38–75 cents above the per share price at the close of the market on September 19. At this point, Pritzker insisted that the Trans Union Board act on his merger proposal within the next three days, stating to Van Gorkom: "We have to have a decision by no later than Sunday [evening, September 21] before the opening of the English stock exchange on Monday morning." Pritzker's lawyer was then instructed to draft the merger documents, to be reviewed by Van Gorkom's lawyer, "sometimes with discussion and sometimes not, in the haste to get it finished."

On Friday, September 19, Van Gorkom, Chelberg, and Pritzker consulted with Trans Union's lead bank regarding the financing of Pritzker's purchase of Trans Union. The bank indicated that it could form a syndicate of banks that would finance the transaction. On the same day, Van Gorkom retained James Brennan, Esquire, to advise Trans Union on the legal aspects of the merger. Van Gorkom did not consult with William Browder, a Vice-President and director of Trans Union and former head of its legal department, or with William Moore, then the head of Trans Union's legal staff.

On Friday, September 19, Van Gorkom called a special meeting of the Trans Union Board for noon the following day. He also called a meeting of the Company's Senior Management to convene at 11:00 a.m., prior to the meeting of the Board. No one, except Chelberg and Peterson, was told the purpose of the meetings. Van Gorkom did not invite Trans Union's investment banker, Salomon Brothers or its Chicago-based partner, to attend.

Of those present at the Senior Management meeting on September 20, only Chelberg and Peterson had prior knowledge of Pritzker's offer. Van Gorkom disclosed the offer and described its terms, but he furnished no copies of the proposed Merger Agreement. Romans announced that his department had done a second study which showed that, for a leveraged buy-out, the price range for Trans Union stock was between $55 and $65 per share. Van Gorkom neither saw the study nor asked Romans to make it available for the Board meeting.

Senior Management's reaction to the Pritzker proposal was completely negative. No member of Management, except Chelberg and Peterson, supported the proposal. Romans objected to the price as being too low[6]. . . .

Ten directors served on the Trans Union Board, five inside (defendants Bonser, O'Boyle, Browder, Chelberg, and Van Gorkom) and five outside (defendants Wallis, Johnson, Lanterman, Morgan and Reneker). All directors were present at the meeting, except O'Boyle who was ill. Of the outside directors, four were corporate chief executive officers and one was the former Dean of the University of Chicago Business School. None was an investment banker or trained financial analyst. All members of the Board were well informed about the Company and its operations as a going concern. They were familiar with the current financial condition of the Company, as well as operating and earnings projections reported in the recent Five Year Forecast. The Board generally received regular and detailed reports and was kept abreast of the accumulated investment tax credit and accelerated depreciation problem.

Van Gorkom began the Special Meeting of the Board with a twenty-minute oral presentation. Copies of the proposed Merger Agreement were delivered too late for study before or during the meeting.[7] He reviewed the Company's ITC and depreciation problems and the efforts theretofore made to solve them. He discussed his initial meeting with Pritzker and his motivation in arranging that meeting. Van Gorkom did not disclose to the Board, however, the methodology by which he alone had arrived at the $55 figure, or the fact that he first proposed the $55 price in his negotiations with Pritzker.

Van Gorkom outlined the terms of the Pritzker offer as follows: Pritzker would pay $55 in cash for all outstanding shares of Trans Union stock upon completion of which Trans Union would be merged into New T Company, a subsidiary wholly-owned by Pritzker and formed to implement the merger; for a period of 90 days, Trans Union could receive, but could not actively solicit, competing offers; the offer had to be acted

---

[6]   Van Gorkom asked Romans to express his opinion as to the $55 price. Romans stated that he "thought the price was too low in relation to what he could derive for the company in a cash sale, particularly one which enabled us to realize the values of certain subsidiaries and independent entities."

[7]   The record is not clear as to the terms of the Merger Agreement. The Agreement, as originally presented to the Board on September 20, was never produced by defendants despite demands by the plaintiffs. Nor is it clear that the directors were given an opportunity to study the Merger Agreement before voting on it. All that can be said is that Brennan had the Agreement before him during the meeting.

on by the next evening, Sunday, September 21; Trans Union could only furnish to competing bidders published information, and not proprietary information; the offer was subject to Pritzker obtaining the necessary financing by October 10, 1980; if the financing contingency were met or waived by Pritzker, Trans Union was required to sell to Pritzker one million newly-issued shares of Trans Union at $38 per share.

Van Gorkom took the position that putting Trans Union "up for auction" through a 90-day market test would validate a decision by the Board that $55 was a fair price. He told the Board that the "free market will have an opportunity to judge whether $55 is a fair price." Van Gorkom framed the decision before the Board not as whether $55 per share was the highest price that could be obtained, but as whether the $55 price was a fair price that the stockholders should be given the opportunity to accept or reject.[8]

Attorney Brennan advised the members of the Board that they might be sued if they failed to accept the offer and that a fairness opinion was not required as a matter of law.

Romans attended the meeting as chief financial officer of the Company. He told the Board that he had not been involved in the negotiations with Pritzker and knew nothing about the merger proposal until the morning of the meeting; that his studies did not indicate either a fair price for the stock or a valuation of the Company; that he did not see his role as directly addressing the fairness issue; and that he and his people "were trying to search for ways to justify a price in connection with such a [leveraged buy-out] transaction, rather than to say what the shares are worth." Romans testified:

> I told the Board that the study ran the numbers at 50 and 60, and then the subsequent study at 55 and 65, and that was not the same thing as saying that I have a valuation of the company at X dollars. But it was a way—a first step towards reaching that conclusion.

Romans told the Board that, in his opinion, $55 was "in the range of a fair price," but "at the beginning of the range." . . .

The Board meeting of September 20 lasted about two hours. Based solely upon Van Gorkom's oral presentation, Chelberg's supporting representations, Romans' oral statement, Brennan's legal advice, and their knowledge of the market history of the Company's stock, the directors approved the proposed Merger Agreement. However, the Board later claimed to have attached two conditions to its acceptance: (1) that Trans Union reserved the right to accept any better offer that was made during the market test period; and (2) that Trans Union could share its proprietary information with any other potential bidders. While the Board now claims to have reserved the right to accept any better offer

---

8   In Van Gorkom's words: The "real decision" is whether to "let the stockholders decide it" which is "all you are being asked to decide today."

received after the announcement of the Pritzker agreement (even though the minutes of the meeting do not reflect this), it is undisputed that the Board did not reserve the right to actively solicit alternate offers.

The Merger Agreement was executed by Van Gorkom during the evening of September 20 at a formal social event that he hosted for the opening of the Chicago Lyric Opera. Neither he nor any other director read the agreement prior to its signing and delivery to Pritzker. . . .

On Monday, September 22, the Company issued a press release announcing that Trans Union had entered into a "definitive" Merger Agreement with an affiliate of the Marmon Group, Inc., a Pritzker holding company. Within 10 days of the public announcement, dissent among Senior Management over the merger had become widespread. Faced with threatened resignations of key officers, Van Gorkom met with Pritzker who agreed to several modifications of the Agreement. Pritzker was willing to do so provided that Van Gorkom could persuade the dissidents to remain on the Company payroll for at least six months after consummation of the merger.

Van Gorkom reconvened the Board on October 8 and secured the directors' approval of the proposed amendments—sight unseen. The Board also authorized the employment of Salomon Brothers, its investment banker, to solicit other offers for Trans Union during the proposed "market test" period.

The next day, October 9, Trans Union issued a press release announcing: (1) that Pritzker had obtained "the financing commitments necessary to consummate" the merger with Trans Union; (2) that Pritzker had acquired one million shares of Trans Union common stock at $38 per share; (3) that Trans Union was now permitted to actively seek other offers and had retained Salomon Brothers for that purpose; and (4) that if a more favorable offer were not received before February 1, 1981, Trans Union's shareholders would thereafter meet to vote on the Pritzker proposal.

It was not until the following day, October 10, that the actual amendments to the Merger Agreement were prepared by Pritzker and delivered to Van Gorkom for execution. As will be seen, the amendments were considerably at variance with Van Gorkom's representations of the amendments to the Board on October 8; and the amendments placed serious constraints on Trans Union's ability to negotiate a better deal and withdraw from the Pritzker agreement. Nevertheless, Van Gorkom proceeded to execute what became the October 10 amendments to the Merger Agreement without conferring further with the Board members and apparently without comprehending the actual implications of the amendments. . . .

Salomon Brothers' efforts over a three-month period from October 21 to January 21 produced only one serious suitor for Trans Union-General Electric Credit Corporation ("GE Credit"), a subsidiary of the

General Electric Company. However, GE Credit was unwilling to make an offer for Trans Union unless Trans Union first rescinded its Merger Agreement with Pritzker. When Pritzker refused, GE Credit terminated further discussions with Trans Union in early January.

In the meantime, in early December, the investment firm Kohlberg, Kravis, Roberts & Co. ("KKR"), the only other concern to make a firm offer for Trans Union, withdrew its offer under circumstances hereinafter detailed.

. . . On January 21, Management's Proxy Statement for the February 10 shareholder meeting was mailed to Trans Union's stockholders. On January 26, Trans Union's Board met and, after a lengthy meeting, voted to proceed with the Pritzker merger. . . .

On February 10, the stockholders of Trans Union approved the Pritzker merger proposal. Of the outstanding shares, 69.9% were voted in favor of the merger; 7.25% were voted against the merger; and 22.85% were not voted.

II.

We turn to the issue of the application of the business judgment rule to the September 20 meeting of the Board.

The Court of Chancery concluded from the evidence that the Board of Directors' approval of the Pritzker merger proposal fell within the protection of the business judgment rule. The Court found that the Board had given sufficient time and attention to the transaction, since the directors had considered the Pritzker proposal on three different occasions, on September 20, and on October 8, 1980 and finally on January 26, 1981. On that basis, the Court reasoned that the Board had acquired, over the four-month period, sufficient information to reach an informed business judgment on the cash-out merger proposal. The Court ruled:

> . . . that given the market value of Trans Union's stock, the business acumen of the members of the board of Trans Union, the substantial premium over market offered by the Pritzkers and the ultimate effect on the merger price provided by the prospect of other bids for the stock in question, that the board of directors of Trans Union did not act recklessly or improvidently in determining on a course of action which they believed to be in the best interest of the stockholders of Trans Union.

The Court of Chancery made but one finding; i.e., that the Board's conduct over the entire period from September 20 through January 26, 1981 was not reckless or improvident, but informed. This ultimate conclusion was premised upon three subordinate findings, one explicit and two implied. The Court's explicit finding was that Trans Union's Board was "free to turn down the Pritzker proposal" not only on September 20 but also on October 8, 1980 and on January 26, 1981. The Court's implied, subordinate findings were: (1) that no legally binding agreement was reached by the parties until January 26; and (2) that if a higher offer were to be forthcoming, the market test would have produced it, and Trans Union would have been contractually free to accept such higher offer. However, the Court offered no factual basis or legal support for any of these findings; and the record compels contrary conclusions. . . .

Under Delaware law, the business judgment rule is the offspring of the fundamental principle, codified in 8 Del.C. § 141(a), that the business and affairs of a Delaware corporation are managed by or under its board of directors. . . . The rule itself "is a presumption that in making a business decision, the directors of a corporation acted on an informed basis, in good faith and in the honest belief that the action taken was in the best interests of the company." . . . [Aronson v. Lewis, 473 A.2d 805, 812 (Del.1984)]. Thus, the party attacking a board decision as uninformed must rebut the presumption that its business judgment was an informed one. Id.

The determination of whether a business judgment is an informed one turns on whether the directors have informed themselves "prior to making a business decision, of all material information reasonably available to them." Id.

Under the business judgment rule there is no protection for directors who have made "an unintelligent or unadvised judgment." Mitchell v. Highland-Western Glass, Del.Ch., 167 A. 831, 833 (1933). . . .

The standard of care applicable to a director's duty of care has also been recently restated by this Court. In Aronson, supra, we stated:

> While the Delaware cases use a variety of terms to describe the applicable standard of care, our analysis satisfies us that under the business judgment rule director liability is predicated upon concepts of gross negligence. (footnote omitted)

473 A.2d at 812.

We again confirm that view. We think the concept of gross negligence is also the proper standard for determining whether a business judgment reached by a board of directors was an informed one. . . .

It is against those standards that the conduct of the directors of Trans Union must be tested, as a matter of law and as a matter of fact, regarding their exercise of an informed business judgment in voting to approve the Pritzker merger proposal.

III. . . .

. . . [T]he question of whether the directors reached an informed business judgment in agreeing to sell the Company, pursuant to the terms of the September 20 Agreement presents, in reality, two questions: (A) whether the directors reached an informed business judgment on September 20, 1980; and (B) if they did not, whether the directors' actions taken subsequent to September 20 were adequate to cure any infirmity in their action taken on September 20. We first consider the directors'

September 20 action in terms of their reaching an informed business judgment.

—A—

On the record before us, we must conclude that the Board of Directors did not reach an informed business judgment on September 20, 1980 in voting to "sell" the Company for $55 per share pursuant to the Pritzker cash-out merger proposal. Our reasons, in summary, are as follows:

The directors (1) did not adequately inform themselves as to Van Gorkom's role in forcing the "sale" of the Company and in establishing the per share purchase price; (2) were uninformed as to the intrinsic value of the Company; and (3) given these circumstances, at a minimum, were grossly negligent in approving the "sale" of the Company upon two hours' consideration, without prior notice, and without the exigency of a crisis or emergency.

As has been noted, the Board based its September 20 decision to approve the cash-out merger primarily on Van Gorkom's representations. None of the directors, other than Van Gorkom and Chelberg, had any prior knowledge that the purpose of the meeting was to propose a cash-out merger of Trans Union. . . .

Without any documents before them concerning the proposed transaction, the members of the Board were required to rely entirely upon Van Gorkom's 20-minute oral presentation of the proposal. No written summary of the terms of the merger was presented; the directors were given no documentation to support the adequacy of $55 price per share for sale of the Company; and the Board had before it nothing more than Van Gorkom's statement of his understanding of the substance of an agreement which he admittedly had never read, nor which any member of the Board had ever seen.

Under 8 Del.C. § 141(e), "directors are fully protected in relying in good faith on reports made by officers." Michelson v. Duncan, Del.Ch., 386 A.2d 1144, 1156 (1978); aff'd in part and rev'd in part on other grounds, Del.Supr., 407 A.2d 211 (1979). See also Graham v. Allis-Chalmers Mfg. Co., Del.Supr., 188 A.2d 125, 130 (1963); Prince v. Bensinger, Del.Ch., 244 A.2d 89, 94 (1968). The term "report" has been liberally construed to include reports of informal personal investigations by corporate officers, Cheff v. Mathes, Del.Supr., 199 A.2d 548, 556 (1964). However, there is no evidence that any "report," as defined under § 141(e), concerning the Pritzker proposal, was presented to the Board on September 20. Van Gorkom's oral presentation of his understanding of the terms of the proposed Merger Agreement, which he had not seen, and Romans' brief oral statement of his preliminary study regarding the feasibility of a leveraged buy-out of Trans Union do not qualify as § 141(e) "reports" for these reasons: The former lacked substance because Van Gorkom was basically uninformed as to the essential provisions of the very document about which he was talking. Romans' statement was irrelevant to the issues before the Board since it did not purport to be a valuation study. At a minimum for a report to enjoy the status conferred by § 141(e), it must be pertinent to the subject matter upon which a board is called to act, and otherwise be entitled to good faith, not blind, reliance. Considering all of the surrounding circumstances—hastily calling the meeting without prior notice of its subject matter, the proposed sale of the Company without any prior consideration of the issue or necessity therefor, the urgent time constraints imposed by Pritzker, and the total absence of any documentation whatsoever—the directors were duty bound to make reasonable inquiry of Van Gorkom and Romans, and if they had done so, the inadequacy of that upon which they now claim to have relied would have been apparent.

The defendants rely on the following factors to sustain the Trial Court's finding that the Board's decision was an informed one: (1) the magnitude of the premium or spread between the $55 Pritzker offering price and Trans Union's current market price of $38 per share; (2) the amendment of the Agreement as submitted on September 20 to permit the Board to accept any better offer during the "market test" period; (3) the collective experience and expertise of the Board's "inside" and "outside" directors; and (4) their reliance on Brennan's legal advice that the directors might be sued if they rejected the Pritzker proposal. We discuss each of these grounds *seriatim:*

(1)

A substantial premium may provide one reason to recommend a merger, but in the absence of other sound valuation information, the fact of a premium alone does not provide an adequate basis upon which to assess the fairness of an offering price. Here, the judgment reached as to the adequacy of the premium was based on a comparison between the historically depressed Trans Union market price and the amount of the Pritzker offer. Using market price as a basis for concluding that the premium adequately reflected the true value of the Company was a clearly faulty, indeed fallacious, premise. . . .

The record is clear that before September 20, Van Gorkom and other members of Trans Union's Board knew that the market had consistently undervalued the worth of Trans Union's stock. . . .

The parties do not dispute that a publicly-traded stock price is solely a measure of the value of a minority position and, thus, market price represents only the value of a single share. Nevertheless, on September 20, the Board assessed the adequacy of the premium over market, offered by Pritzker, solely by comparing it with Trans Union's current and historical stock price. . . .

Indeed, as of September 20, the Board had no other information on which to base a determination of the intrinsic value of Trans Union as a going concern. As of September 20, the Board had made no evaluation of the Company designed to value the entire enterprise, nor had the Board ever previously considered selling the Company or consenting to a buy-out merger. Thus, the adequacy of a premium is indeterminate unless it is assessed in terms of other competent and sound valuation information that reflects the value of the particular business.

Despite the foregoing facts and circumstances, there was no call by the Board, either on September 20 or thereafter, for any valuation study or documentation of the $55 price per share as a measure of the fair value of the Company in a cash-out context. It is undisputed that the major asset of Trans Union was its cash flow. Yet, at no time did the Board call for a valuation study taking into account that highly significant element of the Company's assets.

We do not imply that an outside valuation study is essential to support an informed business judgment; nor do we state that fairness opinions by independent investment bankers are required as a matter of law. Often insiders familiar with the business of a going concern are in a better position than are outsiders to gather relevant information; and under appropriate circumstances, such directors may be fully protected in relying in good faith upon the valuation reports of their management. *See* 8 Del.C. § 141(e). . . .

Here, the record establishes that the Board did not request its Chief Financial Officer, Romans, to make any valuation study or review of the proposal to determine the adequacy of $55 per share for sale of the Company. On the record before us: The Board rested on Romans' elicited response that the $55 figure was within a "fair price range" within the context of a leveraged buy-out. No director sought any further information from Romans. No director asked him why he put $55 at the bottom of his range. No director asked Romans for any details as to his study, the reason why it had been undertaken or its depth. No director asked to see the study; and no director asked Romans whether Trans Union's finance department could do a fairness study within the remaining 36-hour period available under the Pritzker offer. . . .

Thus, the record compels the conclusion that on September 20 the Board lacked valuation information adequate to reach an informed business judgment as to the fairness of $55 per share for sale of the Company.

(2)

This brings us to the post-September 20 "market test" upon which the defendants ultimately rely to confirm the reasonableness of their September 20 decision to accept the Pritzker proposal. In this connection, the directors present a two-part argument: (a) that by making a "market test" of Pritzker's $55 per share offer a condition of their September 20 decision to accept his offer, they cannot be found to have acted impulsively or in an uninformed manner on September 20; and (b) that the adequacy of the $17 premium for sale of the Company was conclusively established over the following 90 to 120 days by the most reliable evidence available—the marketplace. Thus, the defendants impliedly contend that the "market test" eliminated the need for the Board to perform any other form of fairness test either on September 20, or thereafter.

Again, the facts of record do not support the defendants' argument. There is no evidence: (a) that the Merger Agreement was effectively amended to give the Board freedom to put Trans Union up for auction sale to the highest bidder; or (b) that a public auction was in fact permitted to occur. The minutes of the Board meeting make no reference to any of this. Indeed, the record compels the conclusion that the directors had no rational basis for expecting that a market test was attainable, given the terms of the Agreement as executed during the evening of September 20. We rely upon the following facts which are essentially uncontradicted:

The Merger Agreement, specifically identified as that originally presented to the Board on September 20, has never been produced by the defendants, notwithstanding the plaintiffs' several demands for production before as well as during trial. No acceptable explanation of this failure to produce documents has been given to either the Trial Court or this Court. . . .

Van Gorkom states that the Agreement as submitted incorporated the ingredients for a market test by authorizing Trans Union to receive competing offers over the next 90-day period. However, he concedes that the Agreement barred Trans Union from actively soliciting such offers and from furnishing to interested parties any information about the Company other than that already in the public domain. Whether the original Agreement of September 20 went so far as to authorize Trans Union to receive competitive proposals is arguable. The defendants' unexplained failure to produce and identify the original Merger Agreement permits the logical inference that the instrument would not support their assertions in this regard. . . .

The defendant directors assert that they "insisted" upon including two amendments to the Agreement, thereby permitting a market test: (1) to give Trans Union the right to accept a better offer; and (2) to reserve to Trans Union the right to distribute proprietary information on the Company to alternative bidders. Yet, the defendants concede that they did not seek to amend the Agreement to permit Trans Union to solicit competing offers.

Several of Trans Union's outside directors resolutely maintained that the Agreement as submitted was approved on the understanding that, "if we got a better deal, we had a right to take it." Director Johnson so testified; but he then added, "And if they didn't put that in the agreement, then the management did not carry out the conclusion of the Board. And I just don't know whether they did or not." The only clause in the Agreement as finally executed to which the defendants can point as "keeping the door open" is the following underlined statement found in subparagraph (a) of section 2.03 of the Merger Agreement as executed:

> The Board of Directors shall recommend to the stockholders of Trans Union that they approve and adopt the Merger Agreement ("the stockholders' approval") and to use its best efforts to obtain the requisite votes therefor. *GL acknowledges that Trans Union directors may have a competing fiduciary obligation to the shareholders under certain circumstances.*

Clearly, this language on its face cannot be construed as incorporating either of the two "conditions" described above: either the right to accept a better offer or the right to distribute proprietary information to third parties. . . . No reference to either of the so-called "conditions" or of Trans Union's reserved right to test the market appears in any notes of the Board meeting or in the Board Resolution accepting the Pritzker offer or in the Minutes of the meeting itself. . . .

Thus, notwithstanding what several of the outside directors later claimed to have "thought" occurred at the meeting, the record compels the conclusion that Trans Union's Board had no rational basis to conclude on September 20 or in the days immediately following, that the Board's acceptance of Pritzker's offer was conditioned on (1) a "market test" of the offer; and (2) the Board's right to withdraw from the Pritzker Agreement and accept any higher offer received before the shareholder meeting.

(3)

The directors' unfounded reliance on both the premium and the market test as the basis for accepting the Pritzker proposal undermines the defendants' remaining contention that the Board's collective experience and sophistication was a sufficient basis for finding that it reached its September 20 decision with informed, reasonable deliberation. . . .

(4) . . .

We conclude that Trans Union's Board was grossly negligent in that it failed to act with informed reasonable deliberation in agreeing to the Pritzker merger proposal on September 20. . . .

—B—

We now examine the Board's post-September 20 conduct for the purpose of determining first, whether it was informed and not grossly negligent; and second, if informed, whether it was sufficient to legally rectify and cure the Board's derelictions of September 20.[23]

---

[23] As will be seen, we do not reach the second question.

(1)

First, as to the Board meeting of October 8. . . .

The public announcement of the Pritzker merger resulted in an "en masse" revolt of Trans Union's Senior Management. The head of Trans Union's tank car operations (its most profitable division) informed Van Gorkom that unless the merger were called off, fifteen key personnel would resign.

Instead of reconvening the Board, Van Gorkom again privately met with Pritzker, informed him of the developments, and sought his advice. Pritzker then made the following suggestions for overcoming Management's dissatisfaction: (1) that the Agreement be amended to permit Trans Union to solicit, as well as receive, higher offers; and (2) that the shareholder meeting be postponed from early January to February 10, 1981. In return, Pritzker asked Van Gorkom to obtain a commitment from Senior Management to remain at Trans Union for at least six months after the merger was consummated.

Van Gorkom then advised Senior Management that the Agreement would be amended to give Trans Union the right to solicit competing offers through January, 1981, if they would agree to remain with Trans Union. Senior Management was temporarily mollified; and Van Gorkom then called a special meeting of Trans Union's Board for October 8.

Thus, the primary purpose of the October 8 Board meeting was to amend the Merger Agreement, in a manner agreeable to Pritzker, to permit Trans Union to conduct a "market test." Van Gorkom understood that the proposed amendments were intended to give the Company an unfettered "right to openly solicit offers down through January 31." Van Gorkom presumably so represented the amendments to Trans Union's Board members on October 8. In a brief session, the directors approved Van Gorkom's oral presentation of the substance of the proposed amendments, the terms of which were not reduced to writing until October 10. But rather than waiting to review the amendments, the Board again approved them sight unseen and adjourned, giving Van Gorkom authority to execute the papers when he received them.[25] . . .

The next day, October 9, and before the Agreement was amended, Pritzker moved swiftly to off-set the proposed market test amendment. First, Pritzker informed Trans Union that he had completed arrangements for financing its acquisition and that the parties were thereby mutually bound to a firm purchase and sale arrangement. Second, Pritzker announced the exercise of his option to purchase one million shares of Trans Union's treasury stock at $38 per share—75 cents above the current market price. Trans Union's Management responded

---

[25]   We do not suggest that a board must read *in haec verba* every contract or legal document which it approves, but if it is to successfully absolve itself from charges of the type made here, there must be some credible contemporary evidence demonstrating that the directors knew what they were doing, and ensured that their purported action was given effect. That is the consistent failure which cast this Board upon its unredeemable course.

the same day by issuing a press release announcing: (1) that all financing arrangements for Pritzker's acquisition of Trans Union had been completed; and (2) Pritzker's purchase of one million shares of Trans Union's treasury stock at $38 per share.

The next day, October 10, Pritzker delivered to Trans Union the proposed amendments to the September 20 Merger Agreement. Van Gorkom promptly proceeded to countersign all the instruments on behalf of Trans Union without reviewing the instruments to determine if they were consistent with the authority previously granted him by the Board. The amending documents were apparently not approved by Trans Union's Board until a much later date, December 2. The record does not affirmatively establish that Trans Union's directors ever read the October 10 amendments.[26]

The October 10 amendments to the Merger Agreement did authorize Trans Union to solicit competing offers, but the amendments had more far-reaching effects. The most significant change was in the definition of the third-party "offer" available to Trans Union as a possible basis for withdrawal from its Merger Agreement with Pritzker. Under the October 10 amendments, a better *offer* was no longer sufficient to permit Trans Union's withdrawal. Trans Union was now permitted to terminate the Pritzker Agreement and abandon the merger only if, prior to February 10, 1981, Trans Union had either consummated a merger (or sale of assets) with a third party or had entered into a "definitive" merger agreement more favorable than Pritzker's and for a greater consideration—subject only to stockholder approval. Further, the "extension" of the market test period to February 10, 1981 was circumscribed by other amendments which required Trans Union to file its preliminary proxy statement on the Pritzker merger proposal by December 5, 1980 and use its best efforts to mail the statement to its shareholders by January 5, 1981. Thus, the market test period was effectively reduced, not extended. . . .

In our view, the record compels the conclusion that the directors' conduct on October 8 exhibited the same deficiencies as did their conduct on September 20. The Board permitted its Merger Agreement with Pritzker to be amended in a manner it had neither authorized nor intended. . . .

We conclude that the Board acted in a grossly negligent manner on October 8; and that Van Gorkom's representations on which the Board based its actions do not constitute "reports" under § 141(e) on which the directors could reasonably have relied. Further, the amended Merger Agreement imposed on Trans Union's acceptance of a third party offer conditions more onerous than those imposed on Trans Union's acceptance of Pritzker's offer on September 20. After October 10, Trans Union could

---

[26] There is no evidence of record that Trans Union's directors ever raised any objections, procedural or substantive, to the October 10 amendments or that any of them, including Van Gorkom, understood the opposite result of their intended effect—until it was too late.

accept from a third party a better offer only if it were incorporated in a definitive agreement between the parties, and not conditioned on financing or on any other contingency.

The October 9 press release, coupled with the October 10 amendments, had the clear effect of locking Trans Union's Board into the Pritzker Agreement. Pritzker had thereby foreclosed Trans Union's Board from negotiating any better "definitive" agreement over the remaining eight weeks before Trans Union was required to clear the Proxy Statement submitting the Pritzker proposal to its shareholders.

(2)

[On December 2, KKR offered to buy Trans-Union for $60/share. Van Gorkom apparently was resistant to this offer, and KKR withdrew it for reasons that were cloudy. In mid-January, GE Credit Corporation made a proposal which] was not in the form of an offer. Had there been time to do so, GE Credit was prepared to offer between $2 and $5 per share above the $55 per share price which Pritzker offered. But GE Credit needed an additional 60 to 90 days; and it was unwilling to make a formal offer without a concession from Pritzker extending the February 10 "deadline" for Trans Union's stockholder meeting. . . . Pritzker refused to grant such extension. . . .

Our review of the record compels a finding that confirmation of the appropriateness of the Pritzker offer by an unfettered or free market test was virtually meaningless in the face of the terms and time limitations of Trans Union's Merger Agreement with Pritzker as amended October 10, 1980.

. . . [W]e hold that the defendants' post-September conduct did not cure the deficiencies of their September 20 conduct; and that, accordingly, the Trial Court erred in according to the defendants the benefits of the business judgment rule. . . .

V.

The defendants ultimately rely on the stockholder vote of February 10 for exoneration. The defendants contend that the stockholders' "overwhelming" vote approving the Pritzker Merger Agreement had the legal effect of curing any failure of the Board to reach an informed business judgment in its approval of the merger. . . .

[The court rejected the shareholder-approval defense on the ground that Trans Union's stockholders were not fully informed of all facts material to their vote on the Pritzker Merger, and that the Trial Court's ruling to the contrary was clearly erroneous.] . . .

VI.

. . . We hold, therefore, that the Trial Court committed reversible error in applying the business judgment rule in favor of the director defendants in this case.

On remand, the Court of Chancery shall conduct an evidentiary hearing to determine the fair value of the shares represented by the plaintiffs' class, based on the intrinsic value of Trans Union on September 20, 1980. . . . Thereafter, an award of damages may be entered to the extent that the fair value of Trans Union exceeds $55 per share.

Reversed and Remanded for proceedings consistent herewith.

■ MCNEILLY, JUSTICE, dissenting . . .

I have no quarrel with the majority's analysis of the business judgment rule. It is the application of that rule to these facts which is wrong. An overview of the entire record, rather than the limited view of bits and pieces which the majority has exploded like popcorn, convinces me that the directors made an informed business judgment which was buttressed by their test of the market. . . .

At the time of the September 20 meeting the 10 members of Trans Union's Board of Directors were highly qualified and well informed about the affairs and prospects of Trans Union. These directors were acutely aware of the historical problems facing Trans Union which were caused by the tax laws. They had discussed these problems *ad nauseam*. In fact, within two months of the September 20 meeting the board had reviewed and discussed an outside study of the company done by The Boston Consulting Group and an internal five year forecast prepared by management. At the September 20 meeting Van Gorkom presented the Pritzker offer, and the board then heard from James Brennan, the company's counsel in this matter, who discussed the legal documents. Following this, the Board directed that certain changes be made in the merger documents. These changes made it clear that the Board was free to accept a better offer than Pritzker's if one was made. The above facts reveal that the Board did not act in a grossly negligent manner in informing themselves of the relevant and available facts before passing on the merger. To the contrary, this record reveals that the directors acted with the utmost care in informing themselves of the relevant and available facts before passing on the merger. . . .

[The dissenting opinion of Justice Christie is omitted.]

It is reported that after the decision of the Delaware Supreme Court, an agreement was reached to settle *Van Gorkom* by the payment of $23.5 million to the plaintiff class. Of that amount, $10 million, the policy limit, was provided by Trans Union's directors' and officers' liability-insurance carrier. Nearly all of the $13.5 million balance was paid by the Pritzker group on behalf of the Trans Union defendant directors, although the Pritzker group was not a defendant. *See* Manning, Reflections and Practical Tips on Life in the Boardroom After *Van Gorkom*, 41 Bus.Law. 1 (1985).

NOTE ON SUBSTANCE AND PROCESS IN THE DUTY OF CARE

In many areas of law, a distinction is drawn between substance and process. The duty of care may be understood in that way too. In effect, the business judgment rule gives wide latitude to a substantive decision of a director or senior executive if the *process* elements of the duty of care are satisfied. Under this distinction, the process elements of the duty of care, which involve such matters as preparing to make a decision, general monitoring, and following up suspicious circumstances, are governed by a standard of reasonability. However, if the process by which a decision was made satisfies the reasonability standard, the substantive decision itself will be reviewed only under the much looser standard of rationality.

———

C. THE DUTY TO MONITOR, COMPLIANCE PROGRAMS, AND INTERNAL CONTROLS

In re Caremark International Inc. Derivative Litigation

Court of Chancery of Delaware, 1996.
698 A.2d 959.

■ ALLEN, CHANCELLOR.

Pending is a motion pursuant to Chancery Rule 23.1 to approve as fair and reasonable a proposed settlement of a consolidated derivative action on behalf of Caremark International, Inc. ("Caremark"). The suit involves claims that the members of Caremark's board of directors (the "Board") breached their fiduciary duty of care to Caremark in connection with alleged violations by Caremark employees of federal and state laws and regulations applicable to health care providers. As a result of the alleged violations, Caremark was subject to an extensive four year investigation by the United States Department of Health and Human Services and the Department of Justice. In 1994 Caremark was charged in an indictment with multiple felonies. It thereafter entered into a number of agreements with the Department of Justice and others. Those agreements included a plea agreement in which Caremark pleaded guilty to a single felony of mail fraud and agreed to pay civil and criminal fines. Subsequently, Caremark agreed to make reimbursements to various private and public parties. In all, the payments that Caremark has been required to make total approximately $250 million.

This suit was filed in 1994, purporting to seek on behalf of the company recovery of these losses from the individual defendants who constitute the board of directors of Caremark.[1] The parties now propose

---

[1]   Thirteen of the Directors have been members of the Board since November 30, 1992. Nancy Brinker joined the Board in October 1993.

that it be settled and, after notice to Caremark shareholders, a hearing on the fairness of the proposal was held on August 16, 1996.

A motion of this type requires the court to assess the strengths and weaknesses of the claims asserted in light of the discovery record and to evaluate the fairness and adequacy of the consideration offered to the corporation in exchange for the release of all claims made or arising from the facts alleged. The ultimate issue then is whether the proposed settlement appears to be fair to the corporation and its absent shareholders. In this effort the court does not determine contested facts, but evaluates the claims and defenses on the discovery record to achieve a sense of the relative strengths of the parties' positions. Polk v. Good, Del.Supr., 507 A.2d 531, 536 (1986). In doing this, in most instances, the court is constrained by the absence of a truly adversarial process, since inevitably both sides support the settlement and legally assisted objectors are rare. . . .

Legally, evaluation of the central claim made entails consideration of the legal standard governing a board of directors' obligation to supervise or monitor corporate performance. For the reasons set forth below I conclude, in light of the discovery record, that there is a very low probability that it would be determined that the directors of Caremark breached any duty to appropriately monitor and supervise the enterprise. Indeed the record tends to show an active consideration by Caremark management and its Board of the Caremark structures and programs that ultimately led to the company's indictment and to the large financial losses incurred in the settlement of those claims. It does not tend to show knowing or intentional violation of law. Neither the fact that the Board, although advised by lawyers and accountants, did not accurately predict the severe consequences to the company that would ultimately follow from the deployment by the company of the strategies and practices that ultimately led to this liability, nor the scale of the liability, gives rise to an inference of breach of any duty imposed by corporation law upon the directors of Caremark.

I.   BACKGROUND

For these purposes I regard the following facts, suggested by the discovery record, as material. Caremark, a Delaware corporation with its headquarters in Northbrook, Illinois, was created in November 1992 when it was spun-off from Baxter International, Inc. ("Baxter") and became a publicly held company listed on the New York Stock Exchange. The business practices that created the problem pre-dated the spin-off. During the relevant period Caremark was involved in two main health care business segments, providing patient care and managed care services. As part of its patient care business, which accounted for the majority of Caremark's revenues, Caremark provided alternative site health care services, including infusion therapy, growth hormone therapy, HIV/AIDS-related treatments and hemophilia therapy.

Caremark's managed care services included prescription drug programs and the operation of multi-specialty group practices.

A. Events Prior to the Government Investigation

A substantial part of the revenues generated by Caremark's businesses is derived from third party payments, insurers, and Medicare and Medicaid reimbursement programs. The latter source of payments are subject to the terms of the Anti-Referral Payments Law ("ARPL") which prohibits health care providers from paying any form of remuneration to induce the referral of Medicare or Medicaid patients. From its inception, Caremark entered into a variety of agreements with hospitals, physicians, and health care providers for advice and services, as well as distribution agreements with drug manufacturers, as had its predecessor prior to 1992. Specifically, Caremark did have a practice of entering into contracts for services (e.g., consultation agreements and research grants) with physicians at least some of whom prescribed or recommended services or products that Caremark provided to Medicare recipients and other patients. Such contracts were not prohibited by the ARPL but they obviously raised a possibility of unlawful "kickbacks."

As early as 1989, Caremark's predecessor issued an internal "Guide to Contractual Relationships" ("Guide") to govern its employees in entering into contracts with physicians and hospitals. The Guide tended to be reviewed annually by lawyers and updated. Each version of the Guide stated as Caremark's and its predecessor's policy that no payments would be made in exchange for or to induce patient referrals. But what one might deem a prohibited quid pro quo was not always clear. Due to a scarcity of court decisions interpreting the ARPL, however, Caremark repeatedly publicly stated that there was uncertainty concerning Caremark's interpretation of the law.

To clarify the scope of the ARPL, the United States Department of Health and Human Services ("HHS") issued "safe harbor" regulations in July 1991 stating conditions under which financial relationships between health care service providers and patient referral sources, such as physicians, would not violate the ARPL. Caremark contends that the narrowly drawn regulations gave limited guidance as to the legality of many of the agreements used by Caremark that did not fall within the safe-harbor. Caremark's predecessor, however, amended many of its standard forms of agreement with health care providers and revised the Guide in an apparent attempt to comply with the new regulations.

B. Government Investigation and Related Litigation

In August 1991, the HHS Office of the Inspector General ("OIG") initiated an investigation of Caremark's predecessor. Caremark's predecessor was served with a subpoena requiring the production of documents, including contracts between Caremark's predecessor and physicians (Quality Service Agreements ("QSAs")). Under the QSAs, Caremark's predecessor appears to have paid physicians fees for monitoring patients under Caremark's predecessor's care, including Medicare and Medicaid recipients. Sometimes apparently those monitoring patients were referring physicians, which raised ARPL concerns.

In March 1992, the Department of Justice ("DOJ") joined the OIG investigation and separate investigations were commenced by several additional federal and state agencies.[2]

C. Caremark's Response to the Investigation

During the relevant period, Caremark had approximately 7,000 employees and ninety branch operations. It had a decentralized management structure. By May 1991, however, Caremark asserts that it had begun making attempts to centralize its management structure in order to increase supervision over its branch operations.

The first action taken by management, as a result of the initiation of the OIG investigation, was an announcement that as of October 1, 1991, Caremark's predecessor would no longer pay management fees to physicians for services to Medicare and Medicaid patients. Despite this decision, Caremark asserts that its management, pursuant to advice, did not believe that such payments were illegal under the existing laws and regulations.

During this period, Caremark's Board took several additional steps consistent with an effort to assure compliance with company policies concerning the ARPL and the contractual forms in the Guide. In April 1992, Caremark published a fourth revised version of its Guide apparently designed to assure that its agreements either complied with the ARPL and regulations or excluded Medicare and Medicaid patients altogether. In addition, in September 1992, Caremark instituted a policy requiring its regional officers, Zone Presidents, to approve each contractual relationship entered into by Caremark with a physician.

Although there is evidence that inside and outside counsel had advised Caremark's directors that their contracts were in accord with the law, Caremark recognized that some uncertainty respecting the correct interpretation of the law existed. In its 1992 annual report, Caremark disclosed the ongoing government investigations, acknowledged that if penalties were imposed on the company they could have a material adverse effect on Caremark's business, and stated that no assurance could be given that its interpretation of the ARPL would prevail if challenged.

Throughout the period of the government investigations, Caremark had an internal audit plan designed to assure compliance with business

---

[2]   In addition to investigating whether Caremark's financial relationships with health care providers were intended to induce patient referrals, inquiries were made concerning Caremark's billing practices, activities which might lead to excessive and medically unnecessary treatments for patients, potentially improper waivers of patient co-payment obligations, and the adequacy of records kept at Caremark pharmacies.

568 THE DUTY TO ACT WITH CARE, IN GOOD FAITH, AND LAWFULLY CHAPTER 9

and ethics policies. In addition, Caremark employed Price Waterhouse as its outside auditor. On February 8, 1993, the [Audit &] Ethics Committee of Caremark's Board received and reviewed an outside auditors report by Price Waterhouse which concluded that there were no material weaknesses in Caremark's control structure.[3] Despite the positive findings of Price Waterhouse, however, on April 20, 1993, the Audit & Ethics Committee adopted a new internal audit charter requiring a comprehensive review of compliance policies and the compilation of an employee ethics handbook concerning such policies.[4]

The Board appears to have been informed about this project and other efforts to assure compliance with the law. For example, Caremark's management reported to the Board that Caremark's sales force was receiving an ongoing education regarding the ARPL and the proper use of Caremark's form contracts which had been approved by in-house counsel. On July 27, 1993, the new ethics manual, expressly prohibiting payments in exchange for referrals and requiring employees to report all illegal conduct to a toll free confidential ethics hotline, was approved and allegedly disseminated.[5] The record suggests that Caremark continued these policies in subsequent years, causing employees to be given revised versions of the ethics manual and requiring them to participate in training sessions concerning compliance with the law.

During 1993, Caremark took several additional steps which appear to have been aimed at increasing management supervision. These steps included new policies requiring local branch managers to secure home office approval for all disbursements under agreements with health care providers and to certify compliance with the ethics program. In addition, the chief financial officer was appointed to serve as Caremark's compliance officer. In 1994, a fifth revised Guide was published.

D. Federal Indictments Against Caremark and Officers

On August 4, 1994, a federal grand jury in Minnesota issued a 47 page indictment charging Caremark, two of its officers (not the firm's chief officer), an individual who had been a sales employee of Genentech, Inc., and David R. Brown, a physician practicing in Minneapolis, with violating the ARPL over a lengthy period. According to the indictment, over $1.1 million had been paid to Brown to induce him to distribute Protropin, a human growth hormone drug marketed by Caremark.[6] The

---

[3] At that time, Price Waterhouse viewed the outcome of the OIG Investigation as uncertain. After further audits, however, on February 7, 1995, Price Waterhouse informed the Audit & Ethics Committee that it had not become aware of any irregularities or illegal acts in relation to the OIG investigation.

[4] Price Waterhouse worked in conjunction with the Internal Audit Department.

[5] Prior to the distribution of the new ethics manual, on March 12, 1993, Caremark's president had sent a letter to all senior, district, and branch managers restating Caremark's policies that no physician be paid for referrals, that the standard contract forms in the Guide were not to be modified, and that deviation from such policies would result in the immediate termination of employment.

[6] In addition to prescribing Protropin, Dr. Brown had been receiving research grants from Caremark as well as payments for services under a consulting agreement for several years

substantial payments involved started, according to the allegations of the indictment, in 1986 and continued through 1993. Some payments were "in the guise of research grants", Ind. § 20, and others were "consulting agreements", Ind. § 19. The indictment charged, for example, that Dr. Brown performed virtually none of the consulting functions described in his 1991 agreement with Caremark, but was nevertheless neither required to return the money he had received nor precluded from receiving future funding from Caremark. In addition the indictment charged that Brown received from Caremark payments of staff and office expenses, including telephone answering services and fax rental expenses. . . .

Subsequently, five stockholder derivative actions were filed in this court and consolidated into this action. The original complaint, dated August 5, 1994, alleged, in relevant part, that Caremark's directors breached their duty of care by failing adequately to supervise the conduct of Caremark employees, or institute corrective measures, thereby exposing Caremark to fines and liability. . . .

After each complaint was filed, defendants filed a motion to dismiss. According to defendants, if a settlement had not been reached in this action, the case would have been dismissed on two grounds. First, they contend that the complaints fail to allege particularized facts sufficient to excuse the demand requirement under Delaware Chancery Court Rule 23.1. Second, defendants assert that plaintiffs had failed to state a cause of action due to the fact that Caremark's charter eliminates directors' personal liability for money damages, to the extent permitted by law.

E.   Settlement Negotiations

In September, following the announcement of the Ohio indictment, Caremark publicly announced that as of January 1, 1995, it would terminate all remaining financial relationships with physicians in its home infusion, hemophilia, and growth hormone lines of business.[9] In addition, Caremark asserts that it extended its restrictive policies to all of its contractual relationships with physicians, rather than just those involving Medicare and Medicaid patients, and terminated its research grant program which had always involved some recipients who referred patients to Caremark.

Caremark began settlement negotiations with federal and state government entities in May 1995. In return for a guilty plea to a single count of mail fraud by the corporation, the payment of a criminal fine, the payment of substantial civil damages, and cooperation with further federal investigations on matters relating to the OIG investigation, the government entities agreed to negotiate a settlement that would permit

---

before and after the investigation. According to an undated document from an unknown source, Dr. Brown and six other researchers had been providing patient referrals to Caremark valued at $6.55 for each $1 of research money they received.

[9]   On June 1, 1993, Caremark had stopped entering into new contractual agreements in those business segments.

Caremark to continue participating in Medicare and Medicaid programs. On June 15, 1995, the Board approved a settlement ("Government Settlement Agreement") with the DOJ, OIG, U.S. Veterans Administration, U.S. Federal Employee Health Benefits Program, federal Civilian Health and Medical Program of the Uniformed Services, and related state agencies in all fifty states and the District of Columbia.[10] No senior officers or directors were charged with wrongdoing in the Government Settlement Agreement or in any of the prior indictments. In fact, as part of the sentencing in the Ohio action on June 19, 1995, the United States stipulated that no senior executive of Caremark participated in, condoned, or was willfully ignorant of wrongdoing in connection with the home infusion business practices.

The federal settlement included certain provisions in a "Corporate Integrity Agreement" designed to enhance future compliance with law. The parties have not discussed this agreement, except to say that the negotiated provisions of the settlement of this claim are not redundant of those in that agreement.

Settlement negotiations between the parties in this action commenced in May 1995 as well, based upon a letter proposal of the plaintiffs, dated May 16, 1995. These negotiations resulted in a memorandum of understanding ("MOU"), dated June 7, 1995, and the execution of the Stipulation and Agreement of Compromise and Settlement on June 28, 1995, which is the subject of this action.[13] The MOU, approved by the Board on June 15, 1995, required the Board to adopt several resolutions, discussed below, and to create a new compliance committee. The Compliance and Ethics Committee has been reporting to the Board in accord with its newly specified duties. . . .

F.   The Proposed Settlement of this Litigation

In relevant part the terms upon which these claims asserted are proposed to be settled are as follows:

> 1.   That Caremark undertakes that it and its employees and agents not pay any form of compensation to a third party in exchange for the referral of a patient to a Caremark facility or service or the prescription of drugs marketed or distributed by Caremark for which reimbursement may be sought from Medicare, Medicaid, or a similar state reimbursement program;

---

[10]   The agreement, covering allegations since 1986, required a Caremark subsidiary to enter a guilty plea to two counts of mail fraud, and required Caremark to pay $29 million in criminal fines, $129.9 million relating to civil claims concerning payment practices, $3.5 million for alleged violations of the Controlled Substances Act, and $2 million, in the form of a donation, to a grant program set up by the Ryan White Comprehensive AIDS Resources Emergency Act. Caremark also agreed to enter into a compliance agreement with the HHS.

[13]   Plaintiffs' initial proposal had both a monetary component, requiring Caremark's director-officers to relinquish stock options, and a remedial component, requiring management to adopt and implement several compliance related measures. The monetary component was subsequently eliminated.

2. That Caremark undertakes for itself and its employees, and agents not to pay to or split fees with physicians, joint ventures, any business combination in which Caremark maintains a direct financial interest, or other health care providers with whom Caremark has a financial relationship or interest, in exchange for the referral of a patient to a Caremark facility or service or the prescription of drugs marketed or distributed by Caremark for which reimbursement may be sought from Medicare, Medicaid, or a similar state reimbursement program;

3. That the full Board shall discuss all relevant material changes in government health care regulations and their effect on relationships with health care providers on a semi-annual basis;

4. That Caremark's officers will remove all personnel from health care facilities or hospitals who have been placed in such facility for the purpose of providing remuneration in exchange for a patient referral for which reimbursement may be sought from Medicare, Medicaid, or a similar state reimbursement program;

5. That every patient will receive written disclosure of any financial relationship between Caremark and the health care professional or provider who made the referral;

6. That the Board will establish a Compliance and Ethics Committee of four directors, two of which will be non-management directors, to meet at least four times a year to effectuate these policies and monitor business segment compliance with the ARPL, and to report to the Board semi-annually concerning compliance by each business segment; and

7. That corporate officers responsible for business segments shall serve as compliance officers who must report semi-annually to the Compliance and Ethics Committee and, with the assistance of outside counsel, review existing contracts and get advance approval of any new contract forms.

II. LEGAL PRINCIPLES

A. Principles Governing Settlements of Derivative Claims

As noted at the outset of this opinion, this Court is now required to exercise an informed judgment whether the proposed settlement is fair and reasonable in the light of all relevant factors. *Polk v. Good, Del.Supr.*, 507 A.2d 531 (1986). On an application of this kind, this Court attempts to protect the best interests of the corporation and its absent shareholders all of whom will be barred from future litigation on these claims if the settlement is approved. The parties proposing the settlement bear the burden of persuading the court that it is in fact fair and reasonable. Fins v. Pearlman, Del.Supr., 424 A.2d 305 (1980).

B. Directors' Duties To Monitor Corporate Operations

The complaint charges the director defendants with breach of their duty of attention or care in connection with the ongoing operation of the corporation's business. The claim is that the directors allowed a situation to develop and continue which exposed the corporation to enormous legal liability and that in so doing they violated a duty to be active monitors of corporate performance. The complaint thus does not charge either director self-dealing or the more difficult loyalty-type problems arising from cases of suspect director motivation, such as entrenchment or sale of control contexts.[14] The theory here advanced is possibly the most difficult theory in corporation law upon which a plaintiff might hope to win a judgment. . . .

1. *Potential liability for directoral decisions:* Director liability for a breach of the duty to exercise appropriate attention may, in theory, arise in two distinct contexts. First, such liability may be said to follow from a board decision that results in a loss because that decision was ill advised or "negligent". Second, liability to the corporation for a loss may be said to arise from an unconsidered failure of the board to act in circumstances in which due attention would, arguably, have prevented the loss. *See* generally Veasey & Seitz, The Business Judgment Rule in the Revised Model Act . . . 63 Texas L.Rev. 1483 (1985). The first class of cases will typically be subject to review under the director-protective business judgment rule. . . . *See* Aronson v. Lewis, Del.Supr., 473 A.2d 805 (1984); Gagliardi v. TriFoods Int'l, Inc., Del.Ch. 683 A.2d 1049 (July 19, 1996). . . .

2. *Liability for failure to monitor*: The second class of cases in which director liability for inattention is theoretically possible entail circumstances in which a loss eventuates not from a decision but, from unconsidered inaction. Most of the decisions that a corporation, acting through its human agents, makes are, of course, not the subject of director attention. Legally, the board itself will be required only to authorize the most significant corporate acts or transactions: mergers, changes in capital structure, fundamental changes in business, appointment and compensation of the CEO, etc. As the facts of this case graphically demonstrate, ordinary business decisions that are made by officers and employees deeper in the interior of the organization can, however, vitally affect the welfare of the corporation and its ability to achieve its various strategic and financial goals. If this case did not prove the point itself, recent business history would. Recall for example the

---

[14] See Weinberger v. UOP, Inc., Del.Supr., 457 A.2d 701, 711 (1983) (entire fairness test when financial conflict of interest involved); Unitrin, Inc. v. American General Corp., Del.Supr., 651 A.2d 1361, 1372 (1995) (intermediate standard of review when "defensive" acts taken); Paramount Communications, Inc. v. QVC Network, Del.Supr., 637 A.2d 34, 45 (1994) (intermediate test when corporate control transferred).

displacement of senior management and much of the board of Salomon, Inc.;[18] the replacement of senior management of Kidder, Peabody following the discovery of large trading losses resulting from phantom trades by a highly compensated trader;[19] or the extensive financial loss and reputational injury suffered by Prudential Insurance as a result [of] its junior officers' misrepresentations in connection with the distribution of limited partnership interests. Financial and organizational disasters such as these raise the question, what is the board's responsibility with respect to the organization and monitoring of the enterprise to assure that the corporation functions within the law to achieve its purposes?

Modernly this question has been given special importance by an increasing tendency, especially under federal law, to employ the criminal law to assure corporate compliance with external legal requirements, including environmental, financial, employee and product safety as well as assorted other health and safety regulations. In 1991, pursuant to the Sentencing Reform Act of 1984,[21] the United States Sentencing Commission adopted Organizational Sentencing Guidelines which impact importantly on the prospective effect these criminal sanctions might have on business corporations. The Guidelines set forth a uniform sentencing structure for organizations to be sentenced for violation of federal criminal statutes and provide for penalties that equal or often massively exceed those previously imposed on corporations.[22] The Guidelines offer powerful incentives for corporations today to have in place compliance programs to detect violations of law, promptly to report violations to appropriate public officials when discovered, and to take prompt, voluntary remedial efforts.

In 1963, the Delaware Supreme Court in Graham v. Allis-Chalmers Mfg. Co.,[23] addressed the question of potential liability of board members for losses experienced by the corporation as a result of the corporation having violated the anti-trust laws of the United States. There was no claim in that case that the directors knew about the behavior of subordinate employees of the corporation that had resulted in the liability. Rather, as in this case, the claim asserted was that the directors ought to have known of it and if they had known they would have been under a duty to bring the corporation into compliance with the law and thus save the corporation from the loss. The Delaware Supreme Court concluded that, under the facts as they appeared, there was no basis to find that the directors had breached a duty to be informed of the ongoing

---

[18]   See, e.g., Rotten at the Core, the Economist, August 17, 1991, at 69–70; The Judgment of Salomon: An Anticlimax, Bus. Week, June 1, 1992, at 106.

[19]   See Terence P. Pare, Jack Welch's Nightmare on Wall Street, Fortune, Sept. 5, 1994, at 40–48.

[21]   See Sentencing Reform Act of 1984, Pub.L. 98–473, Title II, § 212(a)(2) (1984); 18 U.S.C.A. §§ 3331–4120.

[22]   See United States Sentencing Commission, Guidelines Manual, Chapter 8 (U.S. Government Printing Office November 1994).

[23]   Del.Supr., 188 A.2d 125 (1963).

operations of the firm. In notably colorful terms, the court stated that "absent cause for suspicion there is no duty upon the directors to install and operate a corporate system of espionage to ferret out wrongdoing which they have no reason to suspect exists."[24] The Court found that there were no grounds for suspicion in that case and, thus, concluded that the directors were blamelessly unaware of the conduct leading to the corporate liability.[25]

How does one generalize this holding today? Can it be said today that, absent some ground giving rise to suspicion of violation of law, that corporate directors have no duty to assure that a corporate information gathering and reporting system exists which represents a good faith attempt to provide senior management and the Board with information respecting material acts, events or conditions within the corporation, including compliance with applicable statutes and regulations? I certainly do not believe so. I doubt that such a broad generalization of the Graham holding would have been accepted by the Supreme Court in 1963. The case can be more narrowly interpreted as standing for the proposition that, absent grounds to suspect deception, neither corporate boards nor senior officers can be charged with wrongdoing simply for assuming the integrity of employees and the honesty of their dealings on the company's behalf. *See* 188 A.2d at 130–31.

A broader interpretation of Graham v. Allis-Chalmers—that it means that a corporate board has no responsibility to assure that appropriate information and reporting systems are established by management—would not, in any event, be accepted by the Delaware Supreme Court in 1996, in my opinion. In stating the basis for this view, I start with the recognition that in recent years the Delaware Supreme Court has made it clear—especially in its jurisprudence concerning takeovers, from Smith v. Van Gorkom through *Paramount Communications v. QVC*[26]—the seriousness with which the corporation law views the role of the corporate board. Secondly, I note the elementary fact that relevant and timely information is an essential predicate for satisfaction of the board's supervisory and monitoring role under Section 141 of the Delaware General Corporation Law. Thirdly, I note the potential impact of the federal organizational sentencing guidelines on any business organization. Any rational person attempting in good faith to meet an organizational governance responsibility would be bound to take into account this development and the enhanced penalties and the opportunities for reduced sanctions that it offers.

In light of these developments, it would, in my opinion, be a mistake to conclude that our Supreme Court's statement in *Graham* concerning

---

[24] Id. at 130.

[25] Recently, the *Graham* standard was applied by the Delaware Chancery in a case involving Baxter. In re Baxter International, Inc. Shareholders Litig., Del.Ch., 654 A.2d 1268, 1270 (1995).

[26] E.g., Smith v. Van Gorkom, Del.Supr., 488 A.2d 858 (1985); Paramount Communications v. QVC Network, Del.Supr., 637 A.2d 34 (1994).

"espionage" means that corporate boards may satisfy their obligation to be reasonably informed concerning the corporation, without assuring themselves that information and reporting systems exist in the organization that are reasonably designed to provide to senior management and to the board itself timely, accurate information sufficient to allow management and the board, each within its scope, to reach informed judgments concerning both the corporation's compliance with law and its business performance.

Obviously the level of detail that is appropriate for such an information system is a question of business judgment. And obviously too, no rationally designed information and reporting system will remove the possibility that the corporation will violate laws or regulations, or that senior officers or directors may nevertheless sometimes be misled or otherwise fail reasonably to detect acts material to the corporation's compliance with the law. But it is important that the board exercise a good faith judgment that the corporation's information and reporting system is in concept and design adequate to assure the board that appropriate information will come to its attention in a timely manner as a matter of ordinary operations, so that it may satisfy its responsibility.

Thus, I am of the view that a director's obligation includes a duty to attempt in good faith to assure that a corporate information and reporting system, which the board concludes is adequate, exists, and that failure to do so under some circumstances may, in theory at least, render a director liable for losses caused by non-compliance with applicable legal standards.[27] I now turn to an analysis of the claims asserted with this concept of the directors' duty of care, as a duty satisfied in part by assurance of adequate information flows to the board, in mind.

III. ANALYSIS OF THIRD AMENDED COMPLAINT AND SETTLEMENT

A. The Claims

On balance, after reviewing an extensive record in this case, including numerous documents and three depositions, I conclude that this settlement is fair and reasonable. In light of the fact that the Caremark Board already has a functioning committee charged with overseeing corporate compliance, the changes in corporate practice that are presented as consideration for the settlement do not impress one as very significant. Nonetheless, that consideration appears fully adequate to support dismissal of the derivative claims of director fault asserted, because those claims find no substantial evidentiary support in the

---

[27] Any action seeking recover for losses would logically entail a judicial determination of proximate cause, since, for reasons that I take to be obvious, it could never be assumed that an adequate information system would be a system that would prevent all losses. I need not touch upon the burden allocation with respect to a proximate cause issue in such a suit. See Cede & Co. v. Technicolor, Inc., Del.Supr., 636 A.2d 956 (1994); Cinerama, Inc. v. Technicolor, Inc., Del.Ch., 663 A.2d 1134 (1994), aff'd., Del.Supr., 663 A.2d 1156 (1995). Moreover, questions of waiver of liability under certificate provisions authorized by 8 Del.C. § 102(b)(7) may also be faced.

record and quite likely were susceptible to a motion to dismiss in all events.

In order to show that the Caremark directors breached their duty of care by failing adequately to control Caremark's employees, plaintiffs would have to show either (1) that the directors knew or (2) should have known that violations of law were occurring and, in either event, (3) that the directors took no steps in a good faith effort to prevent or remedy that situation, and (4) that such failure proximately resulted in the losses complained of, although under Cede & Co. v. Technicolor, Inc., Del.Supr., 636 A.2d 956 (1994) this last element may be thought to constitute an affirmative defense. . . .

. . . I turn to a consideration of the [claim based on] . . . director inattention or "negligence." Generally where a claim of directorial liability for corporate loss is predicated upon ignorance of liability creating activities within the corporation, as in *Graham* or in this case, in my opinion only a sustained or systematic failure of the board to exercise oversight—such as an utter failure to attempt to assure a reasonable information and reporting system exits—will establish the lack of good faith that is a necessary condition to liability. Such a test of liability—lack of good faith as evidenced by sustained or systematic failure of a director to exercise reasonable oversight—is quite high. But, a demanding test of liability in the oversight context is probably beneficial to corporate shareholders as a class, as it is in the board decision context, since it makes board service by qualified persons more likely, while continuing to act as a stimulus to good faith performance of duty by such directors.

Here the record supplies essentially no evidence that the director defendants were guilty of a sustained failure to exercise their oversight function. To the contrary, insofar as I am able to tell on this record, the corporation's information systems appear to have represented a good faith attempt to be informed of relevant facts. If the directors did not know the specifics of the activities that lead to the indictments, they cannot be faulted.

The liability that eventuated in this instance was huge. But the fact that it resulted from a violation of criminal law alone does not create a breach of fiduciary duty by directors. The record at this stage does not support the conclusion that the defendants either lacked good faith in the exercise of their monitoring responsibilities or conscientiously permitted a known violation of law by the corporation to occur. The claims asserted against them must be viewed at this stage as extremely weak.

B. The Consideration For Release of Claim

The proposed settlement provides very modest benefits. Under the settlement agreement, plaintiffs have been given express assurances that Caremark will have a more centralized, active supervisory system in the future. Specifically, the settlement mandates duties to be performed by the newly named Compliance and Ethics Committee on an ongoing basis and increases the responsibility for monitoring compliance with the law at the lower levels of management. In adopting the resolutions required under the settlement, Caremark has further clarified its policies concerning the prohibition of providing remuneration for referrals. These appear to be positive consequences of the settlement of the claims brought by the plaintiffs, even if they are not highly significant. Nonetheless, given the weakness of the plaintiffs' claims the proposed settlement appears to be an adequate, reasonable, and beneficial outcome for all of the parties. Thus, the proposed settlement will be approved. . . .

I am today entering an order consistent with the foregoing.

In re Massey Energy Company Derivative and Class Action Litigation

Court of Chancery of Delaware, 2011.
2011 Del. Ch. LEXIS 83.

■ STRINE, VICE CHANCELLOR

The plaintiffs are stockholders of Massey Energy Company, a coal mining corporation with a controversial reputation. Convinced that it knew better than the public authorities charged with enforcing laws designed to make mining a safer and cleaner business, Massey management, with board knowledge, fostered an adversarial relationship with the company's regulators and accepted as ordinary the idea that the company would regularly be accused of violating important safety regulations. On April 5, 2010, a massive explosion occurred at Massey's Upper Big Branch mine in West Virginia and as a result, 29 miners died. Although the worst human and business loss in Massey history, it was not the first time that Massey miners had suffered death and serious injuries. . . .

[Massey is the nation's sixth largest coal mine. From 2000–2010 its CEO was Don Blankenship, who according to subordinates ruled Massey with an "autocratic" management style. Blankenship viewed government safe regulators, such as the federal Mining Safety and Health Administration (MSHA) as nit-pickers and thus Massey took a combative style toward MSHA. Massey had a horrendous safety record with interesting consequences. For example, in a 2007 whistle-blower suit a West Virginia jury awarded $2 million in punitive damages to an in-house safety inspector who was fired in retaliation for his reporting unaddressed safety violations to MSHA. In 2008, Massey pled guilty to criminal charges, including one felony, for willful violation of mandatory safety standards. In that same year, Massey entered into a $20 million settlement with the Environmental Protection Agency involving 4,500 violations of the Clean Water Act.

In 2008, to settle a derivative suit, Massey established a new board committee to oversee compliance with mine safety. While many initiatives to improve mine safety at Massey occurred after the committee's formation, the number of mine safety violations continued to mount (there were 10,653 citations and orders against Massey in 2009, an all-time high among mining firms). And, Blankenship, as well as the board's lead director, continued their strident toward federal regulators.

On April 5, 2010, an explosion at Massey's Upper Big Branch mine killed 29 miners—the deadliest mining accident in 40 years. An investigative report, the McAteer Report, commissioned by the West Virginia governor deplored Massey's compliance with state and federal safety regulations, observing that the Upper Big Branch mine suffered from "chronic" problems that caused the explosion. A report by MSHA reached a similar conclusion.

The present derivative suit alleges the directors continued to disregard their fiduciary duties since the settlement of the earlier derivative suit so that their disregard of mining safety regulations resulted in fines of $27 million.]

[T]he plaintiffs allege that Blankenship knowingly flouted applicable miner safety laws, believing he knew better about how to run mines safely than the MSHA, and more blatantly, made the conscious choice to put miners at risk in order to cut cost-corners and up mining profits. The plaintiffs thus allege that Blankenship himself, and others on his management team, fostered a business strategy expressly designed to put coal production and higher profits over compliance with the law. The plaintiffs argue that Blankenship did not hide his disdain for the company's regulators and caused Massey to take an openly aggressive attitude with the MSHA. Even after Massey had already pled guilty to criminal charges for willful violations of mining safety laws and falsification of evidence, settled a claim with the Environmental Protection Agency for a record sum, and suffered a punitive damages award for firing a whistleblower, Blankenship publicly stated that the idea that governmental safety regulators knew more about mine safety than he did was silly.

. . . Notably, the plaintiffs point to evidence that in the wake of pleading guilty to criminal charges and suffering liability for numerous violations of federal and state safety regulations, Massey mines continued to experience a troubling pattern of major safety violations. But, instead of using their supervisory authority over management to make sure that Massey genuinely changed its culture and made mine safety a genuine priority, the independent directors are alleged to have done nothing of actual substance to change the direction of the company's real policy. In support of that argument, the plaintiffs cite to evidence that Massey was experiencing an increase in 2008 and 2009 in the number of violations of safety regulations; that Massey was continuing to engage in adversarial tactics toward the MSHA; that important safety rules were regularly flouted; . . . and, perhaps most damning of all, to the McAteer Report's conclusion that the Disaster at Upper Big Branch was caused not by a freak and unavoidable accident, but instead by a corporate culture premised on the view that the company's management knew better than the law about what was necessary to run safe mines. . . .

Although the ultimate ability of the plaintiffs to prove that the Massey directors and officers breached their fiduciary duty by knowingly failing to discharge their duty to try to make sure that Massey complied with its legal obligations is difficult to predict, there seems little doubt that a faithful application of the plaintiff-friendly pleading standard would preclude a dismissal of their claims at the pleading stage. . . .

Regrettably, a myriad of particularized facts have been pled that create a pleading-stage inference that the top management of Massey did just that. The objective facts are that Massey had pled guilty to criminal charges, had suffered other serious judgments and settlements as a result of violations of law, had been caught trying to hide violations of law and suppress material evidence, and had miners suffer death and serious injuries at its facilities. Instead of becoming a corporation with a new attitude and commitment to safety that won recognition for that change from its regulators, Massey continued to think it knew better than those charged with enforcing the law, and in fact, often argued with the law itself. Following that continued period of adversarialness, the Upper Big Branch Disaster occurred, Massey miners have lost their lives at other facilities, and the MSHA has alleged that serious safety violations and an attitude of law-flouting has continued at other Massey facilities.

To be plain, when a company already has been proven to have engaged in illegal conduct, it is a high risk strategy for it to embrace the idea that its regulators are wrong-headed and to view itself as simply a victim of a governmental conspiracy. Relatedly, when a company has a "record" as a recidivist, its directors and officers cannot take comfort in the appearance of compliance motion at the pleading stage, when the plaintiffs are able to plead particularized facts creating an inference that the Board and management were aware of a troubling continuing pattern of non-compliance in fact and of a managerial attitude suggestive of a desire to fight with and hide evidence from the company's regulators. . . .

It may well be that after a trial, the Massey directors and officers will be found to have acted in a manner that does not subject them to liability under the *Caremark* standard. But for purposes of this motion, candor requires acknowledging that the plaintiffs have likely pled Derivative Claims that would survive a motion to dismiss, even under the heightened pleading standard applicable under Rule 23.1.

———

Accord: In re Abbott Laboratories Derivative Shareholder Litig., 325 F.3d 795 (7th Cir. 2003) (board aware that during six-year period the pharmaceutical company had received several FDA warnings that culminated in significant government fine and mandated destruction of millions of dollars of inventory); Rich v. Chong, 66 A.3d 963 (Del. Ch. 2013) (self-admitted accounting system failures that resulted in accounting errors of about $130 million and receipt of a NASDAQ warning of delisting unless financial reporting system improved); In re American Int'l Group, Inc., 965 A.2d 763 (Del. Ch. 2009) (complaint supported assertion of a criminal enterprise that produced a variety of financial wrongdoings that were made possible by weak internal controls for which the two defendant senior officers were at least aware and knowingly failed to stop). *Compare* In re Citigroup Inc. Shareholder Derivative Litig., 964 A.2d 106 (Del. Ch. 2009), holding that the business judgment rule insulated the directors against charges they failed to take precautions to avoid the ensuing financial losses arising from Citigroup's large exposure to the subprime lending markets. The suit alleged various red flags such as an economist's forecast that a speculative bubble was nearing its end, a leading subprime lender closing its 229 offices, another lender filing bankruptcy, analysts downgrading subprime mortgages, and a warning of increasing subprime delinquencies by another lender. The court reasoned:

> . . . [The "red flags"]amount to little more than portions of public documents that reflected the worsening conditions in the subprime mortgage market and in the economy generally. Plaintiffs fail to plead particularized facts suggesting that the Board was presented with "red flags" alerting it to potential misconduct. . . . [The plaintiffs] repeatedly make the conclusory allegation that the defendants have breached their duty of oversight, but nowhere do [they] adequately explain what the director defendants actually did or failed to do that would constitute a violation. Even while admitting that Citigroup had a risk monitoring system in place, plaintiffs seem to conclude that, because the director defendants were charged with monitoring Citigroup's risk, then they must be found liable because Citigroup experienced losses as a result of exposure to the subprime mortgage market. The only factual support plaintiffs provide for this conclusion are "red flags" that actually amount to nothing more than signs of continuing deterioration in the subprime mortgage market. These types of conclusory allegations are exactly the kinds of allegation that do not state a claim for relief under *Caremark*.

Id. at 128–130.

———

ABA Section of Business Law, Committee on Corporate Laws, Corporate Director's Guidebook
Sixth ed., 2011.

... COMPLIANCE WITH LAW

The board is responsible for overseeing management's activities in assuring the corporation's compliance with legal requirements in the jurisdictions in which the corporation does business. A well-conceived and properly implemented compliance program can significantly reduce the incidence of violations of laws and corporate policy. It can also reduce or eliminate lawsuits, penalties and criminal prosecution. Although the federal sentencing guidelines greatly increase the penalties for corporations guilty of criminal violations, they also provide for significant fine reductions for corporations with programs in place to prevent and detect such violations. Directors should periodically satisfy themselves that an appropriate process is in place to detect violations and to encourage not only attention to general legal compliance issues and claims against the corporation, but also the timely reporting of significant legal or other compliance matters to the board or an appropriate board committee.

Boards should ensure their companies have formal written policies designed to promote compliance with law and corporate policy. They should review policies periodically for effectiveness, and, if the corporation operates in an industry subject to laws and regulations that demand special compliance procedures and monitoring, the review should be more frequent and intensive. Many public companies assign compliance oversight to the audit committee, others to a governance or risk committee. These committees meet regularly with the company's general counsel or outside counsel to be briefed on compliance and claims. With the increased burdens placed on public company audit committees, some boards have elected to form a separate compliance or legal affairs committee. Directors should consider whether delegating oversight for multiple compliance issues to a single board committee is sufficient for the corporation's legal and regulatory compliance profile.

The board should ensure that employees of the corporation are informed and periodically reminded of corporate policies, including those pertaining to compliance with (i) codes of business conduct and ethics; (ii) anti-discrimination and employment laws; (iii) environmental and health and safety laws; (iv) anti-bribery laws; (v) antitrust and competition laws; (vi) securities laws, particularly those addressing insider trading; and (vii) laws and regulations of other countries as applicable. The major securities markets require their listed companies to adopt codes of business conduct and ethics applicable to all employees, officers and directors. The corporation should have appropriate controls throughout the organization for monitoring compliance with such laws and codes.

Controls may include whistle-blower and hotline policies. The corporation also must establish procedures for addressing violations.

In addition, all compliance personnel should have direct access to the general counsel or other compliance officer to ensure sensitive compliance situations are promptly addressed. Boards should also ensure the compliance program has adequate resources and authority to perform its function.

———

Eisenberg, The Board of Directors and Internal Control

19 Cardozo L. Rev. 237, 1997.

I.   The Meaning of Internal Control

In 1992, the Committee of Sponsoring Organizations (COSO) issued a comprehensive four-volume Report on internal control. The COSO Report defines internal control as "a process, effected by an entity's board of directors, management and other personnel, designed to provide reasonable assurance regarding the achievement of objectives" in three categories: "effectiveness and efficiency of operations, reliability of financial reporting, and compliance with applicable laws and regulations." Internal control over each of these objectives consists of five interrelated components: the control environment, risk assessment, control activities, information and communication, and monitoring. A system of internal control is deemed to be effective only if all five components are functioning effectively. . . .

. . . In 1994, the ABA's Committee on Law and Accounting [stated] that "[t]he COSO Report may well become the standard for defining internal control and its interrelated components, and for measuring the effectiveness of internal control. . . .

———

NOTE ON CIVIL LIABILITY OF DIRECTORS AND OFFICERS TO THIRD PERSONS

Most of the materials in this Section have concerned the liability of directors and officers to the *corporation* for failure to exercise due care. A director or officer may also be civilly liable to *third persons* for acts he commits in a corporate capacity. Robert Thompson has summarized the principles that govern the civil liability of directors and officers to third parties as follows:

> Officers are agents of the corporation who act for the entity in a variety of day-to-day matters. . . . [A]ny individual liability [of officers] for enterprise obligations derives primarily from the common law. These principles, as reflected in the Restatement (Second) of Agency, usually insulate the officer [in the case of

contracts entered into by the officer on the corporation's behalf]. An individual who signs a contract on behalf of the corporation is cloaked in the mantle of the enterprise and is not personally liable for action taken in the corporate name. If the enterprise defaults on an obligation under the contract, the creditor normally cannot proceed against the individual.

However, the same individual who acts for the same corporation in the same capacity in taking action deemed tortious loses the corporate cloak and is held individually liable along with the enterprise. . . .

Thus, as to direct participation, the corporate shield really only works for contracts, a narrowness of protection that may surprise many entrepreneurs who intend to use corporations to avoid liability. Note, however, that the corporate form [normally] does insulate corporate participants in a tort (or contract) setting against vicarious [civil] liability. . . .

Thompson, Unpacking Limited Liability: Direct and Vicarious Liability of Corporate Participants for Torts of the Enterprise, 47 Vand.L.Rev. 1, 6–7, 9, 24 (1994).

D. LIABILITY SHIELDS

In assessing the duties of directors and officers to act with care, account must be taken of three elements that may serve to reduce or eliminate civil liability for breach of those duties: direct limits of liability, insurance, and indemnification. The first element is addressed in this Section. Insurance is addressed in Section 3, infra. Indemnification is addressed in Chapter 13, Section 8.

VIRGINIA CORPORATIONS CODE § 13.1–690

[See Statutory Supplement]

DEL. GEN. CORP. LAW § 102(b)(7)

[See Statutory Supplement]

MODEL BUSINESS CORP. ACT § 2.02(b)(4)

[See Statutory Supplement]

Malpiede v. Townson
Supreme Court of Delaware, 2001.
780 A.2d 1075.

■ VEASEY, CHIEF JUSTICE:

In this appeal, we affirm . . . the granting of a motion to dismiss the plaintiffs' due care claim on the ground that the exculpatory provision in the charter of the target corporation authorized by 8 Del. C. § 102(b)(7), bars any claim for money damages against the director defendants based solely on the board's alleged breach of its duty of care. Accordingly, we affirm the judgment of the Court of Chancery dismissing the amended complaint. . . .

Facts

Frederick's of Hollywood ("Frederick's") is a retailer of women's lingerie and apparel with its headquarters in Los Angeles, California. This case centers on the merger of Frederick's into Knightsbridge Capital Corporation ("Knightsbridge") under circumstances where it became a target in a bidding contest. . . . Two trusts created by the principal founders of Frederick's, Frederick and Harriet Mellinger (the "Trusts"), held a total of about 41% of the outstanding Class A voting shares and a total of about 51% of the outstanding Class B non-voting shares of Frederick's. . . .

On June 13, 1997, the Frederick's board approved an offer from Knightsbridge to purchase all of Frederick's outstanding Class A and Class B shares for $6.14 per share in cash in a two-step merger transaction. The terms of the merger agreement signed by the Frederick's board prohibited the board from soliciting additional bids from third parties, but the agreement permitted the board to negotiate with third party bidders when the board's fiduciary duties required it to do so. . . .

[On August 21, Frederick's received a bid of $7.00 per share from Milton Partners. On August 25, Knightsbridge entered into an agreement to purchase all of the Frederick's shares held by the Trusts for $6.90 per share. On August 27, a third bidder, Veritas Capital Fund, offered $7.75 per share. The Frederick's board then invited Milton and Veritas to continue the bidding process. However, the board conditioned further bidding on their posting a bond of $2.5 million and submitting a written offer within ten days. Veritas posted the bond; Milton did not.

[On September 6, Knightsbridge increased its bid to match the $7.75 Veritas offer, but on the condition that the board accept a variety of terms designed to restrict its ability to pursue superior offers. One of these terms, the so-called "no-talk" provision, prohibited any Frederick's representative from speaking to third party bidders concerning the acquisition of the company. Frederick's board agreed to Knightsbridge's new bid and terms, and thereby effectively ended the bidding process.

Two days later, Knightsbridge acquired enough shares in the open market, at $8.81 per share, to give it majority voting power.]

On September 11, 1997, Veritas increased its cash offer to $9.00 per share. Relying on (1) the "no-talk" provision in the merger agreement, (2) Knightsbridge's stated intention to vote its shares against third party bids, and (3) Veritas' request for an option to dilute Knightsbridge's interest, the board rejected the revised Veritas bid. . . .

[After the Court of Chancery denied the plaintiffs' request for a temporary restraining order, the plaintiffs amended the complaint to seek damages on behalf of the class of shareholders alleging the directors breached their fiduciary duties by terminating the auction and entering in the lower-priced offer with Knightsbridge.]

The Court of Chancery granted the directors' motion to dismiss the amended complaint . . . , concluding that: (1) the complaint did not support a claim of breach of the board's duty of loyalty, [and] (2) the exculpatory provision in the Fredrick's charter precluded money damages against the directors for any breach of the board's duty of care. . . .

Standard of Review

We review de novo the dismissal by the Court of Chancery of a complaint . . . .

The Duty of Loyalty Claim

The central claim in the amended complaint is that the sale of Frederick's to Knightsbridge "constituted a breach of [the Frederick's board's] fiduciary obligation to maximize shareholder value" because the board did not "conduct an auction with a 'level playing field' " as required by Revlon, Inc. v. MacAndrews & Forbes Holdings, Inc.[43] . . .

The Court of Chancery concluded, and the plaintiffs do not appear to contest on appeal, that the amended complaint adequately alleges a conflict of interest with respect to only one of the directors who approved the Knightsbridge merger.[44] The amended complaint does not allege that the lone conflicted director dominated the three other directors who

---

[43]   Del. Supr., 506 A.2d 173, 182–83 (1985).

[44]   See January 2000 Mem. Op., 2000 Del. Ch. LEXIS 19, *17. In particular, the complaint alleges that the Knightsbridge merger agreement provided for several cash payments to George Townson, who was the CEO, President, and Chairman of Frederick's during the relevant period. The personal benefits allegedly received by Townson as a result of the Knightsbridge merger included: (1) a payment of $.05 for each "under water" option held by Townson with an exercise price below the merger price, (2) a severance payment of $750,000 upon consummation of the merger, and (3) a payment of $250,000 on the date of the merger and sixteen quarterly payments of $100,000 under a noncompete and consulting agreement. The complaint also alleges that William Barrett, who was a Frederick's director and a vice president of JMS, the firm's financial advisor, had an interest in the merger transaction. Specifically, the complaint alleges that Barrett's firm received a $2 million fee upon consummation of the Knightsbridge merger. But because Barrett's firm was entitled to receive a fee upon the consummation of any merger and because the fee was proportional to the sale price, the Court of Chancery correctly concluded that the complaint was insufficient to establish a disabling conflict with respect to Barrett. See January 2000 Mem. Op., 2000 Del. Ch. LEXIS 19, *24. . . .

approved the merger on September 6, 1997. The Court of Chancery therefore correctly held that the Knightsbridge merger was approved by a majority of disinterested directors. . . .

The Due Care Claim . . .

Construing the amended complaint most favorably to the plaintiffs, it can be read to allege that the board was grossly negligent in immediately accepting the Knightsbridge offer and agreeing to various restrictions on further negotiations without first determining whether Veritas would issue a counteroffer. Although the board had conducted a search for a buyer over one year, plaintiffs seem to contend that the board was imprudently hasty in agreeing to a restrictive merger agreement on the day it was proposed—particularly where other bidders had recently expressed interest.[45] Although the board's haste, in itself, might not constitute a breach of the board's duty of care because the board had already conducted a lengthy sale process, the plaintiffs argue that the board's decision to accept allegedly extreme contractual restrictions impacted its ability to obtain a higher sale price. Recognizing that, at the end of the day, plaintiffs would have an uphill battle in overcoming the presumption of the business judgment rule, we must give plaintiffs the benefit of the doubt at this pleading stage to determine if they have stated a due care claim. Because of our ultimate decision, however, we need not finally decide this question in this case.

We assume, therefore, without deciding, that a claim for relief based on gross negligence during the board's auction process is stated by the inferences most favorable to plaintiffs that flow from these allegations. The issue then becomes whether the amended complaint may be dismissed upon . . . [a motion to dismiss] by reason of the existence and the legal effect of the exculpatory provision of Article TWELFTH of Frederick's certificate of incorporation, adopted pursuant to 8 Del. C. § 102(b)(7). That provision would exempt directors from personal liability in damages with certain exceptions (e.g., breach of the duty of loyalty) that are not applicable here. . . .[46]

B. Application of *Emerald Partners*

1.   The Court of Chancery Properly Dismissed Claims Based Solely on the Duty of Care

Plaintiffs . . . conceded in oral argument . . . that if a complaint unambiguously and solely asserted only a due care claim, the complaint

---

[45]   Relatedly, the plaintiffs also argue that the board breached its fiduciary duties by favoring Knightsbridge over Veritas in the bidding process.

[46]   Article TWELFTH provides:

TWELFTH. A director of this Corporation shall not be personally liable to the Corporation or its shareholders for monetary damages for breach of fiduciary duty as a director, except for liability (i) for any breach of the director's duty of loyalty to the Corporation or its shareholders, (ii) for acts or omissions not in good faith or which involve intentional misconduct or a knowing violation of law (iii) under Section 174 of the Delaware General Corporation Law, or (iv) for any transaction for which the director derived an improper personal benefit.

is dismissible once the corporation's Section 102(b)(7) provision is invoked. . . .

Plaintiffs contended vigorously, however, that the Section 102(b)(7) charter provision does not apply to bar their claims in this case because the amended complaint alleges breaches of the duty of loyalty and other claims that are not barred by the charter provision. As a result, plaintiffs maintain, this case cannot be boiled down solely to a due care case. They argue, in effect, that their complaint is sufficiently well-pleaded that—as a matter of law—the due care claims are so inextricably intertwined with loyalty and bad faith claims that Section 102(b)(7) is not a bar to recovery of damages against the directors.

We disagree. It is the plaintiffs who have a burden to set forth "a short and plain statement of the claim showing that the pleader is entitled to relief."[47] The plaintiffs are entitled to all reasonable inferences flowing from their pleadings, but if those inferences do not support a valid legal claim, the complaint should be dismissed without the need for the defendants to file an answer and without proceeding with discovery. Here we have assumed, without deciding, that the amended complaint on its face states a due care claim. Because we have determined that the complaint fails properly to invoke loyalty and bad faith claims, we are left with only a due care claim. Defendants had the obligation to raise the bar of Section 102(b)(7) as a defense, and they did. As plaintiffs conceded in oral argument before this Court, if there is only an unambiguous, residual due care claim and nothing else—as a matter of law—then Section 102(b)(7) would bar the claim. Accordingly, the Court of Chancery did not err in dismissing the plaintiffs due care claim in this case.

2.   The Court of Chancery Correctly Applied the Parties' Respective Burdens of Proof

Plaintiffs also assert that the trial court in the case before us incorrectly placed on plaintiffs a pleading burden to negate the elements of the 102(b)(7) charter provision. Plaintiffs argue that this ruling is inconsistent with the statement in *Emerald Partners* [726 A.2d 1215 (Del. 1999)] that "The shield from liability provided by a certificate of incorporation provision adopted pursuant to 8 Del. C. § 102(b)(7) is in the nature of an affirmative defense. . . . Defendants seeking exculpation under such a provision will normally bear the burden of establishing each of its elements."

The procedural posture here is quite different from that in *Emerald Partners*. There the Court stated that it was incorrect for the trial court to grant summary judgment on the record in that case because the defendants had the burden at trial of demonstrating good faith if they were invoking the statutory exculpation provision. In this case, we focus not on trial burdens, but only on pleading issues. A plaintiff must allege well-pleaded facts stating a claim on which relief may be granted. Had

---

[47]   Chancery Rule 8(a).

plaintiff alleged such well-pleaded facts supporting a breach of loyalty or bad faith claim, the Section 102(b)(7) charter provision would have been unavailing as to such claims, and this case would have gone forward.

But we have held that the amended complaint here does not allege a loyalty violation or other violation falling within the exceptions to the Section 102(b)(7) exculpation provision. Likewise, we have held that, even if the plaintiffs had stated a claim for gross negligence, such a well-pleaded claim is unavailing because defendants have brought forth the Section 102(b)(7) charter provision that bars such claims. This is the end of the case.

And rightly so, as a matter of the public policy of this State. Section 102(b)(7) was adopted by the Delaware General Assembly in 1986 following a directors and officers insurance liability crisis and the 1985 Delaware Supreme Court decision in *Smith v. Van Gorkom*. The purpose of this statute was to permit stockholders to adopt a provision in the certificate of incorporation to free directors of personal liability in damages for due care violations, but not duty of loyalty violations, bad faith claims and certain other conduct. Such a charter provision, when adopted, would not affect injunctive proceedings based on gross negligence. Once the statute was adopted, stockholders usually approved charter amendments containing these provisions because it freed up directors to take business risks without worrying about negligence lawsuits.

Our jurisprudence since the adoption of the statute has consistently stood for the proposition that a Section 102(b)(7) charter provision bars a claim that is found to state only a due care violation. Because we have assumed that the amended complaint here does state a due care claim, the exculpation afforded by the statute must affirmatively be raised by the defendant directors.[49] The directors have done so in this case, and the Court of Chancery properly applied the Frederick's charter provision to dismiss the plaintiffs' due care claim. . . .

Accordingly, we affirm the judgment of the Court of Chancery dismissing the amended complaint against the Frederick's board. . . .

————

In *Leal v. Meeks*, 115 A.3d 1173 (Del. 2015), the Delaware Supreme Court clarified the application of Delaware's immunity shield when damages are sought in connection with a transaction with an interested party in which the "entire fairness" standard is applied. The Chancery Court held the immunity shield did not apply to any of the directors so long as the plaintiff had sufficiently pled that the underlying transaction involved

---

[49]   Although an exculpatory charter provision is in the nature of an affirmative defense under *Emerald Partners*, the board is not required to disprove claims based on alleged breaches of the duty of loyalty to gain the protection of the provision with respect to due care claims. Rather, proving the existence of a valid exculpatory provision in the corporate charter entitles directors to dismissal of any claims for money damages against them that are based solely on alleged breaches of the board's duty of care.

self dealing with respect to at least some of the directors. The Supreme Court reversed, reasoning that with respect to a non-interested director of a corporation with immunity shield in its charter, the suit must be dismissed if the plaintiff is unable to plead non-exculpated conduct on the part of such director. It is not, therefore, sufficient for the plaintiff to allege the directors acted in a grossly negligent manner in approving a self-dealing transaction.

E. DIRECTORS' AND OFFICERS'—LIABILITY INSURANCE

———

FORM OF DIRECTORS' AND OFFICERS' LIABILITY INSURANCE

[See Statutory Supplement]

———

NOTES ON DIRECTORS' AND OFFICERS' LIABILITY INSURANCE

1.   Background. Often a director or officer will be entitled to corporate indemnification for losses she incurred in suits against her based on actions that she took in her corporate capacity. See Chapter 13, Section 8. For various reasons, however, a director or officer may not be indemnified for all such losses. For example, the governing law may prohibit indemnification in certain kinds of cases, as where the director's or officer's loss consists of a judgment against her in a duty-of-care action. Or the corporation may be insolvent, or it may refuse to make indemnification where indemnification is discretionary rather than mandatory. Accordingly, corporations will often purchase Directors' and Officers' (D & O) Liability Insurance to cover certain types of non-indemnified losses.

2.   Policy Structure. Typically, a D & O policy has two separate insurance agreements: (i) Corporate reimbursement, which insures the corporation against its potential liability to officers and directors under the latters' right to indemnification from the corporation, and (ii) Personal coverage, which insures the directors and officers themselves against losses based on claims against them for wrongful conduct. The precise scope of the personal coverage varies according to the policy, but all policies would normally cover most liabilities arising in connection with claims based on a violation of the duty of care owed to the corporation, and many or most policies would cover liabilities for duties of care owed to the general public.

3.   Scope of Coverage. D & O insurance does not render directors and officers completely risk-free with regard to claims based on the duty of care. To begin with, a variety of claims are excluded from coverage. For example, many D & O policies contain an insured v. insured exclusion, under which the insurer is not liable in connection with claims made against a director or officer by the corporation, other than a claim made in a shareholder's derivative action (that is, other than a claim made by a shareholder on the corporation's behalf). Also, D & O policy limits typically apply to the combined amount of liability and legal expenses, and in any given case the combination of the two may exceed the policy limit. *See* Helfand v. National Union Fire Ins. Co., 10 Cal.App.4th 869, 13 Cal.Rptr.2d 295 (1992).

Other obstacles may also stand in the way of a recovery under a D & O policy. For example, the insurer is not liable if it can establish any of the following defenses, among others:

(a) The corporation, the directors and officers, or all of them (the "insureds") did not give the insurer notice of the claim against them within the time period specified by the policy. See, e.g., ACE Am. Ins. Co. v. Underwriters at Lloyds & Cos., 971 A.2d 1121 (Pa. 2009). This defense includes cases in which (i) the insureds are given notice of a claim against them, but suit on the claim has not yet been brought; and (ii) the insureds erroneously consider the notice they were given as not sufficiently formal within the meaning of the policy, and they therefore do not notify the insurer of the claim until the time for giving notice has expired.

(b) At the time the policy was issued, the corporation or the directors and officers knew that the event giving rise to the claim against them was likely to occur but did not report that to the insurer.

(c) The claim against the insureds is related to an earlier claim that was pending or completed prior to the inception of the policy. See, e.g., HR Acquisition I Corp. v. Twin City Fire Ins. Co., 2008 WL 4767256 (11th Cir. 2008).

4.   Claims-Made Basis. Another characteristic of D & O insurance that may be relevant to the protection it affords is that such insurance is written on a claims-made basis—that is, the insurance covers only claims made while the policy is in force. To illustrate, suppose C Corporation procured a D & O policy from I Insurance Company for 2010. A claim made in 2010 that is based on events that occurred in 2007 may be covered by the policy even though I was not C's insurer in 2007. Conversely, however, a claim made in 2011 based on events that occurred in 2010 may not be covered by the 2010 policy.

The claims-made nature of D & O insurance is often modified by several features. First, a policy may contain a "retroactive date provision", under which an insured's liability for an event that occurred before a designated date will not be covered by the policy even if a claim based on the event is first made during the policy period. Second, a policy may include a "right of discovery," which allows an insured to extend the coverage to a claim made during a limited period after the policy has terminated, provided the claim is based on wrongful acts that occurred during the term of the policy. Many policies also permit an insured to present a notice of occurrence of a *possible* claim during the policy period, and give such a notice the same effect as an actual claim made against the insured. Subject to these exceptions, an effect of the claims-made nature of D & O insurance is that a director or officer cannot be positive that he will be covered for his present conduct if a claim concerning that conduct arises after the policy has expired or has been canceled.

     5. Insurers Are Not Eager to Pay. Another factor that affects the risk of a director or officer for duty-of-care liability is that D & O insurers often seem to be exceptionally ready to litigate claims brought against them by their insureds. Some of the litigation concerns the interpretation of the policy language, which is often less than crystal clear. In addition, the corporation and the directors and officers who are to be covered under a D & O policy must fill out extensive applications, which include questions on such issues as whether the applicant has knowledge or information of any act, error, or omission that might give rise to a claim under the policy. It is often easy for an insurer to argue that the policy is unenforceable on the ground that a question was not answered accurately. Furthermore, unless the policy otherwise provides, the failure of even one director or officer to answer questions accurately may invalidate the coverage of all officers and directors. *See, e.g.,* Bird v. Penn Central Co., 334 F.Supp. 255 (E.D.Pa.1971), 341 F.Supp. 291 (1972); Shapiro v. American Home Assurance Co., 584 F.Supp. 1245 (D.Mass.1984).

———

2. THE DUTY TO ACT IN GOOD FAITH

In re the Walt Disney Company Derivative Litigation

Supreme Court of State of Delaware, 2006.
906 A.2d 27.

■ JACOBS, JUSTICE:

     [In August 1995, the board of Walt Disney Company entered into an employment agreement with Michael Ovitz under which Ovitz would serve as Disney's president for five years. It soon became apparent that Ovitz was a poor fit, and on December 11, 1996, Ovitz was terminated with a severance package of $140 million. Shareholders then brought a derivative action against Ovitz, the directors, and others. A major element of the complaint was that the directors had not acted in good faith. In particular, the complaint alleged that: (i) Ovitz was hired as a result of pressure from Disney's CEO, Michael Eisner, who had been close friends with Ovitz for 25 years; (ii) Ovitz had never been an executive of a publicly owned entertainment company; (iii) Internal documents had warned that Ovitz was unqualified; (iv) A member of the compensation committee received a $250,000 fee to secure Ovitz's employment; (v) Neither the compensation committee nor, apparently the board, had received, or had an opportunity to review, either the draft or final employment contract with Ovitz in advance of their meetings; (vi) The compensation committee and the board had devoted hardly any time at their meetings to reviewing and approving Ovitz's employment contract; (vii) Eisner had a defining role in the contours of the employment agreement, particularly the timing of the vesting of stock options, which constituted a major portion of Ovitz's severance package; and (viii) The employment agreement was approved by the compensation committee at a one-hour meeting that had other items on its agenda, and a draft of the agreement was not circulated to the committee prior to or at the meeting. The plaintiffs claimed that these facts, taken together, showed that the defendants had violated their fiduciary duty to act in good faith.]

. . . This case . . . is one in which the duty to act in good faith has played a prominent role, yet to date is not a well-developed area of our corporate fiduciary law.[98] Although the good faith concept has recently been the subject of considerable scholarly writing,[99] which includes articles focused on this specific case, the duty to act in good faith is, up to this point relatively uncharted. Because of the increased recognition of the importance of good faith, some conceptual guidance to the corporate community may be helpful. For that reason we proceed to address the merits of the appellants' second argument.

The precise question is whether the Chancellor's articulated standard for bad faith corporate fiduciary conduct—intentional dereliction of duty, a conscious disregard for one's responsibilities—is legally correct. In approaching that question, we note that the Chancellor characterized that definition as "*an* appropriate *(although not the only) standard for determining whether fiduciaries have acted in good faith.*" That observation is accurate and helpful, because as a matter of simple logic, at least three different categories of fiduciary behavior are candidates for the "bad faith" pejorative label.

The first category involves so-called "subjective bad faith," that is, fiduciary conduct motivated by an actual intent to do harm. That such conduct constitutes classic, quintessential bad faith is a proposition so well accepted in the liturgy of fiduciary law that it borders on

---

[98]   The Chancellor observed, after surveying the sparse case law on the subject, that both the meaning and the contours of the duty to act in good faith were "[s]hrouded in the fog of . . . hazy jurisprudence." Post-Trial Op. at *35.

[99]   See, e.g., Hillary A. Sale, Delaware's Good Faith, 89 CORNELL L. REV. 456 (2004); Matthew R. Berry, Does Delaware's Section 102(b)(7) Protect Reckless Directors From Personal Liability? Only if Delaware Courts Act in Good Faith, 79 WASH. L. REV. 1125 (2004); John L. Reed and Matt Neiderman, Good Faith and the Ability of Directors to Assert § 102(b)(7) of the Delaware Corporation Law as a Defense to Claims Alleging Abdication, Lack of Oversight, and Similar Breaches of Fiduciary Duty, 29 DEL. J. CORP. L. 111 (2004); David Rosenberg, Making Sense of Good Faith in Delaware Corporate Fiduciary Law: A Contractarian Approach, 29 DEL. J. CORP. L. 491 (2004); Sean J. Griffith, Good Faith Business Judgment: A Theory of Rhetoric in Corporate Law Jurisprudence, 55 DUKE L. J. 1 (2005) ("Griffith"); Melvin A. Eisenberg, The Duty of Good Faith in Corporate Law, 31 DEL. J. CORP. L. 1 (2005); Filippo Rossi, Making Sense of the Delaware Supreme Court's Triad of Fiduciary Duties (June 22, 2005), available at http://ssrn.com/abstract=755784; Christopher M. Bruner, "Good Faith," State of Mind, and the Outer Boundaries of Director Liability in Corporate Law (Boston Univ. Sch. of Law Working Paper No. 05–19), available at http://ssrn.com/abstract=832944; Sean J. Griffith & Myron T. Steele, On Corporate Law Federalism Threatening the Thaumatrope, 61 BUS. LAW. 1 (2005).

axiomatic.[102] We need not dwell further on this category, because no such conduct is claimed to have occurred, or did occur, in this case.

The second category of conduct, which is at the opposite end of the spectrum, involves lack of due care—that is, fiduciary action taken solely by reason of gross negligence and without any malevolent intent. In this case, appellants assert claims of gross negligence to establish breaches not only of director due care but also of the directors' duty to act in good faith. Although the Chancellor found, and we agree, that the appellants failed to establish gross negligence, to afford guidance we address the issue of whether gross negligence (including a failure to inform one's self of available material facts), without more, can also constitute bad faith. The answer is clearly no.

From a broad philosophical standpoint, that question is more complex than would appear, if only because (as the Chancellor and others have observed) "issues of good faith are (to a certain degree) inseparably and necessarily intertwined with the duties of care and loyalty. . . . "[103] But, in the pragmatic, conduct-regulating legal realm which calls for more precise conceptual line drawing, the answer is that grossly negligent conduct, without more, does not and cannot constitute a breach of the fiduciary duty to act in good faith. The conduct that is the subject of due care may overlap with the conduct that comes within the rubric of good faith in a psychological sense,[104] but from a legal standpoint those duties are and must remain quite distinct. Both our legislative history and our common law jurisprudence distinguish sharply between the duties to exercise due care and to act in good faith, and highly significant consequences flow from that distinction.

The Delaware General Assembly has addressed the distinction between bad faith and a failure to exercise due care (*i.e.*, gross negligence) in two separate contexts. The first is Section 102(b)(7) of the DGCL, which authorizes Delaware corporations, by a provision in the certificate of incorporation, to exculpate their directors from monetary damage liability for a breach of the duty of care.[105] That exculpatory provision affords significant protection to directors of Delaware corporations. The

---

[102] The Chancellor so recognized. *Id.* at *35 ("[A]n action taken with the intent to harm the corporation is a disloyal act in bad faith."). *See McGowan v. Ferro*, 859 A.2d 1012, 1036 (Del. Ch. 2004) ("Bad faith is 'not simply bad judgment or negligence,' but rather 'implies the conscious doing of a wrong because of dishonest purpose or moral obliquity . . . it contemplates a state of mind affirmatively operating with furtive design or ill will.' ") (quoting *Desert Equities, Inc. v. Morgan Stanley Leveraged Equity Fund, II, L.P.*, 624 A.2d 1199, 1208, n. 16 (Del. 1993)).

[103] Post-trial Op. at *31 (citing Griffith, *supra* note 99, at 15).

[104] An example of such overlap might be the hypothetical case where a director, because of subjective hostility to the corporation on whose board he serves, fails to inform himself of, or to devote sufficient attention to, the matters on which he is making decisions as a fiduciary. In such a case, two states of mind coexist in the same person: subjective bad intent (which would lead to a finding of bad faith) and gross negligence (which would lead to a finding of a breach of the duty of care). Although the coexistence of both states of mind may make them indistinguishable from a psychological standpoint, the fiduciary duties that they cause the director to violate—care and good faith—are legally separate and distinct.

[105] 8 *Del. C.* § 102(b)(7).

statute carves out several exceptions, however, including most relevantly, "for acts or omissions not in good faith. . . ."[106] Thus, a corporation can exculpate its directors from monetary liability for a breach of the duty of care, but not for conduct that is not in good faith. To adopt a definition of bad faith that would cause a violation of the duty of care automatically to become an act or omission "not in good faith," would eviscerate the protections accorded to directors by the General Assembly's adoption of Section 102(b)(7).

A second legislative recognition of the distinction between fiduciary conduct that is grossly negligent and conduct that is not in good faith, is Delaware's indemnification statute, found at 8 *Del. C.* § 145. To oversimplify, subsections (a) and (b) of that statute permit a corporation to indemnify (*inter alia*) any person who is or was a director, officer, employee or agent of the corporation against expenses (including attorneys' fees), judgments, fines and amounts paid in settlement of specified actions, suits or proceedings, where (among other things): (i) that person is, was, or is threatened to be made a party to that action, suit or proceeding, and (ii) that person "acted in good faith and in a manner the person reasonably believed to be in or not opposed to the best interests of the corporation. . . ."[107] Thus, under Delaware statutory law a director or officer of a corporation can be indemnified for liability (and litigation expenses) incurred by reason of a violation of the duty of care, but not for a violation of the duty to act in good faith.

Section 145, like Section 102(b)(7), evidences the intent of the Delaware General Assembly to afford significant protections to directors (and, in the case of Section 145, other fiduciaries) of Delaware corporations. To adopt a definition that conflates the duty of care with the duty to act in good faith by making a violation of the former an automatic violation of the latter, would nullify those legislative protections and defeat the General Assembly's intent. There is no basis in policy, precedent or common sense that would justify dismantling the distinction between gross negligence and bad faith.

That leaves the third category of fiduciary conduct, which falls in between the first two categories of (1) conduct motivated by subjective bad intent and (2) conduct resulting from gross negligence. This third category is what the Chancellor's definition of bad faith—intentional dereliction of duty, a conscious disregard for one's responsibilities—is intended to capture. The question is whether such misconduct is properly treated as a non-exculpable, nonindemnifiable violation of the fiduciary duty to act in good faith. In our view it must be, for at least two reasons.

First, the universe of fiduciary misconduct is not limited to either disloyalty in the classic sense (*i.e.*, preferring the adverse self-interest of the fiduciary or of a related person to the interest of the corporation) or

---

[106]   8 *Del. C.* § 102(b)(7)(ii).

[107]   8 *Del. C.* §§ 145(a) & (b).

gross negligence. Cases have arisen where corporate directors have no conflicting self-interest in a decision, yet engage in misconduct that is more culpable than simple inattention or failure to be informed of all facts material to the decision. To protect the interests of the corporation and its shareholders, fiduciary conduct of this kind, which does not involve disloyalty (as traditionally defined) but is qualitatively more culpable than gross negligence, should be proscribed. A vehicle is needed to address such violations doctrinally, and that doctrinal vehicle is the duty to act in good faith. The Chancellor implicitly so recognized in his Opinion, where he identified different examples of bad faith as follows:

> The good faith required of a corporate fiduciary includes not simply the duties of care and loyalty, in the narrow sense that I have discussed them above, but all actions required by a true faithfulness and devotion to the interests of the corporation and its shareholders. A failure to act in good faith may be shown, for instance, where the fiduciary intentionally acts with a purpose other than that of advancing the best interests of the corporation, where the fiduciary acts with the intent to violate applicable positive law, or where the fiduciary intentionally fails to act in the face of a known duty to act, demonstrating a conscious disregard for his duties. There may be other examples of bad faith yet to be proven or alleged, but these three are the most salient.[110]

Those articulated examples of bad faith are not new to our jurisprudence. Indeed, they echo pronouncements our courts have made throughout the decades.[111]

Second, the legislature has also recognized this intermediate category of fiduciary misconduct, which ranks between conduct involving subjective bad faith and gross negligence. Section 102(b)(7)(ii) of the DGCL expressly denies money damage exculpation for "acts or omissions not in good faith or which involve intentional misconduct or a knowing violation of law." By its very terms that provision distinguishes between "intentional misconduct" and a "knowing violation of law" (both examples of subjective bad faith) on the one hand, and "acts . . . not in good faith,"

---

[110] Post-trial Op. at *36 (footnotes omitted).

[111] *See, e.g., Allaun v. Consol. Oil Co.*, 147 A. 257, 261 (Del. Ch. 1929) (further judicial scrutiny is warranted if the transaction results from the directors' "reckless indifference to or a deliberate disregard of the interests of the whole body of stockholders"); *Gimbel v. Signal Cos., Inc.*, 316 A.2d 599, 604 (Del. Ch. 1974), *aff'd*, 316 A.2d 619 (Del. 1974) (injunction denied because, *inter alia*, there was "[n]othing in the record [that] would justify a finding . . . that the directors acted for any personal advantage or out of improper motive or intentional disregard of shareholder interests"); *In re Caremark Int'l Derivative Litig.*, 698 A.2d 959, 971 (Del. Ch. 1996) ("only a sustained or systematic failure of the board to exercise oversight—such as an utter failure to attempt to assure a reasonable information and reporting system exists—will establish the lack of good faith that is a necessary condition to liability."); *Nagy v. Bistricer*, 770 A.2d 43, 48, n.2 (Del. Ch. 2000) (observing that the utility of the duty of good faith "may rest in its constant reminder . . . that, regardless of his motive, a director who consciously disregards his duties to the corporation and its stockholders may suffer a personal judgment for monetary damages for any harm he causes," even if for a reason "other than personal pecuniary interest").

on the other. Because the statute exculpates directors only for conduct amounting to gross negligence, the statutory denial of exculpation for "acts . . . not in good faith" must encompass the intermediate category of misconduct captured by the Chancellor's definition of bad faith.

For these reasons, we uphold the Court of Chancery's definition as a legally appropriate, although not the exclusive, definition of fiduciary bad faith. We need go no further. To engage in an effort to craft (in the Court's words) "a definitive and categorical definition of the universe of acts that would constitute bad faith"[112] would be unwise and is unnecessary to dispose of the issues presented on this appeal.

[The court then affirmed the Chancellor's dismissal of the plaintiffs' remaining claims.]

VI. CONCLUSION

For the reasons stated above, the judgment of the Court of Chancery is affirmed.

Stone v. Ritter

Supreme Court of State of Delaware, 2006.
911 A.2d 362.

■ HOLLAND, JUSTICE

. . . The standard for assessing a director's potential personal liability for failing to act in good faith in discharging his or her oversight responsibilities has evolved beginning with our decision in Graham v. Allis-Chalmers Manufacturing Company, through the Court of Chancery's *Caremark* decision to our most recent decision in *Disney*. A brief discussion of that evolution will help illuminate the standard that we adopt in this case."

Graham and Caremark

Graham was a derivative action brought against the directors of Allis-Chalmers for failure to prevent violations of federal anti-trust laws by Allis-Chalmers employees. There was no claim that the Allis-Chalmers directors knew of the employees' conduct that resulted in the corporation's liability. Rather, the plaintiffs claimed that the Allis-Chalmers directors *should have known* of the illegal conduct by the corporation's employees. In *Graham*, this Court held that '*absent cause for suspicion* there is no duty upon the directors to install and operate a corporate system of espionage to ferret out wrongdoing which they have no reason to suspect exists.' . . .

---

[112] Post-trial Op. at *36. For the same reason, we do not reach or otherwise address the issue of whether the fiduciary duty to act in good faith is a duty that, like the duties of care and loyalty, can serve as an independent basis for imposing liability upon corporate officers and directors. That issue is not before us on this appeal.

In evaluating whether to approve the proposed settlement agreement in *Caremark*, the Court of Chancery narrowly construed our holding in *Graham* 'as standing for the proposition that, absent grounds to suspect deception, neither corporate boards nor senior officers can be charged with wrongdoing simply for assuming the integrity of employees and the honesty of their dealings on the company's behalf.' The *Caremark* Court opined it would be a 'mistake' to interpret this Court's decision in *Graham* to mean that:

> corporate boards may satisfy their obligation to be reasonably informed concerning the corporation, without assuring themselves that information and reporting systems exist in the organization that are reasonably designed to provide to senior management and to the board itself timely, accurate information sufficient to allow management and the board, each within its scope, to reach informed judgments concerning both the corporation's compliance with law and its business performance.

To the contrary, the *Caremark* Court stated, 'it is important that the board exercise a good faith judgment that the corporation's information and reporting system is in concept and design adequate to assure the board that appropriate information will come to its attention in a timely manner as a matter of ordinary operations, so that it may satisfy its responsibility.' The *Caremark* Court recognized, however, that 'the duty to act in good faith to be informed cannot be thought to require directors to possess detailed information about all aspects of the operation of the enterprise.' The Court of Chancery then formulated the following standard for assessing the liability of directors where the directors are unaware of employee misconduct that results in the corporation being held liable:

> Generally where a claim of directorial liability for corporate loss is predicated upon ignorance of liability creating activities within the corporation, as in *Graham* or in this case, . . . only a sustained or systematic failure of the board to exercise oversight—such as an utter failure to attempt to assure a reasonable information and reporting system exists—will establish the lack of good faith that is a necessary condition to liability.

Caremark Standard Approved

As evidenced by the language quoted above, the *Caremark* standard for so-called 'oversight' liability draws heavily upon the concept of director failure to act in good faith. That is consistent with the definition(s) of bad faith recently approved by this Court in its recent *Disney* decision, where we held that a failure to act in good faith requires conduct that is qualitatively different from, and more culpable than, the conduct giving rise to a violation of the fiduciary duty of care (i.e., gross negligence). In *Disney*, we identified the following examples of conduct that would establish a failure to act in good faith:

> A failure to act in good faith may be shown, for instance, where the fiduciary intentionally acts with a purpose other than that of advancing the best interests of the corporation, where the fiduciary acts with the intent to violate applicable positive law, or where the fiduciary intentionally fails to act in the face of a known duty to act, demonstrating a conscious disregard for his duties. There may be other examples of bad faith yet to be proven or alleged, but these three are the most salient.

The third of these examples describes, and is fully consistent with, the lack of good faith conduct that the *Caremark* court held was a 'necessary condition' for director oversight liability, i.e., 'a sustained or systematic failure of the board to exercise oversight—such as an utter failure to attempt to assure a reasonable information and reporting system exists. . . . ' Indeed, our opinion in *Disney* cited *Caremark* with approval for that proposition. Accordingly, the Court of Chancery applied the correct standard in assessing whether demand was excused in this case where failure to exercise oversight was the basis or theory of the plaintiffs' claim for relief.

It is important, in this context, to clarify a doctrinal issue that is critical to understanding fiduciary liability under *Caremark* as we construe that case. The phraseology used in *Caremark* and that we employ here—describing the lack of good faith as a 'necessary condition to liability'—is deliberate. The purpose of that formulation is to communicate that a failure to act in good faith is not conduct that results, *ipso facto*, in the direct imposition of fiduciary liability. The failure to act in good faith may result in liability because the requirement to act in good faith 'is a subsidiary element[,]' i.e., a condition, 'of the fundamental duty of loyalty.' It follows that because a showing of bad faith conduct, in the sense described in *Disney* and *Caremark*, is essential to establish director oversight liability, the fiduciary duty violated by that conduct is the duty of loyalty.

This view of a failure to act in good faith results in two additional doctrinal consequences. First, although good faith may be described colloquially as part of a 'triad' of fiduciary duties that includes the duties of care and loyalty, the obligation to act in good faith does not establish an independent fiduciary duty that stands on the same footing as the duties of care and loyalty. Only the latter two duties, where violated, may directly result in liability, whereas a failure to act in good faith may do so, but indirectly. The second doctrinal consequence is that the fiduciary duty of loyalty is not limited to cases involving a financial or other cognizable fiduciary conflict of interest. It also encompasses cases where the fiduciary fails to act in good faith. As the Court of Chancery aptly put it in *Guttman*, '[a] director cannot act loyally towards the corporation unless she acts in the good faith belief that her actions are in the corporation's best interest.'

We hold that *Caremark* articulates the necessary conditions predicate for director oversight liability: (a) the directors utterly failed to implement any reporting or information system or controls; *or* (b) having implemented such a system or controls, consciously failed to monitor or oversee its operations thus disabling themselves from being informed of risks or problems requiring their attention. In either case, imposition of liability requires a showing that the directors knew that they were not discharging their fiduciary obligations. Where directors fail to act in the face of a known duty to act, thereby demonstrating a conscious disregard for their responsibilities, they breach their duty of loyalty by failing to discharge that fiduciary obligation in good faith.

————

Central Laborers' Pension Fd. and Steamfitters Local 449 Pension Fd. v.
     Dimon

638 Fed. Appx. 34 (2nd Cir. 2016)

The derivative suit complaint alleged that for over twenty years the directors of JP Morgan had "turned a blind eye" to a Ponzi scheme carried out by Bernard Madoff for which JP Morgan served as the primary banker. The Second Circuit affirmed dismissal on the ground of failure to state a *Caremark*-based claim under *Stone v. Ritter*. The court held that *Caremark* proscribes not the lack of a *reasonable* compliance system but proscribes the failure to implement *any* compliance system. The Second Circuit emphasized that *Caremark* itself proscribed "an utter failure to attempt to assure a reasonable information and reporting system exists" and *Stone* similarly specifies that the standard is breached when "directors utterly failed to implement any reporting or information system or controls." The Second Circuit relied on a parallel holding in *In re General Motors Derivative Litig.*, 2015 WL 3958724, at *14–15 (Del. Ch. June 26, 2015):

> Contentions that the Board did not receive specific types of information do not establish that the Board utterly failed to attempt to assure a reasonable information and reporting system exists. . . .

That is, short of pleading that the Board utterly failed to implement any reporting or information system or controls, the complaint is not sufficient to raise a reasonable doubt of the directors' good faith.

————

3. THE DUTY TO ACT LAWFULLY

Miller v. American Telephone & Telegraph Co.

United States Court of Appeals, Third Circuit, 1974.
507 F.2d 759.

■ SEITZ, CHIEF JUDGE.

Plaintiffs, stockholders in American Telephone and Telegraph Company ("AT & T"), brought a stockholders' derivative action in the Eastern District of Pennsylvania against AT & T and all but one of its directors. The suit centered upon the failure of AT & T to collect an outstanding debt of some $1.5 million owed to the company by the Democratic National Committee ("DNC") for communications services provided by AT & T during the 1968 Democratic national convention. Federal diversity jurisdiction was invoked under 28 U.S.C. § 1332.

Plaintiffs' complaint alleged that "neither the officers or directors of AT & T have taken any action to recover the amount owed" from on or about August 20, 1968, when the debt was incurred, until May 31, 1972, the date plaintiffs' amended complaint was filed. The failure to collect was alleged to have involved a breach of the defendant directors' duty to exercise diligence in handling the affairs of the corporation, to have resulted in affording a preference to the DNC in collection procedures in violation of § 202(a) of the Communications Act of 1934, 47 U.S.C. § 202(a) (1970), and to have amounted to AT & T's making a "contribution" to the DNC in violation of a federal prohibition on corporate campaign spending, 18 U.S.C. § 610 (1970).

Plaintiffs sought permanent relief in the form of an injunction requiring AT & T to collect the debt, an injunction against providing further services to the DNC until the debt was paid in full, and a surcharge for the benefit of the corporation against the defendant directors in the amount of the debt plus interest from the due date. A request for a preliminary injunction against the provision of services to the 1972 Democratic convention was denied by the district court after an evidentiary hearing.

On motion of the defendants, the district court dismissed the complaint for failure to state a claim upon which relief could be granted. 364 F.Supp. 648 (E.D.Pa.1973). The court stated that collection procedures were properly within the discretion of the directors whose determination would not be overturned by the court in the absence of an allegation that the conduct of the directors was "plainly illegal, unreasonable, or in breach of a fiduciary duty. . . . " *Id.* at 651. Plaintiffs appeal from dismissal of their complaint.

In viewing the motion to dismiss, we must consider all facts alleged in the complaint and every inference fairly deductible therefrom in the light most favorable to the plaintiffs. A complaint should not be dismissed unless it appears that the plaintiffs would not be entitled to relief under any facts which they might prove in support of their claim. Judging plaintiffs' complaint by these standards, we feel that it does state a claim upon which relief can be granted for breach of fiduciary duty arising from the alleged violation of 18 U.S.C. § 610.

I.

The pertinent law on the question of the defendant directors' fiduciary duties in this diversity action is that of New York, the state of AT & T's incorporation. . . . The sound business judgment rule, the basis of the district court's dismissal of plaintiffs' complaint, expresses the unanimous decision of American courts to eschew intervention in corporate decision-making if the judgment of directors and officers is uninfluenced by personal considerations and is exercised in good faith. Pollitz v. Wabash Railroad Co., 207 N.Y. 113, 100 N.E. 721 (1912); Bayer v. Beran, 49 N.Y.S.2d 2, 4–7 (Sup.Ct.1944); 3 Fletcher, Private Corporations § 1039 (perm. ed. rev. vol. 1965). Underlying the rule is the assumption that reasonable diligence has been used in reaching the decision which the rule is invoked to justify. . . .

Had plaintiffs' complaint alleged only failure to pursue a corporate claim, application of the sound business judgment rule would support the district court's ruling that a shareholder could not attack the directors' decision. *See* United Copper Securities Co. v. Amalgamated Copper Co., 244 U.S. 261, 37 S.Ct. 509, 61 L.Ed. 1119 (1917); Clifford v. Metropolitan Life Insurance Co., 264 App.Div. 168, 34 N.Y.S.2d 693 (2d Dept.1942); 13 Fletcher, Private Corporations § 5822 (perm. ed. rev. vol. 1970). Where, however, the decision not to collect a debt owed the corporation is itself alleged to have been an illegal act, different rules apply. When New York law regarding such acts by directors is considered in conjunction with the underlying purposes of the particular statute involved here, we are convinced that the business judgment rule cannot insulate the defendant directors from liability if they did in fact breach 18 U.S.C. § 610, as plaintiffs have charged.

Roth v. Robertson, 64 Misc. 343, 118 N.Y.S. 351 (Sup.Ct.1909), illustrates the proposition that even though committed to benefit the corporation, illegal acts may amount to a breach of fiduciary duty in New York. In *Roth*, the managing director of an amusement park company had allegedly used corporate funds to purchase the silence of persons who threatened to complain about unlawful Sunday operation of the park. Recovery from the defendant director was sustained on the ground that the money was an illegal payment:

> For reasons of public policy, we are clearly of the opinion that payments of corporate funds for such purposes as those disclosed in this case must be condemned, and officers of a corporation making them held to a strict accountability, and be compelled to refund the amounts so wasted for the benefit of stockholders. . . . To hold any other rule would be establishing a

dangerous precedent, tacitly countenancing the wasting of corporate funds for purposes of corrupting public morals. *Id.* at 346, 118 N.Y.S. at 353.

The plaintiffs' complaint in the instant case alleges a similar "waste" of $1.5 million through an illegal campaign contribution.

Abrams v. Allen, 297 N.Y. 52, 74 N.E.2d 305 (1947), reflects an affirmation by the New York Court of Appeals of the principle of *Roth* that directors must be restrained from engaging in activities which are against public policy. In *Abrams* the court held that a cause of action was stated by an allegation in a derivative complaint that the directors of Remington Rand, Inc., had relocated corporate plants and curtailed production solely for the purpose of intimidating and punishing employees for their involvement in a labor dispute. The Court of Appeals acknowledged that, "depending on the circumstances," proof of the allegations in the complaint might sustain recovery, *inter alia,* under the rule that directors are liable for corporate loss caused by the commission of an "unlawful or immoral act." *Id.* at 55, 74 N.E.2d at 306. In support of its holding, the court noted that the closing of factories for the purpose alleged was opposed to the public policy of the state and nation as embodied in the New York Labor Law and the National Labor Relations Act. *Id.* at 56, 74 N.E.2d at 307.[3]

The alleged violation of the federal prohibition against corporate political contributions not only involves the corporation in criminal activity but similarly contravenes a policy of Congress clearly enunciated in 18 U.S.C. § 610.[4] That statute and its predecessor reflect congressional efforts: (1) to destroy the influence of corporations over elections through financial contributions and (2) to check the practice of using corporate funds to benefit political parties without the consent of the stockholders. United States v. CIO, 335 U.S. 106, 113, 68 S.Ct. 1349, 92 L.Ed. 1849 (1948).

The fact that shareholders are within the class for whose protection the statute was enacted gives force to the argument that the alleged breach of that statute should give rise to a cause of action in those shareholders to force the return to the corporation of illegally contributed funds. Since political contributions by corporations can be checked and shareholder control over the political use of general corporate funds

---

[3] That violation of a federal statute is the basis of the breach of fiduciary duty and that therefore the court is required to interpret the federal statute has not deterred New York courts from entertaining such suits against directors. *See* Knopfler v. Bohen, 15 A.D.2d 922, 225 N.Y.S.2d 609 (2d Dept.1962); *cf.* Simon v. Socony-Vacuum Oil Co., 179 Misc. 202, 38 N.Y.S.2d 270 (Sup.Ct.1942).

[4] We note that prior to June 1, 1974, corporate political contributions made "directly or indirectly" violated New York law. Law of July 20, 1965, ch. 1031, § 43, [1965] N.Y.Laws 1783 (repealed 1974). Furthermore, apart from the statutory prohibition, political donations by corporations were apparently ultra vires acts in New York. *See* People ex rel. Perkins v. Moss, 187 N.Y. 410, 80 N.E. 383 (1907). Corporations or organizations financially supported by corporations doing business in the state are now permitted to make contributions up to $5,000 per year. N.Y. Election Law § 480 (McKinney's Consol.Laws, c. 17, Supp.1974).

effectuated only if directors are restrained from causing the corporation to violate the statute, such a violation seems a particularly appropriate basis for finding breach of the defendant directors' fiduciary duty to the corporation. Under such circumstances, the directors cannot be insulated from liability on the ground that the contribution was made in the exercise of sound business judgment.

Since plaintiffs have alleged actual damage to the corporation from the transaction in the form of the loss of a $1.5 million increment to AT & T's treasury,[5] we conclude that the complaint does state a claim upon which relief can be granted sufficient to withstand a motion to dismiss.[6]

II.

We have accepted plaintiffs' allegation of a violation of 18 U.S.C. § 610 as a shorthand designation of the elements necessary to establish a breach of that statute. This is consonant with the federal practice of notice pleading. *See* Conley v. Gibson, 355 U.S. 41, 47–48, 78 S.Ct. 99, 2 L.Ed.2d 80 (1957); Fed.R.Civ.P. 8(f). That such a designation is sufficient for pleading purposes does not, however, relieve plaintiffs of their ultimate obligation to prove the elements of the statutory violation as part of their proof of breach of fiduciary duty. At the appropriate time, plaintiffs will be required to produce evidence sufficient to establish three distinct elements comprising a violation of 18 U.S.C. § 610: that AT & T (1) made a contribution of money or anything of value to the DNC (2) in connection with a federal election (3) for the purpose of influencing the outcome of that election. *See* United States v. Boyle, 157 U.S.App.D.C. 166, 482 F.2d 755, cert. denied, 414 U.S. 1076, 94 S.Ct. 593, 38 L.Ed.2d 483 (1973); United States v. Lewis Food Co., Inc., 366 F.2d 710 (9th Cir.1966). . . . [7]

The order of the district court will be reversed and the case remanded for further proceedings consistent with this opinion.

NOTES ON CRIMINAL LIABILITIES OF DIRECTORS AND OFFICERS

Miller concerns the civil liability of a director or officer to the corporation on the ground of illegal conduct. An officer (or, more rarely, a director) may also

---

[5] Under New York law, allegation of breach even of a federal statute is apparently insufficient to state a cause of action unless the breach caused independent damage to the corporation. *See* Diamond v. Davis, 263 App.Div. 68, 31 N.Y.S.2d 582 (1st Dept.1941); Borden v. Cohen, 231 N.Y.S.2d 902 (Sup.Ct.1962). *But see* Runcie v. Bankers Trust Co., 6 N.Y.S.2d 623 (Sup.Ct.1938).

[6] We express no opinion today on the question of whether plaintiffs' complaint may also state a cause of action for breach of fiduciary duty arising from the alleged violation of 47 U.S.C. § 202(a).

[7] As amended by the Federal Election Campaign Act of 1971 (effective April 7, 1972), the definition of "contribution" for purposes of 18 U.S.C. § 610 is a gift of money or anything of value "made for the purpose of influencing the nomination for election, or election" of any person to federal office or for influencing the outcome of a primary or national nominating convention. 18 U.S.C. § 591 (1970), as amended (Supp.II 1972).

be criminally liable for such conduct. Two kinds of statute are relevant to the potential criminal liability of officers and directors.

   1.   Nature of the Statute. The first type of statute makes corporate managers criminally liable for unlawful corporate acts if the managers themselves performed or caused the performance of the act. An example is N.Y.Penal Law § 20.25: "A person is criminally liable for conduct constituting an offense which he performs or causes to be performed in the name of or in behalf of a corporation to the same extent as if such conduct were performed in his own name or behalf." A highly publicized case, *People v. Film Recovery Systems, Inc.*, Nos. 83–11091, 84–5064 (Cook County Cir.Ct. of Ill., 1985), arose under an Illinois statute comparable to N.Y.Penal Law § 20.25. Film Recovery reclaimed silver from used photographic film, through a standard process called cyanide leaching, which involves a chemical that gives off poisonous cyanide gas. The ventilation and other conditions at Film Recovery's plant were unsafe, and most of the workers spoke little English and therefore could not read the sodium-cyanide warning label. In December 1982, Stefan Golab, a Polish immigrant, began working at Film Recovery, pumping and stirring the sodium cyanide solution in large vats. In February 1983, Golab complained of headaches and nausea, and asked the plant manager, through an interpreter, to transfer him from the vats. After four more days of working at the vats, Golab died of cyanide inhalation. Film Recovery's president, plant manager, and plant foreman were found guilty of murder, and sentenced to twenty-five years. *See* Note, Corporations Can Kill Too: After *Film Recovery,* Are Individuals Accountable for Corporate Crime?, 19 Loy.L.A.L.Rev. 1411 (1986). In 1990, *Film Recovery* was reversed on a technical ground and remanded for a new trial. *People v. O'Neil,* 194 Ill.App.3d 79, 141 Ill.Dec. 44, 550 N.E.2d 1090 (1990). On remand, the individual defendants pleaded guilty to lesser charges. Two were sentenced to two years, and the third received probation.

   2.   The "Responsible Corporate Officer" Doctrine. A second type of statute makes managers criminally liable for the unlawful acts of employees over whom they have the power of control, even if that power was not exercised. This type of statute gives rise to the "responsible corporate officer" doctrine. The leading case is United States v. Park, 421 U.S. 658, 95 S.Ct. 1903, 44 L.Ed.2d 489 (1975). Acme Markets, Inc., was a national retail food chain with approximately 36,000 employees, 874 retail outlets, and 16 warehouses. Park was Acme's CEO. In April 1970, the FDA formally advised Park of unsanitary conditions, including rodent infestation, in Acme's Philadelphia warehouse. In late 1971, the FDA found that similar conditions existed in the Baltimore warehouse, and in January 1972, the FDA sent a letter to that effect. In March 1972, a second inspection of the Baltimore warehouse showed improvement in the sanitary conditions, but evidence of continued rodent activity and rodent-contaminated food. The Government then brought criminal proceedings against Acme and Park on the ground that food held for sale in Acme's Baltimore warehouse was exposed to contamination by rodents, in violation of 21 U.S.C.A. § 331(k). Park testified that although all of Acme's employees were in a sense under his general direction, under Acme's organizational structure the responsibility for different phases of Acme's operation were assigned to other executives who, in turn, had staff and departments under them. He identified the individuals responsible for sanitation, and stated that upon receipt of the FDA's January 1972 letter, he had conferred with Acme's vice-president for legal affairs, who informed him that the vice-president of Acme's Baltimore division "was investigating the situation immediately and would be taking corrective action and would be preparing a summary of the corrective action to reply to the letter." Park conceded that providing sanitary conditions for food offered for sale to the public was something that he was "responsible for in the entire operation of the company," but said it was one of many phases of the company that he assigned to "dependable subordinates."

Park was convicted, although he had not authorized the violations and the statute did not explicitly impose criminal liability on managers based on the acts of others. The Supreme Court upheld the conviction, relying in part on an earlier case, United States v. Dotterweich:

> In [United States v. Dotterweich, 320 U.S. 277, 64 S.Ct. 134, 88 L.Ed. 48 (1943)], a jury had disagreed as to the corporation, a jobber purchasing drugs from manufacturers and shipping them in interstate commerce under its own label, but had convicted Dotterweich, the corporation's president and general manager. . . .
>
> In reversing the judgment of the Court of Appeals and reinstating Dotterweich's conviction, this Court looked to the purposes of the Act and noted that they "touch phases of the lives and health of people which, in the circumstances of modern industrialism, are largely beyond self-protection." 320 U.S., at 280. It observed that the Act is of "a now familiar type" which "dispenses with the conventional requirement for criminal conduct—awareness of some wrongdoing. In the interest of the larger good it puts the burden of acting at hazard upon a person otherwise innocent but standing in responsible relation to a public danger." Id., at 280–281. . . .
>
> At the same time, however, the Court was aware of the concern which was the motivating factor in the Court of Appeals' decision, that literal enforcement "might operate too harshly by sweeping within its condemnation any person however remotely entangled in the proscribed shipment." Id., at 284. A limiting principle, in the form of "settled doctrines of criminal law" defining those who "are responsible for the commission of a misdemeanor," was available. In this context, the Court concluded, those doctrines dictated that the offense was committed "by all who . . . have . . . a responsible share in the furtherance of the transaction which the statute outlaws." Ibid. . . .
>
> . . . [T]he Act imposes not only a positive duty to seek out and remedy violations when they occur but also, and primarily, a duty to implement measures that will insure that violations will not occur. The requirements of foresight and vigilance imposed on responsible corporate agents are beyond question demanding, and perhaps onerous, but they are no more stringent than the public

has a right to expect of those who voluntarily assume positions of authority in business enterprises whose services and products affect the health and well-being of the public that supports them. . . .

Courts have extended criminal liability under the responsible-corporate-officer doctrine to directors and officers under a broad array of federal criminal statutes, including the Federal Hazardous Substances Act, the Sherman Act, the Economic Stabilization Act of 1970, the Occupational Safety & Health Act and the Federal Water Pollution Control Act. *See* Martin Petrin, Circumscribing the "Prosecutor's Ticket to Tag the Elite"—A Critique of the Responsible Officer Doctrine, 84 Temple L. Rev. 283 (2012); Webb, Molo, and Hurst, Understanding and Avoiding Corporate and Executive Criminal Liability, 49 Bus.Law 617 (1994).

However, *Meyer v. Holley,* 537 U.S. 280, 123 S.Ct. 824, 154 L.Ed.2d 753 (2003), limited the sweep of the doctrine. *Meyer* arose under the Fair Housing Act. That Act forbids racial discrimination in respect to the sale or rental of a dwelling. Triad Inc. was a real estate corporation. David Meyer, Triad's president and sole shareholder, had listed for sale a house in Twenty-Nine Palms, California. Emma and David Holley, an interracial couple, tried to unsuccessfully to buy the house. The Holleys alleged that Grove Crank, a Triad salesman, prevented them from obtaining the house for racially discriminatory reasons, and sued Crank and Triad under the Fair Housing Act. They also sued Meyer on the ground that he was vicariously liable, as Triad's president and sole shareholder, for Crank's unlawful actions. The Ninth Circuit held that the Fair Housing Act made corporate owners and officers liable for the unlawful acts of a corporate employee if the owner or officer controlled or had the right to control the employee's actions. The Supreme Court reversed. The Court pointed out that under traditional principles of agency law, one person, P, is not vicariously liable for the actions of another person, A, unless A was not only under or subject to P's control, but acted for and on P's behalf. Under these traditional principles, an owner or officer of a corporation is usually not vicariously liable for the actions of a corporate employee, because an employee acts on behalf of the corporation, not an owner or an officer:

> . . . Congress said nothing in the statute or on the legislative history about extending vicarious liability in this manner. And Congress' silence, while permitting an inference that Congress intended to apply ordinary background tort principles, cannot show that it intended to apply an unusual modification of those rules. . . .
>
> This Court has applied unusually strict rules only where Congress has specified that such was its intent. *See, e.g.,* United States v. Dotterweich, 320 U.S. 277, 280–281 (1943) (Congress intended that a corporate officer or employee "standing in responsible relation" could be held liable in that capacity for a corporation's violations of the Federal Food, Drug, and Cosmetic Act, congressional intent to impose a duty on "responsible corporate agents"); United States v. Wise, 370 U.S. 405, 411–414 (1962) (discussing 38 Stat. 736, currently 15 U.S.C. § 24, which provides:

"Whenever a corporation shall violate any of the . . . antitrust laws, such violation shall be deemed to be also that of the individual directors, officers, or agents of such corporation who shall have authorized, ordered, or done any of the acts constituting in whole or in part such violation"). . . .

. . . [W]hich "of two innocent people must suffer," *ibid.*, and just when, is a complex matter. We believe that courts ordinarily should determine that matter in accordance with traditional principles of vicarious liability—unless, of course, Congress, better able than courts to weigh the relevant policy considerations, has instructed the courts differently. *Cf., e.g.,* Sykes, the Economics of Vicarious Liability, 93 Yale L.J. 1231, 1236 (1984) (arguing that the expansion of vicarious liability or shifting of liability, due to insurance, may diminish an agent's incentives to police behavior). We have found no different instruction here.

Following *Meyer*, courts when deciding whether to extend the responsible officer doctrine to areas heretofore untouched by the doctrine emphasize whether such an extension is supported by legislative intent. *See e.g., Microsoft Corp. v. ION Technologies Corp.,* 484 F. Supp. 2d 955 (D. Minn. 2007); *State v. Arkell,* 672 N.W. 2d 564 (Minn. 2003).

———

CHAPTER 10

THE DUTY OF LOYALTY

1. SELF-INTERESTED TRANSACTIONS

Gantler v. Stephens

Supreme Court of Delaware, 2009.
965 A.2d 695.

■ JACOBS, JUSTICE:

[The plaintiffs complain that the defendants, officers and directors of First Niles Financial, Inc. ("First Niles" or the "Company") breached their fiduciary duty in rejecting a valuable opportunity to sell the company. First Niles' sole asset was its 100 percent ownership of Home Federal Savings and Loan Association of Niles ("Home Federal" or the "Bank"). Because of the depressed local economy, there was little cause for optimism that the Bank could grow. Nonetheless, because of the prevailing brisk market for local banks like Home Federal, First Niles board believed it was a very good acquisition target. Hence, its board resolved in August 2004 to put the firm up for sale and at that meeting retained a local investment bank, Keefe, Bruyette & Woods (the "Financial Advisor") as well as a law firm, Silver, Freedman & Taft ("Legal Counsel"). At the September board meeting, First Niles management advocated that the board abandon its search for an acquisition partner and instead proceed with management's proposal that the company "privatize" itself which would include ending its Nasdaq listing, converting the bank from a federally chartered to a state chartered bank, and reincorporating in Maryland. No action on this proposal was taken by the board. Staying with its plan produced results; by December 2004, three potential suitors were identified, each offering a premium above First Niles public market share price. One bidder, Farmers National Banc Corp. ("Farmers") stated it had no intention of retaining First Niles board if its bid were accepted; the First Niles board did not further pursue this prospect. Two other bidders, Cortland Bankcorp ("Cortland") and First Place Financial Corp. ("First Place") were more delicate and each submitted due diligence requests. Unknown to the board, management (led by William L. Stephens, chairman of the board and CEO) was not responsive to the due diligence requests. This caused Cortland to withdraw its bid, leaving only First Place. Management then provided to First Place the requested materials for the bidder's due diligence. In the meantime, First Niles stock had declined in value, causing First Place to reduce its offer by approximately $1 per share; however, since First Niles stock had fallen the resulting bid price presented nearly twice the premium as First Place's first offer. At the

March board meeting, Stephens informed the board of First Place's revised offer and suggested that consideration of the offer be put over until the next regularly scheduled board meeting. The Financial Advisor stated that First Place likely would withdraw its offer if the board did not act soon. Stephens, therefore, scheduled a special board meeting to consider the offer. Before that board meeting, First Place increased its bid slightly on a per share basis. At the March 8, 2005, special board meeting, Stephens circulated the Financial Advisor's report that described First Place's bid in glowing terms. Nonetheless, the board voted 4 to 1 to reject the offer. The board thereupon discussed management's privatization plan and instructed Legal Counsel to further investigate the plan.]

C.   The Reclassification Proposal

Five weeks later, on April 18, 2005, Stephens circulated to the Board members a document describing a proposed privatization of First Niles ("Privatization Proposal"). That Proposal recommended reclassifying the shares of holders of 300 or fewer shares of First Niles common stock into a new issue of Series A Preferred Stock on a one-to-one basis (the "Reclassification"). The Series A Preferred Stock would pay higher dividends and have the same liquidation rights as the common stock, but the Preferred holders would lose all voting rights except in the event of a proposed sale of the Company. . . .

On April 20, 2005, the Board appointed Zuzolo to chair a special committee to investigate issues relating to the Reclassification, specifically: (1) reincorporating in a state other than Delaware, (2) changing the Bank's charter from a federal to a state charter, (3) deregistering from NASDAQ, and (4) delisting. However, Zuzolo passed away before any other directors were appointed to the special committee.

On December 5, 2005, Powell Goldstein, First Niles' outside counsel specially retained for the Privatization ("Outside Counsel"), orally presented the Reclassification proposal to the Board. The Board was not furnished any written materials. After the presentation, the Board voted 3 to 1 to direct Outside Counsel to proceed with the Reclassification program. Gantler cast the only dissenting vote.

Thereafter, the makeup of the Board changed. Shaker replaced Zuzolo in January of 2006, and Csontos replaced Gantler in April of 2006. From that point on, the Board consisted of Stephens, Kramer, Eddy, Shaker and Csontos.

On June 5, 2006, the Board determined, based on the advice of Management and First Niles' general counsel, that the Reclassification was fair both to the First Niles shareholders who would receive newly issued Series A Preferred Stock, and to those shareholders who would continue to hold First Niles common stock. On June 19, the Board voted unanimously to amend the Company's certificate of incorporation to reclassify the shares held by owners of 300 or fewer shares of common stock into shares of Series A Preferred Stock that would have the features and terms described in the Privatization Proposal.

D. The Reclassification Proxy and the Shareholder Vote

On June 29, 2006, the Board submitted a preliminary proxy to the United States Securities and Exchange Commission ("SEC"). . . .

In the Reclassification Proxy, the Board represented that the proposed Reclassification would allow First Niles to "save significant legal, accounting and administrative expenses" relating to public disclosure and reporting requirements under the Exchange Act. The Proxy also disclosed the benefits of deregistration as including annual savings of $142,500 by reducing the number of common shareholders, $81,000 by avoiding Sarbanes-Oxley related compliance costs, and $174,000 by avoiding a one-time consulting fee to design a system to improve the Company's internal control structure. The negative features and estimated costs of the transaction included $75,000 in Reclassification-related expenses, reduced liquidity for both the to-be-reclassified preferred and common shares, and the loss of certain investor protections under the federal securities laws.

The Reclassification Proxy also disclosed alternative transactions that the Board had considered, including a cash-out merger, a reverse stock-split, an issue tender offer, expense reduction and a business combination. The Proxy stated that each of the directors and officers of First Niles had "a conflict of interest with respect to [the Reclassification] because he or she is in a position to structure it in such a way that benefits his or her interests differently from the interests of unaffiliated shareholders." The Proxy further disclosed that the Company had received one firm merger offer, and that "[a]fter careful deliberations, the board determined in its business judgment the proposal was not in the best interests of the Company or our shareholders and rejected the proposal."

The Company's shareholders approved the Reclassification on December 14, 2006. Taking judicial notice of the Company's . . . [SEC filing], the trial court concluded that of the 1,384,533 shares outstanding and eligible to vote, 793,092 shares (or 57.3%) were voted in favor and 11,060 shares abstained. Of the unaffiliated shares, however, the proposal passed by a bare 50.28% majority vote.

E. Procedural History . . .

The defendants moved to dismiss the complaint in its entirety. . . .

We first consider the sufficiency of Count I as against the Director Defendants. That Count alleges that those defendants (together with non-party director Zuzolo) improperly rejected a value-maximizing bid from First Place and terminated the Sales Process. Plaintiffs allege that the defendants rejected the First Place bid to preserve personal benefits, including retaining their positions and pay as directors, as well as valuable outside business opportunities. The complaint further alleges that the Board failed to deliberate before deciding to reject the First Place bid and to terminate the Sales Process. Indeed, plaintiffs emphasize, the Board retained the Financial Advisor to advise it on the Sales Process, yet repeatedly disregarded the Financial Advisor's advice.

A board's decision not to pursue a merger opportunity is normally reviewed within the traditional business judgment framework. In that context the board is entitled to a strong presumption in its favor, because implicit in the board's statutory authority to propose a merger, is also the power to decline to do so.

Our analysis of whether the Board's termination of the Sales Process merits the business judgment presumption is two pronged. First, did the Board reach its decision in the good faith pursuit of a legitimate corporate interest? Second, did the Board do so advisedly? For the Board's decision here to be entitled to the business judgment presumption, both questions must be answered affirmatively. . . .

Here, the plaintiffs allege that the Director Defendants had a disqualifying self-interest because they were financially motivated to maintain the status quo. A claim of this kind must be viewed with caution, because to argue that directors have an entrenchment motive solely because they could lose their positions following an acquisition is, to an extent, tautological. By its very nature, a board decision to reject a merger proposal could always enable a plaintiff to assert that a majority of the directors had an entrenchment motive. For that reason, the plaintiffs must plead, in addition to a motive to retain corporate control, other facts sufficient to state a cognizable claim that the Director Defendants acted disloyally.

The plaintiffs have done that here. At the time the Sales Process was terminated, the Board members were Stephens, Kramer, Eddy, Zuzolo and Gander. Only Gantler voted to accept the First Place merger bid. The pled facts are sufficient to establish disloyalty of at least three (*i.e.*, a majority) of the remaining directors, which suffices to rebut the business judgment presumption. First, the Reclassification Proxy itself admits that the Company's directors and officers had "a conflict of interest with respect to [the Reclassification] because he or she is in a position to structure it in a way that benefits his or her interests differently from the interest of the unaffiliated stockholders." Second, a director-specific analysis establishes (for Rule 12(b)(6) purposes) that a majority of the Board was conflicted.

Stephens: Aside from Stephens losing his long held positions as President, Chairman and CEO of First Niles and the Bank, the plaintiffs have alleged specific conduct from which a duty of loyalty violation can reasonably be inferred. Stephens never responded to Cortland's due diligence request. The Financial Advisor noted that Stephens' failure to respond had caused Cortland to withdraw its bid. Even after Cortland had offered First Niles an extension, Stephens did not furnish the necessary due diligence materials, nor did he inform the Board of these due diligence problems until after Cortland withdrew. Cortland had also explicitly stated in its bid letter that the incumbent Board would be terminated if Cortland acquired First Niles. From these alleged facts it may reasonably be inferred that what motivated Stephens' unexplained failure to respond promptly to Cortland's due diligence request was his personal financial interest, as opposed to the interests of the shareholders. That same inference can be drawn from Stephens' response to the First Place bid: Count I alleges that Stephens attempted to "sabotage" the First Place due diligence request in a manner similar to what occurred with Cortland.

Thus, the pled facts provide a sufficient basis to conclude, for purposes of a Rule 12(b)(6) motion to dismiss, that Stephens acted disloyally.

Kramer: Director Kramer's alleged circumstances establish a similar disqualifying conflict. Kramer was the President of William Kramer & Son, a heating and air conditioning company in Niles that provided heating and air conditioning services to the Bank. It is reasonable to infer that Kramer feared that if the Company were sold his firm would lose the Bank as a client. The loss of such a major client would be economically significant, because the complaint alleges that Kramer was a man of comparatively modest means, and that his company had few major assets and was completely leveraged. Because Kramer would suffer significant injury to his personal business interest if the Sales Process went forward, those pled facts are sufficient to support a reasonable inference that Kramer disloyally voted to terminate the Sales Process and support the Privatization Proposal.

Zuzolo: As earlier noted, Director Zuzolo was a principal in a small law firm in Niles that frequently provided legal services to First Niles and the Bank. Zuzolo was also the sole owner of a real estate title company that provided title services in nearly all of Home Federal's real estate transactions. Because Zuzolo, like Kramer, had a strong personal interest in having the Sales Process not go forward, the same reasonable inferences that flow from Kramer's personal business interest can be drawn in Zuzolo's case.

In summary, the plaintiffs have alleged facts sufficient to establish, for purposes of a motion to dismiss, that a majority of the First Niles Board acted disloyally. Because a cognizable claim of disloyalty rebuts the business judgment presumption, we need not reach the separate question of whether, in deciding to terminate the Sales Process, the Director Defendants acted advisedly (*i.e.*, with due care). Because the claim of disloyalty was subject to entire fairness review, the Court of Chancery erred in dismissing Count I as to the Director Defendants on the basis of the business judgment presumption. . . .

The Court of Chancery has held, and the parties do not dispute, that corporate officers owe fiduciary duties that are identical to those owed by corporate directors. That issue—whether or not officers owe fiduciary duties identical to those of directors—has been characterized as a matter of first impression for this Court. In the past, we have implied that officers of Delaware corporations, like directors, owe fiduciary duties of care and loyalty, and that the fiduciary duties of officers are the same as those of directors. We now explicitly so hold. The only question presented here is whether the complaint alleges sufficiently detailed acts of wrongdoing by Stephens and Safarek to state a claim that they breached their fiduciary duties as officers. We conclude that it does.

Stephens and Safarek were responsible for preparing the due diligence materials for the three firms that expressed an interest in acquiring First Niles. The alleged facts that make it reasonable to infer that Stephens violated his duty of loyalty as a director, also establish his violation of that same duty as an officer. It also is reasonably inferable that Safarek aided and abetted Stephens' separate loyalty breach. Safarek, as First Niles' Vice President and Treasurer, depended upon Stephen's continued good will to retain his job and the benefits that it generated. Because Safarek was in no position to act independently of Stephens, it may be inferred that by assisting Stephens to "sabotage" the due diligence process, Safarek also breached his duty of loyalty.

The Court of Chancery found otherwise. Having characterized Safarek's actions as causing "a delay of a matter of days, or at most a couple of weeks," the Vice Chancellor observed that he could not see how that "conceivably could be a breach of Safarek's fiduciary duties." This analysis is inappropriate on a motion to dismiss. The complaint alleges that Safarek never responded to Cortland's due diligence requests and that as a result, Cortland withdrew a competitive bid for First Niles. Those facts support a reasonable inference that Safarek and Stephens attempted to sabotage the Cortland and First Place due diligence process. On a motion to dismiss, the Court of Chancery was not free to disregard that reasonable inference, or to discount it by weighing it against other, perhaps contrary, inferences that might also be drawn. By dismissing Count I as applied to Stephens and Safarek as officers of First Niles, the trial court erred. . . .

CONCLUSION

For the foregoing reasons, the judgment of the Court of Chancery is reversed as to all counts and remanded for proceedings consistent with the rulings in this Opinion

———

Aiding-and-abetting liability has long been a fixture of both criminal and civil law. For example, one who aids and abets another's tort is a co-tortfeasor. Aiding and abetting liability also exists in corporate law. The application of the doctrine in the context of corporate law's duty of loyalty is illustrated by the next case.

———

RBC Capital Mkts., LLC v. Jervis

Delaware Supreme Court, 2015.
129 A.3d 816.

[RBC Capital, an investment bank, was engaged to advise Rural/Metro Corporation in its sale to a private equity firm, Warburg Pincus. RBC was eager for the sale to go forward as it would not only receive fees for advising Rural but also would garner significant fees from Warburg in connection with RBC having facilitated the loan that Warburg needed to complete the acquisition. Rural's special negotiating committee believed that Warburg's offer was inadequate and recommended that the Rural board not accept the offer. Rural had seven directors, although one did not vote on the sale to Warburg. Before the board meeting, RBC aligned itself with Rural's CEO, DeMino, who was also a director; DeMino was eager for the sale to Warburg to proceed as he would be continued in his position following Warburg's purchase. Another board member, Shackelton, was the managing partner of a hedge fund with a substantial ownership position in Rural who was eager to monetize its holdings in Rural through an M&A event. A third director, Davis, was under growing pressure from ISS because he served on too many corporate boards—a dozen; hence, the disappearance of Rural would reduce his board memberships and salve to some extent ISS's concerns that he was "over boarded." These facts caused the court to conclude that each of the three had personal circumstances that inclined them to a near-term sale of the company. Shareholders sued alleging the directors' breached their duty of loyalty and joined RBC as an aider and abettor. The individual defendants settled, paying collectively $11.6 million.

The trial proceeded against RBC. The court found that the directors breached their fiduciary duty by failing to take reasonable steps to attain the best value for the Rural shareholders. The court also found that their breach was facilitated by RBC who, among other actions, deliberately reworked its fairness opinion to lower its appraised value of Rural so that Warburg's offer appeared to be more attractive. It also worked closely with DeMino, Shackelton and Davis in the days between the special committee's recommendation and the board meeting to win approval at the board level. Moreover, RBC was involved in the proxy statement's failure to disclose RBC's own conflicts of interest, so that Rural shareholders were denied this information when approving the sale.

Applying the following four-part test, the court held RBC liable as an aider and abettor of the directors' breaches:

   i)   the existence of a fiduciary relationship;

   ii)   the breach of the fiduciary's duty;

   iii) knowing participation in that breach by the defendant; and

   iv) damages proximately caused by the breach.

The court elaborated on the third element, observing "knowing participation in a board's fiduciary breach requires that the third party act with the knowledge that the conduct advocated or assisted constitutes a breach." *Id.* at 861–62. The Supreme Court reviewed the multiple facts supporting the trial court's finding that RBC acted with the requisite scienter:]

> RBC knowingly induced the breach by exploiting its own conflicted interests to the detriment of Rural and by creating an informational vacuum.[174] RBC's knowing participation included its failure to disclose its interest in obtaining a financing role in the EMS transaction and how it planned to use its engagement as Rural's advisor to capture buy-side financing work from bidders for EMS; its knowledge that the Board and Special Committee were uninformed about Rural's value; and its failure to disclose to the Board its interest in providing the winning bidder in the Rural process with buy-side financing and its eleventh-hour attempts to secure that role while simultaneously leading the negotiations on price. RBC's desire for Warburg's business also manifested itself in its financial analysis, provided by RBC the day the Board approved the merger. RBC's illicit manipulation of the Board's deliberative processes for self-interested purposes was enabled, in part, by the Board's own lack of oversight, affording RBC "the opportunity to indulge in the misconduct which occurred." The Board was unaware of RBC's modifications to the valuation analysis, back-channel communications with Warburg, and eleventh-hour attempt to capture at least a portion of the acquirer's buy-side financing business. RBC made no effort to advise the Rural directors about these contextually shaping points. The result was a poorly-timed sale at a price that was not the product of appropriate efforts to obtain the best value reasonably available and, as the trial court found, a failure to recognize that Rural's stand-alone value exceeded the sale price.

RBC Capital was held liable for nearly $76 million for its role is enabling directors of Rural/Metro Corporation to violate their fiduciary obligations.

———

---

[174]   *Cf. Encite LLC v. Soni*, 2011 Del. Ch. LEXIS 177, 2011 WL 5920896, at *26 (Del. Ch. Nov. 28, 2011) (recognizing that a "plaintiff can prove knowing participation by showing that a [third party] 'attempt[ed] to create or exploit conflicts of interest in the board' or 'conspire[d] in or agree[d] to the fiduciary breach' ") (citation omitted).

Shocking Technologies, Inc. v. Kosowsky

Court of Chancery of Delaware, 2012.
2012 WL 4482838.

[As part of his strategy to gain an additional board seat for a group of investors with whom he believed he shared a common objective, the director [Simon J. Michael], who was aware that the company was in dire financial condition and in need of an infusion of funds, sought to dissuade the only remaining potential investor from investing in the company. In doing so, he shared confidential company information with the potential investor. Michael believed he would be more likely to achieve his goals if either the potential investor withheld any additional investment in the company or the potential investor used the confidential information to get a better deal for its investment. Michael believed that either outcome would undercut the authority of the other members of the company's board of directors and thereby strengthen his ability to persuade them to pursue what he believed was a better plan to revive the company.]

Michael . . . hoped that his disclosure of confidential information to Dickinson would have ultimately resulted in better corporate governance practices for Shocking. That hope, however, cannot outweigh or somehow otherwise counterbalance the foreseeable harm that he would likely cause to Shocking. Notwithstanding his good intentions, his taking steps that would foreseeably cause significant harm to Shocking amounts to nothing less than a breach of fiduciary duty of loyalty.

Michael has referred to this as short-term pain for long-term gain. Perhaps it is a matter of degree. Advancing a policy where short-term adverse effects are outweighed by future benefits may be the product of a prudent and dutiful fiduciary. In theory, there may be something of a continuum on which actions, such as Michael's should be measured. Where the line is between the acceptable and the unacceptable is not readily pinpointed. The circumstances of this case, however, leave little, if any room for doubt. First, the short-term financial consequences of Michael's antics could have caused the demise of Shocking. Such reasonably foreseeable outcomes cannot be reconciled with the exercise of fiduciary duty. Second, the disclosure of confidential information to a potential investor (an adverse party at that particular moment), especially when the director knows (and hopes) that the disclosure would benefit the potential investor to the substantial detriment of the Company, is conduct which, in and of itself, is a breach of the duty of loyalty. In short, a loyal director does not put the company in dire financial circumstances in order to obtain what he perceives as a benefit for himself and his associated investors. That there may be some theoretical improvement in "corporate governance" to the director's liking does not alter this conclusion. . . .

———

Assume the facts in *Shocking Technologies* showed that Michael met with a group of shareholders and learned that they planned to launch a campaign to elect themselves to the board and, if successful, would appoint Michael as the future CEO of the firm. He thereafter provided them with a list of stockholders (including their holdings and addresses) as well as the company bylaws. Would this change the result? *See* Kerbawy v. McDonnell, 2015 WL 4929198 (Del. Ch. Aug. 18, 2015).

———

Matthew D. Cain, Jill E. Fisch, Sean J. Griffith & Steven Davidoff Solomon, How Corporate Governance Is Made: The Case of the Golden Leash

164 U. Pa. L. Rev. 649, 651–655 (2016).

How is corporate governance made? . . .

We use a case study of a corporate governance innovation—the golden leash—to shed light on how corporate governance originates and how it is valued. Activist hedge funds invented the golden leash as a tool for attracting and incentivizing director candidates in a proxy contest. Under the terms of the golden leash, these hedge funds agreed to pay their director nominees millions of dollars if the nominees were successful both in winning board seats and achieving the hedge fund's desired objectives.

The golden leash burst onto the scene in 2012 when JANA Partners, LLC (JANA) offered to pay its nominees to the board of Agrium, Inc. (Agrium) an additional $50,000 each, if elected, plus a collective total of 2.6% of JANA's net gain on the investment. Around the same time, Elliott Management (Elliott) agreed to pay its dissident nominees to the Hess Corp. (Hess) board an additional $30,000, if elected, for each percentage point by which Hess outperformed its peers over a three-year period. . . . [O]pponents of the arrangements dubbed them "golden leashes."

The golden leash was immediately controversial. JANA and Elliott justified the golden leash by the need, first, to get the right people onto their slates and, second, to incentivize those people, once elected, to push the company to outperform. According to this account, golden leashes empower shareholders by providing directors committed to unlocking hidden value and increasing market returns. Critics of the golden leash, however, derided these arrangements as pernicious innovations that merely emboldened those who would "jeopardize a company's ability to generate sustainable long-term returns" and "destroy jobs."

Opponents of activist shareholders soon responded with an innovation of their own. On May 10, 2013, Martin Lipton of Wachtell, Lipton, Rosen & Katz (Wachtell), a prominent law firm known for defending firms against activist interventions and hostile takeovers, issued a public memorandum recommending that corporations adopt bylaws prohibiting golden leash compensation arrangements (the "Wachtell Bylaw"). In relatively short order, more than thirty public companies adopted the Wachtell Bylaw. Moreover, because it could be adopted by any company virtually overnight, the Wachtell Bylaw had a market-wide effect.

The Wachtell Bylaw was challenged, but not in any court of law. Instead, it provoked the wrath of a prominent proxy advisory firm, Institutional Shareholder Services (ISS). On November 12, 2013, ISS recommended that shareholders withhold their votes from directors at Provident Financial Holdings, Inc. (Provident) because the bank had adopted the Wachtell Bylaw. At the subsequent annual meeting, Provident's director nominees received a substantial number of withhold votes, and ISS threatened more withhold recommendations, publishing a list of other firms that had adopted the Wachtell Bylaw.

Corporate America got the message. By May 20, 2014, twenty-eight of the thirty-two companies known to have adopted the Wachtell Bylaw prior to the Provident meeting had removed it in whole or in part. The golden leash, in contrast, is far from dead: it has been used in several recent activist attacks . . . .

The back and forth on the golden leash and the Wachtell Bylaw provides a case study of how corporate governance originates and is tested by the marketplace. The golden leash shows that corporate governance in many cases is a product of "governance intermediaries," each with its own agenda and interests. Activist hedge funds may have invented the golden leash, but the shape of the governance arrangements that ultimately emerged has as much to do with the counseling of a corporate law firm and the advocacy of an institutional proxy advisor as it does with the activists themselves. The success or failure of a governance innovation may often depend upon the position taken by such intermediaries.

While intermediaries may introduce these provisions, the question remains whether they are beneficial to the companies adopting them. With respect to the golden leash, this can be studied empirically. We did so by first examining each company and the circumstances of its adoption and repeal of the golden leash bylaw. We found that while some firms were reacting directly to activist threats, others had no apparent rationale for adopting the Wachtell Bylaw. Second, if the golden leash is economically good or bad, one would expect to see stock price reactions— either positive or negative—in response to firms' adoption and repeal of the Wachtell Bylaw. We therefore ran a time series analysis to determine how the market reacted to firms' adoption and repeal of the new corporate governance terms. We found no statistically significant share price effect for those companies that adopted—and subsequently repealed—the Wachtell Bylaw.

We then looked further. Because a golden leash bylaw can be adopted unilaterally at any time by the board of directors, we posited that what matters is not the actual adoption of the bylaw but rather the bylaw's availability for adoption if and when the board decides that it is needed. Additionally, we reasoned that the availability of a golden leash may not matter for all companies, but only for those that face the imminent prospect of a proxy contest or other activist intervention.

We examined this possibility by looking at the companies that experienced shareholder activism during the period from one year prior to the Wachtell Memorandum to one year after the Provident annual meeting. We assumed market discrimination in pricing corporate governance terms and hypothesized that we would find a share price reaction to the Wachtell Memorandum in this subset of companies. Our results are consistent with our hypothesis. We found a statistically significant decline in the share price of "targeted firms" on the release of the Wachtell Memorandum and a statistically significant increase in share price after the Provident vote. Consistent with our theoretical predictions, these price effects were limited to those companies most affected by the governance innovation in question—that is, those companies most likely to experience activism. Companies not subject to activist intervention had no statistically significant share price reactions.

Our findings contain several important implications for corporate governance. First, they provide evidence that intermediaries play an important role in channeling corporate governance innovation. Second, they show that, at least in this case, corporate governance may be priced by the market. Although our results suggest that investors responded to developments regarding the golden leash, we note that the value assigned by the market may not reflect the economic value of the leash itself, but may instead indicate more general investor or market anticipation of potential activist intervention. Third, our empirical findings provide evidence that investor reactions may be based largely on salience, and governance intermediaries play a critical role in creating this salience.

Ultimately, our findings are cause for caution regarding what constitutes "good" corporate governance and how studies of governance are conducted. While our case study examines only one event, it offers reasons to question the relationship between short-term share price reactions and long-term economic value. More generally, the evolution of corporate governance innovations is a complex story involving the actions and reactions not merely of the firm and its shareholders, but of a variety of intermediaries and interest groups with their own agendas.

———

The obvious concern posed by golden leashes is not just whether the arrangement tethers the leashed director to the shareholders' overlapping interest but the degree to which the shareholders' interests are congruent with those of the leashed director. For a fulsome analysis of these concerns, *see* Gregory H. Shill, The Golden Leash and the

Fiduciary Duty of Loyalty, 64 U.C.L.A. Law Rev. 1246 (2017). What problem arises if the arrangement between the leashed director and the hedge fund is not fully disclosed? Consider *Reading v. Attorney General* examined earlier in Chapter 1, Section 2 C. Disclosure of such a third party payment is mandated for reporting companies by various SEC rules. *See e.g.,* Form 8-K, Item 5.02(d)(5).

———

2. SELF-DEALING TRANSACTIONS

A. COMMON LAW

Marsh, Are Directors Trustees?—Conflicts of Interest and Corporate Morality
22 Bus.Law. 35, 36–43 (1966).

a. *Prohibition.*

In 1880 it could have been stated with confidence that in the United States the general rule was that any contract between a director and his corporation was voidable at the instance of the corporation or its shareholders, without regard to the fairness or unfairness of the transaction. This rule was stated in powerful terms by a number of highly regarded courts and judges in cases which arose generally out of the railroad frauds of the 1860's and 1870's. . . .

Under this rule it mattered not the slightest that there was a majority of so-called disinterested directors who approved the contract. The courts stated that the corporation was entitled to the unprejudiced judgment and advice of all of its directors and therefore it did no good to say that the interested director did not participate in the making of the contract on behalf of the corporation. ". . . the very words in which he asserts his right declare his wrong; he ought to have participated. . . . "[1] Furthermore, the courts said that it was impossible to measure the influence which one director might have over his associates, even though ostensibly abstaining from participation in the discussion or vote. ". . . a corporation, in order to defeat a contract entered into by directors, in which one or more of them had a private interest, is not bound to show that the influence of the director or directors having the private interest determined the action of the board. The law cannot accurately measure the influence of a trustee with his associates, nor will it enter into the inquiry. . . . "[2]

Perhaps the strongest reason for this inflexibility of the law was given by the Maryland Supreme Court which stated that, when a contract is made with even one of the directors, "the remaining directors

---

[1]   Stewart v. Lehigh Valley R.R. Co., 38 N.J.Law 505, at 523 (Ct.Err. & App.1875).
[2]   Munson v. Syracuse, G. & C. Ry. Co., 103 N.Y. 58, at 74, 8 N.E. 355, at 358 (1886).

are placed in the embarrassing and invidious position of having to pass upon, scrutinize and check the transactions and accounts of one of their *own body, with* whom they are associated on terms of equality in the general management of all the affairs of the corporation."[3] Or, as Justice Davies of the New York Supreme Court expressed the same thought: "The moment the directors permit one or more of their number to deal with the property of the stockholders, they surrender their own independence and self control."[4]

This rule applied not only to individual contracts with directors, but also to the situation of interlocking directorates where even a minority of the boards were common to the two contracting corporations. Not only that, it was also applied to the situation where one corporation owned a majority of the stock of another and appointed its directors, even though they might not be the same men as sat on the board of the parent corporation. . . .

This principle, absolutely inhibiting contracts between a corporation and its directors or any of them, appeared to be impregnable in 1880. It was stated in ringing terms by virtually every decided case, with arguments which seemed irrefutable, and it was sanctioned by age. As Justice Davies stated:

> To hold otherwise, would be to overturn principles of equity which have been regarded as well settled since the days of Lord Keeper Bridgman, in the 22nd of Charles Second, to the present time—principles enunciated and enforced by Hardwicke, Thurlow, Loughborough, Eldon, Cranworth, Story and Kent, and which the highest courts in our country have declared to be founded on immutable truth and justice, and to stand upon our great moral obligation to refrain from placing ourselves in relations which excite a conflict between self interest and integrity.

Thirty years later this principle was dead.

b.   *Approval by a disinterested majority of the board.*

It could have been stated with reasonable confidence in 1910 that the general rule was that a contract between a director and his corporation was valid if it was approved by a disinterested majority of his fellow directors and was not found to be unfair or fraudulent by the court if challenged; but that a contract in which a majority of the board was interested was voidable at the instance of the corporation or its shareholders without regard to any question of fairness.

One searches in vain in the decided cases for a reasoned defense of this change in legal philosophy, or for the slightest attempt to refute the powerful arguments which had been made in support of the previous

---

3   Cumberland Coal and Iron Co. v. Parish, 42 Md. 598, at 606 (1875).
4   Cumberland Coal and Iron Co. v. Sherman, 30 Barb. 553, at 573 (N.Y.Sup.Ct.1859).

rule. Did the courts discover in the last quarter of the Nineteenth Century that greed was no longer a factor in human conduct? If so, they did not share the basis of this discovery with the public; nor did they humbly admit their error when confronted with the next wave of corporate frauds arising out of the era of the formation of the "trusts" during the 1890's and early 1900's. . . .

The only explanation which seems to have been given for this change in position was the technical one that a trustee, while forbidden to deal with himself in connection with the trust property, could deal directly with the cestui que trust if he made full disclosure and took no unfair advantage; and that the case of a director who abstained from representing the corporation but dealt in his personal capacity with a majority of disinterested directors was properly analogized to a trustee dealing with the cestui que trust. As the Texas court said:[5]

> . . . we think it is not true that one who holds the position of director is incapable, under all circumstances, of divesting himself of his representative character in a particular transaction, and dealing with the corporation through others competent to represent it, as other trustees may deal directly with the beneficiaries. . . . [T]he company is represented by those who alone can act for it, and, if they are disinterested, he can, we think, deal with them as any other trustee can deal with the cestui que trust, if he makes a full disclosure of all facts known to him about the subject, takes no advantage of his position, deals honestly and openly, and concludes a contract fair and beneficial to the company.

But in no case is there any discussion or attempted refutation of the reasons previously given by the courts as to why it is impossible, in such a situation, for any director to be disinterested. Some courts seem simply to admit that the practice has grown too widespread for them to cope with. In *South Side Trust Co. v. Washington Tin Plate Co.* the Supreme Court of Pennsylvania said:[6] "The interests of corporations are sometimes so interwoven that it is desirable to have joint representatives in their respective managements, and at any rate it is a not uncommon and [therefore?] not unlawful practice." . . .

Under the rule that a disinterested majority of the directors must approve a transaction with one of their number, the question arose whether this meant a disinterested quorum (i.e., normally a majority of the whole board) or merely a disinterested majority of a quorum, so that the interested director or directors could be counted to make up the quorum. Virtually all of the cases held that the interested director could not be counted for quorum purposes. As the California court said, the

---

[5]   Tenison v. Patton, 95 Tex. 284, at 292–93, 67 S.W. 92, at 95 (1902).

[6]   252 Pa. 237 at 241, 97 A. 450 at 451 (1916).

interested director for this purpose was "as much a stranger to the board as if he had never been elected a director. . . ."[7]

c. *Judicial review of the fairness of the transaction.*

By 1960 it could be said with some assurance that the general rule was that no transaction of a corporation with any or all of its directors was automatically voidable at the suit of a shareholder, whether there was a disinterested majority of the board or not; but that the courts would review such a contract and subject it to rigid and careful scrutiny, and would invalidate the contract if it was found to be unfair to the corporation. . . .

B. STATUTORY APPROACH

ALI, PRINCIPLES OF CORPORATE GOVERNANCE
§§ 1.14, 1.25, 5.02, 5.07, 5.08

[See Statutory Supplement]

CAL. CORP. CODE § 310

[See Statutory Supplement]

DEL. GEN. CORP. LAW § 144

[See Statutory Supplement]

REV. MODEL BUS. CORP. ACT §§ 8.60–8.63

[See Statutory Supplement]

N.Y. BUS. CORP. LAW § 713

[See Statutory Supplement]

---

[7]   Curtis v. Salmon River Hydraulic Gold-Mining & Dutch Co., . . . 10 Cal. at 349, 62 P. at 554.

Lewis v. S.L. & E., Inc.

United States Court of Appeals, Second Circuit, 1980.
629 F.2d 764.

■ KEARSE, CIRCUIT JUDGE:

This case arises out of an intra-family dispute over the management of two closely-held affiliated corporations. Plaintiff Donald E. Lewis ("Donald"), a shareholder of S.L. & E., Inc. ("SLE"), appeals from judgments entered against him in the United States District Court for the Western District of New York, Harold P. Burke, Judge, after a bench trial of his derivative claim against directors of SLE, and of a claim asserted against him by the other corporation, Lewis General Tires, Inc. ("LGT"), which intervened in the suit. The defendants Alan E. Lewis ("Alan"), Leon E. Lewis, Jr. ("Leon, Jr."), and Richard E. Lewis ("Richard"), are the brothers of Donald; they were, at pertinent times herein, directors of SLE and officers, directors and shareholders of LGT. Donald charged that his brothers had wasted the assets of SLE by causing SLE to lease business premises to LGT from 1966 to 1972 at an unreasonably low rental. LGT was permitted to intervene in the action, and filed a complaint seeking specific performance of an agreement by Donald to sell his SLE stock to LGT in 1972. The district court held that Donald had failed to prove waste by the defendant directors, and entered judgment in their favor. The court also awarded attorneys' fees to the defendant directors and to SLE, and granted LGT specific performance of Donald's agreement to sell his SLE stock.

On appeal, Donald argues that the district court improperly allocated to him the burden of proving his claims of waste, and that since defendants failed to prove that the transactions in question were fair and reasonable, he was entitled to judgment. Donald also argues that the awards of attorneys' fees were improper. We agree with each of these contentions, and therefore reverse and remand.

I

For many years Leon Lewis, Sr., the father of Donald and the defendant directors, was the principal shareholder of SLE and LGT. LGT, formed in 1933, operated a tire dealership in Rochester, New York. SLE, formed in 1943, owned the land and complex of buildings at 260 East Avenue in Rochester. This property was SLE's only significant asset. Prior to 1956 LGT occupied SLE's premises without benefit of a lease; the rent paid was initially $200 per month, and had increased over the years to $800 per month by 1956, when additional parcels were added. On February 28, 1956, SLE granted LGT a 10-year lease on the newly expanded property ("the Property"), for a rent of $1200 per month, or $14,400 per year. Under the terms of the lease, SLE was responsible for payment of real estate taxes on the Property, while all other current expenses were to be borne by the tenant, LGT.[1]

In 1962, Leon Lewis, Sr., transferred his SLE stock, 90 shares in all, to his six children (defendants Richard, Alan and Leon, Jr., plaintiff Donald, and two daughters, Margaret and Carol), giving 15 shares to each.[2] At that time Richard, Alan and Leon, Jr., were already shareholders, officers and directors of LGT. Contemporaneously with their receipt of SLE stock, all six of the children entered into a "shareholders' agreement" with LGT, under which each child who was not a shareholder of LGT on June 1, 1972 would be required to sell his or her SLE shares to LGT, within 30 days of that date, at a price equal to the book value of the SLE stock as of June 1, 1972.[3]

LGT's lease on the SLE property expired on February 28, 1966. At that time the directors of SLE were Richard, Alan, Leon, Jr., Leon, Sr., and Henry Etsberger; these five were also the directors of LGT. In 1966 Alan owned 44% of LGT, Richard owned 30%, Leon, Jr., owned 19%, and Leon, Sr., owned 7%. From 1967 to 1972 Richard owned 61% of LGT and Leon, Jr., owned the remaining 39%. When the lease expired in 1966, no new lease was entered into. LGT nonetheless continued to occupy the property and to pay SLE at the old rate, $14,400 per year. According to the defendants' testimony at trial, there was never any thought or discussion among the SLE directors of entering into a new lease or of increasing the rent. Richard testified: "We never gave consideration to a new lease." From all that appears, the defendant directors viewed SLE as existing purely for the benefit of LGT. Richard testified, for example, that although real estate taxes rose sharply during the period 1966–1971, from approximately $7,800 to more than $11,000, to be paid by SLE out of its constant $14,400 rental income, raising the rent was never mentioned. He testified that SLE was "only a shell to protect the operating company [LGT]." When this suit was commenced there had not been a formal meeting of either the shareholders or the directors of SLE since 1962. Richard, Alan and Leon, Jr., had largely ignored SLE's separate corporate existence[4] and disregarded the fact that SLE had

---

[1]   It appears that SLE was also responsible for payments due on a mortgage on the Property. In addition, LGT charged SLE for the costs of certain capital improvements, such as the major structural repairs to the principal building's facade, carried out in 1969.

[2]   SLE had 150 shares outstanding, and each child thus received a ten percent interest. At the same time LGT purchased the remaining 60 outstanding shares from the elder Lewis's business partner, Henry Etsberger.

[3]   The agreement specified procedures by which the book value, and hence the price of the shares, would be determined.

[4]   For example, Richard's testimony includes the following statements:

Q   Mr. Lewis, you have always looked at these two corporations as being one and the same, haven't you, Lewis General Tires and S.L. & E.?

A   Yes.

* * *

I never really got into S.L. & E. at all. (Tr. 6/21/78, at 972–73.)

* * *

shareholders who were not shareholders of LGT and who therefore could not profit from actions that used SLE solely for the benefit of LGT.

Neither Donald nor his sisters ever owned LGT stock. As the June 1972 date approached for the required sale of their SLE stock to LGT, Donald apparently came to believe that SLE's book value was lower than it should have been. He sought SLE financial information from Richard, who had been president of SLE since 1967.[5] Richard refused to provide information. Donald therefore refused to sell his SLE shares in 1972,[6] and commenced this shareholders' derivative action in the district court in August 1973, basing jurisdiction on diversity of citizenship. The sole claim raised in the complaint was that the defendant directors had wasted the assets of SLE by "grossly undercharging" LGT for the latter's occupancy and use of the Property. Although the complaint charged such mismanagement for the period 1962 to 1973, plaintiff subsequently limited this claim to the period between February 28, 1966, the date on which the lease expired,[7] and June 1, 1972, the date contractually set for valuation of the SLE shares which plaintiff had agreed to sell to LGT. LGT intervened and demanded specific performance of Donald's agreement to sell his SLE stock. Donald did not contest his ultimate obligation to sell, but took the position that since the book value of the shares would be increased if he prevailed on his derivative claim, specific performance should be granted only after adjudication of that claim.

There ensured an eight-day bench trial, at which plaintiff sought to prove, by the testimony of several expert witnesses, that the fair rental value of the Property was greater than the $14,400 per year that SLE had been paid by LGT. Defendants sought to show that the rental paid was reasonable, by offering evidence concerning the financial straits of LGT, the cost to LGT of operating the Property, the general economic decline of the East Avenue neighborhood, and rentals paid on two other properties in that neighborhood. LGT presented expert testimony that the value of plaintiff's stock as of June 1972, assuming a successful defense of the derivative claims, was $15,650.

The district court subsequently filed lengthy and detailed findings of fact and conclusions of law. Many of the court's findings went to the validity and probative value of the testimony given by plaintiff's expert

---

I don't think I ever looked at an operating statement of S.L. & E. seriously. (*Id.* at 991.)

* * *

I had very little to do with S.L. & E. (Tr. 7/28/78, at 80.)

Alan testified that at no time after 1964 did he participate in any discussions of any increase in rent for SLE. (*Id.* at 160, 164.)

And Leon, Jr., testified, "I didn't have anything to do with running S.L. & E. . . ." (*Id.* at 230.)

[5]   It does not appear that SLE paid salaries to any of its officers or directors.

[6]   Donald's sisters Carol and Margaret sold their SLE shares to LGT in 1972 and 1973 respectively. Alan, who had sold his LGT stock in 1967, sold his SLE stock to LGT in 1972.

[7]   Donald was not a shareholder of SLE in 1956 when the lease was entered into and hence had no standing to challenge its terms. BCL § 626(b); *Bernstein v. Polo Fashions, Inc.,* 55 A.D.2d 530, 389 N.Y.S.2d 368 (1st Dep't 1976).

witnesses, and the court ultimately declined to credit that testimony. On this basis, the court held that Donald had failed to establish the rental value of the Property during the period at issue, and that defendants were therefore entitled to judgment on the derivative claims. Implicit in the district court's ruling, granting judgment for defendants upon plaintiff's failure to prove waste, was a determination that plaintiff bore the burden of proof on that issue. The court also ruled that LGT was entitled to specific performance of Donald's agreement to sell his SLE stock, and that Donald was not entitled to recover attorneys' fees from SLE, but that SLE and the individual defendants were entitled to attorneys' fees from Donald. This appeal followed.

II

Turning first to the question of burden of proof, we conclude that the district court erred in placing upon plaintiff the burden of proving waste. Because the directors of SLE were also officers, directors and/or shareholders of LGT, the burden was on the defendant directors to demonstrate that the transactions between SLE and LGT were fair and reasonable. New York Business Corporation Law ("BCL") § 713(b) (McKinney Supp.1979) (eff. September 1, 1971); BCL § 713(a)(3) (McKinney 1963) (repealed as of September 1, 1971); *see Cohen v. Ayers,* 596 F.2d 733, 739–40 (7th Cir.1979) (construing current BCL § 713); *Remillard Brick Co. v. Remillard-Dandini Co.,* 109 Cal.App.2d 405, 241 P.2d 66, 75 (1952) (construing California Corporations Code § 820, upon which the prior BCL § 713 was patterned).

Under normal circumstances the directors of a corporation may determine, in the exercise of their business judgment, what contracts the corporation will enter into and what consideration is adequate, without review of the merits of their decisions by the courts. The business judgment rule places a heavy burden on shareholders who would attack corporate transactions. *Galef v. Alexander,* 615 F.2d 51, 57–58 (2d Cir.1980); *Auerbach v. Bennett,* 47 N.Y.2d 619, 629, 419 N.Y.S.2d 920, 926, 393 N.E.2d 994, 1000 (1979); 3A Fletcher, *Cyclopedia of the Law of Private Corporations* § 1039 (perm. ed. 1975). But the business judgment rule presupposes that the directors have no conflict of interest. When a shareholder attacks a transaction in which the directors have an interest other than as directors of the corporation, the directors may not escape review of the merits of the transaction. At common law such a transaction was voidable unless shown by its proponent to be fair, and reasonable to the corporation.[11] BCL § 713, in both its current and its prior versions, carries forward this common law principle, and provides special rules for scrutiny of a transaction between the corporation and an entity in which its directors are directors or officers or have a substantial financial interest. . . .

---

[11]   *E.g., Geddes v. Anaconda Copper Co.,* 254 U.S. 590, 599, 41 S.Ct. 209, 65 L.Ed. 425 (1921). . . .

The current version of § 713,* which became effective on September 1, 1971, and governs at least so much of the dealing between SLE and LGT as occurred after that date, expressly provides that a contract between a corporation and an entity in which its directors are interested may be set aside unless the proponent of the contract "shall establish affirmatively that the contract or transaction was fair and reasonable as to the corporation at the time it was approved by the board. . . . " § 713(b). Thus when the transaction is challenged in a derivative action against the interested directors, they have the burden of proving that the transaction was fair and reasonable to the corporation. *Cohen v. Ayers, supra.*

The same was true under the predecessor to § 713(b), former § 713(a)(3), which was in effect prior to September 1, 1971. . . .

During the entire period 1966–1972, Richard, Alan and Leon, Jr., were directors of both SLE and LGT;[14] there were no SLE directors who were not also directors of LGT. Richard, Alan and Leon, Jr., were all shareholders of LGT in 1966, and from 1967 to 1972 Richard and Leon, Jr., were the sole shareholders of LGT. Under BCL § 713, therefore, Richard, Alan and Leon, Jr., had the burden of proving that $14,400 was a fair and reasonable annual rent for the SLE property for the period February 28, 1966 through June 1, 1972.

Our review of the record convinces us that defendants failed to carry their burden. At trial, there was no direct testimony as to what would have been a fair rental during the relevant period, *i.e.,* 1966 to 1972, and the evidence that was introduced fell far short of establishing that $14,400 was a fair annual rental value for those years.

Quite clearly Richard, Alan and Leon, Jr., had made no effort to determine contemporaneously what rental would be fair during the years 1966–1972. Their view was that the rent should simply cover expenses and that SLE existed for the benefit of LGT.[15] During this period no appraisals were made; no attempts were made to sell or rent the Property; no thought whatever was given to whether $14,400 was a fair and reasonable rent even when real estate taxes had risen to consume nearly all of that amount.

Defendants offered instead evidence of rents paid on other properties. Among their best evidence was the expert testimony of Harvey Rosenbloom, a real estate appraiser. Rosenbloom testified that two other East Avenue buildings, which the district court found to be comparable to the 260 East Avenue premises, were leased at lower per-square-foot rentals than was paid by LGT to SLE. However, as to one of these properties, Rosenbloom testified only to rent paid in 1973 and 1974,

---

*   *See* New York Bus.Corp.Law § 713 in the Statutory Supplement. (Footnote by ed.)

14   Alan ceased to be a director in November 1972; Leon, Jr., ceased to be a director in 1977. Richard remains a director.

15   *See* footnote 4 *supra,* and accompanying text.

and did not consider the 1966–1972 period. As to the other property, Rosenbloom described a fifteen year lease that was entered into in 1961. This testimony, while perhaps not wholly irrelevant to the issues in this suit, fell far short of demonstrating what rental the Property could have fetched in 1966, or in any other of the relevant years. Indeed, Rosenbloom himself testified that rental value could well be different for each year of the period. Thus, rentals that Rosenbloom testified were agreed to in 1961 or 1973 might well have been unfair in 1966 or 1967. This evidence thus could not support a finding that defendants acted fairly in maintaining an annual rental of $14,400 during the years from 1966 to 1972.[16]

Defendants also produced considerable evidence that over the relevant period, the East End neighborhood had been on an economic decline; that businesses had been leaving the area; that urban renewal projects and increased crime had depressed property values there; and that the area had, in general, become a less desirable place to do business. There was also evidence of specific developments that had an adverse effect on the Property: for example, the street running along one side of the Property was made a one-way street, thus limiting customers' access to LGT's premises. The district court credited all of this testimony, and it is fair to say that defendants proved that there was a general downward trend in the value of the Property. However, as noted above, defendants did not establish what was a fair rental value for the Property in 1966. Absent such a point of reference, a general downward trend in value is of no assistance in determining whether the rental actually paid was fair and reasonable during the ensuing years.

Moreover, working in reverse, some of defendants' own evidence as to the value of the Property at the end of the relevant period suggested that $14,400 was less than a fair rental in 1966, and that the figure of $38,099, estimated by plaintiff's expert, was perhaps not far off the mark.[17] First, there was a variety of evidence suggesting that in 1972 the Property was worth more than $200,000. An appraisal by defense witness Harold Grunert in 1972 set the fair market value of the Property as of June 30, 1972, at $220,000. In 1972 Leon, Jr., had offered personally to buy the Property for $200,000, an offer which Richard had rejected.[18] And in 1971, Richard had informed Donald that evaluations by another appraiser, Harold Galloway, had set the value of the Property at $200,000 and $236,000. Second, defendants' expert witness Rosenbloom, asked what he would consider a fair rent for the property, given Grunert's

---

[16]   Defendant Richard E. Lewis testified that defendants tried, without success, to sell the Property in 1975, listing it with a realtor for $200,000. In addition he testified that an effort was made to rent the Property in 1973, and that only one offer, for $700 per month, was forthcoming. Since these efforts were made in 1973 and 1975, this evidence, like the evidence as to rentals of other property, was too remote in time to establish a fair rental value, especially as to the earlier years of the 1966–1972 period.

[17]   Plaintiff's expert made his evaluation as of February 1973. He did not make any evaluation for the period 1966–1972.

[18]   Leon, Jr., had just been fired from LGT by Richard.

1972 valuation of $220,000, stated that ten percent of the value would be inadequate and that fifteen to seventeen percent would be closer to adequate. Fifteen percent of $220,000 would have yielded a rent of $33,000 on the basis of the 1972 valuation. Grunert's own expert testimony was entirely consistent with this. While he had made no estimate as to the fair rental value of the property for 1966–1972, he opined that a fair rental as of June 30, 1972, would be $20–21,000 with the tenant paying all expenses including real estate taxes. According to Richard, SLE's real estate taxes in 1972 were about $12,000. Thus Grunert's testimony, too, suggests about $33,000 as the fair rental value in 1972. Finally, consistent with their view of the general downward economic trend, Richard and Alan conceded that, whatever the Property was worth in 1972, it was worth more in 1966.[19] Thus the evidence presented by defendants, far from carrying their burden of showing that $14,400 was a fair and reasonable annual rental in 1966–1972, suggested that the fair rental value of the Property throughout that period exceeded $33,000 per year.

The defendants argued, however, that LGT could not have afforded to pay SLE rent higher than $14,400. They produced evidence designed to show that LGT had made little profit; that this low profitability was due to the expenses of maintenance and upkeep of the 260 East Avenue property; and that LGT therefore would not have been able to pay a higher rent to SLE. The district court credited this evidence, finding that LGT had "experienced a number of years of very severe losses," that during the period from 1962–1973, LGT's overall profit was only $53,876, and that payment of rent at the rate of $39,099 per year during this period could have led to the "demise" of LGT. These findings have only a distorted relationship to this lawsuit.

The period in issue here is 1966–1972. The only "severe" losses shown, totaling nearly $83,000, occurred in 1963 and 1973. Their inclusion in the computation of what LGT could afford to pay in 1966–1972 was patently unfair. In fact LGT's only unprofitable year during the period in issue was 1969 when its loss was small: $1,168. LGT's after-tax profits in 1966–1972 in fact totaled $102,963, or an average of $14,709 per year. Thus, even on paper, LGT could have "afforded" to double its rent payments to SLE during the period in question.

Moreover, the proposition that LGT could not afford to pay as rent more than what its own books showed as profits ignores the fact that LGT was owned and managed by members of the Lewis family, some of whom were also employees of that corporation. It is entirely possible that these family members granted to themselves unusually high salaries or other perquisites, thus reducing LGT's paper profits. For example, in 1966 Richard's salary was approximately $21,000; Leon, Jr.'s compensation was $3,000 salary plus commissions. In 1967, LGT acquired all of Alan's

---

[19]   Leon, Jr., did not know whether the value had decreased from 1966 to 1972, but did not believe it had risen.

LGT stock; and Richard and Leon, Jr., acquired all of the LGT stock of their father, agreeing to pay the purchase price over a ten-year period. Richard and Leon, Jr., thus became LGT's only shareholders, and their LGT salaries were immediately increased by a total of $23,000 per year (Richard's salary went from $21,000 to $36,000; Leon, Jr.'s went from $3,000 to $11,000), to cover the cost of the LGT stock they had just acquired.[20] Defendants bore the burden of proof on the question of a fair and reasonable rental; if they would rely on the proposition that LGT was unable to pay more, it was incumbent on them to demonstrate the fairness of the management and the reasonableness of the conduct of LGT's affairs. It does not appear that they made any effort to do so.

Finally, even if we were to assume that LGT's financial records provided a fair basis for evaluating the SLE-LGT transactions, defendants would not have carried their burden of proof. Defendants did not demonstrate that SLE could not have found some other tenant, stronger financially than LGT, which would have been willing and able to pay a higher rental. Even given the general downward trend of the East Avenue neighborhood, it is entirely possible that at least during the early years of the 1966–1972 period, such a tenant might have been secured. No effort was made during that period to rent to anyone other than LGT.

We conclude, therefore, that defendants failed to prove that the rental paid by LGT to SLE for the years 1966–1972 was fair and reasonable. Thus, Donald is not required to sell his SLE shares to LGT without such upward adjustment in the June 1, 1972, book value of SLE as may be necessary to reflect the amount by which the fair rental value of the Property exceeded $14,400 in any of the years 1966–1972. . . .

We remand to the district court (a) for the entry of judgment in favor of SLE against Richard, Alan and Leon, Jr., jointly and severally, in such amount as the district court shall determine to be equal to the amounts by which the annual fair rental value of the Property exceeded $14,400 in the period February 28, 1966–June 1, 1972, (b) for an accounting as to the value of Donald's SLE shares as of June 1, 1972, in light of such judgment, (c) for an order, following such accounting, of specific performance of the shareholders' agreement, and (d) for such other proceedings as are not inconsistent with this opinion.

---

[20]   Richard had no doubt he could have paid for his newly acquired shares without the increase in his LGT salary. Leon, Jr., apparently lacked other resources from which to pay for the LGT stock (at least after he was fired from LGT in 1972).

Cookies Food Products v. Lakes Warehouse

Supreme Court of Iowa, 1988.
430 N.W.2d 447.

■ NEUMAN, JUSTICE.

This is a shareholders' derivative suit brought by the minority shareholders of a closely held Iowa corporation specializing in barbeque sauce, Cookies Food Products, Inc. (Cookies). The target of the lawsuit is the majority shareholder, Duane "Speed" Herrig and two of his family-owned corporations, Lakes Warehouse Distributing, Inc. (Lakes) and Speed's Automotive Co., Inc. (Speed's). Plaintiffs alleged that Herrig, by acquiring control of Cookies and executing self-dealing contracts, breached his fiduciary duty to the company and fraudulently misappropriated and converted corporate funds. Plaintiffs sought actual and punitive damages. Trial to the court resulted in a verdict for the defendants, the district court finding that Herrig's actions benefited, rather than harmed, Cookies. We affirm.

I. Background. . . .

L.D. Cook of Storm Lake, Iowa, founded Cookies in 1975 to produce and distribute his original barbeque sauce. Searching for a plant site in a community that would provide financial backing, Cook met with business leaders in seventeen Iowa communities, outlining his plans to build a growth-oriented company. He selected Wall Lake, Iowa, persuading thirty-five members of that community, including Herrig and the plaintiffs, to purchase Cookies stock. All of the investors hoped Cookies would improve the local job market and tax base. The record reveals that it has done just that.

Early sales of the product, however, were dismal. After the first year's operation, Cookies was in dire financial straits. . . . Cookies' board of directors approached Herrig with the idea of distributing the company's products. It authorized Herrig to purchase Cookies' sauce for twenty percent under wholesale price, which he could then resell at full wholesale price. Under this arrangement, Herrig began to market and distribute the sauce to his auto parts customers and to grocery outlets from Lakes' trucks as they traversed the regular delivery routes for Speed's Automotive.

In May 1977, Cookies formalized this arrangement by executing an exclusive distribution agreement with Lakes. . . .

Cookies' sales have soared under the exclusive distributorship contract with Lakes. . . .

As sales increased, Cookies' board of directors amended and extended the original distributorship agreement. In 1979, the board amended the original agreement to give Lakes an additional two percent of gross sales to cover freight costs for the ever-expanding market for Cookies' sauce. . . .

In 1981, L.D. Cook, the majority shareholder up to this time, decided to sell his interest in Cookies. He first offered the directors an opportunity to buy his stock, but the board declined to purchase any of his 8100 shares. Herrig then offered Cook and all other shareholders $10 per share for their stock, which was twice the original price. Because of the overwhelming response to these offers, Herrig had purchased enough Cookies stock by January 1982 to become the majority shareholder. . . .

Shortly after Herrig acquired majority control he replaced four of the five members of the Cookies' board with members he selected. This restructuring of authority, following on the heels of an unsuccessful attempt by certain stockholders to prevent Herrig from acquiring majority status, solidified a division of opinion within the shareholder ranks. Subsequent changes made in the corporation under Herrig's leadership formed the basis for this lawsuit.

First, under Herrig's leadership, Cookies' board has extended the term of the exclusive distributorship agreement with Lakes and expanded the scope of services for which it compensates Herrig and his companies. In April 1982, when a sales increase of twenty-five percent over the previous year required Cookies to seek additional short-term storage for the peak summer season, the board accepted Herrig's proposal to compensate Lakes at the "going rate" for use of its nearby storage facilities. The board decided to use Lakes' storage facilities because building and staffing its own facilities would have been more expensive. Later, in July 1982, the new board approved an extension of the exclusive distributorship agreement. Notably, this agreement was identical to the 1980 extension that the former board had approved while four of the plaintiffs in this action were directors.

Second, Herrig moved from his role as director and distributor to take on an additional role in product development. This created a dispute over a royalty Herrig began to receive. Herrig's role in product development began in 1982 when Cookies diversified its product line to include taco sauce. Herrig developed the recipe because he recognized that taco sauce, while requiring many of the same ingredients needed in barbeque sauce, is less expensive to produce. Further, since consumer demand for taco sauce is more consistent throughout the year than the demand for barbeque sauce, this new product line proved to be a profitable method for increasing year-round utilization of production facilities and staff. In August 1982, Cookies' board approved a royalty fee to be paid to Herrig for this taco sauce recipe. This royalty plan was similar to royalties the board paid to L.D. Cook for the barbeque sauce recipe. That plan gives Cook three percent of the gross sales of barbeque sauce; Herrig receives a flat rate per case. Although Herrig's rate is equivalent to a sales percentage slightly higher than what Cook receives, it yields greater profit to Cookies because this new product line is cheaper to produce.

Third, since 1982 Cookies' board has twice approved additional compensation for Herrig. In January 1983, the board authorized payment of a $1000 per month "consultant fee" in lieu of salary, because accelerated sales required Herrig to spend extra time managing the company. Averaging eighty-hour work weeks, Herrig devoted approximately fifteen percent of his time to Cookies and eighty percent to Lakes business. In August, 1983, the board authorized another increase in Herrig's compensation. Further, at the suggestion of a Cookies director who also served as an accountant for Cookies, Lakes, and Speed's, the Cookies board amended the exclusive distributorship agreement to allow Lakes an additional two percent of gross sales as a promotion allowance to expand the market for Cookies products outside of Iowa. As a direct result of this action, by 1986 Cookies regularly shipped products to several states throughout the country.

As we have previously noted, however, Cookies' growth and success has not pleased all its shareholders. The discontent is motivated by two factors that have effectively precluded shareholders from sharing in Cookies' financial success: the fact that Cookies is a closely held corporation, and the fact that it has not paid dividends. Because Cookies' stock is not publicly traded, shareholders have no ready access to buyers for their stock at current values that reflect the company's success. Without dividends, the shareholders have no ready method of realizing a return on their investment in the company. This is not to say that Cookies has improperly refused to pay dividends. The evidence reveals that Cookies would have violated the terms of its loan with the Small Business Administration had it declared dividends before repaying that debt. That SBA loan was not repaid until the month before the plaintiffs filed this action.

Unsatisfied with the status quo, a group of minority shareholders commenced this equitable action in 1985. Based on the facts we have detailed, the plaintiffs claimed that the sums paid Herrig and his companies have grossly exceeded the value of the services rendered, thereby substantially reducing corporate profits and shareholder equity. Through the exclusive distributorship agreements, taco sauce royalty, warehousing fees, and consultant fee, plaintiffs claimed that Herrig breached his fiduciary duties to the corporation and its shareholders because he allegedly negotiated for these arrangements without fully disclosing the benefit he would gain. The plaintiffs sought recovery for lost profits, an accounting to determine the full extent of the damage, attorneys fees, punitive damages, appointment of a receiver to manage the company properly, removal of Herrig from control, and sale of the company in order to generate an appropriate return on their investment.

Having heard the evidence presented on these claims at trial, the district court filed a lengthy ruling that reflected careful attention to the testimony of the twenty-two witnesses and myriad of exhibits admitted. The court . . . found that: (1) the exclusive distributorship arrangement has been the "key to corporate growth and expansion" and the fees under the agreement were appropriate for the diverse services Lakes provided; (2) the warehousing agreement was fair because it allowed Cookies to store its goods at the "going rate" and the board had considered and rejected the idea of constructing its own warehouse as storage at the Lakes facility would be less expensive; (3) the taco sauce royalty agreement appropriately compensated Herrig for the value of his recipe; and (4) the consultant fee "is actually a management fee for services rendered seven days a week" and is "well within reason, considering the success of the business." Additionally, the district court found that Herrig had withheld no information from directors or other shareholders that he was obligated to provide. The court concluded its findings with the following observation:

> The Court believes that the plaintiffs' complaint is not that they have been damaged but that they have not been paid a profit for their investment yet. There is a vast difference. Plaintiffs have made a profit. That profit is in the form of increased value of their stocks rather than in the form of dividends because of the capital considerations of operating the company.

On appeal from this ruling, the plaintiffs challenge: (1) the district court's allocation of the burden of proof with regard to the four claims of self-dealing; (2) the standard employed by the court to determine whether Herrig's self-dealing was fair and reasonable to Cookies; (3) the finding that any self-dealing by Herrig was done in good faith, and with honesty and fairness; (4) the finding that Herrig breached no duty to disclose crucial facts to Cookies' board before it completed deliberations on Herrig's self-dealing transactions; and (5) the district court's denial of restitution and other equitable remedies as compensation for Herrig's alleged breach of his duty of loyalty. . . .

II. Fiduciary Duties.

Herrig, as an officer and director of Cookies, owes a fiduciary duty to the company and its shareholders. . . . Herrig concedes that Iowa law imposed the same fiduciary responsibilities based on his status as majority stockholder. *See Des Moines Bank & Trust Co. v. George M. Bechtel & Co.,* 243 Iowa 1007, 1082–83, 51 N.W.2d 174, 217 (1952) (hereinafter *Bechtel*). . . .

Appellants . . . claim that Herrig violated his duty of loyalty to Cookies. That duty derives from "the prohibition against self-dealing that inheres in the fiduciary relationship." *Norlin,* 744 F.2d at 264. As a fiduciary, one may not secure for oneself a business opportunity that "in fairness belongs to the corporation." *Rowen v. LeMars Mut. Ins. Co. of Iowa,* 282 N.W.2d 639, 660 (Iowa 1979). As we noted in *Bechtel:*

> Corporate directors and officers may under proper circumstances transact business with the corporation including

the purchase or sale of property, but it must be done in the strictest good faith and with full disclosure of the facts to, and the consent of, all concerned. And the burden is upon them to establish their good faith, honesty and fairness. Such transactions are scanned by the courts with skepticism and the closest scrutiny, and may be nullified on slight grounds. It is the policy of the courts to put such fiduciaries beyond the reach of temptation and the enticement of illicit profit. 243 Iowa 1007, 1081, 51 N.W.2d 174, 216 (1952). . . .

self-interested party

Against this common law backdrop, the legislature enacted section 496A.34, quoted here in pertinent part, that establishes three sets of circumstances under which a director may engage in self-dealing without clearly violating the duty of loyalty:

No contract or other transaction between a corporation and one or more of its directors or any other corporation, firm, association or entity in which one or more of its directors are directors or officers or are financially interested, shall be either void or voidable because of such relationship or interest . . . if any of the following occur:

1. The fact of such relationship or interest is disclosed or known to the board of directors or committee which authorizes, approves, or ratifies the contract or transaction . . . without counting the votes . . . of such interested director.

full disclosure

2. The fact of such relationship or interest is disclosed or known to the shareholders entitled to vote [on the transaction] and they authorize . . . such contract or transaction by vote or written consent.

3. The contract or transaction is fair and reasonable to the corporation.

Some commentators have supported the view that satisfaction of any *one* of the foregoing statutory alternatives, in and of itself, would prove that a director has fully met the duty of loyalty. *See* Hansell, Austin, & Wilcox, *Director Liability Under Iowa Law-Duties and Protections*, 13 J.Corp.L. 369, 382. We are obliged, however, to interpret statutes in conformity with the common law wherever statutory language does not directly negate it. . . . Because the common law and section 496A.34 require directors to show "good faith, honesty, and fairness" in self-dealing, we are persuaded that satisfaction of any one of these three alternatives under the statute would merely preclude us from rendering the transaction void or voidable *outright* solely on the basis "of such [director's] relationship or interest." Iowa Code § 496A.34; *see Bechtel*, 243 Iowa at 1081–82, 51 N.W.2d at 216. To the contrary, we are convinced that the legislature did not intend by this statute to enable a court, in a shareholder's derivative suit, to rubber stamp *any* transaction to which a board of directors or the shareholders of a corporation have consented. Such an interpretation would invite those who stand to gain from such transactions to engage in improprieties to obtain consent. We thus require directors who engage in self-dealing to establish the additional element that they have acted in good faith, honesty, and fairness. *Holi-Rest, Inc. v. Treloar,* 217 N.W.2d 517, 525 (Iowa 1974).

III. Burden of Proof.

[The court held that the district court had appropriately placed the burden of proof on Herrig.]

IV. Standard of Law.

Next, appellants claim the district court applied an inappropriate standard of law to determine whether Herrig's conduct was fair and reasonable to Cookies. Appellants correctly assert that self-dealing transactions must have the earmarks of arms-length transactions before a court can find them to be fair or reasonable. *See Bechtel,* 243 Iowa at 1023, 51 N.W.2d at 184. The crux of appellants' claim is that the court should have focused on the fair market value of Herrig's services to Cookies rather than on the success Cookies achieved as a result of Herrig's actions.

We agree with appellants' contention that corporate profitability should not be the sole criteria by which to test the fairness and reasonableness of Herrig's fees. In this connection, appellants cite authority from the Michigan Supreme Court that we find persuasive:

> Given an instance of alleged director enrichment at corporate expense . . . the burden to establish fairness resting on the director requires not only a showing of "fair price" but also a showing of the fairness of the bargain to the interests of the corporation.

Fill Bldgs., Inc. v. Alexander Hamilton Life Ins. Co., 396 Mich. 453, 241 N.W.2d 466, 469 (1976). Applying such reasoning to the record before us, however, we cannot agree with appellants' assertion that Herrig's services were either unfairly priced or inconsistent with Cookies corporate interest.

There can be no serious dispute that the four agreements in issue—for exclusive distributorship, taco sauce royalty, warehousing, and consulting fees—have all benefited Cookies, as demonstrated by its financial success. Even if we assume Cookies could have procured similar services from other vendors at lower costs, we are not convinced that Herrig's fees were therefore unreasonable or exorbitant. Like the district court, we are not persuaded by appellants' expert testimony that Cookies' sales and profits would have been the same under agreements with other vendors. As Cookies' board noted prior to Herrig's takeover, he was the driving force in the corporation's success. Even plaintiffs' expert acknowledged that Herrig has done the work of at least five people— production supervisor, advertising specialist, warehouseman, broker, and salesman. . . . [T]he expert conceded that Herrig may in fact be underpaid for all he has accomplished. We believe the board properly considered this source of Cookies' success when it entered these transactions, as did the district court when it reviewed them. . . .

V. Denial of Equitable Relief.

. . . [T]he record before us aptly demonstrates that all members of Cookies' board were well aware of Herrig's dual ownership in Lakes and Speed's. We are unaware of any authority supporting plaintiffs' contention that Herrig was obligated to disclose to Cookies' board or shareholders the extent of his profits resulting from these distribution and warehousing agreements; nevertheless, the exclusive distribution agreement with Lakes authorized the board to ascertain that information had it so desired. Appellants cannot reasonably claim that Herrig owed Cookies a duty to render such services at no profit to himself or his companies. Having found that the compensation he received from these agreements was fair and reasonable, we are convinced that Herrig furnished sufficient pertinent information to Cookies' board to enable it to make prudent decisions concerning the contracts. . . .

We concur in the trial court's assessment of the evidence presented and affirm its dismissal of plaintiffs' claims.

AFFIRMED.

All Justices concur except SCHULTZ, J., who dissents.

■ SCHULTZ, JUSTICE (dissenting). . . .

I believe that Herrig failed on his burden of proof by what he did not show. He did not produce evidence of the local going rate for distribution contracts or storage fees outside of a very limited amount of self-serving testimony. He simply did not show the fair market value of his services or expense for freight, advertising and storage cost. He did not show that his taco sauce royalty was fair. This was his burden. He cannot succeed on it by merely showing the success of the company.

. . . The appellants have put forth convincing testimony that Herrig has been grossly over compensated for his services based on their fair market value. Appellant's expert witness, a CPA, performed an analysis to show what the company would have earned if it had hired a $65,000 a year executive officer, paid a marketing supervisor and an advertising agency a commission of five percent of the sales each, built a new warehouse and hired a warehouseman. It was compared with what the company actually did make under Herrig's management. The analysis basically shows what the operating cost of this company should be on the open market when hiring out the work to experts. In 1985 alone, the company's income would have doubled what it actually made were these changes made. The evidence clearly shows that the fair market value of those services is considerably less than what Herrig actually has been paid.

Similarly, appellant's food broker expert witness testified that for $110,865, what the CPA analysis stated was the fair market value for brokerage services, his company would have provided all of the services that Herrig had performed. The company actually paid $730,637 for the services, a difference of $620,000 in one year.

In summary, I believe the majority was dazzled by the tales of Herrig's efforts and Cookies' success in these difficult economic times. In the process, however, it is forgotten that Herrig owes a fiduciary duty to the corporation to deal fairly and reasonably with it in his self-dealing transactions. Herrig is not entitled to skim off the majority of the profits through self-dealing transactions unless they are fair to the minority stockholders. At trial, he failed to prove how his charges were in line with what the company could have gotten on the open market. Because I cannot ignore this inequity to the company and its shareholders, I must respectfully dissent.

————

NOTES ON THE EFFECT OF APPROVAL OF SELF-INTERESTED TRANSACTIONS BY DISINTERESTED DIRECTORS

1.   The Utility of Further Review. Even though a self-dealing transaction has been authorized by disinterested directors, there are reasons why the transaction should nevertheless be subject to some review for substantive fairness, although a more limited review than would be applied in the absence of such an authorization.

First, by virtue of their personal relationships, directors are unlikely to treat each other with the degree of wariness they would apply to third parties.

Second, a review of the *substantive* fairness of a self-dealing transaction may be thought of as a surrogate for a review of the fairness of the *process* by which the transaction was approved. In a world of perfect information, a court could always determine, by direct means, whether directors who approved a self-interested transaction involving one or more of their colleagues were objective and impartial, and whether they approached the transaction with that degree of wariness with which they would approach transactions with third parties. In the real world, the courts may need to make these determinations by indirect means. If a self-dealing transaction that has been approved by directors who are technically disinterested is substantively unfair, it can normally be inferred that either the approving directors were not objective and impartial in fact, or that they were not as wary as they should have been because they were dealing with a colleague.

2.   Statutory-Judicial Approaches. Most states have adopted statutes, like those of California, Delaware, New York, and the Model Act, that address the effect of approval of self-dealing transactions by disinterested directors. An important question under these statutes is whether they preclude a judicial inquiry into the fairness of self-dealing transactions that have been so approved. Many of the statutes are susceptible to the interpretation that approval by disinterested directors precludes a judicial inquiry into fairness, but most or all of the statutes can also be interpreted not to preclude such an inquiry. The statutes fall into several categories in this regard:

a). Some of the statutes, such as the California statute, expressly require some form of fairness test even if a transaction has been approved by disinterested directors.

b). Many of the statutes, such as the Delaware statute, explicitly require that approval by disinterested directors be in good faith, and such a requirement can be implied even where it is not explicit. It is often obscure whether a good-faith test is strictly subjective or has an objective content as well. For example, UCC § 2–103 provides that in the case of a merchant, good faith is defined to include "the observance of reasonable commercial standards of fair dealing in the trade." Similarly, in *Sam Wong & Son, Inc. v. New York Mercantile Exchange,* 735 F.2d 653, 671, 678 & n. 32 (2d Cir.1984), Judge Friendly held that the rationality of a decision was relevant in determining whether the decision had been made in good faith. "By this," he added, "we mean only a minimal requirement of some basis in reason. [A]bsent some basis in reason, action could hardly be in good faith even apart from ulterior motive." Even courts that seem to use the term "good faith" in a relatively subjective way characteristically go on to review a decision to determine if it is irrational, egregious, or the like, this shows bad faith. Because of the uncertain meaning of good faith (see Section 2, infra), a good-faith requirement opens the door to some judicial scrutiny of the fairness of self-dealing transactions that have been approved by disinterested directors.

c). Many of the remaining statutes can be interpreted to merely change the common law rule that self-dealing transactions are voidable without regard to fairness, rather than to preclude review for fairness. Thus, some courts have held that such a statute either renders a self-interested transaction not automatically voidable (that is, not voidable even if fair) or shifts the burden of proof. In addition to *Cookies Food Products,* see, e.g., Holi-Rest, Inc. v. Treloar, 217 N.W.2d 517, 525 (Iowa 1974); Cohen v. Ayers, 596 F.2d 733, 740–41 (7th Cir.1979); Remillard Brick Co. v. Remillard-Dandini Co., 109 Cal.App.2d 405, 241 P.2d 66 (1952); Gaillard v. Natomas Co., 208 Cal.App.3d 1250, 256 Cal.Rptr. 702 (1989).

3.   *Delaware.* In contrast, in *Marciano v. Nakash,* 535 A.2d 400 (Del.1987), the Delaware Supreme Court stated that "approval by fully-informed disinterested directors under [Delaware Gen. Corp. Law] section 144(a)(1), or disinterested stockholders under section 144(a)(2), permits invocation of the business judgment rule and limits judicial review to issues of gift or waste with the burden of proof upon the party attacking the transaction." Similarly, in *Oberly v. Kirby,* 592 A.2d 445 (Del.1991) the Delaware Supreme Court said "The key to upholding an interested transaction is the approval of some neutral decision-making body. Under 8 *Del.C.* § 144, a transaction will be sheltered from shareholder challenge if approved by . . . a committee of independent directors [or] the shareholders. . . . "

4. *The Model Act's Regulatory Approach.* By far the most detailed approach to self-dealing transactions is set forth in Subchapter F of the Model Act—MBCA §§ 8.60–8.63. The draftsmen of the Model Act make clear that when a self-dealing transaction that falls within its provisions is approved per the process set forth in the act that the transaction itself will not thereafter be subject to further judicial review and the self-dealing director will not be liable for damages because of such conflict. The comment does observe that despite such approval the transaction may be challenged and the self-dealing director could be liable for damages "on some basis other than the conflict." Section 8.60 broadly defines transactions that fall within the provision as both transactions in which the director "is a party" as well as transactions in which the director has an indirect conflicts of interest through the definition of a "related person," e.g., a director or officer of an entity dealing with the corporation. Notably more rigorous than the earlier generation of conflict of interest statutes, such as the Delaware and New York statutes, the Model Act is very precise in setting forth the requirements that must be met for disinterested director and shareholder approval. *See* MBCA §§ 8.62 & 8.63. Section 8.61 clearly states compliance with either of these two sections insulates the transaction and the conflicted party to challenge because of such conflict.

5. *The ALI Weighs in.* It is widely believed that regardless of the form of the statute, at least outside Delaware, approval by disinterested directors will not prevent a court from reviewing self-interested transactions for obvious unfairness. Section 5.02(a)(2)(B) of the ALI's Principles of Corporate Governance makes this implicit rule explicit, by adopting a test intermediate between the business-judgment rule and a full-fairness test in cases where a self-interested transaction has been approved by disinterested directors. Under that Section, where there has been authorization by disinterested directors, the complainant must show that disinterested directors "could not [have] reasonably . . . believed" the transaction to be fair to the corporation. This test is intended to be easier for the director or senior executive to satisfy than a full-fairness test, although harder to satisfy than the business-judgment standard. Even in Delaware, it may be necessary to show that the directors who approved the transaction were not only disinterested, but independent, and directors who passively approve a manifestly unfair transaction may be deemed to exhibit a lack of independence by virtue of that conduct.

———

NEW YORK STOCK EXCHANGE LISTED
COMPANY MANUAL § 312.03(a)

[See Statutory Supplement]

———

NOTES ON SHAREHOLDER RATIFICATION

An outside limit on the power of even disinterested directors or shareholders is the principle of waste. This principle was defined and explained as follows by Chancellor Allen in *Lewis v. Vogelstein*, 699 A.2d 327, 336 (Del. Ch. 1999):

> The judicial standard for determination of corporate waste is well developed. Roughly, a waste entails an exchange of corporate assets for consideration so disproportionately small as to lie beyond the range at which any reasonable person might be willing to trade. Most often the claim is associated with a transfer of corporate assets that serves no corporate purpose; or for which no consideration at all is received. Such a transfer is in effect a gift. If, however, there is any substantial consideration received by the corporation, and if there is a *good faith judgment* that in the circumstances the transaction is worthwhile, there should be no finding of waste, even if the fact finder would conclude ex post that the transaction was unreasonably risky. Any other rule would deter corporate boards from the optimal rational acceptance of risk, for reasons explained elsewhere. Courts are ill-fitted to attempt to weigh the "adequacy" of consideration under the waste standard or, ex post, to judge appropriate degrees of business risk.

Chancellor Allen's definition was later quoted with approval by the Delaware Supreme Court in *Brehm v. Eisner*, 746 A.2d 244, n. 62 (2000).

The issue of waste therefore overlaps with the issue, what is the effect of shareholder ratification of a conflict-of-interest transaction.

1. *Differing Views on Effect of Ratification.* Former Chancellor Allen, in *Lewis v. Vogelstein*, 699 A.2d 327, 334–336 (1997), thoughtfully examined the possible effects of shareholder ratification of a self-dealing transaction.

> What is the effect under Delaware corporation law of shareholder ratification of an interested transaction? The answer to this apparently simple question appears less clear than one would hope or indeed expect. Four possible effects of shareholder ratification appear logically available: First, one might conclude that an effective shareholder ratification acts as a complete defense to any charge of breach of duty. Second, one might conclude that the effect of such ratification is to shift the substantive test on judicial review of the act from one of fairness that would otherwise obtain (because the transaction is an interested one) to one of waste. Third, one might conclude that the ratification shifts the burden of proof of unfairness to plaintiff, but leaves that shareholder protective test in place. Fourth, one might conclude (perhaps because of great respect for the collective action disabilities that attend shareholder action in public corporations) that shareholder ratification offers no assurance of assent of a character that deserves judicial recognition. Thus, under this approach, ratification on full information would be afforded no effect. Excepting the fourth of these effects, there are cases in this jurisdiction that reflect each of

these approaches to the effect of shareholder voting to approve a transaction. . . .

1. *Ratification generally:* I start with principles broader than those of corporation law. Ratification is a concept deriving from the law of agency which contemplates the ex post conferring upon or confirming of the legal authority of an agent in circumstances in which the agent had no authority or arguably had no authority. Restatement (Second) of Agency § 82 (1958). To be effective, of course, the agent must fully disclose all relevant circumstances with respect to the transaction to the principal prior to the ratification. See, e.g., Breen Air Freight, Ltd. v. Air Cargo, Inc., et al., 470 F.2d 767, 773 (2d Cir.1972); Restatement (Second) of Agency § 91 (1958). Beyond that, since the relationship between a principal and agent is fiduciary in character, the agent in seeking ratification must act not only with candor, but with loyalty. Thus an attempt to coerce the principal's consent improperly will invalidate the effectiveness of the ratification. Restatement (Second) of Agency § 100 (1958). . . .

Assuming that a ratification by an agent is validly obtained, what is its effect? One way of conceptualizing that effect is that it provides, after the fact, the grant of authority that may have been wanting at the time of the agent's act. Another might be to view the ratification as consent or as an estoppel by the principal to deny a lack of authority. See Restatement (Second) of Agency § 103 (1958). In either event the effect of informed ratification is to validate or affirm the act of the agent as the act of the principal. Id. § 82. . . .

2. *Shareholder ratification:* [The] differences between shareholder ratification of director action and classic ratification by a single principal, . . . lead to a difference in the effect of a valid ratification in the shareholder context. The principal novelty added to ratification law generally by the shareholder context, is the idea—no doubt analogously present in other contexts in which common interests are held—that, in addition to a claim that ratification was defective because of incomplete information or coercion, shareholder ratification is subject to a claim by a member of the class that the ratification is ineffectual (1) because a majority of those affirming the transaction had a conflicting interest with respect to it or (2) because the transaction that is ratified constituted a corporate waste. As to the second of these, it has long been held that shareholders may not ratify a waste except by a unanimous vote. Saxe v. Brady, 40 Del.Ch. 474, 184 A.2d 602, 605 (1962). The idea behind this rule is apparently that a transaction that satisfies the high standard of waste constitutes a gift of corporate property and no one should be forced against their will to make a gift of their property. In all events, informed, uncoerced, disinterested shareholder ratification of a transaction in which corporate directors have a material conflict of interest has the effect

of protecting the transaction from judicial review except on the basis of waste. . . .

2. *The Contemporary Delaware Perspective.* The most significant consequence of a transaction constituting waste is that waste cannot be ratified by less than unanimous shareholder approval. Moreover, even this qualification still leaves open to what extent ratification should extend outside the realm of self-dealing transactions. That is, state conflict of interest statutes, such as the N.Y. Bus. Corp. L. § 703 and Del. Gen. Corp. L. § 144, clearly embrace shareholder approval as one of three mechanisms to address self-dealing transactions; the statutes leave open, however, the effect of such approval. And what about claims of self-interest, such as illustrated in *Gantler* and *Shocking Technologies* that appear earlier in this chapter? Would ratification insulate the defendant's conduct in those cases? For the last four decades, despite Allen's erudite analysis, there has been a good deal of confusion in Delaware regarding this matter. J. Travis Laster, The Effect of Stockholder Approval on Enhanced Scrutiny, 40 Wm. Mitchell L. Rev., 1443, 1445 (2014.).

The fog surrounding ratification appears to have been lifted on this question in *Corwin v. KKR Fin. Holdings, LLC*, 125 A.3d 304, 312–314 (Del. 2015), dismissing a claim that directors breached their fiduciary duties diligently to take steps to seek the best offer when selling the company.

> [W]hen . . . [there is no evidence of self-dealing], the long-standing policy of our law has been to avoid the uncertainties and costs of judicial second-guessing when the disinterested stockholders have had the free and informed chance to decide on the economic merits of a transaction for themselves. There are sound reasons for this policy. When the real parties in interest—the disinterested equity owners—can easily protect themselves at the ballot box by simply voting no, the utility of a litigation-intrusive standard of review promises more costs to stockholders in the form of litigation rents and inhibitions on risk-taking than it promises in terms of benefits to them. The reason for that is tied to the core rationale of the business judgment rule, which is that judges are poorly positioned to evaluate the wisdom of business decisions and there is little utility to having them second-guess the determination of impartial decision-makers with more information (in the case of directors) or an actual economic stake in the outcome (in the case of informed, disinterested stockholders). In circumstances, therefore, where the stockholders have had the voluntary choice to accept or reject a transaction, the business judgment rule standard of review is the presumptively correct one and best facilitates wealth creation through the corporate form.

Corwin itself is more fully examined in Chapter 14's treatment of the fiduciary obligations of directors when there is a change of control of the firm.

3. *The Issue of Bundling.* *Corwin* involved the firm selling itself to an unrelated firm. As will be seen in Chapter 15, such transactions require shareholder approval. Under *Corwin's* formulation, we can understand the

shareholder vote as involving two distinct approvals combined into a single vote: approval of the transaction and excusing the directors of their failure to diligently shop for a better offer. While not a Hobson's choice, the choice is a distorted one. The shareholders may well wish both to take the deal that is on the table—especially if there is then no other competing offer—other than not to undertake the sale that provides a modest premium over the status quo and pursue a claim against the directors for breaching their fiduciary obligations. However, *Corwin* holds that their approval of the deal forecloses their pursuing the directors. Earlier, in a part of the *Gantler* decision that was not included in these materials, *Gantler* stated that ratification must be via a vote that is distinct from the one that is undertaken to comply with a statute, e.g., shareholders must approve most mergers. *Corwin* rejected this position, so that ratification can occur as a consequence of the shareholder approval that is mandated for such transactions by statute, provided there is full disclosure and the vote is not coerced. But is bundling in such a context inherently coercive?

4.   *Reach of Ratification Statutes.* Some acts are beyond ratification or even incapable of validation as a matter of equity. This occurs when the act or transaction is deemed void *ab initio* as a result of a failure to comply with the corporate statute or the articles of incorporation. *See e.g.,* STAAR Surgical Co. v. Waggoner, 588 A.2d 1130 (Del. 1991). In 2013, Delaware added Section 204 to the DGCL to provide a process by which corporations can validate such defective corporate acts. Once the steps set forth in Section 204 are completed the earlier defective act is deemed ratified and the ratification relates back to the date the act was originally taken. Breathing life into what was to be legally dead can obviously have uncertain consequences. Thus, a companion provision, DGCL § 205, confers jurisdiction on the Delaware Court of Chancery over the efficacy of, and effects to be accorded, the ratification. New Section 204 does not apply to acts, discussed above, that are *voidable* but not void for which the doctrinal form of ratification is available. *See also,* MBCA §§ 1.46–1.52.

---

3. COMPENSATION

Aggarwal, Executive Compensation and Corporate Controversy
Review 849, 850–56 (2003).

. . . [T]he increase in executive compensation has sparked a growing debate about whether such compensation is excessive, especially when average workers' incomes have been relatively stagnant. Furthermore, the highly publicized bankruptcies . . . [and] the collapse in share prices since 2000 have led some to argue that executive compensation practices, specifically the granting of stock options, are pernicious. Do executive compensation packages provide appropriate incentives to managers, thereby aligning their interests with those of shareholders, or do they actually destroy shareholder value over the medium to long-run?

Much of the discussion in the academic literature has focused on the degree to which managers' interests are aligned with those of shareholders. . . .

II. The Structure of Executive Compensation

In order to understand the determinants of incentives, we must first understand the components of executive compensation. . . .

Total annual compensation can be divided into two categories—short-term components of compensation and long-term components of compensation.

II.1. Short-Term Components of Compensation

Short-term components of compensation include salary, bonus, and other annual compensation. Annual salary is fixed in advance and generally does not have an incentive component associated with it. The exception to this statement is that future increases in salary may in part be determined by current firm performance. Jensen and Murphy (1990) show that the present value of current and future increases in salary and bonuses are a small fraction of total incentives.

Annual bonuses are typically tied to measures of firm performance. Interestingly, the performance measures are often based on accounting information such as earnings, sales, or operating income. Common metrics employed include return on equity (ROE), return on assets (ROA), return on investment (ROI), and economic value added (EVA). Other measures of performance include subjective reports by board members or superiors for lower ranking executives and targets established by the board for investment, product or plant quality (e.g., "zero-defects"), market share, growth rates for income or sales, strategic objectives (e.g., expansion into new lines of business or restructuring of old businesses), and performance relative to that of industry competitors.

There are several points to note about short-term components of compensation. While short-term compensation does have some incentive features (especially the bonus component), it is typically not linked to stock performance in the form of stock returns. Given that shareholders presumably care most about stock returns, this is somewhat surprising. It will become apparent, however, that long-term components of compensation are much more strongly linked to stock returns. For this reason, the right way to think about annual salary and bonuses is that salary provides the executive with a minimum level of income prior to any performance standards or targets being met. Bonuses typically reflect how well the firm or executive has met non-stock return based objectives established by the board. Other annual compensation is usually negligible. . . .

II.2.   Long-Term Components of Compensation

Long-term components of compensation include new grants of restricted stock, new grants of stock options, long-term incentive plan payouts, and all other compensation. All other compensation typically includes gross-ups for tax liabilities, perquisites, preferential discounts on stock purchases, contributions to benefit plans, and severance payments and is usually relatively unimportant.

II.2.a.   Restricted Stock

Restricted stock grants are restricted in the sense that the executive must remain with the firm for a specified amount of time in order not to forfeit the stock grant. Restricted stock grants with a five-year vesting period are typical. There are two practical implications of this restriction. First, the executive has potentially a strong incentive to stay with the firm in order to benefit from the grant. Second, while the vesting period is in effect, the executive cannot sell the stock. She is, in effect, forced to have part of her compensation tied to firm performance over the vesting period. Restricted stock grants clearly align an executive's interests with those of her shareholders. . . .

II.2.b.   Stock Options

Stock options have become the primary mechanism through which managers' interests are aligned with those of shareholders. A stock option gives the manager the right but not the obligation to purchase a share of the firm's stock for a pre-specified price (known as the exercise price) on or before a pre-specified date. Most stock options are granted at the money, which means that the exercise price is set equal to the stock price on the day of the grant. A typical stock option grant has a life of ten years. Since stock prices on average increase from year to year, over time most stock options will move into the money, meaning that the current stock price is greater than the exercise price. Stock options usually have a vesting schedule associated with them, such as 10% of an option grant vests every six months, so that the full grant vests over five years with another five years to maturity. . . .

For tax purposes, I focus on non-qualified options, which are the form of stock options that most executives receive. Non-qualified options have no tax implication at the time that they are issued. When the option is exercised, the executive pays tax on the difference between the stock price and the exercise price at the ordinary income tax rate. The firm deducts the difference between the stock price and the exercise price as compensation expense. If the executive later sells the stock, then the executive pays tax on the difference between the sale price and the market price at exercise of the option at the capital gains tax rate. Because the firm is able to deduct the difference between the stock price at exercise and the exercise price as compensation expense, non-qualified options have favorable tax treatment from the firm's perspective.

Favorable tax treatment is a significant part of the explanation for why the use of stock options has increased so dramatically. . . .

II.2.c.   Long-Term Incentive Plans

Long-term incentive plan payouts are similar to bonuses but are awarded for performance over several years. For example, a long-term incentive plan payout may be triggered if ROA is at least 15% for three consecutive years. In general, long-term incentive plans are not that important on a year to year basis because they occur only when a long-term target is met. . . .

––––––––

NOTE ON TAX TREATMENT OF EXECUTIVE COMPENSATION

The federal income tax helps shape a variety of corporate decisions, including compensation decisions. Under existing tax law, compensation in the form of incentive stock options and non-qualified stock options is given highly favorable treatment. A non-qualified stock option is not taxable when issued, but only when the option is exercised. An incentive stock option is not taxable when issued or when exercised, but only when the stock is sold. Even then, tax is levied at only the capital-gains rate. From the executive's perspective, the tax law therefore provides a push toward using one or more of those forms of compensation.

The multifaceted tax legislation enacted in late 2017 eliminated the exception for "performance-based compensation." As amended, the IRC disallows the deduction of compensation to the extent the amount paid to the CEO, the CFO, and the three most highly compensated officers (other than the CEO and CFO) exceeds $1 million per individual. The provision applies only to public companies.

––––––––

DEL. GEN. CORP. LAW §§ 141(h), 157

[See Statutory Supplement]

––––––––

MODEL BUS. CORP. ACT §§ 6.24, 8.11

[See Statutory Supplement]

––––––––

ALI, PRINCIPLES OF CORPORATE GOVERNANCE § 5.03

[See Statutory Supplement]

––––––––

NEW YORK STOCK EXCHANGE LISTED
COMPANY MANUAL § 312.03(a)

[See Statutory Supplement]

―――――

SEC REGULATION S-K, ITEM 402

[See Statutory Supplement]

―――――

IN RE THE WALT DISNEY COMPANY
DERIVATIVE LITIGATION

[Chapter 9, Section 2, supra]

―――――

In re Inv'rs Bancorp, Inc. Stockholder Litig.

Supreme Court of Delaware, 2017.
177 A.3d 1208.

■ SEITZ, JUSTICE:

In this appeal we consider the limits of the stockholder ratification defense when directors make equity awards to themselves under the general parameters of an equity incentive plan. . . .

For equity incentive plans in which the award terms are fixed and the directors have no discretion how they allocate the awards, the stockholders know exactly what they are being asked to approve. But, other plans—like the equity incentive plan in this appeal—create a pool of equity awards that the directors can later award to themselves in amounts and on terms they decide. The Court of Chancery has recognized a ratification defense for such discretionary plans as long as the plan has "meaningful limits" on the awards directors can make to themselves. If the discretionary plan does not contain meaningful limits, the awards, if challenged, are subject to an entire fairness standard of review. . . .

I.

. . . The defendants fall into two groups—ten non-employee director defendants and two executive director defendants. Investors Bancorp, the nominal defendant, is a Delaware corporation with its principal place of business in Short Hills, New Jersey. Investors Bancorp is a holding company for Investors Bank, a New Jersey chartered savings bank with corporate headquarters in Short Hills, New Jersey. The Company operates 143 banking branches in New Jersey and New York. In 2014, after a mutual-to-stock conversion, Investors Bancorp conducted a second-step offering to the public, which is when the plaintiffs acquired their shares. In this second-step offering, the Company sold 219,580,695 shares and raised about $2.15 billion.

The board sets director compensation based on recommendations of the Compensation and Benefits Committee ("Committee"), composed of seven of the ten non-employee directors. . . . As the Court of Chancery noted, the annual compensation for all non-employee directors ranged from $97,200 to $207,005, with $133,340 as the average amount of compensation per director. . . .

In 2014, Cummings, the Company's President and CEO . . . [compensation] totaled $2,778,700. Cama, the Company's COO and Senior Executive Vice President . . . compensation . . . totaled $1,665,794.

At the end of 2014, following completion of the conversion plan, the Committee met to review 2014 director compensation and set compensation for 2015. Gregory Keshishian, a compensation consultant from GK Partners, Inc., presented to the board a study of director compensation for eighteen publicly held peer companies. According to the study, these companies paid their non-employee directors an average of $157,350 in total compensation. The Company's $133,340 average non-employee director compensation in 2014 fell close to the study average. Following the presentation, the Committee recommended to the board that the non-employee director compensation package remain the same for 2015. . . .

Just a few months after setting the 2015 board compensation, in March, 2015, the board proposed the 2015 EIP [Equity Incentive Plan]. The EIP was intended to "provide additional incentives for [the Company's] officers, employees and directors to promote [the Company's] growth and performance and to further align their interests with those of [the Company's] stockholders . . . and give [the Company] the flexibility [needed] to continue to attract, motivate and retain highly qualified officers, employees and directors."

The Company reserved 30,881,296 common shares for restricted stock awards, restricted stock units, incentive stock options, and non-qualified stock options for the Company's 1,800 officers, employees, non-employee directors, and service providers. The EIP has limits within each category. Of the total shares, a maximum of 17,646,455 can be issued for stock options or restricted stock awards and 13,234,841 for restricted stock units or performance shares. Those limits are further broken down for employee and non-employee directors:

- A maximum of 4,411,613 shares, in the aggregate (25% of the shares available for stock option awards), may be issued or delivered to any one employee pursuant to the exercise of stock options;

- A maximum of 3,308,710 shares, in the aggregate (25% of the shares available for restricted stock awards and restricted stock units), may be issued or delivered to any one employee as a restricted stock or restricted stock unit grant; and

• The maximum number of shares that may be issued or delivered to all non-employee directors, in the aggregate, pursuant to the exercise of stock options or grants of restricted stock or restricted stock units shall be 30% of all option or restricted stock shares available for awards, "all of which may be granted in any calendar year."

According to the proxy sent to stockholders, "[t]he number, types and terms of awards to be made pursuant to the [EIP] are subject to the discretion of the Committee and have not been determined at this time, and will not be determined until subsequent to stockholder approval." At the Company's June 9, 2015 annual meeting, 96.25% of the voting shares approved the EIP (79.1% of the total shares outstanding). . . .

[In the ensuing two weeks, the Committee held four meetings that resulted in the Committee approving awards of restricted stock and stock options to all board members. According to the complaint, these awards were not part of the final 2015 compensation package nor discussed in any prior meetings. The Committee was advised by its outside counsel and relied heavily on its compensation consultant Keshishian; central to their decision was a list of the stock options and awards granted by the 164 companies that underwent mutual-to-stock conversions in the then preceding twenty years. The complaint, however, alleged that the list did not compare five other companies on the list that met the criteria and had more recently undergone conversions—each of which granted significantly lower awards. At the fourth meeting, the directors awarded themselves 7.8 million shares. Non-employee directors each received 250,000 stock options—valued at $780,000—and 100,000 restricted shares—valued at $1,254,000. Peer companies' non-employee awards averaged $175,817. Cummings received 1,333,333 stock options and 1,000,000 restricted shares, valued at $16,699,999 and it was alleged this was 1,759% higher than the peer companies' average compensation for executive directors. Cama received 1,066,666 stock options and 600,000 restricted shares, valued at $13,359,998, an amount alleged to be 2,571% higher than the peer companies' average. According to the complaint, the total fair value of the awards was $51,653,997. . . .]

After the Company disclosed the awards, stockholders filed three separate complaints in the Court of Chancery alleging breaches of fiduciary duty by the directors for awarding themselves excessive compensation. . . .

The Court of Chancery . . . dismissed the plaintiffs' complaint . . . [on the grounds] the EIP contained "meaningful, specific limits on awards to all director beneficiaries" . . . . We review the Court of Chancery decision dismissing the complaint *de novo*.

II.

Unless restricted by the certificate of incorporation or bylaws, Section 141(h) of Delaware General Corporation Law ("DGCL") authorizes the board "to fix the compensation of directors." Although authorized to do so by statute, when the board fixes its compensation, it is self-interested in the decision because the directors are deciding how much they should reward themselves for board service. If no other factors are involved, the board's decision will "lie outside the business judgment rule's presumptive protection, so that, where properly challenged, the receipt of self-determined benefits is subject to an affirmative showing that the compensation arrangements are fair to the corporation." In other words, the entire fairness standard of review will apply.

Other factors do sometimes come into play. When a fully informed, uncoerced, and disinterested majority of stockholders approve the board's authorized corporate action, the stockholders are said to have ratified the corporate act. Stockholder ratification of corporate acts applies in different corporate law settings. Here, we address the affirmative defense of stockholder ratification of director self-compensation decisions. . . .

III.

A.

As ratification has evolved for stockholder-approved equity incentive plans, the courts have recognized the defense in three situations—when stockholders approved the specific director awards; when the plan was self-executing, meaning the directors had no discretion when making the awards; or when directors exercised discretion and determined the amounts and terms of the awards after stockholder approval. The first two scenarios present no real problems. When stockholders know precisely what they are approving, ratification will generally apply. The rub comes, however, in the third scenario, when directors retain discretion to make awards under the general parameters of equity incentive plans. . . .

We think . . . when it comes to the discretion directors exercise following stockholder approval of an equity incentive plan, ratification cannot be used to foreclose the Court of Chancery from reviewing those further discretionary actions when a breach of fiduciary duty claim has been properly alleged. As the Court of Chancery emphasized in *Sample* [*v. Morgan*, 914 A.2d 647 (Del. Ch. 2007)], using an expression coined many years ago, director action is "twice-tested," first for legal authorization, and second by equity.[81] When stockholders approve the general parameters of an equity compensation plan and allow directors to exercise their "broad legal authority" under the plan, they do so "precisely because they know that that authority must be exercised

---

[81] *Sample*, 914 A.2d at 672 (Strine, V.C.) (citing Adolf A. Berle, *Corporate Powers as Powers in Trust*, 44 HARV. L. REV. 1049, 1049 (1931)) ("Corporate acts thus must be 'twice-tested'—once by the law and again by equity.").

consistently with equitable principles of fiduciary duty."[82] The
stockholders have granted the directors the legal authority to make
awards. But, the directors' exercise of that authority must be done
consistent with their fiduciary duties. Given that the actual awards are
self-interested decisions not approved by the stockholders, if the directors
acted inequitably when making the awards, their "inequitable action
does not become permissible simply because it is legally possible"[83] under
the general authority granted by the stockholders.

. . . [W]hen a stockholder properly alleges that the directors breached
their fiduciary duties when exercising their discretion after stockholders
approve the general parameters of an equity incentive plan, the directors
should have to demonstrate that their self-interested actions were
entirely fair to the company.[85]

B.

The Investors Bancorp EIP is a discretionary plan as described
above. It covers about 1,800 officers, employees, non-employee directors,
and service providers. Specific to the directors, the plan reserves
30,881,296 shares of common stock for restricted stock awards, restricted
stock units, incentive stock options, and non-qualified stock options for
the Company's officers, employees, non-employee directors, and service
providers. Of those reserved shares and other equity, the non-employee
directors were entitled to up to 30% of all option and restricted stock
shares, all of which could be granted in any calendar year. But, "[t]he
number, types, and terms of the awards to be made pursuant to the [EIP]
are subject to the discretion of the Committee and have not been
determined at this time, and will not be determined until subsequent to
stockholder approval."

When submitted to the stockholders for approval, the stockholders
were told that "[b]y approving the Plan, stockholders will give [the
Company] the flexibility [it] need[s] to continue to attract, motivate and
retain highly qualified officers, employees and directors by offering a
competitive compensation program that is linked to the performance of
[the Company's] common stock." The complaint alleges that this
representation was reasonably interpreted as forward-looking. In other
words, by approving the EIP, stockholders understood that the directors
would reward Company employees for future performance, not past
services.

---

[82] *Id.* at 584.

[83] *Schnell v. Chris-Craft Ind., Inc.*, 285 A.2d 437, 439 (Del. 1971). As noted in *Desimone v. Barrows*, 924 A.2d 908, 917 (Del. Ch. 2007), "[s]pecifying the precise amount and form of director compensation . . . 'ensure[s] integrity' in the underlying principal-agent relationship between stockholders and directors."

[85] For example, in *Seinfeld* [*v. Slager*, 2012 Del. Ch. LEXIS 139 (Del. Ch. June 29, 2012)], the Court of Chancery refused to extend stockholder approval of the plan to the awards themselves. . . .The directors had the "theoretical ability to award themselves as much as tens of millions of dollars per year, with few limitations." *Id.* The board was also "free to use its absolute discretion . . . with little guidance as to the total pay that can be awarded." *Id.* . . . .

After stockholders approved the EIP, the board eventually approved just under half of the stock options available to the directors and nearly thirty percent of the shares available to the directors as restricted stock awards, based predominately on a five-year going forward vesting period. The plaintiffs argue that the directors breached their fiduciary duties by granting themselves these awards because they were unfair and excessive. According to the plaintiffs, the stockholders were told the EIP would reward future performance, but the Board instead used the EIP awards to reward past efforts for the mutual-to-stock conversion—which the directors had already accounted for in determining their 2015 compensation packages. Also, according to the plaintiffs, the rewards were inordinately higher than peer companies'. As alleged in the complaint, the Board paid each non-employee director more than $2,100,000 in 2015, which "eclips[ed] director pay at every Wall Street firm." This significantly exceeded the Company's non-employee director compensation in 2014, which ranged from $97,200 to $207,005. It also far surpassed the $198,000 median pay at similarly sized companies and the $260,000 median pay at much larger companies. And the awards were over twenty-three times more than the $87,556 median award granted to other companies' non-employee directors after mutual-to-stock conversions.

In addition, according to the complaint, Cama and Cummings' compensation far exceeded their prior compensation and that of peer companies. Cummings' $20,006,957 total compensation in 2015 was seven times more than his 2014 compensation package of $2,778,000. And Cama's $15,318,257 compensation was nine times more than his 2014 compensation package of $1,665,794. Cummings' $16,699,999 award was 3,683% higher than the median award other companies granted their CEOs after mutual-to-stock conversions. And Cama's $13,359,998 award was 5,384% higher than the median other companies granted their second-highest paid executives after the conversions.[99]

The plaintiffs have alleged facts leading to a pleading stage reasonable inference that the directors breached their fiduciary duties in making unfair and excessive discretionary awards to themselves after stockholder approval of the EIP. Because the stockholders did not ratify the specific awards the directors made under the EIP, the directors must demonstrate the fairness of the awards to the Company. . . .

V.

The Investors Bancorp stockholders approved the general parameters of the EIP. The plaintiffs have properly alleged, however, that the directors, when exercising their discretion under the EIP, acted inequitably in granting themselves unfair and excessive awards. Because the stockholders did not ratify the specific awards under the EIP, the

---

[99] The average awards at peer companies were $898,490 for CEOs and $510,435 for the second-highest paid executives. . . .

affirmative defense of ratification cannot not be used to dismiss the complaint. . . . Thus, the Court of Chancery's decision is reversed, and the case is remanded for further proceedings consistent with this opinion.

————

Ryan v. Gifford

Court of Chancery of Delaware, 2007.
918 A.2d 341.

■ CHANDLER, CHANCELLOR.

On March 18, 2006, The Wall Street Journal sparked controversy throughout the investment community by publishing a one-page article, based on an academic's statistical analysis of option grants, which revealed an arguably questionable compensation practice. Commonly known as backdating, this practice involves a company issuing stock options to an executive on one date while providing fraudulent documentation asserting that the options were actually issued earlier. These options may provide a windfall for executives because the falsely dated stock option grants often coincide with market lows. Such timing reduces the strike prices and inflates the value of stock options, thereby increasing management compensation. This practice allegedly violates any stock option plan that requires strike prices to be no less than the fair market value on the date on which the option is granted by the board. Further, this practice runs afoul of many state and federal common and statutory laws that prohibit dissemination of false and misleading information.

After the article appeared in the Journal, Merrill Lynch issued a report demonstrating that officers of numerous companies, including Maxim Integrated Products, Inc., had benefited from so many fortuitously timed stock option grants that backdating seemed the only logical explanation. The report engendered this action.

Plaintiff Walter E. Ryan alleges that defendants breached their duties of due care and loyalty by approving or accepting backdated options that violated the clear letter of the shareholder-approved Stock Option Plan and Stock Incentive Plan ("option plans"). Individual defendants. . . . move to dismiss this action on its merits. . . .

I. FACTS

Maxim Integrated Products, Inc. is a technology leader in design, development, and manufacture of linear and mixed-signal integrated circuits used in microprocessor-based electronic equipment. From 1998 to mid-2002 Maxim's board of directors and compensation committee granted stock options for the purchase of millions of shares of Maxim's common stock . . . . Under the terms of these plans, Maxim contracted and represented that the exercise price of all stock options granted would be no less than the fair market value of the company's common stock, measured by the publicly traded closing price for Maxim stock on the date of the grant. Additionally, the plan identified the board or a committee designated by the board as administrators of its terms.

Ryan is a shareholder of Maxim. . . . He filed this derivative action on June 2, 2006. . . . Ryan alleges that nine specific grants were backdated between 1998 and 2002, as these grants seem too fortuitously timed to be explained as simple coincidence. All nine grants were dated on unusually low (if not the lowest) trading days of the years in question, or on days immediately before sharp increases in the market price of the company.

A. *Genesis of These Claims*

As practices surrounding the timing of options grants for public companies began facing increased scrutiny in early 2006, Merrill Lynch conducted an analysis of the timing of stock option grants from 1997 to 2002 for the semiconductor and semiconductor equipment companies that comprise the Philadelphia Semiconductor Index. Merrill Lynch measured the aggressiveness of timing of option grants by examining the extent to which stock price performance subsequent to options pricing events diverges from stock price performance over a longer period of time. "Specifically, it looked at annualized stock price returns for the twenty day period subsequent to options pricing in comparison to stock price returns for the calendar year in which the options were granted." In theory, companies should not generate systematic excess return in comparison to other investors as a result of the timing of options pricing events. "[I]f the timing of options grants is an arm's length process, and companies have [not] systematically taken advantage of their ability to backdate options within the [twenty] day windows that the law provided prior to the implementation of Sarbanes-Oxley in 2002, there shouldn't be any difference between the two measures." Merrill Lynch failed to take a position on whether Maxim actually backdated; however, it noted that if backdating did not occur, management of Maxim was remarkably effective at timing options pricing events.

With regard to Maxim, Merrill Lynch found that the twenty-day return on option grants to management averaged 14% over the five-year period, an annualized return of 243%, or almost ten times higher than the 29% annualized market returns in the same period. . . .

II. MOTION TO DISMISS

A. *Futility of Demand Under Rule 23.1*

. . . [In order to for the derivative suit to proceed, the Chancellor considered whether sufficient facts were alleged to excuse a pre-suit demand on the board of directors, a subject examined in Chapter 13. A basis for excusing such a demand is that the alleged backdating was not protected by the business judgment rule.]

A board's knowing and intentional decision to exceed the shareholders' grant of express (but limited) authority raises doubt regarding whether such decision is a valid exercise of business judgment. . . .

Plaintiff supports his claim that backdating occurred by pointing to nine option grants over a six-year period where each option was granted during a low point. That is, every challenged option grant occurred during the lowest market price of the month or year in which it was granted. In addition to pointing specifically to highly suspicious timing, plaintiff further supports his allegations with empirical evidence suggesting that backdating occurred. The Merrill Lynch analysis measured the extent to which stock price performance subsequent to options pricing events diverged from stock price performance over a longer period of time to measure the aggressiveness of the timing of option grants and found that Maxim's average annualized return of 243% on option grants to management was almost ten times higher than the 29% annualized market returns in the same period. This timing, by my judgment and by support of empirical data, seems too fortuitous to be mere coincidence. The appearance of impropriety grows even more when one considers the fact that the board granted options, not at set or designated times, but by a sporadic method.[34]

Plaintiff supports his breach of fiduciary duty claim . . . by pointing to the board's decision to ignore limitations set out in the company's stock options plans. The plans do not grant the board discretion to alter the exercise price by falsifying the date on which options were granted. Thus, the alleged facts suggest that the director defendants violated an express provision of two option plans and exceeded the shareholders' grant of express authority.

Plaintiff here points to specific grants, specific language in option plans, specific public disclosures, and supporting empirical analysis to allege knowing and purposeful violations of shareholder plans and intentionally fraudulent public disclosures. . . . [that] provide sufficient particularity in the pleading to survive a motion to dismiss for failure to make demand pursuant to Rule 23.1. . . .

B.   Failure To State a Claim Upon Which Relief Can Be Granted

Defendants assert . . . that in order to survive a motion to dismiss on a fiduciary duty claim, the complaint must rebut the business judgment rule. That is, plaintiff must raise a reason to doubt that the directors were disinterested or independent. Where the complaint does not rebut the business judgment rule, plaintiff must allege waste. Plaintiff here, argue the defendants, fails to do either. Further, there is no evidence that

---

[34]   Defendants argue repeatedly that plaintiff's allegations ultimately rest upon nothing more than statistical abstractions. Nevertheless, this Court is required to draw reasonable inferences and need not be blind to probability. True, the Merrill Lynch report does not state conclusively that Gifford's options were actually backdated. Rather, it emphatically suggests that either defendant directors knowingly manipulated the dates on which options were granted, or their timing was extraordinarily lucky. Given the choice between improbable good fortune and knowing manipulation of option grants, the Court may reasonably infer the latter, even when applying the heightened pleading standards of Rule 23.1.

the defendants acted intentionally, in bad faith, or for personal gain. Therefore, so the argument goes, plaintiff fails to plead facts sufficient to rebut the business judgment rule and cannot maintain an action for breach of fiduciary duties.

Plaintiff responds that . . . the directors' purposeful failure to honor an unambiguous provision of a shareholder approved stock option plan . . . rebuts the business judgment rule for the purpose of a motion to dismiss for failure to state a claim upon which relief can be granted. . . .

1. *The Business Judgment Rule and Bad Faith*

. . . The business affairs of a corporation are to be managed by or under the direction of its board of directors. In an effort to encourage the full exercise of managerial powers, Delaware law protects the managers of a corporation through the business judgment rule. This rule "is a presumption that in making a business decision the directors of a corporation acted on an informed basis, in good faith and in the honest belief that the action taken was in the best interest of the company." Nevertheless, a showing that the board breached either its fiduciary duty of due care or its fiduciary duty of loyalty in connection with a challenged transaction may rebut this presumption. Such a breach may be shown where the board acts intentionally, in bad faith, or for personal gain. . . .

Based on the allegations of the complaint, and all reasonable inferences drawn therefrom, I am convinced that the intentional violation of a shareholder approved stock option plan, coupled with fraudulent disclosures regarding the directors' purported compliance with that plan, constitute conduct that is disloyal to the corporation and is therefore an act in bad faith. Plaintiffs allege the following conduct: Maxim's directors affirmatively represented to Maxim's shareholders that the exercise price of any option grant would be no less than 100% of the fair value of the shares, measured by the market price of the shares on the date the option is granted. Maxim shareholders, possessing an absolute right to rely on those assurances when determining whether to approve the plans, in fact relied upon those representations and approved the plans. Thereafter, Maxim's directors are alleged to have deliberately attempted to circumvent their duty to price the shares at no less than market value on the option grant dates by surreptitiously changing the dates on which the options were granted. To make matters worse, the directors allegedly failed to disclose this conduct to their shareholders, instead making false representations regarding the option dates in many of their public disclosures.

I am unable to fathom a situation where the deliberate violation of a shareholder approved stock option plan and false disclosures, obviously intended to mislead shareholders into thinking that the directors complied honestly with the shareholder-approved option plan, is anything but an act of bad faith. It certainly cannot be said to amount to faithful and devoted conduct of a loyal fiduciary. Well-pleaded allegations of such conduct are sufficient, in my opinion, to rebut the business judgment rule and to survive a motion to dismiss. . . .

————

NOTE ON "SPRING-LOADED" OPTIONS

If we consider option backdating as allowing the executive to bet on a race that has already occurred, then spring-loaded options can be viewed as giving the executive a running head start in that race. Spring-loading refers to the board awarding options to favored individuals with full knowledge that the corporation will shortly make an announcement, e.g., a major product break through, that will materially boost the company's stock price.

Granting spring-loaded options, without explicit authorization from shareholders, clearly involves an indirect deception. A director's duty of loyalty includes the duty to deal fairly and honestly with the shareholders for whom he is a fiduciary. It is inconsistent with such a duty for a board of directors to ask for shareholder approval of an incentive stock option plan and then later to distribute shares to managers in such a way as to undermine the very objectives approved by shareholders. This remains true even if the board complies with the strict letter of a shareholder-approved plan as it relates to strike prices or issue dates.

The question before the Court is not, as plaintiffs suggest, whether spring-loading constitutes a form of insider trading as it would be understood under federal securities law. The relevant issue is whether a director acts in bad faith by authorizing options with a market-value strike price, as he is required to do by a shareholder-approved incentive option plan, at a time when he *knows* those shares are actually worth more than the exercise price. A director who intentionally uses inside knowledge not available to shareholders in order to enrich employees while avoiding shareholder-imposed requirements cannot, in my opinion, be said to be acting loyally and in good faith as a fiduciary.

This conclusion, however, rests upon at least two premises, each of which should be (and, in this case, has been) alleged by a plaintiff in order to show that a spring-loaded option issued by a disinterested and independent board is nevertheless beyond the bounds of business judgment. First, a plaintiff must allege that options were issued according to a shareholder-approved employee compensation plan. Second, a plaintiff must allege that the directors that approved spring-loaded (or bullet-dodging) options (a) possessed material non-public information soon to be released that would impact the company's share price, and (b) issued those options with the intent to circumvent otherwise valid shareholder-approved restrictions upon the exercise price of the options. Such allegations would satisfy a plaintiff's requirement to show adequately at the pleading stage that a director acted disloyally and in bad faith and is therefore unable to claim the protection of the business judgment rule. Of course, it is conceivable that a director might show that shareholders have expressly empowered the board of directors (or relevant committee) to use backdating, spring-loading,   or   bullet-dodging   as   part   of   employee compensation, and that such actions would not otherwise violate applicable law. But defendants make no such assertion here.

In re Tyson Foods, Inc., 919 A.2d 563, 593–593 (Del. Ch. 2007).

———————

NOTES ON CEO COMPENSATION

The issue of executive compensation today has a high place on the corporate and even the national agenda. Most of the concerns have centered on the compensation of the chief executive officers (CEOs) of publicly held corporations. These complaints have fallen into several categories.

1.   *Big But Is It Bad?* One focus of concern is that CEO compensation is too large as an absolute matter. The mean annual compensation of CEOs of the corporations in the S & P 500 index, expressed in constant dollars, grew from $3.1 million in 1992 to $10.1 million in 2014. (The S & P 500 is a group of stocks that is considered representative of the stock market in general.). A. Edmans, X. Gabaix & D. Jenter, Executive Compensation: A Survey of Theory and Evidence 16 (CESifo Working Paper 2017). This growth is not explained by inflation, because the figures are inflation-adjusted. Total executive compensation experienced its greatest growth in the 1990s as a result of increasing portions of executive compensation being derived from stock-based incentive awards. Today, such awards account for more than sixty percent of the compensation in large cap companies, with less than 20 percent of total executive compensation being the executive's fixed salary (the difference between salary and stock-based being bonuses premised on accounting metrics). *Id.* Tbl. 8–10.

A related concern is that there is too much disparity between CEO compensation and average salaries. "In 1992, the average large-company CEO received approximately 140 times the pay of an average worker; in 2003, the separation was about 500:1." Id. Another comparison is the total pay of U.S. CEOs to compensation CEOs receive elsewhere in the world. *See* Joseph A. McCahery & Zacharias Sautner, Institutional Investor Preferences and Executive Compensation in Research Handbook on Executive Pay 241, 248 (Thomas & Hill eds. 2013)('comparative research shows that the total level of CEO pay in the US is roughly double that in any other country, even allowing for differences in purchasing power and taxation). *See also.* Garth Crystal, In Search of Excess 27, 206–09 (1991).

2.   *A Price to Attract Talent.* Complaints about both the absolute and relative levels of CEO compensation leave many unpersuaded, especially in an era in which so many athletes and entertainment stars earn as much or more as the median CEO in the *Journal* survey. It has also been suggested that CEO compensation should be understood as the prize in a tournament,

for which the corporation's vice-presidents joust. "On the day that a given individual is promoted from vice-president to president, his salary may triple. It is difficult to argue that his skills have tripled in that 1-day period. . . . It is not a puzzle, however, when interpreted in the context of a prize. . . . [A CEO's] wage is settled on not necessarily because it reflects his current productivity as president, but rather because it induces that individual and all other individuals to perform appropriately when they are in more junior positions." Edward Lazear, and Sherwin Rosen, Rank-Order Tournaments as Optimum Labor Contracts, 89 Journal of Political Economy 841 (1981). (The tournament theory of compensation has not been empirically verified. See O'Reilly et al., CEO Compensation Tournament and Social Comparison: A Tale of Two Theories, 33 Admin.Sci.Q. 257, 266 (1988).)

   3. *The Public vs. Private Comparison.* By comparing CEO compensation of companies owned by private equity firms and CEO pay in comparable public companies, Professor Jackson provides a powerful insight into likely weaknesses in the pay of public company executives. He finds that overall CEO pay in companies owned by private equity firms is statistically indistinguishable from that of public companies. Nonetheless, on close inspection, he shows that pay packages of CEOs of firms owned by a private equity firm cause the CEO to bear more than twice the cost of shirking or underperformance than would be borne by the CEO of a public company. "[T]he stronger portfolio incentives that we see in private equity-owned companies are not the result of larger stock and option grants at those companies. Rather, the incentives are stronger because of what happens *after* the CEO receives stock and options: Private equity firms restrict CEOs' freedom to unload the equity they receive as compensation. By contrast, public company directors have long allowed CEOs to unload their stock-based pay. . . . After accounting for the effects of unloading, CEO incentives are much stronger in companies owned by private equity than in public companies." Robert J. Jackson, Jr., Private Equity and Executive Compensation, 60 U.C.L.A. L. Rev. 638, 655 (2013).

   4. *A Different Perspective on Executive Compensation.* A more sanguine perspective on executive compensation is taken by Professor Kaplan. He reports that even though CEO pay increased substantially in the 1990s, CEO pay has declined by more than 30 percent from the peak level reached in 2000. And relative to corporate net income, CEO pay levels for S&P 500 firms are the lowest in twenty years and the ratio of large-company CEO pay to firm market value is about the same as it was in the late 1970s. Steven N. Kaplan, CEO Pay and Corporate Governance in the U.S.: Perceptions, Facts and Challenges, 25 J. Applied Corp. Fin. 8 (2013). Is it appropriate to assess CEO pay relative to firm market value? Is the historical evidence relevant? Persuasive?

   5. *Retirement Benefits for Executives.* Senior executives customarily enjoy substantial retirement benefits. There are two competing theories for such benefits. The positive view is that retirement benefits align the executive with the long-term interests of the corporation by essentially making the executive a creditor of the company for that part of her overall employment package. The negative view is that SEC mandated disclosures

for retirement benefits are opaque in critical ways so that their costs are easier to conceal than other forms of compensation. Robert J. Jackson, Jr. & Colleen Honigsberg, The Hidden Nature of Executive Pay, 100 Va. L. Rev. 479 (2014), provides an extensive study of executive pay provided by public companies, finding that most executive retirement plans are anchored in the company's stock so they are better understood as thinly disguised stock-option plans. And, a substantial number of such plans permit the executive to convert the benefits into cash soon after retiring from the firm. Are these features consistent with the long-term alignment as a firm creditor hypothesis? One implication of this study's findings is that retirement plans anchored in a stock-option with a short-term horizon likely enhances an executive's preference for risk above what it would be if the retirement plan truly transformed the executive's perspective of being a long-term creditor.

Harwell Wells, U.S. Executive Compensation in Historical Perspective, in Research Handbook on Executive Pay 41, 48–49, 55

(Thomas & Hill eds. 2013).

Executive compensation remained a minor issue through the 1960s and early 1970s. . . . The composition of pay did change in the 1960s and early 1970s, due in part to legislative changes. The Revenue Act of 1964, for instance, imposed a longer holding requirement on restricted stock options, leading to a decline in their use, while the Act's new, lower marginal rates produced higher after-tax pay for executives. . . . But this did not change the fundamental pattern of executive compensation, whose growth lagged into the 1970s.

The great puzzle of executive compensation during this time—why did it grow so slowly? . . .

Executive compensation began growing at a faster rate in the mid-1970s. . . . The average CEO was paid approximately 24 times more than the average worker in 1965, 35 times the more in 1979, 71 times more in 1989, and 299 times more than the average worker's pay at the end of the century. . . .

As yet, no fully satisfactory explanation for the long-term evolution of executive compensation, and especially for what appears the crucial transition from a low-growth to a high-growth pay regime in the early 1970s, has appeared. . . .

This has led a few scholars to ask what else changed in the early 1970s that may have changed pay and income patterns. . . . The years during which executive pay was restrained were, after all, also the years during which much of the American political economy operated within an informal concordat between labor unions, big business, and the Federal government, an era in which average workers' wages rose relatively rapidly, as political and economic institutions (notable unions) encouraged wide distribution of the fruits of economic growth, and where high tax rates signaled a broader social consensus that high wages should be moderated. . . . the concordat, which some have dubbed the "Treaty of Detroit" or the "New Deal Order," began eroding in the early 1970s, undermined both by economic changes such as stagflation and slowing productivity, and by political developments, notably the erosion of union membership, that shifted political power away from the middle class and may well have further eroded the social norms that also functioned to keep high-end wages down. While the exact link between social, political, and institutional changes of the 1970s and the rise of executive compensation (and more general increases in income inequality) remain unclear, the issue is certainly worthy of further investigation. . . .

———

NOTE ON ADDRESSING EXCESSIVE EXECUTIVE COMPENSATION THROUGH DISCLOSURE AND GOVERNANCE

One response to the problem of executive compensation has been an increased emphasis on disclosure and on the makeup and role of the compensation committee. The SEC has periodically revised the proxy rules to increase enormously the amount of disclosure required in connection with executive compensation, and to establish a critical role to the compensation committee. See Proxy Rules Schedule 14A, Items 8, 10, and Reg. S-K, Item 402, in the Statutory Supplement. Up to now, at least, these changes seem to have had little or no effect. Most recently, in response to Section 953(b) of the Dodd-Frank Act, the SEC amended the disclosure requirements for reporting companies to require annual comparison of the CEO compensation to average worker compensation. Other disclosures have also been enhanced. For example, SEC Rule 402 requires disclosure of the amounts of each component of each senior executive's compensation such as salary, bonuses, options, and even perquisites. *See In the Matter of Polycom, Inc.*, Exchange Act Rel. No. 74613 (Mar. 31, 2015) (company fined $750,000 for nondisclosure of $190,000 in payment of meals, clothing and travel to its CEO).

To be listed on the NYSE and Nasdaq a company must have a compensation committee whose task must include establishing goals and objectives relevant to the CEO's compensation, evaluate the CEO's performance in light of the goals developed, and have the sole authority to determine the CEO's compensation. The compensation committee also must enjoy authority to make recommendations to the board with respect to non-CEO compensation, incentive plans and equity-based plans. SEC Regulation S-K Item 407(e) calls for a good deal of information regarding how the compensation committee performs the tasks assigned to it, including its use of outside consultants.

The Dodd-Frank Wall Street Reform and Consumer Protection Act of 2010 mandates that reporting companies have an advisory vote on their prior year's compensation of the corporation's top five executives. The 2011 proxy season, the first to reflect the effects of Dodd-Frank, showed these patterns:[8]

- Shareholders showed strong support for existing pay practices, with "say on pay" votes garnering on average 91.2% support and voted down only 1.6% of the time (at 37 of the Russell 3000 companies subject to "say on pay" votes).

- Strong predictors of a negative say on pay vote for the individual firm are weak total shareholder return and significant change in overall executive compensation levels from the level of pay in the preceding year. The former suggest that a better title for the advisory vote is "say on performance."

- Equally significant, there is evidence that communications from institutional shareholders and or reaction from proxy advisory firms influenced companies to alter their executive pay programs in advance of circulating the proxy material for a "say on pay" vote, particularly by reducing non-performance-based compensation.

At the same time, in 2011 directors were reelected with the highest average support in five years, suggesting that "say on pay" to a noticeable extent displaced "no" and "withhold" votes as mediums for expressing dissatisfaction with executive pay and performance. SEC Commissioner Luis Aguilar attributes the "say on pay" vote with stimulating greater management attention to shareholder concerns and thereby promoting a more robust dialogue between shareholders and managers. Most vulnerable to a "no" vote are directors serving on compensation committees where the say on pay vote was negative.

Following the 2011 proxy season, companies became proactive in their efforts to avoid a negative say on pay vote.

(1) Most companies targeted by the ISS in 2011 had mostly eliminated "egregious" pay practices, including excessive executive perquisites, "golden parachute" payment tax gross ups," and undue severance pay; (2) companies have been engaging with shareholders through increased disclosure in the CD&A statements; (3) companies have used extra solicitation materials in reply to unfavorable ISS recommendations; (4) more firms have been making "preemptive changes to compensation policies and practices" following consultation with their shareholders and proxy voting advisors; and (5) there are increasing levels of communications between companies and their institutional shareholders.[9]

As commendable and wise as the above practices may be, the aggregate results for 2012, the second proxy season of say-on-pay votes, reveal that

---

[8]   Randall S. Thomas, Alan R. Palmiter and James F. Cotter, Dodd-Frank's Say on Pay: Will It Lead To A Greater Role For Shareholders In Corporate Governance, 97 Cornell L. Rev. 1213 (2012) (examining nearly 2,200 "say on pay" proposals in the 2011 proxy season).

[9]   James F. Cotter, Alan R. Palmiter & Randall S. Thomas, The First Year of Say-on-Pay Under Dodd-Frank: An Empirical Analysis and Look Forward, 81 Geo. Wash. L. Rev. 967, 998–999 (2013).

twice as many Russell 3000 firms had negative votes as were registered in 2011.[10] The influence of proxy advisory firms is also reflected in the 2012 statistics, with ISS advising a negative vote in 14 percent of the S&P 500 firms where roughly 21 percent of those instances the ultimate vote was negative and in instances where say on pay proposal passed the margins were considerably lower if there was a negative ISS recommendation than if there was a positive recommendation.[11]

While a say-on-pay vote formally is a vote on the executive's compensation, is it instead a vote on the firm's performance? *See* Jill Fisch, Darius Palia & Steven Davidoff Solomon, Is Say on Pay All About Pay? The Impact of Firm Performance, 8 Harv. Bus. L. Rev. 107 (2018).

See generally, Steven A. Banks, Brian R. Cheffins & Harwell Wells, Executive Pay: What Worked, 42 J. Corp. L. 59 (2017) (after a close analysis of historical markers the authors conclude that high marginal tax rates, norms among company executives regarding relative pay within the firm, and the influence of labor unions moderated executive compensation through much of the 20th Century, but are unlikely to be effective today).

———

Most courts have held that a failed say on pay vote does not remove the presumption of the business judgment rule; therefore they reason they should not be more disposed to permitting a derivative suit to go forward because the challenges compensation received a negative say-on-pay vote. Agree?

———

4. USE OF CORPORATE ASSETS: THE CORPORATE OPPORTUNITY DOCTRINE

———

MEINHARD v. SALMON

[Chapter 2, Section 7, supra]

———

AMERICAN LAW INSTITUTE, PRINCIPLES OF CORPORATE GOVERNANCE §§ 5.04 & 5.05

[See Statutory Supplement]

———

---

[10] *Id.* at 999–1000.

[11] *Id.* at 1001.

RESTATEMENT (SECOND) OF AGENCY § 388

[See Statutory Supplement]

———

Northeast Harbor Golf Club, Inc. v. Harris

Supreme Judicial Court of Maine, 1995.
661 A.2d 1146.

■ ROBERTS, JUSTICE.

Northeast Harbor Golf Club, Inc., appeals from a judgment entered in the Superior Court (Hancock County, *Atwood, J.*) following a nonjury trial. The Club maintains that the trial court erred in finding that Nancy Harris did not breach her fiduciary duty as president of the Club by purchasing and developing property abutting the golf course. Because we today adopt principles different from those applied by the trial court in determining that Harris's activities did not constitute a breach of the corporate opportunity doctrine, we vacate the judgment.

I.

The Facts

Nancy Harris was the president of the Northeast Harbor Golf Club, a Maine corporation, from 1971 until she was asked to resign in 1990. The Club also had a board of directors that was responsible for making or approving significant policy decisions. The Club's only major asset was a golf course in Mount Desert. During Harris's tenure as president, the board occasionally discussed the possibility of developing some of the Club's real estate in order to raise money. Although Harris was generally in favor of tasteful development, the board always "shied away" from that type of activity.

In 1979, Robert Suminsby informed Harris that he was the listing broker for the Gilpin property, which comprised three noncontiguous parcels located among the fairways of the golf course. The property included an unused right-of-way on which the Club's parking lot and clubhouse were located. It was also encumbered by an easement in favor of the Club allowing foot traffic from the green of one hole to the next tee. Suminsby testified that he contacted Harris because she was the president of the Club and he believed that the Club would be interested in buying the property in order to prevent development.

Harris immediately agreed to purchase the Gilpin property in her own name for the asking price of $45,000. She did not disclose her plans to purchase the property to the Club's board prior to the purchase. She informed the board at its annual August meeting that she had purchased the property, that she intended to hold it in her own name, and that the Club would be "protected." The board took no action in response to the Harris purchase. She testified that at the time of the purchase she had no plans to develop the property and that no such plans took shape until 1988.

In 1984, while playing golf with the postmaster of Northeast Harbor, Harris learned that a parcel of land owned by the heirs of the Smallidge family might be available for purchase. The Smallidge parcel was surrounded on three sides by the golf course and on the fourth side by a house lot. It had no access to the road. With the ultimate goal of acquiring the property, Harris instructed her lawyer to locate the Smallidge heirs. Harris testified that she told a number of individual board members about her attempt to acquire the Smallidge parcel. At a board meeting in August 1985, Harris formally disclosed to the board that she had purchased the Smallidge property.[1] The minutes of that meeting show that she told the board she had no present plans to develop the Smallidge parcel. Harris testified that at the time of the purchase of the Smallidge property she nonetheless thought it might be nice to have some houses there. Again, the board took no formal action as a result of Harris's purchase. Harris acquired the Smallidge property from ten heirs, paying a total of $60,000. In 1990, Harris paid $275,000 for the lot and building separating the Smallidge parcel from the road in order to gain access to the otherwise landlocked parcel.

The trial court expressly found that the Club would have been unable to purchase either the Gilpin or Smallidge properties for itself, relying on testimony that the Club continually experienced financial difficulties, operated annually at a deficit, and depended on contributions from the directors to pay its bills. On the other hand, there was evidence that the Club had occasionally engaged in successful fund-raising, including a two-year period shortly after the Gilpin purchase during which the Club raised $115,000. The Club had $90,000 in a capital investment fund at the time of the Smallidge purchase.

In 1987 or 1988, Harris divided the real estate into 41 small lots, 14 on the Smallidge property and 27 on the Gilpin property. Apparently as part of her estate plan, Harris conveyed noncontiguous lots among the 41 to her children and retained others for herself. In 1991, Harris and her children exchanged deeds to reassemble the small lots into larger parcels. At the time the Club filed this suit, the property was divided into 11 lots, some owned by Harris and others by her children who are also defendants in this case. Harris estimated the value of all the real estate at the time of the trial to be $1,550,000.

In 1988, Harris, who was still president of the Club, and her children began the process of obtaining approval for a five-lot subdivision known as Bushwood on the lower Gilpin property. Even when the board learned of the proposed subdivision, a majority failed to take any action. A group of directors formed a separate organization in order to oppose the

---

[1]   In fact, it appears that Harris did not take title to the property until October 26, 1985. She had only signed a purchase and sale agreement at the time of the August board meeting.

subdivision on the basis that it violated the local zoning ordinance. After Harris's resignation as president, the Club also sought unsuccessfully to challenge the subdivision. *See Northeast Harbor Golf Club, Inc. v. Town of Mount Desert,* 618 A.2d 225 (Me.1992). Plans of Harris and her family for development of the other parcels are unclear, but the local zoning ordinance would permit construction of up to 11 houses on the land as currently divided.

After Harris's plans to develop Bushwood became apparent, the board grew increasingly divided concerning the propriety of development near the golf course. At least two directors, Henri Agnese and Nick Ludington, testified that they trusted Harris to act in the best interests of the Club and that they had no problem with the development plans for Bushwood. Other directors disagreed.

In particular, John Schafer, a Washington, D.C., lawyer and long-time member of the board, took issue with Harris's conduct. He testified that he had relied on Harris's representations at the time she acquired the properties that she would not develop them. According to Schafer, matters came to a head in August 1990 when a number of directors concluded that Harris's development plans irreconcilably conflicted with the Club's interests. As a result, Schafer and two other directors asked Harris to resign as president. In April 1991, after a substantial change in the board's membership, the board authorized the instant lawsuit against Harris for the breach of her fiduciary duty to act in the best interests of the corporation. The board simultaneously resolved that the proposed housing development was contrary to the best interests of the corporation.

The Club filed a complaint against Harris, her sons John and Shepard, and her daughter-in-law Melissa Harris. As amended, the complaint alleged that during her term as president Harris breached her fiduciary duty by purchasing the lots without providing notice and an opportunity for the Club to purchase the property and by subdividing the lots for future development. The Club sought an injunction to prevent development and also sought to impose a constructive trust on the property in question for the benefit of the Club.

The trial court found that Harris had not usurped a corporate opportunity because the acquisition of real estate was not in the Club's line of business. Moreover, it found that the corporation lacked the financial ability to purchase the real estate at issue. Finally, the court placed great emphasis on Harris's good faith. It noted her long and dedicated history of service to the Club, her personal oversight of the Club's growth, and her frequent financial contributions to the Club. The court found that her development activities were "generally ... compatible with the corporation's business." This appeal followed.

II.

The Corporate Opportunity Doctrine

Corporate officers and directors bear a duty of loyalty to the corporations they serve. As Justice Cardozo explained the fiduciary duty in *Meinhard v. Salmon,* 249 N.Y. 458, 164 N.E. 545, 546 (1928):

> A trustee is held to something stricter than the morals of the marketplace. Not honesty alone, but the punctilio of an honor the most sensitive, is then the standard of behavior. As to this there has developed a tradition that is unbending and inveterate.

Maine has embraced this "unbending and inveterate" tradition. Corporate fiduciaries in Maine must discharge their duties in good faith with a view toward furthering the interests of the corporation. They must disclose and not withhold relevant information concerning any potential conflict of interest with the corporation, and they must refrain from using their position, influence, or knowledge of the affairs of the corporation to gain personal advantage. *See Rosenthal v. Rosenthal,* 543 A.2d 348, 352 (Me.1988); 13–A M.R.S.A. § 716 (Supp.1994).

Despite the general acceptance of the proposition that corporate fiduciaries owe a duty of loyalty to their corporations, there has been much confusion about the specific extent of that duty when, as here, it is contended that a fiduciary takes for herself a corporate opportunity. *See, e.g.,* Victor Brudney & Robert C. Clark, *A New Look at Corporate Opportunities,* 94 Harv. L. Rev. 998, 998 (1981) ("Not only are the common formulations vague, but the courts have articulated no theory that would serve as a blueprint for constructing meaningful rules."). This case requires us for the first time to define the scope of the corporate opportunity doctrine in Maine.

Various courts have embraced different versions of the corporate opportunity doctrine. The test applied by the trial court and embraced by Harris is generally known as the "line of business" test. The seminal case applying the line of business test is *Guth v. Loft, Inc.,* 5 A.2d 503 (Del.1939). In *Guth,* the Delaware Supreme Court adopted an intensely factual test stated in general terms as follows:

> [I]f there is presented to a corporate officer or director a business opportunity which the corporation is financially able to undertake, is, from its nature, in the line of the corporation's business and is of practical advantage to it, is one in which the corporation has an interest or a reasonable expectancy, and, by embracing the opportunity, the self-interest of the officer or director will be brought into conflict with that of his corporation, the law will not permit him to seize the opportunity for himself.

Id. at 511. The "real issue" under this test is whether the opportunity "was so closely associated with the existing business activities . . . as to bring the transaction within that class of cases where the acquisition of the property would throw the corporate officer purchasing it into competition with his company." *Id.* at 513. The Delaware court described that inquiry as "a factual question to be decided by reasonable inferences from objective facts." *Id.*

The line of business test suffers from some significant weaknesses. First, the question whether a particular activity is within a corporation's line of business is conceptually difficult to answer. The facts of the instant case demonstrate that difficulty. The Club is in the business of running a golf course. It is not in the business of developing real estate. In the traditional sense, therefore, the trial court correctly observed that the opportunity in this case was not a corporate opportunity within the meaning of the *Guth* test. Nevertheless, the record would support a finding that the Club had made the policy judgment that development of surrounding real estate was detrimental to the best interests of the Club. The acquisition of land adjacent to the golf course for the purpose of preventing future development would have enhanced the ability of the Club to implement that policy. The record also shows that the Club had occasionally considered reversing that policy and expanding its operations to include the development of surrounding real estate. Harris's activities effectively foreclosed the Club from pursuing that option with respect to prime locations adjacent to the golf course.

Second, the *Guth* test includes as an element the financial ability of the corporation to take advantage of the opportunity. The court in this case relied on the Club's supposed financial incapacity as a basis for excusing Harris's conduct. Often, the injection of financial ability into the equation will unduly favor the inside director or executive who has command of the facts relating to the finances of the corporation. Reliance on financial ability will also act as a disincentive to corporate executives to solve corporate financing and other problems. In addition, the Club could have prevented development without spending $275,000 to acquire the property Harris needed to obtain access to the road.

The Massachusetts Supreme Judicial Court adopted a different test in *Durfee v. Durfee & Canning, Inc.*, 323 Mass. 187, 80 N.E.2d 522 (1948). The *Durfee* test has since come to be known as the "fairness test." According to *Durfee*, the

> true basis of governing doctrine rests on the unfairness in the particular circumstances of a director, whose relation to the corporation is fiduciary, taking advantage of an opportunity [for her personal profit] when the interest of the corporation justly call[s] for protection. This calls for application of ethical standards of what is fair and equitable . . . in particular sets of facts.

Id. at 529 (quoting *Ballantine on Corporations* 204–05 (rev. ed. 1946)). As with the *Guth* test, the *Durfee* test calls for a broad-ranging, intensely factual inquiry. The *Durfee* test suffers even more than the *Guth* test from a lack of principled content. It provides little or no practical guidance to the corporate officer or director seeking to measure her obligations.

The Minnesota Supreme Court elected "to combine the 'line of business' test with the 'fairness' test." *Miller v. Miller,* 301 Minn. 207, 222 N.W.2d 71, 81 (1974). It engaged in a two-step analysis, first determining whether a particular opportunity was within the corporation's line of business, then scrutinizing "the equitable considerations existing prior to, at the time of, and following the officer's acquisition." *Id.* The *Miller* court hoped by adopting this approach "to ameliorate the often-expressed criticism that the [corporate opportunity] doctrine is vague and subjects today's corporate management to the danger of unpredictable liability." *Id.* In fact, the test adopted in *Miller* merely piles the uncertainty and vagueness of the fairness test on top of the weaknesses in the line of business test.

Despite the weaknesses of each of these approaches to the corporate opportunity doctrine, they nonetheless rest on a single fundamental policy. At bottom, the corporate opportunity doctrine recognizes that a corporate fiduciary should not serve both corporate and personal interests at the same time. As we observed in *Camden Land Co. v. Lewis,* 101 Me. 78, 97, 63 A. 523, 531 (1905), corporate fiduciaries "owe their whole duty to the corporation, and they are not to be permitted to act when duty conflicts with interest. They cannot serve themselves and the corporation at the same time." The various formulations of the test are merely attempts to moderate the potentially harsh consequences of strict adherence to that policy. It is important to preserve some ability for corporate fiduciaries to pursue personal business interests that present no real threat to their duty of loyalty.

III.

The American Law Institute Approach

In an attempt to protect the duty of loyalty while at the same time providing long-needed clarity and guidance for corporate decisionmakers, the American Law Institute has offered the most recently developed version of the corporate opportunity doctrine. PRINCIPLES OF CORPORATE GOVERNANCE § 5.05 (May 13, 1992), provides as follows:

§ 5.05   **Taking of Corporate Opportunities by Directors or Senior Executives**

(a)   *General Rule.* A director [§ 1.13] or senior executive [§ 1.33] may not take advantage of a corporate opportunity unless:

(1)   The director or senior executive first offers the corporate opportunity to the corporation and makes disclosure concerning the conflict of interest [§ 1.14(a)] and the corporate opportunity [§ 1.14(b)];

(2)   The corporate opportunity is rejected by the corporation; and

(3) Either:

(A) The rejection of the opportunity is fair to the corporation;

(B) The opportunity is rejected in advance, following such disclosure, by disinterested directors [§ 1.15], or, in the case of a senior executive who is not a director, by a disinterested superior, in a manner that satisfies the standards of the business judgment rule [§ 4.01(c)]; or

(C) The rejection is authorized in advance or ratified, following such disclosure, by disinterested shareholders [§ 1.16], and the rejection is not equivalent to a waste of corporate assets [§ 1.42].

(b) *Definition of a Corporate Opportunity.* For purposes of this Section, a corporate opportunity means:

(1) Any opportunity to engage in a business activity of which a director or senior executive becomes aware, either:

(A) In connection with the performance of functions as a director or senior executive, or under circumstances that should reasonably lead the director or senior executive to believe that the person offering the opportunity expects it to be offered to the corporation; or

(B) Through the use of corporate information or property, if the resulting opportunity is one that the director or senior executive should reasonably be expected to believe would be of interest to the corporation; or

(2) Any opportunity to engage in a business activity of which a senior executive becomes aware and knows is closely related to a business in which the corporation is engaged or expects to engage.

(c) *Burden of Proof.* A party who challenges the taking of a corporate opportunity has the burden of proof, except that if such party establishes that the requirements of Subsection (a)(3)(B) or (C) are not met, the director or the senior executive has the burden of proving that the rejection and the taking of the opportunity were fair to the corporation.

(d) *Ratification of Defective Disclosure.* A good faith but defective disclosure of the facts concerning the corporate opportunity may be cured if at any time (but no later than a reasonable time after suit is filed challenging the taking of the corporate opportunity) the original rejection of the corporate opportunity is ratified, following the required disclosure, by the board, the shareholders, or the corporate decisionmaker who initially approved the rejection of the corporate opportunity, or such decisionmaker's successor.

(e) *Special Rule Concerning Delayed Offering of Corporate Opportunities.* Relief based solely on failure to first offer an opportunity to the corporation under Subsection (a)(1) is not available if: (1) such failure resulted from a good faith belief that the business activity did not constitute a corporate opportunity, and (2) not later than a reasonable time after suit is filed challenging the taking of the corporate opportunity, the corporate opportunity is to the extent possible offered to the corporation and rejected in a manner that satisfies the standards of Subsection (a).

The central feature of the ALI test is the strict requirement of full disclosure prior to taking advantage of any corporate opportunity. *Id.,* § 5.05(a)(1). "If the opportunity is not offered to the corporation, the director or senior executive will not have satisfied § 5.05(a)." *Id.,* cmt. to § 5.05(a). The corporation must then formally reject the opportunity. *Id.,* § 505(a)(2). The ALI test is discussed at length and ultimately applied by the Oregon Supreme Court in *Klinicki v. Lundgren,* 298 Or. 662, 695 P.2d 906 (1985). As *Klinicki* describes the test, "full disclosure to the appropriate corporate body is . . . an absolute condition precedent to the validity of any forthcoming rejection as well as to the availability to the director or principal senior executive of the defense of fairness." *Id.* at 920. A "good faith but defective disclosure" by the corporate officer may be ratified after the fact only by an affirmative vote of the disinterested directors or shareholders. PRINCIPLES OF CORPORATE GOVERNANCE § 5.05(d).

The ALI test defines "corporate opportunity" broadly. It includes opportunities "closely related to a business in which the corporation is engaged." *Id.,* § 5.05(b). It also encompasses any opportunities that accrue to the fiduciary as a result of her position within the corporation. *Id.* This concept is most clearly illustrated by the testimony of Suminsby, the listing broker for the Gilpin property, which, if believed by the factfinder, would support a finding that the Gilpin property was offered to Harris specifically in her capacity as president of the Club. If the factfinder reached that conclusion, then at least the opportunity to acquire the Gilpin property would be a corporate opportunity. The state of the record concerning the Smallidge purchase precludes us from intimating any opinion whether that too would be a corporate opportunity.

Under the ALI standard, once the Club shows that the opportunity is a corporate opportunity, it must show either that Harris did not offer the opportunity to the Club or that the Club did not reject it properly. If the Club shows that the board did not reject the opportunity by a vote of the disinterested directors after full disclosure, then Harris may defend her actions on the basis that the taking of the opportunity was fair to the corporation. *Id.,* § 5.05(c). If Harris failed to offer the opportunity at all, however, then she may not defend on the basis that the failure to offer the opportunity was fair. *Id.,* cmt. to § 5.05(c).

The *Klinicki* court viewed the ALI test as an opportunity to bring some clarity to a murky area of the law. *Klinicki,* 695 P.2d at 915. We agree, and today we follow the ALI test. The disclosure-oriented approach provides a clear procedure whereby a corporate officer may insulate herself through prompt and complete disclosure from the possibility of a legal challenge. The requirement of disclosure recognizes the paramount importance of the corporate fiduciary's duty of loyalty. At the same time it protects the fiduciary's ability pursuant to the proper procedure to pursue her own business ventures free from the possibility of a lawsuit.

The importance of disclosure is familiar to the law of corporations in Maine. Pursuant to 13–A M.R.S.A. § 717 (1981), a corporate officer or director may enter into a transaction with the corporation in which she has a personal or adverse interest only if she discloses her interest in the transaction and secures ratification by a majority of the disinterested directors or shareholders. Section 717 is part of the Model Business Corporations Act, adopted in Maine in 1971. P.L.1971, ch. 439, § 1. Like the ALI rule, section 717 was designed to "eliminate the inequities and uncertainties caused by the existing rules." MODEL BUSINESS CORP. ACT § 41, § 2, at 844 (1971).

IV.

Conclusion

The question remains how our adoption of the rule affects the result in the instant case. The trial court made a number of factual findings based on an extensive record.[3] The court made those findings, however, in the light of legal principles that are different from the principles that we today announce. Similarly, the parties did not have the opportunity to develop the record in this case with knowledge of the applicable legal standard. In these circumstances, fairness requires that we remand the case for further proceedings. Those further proceedings may include, at the trial court's discretion, the taking of further evidence.

The entry is:

Judgment vacated.

Remanded for further proceedings consistent with the opinion herein.

All concurring.

———

NOTE ON FURTHER PROCEEDINGS IN NORTHEAST HARBOR GOLF CLUB, INC. V. HARRIS

Following remand, the Superior Court entered judgment for the Club. On appeal, the Maine Supreme Court held that the Gilpin and Smallidge

---

[3] Harris raised the defense of laches and the statute of limitations but the court made no findings on those issues. We do not intimate what result the application of either doctrine would produce in this case. . . .

properties were both corporate opportunities, and that Harris breached her fiduciary obligations by not offering those opportunities to the Club's board:

> "The central feature of the ALI test is the strict requirement of full disclosure prior to taking advantage of any corporate opportunity." Northeast Harbor Golf Club, 661 A.2d at 1151. This feature was designed to prevent individual directors and officers from substituting their own judgment for that of the corporation when determining whether it would be in the corporate interest, or whether the corporation is financially or otherwise able to take advantage of an opportunity. . . . Doubt about the financial capacity of a corporation to pursue an opportunity may affect the incentive of a director or officer to solve corporate financing problems, and evidence regarding the corporation's financial status is often controlled by the usurping corporate director or officer. See Victor Brudney & Robert Charles Clark, A New Look at Corporate Opportunities, 94 Harv. L. Rev. 998, 1020–22 (1981). The ALI approach recognizes the danger in allowing an individual director or officer to determine whether a corporation has the ability to take an opportunity, and accordingly disclosure to the corporation is required.
>
> Full disclosure is likewise important to prevent individual directors and officers from using their own unfettered judgment to determine whether the business opportunity is related to the corporation's business, such that it would be in the corporate interest to take advantage of that opportunity. "The appropriate method to determine whether or not a corporate opportunity exists is to let the corporation decide at the time the opportunity is presented." 3 Fletcher Cyc. Corp. § 861.10, p. 285 (1994). This rule protects individual directors and officers because after disclosing the potential opportunity to the corporation, they can pursue their own business ventures free from the possibility of a lawsuit. If there is doubt as to whether a business opportunity is closely related to the business of the corporation, that doubt must be resolved in favor of the corporation so that the officer or director will have a strong incentive to disclose any business opportunity even remotely related to the business of the corporation.
>
> In this case, the Club's normal business is maintaining and operating a golf course. That business is dependent on having sufficient land for the course itself and ensuring that the activity of golf is not hindered or affected by development of adjacent and surrounding property. The Club had frequently discussed developing some of its own land and on one occasion talked about the possibility of purchasing and developing adjacent land. The purchase of the Smallidge land, surrounded as it is on three sides by the Club's land and adjacent to three of its golf holes, land that could be developed, is, in the circumstances of this case, sufficiently related to the Club's business to constitute a corporate opportunity. . . .

However, the court also concluded that the Club's action was barred by
the statute of limitations.

———

Broz v. Cellular Information Systems, Inc.

Supreme Court of Delaware, 1996.
673 A.2d 148.

[Robert F. Broz was the President and sole stockholder of RFB Cellular,
Inc. (RFBC), a Delaware corporation engaged in the business of providing
cellular telephone service in the Midwest. RFBC held an FCC license
known as the Michigan-4 Rural Service Area Cellular License (Michigan-
4). The license entitled RFBC to provide cellular telephone service to its
service area, a portion of rural Michigan. Broz was also an outside
director of Cellular Information Systems, Inc. (CIS), a publicly held
Delaware corporation and a competitor of RFBC. CIS was at all times
fully aware of Broz's relationship with RFBC.

In April 1994, Mackinac Cellular Corp. wanted to sell its FCC
cellular-phone-license area, known as Michigan-2, which was
immediately adjacent to RFBC's Michigan-4. Mackinac's broker, Daniels,
contacted Broz and broached the subject of RFBC's possible acquisition
of Michigan-2. Daniels did not offer Michigan-2 to CIS. Apparently,
Daniels did not consider CIS to be a viable purchaser for Michigan-2,
because CIS had recently emerged from bankruptcy proceedings and had
made a loan agreement that substantially impaired its ability to
undertake new acquisitions or incur new debt.

On June 1994, Broz spoke with CIS's Chief Executive Officer,
Richard Treibick, concerning Broz's interest in acquiring Michigan-2.
Treibick told Broz that CIS was not interested in Michigan-2. In August
1994, Broz contacted two other CIS directors, who expressed their belief
that CIS had neither the resources nor the inclination to purchase
Michigan-2. Ultimately, all the CIS directors testified at trial that if Broz
had inquired at that time, they each would have expressed the opinion
that CIS was not interested in Michigan-2. In November 1994, Broz
agreed to pay Mackinac $7.2 million for the Michigan-2 license.
Thereafter, the purchase took place.

Meanwhile, between April 1994, when Broz had become aware of the
opportunity to purchase the Michigan-2 license, and November 1994,
when he purchased the license, a third party, PriCellular, Inc. had been
in negotiations to purchase CIS's stock through negotiated transactions
and a tender offer. The tender offer closed nine days after Broz purchased
the license, and PriCellular became the owner of CIS. PriCellular then
caused CIS to sue Broz on the ground that the purchase of the Michigan-
2 license usurped a CIS corporate opportunity. CIS admitted that at the
time the opportunity was offered to Broz, the board of CIS would not have
been interested in Michigan-2, but claimed that Broz was required to look

not just to the interests of CIS at that time, but also to the articulated business plans of PriCellular to determine whether PriCellular would be interested in acquiring Michigan-2. CIS contended that since Broz failed to do this, and instead acquired Michigan-2 without first considering the interests of PriCellular in its capacity as a potential acquiror of CIS, Broz must be held to account for breach of fiduciary duty. The Chancery court entered judgment for CIS. The Delaware Supreme Court reversed.]

The corporate opportunity doctrine, as delineated by [Guth v. Loft, Inc., 5 A.2d 503 (Del. 1939)] and its progeny, holds that a corporate officer or director may not take a business opportunity for his own if: (1) the corporation is financially able to exploit the opportunity; (2) the opportunity is within the corporation's line of business; (3) the corporation has an interest or expectancy in the opportunity; and (4) by taking the opportunity for his own, the corporate fiduciary will thereby be placed in a position inimicable to his duties to the corporation. The Court in *Guth* also derived a corollary which states that a director or officer may take a corporate opportunity if: (1) the opportunity is presented to the director or officer in his individual and not his corporate capacity; (2) the opportunity is not essential to the corporation; (3) the corporation holds no interest or expectancy in the opportunity; and (4) the director or officer has not wrongfully employed the resources of the corporation in pursuing or exploiting the opportunity. *Guth*, 5 A.2d at 509.

Thus, the contours of this doctrine are well established. It is important to note, however, that the tests enunciated in *Guth* and subsequent cases provide guidelines to be considered by a reviewing court in balancing the equities of an individual case. No one factor is dispositive and all factors must be taken into account insofar as they are applicable. Cases involving a claim of usurpation of a corporate opportunity range over a multitude of factual settings. Hard and fast rules are not easily crafted to deal with such an array of complex situations. As this Court noted in Johnston v. Greene, Del.Supr., 121 A.2d 919 (1956), the determination of "[w]hether or not a director has appropriated for himself something that in fairness should belong to the corporation is 'a factual question to be decided by reasonable inference from objective facts.'" Id. at 923 (quoting Guth, 5 A.2d at 513). In the instant case, we find that the facts do not support the conclusion that Broz misappropriated a corporate opportunity....

First, we find that CIS was not financially capable of exploiting the Michigan-2 opportunity....

Second, while it may be said with some certainty that the Michigan-2 opportunity was within CIS' line of business, it is not equally clear that CIS had a cognizable interest or expectancy in the license. Under the third factor laid down by this Court in *Guth*, for an opportunity to be deemed to belong to the fiduciary's corporation, the corporation must have an interest or expectancy in that opportunity. As this Court stated in Johnston, 121 A.2d at 924, "[f]or the corporation to have an actual or expectant interest in any specific property, there must be some tie between that property and the nature of the corporate business." Despite the fact that the nature of the Michigan-2 opportunity was historically close to the core operations of CIS, changes were in process. At the time the opportunity was presented, CIS was actively engaged in the process of divesting its cellular license holdings. CIS' articulated business plan did not involve any new acquisitions. Further, as indicated by the testimony of the entire CIS board, the Michigan-2 license would not have been of interest to CIS even absent CIS' financial difficulties and CIS' then current desire to liquidate its cellular license holdings. Thus, CIS had no interest or expectancy in the Michigan-2 opportunity. . . .

Finally, the corporate opportunity doctrine is implicated only in cases where the fiduciary's seizure of an opportunity results in a conflict between the fiduciary's duties to the corporation and the self-interest of the director as actualized by the exploitation of the opportunity. In the instant case, Broz' interest in acquiring and profiting from Michigan-2 created no duties that were inimicable to his obligations to CIS. Broz, at all times relevant to the instant appeal, was the sole party in interest in RFBC, a competitor of CIS. CIS was fully aware of Broz' potentially conflicting duties. Broz, however, comported himself in a manner that was wholly in accord with his obligations to CIS. Broz took care not to usurp any opportunity which CIS was willing and able to pursue. Broz sought only to compete with an outside entity, PriCellular, for acquisition of an opportunity which both sought to possess. Broz was not obligated to refrain from competition with PriCellular. Therefore, the totality of the circumstances indicates that Broz did not usurp an opportunity that properly belonged to CIS. . . .

In concluding that Broz had usurped a corporate opportunity, the Court of Chancery placed great emphasis on the fact that Broz had not formally presented the matter to the CIS board. The court held that "in such circumstances as existed at the latest after October 14, 1994 (date of PriCellular's option contract on Michigan 2 RSA) it was the obligation of Mr. Broz as a director of CIS to take the transaction to the CIS board for its formal action. . . . " 663 A.2d at 1185. In so holding, the trial court erroneously grafted a new requirement onto the law of corporate opportunity, viz., the requirement of formal presentation under circumstances where the corporation does not have an interest, expectancy or financial ability.

The teaching of *Guth* and its progeny is that the director or officer must analyze the situation ex ante to determine whether the opportunity is one rightfully belonging to the corporation. If the director or officer believes, based on one of the factors articulated above, that the corporation is not entitled to the opportunity, then he may take it for himself. Of course, presenting the opportunity to the board creates a kind of "safe harbor" for the director, which removes the specter of a post hoc judicial determination that the director or officer has improperly usurped a corporate opportunity. Thus, presentation avoids the possibility that an error in the fiduciary's assessment of the situation will create future liability for breach of fiduciary duty. It is not the law of Delaware that presentation to the board is a necessary prerequisite to a finding that a corporate opportunity has not been usurped. . . .

In concluding that Broz usurped an opportunity properly belonging to CIS, the Court of Chancery held that "[f]or practical business reasons CIS's interests with respect to the Mackinac transaction came to merge with those of PriCellular, even before the closing of its tender offer for CIS stock." . . .

We disagree. Broz was under no duty to consider the interests of PriCellular when he chose to purchase Michigan-2. As stated in Guth, a director's right to "appropriate [an] . . . opportunity depends on the circumstances existing at the time it presented itself to him without regard to subsequent events." Guth, 5 A.2d at 513. At the time Broz purchased Michigan-2, PriCellular had not yet acquired CIS. Any plans to do so would still have been wholly speculative. Accordingly, Broz was not required to consider the contingent and uncertain plans of PriCellular in reaching his determination of how to proceed. . . .

Accord: Ostrowski v. Avery, 243 Conn. 355, 703 A.2d 117 (1997).

DEL. GEN. CORP. L. § 122(17)

[See Statutory Supplement]

MODEL BUSINESS CORPORATION ACT
§§ 2.02(b)(6) & 8.70

[See Statutory Supplement]

ALI, PRINCIPLES OF CORPORATE GOVERNANCE
§§ 5.05, 5.06

[See Statutory Supplement]

NOTES ON THE CORPORATE OPPORTUNITY DOCTRINE

1.   Tests. A variety of tests have been formulated to determine whether a director or officer has wrongfully appropriated a corporate opportunity. Among these are three tests discussed in *Northeast Harbor*: (i) The line-of-business test, associated with Guth v. Loft, Inc., 23 Del.Ch. 255, 5 A.2d 503

(1939). (ii) The fairness test, associated with Durfee v. Durfee & Canning, Inc., 323 Mass. 187, 80 N.E.2d 522 (1948). (iii) The two-step test, associated with Miller v. Miller, 301 Minn. 207, 222 N.W.2d 71 (1974). Under another test, associated with Lagarde v. Anniston Lime & Stone Co., 126 Ala. 496, 502, 28 So. 199, 201 (1900), the corporate opportunity doctrine applies only when the director or officer has acquired property in which "the corporation has an interest already existing or in which it has an expectancy growing out of an existing right," or when his "interference will in some degree balk the corporation in effecting the purposes of its creation."

The application of the first branch of the *Lagarde* test (interest or expectancy) is uncertain, because the terms "interest" and "expectancy" have no fixed meaning in this context. See, e.g., Abbott Redmont Thinlite Corp. v. Redmont, 475 F.2d 85, 88–89 (2d Cir.1973). In *Lagarde* itself, the court held that real estate in which the corporation was a tenant constituted a corporate expectancy, but real estate in which the corporation owned an undivided one-third interest did not.

The application of the second branch of the *Lagarde* test (interference with the corporate purpose) is also uncertain. Presumably, it would cover cases in which the corporation's need for the property is very substantial. See, e.g., Harmony Way Bridge Co. v. Leathers, 353 Ill. 378, 187 N.E. 432 (1933) (a director purchased a right of way that was needed as an approach to the corporation's bridge); News-Journal Corp. v. Gore, 147 Fla. 217, 2 So.2d 741 (1941) (a director purchased a tract of land that the corporation leased for its building, and immediately increased the rent).

Insofar as the meaning of the *Lagarde* test can be determined, it is unduly narrow. Even the Alabama Supreme Court may now be seeking more leeway by broadening the second branch of the test:

> The last restriction in *Lagarde,* that which prohibits "balking the corporate purpose," is really quite broad in its formulation, although the case has often been described as restrictive. . . . We think that *Lagarde* when properly read enforces responsibilities for the corporate officer or director comparable to those outlined in *Guth v. Loft, Inc.,* 23 Del.Ch. 255, 5 A.2d 503 (1939), where the Delaware Supreme Court employed the doctrine of corporate opportunity and observed that it
>
> ". . . demands of a corporate officer or director, peremptorily and inexorably, the most scrupulous observance of his duty, not only affirmatively to protect the interests of the corporation committed to his charge, but also to refrain from doing anything that would work injury to the corporation, or to deprive it of profit or advantage which his skill and ability might properly bring to it, or to enable it to make in the reasonable and lawful exercise of its powers. . . .

Morad v. Coupounas, 361 So.2d 6, 8–9 (Ala.1978).

2.   *Data.* A comprehensive analysis of corporate-opportunity cases reported between April 1977 and April 1988 found that disputes concerning corporate opportunities usually occur in close corporations, and that the

opportunity is often directly competitive with the business of the corporation. Chew, Competing Interests in the Corporate Opportunity Doctrine, 67 N. C. L. Rev. 436 (1989).

3.   *Different Types of Corporate Opportunities.* Traditionally, the body of law governing corporate opportunities has lacked clarity in two important respects. To begin with, the corporate-opportunity cases have often tended to lump all kinds of corporate opportunities together. In fact, however, there are two very different kinds of reasons why a *business* opportunity may be a *corporate* opportunity. Call an individual who is a director, officer, employee, or agent of a corporation, *A,* and call the Corporation, *C.* One reason that a business opportunity may be a corporate opportunity is that *A* became aware of the opportunity through the use of corporate property, corporate information, or *A*'s corporate position—that is, through the use of corporate assets. In such cases, the opportunity is Corporation *C*'s property. If *A* took such an opportunity for herself without offering it to Corporation *C,* she has stolen it, just as much as if she had taken or used any other kind of corporate property for her own personal benefit.

A second, very different kind of reason why a business opportunity can constitute a corporate opportunity is that it is closely related to the corporation's business. If that is the *only* reason why an opportunity constitutes a corporate opportunity, then by hypothesis *A* will have found the opportunity on her own, rather than through the use of corporate property, information, or position. If an opportunity that *A* finds on her own constitutes a corporate opportunity, that is not because the discovery of the opportunity is a product of the use of corporate assets—it isn't—but because for some other reason *A* owes Corporation *C* a duty to turn over the opportunity to it.

If *A* is an officer of Corporation *C,* the reason why she might owe *C* the duty to turn over an opportunity that she found on her own is based on her duties not to interfere with, and to advance, *C*'s interests. Whether a given individual owes such duties may depend in part on the individual's position. The higher up in the corporate hierarchy the individual is, the more plausible it is that she owes such duties, and the more demanding the duties will normally be. Although a high-ranking executive can fairly be expected to turn over to the corporation any opportunity that is closely related to the corporation's business solely because it is so related, the same expectation may not apply to a blue-collar or clerical employee.

In short, a business opportunity that is discovered through the use of corporate property, information, or position should be a corporate opportunity regardless of *A*'s corporate position. In contrast, whether a business opportunity that *A* discovers on her own is a corporate opportunity solely because it is closely related to the corporation's business may partly depend on *A*'s corporate position.

4.   *Ability of the Corporation to Take the Opportunity.* Another area in which the traditional law of corporate opportunities has lacked clarity concerns the issue whether and to what extent *A* can raise, as a defense to a suit based on the taking of a business opportunity, that Corporation *C* was unable to take the opportunity. This issue usually, although not always,

arises in the context of whether the corporation had the financial ability to take the relevant opportunity. The courts are all over the place on this issue. At one extreme, some cases, such as *Irving Trust Co. v. Deutsch*, 73 F.2d 121 (2d Cir.1934), hold that the corporation's financial ability should be irrelevant, because it is too easy for executives who take a business opportunity to create a financial-inability excuse through manipulation of the corporation's financial picture. At the other extreme, some cases hold that not only is the corporation's financial ability relevant, but that a plaintiff who claims that a corporate opportunity has been taken has the burden of pleading and proving that the corporation had the financial ability to take the opportunity. See, e.g., Miller v. Miller, supra. Still other courts take some intermediate position between these two extremes. See, e.g., Klinicki v. Lundgren, 298 Or. 662, 695 P.2d 906 (1985) which allows financial inability to serve as a justification for the corporation's rejection of a corporate opportunity. Furthermore, there are a number of shadings on the issue how the corporation's financial ability should be measured in this context. See, e.g., Yiannatsis v. Stephanis, 653 A.2d 275 (Del.1995).

The problem in this area is that the courts have failed to disentangle two very different scenarios in which a corporate-inability defense may play a role. In one scenario, *A* first offers a business opportunity to the board of Corporation *C; C's* board decides to reject the opportunity; and *A* then takes it for herself. A shareholder then brings a derivative action against *A,* and *A* raises as a defense that she did not take the opportunity until *C's* board had rejected it. If, in such a case, the plaintiff puts into issue the fairness or reasonability of the board's rejection of the opportunity, *C's* inability to take the opportunity is relevant, because it may justify the board's rejection.

In the second scenario, *A* takes an opportunity *without* having first offered it to the board of Corporation *C*. When *A* is sued for taking the opportunity, she raises as a defense that *C* did not have the ability to take the opportunity. In this scenario, *C's* inability to take the opportunity should not be a defense, because if a business opportunity would be a corporate opportunity if the issue of the corporation's ability to take the opportunity is put aside, a fiduciary should always be obliged to offer the opportunity to the corporation in the first instance and let the *corporation* decide whether it is or can make itself able to take the opportunity. Business enterprises can be very adaptable when faced with a profitable business opportunity. For example, a corporation that doesn't have the cash to acquire a business opportunity may find that if the opportunity is profitable, a bank will lend the corporation money to acquire it. If *A* does not even offer the opportunity to the corporation, however, there is no way to tell whether the corporation would have been able to raise the money to acquire it by bank financing or otherwise. That being so, it should be presumed against *A* that if she had offered the opportunity, the corporation would have adapted as necessary to take advantage of it. This is essentially the position taken in ALI, Principles of Corporate Governance § 5.05.

   5.   *Private Ordering.* In 2000, Delaware added Section 122(17) authorizing the articles of incorporation to renounce activities or other items that would not be deemed a corporate opportunity. The Model Business

Corporation Act soon followed with a parallel provisions in Sections 2.02(b)(6) & 8.70. The two acts' treatment, however, are not mirror images of one another. The Delaware provision is broader as it applies without qualification to opportunities that are taken by officers, directors and stockholders, whereas under the Model Act officers must obtain the approval of a majority of the disinterested directors. A study of SEC filings reports the wide, and ever growing, adoption of such provisions by public companies. Gabriel Rauterberg & Eric Talley, Contracting Out of Loyalty: An Empirical Analysis of Corporate Opportunity Waivers, 117 Colum. L. Rev. 1075 (2017).

   6.   *The Relationship Between Corporate Opportunities; the Use of Corporate Information, Property, or Position; and Competition with the Corporation.* Three important principles of fiduciary duty overlap in a significant way. These are: (i) The corporate-opportunity principle, which prohibits a corporate fiduciary from taking a corporate opportunity. (ii) The use-of-corporate-assets principle, which prohibits a corporate fiduciary from using corporate property, information, or position for personal gain. (iii) The noncompetition principle, which prohibits a corporate fiduciary from competing with the corporation.

   Often, a given course of conduct violates all three principles. This would be the case, for example, if an executive appropriated a corporate opportunity that she learned of through the use of corporate information, and then exploited that opportunity in a way that competed with the corporation's business. Because of this potential for overlap, it is easy to think that the three principles express different facets of the same basic idea. In fact, however, the three principles express three different ideas, and despite the overlap, one of the principles may apply to a given case although the other principles do not.

   For example, suppose that Officer O of Corporation X takes for herself an opportunity to buy Business B. O learned of the opportunity on her own, but Business B is closely related to A's business. In that case, O may violate the corporate-opportunity doctrine, but not the use-of-corporate-assets principle. Whether O also violates the noncompetition principle may depend on whether O remains in the corporation's employ after taking the opportunity. If O remains in the corporation's employ she may violate the noncompetition principle, because by hypothesis Business B is closely related to the corporation's business. However, if O resigns immediately after acquiring Business B she may not violate the noncompetition principle.

   Suppose now that Business B is not closely related to Corporation X's business, but constituted a corporate opportunity because it came to O's attention through the use of corporate information, property, or position. In that case, if O buys Business B she may violate both the corporate-opportunity principle and the use-of-corporate-assets principle. However, she may not violate the noncompetition principle, even if she remains in the corporation's employ after buying Business B, because Business B might not compete with Corporation X.

   Finally, suppose that O inherits a business that is competitive with that of Corporation X. Here O has not taken a corporate opportunity. However, if

O runs the business without resigning from Corporation X, she may be improperly competing with X. Similarly, suppose that O started a business that originally was not competitive with that of Corporation X, but that later becomes competitive because X itself expands its geographical or product-line reach, so that it begins going head-to-head with O's business. Here too O has not taken a corporate opportunity, but may be improperly competing with X.

In re eBay, Inc. Shareholders Litigation

Court of Chancery of Delaware, 2004.
2004 WL 253521.

... In 1995, defendants Pierre M. Omidyar and Jeffrey Skoll founded nominal defendant eBay, a Delaware corporation, as a sole proprietorship. eBay is a pioneer in online trading platforms, providing a virtual auction community for buyers and sellers to list items for sale and to bid on items of interest. In 1998, eBay retained Goldman Sachs and other investment banks to underwrite an initial public offering of common stock. Goldman Sachs was the lead underwriter. The stock was priced at $18 per share. Goldman Sachs purchased about 1.2 million shares. Shares of eBay stock became immensely valuable during 1998 and 1999, rising to $175 per share in early April 1999. Around that time, eBay made a secondary offering, issuing 6.5 million shares of common stock at $170 per share for a total of $1.1 billion. Goldman Sachs again served as lead underwriter. Goldman Sachs was asked in 2001 to serve as eBay's financial advisor in connection with an acquisition by eBay of PayPal, Inc. For these services, eBay has paid Goldman Sachs over $8 million.

During this same time period, Goldman Sachs 'rewarded' the individual defendants by allocating to them thousands of IPO shares, managed by Goldman Sachs, at the initial offering price. Because the IPO market during this particular period of time was extremely active, prices of initial stock offerings often doubled or tripled in a single day. Investors who were well connected, either to Goldman Sachs or to similarly situated investment banks serving as IPO underwriters, were able to flip these investments into instant profit by selling the equities in a few days or even in a few hours after they were initially purchased.

The essential allegation of the complaint is that Goldman Sachs provided these IPO share allocations to the individual defendants to show appreciation for eBay's business and to enhance Goldman Sachs' chances of obtaining future eBay business. In addition to co-founding eBay, defendant Omidyar has been eBay's CEO, CFO and President. He is eBay's largest stockholder, owning more than 23% of the company's equity. Goldman Sachs allocated Omidyar shares in at least forty IPOs at the initial offering price. Omidyar resold these securities in the public market for millions of dollars in profit. Defendant Whitman owns 3.3%

of eBay stock and has been President, CEO and a director since early 1998. Whitman also has been a director of Goldman Sachs since 2001. Goldman Sachs allocated Whitman shares in over 100 IPOs at the initial offering price. Whitman sold these equities in the open market and reaped millions of dollars in profit. Defendant Skoll, in addition to co-founding eBay, has served in various positions at the company, including Vice-President of Strategic Planning and Analysis and President. He served as an eBay director from December 1996 to March 1998. Skoll is eBay's second largest stockholder, owning about 13% of the company. Goldman Sachs has allocated Skoll shares in at least 75 IPOs at the initial offering price, which Skoll promptly resold on the open market, allowing him to realize millions of dollars in profit. Finally, defendant Robert C. Kagle has served as an eBay director since June 1997. Goldman Sachs allocated Kagle shares in at least 25 IPOs at the initial offering price. Kagle promptly resold these equities, and recorded millions of dollars in profit. . . .

[E]ven if one assumes that IPO allocations like those in question here do not constitute a corporate opportunity, a cognizable claim is nevertheless stated on the common law ground that an agent is under a duty to account for profits obtained personally in connection with transactions related to his or her company. The complaint gives rise to a reasonable inference that the insider directors accepted a commission or gratuity that rightfully belonged to eBay but that was improperly diverted to them. Even if this conduct does not run afoul of the corporate opportunity doctrine, it may still constitute a breach of the fiduciary duty of loyalty. Thus, even if one does not consider Goldman Sachs' IPO allocations to these corporate insiders—allocations that generated millions of dollars in profit—to be a corporate opportunity, the defendant directors were nevertheless not free to accept this consideration from a company, Goldman Sachs, that was doing significant business with eBay and that arguably intended the consideration as an inducement to maintaining the business relationship in the future.

———

5. DUTIES OF CONTROLLING SHAREHOLDERS

As seen earlier in Chapter 4, a characteristic of U.S. capital markets is dispersed ownership in which ownership and management are not only separated but most corporations do not have a dominant stockholder. The dispersed owners frequently face insurmountable costs that make their collective action inefficient. Thus in their celebrated article, Professors Jensen and Meckling rigorously demonstrate that when management and ownership are separated, agency costs arise either in the form of management shirking at the owners' expense or that owners' incur nontrivial expenditures to monitor management performance, or both. Michael C. Jensen & William H. Meckling, Theory of the Firm:

Managerial Behavior, Agency Costs and Ownership Structure, 3 J. Fin. Econ. 305 (1976). The presence of a significant holder is one response to this problem; a large, perhaps even dominant, blockholder has greater incentive than smaller holders to monitor and control management. Indeed, there is evidence that significant blockholders are an increasing phenomenon among U.S. companies. *See* Clifford G. Holderness, The Myth of Diffuse Ownership in the United States, 22 Rev. Fin. Studies 1377 (2009). But the presence of a blockholder who can exercise controlling influence over the firm, while addressing the owner-manager conflict creates the potential for a new conflict between the majority and minority holders. A controlling stockholder can extract value from the firm, minority shareholders, or both. For example, consider what might explain the weight of evidence documenting that control blocks of shares regularly sell at a significant premium suggesting that there are valuable private benefits associated with control. *See e.g.,* Michael J. Barclay & Clifford G. Holderness, Private Benefits of Control of Public Corporation, 25 J. Fin. Econ. 371 (1989). The materials in this section examine not just the fiduciary duties that apply to those in control but illustrate the multiple ways in which control can produce such private benefits.

––––––

ALI, PRINCIPLES OF CORPORATE GOVERNANCE §§ 5.10–5.12

[See Statutory Supplement]

––––––

A. REGULATING THE EXERCISE OF CONTROL

Call a controlling shareholder S, and call the corporation that S controls C. Suppose that S and C have engaged in a transaction between themselves. Assume further that the transaction has been approved by C's board—as will often be the case. A minority shareholder of C who challenges the transaction could, in theory, sue both S and C's directors. As a practical matter, however, although C's directors may be joined as defendants, in many or most cases the real target of such a suit is S, the controlling shareholder, and typically (although not invariably) the court focuses on S's liability rather than on the liability of C's directors.

This phenomenon may be explained on two grounds. First, the controlling shareholder usually has deep pockets; the directors of C may not. Therefore, it may not be worth adding the directors to the suit. Second, C's directors are not self-interested, in the traditional sense, in transactions between C and S, because the directors will not directly profit from the transaction itself. Instead, the directors have a *positional* conflict; that is, it is in the directors' interests, if they want to maintain or augment their positions with C, to go along with S's proposals. Because the law concerning traditional conflicts of interest is better understood than the law concerning positional conflicts, it is easier for the plaintiff and the courts to focus on the liability of the controlling shareholder, who does have a traditional conflict, than on the directors of C, who have only positional conflicts.

Sinclair Oil Corporation v. Levien

Supreme Court of Delaware, 1971.
280 A.2d 717.

■ WOLCOTT, CHIEF JUSTICE. This is an appeal by the defendant, Sinclair Oil Corporation (hereafter Sinclair), from an order of the Court of Chancery, 261 A.2d 911, in a derivative action requiring Sinclair to account for damages sustained by its subsidiary, Sinclair Venezuelan Oil Company (hereinafter Sinven), organized by Sinclair for the purpose of operating in Venezuela, as a result of dividends paid by Sinven, the denial to Sinven of industrial development, and a breach of contract between Sinclair's wholly-owned subsidiary, Sinclair International Oil Company, and Sinven.

Sinclair, operating primarily as a holding company, is in the business of exploring for oil and of producing and marketing crude oil and oil products. At all times relevant to this litigation, it owned about 97% of Sinven's stock. The plaintiff owns about 3000 of 120,000 publicly held shares of Sinven. Sinven, incorporated in 1922, has been engaged in petroleum operations primarily in Venezuela and since 1959 has operated exclusively in Venezuela.

Sinclair nominates all members of Sinven's board of directors. The Chancellor found as a fact that the directors were not independent of Sinclair. Almost without exception, they were officers, directors, or employees of corporations in the Sinclair complex. By reason of Sinclair's domination, it is clear that Sinclair owed Sinven a fiduciary duty. Getty Oil Company v. Skelly Oil Co., 267 A.2d 883 (Del.Supr.1970); Cottrell v. Pawcatuck Co., 35 Del.Ch. 309, 116 A.2d 787 (1955). Sinclair concedes this.

The Chancellor held that because of Sinclair's fiduciary duty and its control over Sinven, its relationship with Sinven must meet the test of intrinsic fairness. The standard of intrinsic fairness involves both a high degree of fairness and a shift in the burden of proof. Under this standard the burden is on Sinclair to prove, subject to careful judicial scrutiny, that its transactions with Sinven were objectively fair. Guth v. Loft, Inc., 23 Del.Ch. 255, 5 A.2d 503 (1939); Sterling v. Mayflower Hotel Corp., 33 Del.Ch. 293, 93 A.2d 107, 38 A.L.R.2d 425 (Del.Supr.1952); Getty Oil Co. v. Skelly Oil Co., supra.

Sinclair argues that the transactions between it and Sinven should be tested, not by the test of intrinsic fairness with the accompanying shift of the burden of proof, but by the business judgment rule under which a court will not interfere with the judgment of a board of directors unless there is a showing of gross and palpable overreaching. Meyerson v. El Paso Natural Gas Co., 246 A.2d 789 (Del.Ch.1967). A board of directors enjoys a presumption of sound business judgment, and its decisions will not be disturbed if they can be attributed to any rational business purpose. A court under such circumstances will not substitute its own notions of what is or is not sound business judgment.

We think, however, that Sinclair's argument in this respect is misconceived. When the situation involves a parent and a subsidiary, with the parent controlling the transaction and fixing the terms, the test of intrinsic fairness, with its resulting shifting of the burden of proof, is applied. Sterling v. Mayflower Hotel Corp., supra; David J. Greene & Co. v. Dunhill International, Inc., 249 A.2d 427 (Del.Ch.1968); Bastian v. Bourns, Inc., 256 A.2d 680 (Del.Ch.1969) aff'd. Per Curiam (unreported) (Del.Supr.1970). The basic situation for the application of the rule is the one in which the parent has received a benefit to the exclusion and at the expense of the subsidiary.

Recently, this court dealt with the question of fairness in parent-subsidiary dealings in Getty Oil Co. v. Skelly Oil Co., supra. In that case, both parent and subsidiary were in the business of refining and marketing crude oil and crude oil products. The Oil Import Board ruled that the subsidiary, because it was controlled by the parent, was no longer entitled to a separate allocation of imported crude oil. The subsidiary then contended that it had a right to share the quota of crude oil allotted to the parent. We ruled that the business judgment standard should be applied to determine this contention. Although the subsidiary suffered a loss through the administration of the oil import quotas, the parent gained nothing. The parent's quota was derived solely from its own past use. The past use of the subsidiary did not cause an increase in the parent's quota. Nor did the parent usurp a quota of the subsidiary. Since the parent received nothing from the subsidiary to the exclusion of the minority stockholders of the subsidiary, there was no self-dealing. Therefore, the business judgment standard was properly applied.

A parent does indeed owe a fiduciary duty to its subsidiary when there are parent-subsidiary dealings. However, this alone will not evoke the intrinsic fairness standard. This standard will be applied only when the fiduciary duty is accompanied by self-dealing—the situation when a parent is on both sides of a transaction with its subsidiary. Self-dealing occurs when the parent, by virtue of its domination of the subsidiary causes the subsidiary to act in such a way that the parent receives something from the subsidiary to the exclusion of, and detriment to, the minority stockholders of the subsidiary.

We turn now to the facts. The plaintiff argues that, from 1960 through 1966, Sinclair caused Sinven to pay out such excessive dividends that the industrial development of Sinven was effectively prevented, and it became in reality a corporation in dissolution.

From 1960 through 1966, Sinven paid out $108,000,000 in dividends ($38,000,000 in excess of Sinven's earnings during the same period). The Chancellor held that Sinclair caused these dividends to be paid during a period when it had a need for large amounts of cash. Although the dividends paid exceeded earnings, the plaintiff concedes that the payments were made in compliance with 8 Del.C. § 170, authorizing payment of dividends out of surplus or net profits. However, the plaintiff attacks these dividends on the ground that they resulted from an improper motive—Sinclair's need for cash. The Chancellor, applying the intrinsic fairness standard, held that Sinclair did not sustain its burden of proving that these dividends were intrinsically fair to the minority stockholders of Sinven.

Since it is admitted that the dividends were paid in strict compliance with 8 Del.C. § 170, the alleged excessiveness of the payments alone would not state a cause of action. Nevertheless, compliance with the applicable statute may not, under all circumstances, justify all dividend payments. If a plaintiff can meet his burden of proving that a dividend cannot be grounded on any reasonable business objective, then the courts can and will interfere with the board's decision to pay the dividend.

Sinclair contends that it is improper to apply the intrinsic fairness standard to dividend payments even when the board which voted for the dividends is completely dominated. In support of this contention, Sinclair relies heavily on American District Telegraph Co. [ADT] v. Grinnell Corp., (N.Y.Sup.Ct.1969) aff'd. 33 A.D.2d 769, 306 N.Y.S.2d 209 (1969). Plaintiffs were minority stockholders of ADT, a subsidiary of Grinnell. The plaintiffs alleged that Grinnell, realizing that it would soon have to sell its ADT stock because of a pending anti-trust action, caused ADT to pay excessive dividends. Because the dividend payments conformed with applicable statutory law, and the plaintiffs could not prove an abuse of discretion, the court ruled that the complaint did not state a cause of action. Other decisions seem to support Sinclair's contention. In Metropolitan Casualty Ins. Co. v. First State Bank of Temple, 54 S.W.2d 358 (Tex.Civ.App.1932), rev'd. on other grounds, 79 S.W.2d 835 (Sup.Ct.1935), the court held that a majority of interested directors does not void a declaration of dividends because all directors, by necessity, are interested in and benefited by a dividend declaration. See, also, Schwartz v. Kahn, 183 Misc. 252, 50 N.Y.S.2d 931 (1944); Weinberger v. Quinn, 264 A.D. 405, 35 N.Y.S.2d 567 (1942).

We do not accept the argument that the intrinsic fairness test can never be applied to a dividend declaration by a dominated board, although a dividend declaration by a dominated board will not inevitably demand the application of the intrinsic fairness standard. Moskowitz v. Bantrell, 41 Del.Ch. 177, 190 A.2d 749 (Del.Supr.1963). If such a dividend is in essence self-dealing by the parent, then the intrinsic fairness standard is the proper standard. For example, suppose a parent dominates a subsidiary and its board of directors. The subsidiary has outstanding two classes of stock, X and Y. Class X is owned by the parent and Class Y is owned by minority stockholders of the subsidiary. If the subsidiary, at the direction of the parent, declares a dividend on its Class X stock only, this might well be self-dealing by the parent. It would be receiving something from the subsidiary to the exclusion of and detrimental to its minority stockholders. This self-dealing, coupled with the parent's fiduciary duty, would make intrinsic fairness the proper standard by which to evaluate the dividend payments.

Consequently it must be determined whether the dividend payments by Sinven were, in essence, self-dealing by Sinclair. The dividends resulted in great sums of money being transferred from Sinven to Sinclair. However, a proportionate share of this money was received by the minority shareholders of Sinven. Sinclair received nothing from Sinven to the exclusion of its minority stockholders. As such, these dividends were not self-dealing. We hold therefore that the Chancellor erred in applying the intrinsic fairness test as to these dividend payments. The business judgment standard should have been applied.

We conclude that the facts demonstrate that the dividend payments complied with the business judgment standard and with 8 Del.C. § 170. The motives for causing the declaration of dividends are immaterial unless the plaintiff can show that the dividend payments resulted from improper motives and amounted to waste. The plaintiff contends only that the dividend payments drained Sinven of cash to such an extent that it was prevented from expanding.

The plaintiff proved no business opportunities which came to Sinven independently and which Sinclair either took to itself or denied to Sinven. As a matter of fact, with two minor exceptions which resulted in losses, all of Sinven's operations have been conducted in Venezuela, and Sinclair had a policy of exploiting its oil properties located in different countries by subsidiaries located in the particular countries.

From 1960 to 1966 Sinclair purchased or developed oil fields in Alaska, Canada, Paraguay, and other places around the world. The plaintiff contends that these were all opportunities which could have been taken by Sinven. The Chancellor concluded that Sinclair had not proved that its denial of expansion opportunities to Sinven was intrinsically fair. He based this conclusion on the following findings of fact. Sinclair made no real effort to expand Sinven. The excessive dividends paid by Sinven resulted in so great a cash drain as to effectively deny to Sinven any ability to expand. During this same period Sinclair actively pursued a company-wide policy of developing through its subsidiaries new sources of revenue, but Sinven was not permitted to participate and was confined in its activities to Venezuela.

However, the plaintiff could point to no opportunities which came to Sinven. Therefore, Sinclair usurped no business opportunity belonging to

Sinven. Since Sinclair received nothing from Sinven to the exclusion of and detriment to Sinven's minority stockholders, there was no self-dealing. Therefore, business judgment is the proper standard by which to evaluate Sinclair's expansion policies.

Since there is no proof of self-dealing on the part of Sinclair, it follows that the expansion policy of Sinclair and the methods used to achieve the desired result must, as far as Sinclair's treatment of Sinven is concerned, be tested by the standards of the business judgment rule. Accordingly, Sinclair's decision absent fraud or gross overreaching, to achieve expansion through the medium of its subsidiaries, other than Sinven, must be upheld.

Even if Sinclair was wrong in developing these opportunities as it did, the question arises, with which subsidiaries should these opportunities have been shared? No evidence indicates a unique need or ability of Sinven to develop these opportunities. The decision of which subsidiaries would be used to implement Sinclair's expansion policy was one of business judgment with which a court will not interfere absent a showing of gross and palpable overreaching. Meyerson v. El Paso Natural Gas Co., 246 A.2d 789 (Del.Ch.1967). No such showing has been made here.

Next, Sinclair argues that the Chancellor committed error when he held it liable to Sinven for breach of contract.

In 1961 Sinclair created Sinclair International Oil Company (hereafter International), a wholly owned subsidiary used for the purpose of coordinating all of Sinclair's foreign operations. All crude purchases by Sinclair were made thereafter through International.

On September 28, 1961, Sinclair caused Sinven to contract with International whereby Sinven agreed to sell all of its crude oil and refined products to International at specified prices. The contract provided for minimum and maximum quantities and prices. The plaintiff contends that Sinclair caused this contract to be breached in two respects. Although the contract called for payment on receipt, International's payments lagged as much as 30 days after receipt. Also, the contract required International to purchase at least a fixed minimum amount of crude and refined products from Sinven. International did not comply with this requirement.

Clearly, Sinclair's act of contracting with its dominated subsidiary was self-dealing. Under the contract Sinclair received the products produced by Sinven, and of course the minority shareholders of Sinven were not able to share in the receipt of these products. If the contract was breached, then Sinclair received these products to the detriment of Sinven's minority shareholders. We agree with the Chancellor's finding that the contract was breached by Sinclair, both as to the time of payments and the amounts purchased.

Although a parent need not bind itself by a contract with its dominated subsidiary, Sinclair chose to operate in this manner. As Sinclair has received the benefits of this contract, so must it comply with the contractual duties.

Under the intrinsic fairness standard, Sinclair must prove that its causing Sinven not to enforce the contract was intrinsically fair to the minority shareholders of Sinven. Sinclair has failed to meet this burden. Late payments were clearly breaches for which Sinven should have sought and received adequate damages. As to the quantities purchased, Sinclair argues that it purchased all the products produced by Sinven. This, however, does not satisfy the standard of intrinsic fairness. Sinclair has failed to prove that Sinven could not possibly have produced or some way have obtained the contract minimums. As such, Sinclair must account on this claim. . . .

We will therefore reverse that part of the Chancellor's order that requires Sinclair to account to Sinven for damages sustained as a result of dividends paid between 1960 and 1966, and by reason of the denial to Sinven of expansion during that period. We will affirm the remaining portion of that order and remand the cause for further proceedings.

Kahn v. Lynch Communication Systems, Inc.

Supreme Court of Delaware, 1994.
638 A.2d 1110.

[In resolving a challenge to a self-dealing acquisition of Lynch Communication Systems by Alcatel U.S.A., the Delaware Supreme Court addressed the impact of the approval by the Lynch directors. In 1981, Alcatel acquired 30.6 percent of Lynch's common stock pursuant to a stock purchase agreement. As part of that agreement, Lynch amended its certificate of incorporation to require an 80 percent affirmative vote of its shareholders for approval of any business combination. In addition, Alcatel obtained proportional representation on the Lynch board of directors and the right to purchase 40 percent of Lynch equity securities in any offering that included third parties. The agreement also precluded Alcatel from holding more than 45 percent of Lynch's stock prior to October 1, 1986. By the time of the contested merger Alcatel owned 43.3 percent of Lynch's outstanding stock and designated five of the eleven members of Lynch's board of directors, two of three members of the executive committee, and two of four members of the compensation committee. To address the self-interest surrounding its acquisition of by Alcatel, Lynch created a three-person committee comprised of non-Alcatel directors to negotiate the terms of the acquisition. Discussions ensued, with Alcatel first offering $14 per share, then $15 per share, and then $15.25. The committee balked, but after Alcatel stated that, if its new offer of $15.50 was not accepted, it would make an unfriendly tender offer at a lower price, the committee agreed. The merger occurred and unhappy Lynch shareholders sued, providing the Delaware Supreme Court to discuss the effect of independent director approval.]

Entire fairness remains the proper focus of judicial analysis in examining an interested merger, irrespective of whether the burden of proof remains upon or is shifted away from the controlling or dominating shareholder, because the unchanging nature of the underlying "interested" transaction requires careful scrutiny. . . .

The initial burden of establishing entire fairness rests upon the party who stands on both sides of the transaction. *Id.* However, an approval of the transaction by an independent committee of directors or an informed majority of minority shareholders shifts the burden of proof on the issue of fairness from the controlling or dominating shareholder to the challenging shareholder-plaintiff. *See Rosenblatt v. Getty Oil Co.,* 493 A.2d at 937–38. Nevertheless, even when an interested cash-out merger transaction receives the informed approval of a majority of minority stockholders or an independent committee of disinterested directors, an entire fairness analysis is the only proper standard of judicial review. . . .

The Alcatel defendants argue that the Independent Committee exercised its "power to say no" in rejecting the three initial offers from Alcatel, and that it therefore cannot be said that Alcatel dictated the terms of the merger or precluded the Independent Committee from exercising real bargaining power. . . .

The Court of Chancery's determination that the Independent Committee "appropriately simulated a third-party transaction, where negotiations are conducted at arm's-length and there is no compulsion to reach an agreement," is not supported by the record. Under the circumstances present in the case sub judice, the Court of Chancery erred in shifting the burden of proof with regard to entire fairness to the contesting Lynch shareholder-plaintiff, Kahn. The record reflects that the ability of the Committee effectively to negotiate at arm's length was compromised by Alcatel's threats to proceed with a hostile tender offer if the $15.50 price was not approved by the Committee and the Lynch board. The fact that the Independent Committee rejected three initial offers, which were well below the Independent Committee's estimated valuation for Lynch and were not combined with an explicit threat that Alcatel was "ready to proceed" with a hostile bid, cannot alter the conclusion that any semblance of arm's length bargaining ended when the Independent Committee surrendered to the ultimatum that accompanied Alcatel's final offer. . . .

Accordingly, the judgment of the Court of Chancery is reversed. This matter is remanded for further proceedings consistent herewith, including a redetermination of the entire fairness of the cash-out merger to Kahn and the other Lynch minority shareholders with the burden of proof remaining on Alcatel, the dominant and interested shareholder.

———

On remand, the Court of Chancery, applying the principles set out in *Kahn*, determined that the merger was entirely fair to the minority shareholders. The Delaware Supreme Court affirmed. Kahn v. Lynch Communication Systems, Inc., 669 A.2d 79 (Del. 1995).

———

Jones v. H. F. Ahmanson Company

Supreme Court of California, 1969.
1 Cal. 3d 93, 81, Cal. Rptr. 592, 460 P.2d 464.

. . . Majority shareholders may not use their power to control corporate activities to benefit themselves alone or in a manner detrimental to the minority. Any use to which they put the corporation or their power to control the corporation must benefit all shareholders proportionately and must not conflict with the proper conduct of the corporation's business. (*Brown v. Halbert, 271 Cal.App.2d 252 [76 Cal.Rptr. 781]; Burt v. Irvine Co., 237 Cal.App.2d 828 [47 Cal.Rptr. 392]; Efron v. Kalmanovitz, 226 Cal.App.2d 546 [38 Cal.Rptr. 148]; Remillard Brick Co. v. Remillard-Dandini Co., 109 Cal.App.2d 405 [241 P.2d 66].*)

The extensive reach of the duty of controlling shareholders and directors to the corporation and its other shareholders was described by the Court of Appeal in *Remillard Brick Co. v. Remillard-Dandini Co., supra,* . . . quoting from the opinion of the United States Supreme Court in *Pepper v. Litton, 308 U.S. 295 [84 L.Ed. 281, 60 S.Ct. 238],* the court held: " 'A director is a fiduciary . . . So is a dominant or controlling stockholder or group of stockholders . . . Their powers are powers of trust . . . Their dealings with the corporation are subjected to rigorous scrutiny . . . . He cannot use his power for his personal advantage and to the detriment of the stockholders and creditors no matter how absolute in terms that power may be and no matter how meticulous he is to satisfy technical requirements. For that power is at all times subject to the equitable limitation that it may not be exercised for the aggrandizement, preference, or advantage of the fiduciary to the exclusion or detriment of the *cestuis*. . . .

———

Should a minority holder ever be subject to a fiduciary duty? For example, how should we analyze a transaction with unquestionable benefits to the corporation and all its shareholders; however, the transaction requires a supermajority vote and a *minority* holder with a sufficient voting power to block approval votes against the transaction in order to obtain a personal benefit not shared by the other stockholders?

———

NOTE ON FAMILY CONTROLLED PUBLIC COMPANIES

On overlooked phenomenon among publicly traded companies are the challenges posed when there is not just a dominant stockholder, but a dominant stockholder who founded the company or members of the founder's family.

> Public companies that are either controlled by individual founders or members of the founder's family or, more loosely, influenced by them, are a significant phenomenon in the United States. . . . [S]uch firms are often said to account for about one third of the Fortune 500. Although that is a minority of the Fortune 500, it represents a substantial minority and a substantial fraction of overall market capitalization. It substantially calls into question the wisdom of premising one's perspective on corporate governance in the United States on a stylized fact of diffuse ownership and then identifying the consequences that stem from a separation between ownership and control as the sole governance concerns for publicly held companies in the United States, in contrast with their counterparts elsewhere. That is, a single focus on diffused ownership and its consequences may tend to slight the governance implications of less typical ownership structures. Moreover, within a cohort of family-controlled public firms, dual-voting structures enable the preservation of control in the absence of a proportionate investment in the firm's equity.

Deborah A. DeMott, Guests at the Table?: Independent Directors in Family-Influenced Public Companies, 33 J. Corp. L. 819, 821 (2008). What possible new concerns do a control stockholder aligned with the firm's founder pose beyond the concerns we believe control stockholders pose generally?

Professor DeMott suggests independent directors of family-dominated firms are well positioned to perform the following functions as something of a counterweight to the influence of controlling stockholders in family firms:

> (1) Vigilance on behalf of the interests of public shareholders; (2) furnishing a reality check that may helpfully complement or challenge the perceptions of management and the controlling family and that may protect the primacy of the firm's business needs and interests, while assuring that high-level decision making is not dominated by spillover from intra family dynamics; (3) serving an intermediary function between the controlling family and senior management, whether or not members of the family; and (4) reinforcing formal institutions and practices of governance.

Id. at 846–847. To what extent are the above functions equally applicable to firms with a controlling stockholder who is not the founder or a member of the founder's family? To what extent can and will the firm's general counsel facilitate the independent directors fulfilling the above functions?

———

B. CLASS WARS

In re Trados Incorporated Shareholder Litigation
Court of Chancery of Delaware, 2013.
73 A.3d 17.

■ LASTER, VICE CHANCELLOR.

TRADOS Inc. ("Trados" or the "Company") obtained venture capital in 2000 to support a growth strategy that could lead to an initial public offering. The VC firms received preferred stock and placed representatives on the Trados board of directors (the "Board"). Afterwards, Trados increased revenue year-over-year but failed to satisfy its VC backers. In 2004, the VC directors began looking to exit. As part of that process, the Board adopted a management incentive plan (the "MIP") that compensated management for achieving a sale even if the transaction yielded nothing for the common stock.

In July 2005, SDL plc acquired Trados for $60 million in cash and stock (the "Merger"). Under Trados's certificate of incorporation, the Merger constituted a liquidation that entitled the preferred stockholders to a liquidation preference of $57.9 million. Without the MIP, the common stockholders would have received $2.1 million. The MIP took the first $7.8 million of the Merger consideration. The preferred stockholders received $52.2 million. The common stockholders received nothing. . . .

[Plaintiff Marc Christen, who owned about 5% of Trados's common stock, sued contending the board breached its fiduciary duty in failing to generate value for the common]

I.   FACTUAL BACKGROUND

. . . [Among the facts developed in the five-day trial was that with the July 2004 hiring of a new CEO, Joseph Campbell, Trados' operations began to improve. Contemporaneous with his hiring the board adopted the MIP. Trados engaged JMP Securities to advise it on shopping the firm and JMP was able to identify 28 potential acquirers. Among that group, SDL made an offer of $40 million to acquire Trados; the board rejected the offer, believing it too low. The rejection did not cool SDL's ardor for Trados; in February 2005, SDL offered to purchase Trados for $60 million]

On June 15, 2005, the Board met to approve the Merger. Under the MIP, the first 13% of the $60 million proceeds ($7.8 million) went to Campbell, Hummel, Budge, and other employees. Campbell's share of the MIP was 30% ($2.34 million). During the Merger negotiations, SDL insisted that Campbell enter into a non-competition agreement, but SDL would not dig any further into its pockets to compensate him for it. To preserve the deal, Campbell agreed to the non-compete. . . . Unlike Campbell, Hummel demanded compensation for his non-competition agreement. His share of the MIP was duly increased from 12% to 14%. Hummel received $1.092 million from the MIP.

At the time of the Merger, the total liquidation preference on the preferred stock was $57.9 million, including accumulated dividends. The proceeds remaining after the MIP payments—approximately $52.2 million—went to satisfy the liquidation preference. Each of the preferred stockholders received less than their full liquidation preference but more than their initial investment. The amounts recovered by the entities affiliated with the directors are shown in the following table:

Preferred Stockholder	Investment in Preferred and Common (ex-dividends)	Allocated Merger Proceeds	Gain
Hg	$16.6 million	$18.9 million	$2.3 million
Wachovia	$6.0 million	$8.1 million	$2.1 million
Invision	$4.0 million	$4.3 million	$0.3 million
Sequoia	$3.8 million	$4.4 million	$0.6 million
Mentor	$191,209	$220,633	$29,424

. . .

All that remained were the necessary stockholder approvals, one by the preferred and one by the common. Trados management anticipated getting both votes handily, as shown by the following table that Budge prepared and Campbell sent to Lancaster:

Shareholder	% of Preferred	% of Total
Large Friendlies:		
Hg Capital	23.20%	14.10%
Sequoia	14.90%	7.70%
Wachovia	13.20%	6.80%
Adastra	7.70%	4.00%
Invision	13.50%	7.00%
Industry Ventures	3.40%	1.80%
Mitsui	4.00%	2.10%
Jochen [Hummel]	0.00%	11.90%
Total Large Friendlies	79.90%	55.40%
Required Percentage	61.00%	50.00%

On June 17, 2005, Trados's stockholders approved the Merger. . . .

II. LEGAL ANALYSIS . . .

[T]he standard of conduct for directors requires that they strive in good faith and on an informed basis to maximize the value of the corporation for the benefit of its residual claimants, the ultimate beneficiaries of the firm's value, not for the benefit of its contractual claimants.[14] In light of this obligation, "it is the duty of directors to pursue the best interests of the corporation and its common stockholders, if that can be done faithfully with the contractual promises owed to the preferred." *LC Capital, 990 A.2d at 452.* . . . Consequently, as this court observed at the motion to dismiss stage, "in circumstances where the interests of the common stockholders diverge from those of the preferred stockholders, it is *possible* that a director could breach her duty by improperly favoring the interests of the preferred stockholders over those of the common stockholders." *Trados I, 2009 Del. Ch. LEXIS 128, 2009 WL 2225958, at *7; accord LC Capital, 990 A.2d at 447* (quoting *Trados I* and remarking that it "summarized the weight of authority very well").[16]

In this case, the directors made the discretionary decision to sell Trados in a transaction that triggered the preferred stockholders'

---

[14]   *See LC Capital, 990 A.2d at 449–50* (holding that the board's duties required the board "to take reasonable efforts to secure the highest price reasonably available for the corporation" and rejecting argument that board had a duty to maximize the value of a liquidation preference and other contractual rights in the certificate of designations governing preferred stock). . . .

[16]   Some scholars have interpreted *Orban v. Field, 1997 Del. Ch. LEXIS 48, 1997 WL 153831 (Del. Ch. Apr. 1, 1997)* (Allen, C.), as supporting a "control-contingent approach" in which a board elected by the common stock owes duties to the common stockholders but not the preferred stock, but a board elected by the preferred stock can promote the interests of the preferred stock at the expense of the common stock. *See, e.g.,* Jesse M. Fried & Mira Ganor, *Agency Costs of Venture Capitalist Control in Startups, 81 N.Y.U. L. Rev. 967, 990–93 (2006)* [hereinafter *Agency Costs*]. The control-contingent interpretation does not comport with how I understand the role of fiduciary duties or the ruling in *Orban,* which I read as a case in which the common stock had no economic value such that a transaction in which the common stockholders received nothing was fair to them. . . . Some scholars also have argued that in lieu of a common stock valuation maximand, directors should have a duty to maximize enterprise value, defined in the common-preferred context as the aggregate value of the returns to the common stock plus the preferred stock, taking into account the preferred stock's contractual rights. *See, e.g.,* William W. Bratton & Michael L. Wachter, *A Theory of Preferred Stock, 161 U. Pa. L. Rev. 1815, 1885–86 (2013)* [hereinafter *Theory of Preferred*]; Douglas G. Baird & M. Todd Henderson, *Other People's Money, 60 Stan. L. Rev. 1309, 1323–28 (2008)*. Among other problems, such an approach does not explain why the duty to maximize enterprise value should encompass certain contract rights (those of preferred) but not others (those of creditors, employees, pensioners, customers, etc.). Moreover, while tolerably clear in the abstract and sometimes in real-world settings, *see, e.g., In re Central Ice Cream Co., 836 F.2d 1068 (7th Cir. 1987),* the enterprise value standard ultimately complicates rather than simplifies the difficult judgments faced by directors acting under conditions of uncertainty and the task confronted by courts who must review their decisions. The enterprise value standard compounds the number of valuation alternatives that must be solved simultaneously, and the resulting multivariate fiduciary calculus quickly devolves into the equitable equivalent of a constituency statute with a concomitant decline in accountability. Delaware case law as I read it does not support the enterprise value theory. As long as a board complies with its legal obligations, the standard of fiduciary conduct calls for the board to maximize the value of the corporation for the benefit of the common stock. *See LC Capital, 990 A.2d at 452* ("[I]t is the duty of directors to pursue the best interests of the corporation and its common stockholders, if that can be done faithfully with the contractual promises owed to the preferred . . . .").

contractual liquidation preference, a right that the preferred stockholders otherwise could not have exercised. The plaintiff contends that the Board should not have agreed to the Merger and had a duty to continue operating Trados on a stand-alone basis, because that alternative had the potential to maximize the value of the corporation for the ultimate benefit of the common stock. The Trados directors, of course, contend that they complied with their fiduciary duties.

2.   The Standards Of Review . . .

Entire fairness, Delaware's most onerous standard, applies when the board labors under actual conflicts of interest. Once entire fairness applies, the defendants must establish "to the court's satisfaction that the transaction was the product of both fair dealing *and* fair price." *Cinerama, Inc. v. Technicolor, Inc. (Technicolor III), 663 A.2d 1156, 1163 (Del. 1995).* . . . "Not even an honest belief that the transaction was entirely fair will be sufficient to establish entire fairness. Rather, the transaction itself must be objectively fair, independent of the board's beliefs." *Gesoff v. IIC Indus., Inc., 902 A.2d 1130, 1145 (Del. Ch. 2006).*

To obtain review under the entire fairness test, the stockholder plaintiff must prove that there were not enough independent and disinterested individuals among the directors making the challenged decision to comprise a board majority. . . . To determine whether the directors approving the transaction comprised a disinterested and independent board majority, the court conducts a director-by-director analysis.

In this case, the plaintiff proved at trial that six of the seven Trados directors were not disinterested and independent, making entire fairness the operative standard. This finding does not mean that the six directors necessarily breached their fiduciary duties, only that entire fairness is the lens through which the court evaluates their actions.

a.   The Management Directors: Campbell And Hummel

Two of the directors—Campbell and Hummel—received personal benefits in the Merger. . . .

At trial, the plaintiff proved that Campbell personally received $2.34 million from the MIP, portions of which were recharacterized as a bonus and as payment for his non-competition agreement. Campbell bargained for and obtained post-transaction employment as SDL's President and Chief Strategy Officer. He also became a member of SDL's board, where he earned $50,000 per year for his service (later bumped to $60,000 per year). . . .

At trial, the plaintiff similarly proved that Hummel personally received material benefits. Hummel's employment with Trados provided his sole source of income between 1984 and 2005; at the time of the Merger, he was earning approximately $190,000 plus an annual bonus. . . . SDL employed Hummel post-transaction at the same level of compensation. Hummel originally was entitled to 12% of the MIP, representing $0.936 million of the Merger proceeds. Just before the Merger, Hummel complained to Campbell about some of the "strings" imposed by the MIP, such as his one year non-competition agreement. After Hummel complained, his MIP percentage increased from 12% to 14% for total proceeds of $1.092 million. Two days later, Budge described Hummel as "obviously a lock" to vote for the Merger. . . .

Taken collectively, the direct financial benefits Hummel received were material to him. He admitted that the $1 million payday was significant. . . .

b.　The VC Directors: Gandhi, Scanlan, And Stone

Three of the directors—Gandhi, Scanlan, and Stone—were fiduciaries for VC funds that received disparate consideration in the Merger in the form of a liquidation preference. . . [Gandhi, Scanlan, and Stone were partners in Sequoia, Wachcovia and Hg, respectively].

The cash flow rights of typical VC preferred stock cause the economic incentives of its holders to diverge from those of the common stockholders. . . . "[T]o the extent that VCs retain their preferred stock, their cash flow rights are debt-like; to the extent that they convert, their preferred stock offers the same cash flow rights as common." *Agency Costs, supra, at 982.* "Because of the preferred shareholders' liquidation preferences, they sometimes gain less from increases in firm value than they lose from decreases in firm value. This effect may cause a board dominated by preferred shareholders to choose lower-risk, lower-value investment strategies over higher-risk, higher-value investment strategies." *Id. at 994.* The different cash flow rights of preferred stockholders are particularly likely to affect the choice between (i) selling or dissolving the company and (ii) maintaining the company as an independent private business. "In particular, preferred dominated boards may favor immediate 'liquidity events' (such as dissolution or sale of the business) even if operating the firm as a stand-alone going concern would generate more value for shareholders."[24] In these situations, "[l]iquidity events promise a certain payout, much [or all] of which the preferred shareholders can capture through their liquidation preferences. Continuing to operate the firm as an independent company may expose the preferred-owning VCs to risk without sufficient opportunity for gain." *Agency Costs, supra, at 993–94.* . . .

The distorting effects "are most likely to arise when, as is often the case, the firm is neither a complete failure nor a stunning success." *Agency Costs, supra, at 996; accord Theory of Preferred, supra, at 1833, 1875.* When the venture is a stunning success (everybody wins) or a complete failure (everybody loses), the outcomes are "cut and dried." William W. Bratton, *Venture Capital on the Downside: Preferred Stock*

---

[24]　*Id.; accord* Darian M. Ibrahim, *The New Exit in Venture Capital*, 65 Vand. L. Rev. 1, 27 (2012) [hereinafter *New Exit*] (noting "traditional exits often do not align the incentives of VCs and entrepreneurs [which] can produce suboptimal outcomes for individual investors that are forced into a premature exit that leaves money on the table"). . . .

and Corporate Control, 100 Mich. L. Rev. 891, 896 (2002) [hereinafter *Downside*]. But in intermediate cases, preferred stockholders have incentives to "act opportunistically." *Agency Costs, supra, at 993.* "The costs of this value-reducing behavior are borne, in the first instance, by common shareholders." *Id. at 995; see Exit Structure, supra, at 351.* "[B]ecause VCs in . . . sales often exit as preferred shareholders with liquidation preferences that must be paid in full before common shareholders receive any payout, common shareholders may receive little (if any) payout. At the same time, the sale eliminates any 'option value' (upside potential) of the common stock." *Carrots & Sticks, supra,* at 3.[25]

ii. Personal Incentives . . .

The timing and form of exit are critical because VCs seek very high rates of return, usually a ten-fold return of capital over a five year period.

Three forms of exit are common. An IPO is the gold standard and most lucrative; liquidation via sale to a larger company (a trade sale) is a second-best solution; and a write-off is the least attractive. "[V]enture capitalists will sometimes liquidate an otherwise viable firm, if its expected returns are not what they (or their investors) expected, or not worth pursuing further, given limited resources and the need to manage other portfolio firms." This may seem irrational, but "it makes perfect economic sense when viewed from the venture capitalist's need to allocate [his] time and resources among various ventures." *Venture Survival, supra, at 110 n.218.* "Although the individual company may be economically viable, the return on time and capital to the individual venture capitalist is less than the opportunity cost." William A. Sahlman, *The Structure and Governance of Venture-Capital Organizations,* 27 J. Fin. Econ. 473, 507 (1990). VC firms strive to avoid a so-called "sideways situation," also known as a "zombie company" or "the living dead," in which the entity is profitable and requires ongoing VC monitoring, but where the growth opportunities and prospects for exit are not high enough to generate an attractive internal rate of return. These companies "are routinely liquidated," usually via trade sales, "by venture capitalists hoping to turn to more promising ventures."

---

[25] Professors Brian J. Broughman and Jesse M. Fried offer a simple illustration: "Consider, for example, a startup with $50 million in aggregate liquidation preferences. Assume there is a 50% likelihood that, within one year, the firm will be worth $90 million and a 50% likelihood that it will be worth $0. A hypothetical risk-neutral buyer content to earn a 0% return would pay $45 million for all of the equity of the startup. Preferred shareholders would get $45 [**94] million; common shareholders would get $0. But if the startup were to remain independent, the common stock would have an expected value of $20 million." Brian J. Broughman & Jesse M. Fried, *Carrots & Sticks: How VCs Induce Entrepreneurial Teams to Sell Startups* . . . [98 Cornell L. Rev. 1319 (2013). [hereinafter *Carrots & Sticks*]. The preferred stockholders will prefer their sure $45 million over the risk-adjusted $25 million. The common stockholders will prefer the opportunity to receive a risk-adjusted $20 million over a sure zero. If the preferred have the power to force a sale, then the $20 million is "the 'option value' of the common stock that is lost in the sale of the firm today for $45 million." *Id.; see also Agency Costs, supra, at 995–97* (providing more detailed examples). Of course, this is not the only possibility. Under other scenarios, the preferred stockholders' incentives can lead to defensible results. *See, e.g., Theory of Preferred, supra, at 1886.*

iii. The Evidence That The VC Directors Faced A Conflict In This Case

. . . At trial, the plaintiff had the burden to prove on the facts of this case, by a preponderance of evidence, that (i) the interests of the VC firms in receiving their liquidation preference as holders of preferred stock diverged from the interests of the common stock and (ii) the VC directors faced a conflict of interest because of their competing duties. . . .

Consistent with Campbell's deposition testimony, the evidence at trial established that Gandhi faced a conflict and acted consistent with Sequoia's interest in exiting from Trados and moving on. . . . As Gandhi explained at trial, when Sequoia invests, it hopes for "really fast" growth and "very large outsized returns." . . . Gandhi had concluded that Trados would not deliver outsized returns . . . Gandhi had decided not to put significant time into Trados beyond Board meetings and only to attend by phone unless meetings were held locally. . . .

Gandhi saw a sale as a means of liquidating Sequoia's investment and moving on to better things. . . .

The evidence at trial established that Scanlan had similar incentives. . . .

Stone's view on exit is best seen in her response to the business plan [for continuing Trados' operations] that Campbell presented on February 2, 2005. . . .[W]hen Stone finally received Campbell's plan, she showed little interest. Within days of the February 2 meeting, she joined the other directors in authorizing Campbell to negotiate a sale to SDL at $60 million. With the prospect of a deal that would return most or all of Hg's liquidation preference, she focused on that alternative. . . . (Stone agreeing that "no one ever took Mr. Campbell's plan a step further from February 2nd") . . . .

Based on this evidence and other materials on which the plaintiff relied, the plaintiff carried his burden to show that Gandhi, Scanlan, and Stone were not independent with respect to the Merger. They wanted to exit, consistent with the interests of the VC firms they represented.

c. The Outside Directors: Laidig And Prang

Two of the directors—Laidig and Prang—were neither members of management nor dual fiduciaries. The plaintiff did not challenge Laidig's disinterestedness and independence. By contrast, the plaintiff contended that (i) Prang was not independent because of his close business relationship with Gandhi and Sequoia, and (ii) he was not disinterested because he beneficially owned preferred stock through Mentor, his investment vehicle, and received a liquidation preference for his shares.

Because of the web of interrelationships that characterizes the Silicon Valley startup community, scholars have argued that "so-called 'independent directors'" on VC-backed startup boards "are often not truly independent of the VCs." *Agency Costs, supra, at 988.* "Many of these directors are chosen by the VCs, who tend to have much larger professional networks than the entrepreneurs or other common shareholders." *Id*. If there is a "conflict of interest" between the VCs and common stockholders, the "independent directors" have incentives to side with the VCs. *Id. at 989*.

> Many of these outside directors have—or can expect to have—long-term professional and business ties with the VCs, who are more likely to be repeat players than are most of the common shareholders. Cooperative outside directors can expect to be recommended for other board seats or even invited to join the VC fund as a "venture partner." . . .

Prang had a long history with Sequoia . . . . The relationship led to Prang investing about $300,000 in three Sequoia funds, including Sequoia X, which owned Trados preferred stock. At the time of the Merger, Prang was also the CEO of Conformia Software, a company backed by Sequoia where Gandhi served on the board. When Sequoia obtained the right to designate two members of Trados's Board, Sequoia designated Gandhi. . . . Having considered these facts as a whole and evaluated Prang's demeanor, I find that Prang's current and past relationships with Gandhi and Sequoia resulted in a sense of "owingness" that compromised his independence for purposes of determining the applicable standard of review.

The plaintiff also introduced sufficient evidence at trial to establish that the $220,633 that Prang received in the Merger (through Mentor) was material to him . . . , representing nearly double Prang's annual salary and 3.7%–5.5% of his estimated net worth, was material to Prang. Prang therefore cannot be counted as disinterested for purposes of determining the applicable standard of review.

3.   Entire Fairness

A reviewing court deploys the entire fairness test to determine whether the members of a conflicted board of directors complied with their fiduciary duties. . . .

"The concept of fairness has two basic aspects: fair dealing and fair price." *Weinberger, 457 A.2d at 711*. Fair dealing "embraces questions of when the transaction was timed, how it was initiated, structured, negotiated, disclosed to the directors, and how the approvals of the directors and the stockholders were obtained." *Id*. Fair price "relates to the economic and financial considerations of the proposed merger, including all relevant factors: assets, market value, earnings, future prospects, and any other elements that affect the intrinsic or inherent value of a company's stock." *Id*. Although the two aspects may be examined separately, "the test for fairness is not a bifurcated one as between fair dealing and price. All aspects of the issue must be examined as a whole since the question is one of entire fairness." *Id*. But "perfection is not possible, or expected. . . ." *Id. at 709 n.7*.

a. Fair Dealing

The evidence pertinent to fair dealing weighed decidedly in favor of the plaintiff. Indeed, there was no contemporaneous evidence suggesting that the directors set out to deal with the common stockholders in a procedurally fair manner. Nor were the defendants able to recharacterize their actions retrospectively to show that they somehow blundered unconsciously into procedural fairness, notwithstanding their vigorous and coordinated efforts at trial to achieve this elusive goal.

i. Transaction Initiation

Fair dealing encompasses an evaluation of how the transaction was initiated. In this case, the VC directors pursued the Merger because Trados did not offer sufficient risk-adjusted upside to warrant either the continuing investment of their time and energy or their funds' ongoing exposure to the possibility of capital loss. An exit addressed these risks by enabling the VCs to devote personal resources to other, more promising investments and by returning their funds' invested capital plus a modest return. The VC directors did not make this decision after evaluating Trados from the perspective of the common stockholders, but rather as holders of preferred stock with contractual cash flow rights that diverged materially from those of the common stock and who sought to generate returns consistent with their VC funds' business model. . . .

Campbell testified that upon joining Trados, he understood that his "mission" was to "help the company understand its future path, which in the mind[s] of the outside board members at that time was some type of either merger or acquisition event." . . . He further understood that the "[preferred investors] who had invested longer were more aggressive to find a path for the company [i.e. the 'merger or acquisition event']." *Id.* Budge, the CFO, testified similarly. . . . It is hardly surprising that Campbell and Budge understood the mission in these terms. The Board was contemporaneously exploring a sale with JMP and authorized Scanlan to design the MIP to ensure that management would benefit from a sale even if the common did not.

To carry out his mission, Campbell recalled coming up with "three scenarios": (i) an immediate sale before the Company ran out of cash, (ii) a 12–18 month managed sale that required at least $2–4 million in additional capital, and (iii) a stand-alone business plan requiring an indeterminate amount of investment. . . . In Campbell's assessment, "[h]alf of the board felt that we should just do something now, take the first offer." . . . None of the VC directors wanted to invest in the Company to support a 12–18 month sale, much less a stand-alone business plan. Campbell was forced to raise venture debt because the "[VC] investors wouldn't kick another round [of investment] in to keep the lights on in December [2004]." *Id.* at 60. Actions speak louder than words, and the VC directors were telling Campbell they wanted out. . . .

ii. Transaction Negotiation And Structure

Fair dealing encompasses questions of how the transaction was negotiated and structured. To analyze these aspects of the Merger requires an understanding of the MIP.

VC-backed portfolio companies commonly adopt plans similar to the MIP to incent management to favor exits. *See Carrots & Sticks, supra*, at 5. . . .

The MIP paid a percentage of the total consideration achieved in any sale to senior management, before any amounts went to the preferred or the common. The percentage payout increased as the value of the deal increased as follows:

Deal Value	MIP Percentage
< $30 million	0%
[>=] $30 million but < $40 million	6%
[>=] $40 million but < $50 million	11%
[>=] $50 million but < $90 million	13%
[>=] $90 million but < $120 million	14%
[>=] $120 million	15%

. . .

As a practical matter, at deal prices below the preferred stockholders' liquidation preference, the preferred bore the entire cost of the MIP because the common would not be entitled to any proceeds. Nothing about that is procedurally or substantively unfair. . . . Once the deal price exceeded the liquidation preference, however, the MIP took value away from the common. At the time of the Merger, for example, the total liquidation preference was $57.9 million. The $60 million in consideration exceeded the preference, so without the MIP, the preferred stockholders would have received $57.9 million and the common stockholders $2.1 million. With the MIP, management received $7.8 million, the preferred stockholders received $52.2 million, and the common stockholders received zero. To fund the MIP, the common stockholders effectively paid $2.1 million, and the preferred stockholders effectively paid $5.7 million. As a result, the common stockholders contributed 100% of their ex-MIP proceeds while the preferred stockholders only contributed 10% ($5.7 million / $57.9 million).

There is no evidence in the record that the Board ever considered how to allocate fairly any incremental dollars above the liquidation preference. Until the Merger proceeds cleared the preference, each dollar was allocated between management and the preferred stockholders, with management receiving its assigned percentage and the preferred taking the rest. But once the consideration topped the preference, thereby implicating the rights of the common, the additional dollars were not fairly allocated. All of the additional dollars went to management and the preferred. The common would not receive anything until the deal price exceeded the preference by more than the MIP payout.

The break-even deal value was $66.5 million. At that point, the MIP payout would be $8.6 million, and the residual proceeds would be sufficient to pay the $57.9 million preference. Above $66.5 million, the common would receive consideration, but would still fund the MIP disproportionately. For example, at $70 million, the MIP receives $9.1 million, the preferred receive $57.9 million, and the common receive $3.0 million. Without the MIP, the preferred would receive $57.9 million, and the common would receive $12.1 million. The common effectively fund the MIP with 75% of the consideration they otherwise would receive, retaining only 25%. The preferred stockholders would not lose a dime. The following graph shows the relative contribution of the common and the preferred at different deal values:

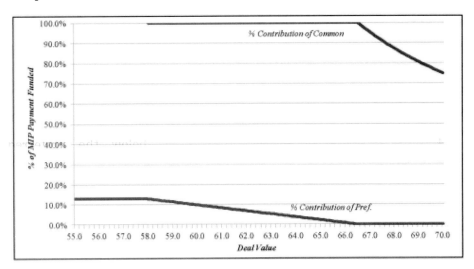

For purposes of fair dealing, the MIP skewed the negotiation and structure of the Merger in a manner adverse to the common stockholders. In February 2005, the Board reached a consensus that Campbell would seek $60 million from SDL. . . . The price target was also influenced significantly by Invision's desire not to take a capital loss by selling below its pre-money entry price of $60 million. . . . At that price, the preferred stockholders would receive back all of their capital and make a nominal profit. There was never any effort to explore prices above $60 million or to consider whether alternatives to the Merger might generate value for the common.

Without the MIP, in a transaction that valued Trados at $60 million, Campbell, Budge, and Hummel would have received nothing for their options. . . .

The MIP ... by reallocating to the MIP recipients 100% of the consideration that the common stockholders would receive in a transaction valued at $66.5 million or less ensured that to the extent any MIP participants might receive consideration at higher deal values in their capacity as equity holders, their MIP payout would be reduced by the amount of the consideration received.... The combination eliminated any financial incentive for senior management to push for a price at which the common stock would receive value or to favor remaining independent with the prospect of a higher valued sale at a later date.

The MIP converted the management team from holders of equity interests aligned with the common stock to claimants whose return profile and incentives closely resembled those of the preferred. Campbell and Hummel in fact acted and voted in a manner that served the preferred stockholders' desire for a near-term sale. Given its design and effect, the MIP is evidence that the Board dealt unfairly with the common when negotiating and structuring the Merger.[36]

iii. Director Approval

Fair dealing encompasses questions of how director approval was obtained. Except for Laidig, all of the directors were financially interested in the Merger or faced a conflict of interest because they owed fiduciary duties to entities whose interests diverged from those of the common stockholders....

During his deposition, Laidig volunteered that the Trados directors never considered the common stockholders....

Conflict blindness and its lesser cousin, conflict denial, have long afflicted the financially sophisticated. Given the directors' intelligence, educational background, and experience, I believe they fully appreciated the diverging interests of the VCs, senior management, and the common stockholders. Despite this reality, the defendants did not consider forming a special committee to represent the interests of the common stockholders.... They also chose not to obtain a fairness opinion to analyze the Merger or evaluate other possibilities from the perspective of the common stockholders.... At trial, the defendants uniformly cited the cost of a fairness opinion, mentioning figures typical of bulge bracket

---

[36] The plaintiff did not try the case on a theory that the defendants breached their duty of loyalty by using the MIP to reallocate consideration from the common to the preferred and management, nor did the plaintiff seek damages for the class on that basis. As with other discretionary exercises of authority, the standard of fiduciary conduct requires that when approving employee compensation arrangements, directors must act to promote the value of the corporation for the ultimate benefit of the common stockholders. *See supra* Part II.A.1. Where, as here, a plaintiff has shown that the board lacked a majority of disinterested and independent directors, the standard of review is entire fairness. *See Gottlieb v. Heyden Chem. Corp., 33 Del. Ch. 177, 91 A.2d 57, 58 (1952); Valeant Pharms. v. Jerney, 921 A.2d 732, 745–46 (Del. Ch. 2007).* It would have been difficult for the defendants to prove that the MIP was fair. A logical remedy would have been for the class to recover its share of the consideration that would have dropped to the residual claimants had the MIP been structured fairly. The plaintiff, however, did not pursue this angle, likely because the resulting damage award would have been relatively small.

institutions and their aspiring competitors. But no one appears to have explored the possibility contemporaneously, even after SDL's counsel expressed "concerns over [the] common stockholders . . . not getting any consideration," . . . and questioned whether Trados needed a "JMP fairness opinion . . . ." One can remain appropriately skeptical of the value of fairness opinions while at the same time recognizing that an outside analysis of the alternatives available to Trados would have improved the record on fair dealing. Taken as a whole, the manner in which director approval was obtained provides evidence of unfair dealing.

iv. Stockholder Approval

Finally, fair dealing encompasses questions of how stockholder approval was obtained. The defendants never considered conditioning the Merger on the vote of a majority of disinterested common stockholders. . . . The vote on the Merger was delivered by the preferred, who controlled a majority of the Company's voting power on an as-converted basis, and other "[l]arge [f]riendlies," such as Hummel. . . . Hummel originally was entitled to 12% of the MIP, but when he seemed to be having second thoughts just before the Merger, his MIP percentage was increased from 12% to 14%. . . . Two days later, Budge described Hummel as "obviously a lock" to vote in favor of the Merger. . . .

"Stockholders in Delaware corporations have a right to control and vote their shares in their own interest." *Bershad v. Curtiss-Wright Corp., 535 A.2d 840, 845 (Del. 1987).* "They are limited only by any fiduciary duty owed to other stockholders. It is not objectionable that their motives may be for personal profit, or determined by whim or caprice, so long as they violate no duty owed [to] other shareholders." *Id.* The fact that the preferred stockholders voted in their own interest is therefore not evidence of unfair dealing. The failure to condition the deal on a vote of the disinterested common stockholders is likewise not evidence of unfairness; it simply deprives the defendants of otherwise helpful affirmative evidence of fairness. The effect of the MIP on Hummel's voting preferences, however, provides some additional evidence of unfairness.

b. Evidence Pertinent To Fair Price

In contrast to the evidence on fair dealing, which decidedly favored the plaintiff, the evidence on fair price was mixed. Consistent with the amount of consideration that the common stockholders received in the Merger, the defendants strived at trial to demonstrate that the common stock had no value. . . .

iv. The Expert Valuations

Both sides introduced expert testimony on the issue of fair price. Gregg A. Jarrell, the defendant's expert, provided a balanced valuation that addressed the central issue in this case: whether Trados could generate positive value for the common stock if operated on a stand-alone basis according to the February 2005 business plan. William Becklean, the plaintiff's expert, did not provide similarly persuasive testimony. . . . [The court then closely reviewed the testimony and methodologies of the two experts.]

Jarrell's DCF valuation addressed the central question of fairness presented by this case. Jarrell made reasonable and plaintiff-friendly assumptions, yet his valuation still did not generate any return for the common. His work provided helpful input on the issue of fair price. Becklean's did not.

c.   The Unitary Determination Of Fairness

Although the defendant directors did not adopt any protective provisions, failed to consider the common stockholders, and sought to exit without recognizing the conflicts of interest presented by the Merger, they nevertheless proved that the transaction was fair. The Delaware Supreme Court has characterized the proper "test of fairness" as whether "the minority stockholder shall receive the substantial equivalent in value of what he had before." *Sterling v. Mayflower Hotel Corp., 33 Del. Ch. 293, 93 A.2d 107, 114 (Del. 1952); accord Rosenblatt v. Getty Oil Co., 493 A.2d 929, 940 (Del. 1985).* If Trados's common stock had no economic value before the Merger, then the common stockholders received the substantial equivalent in value of what they had before, and the Merger satisfies the test of fairness. . . .

Despite the directors' often problematic testimony, they proved that Trados did not have a reasonable prospect of generating value for the common stock. Trados's ability to do so depended on financing its business plan with internally generated cash and the remaining venture debt. To the extent Trados needed outside funds, the Company could not raise them. None of the VC firms would put more money into Trados, and they had no obligation to. *See Equity-Linked, 705 A.2d at 1057* ("[The preferred stockholders] were unwilling to put in more money. The preferred is of course not to be criticized for that. They have every right to send no good dollars after bad ones. Indeed, they had the right to withhold necessary consents to salvage plans unless their demands were satisfied."). As a practical matter no outside VC firm would invest without participation from the Company's existing backers.[49]

---

[49]   . . . Josè M. Padilla, What's Wrong with a Washout?: Fiduciary Duties of the Venture Capitalist Investor in a Washout Financing, 1 Hous. Bus. & Tax L. J. 269, 279–80 (2001) ("[V]enture capitalists will not invest in a company where existing investors do not participate."); Joseph W. Bartlett & Kevin R. Garlitz, Fiduciary Duties in Burnout/Cramdown Financings, 20 J. Corp. L. 593, 601 (1995) ("[O]nce a group of VCs have invested, [**176] it is rare that an issuer will have the ability to raise substantial capital unless the existing investors agree to 'play'—continue to invest—in future rounds of financing. . . . [T]he company can be given the putative opportunity to seek alternative sources, but the venture capital community is small and incestuous, with most managers knowing each other. If the company's existing cadre of VC investors is not willing to continue to support the company, then it is unlikely that any new investor will be interested."). For outside VCs to invest without existing investor participation would run the risk of buying a lemon. See generally George A. Akerlof, The Market for "Lemons": Quality Uncertainty and the Market Mechanism, 84 Q. J. Econ. 488 (1970).

Trados also could not return to the venture debt market. Venture debt providers are not like commercial lenders who rely primarily on the strength of a business and its cash flows. Venture debt providers see themselves as bridging a company to the next round of VC financing or a sale. *See Darian M. Ibrahim, Debt as Venture Capital, 2010 U. Ill. L. Rev. 1169, 1173 (2010).* Trados had played the venture debt card for its stage.

If Trados could not self-fund its business plan, then the Company could not execute it. Even if it could self-fund, Trados had to build value at a rate exceeding the 8% cumulative dividend earned by the preferred to generate a return for the common. Having considered the directors' trial testimony, the documentary record, and Jarrell's DCF analysis, I believe that Trados would not be able to grow at a rate that would yield value for the common. Trados likely could self-fund, avoid bankruptcy, and continue operating, but it did not have a realistic chance of generating a sufficient return to escape the gravitational pull of the large liquidation preference and cumulative dividend. . . .

In light of this reality, the directors breached no duty to the common stock by agreeing to a Merger in which the common stock received nothing. The common stock had no economic value before the Merger, and the common stockholders received in the Merger the substantial equivalent in value of what they had before.

Under the circumstances of this case, the fact that the directors did not follow a fair process does not constitute a separate breach of duty. . . . The defendants' failure to deploy a procedural device such as a special committee resulted in their being forced to prove at trial that the Merger was entirely fair. Having done so, they have demonstrated that they did not commit a fiduciary breach. . . .

III. CONCLUSION

The defendants proved that the decision to approve the Merger was entirely fair. . . .

———

Zahn v. Transamerica Corporation

United States Circuit Court of Appeals, Third Circuit, 1947.
162 F.2d 36.

■ BIGGS, CIRCUIT JUDGE. Zahn, a holder of Class A common stock of Axton-Fisher Tobacco Company, a corporation of Kentucky, sued Transamerica Corporation, a Delaware company, on his own behalf and on behalf of all stockholders similarly situated, in the District Court of the United States for the District of Delaware. His complaint as amended asserts that Transamerica caused Axton-Fisher to redeem its Class A stock at $80.80 per share on July 1, 1943, instead of permitting the Class A stockholders to participate in the assets on the liquidation of their company in June 1944. He alleges in brief that if the Class A stockholders had been allowed to participate in the assets on liquidation of Axton-Fisher and had received their respective shares of the assets, he and the other Class A stockholders would have received $240 per share instead of $80.80. Zahn takes the position that he has two separate causes of action, one based on the Class A shares which were not turned back to the company for redemption; another based on the shares which were redeemed.[1] He prayed the court below to direct Transamerica to pay over to the shareholders who had not surrendered their stock the liquidation value and to pay over to those shareholders who had surrendered their stock the liquidation value less $80.80. Transamerica filed a motion to dismiss. The court below granted the motion holding that Zahn had failed to state a cause of action. See 63 F.Supp. 243. He appealed.

The facts follow as appear from the pleadings, which recite provisions of Axton-Fisher's charter. Prior to April 30, 1943, Axton-Fisher had authorized and outstanding three classes of stock, designated respectively as preferred stock, Class A stock and Class B stock. Each share of preferred stock had a par value of $100 and was entitled to cumulative dividends at the rate of $6 per annum and possessed a liquidation value of $105 plus accrued dividends. The Class A stock, specifically described in the charter as a "common" stock, was entitled to an annual cumulative dividend of $3.20 per share. The Class B stock was next entitled to receive an annual dividend of $1.60 per share. If further funds were made available by action of the board of directors by way of dividends, the Class A stock and the Class B stock were entitled to share equally therein. Upon liquidation of the company and the payment of the sums required by the preferred stock, the Class A stock was entitled to share with the Class B stock in the distribution of the remaining assets, but the Class A stock was entitled to receive twice as much per share as the Class B stock.[2]

Each share of Class A stock was convertible at the option of the shareholder into one share of Class B stock. All or any of the shares of Class A stock were callable by the corporation at any quarterly dividend date upon sixty days' notice to the shareholders, at $60 per share with

---

[1]   The plaintiff was originally the holder of 235 shares of Class A stock purchased on four occasions between July 23 and August 10, 1943, inclusive. Between August 2 and August 20, 1943, the plaintiff surrendered for redemption 215 shares and retained 20 shares.

[2]   The charter provides as follows:

"In the event of the dissolution, liquidation, merger or consolidation of the corporation, or sale of substantially all its assets, whether voluntary or involuntary, there shall be paid to the holders of the preferred stock then outstanding $105 per share, together with all unpaid accrued dividends thereon, before any sum shall be paid to or any assets distributed among the holders of the Class A common stock and/or the holders of the Class B common stock. After such payment to the holders of the preferred stock, and all unpaid accrued dividends on the Class A common stock shall have been paid, then all remaining assets and funds of the corporation shall be divided among and paid to the holders of the Class A common stock and to the holders of the Class B common stock in the ratio of 2 to 1; that is to say, there shall be paid upon each share of Class A common stock twice the amount paid upon each share of Class B common stock, in any such event."

accrued dividends.[3] The voting rights were vested in the Class B stock but if there were four successive defaults in the payment of quarterly dividends, the class or classes of stock as to which such defaults occurred gained voting rights equal share for share with the Class B stock. By reason of this provision the Class A stock had possessed equal voting rights with the Class B stock since on or about January 1, 1937.

On or about May 16, 1941, Transamerica purchased 80,160 shares of Axton-Fisher's Class B common stock. This was about 71.5% of the outstanding Class B stock and about 46.7% of the total voting stocks of Axton-Fisher. By August 15, 1942, Transamerica owned 5,332 shares of Class A stock and 82,610 shares of Class B stock. By March 31, 1943, the amount of Class A stock of Axton-Fisher owned by Transamerica had grown to 30,168 shares or about 66⅔% of the total amount of this stock outstanding, and the amount of Class B stock owned by Transamerica had increased to 90,768 shares or about 80% of the total outstanding. Additional shares of Class B stock were acquired by Transamerica after April 30, 1943, and Transamerica converted the Class A stock owned by it into Class B stock so that on or about the end of May, 1944 Transamerica owned virtually all of the outstanding Class B stock of Axton-Fisher. Since May 16, 1941, Transamerica had control of and had dominated the management, directorate, financial policies, business and affairs of Axton-Fisher. Since the date last stated Transamerica had elected a majority of the board of directors of Axton-Fisher. These individuals are in large part officers or agents of Transamerica.

In the fall of 1942 and in the spring of 1943 Axton-Fisher possessed as its principal asset leaf tobacco which had cost it about $6,361,981. This asset was carried on Axton-Fisher's books in that amount. The value of leaf tobacco had risen sharply and to quote the words of the complaint, "unbeknown to the public holders of . . . Class A common stock of Axton-Fisher, but known to Transamerica, the market value of . . . [the] tobacco had, in March and April of 1943, attained the huge sum of about $20,000,000."

The complaint then alleges the gist of the plaintiff's grievance, viz., that Transamerica, knowing of the great value of the tobacco which Axton-Fisher possessed, conceived a plan to appropriate the value of the tobacco to itself by redeeming the Class A stock at the price of $60 a share plus accrued dividends, the redemption being made to appear as if

---

[3]   The charter provides as follows:

"The whole or any part of the Class A common stock of the corporation, at the option of the Board of Directors, may be redeemed on any quarterly dividend payment date by paying therefor in cash Sixty dollars ($60.00) per share and all unpaid and accrued dividends thereon at the date fixed for such redemption, upon sending by mail to the registered holders of the Class A common stock at least sixty (60) days' notice of the exercise of such option. If at any time the Board of Directors shall determine to redeem less than the whole amount of Class A common stock then outstanding, the particular stock to be so redeemed shall be determined in such manner as the Board of Directors shall prescribe; provided, however, that no holder of Class A common stock shall be preferred over any other holder of such stock."

"incident to the continuance of the business of Axton-Fisher as a going concern," and thereafter, the redemption of the Class A stock being completed, to liquidate Axton-Fisher; that this would result, after the disbursal of the sum required to be paid to the preferred stock, in Transamerica gaining for itself most of the value of the warehouse tobacco. The complaint further alleges that in pursuit of this plan Transamerica, by a resolution of the Board of Directors of Axton-Fisher on April 30, 1943, called the Class A stock at $60 and, selling a large part of the tobacco to Phillip-Morris Company, Ltd., Inc., together with substantially all of the other assets of Axton-Fisher, thereafter liquidated Axton-Fisher, paid off the preferred stock and pocketed the balance of the proceeds of the sale. Warehouse receipts representing the remainder of the tobacco were distributed to the Class B stockholders.

Assuming as we must that the allegations of the complaint are true, it will be observed that agents or representatives of Transamerica constituted Axton-Fisher's board of directors at the times of the happening of the events complained of, and that Transamerica was Axton-Fisher's principal and controlling stockholder at such times. It will be observed also that jurisdiction in the suit at bar is based upon diversity of citizenship and jurisdictional amount. In such a suit the conflict-of-laws rule of Delaware requires the District Court of Delaware to refer to the law of the State of incorporation to determine the extent and nature of relationships between corporation and stockholder, corporate officer or director and stockholder and between stockholders *inter sese*. See Skillman v. Conner, 8 W.W.Harr. 402, 193 A. 563, and Black & Yates v. Mahogany Ass'n, 3 Cir., 129 F.2d 227, 233, 148 A.L.R. 841. As was well stated by the court below in Geller v. Transamerica Corporation, D.C., 53 F.Supp. 625, 629, 630, ". . . under the Delaware conflict of laws rule, the law of the place of the wrong determines the quantum of the breach of duty. . . . It would seem that the place of wrong is where the final act occurred which establishes liability." This court approved that reasoning by affirming per curiam the decision. See, 3 Cir., 151 F.2d 534.

The *loci* of the events complained of in the instant case are not set forth in the complaint. In Black & Yates v. Mahogany Ass'n, 129 F.2d at page 233, we stated, "We think that in the absence of allegations as to the place or places where the acts complained of occurred, the court below would have been entitled to assume that these operative facts took place within the State of Delaware," viz., the state of the forum. It is necessary therefore to assume that the events complained of took place within the State of Delaware. The law of Kentucky determines the existence of fiduciary duty, or the lack of it, between Transamerica (as the board of directors of Axton-Fisher, as its officership or as its controlling stockholder) and Axton-Fisher's minority Class A stockholders, and the law of Delaware determines the extent of the breach of fiduciary duty, if any. [At this point the court stated the case of Taylor v. Axton-Fisher

Tobacco Co., 295 Ky. 226, 173 S.W.2d 377, 148 A.L.R. 834 (Ct.App.1943) which held that the action of the directors of Axton-Fisher in making the call gave the Class B shareholders the right to have the Class A shares redeemed and that a subsequent directors' resolution of June 16, 1943, purporting to give Class A shareholders the option not to have their shares redeemed, was an invalid resolution.]

The circumstances of the case at bar are *sui generis* and we can find no Kentucky decision squarely in point. In our opinion, however, the law of Kentucky imposes upon the directors of a corporation or upon those who are in charge of its affairs by virtue of majority stock ownership or otherwise the same fiduciary relationship in respect to the corporation and to its stockholders as is imposed generally by the laws of Kentucky's sister States or which was imposed by federal law prior to Erie R. Co. v. Tompkins, 304 U.S. 64, 58 S.Ct. 817, 82 L.Ed. 1188, 114 A.L.R. 1487.

The tenor of the federal decisions in respect to the general fiduciary duty of those in control of a corporation is unmistakable. The Supreme Court in Southern Pacific Co. v. Bogert, 250 U.S. 483, 487, 488, 39 S.Ct. 533, 535, 63 L.Ed. 1099, said: "The rule of corporation law and of equity invoked is well settled and has been often applied. The majority has the right to control; but when it does so, it occupies a fiduciary relation toward the minority, as much so as the corporation itself or its officers and directors." In Pepper v. Litton, 308 U.S. 295, 306, 60 S.Ct. 238, 245, 84 L.Ed. 281, the Supreme Court stated: "A director is a fiduciary. . . . So is a dominant or controlling stockholder or group of stockholders. . . . Their powers are powers in trust. . . . Their dealings with the corporation are subjected to rigorous scrutiny and where any of their contracts or engagements with the corporation is challenged the burden is on the director or stockholder not only to prove the good faith of the transaction but also to show its inherent fairness from the viewpoint of the corporation and those interested therein." . . .

It is appropriate to emphasize at this point that the right to call the Class A stock for redemption was confided by the charter of Axton-Fisher to the directors and not to the stockholders of that corporation. We must also reemphasize the statement of the court in Haldeman v. Haldeman, supra, and its reiteration in Kirwan v. Parkway Distillery, supra, that there is a radical difference when a stockholder is voting strictly as a stockholder and when voting as a director; that when voting as a stockholder he may have the legal right to vote with a view of his own benefits and to represent himself only; but that when he votes as a director he represents all the stockholders in the capacity of a trustee for them and cannot use his office as a director for his personal benefit at the expense of the stockholders.

Two theories are presented on one of which the case at bar must be decided: One, vigorously asserted by Transamerica and based on its interpretation of the decision in the Taylor case, is that the board of directors of Axton-Fisher, whether or not dominated by Transamerica, the principal Class B stockholder, at any time and for any purpose, might call the Class A stock for redemption; the other, asserted with equal vigor by Zahn, is that the board of directors of Axton-Fisher as fiduciaries were not entitled to favor Transamerica, the Class B stockholder, by employing the redemption provisions of the charter for its benefit.

We must of course treat the decision of the Court of Appeals of Kentucky in the Taylor case as evidence of what is the law of Kentucky. The Court took the position on that record that the directors at any time might call the Class A stock for redemption and that the redemption provision of the charter was written as much for the benefit of the Class B stock as for the Class A stock. It is argued by Transamerica very persuasively that what the Court of Appeals of Kentucky held was that when the Class A stock received its allocation of $60 a share plus accrued dividends it received its full due and that the directors had the right at any time to eliminate Class A stock from the corporate setup for the benefit of the Class B stock.[4] It does not appear from the opinion of the Court of Appeals of Kentucky whether or not the subsequent liquidation of Axton-Fisher was brought to the attention of the Court. But it is clear from the pleading that the subsequent liquidation was not an issue in the case and from the language of the Court there is some indication that it believed that Axton-Fisher was to continue in existence because Commissioner Stanley spoke of the elimination of the Class A stock, which possessed voting rights, from the management and control of Axton-Fisher. Such surmises are hazardous, however, and are not really apposite since it is our duty to determine the law of Kentucky and not to delve into subjective mental processes. It should be noted that Commissioner Stanley stated the justiciable controversy before the Court of Appeals of Kentucky as follows: "The case presents a novel question of power of the board of directors of a corporation to rescind or modify its action in calling certain stock for redemption or retirement." This, and only this, was the question before the Court. It is notable that Commissioner Stanley said also that the acts of boards of directors "exercised in good faith and not in fraud of the rights of the stockholders" should not be interfered with by the courts and that he spoke as well of the "fair discretion" of directors to be exercised in the same manner as would be the case in the declaration of dividends. . . . We think that it is the settled law of Kentucky that directors may not declare or withhold the declaration of dividends for the purpose of personal profit or, by analogy, take any corporate action for such a purpose.

The difficulty in accepting Transamerica's contentions in the case at bar is that the directors of Axton-Fisher, if the allegations of the complaint be accepted as true, were the instruments of Transamerica, were directors voting in favor of their special interest, that of

---

[4]   The court said: "Manifestly, it was very much to the interest of the holders of Class B stock to have all these priorities, obligations and restrictions on and conditional joint control of the management eliminated. A substantial advantage was given to and acquired by the Class B stockholders. . . . "

Transamerica, could not and did not exercise an independent judgment in calling the Class A stock, but made the call for the purpose of profiting their true principal, Transamerica. In short a puppet-puppeteer relationship existed between the directors of Axton-Fisher and Transamerica.

The act of the board of directors in calling the Class A stock, an act which could have been legally consummated by a disinterested board of directors, was here effected at the direction of the principal Class B stockholder in order to profit it. Such a call is voidable in equity at the instance of a stockholder injured thereby. It must be pointed out that under the allegations of the complaint there was no reason for the redemption of the Class A stock to be followed by the liquidation of Axton-Fisher except to enable the Class B stock to profit at the expense of the Class A stock. As has been hereinbefore stated the function of the call was confided to the board of directors by the charter and was not vested by the charter in the stockholders of any class. It was the intention of the framers of Axton-Fisher's charter to require the board of directors to act disinterestedly if that body called the Class A stock, and to make the call with a due regard for its fiduciary obligations. If the allegations of the complaint be proved, it follows that the directors of Axton-Fisher, the instruments of Transamerica, have been derelict in that duty. Liability which flows from the dereliction must be imposed upon Transamerica which, under the allegations of the complaint, constituted the board of Axton-Fisher and controlled it. . . .

As has been stated the plaintiff has endeavored to set up a "First Cause of Action" and a "Second Cause of Action" in his complaint. The first cause of action is based upon his ownership of shares of Class A stock not surrendered by him to Axton-Fisher for redemption and is asserted not only on his own behalf but also on behalf of other Class A stockholders retaining their stock. The second cause of action is asserted by him on his own behalf and on behalf of other Class A stockholders in respect to the value of the stock which was surrendered for redemption. The two alleged separate causes of action, however, are in reality one. In our opinion, if the allegations of the complaint be proved, Zahn may maintain his cause of action to recover from Transamerica the value of the stock retained by him as that shall be represented by its aliquot share of the proceeds of Axton-Fisher on dissolution. It is also our opinion that he may maintain a cause of action to recover the difference between the amount received by him for the shares already surrendered and the amount which he would have received on liquidation of Axton-Fisher if he had not surrendered his stock. . . .

———

NOTE ON FURTHER PROCEEDINGS IN ZAHN V. TRANSAMERICA CORP.

The Third Circuit's original decision in *Zahn* used some language suggesting that the call of the Class A stock was wrongful in itself. However, in subsequent proceedings the Third Circuit held that the call was rightful even though it benefited the Class B stock and Transamerica and hurt the Class A stock:

> The first and principal question is the one raised by the holders of Class A stock as to the amount of damages to be awarded to them. The Class A stockholders contend that they are entitled to receive their aliquot shares in the liquidation distribution in the two-to-one ratio provided for in the charter for Class A stockholders participating in a liquidation. The district court held, however, that they are entitled only to recover as though they were Class B stockholders for the reason that a disinterested board of directors having knowledge of all the facts could and would have called the Class A stock for redemption in which event all of the Class A stockholders would have exercised their option to convert their shares into Class B stock on a one-for-one basis. We think that the district court was right in so holding.
>
> The Court of Appeals of Kentucky has held that the Axton-Fisher Class A stock, although designated as a common stock was in the nature of a junior preferred stock, and that the provision of the charter for the redemption of the Class A stock was a continuing option allowed to the holders of the Class B common stock which the board of directors could exercise in their favor. This construction of the Axton-Fisher charter by the highest court of the state of its incorporation was, of course, binding on the district court. We agree with the district court that the provisions of the Axton-Fisher charter with respect to liquidation must be read realistically with the provisions for redemption of the Class A stock and its conversion into Class B stock. When so read it becomes apparent that a disinterested board of directors discharging its responsibility to the Class B stockholders in case of liquidation would call the Class A stock for redemption at $60 per share if it appeared that the distribution in liquidation to that stock would exceed that figure on a two-to-one basis. Since the board would have the right to do this and the Class B stockholders would be entitled to such action, the failure to do so would be an arbitrary act which would confer a windfall to which they were not entitled under the charter upon the Class A stockholders at the direct expense of the holders of the Class B stock. The district court was therefore quite right in determining that the damages to be awarded to the Class A stockholders should be measured by what they would have received if they had converted their shares into Class B stock prior to the liquidation.

Speed v. Transamerica Corp., 235 F.2d 369 (3d Cir.1956).

NEMEC v. SHRADER

[Chapter 7, Section 7, supra]

NOTE ON THE DUTY OF DISCLOSURE BY CONTROLLING SHAREHOLDERS UNDER DELAWARE LAW

The Delaware Court has been very rigorous in requiring full disclosure by controlling shareholders when they deal with the minority. In *Lynch v. Vickers Energy Corp.*, 383 A.2d 278 (Del.1977),[1] Vickers, the majority shareholder of TransOcean stock, made a tender offer for the 46% of TransOcean stock held by the public. The trial court held that in preparing the offering circular through which the tender offer was made, Vickers owed a fiduciary duty that required "complete candor" in disclosing fully "all of the facts and circumstances surrounding" the tender offer. The Delaware Supreme Court agreed with that rule, but reversed because the trial court had not applied the rule with sufficient vigor:

> . . . [A]t the time of the offer, defendants were in possession of [an] estimate, prepared by Forrest Harrell, a petroleum engineer and a vice-president of TransOcean, fixing the net asset value [of TransOcean] at $250.8 million, which computes to approximately $20 per share, and from which one could conclude that the value could be as high as $300 million. Both of these estimates were . . . substantially higher than the minimum amount stated in the tender offer.

> The Trial Court closely examined the Harrell report and concluded that nondisclosure thereof was not fatal; the Court reasoned that the [language used in the offering circular] ". . . furnished the TransOcean stockholders with adequate facts on which to make an educated choice. . . . " . . .

> This approach to the controversy was, in our view, mistaken in two respects: First, to reach such a conclusion it was necessary for the Court to weigh the merits of the Harrell report and, in the context of this case, that was error. The Court's function was not to go through Harrell's estimates of oil reserves and recoveries, for example, and make its own judgment about whether these should be "substantially discounted," nor should it have substituted its judgment for Harrell's about the rate which the Federal Power Commission would approve for a sale of natural gas. The stockholders and not the Court should have been permitted to make such qualitative judgments.

---

[1] On subsequent appeal, 429 A.2d 497 (Del.Supr.1981), overruled on another issue, Weinberger v. UOP, Inc., 457 A.2d 701 (Del.Supr.1983).

The Court's duty was to examine what information defendants had and to measure it against what they gave to the minority stockholders, in a context in which "complete candor" is required. In other words, the limited function of the Court was to determine whether defendants had disclosed all information in their possession germane to the transaction in issue. And by "germane" we mean, for present purposes, information such as a reasonable shareholder would consider important in deciding whether to sell or retain stock. . . .

A second reason why we think that the Court of Chancery was mistaken in applying the law was that it incorrectly substituted a "disclosure of adequate facts" standard . . . for the correct standard, which requires disclosure of *all* germane facts. Completeness, not adequacy, is both the norm and the mandate under present circumstances.

In *Rosenblatt v. Getty Oil Co.,* 493 A.2d 929 (Del.1985), the Delaware Court substituted the term "material facts" for the term "germane facts." Subsequently, the Court dropped the "duty of candor" terminology in favor of terminology based on materiality, but made clear that the change in terminology did not signify a change in the underlying concept. Shell Petroleum, Inc. v. Smith, 606 A.2d 112, 113 n. 3 (Del.1992).

In *Shell Petroleum, Inc. v. Smith,* 606 A.2d 112 (Del. 1992), Royal Dutch Petroleum Co. owned 94.6% of Shell Oil Co. Royal Dutch decided to initiate a merger between Shell and SPNV Holdings ("Holdings"). Under the terms of the merger, each Shell minority shareholder would receive $58/share, or $60/share if he waived his right to appraisal before a fixed date. In conjunction with the merger, Holdings distributed several documents to the minority. Due to a computer-programming error, the documents understated Shell's discounted future net cash flows—an important element in the computation of the value of a business—by $3.00 to $3.45 per share. Former minority shareholders of Shell brought a class action. The Court of Chancery awarded damages to the shareholders for material misstatements. Affirmed.

Holdings' duty with respect to disclosure is clear. As the majority shareholder, Holdings bears the burden of showing complete disclosure of all material facts relevant to a minority shareholders' decision whether to accept the short-form merger consideration or seek an appraisal. . . . A fact is considered material if there is a "substantial likelihood that the disclosure of the omitted fact would have been viewed by the reasonable investor as having significantly altered the 'total mix' of information made available." . . . "While it need not be shown that an omission or distortion would have made an investor change his overall view of a proposed transaction, it must be shown that the fact in question would have been relevant to him." . . .

Holdings . . . argues that a $3 per share error was not significant enough to make a reasonable stockholder change his decision and seek an appraisal. However, the question is not whether the information would have changed the stockholder's decision to accept the merger consideration, but whether "the fact in question would have been relevant to him." . . .

See also Zirn v. VLI Corp., 621 A.2d 773, 777 (Del.1993); Arnold v. Society for Savings Bancorp, Inc., 650 A.2d 1270 (Del.1994).

———

C. SALE OF CONTROL

Zetlin v. Hanson Holdings, Inc.
New York Court of Appeals, 1979.
48 N.Y.2d 684, 421 N.Y.S.2d 877, 397 N.E.2d 387.

MEMORANDUM.

The order of the Appellate Division should be affirmed, with costs.

Plaintiff Zetlin owned approximately 2% of the outstanding shares of Gable Industries, Inc., with defendants Hanson Holdings, Inc., and Sylvestri, together with members of the Sylvestri family, owning 44.4% of Gable's shares. The defendants sold their interests to Flintkote Co. for a premium price of $15 per share, at a time when Gable stock was selling on the open market for $7.38 per share. It is undisputed that the 44.4% acquired by Flintkote represented effective control of Gable.

Recognizing that those who invest the capital necessary to acquire a dominant position in the ownership of a corporation have the right of controlling that corporation, it has long been settled law that, absent looting of corporate assets, conversion of a corporate opportunity, fraud or other acts of bad faith, a controlling stockholder is free to sell, and a purchaser is free to buy, that controlling interest at a premium price (see *Barnes v. Brown,* 80 N.Y. 527; *Levy v. American Beverage Corp.,* 265 App.Div. 208; *Essex Universal Corp. v. Yates,* 305 F.2d 572).

Certainly, minority shareholders are entitled to protection against such abuse by controlling shareholders. They are not entitled, however, to inhibit the legitimate interests of the other stockholders. It is for this reason that control shares usually command a premium price. The premium is the added amount an investor is willing to pay for the privilege of directly influencing the corporation's affairs.

In this action plaintiff Zetlin contends that minority stockholders are entitled to an opportunity to share equally in any premium paid for a controlling interest in the corporation. This rule would profoundly affect the manner in which controlling stock interests are now transferred. It would require, essentially, that a controlling interest be transferred only by means of an offer to all stockholders, i.e., a tender offer. This would be contrary to existing law and if so radical a change is to be effected it would best be done by the Legislature. . . .

Order affirmed.

———

Andrews, The Stockholder's Right to Equal Opportunity in the Sale of Shares

78 Harv.L.Rev. 505, 515–22 (1965).

The rule to be considered can be stated thus: whenever a controlling stockholder sells his shares, every other holder of shares (of the same class) is entitled to have an equal opportunity to sell his shares, or a prorata part of them, on substantially the same terms. Or in terms of the correlative duty: before a controlling stockholder may sell his shares to an outsider he must assure his fellow stockholders an equal opportunity to sell their shares, or as high a proportion of theirs as he ultimately sells of his own. There are qualifications in the application of the rule, to which I will return; but for purposes of argument we can begin with this broad statement of it . . .

[*Practical reasons for the proposed rule*] (*a*).—There is a substantial danger that following a transfer of controlling shares corporate affairs may be conducted in a manner detrimental to the interests of the stockholders who have not had an opportunity to sell their shares. The corporation may be looted; it may just be badly run. Or the sale of controlling shares may operate to destroy a favorable opportunity for corporate action. . . .

The equal opportunity rule does not deal directly with the problem of mismanagement, which may occur even after a transfer of control complying with the rule; but enforcement of the rule will remove much of the incentive a purchaser can offer a controlling stockholder to sell on profitable terms. Indeed, in the case of a purchasing looter there is nothing in it for the purchaser unless he can buy less than all the shares; there is no profit in stealing from a solvent corporation if the thief owns all the stock. But the controlling stockholder will be loath to sell only part of his shares (except at a price that compensates him for all of his shares) if he expects the purchaser to destroy the value of what he keeps. The rule forces the controlling stockholder to share equally with his fellow stockholders both the benefits of the price he receives for the shares he sells and the business risks incident to the shares he retains. This will tend strongly to discourage a sale of controlling shares when the risk of looting, or other harm to the corporation, is apparent; and it will provide the seller with a direct incentive to investigate and evaluate with care when the risks are not apparent, since his own financial interest continues to be at stake. . . .

Of course a transfer of control may have advantageous effects for a corporation and its stockholders—and these may be just as subtle as any adverse effects. Many sales of controlling shares come about because the selling stockholders are not doing as well with a business as a purchaser believes he can do; and the belief is often right. Often the sellers are members of a family that has simply run out of managerial talent or interest.

If the rule of equal opportunity would prevent sales in this sort of situation, that would be a high price to pay for the prevention of harm in other cases. . . . For my own part I do not believe the rule of equal opportunity would have much tendency to discourage beneficial transactions. After all, if the purchaser is optimistic—and can convince his bankers to share his optimism—he should be willing to buy out everyone. If the seller is optimistic about the consequences of the transfer, he should be willing to retain some of his shares. If minority stockholders are optimistic, they should be willing to hold their shares. If the financial community is optimistic (in the case of a publicly held corporation), the market itself should offer the minority stockholders a chance to sell at a price that satisfies the rule. Thus, on the face of it the rule would only operate to prevent a sale when all four of these—the seller, the purchaser, the minority stockholders, and the financial community—take a pessimistic view of the transfer. . . .

(b). . . . [A] purchaser attains control of the corporation's business and assets equally whether he purchases all the shares or a smaller controlling block. When a purchaser buys less than all the shares, he is acquiring a business worth more than what he pays in cash, and is financing the difference by leaving the minority shares outstanding. We think of mortgage debts that way; if a person buys property subject to a mortgage and leaves the mortgage outstanding, we recognize that the mortgage provides financing for the purchaser because it has the same effect, substantially, as a new loan with the proceeds of which the purchaser might have paid full value for the property. But stock provides financing just as much as a mortgage does. A purchaser who buys only part of the stock of an enterprise might have accomplished much the same net result by purchasing all the assets in the name of a newly organized corporation in which he takes only a part of the stock. The other stockholders in the new corporation would then be viewed as providing equity financing for the acquisition. The chief difference then between a sale of assets, or of all the stock, and a sale of a controlling block of shares only, is that in the latter case the purchaser has had his acquisition partially financed, perhaps unwillingly, by the stockholders from whom he does not buy. That is no reason to give the minority stockholders less protection than if the purchaser gave them an opportunity to sell, even at a lower price. . . .

(c).—A somewhat broader way of putting the argument is even simpler: each stockholder is entitled to share proportionately in the profits of the enterprise; from the stockholder's point of view a sale of stock is one very important way of realizing a profit on his investment; profits from stock sales ought to be regarded as profits of the enterprise subject to equal sharing among stockholders just as much as profits realized through corporate action.

A minority stockholder must invest largely on the strength of the expectation that decisions will tend to be made for his benefit because of the general identity of interest between him and those in control. This identity of interest is qualified when controlling stockholders have an opportunity to profit by entering into dealings with their corporation; this is permitted because such transactions may be mutually profitable, and there is no way to enforce equality of interest beyond allowing judicial scrutiny of such transactions for fairness. It would be impossible to insist, for example, that a publicly held corporation offer all its stockholders a proportionate opportunity to serve in an executive capacity. But when an opportunity arises for profit by selling shares, there is no such simple practical reason why it cannot be made equally available to all stockholders. . . .

Javaras, Equal Opportunity in the Sale of Controlling Shares: A Reply to Professor Andrews

32 U.Chi.L.Rev. 420, 425–27 (1965).

I believe that the gravest defect in Professor Andrews' theory is a grievous underassessment of the costs of a preventive rule in restraining beneficial transactions. Such restraint would operate on the purchaser by imposing higher required investment—the price of all the shares of the corporation rather than only those owned by the controlling shareholder. Professor Andrews minimizes the effects of this factor on two grounds. First, the controlling shareholder under the rule of equal opportunity, when confronted with a purchaser who wants the controlling shares and no more, may be induced to retain some of his shares and share the sale ratably with the non-controlling shareholders. Admittedly, this requires faith in the management of the purchaser. Second, a beneficial purchaser should be willing to buy all the shares because, after all, the non-controlling shares have the same investment value as the controlling shares. All the purchaser would have to do, therefore, if he did not have the capital is to borrow it. If he could not, that would be a reflection either of superior knowledge in the financial community or dislocations in the capital market.

It is doubtful whether sufficient controlling sellers can be induced to retain their shares so as to eliminate the higher capital requirement. First, . . . sales of securities are not dictated merely by an appraisal of investment value. Many sellers simply want immediate cash. Second, a controlling seller may not wish to hold, say twenty-five per cent as compared to his prior fifty per cent, because of the possibility of his views differing from those of the controlling purchaser in the future. This reticence would partly stem from . . . the controlling sellers assessment of the change in risks when he is deprived of control. The loss of control would subject him to the risk of poor management, which might dictate a lesser investment in this corporation on the principle of risk diversification.

Likewise the purchaser himself might be unwilling that the seller retain some of his shares, particularly where working control (less than fifty per cent) is the subject of the offer. He might well be reluctant to have a large block of stock outstanding whose owners, under conditions of dissension, could mobilize the other shareholders and displace his control of the board of directors.

In effect then, the rule of equal treatment would impose higher capital requirements on beneficial purchasers in a substantial number of transactions. Professor Andrews inappropriately assumes, however, that the purchasers should be willing to meet these higher costs because the investment value of the additional shares is the same. He errs in that his reasoning is incomplete. It is true that the investment value is the same. But even if the capital market did function perfectly and the purchaser could arrange the financing, a rational businessman might not want to buy all the shares at a premium price justified by the investment potential. It might be sensible to decline to buy more than the bare amount necessary for control on the principles of diversification of risk and of opportunity. This might render the equal treatment rule ineffectual as a means of automatically distinguishing "good" and "bad" purchasers. I would think that the number of prospective beneficial purchasers prevented because of a desire to diversify will be much larger than those simply unable to raise the capital. Until empirical evidence is adduced to the contrary, I am predisposed to consider this cost of restraining beneficial transactions substantial when compared with the cases of detriment with which the present law is incompetent to deal. . . .

Perlman v. Feldmann

United States Court of Appeals, Second Circuit, 1955.
219 F.2d 173, cert. denied 349 U.S. 952, 75 S.Ct. 880, 99 L.Ed. 1277.

■ CLARK, CHIEF JUDGE. This is a derivative action brought by minority stockholders of Newport Steel Corporation to compel accounting for, and restitution of, allegedly illegal gains which accrued to defendants as a result of the sale in August, 1950, of their controlling interest in the corporation. The principal defendant, C. Russell Feldmann, who represented and acted for the others, members of his family,[1] was at that time not only the dominant stockholder, but also the chairman of the board of directors and the president of the corporation. Newport, an

---

[1] The stock was not held personally by Feldmann in his own name, but was held by the members of his family and by personal corporations. The aggregate of stock thus [held] amounted to 33% of the outstanding Newport stock and gave working control to the holder. The actual sale included 55,552 additional shares held by friends and associates of Feldmann, so that a total of 37% of the Newport stock was transferred.

Indiana corporation, operated mills for the production of steel sheets for sale to manufacturers of steel products, first at Newport, Kentucky, and later also at other places in Kentucky and Ohio. The buyers, a syndicate organized as Wilport Company, a Delaware corporation, consisted of end-users of steel who were interested in securing a source of supply in a market becoming ever tighter in the Korean War. Plaintiffs contend that the consideration paid for the stock included compensation for the sale of a corporate asset, a power held in trust for the corporation by Feldmann as its fiduciary. This power was the ability to control the allocation of the corporate product in a time of short supply, through control of the board of directors; and it was effectively transferred in this sale by having Feldmann procure the resignation of his own board and the election of Wilport's nominees immediately upon consummation of the sale.

The present action represents the consolidation of three pending stockholders' actions in which yet another stockholder has been permitted to intervene. Jurisdiction below was based upon the diverse citizenship of the parties. Plaintiffs argue here, as they did in the court below, that in the situation here disclosed the vendors must account to the nonparticipating minority stockholders for that share of their profit which is attributable to the sale of the corporate power. Judge Hincks denied the validity of the premise, holding that the rights involved in the sale were only those normally incident to the possession of a controlling block of shares, with which a dominant stockholder, in the absence of fraud or foreseeable looting, was entitled to deal according to his own best interests. Furthermore, he held that plaintiffs had failed to satisfy their burden of proving that the sales price was not a fair price for the stock per se. Plaintiffs appeal from these rulings of law which resulted in the dismissal of their complaint.

The essential facts found by the trial judge are not in dispute. Newport was a relative newcomer in the steel industry with predominantly old installations which were in the process of being supplemented by more modern facilities. Except in times of extreme shortage Newport was not in a position to compete profitably with other steel mills for customers not in its immediate geographical area. Wilport, the purchasing syndicate, consisted of geographically remote end-users of steel who were interested in buying more steel from Newport than they had been able to obtain during recent periods of tight supply. The price of $20 per share was found by Judge Hincks to be a fair one for a control block of stock, although the over-the-counter market price had not exceeded $12 and the book value per share was $17.03. But this finding was limited by Judge Hincks' statement that "[w]hat value the block would have had if shorn of its appurtenant power to control distribution of the corporate product, the evidence does not show." It was also conditioned by his earlier ruling that the burden was on plaintiffs to prove a lesser value for the stock.

Both as director and as dominant stockholder, Feldmann stood in a fiduciary relationship to the corporation and to the minority stockholders as beneficiaries thereof. Pepper v. Litton, 308 U.S. 295, 60 S.Ct. 238, 84 L.Ed. 281; Southern Pac. Co. v. Bogert, 250 U.S. 483, 39 S.Ct. 533, 63 L.Ed. 1099. His fiduciary obligation must in the first instance be measured by the law of Indiana, the state of incorporation of Newport. Rogers v. Guaranty Trust Co. of New York, 288 U.S. 123, 136, 53 S.Ct. 295, 77 L.Ed. 652; Mayflower Hotel Stockholders Protective Committee v. Mayflower Hotel Corp., 89 U.S.App.D.C. 171, 193 F.2d 666, 668. Although there is no Indiana case directly in point, the most closely analogous one emphasizes the close scrutiny to which Indiana subjects the conduct of fiduciaries when personal benefit may stand in the way of fulfillment of trust obligations. In Schemmel v. Hill, 91 Ind.App. 373, 169 N.E. 678, 682, 683, McMahan, J., said: "Directors of a business corporation act in a strictly fiduciary capacity. Their office is a trust. Stratis v. Andreson, 1926, 254 Mass. 536, 150 N.E. 832, 44 A.L.R. 567; Hill v. Nisbet, 1885, 100 Ind. 341, 353. When a director deals with his corporation, his acts will be closely scrutinized. Bossert v. Geis, 1914, 57 Ind.App. 384, 107 N.E. 95. Directors of a corporation are its agents, and they are governed by the rules of law applicable to other agents, and, as between themselves and their principal, the rules relating to honesty and fair dealing in the management of the affairs of their principal are applicable. They must not, in any degree, allow their official conduct to be swayed by their private interest, which must yield to official duty. Leader Publishing Co. v. Grant Trust Co., 1915, 182 Ind. 651, 108 N.E. 121. In a transaction between a director and his corporation, where he acts for himself and his principal at the same time in a matter connected with the relation between them, it is presumed, where he is thus potentially on both sides of the contract, that self-interest will overcome his fidelity to his principal, to his own benefit and to his principal's hurt." And the judge added: "Absolute and most scrupulous good faith is the very essence of a director's obligation to his corporation. The first principal duty arising from his official relation is to act in all things of trust wholly for the benefit of his corporation."

In Indiana, then, as elsewhere, the responsibility of the fiduciary is not limited to a proper regard for the tangible balance sheet assets of the corporation, but includes the dedication of his uncorrupted business judgment for the sole benefit of the corporation, in any dealings which may adversely affect it.... Although the Indiana case is particularly relevant to Feldmann as a director, the same rule should apply to his fiduciary duties as majority stockholder, for in that capacity he chooses and controls the directors, and thus is held to have assumed their liability. Pepper v. Litton, supra, 308 U.S. 295, 60 S.Ct. 238. This, therefore, is the standard to which Feldmann was by law required to conform in his activities here under scrutiny.

It is true, as defendants have been at pains to point out, that this is not the ordinary case of breach of fiduciary duty. We have here no fraud, no misuse of confidential information, no outright looting of a helpless corporation. But on the other hand, we do not find compliance with that high standard which we have just stated and which we and other courts have come to expect and demand of corporate fiduciaries. In the often-quoted words of Judge Cardozo: "Many forms of conduct permissible in a workaday world for those acting at arm's length, are forbidden to those bound by fiduciary ties. A trustee is held to something stricter than the morals of the market place. Not honesty alone, but the punctilio of an honor the most sensitive, is then the standard of behavior. As to this there has developed a tradition that is unbending and inveterate. Uncompromising rigidity has been the attitude of courts of equity when petitioned to undermine the rule of undivided loyalty by the 'disintegrating erosion' of particular exceptions." Meinhard v. Salmon, supra, 249 N.Y. 458, 464, 164 N.E. 545, 546, 62 A.L.R. 1. The actions of defendants in siphoning off for personal gain corporate advantages to be derived from a favorable market situation do not betoken the necessary undivided loyalty owed by the fiduciary to his principal.

The corporate opportunities of whose misappropriation the minority stockholders complain need not have been an absolute certainty in order to support this action against Feldmann. If there was possibility of corporate gain, they are entitled to recover. . . .

. . . In the past Newport had used and profited by its market leverage by operation of what the industry had come to call the "Feldmann Plan." This consisted of securing interest-free advances from prospective purchasers of steel in return for firm commitments to them from future production. The funds thus acquired were used to finance improvements in existing plants and to acquire new installations. In the summer of 1950 Newport had been negotiating for cold-rolling facilities which it needed for a more fully integrated operation and a more marketable product, and Feldmann plan funds might well have been used toward this end.

Further, as plaintiffs alternatively suggest, Newport might have used the period of short supply to build up patronage in the geographical area in which it could compete profitably even when steel was more abundant. Either of these opportunities was Newport's, to be used to its advantage only. Only if defendants had been able to negate completely any possibility of gain by Newport could they have prevailed. It is true that a trial court finding states: "Whether or not, in August, 1950, Newport's position was such that it could have entered into 'Feldmann Plan' type transactions to procure funds and financing for the further expansion and integration of its steel facilities and whether such expansion would have been desirable for Newport, the evidence does not show." This, however, cannot avail the defendants, who—contrary to the ruling below—had the burden of proof on this issue, since fiduciaries always have the burden of proof in establishing the fairness of their dealings with trust property. . . .

Defendants seek to categorize the corporate opportunities which might have accrued to Newport as too unethical to warrant further consideration. It is true that reputable steel producers were not participating in the gray market brought about by the Korean War and were refraining from advancing their prices, although to do so would not have been illegal. But Feldmann plan transactions were not considered within this self-imposed interdiction; the trial court found that around the time of the Feldmann sale Jones & Laughlin Steel Corporation, Republic Steel Company, and Pittsburgh Steel Corporation were all participating in such arrangements. In any event, it ill becomes the defendants to disparage as unethical the market advantages from which they themselves reaped rich benefits.

We do not mean to suggest that a majority stockholder cannot dispose of his controlling block of stock to outsiders without having to account to his corporation for profits or even never do this with impunity when the buyer is an interested customer, actual or potential, for the corporation's product. But when the sale necessarily results in a sacrifice of this element of corporate good will and consequent unusual profit to the fiduciary who has caused the sacrifice, he should account for his gains. So in a time of market shortage, where a call on a corporation's product commands an unusually large premium, in one form or another, we think it sound law that a fiduciary may not appropriate to himself the value of this premium. Such personal gain at the expense of his coventurers seems particularly reprehensible when made by the trusted president and director of his company. In this case the violation of duty seems to be all the clearer because of this triple role in which Feldmann appears, though we are unwilling to say, and are not to be understood as saying, that we should accept a lesser obligation for any one of his roles alone.

Hence to the extent that the price received by Feldmann and his codefendants included such a bonus, he is accountable to the minority stockholders who sue here. Restatement, Restitution §§ 190, 197 (1937); Seagrave Corp. v. Mount, supra, 6 Cir., 212 F.2d 389. And plaintiffs, as they contend, are entitled to a recovery in their own right, instead of in right of the corporation (as in the usual derivative actions), since neither Wilport nor their successors in interest should share in any judgment which may be rendered. See Southern Pacific Co. v. Bogert, 250 U.S. 483, 39 S.Ct. 533, 63 L.Ed. 1099. Defendants cannot well object to this form of recovery, since the only alternative, recovery for the corporation as a whole, would subject them to a greater total liability.

The case will therefore be remanded to the district court for a determination of the question expressly left open below, namely, the value of defendants' stock without the appurtenant control over the corporation's output of steel. We reiterate that on this issue, as on all others relating to a breach of fiduciary duty, the burden of proof must rest on the defendants. Bigelow v. RKO Radio Pictures, 327 U.S. 251, 265–266, 66 S.Ct. 574, 90 L.Ed. 652; Package Closure Corp. v. Sealright Co., 2 Cir., 141 F.2d 972, 979. Judgment should go to these plaintiffs and those whom they represent for any premium value so shown to the extent of their respective stock interests.

The judgment is therefore reversed and the action remanded for further proceedings pursuant to this opinion.

[The dissenting opinion of Judge Swan is omitted.]

____

NOTE ON FURTHER PROCEEDINGS IN PERLMAN V. FELDMANN

On remand, the district court determined the enterprise value of the corporation, based upon its book value and earnings potential, to be $15,825,777, or $14.67 per share. This made the premium $5.33 a share, or $2,126,280. The complaining stockholders, owning sixty-three percent of the stock, were therefore entitled to judgment of $1,339,769, with interest of 6 percent from the sale date, plus costs. Perlman v. Feldmann, 154 F.Supp. 436 (D.Conn.1957).

____

Harris v. Carter

582 A.2d 222, 235 (Del. Ch. 1990)

"[W]hen the circumstances would alert a reasonably prudent person to a risk that his buyer is dishonest or in some material respect not truthful, a duty devolves upon the seller to make such inquiry as a reasonably prudent person would make, and generally to exercise care so that others who will be affected by his actions should not be injured by wrongful conduct."

____

D. THE SALE OF A CORPORATE OFFICE

____

SECURITIES EXCHANGE ACT RULE 14(f)–1

[See Statutory Supplement]

____

ALI, PRINCIPLES OF CORPORATE GOVERNANCE § 5.16

[See Statutory Supplement]

____

Essex Universal Corp. v. Yates

United States Court of Appeals, Second Circuit, 1962.
305 F.2d 572.

■ Before LUMBARD, CHIEF JUDGE, and CLARK and FRIENDLY, CIRCUIT JUDGES.

■ LUMBARD, CHIEF JUDGE.

This appeal from the district court's summary judgment in favor of the defendant raises the question whether a contract for the sale of 28.3 per cent of the stock of a corporation is, under New York law, invalid as against public policy solely because it includes a clause giving the purchaser an option to require a majority of the existing directors to replace themselves, by a process of seriatim resignation, with a majority designated by the purchaser. Despite the disagreement evidenced by the diversity of our opinions, my brethren and I agree that such a provision does not on its face render the contract illegal and unenforceable, and thus that it was improper to grant summary judgment. Judge Friendly would reject the defense of illegality without further inquiry concerning the provision itself (as distinguished from any contention that control could not be safely transferred to the particular purchaser). Judge Clark and I are agreed that on remand, which must be had in any event to consider other defenses raised by the pleadings, further factual issues may be raised by the parties upon which the legality of the clause in question will depend; we disagree, however, on the nature of those factual issues, as our separate opinions reveal. Accordingly, the grant of summary judgment is reversed and the case is remanded for trial of the question of the legality of the contested provision and such further proceedings as may be proper on the other issues raised by the pleadings.

Since we are in agreement on certain preliminary questions, this opinion constitutes the opinion of the court up to the point where it is indicated that it thenceforth states only my individual views.

The defendant Herbert J. Yates, a resident of California, was president and chairman of the board of directors of Republic Pictures Corporation, a New York corporation which at the time relevant to this suit had 2,004,190 shares of common stock outstanding. Republic's stock was listed and traded on the New York Stock Exchange. In August 1957, Essex Universal Corporation, a Delaware corporation owning stock in various diversified businesses, learned of the possibility of purchasing from Yates an interest in Republic. Negotiations proceeded rapidly, and on August 28 Yates and Joseph Harris, the president of Essex, signed a contract in which Essex agreed to buy, and Yates agreed "to sell or cause to be sold" at least 500,000 and not more than 600,000 shares of Republic stock. The price was set at eight dollars a share, roughly two dollars above the then market price on the Exchange. Three dollars per share was to be paid at the closing on September 18, 1957 and the remainder in twenty-four equal monthly payments beginning January 31, 1958. The shares were to be transferred on the closing date, but Yates was to retain the certificates, endorsed in blank by Essex, as security for full payment. In addition to other provisions not relevant to the present motion, the contract contained the following paragraph:

"6.   Resignations.

Upon and as a condition to the closing of this transaction if requested by Buyer at least ten (10) days prior to the date of the closing:

(a)   Seller will deliver to Buyer the resignations of the majority of the directors of Republic.

(b)   Seller will cause a special meeting of the board of directors of Republic to be held, legally convened pursuant to law and the by-laws of Republic, and simultaneously with the acceptance of the directors' resignations set forth in paragraph 6(a) immediately preceding will cause nominees of Buyer to be elected directors of Republic in place of the resigned directors."

Before the date of the closing, as provided in the contract, Yates notified Essex that he would deliver 566,223 shares, or 28.3 per cent of the Republic stock then outstanding, and Essex formally requested Yates to arrange for the replacement of a majority of Republic's directors with Essex nominees pursuant to paragraph 6 of the contract. This was to be accomplished by having eight of the fourteen directors resign seriatim, each in turn being replaced by an Essex nominee elected by the others; such a procedure was *in form* permissible under the charter and by-laws of Republic, which empowered the board to choose the successor of any of its members who might resign.

On September 18, the parties met as arranged for the closing at Republic's office in New York City. Essex tendered bank drafts and cashier's checks totaling $1,698,690, which was the 37½ per cent of the total price of $4,529,784 due at this time. The drafts and checks were payable to one Benjamin C. Cohen, who was Essex' banker and had arranged for the borrowing of the necessary funds. Although Cohen was prepared to endorse these to Yates, Yates upon advice of his lawyer rejected the tender as "unsatisfactory" and said, according to his deposition testimony, "Well, there can be no deal. We can't close it."

Essex began this action in the New York Supreme Court, and it was removed to the district court on account of diversity of citizenship. Essex seeks damages of $2,700,000, claiming that at the time of the aborted closing the stock was in actuality worth more than $12.75 a share.[1] Yates' answer raised a number of defenses, but the motion for summary judgment now before us was made and decided only on the theory that the provision in the contract for immediate transfer of control of the

---

[1]   In 1959, while this action was pending, the stock was sold to another party for ten dollars a share.

board of directors was illegal *per se* and tainted the entire contract. We have no doubt, and the parties agree, that New York law governs.

Appellant's contention that the provision for transfer of director control is separable from the rest of the contract can quickly be rejected. . . .

. . . [W]e hold the provision regarding directors inseparable from the sale of shares, and proceed to a consideration of its legality.

Up to this point my brethren and I are in agreement. The following analysis is my own, except insofar as the separate opinions of Judges Clark and Friendly may indicate agreement.

It is established beyond question under New York law that it is illegal to sell corporate office or management control by itself (that is, accompanied by no stock or insufficient stock to carry voting control). . . . The rationale of the rule is undisputable: persons enjoying management control hold it on behalf of the corporation's stockholders, and therefore may not regard it as their own personal property to dispose of as they wish.[3] Any other rule would violate the most fundamental principle of corporate democracy, that management must represent and be chosen by, or at least with the consent of, those who own the corporation.

Essex was, however, contracting with Yates for the purchase of a very substantial percentage of Republic stock. If, by virtue of the voting power carried by this stock, it could have elected a majority of the board of directors, then the contract was not a simple agreement for the sale of office to one having no ownership interest in the corporation, and the question of its legality would require further analysis. Such stock voting control would incontestably belong to the owner of a majority of the voting stock, and it is commonly known that equivalent power usually accrues to the owner of 28.3% of the stock. For the purpose of this analysis, I shall assume that Essex was contracting to acquire a majority of the Republic stock, deferring consideration of the situation where, as here, only 28.3% is to be acquired.

Republic's board of directors at the time of the aborted closing had fourteen members divided into three classes, each class being "as nearly as may be" of the same size. Directors were elected for terms of three years, one class being elected at each annual shareholder meeting on the first Tuesday in April. Thus, absent the immediate replacement of directors provided for in this contract, Essex as the hypothetical new majority shareholder of the corporation could not have obtained managing control in the form of a majority of the board in the normal course of events until April 1959, some eighteen months after the sale of the stock. The first question before us then is whether an agreement to accelerate the transfer of management control, in a manner legal in form

---

[3]   The cases have made no distinction between contracts by directors or officers to resign and contracts by persons who in actuality control the actions of officers or directors to procure their resignations, and of course none should exist.

under the corporation's charter and by-laws, violates the public policy of New York.

There is no question of the right of a controlling shareholder under New York law normally to derive a premium from the sale of a controlling block of stock. In other words, there was no impropriety *per se* in the fact that Yates was to receive more per share than the generally prevailing market price for Republic stock. Levy v. American Beverage Corp., 265 App.Div. 208, 218, 38 N.Y.S.2d 517, 526 (1st Dept.1942); Stanton v. Schenck, 140 Misc. 621, 251 N.Y.S. 221 (N.Y.County Sup.Ct.1931); see Hill, supra, 70 Harv.L.Rev. at 991–92.

The next question is whether it is legal to give and receive payment for the immediate transfer of management control to one who has achieved majority share control but would not otherwise be able to convert that share control into operating control for some time. I think that it is.

Of course under some circumstances controlling shareholders transferring immediate control may be compelled to account to the corporation for that part of the consideration received by them which exceeds the fair value of the block of stock sold, as well as for the injury which they may cause to the corporation. . . . Gerdes v. Reynolds, 28 N.Y.S.2d 622 (N.Y.County Sup.Ct.1941). . . .

A fair generalization from [Perlman v. Feldmann and other] cases may be that a holder of corporate control will not, as a fiduciary, be permitted to profit from facilitating actions on the part of the purchasers of control which are detrimental to the interests of the corporation or the remaining shareholders. There is, however, no suggestion that the transfer of control over Republic to Essex carried any such threat to the interests of the corporation or its other shareholders.

Our examination of the New York cases . . . gives us no reason to regard as impaired the holding of the early case of Barnes v. Brown, 80 N.Y. 527 (1880), that a bargain for the sale of a majority stock interest is not made illegal by a plan for immediate transfer of management control by a program like that provided for in the Essex-Yates contract. Judge Earl wrote:

> "[The seller] had the right to sell out all his stock and interest in the corporation, . . . and when he ceased to have any interest in the corporation, it was certainly legitimate and right that he should cease to control it . . . It was simply the mode of transferring the control of the corporation to those who by the policy of the law ought to have it, and I am unable to see how any policy of the law was violated, or in what way, upon the evidence, any wrong was thereby done to anyone." 80 N.Y. at 537.

To be sure, in Barnes v. Brown no term of the contract of sale *required* the seller to effectuate the immediate replacement of directors, as did paragraph 6 of the Essex-Yates contract, but Judge Earl stated that "I shall assume that it was the understanding and a part of the scheme that he should do so." 80 N.Y. at 536. . . .

The easy and immediate transfer of corporate control to new interests is ordinarily beneficial to the economy and it seems inevitable that such transactions would be discouraged if the purchaser of a majority stock interest were required to wait some period before his purchase of control could become effective. Conversely it would greatly hamper the efforts of any existing majority group to dispose of its interest if it could not assure the purchaser of immediate control over corporation operations. I can see no reason why a purchaser of majority control should not ordinarily be permitted to make his control effective from the moment of the transfer of stock.

Thus if Essex had been contracting to purchase a majority of the stock of Republic, it would have been entirely proper for the contract to contain the provision for immediate replacement of directors. Although in the case at bar only 28.3 per cent of the stock was involved, it is commonly known that a person or group owning so large a percentage of the voting stock of a corporation which, like Republic, has at least the 1,500 shareholders normally requisite to listing on the New York Stock Exchange, is almost certain to have share control as a practical matter. If Essex was contracting to acquire what in reality would be equivalent to ownership of a majority of stock, i.e., if it would as a practical certainty have been guaranteed of the stock voting power to choose a majority of the directors of Republic in due course, there is no reason why the contract should not similarly be legal.[6] Whether Essex was thus to acquire the equivalent of majority stock control would, if the issue is properly raised by the defendants, be a factual issue to be determined by the district court on remand.

Because 28.3 per cent of the voting stock of a publicly owned corporation is usually tantamount to majority control, I would place the burden of proof on this issue on Yates as the party attacking the legality of the transaction. Thus, unless on remand Yates chooses to raise the question whether the block of stock in question carried the equivalent of majority control, it is my view that the trial court should regard the contract as legal and proceed to consider the other issues raised by the pleadings. If Yates chooses to raise the issue, it will, on my view, be necessary for him to prove the existence of circumstances which would have prevented Essex from electing a majority of the Republic board of directors in due course. It will not be enough for Yates to raise merely hypothetical possibilities of opposition by the other Republic shareholders to Essex' assumption of management control. Rather, it will

---

[6]   The fact that under the Essex-Yates contract only 37½% of the price of the stock was to be paid at the closing and the balance was not to be fully paid for twenty-eight months is irrelevant to this case. There is no indication that Essex did not have sound financial backing sufficient to discharge properly the obligation which had been incurred.

be necessary for him to show that, assuming neutrality on the part of the retiring management, there was at the time some concretely foreseeable reason why Essex' wishes would not have prevailed in shareholder voting held in due course. In other words, I would require him to show that there was at the time of the contract some other organized block of stock of sufficient size to outvote the block Essex was buying, or else some circumstance making it likely that enough of the holders of the remaining Republic stock would band together to keep Essex from control.

Reversed and remanded for further proceedings not inconsistent with the judgment of this court.

■ FRIENDLY, CIRCUIT JUDGE (concurring).

Chief Judge Lumbard's thoughtful opinion illustrates a difficulty, inherent in our dual judicial system, which has led at least one state to authorize its courts to answer questions about its law that a Federal court may ask. Here we are forced to decide a question of New York law, of enormous importance to all New York corporations and their stockholders, on which there is hardly enough New York authority for a really informed prediction what the New York Court of Appeals would decide on the facts here presented, see Cooper v. American Airlines, Inc., 149 F.2d 355, 359, 162 A.L.R. 318 (2 Cir., 1945); Pomerantz v. Clark, 101 F.Supp. 341 (D.Mass.1951); Corbin, The Laws of the Several States, 50 Yale L.J. 762, 775–776 (1941), yet too much for us to have the freedom used to good effect in Perlman v. Feldmann, 219 F.2d 173 (2 Cir.), cert. denied, 349 U.S. 952, 75 S.Ct. 880, 99 L.Ed. 1277 (1955).

I have no doubt that many contracts, drawn by competent and responsible counsel, for the purchase of blocks of stock from interests thought to "control" a corporation although owning less than a majority, have contained provisions like paragraph 6 of the contract *sub judice*. However, developments over the past decades seem to me to show that such a clause violates basic principles of corporate democracy. To be sure, stockholders who have allowed a set of directors to be placed in office, whether by their vote or their failure to vote, must recognize that death, incapacity or other hazard may prevent a director from serving a full term, and that they will have no voice as to his immediate successor. But the stockholders are entitled to expect that, in that event, the remaining directors will fill the vacancy in the exercise of their fiduciary responsibility. A mass seriatim resignation directed by a selling stockholder, and the filling of vacancies by his henchmen at the dictation of a purchaser and without any consideration of the character of the latter's nominees, are beyond what the stockholders contemplated or should have been expected to contemplate. This seems to me a wrong to the corporation and the other stockholders which the law ought not countenance, whether the selling stockholder has received a premium or not. Right in this Court we have seen many cases where sudden shifts of corporate control have caused serious injury; Pettit v. Doeskin Products, Inc., 270 F.2d 95 (2 Cir., 1959), cert. denied, 362 U.S. 910, 80 S.Ct. 660,

4 L.Ed.2d 618 (1960); United States v. Crosby, 294 F.2d 928 (2 Cir., 1961), cert. denied Mittelman v. United States, 368 U.S. 984, 82 S.Ct. 599, 7 L.Ed.2d 523 (1962); and Kirtley v. Abrams, 299 F.2d 341 (2 Cir., 1962), are a few recent examples. To hold the seller for delinquencies of the new directors only if he knew the purchaser was an intending looter is not a sufficient sanction. The difficulties of proof are formidable even if receipt of too high a premium creates a presumption of such knowledge, and, all too often, the doors are locked only after the horses have been stolen. Stronger medicines are needed—refusal to enforce a contract with such a clause, even though this confers an unwarranted benefit on a defaulter, and continuing responsibility of the former directors for negligence of the new ones until an election has been held. Such prophylactics are not contraindicated, as Judge Lumbard suggests, by the conceded desirability of preventing the dead hand of a former "controlling" group from continuing to dominate the board after a sale, or of protecting a would-be purchaser from finding himself without a majority of the board after he has spent his money. A special meeting of stockholders to replace a board may always be called, and there could be no objection to making the closing of a purchase contingent on the results of such an election. I perceive some of the difficulties of mechanics such a procedure presents, but I have enough confidence in the ingenuity of the corporate bar to believe these would be surmounted.

Hence, I am inclined to think that if I were sitting on the New York Court of Appeals, I would hold a provision like [paragraph] 6 violative of public policy save when it was entirely plain that a new election would be a mere formality—i.e., when the seller owned more than 50% of the stock. I put it thus tentatively because, before making such a decision, I would want the help of briefs, including those of *amici curiae,* dealing with the serious problems of corporate policy and practice more fully than did those here, which were primarily devoted to argument as to what the New York law has been rather than what it ought to be. Moreover, in view of the perhaps unexpected character of such a holding, I doubt that I would give it retrospective effect.

As a judge of this Court, my task is the more modest one of predicting how the judges of the New York Court of Appeals would rule, and I must make this prediction on the basis of legal materials rather than of personal acquaintance or hunch. Also, for obvious reasons, the prospective technique is unavailable when a Federal court is deciding an issue of state law. Although Barnes v. Brown, 80 N.Y. 527 (1880), dealt with the sale of a majority interest, I am unable to find any real indication that the doctrine there announced has been thus limited. True, there are New York cases saying that the sale of corporate offices is forbidden; but the New York decisions do not tell us what this means and I can find nothing, save perhaps one unexplained sentence in the opinion of a trial court in Ballantine v. Ferretti, 28 N.Y.S.2d 668, 682 (Sup.Ct.N.Y.Co.1941), to indicate that New York would not apply Barnes

v. Brown to a case where a stockholder with much less than a majority conditioned a sale on his causing the resignation of a majority of the directors and the election of the purchaser's nominees.

Chief Judge Lumbard's proposal goes part of the way toward meeting the policy problem I have suggested. Doubtless proceeding from what, as it seems to me, is the only justification in principle for permitting even a majority stockholder to condition a sale on delivery of control of the board—namely that in such a case a vote of the stockholders would be a useless formality, he sets the allowable bounds at the line where there is "a practical certainty" that the buyer would be able to elect his nominees and, in this case, puts the burden of disproving that on the person claiming illegality.

Attractive as the proposal is in some respects, I find difficulties with it. One is that I discern no sufficient intimation of the distinction in the New York cases, or even in the writers, who either would go further in voiding such a clause, see Berle, "Control" in Corporate Law, 58 Colum.L.Rev. 1212, 1224 (1958); Leech, Transactions in Corporate Control, 104 U.Pa.L.Rev. 725, 809 (1956) [proposing legislation], or believe the courts have not yet gone that far, see Baker & Cary, Corporations: Cases and Materials (3d ed. unabr. 1959) 590. To strike down such a condition only in cases falling short of the suggested line accomplishes little to prevent what I consider the evil; in most instances a seller will not enter into a contract conditioned on his "delivering" a majority of the directors unless he has good reason to think he can do that. When an issue does arise, the "practical certainty" test is difficult to apply. The existence of such certainty will depend not merely on the proportion of the stock held by the seller but on many other factors— whether the other stock is widely or closely held, how much of it is in "street names," what success the corporation has experienced, how far its dividend policies have satisfied its stockholders, the identity of the purchasers, the presence or absence of cumulative voting, and many others. Often, unless the seller has nearly 50% of the stock, whether he has "working control" can be determined only by an election; groups who thought they had such control have experienced unpleasant surprises in recent years. Judge Lumbard correctly recognizes that, from a policy standpoint, the pertinent question must be the buyer's prospects of election, not the seller's—yet this inevitably requires the court to canvass the likely reaction of stockholders to a group of whom they know nothing and seems rather hard to reconcile with a position that it is "right" to insert such a condition if a seller has a larger proportion of the stock and "wrong" if he has a smaller. At the very least the problems and uncertainties arising from the proposed line of demarcation are great enough, and its advantages small enough, that in my view a Federal court would do better simply to overrule the defense here, thereby accomplishing what is obviously the "just" result in this particular case, and leave the development of doctrine in this area to the State, which has primary concern for it.

I would reverse the grant of summary judgment and remand for consideration of defenses other than a claim that the inclusion of paragraph 6 *ex mero motu* renders the contract void.

[The concurring opinion of Judge Clark is omitted.]

———

NOTE ON ESSEX UNIVERSAL CORP. V. YATES

It is not at all clear that a shareholding block of 28.3% necessarily carries control of a publicly held corporation. If not coupled with control of the board. Consider Brannigan, Florida Businessman Seeks to Steer Bank Toward Sale, Wall Street Journal, Sept. 2, 1987, at 27, col. 1: "[Hugh F. Culverhouse] has launched a tender offer for 10% of Florida Commercial Banks Inc's shares, . . . He already holds . . . 39.9% of the bank's shares. Since 1984, Mr. Culverhouse has struggled unsuccessfully to win a seat on the company's board or to acquire control of the concern. As of earlier this year, 28.4% of the company's shares were controlled by a well-entrenched group of officers and directors that has opposed him. . . . "

———

NOTE ON TAG-ALONG AND DRAG-ALONG PROVISIONS

Under modern corporate practice, the problems faced by minority shareholders when controlling shareholders arrange to sell their shares at a premium are often addressed by a *tag-along* provision in a shareholders' agreement. Under such a provision, if a third party offers to buy out the majority shareholders of a corporation, the minority shareholders must be offered the right to sell their shares to the third party on the same terms as those offered to the majority shareholders. Such provisions are only feasible when the corporation still has a small number of shareholders.

Under a related type of provision, known as a *drag-along* provision, minority shareholders agree that if the controlling shareholders sell their shares to a given buyer, the minority shareholders will also sell their shares to the buyer on the same terms. Unlike tag-alongs, the purpose of the drag-alongs is to protect the controlling shareholders in situations where they have lined up a buyer for their shares at an advantageous price, and the buyer insists on acquiring 100% of the shares.

———

CHAPTER 11

THE ANTIFRAUD PROVISION: SECTION 10(b) AND RULE 10b–5

1. AN INTRODUCTION TO SECTION 10(b) AND RULE 10b–5

SECURITIES EXCHANGE ACT § 10(b)

[See Statutory Supplement]

SECURITIES EXCHANGE ACT RULE 10b–5

[See Statutory Supplement]

The Wharf (Holdings) Limited v. United International Holdings, Inc.

Supreme Court of the United States, 2001.
532 U.S. 588, 121 S.Ct. 1776, 149 L.Ed.2d 845.

■ JUSTICE BREYER delivered the opinion of the Court.

This securities fraud action focuses upon a company that sold an option to buy stock while secretly intending never to honor the option. The question before us is whether this conduct violates § 10(b) of the Securities Exchange Act of 1934, which prohibits using "any manipulative or deceptive device or contrivance" "in connection with the purchase or sale of any security." . . . *15 U.S.C. § 78j(b)*. . . . We conclude that it does.

I

Respondent United International Holdings, Inc., a Colorado-based company, sued petitioner The Wharf (Holdings) Limited, a Hong Kong firm, in Colorado's Federal District Court. United said that in October 1992 Wharf had sold it an option to buy 10% of the stock of a new Hong Kong cable system. But, United alleged, at the time of the sale Wharf secretly intended not to permit United to exercise the option. United claimed that Wharf's conduct amounted to a fraud "in connection with the . . . sale of [a] security," prohibited by § 10(b), and violated numerous

741

state laws as well. A jury found in United's favor. The Court of Appeals for the Tenth Circuit upheld that verdict. *210 F.3d 1207 (2000).* And we granted certiorari to consider whether the dispute fell within the scope of § 10(b). . . .

In 1991, the Hong Kong government announced that it would accept bids for the award of an exclusive license to operate a cable television system in Hong Kong. Wharf decided to prepare a bid. Wharf's chairman, Peter Woo, instructed one of its managing directors, Stephen Ng, to find a business partner with cable system experience. Ng found United. And United sent several employees to Hong Kong to help prepare Wharf's application, negotiate contracts, design the system, and arrange financing.

United asked to be paid for its services with a right to invest in the cable system if Wharf should obtain the license. During August and September 1992, while United's employees were at work helping Wharf, Wharf and United negotiated about the details of that payment. Wharf prepared a draft letter of intent that contemplated giving United the right to become a co-investor, owning 10% of the system. But the parties did not sign the letter of intent. And in September, when Wharf submitted its bid, it told the Hong Kong authorities that Wharf would be the system's initial sole owner, although Wharf would also "consider" allowing United to become an investor.*

In early October 1992, Ng met with a United representative, who told Ng that United would continue to help only if Wharf gave United an enforceable right to invest. Ng then orally granted United an option with the following terms: (1) United had the right to buy 10% of the future system's stock; (2) the price of exercising the option would be 10% of the system's capital requirements minus the value of United's previous services (including expenses); (3) United could exercise the option only if it showed that it could fund its 10% share of the capital required for at least the first 18 months; and (4) the option would expire if not exercised within six months of the date that Wharf received the license. The parties continued to negotiate about how to write documents that would embody these terms, but they never reduced the agreement to writing.

In May 1993, Hong Kong awarded the cable franchise to Wharf. United raised $66 million designed to help finance its 10% share. In July or August 1993, United told Wharf that it was ready to exercise its option. But Wharf refused to permit United to buy any of the system's stock. Contemporaneous internal Wharf documents suggested that Wharf had never intended to carry out its promise. . . .

[Various] documents, along with other evidence, convinced the jury that Wharf, through Ng, had orally sold United an option to purchase a 10% interest in the future cable system while secretly intending not to permit United to exercise the option, in violation of § 10(b) of the

---

*   References to transcripts and briefs are omitted. (Footnote by ed.)

Securities Exchange Act and various state laws. The jury awarded United compensatory damages of $67 million . . .

II

Section 10(b) of the Securities Exchange Act makes it "unlawful for any person . . . [t]o use or employ, in connection with the purchase or sale of any security . . . , any manipulative or deceptive device or contrivance in contravention of such rules and regulations as the [SEC] may prescribe." *15 U.S.C. § 78j.*

Pursuant to this provision, the SEC has promulgated Rule 10b–5. That Rule forbids the use, "in connection with the purchase or sale of any security," of (1) "any device, scheme, or artifice to defraud"; (2) "any untrue statement of a material fact"; (3) the omission of "a material fact necessary in order to make the statements made . . . not misleading"; or (4) any other "act, practice, or course of business" that "operates . . . as a fraud or deceit." *17 C.F.R. § 240.10b–5 (2000).*

To succeed in a Rule 10b–5 suit, a private plaintiff must show that the defendant used, in connection with the purchase or sale of a security, one of the four kinds of manipulative or deceptive devices to which the Rule refers, and must also satisfy certain other requirements not at issue here. See, *e.g., 15 U.S.C. § 78j* (requiring the "use of any means or instrumentality of interstate commerce or of the mails, or of any facility of any national securities exchange"); *Ernst & Ernst v. Hochfelder*, 425 U.S. 185, 193, 96 S.Ct. 1375, 47 L.Ed.2d 668 (1976) (requiring scienter, meaning "intent to deceive, manipulate, or defraud"); *Basic Inc. v. Levinson*, 485 U.S. 224, 231–232, 108 S.Ct. 978, 99 L.Ed.2d 194 (1988) (requiring that any misrepresentation be material); *id.*, at 243, 108 S.Ct. 978 (requiring that the plaintiff sustain damages through reliance on the misrepresentation).

In deciding whether the Rule covers the circumstances present here, we must assume that the "security" at issue is not the cable system stock, but the option to purchase that stock. That is because the Court of Appeals found that Wharf conceded this point. *210 F.3d, at 1221* ("Wharf does not contest on appeal the classification of the option as a security"). That concession is consistent with the language of the Securities Exchange Act, which defines "security" to include both "any . . . option . . . on any security" and "any . . . right to . . . purchase" stock. *15 U.S.C. § 78c(a)(10).* . . . Consequently, we must decide whether Wharf's secret intent not to honor the option it sold United amounted to a misrepresentation (or other conduct forbidden by the Rule) in connection with the sale of the option.

Wharf argues that its conduct falls outside the Rule's scope for two basic reasons. First, Wharf points out that its agreement to grant United an option to purchase shares in the cable system was an oral agreement. And it says that § 10(b) does not cover oral contracts of sale. . . .

[There is no] convincing reason to interpret the Act to exclude oral contracts as a class. The Act itself says that it applies to "any contract" for the purchase or sale of a security. *15 U.S.C. §§ 78c(a)(13), (14).* Oral contracts for the sale of securities are sufficiently common that the Uniform Commercial Code and statutes of frauds in every State now consider them enforceable. See U.C.C. § 8–113 (Supp.2000) ("A contract . . . for the sale or purchase of a security is enforceable whether or not there is a writing signed or record authenticated by a party against whom enforcement is sought"). . . . Any exception for oral sales of securities would significantly limit the Act's coverage, thereby undermining its basic purposes. . . .

Second, Wharf argues that a secret reservation not to permit the exercise of an option falls outside § 10(b) because it does not "relat[e] to the value of a security purchase or the consideration paid"; hence it does "not implicate [§ 10(b)'s] policy of full disclosure." Brief for Petitioners 25, 26 (emphasis deleted). But even were it the case that the Act covers only misrepresentations likely to affect the value of securities, Wharf's secret reservation was such a misrepresentation. To sell an option while secretly intending not to permit the option's exercise is misleading, because a buyer normally presumes good faith. Cf., *e.g., Restatement (Second) of Torts § 530*, Comment *c* (1976) ("Since a promise necessarily carries with it the implied assertion of an intention to perform[,] it follows that a promise made without such an intention is fraudulent"). For similar reasons, the secret reservation misled United about the option's value. Since Wharf did not intend to honor the option, the option was, unbeknownst to United, valueless. . . .

For these reasons, the judgment of the Court of Appeals is

Affirmed.

————

What result in *Wharf (Holdings) Limited* if the facts established that only after entering the agreement with United did the defendant decide not to honor its contractual obligation to United? This question invites the application of the "in connection with" element of the antifraud provision. Section 10(b) and Rule 10b–5 proscribe manipulative and deceptive acts that are "in connection with the purchase or sale of any security." Although this language calls for there to be some nexus between a violation of Rule 10b–5 and a purchase or sale, "[t]he courts have interpreted [the term 'in connection with'] broadly. Any statement that is reasonably calculated to affect the investment decision of a reasonable investor will satisfy the 'in connection with' requirement." 3 T. Hazen, Securities Regulation 540–541 (6th ed. 2009). If Wharf decided not to honor its contractual obligations to United after United decided to fulfill its part of the bargain, would Wharf's breach have impacted United's investment decision?

Interesting questions surround the meaning of the "in connection with" requirement. Fraudulent representations to a bank to obtain a loan for which securities are to serve as collateral were not deemed to be "in connection with" the purchase or sale of securities even though a pledge of securities is a sale. *See* Chemical Bank v. Arthur Andersen & Co., 726 F.2d 930 (2d Cir.), *cert. denied*, 469 U.S. 884, 105 S.Ct. 253, 83 L.Ed.2d 190 (1984). And, in Gavin v. AT & T (7th Cir. 2006), the court held the broker had not committed fraud in connection with the sale of securities. In *Gavin* a plan of merger approved by the stockholders of each company provided the stockholders of the disappearing firm with a variety of options by which they would be compensated for their shares. Defendant broker was retained to administer the plan, and sent a notice after the merger's consummation detailing most of the plans, stating that for a $7 fee it would assist any interested stockholders in realizing the option they chose, but without disclosing that one of the options available to the shareholders did not involve any fee to the broker. The court held this omission, although material, was not in connection with the sale of a security which under standard corporate law had occurred earlier following the stockholders' approval and filing of the necessary documents with the secretary of state. On the other hand, in *SEC v. Zandford*, 535 U.S. 813, 122 S.Ct. 1899, 153 L.Ed.2d 1 (2002), a unanimous Supreme Court held that the requisite nexus existed where the broker systematically misappropriated proceeds from sales of his client's securities. The client, who was quite elderly and in poor health, granted the broker full discretion to engage in securities transactions without the client's prior approval. Over a two-year period, the broker repeatedly sold securities from the account and misappropriated the sales proceeds which approximated $343,000. The court found the requisite linkage by reasoning that each sale was made in furtherance of the fraudulent scheme to misappropriate the funds, reasoning rather broadly that the client was "duped into believing . . . [the broker] would 'conservatively invest' their assets in the stock market and that any transaction made on their behalf would be for their benefit. . . . " 535 U.S. at 822, 122 S.Ct. at 1904, 153 L.Ed.2d at 10. What would have been the result had the broker had received funds from the client on the pretense they would be invested in securities, but instead the broker embezzled the funds? *See, e.g.,* VR Global Partners, L.P. v. Bennett, 586 F. Supp. 2d 172 (S.D.N.Y. 2008).

———

NOTE ON PRIVATE ACTIONS UNDER RULE 10b–5

The Wharf (Holdings) Limited v. United International Holdings, Inc. was a private action; that is, it was an action brought by a private party for private relief—damages—rather than an enforcement action brought by the government. Neither Section 10(b) of the Securities Exchange Act nor Rule 10b–5 explicitly provides for private actions. However, there is a long tradition in American law of allowing private parties to bring actions based on violations of statutes or administrative rules in appropriate cases. What kinds of cases are appropriate, for this purpose, is the subject of principles whose content has changed somewhat over time. The most salient principles, for present purposes, are summarized in the descriptions of *J.I. Case Co v. Borak*, *Wyandotte v. United States*, and *Cort v. Ash*, set out at the beginning of Chapter 5, Section 4, supra.

Under these principles, the courts have held that some provisions of the Securities Acts and the rules thereunder give rise to private actions, and others do not. The Supreme Court formally upheld the implied private right of action under section 10(b) and Rule 10b–5 in *Herman & McLean v. Huddleston*, 459 U.S. 375, 103 S.Ct. 683, 74 L.Ed.2d 548 (1983).

––––––––

2.   WHAT CONSTITUTES A MISREPRESENTATION?

The Supreme Court in *Santa Fe Industries, Inc. v. Green*, 430 U.S. 462, 97 S. Ct. 1292, 51 L.Ed.2d 480 (1977), held there can be no violation of Section 10(b) and Rule 10b–5 "without any deception, misrepresentation, or nondisclosure." Therefore, it is paragraph (b) of Rule 10b–5 that does most of the work in litigation under the antifraud provision: among Rule 10b–5's three proscriptions it is paragraph (b) that most clearly reflects *Santa Fe Industries'* holding, as it proscribes material misstatements and omissions made in connection with the purchase or sale of a security.

Misstatements are fairly easy to identity. For example, if a company announces it earned $3 per share in the most recent quarter when in fact it earned substantially less than that amount, it has engaged in a misstatement. Rule 10b–5's proscription of material misstatements can be seen as requiring that when an affirmative statement is made what is affirmatively stated should be correct (subject to other requirements of the rule such as materiality, being in connection with the purchase or sale of a security, etc.). Omissions are also proscribed, but with the qualification that the omitted fact is not just material but needed to be disclosed "in order to make the statements made, in light of the circumstances under which they were made, not misleading." To be observed here is that the materiality of the omitted fact itself does not render the omission of that fact a violation; a violation ensues only if that omitted fact renders what was disclosed materially misleading. Thus, when dealing with an omission, courts focus on whether the defendant had a duty to disclose the omitted material fact. Such violations are generally referred to either an omission or duty to disclose cases.

––––––––

A.   DUTY TO SPEAK

By way of background, consider the three models that government regulation of disclosure might take. First, as we've seen, the Securities

Exchange Act imposes on certain companies a duty of *periodic disclosure* in the form of annual (Form 10-K) and quarterly (Form 10-Q) reporting requirements. Second, disclosure can be mandated for discrete transactions or activities. Such *transactional disclosure* occurs today for the public offerings of securities, the election of directors, or other matters involving the approval of shareholders of public companies. Finally, there is the somewhat utopian world of *continuous disclosure* where companies must disclose material information as soon as the material information arises; this form of disclosure is pretty much limited in the U.S. to the rather tightly configured mandates of Form 8-K for public companies. There is limited evidence of continuous disclosure. To be sure, in the post-Enron era of financial frauds Form 8-K was greatly expanded. However, Form 8-K still compels disclosure upon the occurrence of specified events (entering into or discontinuing a material transaction outside the ordinary course of operations, the resignation of the firm's outside auditor, or the departure of a director) of a reporting company. In addition, stock exchange listing requirements set forth certain duties to disclose important developments and events, although typically the only sanction for noncompliance with those rules would be delisting, and that sanction has seldom or never been imposed for mere nondisclosure.

Also, absent a specific SEC disclosure requirement that needs to be met, such as in the pending Form 10-K, there generally is a good deal of discretion on the part of the company's management. As a leading case on this point emphasized, "the timing of the disclosure [of material facts] is a matter for the business judgment of the corporate officers entrusted with the management of the corporation within the affirmative disclosure requirements promulgated by the exchanges and by the SEC." SEC v. Texas Gulf Sulphur Co., 401 F.2d 833, 850 n. 12 (in banc), *cert. denied*, 394 U.S. 976, 89 S.Ct. 1454, 22 L.Ed.2d 756 (1969). There are four important instances courts regularly find a duty to disclose material information.

1. Half-Truth Statements. A common ground for alleging fraud occurred by non-disclosure is the instance of a half-truth. Recall that Rule 10b–5(b) includes among its prohibitions an omission "to state a material fact necessary in order to make the statements made, in the light of the circumstances under which they were made, not misleading." Thus, a duty to disclose can flow from omitting a fact that was necessary to prevent from what was stated being materially misleading. For example, Twitter committed a misrepresentation when it announced continued growth in the total number of users of its service but did not disclose that average daily use had declined, in light of the fact that average daily use was found to be important by stock analysts). *Shenwick v. Twitter, Inc.*, 282 F. Supp.3d 1115 (N.D. Cal. 2017). *See* Donald C. Langevoort, Half-Truths: Protecting Mistaken Inferences by Investors and Others, 52 Stan. L. Rev. 87 (1999).

2. Duty to Correct. If the corporation makes a statement that is misleading—inaccurate—when made, even though not intentionally or recklessly so, and the corporation later learns that the statement was misleading, it is under a duty to correct the statement if the statement is still "alive," rather than "stale"—that is, if the statement would still be likely to be material to investors. See, e.g., Backman v. Polaroid Corp., 910 F.2d 10 (1st Cir.1990) (en banc). *In re Burlington Coat Factory Sec. Litig.,* 114 F.3d 1410, 1431 (3rd Cir. 1997) explains the duty as follows:

> [T]he duty to correct can also apply to a certain narrow set of forward-looking statements. We will attempt to illustrate the kinds of circumstances we have in mind with an example. Imagine the following situation. A public company in Manhattan makes a forecast that appears to it to be reasonable at the time made. Subsequently, the company discovers that it misread a vital piece of data that went into its forecast. Perhaps a fax sent by the company's factory manager in some remote location was blurry and was reasonably misread by management in Manhattan as representing sales for the past quarter as 100,000 units as opposed to 10,000 units. Manhattan management then makes an erroneous forecast based on the information it has at the time. A few weeks later, management receives the correct sales figures by mail. So long as the correction in the sales figures was material to the forecast that was discussed earlier, we think there would likely be a duty on the part of the company to disclose either the corrected figures or a corrected forecast. In other words, there is an implicit representation in any forecast (or statement of historical fact) that errors of the type we have identified will be corrected. This duty derives from the implicit factual representation that a public company makes whenever it makes a forecast, i.e., that the forecast was reasonable at the time made. What is crucial to recognize is that the error, albeit an honest one, was one that had to do with information available at the time the forecast was made and that the error in the information was subsequently discovered. . . .

3. Duty to Update. A more difficult question is whether a corporation has a duty to *update* an earlier forward-looking statement that was correct—or more accurately, reasonable—when made but later comes to be materially misleading. Several courts have held that if a corporation makes a public statement that is correct when made, but that becomes materially misleading in light of subsequent events, the corporation may have a duty to update the statement. For example, in *Greenfield v. Heublein, Inc.,* 742 F.2d 751, 758 (3d Cir.1984), cert. denied 469 U.S. 1215, 105 S.Ct. 1189, 84 L.Ed.2d 336 (1985), the court said, "[a]lthough a corporation may be under no duty to disclose . . . , if a corporation voluntarily makes a public statement that is correct when issued, [the corporation] has a duty to update the statement if it becomes materially misleading in light of subsequent events." See also In re Time Warner Inc. Securities Litigation, 9 F.3d 259, 267 (2d Cir.1993), cert. denied 511 U.S. 1017, 114 S.Ct. 1397, 128 L.Ed.2d 70 (1994) ("a duty to update opinions and projections may arise if the original opinions or projections have become misleading as the result of intervening events").

4. *Insider Trading.* As examined fully in the next chapter, insiders who trade on, or selectively disclose to others, material non-public information violate the antifraud provision; this occurs under the so-called "disclose or abstain" doctrine which holds that such individuals must either abstain from trading when in possession of material non public information or disclose that information. Hence, insider trading regulation has its own mechanism for imposing a duty to disclose.

5. *Entanglement.* A corporation may so involve itself in the preparation of statements about the corporation by outsiders—such as analysts' reports or earnings projections—that it assumes a duty to correct material errors in those statements. Such a duty "may occur when officials of the company have, by their activity, made an implied representation that the information they have reviewed is true or at least in accordance with the company's views." Elkind v. Liggett & Myers, Inc., 635 F.2d 156, 163 (2d Cir.1980). Similarly, A corporation may be under a duty to correct erroneous rumors resulting from leaks by the corporation or its agents. See, e.g., State Teachers Retirement Board v. Fluor Corp., 654 F.2d 843, 850 (2d Cir.1981) (dictum).

———

B. OPINION STATEMENTS

Rule 10b–5 speaks in terms of a misstatement or omission of a material *fact.* A perplexing question is whether an expression of opinion is a *fact.* At many locations, the SEC's mandatory disclosure rules call for corporations and their senior executives to provide opinions regarding certain matters. More frequently, public statements regarding corporate transactions or developments are statements of opinion.

Omnicare, Inc. v. Laborers Dist. Council Constr. Indus. Pension Fund, ___ U.S. ___, 135 S.Ct. 1318, 191 L.Ed.2d 253 (2015), illustrates the courts' approaches to such statements. In that case, Omnicare, Inc. made two statements regarding its compliance program, stating it believed its arrangements with suppliers and customers were in compliance with state and federal law, and adding that they were legal arrangements. They were not in compliance and a securities fraud was brought after its unlawful practices caused its stock price to decline. Justice Kagan examined how the statements could be actionable both as a misstatement and omission of material facts. The claim of compliance can be a misstatement if the speaker does not actually believe the opinion stated, i.e., the speaker knows the company's arrangements and contracts with customers and vendors are not lawful.

A company's CEO states: "The TVs we manufacture have the highest resolution available on the market." Or, alternatively, the CEO transforms that factual statement into one of opinion: "I *believe*" (or "I think") "the TVs we manufacture have the highest resolution available on the market." The first version would be an untrue statement of fact if a competitor had introduced a higher resolution TV a month before—even assuming the CEO had not yet learned of the new product. The CEO's assertion, after all, is not mere puffery, but a determinate, verifiable statement about her company's TVs; and the CEO, however innocently, got the facts wrong. But in the same set of circumstances, the second version would remain true. Just as she said, the CEO really did believe, when she made the statement, that her company's TVs had the sharpest picture around. And although a plaintiff could later prove that opinion erroneous, the words "I believe" themselves admitted that possibility, thus precluding liability for an untrue statement of fact. That remains the case if the CEO's opinion, as here, concerned legal compliance. If, for example, she said, "I believe our marketing practices are lawful," and actually did think that, she could not be liable for a false statement of fact—even if she afterward discovered a longtime violation of law. Once again, the statement would have been true, because all she expressed was a view, not a certainty, about legal compliance.

. . . As even Omnicare acknowledges, every such statement explicitly affirms one fact: that the speaker actually holds the stated belief. . . . For that reason, the CEO's statement about product quality ("I believe our TVs have the highest resolution available on the market") would be an untrue statement of fact—namely, the fact of her own belief—if she knew that her company's TVs only placed second. And so too the statement about legal compliance ("I believe our marketing practices are lawful") would falsely describe her own state of mind if she thought her company was breaking the law

A statement of opinion can also be actionable fact on the ground it omitted certain facts needed to prevent what was said from being materially misleading.

[A]n investor cannot state a claim by alleging only that an opinion was wrong; the complaint must as well call into question the issuer's basis for offering the opinion. . . . To be specific: The investor must identify particular (and material) facts going to the basis for the issuer's opinion—facts about the inquiry the issuer did or did not conduct or the knowledge it did or did not have—whose omission makes the opinion statement at issue

misleading to a reasonable person reading the statement fairly
and in context. . . .

Thus, if at the time of making the claim of compliance with the law the
speaker was aware the firm's general counsel had warned that some of
the arrangements as violating certain state and federal requirements
that could give rise to misrepresentation of opinion. But the Court
observed this is tricky as it expressed doubt there would have been a
misrepresentation if the warning had come from a very junior attorney.

————

C. FORWARD LOOKING STATEMENTS

A universal quality about the future is that it is hard to predict
accurately. When a company estimates that it will earn $3 in the next
year and ultimately earns materially less, was its earlier statement
materially misleading? What would render the statement actionable
under rule 10b–5? Are there risks that the determination of fault will be
made via hindsight so that earlier assumptions in formulating the
forecast will be viewed differently by the trier of fact? For example, what
if the earlier prediction assumed that materials and labor costs would not
rise, but in retrospect that assumption appears grossly optimistic? *See
e.g.* Financial Indus. Fund v. McDonnell Corp., 474 F.2d 514 (10th Cir.),
cert. denied, 414 U.S. 874, 94 S.Ct. 155, 38 L.Ed.2d 114 (1973).

   1. Statutory Safe Harbor for Forward-Looking Statements. In
1995, with the enactment of the Private Securities Litigation Reform Act,
discussed more fully later in this chapter, Congress provided special "safe
harbors" in the securities acts for most "forward-looking statements"—
that is, statements about the future (for example, predictions of
earnings).

   Section 21E(c)(1) provides two safe harbors against civil liability for
written forward-looking statements, as defined, that are made (1) by a
corporation that either has a security registered under section 12 of the
Act or has filed a registration statement as described in section 15(d), or
(2) by certain persons acting on behalf of such a corporation. Under the
first safe harbor, there is no liability if the statement is identified as a
forward-looking statement and is accompanied by "meaningful
cautionary" statements identifying important factors that could cause
actual results to differ materially from those in the statement. Under the
second safe harbor, there is no liability if the plaintiff fails to prove that
the statement was made with actual knowledge—not simply with
recklessness—that the statement was false or misleading. Accordingly,
Section 21E eliminates recklessness as sufficient scienter under Rule
10b–5 for forward-looking statements, although it does not affect
omissions or statements that purport to concern historical or existing
facts or forward-looking statements expressly excluded from the section
21E safe harbor. Section 21E(c)(2) provides a special additional safe

harbor applicable only to oral statements. (Comparable provisions are found in the Securities Act of 1933).

    2.   *"Bespeaks Caution" Doctrine.* Independent of the statutory safe harbor is a doctrine known as "bespeaks caution" that provides that a forward-looking statement does not give rise to liability, even though, if taken in isolation, it is misleading, if the document in which the statement is contained includes "meaningful cautionary language." The applicability of the bespeaks-caution doctrine is highly fact-specific. To some extent, it is also court-specific; different circuits have been either more or less ready to conclude that cautionary language was sufficient to protect against liability. It is fairly clear, however, that a generic, boiler-plate warning will not suffice. To have the desired effect, the cautionary language must be "tailored the specific future projections, estimates or opinions . . . which the plaintiffs challenge." Trump Casino Securities Litigation, 7 F.3d 357 (3d Cir. 1993), cert. denied sub nom. Gollomp v. Trump, 510 U.S. 1178, 114 S.Ct. 1219, 127 L.Ed.2d 565 (1994). By its terms, the bespeaks-caution doctrine, like the safe-harbor provisions in the Section 21E, is directed only to forward-looking statements, not to statements of present or historical facts. See EP MedSystems, Inc. v. EchoCath, Inc., 235 F.3d 865 (3d Cir. 2000). The doctrine is of special relevance when a forward-looking statement is made by a corporation or other person who is not within the safe harbor provided by Securities Exchange Act section 21E because the statement was made in the context of one of the many exceptions in section 21E—for example, a corporation that does not have a class of stock registered under section 12, the statement was made in connection with an initial public offering or the statement was made in connection with a tender offer.

––––––

3. MATERIALITY

––––––

TSC INDUSTRIES, INC. v. NORTHWAY, INC.

[Chapter 5, Section 4, *supra*]

––––––

Basic Inc. v. Levinson

Supreme Court of the United States, 1988.
485 U.S. 224, 108 S.Ct. 978, 99 L.Ed.2d 194.

■ JUSTICE BLACKMUN delivered the opinion of the Court.

    This case requires us to apply the materiality requirement of § 10(b) of the Securities Exchange Act of 1934 . . . Rule 10b–5 . . . in the context of preliminary corporate merger discussions. We must also determine whether a person who traded a corporation's shares on a securities exchange after the issuance of a materially misleading statement by the corporation may invoke a rebuttable presumption that, in trading, he relied on the integrity of the price set by the market.

I

Prior to December 20, 1978, Basic Incorporated was a publicly traded company primarily engaged in the business of manufacturing chemical refractories for the steel industry. . . .

Beginning in September 1976, Combustion representatives had meetings and telephone conversations with Basic officers and directors, including petitioners here, concerning the possibility of a merger. During 1977 and 1978, Basic made three public statements denying that it was engaged in merger negotiations.[4] On December 18, 1978, Basic asked the New York Stock Exchange to suspend trading in its shares and issued a release stating that it had been "approached" by another company concerning a merger. *Id.,* at 413. On December 19, Basic's board endorsed Combustion's offer of $46 per share for its common stock, *id.,* at 335, 414–416, and on the following day publicly announced its approval of Combustion's tender offer for all outstanding shares.

Respondents are former Basic shareholders who sold their stock after Basic's first public statement of October 21, 1977, and before the suspension of trading in December 1978. Respondents brought a class action against Basic and its directors, asserting that the defendants issued three false or misleading public statements and thereby were in violation of § 10(b) of the 1934 Act and of Rule 10b–5. Respondents alleged that they were injured by selling Basic shares at artificially depressed prices in a market affected by petitioners' misleading statements and in reliance thereon.

The District Court adopted a presumption of reliance by members of the plaintiff class upon petitioners' public statements that enabled the court to conclude that common questions of fact or law predominated over particular questions pertaining to individual plaintiffs. See Fed.Rule

---

[4]　On October 21, 1977, after heavy trading and a new high in Basic stock, the following news item appeared in the Cleveland Plain Dealer:

"[Basic] President Max Muller said the company knew no reason for the stock's activity and that no negotiations were under way with any company for a merger. He said Flintkote recently denied Wall Street rumors that it would make a tender offer of $25 a share for control of the Cleveland-based maker of refractories for the steel industry." App. 363.

On September 25, 1978, in reply to an inquiry from the New York Stock Exchange, Basic issued a release concerning increased activity in its stock and stated that

"management is unaware of any present or pending company development that would result in the abnormally heavy trading activity and price fluctuation in company shares that have been experienced in the past few days." *Id.,* at 401.

On November 6, 1978, Basic issued to its shareholders a "Nine Months Report 1978." This Report stated:

"With regard to the stock market activity in the Company's shares we remain unaware of any present or pending developments which would account for the high volume of trading and price fluctuations in recent months." *Id.,* at 403.

Civ.Proc. 23(b)(3). The District Court therefore certified respondents' class. On the merits, however, the District Court granted summary judgment for the defendants. It held that, as a matter of law, any misstatements were immaterial: there were no negotiations ongoing at the time of the first statement, and although negotiations were taking place when the second and third statements were issued, those negotiations were not "destined, with reasonable certainty, to become a merger agreement in principle." App. to Pet. for Cert. 103a.

The United States Court of Appeals for the Sixth Circuit affirmed the class certification, but reversed the District Court's summary judgment, and remanded the case. 786 F.2d 741 (1986). The court reasoned that while petitioners were under no general duty to disclose their discussions with Combustion, any statement the company voluntarily released could not be " 'so incomplete as to mislead.' "*Id.,* at 746, quoting SEC v. Texas Gulf Sulphur Co., 401 F.2d 833, 862 (C.A.2 1968) (en banc), cert. denied *sub nom.* Coates v. SEC, 394 U.S. 976 (1969). In the Court of Appeals' view, Basic's statements that no negotiations were taking place, and that it knew of no corporate developments to account for the heavy trading activity, were misleading. With respect to materiality, the court rejected the argument that preliminary merger discussions are immaterial as a matter of law, and held that "once a statement is made denying the existence of any discussions, even discussions that might not have been material in absence of the denial are material because they make the statement made untrue." 786 F.2d, at 749.

The Court of Appeals joined a number of other circuits in accepting the "fraud-on-the-market theory" to create a rebuttable presumption that respondents relied on petitioners' material misrepresentations, noting that without the presumption it would be impractical to certify a class under Fed.Rule Civ.Proc. 23(b)(3). See 786 F.2d, at 750–751.

We granted certiorari, 479 U.S. 1083 (1987), to resolve the split, see Part III, *infra,* among the Courts of Appeals as to the standard of materiality applicable to preliminary merger discussions, and to determine whether the courts below properly applied a presumption of reliance in certifying the class, rather than requiring each class member to show direct reliance on Basic's statements.

II. . . .

. . . The Court . . . explicitly has defined a standard of materiality under the securities laws, see *TSC Industries, Inc. v. Northway, Inc.,* 426 U.S. 438 (1976), concluding in the proxy-solicitation context that "[a]n omitted fact is material if there is a substantial likelihood that a reasonable shareholder would consider it important in deciding how to vote." *Id.,* at 449.[7] Acknowledging that certain information concerning

---

[7]   *TSC Industries* arose under § 14(a), as amended, of the 1934 Act, 15 U.S.C. § 78n(a), and Rule 14a–9, 17 CFR § 240.14a–9 (1975).

corporate developments could well be of "dubious significance," *id.*, at 448, the Court was careful not to set too low a standard of materiality; it was concerned that a minimal standard might bring an overabundance of information within its reach, and lead management "simply to bury the shareholders in an avalanche of trivial information—a result that is hardly conducive to informed decisionmaking." *Id.*, at 448–449. It further explained that to fulfill the materiality requirement "there must be a substantial likelihood that the disclosure of the omitted fact would have been viewed by the reasonable investor as having significantly altered the 'total mix' of information made available." *Id.*, at 449. We now expressly adopt the *TSC Industries* standard of materiality for the § 10(b) and Rule 10b–5 context.

III

The application of this materiality standard to preliminary merger discussions is not self-evident. Where the impact of the corporate development on the target's fortune is certain and clear, the *TSC Industries* materiality definition admits straightforward application. Where, on the other hand, the event is contingent or speculative in nature, it is difficult to ascertain whether the "reasonable investor" would have considered the omitted information significant at the time. Merger negotiations, because of the ever-present possibility that the contemplated transaction will not be effectuated, fall into the latter category. . . .

Petitioners urge upon us a Third Circuit test for resolving this difficulty. . . . Under this approach, preliminary merger discussions do not become material until "agreement-in-principle" as to the price and structure of the transaction has been reached between the would-be merger partners. See *Greenfield v. Heublein, Inc.,* 742 F.2d 751, 757 (C.A.3 1984), cert. denied, 469 U.S. 1215 (1985). By definition, then, information concerning any negotiations not yet at the agreement-in-principle stage could be withheld or even misrepresented without a violation of Rule 10b–5.

[The Court rejected the "agreement in principle" test, concluding "We . . . find no valid justification for artificially excluding from the definition of materiality information concerning merger discussions, which would otherwise be considered significant to the trading decision of a reasonable investor, merely because agreement-in-principle as to price and structure has not yet been reached by the parties or their representatives."] . . .

Even before this Court's decision in *TSC Industries,* the Second Circuit had explained the role of the materiality requirement of Rule 10b–5, with respect to contingent or speculative information or events, in a manner that gave that term meaning that is independent of the other provisions of the Rule. Under such circumstances, materiality "will depend at any given time upon a balancing of both the indicated probability that the event will occur and the anticipated magnitude of the event in light of the totality of the company activity." *SEC v. Texas Gulf Sulphur Co.,* 401 F.2d, at 849. Interestingly, neither the Third Circuit decision adopting the agreement-in-principle test nor petitioners here take issue with this general standard. Rather, they suggest that with respect to preliminary merger discussions, there are good reasons to draw a line at agreement on price and structure.

In a subsequent decision, the late Judge Friendly, writing for a Second Circuit panel, applied the *Texas Gulf Sulphur* probability/magnitude approach in the specific context of preliminary merger negotiations. After acknowledging that materiality is something to be determined on the basis of the particular facts of each case, he stated:

> "Since a merger in which it is bought out is the most important event that can occur in a small corporation's life, to wit, its death, we think that inside information, as regards a merger of this sort, can become material at an earlier stage than would be the case as regards lesser transactions—and this even though the mortality rate of mergers in such formative stages is doubtless high."

SEC v. Geon Industries, Inc., 531 F.2d 39, 47–48 (C.A.2 1976). We agree with that analysis.

Whether merger discussions in any particular case are material therefore depends on the facts. Generally, in order to assess the probability that the event will occur, a factfinder will need to look to indicia of interest in the transaction at the highest corporate levels. Without attempting to catalog all such possible factors, we note by way of example that board resolutions, instructions to investment bankers, and actual negotiations between principals or their intermediaries may serve as indicia of interest. To assess the magnitude of the transaction to the issuer of the securities allegedly manipulated, a factfinder will need to consider such facts as the size of the two corporate entities and of the potential premiums over market value. No particular event or factor short of closing the transaction need be either necessary or sufficient by itself to render merger discussions material.

As we clarify today, materiality depends on the significance the reasonable investor would place on the withheld or misrepresented information. The fact-specific inquiry we endorse here is consistent with the approach a number of courts have taken in assessing the materiality of merger negotiations. Because the standard of materiality we have adopted differs from that used by both courts below, we remand the case for reconsideration of the question whether a grant of summary judgment is appropriate on this record.

————

NOTE: MORE ON THE PROBABILITY-MAGNITUDE APPROACH TO MATERIALITY

In *Matrixx Initiatives, Inc. v. Siracusano*, 563 U.S. 27, 131 S. Ct. 1309, 179 L.Ed.2d 398 (2011), the Supreme Court once again visited the materiality of uncertain consequences of known activity. Matrixx's leading product was Zicam which accounted for seventy percent of its sales. In late 2003, Matrixx received reports from three physicians that after using Zicam their patients (ten in total) suffered anosmia, the permanent loss of the sense of smell. During the period it received the reports from the doctors, Matrixx issued a series of rosy forecasts regarding its financial performance and in early January 2004 it even increased by eighty percent an earlier earnings prediction. On January 30, 2004, the press reported that the FDA was looking into complaints that Zicam caused anosmia. Thereupon Matrixx shares declined 12 percent. The Supreme Court addressed the defense that under *Basic's* probability-magnitude test such reports were not material unless supported by a study documenting their statistical significance:

> Matrixx's argument rests on the premise that statistical significance is the only reliable indication of causation. This premise is flawed: As the SEC points out, "medical researchers. . .consider multiple factors in assessing causation." . . .

> Not only does the FDA rely on a wide range of evidence of causation, it sometimes acts on the basis of evidence that suggests, but does not prove, causation. For example, the FDA requires manufacturers of over-the-counter drugs to revise their labeling "to include a warning as soon as there is reasonable evidence of an association of a serious hazard with a drug; a causal relationship need not have been proved." 21 CFR § 201.80(e). More generally, the FDA may make regulatory decisions against drugs based on postmarketing evidence that gives rise to only a suspicion of causation. . . .

> Given that medical professionals and regulators act on the basis of evidence of causation that is not statistically significant, it stands to reason that in certain cases reasonable investors would as well. . . . As a result, assessing the materiality of adverse event reports is a "fact-specific" inquiry, . . . that requires consideration of the source, content, and context of the reports. This is not to say that statistical significance (or the lack thereof) is irrelevant—only that it is not dispositive of every case.

> Application of *Basic's* "total mix" standard does not mean that pharmaceutical manufacturers must disclose all reports of adverse events. . . . [T]he mere existence of reports of adverse events— which says nothing in and of itself about whether the drug is causing the adverse events—will not satisfy this standard. Something more is needed, but that something more is not limited to statistical significance . . .

> Applying *Basic's* "total mix" standard in this case, we conclude that respondents have adequately pleaded materiality. . . . Matrixx

received information that plausibly indicated a reliable causal link between Zicam and anosmia. That information included reports from three medical professionals and researchers about more than 10 patients who had lost their sense of smell after using Zicam. . . . Matrixx had received additional reports of anosmia. (In addition, during the class period, nine plaintiffs commenced four product liability lawsuits against Matrixx alleging a causal link between Zicam use and anosmia.) Further, Matrixx knew that . . . [two researchers] had presented their findings about a causal link between Zicam and anosmia to a national medical conference devoted to treatment of diseases of the nose. Their presentation described a patient who experienced severe burning in his nose, followed immediately by a loss of smell, after using Zicam— suggesting a temporal relationship between Zicam use and anosmia.

Critically, both . . . [researchers] had also drawn Matrixx's attention to previous studies that had demonstrated a biological causal link between intranasal application of zinc and anosmia. . . .

The information provided to Matrixx by medical experts revealed a plausible causal relationship between Zicam Cold Remedy and anosmia. . . .

It is substantially likely that a reasonable investor would have viewed this information " 'as having significantly altered the "total mix" of information made available.' " *Basic*, 485 U.S., at 232 . . . . Matrixx told the market that revenues were going to rise 50 and then 80 percent. Assuming the complaint's allegations to be true, however, Matrixx had information indicating a significant risk to its leading revenue-generating product. Matrixx also stated that reports indicating that Zicam caused anosmia were " 'completely unfounded and misleading' " and that " 'the safety and efficacy of zinc gluconate for the treatment of symptoms related to the common cold have been well established.' " . . .

––––––––

4. SCIENTER

1. The Call for Scienter. In *Ernst & Ernst v. Hochfelder*, 425 U.S. 185, 96 S.Ct. 1375, 47 L.Ed.2d 668 (1976), the Supreme Court held that a private action for damages under Rule 10b–5 does not exist "in the absence of any allegation of 'scienter,' " which the Court defined as an "intent to deceive, manipulate, or defraud" on the defendant's part. Loss and Seligman comment on this ruling as follows: "It is necessary [given the language of Section 10(b)] that some sort of watered-down scienter requirement be read into Clause (2) [of Rule 10b–5]. But why—in construing a fraud provision that was designed to *raise* the standards of securities trading, and that the courts have repeatedly interpreted as not limited to circumstances that would amount to common law deceit—did the majority opinion reach back in history to the strictest common law definition: not merely knowing falsity, but 'intent to deceive, manipulate, or defraud'?" 8 L. Loss & J. Seligman, Securities Regulation 3664 (3d ed. 1991).

　　2.　*Recklessness.* In footnote 12 of *Ernst & Ernst,* the Court stated:

> In this opinion the term "scienter" refers to a mental state embracing intent to deceive, manipulate, or defraud. In certain areas of the law recklessness is considered to be a form of intentional conduct for purposes of imposing liability for some act. We need not address here the question whether, in some circumstances, reckless behavior is sufficient for civil liability under § 10(b) and Rule 10b–5.

Decisions since *Ernst & Ernst* have unanimously held that recklessness satisfies the scienter requirement. What constitutes recklessness for purposes of Rule 10b–5 is less clear. Various courts have adopted, or cited with approval, observations in *Sundstrand Corp. v. Sun Chemical Corp.*, 553 F.2d 1033 (7th Cir.1977), cert. denied 434 U.S. 875, 98 S.Ct. 224, 54 L.Ed.2d 155, and *Sanders v. John Nuveen & Co., Inc.*, 554 F.2d 790 (7th Cir.1977). In *Sundstrand,* the court said:

> [R]eckless conduct may be defined as [highly unreasonable conduct], involving not merely simple, or even inexcusable negligence, but an extreme departure from the standards of ordinary care, and which presents a danger of misleading buyers or sellers that is either known to the defendant or is so obvious that the actor must have been aware of it.

553 F.2d at 1045. According to a gloss put on this test in *Mansbach v. Prescott, Ball & Turben,* 598 F.2d 1017, 1025 (6th Cir.1979), "[w]hile the danger need not be known, it must at least be so obvious that any reasonable man would have known of it." In *Sanders,* the court, after referring to the *Sundstrand* test, said:

> In view of the Supreme Court's analysis in *Hochfelder* of the statutory scheme of implied private remedies and express remedies, the definition of "reckless behavior" should not be a liberal one lest any discernible distinction between "scienter" and "negligence" be obliterated for these purposes. We believe "reckless" in these circumstances comes closer to being a lesser form of intent than merely a greater degree of ordinary negligence. We perceive it to be not just a difference in degree, but also in kind.

554 F.2d at 793. Thus, the pleading standard for recklessness was met when the complaint alleged the company's senior executives reported the automotive parts manufacturer was having "gangbuster earnings" as a result of cost efficiencies even though the entire auto industry was spiraling toward bankruptcy and during the period of the optimistic reports the executives were negotiating a loan which surely would have

been denied if the true financial status of the firm was known. Frank v. Dana Corp., 646 F.3d 954 (6th Cir. 2011).

3.   *Injunctive Relief.* In *Aaron v. SEC,* 446 U.S. 680, 100 S.Ct. 1945, 64 L.Ed.2d 611 (1980), the Supreme Court held that a showing of scienter was a requirement in an injunctive action under Rule 10b–5.

———

5. PRIMARY PARTICIPANTS AFTER *CENTRAL BANK*

Section 10(b) and Rule 10b–5 each expressly proscribe misconduct of "any person." At one time this meant liability reached both primary participants as well as those who aided and abetted their misbehavior. *See e.g.,* Roberts v. Peat, Marwick, Mitchell & Co., 857 F.2d 646 (9th Cir. 1988). Indeed, all circuits recognized that aiding and abetting was within the reach of section 10(b) and Rule 10b–5. That world changed, and changed dramatically, for private suits with *Central Bank of Denver v. First Interstate Bank of Denver,* 511 U.S. 164, 114 S.Ct. 1439, 128 L.Ed.2d 119 (1994).

In rejecting aiding and abetting liability under the antifraud provision, the *Central Bank* majority was not persuaded by the "directly or indirectly" language of Section 10(b). The Court reasoned this would extend liability to those whose conduct itself is not proscribed by the antifraud provision. Moreover, the Court pointed out that the "directly or indirectly" language is used in many other provisions, such as Section 16(a) of the Exchange Act, which clearly do not contemplate aiding and abetting liability. The Court drew further strength for its position by emphasizing that none of the express liability provisions of the Securities Act or the Exchange Act proscribe aiders and abettors. It thus inferred from Congress' refusal to proscribe aiding and abetting in the express liability provisions the likely intent not to proscribe aiding and abetting in an implied cause of action.

> It is inconsistent with settled methodology in § 10(b) cases to extend liability beyond the scope of conduct prohibited by the statutory text. . . .
>
> As in earlier cases considering conduct prohibited by § 10(b), we again conclude that the statute prohibits only the making of a material misstatement (or omission) or the commission of a manipulative act. *See Santa Fe Industries,* 430 U.S. at 473 ("language of § 10(b) gives no indication that Congress meant to prohibit any conduct not involving manipulation or deception"). . . . The proscription does not include giving aid to a person who commits a manipulative or deceptive act. We cannot amend the statute to create liability for acts that are not themselves manipulative or deceptive within the meaning of the statute. . . .

Our reasoning is confirmed by the fact that respondents' argument would impose 10b–5 aiding and abetting liability when at least one element critical for recovery under 10b–5 is absent: reliance. A plaintiff must show reliance on the defendant's misstatement or omission to recover under 10b–5. *Basic Inc. v. Levinson,* supra, at 243. Were we to allow the aiding and abetting action proposed in this case, the defendant could be liable without any showing that the plaintiff relied upon the aider and abettor's statements or actions. . . . Allowing plaintiffs to circumvent the reliance requirement would disregard the careful limits on 10b–5 recovery mandated by our earlier cases. . . .

Because the text of § 10(b) does not prohibit aiding and abetting, we hold that a private plaintiff may not maintain an aiding and abetting suit under § 10(b). The absence of § 10(b) aiding and abetting liability does not mean that secondary actors in the securities markets are always free from liability under the securities acts. Any person or entity, including a lawyer, accountant, or bank, who employs a manipulative device or makes a material misstatement (or omission) on which a purchaser or seller of securities relies may be liable as a primary violator under 10b–5, assuming all of the requirements for primary liability under Rule 10b–5 are met. *See* Fischel, 69 Cal. L. Rev., at 107–108. In any complex securities fraud, moreover, there are likely to be multiple violators; in this case, for example, respondents named four defendants as primary violators. . . .

511 U.S. at 177–181, 114 S.Ct. at 1448–51, 128 L.Ed.2d at 132–135.

The Supreme Court returned to the meaning of "make," in the context of making false statements, in *Janus Capital Group, Inc. v. First Derivative Traders*, 564 U.S. 135, 143–44, 131 S.Ct. 2296, 2302–03 180 L.Ed.2d 166, 175–76 (2011). Janus Capital Group, Inc. (Janus) was a publicly traded company whose wholly owned subsidiary, Janus Capital Management LLC (JCM), provided investment advisory services to various mutual funds that Janus created. Mutual funds pool cash received from their investors and manage the pooled funds according to the investment strategy that distinguishes each particular fund. Each mutual fund is a separate corporation with its own board of directors, but without its own management, employees, or for that matter tangible assets other than the securities held in its portfolio. The most important function of the board of directors of a mutual fund is the annual approval of a management contract with the fund's advisor, for example JCM. Such approvals are perfunctory given that Janus created the fund for the purpose of the fund attracting investors whose pooled investments would be managed by JCM for which JCM (and hence indirectly its parent) would earn fees. Mutual fund fees are paid quarterly and are based on a percentage, e.g., 0.5%, of assets under management. Thus the more pooled money in a Janus fund the more profitable is Janus itself.

In 2003, it was revealed that one of the Janus funds, Janus Investment Fund (JIF), despite claims to the contrary in several of its quarterly reports to its investors, had engaged in a series of clandestine activities that harmed fund investors. The quarterly reports were prepared by personnel of JCM (recall that JIF as a mutual fund had no employees) and were filed with the approval of JIF's board of directors. The revelation caused a mass withdrawal of investor funds from JIF as well as several other Janus funds. This in turn resulted in a decline in income to publicly traded Janus, causing its stock price to decline. The SEC investigated, and eventually Janus settled with the SEC, agreeing to reduce its fees by a total of $125 million, pay a $50 million fine, and disgorge $50 million to fund investors. A parallel class action on behalf of Janus stockholders failed because the defendants, Janus and JCM, were not primary participants under the following formulation:

> For purposes of *Rule 10b–5*, the maker of a statement is the person or entity with ultimate authority over the statement, including its content and whether and how to communicate it. Without control, a person or entity can merely suggest what to say, not "make" a statement in its own right. One who prepares or publishes a statement on behalf of another is not its maker. And in the ordinary case, attribution within a statement or implicit from surrounding circumstances is strong evidence that a statement was made by—and only by—the party to whom it is attributed. This rule might best be exemplified by the relationship between a speechwriter and a speaker. Even when a speechwriter drafts a speech, the content is entirely within the control of the person who delivers it. And it is the speaker who takes credit—or blame—for what is ultimately said.
>
> . . . A broader reading of "make," including persons or entities without ultimate control over the content of a statement, would substantially undermine *Central Bank*. If persons or entities without control over the content of a statement could be considered primary violators who "made" the statement, then aiders and abettors would be almost nonexistent.

Attempts to repackage aiding and abetting liability by invoking Rule 10b–5's reference to "any . . . scheme" was rejected by the Supreme Court. See Stoneridge Investment Partners, LLC, Petitioner v. Scientific-Atlanta, Inc., 552 U.S. 148, 128 S.Ct. 761, 169 L.Ed.2d 627 (2008) (vendors who cooperate with their customer to create fictitious purchases for the purpose of inflating the customer's revenues are too remote from the customer's false financial statements, so that their misdeeds—which included false invoices and other documents intended to prevent the customer's auditor from learning of their chicanery—cannot be said to have been relied upon by investors when they purchased the customer's stock at prices inflated by the false financial reports).

Post-*Central Bank,* Section 20(e) to the Securities Exchange Act has been twice amended to authorize SEC enforcement actions against any person who "knowingly or recklessly provides substantial assistance to another person in violation of a provision" of the act.

———

Lorenzo v. SEC

Supreme Court of the Supreme Court of the United States, 2019.
139 S.Ct. 1094.

■ JUSTICE BREYER delivered the opinion of the Court. . . .

In *Janus Capital Group, Inc.* v. *First Derivative Traders*, 564 U. S. 135 . . . (2011), we examined the second of these provisions, Rule 10b–5(b), which forbids the "mak[ing]" of "any untrue statement of a material fact." We held that the "*maker* of a statement is the person or entity with ultimate authority over the statement, including its content and whether and how to communicate it." *Id.*, at 142 . . . (emphasis added). We said that "[w]ithout control, a person or entity can merely suggest what to say, not 'make' a statement in its own right." *Ibid.* And we illustrated our holding with an analogy: "[W]hen a speechwriter drafts a speech, the content is entirely within the control of the person who delivers it. And it is the speaker who takes credit—or blame—for what is ultimately said." *Id.*, at 143 . . . . On the facts of *Janus*, this meant that an investment adviser who had merely "participat[ed] in the drafting of a false statement" "made" by another could not be held liable in a private action under subsection (b) of Rule 10b–5. *Id.*, at 145 . . . .

In this case, we consider whether those who do not "make" statements (as *Janus* defined "make"), but who disseminate false or misleading statements to potential investors with the intent to defraud, can be found to have violated the *other* parts of Rule 10b–5, subsections (a) and (c) . . . We believe that they can.

I

A . . .

Francis Lorenzo, the petitioner, was the director of investment banking at Charles Vista, LLC, a registered broker-dealer in Staten Island, New York. Lorenzo's only investment banking client at the time was Waste2Energy Holdings, Inc., a company developing technology to convert "solid waste" into "clean renewable energy."

In a June 2009 public filing, Waste2Energy stated that its total assets were worth about $14 million. This figure included intangible assets, namely, intellectual property, valued at more than $10 million. Lorenzo was skeptical of this valuation, later testifying that the intangibles were a "dead asset" because the technology "didn't really work."

During the summer and early fall of 2009, Waste2Energy hired Lorenzo's firm, Charles Vista, to sell to investors $15 million worth of debentures, a form of "debt secured only by the debtor's earning power, not by a lien on any specific asset," Black's Law Dictionary 486 (10th ed. 2014).

In early October 2009, Waste2Energy publicly disclosed, and Lorenzo was told, that its intellectual property was worthless, that it had " ' "[w]rit[ten] off . . . all [of its] intangible assets," ' " and that its total assets (as of March 31, 2009) amounted to $370,552.

Shortly thereafter, on October 14, 2009, Lorenzo sent two e-mails to prospective investors describing the debenture offering. According to later testimony by Lorenzo, he sent the e-mails at the direction of his boss, who supplied the content and "approved" the messages. The e-mails described the investment in Waste2Energy as having "3 layers of protection," including $10 million in "confirmed assets." The e-mails nowhere revealed the fact that Waste2Energy had publicly stated that its assets were in fact worth less than $400,000. Lorenzo signed the e-mails with his own name, he identified himself as "Vice President— Investment Banking," and he invited the recipients to "call with any questions."

B

In 2013, the Securities and Exchange Commission instituted proceedings against Lorenzo (along with his boss and Charles Vista). The Commission charged that Lorenzo had violated Rule 10b–5, § 10(b) of the Exchange Act . . . . Ultimately, the Commission found that Lorenzo had run afoul of these provisions by sending false and misleading statements to investors with intent to defraud. As a sanction, it fined Lorenzo $15,000, ordered him to cease and desist from violating the securities laws, and barred him from working in the securities industry for life.

Lorenzo appealed [to the Court of Appeals for the District of Columbia], arguing primarily that in sending the e-mails he lacked the intent required to establish a violation of Rule 10b–5, § 10(b), and § 17(a)(1), which we have characterized as " 'a mental state embracing intent to deceive, manipulate, or defraud.' " *Aaron* v. *SEC*, 446 U. S. 680 . . . . With one judge dissenting, the Court of Appeals panel rejected Lorenzo's lack-of-intent argument. 872 F. 3d 578, 583 (CADC 2017). Lorenzo does not challenge the panel's scienter finding. . . .

Lorenzo also argued that, in light of *Janus*, he could not be held liable under subsection (b) of Rule 10b–5. 872 F. 3d, at 586–587. The panel agreed. Because his boss "asked Lorenzo to send the emails, supplied the central content, and approved the messages for distribution," *id.*, at 588, it was the boss that had "ultimate authority" over the content of the statement "and whether and how to communicate it," *Janus*, 563 U. S., at 142, 131 S. Ct. 2296, 180 L. Ed. 2d 166. (We took this case on the assumption that Lorenzo was not a "maker" under subsection (b) of Rule 10b–5, and do not revisit the court's decision on this point.)

The Court of Appeals nonetheless sustained (with one judge dissenting) the Commission's finding that, by knowingly disseminating false information to prospective investors, Lorenzo had violated other parts of Rule 10b–5, subsections (a) and (c), as well as § 10(b) . . . .

Lorenzo then filed a petition for certiorari in this Court. We granted review to resolve disagreement about whether someone who is not a "maker" of a misstatement under *Janus* can nevertheless be found to have violated the other subsections of Rule 10b–5 and related provisions of the securities laws, when the only conduct involved concerns a misstatement. . . .

II

A

At the outset, we review the relevant provisions of Rule 10b–5 and of the statutes. See Appendix, *infra*. As we have said, subsection (a) of the Rule makes it unlawful to "employ any device, scheme, or artifice to defraud." Subsection (b) makes it unlawful to "make any untrue statement of a material fact." And subsection (c) makes it unlawful to "engage in any act, practice, or course of business" that "operates . . . as a fraud or deceit." See 17 CFR § 240.10b–5. . . .

B . . .

It would seem obvious that the words in these provisions are, as ordinarily used, sufficiently broad to include within their scope the dissemination of false or misleading information with the intent to defraud. By sending emails he understood to contain material untruths, Lorenzo "employ[ed]" a "device," "scheme," and "artifice to defraud" within the meaning of subsection (a) of the Rule, § 10(b) . . . . By the same conduct, he "engage[d] in a[n] act, practice, or course of business" that "operate[d] . . . as a fraud or deceit" under subsection (c) of the Rule. Recall that Lorenzo does not challenge the appeals court's scienter finding, so we take for granted that he sent the emails with "intent to deceive, manipulate, or defraud" the recipients. *Aaron*, 446 U. S., at 686, n. 5 . . . . Under the circumstances, it is difficult to see how his actions could escape the reach of those provisions. . . .

These provisions capture a wide range of conduct. Applying them may present difficult problems of scope in borderline cases. Purpose, precedent, and circumstance could lead to narrowing their reach in other contexts. But we see nothing borderline about this case, where the relevant conduct (as found by the Commission) consists of disseminating false or misleading information to prospective investors with the intent to defraud. And while one can readily imagine other actors tangentially involved in dissemination—say, a mailroom clerk—for whom liability would typically be inappropriate, the petitioner in this case sent false statements directly to investors, invited them to follow up with questions, and did so in his capacity as vice president of an investment banking company.

C

Lorenzo argues that, despite the natural meaning of these provisions, they should not reach his conduct. This is so, he says, because the only way to be liable for false statements is through those provisions that refer *specifically* to false statements. Other provisions, he says, concern "scheme liability claims" and are violated only when conduct other than misstatements is involved. . . .

The premise of this argument is that each of these provisions should be read as governing different, mutually exclusive, spheres of conduct. But this Court and the Commission have long recognized considerable overlap among the subsections of the Rule and related provisions of the securities laws. See *Herman & MacLean* v. *Huddleston*, 459 U. S. 375, 383, 103 S. Ct. 683, 74 L. Ed. 2d 548 (1983) ("[I]t is hardly a novel proposition that" different portions of the securities laws "prohibit some of the same conduct" (internal quotation marks omitted)). . . . It is "understandable, therefore," that "in declaring certain practices unlawful," it was thought prudent "to include both a general proscription against fraudulent and deceptive practices and, out of an abundance of caution, a specific proscription against nondisclosure" even though "a specific proscription against nondisclosure" might in other circumstances be deemed "surplusage." *Id.*, at 198–199 . . . .

Coupled with the Rule's expansive language, which readily embraces the conduct before us, this considerable overlap suggests we should not hesitate to hold that Lorenzo's conduct ran afoul of subsections (a) and (c), as well as the related statutory provisions. Our conviction is strengthened by the fact that we here confront behavior that, though plainly fraudulent, might otherwise fall outside the scope of the Rule. Lorenzo's view that subsection (b), the making-false-statements provision, *exclusively* regulates conduct involving false or misleading statements would mean those who disseminate false statements with the intent to cheat investors might escape liability under the Rule altogether. But using false representations to induce the purchase of securities would seem a paradigmatic example of securities fraud. We do not know why Congress or the Commission would have wanted to disarm enforcement in this way. And we cannot easily reconcile Lorenzo's approach with the basic purpose behind these laws: "to substitute a philosophy of full disclosure for the philosophy of *caveat emptor* and thus to achieve a high standard of business ethics in the securities industry." *Capital Gains*, 375 U. S., at 186 . . . .

III

Lorenzo and the dissent make a few other important arguments. They contend that applying subsections (a) or (c) of Rule 10b–5 to conduct like his would render our decision in *Janus* . . .) "a dead letter". But we do not see how that is so. In *Janus*, we considered the language in subsection (b), which prohibits the "mak[ing]" of "any untrue statement of a material fact." See 564 U. S., at 141–143 . . . We held that the "maker" of a "statement" is the "person or entity with ultimate authority over the statement." *Id.*, at 142 . . . . And we found that subsection (b) did not (under the circumstances) cover an investment adviser who helped *draft* misstatements issued by a *different* entity that controlled the statements' content. *Id.*, at 146–148 . . . . We said nothing about the Rule's application to the dissemination of false or misleading information. And we can assume that *Janus* would remain relevant (and preclude liability) where an individual neither *makes* nor *disseminates* false information— provided, of course, that the individual is not involved in some other form of fraud.

Next, Lorenzo points to the statute's "aiding and abetting" provision. 15 U. S. C. § 78t(e). This provision, enforceable only by the Commission (and not by private parties), makes it unlawful to "knowingly or recklessly . . . provid[e] substantial assistance to another person" who violates the Rule. *Ibid.* . . . Lorenzo claims that imposing primary liability upon his conduct would erase or at least weaken what is otherwise a clear distinction between primary and secondary (*i.e.*, aiding and abetting) liability. He emphasizes that, under today's holding, a disseminator might be a primary offender with respect to subsection (a) of Rule 10b–5 (by employing a "scheme" to "defraud") and also secondarily liable as an aider and abettor with respect to subsection (b) (by providing substantial assistance to one who "makes" a false statement). And he refers to two cases that, in his view, argue in favor of circumscribing primary liability. . . .

We do not believe, however, that our decision creates a serious anomaly or otherwise weakens the distinction between primary and secondary liability. For one thing, it is hardly unusual for the same conduct to be a primary violation with respect to one offense and aiding and abetting with respect to another. John, for example, might sell Bill an unregistered firearm in order to help Bill rob a bank, under circumstances that make him primarily liable for the gun sale and secondarily liable for the bank robbery.

For another, the cases to which Lorenzo refers do not help his cause. Take *Central Bank*, where we held that Rule 10b–5's private right of action does not permit suits against secondary violators. 511 U. S., at 177 . . . . The holding of *Central Bank*, we have said, suggests the need for a "clean line" between conduct that constitutes a primary violation of Rule 10b–5 and conduct that amounts to a secondary violation. . . . The line we adopt today is just as administrable. Those who disseminate false statements with intent to defraud are primarily liable under Rules 10b–5(a) and (c), § 10(b)..., even if they are secondarily liable under Rule 10b–5(b). Lorenzo suggests that classifying dissemination as a primary violation would inappropriately subject peripheral players in fraud (including him, naturally) to substantial liability. We suspect the investors who received Lorenzo's e-mails would not view the deception so favorably. And as *Central Bank* itself made clear, even a bit participant in the securities markets "may be liable as a primary violator under [Rule] 10b–5" so long as "all of the requirements for primary liability... are met." *Id.,* at 191 ....

Lorenzo's reliance on *Stoneridge* is even further afield. There, we held that private plaintiffs could not bring suit against certain securities defendants based on *undisclosed* deceptions upon which the plaintiffs could not have relied. 552 U. S., at 159 .... But the Commission, unlike private parties, need not show reliance in its enforcement actions. And even supposing reliance were relevant here, Lorenzo's conduct involved the direct transmission of false statements to prospective investors intended to induce reliance—far from the kind of concealed fraud at issue in *Stoneridge*.

As for Lorenzo's suggestion that those like him ought to be held secondarily liable, this offer will, far too often, prove illusory. In instances where a "maker" of a false statement does *not* violate subsection (b) of the Rule (perhaps because he lacked the necessary intent), a disseminator of those statements, even one knowingly engaged in an egregious fraud, could not be held to have violated the "aiding and abetting" statute. That is because the statute insists that there be a primary violator to whom the secondary violator provided "substantial assistance." 15 U. S. C. § 78t(e). And the latter can be "deemed to be in violation" of the provision only "to the same extent as the person to whom such assistance is provided." *Ibid.* In other words, if Acme Corp. could not be held liable under subsection (b) for a statement it made, then a knowing disseminator of those statements could not be held liable for aiding and abetting Acme under subsection (b). And if, as Lorenzo claims, the disseminator has not primarily violated other parts of Rule 10b–5, then such a fraud, whatever its intent or consequences, might escape liability altogether.

That is not what Congress intended. Rather, Congress intended to root out all manner of fraud in the securities industry. And it gave to the Commission the tools to accomplish that job.

For these reasons, the judgment of the Court of Appeals is affirmed.

So ordered.

■ JUSTICE KAVANAUGH took no part in the consideration or decision of this case.

■ JUSTICE THOMAS, with whom JUSTICE GORSUCH joins, dissenting. (dissenting opinion omitted)

———

West Virginia Pipe Trades Health & Welfare Fund v. Medtronic, Inc.

United States Court of Appeals, Eighth Circuit, 2016.
845 F.3d 384.

. . . Medtronic developed INFUSE as an alternative to bone grafting procedures, and the FDA approved it for use in lower back spinal fusion surgeries in 2002. [FDA approval was based on thirteen published articles concerning clinical trials sponsored by Medtronic; each article, however, was by a physician who had a financial interest in INFUSE. Following FDA approval, patients treated with INFUSE began incurring serious health problems. Soon the national press reported the dire health issues surround use of INFUSE as well as that the physicians authoring the articles leading to FDA approval stood to benefit and did benefit from INFUSE's approval. Congressional hearings ensued, Medtronic share price fell, and a securities class action based on misrepresentations in the published articles was filed. The suit alleged that Medtronic had engaged in a *scheme* to defraud. The district court's granted Medtronic's summary judgment on the ground that it did not meet the *Janus* test as a primary participant in the misrepresentations linked to the published articles. The Eighth Circuit reversed.]

The broader scope of scheme liability under Rule 10b–5(a) and (c) potentially offers plaintiffs a means to circumvent *Janus*—a situation we encountered in *Public Pension Fund Group v. KV Pharmaceutical Co.,* 679 F.3d 972 (8th Cir. 2012). In that case, investors asserted false statement claims against a pharmaceutical company for misrepresenting its compliance with FDA regulations in its SEC filings. The investors also attempted to assert a scheme liability claim against two of the pharmaceutical company's officers, alleging only that the officers had knowledge of the company's misrepresentations. We rejected the scheme liability claim, emphasizing that "a scheme liability claim must be based on conduct beyond misrepresentations or omissions actionable under Rule 10b–5(b)." *Id.* at 987. Otherwise, plaintiffs could simply recast false statement claims barred under *Janus* as scheme liability claims. *See id.* Without alleging that the officers engaged in conduct beyond misrepresentations, allegations that the officers simply knew about the company's misrepresentations were insufficient to support a scheme liability claim. *Id.* Accordingly, a plaintiff cannot support a scheme liability claim by simply repackaging a fraudulent misrepresentation as a scheme to defraud. Rather, a plaintiff must allege some deceptive act other than the fraudulent misrepresentation. . . .

Here, Appellants allege conduct beyond mere misrepresentations or omissions actionable under Rule 10b–5(b). Appellants' scheme liability claim alleges that Medtronic shaped the content of medical journals by "pa[ying] physicians . . . to induce their complicity in concealing adverse events and side effects associated with the use of INFUSE and overstating the disadvantages of alternative bone graft procedures." Although the scheme liability claim also includes allegations that Medtronic edited language in the clinical studies that the physicians ultimately published, the act of paying physicians to induce their complicity is the allegation at the heart of the scheme liability claim. Paying someone else to make a misrepresentation is not itself a misrepresentation. Thus, Appellants do not merely repackage allegations of misrepresentation as allegations of a scheme. *Janus* and *KV Pharmaceuticals* require some conduct other than a misrepresentation to support a scheme liability claim. They do not hold that the alleged scheme can never involve any misrepresentation in order for the scheme liability claim to survive. *See, e.g., In re Smith Barney*, 884 F. Supp. 2d at 161 (sustaining scheme liability claim where alleged conduct included but was not limited to misleadingly disclosing fees). Accordingly, because Medtronic's alleged deceptive conduct goes beyond mere misrepresentations or omissions, *Janus* does not bar Appellants' scheme liability claim.

The second part of Medtronic's argument concerns whether Appellants have sufficiently pleaded that the market relied on Medtronic's conduct as a matter of law. In *Stoneridge*, Charter Communications and its suppliers engaged in sham transactions designed to enable Charter to falsify its financial statements. 552 U.S. at 152–55. Investors sued the suppliers, asserting both a false statement claim and a scheme liability claim. While the investors argued that the suppliers' participation in the sham transactions enabled Charter to falsify its statements, the Supreme Court held that the investors could not demonstrate that they relied on the suppliers' conduct. *Id.* at 159. "Reliance by the plaintiff upon the defendant's deceptive acts is an essential element of the § 10(b) private cause of action. It ensures that, for liability to arise, the 'requisite causal connection between a defendant's misrepresentation and a plaintiff's injury' exists as a predicate for liability." *Id.* . . .

Unlike the conduct at issue in *Stoneridge*, the causal connection between Medtronic's alleged deceptive conduct and the information on which the market relied is not too remote to support a finding of reliance. Medtronic's alleged deceptive conduct consists of manipulating the clinical trials by paying the physician-authors to conceal adverse effects and to overstate the disadvantages of alternative procedures. Appellants alleged in their complaint that investors directly relied on the resulting favorable clinical trials. Indeed, according to the Appellants' amended complaint, in speaking with potential investors, Medtronic's CEO specifically emphasized that the company's products' strong clinical trial performance undergirded Medtronic's competitiveness and sustainability. As a result, taking the allegations as true, Medtronic's deceptive conduct directly caused the production of the information on which the market relied. Unlike the suppliers' conduct in *Stoneridge*, Medtronic's purported conduct would not merely assist or enable the physician-authors to deceive the market. Rather, Medtronic's alleged conduct would deceive the market with the assistance of the physician-authors. A company cannot instruct individuals to take a certain action, pay to induce them to do it, and then claim any causal connection is too remote when they follow through. In this way, Medtronic's alleged manipulative conduct directly caused the biased clinical trial results that the market relied upon. This alleged causal connection is sufficient to support a finding of reliance. . . .

III.

For the reasons discussed above, we vacate summary judgment and remand for proceedings not inconsistent with this opinion.

---

6.   STANDING TO SUE

In *Blue Chip Stamps v. Manor Drug Stores,* 421 U.S. 723, 95 S.Ct. 1917, 44 L.Ed.2d 539 (1975), the Supreme Court held that under the "in connection with" clause of § 10(b), only a person who had purchased or sold stock had standing to bring a private action under Rule 10b–5. The purchaser-seller requirement had been adopted by the Second Circuit some years earlier in a widely followed opinion, Birnbaum v. Newport Steel Corp., 193 F.2d 461 (1952), cert. denied 343 U.S. 956, 72 S.Ct. 1051, 96 L.Ed. 1356. *Blue Chip Stamps* decision the Ninth Circuit held the facts justified what it considered a slight departure from *Birnbaum's* purchaser-seller requirement. As part of a consent decree ending a government antitrust settlement, Blue Chip Stamps was required to reorganize itself by undertaking a public offering of its shares to numerous retailers identified in the decree. The precise number of shares each retailer could acquire was determined according to a formula agreed to in the settlement. Plaintiffs were retailers included in the decree but did not exercise their right to acquire the offered shares. They alleged Blue Chip Stamps intentionally made the prospectus overly pessimistic in order to discourage retailers from accepting what was to be a bargain offer, so that the rejected shares could later be sold to the public at a higher price. The plaintiffs further alleged that they relied on the false pessimistic information and therefore did not purchase the offered units. The Ninth Circuit reasoned the facts justified a departure from the rigid purchaser-seller requirement. The Supreme Court's opinion, by Justice Rehnquist, reversed. It recognized that the language of section 10(b) was not conclusive on the issue, but supported its reversal on the basis of policy considerations:

> There has been widespread recognition that litigation under Rule 10b–5 presents a danger of vexatiousness different

in degree and in kind from that which accompanies litigation in general. . . .

We believe that the concern expressed for the danger of vexatious litigation which could result from a widely expanded class of plaintiffs under Rule 10b–5 is founded in something more substantial than the common complaint of the many defendants who would prefer avoiding lawsuits entirely to either settling them or trying them. These concerns have two largely separate grounds.

The first of these concerns is that in the field of federal securities laws governing disclosure of information even a complaint which by objective standards may have very little chance of success at trial has a settlement value to the plaintiff out of any proportion to its prospect of success at trial so long as he may prevent the suit from being resolved against him by dismissal or summary judgment. The very pendency of the lawsuit may frustrate or delay normal business activity of the defendant which is totally unrelated to the lawsuit. . . .

The potential for possible abuse of the liberal discovery provisions of the Federal Rules of Civil Procedure may likewise exist in this type of case to a greater extent than they do in other litigation. The prospect of extensive deposition of the defendant's officers and associates and the concomitant opportunity for extensive discovery of business documents, is a common occurrence in this and similar types of litigation. To the extent that this process eventually produces relevant evidence which is useful in determining the merits of the claims asserted by the parties, it bears the imprimatur of those Rules and of the many cases liberally interpreting them. But to the extent that it permits a plaintiff with a largely groundless claim to simply take up the time of a number of other people, with the right to do so representing an *in terrorem* increment of the settlement value, rather than a reasonably founded hope that the process will reveal relevant evidence, it is a social cost rather than a benefit. Yet to broadly expand the class of plaintiffs who may sue under Rule 10b–5 would appear to encourage the least appealing aspect of the use of the discovery rules.

Without the *Birnbaum* rule, an action under Rule 10b–5 will turn largely on which oral version of a series of occurrences the jury may decide to credit, and therefore no matter how improbable the allegations of the plaintiff, the case will be virtually impossible to dispose of prior to trial other than by settlement. . . .

The second ground for fear of vexatious litigation is based on the concern that, given the generalized contours of liability, the abolition of the *Birnbaum* rule would throw open to the trier of fact many rather hazy issues of historical fact the proof of which depended almost entirely on oral testimony. We in no way disparage the worth and frequent high value of oral testimony when we say that dangers of its abuse appear to exist in this type of action to a peculiarly high degree. . . .

The most significant bite of the *Blue Chip* doctrine is to bar private actions by persons who claim they *would have sold* stock that they owned had they not been induced to retain the stock by misrepresentations, or omissions, that violated Rule 10b–5. There are some notable "wrinkles" to the doctrine:

1. *SEC Proceedings.* The *Blue Chip* doctrine does not affect the standing of the SEC to bring proceedings under Rule 10b–5 even though the SEC was neither a purchaser nor a seller (as it never would be).

2. *Injunctive Relief.* Several pre-*Blue Chip Stamp* cases held that a plaintiff in a private action for injunctive relief need not be a purchaser or a seller. See Kahan v. Rosenstiel, 424 F.2d 161, 173 (3d Cir.1970), cert. denied sub nom. Glen Alden Corp. v. Kahan, 398 U.S. 950, 90 S.Ct. 1870, 26 L.Ed.2d 290 (1970); Mutual Shares Corp. v. Genesco, Inc., 384 F.2d 540, 546–47 (2d Cir.1967). Although a few post-*Blue Chip Stamp* decisions have assumed this exception was unaffected by the 1975 decision, *See e.g.,* Warner Communications Inc. v. Murdoch, 581 F.Supp. 1482, 1494 (D. Del. 1984), the overall response is more restrained. For example, in Advanced Resources International v. Tri-Star Petroleum Co., 4 F.3d 327 (4th Cir.1993), the Fourth Circuit reasoned that *Blue Chip Stamp* requires the plaintiff in an injunctive action to be a purchaser or seller, unless absent obtaining an injunction the plaintiff would suffer a future monetary loss. More restrictive yet is Cowin v. Bresler, 741 F.2d 410 (D.C. Cir. 1984), holding there is no exception to the purchaser-seller requirement for injunctive relief.

3. *Defendants.* It is well established that although the *plaintiff* in a private action under Rule 10b–5 must be a buyer or a seller, the *defendants* need not be. Moreover, "where the alleged fraud involves the public dissemination of information in a medium upon which investors would presumably rely, the 'in connection with' element may be established by proof of materiality of the misrepresentation and the means of its dissemination. . . . Under that standard, it is irrelevant that the misrepresentations were not made for the purpose or object of influencing the investment decisions of market participants." Semerenko v. Cendant Corp., 223 F.3d 165, 176 (3d Cir. 2000).

————

7. THE PRIVATE SECURITIES LITIGATION REFORM ACT AND SECURITIES LITIGATION UNIFORM STANDARDS ACT

Twice in the last few decades Congress has enacted sweeping changes that restrain private securities fraud actions. It is unlikely Congress would have acted if suits were all like the suit in *Wharf Holdings,* involving only disputes between business partners rather than a class actions on behalf of thousands of investors. What prompted Congress to act was the burgeoning number of securities class actions that Congress believed were largely nuisance suits initiated to extract settlements that benefitted only the class action lawyers, produced small rewards to investors alleged harmed by the fraud, and rendered the U.S. capital markets anticompetitive versus rival foreign markets (where class action procedures generally do not exist, contingency fee arrangements are generally not allowed, and the loser pay rule is the norm).

1. Lead Plaintiff. The Private Securities Litigation Reform Act of 1995 introduced a variety of reforms for securities fraud actions. The centerpiece of the legislation was adding Section 21D(a)(3) to the Securities Exchange Act, establishing a procedure for the court to appoint a "lead plaintiff" for the suit. Pursuant to this provision, soon after the filing of the complaint, notice is publicized inviting interested parties to become the suit's plaintiff. There is a rebuttable presumption that the petitioner with the largest loss suffered is the most adequate plaintiff. The lead plaintiff provision reflected Congress' view that the menacing features of the securities class action flowed from the suits being lawyer driven. The PSLRA thus seeks to provide the suit's attorney with a real client.

The PSLRA's legislative history clearly reflects that the lead plaintiff provision was adopted in order to encourage financial institutions to step forward as the class' representative. The expectation was that such a plaintiff would actively monitor the conduct of a securities fraud class action so as to reduce the litigation agency costs that may arise when class counsel's interests diverge from those of the shareholder class. The Congress clearly envisioned that various types of financial institutions—pension funds, insurance companies, mutual funds—were the most likely type of investors who could combine a large financial stake in the suit's outcome with the sophistication to guide the suit to an appropriate outcome, including a decision whether the suit should be maintained at all. Overall, proponents of the provision believed there would be substantial benefits from having institutional investors serve as lead plaintiffs, including more favorable settlement terms, lower attorneys' fees for class counsel, fewer strike suits, more adjudications of class actions, and greater deterrence of securities fraud.

Once appointed, the lead plaintiff, subject to approval by the court, appoints the class's counsel. The impetus for the lead plaintiff provision was not just the general belief that securities class action suits were lawyer driven, but that in many suits institutional investors had a sufficient enough stake in the suit's prosecution so that they had natural economic incentives to monitor counsel's prosecution of the suit. An important study that preceded Congress' enactment of the PSLRA reported that in 82 examined securities class action settlements the 50 largest claimants had average allowable losses of $597,000 and represented 57.5 percent of all allowable losses in the settlement. Elliott Weiss and John Beckerman, Let the Money Do the Monitoring: How Institutional Investors Can Reduce Agency Costs in Securities Class Actions, 104 Yale L. J. 2053, 2089–2090 (1995).

2. *Some Other Reforms.* Among the other provisions added by the PSLRA are a broad embrace of proportionate fault, so that in general a single defendant is not jointly and severally liable for all the losses suffered by the plaintiff at the hands of multiple wrongdoers; pursuant to the PSLRA, and subject to some exceptions, a defendant is only liable for that portion of the plaintiff's loss that is attributable to that defendant's misconduct. There is a bar of "professional plaintiffs" that prohibits any person serving as a lead plaintiff more than five times in three years. And, at the conclusion of the suits, the presiding judge is to determine whether Rule 11 sanctions should be imposed on any attorney. Recall that in other contexts Rule 11 sanctions are in response to a motion by one of the litigants so that whatever misconduct a litigant might have believed the other party's attorney engaged in is customarily dropped as part of the case's settlement. Under the PSLRA the judge, regardless of any party's motion, is required to determine whether Rule 11 sanctions are to be imposed.

3. *SLUSA Closes State Bypass.* After the PSLRA's enactment there was a noticeable increase in securities fraud cases filed in state courts, for the apparent purpose of escaping the dual effects of the PSLRA's heightened pleading requirement and its discovery bar. This prompted Congress in 1998 to return to the subject of securities class actions by enacting the Securities Litigation Uniform Standards Act (SLUSA). The Act amended section 28(f) of the Securities Exchange Act to confer exclusive jurisdiction to federal courts for class actions involving misrepresentation or manipulative acts in connection with the purchase or sale of a "covered security." SLUSA defines "class action" as any suit seeking relief on behalf of 50 or more persons. A covered security is technically defined in section 18(b) of the Securities Act and includes securities listed on a national exchange as well as securities that are privately placed. Among the notable exclusions from the preemptive reach of section 28(f) is the so-called "Delaware carve-out" that preserves state court jurisdiction for suits focused on misrepresentations by a firm's officers, directors, and control persons. Such actions arise primarily in connection with statements made in connection with tender offers, mergers and other transactions that involve shareholder approval where

the officers, directors, or controlling stockholders allegedly committed a misrepresentation in connection with the transactions for which shareholder approval is sought, either in the form of voting their shares or tendering them to a bidder.

  4. SLUSA and the Purchaser-Seller Requirement. Merrill Lynch, Pierce, Fenner & Smith v. Dabit, 547 U.S. 71, 126 S.Ct. 1503, 164 L.Ed.2d 179 (2006), involved a class action initially filed in the state court of Oklahoma alleging various Oklahoma laws were violated by Merrill Lynch's scheme that included false analysts' recommendations. The class was made up of individuals who, in reliance on the analysts' recommendations, continued to hold the affected stocks. They suffered a loss when the stocks declined and the brokerage firm's scheme was discovered by government investigators. Merrill Lynch invoked SLUSA to remove the case to the federal court and pursuant to the multidistrict panel the suit was directed to the District Court for Southern District of New York. After skirmishing there, the suit reached the Second Circuit which held that SLUSA applied only to suits that could substantively be maintained in the federal court. Since the plaintiffs' complaint was that the fraudulent analysts' reports and other conduct caused them to retain their shares, the Second Circuit held the suit was improperly removed to the federal court. The Supreme Court vacated the opinion, reasoning that SLUSA's use of the parallel "in connection with the purchase or sale of a security" language meant that Congress intended the expression to have the same meaning in SLUSA as it has in Rule 10b–5. Accordingly it held SLUSA preempted the state law holder class action claims of the kind alleged in the suit by Dabit. Does this mean the holders in *Dabit* are without a remedy? Is that an efficient remedy?

NOTES ON PLEADING SCIENTER AFTER THE PSLRA

As discussed scienter is a necessary part of the plaintiff's case. Scienter takes one of two forms of conscious misbehavior: either the defendant had a specific intent to mislead or he acted recklessly. It has long been a requirement of Federal Rule of Civil Procedure 9(b) that all types of fraud must be pleaded with "particularity." Before the PSLRA, the most stringent pleading standard in securities-act fraud cases under the requirement of Rule 9(b) was a standard established by the Second Circuit. This standard required the plaintiff to state with particularity facts that gave rise to a "strong inference" of the requisite intent, that is, of scienter. Under the Second Circuit test for applying that standard, the plaintiff could establish the required strong inference by detailed factual allegations that showed either direct evidence of scienter (conscious misbehavior or recklessness), circumstantial evidence of scienter, or that the defendant had the motive and opportunity to commit fraud.

  To satisfy the motive element of the second branch of this test, it was not enough for a plaintiff to merely allege that the defendant had a motive of a kind possessed by virtually all corporate insiders, such as the desire to sustain the appearance of corporate profitability. Rather, the plaintiff had to allege that the defendant benefited in some concrete and personal way from his purported fraud. This requirement was normally satisfied when a corporate insider was alleged to have publicly misrepresented material facts about the corporation's performance or prospects to keep the stock price artificially high while he sold his own shares at a profit. Congress in 1995 greatly enhanced the role of a pleading requirement for securities fraud suits by making one of the cornerstones of the Private Securities Litigation Reform Act ("PSLRA") a heightened pleading standard.

With the PSLRA Congress adopted the Second Circuit's "strong inference" standard, but the legislative reports accompanying the legislation made clear that Congress was not necessarily adopting the motive-and-opportunity test the Second Circuit had employed. Securities Exchange Act § 21D(b)(2) provides that a plaintiff who alleges securities fraud must "state with particularity facts giving rise to a strong inference that the defendant acted with the required state of mind"—that is, scienter.

Tellabs, Inc. v. Makor Issues & Rights, Ltd., 551 U.S. 308, 127 S.Ct. 2499, 168 L.Ed.2d 179 (2007), offers the following guidance regarding the heightened pleading requirement:

> We establish the following prescriptions: *First*, faced with a *Rule 12(b)(6)* motion to dismiss a *§ 10(b)* action, courts must, as with any motion to dismiss for failure to plead a claim on which relief can be granted, accept all factual allegations in the complaint as true. . . .

> *Second*, courts must consider the complaint in its entirety, as well as other sources courts ordinarily examine when ruling on *Rule 12(b)(6)* motions to dismiss, in particular, documents incorporated into the complaint by reference, and matters of which a court may take judicial notice. See 5B Wright & Miller § 1357 (3d ed. 2004 and Supp. 2007). The inquiry, as several Courts of Appeals have recognized, is whether *all* of the facts alleged, taken collectively, give rise to a strong inference of scienter, not whether any individual allegation, scrutinized in isolation, meets that standard. . . .

> *Third*, in determining whether the pleaded facts give rise to a "strong" inference of scienter, the court must take into account plausible opposing inferences. The Seventh Circuit expressly declined to engage in such a comparative inquiry. A complaint could survive, that court said, as long as it "alleges facts from which, if true, a reasonable person could infer that the defendant acted with the required intent"; in other words, only "[i]f a reasonable person could not draw such an inference from the alleged facts" would the defendant prevail on a motion to dismiss. *437 F.3d at 602*. But in *§ 21D(b)(2)*, Congress did not merely require plaintiffs to "provide a factual basis for [their] scienter allegations,". . . . Instead, Congress required plaintiffs to plead

with particularity facts that give rise to a "strong"—*i.e.*, a powerful or cogent—inference. See American Heritage Dictionary 1717 (4th ed. 2000) (defining "strong" as "[p]ersuasive, effective, and cogent"); 16 Oxford English Dictionary 949 (2d ed. 1989) (defining "strong" as "[p]owerful to demonstrate or convince" (definition 16b)); cf. 7 *id.,* at 924 (defining "inference" as "a conclusion [drawn] from known or assumed facts or statements"; "reasoning from something known or assumed to something else which follows from it").

The strength of an inference cannot be decided in a vacuum. The inquiry is inherently comparative: How likely is it that one conclusion, as compared to others, follows from the underlying facts? To determine whether the plaintiff has alleged facts that give rise to the requisite "strong inference" of scienter, a court must consider plausible, nonculpable explanations for the defendant's conduct, as well as inferences favoring the plaintiff. The inference that the defendant acted with scienter need not be irrefutable, *i.e.,* of the "smoking-gun" genre, or even the "most plausible of competing inferences," *Fidel, 392 F.3d at 227* (quoting *Helwig v. Vencor, Inc., 251 F.3d 540, 553 (CA6 2001)* (en banc)). Recall in this regard that *§ 21D(b)*'s pleading requirements are but one constraint among many the PSLRA installed to screen out frivolous suits, while allowing meritorious actions to move forward. . . . Yet the inference of scienter must be more than merely "reasonable" or "permissible"—it must be cogent and compelling, thus strong in light of other explanations. A complaint will survive, we hold, only if a reasonable person would deem the inference of scienter cogent and at least as compelling as any opposing inference one could draw from the facts alleged.

551 U.S. at 322–323, 127 S.Ct. at 2509–10, 168 L.Ed.2d 192–194.

———

8.   CAUSAL RELATIONSHIP

In principle, it is well-established that causation and reliance are required elements of a private action under Rule 10b–5. In practice, however, those requirements have sometimes proved to be elusive or even illusory. As developed below, the courts have required the plaintiff in private actions to establish both transaction causation and loss causation.

Transaction causation means that there must be a causal connection between the defendant's violation of Rule 10b–5 and the plaintiff's decision to purchase or sell a security. To satisfy this requirement, a violation of Rule 10b–5 must have caused the plaintiff to engage in the transaction in question. Schlick v. Penn-Dixie Cement Corp., 507 F.2d 374 (2d Cir. 1974). Accordingly, the plaintiff must allege and show that but for the fraudulent statement or omission, she would not have entered into the transaction. Transaction causation has been analogized to reliance. See Currie v. Cayman Resources Corp., 835 F.2d 780, 785 (11th Cir.1988). *Loss causation* generally refers to establishing that the misrepresentation proximately caused an economic loss to the plaintiff.

———

A. LITIGATING TRANSACTION CAUSATION

The requirement of causation arises only in private suits under Rule 10b–5; it does not apply to actions by the SEC. Accordingly, the SEC can bring an action for injunctive or other appropriate relief based on a misrepresentation that violates Rule 10b–5 even if no investors have relied upon the statement—because, for example, trading in the relevant stock was suspended immediately after the statement was made. SEC v. Rana Research, Inc., 8 F.3d 1358 (1993).

Proving transaction causation in a pure omission case is problematic. We can say that *A* acted—bought or sold at a given price— in reliance on what *B* told him, but we can seldom say that *A* acted in reliance on *B*'s silence. What we *can* say in the latter case is that a reasonable investor who knew the omitted fact probably would or would not have bought or sold at the given price. In *TSC Industries v. Northway, Inc.*, the Supreme Court held that the standard of materiality in a nondisclosure case is satisfied by "a showing of a substantial likelihood that, under all the circumstances, the omitted fact would have assumed actual significance in the deliberations of the reasonable shareholder." 426 U.S. 438, 449, 96 S.Ct. 2126, 2132, 48 L.Ed.2d 757 (1976). At first glance, this standard is so close to what must be shown to prove causation in a nondisclosure case that for all intents and purposes, causation in such a case collapses into materiality. In its formulation of materiality *TSC* also observes that the showing of significance "does not require proof of a substantial likelihood that disclosure of the omitted fact would have caused the reasonable investor to change his vote" or decision to purchase. Thus, an inquiry into transaction causation that is premised only on a finding of materiality could in many instances find such causation even in instances in which the investor would not have altered the decision to purchase (or to sell) if all the facts were honestly presented. Consider how well the Supreme Court dealt with these questions in the next case.

———

Affiliated Ute Citizens v. United States

Supreme Court of the United States, 1972.
406 U.S. 128, 92 S.Ct. 1456, 31 L.Ed.2d 741.

■ MR. JUSTICE BLACKMUN delivered the opinion of the Court. . . .

[Pursuant to the Ute Partition Act, Ute Distribution Corporation (UDC) was created to facilitate the federal government's withdrawal from its supervision of various assets of mixed and full blood members of the Ute tribe and to make an equitable distribution of property claims between the two groups. The primary assets of the UDC were oil, gas and other mineral rights owned by members of the tribe. To carry out the partition, UDC issued 10 shares of capital stock to each mixed-blood Ute and the plan provided that First Security Bank of Utah would serve as transfer agent for the shares and would hold the shares for the members of the Ute tribe. Members wishing to dispose of their shares, therefore, were required to do so through the Bank. Defendants, Gale and Haslam, were employees of the Bank and at various times in 1963 and 1964 purchased 1,387 shares from mixed-bloods members without disclosing that non-tribal members were trading the shares at prices significantly higher than the defendants were offering the tribal members for their shares. Only 113 of these shares were acquired personally by Gale and Haslam and the other shares were acquired by non-tribal members, many of whom not only had standing orders with Gale and Haslam to purchase the shares but also had deposited funds with the Bank so their purchases could be swiftly executed once the Bank learned that a member wished to sell.

The District Court awarded damages based on its determination that the fair value of the shares was $1500, much above the member's selling price which ranged between $300 to $700. The Tenth Circuit reversed, partially; it upheld liability for the shares Gale and Haslam had acquired for themselves, but held that with respect to purchases by others that there was insufficient evidence of reliance by the selling members on any statement of conduct of the defendants.]

B. *Gale and Haslem. . . .*

[The proscriptions of Section 10(b) and Rule 10b–5] are broad and, by repeated use of the word "any," are obviously meant to be inclusive. The Court has said that the 1934 Act and its companion legislative enactments embrace a "fundamental purpose . . . to substitute a philosophy of full disclosure for the philosophy of *caveat emptor* and thus to achieve a high standard of business ethics in the securities industry." *SEC v. Capital Gains Research Bureau, 375 U.S. 180, 186 (1963).* In the case just cited the Court noted that Congress intended securities legislation enacted for the purpose of avoiding frauds to be construed "not technically and restrictively, but flexibly to effectuate its remedial purposes." *Id., at 195. . . .*

In the light of the congressional philosophy and purpose, . . . we conclude that the Court of Appeals viewed too narrowly the activities of defendants Gale and Haslam. We would agree that if the two men and the employer bank had functioned merely as a transfer agent, there would have been no duty of disclosure here. But, as the Court of Appeals itself observed, the record shows that Gale and Haslam "were active in encouraging a market for the UDC stock among non-Indians." *431 F.2d, at 1345.* They did this by soliciting and accepting standing orders from non-Indians. They and the bank, as a result, received increased deposits because of the development of this market. The two men also received commissions and gratuities from the expectant non-Indian buyers. The men, and hence the bank, as the Court found, were "entirely familiar with the prevailing market for the shares at all material times." *431 F.2d, at 1347.* The bank itself had acknowledged, by letter to AUC in January 1958, that "it would be our duty to see that these transfers were properly made" and that, with respect to the sale of shares, "the bank would be acting for the individual stockholders." The mixed-blood sellers "considered these defendants to be familiar with the market for the shares of stock and relied upon them when they desired to sell their shares." *431 F.2d, at 1347. . . .*

We conclude . . . that the Court of Appeals erred when it held that there was no violation of the Rule unless the record disclosed evidence of reliance on material fact misrepresentations by Gale and Haslem. *431 F.2d, at 1348.* We do not read *Rule 10b–5* so restrictively. To be sure, the second subparagraph of the rule specifies the making of an untrue statement of a material fact and the omission to state a material fact. The first and third subparagraphs are not so restricted. These defendants' activities, outlined above, disclose, within the very language of one or the other of those subparagraphs, a "course of business" or a "device, scheme, or artifice" that operated as a fraud upon the Indian sellers. . . . This is so because the defendants devised a plan and induced the mixed-blood holders of UDC stock to dispose of their shares without disclosing to them material facts that reasonably could have been expected to influence their decisions to sell. The individual defendants, in a distinct sense, were market makers, not only for their personal purchases constituting 81/3% of the sales, but for the other sales their activities produced. This being so, they possessed the affirmative duty under the Rule to disclose this fact to the mixed-blood sellers. See *Chasins v. Smith, Barney & Co., 438 F.2d 1167 (CA2 1970).* It is no answer to urge that, as to some of the petitioners, these defendants may have made no positive representation or recommendation. The defendants may not stand mute while they facilitate the mixed-bloods' sales to those seeking to profit in the non-Indian market the defendants had developed and encouraged and with which they were fully familiar. The sellers had the right to know that the defendants were in a position to gain financially from their sales and that their shares were selling for a higher price in that market. . . .

Under the circumstances of this case, involving primarily a failure to disclose, positive proof of reliance is not a prerequisite to recovery. All that is necessary is that the facts withheld be material in the sense that a reasonable investor might have considered them important in the making of this decision. . . . This obligation to disclose and this withholding of a material fact establish the requisite element of causation in fact. . . .

Gale and Haslem engaged in more than ministerial functions. Their acts were clearly within the reach of *Rule 10b–5*. And they were acts performed when they were obligated to act on behalf of the mixed-blood sellers.

C. *The Bank*. The liability of the bank, of course, is coextensive with that of Gale and Haslem. . . .

———

On its face, *Ute* appears to eliminate any requirement of reliance in a case of nondisclosure. In general, however, the cases have held that *Ute* "merely established a presumption that made it possible for the plaintiffs to meet their burden." Shores v. Sklar, 647 F.2d 462, 468 (5th Cir.1981) (en banc), cert. denied 459 U.S. 1102, 103 S.Ct. 722, 74 L.Ed.2d 949 (1983). The defendant can rebut this presumption "by showing that the . . . plaintiff would have followed the same course of conduct even with full and honest disclosure, [so that] the defendant's action (or lack thereof) cannot be said to have caused plaintiff's loss." Id. The defendant might carry this burden by showing, for example, that the plaintiff learned the omitted fact from an independent source before making his investment decision, so that the decision could not have been caused by the defendant's nondisclosure. Although the cases continue to use the language of "reliance" in the nondisclosure context, the real question is causation. When the question is properly framed in causation terms, once the plaintiff has shown that defendant omitted to disclose a material fact he was obliged to disclose, the burden is on the defendant to prove that the plaintiff would have made the same investment decision even if disclosure had been made.

Even though *Ute* diluted the requirement of reliance in the case of nondisclosure, the requirement of reliance remains meaningful in the vast majority of misstatement cases. For example, in a face-to-face case the defendant might be able to show that the plaintiff did not rely on a misstatement because he knew from other sources that the representation was false. Reliance can be established circumstantially. People who trade soon after material misstatement has been made to them will have almost always have relied on the misrepresentations. Accordingly, once the plaintiff shows that a material misrepresentation was made to him, and that he traded *soon* thereafter, as a practical matter reliance will normally be presumed, and the burden will shift to the defendant to show that the plaintiff did not rely on the misrepresentation. The strength of the reliance claim, however, is weakened as the time between the misstatement and the investor's trade lengthens. Thus, in some instances the misstatement case can be seen as similar to the nondisclosure case—that is, as a practical matter, once the plaintiff makes a showing of materiality the burden shifts to the defendant to show that the plaintiff did not rely on the misrepresentation. But in other instances, the link between the material misstatement and the trade provides less circumstantial support for the latter being dependent on the former.

————

Halliburton Co. v. Erica P. John Fund, Inc.

Supreme Court of the United States, 2014.
573 U.S. 258, 134 S.Ct. 2398, 189 L.Ed.2d 339.

■ ROBERTS, C. J.

I

Respondent Erica P. John Fund, Inc. (EPJ Fund), is the lead plaintiff in a putative class action against Halliburton and one of its executives (collectively Halliburton) alleging violations of *section 10(b)* of the Securities Exchange Act of 1934 . . . and Securities and Exchange Commission *Rule 10b–5* . . . . According to EPJ Fund, between June 3, 1999, and December 7, 2001, Halliburton made a series of misrepresentations regarding its potential liability in asbestos litigation, its expected revenue from certain construction contracts, and the anticipated benefits of its merger with another company—all in an attempt to inflate the price of its stock. Halliburton subsequently made a number of corrective disclosures, which, EPJ Fund contends, caused the company's stock price to drop and investors to lose money. . . .

II

Halliburton urges us to overrule . . . presumption of reliance [of *Basic Inc. v. Levinson*, 485 U.S. 224 (1988)] and to instead require every securities fraud plaintiff to prove that he actually relied on the defendant's misrepresentation in deciding to buy or sell a company's stock. . . .

A

The reliance element " 'ensures that there is a proper connection between a defendant's misrepresentation and a plaintiff's injury.' " 568 U.S., at ___ . . . (quoting *Halliburton I*, 563 U.S., at ___ . . . . "The traditional (and most direct) way a plaintiff can demonstrate reliance is by showing that he was aware of a company's statement and engaged in a relevant transaction—*e.g.*, purchasing common stock—based on that specific misrepresentation." *Id.*, at ___ (slip op., at 4).

In *Basic*, however, we recognized that requiring such direct proof of reliance "would place an unnecessarily unrealistic evidentiary burden on the *Rule 10b–5* plaintiff who has traded on an impersonal market." *485 U.S., at 245.* That is because, even assuming an investor could prove that he was aware of the misrepresentation, he would still have to "show a speculative state of facts, *i.e.*, how he would have acted . . . if the misrepresentation had not been made." *Ibid.*

We also noted that "[r]equiring proof of individualized reliance" from every securities fraud plaintiff "effectively would . . . prevent[ ][plaintiffs] from proceeding with a class action" in *Rule 10b–5* suits. If every plaintiff had to prove direct reliance on the defendant's misrepresentation, "individual issues then would . . . overwhelm[ ] the common ones," making certification under *Rule 23(b)(3)* inappropriate.

To address these concerns, *Basic* held that securities fraud plaintiffs can in certain circumstances satisfy the reliance element of a *Rule 10b–5* action by invoking a rebuttable presumption of reliance, rather than proving direct reliance on a misrepresentation. The Court based that presumption on what is known as the "fraud-on-the-market" theory, which holds that "the market price of shares traded on well-developed markets reflects all publicly available information, and, hence, any material misrepresentations." *Id., at 246*. The Court also noted that, rather than scrutinize every piece of public information about a company for himself, the typical "investor who buys or sells stock at the price set by the market does so in reliance on the integrity of that price"—the belief that it reflects all public, material information. *Id., at 247*. As a result, whenever the investor buys or sells stock at the market price, his "reliance on any public material misrepresentations . . . may be presumed for purposes of a *Rule 10b–5* action." *Ibid.* . . .

At the same time, *Basic* emphasized that the presumption of reliance was rebuttable rather than conclusive. Specifically, "[a]ny showing that severs the link between the alleged misrepresentation and either the price received (or paid) by the plaintiff, or his decision to trade at a fair market price, will be sufficient to rebut the presumption of reliance." *485 U.S., at 248*. So for example, if a defendant could show that the alleged misrepresentation did not, for whatever reason, actually affect the market price, or that a plaintiff would have bought or sold the stock even had he been aware that the stock's price was tainted by fraud, then the presumption of reliance would not apply. *Id., at 248–249*. In either of those cases, a plaintiff would have to prove that he directly relied on the defendant's misrepresentation in buying or selling the stock.

B

. . .

2

Halliburton's primary argument for overruling *Basic* is that the decision rested on two premises that can no longer withstand scrutiny. The first premise concerns what is known as the "efficient capital markets hypothesis." *Basic* stated that "the market price of shares traded on well-developed markets reflects all publicly available information, and, hence, any material misrepresentations." *Id., at 246*. From that statement, Halliburton concludes that the *Basic* Court espoused "a robust view of market efficiency" that is no longer tenable, for " 'overwhelming empirical evidence' now 'suggests that capital markets are not fundamentally efficient.' " Brief for Petitioners 14–16 (quoting Lev & de Villiers, Stock Price Crashes and 10b–5 Damages: A Legal, Economic, and Policy Analysis, *47 Stan. L. Rev 7, 20 (1994)*). To support this contention, Halliburton cites studies purporting to show that "public information is often not incorporated immediately (much less rationally) into market prices." . . .

Halliburton does not, of course, maintain that capital markets are *always* inefficient. Rather, in its view, *Basic*'s fundamental error was to ignore the fact that " 'efficiency is not a binary, yes or no question.' " . . . The markets for some securities are more efficient than the markets for others, and even a single market can process different kinds of information more or less efficiently, depending on how widely the information is disseminated and how easily it is understood. . . . Yet *Basic*, Halliburton asserts, glossed over these nuances, assuming a false dichotomy that renders the presumption of reliance both underinclusive and overinclusive: A misrepresentation can distort a stock's market price even in a generally inefficient market, and a misrepresentation can leave a stock's market price unaffected even in a generally efficient one. . . .

Halliburton's criticisms fail to take *Basic* on its own terms. Halliburton focuses on the debate among economists about the degree to which the market price of a company's stock reflects public information about the company—and thus the degree to which an investor can earn an abnormal, above-market return by trading on such information. . . . That debate is not new. Indeed, the *Basic* Court acknowledged it and declined to enter the fray, declaring that "[w]e need not determine by adjudication what economists and social scientists have debated through the use of sophisticated statistical analysis and the application of economic theory." *485 U.S., at 246–247, n. 24.* To recognize the presumption of reliance, the Court explained, was not "conclusively to adopt any particular theory of how quickly and completely publicly available information is reflected in market price." *Id., at 248, n. 28.* The Court instead based the presumption on the fairly modest premise that "market professionals generally consider most publicly announced material statements about companies, thereby affecting stock market prices." *Id., at 247, n. 24. Basic*'s presumption of reliance thus does not rest on a "binary" view of market efficiency. Indeed, in making the presumption rebuttable, *Basic* recognized that market efficiency is a matter of degree and accordingly made it a matter of proof.

The academic debates discussed by Halliburton have not refuted the modest premise underlying the presumption of reliance. Even the foremost critics of the efficient-capital-markets hypothesis acknowledge that public information generally affects stock prices. . . .

Halliburton also contests a second premise underlying the *Basic* presumption: the notion that investors "invest 'in reliance on the integrity of [the market] price.' " . . . Halliburton identifies a number of classes of investors for whom "price integrity" is supposedly "marginal or irrelevant." . . . The primary example is the value investor, who believes that certain stocks are undervalued or overvalued and attempts to "beat the market" by buying the undervalued stocks and selling the overvalued ones. . . .

But *Basic* never denied the existence of such investors. As we recently explained, *Basic* concluded only that "it is reasonable to presume that *most* investors—knowing that they have little hope of outperforming the market in the long run based solely on their analysis of publicly available information—will rely on the security's market price as an unbiased assessment of the security's value in light of all public information." *Amgen*, 568 U.S., at ___ . . . (emphasis added).

In any event, there is no reason to suppose that even Halliburton's main counterexample—the value investor—is as indifferent to the integrity of market prices as Halliburton suggests. Such an investor implicitly relies on the fact that a stock's market price will eventually reflect material information—how else could the market correction on which his profit depends occur? To be sure, the value investor "does not believe that the market price accurately reflects public information *at the time he transacts*." *Post*, at 11. But to indirectly rely on a misstatement in the sense relevant for the *Basic* presumption, he need only trade stock based on the belief that the market price will incorporate public information within a reasonable period. The value investor also presumably tries to estimate *how* undervalued or overvalued a particular stock is, and such estimates can be skewed by a market price tainted by fraud. . . .

C . . .

Finally, Halliburton and its *amici* contend that, by facilitating securities class actions, the *Basic* presumption produces a number of serious and harmful consequences. Such class actions, they say, allow plaintiffs to extort large settlements from defendants for meritless claims; punish innocent shareholders, who end up having to pay settlements and judgments; impose excessive costs on businesses; and consume a disproportionately large share of judicial resources. . . .

These concerns are more appropriately addressed to Congress, which has in fact responded, to some extent, to many of the issues raised by Halliburton and its *amici*. Congress has, for example, enacted the Private Securities Litigation Reform Act of 1995 (PSLRA) . . . [and] also enacted the Securities Litigation Uniform Standards Act of 1998. . . . Such legislation demonstrates Congress's willingness to consider policy concerns of the sort that Halliburton says should lead us to overrule *Basic*.

III

Halliburton proposes two alternatives to overruling *Basic* that would alleviate what it regards as the decision's most serious flaws. The first alternative would require plaintiffs to prove that a defendant's misrepresentation actually affected the stock price—so-called "price impact"—in order to invoke the *Basic* presumption. . . . Halliburton's second proposed alternative would allow defendants to rebut the presumption of reliance with evidence of a *lack* of price impact, not only at the merits stage—which all agree defendants may already do—but also before class certification.

A

. . . [T]o invoke the *Basic* presumption, a plaintiff must prove that: (1) the alleged misrepresentations were publicly known, (2) they were material, (3) the stock traded in an efficient market, and (4) the plaintiff traded the stock between when the misrepresentations were made and when the truth was revealed. . . . The first three prerequisites are directed at price impact—"whether the alleged misrepresentations affected the market price in the first place." *Halliburton I* . . . . In the absence of price impact, *Basic*'s fraud-on-the-market theory and presumption of reliance collapse. . . . Halliburton argues that since the *Basic* presumption hinges on price impact, plaintiffs should be required to prove it directly in order to invoke the presumption. . . .

Far from a modest refinement of the *Basic* presumption, this proposal would radically alter the required showing for the reliance element of the *Rule 10b–5* cause of action. What is called the *Basic* presumption actually incorporates two constituent presumptions: First, if a plaintiff shows that the defendant's misrepresentation was public and material and that the stock traded in a generally efficient market, he is entitled to a presumption that the misrepresentation affected the stock price. Second, if the plaintiff also shows that he purchased the stock at the market price during the relevant period, he is entitled to a further presumption that he purchased the stock in reliance on the defendant's misrepresentation.

By requiring plaintiffs to prove price impact directly, Halliburton's proposal would take away the first constituent presumption. Halliburton's argument for doing so is the same as its primary argument for overruling the *Basic* presumption altogether: Because market efficiency is not a yes-or-no proposition, a public, material misrepresentation might not affect a stock's price even in a generally efficient market. But as explained, *Basic* never suggested otherwise; that is why it affords defendants an opportunity to rebut the presumption by showing, among other things, that the particular misrepresentation at issue did not affect the stock's market price. For the same reasons we declined to completely jettison the *Basic* presumption, we decline to effectively jettison half of it by revising the prerequisites for invoking it.

B

Even if plaintiffs need not directly prove price impact to invoke the *Basic* presumption, Halliburton contends that defendants should at least be allowed to defeat the presumption at the class certification stage through evidence that the misrepresentation did not in fact affect the stock price. We agree.

1

There is no dispute that defendants may introduce such evidence at the merits stage to rebut the *Basic* presumption. *Basic* itself "made clear that the presumption was just that, and could be rebutted by appropriate evidence," including evidence that the asserted misrepresentation (or its correction) did not affect the market price of the defendant's stock. . . . Nor is there any dispute that defendants may introduce price impact evidence at the class certification stage, so long as it is for the purpose of countering a plaintiff's showing of market efficiency, rather than directly rebutting the presumption. . . .

After all, plaintiffs themselves can and do introduce evidence of the *existence* of price impact in connection with "event studies"—regression analyses that seek to show that the market price of the defendant's stock tends to respond to pertinent publicly reported events. See Brief for Law Professors as *Amici Curiae* 25–28. In this case, for example, EPJ Fund submitted an event study of various episodes that might have been expected to affect the price of Halliburton's stock, in order to demonstrate that the market for that stock takes account of material, public information about the company. See App. 217–230 (describing the results of the study). The episodes examined by EPJ Fund's event study included one of the alleged misrepresentations that form the basis of the Fund's suit. . . .

Defendants—like plaintiffs—may accordingly submit price impact evidence prior to class certification. . . .

Suppose a defendant at the certification stage submits an event study looking at the impact on the price of its stock from six discrete events, in an effort to refute the plaintiffs' claim of general market efficiency. All agree the defendant may do this. Suppose one of the six events is the specific misrepresentation asserted by the plaintiffs. All agree that this too is perfectly acceptable. Now suppose the district court determines that, despite the defendant's study, the plaintiff has carried its burden to prove market efficiency, but that the evidence shows no price impact with respect to the specific misrepresentation challenged in the suit. The evidence at the certification stage thus shows an efficient market, on which the alleged misrepresentation had no price impact. . . . [U]nder EPJ Fund's view, the plaintiffs' action should be certified and proceed as a class action (with all that entails), even though the fraud-on-the-market theory does not apply and common reliance thus cannot be presumed.

Such a result is inconsistent with *Basic*'s own logic. Under *Basic*'s fraud-on-the-market theory, market efficiency and the other prerequisites for invoking the presumption constitute an indirect way of showing price impact. As explained, it is appropriate to allow plaintiffs to rely on this indirect proxy for price impact, rather than requiring them to prove price impact directly, given *Basic*'s rationales for recognizing a presumption of reliance in the first place. . . .

But an indirect proxy should not preclude direct evidence when such evidence is available. As we explained in *Basic*, "[a]ny showing that severs the link between the alleged misrepresentation and . . . the price received (or paid) by the plaintiff . . . will be sufficient to rebut the presumption of reliance" because "the basis for finding that the fraud had been transmitted through market price would be gone." *485 U.S., at 248.* And without the presumption of reliance, a *Rule 10b–5* suit cannot proceed as a class action: Each plaintiff would have to prove reliance individually, so common issues would not "predominate" over individual ones, as required by *Rule 23(b)(3). Id., at 242.* Price impact is thus an essential precondition for any *Rule 10b–5* class action. While *Basic* allows plaintiffs to establish that precondition indirectly, it does not require courts to ignore a defendant's direct, more salient evidence showing that the alleged misrepresentation did not actually affect the stock's market price and, consequently, that the *Basic* presumption does not apply. . . .

Our choice in this case, then, is not between allowing price impact evidence at the class certification stage or relegating it to the merits. Evidence of price impact will be before the court at the certification stage in any event. The choice, rather, is between limiting the price impact inquiry before class certification to indirect evidence, or allowing consideration of direct evidence as well. As explained, we see no reason to artificially limit the inquiry at the certification stage to indirect evidence of price impact. Defendants may seek to defeat the *Basic* presumption at that stage through direct as well as indirect price impact evidence.

More than 25 years ago, we held that plaintiffs could satisfy the reliance element of the *Rule 10b–5* cause of action by invoking a presumption that a public, material misrepresentation will distort the price of stock traded in an efficient market, and that anyone who purchases the stock at the market price may be considered to have done so in reliance on the misrepresentation. We adhere to that decision and decline to modify the prerequisites for invoking the presumption of reliance. But to maintain the consistency of the presumption with the class certification requirements of *Federal Rule of Civil Procedure 23*, defendants must be afforded an opportunity before class certification to defeat the presumption through evidence that an alleged misrepresentation did not actually affect the market price of the stock.

Because the courts below denied Halliburton that opportunity, we vacate the judgment of the Court of Appeals for the Fifth Circuit and remand the case for further proceedings consistent with this opinion.

It is so ordered.

■ JUSTICE GINSBURG, with whom JUSTICE BREYER and JUSTICE SOTOMAYOR join, concurring.

Advancing price impact consideration from the merits stage to the certification stage may broaden the scope of discovery available at certification. . . . But the Court recognizes that it is incumbent upon the defendant to show the absence of price impact. . . . The Court's judgment, therefore, should impose no heavy toll on securities-fraud plaintiffs with tenable claims. On that understanding, I join the Court's opinion.

■ JUSTICE THOMAS, with whom JUSTICE SCALIA and JUSTICE ALITO join, concurring in the judgment. (opinion omitted).

————

NOTES ON THE FORENSICS OF FRAUD-ON-THE-MARKET

1. Indicia of an "Efficient Market." Cammer v. Bloom, 711 F.Supp. 1264 (D.N.J. 1989), is a leading case regarding factors considered in determining whether a security likely traded in an efficient market so that the fraud-on-the-market approach to transaction causation can be used to certify the class. The factors it lists are (1) percentage of shares traded weekly, (2) analysts following, (3) presence of market makers and arbitrageurs, (4) eligibility to take advantage of the SEC's integrated disclosure procedures pursuant to Form S-3 for engaging in public offerings, and (5) responsiveness of security's price to new information. As in any factor analysis, the courts tend not to require all factors to be present, and some courts have added considerations such as the market capitalization of the firm (i.e., number of shares outstanding multiplied by their market price), bid-ask spreads, percentage of stock held by insiders, and institutional share ownership. See Fisher, Does the Efficient Market Theory Help Us Do Justice in a Time of Madness?, 54 Emory L.J. 843, 859–866 (2005). Why are these factors consistent with market efficiency? Why is market efficiency a precondition for the plaintiff's to invoke the fraud on the market approach to causation? Why is this approach necessary for the suit to proceed as a class action?

2. The Price Impact Inquiry. The inquiry into the price impact of an alleged misrepresentation in fraud on the market cases frequently occurs in the context of an event study, a statistical method for determining whether some corporate event, e.g., the announcement of earnings, is associated with a statistically significant change in the price of a company's stock. The main inputs for any event study are benchmark returns provided by a broad index such as the S&P Industrial 500, the historical stock return of the company or companies being observed, and standard statistical methods to measure statistical significance. As originally developed by financial economists, event studies observed phenomenon shared by a portfolio of companies, e.g., they each announced an earnings increase. Event studies in securities litigation, however, almost always involve only a single firm as they seek to isolate and measure price moves of a particular (defendant) firm involved in the litigation. Importing a methodology long-used by economists for studies of phenomena shared by multiple firms into a single-firm context raises profound methodological concerns, namely in terms of the model's predictive power. *See e.g.,* J. B. Heaton & Alon Brav, Event Studies in Securities Litigation: Low Power, Confounding Effects, and Bias, 93 Wash. U. L. Rev. 583 (2015). This concern is beginning to be reflected in court decisions. *In re Petrobras Securities Litig.,* 862 F.3d 250 (2nd Cir. 2017), held the defendants could not use an event study to establish—without consideration of other evidence—that an alleged securities fraud had no impact on a stock price of the defendant company. Judge Garaufis in his decision notes that "event studies offer the seductive promise of hard numbers and dispassionate truth, but methodological constraints limit their utility in the context of single-firm analyses. *Id.* at 278. Recall that the fifth *Cammer* factor for determining whether a particular security trades in an efficient market is the security's responsiveness to new information. *Waggoner v. Barclays PLC*, 875 F.3d 79 (2nd Cir. 2017), held that when the weight of other factors support a finding that a particular security traded in an efficient market there is no need to consider the absence of price impact from an event study.

     3.   *Value Investors.* In *GAMCO Investors v. Vivendi Universal*, 838 F.3d 214 (2d Cir. 2016), plaintiffs had opted out of a class action against Vivendi and pursued their individual claims alleging that during the time of their purchases Vivendi had engaged in a series of misrepresentations that concealed various "liquidity" problems the firm was having and such concealment had the effect of inflating shares' market price above what the price would have been had the various liquidity issues not be concealed. Plaintiffs were so-called "value investors" who purchased their shares in the belief that the market price of Vivendi shares were less than value the plaintiffs believed the shares were worth. The district court dismissal of the case was affirmed by the Second Circuit on the basis that evidence produced by the defendant established that the plaintiff's valuation model did not focus on such liquidity concerns so that the plaintiffs would have purchased Vivendi shares even if the liquidity issues had been disclosed. The plaintiffs' case was not assisted by the fact that even after they became aware of the fraud they continued to purchase Vivendi shares.

————

NOTE ON CLASS CERTIFICATION IN FRAUD ON THE MARKET CASES

Erica P. John Fund, Inc. v. Halliburton, 563 U.S. 804, 131 S. Ct. 2179, 180 L.Ed.2d 24 (2011) (Halliburton I), held that class certification in a fraud on the market case is not dependent on the plaintiff establishing loss causation. The defendant had argued the plaintiff's inability to provide loss causation prevented the plaintiff from invoking a rebuttable presumption of reliance. The court rejected this, reasoning, "[s]uch a rule contravenes Basic's fundamental premise—that an investor presumptively relies on a misrepresentation so long as it was reflected in the market price at the time of his transaction. The fact that a subsequent loss may have been caused by factors other than the revelation of a misrepresentation has nothing to do with whether an investor relied on the misrepresentation in the first place."

A divided Supreme Court in *Amgen Inc. v. Connecticut Retirement Plans and Trust Funds,* 586 U.S.804, 133 S. Ct. 1184, 185 L.Ed.2d 308 (2013), held that in order to obtain class certification based on fraud on the market investors are not required to prove (and defendants are not allowed to introduce evidence rebutting) the materiality of the defendant's alleged misrepresentation. The majority reasoned that class certification does not require plaintiffs to establish each element of their claim; rather the majority believed that for class certification the focus is on whether, among the issues in dispute, the issues that are common to the class predominate over individual issues that may exist. The majority reasoned that "the question of materiality is an objective one that is common to all members of the class" so that for class certification no further inquiry into materiality is required. Furthermore, to require proof of materiality of the alleged misrepresentation as a condition to certifying the class would "put the cart before the horse."

B. LOSS CAUSATION

The best interpretation of *loss causation* is that the defendant's wrongful act not only must have caused the plaintiff to buy or sell a security (transaction causation); it must also have been the cause of the plaintiff's economic *loss* on the security. In contrast to transaction causation, loss causation requires a showing that the violation of Rule 10b–5 caused the economic harm of which the plaintiff complains. While transaction causation is generally understood as the investor's reliance on the misrepresentation, loss causation has often been described as proximate cause, meaning in part that the damages suffered by plaintiff must be a foreseeable consequence of any misrepresentation or material omission. An alternative formulation of loss causation is that it requires that "the misrepresentation touches upon the reasons for the investment's decline in value." Binder v. Gillespie, 184 F.3d 1059 (9th Cir. 1999). As stated in *Suez Equity v. Toronto-Dominion Bank*, 250 F.3d 87 (2d Cir. 2001), "[t]he loss causation inquiry typically examines how directly the subject of the [violation] caused the loss, and whether the resulting loss was a foreseeable outcome of the [violation]," while also taking into account issues such as the presence of intervening causes and the lapse of time between the behavior complained of and the loss.

Metzler Investment GMBH v. Corinthian Colleges, Inc.

United States Court of Appeals, Ninth Circuit, 2008.
540 F.3d 1049.

■ B. FLETCHER, CIRCUIT JUDGE: . . .

Metzler alleges that Corinthian's colleges are pervaded by fraudulent practices designed to maximize the amount of federal Title IV funding—a major source of Corinthian's revenue—that those schools receive. The TAC [the Third Amended Complaint] alleges that Corinthian engaged in a variety of false or deceptive schemes falsifying financial aid applications to obtain federal funds and increase federal award entitlements; encouraging students to falsify federal student aid forms themselves; manipulating student enrollment by counting students not yet enrolled (referred to in the TAC as "false starts"); manipulating or falsifying student grades to maintain federal funding eligibility; exposing the company to bad debt in order to meet regulatory requirements for continued federal funding; delaying notification to federal officials of dropped students and delaying refunds to the federal government after students had dropped; and manipulating job placement data in order-to satisfy federal and state regulatory requirements. According to the TAC, the net effect of these practices was that "at numerous Corinthian campuses, as many as 50% to 60% of the people defendants represented to the U.S. government as being qualified, attending 'students' were either 'no shows' in class or unqualified for admission and federal funds from the outset." . . . Thus, according to the TAC, Corinthian's public face to the market—one of growth and financial success premised on increasing student enrollment and successful placement rates—masked extensive fraud. The TAC alleges that this fraud resulted in an artificial inflation of Corinthian's stock price. . . .

Because Corinthian campuses were allegedly pervaded by fraudulent admission practices, the TAC alleges that virtually every Class Period statement discussing Corinthian's financial status was false. Specifically, the TAC alleges that public statements in regulatory disclosures and related documents regarding the company's financial performance were rendered false by the fact that Corinthian's underlying fraudulent practices remained hidden. . . .

The TAC thus alleges that any positive financial statement released by the company created the decidedly false impression among investors that Corinthian's success was due to "legitimate business means that could be expected to continue," when in fact its "financial performance was materially driven by fraudulent manipulation of the Title IV funding program and could cease at any time if exposed." TAC P 147(a). . . .

C. The TAC's allegations that Corinthian's fraud was revealed to the market, causing Metzler's losses.

The TAC points to two specific disclosures that purportedly revealed Corinthian's fraudulent student enrollment and financial aid practices to the market: (1) the June 24, 2004 *Financial Times* story reporting the DOE investigation at the Bryman campus, and (2) an August 2, 2004 press release disclosing reduced earnings and earning projections. According to the TAC, when read in tandem these two disclosures revealed "the truth regarding [Corinthian's] fraudulent practices and deception," and precipitated considerable drops in the value of Corinthian stock. . . .

As described above, the June 24 *Financial Times* story revealed that the DOE investigated Corinthian's Bryman campus in December 2003, and as a result that campus had been placed on reimbursement status. The *Financial Times* story further reported, however, that the DOE review and Bryman's placement on reimbursement status, "does not affect the status of other Corinthian schools." Nonetheless, Corinthian stock fell $2.55 on June 24, losing 10% of its value and closing at $22.51. Corinthian's stock rebounded within three trading days and by June 29, 2004, it rose to $25.11, an amount that exceeded the stock's value before the June 24 *Financial Times* story.

The second alleged disclosure occurred on August 2, 2004, when Corinthian issued a press release announcing that it had cut its revenue and earnings projections for the fourth quarter of 2004 and all of fiscal year 2005. That press release also revealed that the company had participated in a meeting with the California Attorney General regarding Corinthian's business practices. The release announced revised earnings per share ("EPS") for fiscal year 2004 of 86 to 87 cents, down from earlier projections of 94 cents EPS. The company also lowered guidance for all of fiscal year 2005. CEO Moore attributed the reduced earnings and accompanying projections to a number of factors:

> During the fourth quarter [FY 2004] we achieved a remarkable growth rate in student enrollments, although below our expectations. Strong growth, unfortunately, sometimes brings challenges, and there were several during the past quarter that we now believe caused our revenue to fall short of our expectations and earlier guidance. Those factors included changes in lead flow mix among television leads, direct mail leads, newspaper leads and Internet leads; higher than anticipated attrition; negative publicity related to student litigation in Florida; and later than anticipated new branch campus openings.

After the August 2, 2004 earnings miss, Corinthian's stock dropped 45% to $10.29. . . .

. . . [The district court granted the defendants' motion to dismiss.]

III. DISCUSSION

A. The TAC does not adequately plead "loss causation."

As explained by the Supreme Court in *Dura Pharmaceuticals [Inc. v. Broudo, 544 U.S. 336, 125 S.Ct. 1627, 161 L.Ed. 577 (2005)],* loss causation is the "causal connection between the [defendant's] material misrepresentation and the [plaintiff's] loss." *544 U.S. at 342* (citation omitted). A complaint fails to allege loss causation if it does not "provide[ ] [a defendant] with notice of what the relevant economic loss might be or of what the causal connection might be between that loss and the misrepresentation[.]" *Id. at 347.* Stated in the affirmative, the complaint must allege that the defendant's "share price fell significantly after the truth became known." *Id.* A plaintiff does not, of course, need to *prove* loss causation in order to avoid dismissal; but the plaintiff must properly allege it. *Id. at 346. . . .*

The principal Ninth Circuit case applying *Dura's* loss causation standards is *In re Daou Systems. 411 F.3d 1006. . . .*

In *Daou* the plaintiffs' theory of fraud was that the defendant was systematically recognizing revenue on contracts that had not been completed. *Id. at 1012–13.* Plaintiffs adequately pled loss causation in *Daou* because their complaint alleged that the market learned of and reacted to this fraud, as opposed to merely reacting to reports of the defendant's poor financial health generally. *Id. at 1026 . . .*

Here, Metzler relies on the June 24 *Financial Times* story disclosing the DOE investigation at the Bryman campus and the August 2 earnings announcement. In doing so, Metzler fails to adequately plead loss causation. The TAC does not allege that the June 24 and August 2 announcements disclosed—or even suggested—to the market that Corinthian was manipulating student enrollment figures company-wide in order to procure excess federal funding, which is the fraudulent activity that Metzler contends forced down the stock that caused its losses. Neither the June 24 *Financial Times* story nor the August 2 press release regarding earnings can be reasonably read to reveal widespread financial aid manipulation by Corinthian, and the TAC does not otherwise adequately plead that these releases did so.

As for the *Financial Times* story, it does reveal a DOE investigation at the Bryman campus and the campus's placement on reimbursement status as a result of improper financial aid practices; but it simultaneously notes that the investigation there "does not affect the status of other Corinthian schools." The TAC does not allege that all, or even some appreciable number, of Corinthian's schools were being investigated or placed on reimbursement status. Only the Bryman campus was subject to that sanction. Indeed, the TAC itself discredits the notion that the June 24 disclosure revealed company-wide manipulation of student enrollment, by describing the June 24 disclosure as revealing to investors "the *potential* but real *risk* of all 88 colleges being placed on reimbursement status, which would have delayed Title IV funding and increased accounts receivable by up to $135 million company-wide." TAC P 159 (emphases added) . . . But neither *Daou* nor *Dura* support the notion that loss causation is pled where a defendant's disclosure reveals a "risk" or "potential" for widespread fraudulent conduct. In *Daou* the defendant disclosed that the company actually had $10 million in unbilled receivables, not merely that there was some risk it might accrue such receivables. *411 F.3d at 1026.* Moreover, as Corinthian notes, its stock recovered very shortly after the modest 10% drop that accompanied the June 24 announcement.

The TAC's characterization of the August 2 earnings announcement similarly fails to allege that the market became aware of, and the resulting stock drop resulted from, widespread enrollment fraud. At best, the TAC contends that the reference in the August 2 announcement to "higher than anticipated attrition" was understood by the market as Corinthian's "euphemism for an admission that they had enrolled students who should not have been signed up at all, resulting in a 45% stock drop." TAC P 48. Metzler's appellate brief asserts that the August 2 disclosure made investors "realize that Corinthian's improper manipulation of student and enrollment records was not limited to [the Bryman campus at] San Jose, nor was it immaterial." But the TAC does not allege facts to suggest that on August 2 the market became aware that Corinthian was manipulating student records company-wide, other than an undocumented assertion that Corinthian's August 2 stock drop was, by necessity, a result of this market "realization."[8]

Metzler is correct to observe that neither *Daou* nor *Dura* require an admission or finding of fraud before loss causation can be properly pled. *Dura Pharms., Inc., 544 U.S. at 346*; *Daou, 411 F.3d at 1025*. But that does not allow a plaintiff to plead loss causation through "euphemism" and thereby avoid alleging the necessary connection between defendant's fraud and the actual loss. So long as there is a drop in a stock's price, a plaintiff will always be able to contend that the market "understood" a defendant's statement precipitating a loss as a coded message revealing the fraud. Enabling a plaintiff to proceed on such a theory would effectively resurrect what *Dura* discredited—that loss causation is established through an allegation that a stock was purchased at an inflated price. *544 U.S. at 347*. Loss causation requires more. . . .

Finally, while the court assumes that the facts in a complaint are true, it is not required to indulge unwarranted inferences in order to save a complaint from dismissal. . . . The TAC's allegation that the market understood the June 24 and August 2 disclosures as a revelation of Corinthian's systematic manipulation of student enrollment is not a "fact." It is an inference that Metzler believes is warranted from the facts that are alleged. But Corinthian persuasively explains why this is not the case. As to the June 24 disclosure, Corinthian points out that its stock quickly recovered from the 10% drop that followed the *Financial Times* story. Similarly, the August 2 announcement contained a far more plausible reason for the resulting drop in Corinthian's stock price—the company failed to hit prior earnings estimates. The August 2 announcement simultaneously reported that student population growth was up nearly 50% overall and same-school population increased 15%, making it even further unwarranted to infer that the reference to

---

8   Nor do the June 24 and August 2 disclosures become adequate when viewed in tandem. The June 24 *Financial Times* story discusses impropriety regarding the financial aid practices at one school; the August 2 release contains one reference to attrition. The combined force of these statements does not suggest that the market was alerted to widespread enrollment and admissions fraud at Corinthian schools nationwide. Nor does the TAC allege any genuine causal connection between the August 2 earnings miss and the allegations that Corinthian had manipulated student enrollment in order to receive excess federal funds, or that the earnings miss was caused by slashed federal funding.

"attrition" was understood by the market to mean that Corinthian had revealed widespread misrepresentation of student enrollment to fraudulently procure excess federal funding. The TAC thus fails to allege loss causation based on the June 24 and August 2 disclosures. . . .

IV. CONCLUSION

The TAC's allegations, although not lacking in breadth or numerosity, ultimately fail to meet the PSLRA's exacting requirements and the standards for pleading loss causation. The disclosures that the TAC relies on simply do not identify the requisite causal connection between Metzler's claims of fraudulent student admission and financial aid practices, and a resulting drop in Corinthian's stock price. . . . For these reasons, we affirm.

―――――

First Solar, Inc., one of the world's largest producers of photovoltaic solar panel modules, discovered a manufacturing defect causing field power loss and a design defect causing faster power loss in hot climates, but concealed the problems from investors, covering up the cost and scope of the defects and reported false information on their financial statements. Months later it announced a serious decline in earnings, causing its stock to fall precipitously. *Mineworkers Pension Scheme v. First Solar, Inc.*, 881 F.3d 750, 754 (9th Cir. 2018), held that loss causation was sufficiently established by the price decline accompanying the announcement of earnings decline, even though that announcement did not reveal the earlier fraudulent concealment. The court applied a proximate cause test whereby the ultimate issue is whether the defendant's misstatement, as opposed to some other fact, foreseeably caused the plaintiff's loss.

―――――

NOTE ON BUNDLING AND ITS CONSEQUENCES

"Got any other material news, be it good or bad news, we can disclose?" This may well be the wise response of defense counsel upon learning the client, a publicly traded company, has previously committed a material misrepresentation. This defensive strategy in anticipation of possible securities law private actions is baked into the loss causation requirement mandated by *Dura Pharmaceuticals, Inc.* and applied in *Metzler*. Minimally disentangling the actionable statements from other statements released in the same announcement is a formidable undertaking for even the most talented forensic economist. But it has other consequences as well. *See* Barbara Bliss, Frank Partnoy & Michael Furchgott, Information Bundling and Securities Litigation, 65 J. Acctg. & Econ. 61 (2018) (finding strong negative correlation between likelihood of litigation (as well as settlement amount) and the bundling (inclusion) of good or bad news in the announcement that first discloses information reflecting the company earlier had committed a material misrepresentation).

―――――

9. THE JUNCTION OF BREACHES OF FIDUCIARY DUTY AND RULE 10b–5

Santa Fe Industries, Inc. v. Green

Supreme Court of the United States, 1977.
430 U.S. 462, 97 S.Ct. 1292, 51 L.Ed.2d 480.

■ MR. JUSTICE WHITE delivered the opinion of the Court.

The issue in this case involves the reach and coverage of § 10(b) of the Securities Exchange Act of 1934 and Rule 10b–5 thereunder in the context of a Delaware short-form merger transaction used by the majority stockholder of a corporation to eliminate the minority interest.

I

In 1936, petitioner Santa Fe Industries, Inc. (Santa Fe), acquired control of 60% of the stock of Kirby Lumber Corp. (Kirby), a Delaware corporation. Through a series of purchases over the succeeding years, Santa Fe increased its control of Kirby's stock to 95%; the purchase prices during the period 1968–1973 ranged from $65 to $92.50 per share. In 1974, wishing to acquire 100% ownership of Kirby, Santa Fe availed itself of § 253 of the Delaware Corporation Law, known as the "short-form merger" statute. Section 253 permits a parent corporation owning at least 90% of the stock of a subsidiary to merge with that subsidiary, upon approval by the parent's board of directors, and to make payment in cash for the shares of the minority stockholders. The statute does not require the consent of, or advance notice to, the minority stockholders. However, notice of the merger must be given within 10 days after its effective date, and any stockholder who is dissatisfied with the terms of the merger may petition the Delaware Court of Chancery for a decree ordering the surviving corporation to pay him the fair value of his shares, as determined by a court-appointed appraiser subject to review by the court. Del.Code Ann., Tit. 8, §§ 253, 262 (1975 ed. and Supp.1976).

Santa Fe obtained independent appraisals of the physical assets of Kirby—land, timber, buildings, and machinery—and of Kirby's oil, gas, and mineral interests. These appraisals, together with other financial information, were submitted to Morgan Stanley & Co. (Morgan Stanley), an investment banking firm retained to appraise the fair market value of Kirby stock. Kirby's physical assets were appraised at $320 million (amounting to $640 for each of the 500,000 shares); Kirby's stock was valued by Morgan Stanley at $125 per share. Under the terms of the merger, minority stockholders were offered $150 per share.

The provisions of the short-form merger statute were fully complied with. The minority stockholders of Kirby were notified the day after the merger became effective and were advised of their right to obtain an appraisal in Delaware court if dissatisfied with the offer of $150 per share. They also received an information statement containing, in addition to the relevant financial data about Kirby, the appraisals of the value of Kirby's assets and the Morgan Stanley appraisal concluding that the fair market value of the stock was $125 per share.

Respondents, minority stockholders of Kirby, objected to the terms of the merger, but did not pursue their appraisal remedy in the Delaware Court of Chancery.[4] Instead, they brought this action in federal court on behalf of the corporation and other minority stockholders, seeking to set aside the merger or to recover what they claimed to be the fair value of their shares. The amended complaint asserted that, based on the fair market value of Kirby's physical assets as revealed by the appraisal included in the information statement sent to minority shareholders, Kirby's stock was worth at least $772 per share.[5] The complaint alleged further that the merger took place without prior notice to minority stockholders; that the purpose of the merger was to appropriate the difference between the "conceded pro rata value of the physical assets," App. 103a, and the offer of $150 per share—to "freez[e] out the minority stockholders at a wholly inadequate price," *id.,* at 100a; and that Santa Fe, knowing the appraised value of the physical assets, obtained a "fraudulent appraisal" of the stock from Morgan Stanley and offered $25 above that appraisal "in order to lull the minority stockholders into erroneously believing that [Santa Fe was] generous." *Id.,* at 103a. This course of conduct was alleged to be "a violation of Rule 10b–5 because defendants employed a 'device, scheme, or artifice to defraud' and engaged in an 'act, practice or course of business which operates or would operate as a fraud or deceit upon any person, in connection with the purchase or sale of any security.'" *Ibid.* Morgan Stanley assertedly participated in the fraud as an accessory by submitting its appraisal of $125 per share although knowing the appraised value of the physical assets. . . .

The District Court dismissed the complaint for failure to state a claim upon which relief could be granted. 391 F.Supp. 849 (S.D.N.Y.1975). . . .

As for the claim that actionable fraud inhered in the allegedly gross undervaluation of the minority shares, the District Court observed that respondents valued their shares at a minimum of $772 per share, "basing this figure on the *pro rata* value of Kirby's physical assets." *Id.,* at 853. Accepting this valuation for purposes of the motion to dismiss, the District Court further noted that, as revealed by the complaint, the

---

4   On August 21, 1974, respondents petitioned for an appraisal of their Kirby stock, but they withdrew that petition on September 9 and the next day commenced this lawsuit.

5   The figure of $772 per share was calculated as follows:

"The difference of $311,000,000 ($622 per share) between the fair market value of Kirby's land and timber, alone, as per the defendants' own appraisal thereof at $320,000,000 and the $9,000,000 book value of said land and timber, added to the $150 per share, yields a pro rata share of the value of the physical assets of Kirby of at least $772 per share. The value of the stock was at least the pro rata value of the physical assets." App. 102a.

physical asset appraisal, along with other information relevant to Morgan Stanley's valuation of the shares, had been included with the information statement sent to respondents within the time required by state law. It thought that if "full and fair disclosure is made, transactions eliminating minority interests are beyond the purview of Rule 10b–5," and concluded that the "complaint fail[ed] to allege an omission, misstatement or fraudulent course of conduct that would have impeded a shareholder's judgment of the value of the offer." *Id.,* at 854. The complaint therefore failed to state a claim and was dismissed.

A divided Court of Appeals for the Second Circuit reversed. 533 F.2d 1283 (1976). . . . The court [held] that the complaint, taken as a whole, stated a cause of action under the Rule:

> "We hold that a complaint alleges a claim under Rule 10b–5 when it charges, in connection with a Delaware short-form merger, that the majority has committed a breach of its fiduciary duty to deal fairly with minority shareholders by effecting the merger without any justifiable business purpose. The minority shareholders are given no prior notice of the merger, thus having no opportunity to apply for injunctive relief, and the proposed price to be paid is substantially lower than the appraised value reflected in the Information Statement." *Id.,* at 1291. . . .

We granted the petition for certiorari challenging this holding because of the importance of the issue involved to the administration of the federal securities laws. 429 U.S. 814 (1976). We reverse.

II

Section 10(b) of the 1934 Act makes it "unlawful for any person . . . to use or employ . . . any manipulative or deceptive device or contrivance in contravention of [Securities and Exchange Commission rules]"; Rule 10b–5, promulgated by the SEC under § 10(b), prohibits, in addition to nondisclosure and misrepresentation, any "artifice to defraud" or any act "which operates or would operate as a fraud or deceit." . . . The Court of Appeals' approach to the interpretation of Rule 10b–5 is inconsistent with that taken by the Court last Term in Ernst & Ernst v. Hochfelder, 425 U.S. 185 . . . (1976). . . .

The language of § 10(b) gives no indication that Congress meant to prohibit any conduct not involving manipulation or deception. Nor have we been cited to any evidence in the legislative history that would support a departure from the language of the statute. "When a statute speaks so specifically in terms of manipulation and deception, . . . and when its history reflects no more expansive intent, we are quite unwilling to extend the scope of the statute. . . . " *Id.,* at 214. Thus the claim of fraud and fiduciary breach in this complaint states a cause of action under any part of Rule 10b–5 only if the conduct alleged can be fairly viewed as "manipulative or deceptive" within the meaning of the statute.

III

It is our judgment that the transaction, if carried out as alleged in the complaint, was neither deceptive nor manipulative and therefore did not violate either § 10(b) of the Act or Rule 10b–5.

As we have indicated, the case comes to us on the premise that the complaint failed to allege a material misrepresentation or material failure to disclose. The finding of the District Court, undisturbed by the Court of Appeals, was that there was no "omission" or "misstatement" in the information statement accompanying the notice of merger. On the basis of the information provided, minority shareholders could either accept the price offered or reject it and seek an appraisal in the Delaware Court of Chancery. Their choice was fairly presented, and they were furnished with all relevant information on which to base their decision.

We therefore find inapposite the cases relied upon by respondents and the court below, in which the breaches of fiduciary duty held violative of Rule 10b–5 included some element of deception. Those cases forcefully reflect the principle that "[§]10(b) must be read flexibly, not technically and restrictively" and that the statute provides a cause of action for any plaintiff who "suffer[s] an injury as a result of deceptive practices touching its sale [or purchase] of securities. . . ." *Superintendent of Insurance v. Bankers Life & Cas. Co.,* 404 U.S. 6, 12–13 . . . (1971). But the cases do not support the proposition, adopted by the Court of Appeals below and urged by respondents here, that a breach of fiduciary duty by majority stockholders, without any deception, misrepresentation, or nondisclosure, violates the statute and the Rule.

It is also readily apparent that the conduct alleged in the complaint was not "manipulative" within the meaning of the statute. "Manipulation" is "virtually a term of art when used in connection with securities markets." *Ernst & Ernst,* 425 U.S., at 199. The term refers generally to practices, such as wash sales, matched orders, or rigged prices, that are intended to mislead investors by artificially affecting market activity. . . . Section 10(b)'s general prohibition of practices deemed by the SEC to be "manipulative"—in this technical sense of artificially affecting market activity in order to mislead investors—is fully consistent with the fundamental purpose of the 1934 Act " 'to substitute a philosophy of full disclosure for the philosophy of *caveat emptor.* . . .' " *Affiliated Ute Citizens v. United States,* 406 U.S. 128 . . . (1972), quoting *SEC v. Capital Gains Research Bureau,* 375 U.S. 180 . . . (1963). Indeed, nondisclosure is usually essential to the success of a manipulative scheme. 3 Loss, *supra,* at 1565. No doubt Congress meant to prohibit the full range of ingenious devices that might be used to manipulate securities prices. But we do not think it would have chosen this "term of art" if it had meant to bring within the scope of § 10(b) instances of corporate mismanagement such as this, in which the essence of the complaint is that shareholders were treated unfairly by a fiduciary.

IV

The language of the statute is, we think, "sufficiently clear in its context" to be dispositive here, *Ernst & Ernst, supra,* at 201; but even if it were not, there are additional considerations that weigh heavily against permitting a cause of action under Rule 10b–5 for the breach of corporate fiduciary duty alleged in this complaint. Congress did not expressly provide a private cause of action for violations of § 10(b). Although we have recognized an implied cause of action under that section in some circumstances, *Superintendent of Insurance v. Bankers Life & Cas. Co., supra,* at 13 n. 9, we have also recognized that a private cause of action under the antifraud provisions of the Securities Exchange Act should not be implied where it is "unnecessary to ensure the fulfillment of Congress' purposes" in adopting the Act. *Piper v. Chris-Craft Industries, ante,* at 41. Cf. *J.I. Case Co. v. Borak,* 377 U.S. 426, 431–433 . . . (1964). As we noted earlier, . . . the Court repeatedly has described the "fundamental purpose" of the Act as implementing a "philosophy of full disclosure"; once full and fair disclosure has occurred, the fairness of the terms of the transaction is at most a tangential concern of the statute. . . . As in *Cort v. Ash,* 422 U.S. 66, 80 . . . (1975), we are reluctant to recognize a cause of action here to serve what is "at best a subsidiary purpose" of the federal legislation.

A second factor in determining whether Congress intended to create a federal cause of action in these circumstances is "whether 'the cause of action [is] one traditionally relegated to state law. . . .' " *Piper v. Chris-Craft Industries, Inc., ante,* at 40, quoting *Cort v. Ash, supra,* at 78. The Delaware Legislature has supplied minority shareholders with a cause of action in the Delaware Court of Chancery to recover the fair value of shares allegedly undervalued in a short-form merger. . . . Of course, the existence of a particular state-law remedy is not dispositive of the question whether Congress meant to provide a similar federal remedy, but as in *Cort* and *Piper,* we conclude that "it is entirely appropriate in this instance to relegate respondent and others in his situation to whatever remedy is created by state law." 422 U.S., at 84; *ante,* at 41.

The reasoning behind a holding that the complaint in this case alleged fraud under Rule 10b–5 could not be easily contained. It is difficult to imagine how a court could distinguish, for purposes of Rule 10b–5 fraud, between a majority stockholder's use of a short-form merger to eliminate the minority at an unfair price and the use of some other device, such as a long-form merger, tender offer, or liquidation, to achieve the same result; or indeed how a court could distinguish the alleged abuses in these going private transactions from other types of fiduciary self-dealing involving transactions in securities. The result would be to bring within the Rule a wide variety of corporate conduct traditionally left to state regulation. In addition to posing a "danger of vexatious litigation which could result from a widely expanded class of plaintiffs under Rule 10b–5," *Blue Chip Stamps v. Manor Drug Stores,* 421 U.S., at

740, this extension of the federal securities laws would overlap and quite possibly interfere with state corporate law. Federal courts applying a "federal fiduciary principle" under Rule 10b–5 could be expected to depart from state fiduciary standards at least to the extent necessary to ensure uniformity within the federal system.[16] Absent a clear indication of congressional intent, we are reluctant to federalize the substantial portion of the law of corporations that deals with transactions in securities, particularly where established state policies of corporate regulation would be overridden. As the Court stated in *Cort v. Ash, supra:* "Corporations are creatures of state law, and investors commit their funds to corporate directors on the understanding that, except where federal law *expressly* requires certain responsibilities of directors with respect to stockholders, state law will govern the internal affairs of the corporation." 422 U.S., at 84 (emphasis added).

We thus adhere to the position that "Congress by § 10(b) did not seek to regulate transactions which constitute no more than internal corporate mismanagement." *Superintendent of Insurance v. Bankers Life & Cas. Co.,* 404 U.S., at 12. There may well be a need for uniform federal fiduciary standards to govern mergers such as that challenged in this complaint. But those standards should not be supplied by judicial extension of § 10(b) and Rule 10b–5 to "cover the corporate universe."

The judgment of the Court of Appeals is reversed, and the case is remanded for further proceedings consistent with this opinion.

So ordered.

[The dissenting opinion of Justice Brennan is omitted.]

■ MR. JUSTICE BLACKMUN, concurring in part.

Like MR. JUSTICE STEVENS, I refrain from joining Part IV of the Court's opinion. I, too, regard that part as unnecessary for the decision in the instant case. . . . I, however, join the remainder of the Court's opinion and its judgment.

■ MR. JUSTICE STEVENS, concurring in part.

. . . [T]he entire discussion in Part IV is unnecessary to the decision of this case. Accordingly, I join only Parts I, II, and III of the Court's opinion. I would also add further emphasis to the fact that the controlling stockholders in this case did not breach any duty owed to the minority shareholders because (a) there was complete disclosure of the relevant

---

16   For example, some States apparently require a "valid corporate purpose" for the elimination of the minority interest through a short-form merger, whereas other States do not. Compare *Bryan v. Brock & Blevins Co.,* 490 F.2d 563 (CA5), cert. denied, 419 U.S. 844, 95 S.Ct. 77, 42 L.Ed.2d 72 (1974) (merger arranged by controlling stockholder for no business purpose except to eliminate 15% minority stockholder violated Georgia short-form merger statute) with *Stauffer v. Standard Brands, Inc.,* 41 Del.Ch. 7, 187 A.2d 78 (1962) (Delaware short-form merger statute allows majority stockholder to eliminate the minority interest without any corporate purpose and subject only to an appraisal remedy). Thus to the extent that Rule 10b–5 is interpreted to require a valid corporate purpose for elimination of minority shareholders as well as a fair price for their shares, it would impose a stricter standard of fiduciary duty than that required by the law of some States.

facts, and (b) the minority are entitled to receive the fair value of their shares.[2] The facts alleged in the complaint do not constitute "fraud" within the meaning of Rule 10b–5.

————

Would the plaintiff prevail in *Santa Fe* if there had been no disclosure of Kirby Lumber's book value? *See* Virginia Bankshares, Inc. v. Sandberg, 501 U.S. 1083, 111 S.Ct. 2749, 115 L.Ed.2d 929 (1991). Should the answer to this question depend on whether the applicable state corporate law provides minority holders an appraisal remedy, discuss in Chapter 14 section 1, whereby, instead of receiving what is offered in the merger, a shareholder can elect to have her shares independently appraised and receive cash equal to the resulting fair value of the appraised shares? *See* Wilson v. Great American Industries, Inc., 979 F.2d 924 (2d Cir. 1992); Howing Co. v. Nationwide Corp., 972 F.2d 700 (6th Cir. 1992), *cert. denied*, 507 U.S. 1004, 113 S.Ct. 1645, 123 L.Ed.2d 266 (1993).

————

---

[2]   The motivation for the merger is a matter of indifference to the minority stockholders because they retain no interest in the corporation after the merger is consummated.

CHAPTER 12

INSIDER TRADING

1. THE COMMON LAW BACKGROUND

NOTES ON THE DUTIES OF DIRECTORS AND OFFICERS UNDER THE COMMON LAW WHEN TRADING IN THEIR CORPORATION'S STOCK

1. *Majority Rule.* At common law, the majority rule was that a director or officer of a corporation could trade in its stock without disclosing material nonpublic information concerning the corporation that he had acquired through his position—a type of information now referred to as *inside information.* A leading case was *Goodwin v. Agassiz,* 283 Mass. 358, 186 N.E. 659 (1933).

2. *"Special Facts."* Perhaps the most important exception to the majority rule was the "special facts" exception, adopted in *Strong v. Repide,* 213 U.S. 419, 29 S.Ct. 521, 53 L.Ed. 853 (1909) and later in many other cases. Repide was a director, the administrator general, and owner of nearly three-fourths of the shares, of Philippine Sugar. Strong, who owned shares in Philippine Sugar, had given Jones a power of attorney to sell her shares. Philippine Sugar owned certain lands in the Philippines that the United States government wished to buy. The corporation was without funds, and the value of its shares was wholly dependent on making an advantageous sale of its properties to the government. Repide was in charge of the negotiations with the government, which dragged on for months, primarily because Repide was holding out for a higher price. While negotiations with the government were pending, Repide, knowing that a sale to the government was probable, used an intermediary to employ a broker to purchase Strong's shares from Jones. Jones was given no information as to the state of the negotiations with the government, and neither Strong nor Jones knew that Repide was the purchaser. The price paid to Strong was about one-tenth what the shares became worth less than three months later, when the sale of the corporation's property to the government was consummated.

The Supreme Court affirmed an award of damages to Strong, on the ground that even if a director has no general duty to disclose facts known to him before he purchases shares, "there are cases where, by reason of the special facts, such duty exists." Id. at 431, 29 S.Ct. at 525.

Since there was no meaningful way to differentiate those cases that involved "special facts" from those that didn't, the special-facts exception either ate up the majority rule or made the rule impossible to administer in a consistent fashion. At bottom, the exception was inconsistent with the majority rule, and was employed by the courts as a mechanism to escape from that rule while purporting to follow it.

3.   Atrophy. The common law rule concerning disclosure in the sale of securities atrophied after the 1940's, due to the development of Rule 10b–5 under the Securities Exchange Act, which came to occupy most of the field.

---

2.   THE FEDERAL DISCLOSE OR ABSTAIN REQUIREMENT

In the Matter of Cady, Roberts & Co.

40 S.E.C. 907, 911–12 (1961)

In an SEC disciplinary proceeding against a broker who sold publicly traded shares on behalf of his clients after tipping them of his confidential knowledge that the company would soon reduce its dividend, SEC Chairman Cary offered the following regarding the antifraud provision's proscription of insider trading and tipping: "[Rule 10b–5 applies] to securities transactions by 'any person.' Misrepresentations will lie within [its] ambit, no matter who the speaker may be. An affirmative duty to disclose material information has been traditionally imposed on corporate 'insiders,' particularly officers, directors, or controlling stockholders. We, and the courts have consistently held that insiders must disclose material facts which are known to them by virtue of their position but which are not known to persons with whom they deal and which, if known, would affect their investment judgment. Failure to make disclosure in these circumstances constitutes a violation of the anti-fraud provisions. If, on the other hand, disclosure prior to effecting a purchase or sale would be improper or unrealistic under the circumstances, we believe the alternative is to forego the transaction. . . .

"We have already noted that the anti-fraud provisions are phrased in terms of 'any person' and that a special obligation has been traditionally required of corporate insiders, e.g., officers, directors and controlling stockholders. These three groups, however, do not exhaust the classes of persons upon whom there is such an obligation. Analytically, the obligation rests on two principal elements; first, the existence of a relationship giving access, directly or indirectly, to information intended to be available only for a corporate purpose and not for the personal benefit of anyone, and second, the inherent unfairness involved where a party takes advantage of such information knowing it is unavailable to those with whom he is dealing. In considering these elements under the broad language of the anti-fraud provisions we are not to be circumscribed by fine distinctions and rigid classifications. Thus our task here is to identify those persons who are in a special relationship with a company and privy to its internal affairs, and thereby suffer correlative duties in trading in its securities. Intimacy demands restraint lest the uninformed be exploited."

Securities and Exchange Commission v.
Texas Gulf Sulphur Co.

United States Court of Appeals, Second Circuit, 1968.
401 F.2d 833 (in banc), cert. denied 394 U.S. 976, 89 S.Ct. 1454, 22 L.Ed.2d 756 (1969).

■ WATERMAN, CIRCUIT JUDGE:

[This was an action brought by the S.E.C. against Texas Gulf Sulphur (TGS) based on the issuance of a misleading press release, and against certain officers and employees of TGS based on their trading and tipping. The case grew out of an important mineral discovery by TGS. Four of the individual defendants were members of the geological exploration group that made the discovery: Mollison, a vice-president and mining engineer who headed the exploration group; Holyk, TGS' chief geologist; Clayton, an electrical engineer and geophysicist, and Darke, a geologist. The other individual defendants included Stephens, who was TGS's President; Fogarty, its Executive Vice-President; Kline, its Vice-President and General Counsel; and Coates, a director.

[Those portions of the opinion dealing with the liability of TGS for the misleading press release and the liability of individual defendants for tipping have been omitted, because the discussion of those issues has been largely superseded by later Supreme Court cases, examined later in this Chapter.]

This action derives from the exploratory activities of TGS begun in 1957 on the Canadian Shield in eastern Canada. In March of 1959, aerial geophysical surveys were conducted over more than 15,000 square miles of this area by a group led by defendant Mollison, a mining engineer and a Vice President of TGS. The group included defendant Holyk, TGS's chief geologist, defendant Clayton, an electrical engineer and geophysicist, and defendant Darke, a geologist. These operations resulted in the detection of numerous anomalies, i.e., extraordinary variations in the conductivity of rocks, one of which was on the Kidd 55 segment of land located near Timmins, Ontario.

On October 29 and 30, 1963, Clayton conducted a ground geophysical survey on the northeast portion of the Kidd 55 segment which confirmed the presence of an anomaly and indicated the necessity of diamond core drilling for further evaluation. Drilling of the initial hole, K–55–1, at the strongest part of the anomaly was commenced on November 8 and terminated on November 12 at a depth of 655 feet. Visual estimates by Holyk of the core of K–55–1 indicated an average copper content of 1.15% and an average zinc content of 8.64% over a length of 599 feet. This visual estimate convinced TGS that it was desirable to acquire the remainder of the Kidd 55 segment, and in order to facilitate this acquisition TGS President Stephens instructed the exploration group to keep the results of K–55–1 confidential and undisclosed even as to other officers, directors, and employees of TGS. The hole was concealed and a barren core was intentionally drilled off the anomaly. Meanwhile, the core of K–

55–1 had been shipped to Utah for chemical assay which, when received in early December, revealed an average mineral content of 1.18% copper, 8.26% zinc, and 3.94% ounces of silver per ton over a length of 602 feet. These results were so remarkable that neither Clayton, an experienced geophysicist, nor four other TGS expert witnesses, had ever seen or heard of a comparable initial exploratory drill hole in a base metal deposit. So, the trial court concluded, "There is no doubt that the drill core of K–55–1 was unusually good and that it excited the interest and speculation of those who knew about it." Id. at 282. By March 27, 1964, TGS decided that the land acquisition program had advanced to such a point that the company might well resume drilling, and drilling was resumed on March 31.

During this period, from November 12, 1963 when K–55–1 was completed, to March 31, 1964 when drilling was resumed certain of the individual defendants . . . and persons . . . said to have received "tips" from them, purchased TGS stock or calls thereon. Prior to these transactions these persons had owned 1135 shares of TGS stock and possessed no calls; thereafter they owned a total of 8235 shares and possessed 12,300 calls.

On February 20, 1964, also during this period, TGS issued stock options to 26 of its officers and employees whose salaries exceeded a specified amount, five of whom were the individual defendants Stephens, Fogarty, Mollison, Holyk, and Kline. Of these, only Kline was unaware of the detailed results of K–55–1, but he, too, knew that a hole containing favorable bodies of copper and zinc ore had been drilled in Timmins. At this time, neither the TGS Stock Option Committee nor its Board of Directors had been informed of the results of K–55–1, presumably because of the pending land acquisition program which required confidentiality. All of the foregoing defendants accepted the options granted them.

When drilling was resumed on March 31, hole K–55–3 was commenced 510 feet west of K–55–1 and was drilled easterly at a 45 degrees angle so as to cross K–55–1 in a vertical plane. Daily progress reports of the drilling of this hole K–55–3 and of all subsequently drilled holes were sent to defendants Stephens and Fogarty (President and Executive Vice President of TGS) by Holyk and Mollison. Visual estimates of K–55–3 revealed an average mineral content of 1.12% copper and 7.93% zinc over 641 of the hole's 876-foot length. On April 7, drilling of a third hole, K–55–4, 200 feet south of and parallel to K–55–1 and westerly at a 45 degrees angle, was commenced and mineralization was encountered over 366 of its 579-foot length. Visual estimates indicated an average content of 1.14% copper and 8.24% zinc. Like K–55–1, both K–55–3 and K–55–4 established substantial copper mineralization on the eastern edge of the anomaly. On the basis of these findings relative to the foregoing drilling results, the trial court concluded that the vertical plane created by the intersection of K–55–1 and K–55–3, which measured at least 350 feet wide by 500 feet deep extended southward 200 feet to its intersection with K–55–4, and that "There was real evidence that a body of commercially mineable ore might exist." Id. at 281–82.

On April 8 TGS began with a second drill rig to drill another hole, K–55–6, 300 feet easterly of K–55–1. This hole was drilled westerly at an angle of 60—and was intended to explore mineralization beneath K–55–1. While no visual estimates of its core were immediately available, it was readily apparent by the evening of April 10 that substantial copper mineralization had been encountered over the last 127 feet of the hole's 569-foot length. On April 10, a third drill rig commenced drilling yet another hole, K–55–5, 200 feet north of K–55–1, parallel to the prior holes, and slanted westerly at a 45 degrees angle. By the evening of April 10 in this hole, too, substantial copper mineralization had been encountered over the last 42 feet of its 97-foot length.

Meanwhile, rumors that a major ore strike was in the making had been circulating throughout Canada. On the morning of Saturday, April 11, Stephens at his home in Greenwich, Conn. read in the New York Herald Tribune and in the New York Times unauthorized reports of the TGS drilling which seemed to infer a rich strike from the fact that the drill cores had been flown to the United States for chemical assay. Stephens immediately contacted Fogarty at his home in Rye, N.Y., who in turn telephoned and later that day visited Mollison at Mollison's home in Greenwich to obtain a current report and evaluation of the drilling progress.[7] The following morning, Sunday, Fogarty again telephoned Mollison, inquiring whether Mollison had any further information and told him to return to Timmins with Holyk, the TGS Chief Geologist, as soon as possible "to move things along." With the aid of one Carroll, a public relations consultant, Fogarty drafted a press release designed to quell the rumors, which release, after having been channeled through Stephens and Huntington, a TGS attorney, was issued at 3:00 P.M. on Sunday, April 12, and which appeared in the morning newspapers of general circulation on Monday, April 13. It read in pertinent part as follows:

New York, April 12—The following statement was made today by Dr. Charles F. Fogarty, executive vice president of Texas Gulf Sulphur Company, in regard to the company's drilling operations near Timmins, Ontario, Canada. Dr. Fogarty said:

"During the past few days, the exploration activities of Texas Gulf Sulphur in the area of Timmins, Ontario, have been widely reported in the press, coupled with rumors of a substantial copper discovery there.

---

[7] Mollison had returned to the United States for the weekend. Friday morning April 10, he had been on the Kidd tract "and had been advised by defendant Holyk as to the drilling results to 7:00 p.m. on April 10. At that time drill holes K–55–1, K–55–3 and K–55–4 had been completed; drilling of K–55–5 had started on Section 2200 S and had been drilled to 97 feet, encountering mineralization on the last 42 feet; and drilling of K–55–6 had been started on Section 2400 S and had been drilled to 569 feet, encountering mineralization over the last 127 feet." Id. at 294.

These reports exaggerate the scale of operations, and mention plans and statistics of size and grade of ore that are without factual basis and have evidently originated by speculation of people not connected with TGS.

"The facts are as follows. TGS has been exploring in the Timmins area for six years as part of its overall search in Canada and elsewhere for various minerals—lead, copper, zinc, etc. During the course of this work, in Timmins as well as in Eastern Canada, TGS has conducted exploration entirely on its own, without the participation by others. Numerous prospects have been investigated by geophysical means and a large number of selected ones have been core-drilled. These cores are sent to the United States for assay and detailed examination as a matter of routine and on advice of expert Canadian legal counsel. No inferences as to grade can be drawn from this procedure.

"Most of the areas drilled in Eastern Canada have revealed either barren pyrite or graphite without value; a few have resulted in discoveries of small or marginal sulphide ore bodies.

"Recent drilling on one property near Timmins has led to preliminary indications that more drilling would be required for proper evaluation of this prospect. The drilling done to date has not been conclusive, but the statements made by many outside quarters are unreliable and include information and figures that are not available to TGS.

"The work done to date has not been sufficient to reach definite conclusions and any statement as to size and grade of ore would be premature and possibly misleading. When we have progressed to the point where reasonable and logical conclusions can be made, TGS will issue a definite statement to its stockholders and to the public in order to clarify the Timmins project."

* * *

The release purported to give the Timmins drilling results as of the release date, April 12. From Mollison Fogarty had been told of the developments through 7:00 P.M. on April 10, and of the remarkable discoveries made up to that time, detailed supra, which discoveries, according to the calculations of the experts who testified for the SEC at the hearing, demonstrated that TGS had already discovered 6.2 to 8.3 million tons of proven ore having gross assay values from $26 to $29 per ton. TGS experts, on the other hand, denied at the hearing that proven or probable ore could have been calculated on April 11 or 12 because there was then no assurance of continuity in the mineralized zone.

The evidence as to the effect of this release on the investing public was equivocal and less than abundant. On April 13 the New York Herald Tribune in an article head-noted "Copper Rumor Deflated" quoted from the TGS release of April 12 and backtracked from its original April 11 report of a major strike but nevertheless inferred from the TGS release that "recent mineral exploratory activity near Timmins, Ontario, has provided preliminary favorable results, sufficient at least to require a step-up in drilling operations." Some witnesses who testified at the hearing stated that they found the release encouraging. On the other hand, a Canadian mining security specialist, Roche, stated that "earlier in the week [before April 16] we had a Dow Jones saying that they [TGS] didn't have anything basically" and a TGS stock specialist for the Midwest Stock Exchange became concerned about his long position in the stock after reading the release. The trial court stated only that "While, in retrospect, the press release may appear gloomy or incomplete, this does not make it misleading or deceptive on the basis of the facts then known." Id. at 296.

Meanwhile, drilling operations continued. . . .

While drilling activity ensued to completion, TGS officials were taking steps toward ultimate disclosure of the discovery. On April 13, a previously-invited reporter for The Northern Miner, a Canadian mining industry journal, visited the drillsite, interviewed Mollison, Holyk and Darke, and prepared an article which confirmed a 10 million ton ore strike. This report, after having been submitted to Mollison and returned to the reporter unamended on April 15, was published in the April 16 issue. A statement relative to the extent of the discovery, in substantial part drafted by Mollison, was given to the Ontario Minister of Mines for release to the Canadian media. Mollison and Holyk expected it to be released over the airways at 11 P.M. on April 15th, but, for undisclosed reasons, it was not released until 9:40 A.M. on the 16th. An official detailed statement, announcing a strike of at least 25 million tons of ore, based on the drilling data set forth above, was read to representatives of American financial media from 10:00 A.M. to 10:10 or 10:15 A.M. on April 16, and appeared over Merrill Lynch's private wire at 10:29 A.M. and, somewhat later than expected, over the Dow Jones ticker tape at 10:54 A.M.

Between the time the first press release was issued on April 12 and the dissemination of the TGS official announcement on the morning of April 16, the only defendants before us on appeal who engaged in market activity were Clayton and Crawford and TGS director Coates. Clayton ordered 200 shares of TGS stock through his Canadian broker on April 15 and another 300 shares at 8:30 A.M. the next day, and these orders were executed over the Midwest Exchange in Chicago at its opening on April 16. Coates left the TGS press conference and called his broker son-in-law Haemisegger shortly before 10:20 A.M. on the 16th and ordered 2,000 shares of TGS for family trust accounts of which Coates was a trustee but not a beneficiary; Haemisegger executed this order over the New York and Midwest Exchanges, and he and his customers purchased 1500 additional shares.

During the period of drilling in Timmins, the market price of TGS stock fluctuated but steadily gained overall. On Friday, November 8, when the drilling began, the stock closed at 17³/₈; on Friday, November

15, after K–55–1 had been completed, it closed at 18. After a slight decline to 16³/₈ by Friday, November 22, the price rose to 20⁷/₈ by December 13, when the chemical assay results of K–55–1 were received, and closed at a high of 24¹/₈ on February 21, the day after the stock options had been issued. It had reached a price of 26 by March 31, after the land acquisition program had been completed and drilling had been resumed, and continued to ascend to 30¹/₈ by the close of trading on April 10, at which time the drilling progress up to then was evaluated for the April 12th press release. On April 13, the day on which the April 12 release was disseminated, TGS opened at 30¹/₈, rose immediately to a high of 32 and gradually tapered off to close at 30⁷/₈. It closed at 30¼ the next day, and at 29³/₈ on April 15. On April 16, the day of the official announcement of the Timmins discovery, the price climbed to a high of 37 and closed at 36³/₈. By May 15, TGS stock was selling at 58¼. . . .*

---

* [Footnote by the court; relocated by the editor.]

Purchase		Shares		Calls	
Date	Purchaser	Number	Price	Number	Price
Hole K–55–1 Completed November 12, 1963					
1963					
Nov. 12	Fogarty	300	17¾–18		
15	Clayton	200	17¾		
15	Fogarty	700	17⁵/₈–17⁷/₈		
15	Mollison	100	17⁷/₈		
19	Fogarty	500	18¹/₈		
26	Fogarty	200	17¾		
29	Holyk	50	18		
Chemical Assays of Drill Core of K–55–1 Received December 9–13, 1963					
Dec. 10	Holyk (Mrs.)	100	20³/₈		
12	Holyk (or wife)			200	21
13	Mollison	100	21¹/₈		
30	Fogarty	200	22		
31	Fogarty	100	23¼		
1964					
Jan. 6	Holyk (or wife)			100	23⁵/₈
8	Murray			400	23¼
24	Holyk (or wife)			200	22¼–22³/₈
Feb. 10	Fogarty	300	22¹/₈–22¼		
20	Darke	300	24¹/₈		
24	Clayton	400	23⁷/₈		
24	Holyk (or wife)			200	24¹/₈
26	Holyk (or wife)			200	23³/₈
26	Huntington	50	23¼		
27	Darke (Moran as nominee)			1000	22⁵/₈–22¾
Mar. 2	Holyk (Mrs.)	200	22³/₈		
3	Clayton	100	22¼		
16	Huntington			100	22³/₈
16	Holyk (or wife)			300	23¼
17	Holyk (Mrs.)	100	23⁷/₈		
23	Darke			1000	24¾
26	Clayton	200	25		

I.   The Individual Defendants

A. *Introductory*

... Whether predicated on traditional fiduciary concepts, see, e.g., Hotchkiss v. Fisher, 136 Kan. 530, 16 P.2d 531 (Kan.1932), or on the "special facts" doctrine, see, e.g., Strong v. Repide, 213 U.S. 419, 29 S.Ct. 521, 53 L.Ed. 853 (1909), ... Rule [10b–5] is based in policy on the justifiable expectation of the securities marketplace that all investors trading on impersonal exchanges have relatively equal access to material information, see Cary, Insider Trading in Stocks, 21 Bus.Law. 1009, 1010 (1966), Fleischer, Securities Trading and Corporation Information Practices: The Implications of the Texas Gulf Sulphur Proceeding, 51 Va.L.Rev. 1271, 1278–80 (1965). The essence of the Rule is that anyone who, trading for his own account in the securities of a corporation has "access, directly or indirectly, to information intended to be available only for a corporate purpose and not for the personal benefit of anyone" may not take "advantage of such information knowing it is unavailable to those with whom he is dealing," i.e., the investing public. Matter of Cady, Roberts & Co., 40 SEC 907, 912 (1961). Insiders, as directors or management officers are, of course, by this Rule, precluded from so unfairly dealing, but the Rule is also applicable to one possessing the information who may not be strictly termed an "insider" within the meaning of Sec. 16(b) of the Act. Cady, Roberts, supra. Thus, anyone in possession of material inside information must either disclose it to the investing public, or, if he is disabled from disclosing it in order to protect a corporate confidence, or he chooses not to do so, must abstain from trading in or recommending the securities concerned while such inside information remains undisclosed. So, it is here no justification for insider activity that disclosure was forbidden by the legitimate corporate objective of acquiring options to purchase the land surrounding the exploration site; if the information was, as the SEC contends, material,

---

Land Acquisition Completed March 27, 1964

Mar.	30	Darke			100	25½
	30	Holyk (Mrs.)	100	25⅞		

Core Drilling of Kidd Segment Resumed March 31, 1964

April	1	Clayton	60	26½
	1	Fogarty	400	26½
	2	Clayton	100	26⅞
	6	Fogarty	400	28⅛–28⅞
	8	Mollison (Mrs.)	100	28⅛

First Press Release Issued April 12, 1964

April	15	Clayton	200	29⅜
	16	Crawford (and wife)	600	30⅛–30¼

Second Press Release Issued 10:00–10:10 or 10:15 A.M., April 16, 1964 ...

1963
April	16	(app. 10:20 A.M.)		
		Coates (for family trusts)	2000	31–31⅝

its possessors should have kept out of the market until disclosure was accomplished. Cady, Roberts, supra at 911.

B. *Material Inside Information*

An insider is not, of course, always foreclosed from investing in his own company merely because he may be more familiar with company operations than are outside investors. An insider's duty to disclose information or his duty to abstain from dealing in his company's securities arises only in "those situations which are essentially extraordinary in nature and which are reasonably certain to have a substantial effect on the market price of the security if [the extraordinary situation is] disclosed." Fleischer, Securities Trading and Corporate Information Practices: The Implications of the Texas Gulf Sulphur Proceeding, 51 Va.L.Rev. 1271, 1289.

Nor is an insider obligated to confer upon outside investors the benefit of his superior financial or other expert analysis by disclosing his educated guesses or predictions. 3 Loss, op. cit. supra at 1463. The only regulatory objective is that access to material information be enjoyed equally, but this objective requires nothing more than the disclosure of basic facts so that outsiders may draw upon their own evaluative expertise in reaching their own investment decisions with knowledge equal to that of the insiders.

This is not to suggest, however, as did the trial court, that "the test of materiality must necessarily be a conservative one, particularly since many actions under Section 10(b) are brought on the basis of hindsight," 258 F.Supp. 262 at 280, in the sense that the materiality of facts is to be assessed solely by measuring the effect the knowledge of the facts would have upon prudent or conservative investors. As we stated in List v. Fashion Park, Inc., 340 F.2d 457, 462, "The basic test of materiality . . . is whether a *reasonable* man would attach importance . . . in determining his choice of action in the transaction in question. Restatement, Torts § 538(2)(a); accord Prosser, Torts 554–55; I Harper & James, Torts 565–66." (Emphasis supplied.) . . . [M]aterial facts include not only information disclosing the earnings and distributions of a company but also those facts which affect the probable future of the company and those which may affect the desire of investors to buy, sell, or hold the company's securities.

In each case, then, whether facts are material within Rule 10b–5 when the facts relate to a particular event and are undisclosed by those persons who are knowledgeable thereof will depend at any given time upon a balancing of both the indicated probability that the event will occur and the anticipated magnitude of the event in light of the totality of the company activity. Here, notwithstanding the trial court's conclusion that the results of the first drill core, K–55–1, were "too 'remote' . . . to have had any significant impact on the market, i.e., to be deemed material," 258 F.Supp. at 283, knowledge of the possibility, which surely was more than marginal, of the existence of a mine of the vast magnitude indicated by the remarkably rich drill core located rather close to the surface (suggesting mineability by the less expensive open pit method) within the confines of a large anomaly (suggesting an extensive region of mineralization) might well have affected the price of TGS stock and would certainly have been an important fact to a reasonable, if speculative, investor in deciding whether he should buy, sell, or hold. After all, this first drill core was "unusually good and . . . excited the interest and speculation of those who knew about it." 258 F.Supp. at 282.

. . . Our survey of the facts found below conclusively establishes that knowledge of the results of the discovery hole, K–55–1, would have been important to a reasonable investor and might have affected the price of the stock.[2] On April 16, The Northern Miner, a trade publication in wide circulation among mining stock specialists, called K–55–1, the discovery hole, "one of the most impressive drill holes completed in modern times." Roche, a Canadian broker whose firm specialized in mining securities, characterized the importance to investors of the results of K–55–1. He stated that the completion of "the first drill hole" with "a 600 foot drill core is very very significant . . . anything over 200 feet is considered very significant and 600 feet is just beyond your wildest imagination." He added, however, that it "is a natural thing to buy more stock once they give you the first drill hole." Additional testimony revealed that the prices of stocks of other companies, albeit less diversified, smaller firms, had increased substantially solely on the basis of the discovery of good anomalies or even because of the proximity of their lands to the situs of a potentially major strike.

Finally, a major factor in determining whether the K–55–1 discovery was a material fact is the importance attached to the drilling results by those who knew about it. In view of other unrelated recent developments favorably affecting TGS, participation by an informed person in a regular stock-purchase program, or even sporadic trading by an informed person, might lend only nominal support to the inference of the materiality of the K–55–1 discovery; nevertheless, the timing by those who knew of it of their stock purchases and their purchases of *short-term* calls—purchases in some cases by individuals who had never before purchased calls or even TGS stock—virtually compels the inference that the insiders were influenced by the drilling results. This insider trading activity, which surely constitutes highly pertinent evidence and the only truly objective evidence of the materiality of the K–55–1 discovery, was apparently disregarded by the court below in favor of the testimony of defendants'

---

[2]   We do not suggest that material facts must be disclosed immediately; the timing of disclosure is a matter for the business judgment of the corporate officers entrusted with the management of the corporation within the affirmative disclosure requirements promulgated by the exchanges and by the SEC. Here, a valuable corporate purpose was served by delaying the publication of the K–55–1 discovery. We do intend to convey, however, that where a corporate purpose is thus served by withholding the news of a material fact, those persons who are thus quite properly true to their corporate trust must not during the period of non-disclosure deal personally in the corporation's securities or give to outsiders confidential information not generally available to all the corporations' stockholders and to the public at large.

expert witnesses, all of whom "agreed that one drill core does not establish an ore body, much less a mine," 258 F.Supp. at 282–283. Significantly, however, the court below, while relying upon what these defense experts said the defendant insiders *ought* to have thought about the worth to TGS of the K–55–1 discovery, and finding that from November 12, 1963 to April 6, 1964 Fogarty, Murray, Holyk and Darke spent more than $100,000 in purchasing TGS stock and calls on that stock, made no finding that the insiders were motivated by any factor other than the extraordinary K–55–1 discovery when they bought their stock and their calls. No reason appears why outside investors, perhaps better acquainted with speculative modes of investment and with, in many cases, perhaps more capital at their disposal for intelligent speculation, would have been less influenced, and would not have been similarly motivated to invest if they had known what the insider investors knew about the K–55–1 discovery.

Our decision to expand the limited protection afforded outside investors by the trial court's narrow definition of materiality is not at all shaken by fears that the elimination of insider trading benefits will deplete the ranks of capable corporate managers by taking away an incentive to accept such employment. Such benefits, in essence, are forms of secret corporate compensation, see Cary, Corporate Standards and Legal Rules, 50 Calif.L.Rev. 408, 409–10 (1962), derived at the expense of the uninformed investing public and not at the expense of the corporation which receives the sole benefit from insider incentives. Moreover, adequate incentives for corporate officers may be provided by properly administered stock options and employee purchase plans of which there are many in existence. In any event, the normal motivation induced by stock ownership, i.e., the identification of an individual with corporate progress, is ill-promoted by condoning the sort of speculative insider activity which occurred here; for example, some of the corporation's stock was sold at market in order to purchase short-term calls upon that stock, calls which would never be exercised to increase a stockholder equity in TGS unless the market price of that stock rose sharply.

The core of Rule 10b–5 is the implementation of the Congressional purpose that all investors should have equal access to the rewards of participation in securities transactions. It was the intent of Congress that all members of the investing public should be subject to identical market risks,—which market risks include, of course the risk that one's evaluative capacity or one's capital available to put at risk may exceed another's capacity or capital. The insiders here were not trading on an equal footing with the outside investors. They alone were in a position to evaluate the probability and magnitude of what seemed from the outset to be a major ore strike; they alone could invest safely, secure in the expectation that the price of TGS stock would rise substantially in the event such a major strike should materialize, but would decline little, if at all, in the event of failure, for the public, ignorant at the outset of the favorable probabilities would likewise be unaware of the unproductive exploration, and the additional exploration costs would not significantly affect TGS market prices. Such inequities based upon unequal access to knowledge should not be shrugged off as inevitable in our way of life, or, in view of the congressional concern in the area, remain uncorrected.

We hold, therefore, that all transactions in TGS stock or calls by individuals apprised of the drilling results[14] of K–55–1 were made in violation of Rule 10b–5.[15] Inasmuch as the visual evaluation of that drill core (a generally reliable estimate though less accurate than a chemical assay) constituted material information, those advised of the results of the visual evaluation as well as those informed of the chemical assay traded in violation of law. The geologist Darke possessed undisclosed material information and traded in TGS securities. Therefore we reverse the dismissal of the action as to him and his personal transactions. . . .

With reference to Huntington, the trial court found that he "had no detailed knowledge as to the work" on the Kidd–55 segment, 258 F.Supp. 281. Nevertheless, the evidence shows that he knew about and participated in TGS's land acquisition program which followed the receipt of the K–55–1 drilling results, and that on February 26, 1964 he purchased 50 shares of TGS stock. Later, on March 16, he helped prepare a letter for Dr. Holyk's signature in which TGS made a substantial offer for lands near K–55–1, and on the same day he, who had never before purchased calls on any stock, purchased a call on 100 shares of TGS stock. We are satisfied that these purchases in February and March, coupled with his readily inferable and probably reliable, understanding of the highly favorable nature of preliminary operations on the Kidd segment, demonstrate that Huntington possessed material inside information such as to make his purchase violative of the Rule and the Act.

C. *When May Insiders Act?*

Appellant Crawford, who ordered[17] the purchase of TGS stock shortly before the TGS April 16 official announcement, and defendant

---

[14] The trial court found that defendant Murray "had no detailed knowledge as to the work" on the Kidd–55 segment. There is no evidence in the record suggesting that Murray purchased his stock on January 8, 1964, on the basis of material undisclosed information, and the disposition below is undisturbed as to him.

[15] Even if insiders were in fact ignorant of the broad scope of the Rule and acted pursuant to a mistaken belief as to the applicable law such an ignorance does not insulate them from the consequences of their acts. Tager v. SEC, 344 F.2d 5, 8 (2 Cir.1965).

[17] The effective protection of the public from insider exploitation of advance notice of material information requires that the time that an insider places an order, rather than the time of its ultimate execution, be determinative for Rule 10b–5 purposes. Otherwise, insiders would be able to "beat the news," cf. Fleischer, supra, 51 Va.L.Rev. at 1291, by requesting in advance that their orders be executed immediately after the dissemination of a major news release but before outsiders could act on the release. Thus it is immaterial whether Crawford's orders were executed before or after the announcement was made in Canada (9:40 A.M., April 16) or in the United States (10:00 A.M.) or whether Coates's order was executed before or after the news appeared over the Merrill Lynch (10:29 A.M.) or Dow Jones (10:54 A.M.) wires.

Coates, who placed orders with and communicated the news to his broker immediately after the official announcement was read at the TGS-called press conference, concede that they were in possession of material information. They contend, however, that their purchases were not proscribed purchases for the news had already been effectively disclosed. We disagree.

Crawford telephoned his orders to his Chicago broker about midnight on April 15 and again at 8:30 in the morning of the 16th, with instructions to buy at the opening of the Midwest Stock Exchange that morning. The trial court's finding that "he sought to, and did, 'beat the news,'" 258 F.Supp. at 287, is well documented by the record. The rumors of a major ore strike which had been circulated in Canada and, to a lesser extent, in New York, had been disclaimed by the TGS press release of April 12, which significantly promised the public an official detailed announcement when possibilities had ripened into actualities. The abbreviated announcement to the Canadian press at 9:40 A.M. on the 16th by the Ontario Minister of Mines and the report carried by The Northern Miner, parts of which had sporadically reached New York on the morning of the 16th through reports from Canadian affiliates to a few New York investment firms, are assuredly not the equivalent of the official 10–15 minute announcement which was not released to the American financial press until after 10:00 A.M. Crawford's orders had been placed before that. Before insiders may act upon material information, such information must have been effectively disclosed in a manner sufficient to insure its availability to the investing public. Particularly here, where a formal announcement to the entire financial news media had been promised in a prior official release known to the media, all insider activity must await dissemination of the promised official announcement.

Coates was absolved by the court below because his telephone order was placed shortly before 10:20 A.M. on April 16, which was after the announcement had been made even though the news could not be considered already a matter of public information. 258 F.Supp. at 288. This result seems to have been predicated upon a misinterpretation of dicta in *Cady, Roberts,* where the SEC instructed insiders to "keep out of the market until the established procedures for public release of the information are *carried out* instead of hastening to execute transactions in advance of, and in frustration of, the objectives of the release," 40 SEC at 915 (emphasis supplied). The reading of a news release, which prompted Coates into action, is merely the first step in the process of dissemination required for compliance with the regulatory objective of providing all investors with an equal opportunity to make informed investment judgments. Assuming that the contents of the official release could instantaneously be acted upon,[18] at the minimum Coates should

---

[18]   Although the only insider who acted after the news appeared over the Dow Jones broad tape is not an appellant and therefore we need not discuss the necessity of considering the

have waited until the news could reasonably have been expected to appear over the media of widest circulation, the Dow Jones broad tape, rather than hastening to insure an advantage to himself and his broker son-in-law.[19] . . .

E. May Insiders Accept Stock Options Without Disclosing Material Information to the Issuer?

On February 20, 1964, defendants Stephens, Fogarty, Mollison, Holyk and Kline accepted stock options issued to them and a number of other top officers of TGS, although not one of them had informed the Stock Option Committee of the Board of Directors or the Board of the results of K–55–1, which information we have held was then material. The SEC sought rescission of these options. The trial court, in addition to finding the knowledge of the results of the K–55 discovery to be immaterial, held that Kline had no detailed knowledge of the drilling progress and that Holyk and Mollison could reasonably assume that their superiors, Stephens and Fogarty, who were directors of the corporation, would report the results if that was advisable; indeed all employees had been instructed not to divulge this information pending completion of the land acquisition program, 258 F.Supp. at 291. Therefore, the court below concluded that only directors Stephens and Fogarty, of the top management, would have violated the Rule by accepting stock options without disclosure, but it also found that they had not acted improperly as the information in their possession was not material. 258 F.Supp. at 292. In view of our conclusion as to materiality we hold that Stephens and Fogarty violated the Rule by accepting them. However, as they have surrendered the options and the corporation has canceled them, supra at 292, n. 17, we find it unnecessary to order that the injunctions prayed for be actually issued. We point out, nevertheless, that the surrender of these options after the SEC commenced the case is not a satisfaction of the SEC claim, and a determination as to whether the issuance of injunctions against Stephens and Fogarty is advisable in order to prevent or deter future violations of regulatory provisions is remanded for the exercise of discretion by the trial court.

Contrary to the belief of the trial court that Kline had no duty to disclose his knowledge of the Kidd project before accepting the stock

---

advisability of a "reasonable waiting period" during which outsiders may absorb and evaluate disclosures, we note in passing that, where the news is of a sort which is not readily translatable into investment action, insiders may not take advantage of their advance opportunity to evaluate the information by acting immediately upon dissemination. In any event, the permissible timing of insider transactions after disclosures of various sorts is one of the many areas of expertise for appropriate exercise of the SEC's rule-making power, which we hope will be utilized in the future to provide some predictability of certainty for the business community.

[19]   The record reveals that news usually appears on the Dow Jones broad tape 2–3 minutes after the reporter completes dictation. Here, assuming that the Dow Jones reporter left the press conference as early as possible, 10:10 A.M., the 10–15 minute release (which took at least that long to dictate) could not have appeared on the wire before 10:22, and for other reasons unknown to us did not appear until 10:54. Indeed, even the abbreviated version of the release reported by Merrill Lynch over its private wire did not appear until 10:29. Coates, however, placed his call no later than 10:20.

option offered him, we believe that he, a vice president, who had become the general counsel of TGS in January 1964, but who had been secretary of the corporation since January 1961, and was present in that capacity when the options were granted, and who was in charge of the mechanics of issuance and acceptance of the options, was a member of top management and under a duty before accepting his option to disclose any material information he may have possessed, and, as he did not disclose such information to the Option Committee we direct rescission of the option he received.[24] As to Holyk and Mollison, the SEC has not appealed the holding below that they, not being then members of top management (although Mollison was a vice president) had no duty to disclose their knowledge of the drilling before accepting their options. Therefore, the issue of whether, by accepting, they violated the Act, is not before us, and the holding below is undisturbed. . . .

■ FRIENDLY, CIRCUIT JUDGE (concurring):

Agreeing with the result reached by the majority and with most of Judge Waterman's searching opinion, I take a rather different approach to two facets of the case.

I.

The first is a situation that will not often arise, involving as it does the acceptance of stock options during a period when inside information likely to produce a rapid and substantial increase in the price of the stock was known to some of the grantees but unknown to those in charge of the granting. I suppose it would be clear, under Ruckle v. Roto American Corp., 339 F.2d 24 (2 Cir.1964), that if a corporate officer having such knowledge persuaded an unknowing board of directors to grant him an option at a price approximating the current market, the option would be rescindable in an action under Rule 10b–5. It would seem, by the same token, that if, to make the pill easier to swallow, he urged the directors to include others lacking the knowledge he possessed, he would be liable for all the resulting damage. The novel problem in the instant case is to

---

[24] The options granted on February 20, 1964 to Mollison, Holyk, and Kline were ratified by the Texas Gulf directors on July 15, 1965 after there had been, of course, a full disclosure and after this action had been commenced. However, the ratification is irrelevant here, for we would hold with the district court that a member of top management, as was Kline, is required, before accepting a stock option, to disclose material inside information which, if disclosed, might affect the price of the stock during the period when the accepted option could be exercised. Kline had known since November 1962 that K–55–1 had been drilled, that the drilling had intersected a sulphide body containing copper and zinc, and that TGS desired to acquire adjacent property.

Of course, if any of the five knowledgeable defendants had rejected his option there might well have been speculation as to the reason for the rejection. Therefore, in a case where disclosure to the grantors of an option would seriously jeopardize corporate security, it could well be desirable, in order to protect a corporation from selling securities to insiders who are in a position to appreciate their true worth at a price which may not accurately reflect the true value of the securities and at the same time to preserve when necessary the secrecy of corporate activity, not to require that an insider possessed of undisclosed material information reject the offer of a stock option, but only to require that he abstain from exercising it until such time as there shall have been a full disclosure and, after the full disclosure, a ratification such as was voted here. However, as this suggestion was not presented to us, we do not consider it or make any determination with reference to it.

define the responsibility of officers when a directors' committee administering a stock option plan proposes of its own initiative to make options available to them and others at a time when they know that the option price, geared to the market value of the stock, did not reflect a substantial increment likely to be realized in short order and was therefore unfair to the corporation.

A rule requiring a minor officer to reject an option so tendered would not comport with the realities either of human nature or of corporate life. If the SEC had appealed the ruling dismissing this portion of the complaint as to Holyk and Mollison, I would have upheld the dismissal quite apart from the special circumstance that a refusal on their part could well have broken the wall of secrecy it was important for TGS to preserve. Whatever they knew or didn't know about Timmins, they were entitled to believe their superiors had reported the facts to the Option Committee unless they had information to the contrary. Stephens, Fogarty and Kline stand on an altogether different basis; as senior officers they had an obligation to inform the Committee that this was not the right time to grant options at 95% of the current price. Silence, when there is a duty to speak, can itself be a fraud. I am unimpressed with the argument that Stephens, Fogarty and Kline could not perform this duty on the peculiar facts of this case, because of the corporate need for secrecy during the land acquisition program. Non-management directors would not normally challenge a recommendation for postponement of an option plan from the President, the Executive Vice President, and the Vice President and General Counsel. Moreover, it should be possible for officers to communicate with directors, of all people, without fearing a breach of confidence. Hence, as one of the foregoing hypotheticals suggests, I am not at all sure that a company in the position of TGS might not have a claim against top officers who breached their duty of disclosure for the entire damage suffered as a result of the untimely issuance of options, rather than merely one for rescission of the options issued to them.[2] Since that issue is not before us, I merely make the reservation of my position clear. . . .

[The opinions of Judges Kaufman and Anderson (concurring), Judge Hays (concurring in part and dissenting in part), and Judges Moore and Lumbard (dissenting) are omitted.]

----

[2]   Though the Board of Directors of TGS ratified the issuance of the options after the Timmins discovery had been fully publicized, it obviously was of the belief that Kline had committed no serious wrong in remaining silent. Throughout this litigation TGS has supported the legality of the actions of all the defendants—the company's counsel having represented, among others, Stephens, Fogarty and Kline. Consequently, I agree with the majority in giving the Board's action no weight here. If a fraud of this kind may ever be cured by ratification, compare Continental Securities Co. v. Belmont, 206 N.Y. 7, 99 N.E. 138, 51 L.R.A., N.S., 112 (1912), with Claman v. Robertson, 164 Ohio St. 61, 128 N.E.2d 429 (1955); cf. Wilko v. Swan, 346 U.S. 427, 74 S.Ct. 182, 98 L.Ed. 168 (1953), that cannot be done without an appreciation of the illegality of the conduct proposed to be excused, cf. United Hotels Co. v. Mealey, 147 F.2d 816, 819 (2 Cir.1945).

NOTE ON THE "USE" TEST UNDER RULE 10b–5

In 1998, the Ninth and Eleventh Circuits held that Rule 10b–5 is not violated unless the defendant not only *possessed* material inside information when she traded, but actually *used* the information in deciding to buy or sell. These decisions rested on the theory that having inside information in one's possession when trading does not wrongfully cause harm; only using such information wrongfully causes harm. SEC v. Adler, 137 F.3d 1325 (11th Cir.1998); United States v. Smith, 155 F.3d 1051 (9th Cir.1998).

This esoteric distinction between possession and use of inside information had earlier been rejected by the Second Circuit in 1993, in United States v. Teicher, 987 F.2d 112. There the court said:

> . . . [A] "knowing possession" standard has the attribute of simplicity. It recognizes that one who trades while knowingly possessing material inside information has an informational advantage over other traders. Because the advantage is in the form of information, it exists in the mind of the trader. Unlike a loaded weapon which may stand ready but unused, material information can not lay idle in the human brain. The individual with such information may decide to trade upon that information, to alter a previously decided-upon transaction, to continue with a previously planned transaction even though publicly available information would now suggest otherwise, or simply to do nothing. In our increasingly sophisticated securities markets, where subtle shifts in strategy can produce dramatic results, it would be a mistake to think of such decisions as merely binary choices—to buy or to sell.

In 2000, the SEC promulgated Rule 10b5–1, which addresses the issue of whether liability under Rule 10b–5 is based on trading while in the knowing possession of material nonpublic information, or on using such information to trade. Rule 10b5–1(b) defines a purchase or sale being "on the basis of" material nonpublic information "if the person making the purchase or sale was *aware* of material nonpublic information when the person made the purchase or sale." (emphasis added). However, the general rule is subject to an affirmative defense where the trade is made pursuant to a written contract instructing another to purchase or sell securities (either identifying a specific amount or setting forth an algorithm for determining such amount) for the instructing person's account, provided the contract is entered into before becoming aware of the information. Why would company officers wish to have a plan setting forth when company shares would be purchased or sold in the future? Rule 10b5–1 provides that disclosure of the existence of a Rule 10b5–1 plan is optional. Why might executives choose to voluntarily disclose the existence of their plan?

Can executives with Rule 10b5–1 plans game the provision's safe harbor to maximize their wealth on the basis of inside information? *See* Alan Horwich, The Origin, Application, Validity, and Potential Misuse of Rule 10b5–1, 62 Bus. Law. 913, 936–953 (2007). Several reports have raised questions whether insiders adopt Rule 10b5–1 plans when they are aware of non-public information and engage in other abuses. See *e.g.,* Susan Pulliam

& Rob Barry, *Executives' Good Luck in Trading Own Stock*, Wall. St. J., A-1 (Nov. 27, 2012). The articles report that insiders frequently cancel or amend plans, thus raising questions whether the plan was initially adopted in good faith. Executives sometimes have multiple Rule 10b5–1 plans. And, journalists report frequent instances where substantial trading occurred just days after a plan was adopted, thus raising questions whether the plan was adopted when the insider was in possession of material non-public information. Following such press stories, the SEC launched an inquiry whether corporate insiders have systematically abused Rule 10b5–1 plans to garner profits on the basis of their access to inside information.

————

Chiarella v. United States

United States Supreme Court, 1980.
445 U.S. 222, 100 S.Ct. 1108, 63 L.Ed.2d 348.

■ MR. JUSTICE POWELL, delivered the opinion of the Court.

The question in this case is whether a person who learns from the confidential documents of one corporation that it is planning an attempt to secure control of a second corporation violates § 10(b) of the Securities Exchange Act of 1934 if he fails to disclose the impending takeover before trading in the target company's securities.

I

Petitioner is a printer by trade. In 1975 and 1976, he worked as a "markup man" in the New York composing room of Pandick Press, a financial printer. Among documents that petitioner handled were five announcements of corporate takeover bids. When these documents were delivered to the printer, the identities of the acquiring and target corporations were concealed by blank spaces or false names. The true names were sent to the printer on the night of the final printing.

The petitioner, however, was able to deduce the names of the target companies before the final printing from other information contained in the documents. Without disclosing his knowledge, petitioner purchased stock in the target companies and sold the shares immediately after the takeover attempts were made public. By this method, petitioner realized a gain of slightly more than $30,000 in the course of 14 months. Subsequently, the Securities and Exchange Commission (Commission or SEC) began an investigation of his trading activities. In May 1977, petitioner entered into a consent decree with the Commission in which he agreed to return his profits to the sellers of the shares. On the same day, he was discharged by Pandick Press.

In January 1978, petitioner was indicted on 17 counts of violating § 10(b) of the Securities Exchange Act of 1934 (1934 Act) and SEC Rule 10b–5. After petitioner unsuccessfully moved to dismiss the indictment, he was brought to trial and convicted on all counts.

The Court of Appeals for the Second Circuit affirmed petitioner's conviction. 588 F.2d 1358 (2d Cir.1978). We granted certiorari, 441 U.S. 942, 99 S.Ct. 2158, 60 L.Ed.2d 1043 (1979), and we now reverse.

II . . .

This case concerns the legal effect of the petitioner's silence. The District Court's charge permitted the jury to convict the petitioner if it found that he willfully failed to inform sellers of target company securities that he knew of a forthcoming takeover bid that would make their shares more valuable. In order to decide whether silence in such circumstances violates § 10(b), it is necessary to review the language and legislative history of that statute as well as its interpretation by the Commission and the federal courts.

Although the starting point of our inquiry is the language of the statute, *Ernst & Ernst v. Hochfelder,* 425 U.S. 185, 197, 96 S.Ct. 1375, 47 L.Ed.2d 668 (1976), § 10(b) does not state whether silence may constitute a manipulative or deceptive device. Section 10(b) was designed as a catchall clause to prevent fraudulent practices. 425 U.S., at 202, 206. But neither the legislative history nor the statute itself affords specific guidance for the resolution of this case. When Rule 10b–5 was promulgated in 1942, the SEC did not discuss the possibility that failure to provide information might run afoul of § 10(b).

The SEC took an important step in the development of § 10(b) when it held that a broker-dealer and his firm violated that section by selling securities on the basis of undisclosed information obtained from a director of the issuer corporation who was also a registered representative of the brokerage firm. In *Cady, Roberts & Co.,* 40 S.E.C. 907 (1961), the Commission decided that a corporate insider must abstain from trading in the shares of his corporation unless he has first disclosed all material inside information known to him. The obligation to disclose or abstain derives from

> "[a]n affirmative duty to disclose material information[, which] has been traditionally imposed on corporate 'insiders,' particularly officers, directors, or controlling stockholders. We, and the courts have consistently held that insiders must disclose material facts which are known to them by virtue of their position but which are not known to persons with whom they deal and which, if known, would affect their investment judgment." *Id.,* at 911.

The Commission emphasized that the duty arose from (i) the existence of a relationship affording access to inside information intended to be available only for a corporate purpose, and (ii) the unfairness of allowing a corporate insider to take advantage of that information by trading without disclosure. *Id.,* at 912, and n. 15.[8]

---

[8]   . . . The transaction in *Cady, Roberts* involved sale of stock to persons who previously may not have been shareholders in the corporation. 40 S.E.C., at 913, and n. 21. The Commission

That the relationship between a corporate insider and the stockholders of his corporation gives rise to a disclosure obligation is not a novel twist of the law. At common law, misrepresentation made for the purpose of inducing reliance upon the false statement is fraudulent. But one who fails to disclose material information prior to the consummation of a transaction commits fraud only when he is under a duty to do so. And the duty to disclose arises when one party has information "that the other [party] is entitled to know because of a fiduciary or other similar relation of trust and confidence between them."[9] In its *Cady, Roberts* decision, the Commission recognized a relationship of trust and confidence between the shareholders of a corporation and those insiders who have obtained confidential information by reason of their position with that corporation. This relationship gives rise to a duty to disclose because of the "necessity of preventing a corporate insider from . . . tak[ing] unfair advantage of the uninformed minority stockholders." *Speed v. Transamerica Corp.,* 99 F.Supp. 808, 829 (Del.1951).

The federal courts have found violations of § 10(b) where corporate insiders used undisclosed information for their own benefit. *E.g., SEC v. Texas Gulf Sulphur Co.,* 401 F.2d 833 (C.A.2 1968), cert. denied, 404 U.S. 1005 (1971). The cases also have emphasized, in accordance with the common-law rule, that "[t]he party charged with failing to disclose market information must be under a duty to disclose it." *Frigitemp Corp. v. Financial Dynamics Fund, Inc.,* 524 F.2d 275, 282 (C.A.2 1975). Accordingly, a purchaser of stock who has no duty to a prospective seller because he is neither an insider nor a fiduciary has been held to have no obligation to reveal material facts. See *General Time Corp. v. Talley Industries, Inc.,* 403 F.2d 159, 164 (C.A.2 1968), cert. denied, 393 U.S. 1026, 89 S.Ct. 631, 21 L.Ed.2d 570 (1969). . . .

Thus, administrative and judicial interpretations have established that silence in connection with the purchase or sale of securities may operate as a fraud actionable under § 10(b) despite the absence of statutory language or legislative history specifically addressing the legality of nondisclosure. But such liability is premised upon a duty to disclose arising from a relationship of trust and confidence between parties to a transaction. Application of a duty to disclose prior to trading guarantees that corporate insiders, who have an obligation to place the

---

embraced the reasoning of Judge Learned Hand that "the director or officer assumed a fiduciary relation to the buyer by the very sale; for it would be a sorry distinction to allow him to use the advantage of his position to induce the buyer into the position of a beneficiary although he was forbidden to do so once the buyer had become one." *Id.,* at 914, n. 23, quoting *Gratz v. Claughton,* 187 F.2d 46, 49 (CA2), cert. denied, 341 U.S. 920, 71 S.Ct. 741, 95 L.Ed. 1353 (1951).

[9]   Restatement (Second) of Torts § 551(2)(a) (1976). See James & Gray, Misrepresentation—Part II, 37 Md.L.Rev. 488, 523–527 (1978). As regards securities transactions, the American Law Institute recognizes that "silence when there is a duty to . . . speak may be a fraudulent act." ALI, Federal Securities Code § 262(b) (Prop.Off.Draft 1978).

shareholder's welfare before their own, will not benefit personally through fraudulent use of material, nonpublic information.[12]

III

In this case, the petitioner was convicted of violating § 10(b) although he was not a corporate insider and he received no confidential information from the target company. Moreover, the "market information" upon which he relied did not concern the earning power or operations of the target company, but only the plans of the acquiring company. Petitioner's use of that information was not a fraud under § 10(b) unless he was subject to an affirmative duty to disclose it before trading. In this case, the jury instructions failed to specify any such duty. In effect, the trial court instructed the jury that petitioner owed a duty to everyone; to all sellers, indeed, to the market as a whole. The jury simply was told to decide whether petitioner used material, nonpublic information at a time when "he knew other people trading in the securities market did not have access to the same information." Record 677.

The Court of Appeals affirmed the conviction by holding that "[a]*nyone*—corporate insider or not—who regularly receives material nonpublic information may not use that information to trade in securities without incurring an affirmative duty to disclose." 588 F.2d, at 1365 (emphasis in original). Although the court said that its test would include only persons who regularly receive material, nonpublic information, *id.,* at 1366, its rationale for that limitation is unrelated to the existence of a duty to disclose.[14] The Court of Appeals, like the trial court, failed to identify a relationship between petitioner and the sellers that could give rise to a duty. Its decision thus rested solely upon its belief that the federal securities laws have "created a system providing equal access to information necessary for reasoned and intelligent investment decisions." *Id.,* at 1362. The use by anyone of material information not generally available is fraudulent, this theory suggests, because such information gives certain buyers or sellers an unfair advantage over less informed buyers and sellers.

This reasoning suffers from two defects. First, not every instance of financial unfairness constitutes fraudulent activity under § 10(b). See *Santa Fe Industries, Inc. v. Green,* 430 U.S. 462, 474–477, 97 S.Ct. 1292, 51 L.Ed.2d 480 (1977). Second, the element required to make silence

---

[12] "Tippees" of corporate insiders have been held liable under § 10(b) because they have a duty not to profit from the use of inside information that they know is confidential and know or should know came from a corporate insider, *Shapiro v. Merrill Lynch, Pierce, Fenner & Smith, Inc.,* 495 F.2d 228, 237–238 (C.A.2 1974). The tippee's obligation has been viewed as arising from his role as a participant after the fact in the insider's breach of a fiduciary duty. . . .

[14] The Court of Appeals said that its "regular access to market information" test would create a workable rule embracing "those who occupy . . . strategic places in the market mechanism." 588 F.2d, at 1365. These considerations are insufficient to support a duty to disclose. A duty arises from the relationship between parties, see nn. 9 and 10, *supra,* and accompanying text, and not merely from one's ability to acquire information because of his position in the market. . . .

fraudulent—a duty to disclose—is absent in this case. No duty could arise from petitioner's relationship with the sellers of the target company's securities, for petitioner had no prior dealings with them. He was not their agent, he was not a fiduciary, he was not a person in whom the sellers had placed their trust and confidence. He was, in fact, a complete stranger who dealt with the sellers only through impersonal market transactions.

We cannot affirm petitioner's conviction without recognizing a general duty between all participants in market transactions to forgo actions based on material, nonpublic information. Formulation of such a broad duty, which departs radically from the established doctrine that duty arises from a specific relationship between two parties, see n. 9, *supra,* should not be undertaken absent some explicit evidence of congressional intent.

As we have seen, no such evidence emerges from the language or legislative history of § 10(b). Moreover, neither the Congress nor the Commission ever has adopted a parity-of-information rule. Instead the problems caused by misuse of market information have been addressed by detailed and sophisticated regulation that recognizes when use of market information may not harm operation of the securities markets. For example, the Williams Act[15] limits but does not completely prohibit a tender offeror's purchases of target corporation stock before public announcement of the offer. Congress' careful action in this and other areas contrasts, and is in some tension, with the broad rule of liability we are asked to adopt in this case. . . .

. . . As we have emphasized before, the 1934 Act cannot be read " 'more broadly than its language and the statutory scheme reasonably permit.' " *Touche Ross & Co. v. Redington,* 442 U.S. 560, 578, 99 S.Ct. 2479, 61 L.Ed.2d 82 (1979), quoting *SEC v. Sloan,* 436 U.S. 103, 116, 98 S.Ct. 1702, 56 L.Ed.2d 148 (1978). Section 10(b) is aptly described as a catchall provision, but what it catches must be fraud. When an allegation of fraud is based upon nondisclosure, there can be no fraud absent a duty to speak. We hold that a duty to disclose under § 10(b) does not arise from the mere possession of nonpublic market information. The contrary result is without support in the legislative history of § 10(b) and would be inconsistent with the careful plan that Congress has enacted for regulation of the securities markets. Cf. *Santa Fe Industries, Inc. v. Green,* 430 U.S., at 479.[20]

---

[15] Title 15 U.S.C. § 78m(d)(1) (1976 ed., Supp. II) permits a tender offeror to purchase 5% of the target company's stock prior to disclosure of its plan for acquisition.

[20] . . . It is worth noting that this is apparently the first case in which criminal liability has been imposed upon a purchaser for § 10(b) nondisclosure. Petitioner was sentenced to a year in prison, suspended except for one month, and a 5-year term of probation. 588 F.2d, at 1373, 1378 (Meskill, J., dissenting).

IV

In its brief to this Court, the United States offers an alternative theory to support petitioner's conviction. It argues that petitioner breached a duty to the acquiring corporation when he acted upon information that he obtained by virtue of his position as an employee of a printer employed by the corporation. The breach of this duty is said to support a conviction under § 10(b) for fraud perpetrated upon both the acquiring corporation and the sellers.

We need not decide whether this theory has merit for it was not submitted to the jury. . . .

The jury instructions demonstrate that petitioner was convicted merely because of his failure to disclose material, nonpublic information to sellers from whom he bought the stock of target corporations. The jury was not instructed on the nature or elements of a duty owed by petitioner to anyone other than the sellers. Because we cannot affirm a criminal conviction on the basis of a theory not presented to the jury, *Rewis v. United States,* 401 U.S. 808, 814, 91 S.Ct. 1056, 28 L.Ed.2d 493 (1971), see *Dunn v. United States,* 442 U.S. 100, 106, 99 S.Ct. 2190, 60 L.Ed.2d 743 (1979), we will not speculate upon whether such a duty exists, whether it has been breached, or whether such a breach constitutes a violation of § 10(b).

The judgment of the Court of Appeals is

Reversed.

[The concurring opinions of Justices Stevens and Brennan are omitted.]

■ MR. CHIEF JUSTICE BURGER, dissenting.

I believe that the jury instructions in this case properly charged a violation of § 10(b) and Rule 10b–5, and I would affirm the conviction.

I

As a general rule, neither party to an arm's-length business transaction has an obligation to disclose information to the other unless the parties stand in some confidential or fiduciary relation. See W. Prosser, Law of Torts § 106 (2d ed. 1955). This rule permits a businessman to capitalize on his experience and skill in securing and evaluating relevant information; it provides incentive for hard work, careful analysis, and astute forecasting. But the policies that underlie the rule also should limit its scope. In particular, the rule should give way when an informational advantage is obtained, not by superior experience, foresight, or industry, but by some unlawful means. One commentator has written:

> "[T]he way in which the buyer acquires the information which he conceals from the vendor should be a material circumstance. The information might have been acquired as the result of his bringing to bear a superior knowledge, intelligence, skill or

technical judgment; it might have been acquired by mere chance; or it might have been acquired by means of some tortious action on his part. . . . *Any time information is acquired by an illegal act it would seem that there should be a duty to disclose that information.*" Keeton, Fraud—Concealment and Non-Disclosure, 15 Texas L.Rev. 1, 25–26 (1936) (emphasis added).

I would read § 10(b) and Rule 10b–5 to encompass and build on this principle: to mean that a person who has misappropriated nonpublic information has an absolute duty to disclose that information or to refrain from trading.

II

The Court's opinion, as I read it, leaves open the question whether § 10(b) and Rule 10b–5 prohibit trading on misappropriated nonpublic information.[4] Instead, the Court apparently concludes that this theory of the case was not submitted to the jury. In the Court's view, the instructions given the jury were premised on the erroneous notion that the mere failure to disclose nonpublic information, however acquired, is a deceptive practice. . . .

The Court's reading of the District Court's charge is unduly restrictive. Fairly read as a whole and in the context of the trial, the instructions required the jury to find that Chiarella obtained his trading advantage by misappropriating the property of his employer's customers. . . . [t]he evidence shows beyond all doubt that Chiarella, working literally in the shadows of the warning signs in the printshop, misappropriated—stole to put it bluntly—valuable nonpublic information entrusted to him in the utmost confidence. He then exploited his ill-gotten informational advantage by purchasing securities in the market. In my view, such conduct plainly violates § 10(b) and Rule 10b–5. Accordingly, I would affirm the judgment of the Court of Appeals.

■ JUSTICES BLACKMUN with whom JUSTICE MARSHALL joins, dissenting.

Although I agree with much of what is said in Part I of the dissenting opinion of The Chief Justice, I write separately because, in my view, it is unnecessary to rest petitioner's conviction on a "misappropriation" theory. The fact that petitioner Chiarella purloined, or, to use The Chief Justice's word, "stole," information concerning pending tender offers certainly is the most dramatic evidence that petitioner was guilty of fraud. He has conceded that knew it was wrong, and he and his co-workers in the print shop wee specifically warned by their employer that

---

[4]   There is some language in the Court's opinion to suggest that only "a relationship between petitioner and the sellers . . . could give rise to a duty [to disclose]." . . . The Court's holding, however, is much more limited, namely, that mere possession of material, nonpublic information is insufficient to create a duty to disclose or to refrain from trading. . . . Accordingly, it is my understanding that the Court has not rejected the view, advanced above, that an absolute duty to disclose or refrain arises from the very act of misappropriating nonpublic information.

actions of this kind were improper and forbidden. But I also would find petitioner's conduct fraudulent within the meaning of § 10(b) [and] Rule 10b–5, even if he had obtained the blessing of his employer's principals before embarking on his profiteering scheme. I think petitioner's brand of manipulative trading, with or without such approval, lies close to the heart of what the securities laws are intended to prohibit. . . .

The Court continues to pursue a course, charted in certain recent decisions, designed to transform § 10(b) from an intentionally elastic "catchall" provision to one that catches relatively little of the misbehavior that all too often makes investment in securities needlessly risky business for the uninitiated investor. . . .

Whatever the outer limits of the Rule, petitioner Chiarella's case fits neatly near the center of its analytical framework. He occupied a relationship to the takeover companies giving him intimate access to concededly material information that was sedulously guarded from public access. The information, in the words of Cady Roberts & Co., 40 SEC, at 912, was "intended to be available only for a corporate purpose and not for the personal benefit of anyone." Petitioner, moreover, knew that the information was unavailable to those with whom he dealt. And, he took full, virtually riskless advantage of this artificial information gap by selling the stocks shortly after each takeover bid was announced. By any reasonable definition, his trading was "inherent[ly] unfair[r]." This misuse of confidential information was clearly before the jury. Petitioner's conviction, therefore, should be upheld and I dissent from the Court's upsetting that conviction.

––––––

SECURITIES EXCHANGE ACT § 14(e) AND RULE 14(e)(3)

[See Statutory Supplement]

––––––

United States v. O'Hagan

United States Supreme Court, 1997.
521 U.S. 642, 117 S.Ct. 2199, 138 L.Ed.2d 724.

■ JUSTICE GINSBURG delivered the opinion of the Court.

This case concerns the interpretation and enforcement of § 10(b) and § 14(e) of the Securities Exchange Act of 1934, and rules made by the Securities and Exchange Commission pursuant to these provisions, Rule 10b–5 and Rule 14e–3(a). Two prime questions are presented. The first relates to the misappropriation of material, nonpublic information for securities trading; the second concerns fraudulent practices in the tender offer setting. In particular, we address and resolve these issues: (1) Is a person who trades in securities for personal profit, using confidential information misappropriated in breach of a fiduciary duty to the source of the information, guilty of violating § 10(b) and Rule 10b–5? (2) Did the Commission exceed its rulemaking authority by adopting Rule 14e–3(a), which proscribes trading on undisclosed information in the tender offer setting, even in the absence of a duty to disclose? Our answer to the first question is yes, and to the second question, viewed in the context of this case, no.

I

Respondent James Herman O'Hagan was a partner in the law firm of Dorsey & Whitney in Minneapolis, Minnesota. In July 1988, Grand Metropolitan PLC (Grand Met), a company based in London, England, retained Dorsey & Whitney as local counsel to represent Grand Met regarding a potential tender offer for the common stock of the Pillsbury Company, headquartered in Minneapolis. Both Grand Met and Dorsey & Whitney took precautions to protect the confidentiality of Grand Met's tender offer plans. O'Hagan did no work on the Grand Met representation. Dorsey & Whitney withdrew from representing Grand Met on September 9, 1988. Less than a month later, on October 4, 1988, Grand Met publicly announced its tender offer for Pillsbury stock.

On August 18, 1988, while Dorsey & Whitney was still representing Grand Met, O'Hagan began purchasing call options for Pillsbury stock. Each option gave him the right to purchase 100 shares of Pillsbury stock by a specified date in September 1988. Later in August and in September, O'Hagan made additional purchases of Pillsbury call options. By the end of September, he owned 2,500 unexpired Pillsbury options, apparently more than any other individual investor. See App. 85, 148. O'Hagan also purchased, in September 1988, some 5,000 shares of Pillsbury common stock, at a price just under $39 per share. When Grand Met announced its tender offer in October, the price of Pillsbury stock rose to nearly $60 per share. O'Hagan then sold his Pillsbury call options and common stock, making a profit of more than $4.3 million.

The Securities and Exchange Commission (SEC or Commission) initiated an investigation into O'Hagan's transactions, culminating in a 57-count indictment. The indictment alleged that O'Hagan defrauded his law firm and its client, Grand Met, by using for his own trading purposes material, nonpublic information regarding Grand Met's planned tender offer. Id., at 8. According to the indictment, O'Hagan used the profits he gained through this trading to conceal his previous embezzlement and conversion of unrelated client trust funds. Id., at 10.[2] O'Hagan was charged with 20 counts of mail fraud, in violation of 18 U.S.C. § 1341; 17 counts of securities fraud, in violation of § 10(b) of the Securities Exchange Act of 1934 (Exchange Act) . . . and SEC Rule 10b–5 . . . ; 17 counts of fraudulent trading in connection with a tender offer, in violation

---

[2] O'Hagan was convicted of theft in state court, sentenced to 30 months' imprisonment, and fined. See State v. O'Hagan, 474 N.W.2d 613, 615, 623 (Minn.App.1991). The Supreme Court of Minnesota disbarred O'Hagan from the practice of law. See In re O'Hagan, 450 N.W.2d 571 (Minn.1990).

of § 14(e) of the Exchange Act . . . and SEC Rule 14e–3(a) . . . (1996); and 3 counts of violating federal money laundering statutes, 18 U.S.C. §§ 1956(a)(1)(B)(i), 1957. . . . A jury convicted O'Hagan on all 57 counts, and he was sentenced to a 41-month term of imprisonment.

A divided panel of the Court of Appeals for the Eighth Circuit reversed all of O'Hagan's convictions. 92 F.3d 612 (1996). Liability under § 10(b) and Rule 10b–5, the Eighth Circuit held, may not be grounded on the "misappropriation theory" of securities fraud on which the prosecution relied. Id., at 622. The Court of Appeals also held that Rule 14e–3(a)—which prohibits trading while in possession of material, nonpublic information relating to a tender offer—exceeds the SEC's § 14(e) rulemaking authority because the rule contains no breach of fiduciary duty requirement. Id., at 627. The Eighth Circuit further concluded that O'Hagan's mail fraud and money laundering convictions rested on violations of the securities laws, and therefore could not stand once the securities fraud convictions were reversed. Id., at 627–628. Judge Fagg, dissenting, stated that he would recognize and enforce the misappropriation theory, and would hold that the SEC did not exceed its rulemaking authority when it adopted Rule 14e–3(a) without requiring proof of a breach of fiduciary duty. Id., at 628.

Decisions of the Courts of Appeals are in conflict on the propriety of the misappropriation theory under § 10(b) and Rule 10b–5, see infra this page and n. 3, and on the legitimacy of Rule 14e–3(a) under § 14(e). . . . We granted certiorari, 519 U.S. 1037 (1997), and now reverse the Eighth Circuit's judgment.

II

We address first the Court of Appeals' reversal of O'Hagan's convictions under § 10(b) and Rule 10b–5. Following the Fourth Circuit's lead, see United States v. Bryan, 58 F.3d 933, 943–959 (1995), the Eighth Circuit rejected the misappropriation theory as a basis for § 10(b) liability. We hold, in accord with several other Courts of Appeals, that criminal liability under § 10(b) may be predicated on the misappropriation theory.[4]

A . . .

[Section] 10(b) of the Exchange Act proscribes (1) using any deceptive device (2) in connection with the purchase or sale of securities, in contravention of rules prescribed by the Commission. The provision,

---

[4]   Twice before we have been presented with the question whether criminal liability for violation of § 10(b) may be based on a misappropriation theory. In Chiarella v. United States, 445 U.S. 222, 235–237 (1980), the jury had received no misappropriation theory instructions, so we declined to address the question. . . . In Carpenter v. United States, 484 U.S. 19, 24 (1987), the Court divided evenly on whether, under the circumstances of that case, convictions resting on the misappropriation theory should be affirmed. See Aldave, The Misappropriation Theory: Carpenter and Its Aftermath, 49 Ohio St. L.J. 373, 375 (1988) (observing that "Carpenter was, by any reckoning, an unusual case," for the information there misappropriated belonged not to a company preparing to engage in securities transactions, e.g., a bidder in a corporate acquisition, but to the Wall Street Journal).

as written, does not confine its coverage to deception of a purchaser or seller of securities, see United States v. Newman, 664 F.2d 12, 17 (C.A.2 1981); rather, the statute reaches any deceptive device used "in connection with the purchase or sale of any security."

Pursuant to its § 10(b) rulemaking authority, the Commission has adopted Rule 10b–5. . . .

Under the "traditional" or "classical theory" of insider trading liability, § 10(b) and Rule 10b–5 are violated when a corporate insider trades in the securities of his corporation on the basis of material, nonpublic information. Trading on such information qualifies as a "deceptive device" under § 10(b), we have affirmed, because "a relationship of trust and confidence [exists] between the shareholders of a corporation and those insiders who have obtained confidential information by reason of their position with that corporation." Chiarella v. United States, 445 U.S. 222, 228 (1980). That relationship, we recognized, "gives rise to a duty to disclose [or to abstain from trading] because of the 'necessity of preventing a corporate insider from . . . taking unfair advantage of . . . uninformed . . . stockholders.' " Id., at 228–229 (citation omitted). The classical theory applies not only to officers, directors, and other permanent insiders of a corporation, but also to attorneys, accountants, consultants, and others who temporarily become fiduciaries of a corporation. See Dirks v. SEC, 463 U.S. 646, 655, n. 14 (1983).

The "misappropriation theory" holds that a person commits fraud "in connection with" a securities transaction, and thereby violates § 10(b) and Rule 10b–5, when he misappropriates confidential information for securities trading purposes, in breach of a duty owed to the source of the information. See Brief for United States 14. Under this theory, a fiduciary's undisclosed, self-serving use of a principal's information to purchase or sell securities, in breach of a duty of loyalty and confidentiality, defrauds the principal of the exclusive use of that information. In lieu of premising liability on a fiduciary relationship between company insider and purchaser or seller of the company's stock, the misappropriation theory premises liability on a fiduciary-turned-trader's deception of those who entrusted him with access to confidential information.

The two theories are complementary, each addressing efforts to capitalize on nonpublic information through the purchase or sale of securities. The classical theory targets a corporate insider's breach of duty to shareholders with whom the insider transacts; the misappropriation theory outlaws trading on the basis of nonpublic information by a corporate "outsider" in breach of a duty owed not to a trading party, but to the source of the information. The misappropriation theory is thus designed to "protect the integrity of the securities markets against abuses by 'outsiders' to a corporation who have access to confidential information that will affect the corporation's security price when revealed, but who owe no fiduciary or other duty to that corporation's shareholders." Ibid.

In this case, the indictment alleged that O'Hagan, in breach of a duty of trust and confidence he owed to his law firm, Dorsey & Whitney, and to its client, Grand Met, traded on the basis of nonpublic information regarding Grand Met's planned tender offer for Pillsbury common stock. App. 16. This conduct, the Government charged, constituted a fraudulent device in connection with the purchase and sale of securities.[5]

B

We agree with the Government that misappropriation, as just defined, satisfies § 10(b)'s requirement that chargeable conduct involve a "deceptive device or contrivance" used "in connection with" the purchase or sale of securities. We observe, first, that misappropriators, as the Government describes them, deal in deception. A fiduciary who "[pretends] loyalty to the principal while secretly converting the principal's information for personal gain," Brief for United States 17, "dupes" or defrauds the principal. See Aldave, Misappropriation: A General Theory of Liability for Trading on Nonpublic Information, 13 Hofstra L.Rev. 101, 119 (1984).

We addressed fraud of the same species in Carpenter v. United States, 484 U.S. 19 (1987), which involved the mail fraud statute's proscription of "any scheme or artifice to defraud," 18 U.S.C. § 1341. Affirming convictions under that statute, we said in Carpenter that an employee's undertaking not to reveal his employer's confidential information "became a sham" when the employee provided the information to his co-conspirators in a scheme to obtain trading profits. 484 U.S. at 27. A company's confidential information, we recognized in Carpenter, qualifies as property to which the company has a right of exclusive use. Id., at 25–27. The undisclosed misappropriation of such information, in violation of a fiduciary duty, the Court said in Carpenter, constitutes fraud akin to embezzlement—" 'the fraudulent appropriation to one's own use of the money or goods entrusted to one's care by another.' " Id., at 27 (quoting Grin v. Shine, 187 U.S. 181, 189 (1902)); see Aldave, 13 Hofstra L.Rev., at 119. Carpenter's discussion of the fraudulent misuse of confidential information, the Government notes, "is a particularly apt source of guidance here, because [the mail fraud statute] (like Section 10(b)) has long been held to require deception, not merely the breach of a fiduciary duty." Brief for United States 18, n. 9 (citation omitted).

---

[5]   The Government could not have prosecuted O'Hagan under the classical theory, for O'Hagan was not an "insider" of Pillsbury, the corporation in whose stock he traded. Although an "outsider" with respect to Pillsbury, O'Hagan had an intimate association with, and was found to have traded on confidential information from Dorsey & Whitney, counsel to tender offeror Grand Met. Under the misappropriation theory, O'Hagan's securities trading does not escape Exchange Act sanction, as it would under the dissent's reasoning, simply because he was associated with, and gained nonpublic information from, the bidder, rather than the target.

Deception through nondisclosure is central to the theory of liability for which the Government seeks recognition. As counsel for the Government stated in explanation of the theory at oral argument: "To satisfy the common law rule that a trustee may not use the property that [has] been entrusted [to] him, there would have to be consent. To satisfy the requirement of the Securities Act that there be no deception, there would only have to be disclosure." Tr. of Oral Arg. 12; see generally Restatement (Second) of Agency §§ 390, 395 (1958) (agent's disclosure obligation regarding use of confidential information).[6]

. . . [F]ull disclosure forecloses liability under the misappropriation theory: Because the deception essential to the misappropriation theory involves feigning fidelity to the source of information, if the fiduciary discloses to the source that he plans to trade on the nonpublic information, there is no "deceptive device" and thus no § 10(b) violation— although the fiduciary-turned-trader may remain liable under state law for breach of a duty of loyalty.[7]

We turn next to the § 10(b) requirement that the misappropriator's deceptive use of information be "in connection with the purchase or sale of [a] security." This element is satisfied because the fiduciary's fraud is consummated, not when the fiduciary gains the confidential information, but when, without disclosure to his principal, he uses the information to purchase or sell securities. The securities transaction and the breach of duty thus coincide. This is so even though the person or entity defrauded is not the other party to the trade, but is, instead, the source of the nonpublic information. See Aldave, 13 Hofstra L.Rev., at 120 ("a fraud or deceit can be practiced on one person, with resultant harm to another person or group of persons"). A misappropriator who trades on the basis of material, nonpublic information, in short, gains his advantageous market position through deception; he deceives the source of the information and simultaneously harms members of the investing public. See id., at 120–121, and n. 107.

The misappropriation theory targets information of a sort that misappropriators ordinarily capitalize upon to gain no-risk profits through the purchase or sale of securities. Should a misappropriator put such information to other use, the statute's prohibition would not be implicated. The theory does not catch all conceivable forms of fraud

---

[6]   Under the misappropriation theory urged in this case, the disclosure obligation runs to the source of the information, here, Dorsey & Whitney and Grand Met. Chief Justice Burger, dissenting in Chiarella, advanced a broader reading of § 10(b) and Rule 10b–5; the disclosure obligation, as he envisioned it, ran to those with whom the misappropriator trades. 445 U.S., at 240 ("a person who has misappropriated nonpublic information has an absolute duty to disclose that information or to refrain from trading"); see also id., at 243, n. 4. The Government does not propose that we adopt a misappropriation theory of that breadth.

[7]   Where, however, a person trading on the basis of material, nonpublic information owes a duty of loyalty and confidentiality to two entities or persons—for example, a law firm and its client—but makes disclosure to only one, the trader may still be liable under the misappropriation theory.

involving confidential information; rather, it catches fraudulent means of capitalizing on such information through securities transactions.

The Government notes another limitation on the forms of fraud § 10(b) reaches: "The misappropriation theory would not . . . apply to a case in which a person defrauded a bank into giving him a loan or embezzled cash from another, and then used the proceeds of the misdeed to purchase securities." Brief for United States 24, n. 13. In such a case, the Government states, "the proceeds would have value to the malefactor apart from their use in a securities transaction, and the fraud would be complete as soon as the money was obtained." Ibid. In other words, money can buy, if not anything, then at least many things; its misappropriation may thus be viewed as sufficiently detached from a subsequent securities transaction that § 10(b)'s "in connection with" requirement would not be met. Ibid. . . .

The misappropriation theory comports with § 10(b)'s language, which requires deception "in connection with the purchase or sale of any security," not deception of an identifiable purchaser or seller. The theory is also well-tuned to an animating purpose of the Exchange Act: to insure honest securities markets and thereby promote investor confidence. See 45 Fed.Reg. 60412 (1980) (trading on misappropriated information "undermines the integrity of, and investor confidence in, the securities markets"). Although informational disparity is inevitable in the securities markets, investors likely would hesitate to venture their capital in a market where trading based on misappropriated nonpublic information is unchecked by law. An investor's informational disadvantage vis-a-vis a misappropriator with material, nonpublic information stems from contrivance, not luck; it is a disadvantage that cannot be overcome with research or skill. See Brudney, Insiders, Outsiders, and Informational Advantages Under the Federal Securities Laws, 93 Harv.L.Rev. 322, 356 (1979) ("If the market is thought to be systematically populated with . . . transactors [trading on the basis of misappropriated information] some investors will refrain from dealing altogether, and others will incur costs to avoid dealing with such transactors or corruptly to overcome their unerodable informational advantages."); Aldave, 13 Hofstra L.Rev., at 122–123.

In sum, considering the inhibiting impact on market participation of trading on misappropriated information, and the congressional purposes underlying § 10(b), it makes scant sense to hold a lawyer like O'Hagan a § 10(b) violator if he works for a law firm representing the target of a tender offer, but not if he works for a law firm representing the bidder. The text of the statute requires no such result.[9] The misappropriation at

---

[9] As noted earlier, however, see supra, at 9–10, the textual requirement of deception precludes § 10(b) liability when a person trading on the basis of nonpublic information has disclosed his trading plans to, or obtained authorization from, the principal—even though such conduct may affect the securities markets in the same manner as the conduct reached by the misappropriation theory. . . . [T]he fact that § 10(b) is only a partial antidote to the problems it was designed to alleviate does not call into question its prohibition of conduct that falls within

issue here was properly made the subject of a § 10(b) charge because it meets the statutory requirement that there be "deceptive" conduct "in connection with" securities transactions.

C

... [T]he misappropriation theory, as we have examined and explained it in this opinion, is both consistent with the statute and with our precedent.[11] ...

The Eighth Circuit erred in holding that the misappropriation theory is inconsistent with § 10(b). The Court of Appeals may address on remand O'Hagan's other challenges to his convictions under § 10(b) and Rule 10b–5.

III

We consider next the ground on which the Court of Appeals reversed O'Hagan's convictions for fraudulent trading in connection with a tender offer, in violation of § 14(e) of the Exchange Act and SEC Rule 14e–3(a). A sole question is before us as to these convictions: Did the Commission, as the Court of Appeals held, exceed its rulemaking authority under § 14(e) when it adopted Rule 14e–3(a) without requiring a showing that the trading at issue entailed a breach of fiduciary duty? We hold that the Commission, in this regard and to the extent relevant to this case, did not exceed its authority.

The governing statutory provision, § 14(e) of the Exchange Act, reads in relevant part:

"It shall be unlawful for any person ... to engage in any fraudulent, deceptive, or manipulative acts or practices, in connection with any tender offer.... The [SEC] shall, for the purposes of this subsection, by rules and regulations define, and prescribe means reasonably designed to prevent, such acts and practices as are fraudulent, deceptive, or manipulative." 15 U.S.C. § 78n(e).

---

its textual proscription. Moreover, once a disloyal agent discloses his imminent breach of duty, his principal may seek appropriate equitable relief under state law. Furthermore, in the context of a tender offer, the principal who authorizes an agent's trading on confidential information may, in the Commission's view, incur liability for an Exchange Act violation under Rule 14e–3(a).

[11] The United States additionally argues that Congress confirmed the validity of the misappropriation theory in the Insider Trading and Securities Fraud Enforcement Act of 1988 (ITSFEA), § 2(1), 102 Stat. 4677, note following 15 U.S.C. § 78u–1. See Brief for United States 32–35. ITSFEA declares that "the rules and regulations of the Securities and Exchange Commission under the Securities Exchange Act of 1934 ... governing trading while in possession of material, nonpublic information are, as required by such Act, necessary and appropriate in the public interest and for the protection of investors." Note following 15 U.S.C. § 78u–1. ITSFEA also includes a new § 20A(a) of the Exchange Act expressly providing a private cause of action against persons who violate the Exchange Act "by purchasing or selling a security while in possession of material, nonpublic information", such an action may be brought by "any person who, contemporaneously with the purchase or sale of securities that is the subject of such violation, has purchased ... or sold ... securities of the same class." 15 U.S.C. § 78r–1(a). Because we uphold the misappropriation theory on the basis of § 10(b) itself, we do not address ITSFEA's significance for cases of this genre.

Section 14(e)'s first sentence prohibits fraudulent acts in connection with a tender offer. This self-operating proscription was one of several provisions added to the Exchange Act in 1968 by the Williams Act, 82 Stat. 454. The section's second sentence delegates definitional and prophylactic rulemaking authority to the Commission. Congress added this rulemaking delegation to § 14(e) in 1970 amendments to the Williams Act. See § 5, 84 Stat. 1497. . . .

Relying on § 14(e)'s rulemaking authorization, the Commission, in 1980, promulgated Rule 14e–3(a). That measure provides:

> "(a) If any person has taken a substantial step or steps to commence, or has commenced, a tender offer (the 'offering person'), it shall constitute a fraudulent, deceptive or manipulative act or practice within the meaning of section 14(e) of the [Exchange] Act for any other person who is in possession of material information relating to such tender offer which information he knows or has reason to know is nonpublic and which he knows or has reason to know has been acquired directly or indirectly from:

> > "(1) The offering person,

> > "(2) The issuer of the securities sought or to be sought by such tender offer, or

> > "(3) Any officer, director, partner or employee or any other person acting on behalf of the offering person or such issuer,

> to purchase or sell or cause to be purchased or sold any of such securities or any securities convertible into or exchangeable for any such securities or any option or right to obtain or to dispose of any of the foregoing securities, unless within a reasonable time prior to any purchase or sale such information and its source are publicly disclosed by press release or otherwise." 17 CFR § 240.14e–3(a) (1996).

As characterized by the Commission, Rule 14e–3(a) is a "disclose or abstain from trading" requirement. 45 Fed.Reg. 60410 (1980).[15] The Second Circuit concisely described the rule's thrust:

> "One violates Rule 14e–3(a) if he trades on the basis of material nonpublic information concerning a pending tender offer that he knows or has reason to know has been acquired 'directly or indirectly' from an insider of the offeror or issuer, or someone working on their behalf. Rule 14e–3(a) is a disclosure provision. It creates a duty in those traders who fall within its ambit to abstain or disclose, without regard to whether the

---

[15]   The rule thus adopts for the tender offer context a requirement resembling the one Chief Justice Burger would have adopted in Chiarella for misappropriators under § 10(b). See supra, at 10, n. 6.

trader owes a pre-existing fiduciary duty to respect the confidentiality of the information." United States v. Chestman, 947 F.2d 551, 557 (1991) (en banc) (emphasis added), cert. denied, 503 U.S. 1004 (1992).

See also SEC v. Maio, 51 F.3d 623, 635 (C.A.7 1995) ("Rule 14e–3 creates a duty to disclose material nonpublic information, or abstain from trading in stocks implicated by an impending tender offer, regardless of whether such information was obtained through a breach of fiduciary duty.") (emphasis added); SEC v. Peters, 978 F.2d 1162, 1165 (C.A.10 1992) (as written, Rule 14e–3(a) has no fiduciary duty requirement).

In the Eighth Circuit's view, because Rule 14e–3(a) applies whether or not the trading in question breaches a fiduciary duty, the regulation exceeds the SEC's § 14(e) rulemaking authority. . . .

The Eighth Circuit homed in on the essence of § 14(e)'s rulemaking authorization: "The statute empowers the SEC to 'define' and 'prescribe means reasonably designed to prevent' 'acts and practices' which are 'fraudulent.'" Id., at 624. All that means, the Eighth Circuit found plain, is that the SEC may "identify and regulate," in the tender offer context, "acts and practices" the law already defines as "fraudulent"; but, the Eighth Circuit maintained, the SEC may not "create its own definition of fraud." Ibid. (internal quotation marks omitted). . . .

We need not resolve in this case whether the Commission's authority under § 14(e) to "define . . . such acts and practices as are fraudulent" is broader than the Commission's fraud-defining authority under § 10(b), for we agree with the United States that Rule 14e–3(a), as applied to cases of this genre, qualifies under § 14(e) as a "means reasonably designed to prevent" fraudulent trading on material, nonpublic information in the tender offer context. A prophylactic measure, because its mission is to prevent, typically encompasses more than the core activity prohibited. . . . [Section] 14(e)'s rulemaking authorization gives the Commission "latitude," even in the context of a term of art like "manipulative," "to regulate nondeceptive activities as a 'reasonably designed' means of preventing manipulative acts, without suggesting any change in the meaning of the term 'manipulative' itself." 472 U.S., at 11, n. 11. We hold, accordingly, that under § 14(e), the Commission may prohibit acts, not themselves fraudulent under the common law or § 10(b), if the prohibition is "reasonably designed to prevent . . . acts and practices [that] are fraudulent." 15 U.S.C. § 78n(c). . . .

[I]t is a fair assumption that trading on the basis of material, nonpublic information [in connection with a tender offer] will often involve a breach of a duty of confidentiality to the bidder or target company or their representatives. The SEC, cognizant of the proof problem that could enable sophisticated traders to escape responsibility, placed in Rule 14e–3(a) a "disclose or abstain from trading" command that does not require specific proof of a breach of fiduciary duty. That prescription, we are satisfied, applied to this case, is a "means reasonably designed to prevent" fraudulent trading on material, nonpublic information in the tender offer context. See Chestman, 947 F.2d, at 560 ("While dispensing with the subtle problems of proof associated with demonstrating fiduciary breach in the problematic area of tender offer insider trading, [Rule 14e–3(a)] retains a close nexus between the prohibited conduct and the statutory aims."); accord, Maio, 51 F.3d, at 635, and n. 14; Peters, 978 F.2d, at 1167. Therefore, insofar as it serves to prevent the type of misappropriation charged against O'Hagan, Rule 14e–3(a) is a proper exercise of the Commission's prophylactic power under § 14(e).

As an alternate ground for affirming the Eighth Circuit's judgment, O'Hagan urges that Rule 14e–3(a) is invalid because it prohibits trading in advance of a tender offer—when "a substantial step . . . to commence" such an offer has been taken—while § 14(e) prohibits fraudulent acts "in connection with any tender offer." See Brief for Respondent 41–42. O'Hagan further contends that, by covering pre-offer conduct, Rule 14e–3(a) "fails to comport with due process on two levels": The rule does not "give fair notice as to when, in advance of a tender offer, a violation of § 14(e) occurs," id., at 42; and it "disposes of any scienter requirement," id., at 43. The Court of Appeals did not address these arguments, and O'Hagan did not raise the due process points in his briefs before that court. We decline to consider these contentions in the first instance.[23] The Court of Appeals may address on remand any arguments O'Hagan has preserved. . . .

The judgment of the Court of Appeals for the Eighth Circuit is reversed, and the case is remanded for further proceedings consistent with this opinion.

It is so ordered.

■ DISSENT: JUSTICE SCALIA, concurring in part and dissenting in part.

I join Parts I, III, and IV of the Court's opinion. I do not agree, however, with Part II of the Court's opinion, containing its analysis of respondent's convictions under § 10(b) and Rule 10b–5. . . .

While the Court's explanation of the scope of § 10(b) and Rule 10b–5 would be entirely reasonable in some other context, it does not seem to accord with the principle of lenity we apply to criminal statutes. . . .

In light of that principle, it seems to me that the unelaborated statutory language: "to use or employ in connection with the purchase or sale of any security . . . any manipulative or deceptive device or contrivance," § 10(b), must be construed to require the manipulation or deception of a party to a securities transaction.

---

[23]   As to O'Hagan's scienter argument,. . . . 15 U.S.C. § 78ff(a) requires the Government to prove "willful violation" of the securities laws, and that lack of knowledge of the relevant rule is an affirmative defense to a sentence of imprisonment. . . .

[The opinion of Justice Thomas, concurring with the majority on the Mail Fraud Act issue, but dissenting on the Rule 10b–5 and Rule 14e–3(a) issues, is omitted. Chief Justice Rehnquist concurred in Justice Thomas's opinion.]

———

NOTE ON WHO'S A MISAPPROPRIATOR?

What relationship provides the appropriate bond from which the misappropriation theory operates? *United States v. Chestman*, 947 F.2d 551 (2d Cir. 1991) (en banc), *cert. denied,* 503 U.S. 1004, 112 S.Ct. 1759, 118 L.Ed.2d 422 (1992), believed the requisite fiduciary duty upon which the misappropriation theory rests must be a fiduciary or similar relationship. It recognized "hornbook fiduciary relations are those existing between attorney and client, executor and heir, guardian and ward, principal and agent, trustee and trust beneficiary, and senior corporate official and shareholder." *Id.* at 568. It then reasoned that the misappropriation theory is premised on there being a special relationship of trust and confidence and this relationship must itself be the functional equivalent of a fiduciary relationship. It also believed it necessary to restrain somewhat the scope of the misappropriation theory. It therefore considered what it believed to be the basic contours of a fiduciary relationship:

> A fiduciary relationship involves discretionary authority and dependency. One person depends on another—the fiduciary—to serve his interests. In relying on a fiduciary to act for his benefit, the beneficiary of the relationship may entrust the fiduciary with custody over property of one sort or another. Because the fiduciary obtains access to this property to serve the ends of the fiduciary relationship he becomes duty-bound not to appropriate the property for his own use. What has been said of an agent's duty of confidentiality applies with equal force to other fiduciary relations: "an agent is subject to a duty to the principal not to use or to communicate information confidentially given him by the principal or acquired by him during the course of or on account of his agency." Restatement (Second) of Agency § 395 (1958). These characteristics represent the measure of the paradigmatic fiduciary relationship. A similar relationship of trust and confidence consequently must share these qualities.

947 F.2d at 569. The bare majority in the en banc decision applied the above standard to conclude that the husband who learned from his wife (whose family had founded what had become a publicly traded firm) that the company would soon be acquired at a premium was not a wrongful misappropriator when he traded on this information, even though he was told by his wife not to share the information with anyone because "it could possibly ruin the sale." The majority reasoned the disclosure to the defendant was made gratuitously and that there was no evidence that such confidences were shared because of any dependence by the family or the wife to act on

the confidential information in serving their interest. Moreover, there was no express agreement of confidentiality.

How easily do the following cases fall within the fiduciary relationship set forth by the *Chestman* majority? The psychiatrists that learns confidential information during sessions with the spouse of a public company's CEO. United States v. Willis, 778 F.Supp. 205 (S.D.N.Y. 1991); a journalists of the Wall Street Journal's Heard on the Street column who tipped others on his advance knowledge of what companies would appear in the market-moving column. United States v. Carpenter, 791 F.2d 1024 (2d Cir. 1986), *aff'd*, 484 U.S. 19, 108 S.Ct. 316, 98 L.Ed.2d 275 (1987).

Since the above decisions dealing with a trading husband and psychiatrist and the tipping journalist, the SEC has adopted Rule 10b5–2, described in the adopting SEC release as follows:

> ... [A]n unsettled issue in insider trading law has been under what circumstances certain non-business relationships, such as family and personal relationships, may provide the duty of trust or confidence required under the misappropriation theory. Case law has produced the following anomalous result. A family member who receives a "tip" (within the meaning of Dirks) and then trades violates Rule 10b–5. A family member who trades in breach of an express promise of confidentiality also violates Rule 10b–5. A family member who trades in breach of a reasonable expectation of confidentiality, however, does not necessarily violate Rule 10b–5.

> ... [W]e think that this anomalous result harms investor confidence in the integrity and fairness of the nation's securities markets. The family member's trading has the same impact on the market and investor confidence in the third example as it does in the first two examples. In all three examples, the trader's informational advantage stems from "contrivance, not luck," and the informational disadvantage to other investors "cannot be overcome with research or skill." Additionally, the need to distinguish among the three types of cases may require an unduly intrusive examination of the details of particular family relationships. Accordingly, we believe there is good reason for the broader approach we adopt today for determining when family or personal relationships create "duties of trust or confidence" under the misappropriation theory.

> Some of the commenters ... expressed concern that the rule would erode standards of personal and family privacy. ... [W]e do not believe that the rule will require a more intrusive examination of family relationships than would be required under existing case law without the rule. Current case law, such as United States v. Chestman ... already establishes a regime under which questions of liability turn on the nature of the details of the relationships between family members, such as their prior history and patterns of sharing confidences. By providing more of a bright-line test for certain enumerated close family relationships, we believe the rule

will mitigate, to some degree, the need to examine the details of particular relationships in the course of investigating suspected insider trading. . . .

The rule sets forth a non-exclusive list of three situations in which a person has a duty of trust or confidence for purposes of the "misappropriation" theory of the Exchange Act and Rule 10b–5 thereunder.

First, . . . we provide that a duty of trust or confidence exists whenever a person agrees to maintain information in confidence.

Second, we provide that a duty of trust or confidence exists when two people have a history, pattern, or practice of sharing confidences such that the recipient of the information knows or reasonably should know that the person communicating the material nonpublic information expects that the recipient will maintain its confidentiality. This is a "facts and circumstances" test based on the expectation of the parties in light of the overall relationship. Some commenters were concerned that, as proposed, this provision examined the reasonable expectation of confidentiality of the person communicating the material nonpublic information rather than examining the expectations of the recipient of the information and/or both parties to the communication. . . . [W]e have revised the provision to make this mutuality explicit. . . .

Third, we are adopting as proposed a bright-line rule that states that a duty of trust or confidence exists when a person receives or obtains material nonpublic information from certain enumerated close family members: spouses, parents, children, and siblings. An affirmative defense permits the person receiving or obtaining the information to demonstrate that under the facts and circumstances of that family relationship, no duty of trust or confidence existed. . . .

SEC, Selective Disclosure and Insider Trading, Securities Act Rel. No. 7881 (August 15, 2000).

Assume in *O'Hagan* that Bill "hacked" into Dorsey Whitney's computer system and as a result learned of the forthcoming bid for Pillsbury. On the basis of this purloined information Bill purchased a significant number of Pillsbury shares. Is Bill's conduct proscribed by Rule 10b–5? Rule 14 e–3? In resolving these questions should it matter whether Bill, in order to circumvent the law firm's encryption system, "planted" in the system a false password within the system and then used that password to access Dorsey Whitney files? See Securities and Exchange Commission v. Dorozhko, 574 F.3d 42 (2nd Cir. 2009).

Finally, consider the social implications of premising federal regulation of inside trading on the private relations of trust and confidence between the creator/owner of the nonpublic information and the person that trades on that information. Observe that under *O'Hagan* the wrongfulness of the defendant's act does not turn on any social harm to markets or investors generally, but rather on the harm to the party from who the confidential information was obtained. Does this run the risk that such a privatized view of why and how inside trading is regulated will lead to our more broadly based concerns for preserving the integrity of fair and efficient capital markets to be subordinated to the vagaries of private arrangements. For example, after *Chiarella* and *O'Hagan* could an oil company, in order to incent the firm's geologists, permit all its geologists to trade in the firm's stock on the basis of any information they obtain through their employment position? *See generally* James D. Cox, Insider Trading And Contracting: A Critical Response To The "Chicago School," 1986 Duke L. J. 628, 653–659. A related issue is the enforceability of so-called "big boy" letters where the privately negotiated contract for the purchase-sale of securities expressly provides that the selling (buying) party might be in possession of material nonpublic information that is not disclosed to the other party and the parties agree to this condition. *See* Edwin D. Eshmoili, Note, Big boy Letters: Trading On Inside Information, 94 Cornell L. Rev. 133 (2008). To what extent are such private licensing and waiver efforts effective under Rule 14e–3?

For a thoughtful review of how the experiences as a practitioner influenced Justice Powell, the author of the majority opinions in *Chiarella and Dirks,* in his many decisions constricting the scope Rule 10b–5, *see* A.C. Pritchard, Justice Lewis F. Powell, Jr., And The Counterrevolution In the Federal Securities Laws, 52 Duke L.J. 841 (2003).

———

SEC RULE 10b5–2

[See Statutory Supplement]

———

Dirks v. Securities and Exchange Commission

Supreme Court of the United States, 1983.
463 U.S. 646, 103 S.Ct. 3255, 77 L.Ed.2d 911.

■ JUSTICE POWELL delivered the opinion of the Court.

Petitioner Raymond Dirks received material nonpublic information from "insiders" of a corporation with which he had no connection. He disclosed this information to investors who relied on it in trading in the shares of the corporation. The question is whether Dirks violated the antifraud provisions of the federal securities laws by this disclosure.

I

In 1973, Dirks was an officer of a New York broker-dealer firm who specialized in providing investment analysis of insurance company securities to institutional investors. On March 6, Dirks received information from Ronald Secrist, a former officer of Equity Funding of America. Secrist alleged that the assets of Equity Funding, a diversified corporation primarily engaged in selling life insurance and mutual funds, were vastly overstated as the result of fraudulent corporate practices. Secrist also stated that various regulatory agencies had failed to act on similar charges made by Equity Funding employees. He urged Dirks to verify the fraud and disclose it publicly.

Dirks decided to investigate the allegations. He visited Equity Funding's headquarters in Los Angeles and interviewed several officers and employees of the corporation. The senior management denied any wrongdoing, but certain corporation employees corroborated the charges of fraud. Neither Dirks nor his firm owned or traded any Equity Funding stock, but throughout his investigation he openly discussed the information he had obtained with a number of clients and investors. Some of these persons sold their holdings of Equity Funding securities, including five investment advisers who liquidated holdings of more than $16 million.[2]

While Dirks was in Los Angeles, he was in touch regularly with William Blundell, the Wall Street Journal's Los Angeles bureau chief. Dirks urged Blundell to write a story on the fraud allegations. Blundell did not believe, however, that such a massive fraud could go undetected and declined to write the story. He feared that publishing such damaging hearsay might be libelous.

During the two-week period in which Dirks pursued his investigation and spread word of Secrist's charges, the price of Equity Funding stock fell from $26 per share to less than $15 per share. This led the New York Stock Exchange to halt trading on March 27. Shortly thereafter California insurance authorities impounded Equity Funding's records and uncovered evidence of the fraud. Only then did the Securities and Exchange Commission (SEC) file a complaint against Equity Funding[3] and only then, on April 2, did the Wall Street Journal publish a front-page story based largely on information assembled by Dirks. Equity Funding immediately went into receivership.[4]

The SEC began an investigation into Dirks' role in the exposure of the fraud. After a hearing by an administrative law judge, the SEC found

---

[2] Dirks received from his firm a salary plus a commission for securities transactions above a certain amount that his clients directed through his firm. See 21 S.E.C. Docket, at 1402, n. 3. But "[i]t is not clear how many of those with whom Dirks spoke promised to direct some brokerage business through [Dirks' firm] to compensate Dirks, or how many actually did so." 220 U.S.App.D.C., at 316, 681 F.2d, at 831. The Boston Company Institutional Investors, Inc., promised Dirks about $25,000 in commissions, but it is unclear whether Boston actually generated any brokerage business for his firm. See App. 199, 204–205; 21 S.E.C. Docket, at 1404, n. 10; 220 U.S.App.D.C., at 316, n. 5, 681 F.2d, at 831, n. 5.

[3] As early as 1971, the SEC had received allegations of fraudulent accounting practices at Equity Funding. Moreover, on March 9, 1973, an official of the California Insurance Department informed the SEC's regional office in Los Angeles of Secrist's charges of fraud. Dirks himself voluntarily presented his information at the SEC's regional office beginning on March 27.

[4] A federal grand jury in Los Angeles subsequently returned a 105-count indictment against 22 persons, including many of Equity Funding's officers and directors. All defendants were found guilty of one or more counts, either by a plea of guilty or a conviction after trial. See Brief for Petitioner 15; App. 149–153.

that Dirks had aided and abetted violations of § 17(a) of the Securities Act of 1933 . . . § 10(b) of the Securities Exchange Act of 1934 . . . and SEC Rule 10b–5 . . . by repeating the allegations of fraud to members of the investment community who later sold their Equity Funding stock. The SEC concluded: "Where 'tippees'—regardless of their motivation or occupation—come into possession of material 'information that they know is confidential and know or should know came from a corporate insider,' they must either publicly disclose that information or refrain from trading." 21 S.E.C. Docket 1401, 1407 (1981) (footnote omitted) (quoting Chiarella v. United States, 445 U.S. 222, 230 n. 12, 100 S.Ct. 1108, 1115 n. 12, 63 L.Ed.2d 348 (1980)). Recognizing, however, that Dirks "played an important role in bringing [Equity Funding's] massive fraud to light," 21 S.E.C. Docket, at 1412, the SEC only censured him.

Dirks sought review in the Court of Appeals for the District of Columbia Circuit. The court entered judgment against Dirks. . . .

In view of the importance to the SEC and to the securities industry of the question presented by this case, we granted a writ of certiorari. 459 U.S. 1014 . . . (1982). We now reverse.

II

In the seminal case of In re Cady, Roberts & Co., 40 S.E.C. 907 (1961), the SEC recognized that the common law in some jurisdictions imposes on "corporate 'insiders,' particularly officers, directors, or controlling stockholders" an "affirmative duty of disclosure . . . when dealing in securities." Id., at 911, and n. 13.[10] The SEC found that not only did breach of this common-law duty also establish the elements of a Rule 10b–5 violation, but that individuals other than corporate insiders could be obligated either to disclose material non-public information before trading or to abstain from trading altogether. Id., at 912. In *Chiarella,* we accepted the two elements set out in *Cady, Roberts* for establishing a Rule 10b–5 violation: "(i) the existence of a relationship affording access to inside information intended to be available only for a corporate purpose, and (ii) the unfairness of allowing a corporate insider to take advantage of that information by trading without disclosure." 445 U.S., at 227. . . . In examining whether Chiarella had an obligation to disclose or abstain, the Court found that there is no general duty to disclose before trading on material nonpublic information, and held that "a duty to disclose under § 10(b) does not arise from the mere possession of nonpublic market information." Id., at 235. . . . Such a duty arises rather from the existence of a fiduciary relationship. See id., at 227–235. . . .

---

[10]   The duty that insiders owe to the corporation's shareholders not to trade on inside information differs from the common-law duty that officers and directors also have to the corporation itself not to mismanage corporate assets, of which confidential information is one. . . . In holding that breaches of this duty to shareholders violated the Securities Exchange Act, the *Cady, Roberts* Commission recognized, and we agree, that "[a] significant purpose of the Exchange Act was to eliminate the idea that use of inside information for personal advantage was a normal emolument of corporate office." See 40 S.E.C., at 912, n. 15.

Not "all breaches of fiduciary duty in connection with a securities transaction," however, come within the ambit of Rule 10b–5. Santa Fe Industries, Inc. v. Green, 430 U.S. 462, 472 . . . (1977). There must also be "manipulation or deception." Id., at 473, 97 S.Ct., at 1300. In an inside-trading case this fraud derives from the "inherent unfairness involved where one takes advantage" of "information intended to be available only for a corporate purpose and not for the personal benefit of anyone." In re Merrill Lynch, Pierce, Fenner & Smith, Inc., 43 S.E.C. 933, 936 (1968). Thus, an insider will be liable under Rule 10b–5 for inside trading only where he fails to disclose material nonpublic information before trading on it and thus makes "secret profits." Cady, Roberts, 40 S.E.C., at 916, n. 31.

<h1 style="text-align:center">III</h1>

We were explicit in Chiarella in saying that there can be no duty to disclose where the person who has traded on inside information "was not [the corporation's] agent, . . . was not a fiduciary, [or] was not a person in whom the sellers [of the securities] had placed their trust and confidence." 445 U.S., at 232. . . . Not to require such a fiduciary relationship, we recognized, would "depar[t] radically from the established doctrine that duty arises from a specific relationship between two parties" and would amount to "recognizing a general duty between all participants in market transactions to forgo actions based on material, nonpublic information." Id., at 232, 233. . . . This requirement of a specific relationship between the shareholders and the individual trading on inside information has created analytical difficulties for the SEC and courts in policing tippees who trade on inside information. Unlike insiders who have independent fiduciary duties to both the corporation and its shareholders, the typical tippee has no such relationships.[14] In view of this absence, it has been unclear how a tippee acquires the Cady, Roberts duty to refrain from trading on inside information. . . .

---

[14] Under certain circumstances, such as where corporate information is revealed legitimately to an underwriter, accountant, lawyer, or consultant working for the corporation, these outsiders may become fiduciaries of the shareholders. The basis for recognizing this fiduciary duty is not simply that such persons acquired nonpublic corporate information, but rather that they have entered into a special confidential relationship in the conduct of the business of the enterprise and are given access to information solely for corporate purposes. See SEC v. Monarch Fund, 608 F.2d 938, 942 (C.A.2 1979); In re Investors Management Co., 44 S.E.C. 633, 645 (1971); In re Van Alystne, Noel & Co., 43 S.E.C. 1080, 1084–1085 (1969); In re Merrill Lynch, Pierce, Fenner & Smith, Inc., 43 S.E.C. 933, 937 (1968); Cady, Roberts, 40 S.E.C., at 912. When such a person breaches his fiduciary relationship, he may be treated more properly as a tipper than a tippee. See Shapiro v. Merrill Lynch, Pierce, Fenner & Smith, Inc., 495 F.2d 228, 237 (C.A.2 1974) (investment banker had access to material information when working on a proposed public offering for the corporation). For such a duty to be imposed, however, the corporation must expect the outsider to keep the disclosed nonpublic information confidential, and the relationship at least must imply such a duty.

A

The SEC's position, as stated in its opinion in this case, is that a tippee "inherits" the *Cady, Roberts* obligation to shareholders whenever he receives inside information from an insider . . .

. . . This [position] conflicts with the principle set forth in *Chiarella* that only some persons, under some circumstances, will be barred from trading while in possession of material nonpublic information. . . . See *Chiarella,* 445 U.S., at 235, n. 20. . . . We reaffirm today that "[a] duty [to disclose] arises from the relationship between parties . . . and not merely from one's ability to acquire information because of his position in the market." [Chiarella,] 445 U.S., at 232–233, n. 14. . . .

Imposing a duty to disclose or abstain solely because a person knowingly receives material nonpublic information from an insider and trades on it could have an inhibiting influence on the role of market analysts, which the SEC itself recognizes is necessary to the preservation of a healthy market. It is commonplace for analysts to "ferret out and analyze information," 21 S.E.C., at 1406,[18] and this often is done by meeting with and questioning corporate officers and others who are insiders. And information that the analysts obtain normally may be the basis for judgments as to the market worth of a corporation's securities. The analyst's judgment in this respect is made available in market letters or otherwise to clients of the firm. It is the nature of this type of information, and indeed of the markets themselves, that such information cannot be made simultaneously available to all of the corporation's stockholders or the public generally.

B

The conclusion that recipients of inside information do not invariably acquire a duty to disclose or abstain does not mean that such tippees always are free to trade on the information. The need for a ban on some tippee trading is clear. Not only are insiders forbidden by their fiduciary relationship from personally using undisclosed corporate information to their advantage, but they may not give such information to an outsider for the same improper purpose of exploiting the information for their personal gain. See 15 U.S.C. § 78t(b) (making it unlawful to do indirectly "by means of any other person" any act made unlawful by the federal securities laws). Similarly, the transactions of

---

[18] On its facts, this case is the unusual one. Dirks is an analyst in a broker-dealer firm, and he did interview management in the course of his investigation. He uncovered, however, startling information that required no analysis or exercise of judgment as to its market relevance. Nonetheless, the principle at issue here extends beyond these facts. The SEC's rule—applicable without regard to any breach by an insider—could have serious ramifications on reporting by analysts of investment views.

Despite the unusualness of Dirks' "find," the central role that he played in uncovering the fraud at Equity Funding, and that analysts in general can play in revealing information that corporations may have reason to withhold from the public, is an important one. Dirks' careful investigation brought to light a massive fraud at the corporation. And until the Equity Funding fraud was exposed, the information in the trading market was grossly inaccurate. But for Dirks' efforts, the fraud might well have gone undetected longer. See n. 8, supra.

those who knowingly participate with the fiduciary in such a breach are "as forbidden" as transactions "on behalf of the trustee himself." Mosser v. Darrow, 341 U.S. 267, 272. . . . As the Court explained in *Mosser,* a contrary rule "would open up opportunities for devious dealings in the name of the others that the trustee could not conduct in his own." 341 U.S., at 271. . . . See SEC v. Texas Gulf Sulphur Co., 446 F.2d 1301, 1308 (CA2), cert. denied, 404 U.S. 1005, 92 S.Ct. 561, 30 L.Ed.2d 558 (1971). Thus, the tippee's duty to disclose or abstain is derivative from that of the insider's duty. See Tr. of Oral Arg. 38. Cf. *Chiarella,* 445 U.S., at 246, n. 1 . . . (Blackmun, J., dissenting). As we noted in *Chiarella,* "[t]he tippee's obligation has been viewed as arising from his role as a participant after the fact in the insider's breach of a fiduciary duty." 445 U.S., at 230, n. 12. . . .

Thus, some tippees must assume an insider's duty to the shareholders not because they receive inside information, but rather because it has been made available to them *improperly.* And for Rule 10b–5 purposes, the insider's disclosure is improper only where it would violate his *Cady, Roberts* duty. Thus, a tippee assumes a fiduciary duty to the shareholders of a corporation not to trade on material nonpublic information only when the insider has breached his fiduciary duty to the shareholders by disclosing the information to the tippee and the tippee knows or should know that there has been a breach. As Commissioner Smith perceptively observed in *Investors Management Co.:* "[T]ippee responsibility must be related back to insider responsibility by a necessary finding that the tippee knew the information was given to him in breach of a duty by a person having a special relationship to the issuer not to disclose the information. . . . " 44 S.E.C., at 651 (concurring in the result). Tipping thus properly is viewed only as a means of indirectly violating the *Cady, Roberts* disclose-or-abstain rule.

C

In determining whether a tippee is under an obligation to disclose or abstain, it thus is necessary to determine whether the insider's "tip" constituted a breach of the insider's fiduciary duty. All disclosures of confidential corporate information are not inconsistent with the duty insiders owe to shareholders. In contrast to the extraordinary facts of this case, the more typical situation in which there will be a question whether disclosure violates the insider's *Cady, Roberts* duty is when insiders disclose information to analysts. See n. 16, supra. In some situations, the insider will act consistently with his fiduciary duty to shareholders, and yet release of the information may affect the market. For example, it may not be clear—either to the corporate insider or to the recipient analyst—whether the information will be viewed as material nonpublic information. Corporate officials may mistakenly think the information already has been disclosed or that it is not material enough to affect the market. Whether disclosure is a breach of duty therefore depends in large part on the purpose of the disclosure. This standard was identified by the

SEC itself in *Cady, Roberts:* a purpose of the securities laws was to eliminate "use of inside information for personal advantage." 40 S.E.C., at 912, n. 15. See n. 10, *supra.* Thus, the test is whether the insider personally will benefit, directly or indirectly, from his disclosure. Absent some personal gain, there has been no breach of duty to stockholders. And absent a breach by the insider, there is no derivative breach. As Commissioner Smith stated in *Investors Management Co.* "It is important in this type of case to focus on policing insiders and what they do . . . rather than on policing information *per se* and its possession. . . . " 44 S.E.C., at 648 (concurring in the result).

The SEC argues that, if inside-trading liability does not exist when the information is transmitted for a proper purpose but is used for trading, it would be a rare situation when the parties could not fabricate some ostensibly legitimate business justification for transmitting the information. We think the SEC is unduly concerned. In determining whether the insider's purpose in making a particular disclosure is fraudulent, the SEC and the courts are not required to read the parties' minds. Scienter in some cases is relevant in determining whether the tipper has violated his *Cady, Roberts* duty. But to determine whether the disclosure itself "deceive[s], manipulate[s], or defraud[s]" shareholders, Aaron v. SEC, 446 U.S. 680, 686 . . . (1980), the initial inquiry is whether there has been a breach of duty by the insider. This requires courts to focus on objective criteria, i.e., whether the insider receives a direct or indirect personal benefit from the disclosure, such as a pecuniary gain or a reputational benefit that will translate into future earnings. Cf. 40 S.E.C., at 912, n. 15; Brudney, Insiders, Outsiders, and Informational Advantages Under the Federal Securities Laws, 93 Harv.L.Rev. 324, 348 (1979) ("The theory . . . is that the insider, by giving the information out selectively, is in effect selling the information to its recipient for cash, reciprocal information, or other things of value for himself . . . "). There are objective facts and circumstances that often justify such an inference. For example, there may be a relationship between the insider and the recipient that suggests a *quid pro quo* from the latter, or an intention to benefit the particular recipient. The elements of fiduciary duty and exploitation of nonpublic information also exist when an insider makes a gift of confidential information to a trading relative or friend. The tip and trade resemble trading by the insider himself followed by a gift of the profits to the recipient.

Determining whether an insider personally benefits from a particular disclosure, a question of fact, will not always be easy for courts. But it is essential, we think, to have a guiding principle for those whose daily activities must be limited and instructed by the SEC's inside-trading rules, and we believe that there must be a breach of the insider's fiduciary duty before the tippee inherits the duty to disclose or abstain. In contrast, the rule adopted by the SEC in this case would have no limiting principle.

IV

Under the inside-trading and tipping rules set forth above, we find that there was no actionable violation by Dirks. It is undisputed that Dirks himself was a stranger to Equity Funding, with no pre-existing fiduciary duty to its shareholders. He took no action, directly or indirectly, that induced the shareholders or officers of Equity Funding to repose trust or confidence in him. There was no expectation by Dirks' sources that he would keep their information in confidence. Nor did Dirks misappropriate or illegally obtain the information about Equity Funding. Unless the insiders breached their *Cady, Roberts* duty to shareholders in disclosing the nonpublic information to Dirks, he breached no duty when he passed it on to investors as well as to the Wall Street Journal.

It is clear that neither Secrist nor the other Equity Funding employees violated their *Cady, Roberts* duty to the corporation's shareholders by providing information to Dirks. The tippers received no monetary or personal benefit for revealing Equity Funding's secrets, nor was their purpose to make a gift of valuable information to Dirks. As the facts of this case clearly indicate, the tippers were motivated by a desire to expose the fraud. . . . In the absence of a breach of duty to shareholders by the insiders, there was no derivative breach by Dirks. See n. 20, supra. Dirks therefore could not have been "a participant after the fact in [an] insider's breach of a fiduciary duty." *Chiarella,* 445 U.S., at 230, n. 12. . . .

V

We conclude that Dirks, in the circumstances of this case, had no duty to abstain from use of the inside information that he obtained. The judgment of the Court of Appeals therefore is reversed.

■ JUSTICE BLACKMUN, with whom JUSTICE BRENNAN and JUSTICE MARSHALL join, dissenting.

The Court today takes still another step to limit the protections provided investors by § 10(b) of the Securities Exchange Act of 1934. . . . The device employed in this case engrafts a special motivational requirement on the fiduciary duty doctrine. This innovation excuses a knowing and intentional violation of an insider's duty to shareholders if the insider does not act from a motive of personal gain. Even on the extraordinary facts of this case, such an innovation is not justified.

I

As the Court recognizes, . . . the facts here are unusual. After a meeting with Ronald Secrist, a former Equity Funding employee, on March 7, 1973, App. 226, petitioner Raymond Dirks found himself in possession of material nonpublic information of massive fraud within the company.[2] In the Court's words, "[h]e uncovered . . . startling information

---

[2] Unknown to Dirks, Secrist also told his story to New York insurance regulators the same day. App. 23. They immediately assured themselves that Equity Funding's New York subsidiary had sufficient assets to cover its outstanding policies and then passed on the information to California regulators who in turn informed Illinois regulators. Illinois

that required no analysis or exercise of judgment as to its market relevance." . . . In disclosing that information to Dirks, Secrist intended that Dirks would disseminate the information to his clients, those clients would unload their Equity Funding securities on the market, and the price would fall precipitously, thereby triggering a reaction from the authorities. App. 16, 25, 27.

Dirks complied with his informant's wishes. Instead of reporting that information to the Securities and Exchange Commission (SEC or Commission) or to other regulatory agencies, Dirks began to disseminate the information to his clients and undertook his own investigation. One of his first steps was to direct his associates at Delafield Childs to draw up a list of Delafield clients holding Equity Funding securities. On March 12, eight days before Dirks flew to Los Angeles to investigate Secrist's story, he reported the full allegations to Boston Company Institutional Investors, Inc., which on March 15 and 16 sold approximately $1.2 million of Equity securities.[4] See id., at 199. As he gathered more information, he selectively disclosed it to his clients. To those holding Equity Funding securities he gave the "hard" story—all the allegations; others received the "soft" story—a recitation of vague factors that might reflect adversely on Equity Funding's management. See id., at 211, n. 24.

Dirks' attempts to disseminate the information to nonclients were feeble, at best. On March 12, he left a message for Herbert Lawson, the San Francisco bureau chief of The Wall Street Journal. Not until March 19 and 20 did he call Lawson again, and outline the situation. William Blundell, a Journal investigative reporter based in Los Angeles, got in touch with Dirks about his March 20 telephone call. On March 21, Dirks met with Blundell in Los Angeles. Blundell began his own investigation, relying in part on Dirks' contacts, and on March 23 telephoned Stanley Sporkin, the SEC's Deputy Director of Enforcement. On March 26, the next business day, Sporkin and his staff interviewed Blundell and asked to see Dirks the following morning. Trading was halted by the New York Stock Exchange at about the same time Dirks was talking to Los Angeles SEC personnel. The next day, March 28, the SEC suspended trading in Equity Funding securities. By that time, Dirks' clients had unloaded close to $15 million of Equity Funding stock and the price had plummeted from $26 to $15. The effect of Dirks' selective dissemination of Secrist's information was that Dirks' clients were able to shift the losses that were

---

investigators, later joined by California officials, conducted a surprise audit of Equity Funding's Illinois subsidiary, id., at 87–88, to find $22 million of the subsidiary's assets missing. On March 30, these authorities seized control of the Illinois subsidiary. Id., at 271.

[4] The Court's implicit suggestion that Dirks did not gain by this selective dissemination of advice, ante, at . . . n. 2, is inaccurate. The [Administrative Law Judge] found that because of Dirks' information, Boston Company Institutional Investors, Inc., directed business to Delafield Childs that generated approximately $25,000 in commissions. App. 199, 204–205. While it is true that the exact economic benefit gained by Delafield Childs due to Dirks' activities is unknowable because of the structure of compensation in the securities market, there can be no doubt that Delafield and Dirks gained both monetary rewards and enhanced reputations for "looking after" their clients.

inevitable due to the Equity Funding fraud from themselves to uninformed market participants.

II

A

No one questions that Secrist himself could not trade on his inside information to the disadvantage of uninformed shareholders and purchasers of Equity Funding securities. See Brief for United States as *Amicus Curiae* 19, n. 12. Unlike the printer in *Chiarella,* Secrist stood in a fiduciary relationship with these shareholders. . . .

The Court also acknowledges that Secrist could not do by proxy what he was prohibited from doing personally. . . . Mosser v. Darrow, 341 U.S. 267, 272 . . . (1951). But this is precisely what Secrist did. Secrist used Dirks to disseminate information to Dirks' clients, who in turn dumped stock on unknowing purchasers. Secrist thus intended Dirks to injure the purchasers of Equity Funding securities to whom Secrist had a duty to disclose. Accepting the Court's view of tippee liability,[5] it appears that Dirks' knowledge of this breach makes him liable as a participant in the breach after the fact. . . . ; *Chiarella,* 445 U.S., at 230, n. 12. . . .

B

The Court holds, however, that Dirks is not liable because Secrist did not violate his duty; according to the Court, this is so because Secrist did not have the improper purpose of personal gain. . . . In so doing, the Court imposes a new, subjective limitation on the scope of the duty owed by insiders to shareholders. The novelty of this limitation is reflected in the Court's lack of support for it. . . .

C

The fact that the insider himself does not benefit from the breach does not eradicate the shareholder's injury. Cf. Restatement (Second) of Trusts § 205, Comments c and d (1959) (trustee liable for acts causing diminution of value of trust); 3 A. Scott on Trusts § 205, p. 1665 (1967) (trustee liable for any losses to trust caused by his breach). It makes no difference to the shareholder whether the corporate insider gained or intended to gain personally from the transaction; the shareholder still has lost because of the insider's misuse of nonpublic information. The duty is addressed not to the insider's motives, but to his actions and their consequences on the shareholder. Personal gain is not an element of the breach of this duty.[11] . . .

---

[5] I interpret the Court's opinion to impose liability on tippees like Dirks when the tippee knows or has reason to know that the information is material and nonpublic and was obtained through a breach of duty by selective revelation or otherwise. See In re Investors Management Co., 44 S.E.C. 633, 641 (1971).

[11] The Court seems concerned that this case bears on insiders' contacts with analysts for valid corporate reasons. . . . When the disclosure is to an investment banker or some other adviser, however, there is normally no breach because the insider does not have scienter: he does not intend that the inside information be used for trading purposes to the disadvantage of shareholders. . . .

Although Secrist's general motive to expose the Equity Funding fraud was laudable, the means he chose were not. Moreover, even assuming that Dirks played a substantial role in exposing the fraud,[15] he and his clients should not profit from the information they obtained from Secrist. . . .

IV

In my view, Secrist violated his duty to Equity Funding shareholders by transmitting material nonpublic information to Dirks with the intention that Dirks would cause his clients to trade on that information. Dirks, therefore, was under a duty to make the information publicly available or to refrain from actions that he knew would lead to trading. Because Dirks caused his clients to trade, he violated § 10(b) and Rule 10b–5. Any other result is a disservice to this country's attempt to provide fair and efficient capital markets. I dissent.

———

Scienter is an obvious requirement for establishing a violation of the antifraud provision as a tippee. But what does scienter require the tippee know? In *United States v. Newman*, 773 F.3d 438 (2nd Cir. 2014), the Second Circuit reversed the convictions of two portfolio managers who traded on the basis of material non-public information they received indirectly from company insiders. The Second Circuit held:

> [T]o sustain an insider trading conviction against a tippee, the Government must prove each of the following elements beyond a reasonable doubt: that (1) the corporate insider was entrusted with a fiduciary duty; (2) the corporate insider breached his fiduciary duty by (a) disclosing confidential information to a tippee (b) in exchange for a personal benefit; (3) the tippee knew of the tipper's breach, that is, he knew the information was confidential and divulged for personal benefit; and (4) the tippee still used that information to trade in a security or tip another individual for personal benefit.

773 F. 3d at 450. The Second Circuit reversed the defendants' convictions because the district court did not instruct the jury that the defendants must know that the insider disclosed the confidential information in exchange for a personal benefit. This was widely seen, at least among prosecutors, as imposing an insurmountable burden in prosecuting tippees, especially those who are two or even three steps removed from the insider who initiated the selective disclosure.

The situation here, of course, is radically different. . . . Secrist divulged the information for the precise purpose of causing Dirks' clients to trade on it. I fail to understand how imposing liability on Dirks will affect legitimate insider-analyst contacts.

[15]   The Court uncritically accepts Dirks' own view of his role in uncovering the Equity Funding fraud. . . . It ignores the fact that Secrist gave the same information at the same time to state insurance regulators, who proceeded to expose massive fraud in a major Equity Funding subsidiary. The fraud surfaced before Dirks ever spoke to the SEC.

––––––

Salman v. United States

Supreme Court of the United States, 2016.
___ U.S. ___, 137 S.Ct. 420, 196 L.Ed.2d 351.

■ JUSTICE ALITO delivered the opinion of the Court.

Section 10(b) of the Securities Exchange Act of 1934 and the Securities and Exchange Commission's Rule 10b–5 prohibit undisclosed trading on inside corporate information by individuals who are under a duty of trust and confidence that prohibits them from secretly using such information for their personal advantage. . . . Individuals under this duty may face criminal and civil liability for trading on inside information (unless they make appropriate disclosures ahead of time).

These persons also may not tip inside information to others for trading. The tippee acquires the tipper's duty to disclose or abstain from trading if the tippee knows the information was disclosed in breach of the tipper's duty, and the tippee may commit securities fraud by trading in disregard of that knowledge. In *Dirks* v. *SEC*, 463 U.S. 646 . . . , this Court explained that a tippee's liability for trading on inside information hinges on whether the tipper breached a fiduciary duty by disclosing the information. A tipper breaches such a fiduciary duty, we held, when the tipper discloses the inside information for a personal benefit. And, we went on to say, a jury can infer a personal benefit—and thus a breach of the tipper's duty—where the tipper receives something of value in exchange for the tip or "makes a gift of confidential information to a trading relative or friend." *Id.,* at 664. . . .

I

Maher Kara was an investment banker in Citigroup's healthcare investment banking group. He dealt with highly confidential information about mergers and acquisitions involving Citigroup's clients. Maher enjoyed a close relationship with his older brother, Mounir Kara (known as Michael). After Maher started at Citigroup, he began discussing aspects of his job with Michael. At first he relied on Michael's chemistry background to help him grasp scientific concepts relevant to his new job. Then, while their father was battling cancer, the brothers discussed companies that dealt with innovative cancer treatment and pain management techniques. Michael began to trade on the information Maher shared with him. At first, Maher was unaware of his brother's trading activity, but eventually he began to suspect that it was taking place.

Ultimately, Maher began to assist Michael's trading by sharing inside information with his brother about pending mergers and acquisitions. Maher sometimes used code words to communicate corporate information to his brother. Other times, he shared inside information about deals he was not working on in order to avoid detection. . . . Without his younger brother's knowledge, Michael fed the information to others—including [Bassam] Salman, Michael's friend and Maher's brother-in-law. By the time the authorities caught on, Salman had made over $1.5 million in profits that he split with another relative who executed trades via a brokerage account on Salman's behalf.

Salman was indicted on one count of conspiracy to commit securities fraud, see 18 U.S.C. § 371, and four counts of securities fraud, see 15 U.S.C. §§ 78j(b) . . . [and] 17 CFR § 240.10b–5. Facing charges of their own, both Maher and Michael pleaded guilty and testified at Salman's trial.

The evidence at trial established that Maher and Michael enjoyed a "very close relationship." . . . Maher testified that he shared inside information with his brother to benefit him and with the expectation that his brother would trade on it. While Maher explained that he disclosed the information in large part to appease Michael (who pestered him incessantly for it), he also testified that he tipped his brother to "help him" and to "fulfil[l] whatever needs he had." . . . For instance, Michael once called Maher and told him that "he needed a favor." . . . Maher offered his brother money but Michael asked for information instead. Maher then disclosed an upcoming acquisition. *Ibid.* Although he instantly regretted the tip and called his brother back to implore him not to trade, Maher expected his brother to do so anyway. . . .

Michael testified that he became friends with Salman when Maher was courting Salman's sister and later began sharing Maher's tips with Salman. As he explained at trial, "any time a major deal came in, [Salman] was the first on my phone list." *Id.*, at 258. Michael also testified that he told Salman that the information was coming from Maher. . . .

After a jury trial in the Northern District of California, Salman was convicted on all counts. He was sentenced to 36 months of imprisonment, three years of supervised release, and over $730,000 in restitution. . . . Salman appealed to the Ninth Circuit. While his appeal was pending, the Second Circuit issued its opinion in *United States* v. *Newman*, 773 F.3d 438 (2014), cert. denied, 577 U.S. ___, 136 S. Ct. 242, 193 L. Ed. 2d 133 (2015). There, the Second Circuit reversed the convictions of two portfolio managers who traded on inside information. The *Newman* defendants were "several steps removed from the corporate insiders" and the court found that "there was no evidence that either was aware of the source of the inside information." 773 F.3d, at 443. The court acknowledged that *Dirks* and Second Circuit case law allow a factfinder to infer a personal benefit to the tipper from a gift of confidential information to a trading relative or friend. 773 F.3d, at 452. But the court concluded that, "[t]o the extent" *Dirks* permits "such an inference," the inference "is impermissible in the absence of proof of a meaningfully close personal relationship that generates an exchange that is objective, consequential, and represents at least a potential gain of a pecuniary or similarly valuable nature." 773 F.3d, at 452.[1]

Pointing to *Newman*, Salman argued that his conviction should be reversed. While the evidence established that Maher made a gift of trading information to Michael and that Salman knew it, there was no evidence that Maher received anything of "a pecuniary or similarly valuable nature" in exchange—or that Salman knew of any such benefit. The Ninth Circuit disagreed and affirmed Salman's conviction. 792 F.3d 1087. The court reasoned that the case was governed by *Dirks*'s holding that a tipper benefits personally by making a gift of confidential information to a trading relative or friend. . . .

We granted certiorari to resolve the tension between the Second Circuit's *Newman* decision and the Ninth Circuit's decision in this case.[2] . . .

II

A

In this case, Salman contends that an insider's "gift of confidential information to a trading relative or friend," *Dirks*, 463 U.S., at 664, 103 S. Ct. 3255, 77 L. Ed. 2d 911, is not enough to establish securities fraud. Instead, Salman argues, a tipper does not personally benefit unless the tipper's goal in disclosing inside information is to obtain money, property, or something of tangible value. . . . Salman contends that gift situations create especially troubling problems for remote tippees—that is, tippees who receive inside information from another tippee, rather than the tipper—who may have no knowledge of the relationship between the original tipper and tippee and thus may not know why the tipper made the disclosure. . . .

The Government disagrees and argues that a gift of confidential information to anyone, not just a "trading relative or friend," is enough to prove securities fraud. . . . Under the Government's view, a tipper

---

[1] The Second Circuit also reversed the *Newman* defendants' convictions because the Government introduced no evidence that the defendants knew the information they traded on came from insiders or that the insiders received a personal benefit in exchange for the tips. 773 F.3d, at 453–454. This case does not implicate those issues.

[2] *Dirks* v. *SEC*, 463 U.S. 646, 103 S. Ct. 3255, 77 L. Ed. 2d 911 (1983), established the personal-benefit framework in a case brought under the classical theory of insider-trading liability, which applies "when a corporate insider" or his tippee "trades in the securities of [the tipper's] corporation on the basis of material, nonpublic information." *United States* v. *O'Hagan*, 521 U.S. 642, 651–652, 117 S. Ct. 2199, 138 L. Ed. 2d 724 (1997). In such a case, the defendant breaches a duty to, and takes advantage of, the shareholders of his corporation. By contrast, the misappropriation theory holds that a person commits securities fraud "when he misappropriates confidential information for securities trading purposes, in breach of a duty owed to the source of the information" such as an employer or client. *Id.,* at 652, 117 S. Ct. 2199, 138 L. Ed. 2d 724. In such a case, the defendant breaches a duty to, and defrauds, the source of the information, as opposed to the shareholders of his corporation. The Court of Appeals observed that this is a misappropriation case, 792 F.3d, 1087, 1092, n. 4 (CA9 2015), while the Government represents that both theories apply on the facts of this case, Brief for United States 15, n. 1. We need not resolve the question. The parties do not dispute that *Dirks*'s personal-benefit analysis applies in both classical and misappropriation cases, so we will proceed on the assumption that it does.

personally benefits whenever the tipper discloses confidential trading information for a noncorporate purpose. Accordingly, a gift to a friend, a family member, or anyone else would support the inference that the tipper exploited the trading value of inside information for personal purposes and thus personally benefited from the disclosure. . . .

The Government also argues that Salman's concerns about unlimited and indeterminate liability for remote tippees are significantly alleviated by other statutory elements that prosecutors must satisfy to convict a tippee for insider trading. The Government observes that, in order to establish a defendant's criminal liability as a tippee, it must prove beyond a reasonable doubt that the tipper expected that the information being disclosed would be used in securities trading. . . . The Government also notes that, to establish a defendant's criminal liability as a tippee, it must prove that the tippee knew that the tipper breached a duty—in other words, that the tippee knew that the tipper disclosed the information for a personal benefit and that the tipper expected trading to ensue. . . .

B

We adhere to *Dirks,* which easily resolves the narrow issue presented here.

In *Dirks*, we explained that a tippee is exposed to liability for trading on inside information only if the tippee participates in a breach of the tipper's fiduciary duty. Whether the tipper breached that duty depends "in large part on the purpose of the disclosure" to the tippee. 463 U.S., at 662 . . . . "[T]he test," we explained, "is whether the insider personally will benefit, directly or indirectly, from his disclosure." *Ibid.* Thus, the disclosure of confidential information without personal benefit is not enough. In determining whether a tipper derived a personal benefit, we instructed courts to "focus on objective criteria, *i.e.,* whether the insider receives a direct or indirect personal benefit from the disclosure, such as a pecuniary gain or a reputational benefit that will translate into future earnings." *Id.,* at 663 . . . . This personal benefit can "often" be inferred "from objective facts and circumstances," we explained, such as "a relationship between the insider and the recipient that suggests a *quid pro quo* from the latter, or an intention to benefit the particular recipient." *Id.,* at 664 . . . . In particular, we held that "[t]he elements of fiduciary duty and exploitation of nonpublic information also exist *when an insider makes a gift of confidential information to a trading relative or friend*." *Ibid.* (emphasis added). In such cases, "[t]he tip and trade resemble trading by the insider followed by a gift of the profits to the recipient." *Ibid.* We then applied this gift-giving principle to resolve *Dirks* itself, finding it dispositive that the tippers "received no monetary or personal benefit" from their tips to Dirks, "*nor was their purpose to make a gift of valuable information to Dirks.*" *Id.,* at 667 . . . (emphasis added).

Our discussion of gift giving resolves this case. Maher, the tipper, provided inside information to a close relative, his brother Michael. *Dirks* makes clear that a tipper breaches a fiduciary duty by making a gift of confidential information to "a trading relative," and that rule is sufficient to resolve the case at hand. As Salman's counsel acknowledged at oral argument, Maher would have breached his duty had he personally traded on the information here himself then given the proceeds as a gift to his brother. Tr. of Oral Arg. 3–4. It is obvious that Maher would personally benefit in that situation. But Maher effectively achieved the same result by disclosing the information to Michael, and allowing him to trade on it. *Dirks* appropriately prohibits that approach, as well. . . . *Dirks* specifies that when a tipper gives inside information to "a trading relative or friend," the jury can infer that the tipper meant to provide the equivalent of a cash gift. In such situations, the tipper benefits personally because giving a gift of trading information is the same thing as trading by the tipper followed by a gift of the proceeds. Here, by disclosing confidential information as a gift to his brother with the expectation that he would trade on it, Maher breached his duty of trust and confidence to Citigroup and its clients—a duty Salman acquired, and breached himself, by trading on the information with full knowledge that it had been improperly disclosed.

To the extent the Second Circuit held that the tipper must also receive something of a "pecuniary or similarly valuable nature" in exchange for a gift to family or friends, *Newman*, 773 F.3d, at 452, we agree with the Ninth Circuit that this requirement is inconsistent with *Dirks*.

C

Salman points out that many insider-trading cases—including several that *Dirks* cited—involved insiders who personally profited through the misuse of trading information. But this observation does not undermine the test *Dirks* articulated and applied. . . . Making a gift of inside information to a relative like Michael is little different from trading on the information, obtaining the profits, and doling them out to the trading relative. The tipper benefits either way. The facts of this case illustrate the point: In one of their tipper-tippee interactions, Michael asked Maher for a favor, declined Maher's offer of money, and instead requested and received lucrative trading information.

. . .

III

Salman's jury was properly instructed that a personal benefit includes "the benefit one would obtain from simply making a gift of confidential information to a trading relative." . . . As the Court of Appeals noted, "the Government presented direct evidence that the disclosure was intended as a gift of market-sensitive information." 792 F.3d, at 1094. And, as Salman conceded below, this evidence is sufficient to sustain his conviction under our reading of *Dirks*. . . . Accordingly, the Ninth Circuit's judgment is affirmed.

It is so ordered.

SEC, Selective Disclosure and Insider Trading
Securities Act Rel. No. 7881 (August 15, 2000).

I. Executive Summary

We are adopting new rules and amendments to address the selective disclosure of material nonpublic information by issuers and to clarify two issues under the law of insider trading. In response to the comments we received on the proposal, we have made several modifications, as discussed below, in the final rules.

Regulation FD (Fair Disclosure) is a new issuer disclosure rule that addresses selective disclosure. The regulation provides that when an issuer, or person acting on its behalf, discloses material nonpublic information to certain enumerated persons (in general, securities market professionals and holders of the issuer's securities who may well trade on the basis of the information), it must make public disclosure of that information. The timing of the required public disclosure depends on whether the selective disclosure was intentional or non-intentional; for an intentional selective disclosure, the issuer must make public disclosure simultaneously; for a non-intentional disclosure, the issuer must make public disclosure promptly. Under the regulation, the required public disclosure may be made by filing or furnishing a Form 8-K, or by another method or combination of methods that is reasonably designed to effect broad, non-exclusionary distribution of the information to the public.

II. Selective Disclosure: Regulation FD

A. Background

. . . [W]e have become increasingly concerned about the selective disclosure of material information by issuers. As reflected in recent publicized reports, many issuers are disclosing important nonpublic information, such as advance warnings of earnings results, to securities analysts or selected institutional investors or both, before making full disclosure of the same information to the general public. Where this has happened, those who were privy to the information beforehand were able to make a profit or avoid a loss at the expense of those kept in the dark.

We believe that the practice of selective disclosure leads to a loss of investor confidence in the integrity of our capital markets. Investors who see a security's price change dramatically and only later are given access to the information responsible for that move rightly question whether they are on a level playing field with market insiders.

Issuer selective disclosure bears a close resemblance in this regard to ordinary "tipping" and insider trading. In both cases, a privileged few gain an informational edge—and the ability to use that edge to profit—from their superior access to corporate insiders, rather than from their skill, acumen, or diligence. Likewise, selective disclosure has an adverse impact on market integrity that is similar to the adverse impact from illegal insider trading: investors lose confidence in the fairness of the markets when they know that other participants may exploit "unerodable informational advantages" derived not from hard work or insights, but from their access to corporate insiders. The economic effects of the two practices are essentially the same. Yet, as a result of judicial interpretations, tipping and insider trading can be severely punished under the antifraud provisions of the federal securities laws, whereas the status of issuer selective disclosure has been considerably less clear.

Regulation FD is also designed to address another threat to the integrity of our markets: the potential for corporate management to treat material information as a commodity to be used to gain or maintain favor with particular analysts or investors. As noted in the Proposing Release, in the absence of a prohibition on selective disclosure, analysts may feel pressured to report favorably about a company or otherwise slant their analysis in order to have continued access to selectively disclosed information. We are concerned, in this regard, with reports that analysts who publish negative views of an issuer are sometimes excluded by that issuer from calls and meetings to which other analysts are invited.

Finally, . . . technological developments have made it much easier for issuers to disseminate information broadly. Whereas issuers once may have had to rely on analysts to serve as information intermediaries, issuers now can use a variety of methods to communicate directly with the market. In addition to press releases, these methods include, among others, Internet webcasting and teleconferencing. Accordingly, technological limitations no longer provide an excuse for abiding the threats to market integrity that selective disclosure represents.

———

On the question of what constitutes appropriate public disclosure, *see* Netflix, Inc., Exchange Act Rel. No. 69279 (Apr. 2, 2013) (personal media sites are not ordinarily assumed to be a medium by which companies release information, so that CEO's posting on Facebook material company information was not deemed an accepted method of disclosure unless investors receive advance notice that the site may be used).

———

NOTE ON INSIDER TRADING ENFORCEMENT

The heavy lifting with respect to insider trading is carried out by the government, either through civil enforcement by the SEC or criminal enforcement by the Department of Justice. The SEC enjoys a full panoply of remedies for violation of the securities laws. Most frequently invoked in insider trading cases. The authority to seek up to treble the insider trading profits was added by the Insider Trading Sanctions Act of 1984 amending section 21A(a)(2) to the Securities Exchange Act authorizing the SEC. In addition, the SEC can seek fairly substantial fines against violators. See Securities Exchange Act section 21(d)(3)(B). Interestingly, although little used, section 21A(e) authorizes the award of bounties to those who provide information in detecting and prosecuting violators. Because the sanctions (including the fines) that the SEC can impose are civil rather than criminal, the relevant standard of proof is whether the defendant's wrong has been established by a preponderance of the evidence, rather than whether it has been established beyond a reasonable doubt. The Department of Justice can proceed criminally under Section 32(a) of the Securities Exchange Act for knowing violations of any Exchange Act provision or violation. Criminal actions can also be maintained under the mail and wire fraud statutes. *See e.g.,* Carpenter v. United States, 484 U.S. 19, 108 S.Ct. 316, 98 L.Ed.2d 275 (1987) (financial columnist who tipped outsiders regarding what companies would be mentioned in his forthcoming market-moving column violated the mail and wire fraud statutes as a wrongful misappropriation of confidential information from his employer). Currently the mail and wire fraud statutes proscribe any scheme or artifice to deprive another of the intangible right to honest services. 18 U.S.C. § 1364.

Suppose, finally, that the plaintiff has purchased or sold publicly held stock at a time when the defendant wrongfully failed to disclose a material fact? Section 20A(a) of the Securities Exchange Act provides that any person who violates the Act or the Rules thereunder by purchasing or selling a security while in possession of material, nonpublic information shall be liable to any person who, contemporaneously with the purchase has sold, or contemporaneously with the sale has purchased, securities of the same class. Section 20A(b)(1) then qualifies section 20A(a) by providing that the amount of damages imposed under that section shall not exceed the profit gained or loss avoided in the transaction that is the subject of the violation.

It should be noted that § 20A(b) does not limit the liability of defendants in Rule 10b–5 actions that do not fall within § 20A, because § 20A is expressly made nonexclusive by § 20A(d). "The principal intent of this language is to assure that persons other than open market traders (i.e., sources of the information defrauded under the misappropriation theory) are not prevented from seeking a separate remedy for harm. . . . Although the matter is hardly clear . . . the strong inference from the legislative history is that . . . [open market purchasers relying]on the abstain or disclose principle . . . are limited to the Section 20A remedy." Donald C. Langevoort, Insider Trading: Regulation, Enforcement & Prevention 9–16 (2002).

———

3. LIABILITY FOR SHORT-SWING TRADING UNDER § 16(b) OF THE SECURITIES EXCHANGE ACT

SECURITIES EXCHANGE ACT § 16

[See Statutory Supplement]

SECURITIES EXCHANGE ACT RULES 3A–11–1, 3b–2, 16a–1, 16a–2, 16a–3, 16a–10, 16b–3, 16b–5, 16b–6, 16b–7, 16b–9; FORM 3; FORM 4; FORM 5

[See Statutory Supplement]

Section 16(a) mandates that officers, directors and beneficial owners of more than 10 percent of an equity security registered pursuant to section 12 reporting company must report changes in their beneficial ownership of any equity security of the company. In the context of section 16 they are frequently referred to as "statutory insiders." A change in ownership report must be filed electronically with the SEC before the end of the second business day following the date the reportable transaction occurred. Moreover, within one business day of the SEC filing the report should be placed on the firm's website if it maintains such a website.

The report of the officer's, director's or beneficial owner's trade serves several functions. First, information that an officer, director or owner of more than ten percent has increased or decreased holdings in the firm itself reveals information that can be useful to investors. For example, knowledge that an officer or director is increasing or decreasing her holdings in the firm can be seen as reflecting the statutory insiders' optimism or pessimism regarding the firm's future prospects. This may prompt investors to following the insider's lead and increase or decrease their ownership of the firm's shares. And, knowledge of changes in share ownership can suggest changes in control. Second, and most significantly from the perspective of section 16's purpose, the reported changes in the statutory insider's holdings complements the operation of subsection (b). Section 16(b) imposes absolute liability on statutory insiders for the profits they obtain by the purchase and sale (as well as by the sale and purchase) when such purchase and sale are within a period of less than six months of one another. The resulting profit, called short-swing profit, is recoverable by the issuer without the need to prove the abuse of inside information.

In *Gollust v. Mendell*, 501 U.S. 115, 111 S.Ct. 2173, 115 L.Ed.2d 109 (1991), the Supreme Court made the following observations on the procedural aspects of § 16(b):

To enforce this strict liability rule on insider trading, Congress chose to rely solely on the issuers of stock and their security holders. Unlike most of the federal securities laws, § 16(b) does not confer enforcement authority on the Securities and Exchange Commission. It is, rather, the security holders of an issuer who have the ultimate authority to sue for enforcement of § 16(b). If the issuer declines to bring a § 16(b) action within 60 days of a demand by a security holder, or fails to prosecute the action "diligently" . . . then the security holder may "institut[e]" an action to recover insider short-swing profits for the issuer. . . .

Although plaintiffs seeking to sue under the statute must own a "security," § 16(b) places no significant restriction on the type of security adequate to confer standing. "[A]ny security" will suffice, . . . the statutory definition being broad enough to include stock, notes, warrants, bonds, debentures, puts, calls, and a variety of other financial instruments; it expressly excludes only "currency or any note, draft, bill of exchange, or banker's acceptance which has a maturity at the time of issuance of not exceeding nine months. . . ."

Only private suits are authorized for recovering short-swing profits. Section 16(c) provides a limitations period so that suit must commence, "within one year of discovery of the facts constituting the cause of action and within three years after such cause of action accrued." *Credit Suisse Securities LLC v. Simmonds,* 566 U.S. 221, 132 S. Ct. 1414, 182 L. Ed. 3d 446 (2012), held that the statute is not tolled automatically by the insider's failure to file the mandated Section 16(a) report; the court was evenly divided whether the three-year limitations period is a period of repose so that no equitable tolling would be available so as to permit a suit to proceed if it is initiated more than three years after the trade giving rise to a claim of short-swing profits.

When enacted in 1934, section 16 of the Securities Exchange Act, was the federal securities laws' sole means to deter insider trading. As part of the original legislation, its presence was a sensible response to a world where computer surveillance and other sophisticated techniques for detecting inside trading were not at hand so that Congress was dubious whether any actual abuse by insiders could be detected. Congress therefore opted for a prophylactic approach that continues today. However, as seen in the materials in this chapter, there now is a well-established body of law that arms the SEC to prosecute insider trading cases. Indeed, roughly in any year slightly more than ten percent of the SEC's enforcement efforts are focused on insider trading and tipping cases. Further consider that, unlike the procedural setting in 1934, the modern class action and well-financed plaintiff's bar stand eager to step forward in instances where the SEC has not already acted.

Thus, what justifies in today's legal setting continuing section 16(b)'s disgorgement remedy for short-swing profits?

———

NOTES ON THE COMPUTATION OF PROFITS UNDER § 16(b)

1. *The Smolowe Approach.* In *Smolowe v. Delendo Corporation*, 136 F.2d 231 (2d Cir.1943), cert. denied 320 U.S. 751, 64 S.Ct. 56, 88 L.Ed. 446, the court considered and rejected several formulas for computing profits under § 16(b):

> Once the principle of [measuring damages based on the identification of the stock certificates involved] is rejected, its corollary, the first-in, first-out rule, is left at loose ends. . . . Its rationalization is the same as that for the identification rule, for which it operates as a presumptive principle; and it has no other support. If we reject one, we reject the other and for like reasons. Its application would render the large stockholder with a backlog of stock not immediately devoted to trading immune from the Act. Further, we should note that it does not fit the broad statutory language; a purchase followed immediately by a sale, albeit a transaction within the exact statutory language, would often be held immune from the statutory penalty because the purchase would be deemed by arbitrary rule to have been made at an earlier date; while a sale followed by purchase would never even be within the terms of the rule. . . .

> Another possibility might be the striking of an average purchase price and an average sale price during the period, and using these as bases of computation. What this rule would do in concrete effect is to allow as offsets all losses made by such trading. This in effect the district court first planned to do. . . . But it corrected this in its supplemental opinion, properly pointing out that the statute provided for the recovery of "any" profit realized and obviously precluded a setting off of losses. Even had the statutory language been more uncertain, this rule seems one not to be favored in the light of the statutory purpose. Compared to other possible rules, it tends to stimulate more active trading by reducing the chance of penalty. . . . Its application to a case where trading continued more than six months might be most uncertain, depending upon how the beginning of each six months' period was ascertained. It is not a clear-cut taking of "any profit" for the corporation, and we agree with the district court in rejecting it.

See generally Andrew Chin, The Learned Hand Unformula for Short-Swing Liability, 91 Wash. L. Rev. 1523 (2016) (after closely examining the transactions in *Gratz* in which there were 400 transactions over 21 months causing Judge Hand to defer to a special master, Professor Chin concludes that the special master's calculation (done in an era before sophisticated calculators) seriously understated maximum profits by 19 percent).

2.   *Smolowe Illustrated.* The formula adopted in *Smolowe* has been generally approved by the courts. It is often referred to the "lowest purchase price, highest sale price" method. See, e.g., Whittaker v. Whittaker Corp., 639 F.2d 516, 530 (9th Cir.1981). Here are three illustrations of this method. Assume in all three illustrations that D is a director of C Corporation, whose stock is traded on a national securities exchange.

a).   On January 2, D purchases 1,000 shares of C at $10. On April 1, D sells 1,000 shares of C at $15. This is a short-swing "purchase and sale," and D is liable under § 16(b) for his profit of $5,000.

b).   On January 2, D purchases 1,000 shares of C at $10. On August 1, D sells 1,000 shares at $15. On November 1, D purchases 1,000 shares at $10. D has no § 16(b) liability on the basis of the January–August swing, because the two ends of the swing did not occur within six months. However, the August and November transactions constitute a short-swing "sale and purchase," and D would be liable under § 16(b) for a profit of $5,000 on these two transactions. Why has D made a $5,000 "profit"? Because after D's November 1 purchase, his position in C Corporation's stock is exactly as it was just before August 1 (that is, he owns 1,000 C shares) but he has also added $5,000 cash to his bank account. D may have accomplished this result by using inside information. The sale at $15 may have been made on the basis of undisclosed bad news. The purchase at $10 may have been made on the basis of undisclosed good news.

c).   D engages in the following pattern of activity:

Date	Action	Amount	Price
2/1	Purchase	1,000	$30
3/1	Sale	1,000	$25
4/1	Purchase	1,000	$20
5/1	Sale	1,000	$15

Under the *Smolowe* formula, D has a profit of $5,000, because the purchase at $20 on 4/1 can be matched with the sale at $25 on 3/1. At first glance, this looks counterintuitive: it seems that D has a $10,000 loss in his total trading, not a $5,000 profit. But it may be that except for inside information, D would not have sold on 3/1, and instead would have ridden the C stock all the way down from $30 to $15, for a loss of $15,000. Accordingly, there is a possibility (which is all that § 16(b) requires) that D has profited by $5,000 by holding his loss to $10,000 through the use of inside information.[1]

---

[1]   For a hypothetical in which a finding of profits under the *Smolowe/Gratz* formula does seem counterintuitive, see Lowenfels, Section 16(b): A New Trend in Regulating Insider Trading, 54 Cornell L.Rev. 45, 46–47 n. 6 (1968).

NOTE ON THE INTERPRETATION OF § 16(b)

The courts have tended to use two somewhat different approaches in cases in which the applicability of § 16(b) is contestable. Until the early 1960s, the predominant theory of interpreting § 16(b) was that the section should be construed to cover all transactions within its literal reach. "[T]he statute was intended to be thoroughgoing, to squeeze all possible profits out of stock transactions, and thus to establish a standard so high as to prevent any conflict between the selfish interest of [an insider] and the faithful performance of his duty." Smolowe v. Delendo Corp., 136 F.2d 231, 239 (2d Cir.1943), cert. denied 320 U.S. 751, 64 S.Ct. 56, 88 L.Ed. 446. This theory of interpreting § 16(b) was known as the "objective" approach, although it has been aptly suggested that "automatic" would be more descriptive. Blau v. Lamb, 363 F.2d 507, 520 (2d Cir.1966), cert. denied 385 U.S. 1002, 87 S.Ct. 707, 17 L.Ed.2d 542 (1967).

Beginning in the mid-1960s, § 16(b) came to be perceived by some as overly harsh, because it operates without regard to fault. A different theory of interpretation, known as the "subjective" or "pragmatic" approach, then set in. Under this approach, in *borderline* cases—particularly cases involving an *"unorthodox"* transaction, rather than a garden-variety purchase or sale—the statute would be interpreted to impose liability only if the insider actually had access to inside information, or the transaction was of a type that carries a potential for insider abuse. See Whittaker v. Whittaker Corp., 639 F.2d 516, 522 (9th Cir.1981), cert. denied, 454 U.S. 1031, 102 S.Ct. 566, 70 L.Ed.2d 473; Lowenfels, Section 16(b): A New Trend in Regulating Insider Trading, 54 Cornell L.Rev. 45 (1968).

The names given to these two approaches are misleading. The "subjective" approach does not turn, as its name suggests, on the defendant's subjective intent to use inside information. Conversely, the "objective" approach can be just as pragmatic as the "pragmatic" approach. If the names of the two approaches are put aside, the conflict is between an approach that treats § 16(b) as a prophylactic rule of thumb, whose purpose would be defeated if defendants could escape liability on the ground that in their particular case no abuse could have occurred, and an approach that treats § 16(b) as inviting an inquiry into the possibility of abuse, at least in borderline cases. To a certain extent, which approach is adopted in a given case may depend on whether the court perceives § 16(b) as a good idea or a bad idea.

It should be emphasized that, although the tension between the approaches to the interpretation of § 16(b) is real and important, it is a tension only at the margins. In the great bulk of potential cases, the application of § 16(b) is relatively straightforward. As pointed out in *Whittaker,* supra:

> [T]he pragmatic approach has not ousted the objective view. Rather, the pragmatic approach is used to determine the boundaries of the statute's definitional scope in borderline situations, especially unorthodox transactions. . . . For a garden-variety transaction which cannot be regarded as unorthodox, the

pragmatic approach is not applicable. . . . In such cases, if the situation is within the requirements established by Congress for § 16, then the mechanical, "objective," operation of the statute imposes liability.

―――――

NOTE ON "UNORTHODOX" TRANSACTIONS UNDER § 16(b)

Kern County Land Co. v. Occidental Petroleum Corp., 411 U.S. 582, 93 S. Ct. 1736, 36 L. Ed.2d 503 (1973), concerned what is known, for Section 16(b) purposes, as an "unorthodox transaction," that is, a transaction other than a straight purchase and sale that nevertheless can fall within Section 16(b). The case arose from the unsuccessful attempt of Occidental to acquire Kern via a hostile takeover. Kern's defensive response to Occidental's offer was to enter into a friendly merger with Tenneco Corporation. As a result of that merger, Occidental received Tenneco preferred stock for the substantial number of Kern common shares it had acquired through its open market purchases and its tender offer within six months of the Kern-Tenneco merger. Occidental, not wishing to own shares in a competitor, granted Tenneco an option to acquire the preferred shares. The option stated it could not be exercised within six months of the Kern-Tenneco merger. Thereafter, Kern asserted that Occidental was required under section 16(b) to disgorge its short-swing profits.

The Supreme Court thus had to decide (1) whether Occidental's exchange of its Kern shares for the Tenneco preferred shares pursuant to the merger was a "sale" and (2) whether the subsequent option resulted in a "sale" within six months of the "purchase" of the Tenneco preferred shares. The Supreme Court embraced the pragmatic approach, reasoning as follows:

> In deciding whether borderline [unorthodox] transactions are within the reach of the statute, the courts have come to inquire whether the transaction may serve as a vehicle for the evil which Congress sought to prevent—the realization of short-swing profits based upon access to inside information—thereby endeavoring to implement congressional objectives without extending the reach of the statute beyond its intended limits.

411 U.S. at 594–595. Because Occidental was not only an outsider, but one hostile to the management of both Kern and Tenneco, the court concluded there was no chance that Occidental's purchase or sale were tainted by its use of inside information. It therefore concluded that the purpose of section 16(b) would not be furthered by treating the forced exchange of its Kern shares for Tenneco shares was either a sale of Kern common shares or a purchase of Tenneco preferred shares.

―――――

NOTE ON ATTRIBUTION OF OWNERSHIP UNDER SECTIONS 16(a) AND (b)

Sections 16(a) and (b) use the term or the concept of "beneficial ownership" for several different purposes.

Under § 16(a), a person who is either "a beneficial owner of more than 10 per centum of any class of equity security" (hereafter, a "more-than-10-percent owner"), or an officer or director, must report the amount of all equity securities of the issuer "of which he is the beneficial owner."

Under § 16(b), a director, officer, or more-than-10-percent owner is liable for short-swing profits "realized by him from any purchase and sale, or any sale and purchase, of any equity security" of the issuer. Given both the purpose of the statute and the context, § 16(b) seems generally intended to cover the purchase and sale of those equity securities of which a person is a beneficial owner for purposes of § 16(a).

If a person is the record owner of an equity security and also has a pecuniary interest in the security, he is undoubtedly a beneficial owner for all purposes under § 16. Problems of interpretation arise, however, if a person is a record owner of shares but has no pecuniary interest; or if a person has a pecuniary interest but is not the record owner; or if a person is neither the record owner nor has a pecuniary interest, but there is nevertheless an important relationship between the person and the security, such as the right to control the security. For most although not all practical purposes, the problem can be stated as follows: when should an equity security that is not legally owned by a person, in the conventional sense, nevertheless be *attributed* to the person under § 16, so that either (i) the security counts toward determining whether the person's ownership crosses the 10-percent-beneficial-ownership line, (ii) the person's transactions in the security must be reported under § 16(a), or (iii) the person's transactions in the security may subject him to liability under § 16(b)?

These problems are addressed in detail by the Rules under § 16. Those Rules draw a distinction between (1) what constitutes beneficial ownership for purposes of determining whether a person is a more-than-10-percent owner, and (2) what constitutes beneficial ownership for purposes of determining whether a person who *is* a more-than-10-percent owner, or a director or officer, must report under § 16(a) and may be liable for short-swing profits under § 16(b).

As to the first problem (whether a person is a more-than-10-percent owner), Rule 16a–1(a)(1) provides that, with certain exceptions, *"solely for purposes of determining whether a person is a beneficial owner of more than ten percent of* any class of equity securities registered pursuant to § 12 of the Act, the term 'beneficial owner' shall mean any person who is deemed a beneficial owner pursuant to § 13(d) of the Act and the rules thereunder. . . ." (emphasis added). Rule 13d–3, in turn, provides that a beneficial owner of a security includes "any person who, directly or indirectly, through any contract, arrangement, understanding, relationship, or otherwise has or shares: (1) *Voting power* which includes the power to vote, or to direct the voting of, such security; and/or, (2) *Investment power* which includes the power to dispose, or to direct the disposition of, such security." (Emphasis added.) In short, in determining *whether* a person is a more-than-10-percent owner of stock, the emphasis, under Rule 16a–1, is on the person's *control* over the stock. Of special note is Rule 13d–5(b)(1) which provides "when two or more persons agree to act together for the purpose of acquiring, holding, voting or disposing of equity securities of an issuer, the group formed thereby shall be deemed to have acquired beneficial ownership. . . ." Roth v. Jennings, 489 F.3d 499 (2d Cir. 2007) illustrates how liability can arise under section 16(b) when one's purchases and sales are seen as part of a group. Jennings acquired in the open market 8.3 percent of Metal Management about two weeks after EMR, through open market purchases, acquired 14.8 percent of Metal Management. Jennings had borrowed the funds to purchase the shares from EMR. It was an astute move, as a few weeks after his purchase, Jennings garnered a $4.25 million profit by selling the Metal Management shares. The plaintiff argued that Jennings and EMR were acting in concert to change control of Metal Management. Relying on the disjunctive used in Rule 13d–5(b)(1), the Second Circuit reasoned that a group is formed if two or more persons come together to acquire, hold *or* dispose of stock. Believing factual issues existed whether they continued to be a group when the shares were sold, the court reversed the trial court's grant of the defendant's motion to dismiss and remanded the case to determine whether Jennings and EMR acted together for a common purpose.

As to the second problem (what constitutes beneficial ownership for *reporting* and *liability* purposes), Rule 16a–1(a)(2) provides that as a general principle, with certain exceptions and elaborations, (1) *"other than for purposes of determining whether a person is a beneficial owner of more than ten percent of any class of equity securities* registered under § 12 of the Act, the term 'beneficial owner' shall mean any person who, directly or indirectly, through any contract, arrangement, understanding, relationship or otherwise, has or shares a direct or indirect *pecuniary interest* in the equity securities. . . ."; and (2) "[t]he term 'pecuniary interest' in any class of equity securities shall mean the opportunity, directly or indirectly, *to profit or share in any profit* derived from a transaction in the subject securities." (Emphasis added.) In short, unlike Rule 16a–1(a)(1), which emphasizes *control* for purposes of determining who is a more-than-10-percent owner, Rule 16a–1(a)(2) emphasizes *pecuniary interest* for purposes of determining what transactions in equity securities must be reported and may give rise to liability.

After stating the pecuniary-interest test as a general principle to govern the determination of beneficial ownership for reporting and liability purposes, Rule 16a–1(a)(2) then goes on to deal with certain recurring cases in which problems of attribution based on a pecuniary interest may arise. Some of these cases are as follows:

Family members. Rule 16a–1(a)(2)(ii)(A) provides that "[t]he term 'indirect pecuniary interest' [under Rule 16a–2] in any class of equity securities shall include, but not be limited to . . . securities held by members of a person's immediate family sharing the same household; *provided, however,* that the presumption of such beneficial ownership may be rebutted. . . . " Rule 16a–1(e) then provides that "[t]he term 'immediate family', shall mean any child, stepchild, grandchild, parent, stepparent, grandparent, spouse, sibling, mother-in-law, father-in-law, son-in-law, daughter-in-law, brother-in-law, or sister-in-law, and shall include adoptive relationships."

Partnerships. Rule 16a–1(a)(2)(ii)(B) provides that the term "indirect pecuniary interest" [under Rule 16a–1(a)(2)] includes "a general partner's proportionate interest in the portfolio securities held by a general or limited partnership."

Corporations. Rule 16a–1(a)(2)(iii) provides that "[a] shareholder shall not be deemed to have a pecuniary interest in the portfolio securities held by a corporation or similar entity in which the person owns securities if the shareholder is not a controlling shareholder of the entity and does not have or share investment control over the entity's portfolio. . . . " Note that this Rule does not specify a general principle for determining when a corporation's portfolio securities will be attributed to shareholders in the corporation, but only provides a safe harbor in the cases that the rule specifies.

The Rules under § 16 also contain elaborate provisions dealing with such matters as when a trustee is a beneficial owner for reporting and liability purposes, and when the ownership of a derivative security makes a person the beneficial owner of the derivative security.

NOTE ON STATUTORY INSIDER STATUS AT ONLY ONE END OF A SWING

The last sentence of § 16(b) sets out an exemptive provision under which "[T]his subsection shall not be construed to cover any transaction where [a more-than-10-percent] beneficial owner was not such both at the time of the purchase and sale, or the sale and purchase, of the security involved." Suppose a person, S, owns a more-than-10-percent block, but is not a director or officer. S makes a sale that reduces his block to less than 10 percent, but leaves him with the remainder. Are S's later sales of some or all of the remainder of his block, covered by § 16? The Supreme Court has held that the later sales are not covered, because the person is not a 10 percent owner at the time of those sales. Reliance Electric Co. v. Emerson Electric Co., 404 U.S. 418, 92 S.Ct. 596, 30 L.Ed.2d 575 (1972). This result is codified in Rule 16a–2(c).

What about the very purchase that makes a person a more-than-10-percent beneficial owner? Can that purchase be matched with a subsequent sale within six months? In *Foremost-McKesson, Inc. v. Provident Securities Co.*, 423 U.S. 232, 96 S.Ct. 508, 46 L.Ed.2d 464 (1976) the Supreme Court held, largely on the basis of the exemptive provision and legislative history, that in the case of a *purchase-sale sequence*, a more-than-10-percent beneficial owner is not liable unless he was such *before* he made the purchase in question. To put this differently, the purchase that first lifts a beneficial owner above 10 percent cannot be matched with a subsequent sale under § 16(b).

Suppose a person who is a more-than-10-percent owner sells enough stock to get below the 10 percent line, and then buys stock within six months after that sale? This kind of case is called a sale-repurchase sequence. The *Foremost* opinion did not cover this case, and left considerable room for arguing that this sequence should result in liability under § 16(b).

Suppose a person is a director or officer at only one end of a swing? Since the exemptive clause provides that "this subsection shall not be construed to cover any transaction where [*a more-than-10-percent*] *beneficial owner* was not such both at the time of the purchase and sale, or the sale and purchase" (emphasis added), the clear implication is that § 16(b) *does* apply to a short-swing transaction by a director or officer even where the director or officer "was not such both at the time of purchase and sale, or the sale and purchase." In *Feder v. Martin Marietta Corp.*, 406 F.2d 260 (2d Cir.1969), cert. denied 396 U.S. 1036, 90 S.Ct. 678, 24 L.Ed.2d 681 (1970), the court held that a director or officer who purchases, resigns, and then sells within six months of the purchase, is liable under § 16(b). However, no liability will be imposed if both ends of a swing occur after the director or officer resigns. Lewis v. Mellon Bank, N.A., 513 F.2d 921 (3d Cir.1975); Lewis v. Varnes, 505 F.2d 785 (2d Cir.1974). Prior to 1991, it had been held that § 16(b) applies to a purchase or sale of shares by a person who becomes a director or officer after the transaction, and engages in a matching transaction within six months of the original transaction. In such a case, the director or officer will have had an opportunity to utilize inside information at the second end of the swing, but not at the first. This issue is now governed by Rule 16a–2(a), adopted by the SEC in 1991, which provides that purchases and sales by a director or officer before she became a director or officer are not subject to § 16.

NOTE ON WHO IS AN "OFFICER" UNDER § 16(b)

The battle between "objective" and "subjective" approaches to the interpretations of Section 16(b) has played a dramatic role in the question who is an "officer" for purposes of that Section. Under the objective view, an officer *title* would give rise to § 16(b) liability. Under the subjective view, liability would depend on whether the person had access to inside information by virtue of her position. An intermediate view is that liability should turn on a person's corporate role or function (rather than her title), but that the issue is whether the function is "officer-like," not whether the person's corporate function gives her access to inside information.

For many years, SEC Rule 3b–2 provided that the term officer "means a president, vice president, secretary, treasurer or principal financial officer, comptroller or principal accounting officer, and any person routinely performing corresponding functions with respect to any organization whether incorporated or unincorporated."

Eventually, the SEC adopted a new definition of "officer" which is essentially function-based, and much more limited in its coverage than was Rule 3b–2. The new rule, Rule 16a–1(f), provides that:

> [T]he term "officer" shall mean an issuer's president, principal financial officer, or principal accounting officer (or, if there is no such accounting officer, the controller), any vice-president of the issuer in charge of a principal business unit, division or function (such as sales, administration or finance), any other officer who performs a policy-making function, or any other person who performs similar policy-making functions for the issuer.

In a note to Rule 16a–1(f), the SEC states that the term "policy-making function" is not intended to include policy-making functions that are not significant.

The Chairman of the SEC, in his opening remarks at the meeting at which the new rule was adopted, stated that:

> The definition of officer has been revised to make clear that a person's functions and not simply title will determine the applicability of Section 16. The definition . . . is intended to make clear that individuals with executive functions do not avoid liability under Section 16 simply by foregoing title, and those with a title but no significant executive responsibilities are not subject to the automatic short-swing profit liability of Section 16(b). Thus, for example, a vice-president of a bank, who has no policy-making responsibility would not have to be concerned with possible liability under Section 16(b), if because of an unexpected family emergency, he needed to sell securities.

Barron, Control and Restricted Securities, 19 Sec.Reg.L.J. 292, 294–95 (1991).

---

4. CORPORATE RECOVERIES FOR INSIDE TRADING UNDER STATE LAW

Diamond v. Oreamuno
New York Court of Appeals, 1969.
24 N.Y.2d 494, 301 N.Y.S.2d 78, 248 N.E.2d 910.

■ CHIEF JUDGE FULD. Upon this appeal from an order denying a motion to dismiss the complaint as insufficient on its face, the question presented—one of first impression in this court—is whether officers and directors may be held accountable to their corporation for gains realized by them from transactions in the company's stock as a result of their use of material inside information.

The complaint was filed by a shareholder of Management Assistance, Inc. (MAI) asserting a derivative action against a number of its officers and directors to compel an accounting for profits allegedly acquired as a result of a breach of fiduciary duty. It charges that two of the defendants—Oreamuno, chairman of the board of directors, and Gonzalez, its president—had used inside information, acquired by them solely by virtue of their positions, in order to reap large personal profits from the sale of MAI shares and that these profits rightfully belong to the corporation. Other officers and directors were joined as defendants on the ground that they acquiesced in or ratified the assertedly wrongful transactions.

MAI is in the business of financing computer installations through sale and lease back arrangements with various commercial and industrial users. Under its lease provisions, MAI was required to maintain and repair the computers but, at the time of this suit, it lacked the capacity to perform this function itself and was forced to engage the manufacturer of the computers, International Business Machines (IBM), to service the machines. As a result of a sharp increase by IBM of its charges for such service, MAI's expenses for August of 1966 rose considerably and its net earnings declined from $262,253 in July to $66,233 in August, a decrease of about 75%. This information, although earlier known to the defendants, was not made public until October of 1966. Prior to the release of the information, however, Oreamuno and Gonzalez sold off a total of 56,500 shares of their MAI stock at the then current market price of $28 a share.

After the information concerning the drop in earnings was made available to the public, the value of a share of MAI stock immediately fell from the $28 realized by the defendants to $11. Thus, the plaintiff alleges, by taking advantage of their privileged position and their access to confidential information, Oreamuno and Gonzalez were able to realize $800,000 more for their securities than they would have had this inside information not been available to them. Stating that the defendants were "forbidden to use [such] information . . . for their own personal profit or gain", the plaintiff brought this derivative action seeking to have the defendants account to the corporation for this difference. A motion by the defendants to dismiss the complaint—pursuant to CPLR 3211 (subd. [a], par. 7)—for failure to state a cause of action was granted by the court at Special Term. The Appellate Division, with one dissent, modified Special Term's order by reinstating the complaint as to the defendants Oreamuno and Gonzalez. The appeal is before us on a certified question.

In reaching a decision in this case, we are, of course, passing only upon the sufficiency of the complaint and we necessarily accept the charges contained in that pleading as true.

It is well established, as a general proposition, that a person who acquires special knowledge or information by virtue of a confidential or fiduciary relationship with another is not free to exploit that knowledge or information for his own personal benefit but must account to his principal for any profits derived therefrom. (See, e.g., *Byrne v. Barrett,*

268 N.Y. 199.) This, in turn, is merely a corollary of the broader principle, inherent in the nature of the fiduciary relationship, that prohibits a trustee or agent from extracting secret profits from his position of trust.

In support of their claim that the complaint fails to state a cause of action, the defendants take the position that, although it is admittedly wrong for an officer or director to use his position to obtain trading profits for himself in the stock of his corporation, the action ascribed to them did not injure or damage MAI in any way. Accordingly, the defendants continue, the corporation should not be permitted to recover the proceeds. They acknowledge that, by virtue of the exclusive access which officers and directors have to inside information, they possess an unfair advantage over other shareholders and, particularly, the persons who had purchased the stock from them but, they contend, the corporation itself was unaffected and, for that reason, a derivative action is an inappropriate remedy.

It is true that the complaint before us does not contain any allegation of damages to the corporation but this has never been considered to be an essential requirement for a cause of action founded on a breach of fiduciary duty. (See, e.g., *Matter of People* [*Bond & Mtge. Guar. Co.*], 303 N.Y. 423, 431; *Wendt v. Fischer,* 243 N.Y. 439, 443; *Dutton v. Willner,* 52 N.Y. 312, 319.) This is because the function of such an action, unlike an ordinary tort or contract case, is not merely to *compensate* the plaintiff for wrongs committed by the defendant but, as this court declared many years ago (*Dutton v. Willner,* 52 N.Y. 312, 319, *supra*), "to *prevent* them, by removing from agents and trustees all inducement to attempt dealing for their own benefit in matters which they have undertaken for others, or to which their agency or trust relates." (Emphasis supplied.)

Just as a trustee has no right to retain for himself the profits yielded by property placed in his possession but must account to his beneficiaries, a corporate fiduciary, who is entrusted with potentially valuable information, may not appropriate that asset for his own use even though, in so doing, he causes no injury to the corporation. The primary concern, in a case such as this, is not to determine whether the corporation has been damaged but to decide, as between the corporation and the defendants, who has a higher claim to the proceeds derived from the exploitation of the information. In our opinion, there can be no justification for permitting officers and directors, such as the defendants, to retain for themselves profits which, it is alleged, they derived solely from exploiting information gained by virtue of their inside position as corporate officials.

In addition, it is pertinent to observe that, despite the lack of any specific allegation of damage, it may well be inferred that the defendants' actions might have caused some harm to the enterprise. Although the corporation may have little concern with the day-to-day transactions in its shares, it has a great interest in maintaining a reputation of integrity, an image of probity, for its management and in insuring the continued public acceptance and marketability of its stock. When officers and directors abuse their position in order to gain personal profits, the effect may be to cast a cloud on the corporation's name, injure stockholder relations and undermine public regard for the corporation's securities. As Presiding Justice BOTEIN aptly put it, in the course of his opinion for the Appellate Division, "[t]he prestige and good will of a corporation, so vital to its prosperity, may be undermined by the revelation that its chief officers had been making personal profits out of corporate events which they had not disclosed to the community of stockholders." (29 A.D.2d, at p. 287.)

The defendants maintain that extending the prohibition against personal exploitation of a fiduciary relationship to officers and directors of a corporation will discourage such officials from maintaining a stake in the success of the corporate venture through share ownership, which, they urge, is an important incentive to proper performance of their duties. There is, however, a considerable difference between corporate officers who assume the same risks and obtain the same benefits as other shareholders and those who use their privileged position to gain special advantages not available to others. The sale of shares by the defendants for the reasons charged was not merely a wise investment decision which any prudent investor might have made. Rather, they were assertedly able in this case to profit solely because they had information which was not available to anyone else—including the other shareholders whose interests they, as corporate fiduciaries, were bound to protect.

Although no appellate court in this State has had occasion to pass upon the precise question before us, the concept underlying the present cause of action is hardly a new one. (See, e.g., Securities Exchange Act of 1934 [48 U.S.Stat. 881], § 16[b]; U.S.Code, tit. 15, § 78p, subd. [b]; *Brophy v. Cities Serv. Co.,* 31 Del.Ch. 241; Restatement, 2d, Agency, § 388, comment *c*; Israels, A New Look at Corporate Directorship, 24 Business Lawyer 727, 732 *et seq.;* Note, 54 Cornell L.Rev. 306, 309–312.) Under Federal law (Securities Exchange Act of 1934, § 16[b]), for example, it is conclusively presumed that, when a director, officer or 10% shareholder buys and sells securities of his corporation within a six-month period, he is trading on inside information. The remedy which the Federal statute provides in that situation is precisely the same as that sought in the present case under State law, namely, an action brought by the corporation or on its behalf to recover all profits derived from the transactions.

In providing this remedy, Congress accomplished a dual purpose. It not only provided for an efficient and effective method of accomplishing its primary goal—the protection of the investing public from unfair treatment at the hands of corporate insiders—but extended to the corporation the right to secure for itself benefits derived by those insiders from their exploitation of their privileged position. The United States

Court of Appeals for the Second Circuit has stated the policy behind section 16(b) in the following terms (*Adler v. Klawans*, 267 F.2d 840, 844):

> "The undoubted congressional intent in the enactment of § 16(b) was to discourage what was reasonably thought to be a widespread abuse of a fiduciary relationship—specifically to discourage if not prevent three classes of persons from making private and gainful use of information acquired by them by virtue of their official relationship to a corporation."

Although the provisions of section 16(b) may not apply to all cases of trading on inside information, it demonstrates that a derivative action can be an effective method for dealing with such abuses which may be used to accomplish a similar purpose in cases not specifically covered by the statute. In *Brophy v. Cities Serv. Co.* (31 Del.Ch. 241, *supra*), for example, the Chancery Court of Delaware allowed a similar remedy in a situation not covered by the Federal legislation. One of the defendants in that case was an employee who had acquired inside information that the corporate plaintiff was about to enter the market and purchase its own shares. On the basis of this confidential information, the employee, who was not an officer and, hence, not liable under Federal law, bought a large block of shares and, after the corporation's purchases had caused the price to rise, resold them at a profit. The court sustained the complaint in a derivative action brought for an accounting, stating that "[p]ublic policy will not permit an employee occupying a position of trust and confidence toward his employer to abuse that relation to his own profit, regardless of whether his employer suffers a loss" (31 Del.Ch., at p. 246). And a similar view has been expressed in the Restatement, 2d, Agency (§ 388, comment *c*):

> "*c. Use of confidential information.* An agent who acquires confidential information in the course of his employment or in violation of his duties has a duty . . . to account for any profits made by the use of such information, although this does not harm the principal. . . . So, if [a corporate officer] has 'inside' information that the corporation is about to purchase or sell securities, or to declare or to pass a dividend, profits made by him in stock transactions undertaken because of his knowledge are held in constructive trust for the principal."

In the present case, the defendants may be able to avoid liability to the corporation under section 16(b) of the Federal law since they had held the MAI shares for more than six months prior to the sales. Nevertheless, the alleged use of the inside information to dispose of their stock at a price considerably higher than its known value constituted the same sort of "abuse of a fiduciary relationship" as is condemned by the Federal law. Sitting as we are in this case as a court of equity, we should not hesitate to permit an action to prevent any unjust enrichment realized by the defendants from their allegedly wrongful act.

The defendants recognize that the conduct charged against them directly contravened the policy embodied in the Securities Exchange Act but, they maintain, the Federal legislation constitutes a comprehensive and carefully wrought plan for dealing with the abuse of inside information and that allowing a derivative action to be maintained under State law would interfere with the Federal scheme. Moreover, they urge, the existence of dual Federal and State remedies for the same act would create the possibility of double liability.

An examination of the Federal regulatory scheme refutes the contention that it was designed to establish any particular remedy as exclusive. In addition to the specific provisions of section 16(b), the Securities and Exchange Act contains a general anti-fraud provision in section 10(b), (U.S.Code, tit. 15, § 78j, subd. [b]) which, as implemented by rule 10b–5 (Code of Fed.Reg., tit. 17, § 240.10b–5) under that section, renders it unlawful to engage in a variety of acts considered to be fraudulent. In interpreting this rule, the Securities and Exchange Commission and the Federal courts have extended the common-law definition of fraud to include not only affirmative misrepresentations, relied upon by the purchaser or seller, but also a failure to disclose material information which might have affected the transaction. (See, e.g., *Securities & Exch. Comm. v. Texas Gulf Sulphur Co.,* 401 F.2d 833, 847–848; *Myzel v. Fields,* 386 F.2d 718, 733–735.)

Accepting the truth of the complaint's allegations, there is no question but that the defendants were guilty of withholding material information from the purchasers of the shares and, indeed, the defendants acknowledge that the facts asserted constitute a violation of rule 10b–5. The remedies which the Federal law provides for such violation, however, are rather limited. An action could be brought, in an exceptional case, by the SEC for injunctive relief. This, in fact, is what happened in the *Texas Gulf Sulphur* case (401 F.2d 833, *supra*). The purpose of such an action, however, would appear to be more to establish a principle than to provide a regular method of enforcement. A class action under the Federal rule might be a more effective remedy but the mechanics of such an action have, as far as we have been able to ascertain, not yet been worked out by the Federal courts and several questions relating thereto have never been resolved. These include the definition of the class entitled to bring such an action, the measure of damages, the administration of the fund which would be recovered and its distribution to the members of the class. (See Note, 54 Cornell L.Rev. 306, 309, *supra*.) Of course, any individual purchaser, who could prove his own injury as a result of a rule 10b–5 violation can bring an action for rescission but we have not been referred to a single case in which such an action has been successfully prosecuted where the public sale of securities is involved. The reason for this is that sales of securities, whether through a stock exchange or over-the-counter, are characteristically anonymous transactions, usually handled through brokers, and the matching of the ultimate buyer with the ultimate seller presents virtually insurmountable obstacles. Thus, unless a section 16(b) violation is also present, the Federal law does not yet provide a really effective remedy.

In view of the practical difficulties inherent in an action under the Federal law, the desirability of creating an effective common-law remedy is manifest. "Dishonest directors should not find absolution from retributive justice", Ballantine observed in his work on Corporations ([rev. ed., 1946], p. 216), "by concealing their identity from their victims under the mask of the stock exchange." There is ample room in a situation such as is here presented for a "private Attorney General" to come forward and enforce proper behavior on the part of corporate officials through the medium of the derivative action brought in the name of the corporation. (See, e.g., *Associated Ind. v. Ickes,* 134 F.2d 694, 704; *Cherner v. Transitron Electronic Corp.,* 201 F.Supp. 934, 936.) Only by sanctioning such a cause of action will there be any effective method to prevent the type of abuse of corporate office complained of in this case.

There is nothing in the Federal law which indicates that it was intended to limit the power of the States to fashion additional remedies to effectuate similar purposes. Although the impact of Federal securities regulation has on occasion been said to have created a "Federal corporation law," in fact, its effect on the duties and obligations of directors and officers and their relation to the corporation and its shareholders is only occasional and peripheral. The primary source of the law in this area ever remains that of the State which created the corporation. Indeed, Congress expressly provided against any implication that it intended to pre-empt the field by declaring, in section 28(a) of the Securities Exchange Act of 1934 (48 U.S.Code 903), that "[t]he rights and remedies provided by this title shall be in addition to any and all other rights and remedies that may exist at law or in equity".

Nor should we be deterred, in formulating a State remedy, by the defendants' claim of possible double liability. Certainly, as already indicated, if the sales in question were publicly made, the likelihood that a suit will be brought by purchasers of the shares is quite remote. But, even if it were not, the mere possibility of such a suit is not a defense nor does it render the complaint insufficient. It is not unusual for an action to be brought to recover a fund which may be subject to a superior claim by a third party. If that be the situation, a defendant should not be permitted to retain the fund for his own use on the chance that such a party may eventually appear. A defendant's course, if he wishes to protect himself against double liability, is to interplead any and all possible claimants and bind them to the judgment (CPLR 1006, subd. [b]).

In any event, though, no suggestion has been made either in brief or on oral argument that any purchaser has come forward with a claim against the defendants or even that anyone is in a position to advance such a claim.[1] As we have stated, the defendants' assertion that such a party may come forward at some future date is not a basis for permitting them to retain for their own benefit the fruits of their allegedly wrongful acts. For all that appears, the present derivative action is the only effective remedy now available against the abuse by these defendants of their privileged position.

As we have previously indicated, what we have written must be read in the light of the charges contained in the complaint, and it must be borne in mind that "it will be incumbent upon the plaintiff, if he is to succeed, to prove upon the trial the truth and correctness of his allegations." (*Walkovszky v. Carlton,* 23 N.Y.2d 714, 715.)

The order appealed from should be affirmed, with costs, and the question certified answered in the affirmative.

■ JUDGES BURKE, SCILEPPI, BERGAN, KEATING, BREITEL and JASEN concur.

Order affirmed, etc.

———

In *Kahn v. Kohlberg Kravis Roberts & Co.,* 23 A.3d 831, 837–840 (Del. 2011), the Delaware Supreme Court broadly embraced the sweeping fiduciary obligations supporting the disgorgement remedy awarded in *Brophy v. Cities Service Co.,* 31 Del.Ch. 241, 70 A.2d 5 (1945)—an opinion relied upon in *Oreamuno*—and rejected the qualifications suggested by Pfeiffer v. Toll, 989 A.2d 683, 699 (Del. Ch. 2010)("trading in the market typically does not involve the usurpation of a corporate opportunity, where disgorgement has been the preferred remedy"):

> We decline to adopt *Pfeiffer*'s interpretation that would limit the disgorgement remedy to a usurpation of corporate opportunity or cases where the insider used confidential corporate information to compete directly with the corporation. *Brophy* was not premised on either of those rationales. Rather, *Brophy* focused on the public policy of preventing unjust enrichment based on the misuse of confidential corporate information.

> ... *Pfeiffer*'s holding—which requires a plaintiff to show that the corporation suffered actual harm before bringing a *Brophy* claim—is not a correct statement of our law. To the extent *Pfeiffer v. Toll* conflicts with our current interpretation of *Brophy v. Cities Service Co., Pfeiffer* cannot be Delaware law. Thus, actual harm to the corporation is not required for a plaintiff to state a claim under *Brophy*. In *Brophy*, the court relied on the principles of restitution and equity, citing the

---

[1]   In the absence of any such appearance by adverse claimants, we need not now decide whether the corporation's recovery would be affected by any amounts which might have to be refunded by the defendant to the injured purchasers.

Restatement of the Law of Restitution § 200, comment a, for the proposition that a fiduciary cannot use confidential corporate information for his own benefit. As the court recognized in *Brophy*, it is inequitable to permit the fiduciary to profit from using confidential corporate information. Even if the corporation did not suffer actual harm, equity requires disgorgement of that profit.

. . . We also disagree with the *Pfeiffer* court's conclusion that the purpose of *Brophy* is to "remedy harm to the corporation." In fact, *Brophy* explicitly held that the corporation did not need to suffer an actual loss for there to be a viable claim. Importantly, *Brophy* focused on preventing a fiduciary wrongdoer from being unjustly enriched. Moreover, we have found no cases requiring that the corporation suffer actual harm for a plaintiff to bring a *Brophy* claim. To read *Brophy* as applying only where the corporation has suffered actual harm improperly limits its holding.

Contra: Freeman v. Decio, 584 F.2d 186 (7th Cir. 1978) (applying Indiana law in holding that corporate recovery may occur only when the fiduciary's trading interferes with the corporation's ability to secretly use the same information to its own advantage); Schein v. Chasen, 313 So.2d 739 (Fla. 1975) (corporate recovery permitted only if the fiduciary trading harmed the corporation).

———

CHAPTER 13

SHAREHOLDER SUITS

1. INTRODUCTION

BACKGROUND NOTE

If the fiduciary duties owed by directors, officers, and controlling shareholders could be enforced only in suits by the corporation, many wrongs would never be remedied. If a controlling shareholder breaches its duty, it will normally cause the corporation to not institute litigation to remedy the wrong. Similarly, directors will seldom bring suit against one of their colleagues or top executives for such a breach. To overcome these obstacles, and hold wrongdoing managers and controlling shareholders to account, the law permits shareholders to bring suit for breach of fiduciary duty on the corporation's behalf.

In *Ross v. Bernhard,* 396 U.S. 531, 534–35, 90 S.Ct. 733, 735–6, 24 L.Ed.2d 729 (1970), the Supreme Court sketched the background and nature of such suits in the following terms:

> The common law refused . . . to permit stockholders to call corporate managers to account in actions at law. The possibilities for abuse, thus presented, were not ignored by corporate officers and directors. Early in the 19th century, equity provided relief both in this country and in England. Without detailing these developments, it suffices to say that the remedy in this country, first dealt with by this Court in Dodge v. Woolsey, 18 How. 331, 15 L.Ed. 401 (1855), provided redress . . . against faithless officers and directors. . . . The remedy made available in equity was the derivative suit, viewed in this country as a suit to enforce a *corporate* cause of action against officers, directors, and third parties. As elaborated in the cases, one precondition for the suit was a valid claim on which the corporation could have sued; another was that the corporation itself had refused to proceed after suitable demand, unless excused by extraordinary conditions. Thus the dual nature of the stockholder's action: first, the plaintiff's right to sue on behalf of the corporation and, second, the merits of the corporation's claim itself.

This type of suit is commonly known as a *derivative action,* since the shareholder's right to bring the suit derives from the corporation.

Two features of the derivative action warrant highlighting at the outset. First is the extraordinary procedural complexity inherent in such actions—complexity involving, for example, proper parties and their alignment, jurisdiction, demand on the board, demand on the shareholders, right to sue, intervention, settlement, and dismissal. Second is the difficult problem of social policy raised by such actions, particularly in the publicly held corporation. Through the derivative action, a shareholder with a tiny investment can force an expenditure by the corporation of a large amount of funds and executive time. The question is whether the overall benefits of such actions justify their overall costs, which are, in effect, borne involuntarily by the noncomplaining shareholders.

Where the corporation is publicly held, the plaintiff-shareholder's gain is not only indirect, but usually very small and often infinitesimal. For example, the defendants' briefs in *Hornstein v. Paramount Pictures, Inc.,* 37 N.Y.S.2d 404 (Sup.Ct. 1942), aff'd, 266 App.Div. 659, 41 N.Y.S.2d 210 (1943), aff'd 292 N.Y. 468, 55 N.E.2d 740 (1944), asserted that the five plaintiffs in that case stood to gain $3.57, $.41, $2.41, $.17 and $.65, respectively. In another well-known case, Winkelman v. General Motors Corp., 44 F.Supp. 960 (S.D.N.Y.1942), the three plaintiffs gained 8⟩ share for the ninety shares held between them.

A more recent approach to considering the adequacy of the plaintiff focuses not on the individual plaintiff's "stake" in the litigation but rather considers the substantive claims of the suit, particularly the plaintiff's understanding of those claims. For example, the plaintiff was deemed adequate in Asbury Auto Group, Inc. v. Palasack, 366 Ark. 601, 237 S.W. 3d 462 (Ark. 2006), even though unaware of the suit before being contacted by the suit's counsel to serve as its plaintiff as the court was impressed the plaintiff had conducted some research into the legitimacy of the claims before agreeing to become the suit's plaintiff. On the other hand, a quickly filed and poorly drafted complaint can be the basis for deeming the suit's plaintiff inadequate, being but a tool of the suit's counsel. *See e.g.,* South v. Baker, 62 A. 3d 1, 23 (Del. Ch. 2012).

In contrast, the plaintiff's lawyer stands to be awarded a very substantial fee out of the proceeds of any judgment or settlement—a fee that often runs into many hundreds of thousands, or even millions, of dollars. Furthermore, defendants in derivative actions are sometimes able to make settlements involving the illicit use of corporate funds to discharge their own liabilities. As a result of these elements, a concern exists that unscrupulous lawyers will exploit either the nuisance value of a nonmeritorious claim, or management's desire to cover up its own wrongdoing, through the institution of suits essentially brought to extract an exorbitant attorneys' fee.

Many or most of the issues to be considered in this chapter, although couched in technical terms, reflect an underlying tension between a concern that managers be held accountable for their wrongdoing, on the one hand, and a concern with the abusive or *strike suit* potential of derivative actions, on the other. Emphasis on the former element leads to liberality in permitting derivative actions; emphasis on the latter leads to rules that restrict such actions. In weighing these opposed concerns, it should be borne in mind that the derivative action and the disclosure requirements of the securities acts constitute the two major legal bulwarks against managerial self-dealing. In considering the various rules taken up in this chapter, it is therefore critical to evaluate the extent to which each rule cuts into the effectiveness of the derivative action, and whether the benefits of the rule justify that cost.

It should also be kept in mind, when considering the problems raised in this chapter, that significant substantive consequences often turn on the success of a motion to dismiss a derivative action on procedural grounds. If the plaintiff can survive such a motion, the facts that he already knows, together with the material that he can develop through discovery, will often lead to a substantial settlement. If the defendant can get the case dismissed on procedural grounds, however, no other plaintiff may come forward— either because no other shareholder who would bring suit knows all the relevant facts, or because the statute of limitations has run. Accordingly, for practical purposes many derivative actions will be won or lost on the basis of procedural issues that do not go to the merits of the case.

————

FEDERAL RULES OF CIVIL PROCEDURE, RULE 11

[See Statutory Supplement]

————

AMERICAN LAW INSTITUTE, PRINCIPLES OF CORPORATE GOVERNANCE §§ 7.04(a)(1), (b), (d) & 7.15

[See Statutory Supplement]

————

NOTES ON WHO CAN BRING A DERIVATIVE ACTION

1.   Shareholder Status. It is generally agreed that the plaintiff in a derivative action must be a shareholder at the time the action is begun, e.g., Vista Fund v. Garis, 277 N.W.2d 19 (Minn.1979), and must remain a shareholder during the pendency of the action, see, e.g., Schilling v. Belcher, 582 F.2d 995 (5th Cir.1978). An implication of this rule is that if S, a shareholder of C Corporation, brings a derivative action on C's behalf, and C then merges into T Corporation, which is the survivor of the merger, S loses standing to continue prosecuting the action, since she is no longer a shareholder in C. This rule was adopted in Delaware in the leading case of Lewis v. Anderson, 477 A.2d 1040 (Del. 1984). *See also* Lewis v. Ward, 852 A.2d 896 (Del. 2004) (affirming the position taken earlier in *Lewis*). However, both cases recognize two exceptions: (1) Where the merger is subject to the claim that it was perpetrated merely to deprive shareholders of the right to bring a derivative action; and (2) Where the merger is in reality a reorganization that does not affect the plaintiff's ownership of the business enterprise. A distinct minority of the courts permit a suit initiated before the merger terminated the plaintiff's holdings in the derivative suit corporation. *See* Duffy v. Cross Country Ind., 395 N.Y.S.2d 852 (1977). Some courts permit the suit to continue provided the plaintiff first makes a demand on the acquiring corporation's board. *See* Professional Management Assoc. Inc. v. Coss, 598 N.W.2d 406 (Minn. Ct. App. 1999).

What constitutes shareholdership for derivative-action purposes? In a few states, a statute or rule speaks to the issue directly. For example, N.Y.Bus.Corp.Law § 626(a) provides that the plaintiff in a derivative suit must be "a holder of shares or of voting trust certificates . . . or of a beneficial interest in such shares or certificates." Where the statute is silent, courts normally define shareholdership in a very expansive manner. First, record ownership is generally not required; an unregistered shareholder will qualify. See, e.g., Rosenthal v. Burry Biscuit Corp., 30 Del.Ch. 299, 60 A.2d 106 (Ch.1948). Second, legal ownership is not required—equitable ownership suffices. The latter category has been held to include, among others, an owner of stock held by a broker in a margin account in the broker's street name, a pledgee, the beneficiary of a trust, a legatee, a surviving spouse with a community interest in stock held in the deceased spouse's name, and a person who has contracted to purchase stock.

It is also established that in an appropriate case a shareholder in a parent corporation can bring a derivative action on behalf of a subsidiary, despite the fact that he is not a shareholder in the subsidiary. See Painter, Double Derivative Suits and Other Remedies With Regard to Damaged Subsidiaries, 36 Ind.L.J. 143, 147–49 (1961).

2.   Creditors. An implication from the rule that the plaintiff in a derivative action must be a shareholder at the time he brings suit is that a creditor (including a bondholder) ordinarily has no right to bring a derivative action. The bondholder's status was not improved where the bond was convertible into equity shares. See, e.g., Harff v. Kerkorian, 324 A.2d 215 (Del.Ch.1974), aff'd in pertinent part 347 A.2d 133 (Del.1975). Professor DeMott comments, "Convertible debentures present a more complicated problem. Some courts have held that the holder lacks standing to sue derivatively until the debenture has been converted, while others have held that the conversion feature provides the holder a sufficient equity interest to confer standing to sue derivatively—or have recognized that the question is disputed. More generally, in analyzing the status of holders of rights related to stocks, most courts focus on whether the holder has the right or an obligation to acquire shares of stock." Deborah DeMott, Shareholder Derivative Actions § 4:3 (2003).

Moreover, any claim based on misconduct that occurred prior to the corporation filing bankruptcy becomes the property of the bankruptcy estate and hence falls under the control of the trustee or debtor in possession. When the debtor in possession includes the defendants in the earlier initiated derivative suit an interesting question arises regarding who should control the suit. *See* David A. Skeel, Rethinking The Line Between Corporate Law and Corporate Bankruptcy, 72 Tex. L. Rev. 471 (1994).

3.   Should Creditors Have Standing? Chancellor William Allen famously observed in *Credit Lyonnais Bank Nederland N.V. v. Pathe Comm. Corp.,* 1991 WL 277613 (Del. Ch. 1991) that when a corporation was in the "zone of insolvency," creditors should enjoy standing to raise fiduciary duty claims, reasoning:

> [W]here a corporation is operating in the vicinity of insolvency, a board of directors is not merely the agent of the residual risk bearers, but owes its duty to the corporate enterprise ... [T]he board ... had an obligation to the community of interest that sustained the corporation, to exercise judgment in an informed, good faith effort to maximize the corporation's long-term wealth creating capacity.

Id. at 26. The Delaware Supreme court in *North American Catholic Education Programming Fdn. v. Gheewalla*, 930 A.2d 92 (Del. 2007) rejected *Credit Lyonnais's* reasoning; the court instead concluded that creditors do not need protections beyond those they can secure through carefully crafted lending covenants and the panoply of remedies they enjoy under various creditor rights laws at the state and federal level. Nonetheless, some modest protections for creditors do exist under state corporate law and are summarized in *Quadrant Structured Products Co., Ltd. v. Vertin*, 115 A.3d 535 (Del.Ch. 2015):

i)   Directors owe a fiduciary duty to creditors only once a corporation is actually insolvent;

ii)   Creditors may only bring a derivative claim to enforce the directors' fiduciary duties;

iii) Directors do not owe any particular duties to creditors, as their duty runs to the corporation for the benefit of all of its residual claimants that include the creditors of the insolvent firm;

iv)   Directors acting within their business judgment, can "favor certain non-insider creditors over others of similar priority;"

v)   Directors' ownership of stock does not alone give rise to a conflict of interest; and

vi)   The theory of deepening insolvency (where directors are alleged to breach their fiduciary duty by continuing to operate the firm with the consequence of increasing the losses to creditors) is rejected.

See also, Weinstein v. Colborne Foodbotics, 302 P.3d 263 (Colo. 2013) (fiduciary duty not owed to creditors of firm even when it is in the vicinity of insolvency).

4.   *Directors.* Occasionally a statute gives an officer or director the right to bring a derivative action. See N.Y.Bus.Corp.Law § 720(b). Absent such express statutory authorization, directors and officers lack standing to sue derivatively in their capacity as a director or officer. *See* Schoon v. Smith, 953 A.2d 196 (Del. 2008).

NOTE ON THE CORPORATION AS AN INDISPENSABLE PARTY

It is well established that the corporation is an indispensable party to a derivative action, and therefore must be joined in the suit:

> If the defendants account, it must be to the corporation and not to the shareholders. As to the defendants charged with defrauding it, the corporation is an indispensable party. . . . Furthermore, the decree must protect the defendants against any further suit by the corporation, and this will not be true unless it properly be made a party to the action. . . . The usual American practice is to name the beneficiary corporation as a party defendant, although in substance it is a party plaintiff; the flexibility of equity procedure permits an affirmative judgment to be entered in favor of one defendant against other defendants.

Dean v. Kellogg, 294 Mich. 200, 207–08, 292 N.W. 704, 707–08 (1940).

———

2.   THE NATURE OF THE DERIVATIVE ACTION

Tooley v. Donaldson, Lufkin, & Jenrette, Inc.
Supreme Court of Delaware, 2004.
845 A.2d 1031.

■ VEASEY, CHIEF JUSTICE:

Plaintiff-stockholders brought a purported class action in the Court of Chancery, alleging that the members of the board of directors of their corporation breached their fiduciary duties by agreeing to a 22-day delay in closing a proposed merger. Plaintiffs contend that the delay harmed them due to the lost time-value of the cash paid for their shares. The Court of Chancery granted the defendants' motion to dismiss on the sole ground that the claims were, "at most," claims of the corporation being asserted derivatively. They were, thus, held not to be direct claims of the stockholders, individually. Thereupon, the Court held that the plaintiffs lost their standing to bring this action when they tendered their shares in connection with the merger.

. . . We set forth in this Opinion the law to be applied henceforth in determining whether a stockholder's claim is derivative or direct. That issue must turn *solely* on the following questions: (1) who suffered the alleged harm (the corporation or the suing stockholders, individually); and (2) who would receive the benefit of any recovery or other remedy (the corporation or the stockholders, individually)? . . .

Facts

Patrick Tooley and Kevin Lewis are former minority stockholders of Donaldson, Lufkin & Jenrette, Inc. (DLJ), a Delaware corporation engaged in investment banking. DLJ was acquired by Credit Suisse Group (Credit Suisse) in the Fall of 2000. Before that acquisition, AXA

Financial, Inc.(AXA), which owned 71% of DLJ stock, controlled DLJ. Pursuant to a stockholder agreement between AXA and Credit Suisse, AXA agreed to exchange with Credit Suisse its DLJ stockholdings for a mix of stock and cash. The consideration received by AXA consisted primarily of stock. Cash made up one-third of the purchase price. Credit Suisse intended to acquire the remaining minority interests of publicly-held DLJ stock through a cash tender offer, followed by a merger of DLJ into a Credit Suisse subsidiary.

The tender offer price was set at $90 per share in cash. The tender offer was to expire 20 days after its commencement. The merger agreement, however, authorized two types of extensions. First, Credit Suisse could unilaterally extend the tender offer if certain conditions were not met, such as SEC regulatory approvals or certain payment obligations. Alternatively, DLJ and Credit Suisse could agree to postpone acceptance by Credit Suisse of DLJ stock tendered by the minority stockholders.

Credit Suisse availed itself of both types of extensions to postpone the closing of the tender offer. The tender offer was initially set to expire on October 5, 2000, but Credit Suisse invoked the five-day unilateral extension provided in the agreement. Later, by agreement between DLJ and Credit Suisse, it postponed the merger a second time so that it was then set to close on November 2, 2000.

Plaintiffs challenge the second extension that resulted in a 22-day delay. They contend that this delay was not properly authorized and harmed minority stockholders while improperly benefitting AXA. They claim damages representing the time-value of money lost through the delay.

The Decision of the Court of Chancery

. . . The Court of Chancery, relying upon our confusing jurisprudence on the direct/derivative dichotomy, based its dismissal on the following ground: "Because this delay affected all DLJ shareholders equally, plaintiffs' injury was not a special injury, and this action is, thus, a derivative action, at most."

Plaintiffs argue that they have suffered a "special injury" because they had an alleged contractual right to receive the merger consideration of $90 per share without suffering the 22-day delay arising out of the extensions under the merger agreement. But the trial court's opinion convincingly demonstrates that plaintiffs had no such contractual right that had ripened at the time the extensions were entered into:

> *Here, it is clear that plaintiffs have no separate contractual right to bring a direct claim, and they do not assert contractual rights under the merger agreement.* First, the merger agreement specifically disclaims any persons as being third party beneficiaries to the contract. Second, any contractual shareholder right to payment of the merger consideration did

not ripen until the conditions of the agreement were met. The agreement stated that Credit Suisse Group was not required to accept any shares for tender, or could extend the offer, under certain conditions—one condition of which included an extension or termination by agreement between Credit Suisse Group and DLJ. *Because Credit Suisse Group and DLJ did in fact agree to extend the tender offer period, any right to payment plaintiffs could have did not ripen until this newly negotiated period was over. The merger agreement only became binding and mutually enforceable at the time the tendered shares ultimately were accepted for payment by Credit Suisse Group.* It is at that moment in time, November 3, 2000, that the company became bound to purchase the tendered shares, making the contract mutually enforceable. *DLJ stockholders had no individual contractual right to payment until November 3, 2000, when their tendered shares were accepted for payment.* Thus, they have no contractual basis to challenge a delay in the closing of the tender offer up until November 3. *Because this is the date the tendered shares were accepted for payment, the contract was not breached and plaintiffs do not have a contractual basis to bring a direct suit.* . . .

That conclusion could have ended the case because it portended a definitive ruling that plaintiffs have no claim whatsoever on the facts alleged. But the defendants chose to argue, and the trial court chose to decide, the standing issue, which is predicated on an assertion that this claim is a derivative one asserted on behalf of the corporation, DLJ. . . .

The trial court's analysis was hindered, however, because it focused on the confusing concept of "special injury" as the test for determining whether a claim is derivative or direct. The trial court's premise was as follows:

> In order to bring a *direct* claim, a plaintiff must have experienced some "special injury." [citing *Lipton v. News Int'l,* 514 A.2d 1075, 1079 (Del.1986)]. A special injury is a wrong that "is separate and distinct from that suffered by other shareholders, . . . or a wrong involving a contractual right of a shareholder, such as the right to vote, or to assert majority control, which exists independently of any right of the corporation." [citing *Moran v. Household Int'l. Inc.,* 490 A.2d 1059, 1070 (Del.Ch.1985), *aff'd* 500 A.2d 1346 (Del.1986 [1985])].

In our view, the concept of "special injury" that appears in some Supreme Court and Court of Chancery cases is not helpful to a proper analytical distinction between direct and derivative actions. We now disapprove the use of the concept of "special injury" as a tool in that analysis.

The Proper Analysis to Distinguish Between
Direct and Derivative Actions

The analysis must be based solely on the following questions: Who suffered the alleged harm—the corporation or the suing stockholder individually—and who would receive the benefit of the recovery or other remedy? This simple analysis is well imbedded in our jurisprudence,[3] but some cases have complicated it by injection of the amorphous and confusing concept of "special injury."

The Chancellor, in the very recent *Agostino* case,[4] correctly points this out and strongly suggests that we should disavow the concept of "special injury." In a scholarly analysis of this area of the law, he also suggests that the inquiry should be whether the stockholder has demonstrated that he or she has suffered an injury that is not dependent on an injury to the corporation. In the context of a claim for breach of fiduciary duty, the Chancellor articulated the inquiry as follows: "Looking at the body of the complaint and considering the nature of the wrong alleged and the relief requested, has the plaintiff demonstrated that he or she can prevail without showing an injury to the corporation?"[5] We believe that this approach is helpful in analyzing the first prong of the analysis: what person or entity has suffered the alleged harm? The second prong of the analysis should logically follow.

A Brief History of Our Jurisprudence

. . . Because a derivative suit is being brought on behalf of the corporation, the recovery, if any, must go to the corporation. A stockholder who is directly injured, however, does retain the right to bring an individual action for injuries affecting his or her legal rights as a stockholder. Such a claim is distinct from an injury caused to the corporation alone. In such individual suits, the recovery or other relief flows directly to the stockholders, not to the corporation.

Determining whether an action is derivative or direct is sometimes difficult and has many legal consequences, some of which may have an expensive impact on the parties to the action. For example, if an action is derivative, the plaintiffs are then required to comply with the requirements of Court of Chancery Rule 23.1, that the stockholder: (a) retain ownership of the shares throughout the litigation; (b) make presuit

---

[3]   *See, e.g., Kramer v. Western Pacific Industries, Inc.,* 546 A.2d 348 (Del.1988).

[4]   *Agostino v. Hicks,* No. Civ. A. 20020–NC, 2004 WL 443987 (Del.Ch. March 11, 2004).

[5]   *Agostino,* 2004 WL 443987, at * 7. The Chancellor further explains that the focus should be on the person or entity to whom the relevant duty is owed. *Id.* at *7 n. 54. As noted in *Agostino, id.,* this test is similar to that articulated by the American Law Institute (ALI), a test that we cited with approval in *Grimes v. Donald,* 673 A.2d 1207 (Del.1996). The ALI test is as follows:

> A direct action may be brought in the name and right of a holder to redress an injury sustained by, or enforce a duty owed to, the holder. An action in which the holder can prevail without showing an injury or breach of duty to the corporation should be treated as a direct action that may be maintained by the holder in an individual capacity.

2 American Law Institute, PRINCIPLES OF CORPORATE GOVERNANCE: ANALYSIS AND RECOMMENDATIONS § 7.01(b) at 17.

demand on the board; and (c) obtain court approval of any settlement. Further, the recovery, if any, flows only to the corporation. The decision whether a suit is direct or derivative may be outcome-determinative. Therefore, it is necessary that a standard to distinguish such actions be clear, simple and consistently articulated and applied by our courts.

In *Elster v. American Airlines, Inc.,*[7] the stockholder sought to enjoin the grant and exercise of stock options because they would result in a dilution of her stock personally. In *Elster,* the alleged injury was found to be derivative, not direct, because it was essentially a claim of mismanagement of corporate assets. Then came the complication in the analysis: The Court held that where the alleged injury is to both the corporation *and* to the stockholder, the stockholder must allege a "special injury" to maintain a direct action. The Court did not define "special injury," however. By implication, decisions in later cases have interpreted *Elster* to mean that a "special injury" is alleged where the wrong is inflicted upon the stockholder alone or where the stockholder complains of a wrong affecting a particular right. Examples would be a preemptive right as a stockholder, rights involving control of the corporation or a wrong affecting the stockholder, qua individual holder, and not the corporation.

In *Bokat v. Getty Oil Co.,*[8] a stockholder of a subsidiary brought suit against the director of the parent corporation for causing the subsidiary to invest its resources wastefully, resulting in a loss to the subsidiary. The claim in *Bokat* was essentially for mismanagement of corporate assets. Therefore, the Court held that any recovery must be sought on behalf of the corporation, and the claim was, thus, found to be derivative.

In describing how a court may distinguish direct and derivative actions, the *Bokat* Court stated that a suit must be maintained derivatively if the injury falls equally upon all stockholders. Experience has shown this concept to be confusing and inaccurate. It is confusing because it appears to have been intended to address the fact that an injury to the corporation tends to diminish each share of stock equally because corporate assets or their value are diminished. In that sense, the *indirect* injury to the stockholders arising out of the harm to the corporation comes about solely by virtue of their stockholdings. It does not arise out of any independent or direct harm to the stockholders, individually. That concept is also inaccurate because a direct, individual claim of stockholders that does not depend on harm to the corporation can also fall on all stockholders equally, without the claim thereby becoming a derivative claim.

In *Lipton v. News International, Plc.,*[9] this Court applied the "special injury" test. There, a stockholder began acquiring shares in the

---

[7]   100 A.2d 219, 222 (Del.Ch.1953).

[8]   262 A.2d 246 (Del.1970).

[9]   . . . . 514 A.2d at 1078 [Del. 1988].

defendant corporation presumably to gain control of the corporation. In response, the defendant corporation agreed to an exchange of its shares with a friendly buyer. Due to the exchange and a supermajority voting requirement on certain stockholder actions, the management of the defendant corporation acquired a veto power over any change in management.

The *Lipton* Court concluded that the critical analytical issue in distinguishing direct and derivative actions is whether a "special injury" has been alleged. There, the Court found a "special injury" because the board's manipulation worked an injury upon the plaintiff-stockholder unlike the injury suffered by other stockholders. That was because the plaintiff-stockholder was actively seeking to gain control of the defendant corporation. Therefore, the Court found that the claim was direct. Ironically, the Court could have reached the same correct result by simply concluding that the manipulation directly and individually harmed the stockholders, without injuring the corporation. . . .

Thus, two confusing propositions have encumbered our caselaw governing the direct/derivative distinction. The "special injury" concept, applied in cases such as *Lipton,* can be confusing in identifying the nature of the action. The same is true of the proposition that stems from *Bokat*— that an action cannot be direct if all stockholders are equally affected or unless the stockholder's injury is separate and distinct from that suffered by other stockholders. The proper analysis has been and should remain that stated in *Grimes.* . . . That is, a court should look to the nature of the wrong and to whom the relief should go. The stockholder's claimed direct injury must be independent of any alleged injury to the corporation. The stockholder must demonstrate that the duty breached was owed to the stockholder and that he or she can prevail without showing an injury to the corporation.

Standard to Be Applied in This Case

In this case it cannot be concluded that the complaint alleges a derivative claim. There is no derivative claim asserting injury to the corporate entity. There is no relief that would go the corporation. Accordingly, there is no basis to hold that the complaint states a derivative claim.

But, it does not necessarily follow that the complaint states a direct, individual claim. While the complaint purports to set forth a direct claim, in reality, it states no claim at all. The trial court analyzed the complaint and correctly concluded that it does not claim that the plaintiffs have any rights that have been injured. Their rights have not yet ripened. The contractual claim is nonexistent until it is ripe, and that claim will not be ripe until the terms of the merger are fulfilled, including the extensions of the closing at issue here. Therefore, there is no direct claim stated in the complaint before us.

Accordingly, the complaint was properly dismissed. But, due to the reliance on the concept of "special injury" by the Court of Chancery, the ground set forth for the dismissal is erroneous, there being no derivative claim. That error is harmless, however, because, in our view, there is no direct claim either.

Conclusion

. . . We affirm the judgment of the Court of Chancery dismissing the complaint, although on a different ground from that decided by the Court of Chancery. . . .

Int'l Brotherhood of Electrical Workers Local No. 129 Benefit Fund v. Tucci

Supreme Judicial Court of Massachusetts, 2017.
476 Mass. 553, 70 N.E.3d 918.

■ BOTSFORD, J. . . . [S]hareholders of a publicly traded corporation claim that a merger transaction proposed by the board of directors will result in the effective sale of the corporation for an inadequate price. The question we consider is whether they may bring that claim directly against the board members, or must bring it as a derivative claim on behalf of the corporation. . . .

Background. The plaintiffs . . . [allege] breaches of fiduciary duty by the board of directors of EMC Corporation (EMC) arising from a merger between EMc and . . . Dell. . . . The plaintiffs' complaint alleged that they brought the actions on behalf of a class consisting of "all other shareholders of EMC . . . who are or will be deprived of the opportunity to maximize the value of their shares of EMC as a result of the [directors'] breaches of fiduciary duty and other misconduct." The plaintiffs asserted that the members of EMC's board of directors violated their fiduciary duties, allegedly owed to both EMC and the shareholders, by "(i) failing to take steps to maximize the value of EMC stock; and (ii) agreeing to unreasonably preclusive deal protection provisions, thereby hindering any potential bid that may have been superior" to the sale of EMC to Dell. . . .

EMC has a federation structure; that is, it acts as parent company to numerous related but independently functioning businesses. The defendant Joseph M. Tucci, the longtime chief executive officer of EMC and the architect of this federated structure, wanted to keep the federation of companies together. This caused EMC's shares to trade at a "conglomerate discount" because investors valued the large company less than they would its individual components. . . . Tucci had scheduled his retirement several times, but continually extended the date. He negotiated the sale of EMC and all its subsidiaries to Dell via his longtime friend and business associate, Michael Dell, in order to keep the company's federated structure intact. Tucci is to receive approximately $27 million in "change-in-control" benefits as a result of selling the entire company, a sum that Tucci would not have received if he had retired as planned. The proposed transaction also permits Dell to shelter significant tax liability and to retain the value locked in the subsidiaries through a potential break-up of the EMC federation in the future.

In October, 2015, Tucci announced that Dell agreed to acquire all of EMC for approximately $67 billion. Tucci used his influence over the other board members to convince them to approve the merger. The transaction was unanimously approved by the board and announced on October 12, 2015. In approving the proposed merger, the board also agreed to termination fees that further dissuaded competing companies from placing a higher bid on EMC than Dell: the merger agreement between EMC and Dell included a $2 billion termination fee that any higher bidder would have to pay before it could top the Dell bid. . . .[7]

Discussion. The parties agree that EMC is a large, publicly traded Massachusetts corporation . . .

1.   *Derivative actions and claims.* "The derivative form of action permits an individual shareholder to bring 'suit to enforce a *corporate* cause of action against officers, directors, and third parties.' . . . Devised as a suit in equity, the purpose of the derivative action was to place in the hands of the individual shareholder a means to protect the interests of the corporation from the misfeasance and malfeasance of 'faithless directors and managers.'" . . . To determine whether a claim belongs to the corporation, and is therefore derivative, "a court must inquire whether the shareholders' injury is distinct from the injury suffered generally by the shareholders as owners of corporate stock" *Stegall* v. *Ladner*, 394 F. Supp. 2d 358, 364 (D. Mass. 2005) (applying Massachusetts law).

2.   *Direct versus derivative.* As the plaintiffs recognize, whether a claim asserted by stockholders of a Massachusetts corporation is one that may be pursued directly by them against the corporation's directors or must be pursued derivatively depends on whether the harm they claim to have suffered resulted from a breach of duty owed directly to them, or whether the harm claimed was derivative of a breach of duty owed to the corporation. . . . The plaintiffs also recognize that the act's provisions defining the standards of conduct applicable to corporate directors governs, or at least has a direct bearing on, the determination whether corporate directors owe a fiduciary duty directly to the corporation's shareholders. We turn to the act.

3.   *The Act.* Section 8.30 of the act defines the standards of conduct a director of a Massachusetts corporation is required to follow. The section provides in relevant part:

---

[7]   The defendants inform us in their brief that at a special shareholder meeting held on July 19, 2016, ninety-eight per cent of voting EMC shareholders voted to approve the merger transaction. . . .

"(a) A director shall discharge his duties as a director, including his duties as a member of a committee:

"(1) in good faith;

"(2) with the care that a person in a like position would reasonably believe appropriate under similar circumstances; and

"(3) in a manner the director reasonably believes to be in the best interests of the corporation. In determining what the director reasonably believes to be in the best interests of the corporation, a director may consider the interests of the corporation's employees, suppliers, creditors and customers, the economy of the state, the region and the nation, community and societal considerations, and the long-term and short-term interests of the corporation and its shareholders, including the possibility that these interests may be best served by the continued independence of the corporation.

". . .

G. L. c. 156D, § 8.30. . . .

[A]lthough § 8.30 (a) (3) makes clear that a director may consider, among other interests, "the long-term and short-term interests of the corporation *and its shareholders*" (emphasis added), it first specifies that the director may do so only in the context of "determining what the director reasonably believes to be in the best interests of the corporation." Particularly in light of this specification, the plaintiffs' proposed interpretation of § 8.30 (a) as implicitly imposing or recognizing a fiduciary duty owed by a corporate director directly to the shareholders must fail.

4.   *Massachusetts corporate law principles.* As reflected in § 8.30 (a), its antecedent statute, G. L. c. 156B, § 65, and decisions reflecting our common-law principles, the general rule of Massachusetts corporate law is that a director of a Massachusetts corporation owes a fiduciary duty to the corporation itself, and not its shareholders—although . . . there are at least two exceptions. First, there is a special rule for close corporations: . . . See *Donahue* v. *Rodd Electrotype Co. of New England*, 367 Mass. 578, 593–594, 328 N.E.2d 505 (1975). . . . Second, where a controlling shareholder who also is a director proposes and implements a self-interested transaction that is to the detriment of minority shareholders, a direct action by the adversely affected shareholders may proceed. *Coggins* v. *New England Patriots Football Club, Inc.*, 397 Mass. 525, 532–533, 492 N.E.2d 1112 (1986). . . Neither of these exceptions, however, applies in this case. . . . As the motion judge noted, the wrong alleged by the plaintiffs, undervaluing EMC to secure the merger and sale of the federation of companies, qualifies as a direct injury to the corporation, the entity to which the directors clearly owed a fiduciary duty of good faith and loyalty. Flowing from that alleged injury is a claimed derivative

injury to each shareholder, whose individual shares, as a consequence of the asserted undervaluing of EMC itself, are consequently undervalued as well. . . . Because the plaintiffs did not bring their claim as a derivative action, their complaint was properly dismissed.

5. *Delaware law.* . . . The plaintiffs have a response, however, which is that we should change our approach and follow those corporate law jurisdictions, including in particular Delaware . . . . We decline to do so. Delaware's General Corporation Law . . . differs from the act, and has no equivalent of § 8.30. Delaware also has a history of asserting that directors stand in a fiduciary relation to stockholders of the company, in contrast to our own precedent. See *In re MONY Group, Inc. Shareholder Litig.,* 853 A.2d 661, 676 (Del. Ch. 2004) (board of directors "owes its fiduciary duties to corporation and its stockholders") . . . .

6. *Equitable relief.* The plaintiffs claim that the result we reach is unjust because even if they had sought to follow the statutory procedures governing derivative claims, see G. L. c. 156D, §§ 7.40–7.47, it was likely that the defendants would have taken steps to assure that the merger occurred before any derivative suit could be concluded and, under our law, once the plaintiffs were no longer shareholders, they could not have continued to seek derivative relief because their ownership rights in EMC would have been extinguished. We agree that if a shareholder no longer owns shares in a corporation, as a general rule, the shareholder would no longer have standing to pursue a derivative claim on behalf of the corporation. See *Billings* v. *GTFM, LLC,* 449 Mass. 281, 296, 867 N.E.2d 714 (2007). But we disagree that this means it is unfair or inequitable . . . .

The act clearly illustrates the procedures to follow to bring a derivative claim. A shareholder must make a demand pursuant to G. L. c. 156D, § 7.42. The corporation then must determine whether it would be in the best interests of the corporation to take over the shareholder's claim, and the statute specifies alternative ways that the corporation may undertake to make this determination. G. L. c. 156D, § 7.44 (*b*). If the demand is rejected, the shareholder may commence suit, in accordance with the time requirements in § 7.42 (2). In this case, at any time between the time the proposed merger transaction was announced on October 12, 2015, and the date the merger transaction was completed, September 7, 2016, the plaintiffs could have made a derivative demand on EMC. They did not do so.[15] We find nothing in the statutory provisions governing derivative proceedings to indicate or suggest that it offered the plaintiffs here, and other shareholders in the plaintiffs' position, a hollow or inadequate form of relief.

---

[15]   Moreover, if the plaintiffs had filed suit after having made such a demand that was rejected, and it appeared that the proposed merger might likely be completed while the suit was pending, the plaintiffs could have sought preliminary injunctive relief.

Conclusion. For the foregoing reasons, the Superior Court's order dismissing the plaintiffs' complaint is affirmed.

So ordered.

————

AMERICAN LAW INSTITUTE, PRINCIPLES OF CORPORATE GOVERNANCE § 7.01

[See Statutory Supplement]

————

Barth v. Barth

Supreme Court of Indiana, 1995.
659 N.E.2d 559.

■ SULLIVAN, JUSTICE.

Background

This lawsuit was brought against defendants Barth Electric Co., Inc., and its president and majority shareholder Michael G. Barth, Jr., by plaintiff minority shareholder Robert Barth individually (rather than derivatively on behalf of the corporation).[3] Plaintiff Robert Barth alleged that defendant Michael Barth had taken certain actions which had the effect of "substantially reducing the value of Plaintiff's shares of common stock" in the corporation. Specifically, plaintiff contended that defendant Michael Barth had: (1) paid excessive salaries to himself and to members of his immediate family; (2) used corporate employees to perform services on his and his son's homes without compensating the corporation; (3) dramatically lowered dividend payments; and (4) appropriated corporate funds for personal investments. . . . Michael Barth and the corporation moved to dismiss Robert Barth's complaint for the failure to state a claim upon which relief can be granted, . . . arguing that a derivative action was required to redress claims of this nature. The trial court granted the motion to dismiss. The Court of Appeals acknowledged that the "well-established general rule" prohibits a shareholder from maintaining an action in the shareholder's own name but found that requiring a derivative action here would "exalt form over substance" since Robert Barth could have satisfied the requirements for bringing a derivative action and that none of the reasons underlying the general derivative action requirement were present. *Barth v. Barth*, 651 N.E.2d at 293. The Court of Appeals reversed the trial court; the corporation and Michael Barth seek transfer.

---

[3]   Michael Barth owns 51% of the shares of the corporation. Robert Barth owns 29.8%. A third individual owns the remaining shares.

Discussion

As the Court of Appeals made clear, the well-established general rule is that shareholders of a corporation may not maintain actions at law in their own names to redress an injury to the corporation even if the value of their stock is impaired as a result of the injury. *Moll v. South Central Solar Systems, Inc.* (Ind.App.1981), 419 N.E.2d 154, 161. . . . In *Moll,* Judge Ratliff discussed the purpose of the rule in the following terms:

> The rationale supporting this rule is based on sound public policy considerations. It is recognized that authorization of shareholder actions in such cases would constitute authorization of multitudinous litigation and disregard for the corporate entity. . . . Sound policy considerations have been said to require that a single action be brought rather than to permit separate suits by each shareholder even when the corporation and the shareholder are the same. . . .

Moll, 419 N.E.2d at 161. In W & W Equipment Co., Inc. v. Mink (1991), Ind.App., 568 N.E.2d 564, Judge Baker set forth additional reasons for this rule: the protection of corporate creditors by putting the proceeds of the recovery back in the corporation; the protection of the interests of all the shareholders rather than allowing one shareholder to prejudice the interests of other shareholders; and the adequate compensation of the injured shareholder by increasing the value of the shares when recovery is put back into the corporation. *Id.,* 568 N.E.2d at 571. . . .

While we affirm the general rule requiring a shareholder to bring a derivative rather than direct action when seeking redress for injury to the corporation, we nevertheless observe two reasons why this rule will not always apply in the case of closely-held corporations.[5] First, shareholders in a close corporation stand in a fiduciary relationship to each other, and as such, must deal fairly, honestly, and openly with the corporation and with their fellow shareholders. *W & W Equipment Co.,* 568 N.E.2d at 570; *Krukemeier v. Krukemeier Machine and Tool Co., Inc.* (Ind.App.1990), 551 N.E.2d 885; *Garbe v. Excel Mold, Inc.* (Ind.App.1979), 397 N.E.2d 296.[6] Second, shareholder litigation in the closely-held corporation context will often not implicate the policies that mandate requiring derivative litigation when more widely-held corporations are involved. W & W Equipment Co., Inc. v. Mink is a leading case in this regard. There our Court of Appeals was faced with a lawsuit filed by one of two 50% shareholders of a corporation after the

---

[5]   A closely-held corporation is one which typically has relatively few shareholders and whose shares are not generally traded in the securities market. *W & W Equipment Co., Inc. v. Mink* (Ind.App.1991), 568 N.E.2d 564, 570 (citing F. Hodge O'Neal & Robert B. Thompson, O'Neal's Close Corporations § 1.02 (3d ed.)). Accord, American Law Institute, Principles of Corporate Governance: Analysis and Recommendations § 1.06 (1994).

[6]   This principle of Indiana corporate law mirrors that reached by the Supreme Judicial Court of Massachusetts in. . . . *Donahue v. Rodd Electrotype Co. of New England, Inc.,* 367 Mass. 578, 328 N.E.2d 505, 515 (Mass.1975). . . .

other shareholder joined with nonshareholder directors to fire the plaintiff shareholder and arrange for the payment of certain corporate assets to the other shareholder. The court concluded that no useful purpose would be served by forcing the plaintiff to proceed derivatively where the policies favoring derivative actions were not implicated—direct corporate recovery was not necessary to protect absent shareholders or creditors as none existed. *Id.,* 568 N.E.2d at 571.

Because shareholders of closely-held corporations have very direct obligations to one another and because shareholder litigation in the closely-held corporation context will often not implicate the principles which gave rise to the rule requiring derivative litigation, courts in many cases are permitting direct suits by shareholders of closely-held corporations where the complaint is one that in a public corporation would have to be brought as a derivative action. See F. Hodge O'Neal & Robert B. Thompson, O'Neal's Close Corporations § 8.16 n. 32 (3d ed. & 1995 Cum.Supp.) (collecting cases); American Law Institute, Principles of Corporate Governance: Analysis and Recommendations § 7.01, reporter's n. 4 (1994) (collecting cases). However, it is important to keep in mind that the principles which gave rise to the rule requiring derivative actions will sometimes be present even in litigation involving closely-held corporations. For example, because a corporate recovery in a derivative action will benefit creditors while a direct recovery by a shareholder will not, the protection of creditors principle could well be implicated in a shareholder suit against a closely-held corporation with debt. . . .

In its recently-completed corporate governance project, the American Law Institute proposed the following rule for determining when a shareholder of a closely-held corporation may proceed by direct or derivative action:

> In the case of a closely held corporation, the court in its discretion may treat an action raising derivative claims as a direct action, exempt it from those restrictions and defenses applicable only to derivative actions, and order an individual recovery, if it finds that to do so will not (i) unfairly expose the corporation or the defendants to a multiplicity of actions, (ii) materially prejudice the interests of creditors of the corporation, or (iii) interfere with a fair distribution of the recovery among all interested persons.

A.L.I., Principles of Corporate Governance § 7.01(d). We have studied this rule and find that it is consistent with the approach taken by our Court of Appeals and by most other jurisdictions in similar cases and that it represents a fair and workable approach for balancing the relative interests in closely-held corporation shareholder litigation.

In determining that a trial court has discretion to decide whether a plaintiff must proceed by direct or by derivative action, we make the following observations, drawn largely from the Comment to § 7.01(d).

First, permitting such litigation to proceed as a direct action will exempt the plaintiff from the requirements of Ind.Code § 23–1–32–1 et seq., including the provisions that permit a special committee of the board of directors to recommend dismissal of the lawsuit. Ind.Code § 23–1–32–4. As such, the court in making its decision should consider whether the corporation has a disinterested board that should be permitted to consider the lawsuit's impact on the corporation. A.L.I., Corporate Governance Project § 7.01 comment e. Second, in some situations it may actually be to the benefit of the corporation to permit the plaintiff to proceed by direct action. This will permit the defendant to file a counterclaim against the plaintiff, whereas counterclaims are generally prohibited in derivative actions. Also, in a direct action each side will normally be responsible for its own legal expenses; the plaintiff, even if successful, cannot ordinarily look to the corporation for attorney's fees. Id.

Conclusion

We grant transfer, vacate the opinion of the Court of Appeals, and remand this cause to the trial court for reconsideration of its order of dismissal in light of the rule adopted in this opinion.

■ SHEPARD, C.J., and DEBRULER, DICKSON and SELBY, JJ., concur.

---

3. INDIVIDUAL RECOVERY IN DERIVATIVE ACTIONS

Glenn v. Hoteltron Systems, Inc.

Court of Appeals of New York, 1989.
74 N.Y.2d 386, 547 N.Y.S.2d 816, 547 N.E.2d 71.

■ WACHTLER, CHIEF JUDGE. . . .

The dispute here is between Jacob Schachter and Herbert Kulik, the founders of Ketek Electric Corporation. Schachter and Kulik each own 50% of the corporation's shares and serve as the corporation's only officers. . . . [T]he Appellate Division, on [a] prior appeal, found Schachter liable for diverting Ketek assets and opportunities to Hoteltron Systems, Inc., a corporation wholly owned by Schachter.

Following the trial on damages, Supreme Court concluded that Hoteltron had earned profits of $362,242.84 from Schachter's usurpation of Ketek assets and opportunities. . . .

On Schachter's appeal, the Appellate Division . . . concluded that the Hoteltron profits should be awarded to the injured corporation, Ketek, rather than the innocent shareholder Kulik. . . .

It is the general rule that, because a shareholders' derivative suit seeks to vindicate a wrong done to the corporation through enforcement of a corporate cause of action, any recovery obtained is for the benefit of the injured corporation. . . .

Kulik argues that this result is inequitable because Schachter, as a shareholder of Ketek, will ultimately share in the proceeds of the damage award. But that prospect exists in any successful derivative action in which the wrongdoer is a shareholder of the injured corporation. An exception based on that fact alone would effectively nullify the general rule that damages for a corporate injury should be awarded to the corporation.

It is true that this anomaly is magnified in cases involving closely held corporations, because the errant fiduciary is likely to own a large share of the corporation—as Schachter owns 50% of Ketek—and will share proportionately in the restitution to the corporation generated by a successful suit against him. Thus, it may be argued that in such circumstances an award of damages to the corporation does not provide a sufficient deterrent to the potential wrongdoer. We conclude, however, that this consideration does not require a different damage rule for close corporations.

While awarding damages directly to the innocent shareholder may seem equitable with respect to the parties before the court, other interests, particularly those of the corporation's creditors, should not be overlooked. The fruits of a diverted corporate opportunity are properly a corporate asset. Awarding that asset directly to a shareholder could impair the rights of creditors whose claims may be superior to that of the innocent shareholder. . . .

Thus, while we do not rule out the possibility that an award to innocent shareholders rather than to the corporation would be appropriate in some circumstances, we find no need to invoke such an exception here.

Accordingly, the order of the Appellate Division should be affirmed, without costs.

■ SIMONS, KAYE, ALEXANDER, TITONE, HANCOCK and BELLACOSA, JJ., concur.

Order affirmed, without costs.

———

PERLMAN v. FELDMANN

[Chapter 10, supra.]

———

4. THE CONTEMPORANEOUS-OWNERSHIP RULE

———

FEDERAL RULES OF CIVIL PROCEDURE, RULE 23.1

[See Statutory Supplement]

———

DELAWARE GEN. CORP. LAW § 327

[See Statutory Supplement]

———

MODEL BUS. CORP. ACT § 7.41

[See Statutory Supplement]

———

CAL. CORP. CODE § 800(b)(1)

[See Statutory Supplement]

———

ALI, PRINCIPLES OF CORPORATE GOVERNANCE § 7.02(a)

[See Statutory Supplement]

———

Bangor Punta Operations, Inc.
v. Bangor & Aroostook R.R.

Supreme Court of the United States, 1974.
417 U.S. 703, 94 S.Ct. 2578, 41 L.Ed.2d 418.

■ MR. JUSTICE POWELL delivered the opinion of the Court. . . .

I

[Prior to October 1964, Bangor & Aroostook Corporation ("B & A")
held 98.3% of the stock of the Bangor & Aroostook Railroad Company
("BAR"), a Maine corporation. In October 1964, B & A sold its BAR stock
to Bangor Punta, a Delaware corporation. Bangor Punta held the stock
for five years, and then sold it in October 1969 to Amoskeag Co. for $5
million. Amoskeag later acquired additional shares which gave it
ownership of more than 99% (but less than 100%) of BAR.]*

———

* In the interests of clarity, the statement of facts eliminates subsidiaries that do not
figure in the opinion. (Footnote by ed.)

In 1971, BAR . . . filed the present action against Bangor Punta . . . in the United States District Court for the District of Maine. The complaint specified 13 counts of alleged mismanagement, misappropriation, and waste of BAR's corporate assets occurring during the period from 1960 through 1967 when B & A and then Bangor Punta controlled BAR.[1] Damages were sought in the amount of $7,000,000 for violations of both federal and state laws. The federal statutes and regulations alleged to have been violated included § 10 of the Clayton Act, 15 U.S.C.A. § 20; § 10(b) of the Securities Exchange Act of 1934 . . . and Rule 10b–5. . . . The state claims were grounded on § 104 of the Maine Public Utilities Act, Maine Rev.Stat.Ann., Tit. 35, § 104 (1965), and the common law of Maine. . . .

The District Court granted petitioners' motion for summary judgment and dismissed the action. 353 F.Supp. 724 (1972). The court first observed that although the suit purported to be a primary action brought in the name of the corporation, the real party in interest and hence the actual beneficiary of any recovery, was Amoskeag, the present owner of more than 99% of the outstanding stock of BAR. The court then noted that Amoskeag had acquired all of its BAR stock long after the alleged wrongs occurred and that Amoskeag did not contend that it had not received full value for its purchase price, or that the purchase transaction was tainted by fraud or deceit. Thus, any recovery on Amoskeag's part would constitute a windfall because it had sustained no injury. With this in mind, the court then addressed the claims based on federal law and determined that Amoskeag would have been barred from maintaining a shareholder derivative action because of its failure to satisfy the "contemporaneous ownership" requirement of Fed.Rule Civ.Proc. 23.1(1).[3] Finding that equitable principles prevented the use of the corporate fiction to evade the proscription of Rule 23.1, the court concluded that Amoskeag's efforts to recover under the Securities Exchange Act and the Clayton Act must fail. Turning to the claims based on state law, the court recognized that the applicability of Rule 23.1(1) has been questioned where federal jurisdiction is based on diversity of citizenship.[4] The court found it unnecessary to resolve this issue,

---

[1] Several of the alleged acts of corporate mismanagement occurred between 1960 and 1964 when B & A . . . was in control of the railroad. Liability for these acts was nevertheless sought to be imposed on Bangor Punta, even though it had no interest in either BAR or B & A during this period. The apparent basis for liability was the 1964 purchase agreement between B & A and Bangor Punta. The complaint in the instant case alleged that under the agreement Bangor Punta, through its subsidiary, assumed "all . . . debts, obligations, contracts and liabilities" of B & A.

[3] Rule 23.1(1), which specifies the requirements applicable to shareholder derivative actions, states that the complaint shall aver that "the plaintiff was a shareholder or member at the time of the transaction of which he complains. . . ." This provision is known as the "contemporaneous ownership" requirement. See 3B J. Moore, Federal Practice § 23.1 et seq. (2d ed. 1974).

[4] The "contemporaneous ownership" requirement in shareholder derivative actions was first announced in Hawes v. Oakland, 104 U.S. 450, 26 L.Ed. 827 (1881), and soon thereafter adopted as Equity Rule 97. This provision was later incorporated in Equity Rule 27 and finally in the present Rule 23.1. After the decision in Erie R. Co. v. Tompkins, 304 U.S. 64, 58 S.Ct.

however, since its examination of state law indicated that Maine probably followed the "prevailing rule" requiring contemporaneous ownership in order to maintain a shareholder derivative action. Thus, whether the federal rule or state substantive law applied, the present action could not be maintained.

The United States Court of Appeals for the First Circuit reversed. . . .

We granted petitioners' application for certiorari. 414 U.S. 1127 (1974). We now reverse.

II

A

We first turn to the question whether respondent corporations* may maintain the present action under § 10 of the Clayton Act . . . and § 10(b) of the Securities Exchange Act of 1934 . . . and Rule 10b–5. . . . The resolution of this issue depends upon the applicability of the settled principle of equity that a shareholder may not complain of acts of corporate mismanagement if he acquired his shares from those who participated or acquiesced in the allegedly wrongful transactions. See, e.g., Bloodworth v. Bloodworth, 225 Ga. 379, 387, 169 S.E.2d 150, 156–157 (1969). . . .[5] This principle has been invoked with special force where a shareholder purchases all or substantially all the shares of a corporation from a vendor at a fair price, and then seeks to have the corporation recover against that vendor for prior corporate mismanagement. See, e.g., Matthews v. Headley Chocolate Co., 130 Md. 523, 532–535, 100 A. 645, 650–651 (1917); Home Fire Insurance Co. v. Barber, 67 Neb. 644, 661–662, 93 N.W. 1024, 1030–1031 (1903). . . . The equitable considerations precluding recovery in such cases were explicated long ago by Dean (then Commissioner) Roscoe Pound in Home Fire Insurance Co. v. Barber, supra. Dean Pound, writing for the Supreme Court of Nebraska, observed that the shareholders of the plaintiff corporation in that case had sustained no injury since they had acquired their shares from the alleged wrongdoers after the disputed transactions occurred and had received full value for their purchase price. Thus, any recovery on their part would constitute a windfall, for it would enable them to obtain funds to which they had no just title or claim. Moreover, it would in effect allow the shareholders to recoup a large part of the price they agreed to pay for their shares, notwithstanding the fact that they received all they had bargained for.

817, 82 L.Ed. 1188 (1938), the question arose whether the contemporaneous-ownership requirement was one of procedure or substantive law. If the requirement were substantive, then under the regime of *Erie* it could not be validly applied in federal diversity cases where state law permitted a noncontemporaneous shareholder to maintain a derivative action. See 3B J. Moore, Federal Practice §§ 23.1.01–23.1.15[2] (2d ed. 1974). Although most cases treat the requirement as one of procedure, this Court has never resolved the issue. Ibid.

    *   The respondents were BAR and a wholly owned subsidiary. (Footnote by ed.)

    5   This principle obtains in the great majority of jurisdictions. See, e.g., Russell v. Louis Melind Co., 331 Ill.App. 182, 72 N.E.2d 869 (1947).

Finally, it would permit the shareholders to reap a profit from wrongs done to others, thus encouraging further such speculation. Dean Pound stated that these consequences rendered any recovery highly inequitable and mandated dismissal of the suit.

The considerations supporting the *Home Fire* principle are especially pertinent in the present case. As the District Court pointed out, Amoskeag, the present owner of more than 99% of the BAR shares, would be the principal beneficiary of any recovery obtained by BAR. Amoskeag, however, acquired 98.3% of the outstanding shares of BAR from petitioner Bangor Punta in 1969, well after the alleged wrongs were said to have occurred. Amoskeag does not contend that the purchase transaction was tainted by fraud or deceit, or that it received less than full value for its money. Indeed, it does not assert that it has sustained any injury at all. Nor does it appear that the alleged acts of prior mismanagement have had any continuing effect on the corporations involved or the value of their shares.[6] Nevertheless, by causing the present action to be brought in the name of respondent corporations, Amoskeag seeks to recover indirectly an amount equal to the $5,000,000 it paid for its stock, plus an additional $2,000,000. All this would be in the form of damages for wrongs petitioner Bangor Punta is said to have inflicted, not upon Amoskeag, but upon respondent corporations during the period in which Bangor Punta owned 98.3% of the BAR shares. In other words, Amoskeag seeks to recover for wrongs Bangor Punta did to *itself* as owner of the railroad.[7] At the same time it reaps this windfall, Amoskeag desires to retain all its BAR stock. Under *Home Fire,* it is evident that Amoskeag would have no standing in equity to maintain the present action.[8]

We are met with the argument, however, that since the present action is brought in the name of respondent corporations, we may not

---

[6]   In *Home Fire,* Dean Pound suggested that equitable principles might not prevent recovery where the effects of the wrongful acts continued and resulted in injury to present shareholders. 67 Neb. 644, 662, 93 N.W. 1024, 1031. In their complaint in the instant case, respondents alleged that "[t]he injury to BAR is a continuing one surviving the aforesaid sale [from petitioner BPO] to Amoskeag." The District Court noted that respondents alleged no facts to support this contention and therefore found any such exception inapplicable. 353 F.Supp. 724, 727 n. 1 (1972). Respondents apparently did not renew this contention on appeal.

[7]   Similarly, as to the period before October 1964, Amoskeag seeks to recover for wrongs B & A and its shareholders did to *themselves* as owners of the railroad.

[8]   Conceding the lack of equity in any recovery by Amoskeag, the dissent argues that the present action can nevertheless be maintained because there are 20 minority shareholders, holding less than 1% of the BAR stock, who owned their shares "during the period from 1960 through 1967 when the transactions underlying the railroad's complaint took place, and who still owned that stock in 1971 when the complaint was filed." . . . The dissent would conclude that the existence of these innocent minority shareholders entitled BAR, and hence Amoskeag, to recover the entire $7,000,000 amount of alleged damages.

Aside from the illogic of such an approach, the dissent's position is at war with the precedents, for the *Home Fire* principle has long been applied to preclude full recovery by a corporation even where there are innocent minority shareholders who acquired their shares prior to the alleged wrongs. See cases cited at n. 5, supra, and accompanying text. The dissent also mistakes the factual posture of this case, since the respondent corporations did not institute this action for the benefit of the minority shareholders. See discussion at n. 15, infra.

look behind the corporate entity to the true substance of the claims and the actual beneficiaries. The established law is to the contrary. Although a corporation and its shareholders are deemed separate entities for most purposes, the corporate form may be disregarded in the interests of justice where it is used to defeat an overriding public policy. New Colonial Ice Co. v. Helvering, 292 U.S. 435, 442, 54 S.Ct. 788, 78 L.Ed. 1348 (1934); Chicago, M. & St. P.R. Co. v. Minneapolis Civic Assn., 247 U.S. 490, 501, 38 S.Ct. 553, 62 L.Ed. 1229 (1918). In such cases, courts of equity, piercing all fictions and disguises, will deal with the substance of the action and not blindly adhere to the corporate form. Thus, where equity would preclude the shareholders from maintaining an action in their own right, the corporation would also be precluded. Amen v. Black, supra; Capitol Wine & Spirit Corp. v. Pokrass, 277 App.Div. 184, 98 N.Y.S.2d 291 (1950), aff'd, 302 N.Y. 734, 98 N.E.2d 704 (1951); Matthews v. Headley Chocolate Co., supra; Home Fire Insurance Co. v. Barber, supra. It follows that Amoskeag, the principal beneficiary of any recovery and itself estopped from complaining of petitioners' alleged wrongs, cannot avoid the command of equity through the guise of proceeding in the name of respondent corporations which it owns and controls.

B

Respondents fare no better in their efforts to maintain the present actions under state law, specifically § 104 of the Maine Public Utilities Act, Maine Rev.Stat.Ann., Tit. 35, § 104 (1965), and the common law of Maine. In Forbes v. Wells Beach Casino, Inc., 307 A.2d 210, 223 n. 10 (1973), the Maine Supreme Judicial Court recently declared that it had long accepted the equitable principle that a "stockholder has no standing if either he or his vendor participated or acquiesced in the wrong. . . ." See Hyams v. Old Dominion Co., 113 Me. 294, 302, 93 A. 747, 750 (1915).[9]
. . .

III

In reaching the contrary conclusion, the Court of Appeals stated that it could not accept the proposition that Amoskeag would be the "sole beneficiary" of any recovery by BAR. 482 F.2d, at 868. The court noted that in view of the railroad's status as a "quasi-public" corporation and the essential nature of the services it provides, the public had an identifiable interest in BAR's financial health. Thus, any recovery by BAR would accrue to the benefit of the public through the improvement

---

[9] In addition, the new Maine Business Corporation Act adopts the contemporaneous-ownership requirement for shareholder derivative actions. See Maine Rev.Stat.Ann., Tit. 13–A, § 627.1.A (1974). This provision apparently became effective two days after the present action was filed. As the District Court noted, it is an open question whether Maine in fact had a contemporaneous-ownership requirement prior to that time. 353 F.Supp., at 727. See R. Field, V. McKusick & L. Wroth, Maine Civil Practice § 23.2, p. 393 (2d ed. 1970). In the absence of any indication that Maine would not have followed the "prevailing view," the District Court determined that the contemporaneous-ownership requirement of Fed.Rule Civ.Proc. 23.1 applied.

in BAR's economic position and the quality of its services. The court thought that this factor rendered any windfall to Amoskeag irrelevant.

At the outset, we note that the Court of Appeals' assumption that any recovery would necessarily benefit the public is unwarranted. As that court explicitly recognized, any recovery by BAR could be diverted to its shareholders, namely Amoskeag, rather than re-invested in the railroad for the benefit of the public. . . .

The Court of Appeals' position also appears to overlook the fact that Amoskeag, the actual beneficiary of any recovery through its ownership of more than 99% of the BAR shares, would be unjustly enriched since it has sustained no injury. . . .

The Court of Appeals further stated that it was important to insure that petitioners would not be immune from liability for their wrongful conduct and noted that BAR's recovery would provide a needed deterrent to mismanagement of railroads. Our difficulty with this argument is that it proves too much. If deterrence were the only objective, then in logic any plaintiff willing to file a complaint would suffice. No injury or violation of a legal duty to the particular plaintiff would have to be alleged. The only prerequisite would be that the plaintiff agree to accept the recovery, lest the supposed wrongdoer be allowed to escape a reckoning. Suffice it to say that we have been referred to no authority which would support so novel a result, and we decline to adopt it.

We therefore conclude that respondent corporations may not maintain the present action.[15] The judgment of the Court of Appeals is reversed.

■ MR. JUSTICE MARSHALL, with whom MR. JUSTICE DOUGLAS, MR. JUSTICE BRENNAN, and MR. JUSTICE WHITE join, dissenting. . . .

The majority places primary reliance on Dean Pound's decision in *Home Fire Insurance Co. v. Barber*, supra. In that case, *all* of the shares of the plaintiff corporation had been acquired from the alleged wrongdoers after the transactions giving rise to the causes of action

---

[15] Our decision rests on the conclusion that equitable principles preclude recovery by Amoskeag, the present owner of more than 99% of the BAR shares. The record does not reveal whether the minority shareholders who hold the remaining fraction of 1% of the BAR shares stand in the same position as Amoskeag. Some courts have adopted the concept of a pro-rata recovery where there are innocent minority shareholders. Under this procedure, damages are distributed to the minority shareholders individually on a proportional basis, even though the action is brought in the name of the corporation to enforce primary rights. See, e.g., Matthews v. Headley Chocolate Co., 130 Md. 523, 536–540, 100 A. 645, 650–652 (1917). In the present case, respondents have expressly disavowed any intent to obtain a pro-rata recovery on behalf of the 1% minority shareholders of BAR. We therefore do not reach the question whether such recovery would be appropriate.

The dissent asserts that the alleged acts of corporate mismanagement have placed BAR "close to the brink of bankruptcy" and that the present action is maintained for the benefit of BAR's creditors. . . . With all respect, it appears that the dissent has sought to redraft respondents' complaint. As the District Court noted, respondents have not brought this action on behalf of any creditors. 353 F.Supp., at 726. Indeed, they have never so contended. Moreover, respondents have conceded that the financial health of the railroad is excellent. Tr. of Oral Arg. 18.

stated in the complaint. Since none of the corporation's shareholders held stock at the time of the alleged wrongful transactions, none had been injured thereby. Dean Pound therefore held that equity barred the corporation from pursuing a claim where none of its shareholders could complain of injury.

Dean Pound thought it clear, however, that the opposite result would obtain if *any* of the present shareholders

> "are entitled to complain of the acts of the defendant and of his past management of the company; for if any of them are so entitled, there can be no doubt of the right and duty of the corporation to maintain this suit. It would be maintainable in such a case even though the wrongdoers continued to be stockholders and would share in the proceeds." 67 Neb., at 655, 93 N.W., at 1028.

Cf. Capitol Wine & Spirit Corp. v. Pokrass, 277 App.Div. 184, 186, 98 N.Y.S.2d 291, 293 (1950), aff'd, 302 N.Y. 734, 98 N.E.2d 704 (1951).

The rationale for the distinction drawn by Dean Pound is simple enough. The sole shareholder who defrauds or mismanages his own corporation hurts only himself. For the corporation to sue him for his wrongs is simply to take money out of his right pocket and put it in his left. It is therefore appropriate for equity to intervene to pierce the corporate veil. But where there are minority shareholders, misappropriation and conversion of corporate assets injure their interests as well as the interest of the majority shareholder. The law imposes upon the directors of a corporation a fiduciary obligation to all of the corporation's shareholders, and part of that obligation is to use due care to ensure that the corporation seek redress where a majority shareholder has drained the corporation's resources for his own benefit and to the detriment of minority shareholders.[1] . . .

Rifkin v. Steele Platt

Colorado Court of Appeals, 1991.
824 P.2d 32.

■ Opinion by JUDGE PLANK. . . .

This matter involves the sale of the controlling shares of the corporation [The Boiler Room], which owns a restaurant. . . . Plaintiffs include the corporation and its present principal shareholders, Robert C.

---

[1] Under a separate rule, the plaintiff must be a shareholder at the time the action is brought. See Note on Who Can Bring a Derivative Action, Section 1, supra. The two rules are bridged by a third rule requiring that the plaintiff's ownership between the time of the wrong and the time of the suit must be uninterrupted. Vista Fund v. Garis, 277 N.W.2d 19 (Minn.1979); Gresov v. Shattuck Denn Mining Corp., 40 Misc.2d 569, 243 N.Y.S.2d 760 (1963).

Rifkin, Gerald N. Kernis, and Gary G. Kortz (buyers). Sellers [Mr. Steele Platt and Fas-Wok, Inc.] are the former controlling shareholders.

Buyers and sellers executed a Stock Purchase Agreement to effectuate the sale of the corporation. . . .

The complaint alleged, in part, that Platt, as officer and director of the corporation, had misappropriated funds from it and that certain assets on the balance sheet were actually owned by Platt or other entities that he controlled. . . .

After a trial to the court, judgment was entered in favor of . . . the corporation on the breach of fiduciary duty claim. The court also awarded attorney fees pursuant to the agreement. Sellers do not appeal that part of the judgment concerning the breach of contract claim. . . .

Sellers . . . contend that the trial court erred in awarding the corporation damages for breach of fiduciary duty for conduct which occurred prior to buyers' acquisition of stock. They cite *Bangor Punta Operations, Inc. v. Bangor & Aroostook R. Co.,* 417 U.S. 703, 94 S.Ct. 2578, 41 L.Ed.2d 418 (1974) in support of this argument. We agree that *Bangor Punta* raises issues which must be resolved in this matter.

In *Bangor Punta,* the new shareholders of the corporation, in the name of the corporation, sought damages from the former shareholders for violations of state and federal law which occurred before the sale. The United States Supreme Court held that the corporation could not maintain the action for wrongs that occurred before the new shareholders' acquisition of the shares. The court reasoned that the real parties that would gain from a successful lawsuit would be the new shareholders. It presumed that the purchase price that they paid reflected the prior wrongdoings. Thus, the shareholders would improperly receive a windfall if allowed to recover damages.

Here, it is undisputed that the acts which constituted Platt's breach of fiduciary duty occurred prior to the buyers' acquisition of stock in The Boiler Room. However, the parties dispute whether the purchase price reflected the prior wrongdoings. The trial court did not make a finding on this issue. Therefore, we remand it to the trial court for further findings. *See El Dorado Bancshares v. Martin,* 701 F.Supp. 1515 (D.Kan.1988).

If on review the court finds that the price, in fact, reflected Platt's wrongdoings, it must dismiss the breach of fiduciary duty claim. If, on the other hand, it finds that the purchase price of the shares did not reflect the wrongdoings, then the corporation's previous damage award may stand. . . .

■ HUME and NEY, JJ., concur.

NOTES ON THE CONTEMPORANEOUS-OWNERSHIP RULE

1. *The Basic Rule and Three Standard Exceptions.* At early common law, the cases were divided on whether a shareholder was barred from bringing a derivative action if he was not a "contemporaneous shareholder"—that is, if he did not hold his shares when the wrong occurred. Today, however, most jurisdictions have adopted some version of the contemporaneous-ownership rule by case-law, statute, or court rule. What justifies this requirement? Consider that the American Law Institute accords standing to a non-contemporaneous holder who became a holder "before the material facts relating to the alleged wrong were publicly disclosed or were known by, or specifically communicated to the holder." A.L.I., 2 Principles of Corporate Governance: Analysis and Recommendations § 7.02(a)(1) (1992).

In forums where the contemporaneous rule exists it is subject to several important exceptions:

a). *Devolution by Operation of Law.* A non-contemporaneous shareholder is normally allowed to bring a derivative action if his shares devolved upon him "by operation of law"—for example, by inheritance. (This exception is sometimes made applicable only where the shares have devolved from a person who was a shareholder at the time of the wrong.)

b). *Continuing-Wrong Theory.* Under the continuing-wrong theory, a plaintiff can bring an action to challenge a wrong that began before he acquired his shares but continued thereafter. In principle this may not seem to be an exception at all, since the plaintiff is only complaining about what happened after he became a shareholder. In practice, however, it is often difficult to distinguish between a wrongful continuing course of conduct, on the one hand, and the continued effect of a completed wrongful transaction, on the other. Therefore, while the continuing-wrong exception is widely accepted in principle, in practice there is considerable divergence in the way it is applied, and different cases often seem to come out differently on virtually the same facts.

For example, in *Forbes v. Wells Beach Casino, Inc.*, 307 A.2d 210 (Me.1973), the continuing-wrong theory was deemed applicable, and the plaintiff was allowed to bring suit, where the plaintiff had purchased his stock after a fiduciary had wrongfully taken possession of corporate property, but while the fiduciary continued to hold the property. In contrast, in *Weinhaus v. Gale,* 237 F.2d 197 (7th Cir.1956), the continuing-wrong theory was deemed inapplicable, and the plaintiff was not allowed to bring suit, where the plaintiff had purchased his stock after a subsidiary had sold stock to its parent at a price alleged to be unfairly low, but before the parent had resold the stock. In *Palmer v. Morris,* 316 F.2d 649 (5th Cir.1963), the continuing-wrong theory was deemed applicable, and the plaintiff was allowed to bring suit, where the plaintiff had purchased his stock after an allegedly wrongful deal had been made, but while payments under the deal continued. In contrast, in *Chaft v. Kass,* 19 A.D.2d 610, 241 N.Y.S.2d 284 (1963), the continuing-wrong theory was deemed inapplicable, and the plaintiff was not allowed to bring suit, where the plaintiff purchased his stock after the corporation had entered into an allegedly invalid contract, but while payments under the contract were still being made.

Some statutes provide that the plaintiff must allege that he was a shareholder at the time of the transaction "or any part thereof." *See e.g.*, Cal. § 800(b)(1). Where there is a close question whether the continuing-wrong theory applies to a given case, such a statute might tip the scale in the plaintiff's favor.

————

5. THE DEMAND REQUIREMENT

————

MODEL BUSINESS CORPORATION ACT §§ 7.42–7.44

[See Statutory Supplement]

————

AMERICAN LAW INSTITUTE, PRINCIPLES OF CORPORATE GOVERNANCE §§ 7.03, 7.04, 7.08–7.13

[See Statutory Supplement]

————

CAL. CORP. CODE § 800(b)(2)

[See Statutory Supplement]

————

FEDERAL RULES OF CIVIL PROCEDURE RULE 23.1

[See Statutory Supplement]

————

INTRODUCTORY NOTE

Recall that the derivative suit is a suit prosecuting the claim of the corporation that procedurally is brought on the corporation's behalf by one of its shareholders. This procedure coexists with the provision in all corporate statutes which provide that the affairs of the corporation are managed or under the direction of a corporation's board of directors. From such statutes arises the demand requirement whereby before bringing a derivative action, a shareholder is required to make a demand on the board, unless demand was excused. This is the so-called demand requirement. The cases and materials in this section explore the many modern developments surrounding the demand requirement.

————

Marx v. Akers

New York Court of Appeals, 1996.
88 N.Y.2d 189, 644 N.Y.S.2d 121, 666 N.E.2d 1034.

■ SMITH, J.:

Plaintiff commenced this shareholder derivative action against International Business Machines Corporation (IBM) and IBM's board of directors without first demanding that the board initiate a lawsuit. The amended complaint (complaint) alleges that the board wasted corporate assets by awarding excessive compensation to IBM's executives and outside directors. The issues raised on this appeal are whether the Appellate Division abused its discretion by dismissing plaintiff's complaint for failure to make a demand and whether plaintiff's complaint fails to state a cause of action. We affirm the order of the Appellate Division because we conclude that plaintiff was not excused from making a demand with respect to the executive compensation claim and that plaintiff has failed to state a cause of action for corporate waste in connection with the allegations concerning payments to IBM's outside directors.

Facts and Procedural History

The complaint alleges that during a period of declining profitability at IBM the director defendants engaged in self-dealing by awarding excessive compensation to the 15 outside directors on the 18-member board. Although the complaint identifies only one of the three inside directors as an IBM executive (defendant Akers is identified as a former chief executive officer of IBM), plaintiff also appears to allege that the director defendants violated their fiduciary duties to IBM by voting for unreasonably high compensation for IBM executives.[2]

Defendants moved to dismiss the complaint for (1) failure to state a cause of action, and (2) failure to serve a demand on IBM's board to initiate a lawsuit based on the complaint's allegations. The Supreme Court dismissed, holding that plaintiff failed to establish the futility of a demand. Supreme Court concluded that excusing a demand here would render Business Corporation Law § 626(c) "virtually meaningless in any shareholders' derivative action in which all members of a corporate board are named as defendants." Having decided the demand issue in favor of defendants, the court did not reach the issue of whether plaintiff's complaint stated a cause of action. The Appellate Division affirmed the dismissal, concluding that the complaint did not contain any details from which the futility of a demand could be inferred. The Appellate Division found that plaintiff's objections to the level of compensation were not

---

[2] Executives at IBM are compensated through a fixed salary and performance incentives. Payouts on the performance incentives are based on IBM's earnings per share, return on equity and cash flow. Plaintiff's complaint criticizes only the performance incentive component of executive compensation as excessive because of certain accounting practices which plaintiff alleges artificially inflate earnings, return on equity and cash flow.

stated with sufficient particularity in light of statutory authority permitting directors to set their own compensation.

Background

A shareholder's derivative action is an action "brought in the right of a domestic or foreign corporation to procure a judgment in its favor, by a holder of shares or of voting trust certificates of the corporation or of a beneficial interest in such shares or certificates" (Business Corporation Law § 626[a]). "Derivative claims against corporate directors belong to the corporation itself" (Auerbach v. Bennett, 47 N.Y. 2d 619, 631).

> "The remedy sought is for wrong done to the corporation; the primary cause of action belongs to the corporation; recovery must enure to the benefit of the corporation. The stockholder brings the action, in behalf of others similarly situated, to vindicate the corporate rights and a judgment on the merits is a binding adjudication of these rights (citations omitted)" (Isaac v. Marcus, 258 N.Y. 257, 264).

. . . Business Corporation Law § 626(c) provides that in any shareholders' derivative action, "the complaint shall set forth with particularity the efforts of the plaintiff to secure the initiation of such action by the board or the reasons for not making such effort." Enacted in 1961 (L 1961, ch 855), section 626(c) codified a rule of equity developed in early shareholder derivative actions requiring plaintiffs to demand that the corporation initiate an action, unless such demand was futile, before commencing an action on the corporation's behalf (Barr v. Wackman, 36 N.Y. 2d 371, 377). The purposes of the demand requirement are to (1) relieve courts from deciding matters of internal corporate governance by providing corporate directors with opportunities to correct alleged abuses, (2) provide corporate boards with reasonable protection from harassment by litigation on matters clearly within the discretion of directors, and (3) discourage "strike suits" commenced by shareholders for personal gain rather than for the benefit of the corporation (Barr, 36 NY2d at 378). "The demand is generally designed to weed out unnecessary or illegitimate shareholder derivative suits" (id.).

By their very nature, shareholder derivative actions infringe upon the managerial discretion of corporate boards. "As with other questions of corporate policy and management, the decision whether and to what extent to explore and prosecute such [derivative] claims lies within the judgment and control of the corporation's board of directors" (Auerbach, supra, 47 NY2d at 631). Consequently, we have historically been reluctant to permit shareholder derivative suits, noting that the power of courts to direct the management of a corporation's affairs should be "exercised with restraint" (Gordon v. Elliman, 306 N.Y. 456, 462).

In permitting a shareholder derivative action to proceed because a demand on the corporation's directors would be futile, "the object is for the court to chart the course for the corporation which the directors should have selected, and which it is presumed that they would have chosen if they had not been actuated by fraud or bad faith. Due to their misconduct, the court substitutes its judgment ad hoc for that of the directors in the conduct of its business" (id. at 462).

Achieving a balance between preserving the discretion of directors to manage a corporation without undue interference, through the demand requirement, and permitting shareholders to bring claims on behalf of the corporation when it is evident that directors will wrongfully refuse to bring such claims, through the demand futility exception, has been accomplished by various jurisdictions in different ways. One widely cited approach to demand futility which attempts to balance these competing concerns has been developed by Delaware courts and applies a two-pronged test to each case to determine whether a failure to serve a demand is justified. At the other end of the spectrum is a universal demand requirement which would abandon particularized determinations in favor of requiring a demand in every case before a shareholder derivative suit may be filed.

The Delaware Approach

Delaware's demand requirement, codified in Delaware Chancery Court Rule 23.1, provides, in relevant part,

"In a derivative action brought by 1 or more shareholders or members to enforce a right of a corporation * * * [the complaint shall allege] with particularity the efforts, if any, made by the plaintiff to obtain the action the plaintiff desires from the directors or comparable authority and the reasons for the plaintiff's failure to obtain the action or for not making the effort."

Interpreting Rule 23.1, the Delaware Supreme Court in Aronson v. Lewis (473 A.2d 805) developed a two-prong test for determining the futility of a demand. Plaintiffs must allege particularized facts which create a reasonable doubt that,

"(1) the directors are disinterested and independent and (2) the challenged transaction was otherwise the product of a valid exercise of business judgment. Hence, the Court of Chancery must make two inquiries, one into the independence and disinterestedness of the directors and the other into the substantive nature of the challenged transaction and the board's approval thereof" (473 A2d at 814).

The two branches of the *Aronson* test are disjunctive (see, Levine v. Smith, 591 A.2d 194, 205). Once director interest has been established, the business judgment rule becomes inapplicable and the demand excused without further inquiry (*Aronson,* 473 A2d at 814). Similarly, a director whose independence is compromised by undue influence exerted by an interested party cannot properly exercise business judgment and the loss of independence also justifies the excusal of a demand without further inquiry (see, Levine, supra, 591 A2d at 205–206). Whether a board has validly exercised its business judgment must be evaluated by determining whether the directors exercised procedural (informed decision) and substantive (terms of the transaction) due care (Grobow v. Perot, 539 A.2d 180, 189).

The reasonable doubt threshold of Delaware's two-fold approach to demand futility has been criticized. The use of a standard of proof which is the heart of a jury's determination in a criminal case has raised questions concerning its applicability in the corporate context (see, Starrels v. First Natl. Bank, 870 F.2d 1168, 1175 (7th Cir.)) [Easterbrook, J, concurring]. The reasonable doubt standard has also been criticized as overly subjective, thereby permitting a wide variance in the application of Delaware law to similar facts (2 American Law Institute, Principles of Corporate Governance: Analysis and Recommendations § 7.03, Comment d at 57 [1992]).

Universal Demand

A universal demand requirement would dispense with the necessity of making case-specific determinations and impose an easily applied bright line rule. The Business Law Section of the American Bar Association has proposed requiring a demand in all cases, without exception, and permits the commencement of a derivative proceeding within 90 days of the demand unless the demand is rejected earlier (Model Business Corporation Act § 7.42[1] [1995 Supplement]). However, plaintiffs may file suit before the expiration of 90 days, even if their demand has not been rejected, if the corporation would suffer irreparable injury as a result (Model Business Corporation Act § 7.42[2]).

The American Law Institute (ALI) has also proposed a "universal" demand. Section 7.03 of ALI's Principles of Corporate Governance would require shareholder derivative action plaintiffs to serve a written demand on the corporation unless a demand is excused because "the plaintiff makes a specific showing that irreparable injury to the corporation would otherwise result" (2 American Law Institute, Principles of Corporate Governance: Analysis and Recommendations, § 7.03[b] at 53–54, [1992]). Once a demand has been made and rejected, however, the ALI would subject the board's decision to "an elaborate set of standards that calibrates the deference afforded the decision of the directors to the character of the claim being asserted" (Kamen v. Kemper Financial Services, Inc., 500 U.S. 90, 104).

At least 11 states have adopted, by statute, the universal demand requirement proposed in the Model Business Corporation Act. Georgia, Michigan, Wisconsin, Montana, Virginia, New Hampshire, Mississippi, Connecticut, Nebraska and North Carolina require shareholders to wait 90 days after serving a demand before filing a derivative suit unless the demand is rejected before the expiration of the 90 days, or irreparable injury to the corporation would result. . . . Arizona additionally permits shareholders to file suit before the expiration of 90 days if the statute of limitations would expire during the 90 day period. . . . Florida also appears to have adopted a universal demand requirement, although the statutory language does not track the Model Business Corporation Act. Florida's statute provides, "A complaint in a proceeding brought in the right of a corporation must be verified and allege with particularity the demand made to obtain action by the board of directors and that the demand was refused or ignored (emphasis added)". . . .

New York State has also considered and continues to consider implementing a universal demand requirement. However, even though bills to adopt a universal demand have been presented over three legislative sessions, the Legislature has yet to enact a universal demand requirement. . . .

New York's Approach to Demand Futility

Although instructive, neither the universal demand requirement nor the Delaware approach to demand futility is adopted here. Since New York's demand requirement is codified in Business Corporation Law § 626(c), a universal demand can only be adopted by the Legislature. Delaware's approach, which resembles New York law in some respects, incorporates a "reasonable doubt" standard which, as we have already pointed out, has provoked criticism as confusing and overly subjective. An analysis of the *Barr* decision compels the conclusion that in New York, a demand would be futile if a complaint alleges with particularity that (1) a majority of the directors are interested in the transaction, or (2) the directors failed to inform themselves to a degree reasonably necessary about the transaction, or (3) the directors failed to exercise their business judgment in approving the transaction.

In Barr v. Wackman (36 N.Y. 2d 371, supra), we considered whether the plaintiff was excused from making a demand where the board of Talcott National Corporation (Talcott), consisting of 13 outside directors, a director affiliated with a related company and four interested inside directors, rejected a merger proposal involving Gulf & Western Industries (Gulf & Western) in favor of another proposal on allegedly less favorable terms for Talcott and its shareholders. The merger proposal, memorialized in a board-approved "agreement in principle," proposed exchanging one share of Talcott common stock for approximately $24.00 consisting of $17.00 in cash and 0.6 of a warrant to purchase Gulf & Western stock, worth approximately $7.00. This proposal was abandoned in favor of a cash tender offer for Talcott shares by Associated First Capital Corporation (a Gulf & Western subsidiary) at $20.00 per share— four dollars less than proposed for the merger.

The plaintiff in *Barr* alleged that Talcott's board discarded the merger proposal after the four "controlling" inside directors received pecuniary and personal benefits from Gulf & Western in exchange for ceding control of Talcott on terms less favorable to Talcott's shareholders.

As alleged in the complaint, these benefits included new and favorable employment contracts for nine Talcott officers, including five-year employment contracts for three of the controlling directors. In addition to his annual salary of $125,000 with Talcott, defendant Silverman (a controlling director) would allegedly receive $60,000 a year under a five year employment contract with Associated First Capital, and an aggregate of $275,000 for the next five years in an arrangement with Associated First Capital to serve as a consultant. This additional compensation would be awarded to Silverman after control of Talcott passed to Associated First Capital and Gulf & Western. Plaintiff also alleged that Gulf & Western and Associated First Capital paid an excessive "finder's fee" of $340,000 to a company where Silverman's son was an executive vice president. In addition to alleging that the controlling defendants obtained personal benefits, the complaint also alleged that Talcott's board agreed to sell a Talcott subsidiary at a net loss of $6,100,000 solely to accommodate Gulf & Western.

In *Barr,* we held that insofar as the complaint attacked the controlling directors' acts in causing the corporation to enter into a transaction for their own financial benefit, demand was excused because of the self-dealing, or self-interest of those directors in the challenged transaction. Specifically, we pointed to the allegation that the controlling directors "breached their fiduciary obligations to Talcott in return for personal benefits" (id., at 376).

We also held in *Barr,* however, that as to the disinterested outside directors, demand could be excused even in the absence of their receiving any financial benefit from the transaction. That was because the complaint alleged that, by approving the terms of the less advantageous offer, those directors were guilty of a "breach of their duties of due care and diligence to the corporation" (id., at 380). Their performance of the duty of care would have "put them on notice of the claimed self-dealing of the affiliated directors" (id.). The complaint charged that the outside directors failed "to do more than passively rubber stamp the decisions of the active managers" (id., at 381) resulting in corporate detriment. These allegations, the *Barr* Court concluded, also excused demand as to the charges against the disinterested directors.

Barr also makes clear that "it is not sufficient * * * merely to name a majority of the directors as parties defendant with the conclusory allegation of wrongdoing or control by wrongdoers" (id., at 379) to justify failure to make a demand. Thus, *Barr* reflects the statutory requirement that the complaint "must set forth with particularity the * * * reasons for not making such effort" (Business Corporation Law § 626[c]).

Unfortunately, various courts have overlooked the explicit warning that conclusory allegations of wrongdoing against each member of the board are not sufficient to excuse demand and have misinterpreted *Barr* as excusing demand whenever a majority of the board members who approved the transaction are named as defendants (see, Miller v.

Schreyer, 200 A.D. 2d 492; Curreri v. Verni, 156 A.D. 2d 420; MacKay v. Pierce, 86 A.D. 2d 655; Joseph v. Amrep Corp., 59 A.D. 2d 841; see also, Allison Publications Incorporated v. Mutual Benefit Life Insurance, 197 A.D. 2d 463). As stated most recently, "the rule is clear in this State that no demand is necessary 'if the complaint alleges acts for which a majority of the directors may be liable and plaintiff reasonably concluded that the board would not be responsive to a demand'" (Miller v. Schreyer, supra, at 494 [quoting from *Barr,* supra, 36 N.Y.2d at 371]; but see, Lewis v. Welch, 126 A.D. 2d 519, 521). The problem with such an approach is that it permits plaintiffs to frame their complaint in such a way as to automatically excuse demand, thereby allowing the exception to swallow the rule.

We thus deem it necessary to offer the following elaboration of *Barr's* demand/futility standard. (1) Demand is excused because of futility when a complaint alleges with particularity that a majority of the board of directors is interested in the challenged transaction. Director interest may either be self-interest in the transaction at issue (see, Barr v. Wackman, supra, at 376 [receipt of "personal benefits"]), or a loss of independence because a director with no direct interest in a transaction is "controlled" by a self-interested director. (2) Demand is excused because of futility when a complaint alleges with particularity that the board of directors did not fully inform themselves about the challenged transaction to the extent reasonably appropriate under the circumstances (see, *Barr,* supra, at 380, 368 N.Y.S.2d 497, 329 N.E.2d 180). The "long-standing rule" is that a director "does not exempt himself from liability by failing to do more than passively rubber-stamp the decisions of the active managers" (id., at 381). (3) Demand is excused because of futility when a complaint alleges with particularity that the challenged transaction was so egregious on its face that it could not have been the product of sound business judgment of the directors.

The Current Appeal

Plaintiff argues that the demand requirement was excused both because the outside directors awarded themselves generous compensation packages and because of the acquiescence of the disinterested directors in the executive compensation schemes. The complaint states:

> "Plaintiff has made no demand upon the directors of IBM to institute this lawsuit because such demand would be futile. As set forth above, each of the directors authorized, approved, participated and/or acquiesced in the acts and transactions complained of herein and are liable therefor. Further, each of the Non-Employee [outside] Directors has received and retained the benefit of his excessive compensation and each of the other directors has received and retained the benefit of the incentive compensation described above. The defendants cannot be expected to vote to prosecute an action against themselves.

Demand upon the company to bring action (sic) to redress the wrongs herein is therefore unnecessary."

. . . Defendant's motion to dismiss for failure to make a demand as to the allegations concerning the compensation paid to IBM's executive officers was properly granted. A board is not interested "in voting compensation for one of its members as an executive or in some other nondirectorial capacity, such as a consultant to the corporation," although "so-called 'back-scratching' arrangements, pursuant to which all directors vote to approve each other's compensation as officers or employees, do not constitute disinterested directors' action" (1 ALI, supra, at 250). Since only three directors are alleged to have received the benefit of the executive compensation scheme, plaintiff has failed to allege that a majority of the board was interested in setting executive compensation. Nor do the allegations that the board used faulty accounting procedures to calculate executive compensation levels move beyond "conclusory allegations of wrongdoing" (Barr v. Wackman, supra, at 379) which are insufficient to excuse demand. The complaint does not allege particular facts in contending that the board failed to deliberate or exercise its business judgment in setting those levels. Consequently, the failure to make a demand regarding the fixing of executive compensation was fatal to [the] portion of the complaint challenging that transaction.

However, a review of the complaint indicates that plaintiff also alleged that a majority of the board was self-interested in setting the compensation of outside directors because the outside directors comprised a majority of the board.

Directors are self-interested in a challenged transaction where they will receive a direct financial benefit from the transaction which is different from the benefit to shareholders generally (see, Rales v. Blasband, 634 A.2d 927, 936 [Del Sup Ct]; Bergstein v. Texas Intern. Co., 453 A.2d 467, 472–473 [Del Ch]; ALI, Principles of Corporate Governance § 1.23, at 25; 13 Fletcher, Cyclopedia Corporations § 5965, at 138). A director who votes him or herself a raise in directors' compensation is always "interested" because that person will receive a personal financial benefit from the transaction not shared in by stockholders (see, 1 ALI Principles of Corporate Governance § 5.03, comment g, at 250 ["if the board votes directorial compensation for itself, the board is interested"]; see also, Steiner v. Meyerson, [1995 Transfer Binder], Fed. Sec. L. Rep. P 98857 [Del Ch], 1995 WL 441999, at 12 ["As the outside directors comprise a majority of the Telxon board and are personally interested in their compensation levels, demand upon them to challenge or decrease their own compensation is excused"]). Consequently, a demand was excused as to plaintiff's allegations that the compensation set for outside directors was excessive.

Corporate Waste

Our conclusion that demand should have been excused as to the part of the complaint challenging the fixing of directors' compensation does not end our inquiry, however. We must also determine whether plaintiff has stated a cause of action regarding that transaction, i.e., some wrong to the corporation. We conclude that plaintiff has not, and thus dismiss the complaint in its entirety.

Historically, directors did not receive any compensation for their work as directors (see, Fletcher, Cyclopedia Corporations, § 2109). Thus, a bare allegation that corporate directors voted themselves excessive compensation was sufficient to state a cause of action (e.g., Walsh v. Van Ameringen-Haebler, Inc., 257 N.Y. 478, 480; Jacobson v. Brooklyn Lumber Co., 184 N.Y. 152, 162). Many jurisdictions, including New York, have since changed the common law rule by statute providing that a corporation's board of directors has the authority to fix director compensation unless the corporation's charter or bylaws provides otherwise. Thus, the allegation that directors have voted themselves compensation is clearly no longer an allegation which gives rise to a cause of action, as the directors are statutorily entitled to set those levels. Nor does a conclusory allegation that the compensation directors have set for themselves is excessive give rise to a cause of action.

> The courts will not undertake to review the fairness of the official salaries, at the suit of a shareholder attacking them as excessive, unless wrongdoing and oppression or possible abuse of a fiduciary position are shown. However, the courts will take a hand in the matter at the instance of the corporation or of shareholders in extreme cases. A case of fraud is presented where directors increase their collective salaries so as to use up nearly the entire earnings of a company; where directors or officers appropriate the income so as to deprive shareholders of reasonable dividends, or perhaps so reduce to assets as to threaten the corporation with insolvency * * * (Fletcher, Cyclopedia Corporations, § 2122, at 46–47).

Thus, a complaint challenging the excessiveness of director compensation must—to survive a dismissal motion—allege compensation rates excessive on their face or other facts which call into question whether the compensation was fair to the corporation when approved, the good faith of the directors setting those rates, or that the decision to set the compensation could not have been a product of valid business judgment.[6]

Applying the foregoing principles to plaintiff's complaint, it is clear that it must be dismissed. The complaint alleges that the directors increased their compensation rates from a base of $20,000 plus $500 for

---

[6] There is general agreement that the allocation of the burden of proof differs depending on whether the compensation was approved by disinterested directors or shareholders, or by interested directors. Plaintiffs must prove wrongdoing or waste as to compensation arrangements regarding disinterested directors or shareholders, but directors who approve their own compensation bear the burden of proving that the transaction was fair to the corporation (see, Block, et al., The Business Judgment Rule, at 149 [4th ed.]; Fletcher, supra, § 514.1, 632; ALI, supra, § 5.03). However, at the pleading stage we are not concerned with burdens of proof.

each meeting attended to a retainer of $55,000 plus 100 shares of IBM stock over a five-year period. The complaint also alleges that "this compensation bears little relation to the part-time services rendered by the Non-Employee Directors or to the profitability of IBM. The board's responsibilities have not increased, its performance, measured by the company's earnings and stock price, has been poor yet its compensation has increased far in excess of the cost of living."

These conclusory allegations do not state a cause of action. There are no factually-based allegations of wrongdoing or waste which would, if true, sustain a verdict in plaintiff's favor. Plaintiff's bare allegations that the compensation set lacked a relationship to duties performed or to the cost of living are insufficient as a matter of law to state a cause of action.

Accordingly, the order of the Appellate Division should be affirmed, with costs.

———

Del. County Employees Ret. Fund v. Sanchez
Supreme Court of State of Delaware, 2015.
124 A.3d 1017.

■ STRINE, CHIEF JUSTICE:

. . .

This case involves an appeal from a complicated transaction between a private company whose equity is wholly owned by the family of A.R. Sanchez, Jr., Sanchez Resources, LLC (hereinafter, the "Private Sanchez Company"), and a public company in which the Sanchez family constitutes the largest stockholder bloc with some 16% of the shares and that is dependent on the Private Sanchez Company for all of its management services, Sanchez Energy Corporation (the "Sanchez Public Company"). The transaction at issue required the Sanchez Public Company to pay $78 million to: i) help the Private Sanchez Company buy out the interests of a private equity investor; ii) acquire an interest in certain properties with energy-producing potential from the Private Sanchez Company; iii) facilitate the joint production of 80,000 acres of property between the Sanchez Private and Public Companies; and iv) fund a cash payment of $14.4 million to the Private Sanchez Company. In this derivative action, the plaintiffs allege that this transaction involved a gross overpayment by the Sanchez Public Company, which unfairly benefited the Private Sanchez Company by allowing it to use the Sanchez Public Company's funds to buy out their private equity partner, obtain a large cash payment for itself, and obtain a contractual right to a lucrative royalty stream that was unduly favorable to the Private Sanchez Company and thus unfairly onerous to the Sanchez Public Company. . . .

The Court of Chancery dismissed the complaint, finding that the defendants were correct in their contention that the plaintiffs had not pled demand excusal under *Aronson [v. Lewis*, 473 A.2d 805 (Del. 1984)]. . . .

[I]n resolving this appeal, we focus on only one issue, which is outcome-determinative. The parties agree that two of the five directors on the Sanchez Public Company board were not disinterested in the transaction: A.R. Sanchez, Jr., the Public Company's Chairman [Chairman Sanchez]; and his son, Antonio R. Sanchez, III, the Sanchez Public Company's President and CEO. . . .

The question for *Aronson* purposes was therefore whether the plaintiffs had pled particularized facts raising a pleading-stage doubt about the independence of one of the other Sanchez Public Company directors. If they had, the defendants and the Court of Chancery itself recognized that the plaintiffs would have pled grounds for demand excusal under *Aronson*.

III. ANALYSIS

To plead demand excusal under Rule 23.1, a plaintiff in a derivative action must plead particularized facts creating a "reasonable doubt" that either "(1) the directors are disinterested and independent or (2) the challenged transaction was otherwise the product 4 of a valid exercise of business judgment." Although there is a heightened burden under Rule 23.1 to plead particularized facts, when a motion to dismiss for failure to make a demand is made, all reasonable inferences from the pled facts must nonetheless be drawn in favor of the plaintiff in determining whether the plaintiff has met its burden under *Aronson*.

The closest question below centered on director Alan Jackson. The complaint bases its challenge to Jackson's independence on two related grounds. First, it pleads that "[Chairman] Sanchez and Jackson have been close friends for more than five decades." Consistent with this allegation, the complaint indicates that when Chairman Sanchez ran for Governor of Texas in 2012, Jackson donated $12,500 to his campaign.

Second, the complaint pleads facts supporting an inference that Jackson's personal wealth is largely attributable to business interests over which Chairman Sanchez has substantial influence. According to the complaint, Jackson's full-time job and primary source of income is as an executive at IBC Insurance Agency, Ltd. IBC Insurance provides insurance brokerage services to the Sanchez Public Company and other Sanchez affiliates. But even more importantly, IBC Insurance is a wholly owned subsidiary of International Bancshares Corporation ("IBC"), a company of which Chairman Sanchez is the largest stockholder and a director who IBC's board has determined is not independent under the NASDAQ Marketplace Rules. Not only does Jackson work full-time for IBC Insurance, so too does his brother. Both of them service the work that IBC Insurance does for the Sanchez Public and Private Companies.

The complaint also alleges that the approximately $165,000 Jackson earned as a Sanchez Public Company director constituted "30–40% of Jackson's total income for 2012."

. . .

[E]mploying the *de novo* review that governs this appeal, we do not come to the same conclusion as the Court of Chancery. The reason for that is that the Court of Chancery's analysis seemed to consider the facts the plaintiffs pled about Jackson's personal friendship with Sanchez and the facts they pled regarding his business relationships as entirely separate issues. Having parsed them as categorically distinct, the Court of Chancery appears to have then concluded that neither category of facts on its own was enough to compromise Jackson's independence for purposes of demand excusal.

The problem with that approach is that our law requires that all the pled facts regarding a director's relationship to the interested party be considered in full context . . . . In that consideration . . . [the court is] bound to draw all inferences from those particularized facts in favor of the plaintiff, not the defendant, when dismissal of a derivative complaint is sought.

Here, the plaintiffs did not plead the kind of thin social-circle friendship, for want of a better way to put it, which was at issue in *Beam*. In that case, we held that allegations that directors "moved in the same social circles, attended the same weddings, developed business relationships before joining the board, and described each other as 'friends,' . . . are insufficient, without more, to rebut the presumption of independence." In saying that, we did not suggest that deeper human friendships could not exist that would have the effect of compromising a director's independence. When, as here, a plaintiff has pled that a director has been close friends with an interested party for a half century, the plaintiff has pled facts quite different from those at issue in *Beam*. Close friendships of that duration are likely considered precious by many people, and are rare. People drift apart for many reasons, and when a close relationship endures for that long, a pleading stage inference arises that it is important to the parties.

The plaintiffs did not rely simply on that proposition, however. They pled facts regarding the economic relations of Jackson and Chairman Sanchez that buttress their contention that they are confidantes and that there is a reasonable doubt that Jackson can act impartially in a matter of economic importance to Sanchez personally. It may be that it is entirely coincidental that Jackson's full-time job is as an executive at a subsidiary of a corporation over which Chairman Sanchez has substantial influence, as the largest stockholder, director, and the Chairman of an important source of brokerage work. It may be that it is also coincidental that Jackson's brother also works there. It may be coincidental that Jackson and his brother both work on insurance brokerage work for the Sanchez Public and Private Companies there.

And it may be coincidental that Jackson finds himself a director of the Sanchez Public Company. But rather certainly, there arises a pleading stage inference that Jackson's economic positions derive in large measure from his 50-year close friendship with Chairman Sanchez, and that he is in these positions because Sanchez trusts, cares for, and respects him. . . . [W]here the question is whether the plaintiffs have met their pleading burden to plead facts suggesting that Jackson cannot act independently of Chairman Sanchez, these obvious inferences that arise from the pled facts require that the defendants' motion to dismiss be denied. In other words, using the precise parlance of *Aronson*, the plaintiffs pled particularized facts, that when considered in the plaintiff-friendly manner required, create a reasonable doubt about Jackson's independence.

. . .

Therefore, the judgment of the Court of Chancery of November 25, 2014 dismissing this case is reversed, and this case is remanded for further proceedings consistent with this opinion.

———

THE DEMAND REQUIREMENT AND PRECLUSION IN MULTI-FORUM LITIGATION

Evidence of possible management misconduct frequently prompts litigation in multiple forums. Following a New York Times story detailing extensive bribery of Mexican officials and a coverup by senior executives of a Wal-Mart subsidiary, derivative suits were filed against certain Wal-Mart executives in the Delaware Chancery Court and the federal district court in Arkansas, Wal-Mart's headquarters. Different plaintiffs and law firms were involved in both the suits, but the complaints in both cases relied on facts set forth in the Times story. The Delaware proceeding was stayed after the Chancellor admonished its lawyers to "use the tools at hand," i.e., launch a books and records request, to sustain the otherwise weakly supported allegations in the complaint, as otherwise the suit would not likely survive a motion to dismiss. Nearly three years passed due to the fierce resistance of Wal-Mart to the inspection request. During this period, the parallel suit in Arkansas was also stayed. However, the Eighth Circuit Court of Appeals ultimately vacated the stay and soon thereafter the Arkansas district court held that a pre-suit demand on the board of directors was necessary, had not been made, and dismissed the suit with prejudice. Wal-Mart thereupon moved for dismissal of the Delaware proceeding, arguing the Delaware plaintiff was collaterally estopped by the Arkansas holding from relitigating demand futility.

California State Teachers Ret. Sys. v. Alvarez, 179 A.3d 824 (Del. 2018), held that because the corporation is the real plaintiff in the derivative suit, privity thereby existed between the litigants in the two forums; the court further reasoned that Due Process is satisfied by the court scrutinizing the adequacy of representation in the Arkansas proceeding. Finding that counsel in that proceeding was adequate, the court held that Delaware plaintiff could not relitigate demand futility.

————

NOTE ON MODEL ACT'S UNIVERSAL DEMAND

The Model Act embraces universal demand. Section 7.42 requires a demand on the corporation in all cases and provides that suit may not commence within ninety days of making such demand, "unless irreparable injury to the corporation would result by waiting for the expiration of the 90-day period." As the Introductory Comment explains: "It is believed that this provision will eliminate the often excessive time and expense for both litigants and the court in litigating the question whether demand is required. . . . " The corporation may, under section 7.43, request a further stay of the proceeding if, for example, more time is needed to assess the allegations and the corporate interest in the suit's continuance. Section 7.44 sets forth the mechanics (e.g., criteria for dismissal and burden of proof in meeting the criteria) by which "qualified directors" can obtain dismissal of the suit if they believe that maintenance of the suit is not in best interests of the corporation. "Qualified directors" is defined in section 1.43.

Utah is among the states following adopting the Model Act's universal demand provision. *Brewster v. Brewster* (2013), 241 P.3d 357 (Utah Ct. App. 2010), reversed the trial court's refusal to dismiss the suit alleging usurpation of a corporate opportunity. Although the trial court believed that the board's third party investigator retained had carried out a detailed investigation in good faith, the court held the suit should continue because more consideration could have been given by the investigator to one of the nine factors advanced by the investigator as bases—that the company lacked resources to pursue the opportunity—to believe the derivative suit was not in the corporation's interest. The appellate court reversed, reasoning that the trial court had gone beyond the scope of review permitted under Model Act as the record supported finding there had been a reasonable and independent investigation carried out in good faith.

————

Auerbach v. Bennett

Court of Appeals of New York, 1979.
47 N.Y.2d 619, 419 N.Y.S.2d 920, 393 N.E.2d 994.

■ JONES, JUDGE. . . .

In the summer of 1975 the management of General Telephone & Electronics Corporation, in response to reports that numerous other multinational companies had made questionable payments to public officials or political parties in foreign countries, directed that an internal preliminary investigation be made to ascertain whether that corporation had engaged in similar transactions. On the basis of the report of this survey, received in October, 1975, management brought the issue to the attention of the corporation's board of directors. At a meeting held on November 6 of that year the board referred the matter to the board's audit committee. The audit committee retained as its special counsel the Washington, D.C., law firm of Wilmer, Cutler & Pickering which had not previously acted as counsel to the corporation. With the assistance of such special counsel and Arthur Andersen & Co., the corporation's outside auditors, the audit committee engaged in an investigation into the corporation's worldwide operations, focusing on whether, in the period January 1, 1971 to December 31, 1975, corporate funds had been (1) paid directly or indirectly to any political party or person or to any officer, employee, shareholder or director of any governmental or private customer, or (2) used to reimburse any officer of the corporation or other person for such payments.

On March 4, 1976 the audit committee released its report which was filed with the Securities and Exchange Commission and disclosed to the corporation's shareholders in a proxy statement prior to the annual meeting of shareholders held in April, 1976. The audit committee reported that it had found evidence that in the period from 1971 to 1975 the corporation or its subsidiaries had made payments abroad and in the United States constituting bribes and kickbacks in amounts perhaps totaling more than 11 million dollars and that some of the individual defendant directors had been personally involved in certain of the transactions.

Almost immediately Auerbach, a shareholder in the corporation, instituted the present shareholders' derivative action on behalf of the corporation against the corporation's directors, Arthur Andersen & Co. and the corporation. The complaint alleged that in connection with the transactions reported by the audit committee defendants, present and former members of the corporation's board of directors and Arthur Andersen & Co., are liable to the corporation for breach of their duties to the corporation and should be made to account for payments made in those transactions.

On April 21, 1976 the board of directors of the corporation adopted a resolution creating a special litigation committee "for the purpose of establishing a point of contact between the Board of Directors and the Corporation's General Counsel concerning the position to be taken by the Corporation in certain litigation involving shareholder derivative claims on behalf of the Corporation against certain of its directors and officers" and authorizing that committee "to take such steps from time to time as it deems necessary to pursue its objectives including the retention of special outside counsel." The special committee comprised three disinterested directors who had joined the board after the challenged transactions had occurred. The board subsequently additionally vested in the committee "all of the authority of the Board of Directors to determine, on behalf of the Board, the position that the Corporation shall take with respect to the derivative claims alleged on its behalf" in the present and similar shareholder derivative actions.

The special litigation committee reported under date of November 22, 1976. It found that defendant Arthur Andersen & Co. had conducted its examination of the corporation's affairs in accordance with generally accepted auditing standards and in good faith and concluded that no proper interest of the corporation or its shareholders would be served by the continued assertion of a claim against it. The committee also concluded that none of the individual defendants had violated the New York State statutory standard of care, that none had profited personally or gained in any way, that the claims asserted in the present action are without merit, that if the action were allowed to proceed the time and talents of the corporation's senior management would be wasted on lengthy pretrial and trial proceedings, that litigation costs would be inordinately high in view of the unlikelihood of success, and that the continuing publicity could be damaging to the corporation's business. The committee determined that it would not be in the best interests of the corporation for the present derivative action to proceed, and, exercising the authority delegated to it, directed the corporation's general counsel to take that position in the present litigation as well as in pending comparable shareholders' derivative actions.

On December 17, 1976 the corporation and the four individual defendants . . . moved for an order . . . dismissing the complaint . . . On January 7, 1977 Arthur Andersen & Co. made a similar motion. On May 13, 1977 Supreme Court, Special Term, granted the motions of all defendants and dismissed the complaint on the merits. . . .

As all parties and both courts below recognize, the disposition of this case on the merits turns on the proper application of the business judgment doctrine, in particular to the decision of a specially appointed committee of disinterested directors acting on behalf of the board to terminate a shareholders' derivative action. That doctrine bars judicial inquiry into actions of corporate directors taken in good faith and in the exercise of honest judgment in the lawful and legitimate furtherance of corporate purposes. . . ."

In this instance our inquiry, to the limited extent to which it may be pursued, has a two-tiered aspect. The complaint initially asserted liability on the part of defendants based on the payments made to foreign governmental customers and privately owned customers, some unspecified portions of which were allegedly passed on to officials of the customers, i.e., the focus was on first-tier bribes and kickbacks. Then subsequent to the service of the complaint there came the report of a special litigation committee, particularly appointed by the corporation's board of directors to consider the merits of the present and similar shareholders' derivative actions, and its determination that it would not be in the best interests of the corporation to press claims against defendants based on their possible first-tier liability. The motions for summary judgment were predicated principally on the report and determination of the special litigation committee and on the contention that this second-tier corporate action insulated the first-tier transactions from judicial inquiry and was itself subject to the shelter of the business judgment doctrine. . . .

It appears to us that the business judgment doctrine, at least in part, is grounded in the prudent recognition that courts are ill equipped and infrequently called on to evaluate what are and must be essentially business judgments. The authority and responsibilities vested in corporate directors both by statute and decisional law proceed on the assumption that inescapably there can be no available objective standard by which the correctness of every corporate decision may be measured, by the courts or otherwise. Even if that were not the case, by definition the responsibility for business judgments must rest with the corporate directors; their individual capabilities and experience peculiarly qualify them for the discharge of that responsibility. Thus, absent evidence of bad faith or fraud (of which there is none here) the courts must and properly should respect their determinations. . . .

In the present case we confront a special instance of the application of the business judgment rule and inquire whether it applies in its full vigor to shield from judicial scrutiny the decision of a three-person minority committee of the board acting on behalf of the full board not to prosecute a shareholder's derivative action. The record in this case reveals that the board is a 15-member board, and that the derivative suit was brought against four of the directors. Nothing suggests that any of the other directors participated in any of the challenged first-tier transactions. Indeed the report of the audit committee on which the complaint is based specifically found that no other directors had any prior knowledge of or were in any way involved in any of these transactions. Other directors had, however, been members of the board in the period during which the transactions occurred. Each of the three director members of the special litigation committee joined the board thereafter.

The business judgment rule does not foreclose inquiry by the courts into the disinterested independence of those members of the board chosen by it to make the corporate decision on its behalf—here the members of the special litigation committee. Indeed the rule shields the deliberations and conclusions of the chosen representatives of the board only if they possess a disinterested independence and do not stand in a dual relation which prevents an unprejudicial exercise of judgment. . . .

It is not disputed that the members of the special litigation committee were not members of the corporation's board of directors at the time of the first-tier transactions in question. . . . None of the three had had any prior affiliation with the corporation. . . .

The contention . . . that any committee authorized by the board of which defendant directors were members must be held to be legally infirm and may not be delegated power to terminate a derivative action must be rejected. . . . The board in this instance, with slight adaptation, followed prudent practice in observing the general policy that when individual members of a board of directors prove to have personal interests which may conflict with the interests of the corporation, such interested directors must be excluded while the remaining members of the board proceed to consideration and action. (Cf. Business Corporation Law, § 713, which contemplates such situations and provides that the interested directors may nonetheless be included in the quorum count.) Courts have consistently held that the business judgment rule applies where some directors are charged with wrongdoing, so long as the remaining directors making the decision are disinterested and independent . . .

To accept the assertions of the intervenor and to disqualify the entire board would be to render the corporation powerless to make an effective business judgment with respect to prosecution of the derivative action. . . .

We turn then to the action of the special litigation committee itself which comprised two components. First, there was the selection of procedures appropriate to the pursuit of its charge, and second, there was the ultimate substantive decision; predicated on the procedures chosen and the data produced thereby, not to pursue the claims advanced in the shareholders' derivative actions. The latter, substantive decision falls squarely within the embrace of the business judgment doctrine, involving as it did the weighing and balancing of legal, ethical, commercial, promotional, public relations, fiscal and other factors familiar to the resolution of many if not most corporate problems. To this extent the conclusion reached by the special litigation committee is outside the scope of our review. Thus, the courts cannot inquire as to which factors were considered by that committee or the relative weight accorded them in reaching that substantive decision—"the reasons for the payments, the advantages or disadvantages accruing to the corporation by reason of the transactions, the extent of the participation or profit by the respondent directors and the loss, if any, of public confidence in the corporation which might be incurred" (64 A.D.2d, at p. 107, 408 N.Y.S.2d at pp. 87–88). Inquiry into such matters would go to the very core of the business judgment made by the committee. To permit judicial probing of such issues would be to emasculate the business judgment doctrine as applied to the actions and determinations of the special litigation committee. Its substantive evaluation of the problems posed and its judgment in their resolution are beyond our reach.

As to the other component of the committee's activities, however, the situation is different, and here we agree with the Appellate Division. As to the methodologies and procedures best suited to the conduct of an investigation of facts and the determination of legal liability, the courts are well equipped by long and continuing experience and practice to make determinations. In fact they are better qualified in this regard than are corporate directors in general. Nor do the determinations to be made in the adoption of procedures partake of the nuances or special perceptions or comprehensions of business judgment or corporate activities or interests. The question is solely how appropriately to set about to gather the pertinent data.

While the court may properly inquire as to the adequacy and appropriateness of the committee's investigative procedures and methodologies, it may not under the guise of consideration of such factors trespass in the domain of business judgment. At the same time those responsible for the procedures by which the business judgment is reached may reasonably be required to show that they have pursued their chosen investigative methods in good faith. What evidentiary proof may be required to this end will, of course, depend on the nature of the particular investigation, and the proper reach of disclosure at the instance of the shareholders will in turn relate inversely to the showing made by the corporate representatives themselves. The latter may be expected to show that the areas and subjects to be examined are reasonably complete and that there has been a good-faith pursuit of inquiry into such areas and subjects. What has been uncovered and the relative weight accorded in evaluating and balancing the several factors and considerations are beyond the scope of judicial concern. Proof, however, that the investigation has been so restricted in scope, so shallow in execution, or otherwise so *pro forma* or halfhearted as to constitute a pretext or sham, consistent with the principles underlying the application of the business judgment doctrine, would raise questions of good faith or conceivably fraud which would never be shielded by that doctrine.

In addition to the issue of the disinterested independence of the special litigation committee, addressed above, the disposition of the present appeal . . . [depends on whether the derivative suit plaintiff] has shown facts sufficient to require a trial of any material issue of fact as to the adequacy or appropriateness of the *modus operandi* of that committee or has demonstrated acceptable excuse for failure to make such tender. . . . We conclude that the requisite showing has not been made on this record. . . .

On the submissions made by defendants in support of their motions, we do not find either insufficiency or infirmity as to the procedures and methodologies chosen and pursued by the special litigation committee. That committee promptly engaged eminent special counsel to guide its deliberations and to advise it. The committee reviewed the prior work of the audit committee, testing its completeness, accuracy and thoroughness by interviewing representatives of Wilmer, Cutler & Pickering, reviewing transcripts of the testimony of 10 corporate officers and employees before the Securities and Exchange Commission, and studying documents collected by and work papers of the Washington law firm. Individual interviews were conducted with the directors found to have participated in any way in the questioned payments, and with representatives of Arthur Andersen & Co. Questionnaires were sent to and answered by each of the corporation's nonmanagement directors. At the conclusion of its investigation the special litigation committee sought and obtained pertinent legal advice from its special counsel. The selection of appropriate investigative methods must always turn on the nature and characteristics of the particular subject being investigated, but we find nothing in this record that requires a trial of any material issue of fact concerning the sufficiency or appropriateness of the procedures chosen by this special litigation committee. Nor is there anything in this record to raise a triable issue of fact as to the good-faith pursuit of its examination by that committee. . . .

For the reasons stated the order of the Appellate Division should be modified, with costs to defendants, by reversing so much thereof as reversed the order of Supreme Court, and, as so modified, affirmed.

[The dissenting opinion of Chief Judge Cooke is omitted.]

■ JASEN, WACHTLER, FUCHSBERG and MEYER, JJ., concur with JONES, J.

■ COOKE, C.J., dissents and votes to affirm in a separate opinion.

■ GABRIELLI, J., taking no part. . . .

———

Zapata Corp. v. Maldonado

Supreme Court of Delaware, 1981.
430 A.2d 779.

■ Before DUFFY, QUILLEN and HORSEY, JJ.

[The claims on which this case was apparently based are stated as follows in Maldonado v. Flynn, 597 F.2d 789 (2d Cir.1979): A stock-option plan had been adopted by the board of Zapata Corporation in 1970 and approved by Zapata's shareholders in 1971. The board was authorized to amend the plan freely. The options were exercisable in five equal installments; the last exercise date was July 14, 1974. Flynn, the chief executive officer and a director of Zapata, as well as other senior officers of Zapata, were granted options under the plan to purchase Zapata stock at $12.15 per share.

[In 1974, Flynn and the board had decided Zapata should make a cash tender offer for its own stock at $25–$30 per share. Since Zapata stock was then trading at only $19 per share, the announcement of the tender offer would trigger a sharp rise in the price of Zapata stock. The tender offer was to be publicly announced on July 2, 1974. Early that day, trading in Zapata stock on the New York Stock Exchange was suspended at the request of Zapata's management, pending the announcement. Before trading resumed, the board accelerated the final exercise date for the options held by Flynn and the other senior officers from July 14, 1974 to July 2, 1974. The board also modified the plan to authorize Zapata to make interest-free loans to Flynn and the other senior officers in the amount of (i) the purchase price of the options they exercised and (ii) the tax liability they would incur by exercising the options. The purpose and effect of these amendments were to permit Flynn and the other senior officers to benefit at Zapata's expense. Under applicable federal tax laws, on the exercise of the option Flynn and the other senior officers would realize ordinary income in the amount of the spread between the option price and the fair market price of the stock at the time the option was exercised. Correspondingly, Zapata could deduct the amount of that spread as a business expense. By accelerating the last exercise date, and allowing Flynn and the other senior officers to exercise their options before the market price of the stock rose as a result of the tender offer, the board permitted the optionees to save a considerable amount of taxes but correlatively prevented Zapata from enjoying a higher tax deduction.]

■ QUILLEN, JUSTICE. This is an interlocutory appeal from an order entered on April 9, 1980, by the Court of Chancery denying appellant-defendant Zapata Corporation's (Zapata) alternative motions to dismiss the complaint or for summary judgment. The issue to be addressed has reached this Court by way of a rather convoluted path.

In June, 1975, William Maldonado, a stockholder of Zapata, instituted a derivative action in the Court of Chancery on behalf of Zapata against ten officers and/or directors of Zapata, alleging, essentially, breaches of fiduciary duty. Maldonado did not first demand that the board bring this action, stating instead such demand's futility because all directors were named as defendants and allegedly participated in the acts specified.[1] In June, 1977, Maldonado commenced an action in the United States District Court for the Southern District of New York against the same defendants, save one, alleging federal security law violations as well as the same common law claims made previously in the Court of Chancery.

By June, 1979, four of the defendant-directors were no longer on the board, and the remaining directors appointed two new outside directors to the board. The board then created an "Independent Investigation Committee" (Committee), composed solely of the two new directors, to investigate Maldonado's actions . . . and to determine whether the corporation should continue any or all of the litigation. The Committee's determination was stated to be "final, . . . not . . . subject to review by the Board of Directors and . . . in all respects . . . binding upon the Corporation."

Following an investigation, the Committee concluded, in September, 1979, that each action should "be dismissed forthwith as their continued

---

[1]   Court of Chancery Rule 23.1 states in part: "The complaint shall also allege with particularity the efforts, if any, made by the plaintiff to obtain the action he desires from the directors or comparable authority and the reasons for his failure to obtain the action or for not making the effort."

maintenance is inimical to the Company's best interests. . . ."
Consequently, Zapata moved for dismissal or summary judgment. . . .

On March 18, 1980, the Court of Chancery, in a reported opinion, the
basis for the order of April 9, 1980, denied Zapata's motions, holding that
Delaware law does not sanction this means of dismissal. . . .

[T]he focus in this case is on the power to speak for the corporation
as to whether the lawsuit should be continued or terminated. As we see
it, this issue in the current appellate posture of this case . . . [concerns]
the corporate power under Delaware law of an authorized board
committee to cause dismissal of litigation instituted for the benefit of the
corporation; and the role of the Court of Chancery in resolving conflicts
between the stockholder and the committee. . . .

Consistent with the purpose of requiring a demand, a board decision
to cause a derivative suit to be dismissed as detrimental to the company,
after demand has been made and refused, will be respected unless it was
wrongful.[10] . . . A claim of a wrongful decision not to sue is thus the first
exception and the first context of dispute. Absent a wrongful refusal, the
stockholder in such a situation simply lacks legal managerial power.

But it cannot be implied that, absent a wrongful board refusal, a
stockholder can never have an individual right to initiate an action. For,
as is stated in *[McKee]*, a "well settled" exception exists to the general
rule.

> "[A] stockholder may sue in equity in his derivative right to
> assert a cause of action in behalf of the corporation, *without
> prior demand* upon the directors to sue, when it is apparent that
> a demand would be futile, that the officers are under an
> influence that sterilizes discretion and could not be proper
> persons to conduct the litigation."

156 A. at 193 (emphasis added). . . . [11]

These comments in *McKee* . . . make obvious sense. A demand, when
required and refused (if not wrongful), terminates a stockholder's legal
ability to initiate a derivative action. But where demand is properly
excused, the stockholder does possess the ability to initiate the action on
his corporation's behalf.

These conclusions, however, do not determine the question before us.
Rather, they merely bring us to the question to be decided. . . .

The question to be decided becomes: When, if at all, should an
authorized board committee be permitted to cause litigation, properly

---

[10]   In other words, when stockholders, after making demand and having their suit rejected,
attack the board's decision as improper, the board's decision falls under the "business judgment"
rule and will be respected if the requirements of the rule are met. . . . That situation should be
distinguished from the instant case, where demand was not made, and the *power* of the board
to seek a dismissal, due to disqualification, presents a threshold issue. . . .

[11]   These statements are consistent with Rule 23.1's "reasons for . . . failure" to make
demand. . . .

initiated by a derivative stockholder in his own right, to be dismissed? As noted above, a board has the power to choose not to pursue litigation when demand is made upon it, so long as the decision is not wrongful. If the board determines that a suit would be detrimental to the company, the board's determination prevails. Even when demand is excusable, circumstances may arise when continuation of the litigation would not be in the corporation's best interests. Our inquiry is whether, under such circumstances, there is a permissible procedure under § 141(a) by which a corporation can rid itself of detrimental litigation. If there is not, a single stockholder in an extreme case might control the destiny of the entire corporation. This concern was bluntly expressed by the Ninth Circuit in Lewis v. Anderson, 9th Cir., 615 F.2d 778, 783 (1979), cert. denied, 449 U.S. 869, 101 S.Ct. 206, 66 L.Ed.2d 89 (1980): "To allow one shareholder to incapacitate an entire board of directors merely by leveling charges against them gives too much leverage to dissident shareholders." But, when examining the means, including the committee mechanism examined in this case, potentials for abuse must be recognized. This takes us to the second and third aspects of the issue on appeal. . . .

The corporate power inquiry then focuses on whether the board, tainted by the self-interest of a majority of its members, can legally delegate its authority to a committee of two disinterested directors. We find our statute clearly requires an affirmative answer to this question. As has been noted, under an express provision of the statute, § 141(c), a committee can exercise all of the authority of the board to the extent provided in the resolution of the board. Moreover, at least by analogy to our statutory section on interested directors, 8 Del.C. § 141, it seems clear that the Delaware statute is designed to permit disinterested directors to act for the board.[14] . . .

We do not think that the interest taint of the board majority is per se a legal bar to the delegation of the board's power to an independent committee composed of disinterested board members. The committee can properly act for the corporation to move to dismiss derivative litigation that is believed to be detrimental to the corporation's best interest.

Our focus now switches to the Court of Chancery which is faced with a stockholder assertion that a derivative suit, properly instituted, should continue for the benefit of the corporation and a corporate assertion, properly made by a board committee acting with board authority, that the same derivative suit should be dismissed as inimical to the best interests of the corporation.

At the risk of stating the obvious, the problem is relatively simple. If, on the one hand, corporations can consistently wrest bona fide derivative actions away from well-meaning derivative plaintiffs through the use of the committee mechanism, the derivative suit will lose much,

---

[14]   [The court quoted Del. § 144.]

if not all, of its generally-recognized effectiveness as an intra-corporate means of policing boards of directors. See Dent, [supra note 5,] 75 Nw.U.L.Rev. at 96 & n. 3, 144 & n. 241. If, on the other hand, corporations are unable to rid themselves of meritless or harmful litigation and strike suits, the derivative action, created to benefit the corporation, will produce the opposite, unintended result. . . . It thus appears desirable to us to find a balancing point where bona fide stockholder power to bring corporation causes of action cannot be unfairly trampled on by the board of directors, but the corporation can rid itself of detrimental litigation.

[T]he question has been treated by other courts as one of the "business judgment" of the board committee. If a "committee, composed of independent and disinterested directors, conducted a proper review of the matters before it, considered a variety of factors and reached, in good faith, a business judgment that [the] action was not in the best interest of [the corporation]", the action must be dismissed. See, e.g., Maldonado v. Flynn, . . . 485 F.Supp. at 282, 286. The issues become solely independence, good faith, and reasonable investigation. The ultimate conclusion of the committee, under that view, is not subject to judicial review.

We are not satisfied, however, that acceptance of the "business judgment" rationale at this stage of derivative litigation is a proper balancing point. While we admit an analogy with a normal case respecting board judgment, it seems to us that there is sufficient risk in the realities of a situation like the one presented in this case to justify caution beyond adherence to the theory of business judgment.

The context here is a suit against directors where demand on the board is excused. We think some tribute must be paid to the fact that the lawsuit was properly initiated. It is not a board refusal case. Moreover, this complaint was filed in June of 1975 and, while the parties undoubtedly would take differing views on the degree of litigation activity, we have to be concerned about the creation of an "Independent Investigation Committee" four years later, after the election of two new outside directors. Situations could develop where such motions could be filed after years of vigorous litigation for reasons unconnected with the merits of the lawsuit.

Moreover, notwithstanding our conviction that Delaware law entrusts the corporate power to a properly authorized committee, we must be mindful that directors are passing judgment on fellow directors in the same corporation and fellow directors, in this instance, who designated them to serve both as directors and committee members. The question naturally arises whether a "there but for the grace of God go I" empathy might not play a role. And the further question arises whether inquiry as to independence, good faith and reasonable investigation is sufficient safeguard against abuse, perhaps subconscious abuse.

There is another line of exploration besides the factual context of this litigation which we find helpful. The nature of this motion finds no ready pigeonhole, as perhaps illustrated by its being set forth in the alternative. It is perhaps best considered as a hybrid summary judgment motion for dismissal because the stockholder plaintiff's standing to maintain the suit has been lost. But it does not fit neatly into a category described in Rule 12(b) of the Court of Chancery Rules nor does it correspond directly with Rule 56 since the question of genuine issues of fact on the merits of the stockholder's claim are not reached.

It seems to us that there are two other procedural analogies that are helpful in addition to reference to Rules 12 and 56. There is some analogy to a settlement in that there is a request to terminate litigation without a judicial determination of the merits. See Perrine v. Pennroad Corp., Del.Supr., 47 A.2d 479, 487 (1946). "In determining whether or not to approve a proposed settlement of a derivative stockholders' action [when directors are on both sides of the transaction], the Court of Chancery is called upon to exercise its own business judgment." Neponsit Investment Co. v. Abramson, Del.Supr., 405 A.2d 97, 100 (1979) and cases therein cited. In this case, the litigating stockholder plaintiff facing dismissal of a lawsuit properly commenced ought, in our judgment, to have sufficient status for strict Court review.

Finally, if the committee is in effect given status to speak for the corporation as the plaintiff in interest, then it seems to us there is an analogy to Court of Chancery Rule 41(a)(2) where the plaintiff seeks a dismissal after an answer. Certainly, the position of record of the litigating stockholder is adverse to the position advocated by the corporation in the motion to dismiss. Accordingly, there is perhaps some wisdom to be gained by the direction in Rule 41(a)(2) that "an action shall not be dismissed at the plaintiff's instance save upon order of the Court and upon such terms and conditions as the Court deems proper."

Whether the Court of Chancery will be persuaded by the exercise of a committee power resulting in a summary motion for dismissal of a derivative action, where a demand has not been initially made, should rest, in our judgment, in the independent discretion of the Court of Chancery. We thus steer a middle course between those cases which yield to the independent business judgment of a board committee and this case as determined below which would yield to unbridled plaintiff stockholder control. In pursuit of the course, we recognize that "[t]he final substantive judgment whether a particular lawsuit should be maintained requires a balance of many factors—ethical, commercial, promotional, public relations, employee relations, fiscal as well as legal." Maldonado v. Flynn, [supra,] 485 F.Supp. at 285. But we are content that such factors are not "beyond the judicial reach" of the Court of Chancery which regularly and competently deals with fiduciary relationships, disposition of trust property, approval of settlements and scores of similar problems. We recognize the danger of judicial overreaching but the alternatives seem to us to be outweighed by the fresh view of a judicial outsider. Moreover, if we failed to balance all the interests involved, we would in the name of practicality and judicial economy foreclose a judicial decision on the merits. At this point, we are not convinced that is necessary or desirable.

After an objective and thorough investigation of a derivative suit, an independent committee may cause its corporation to file a pretrial motion to dismiss in the Court of Chancery. The basis of the motion is the best interests of the corporation, as determined by the committee. The motion should include a thorough written record of the investigation and its findings and recommendations. Under appropriate court supervision, akin to proceedings on summary judgment, each side should have an opportunity to make a record on the motion. As to the limited issues presented by the motion noted below, the moving party should be prepared to meet the normal burden under Rule 56 that there is no genuine issue as to any material fact and that the moving party is entitled to dismiss as a matter of law.[15] The Court should apply a two-step test to the motion.

First, the Court should inquire into the independence and good faith of the committee and the bases supporting its conclusions. Limited discovery may be ordered to facilitate such inquiries. The corporation should have the burden of proving independence, good faith and a reasonable investigation, rather than presuming independence, good faith and reasonableness.[17] If the Court determines that the committee is not independent or has not shown reasonable bases for its conclusions, or, if the Court is not satisfied for other reasons relating to the process, including but not limited to the good faith of the committee, the Court shall deny the corporation's motion. If, however, the Court is satisfied under Rule 56 standards that the committee was independent and showed reasonable bases for good faith findings and recommendations, the Court may proceed, in its discretion, to the next step.

The second step provides, we believe, the essential key in striking the balance between legitimate corporate claims as expressed in a derivative stockholder suit and a corporation's best interests as expressed by an independent investigating committee. The Court should determine, applying its own independent business judgment, whether

[15]   We do not foreclose a discretionary trial of factual issues but that issue is not presented in this appeal. See Lewis v. Anderson, supra, 615 F.2d at 780. Nor do we foreclose the possibility that other motions may proceed or be joined with such a pretrial summary judgment motion to dismiss, e.g., a partial motion for summary judgment on the merits.

[17]   Compare Auerbach v. Bennett, 47 N.Y.2d 619, 419 N.Y.S.2d 920, 928–29, 393 N.E.2d 994 (1979). Our approach here is analogous to and consistent with the Delaware approach to "interested director" transactions, where the directors, once the transaction is attacked, have the burden of establishing its "intrinsic fairness" to a court's careful scrutiny. See, e.g., Sterling v. Mayflower Hotel Corp., Del.Supr., 93 A.2d 107 (1952).

the motion should be granted.[18] This means, of course, that instances could arise where a committee can establish its independence and sound bases for its good faith decisions and still have the corporation's motion denied. The second step is intended to thwart instances where corporate actions meet the criteria of step one, but the result does not appear to satisfy its spirit, or where corporate actions would simply prematurely terminate a stockholder grievance deserving of further consideration in the corporation's interest. The Court of Chancery of course must carefully consider and weigh how compelling the corporate interest in dismissal is when faced with a nonfrivolous lawsuit. The Court of Chancery should, when appropriate, give special consideration to matters of law and public policy in addition to the corporation's best interests.

If the Court's independent business judgment is satisfied, the Court may proceed to grant the motion, subject, of course, to any equitable terms or conditions the Court finds necessary or desirable.

The interlocutory order of the Court of Chancery is reversed and the cause is remanded for further proceedings consistent with this opinion.

Boland v. Boland Trane Associates, Inc.

Court of Appeals of Maryland, 2011.
423 Md. 296; 31 A.3d 529.

[This derivative suit focused on stock transactions in a family business owned primarily by eight siblings. Four of the siblings were directors and officers of two family corporations; the other siblings were not actively involved in management. The derivative suit questioned several stock transactions in which three directors had acquired additional corporate stock. Believing these transaction had harmed them and the corporation, John and Kevin Boland, two of the non-director siblings, sent a demand for litigation to the corporation and thereafter filed a derivative action alleging self-dealing and a breach of fiduciary duty. The corporation appointed a special litigation committee ("SLC"), consisting of two newly recruited "independent directors" to examine the claims. After an extended study, the SLC issued a report concluding that the stock transactions were legitimate. The Circuit Court, deferring to the judgment of the SLC, granted summary judgment in favor of the corporations in the derivative action. On appeal, the Court of Special Appeals upheld the Circuit Court's grant of summary judgment, agreeing that the SLC's report properly disposed of the matter. The plaintiff sought review.]

---

[18]　This step shares some of the same spirit and philosophy of the statement by the Vice Chancellor: "Under our system of law, courts and not litigants should decide the merits of litigation." 413 A.2d at 1263.

■ ADKINS, J.

We disagree ... that *Auerbach's* inquiry must necessarily be a "rubber stamp" review. Although *Auerbach* held that an SLC's substantive decisions are presumed reasonable, it did not presume that the SLC was independent, acted in good faith, or followed reasonable procedures. We conclude that there should be no presumption on these issues. Rather, the court should not grant summary judgment on the basis of an SLC's decision unless the directors have stated how they chose the SLC members and come forward with some evidence that the SLC followed reasonable procedures and that no substantial business or personal relationships impugned the SLC's independence and good faith. This places a minimal burden on the directors, as these assertions can be made in an affidavit. If the corporate directors have met this burden, then the burden shifts to the derivative plaintiffs to come forward with evidence regarding these issues sufficient to survive summary judgment. If the plaintiff survives summary judgment, at trial, the burden is on the directors to prove that the SLC was independent, acted in good faith, and made a reasonable investigation and principled, factually supported conclusions. . . .

Regarding the first prong of the *Auerbach* inquiry (the SLC's independence and good faith), judicial inquiry can involve an investigation of the SLC's composition and its members' relation to the director-defendants. *Auerbach, 393 N.E.2d at 1002–03* (stating that courts should examine the SLC's "disinterested independence" and "the adequacy and appropriateness of the committee's investigative procedures and methodologies"). . . .

We now apply the above standards to the Circuit Court's review of the SLC opinion in this case.

A. The SLC's Independence and Good Faith

Under our standard of review, the circuit court must first conclude that the SLC was independent and acted in good faith. As explained above, the SLC members are entitled to no presumption of independence and good faith, and the corporations must state in a motion for summary judgment how they chose the SLC members and come forward with some evidence that no significant relationships or influences impugned their "disinterested independence." *See Auerbach, 393 N.E.2d at 1003.* . . .

Here, the directors never attested to how they chose the SLC members or that the SLC members had no significant business, personal, or social relationships with the directors. Instead, they argued that the SLC was entitled to a presumption of independence and good faith, and from then on simply stated, without proving, that the SLC was independent. Thus, as explained above, the Circuit Court did not have sufficient grounds for summary judgment on the basis of the SLC's report, and we therefore vacate its judgment and remand for further proceedings. On remand, to create sufficient grounds on this issue, the directors would need to state how they chose the SLC members and assert that no significant business, personal, or social relationships impugned the SLC's independence or good faith. Then, if the plaintiffs raises a genuine issue of material fact, the court should complete a thorough investigation.[41]

. . .

The court should require that the directors at least attest to the lack of a significant business, personal, or social relationship with the SLC members and state why they chose the SLC members and how they learned of them. Inquiring only into the SLC members' formal or financial ties with the defendants is inadequate. Nonetheless, the independence inquiry does not require the directors to show, beyond all doubt, that no conceivable theory of influence exists between them and the SLC. The defendants should state the nature of their prior relations with the SLC members. The defendants should address whether the SLC members have any joint pursuits outside of the business world, whether in recreational, social, religious, or non-profit organizations. Once the court has this information, it should be able to determine whether there were any further questions regarding the ability of the SLC to render an independent opinion on behalf of the corporation. But these questions must be addressed, and therefore we remand.

B.　The Reasonableness of the SLC's Methodology

. . .

The reviewing court must examine the methodologies and procedures of the SLC's investigation, and whether there was a reasonable basis for its conclusions. Again, the SLC is not entitled to a presumption that its investigation and conclusions were reasonable. Indeed, the court may find evidence of procedural unreasonableness in the report itself. . . . Moreover, the mere length of the report and the sheer volume of items considered should not be given undue weight by the court. Page totals are a shallow metric, especially given the "relative ease with which a committee could construct a record of apparently diligent investigation after having predetermined the outcome of the investigation." *Abella, 546 F. Supp. at 799. See also Oracle, 824 A.2d at 925 . . .*

Under our standards, although the court should not question the SLC's substantive conclusions, it should examine what issues the SLC actually set out to address. The SLC cannot arrive at a reasonable answer if it addresses the wrong issues. Thus, addressing the wrong issues is an example of unreasonable methodology. . . .

---

[41]　Although we remand on this issue solely because the directors did not make the statements of independence and good faith necessary to support a motion for summary judgment, we observe as well that the Circuit Court's inquiry into the SLC's independence and good faith was improperly narrow. Specifically, the court failed to address whether the directors had any significant business, social, or personal relationships with the SLC members. . . .

Applying our above-described standards, we observe that the Circuit Court incorrectly applied a presumption that the SLC's methodology was reasonable. . . . The court, however, stated that "the business judgment standard requires this Court to examine the work of the SLC *with the presumption . . . that its investigation was conducted within sound business judgment"* (emphasis added) . . . .

As its opinion shows, the court believed that any further investigation into the SLC's report was unnecessary. While courts must defer to the SLC's *substantive conclusions*, they cannot afford any presumption of reasonableness to its methodology.

. . . [A] close examination of the SLC's report raises serious questions regarding the standard of review used by the SLC investigation, and seems to suggest that the SLC itself applied a deferential standard to the Board's previous actions, rather than stepping into the shoes of the corporation and making an independent decision. In reviewing the stock sales to the directors, the SLC concluded:

> **The Board determined that the stock sales were to further solidify successful management for the future well being of the corporation.** It goes without saying that it is common for corporations to give stock or stock options as part of compensation. Here, it has the purposes of further binding management and encouraging performance to enhance personal dividend income.
>
> * * *
>
> The enhancement of control is a positive benefit for the corporations. **The SLC finds those transactions to be well within the business judgment and done in good faith for the benefit of the corporation.** See Cummings v. United Artists Theatre Circuit, Inc., 237 Md. 1, 22, 204 A.2d 795 (1964); Mountain Manor Realty, Inc. v. Buccheri, 55 Md. App. 185, 198, 461 A.2d 45, 53 (1983).
>
> But an issue of the stock that has the collateral effect of enhancing the power of incumbent management is not invalid if the transaction has as its principal purpose some proper corporate goal. . . .
>
> Further, the price received for those shares is more than in dollars. It rewards and expects services to be performed for the corporation. (emphasis added)

It is unclear, from the above passage, whether the SLC independently determined that the stock sales were fair to the corporation or, as the emphasized language suggests, merely gave deference to the Board's determination under the business judgment rule.

Comparing the Circuit Court's review with the standards described above, we are unable to give our blessing to its decision. The report, as submitted, did not provide sufficient explanation of its methodology to allow meaningful judicial review of the methodology's reasonableness. Therefore, the court should not have granted summary judgment, which it apparently did based on a presumption that the SLC's methodology was reasonable. . . . On remand, the Circuit Court shall analyze the thoroughness of the SLC's investigation and the reasonableness of the methodology it employed, consistent with our above-described standards.

. . .

Dissenting Opinion by BATTAGLIA, J.

. . .

The majority's adoption of "enhanced *Auerbach*," also known as the first prong of the *Zapata* standard, removes the presumption of our traditional business judgment rule in favor of the corporation. This ruling is contrary to our jurisprudence and the goal of acknowledging the will of the majority, absent a showing of director abuse by the plaintiff shareholder; our standard, like New York's *Auerbach* standard, has placed the burden on the plaintiff shareholder to demonstrate that the director action, including a demand refusal, was made unreasonably, in bad faith, or while the director was on both sides of the transaction and thus interested. . . .

In the case . . . The circuit court held, and the Court of Special Appeals agreed in its reported opinion, that John and Kevin as derivative plaintiffs failed to rebut the presumption that the SLC, as the disinterested directors for the corporations, acted in the best interests of the companies. Just as did our colleagues on the Court of Special Appeals, I would affirm the reasoned application by the circuit court of the business judgment rule. . . .

The independence of the SLC members and their counsel only should turn on whether they are financially interested in the board of directors's action or decision at issue. Rather than a review of the multifarious personal and professional relationships that will become unworkable and unnecessarily intrusive, a review of the members' financial relationship with the challenged transaction serves as a bright-line per capita approach to director independence. . . .

I respectfully dissent.

———

Oliveira v. Sugarman, 451 Md. 208, 152 A.3d 728 (Md. 2017), held that the heightened review applied in *Boland* applies only when the board does not have a disinterested majority. When a majority of the directors do not benefit from the transaction challenged in the suit, the business judgment rule is applied to the board's rejection of the demand by the derivative suit plaintiff. In that inquiry, the board's decision will be upset only if the facts in a well-pleaded complaint, if true, supports a cause of action.

In re PSE & G Shareholder Litigation

173 N.J. 258, 801 A.2d 295 (2002)

Plaintiffs filed derivative actions. The board directed an investigation by a law firm, and, based on the law firm's report, moved for summary judgment. The New Jersey court adopted the following standard of review: "We believe that the trial court correctly declined to apply the traditional business judgment rule in this case. Instead, we shall apply a modified business judgment rule that imposes an initial burden on a corporation to demonstrate that in deciding to reject or terminate a shareholder's suit the members of the board (1) were independent and disinterested, (2) acted in good faith and with due care in their investigation of the shareholder's allegations, and that (3) the board's decision was reasonable. . . . All three elements must be satisfied. Moreover, shareholders in these circumstances must be permitted access to corporate documents and other discovery 'limited to the narrow issue of what steps the directors took to inform themselves of the shareholder demand and the reasonableness of its decision.' " . . .

---

6. DEMAND ON THE SHAREHOLDERS

The Federal Rule of Civil Procedure 23.1 provides that the plaintiff's complaint must set forth the efforts to obtain action from the stockholder "if necessary.". "The rationale for demand on other shareholders is that such a requirement allows the majority of shareholders to determine whether legal action is in the corporation's best interest." Harhen v. Brown, 431 Mass. 838, 730 N.E.2d 859 (Mass. 2000). This requirement, however, is a matter of substantive state law, except where the making of a demand would prove inconsistent with federal policy underlying any federal question raised in the derivative suit. *See* Burks v. Lasker, 441 U.S. 471, 99 S.Ct. 1831, 60 L.Ed.2d 404 (1979). Under the law of most states, demand on shareholders is not required. For example, the California and New York statutory counterparts to FRCP 23.1 omit any reference to demand on the shareholders, and it is clear that this omission was deliberate. See Syracuse Television, Inc. v. Channel 9, Syracuse, Inc., 51 Misc.2d 188, 273 N.Y.S.2d 16 (1966). And, where the statutes are not definitive, the requirement of a demand on the shareholders is largely overtaken by numerous exceptions, so that the failure to make a demand on the shareholders is rarely a successful in scuttling the derivative suit. Among the exceptions are i) the suit's defendant controls the corporation, ii) the large number of shareholders would visit high cost and much delay in making a demand on the shareholders, and iii) the misconduct to be pursued in the derivative suit is of the type that cannot be ratified by the shareholders.

7. INDEMNIFICATION AND INSURANCE

A. INDEMNIFICATION

The right of a director or officer to indemnification under the common law was not completely clear. *New York Dock Co. v. McCollom,* 173 Misc. 106, 16 N.Y.S.2d 844 (1939), decided prior to the enactment of the New York indemnification statute, held that, even though the directors had successfully defended themselves in a derivative suit, they were not entitled to reimbursement of their counsel fees absent proof that their defense benefitted the corporation. Later decisions in other jurisdictions, however, upheld the common law right of a vindicated director to recover the expenses of his defense without any showing of a specific benefit to the corporation. In re E.C. Warner Co., 232 Minn. 207, 45 N.W.2d 388 (1950); Solimine v. Hollander, 129 N.J.Eq. 264, 19 A.2d 344 (Ch.1941). The policy reasons why the corporation should indemnify a director, as set forth in *Solimine,* are (1) to encourage innocent directors to resist unjust charges and provide them an opportunity to hire competent counsel; (2) to induce "responsible business men to accept the post of directors": and (3) "to discourage in large measure stockholders' litigation of the strike variety." Id. at 272, 19 A.2d at 348. Today, virtually every state has an indemnification statute, but the statutes vary widely in detail.

DEL. GEN. CORP. LAW § 145

[See Statutory Supplement]

MODEL BUS. CORP. ACT §§ 8.50–8.59

[See Statutory Supplement]

N.Y. BUS. CORP. LAW §§ 721–726

[See Statutory Supplement]

CAL. CORP. CODE § 317

[See Statutory Supplement]

ALI, PRINCIPLES OF CORPORATE GOVERNANCE § 7.20

[See Statutory Supplement]

———

Waltuch v. Conticommodity Services, Inc.

United States Court of Appeals, Second Circuit, 1996.
88 F.3d 87.

■ JACOBS, CIRCUIT JUDGE:

Famed silver trader Norton Waltuch spent $2.2 million in unreimbursed legal fees to defend himself against numerous civil lawsuits and an enforcement proceeding brought by the Commodity Futures Trading Commission (CFTC). In this action under Delaware law, Waltuch seeks indemnification of his legal expenses from his former employer. The district court denied any indemnity, and Waltuch appeals.

As vice-president and chief metals trader for Conticommodity Services, Inc., Waltuch traded silver for the firm's clients, as well as for his own account. In late 1979 and early 1980, the silver price spiked upward as the then-billionaire Hunt brothers and several of Waltuch's foreign clients bought huge quantities of silver futures contracts. Just as rapidly, the price fell until (on a day remembered in trading circles as "Silver Thursday") the silver market crashed. Between 1981 and 1985, angry silver speculators filed numerous lawsuits against Waltuch and Conticommodity, alleging fraud, market manipulation, and antitrust violations. All of the suits eventually settled and were dismissed with prejudice, pursuant to settlements in which Conticommodity paid over $35 million to the various suitors. Waltuch himself was dismissed from the suits with no settlement contribution. His unreimbursed legal expenses in these actions total approximately $1.2 million.

Waltuch was also the subject of an enforcement proceeding brought by the CFTC, charging him with fraud and market manipulation. The proceeding was settled, with Waltuch agreeing to a penalty that included a $100,000 fine and a six-month ban on buying or selling futures contracts from any exchange floor. Waltuch spent $1 million in unreimbursed legal fees in the CFTC proceeding.[1]

Waltuch brought suit in the United States District Court for the Southern District of New York (Lasker, J.) against Conticommodity and its parent company, Continental Grain Co. (together "Conti"), for

---

[1]   The parties have stipulated that Waltuch's "reasonable attorney's fees and costs" for the private lawsuits totaled $1,228,586.67, and that the comparable expenses for the CFTC proceeding are an even $1 million.

indemnification of his unreimbursed expenses.[2] Only two of Waltuch's claims reach us on appeal.

Waltuch first claims that Article Ninth of Conticommodity's articles of incorporation requires Conti to indemnify him for his expenses in both the private and CFTC actions. Conti responds that this claim is barred by subsection (a) of § 145 of Delaware's General Corporation Law, which permits indemnification only if the corporate officer acted "in good faith," something that Waltuch has not established. Waltuch counters that subsection (f) of the same statute permits a corporation to grant indemnification rights outside the limits of subsection (a), and that Conticommodity did so with Article Ninth (which has no stated good-faith limitation). The district court held that, notwithstanding § 145(f), Waltuch could recover under Article Ninth only if Waltuch met the "good faith" requirement of § 145(a).[3] 833 F.Supp. 302, 308–09 (S.D.N.Y.1993). On the factual issue of whether Waltuch had acted "in good faith," the court denied Conti's summary judgment motion and cleared the way for trial. Id. at 313. The parties then stipulated that they would forgo trial on the issue of Waltuch's "good faith," agree to an entry of final judgment against Waltuch on his claim under Article Ninth and § 145(f), and allow Waltuch to take an immediate appeal of the judgment to this Court. Thus, as to Waltuch's first claim, the only question left is how to interpret §§ 145(a) and 145(f), assuming Waltuch acted with less than "good faith." As we explain in part I below, we affirm the district court's judgment as to this claim and hold that § 145(f) does not permit a corporation to bypass the "good faith" requirement of § 145(a).

Waltuch's second claim is that subsection (c) of § 145 requires Conti to indemnify him because he was "successful on the merits or otherwise" in the private lawsuits.[4] The district court ruled for Conti on this claim as well. The court explained that, even though all the suits against Waltuch were dismissed without his making any payment, he was not "successful on the merits or otherwise," because Conti's settlement payments to the plaintiffs were partially on Waltuch's behalf. Id. at 311. For the reasons stated in part II below, we reverse this portion of the district court's ruling, and hold that Conti must indemnify Waltuch under § 145(c) for the $1.2 million in unreimbursed legal fees he spent in defending the private lawsuits.

---

[2] Conticommodity and Continental Grain are incorporated in Delaware and have their principal places of business in New York; Waltuch is a New Jersey citizen. We therefore have diversity jurisdiction under 28 U.S.C. § 1332. All parties agree that Delaware law governs.

[3] A Special Committee of Continental Grain Co.'s Board of Directors reached the same conclusion in November 1991. Waltuch filed his complaint two months later. In the district court, Conti argued that under the business judgment rule, the Special Committee's decision was immune from challenge, an argument the district court rejected. 833 F.Supp. at 305. Although the parties signed a stipulation preserving Conti's right to contest the district court's ruling on this issue, Conti has abandoned its business judgment rule argument on appeal.

[4] The district court held that Waltuch was not successful "on the merits or otherwise" in the CFTC proceeding. 833 F.Supp. at 311. Waltuch does not appeal this aspect of the court's ruling.

I

Article Ninth, on which Waltuch bases his first claim, is categorical and contains no requirement of "good faith":

> The Corporation shall indemnify and hold harmless each of its incumbent or former directors, officers, employees and agents . . . against expenses actually and necessarily incurred by him in connection with the defense of any action, suit or proceeding threatened, pending or completed, in which he is made a party, by reason of his serving in or having held such position or capacity, except in relation to matters as to which he shall be adjudged in such action, suit or proceeding to be liable for negligence or misconduct in the performance of duty.[5]

Conti argues that § 145(a) of Delaware's General Corporation Law, which does contain a "good faith" requirement, fixes the outer limits of a corporation's power to indemnify; Article Ninth is thus invalid under Delaware law, says Conti, to the extent that it requires indemnification of officers who have acted in bad faith. The affirmative grant of power in § 145(a) is as follows:

> *A corporation shall have power to indemnify* any person who was or is a party or is threatened to be made a party to any threatened, pending or completed action, suit or proceeding, whether civil, criminal, administrative or investigative (other than an action by or in the right of the corporation) by reason of the fact that he is or was a director, officer, employee or agent of the corporation, or is or was serving at the request of the corporation as a director, officer, employee or agent of another corporation, partnership, joint venture, trust or other enterprise, against expenses (including attorneys' fees), judgments, fines and amounts paid in settlement actually and reasonably incurred by him in connection with such action, suit or proceeding *if he acted in good faith and in a manner he reasonably believed to be in or not opposed to the best interests of the corporation,* and, with respect to any criminal action or proceeding, had no reasonable cause to believe his conduct was unlawful.

56 Del.Laws 50, § 1 at 170–71 (1967) (emphasis added) (rewriting Delaware's General Corporation Law, title 8, chapter 1 of the Delaware Code), *codified at* 8 Del.Code Ann. tit. 8, § 145(a) (Michie 1991). Key language in the Delaware Code Annotated's version of this subsection is in error, as explained in the margin.[6]

---

[5]   Because the private suits and the CFTC proceeding were settled, it is undisputed that Waltuch was not "adjudged . . . to be liable for negligence or misconduct in the performance of duty."

[6]   There is some confusion about whether this subsection begins, "A corporation *shall have power* to indemnify . . . " or "A corporation *may* indemnify . . . ". As originally enacted, § 145(a) contained the phrase "shall have power". 56 Del.Laws 50, § 1 at 170 (1967). According

In order to escape the "good faith" clause of § 145(a), Waltuch argues that § 145(a) is not an *exclusive* grant of indemnification power, because § 145(f) expressly allows corporations to indemnify officers in a manner broader than that set out in § 145(a). The "nonexclusivity" language of § 145(f) provides:

> The indemnification and advancement of expenses provided by, or granted pursuant to, the other subsections of this section *shall not be deemed exclusive of any other rights* to which those seeking indemnification or advancement of expenses may be entitled under any bylaw, agreement, vote of stockholders or disinterested directors or otherwise, both as to action in his official capacity and as to action in another capacity while holding such office.

56 Del.Laws 50, § 1 at 172 (emphasis added), *as amended and codified* at 8 Del.Code Ann. tit. 8, § 145(f). Waltuch contends that the "nonexclusivity" language in § 145(f) is a separate grant of indemnification power, not limited by the good faith clause that governs the power granted in § 145(a). Conti on the other hand contends that § 145(f) must be limited by "public policies," one of which is that a corporation may indemnify its officers only if they act in "good faith."

In a thorough and scholarly opinion, Judge Lasker agreed with Conti's reading of § 145(f), writing that "it has been generally agreed that there are public policy limits on indemnification under Section 145(f)," although it was "difficult . . . to define precisely what limitations on indemnification public policy imposes." 833 F.Supp. at 307, 308. After reviewing cases from Delaware and elsewhere and finding that they provided no authoritative guidance, Judge Lasker surveyed the numerous commentators on this issue and found that they generally

---

to the annotations in the *Delaware Code Annotated* (and confirmed by a review of the legislative records since 1967), § 145(a) has never been amended. *See* 8 Del.Code Ann. tit. 8, § 145(a) (1991 & 1995 Supp.).

Nevertheless, the *Delaware Code Annotated,* a private compilation by the Michie Company of all Delaware legislative acts, at some point began using the phrase "may" in place of "shall have power". *See* 8 Del.Code Ann. tit. 8, § 145(a) (1974). We have not been able to explain this non-legislative change in statutory language. The *Delaware Corporation Law Annotated,* published by the Corporation Trust Company, continues to use the phrase "shall have power". Del.Corp.L.Ann. § 145(a) (20th ed. Corp.Trust Co.1991).

One treatise uses the phrase "shall have power", *see* Ernest L. Folk, III, et al., *Folk on the Delaware General Corporation Law* at 145:1 (3d ed. 1994), while another uses "may". *See* 5 R. Franklin Balotti & Jesse A. Finkelstein, *The Delaware Law of Corporations and Business Organizations* at 100 (1990 & 1993 Supp.) ("Balotti & Finkelstein"). The parties to this appeal perpetuate the confusion: their joint appendix contains a version of § 145(a) that says "shall have power", but one of the briefs quotes a version that says "may".

When there is a conflict between an original enactment of the Delaware Legislature and the codification of the law, the original enactment controls. *Elliott v. Blue Cross & Blue Shield,* 407 A.2d 524, 528 (Del.1979); *Kimmey v. Farmers Bank,* 373 A.2d 569, 570 (Del.1977). We therefore employ the Legislature's version of § 145(a), which says "shall have power".

We are indebted to Lesley Lawrence and the staff at the Third Circuit library in Wilmington for their assistance on this issue.

agreed with Conti's position. *Id.* at 308–09. He also found that Waltuch's reading of § 145(f) failed to make sense of the statute as a whole:

> [T]here would be no point to the carefully crafted provisions of Section 145 spelling out the permissible scope of indemnification under Delaware law if subsection (f) allowed indemnification in additional circumstances without regard to these limits. The exception would swallow the rule.

Id. at 309. The fact that § 145(f) was limited by § 145(a) did not make § 145(f) meaningless, wrote Judge Lasker, because § 145(f) "still 'may authorize the adoption of various procedures and presumptions to make the process of indemnification more favorable to the indemnitee without violating the statute.'" *Id.* at 309 (quoting 1 Balotti & Finkelstein § 4.16 at 4–321). As will be evident from the discussion below, we adopt much of Judge Lasker's analysis.

A.   Delaware Cases

No Delaware court has decided the very issue presented here; but the applicable cases tend to support the proposition that a corporation's grant of indemnification rights cannot be *inconsistent* with the substantive statutory provisions of § 145, notwithstanding § 145(f). We draw this rule of "consistency" primarily from our reading of the Delaware Supreme Court's opinion in *Hibbert v. Hollywood Park, Inc.*, 457 A.2d 339 (Del.1983). In that case, Hibbert and certain other directors sued the corporation and the remaining directors, and then demanded indemnification for their expenses and fees related to the litigation. The company refused indemnification on the ground that directors were entitled to indemnification only as *defendants* in legal proceedings. The court reversed the trial court and held that Hibbert was entitled to indemnification under the plain terms of a company bylaw that did not draw an express distinction between plaintiff directors and defendant directors. *Id.* at 343. The court then proceeded to test the bylaw for consistency with § 145(a):

> Furthermore, *indemnification here is consistent with current Delaware law.* Under 8 Del.C. § 145(a) . . . , "a corporation may indemnify any person who was or is a party or is threatened to be made a party to any threatened, pending or completed" derivative or third-party action. By this language, indemnity is *not limited to* only those who stand as a defendant in the main action. The corporation can also grant indemnification rights beyond those provided by statute. 8 Del.C. § 145(f).

Id. at 344 (emphasis added and citations omitted). *See supra* note 6 (explaining the error in the *Delaware Code Annotated*'s use of the phrase "may indemnify" in § 145(a)). This passage contains two complementary propositions. Under § 145(f), a corporation may provide indemnification rights that go "beyond" the rights provided by § 145(a) and the other substantive subsections of § 145. At the same, any such indemnification rights provided by a corporation must be "consistent with" the substantive provisions of § 145, including § 145(a). In *Hibbert,* the corporate bylaw was "consistent with" § 145(a), because this subsection was "not limited to" suits in which directors were defendants. *Hibbert's* holding may support an inverse corollary that illuminates our case: if § 145(a) had been expressly limited to directors who were named as defendants, the bylaw could not have stood, regardless of § 145(f), because the bylaw would not have been "consistent with" the substantive statutory provision.[7] . . .

B.   Statutory Reading

The "consistency" rule suggested by [the] Delaware cases is reinforced by our reading of § 145 as a whole. Subsections (a) (indemnification for third-party actions) and (b) (similar indemnification for derivative suits) expressly grant a corporation the power to indemnify directors, officers, and others, if they "acted in good faith and in a manner reasonably believed to be in or not opposed to the best interest of the corporation." These provisions thus limit the scope of the power that they confer. They are permissive in the sense that a corporation may exercise less than its full power to grant the indemnification rights set out in these provisions. *See Essential Enter. Corp. v. Dorsey Corp.,* 182 A.2d 647, 653 (Del.Ch.1962). By the same token, subsection (f) permits the corporation to grant additional rights: the rights provided in the rest of § 145 "shall not be deemed exclusive of any other rights to which those seeking indemnification may be entitled." But crucially, subsection (f) merely acknowledges that one seeking indemnification may be entitled to "other rights" (of indemnification or otherwise); it does not speak in terms of corporate power, and therefore cannot be read to free a corporation from the "good faith" limit explicitly imposed in subsections (a) and (b).

An alternative construction of these provisions would effectively force us to ignore certain explicit terms of the statute. Section 145(a) gives Conti the power to indemnify Waltuch "*if* he acted in good faith and in a manner reasonably believed to be in or not opposed to the best interest of the corporation." 56 Del.Laws 50, § 1 at 171 (emphasis added). This statutory limit must mean that there is *no power* to indemnify

---

[7]   The *Hibbert* court cites to a 1978 article by Samuel Arsht, chairman of the committee of experts that drafted Delaware's General Corporation Law in 1967, *id.,* which supports our conclusion that indemnification rights permitted under § 145(f) must be consistent with the other substantive provisions of § 145. At the pages cited by the court, Arsht writes:

> The question most frequently asked by practicing lawyers is what subsection (f), the nonexclusive clause, means. . . . The question which subsection (f) invariably raises is whether a corporation can adopt a by-law or make a contract with its directors providing that they will be indemnified for whatever they may have to pay if they are sued and lose or settle. The answer to this question is "no." Subsection (f) . . . permits additional rights to be created, but *it is not a blanket authorization to indemnify directors* against all expenses, fines, or settlements of whatever nature and *regardless of the directors' conduct.* The statutory language is circumscribed by limits of public policy. . . .

S. Samuel Arsht, *Indemnification Under Section 145 of Delaware General Corporation Law,* 3 Del.J.Corp.L. 176, 176–77 (1978) (emphasis added).

Waltuch if he did not act in good faith. Otherwise, as Judge Lasker pointed out, § 145(a)—and its good faith clause—would have no meaning: a corporation could indemnify whomever and however it wished regardless of the good faith clause or anything else the Delaware Legislature wrote into § 145(a).

When the Legislature intended a subsection of § 145 to augment the powers limited in subsection (a), it set out the additional powers expressly. Thus subsection (g) explicitly allows a corporation to circumvent the "good faith" clause of subsection (a) by purchasing a directors and officers liability insurance policy. Significantly, that subsection is framed as a grant of corporate power:

> A corporation shall have power to purchase and maintain insurance on behalf of any person who is or was a director, officer, employee or agent of the corporation . . . against any liability asserted against him and incurred by him in any such capacity, or arising out of his status as such, *whether or not the corporation would have the power to indemnify him against such liability under this section.*

56 Del.Laws 50, § 1 at 172 (1967) (emphasis added), *codified at* 8 Del.Code Ann. tit. 8, § 145(g) (Michie 1991). The italicized passage reflects the principle that corporations have the power under § 145 to indemnify in some situations and not in others. Since § 145(f) is neither a grant of corporate power nor a limitation on such power, subsection (g) must be referring to the limitations set out in § 145(a) and the other provisions of § 145 that describe corporate power. If § 145 (through subsection (f) or another part of the statute) gave corporations unlimited power to indemnify directors and officers, then the final clause of subsection (g) would be unnecessary: that is, its grant of "power to purchase and maintain insurance" (exercisable regardless of whether the corporation itself would have the power to indemnify the loss directly) is meaningful only because, in some insurable situations, the corporation simply lacks the power to indemnify its directors and officers directly.

A contemporaneous account from the principal drafter of Delaware's General Corporation Law confirms what an integral reading of § 145 demonstrates: the statute's affirmative grants of power also impose limitations on the corporation's power to indemnify. Specifically, the good faith clause (unchanged since the Law's original enactment in 1967) was included in subsections (a) and (b) as a carefully calculated improvement on the prior indemnification provision and as an explicit limit on a corporation's power to indemnify:

> During the three years of the Revision Committee's study, no subject was more discussed among members of the corporate bar than the subject of indemnification of officers and directors. As far as Delaware law was concerned, the existing statutory provision on the subject had been found inadequate. Numerous by-laws and charter provisions had been adopted clarifying and

extending its terms, but *uncertainty existed in many instances as to whether such provisions transgressed the limits* which the courts had indicated they would establish based on public policy. . . .

It was . . . apparent that revision was appropriate with respect to *the limitations which must necessarily be placed on the power to indemnify* in order to prevent the statute from undermining the substantive provisions of the criminal law and corporation law. . . .

[There was a] need for a . . . provision to protect the corporation law's requirement of loyalty to the corporation. . . . Ultimately, it was decided that *the power to indemnify should not be granted unless* it appeared that the person seeking indemnification had "acted in good faith and in a manner reasonably believed to be in or not opposed to the best interest of the corporation."

S. Samuel Arsht & Walter K. Stapleton, *Delaware's New General Corporation Law: Substantive Changes,* 23 Bus.Law. 75, 77–78 (1967).[9] This passage supports *Hibbert's* rule of "consistency" and makes clear that a corporation has no power to transgress the indemnification limits set out in the substantive provisions of § 145.

Waltuch argues at length that reading § 145(a) to bar the indemnification of officers who acted in bad faith would render § 145(f) meaningless. This argument misreads § 145(f). That subsection refers to "any other rights to which those seeking indemnification or advancement of expenses may be entitled." Delaware commentators have identified various indemnification rights that are "beyond those provided by statute," *Hibbert,* 457 A.2d at 344, and that are at the same time consistent with the statute:

[S]ubsection (f) provides general authorization for the adoption of various procedures and presumptions making the process of indemnification more favorable to the indemnitee. For example, indemnification agreements or by-laws could provide for: (i) mandatory indemnification unless prohibited by statute; (ii) mandatory advancement of expenses, which the indemnitee can, in many instances, obtain on demand; (iii) accelerated procedures for the "determination" required by section 145(d) to be made in the "specific case"; (iv) litigation "appeal" rights of the indemnitee in the event of an unfavorable determination; (v) procedures under which a favorable determination will be deemed to have been made under circumstances where the

---

[9] Delaware commentators consider this article to be part of (if not all of) "[t]he legislative history of Section 145." A. Gilchrist Sparks, III, et al., *Indemnification, Directors and Officers Liability Insurance and Limitations of Director Liability Pursuant to Statutory Authorization: The Legal Framework Under Delaware Law,* 696 PLI/Corp. 941 (1990) (at page 10 out of 123 on WESTLAW). . . .

board fails or refuses to act; [and] (vi) reasonable funding mechanisms.

E. Norman Veasey, et al., *Delaware Supports Directors With a Three-Legged Stool of Limited Liability, Indemnification, and Insurance,* 42 Bus.Law. 399, 415 (1987).[10] Moreover, subsection (f) may reference nonindemnification rights, such as advancement rights or rights to other payments from the corporation that do not qualify as indemnification.

We need not decide in this case the precise scope of those "other rights" adverted to in § 145(f). We simply conclude that § 145(f) is not rendered meaningless or inoperative by the conclusion that a Delaware corporation lacks power to indemnify an officer or director "unless [he] 'acted in good faith and in a manner reasonably believed to be in or not opposed to the best interest of the corporation.'" *See* Arsht & Stapleton, 23 Bus.Law. at 78. As a result, we hold that Conti's Article Ninth, which would require indemnification of Waltuch even if he acted in bad faith, is inconsistent with § 145(a) and thus exceeds the scope of a Delaware corporation's power to indemnify. Since Waltuch has agreed to forgo his opportunity to prove at trial that he acted in good faith, he is not entitled to indemnification under Article Ninth for the $2.2 million he spent in connection with the private lawsuits and the CFTC proceeding. We therefore affirm the district court on this issue.

II

Unlike § 145(a), which grants a discretionary indemnification power, § 145(c) affirmatively *requires* corporations to indemnify its officers and directors for the "successful" defense of certain claims:

> To the extent that a director, officer, employee or agent of a corporation has been successful on the merits or otherwise in defense of any action, suit or proceeding referred to in subsections (a) and (b) of this section, or in defense of any claim, issue or matter therein, he shall be indemnified against expenses (including attorneys' fees) actually and reasonably incurred by him in connection therewith.

56 Del.Laws 50, § 1 at 171 (1967), *codified at* 8 Del.Code Ann. tit. 8, § 145(c) (Michie 1991). Waltuch argues that he was "successful on the merits or otherwise" in the private lawsuits, because they were dismissed with prejudice without any payment or assumption of liability by him. Conti argues that the claims against Waltuch were dismissed only because of Conti's $35 million settlement payments, and that this payment was contributed, in part, "on behalf of Waltuch."[11]

---

[10] Veasey is now Chief Justice of the Delaware Supreme Court. *See also* 1 Balotti & Finkelstein § 4.16 at 4–321, which makes the same suggestions. Other suggestions are made in Joseph F. Johnston, Jr., *Corporate Indemnification and Liability Insurance for Directors and Officers,* 33 Bus.Law. 1993, 1996, 2009–10 (1978).

[11] Although this is not essential to our holding, we note that Conti points to no evidence in support of its contention that the plaintiffs would have continued to pursue their suits as to Waltuch if Conti had paid some lesser amount.

The district court agreed with Conti that "the successful settlements cannot be credited to Waltuch but are attributable solely to Conti's settlement payments. It was not Waltuch who was successful, but Conti who was successful for him." 833 F.Supp. at 311. The district court held that § 145(c) mandates indemnification when the director or officer "is vindicated," but that there was no vindication here:

> Vindication is also ordinarily associated with a dismissal with prejudice without any payment. However, a director or officer is not vindicated when the reason he did not have to make a settlement payment is because someone else assumed that liability. Being bailed out is not the same thing as being vindicated.

Id. We believe that this understanding and application of the "vindication" concept is overly broad and is inconsistent with a proper interpretation of § 145(c).

No Delaware court has applied § 145(c) in the context of indemnification stemming from the settlement of civil litigation. One lower court, however, has applied that subsection to an analogous case in the criminal context, and has illuminated the link between "vindication" and the statutory phrase, "successful on the merits or otherwise." In *Merritt-Chapman & Scott Corp. v. Wolfson,* 321 A.2d 138 (Del.Super.Ct.1974), the corporation's agents were charged with several counts of criminal conduct. A jury found them guilty on some counts, but deadlocked on the others. The agents entered into a "settlement" with the prosecutor's office by pleading nolo contendere to one of the counts in exchange for the dropping of the rest. *Id.* at 140. The agents claimed entitlement to mandatory indemnification under § 145(c) as to the counts that were dismissed. In opposition, the corporation raised an argument similar to the argument raised by Conti:

> [The corporation] argues that the statute and sound public policy require indemnification only where there has been vindication by a finding or concession of innocence. *It contends that the charges against [the agents] were dropped for practical reasons,* not because of their innocence. . . .
>
> The statute requires indemnification to the extent that the claimant "has been successful on the merits or otherwise." *Success is vindication.* In a criminal action, any result other than conviction must be considered success. *Going behind the result,* as [the corporation] attempts, is neither authorized by subsection (c) nor consistent with the presumption of innocence.

Id. at 141 (emphasis added).

Although the underlying proceeding in *Merritt* was criminal, the court's analysis is instructive here. The agents in *Merritt* rendered consideration—their guilty plea on one count—to achieve the dismissal of the other counts. The court considered these dismissals both "success" and (therefore) "vindication," and refused to "go[ ] behind the result" or to appraise the reason for the success. In equating "success" with "vindication," the court thus rejected the more expansive view of vindication urged by the corporation. Under *Merritt*'s holding, then, vindication, when used as a synonym for "success" under § 145(c), does not mean moral exoneration. Escape from an adverse judgment or other detriment, for whatever reason, is determinative. According to *Merritt*, the only question a court may ask is what the result was, not why it was.[12]

Conti's contention that, because of its $35 million settlement payments, Waltuch's settlement without payment should not really count as settlement without payment, is inconsistent with the rule in *Merritt*. Here, Waltuch was sued, and the suit was dismissed without his having paid a settlement. Under the approach taken in *Merritt*, it is not our business to ask why this result was reached. Once Waltuch achieved his settlement gratis, he achieved success "on the merits or otherwise." And, as we know from *Merritt*, success is sufficient to constitute vindication (at least for the purposes of § 145(c)). Waltuch's settlement thus vindicated him.

The concept of "vindication" pressed by Conti is also inconsistent with the fact that a director or officer who is able to defeat an adversary's claim by asserting a technical defense is entitled to indemnification under § 145(c). *See* 1 Balotti & Finkelstein, § 4.13 at 4–302. In such cases, the indemnitee has been "successful" in the palpable sense that he has won, and the suit has been dismissed, whether or not the victory is deserved in merits terms. If a technical defense is deemed "vindication" under Delaware law, it cannot matter why Waltuch emerged unscathed, or whether Conti "bailed [him] out", or whether his success was deserved. Under § 145(c), mere success is vindication enough.

This conclusion comports with the reality that civil judgments and settlements are ordinarily expressed in terms of cash rather than moral victory. No doubt, it would make sense for Conti to buy the dismissal of the claims against Waltuch along with its own discharge from the case, perhaps to avoid further expense or participation as a non-party, potential cross-claims, or negative publicity. But Waltuch apparently did

---

[12] Our adoption of *Merritt*'s interpretation of the statutory term "successful" does not necessarily signal our endorsement of the result in that case. The *Merritt* court sliced the case into individual counts, with indemnification pegged to each count independently of the others. We are not faced with a case in which the corporate officer claims to have been "successful" on some parts of the case but was clearly "unsuccessful" on others, and therefore take no position on this feature of the *Merritt* holding.

We also do not mean our discussion of *Merritt* to suggest that the line between success and failure in a criminal case may be drawn in the same way in the civil context. In a criminal case, conviction on a particular count is obvious failure, and dismissal of the charge is obvious success. In a civil suit for damages, however, there is a monetary continuum between complete success (dismissal of the suit without any payment) and complete failure (payment of the full amount of damages requested by the plaintiff). Because Waltuch made no payment in connection with the dismissal of the suits against him, we need not decide whether a defendant's settlement payment automatically renders that defendant "unsuccessful" under § 145(c).

not accede to that arrangement, and Delaware law cannot allow an indemnifying corporation to escape the mandatory indemnification of subsection (c) by paying a sum in settlement on behalf of an unwilling indemnitee.

. . . In *Wisener v. Air Express Int'l Corp.*, 583 F.2d 579 (2d Cir.1978), we construed an Illinois indemnification statute that was intentionally enacted as a copy of Delaware's § 145. *See id.* at 582 n. 3; 1 Balotti & Finkelstein, § 4.12 at 4–296 n. 1048 (§ 145 was the "prototype" for Illinois's indemnification statute). Our holding in that case is perfectly applicable here:

> It is contended that [the director] was not "successful" in the litigation, since the third-party claims against him never proceeded to trial. The statute, however, refers to success "on the merits or otherwise," which surely is broad enough to cover a termination of claims by agreement without any payment or assumption of liability.

583 F.2d at 583. It is undisputed that the private lawsuits against Conti and Waltuch were dismissed with prejudice, "without any payment of assumption of liability" by Waltuch. Applying the analysis of *Wisener,* Conti must indemnify Waltuch for his expenses in connection with the private lawsuits.

. . . [T]he extent of Waltuch's success] is not lessened by Conti's payments, even if it is true (as it stands to reason) that his success was achieved because Conti was willing to pay. Whatever the impetus for the plaintiffs' dismissal of their claims against Waltuch, he still walked away without liability and without making a payment. This constitutes a success that is untarnished by the process that achieved it.

For all of these reasons, we agree with Waltuch that he is entitled to indemnification under § 145(c) for his expenses pertaining to the private lawsuits.

III

The judgment of the district court is affirmed in part and reversed in part. This case is remanded to the district court so that judgment may be entered in favor of Waltuch on his claim for $1,228,586.67, representing the unreimbursed expenses from the private lawsuits. *See supra* note 1.

———

If Norton Waltuch's good faith had been an issue in *Waltuch*, how would this have been resolved? *See* In re Landmark Land Co., 76 F.3d 553, 565 (4th Cir. 1996).

> An agent who has intentionally participated in illegal activity or wrongful conduct against third persons cannot be said to have acted in good faith, even if the conduct benefits the corporation. *Plate [v. Sun-Diamond Growers], 275 Cal.Rptr. at 672.* "For

example, corporate executives who participate in a deliberate price-fixing conspiracy with competing firms could not be found to have acted in good faith, even though they may have reasonably believed that a deliberate flouting of the antitrust laws would increase the profits of the corporation." 1 Harold Marsh, Jr. and R. Roy Finkle, Marsh's California Corporation Law (3d ed.) § 10.43, at 751; see *Plate, 275 Cal.Rptr. at 672* (citing same language from second edition). . . . [A] deliberate attempt to undermine the regulatory authority of a government agency cannot constitute good faith conduct, even if such actions benefit the corporation.

See also Biondi v. Beekman Hill House Apartment Corp., 731 N.E.2d 577, 581 (N.Y. 2000) (denying indemnification for punitive damage claims reasoning that officer who intentionally denied lease application on the basis of the applicant's race thereby knowingly subjected the corporation to liability under the civil rights laws and, hence, his actions "cannot be considered an act in the corporation's best interests").

Do the same public policy considerations apply when the conduct to be indemnified is not willful but rather bumbling? In Globus v. Law Research Service, Inc., 418 F.2d 1276 (2d Cir.1969), cert. denied 397 U.S. 913, 90 S.Ct. 913, 25 L.Ed.2d 93 (1970) plaintiffs, who had purchased stock under an allegedly misleading offering circular, brought actions under § 17(a) of the 1933 Act and Rule 10b–5 against the issuer, the underwriter, and the issuer's president. The underwriter cross-claimed against the issuer pursuant to an agreement under which the issuer had promised to indemnify the underwriter for any loss arising out of defects in the offering circular, except for those attributable to the underwriter's "willful misfeasance, bad faith or gross negligence . . . or . . . reckless disregard of its obligations under the agreement." Id. at 1287. The court concluded that the underwriter had actual knowledge of material misstatements in the circular, and denied the cross-claim both because it fell within the exception to the agreement and on grounds of public policy:

> Given [the underwriter's actual knowledge of material misstatements],. . . . to tolerate indemnity under these circumstances would encourage flouting the policy of the common law and the Securities Act. . . .
>
> Civil liability under section 11 and similar provisions was designed not so much to compensate the defrauded purchaser as to promote enforcement of the Act and to deter negligence by providing a penalty for those who fail in their duties. And Congress intended to impose a "high standard of trusteeship" on underwriters. Thus, what Professor Loss terms the "*in terrorem* effect" of civil liability might well be thwarted if underwriters were free to pass their liability on to the issuer. Underwriters who knew they could be indemnified simply by showing that the issuer was "more liable" than they (a process not too difficult

when the issuer is inevitably closer to the facts) would have a tendency to be lax in their independent investigations. Cases upholding indemnity for negligence in other fields are not necessarily apposite. The goal in such cases is to compensate the injured party. But the Securities Act is more concerned with prevention than cure.

Globus involved "a sin graver than ordinary negligence," and left open the propriety of indemnification for negligence or other lesser sins. Some later cases have held that the policy of the Securities Acts bars indemnification for negligence; others have held indemnification for negligence permissible under the Securities Acts where the indemnitor's conduct was significantly more wrongful than that of the indemnitee. See Donaldson Lufkin & Jenrette Securities Corp. v. Star Technologies, 148 Misc.2d 880, 561 N.Y.S.2d 371 (1990), aff'd, Donaldson, Lufkin & Jenrette Sec. Corp. v. Star Technologies, Inc., 180 A.D.2d 495, 580 N.Y.S.2d 657 (1st Dep't 1992) (reviewing cases); ALI, Principles of Corporate Governance § 7.20, Reporter's Note 7. It has been held that indemnification for liability under section 16(b) would violate public policy, even though section 16(b) does not require proof of fraudulent intent. See First Golden Bancorporation v. Weiszmann, 942 F.2d 726 (10th Cir.1991).

Under SEC Regulation S-K, Item 512(h), if a registrant seeks acceleration of a prospectus (as most registrants do), and any provision or agreement exists under which the registrant may indemnify a director or officer against liabilities arising under the Securities Act, then unless the right to indemnification is waived, the registrant must include the following statement in the Prospectus:

> Insofar as indemnification for liabilities arising under the Securities Act of 1933 may be permitted to directors, officers and controlling persons of the registrant pursuant to the foregoing provisions, or otherwise, the registrant has been advised that in the opinion of the Securities and Exchange Commission such indemnification is against public policy as expressed in the Act and is, therefore, unenforceable. In the event that a claim for indemnification against such liabilities (other than the payment by the registrant of expenses incurred or paid by a director, officer or controlling person of the registrant in the successful defense of any action, suit or proceeding) is asserted by such director, officer or controlling person in connection with the securities being registered, the registrant will, unless in the opinion of its counsel the matter has been settled by controlling precedent, submit to a court of appropriate jurisdiction the question whether such indemnification by it is against public policy as expressed in the Act and will be governed by the final adjudication of such issue.

NOTE ON THE SCOPE OF INDEMNIFICATION PROVISIONS

Indemnity statutes, bylaws and board resolutions frequently provide indemnification and advancement of litigation costs to "agents." Such provisions have spawned a good deal of litigation whether the individual seeking indemnification or an advance was an agent. Can a company's outside lawyer also be its "agent? *See* Cohen v. Southbridge Park, 369 N.J.Super. 156, 848 A.2d 781 (N.J. Super. App. Div. 2004) (attorney who represented corporation in its negotiations with a departing officer and later was sued for malpractice in attorney's representation of the company is not an agent within the scope of the indemnification provision because he was not cloaked with any management authority); Zaman v. Amedeo Holdings, Inc., 2008 WL 2168397 (Del.Ch.) (attorneys who were retained to look after client's American companies were at least agents of the corporation since they enjoyed powers co-equal to that of directors). Another heavily litigated issue is whether the act prompting the quest for indemnification or an advance was an act committed in an official capacity as an officer, director or even agent. In *Vergopia v. Shaker,* 922 A.2d 1238 (N.J. 2007), the outside attorney who served as the company's secretary was sued for slander and emotional distress flowing from an employee's dismissal that was described in SEC filings that were reviewed and edited by the attorney. Although the bylaws conditioned indemnification on the act giving rise to indemnification occurring within the officer's official capacity, a majority of the New Jersey Supreme Court held that this limitation, because it only appeared in the company's bylaws, did not qualify the broader right's granted in the articles of incorporation (which did not contain the limiting language). It therefore awarded indemnification. Some conduct is inherently individual and not in a corporate or representative capacity.

———

NOTE ON ADVANCES

In *Advanced Mining Systems, Inc. v. Fricke,* 623 A.2d 82 (Del.Ch.1992), the Delaware court held that indemnification rights and advancement rights stand apart as two "distinct types of legal rights," so that a bylaw provision that required a corporation to "indemnify . . . to the extent permitted" under Delaware law did not wrest from a corporation the ability to refuse advances. See also Rev. Model Bus. Corp. Act § 8.58(a) and Official Comment.

———

B. INSURANCE

[See Chapter 9.]

———

8. THE ROLE OF CORPORATE COUNSEL

Bell Atlantic Corp. v. Bolger

United States Court of Appeals, Third Circuit, 1993.
2 F.3d 1304.

■ SCIRICA, CIRCUIT JUDGE . . .

[The Pennsylvania Attorney General sued Bell Atlantic alleging it had defrauded consumers. After some initial skirmishing, Bell Atlantic settled the matter, paying $40 million in customer rebates, making contributions to a consumer education trust, and reimbursing the legal costs of the Attorney General. Following the settlement of the government's suit, a derivative suit was filed seeking to recoup from the Bell Atlantic directors the sums paid to consumers and the attorney general. The derivative suit plaintiff alleged that the misconduct prompting the state's successful action was the result of mismanagement and a breach of the directors' fiduciary duties to the corporation. Bell Atlantic's board appointed a special litigation committee that, after a thorough investigation, opined that the suit was not in the Bell Atlantic's best interests. The derivative suit was ultimately settled on the eve of the trial; the proposed settlement required Bell Atlantic to establish and follow new procedures to monitor sales and marketing programs and to pay plaintiff's counsel fees in an amount not to exceed $450,000. Seymour Lazar, a Bell Atlantic shareholder, objected to the settlement. The district court approved the settlement. Although Lazar did not formerly seek to intervene in the derivative action, the Third Circuit nevertheless held Lazur had standing to appeal the district court's approval of the settlement.]

Lazar impugns the settlement agreement as resulting from conflicts of interest. He attacks Dechert, Price & Rhoads's joint representation of Bell Atlantic (nominal defendant but real party in interest) and the individual defendants. The district court found no disqualifying conflict, relying on *Otis & Co. v. Pennsylvania R.R. Co., 57 F. Supp. 680, 684 (E.D. Pa. 1944), aff'd per curiam, 155 F.2d 522 (3d Cir. 1946)*, and *Hornsby v. Lohmeyer, 364 Pa. 271, 279, 72 A.2d 294, 299 (1950)*. Both cases rejected plaintiffs' challenges to counsels' dual representation of corporate and individual defendants.

More recent cases perceive problems with this form of dual representation. For example, *Messing v. FDI, Inc., 439 F. Supp. 776 (D.N.J. 1977)*, involved a derivative action charging certain inside directors in a merger with fraud which resulted in their being overcompensated for stock they owned in the acquired corporation. The outside directors were charged with negligence in connection with this merger. The same counsel initially represented the corporation, two of the outside directors, and all of the inside directors. *Messing* observed some courts have allowed directors in the corporation to be represented by the same counsel in cases that do not involve "any allegations of breach of confidence or trust" or fraud. *439 F. Supp. at 781.* Yet *Messing* nonetheless found that irrespective of the allegation against the director, be it fraud or negligence, the interests of the two will always be diverse. *Id. at 782. Messing* required the corporation to retain independent counsel other than the attorney who represented the individual defendants.

Other courts have required independent counsel where directors are alleged to have defrauded the corporation. *See Cannon v. U.S. Acoustics Co., 398 F. Supp. 209 (N.D. Ill. 1975), aff'd in relevant part per curiam, 532 F.2d 1118, 1119 (7th Cir. 1976)* (district court disqualified counsel from simultaneously representing the corporation and the individual directors accused of fraud; conflict of interests among defendants and risk that confidences obtained from one client would be used against another); *Lewis v. Shaffer Stores Co., 218 F. Supp. 238 (S.D.N.Y. 1963)* (corporation could not share counsel with individual directors accused of defrauding the corporation).

Thus, as a general matter, the case law is not uniform on the issue of joint representation of the corporation and individual defendants. Commentators are more certain. In a representative observation, one commentator says,

> There is some conflict as to the propriety of an attorney or law firm simultaneously representing a corporation and its officers and directors in a stockholders' derivative action. But the modern view is that it is generally improper due to conflict of interests for counsel to attempt to represent the corporation, on whose behalf the action has been instituted, while also representing the individuals charged with harming the corporation for their wrongful conduct.

13 William M. Fletcher, *Fletcher Cyclopedia of the Law of Private Corporations* § 6025, at 442 (perm. ed. rev. vol. 1991); *see also* Harry G. Henn & John R. Alexander, *Laws of Corporations* § 370, at 1082 (1983). But these commentators recognize that "even under the modern rule, independent counsel may not be required if the derivative claim is obviously or patently frivolous." Fletcher, *Fletcher Cyclopedia* § 6025, at 443.

The ethical standards imposed upon attorneys in federal court are a matter of federal law. *County of Suffolk v. Long Island Lighting Co., 710 F. Supp. 1407, 1413 (E.D.N.Y. 1989), aff'd, 907 F.2d 1295 (2d Cir. 1990).* We look to the Model Rules of Professional Conduct to furnish the appropriate ethical standard. *Id. at 1414.* Under Rule 1.13(a), a lawyer's obligation runs to the entity. The commentary to Rule 1.13 provides:

> The question can arise whether counsel for the organization may defend [a derivative] action. The proposition that the organization is the lawyer's client does not alone resolve the

issue. Most derivative actions are a normal incident of an organization's affairs, to be defended by the organization's lawyer like any other suit. However, if the claim involves serious charges of wrongdoing by those in control of the organization, a conflict may arise between the lawyer's duty to the organization and the lawyer's relationship with the board. In those circumstances, Rule 1.7 governs who should represent the directors and the organization.

American Bar Ass'n, *Annotated Model Rules of Professional Conduct* (2d ed. 1992).

We believe serious charges of wrongdoing have not been levelled against the individual defendants. We say this because plaintiffs have alleged only mismanagement, a breach of the fiduciary *duty of care*. . . . But we do not understand plaintiffs to have accused defendants of breaching their *duty of loyalty* which requires a director to act in good faith and in the honest belief that the action taken is in the corporation's best interests. . . . There are no allegations of self-dealing, stealing, fraud, intentional misconduct, conflicts of interest, or usurpation of corporate opportunities by defendant directors. Indeed the district court found the directors acted in good faith in investigating plaintiffs' demands. As noted, Bell Atlantic's board charged a special committee along with independent counsel to investigate the shareholder plaintiffs' demands. The special committee and independent counsel found prosecution of these demands not in Bell Atlantic's interest. This suggests a relative (though not complete) convergence of individual and corporate interests in defending and settling the litigation. Although not dispositive, it is important that early in the litigation, independent counsel, after undertaking an exhaustive investigation, determined the corporation's interests were more in line with those of the defendants than plaintiffs. Of greater significance, however, is the absence of allegations of fraud, intentional misconduct, or self-dealing.

We have no hesitation in holding that—except in patently frivolous cases—allegations of directors' fraud, intentional misconduct, or self-dealing require separate counsel. We recognize that corporate law has traditionally distinguished between breach of the duty of care and breach of the duty of loyalty, the latter being more grave. *See Del. Code Ann. tit. 8 § 102(b)(7)* (charter amendment provision allowed to limit director liability for breaches of duty of care but "such provision shall not eliminate or limit the liability of a director: . . . for any breach of the director's duty of loyalty"). . . . But drawing the line between breaches of care and loyalty may be difficult in many cases. *See* Frank H. Easterbrook & Daniel R. Fischel, *The Economic Structure of Corporate Law* 103 (1991) ("Ultimately, though, there is no sharp line between the duty of care and the duty of loyalty."). We do not believe the district court abused its discretion in allowing common counsel here. We note, however, that in cases where the line is blurred between duties of care and loyalty, the better practice is to obtain separate counsel for individual and corporate defendants.[17] . . .

If separate counsel is ordered for the corporation and the real defendants, who should be required to obtain new counsel? If the court believes it is the corporation who should retain new counsel, who hires that counsel (assuming, as is frequently the case, that senior management are the suit's defendants)? Who does the corporation's counsel advise on, for example, whether to accept a settlement offered by the real defendants? Recall that state indemnification statutes set forth procedural steps and substantive standards for indemnifying officers and directors. Does the same lawyer representing both the corporation and a director or officer pose a threat (opportunity) of circumventing these procedural steps and substantive standards for awarding indemnification?

Independent of the question of dual representation, can the counsel representing the corporation question the suit's plaintiff as an adequate representative? Raise the failure to make a demand on the board? Question whether plaintiff meets the contemporaneous ownership requirement? Enter a defense on the substantive defense on the merits? Should the latter be guided by the same considerations that *Bell Atlantic* and other courts have relied upon for determining when the same counsel can represent the real and nominal defendants? *See* Otis & Co. v. Pennsylvania R.R., 57 F.Supp. 680 (E.D. Pa. 1944), *aff'g*, 155 F.2d 522 (3d Cir. 1946) (corporation allowed to answer derivative suit complaint alleging mismanagement by directors and officers by their adherence to long-followed practice for placing bonds without competitive bidding).

NOTES ON PROBLEMS CONCERNING THE LAW GOVERNING LAWYERS IN DERIVATIVE ACTIONS

1.   *Attorney Conflicts of Interest in Derivative Litigation; Garner v. Wolfinbarger.* Partly because of their complex four-party structure—involving nominal plaintiffs, entrepreneurial attorneys, the corporation, and defendants who in their director or officer capacities have or share control of the corporation—derivative actions present a number of severe problems that fall under the heading of the law governing lawyers.

On one side of the case, there may be a conflict between the interests of the shareholders as a class, who are the ultimate beneficiaries of a derivative action, and the interests of the entrepreneurial attorney who brings the action. On the other side, the interests of the corporation may diverge from the interests of defendants who control the corporation, and the corporation's

---

[17]   *See* Edited Transcript of Proceedings of the Business Roundtable, 71 Corn. L. Rev. 367–71 (L. Ribstein ed. 1985) (debating merits of distinction).

lawyers may as a practical matter regard themselves as working for the latter.

Against this background, problems may also arise concerning the lawyer-client and work-product privileges. In doctrinal terms, the issue can be phrased in terms of whether the corporation's attorney can assert the privilege in a way that favors the defendants even though at least nominally the attorney's client was not the defendants, but rather the corporation in whose right the action is brought. In substantive terms, the issue can be phrased as whether which one of the following rules best serves the interests of the shareholder-owners: (1) A rule that gives inviolate protection to management communications with lawyers, on the ground that to do so will make managers more secure in seeking advice from corporate counsel. (2) A rule that permits exceptions when the very issue is whether a manager's conduct injured rather than served the corporation by whom the attorney was retained or employed.

In *Garner v. Wolfinbarger,* 430 F.2d 1093 (5th Cir.1970), cert. denied 401 U.S. 974, 91 S.Ct. 1191, 28 L.Ed.2d 323 (1971), the court attempted to balance the various interests involved by adopting the rule that in a derivative action, invocation of the attorney-client privilege was subject to the right of the plaintiff-shareholders to show good cause why the privilege should not be invoked:

> It is urged that disclosure is injurious to both the corporation and the attorney. Corporate management must manage. It has the duty to do so and requires the tools to do so. Part of the managerial task is to seek legal counsel when desirable, and, obviously, management prefers that it confer with counsel without the risk of having the communications revealed at the instance of one or more dissatisfied stockholders. The managerial preference is a rational one, because it is difficult to envision the management of any sizeable corporation pleasing all of its stockholders all of the time, and management desires protection from those who might second-guess or even harass in matters purely of judgment.

> But in assessing management assertions of injury to the corporation it must be borne in mind that management does not manage for itself and that the beneficiaries of its action are the stockholders. Conceptualistic phrases describing the corporation as an entity separate from its stockholders are not useful tools of analysis. They serve only to obscure the fact that management has duties which run to the benefit ultimately of the stockholders. For example, it is difficult to rationally defend the assertion of the privilege if all, or substantially all, stockholders desire to inquire into the attorney's communications with corporate representatives who have only nominal ownership interests, or even none at all. There may be reasonable differences over the manner of characterizing in legal terminology the duties of management, and over the extent to which corporate management is less of a fiduciary than the common law trustee. There may be many situations in which the corporate entity or its management, or both,

have interests adverse to those of some or all stockholders. But when all is said and done management is not managing for itself. . . .

In summary, we say this. The attorney-client privilege still has viability for the corporate client. The corporation is not barred from asserting it merely because those demanding information enjoy the status of stockholders. But where the corporation is in suit against its stockholders on charges of acting inimically to stockholder interests, protection of those interests as well as those of the corporation and of the public require that the availability of the privilege be subject to the right of the stockholders to show cause why it should not be invoked in the particular instance. . . .

There are many indicia that may contribute to a decision of presence or absence of good cause, among them the number of shareholders and the percentage of stock they represent; the bona fides of the shareholders; the nature of the shareholders' claim and whether it is obviously colorable; the apparent necessity or desirability of the shareholders having the information and the availability of it from other sources; whether, if the shareholders' claim is of wrongful action by the corporation, it is of action criminal, or illegal but not criminal, or of doubtful legality; whether the communication related to past or to prospective actions; whether the communication is of advice concerning the litigation itself; the extent to which the communication is identified versus the extent to which the shareholders are blindly fishing; the risk of revelation of trade secrets or other information in whose confidentiality the corporation has an interest for independent reasons. The court can freely use *in camera* inspection or oral examination and freely avail itself of protective orders, a familiar device to preserve confidentiality in trade secret and other cases where the impact of revelation may be as great as in revealing a communication with counsel.

On remand, the district court held that the lawyer-client privilege was inapplicable under the standards *Garner* set out. Garner v. Wolfinbarger, 56 F.R.D. 499 (S.D.Ala.1972). The Delaware Supreme Court in *Wal-Mart Stores, Inc. v. Ind. Elec. Workers Pensino Trust Fund IBEW*, 95 A.3d 1264 (Del. 2014), applied the *Garner* doctrine to permit a shareholder to review certain internal files that concerned what Wal-Mart directors knew regarding claims executives had paid bribes to facilitated business in Mexico. The shareholder document request was pursuant to shareholder inspection rights under Section 220 of the Delaware statute. Delaware previously had invoked *Garner* only in dicta.

There is a split among the Circuits concerning whether the *Garner* principle is applicable to shareholder class actions. Compare Weil v. Investment/Indicators, Research & Management, 647 F.2d 18 (9th Cir. 1981) (*Garner* is not applicable to class actions), with Ward v. Succession of Freeman, 854 F.2d 780 (5th Cir. 1988), cert. denied, 490 U.S. 1065, 109 S.Ct. 2064, 104 L.Ed.2d 629 (1989) (*Garner* is applicable to class actions) and

Fausek v. White, 965 F.2d 126 (6th Cir.), cert. denied, 506 U.S. 1034, 113 S.Ct. 814, 121 L.Ed.2d 686 (1992) (same).

    2.   *Upjohn.* In *Upjohn Co. v. United States,* 449 U.S. 383, 101 S.Ct. 677, 66 L.Ed.2d 584 (1981), Upjohn's independent accountant discovered that an Upjohn subsidiary had made improper payments to secure foreign government business. After consultation among Upjohn's general counsel, outside counsel, and chairman of the board, it was decided that the company would conduct an internal investigation of "questionable payments." As part of this investigation the attorneys prepared a letter containing a questionnaire which was sent to "All Foreign General and Area Managers" over the chairman's signature. Subsequently, the Internal Revenue Service issued a summons demanding production of certain records, including the questionnaires. The Supreme Court held that the questionnaires were protected from disclosure by the attorney-client privilege. Unlike *Garner, Upjohn* involved an action by a third party against the corporation, rather than a derivative action on the corporation's behalf against some of its managers.

    3.   *Work-Product.* In *In re International Systems & Controls Corp. Securities Litigation,* 693 F.2d 1235 (5th Cir.1982), the court held that the good-cause standard of *Garner* is inapplicable to material covered by the work-product immunity, that is, material prepared in anticipation of litigation, as opposed to the communications between managers and counsel in the course of business decisionmaking. The court said the discoverability of work product in this context is governed by the general principle concerning the discoverability of work product under FRCP Rule 26(b)(3), which turns on a general principle concerning substantial need/undue hardship test. See also *Upjohn,* supra; Cox v. Administrator U.S. Steel & Carnegie, 17 F.3d 1386, 1423 (11th Cir.1994). Courts are, however, badly divided on what constitutes the attorney's work product. *See* United States v. Adlman, 134 F.3d 1194, 1195 (2d Cir. 1998) (documents are work product if they were prepared "because of anticipated litigation and would not have been prepared in substantially similar form but for the prospect of that litigation"); United States v. El Paso Co., 682 F.2d 530, 542 (5th Cir. 1982) (document is attorney's work product if "the primary motivating purpose behind the creation of the document was to aid in possible future litigation"); United States v. Textron, Inc., 577 F.3d 21, 29 (1st Cir. 2009) (en banc) (doctrine extends only to documents "prepared for use in possible litigation" and therefore did not extend to attorney's analysis of risks of disallowance by the IRS of client's method of reporting on its tax return certain transactions).

————

ABA MODEL RULES OF PROFESSIONAL CONDUCT, RULES 1.6, 1.7, 1.13

[See Statutory Supplement]

————

AMERICAN LAW INSTITUTE, PRINCIPLES OF
CORPORATE GOVERNANCE, INTRODUCTION
TO PART VII, REPORTER'S NOTE

[See Statutory Supplement]

————

9. "DEAL LITIGATION" AND SETTLEMENTS

NOTE ON DELAWARE'S ANTIDOTE FOR THE EPIDEMIC OF DEAL LITIGATION

Section 1 of this chapter set forth startling statistics regarding the high frequency of shareholder suits in connection with M&A deals; depending on the particular year 70–90 percent of transactions exceeding $100 million are subject to a shareholder suit. Jill E. Fisch, Sean J. Griffith & Steven Davidoff Solomon, Confronting the Peppercorn Settlement in Merger Litigation: An Empirical Analysis and A Proposal for Reform, 93 Tex. L. Rev. 557 (2015), examined three types of relief flowing from challenged mergers: 1) amendment of the terms, 2) disclosure-only settlement, and 3) increase in merger consideration. The authors examined transactions involving 453 firms in the 2005–2013 time period, of which 319 experienced litigation, resulting in 191 instances of some type of remedy. They found that amendment-only and disclosure settlements did not have an impact on ultimate shareholder vote and there is only weak evidence that an increase in consideration impacts shareholder vote. They also tested other variables, finding that transaction value and the position of proxy advisors had significant effect. The authors recommend that state courts should, correlative with *Santa Fe v. Green*, 430 U.S. 462 (1977), *supra* Chapter 11, withdraw from disclosure-only challenges and thus remit such suits to more experienced and institutionally equipped federal courts under the federal securities laws.

Disclosure-only settlements have caught the attention of the Delaware judiciary. Chancellor Bouchard provides a template for closer scrutiny of such settlements with in *In re Trulia, Inc. Stockholder Litig.*, 129 A.3d 884 (Del. Ch. 2016):

> [D]isclosure settlements are likely to be met with continued disfavor in the future unless the supplemental disclosures address a plainly material misrepresentation or omission, and the subject matter of the proposed release is narrowly circumscribed to encompass nothing more than the disclosure claims and fiduciary duty claims concerning the sale, if the record shows that such claims have been investigated sufficiently. In using the term "plainly material," I mean that it should not be a close call that the supplemental information is material as that term is defined under Delaware law. Where the supplemental information is not material, it may be appropriate for the Court to appoint an *amicus curiae* to assess the Court in its evaluation of the alleged benefits

of the supplemental disclosures given the challenges posed by the non-adversarial nature of the typical disclosure settlement hearing.

Id. at 898–99.

The complaint in *Trulia, Inc.* alleged the directors breached their fiduciary duties in approving a merger with a single bidder that allegedly failed to obtain the highest exchange ratio for the shareholders. Soon after the complaint was filed, opposing counsel reached an agreement in time for several supplemental disclosures to be added to the proxy statement circulated among the shareholders; the proposed settlement also provided the defendants would not oppose a fee request that did not exceed $375,000 and the plaintiff class would broadly release any claims that could conceivably arise from the merger (except such claims that may exist under specified antitrust laws). The merger was ultimately approved by 79.52 percent of the shares entitled to vote (99.15 percent of the votes cast). Following the merger's completion, the parties sought approval of the settlement, which included any other claims that could be brought against the company's directors. Chancellor Bouchard closely examined each of the supplementary disclosures regarding distinct features of the valuation process used by the investment bank in its fairness opinion to the board. He found the supplementary disclosures were not meaningful in light of all the other information the company disclosed regarding the valuation process. He therefore rejected the settlement, thereby leaving the suit where it had started, a bald accusation of breach of fiduciary obligation.

Compare In re Walgreen, 832 F.3d 718, 726 (7th Cir. 2016) (J. Posner) (rejecting disclosure-only settlement where disclosures were characterized as "worthless" by the court that also concluded that "class counsel has failed to represent the class fairly and adequately" so that the district court on remand should give serious consideration to either appointing new class counsel . . . or dismissing the suit). *But see Gordon v. Verizon Communications, Inc.,* 148 A.D. 3d 146, 161–62 (N.Y. App. Div. 2017) (in approving a fee award applied the standard whether the settlement was in the best interest of the class and the corporation and thus awarded a fee even though disclosure was believed to provide minimal benefit other than exposing the corporation to additional costs of litigation).

Of additional interest in *Trulia, Inc.* is that the complaint did not allege that any disclosure violation on the part of the directors had occurred; the complaint essentially alleged the directors breached their *Revlon* duty, discussed in Chapter 14, in failing to aggressively shop the firm to obtain the best offer was received for the shareholders. Moreover, the settlement would release all (but certain antitrust) claims the class members may have against anyone arising from the merger. *Id.* at 890.

Trulia, Inc.'s likely reflects growing cynicism of deal-related litigation particularly the seemingly cosmetic recoveries their settlements produce. By way of background, consider that in 1999 and 2000 only 12 percent of deals produced litigation; in that era most of the deal litigation not only involved Delaware firms but also took place in Delaware. C.N.V. Krishnan, Ronald

W. Masulis, Randall S. Thomas & Robert B. Thompson, Shareholder Litigation in Mergers and Acquisitions, 18 J. CORP. FIN. 1248, 1250–54 (2012). Suits in that era were consequential because firms that were sued experienced a statistically significant higher incidence of deals that did not close, and litigated deals that closed yielded their shareholders increased returns. Hence, the deal-focused suits in that former era could be seen, on the whole, as positive. Times have since changed. For example, Robert M. Daines & Olga Koumrian, Cornerstone Research, Shareholder Litigation Involving Mergers and Acquisitions: Review of 2012 M&A Litigation 1 (2013), reports that for deals valued over $100 million, 93 percent were challenged, with an average of 4.8 lawsuits filed per deal with a single deal often giving rise to litigation in more than one jurisdictions. Thus, unless we believe the mores within executive suites changed, and rapidly, the rapid increase in deal litigation more than likely points toward an abuse of process.

In a study of merger litigation in 2016 and 2017, Matthew Cain, Jill Fisch, Steven Davidoff Solomon & Randall S. Thomas, The Shifting Tides of Merger Litigation, 71 Vand. L. Rev. 603, 621–629 (2018), find that *Trulia, Inc.* and the wide adoption of forum selection clauses (bylaw provision that empower a corporation's board of directors to choose which forum a shareholder suit can proceed when the same transaction has spawned in multiple forums, a topic discussed later in this chapter) are associated with an outflow of suits from Delaware particularly toward federal courts involving Rule 14a–9 disclosure claims. Moreover, awards of fees in the cases also declined while dismissals have increased.

————

10. PLAINTIFF'S COUNSEL FEES

————

ALI, PRINCIPLES OF CORPORATE GOVERNANCE § 7.17

[See Statutory Supplement]

————

Tandycrafts, Inc. v. Initio Partners
Supreme Court of Delaware, 1989.
562 A.2d 1162.

[Initio Partners, a limited partnership, was the largest independent shareholder of Tandycrafts, Inc., owning 9.9% of Tandycraft's stock. Tandycraft proposed to amend its charter, and issued a proxy statement in connection with the vote on the proposed amendment at the annual meeting. Initio sought a temporary injunction against holding Tandycraft's annual meeting, on the ground that the proxy statement was materially misleading.

Tandycraft then prepared a supplement to its proxy statement that made clarifications and new disclosures on the subjects Initio had complained of. The annual meeting was held, and the charter amendments were soundly defeated. Initio then moved for the award of counsel fees and expenses. Tandycraft opposed the motion, on the grounds that the changes in the proxy statement were not attributable to Initio's litigation and that counsel fees could not be awarded to a plaintiff that had sued on its own behalf (as had Initio), rather than derivatively or on behalf of a class. The Vice Chancellor awarded counsel fees to Initio. Affirmed.]

In the realm of corporate litigation, the Court may order the payment of counsel fees and related expenses to a plaintiff whose efforts result in the creation of a common fund . . . or the conferring of a corporate benefit. . . . Typically, successful derivative or class action suits which result in the recovery of money or property wrongfully diverted from the corporation, or which result in the imposition of changes in internal operating procedures that are designed to produce such monetary savings in the future, are viewed as fund creating actions. . . .

The definition of a corporate benefit, however, is much more elastic. While the benefit achieved may have an indirect economic effect on the corporation, in the sense that the interests of the plaintiff class reflect a value not theretofore apparent, the benefit need not be measurable in economic terms. Changes in corporate policy or, as here, a heightened level of corporate disclosure, if attributable to the filing of a meritorious suit, may justify an award of counsel fees. *See* Chrysler Corp. v. Dann, 223 A.2d at 386; Allied Artists Pictures Corp. v. Baron, 413 A.2d at 878.

Once it is determined that action benefiting the corporation chronologically followed the filing of a meritorious suit, the burden is upon the corporation to demonstrate 'that the lawsuit did not in any way cause their action.' Allied Artists Pictures Corp. v. Baron, 413 A.2d at 880. . . .

Although this Court has not adopted an expansive approach to fee shifting in corporate litigation, the critical inquiry is not the status of the plaintiff but the nature of the corporate or class benefit which is causally related to the filing of suit. It is to be expected that litigation to force compliance with fiduciary standards or statutory duties will be initiated by a shareholder who has standing to sue for the benefit of the corporation. For the most part, such claims are clearly derivative, or class based. But where the shareholder's individual interests are directly and equally implicated, as in proxy contests, the distinction between individual and representative claims may become blurred. Indeed, the same wrong may give rise to both an individual and derivative action. . . .

Having concluded that, under these circumstances, Initio had standing to seek an award of counsel fees as an individual plaintiff, we summarily address Tandycrafts' claim that the Vice Chancellor abused his discretion in the fee allowance. The sequence of events is not in dispute and the correction or clarification of the proxy material chronologically followed the filing of the Initio suit attacking the accuracy of the material. It was thus incumbent upon Tandycrafts to demonstrate that there was no causal connection between the suit and the subsequent action. . . . Although Tandycrafts argues that the corrective action would have been taken in any event, we are not persuaded that the Vice Chancellor abused his discretion in ruling to the contrary.

———

Sugarland Ind., Inc. v. Thomas

Supreme Court of Delaware, 1980.
420 A.2d 142.

[Mr. and Mrs. Harris, shareholders in Sugarland, Industries, Inc., retained an attorney to represent them when they learned that the Sugarland board was considering the sale to White and Hill of substantial acreage (referred to as the South Tract) the company owned for $23.8 million. They believed the price was inadequate. Partly as a result of Harris's efforts, another bidder, R-S-C offered to purchase the land for $27 million. Nonetheless, the Sugarland board continued to favor the lower White and Hill offer. The Harris' ultimately initiated a derivative suit and the Chancellor ordered that the board entertain competitive bids for the property. Among the sealed bids, Hines was the winner, offering approximately $32.2 million for the property. Hines pushed to acquire the adjacent North Tract which led to more sealed bids and once again Hines won, having bid $1.25 million more than the next highest bid. Thus, both tracts were sold to Hines for $44 million. The attorney representing Mr. and Mrs. Harris sought a fee from Sugarland.]

It is crystal clear from the record that the services of petitioners benefited Sugarland to the extent of the difference between the White and Hill offer of $23,800,000 and the $27,000,000 which was submitted by R-S-C. But how one should view the amount received by Sugarland in excess of the $27,000,000 is not so clear. Petitioners had sought the best price obtainable and but for their initiative (and success) at the injunctive stage, Sugarland might not have received anything over the White and Hill offer. Thus, there is, as we have noted, "some" cause and effect between what petitioners did and the ultimate price received. But petitioners are attorneys seeking compensation for services rendered in litigation. They are not brokers or real estate agents seeking a commission or a percentage of sale price for having produced a buyer. And how much anyone would pay, at least in excess of the $27,000,000 offered by R-S-C, was a circumstance neither caused nor influenced by petitioners. The highest offer eventually made has in it something in the nature of [a] "windfall". . . . [P]etitioners here cannot take full credit for the price which Hines was willing to pay for both tracts. . . .

In making the award, the Chancellor used a 20%-of-benefit factor and that seems reasonable to us when applied to the difference between the respective offers. But for the reasons we have discussed, it is unreasonable when applied to the amounts paid by the buyer in excess of the $27,000,000. We have held that petitioners are entitled to some credit for the benefit received in excess of that sum and, in view of the circumstances, any percentage is arguably fair or not, depending on one's point of view. In our judgment, based on the various factors we have noted, compensation at the rate of 5% of the benefit achieved is fair and should be applied to the additional benefits Sugarland received from the sale of both the North and South Tracts. Given the fee which that percentage generates (about $573,609 in all), we conclude that it is reasonable (and perhaps generous) compensation for the significant skills and expertise which petitioners demonstrated in identifying an inadequate price for the Tracts, in stimulating the competitive offer from R-S-C, in quickly initiating the litigation, in successfully carrying it to a conclusion against highly competent counsel and thus opening the door for entry by the Hines Interests with their offers. . . .

[A fee was awarded of $1,213,609, reflecting 20 percent on the difference between the White and Hill offer and the R-S-C offer and 5 percent of the improvement in the sales price reflected via competitive bidding].

———

BACKGROUND NOTE ON THE AWARD OF COUNSEL FEES TO SUCCESSFUL DERIVATIVE-ACTION PLAINTIFFS

The derivative action constitutes a major legal bulwark against managerial self-dealing. As a practical matter this means that the rules governing plaintiffs' legal fees are critical to the operation of the corporate system: Because very few shareholders would pay, out of their own pockets, the attorney's fee for a suit that is brought on the corporation's behalf and will benefit all shareholders, with only a slight and indirect benefit for the plaintiff, very few derivative actions would be brought if the law did not allow the plaintiff's attorney to be compensated by a contingent fee payable out of the corporate recovery.

As a conceptual matter, the award of counsel fees to successful plaintiffs in derivative actions has been justified by several overlapping rationales, none of which is unique to derivative actions. The most important of these is the "common fund" theory, under which a plaintiff who has successfully established a fund under the control of the court, from which many besides himself will benefit, may recover his counsel fees out of that fund. As stated in the seminal case of *Trustees v. Greenough,* 105 U.S. (15 Otto) 527, 532, 26 L.Ed. 1157 (1881), to deny an allowance for fees in such circumstances "would not only be unjust to [plaintiff], but . . . would give to the other parties entitled to participate in the benefits of the fund an unfair advantage." This theory was later elaborated, under the heading of the "substantial benefit" or "common benefit" theory, to cover cases where the plaintiff had not brought a fund into the court's control but had established a right to a fund from which others would benefit. See Sprague v. Ticonic Nat. Bank, 307 U.S. 161, 59 S.Ct. 777, 83 L.Ed. 1184 (1939). Eventually, the common-benefit theory was extended to cover cases involving the establishment of nonpecuniary benefits.

Another basic rationale for the award of attorneys' fees to successful plaintiffs in derivative actions is the "private attorney-general" doctrine—that plaintiff's counsel fees should be awarded in appropriate cases to encourage the initiation of private actions that vindicate important legal policies. See Newman v. Piggie Park Enterprises, Inc., 390 U.S. 400, 402, 88 S.Ct. 964, 966, 19 L.Ed.2d 1263 (1968).

In the corporate area, this doctrine is important chiefly as a reinforcement to the common-fund or common-benefit theory, particularly where the benefit is not pecuniary. For example, in *Mills v. Electric Auto-Lite Co.*, 396 U.S. 375, 90 S.Ct. 616, 24 L.Ed.2d 593 (1970), plaintiffs, who were former Auto-Lite shareholders, alleged that defendants had violated the Proxy Rules in connection with a merger of Auto-Lite into Mergenthaler. The Court held that plaintiffs were entitled to summary judgment on the merits. It then went on to award interim counsel fees, although it recognized that if on remand the merger were found to be fair, there might be no feasible way to remedy the violation, and therefore no economically measurable benefit to either Auto-Lite or its shareholders. The opinion began by attempting to bring the case within the common-benefit rule: "In many suits under § 14(a) . . . it may be impossible to assign monetary value to the benefit. Nevertheless, the stress placed by Congress on the importance of fair and informed corporate suffrage leads to the conclusion that, in vindicating the statutory policy, petitioners have rendered a substantial service to the corporation and its shareholders." However, the Court then seemed to shift rationales by stressing that the action conferred a benefit on a subsector of the public, that is, shareholders as a class.

In *Alyeska Pipeline Service Co. v. Wilderness Society,* 421 U.S. 240, 95 S.Ct. 1612, 44 L.Ed.2d 141 (1975), the Supreme Court held that in the absence of statutory authorization, attorney's fees may not be awarded on the private-attorney-general theory in suits brought under federal statutes. While the opinion left the common-fund theory (and its derivative, the common-benefit theory) undisturbed, and cited *Sprague* and *Mills* with approval, it is open to question whether the Supreme Court would again go as far as it did in *Mills* in determining what constitutes a benefit for these purposes in a suit brought under federal law.

Consistent with these views, it is now well-established that attorneys' fees can be awarded to a plaintiff on the basis of a common but nonmonetary benefit, such as the corporation's agreement to change its governance structure, as opposed to the creation of a common fund. This rule has two important implications in derivative actions.

First, it is often very difficult to attribute any realistic value to nonmonetary benefits. As a result, in such cases attorney's fees usually are measured under the lodestar method, even by courts that employ the percentage-of-the-benefit test in common-fund cases.

Second, the rule that a plaintiff's attorney is entitled to a fee for producing a nonmonetary benefit opens the door to the possibility of collusive settlements in which the real defendants in a derivative action (the directors or officers) pay little or nothing; the corporation agrees to a change that is largely cosmetic; plaintiff's attorney and the corporation join hands to inflate the importance of the change; and plaintiff's attorney is then paid a fee that is supposed to be justified by that importance, but is really a bribe to drop the case. The real defendants are happy, because they get a release although they have paid little or nothing. Plaintiff's counsel is happy, because she gets a very nice fee. The shareholders aren't unhappy, because they don't realize what happened. If they did realize what happened, they would be very unhappy.

This doesn't mean that every settlement involving only a nonmonetary benefit is collusive. Nevertheless, the possibility that settlements involving only nonmonetary benefits may be collusive suggests that the courts should be especially cautious in reviewing such settlements.

Consider here the following: "[I]f the plaintiff had sought in its complaint [a change in various aspects of the firm's corporate governance] to the exclusion of all other relief, including monetary damages, is it not likely that the defendants would have settled immediately? Assuming the answer is 'yes,' then perhaps the corporate defendant should only have to pay for the value of the benefit, largely ignoring the litigation costs of the plaintiff." Mark J. Loewenstein, Shareholder Derivative Litigation and Corporate Governance, 24 Del. J. Corp. L. 1, 13, 22 (1999).

———

Goodrich v. E.F. Hutton Group

681 A.2d 1039 (Del.1996)

The court here summarized what continues to be the approach taken in awarding counsel fees in actions before the federal courts:

> In the 1970s, courts began to use the 'lodestar' approach to calculate fee awards in common fund cases. *Lindy Bros. Builders, Inc. of Phila. v. American Radiator & Standard Sanitary Corp.*, 487 F.2d 161, 167–68 (3d Cir.1973). *See* Report of the Third Circuit Task Force, *Court Awarded Attorney Fees,* 108 F.R.D. 237, 242 (1985). That method requires a court to calculate the product of an attorney's reasonable hours expended on the litigation and reasonable hourly rate to arrive at the 'lodestar.' *Swedish Hosp. Corp. v. Shalala,* 1 F.3d at 1266. That lodestar calculation can then be adjusted, through application of a 'multiplier' or fee enhancer, to account for additional factors, *e.g.,* the contingent nature of the case and the quality of an attorney's work. *Lindy Bros. Builders, Inc. of Phila. v. American Radiator & Standard Sanitary Corp.,* 540 F.2d 102,

112 (3d Cir.1976); *Swedish Hosp. Corp. v. Shalala,* 1 F.3d at
1266. During the 1970s, the 'lodestar/multiplier' method of
awarding fees was frequently invoked in common fund cases,
instead of determining a reasonable percentage of recovery from
the fund, based upon a multifactor analysis. *Johnson v. Georgia
Highway Express, Inc.,* 488 F.2d 714, 716–19 (5th Cir.1974)
(*'Johnson'* factors); *Lindy Bros. Builders, Inc. v. American
Radiator & Standard Sanitary Corp.,* 487 F.2d at 164–69
(*'Lindy'* factors).

In the 1980s, however, two events led to a reconsideration
of the lodestar method of calculating common fund fee awards.
First, in 1984, the Supreme Court distinguished the calculation
of awards under fee-shifting statutes from the calculation of
attorney's fees under the common fund doctrine. In doing so, the
Supreme Court suggested that an award in a common fund case
should be based upon a percentage of the fund:

> Unlike the calculation of attorney's fees under the
> 'common fund doctrine,' where a reasonable fee is based on
> a percentage of the fund bestowed on the class, a reasonable
> fee under [42 U.S.C.] § 1988 reflects the amount of attorney
> time reasonably expended on the litigation.

Blum v. Stenson, 465 U.S. 886, 900 n. 16, 104 S.Ct. 1541, 1550
n. 16, 79 L.Ed.2d 891 (1984). Footnote 16 in *Blum* has been cited
for the proposition that the Supreme Court's approval of the
lodestar method in the fee-shifting context was not intended to
overrule decisions which had approved percentage of the fund
awards of attorney's fees in common fund cases. Swedish Hosp.,
1 F.3d at 1268. See, e.g., Sprague v. Ticonic National Bank, 307
U.S. 161, 59 S.Ct. 777, 83 L.Ed. 1184 (1939); Central Railroad
& Banking Co. v. Pettus, 113 U.S. 116, 5 S.Ct. 387, 28 L.Ed. 915
(1885). That interpretation of *Blum* did not change when the
Supreme Court held that the lodestar should not be enhanced
through the use of a multiplier in statutory fee-shifting cases.
City of Burlington v. Dague, 505 U.S. 557, 565–67, 112 S.Ct.
2638, 2642–44, 120 L.Ed.2d 449 (1992).

The second significant event in the 1980s was the report
issued in 1985 by a Task Force the Third Circuit had appointed
to evaluate the practical effectiveness of the lodestar method in
making attorney fee awards. *See* Report of the Third Circuit
Task Force, Court Awarded Attorney Fees, 108 F.R.D. 237
(1985). The Task Force recommended continued use of the
lodestar technique in statutory fee-shifting cases. *Id.* See also
City of Burlington v. Dague, 505 U.S. at 562, 112 S.Ct. at 2641
(acknowledging, in the statutory fee-shifting context, 'a strong
presumption that the lodestar represents the reasonable fee').
The Task Force concluded, however, that all attorney fee awards

in common fund cases should be structured as a percentage of the fund. Report of the Third Circuit Task Force, Court Awarded Attorney Fees, 108 F.R.D. at 255.

At the present time, the majority of federal courts use a reasonable percentage of the fund method when making attorney fee awards in common fund cases. See Swedish Hosp. Corp. v. Shalala, 1 F.3d at 1266 (chronicling history of the methodologies). *See also* FEDERAL JUDICIAL CENTER, AWARDING ATTORNEYS' FEES AND MANAGING FEE LITIGATION 63–64 (1994) (canvassing case law.) The Third Circuit has recently held that the percentage of the fund is generally the preferable method for awarding fees in common fund cases, but noted that a lodestar analysis might be used to cross check the propriety of the award (a 'hybrid' approach). See In re General Motors Corp. Pick-Up Truck Fuel Tank Products Liability Litigation, 55 F.3d at 821. Ultimately, however, the Third Circuit permits the trial court to exercise its discretion in choosing *either* the percentage method *or* the lodestar method, *or* some combination or hybrid, as the circumstances warrant, in making common fund fee awards.

———

11. SECURITY FOR EXPENSES

———

N.Y. BUS. CORP. LAW § 627

[See Statutory Supplement]

———

CAL. CORP. CODE § 800(c)–(f)

[See Statutory Supplement]

———

SECURITIES ACT § 11(e), 27(c)

[See Statutory Supplement]

———

SECURITIES EXCHANGE ACT § 21D(c)

[See Statutory Supplement]

———

West Hills Farms, Inc. v. RCO AG Credit, Inc.

California Court of Appeal, Fifth District, 2009.
170 Cal.App.4th 710, 88 Cal.Rptr.3d 458.

■ **KANE, J.**—In this derivative action, defendant RCO Ag Credit, Inc., was sued by two of its shareholders, plaintiffs West Hills Farms, Inc., and California Pistachio, LLC, based on allegedly unnecessary fees paid by defendant to a related corporate entity. Defendant made a motion under *Corporations Code section 800* to require plaintiffs to furnish a bond in the amount of $50,000 as security for defendant's anticipated litigation expenses to defend the action. The motion was granted and plaintiffs furnished the required bond. Defendant ultimately prevailed in the action and, following entry of judgment, moved for an award of *all* of its attorney fees and costs incurred, totaling over $350,000. The trial court's order limited the award of attorney fees and costs to $50,000, the amount of the bond. Defendant appeals from that order, contending that under *section 800* it was entitled to recover *all* of its attorney fees and costs, regardless of the amount of the bond. We disagree. . . . Accordingly, we affirm the trial court's order. . . .

Section 800 addresses the terms and conditions under which a shareholder derivative action may be maintained. . . . The statute includes the provision at issue here that a plaintiff-shareholder may be compelled to furnish a bond as security for a defendant's anticipated litigation expenses, including attorney fees, which may be incurred in defense of the derivative action. (*§ 800, subds. (c), (d)*.) "[T]he essential purpose of the *section 800* bond statute is to create a deterrent to unwarranted shareholder derivative lawsuits by providing a mechanism for securing a prevailing defendant's expenses up to $50,000." (*Donner Management Co. v. Schaffer (2006) 142 Cal.App.4th 1296, 1308 [48 Cal. Rptr. 3d 534]*.) According to the statute, a defendant-corporation's motion to require a bond will be granted on a showing that "there is no reasonable possibility that the prosecution of the cause of action alleged in the complaint against the moving party will benefit the corporation or its shareholders." (*§ 800, subd. (c)(1)*.) Additionally, the same relief will be extended to a defendant who is an officer or director of the corporation if it is shown that said "moving party, if other than the corporation, did not participate in the transaction complained of in any capacity." (*§ 800, subd. (c)(2)*.)

Subdivision (d) of section 800 sets forth the particulars of the relief afforded by the motion as follows: "At the hearing upon any motion pursuant to subdivision (c), the court shall consider such evidence . . . , as may be material (1) to the ground or grounds upon which the motion is based, or (2) to a determination of the probable reasonable expenses, including attorneys' fees, of the corporation . . . which will be incurred in the defense of the action. If the court determines, after hearing the evidence adduced by the parties, that the moving party has established a probability in support of any of the grounds upon which the motion is based, *the court shall fix the amount of the bond, not to exceed fifty thousand dollars ($50,000), to be furnished by the plaintiff for reasonable expenses, including attorneys' fees, which may be incurred by the . . . corporation in connection with the action,* including expenses for which the corporation may become liable pursuant to Section 317. A ruling by the court on the motion shall not be a determination of any issue in the action or of the merits thereof. If the court, upon the motion, makes a determination that a bond shall be furnished by the plaintiff as to any one or more defendants, the action shall be dismissed as to the defendant or defendants, unless the bond required by the court has been furnished within such reasonable time as may be fixed by the court." (Italics added.) . . .

Aside from this bond protection, however, *section 800* makes no mention at all of attorney fees or expenses. Indeed, the *only* references in the statute to attorney fees or other expenses are within the limited context of describing what the bond will secure. (*§ 800, subds. (d), (e)*.) There is simply nothing in the language of *section 800* to suggest that the Legislature intended to create an independent basis for recovery of attorney fees or costs *apart from recourse to the bond*. Of course, the Legislature is quite capable of drafting statutes that authorize awards to prevailing parties of all reasonable attorney fees or costs incurred in an action without limitation. . . . Here, however, the Legislature did not do so. . . .

————

BACKGROUND NOTE ON SECURITY-FOR-EXPENSES STATUTES

Security-for-expenses statutes must be considered against the background of the general American rule that the losing party in a lawsuit does not have to pay the winner's expenses, except for "taxable costs," such as clerk's, witness, docket, and transcript fees. Accordingly, security-for-expenses statutes are normally not interpreted to impose *individual* liability on the plaintiff for expenses—that is, liability beyond the amount of his bond.

A shareholder who wants to bring a derivative action in a state that has a security-for-expenses statute is under heavy pressure to find some way to bring suit without posting security. Since the statutes are normally interpreted to be inapplicable to direct (as opposed to derivative) actions, one alternative is to frame the suit as a direct action. A second alternative is to bring the action under some provision of federal law, such as the Proxy Rules or Rule 10b–5. The security-for-expenses requirement may also be avoided in certain types of cases by petitioning for dissolution or the appointment of a receiver. See Leibert v. Clapp, 13 N.Y.2d 313, 247 N.Y.S.2d 102, 196 N.E.2d 540 (1963).

————

12. PRIVATE ORDERING AND SHAREHOLDER SUITS

Consider the policy implications of the contemporary debate on the efficacy and desirability of articles of incorporation or bylaws including provisions that either require intra-firm disputes be arbitrated or litigated only in the courts of a specific state ("forum selection" provision). The typical forum selection bylaw empowers the board of directors to choose between a favored forum, e.g., Delaware, set forth in the document or choose among the forums in which a suit is pending in which a shareholder suit can proceed. Forum selection bylaws were upheld in *Boilermakers Local 154 Ret. Fd. v. Chevron*, 73 A.3d 934 (Del. Ch. 2013), Chancellor Strine held that Section 109 of the Delaware statute empowers boards to adopt forum selection bylaws:

> *8 Del. C. § 109(b)* has long been understood to allow the corporation to set "self-imposed rules and regulations [that are] deemed expedient for its convenient functioning." The forum selection bylaws here fit this description. They are process-oriented, because they regulate *where* stockholders may file suit, not *whether* the stockholder may file suit or the kind of remedy that the stockholder may obtain on behalf of herself or the corporation. The bylaws also clearly address cases of the kind that address "the business of the corporation, the conduct of its affairs, and . . . the rights or powers of its stockholders, directors, officers or employees," because they govern where internal affairs cases governed by state corporate law may be heard. These are the kind of claims most central to the relationship between those who manage the corporation and the corporation's stockholders.

Furthermore, *Boilermakers* deployed the view that the company's bylaws are part of a "web of contracts" that can limit rights shareholders may otherwise have:

> In an unbroken line of decisions dating back several generations, our Supreme Court has made clear that the bylaws constitute a binding part of the contract between a Delaware corporation and its stockholders. Stockholders are on notice that, as to those subjects that are subject of regulation by bylaw under *8 Del. C. § 109(b)*, the board itself may act unilaterally to adopt bylaws addressing those subjects. Such a change by the board is not extra-contractual simply because the board acts unilaterally; rather it is the kind of change that the overarching statutory and contractual regime the stockholders buy into explicitly allows the board to make on its own. In other words, the Chevron and FedEx stockholders have assented to a contractual framework established by the DGCL and the certificates of incorporation that explicitly recognizes that stockholders will be bound by bylaws adopted unilaterally by

their boards. Under that clear contractual framework, the stockholders assent to not having to assent to board-adopted bylaws. . . .

[T]he statutory regime provides protections for the stockholders, through the indefeasible right of the stockholders to adopt and amend bylaws themselves. "[B]y its terms *Section 109(a)* vests in the shareholders a power to adopt, amend or repeal bylaws that is legally sacrosanct, *i.e.*, the power cannot be non-consensually eliminated or limited by anyone other than the legislature itself." Thus, even though a board may, as is the case here, be granted authority to adopt bylaws, stockholders can check that authority by repealing board-adopted bylaws. And, of course, because the DGCL gives stockholders an annual opportunity to elect directors, stockholders have a potent tool to discipline boards who refuse to accede to a stockholder vote repealing a forum selection clause. Thus, a corporation's bylaws are part of an inherently flexible contract between the stockholders and the corporation under which the stockholders have powerful rights they can use to protect themselves if they do not want board-adopted forum selection bylaws to be part of the contract between themselves and the corporation. . . .

And, as noted, precisely because forum selection bylaws are part of a larger contract between the corporation and its stockholders, and because bylaws are interpreted using contractual principles, the bylaws will also be subject to scrutiny under the principles for evaluating contractual forum selection clauses established by the Supreme Court of the United States in *The Bremen v. Zapata Off-Shore Co.*, [407 U.S. 1 (1972)] and adopted by our Supreme Court. In *Bremen*, the Court held that forum selection clauses are valid provided that they are "unaffected by fraud, undue influence, or overweening bargaining power," and that the provisions "should be enforced unless enforcement is shown by the resisting party to be 'unreasonable.'"

Subsequent to *Boilermakers*, relying on the contract-orientation that was emphasized in *Boilermakers*, the Delaware Supreme Court held that a non-stock Delaware corporation's board of directors could adopt and enforce a bylaw that shifted the defense's litigation costs to the plaintiff when the suit was not substantially successful. *ATP Tour, Inc. v. Deutscher Tennis Bund*, 91 A. 3d 554 (Del. 2014). It should be noted that Delaware non-stock corporations, although not having stockholders but members, are subject to the Delaware General Corporation Law.

To some extent, *Boilermakers and ATP Tour, Inc.* have now been overtaken by legislative developments, at least in Delaware. In 2015, the Delaware legislature amended the Delaware General Corporation Law to expressly authorize forum selection bylaws, Del. Gen. Corp. L. § 115, but the same legislature acted to prohibit fee shifting provisions, such as was involved in *ATP Tour, Inc.*, Del. Gen. Corp. L. § 102(f) (which prohibits the provision in the charter and by virtue of section 109(b) a fee shifting provision is also prohibited in the bylaws). Neither provision addresses another lurking development, bylaws calling for shareholder disputes to be arbitrated. *See* Ann Lipton, Manufactured Consent: The Problem of Arbitration Clauses in Corporate Charters and Bylaws, 104 Geo. L. J. 583 (2016).

Commentators have also challenged the contractual basis for provisions affecting shareholder litigation via unilateral action by the board of directors. *See* James D. Cox, Corporate Law and the Limits of Private Ordering, 93 Wash. U. L. Rev. 257 (2015); Deborah A. DeMott, Forum Selection Bylaws Refracted Through the Agency Lens, 57 Ariz. L. Rev. 269 (2015); Lawrence A. Hamermesh, Consent in Corporate Law, 70 Bus. Law. 161 (2014). *But see* Joseph A. Grundfest & Kristen A. Savelle, The Brouhaha over Intra-Corporate Forum Selection Provisions: A Legal, Economic, and Political Analysis, 68 Bus. Law. 325, 335 (2013). A separate concern is the scope of such litigation-focused bylaws. For example, Sciabacucchi v. Salzburg, 2018 WL 6719718 (Del. Ch., Dec. 19, 2018), considered the validity of a provision in the articles of incorporation providing that any securities fraud claim under the Federal Securities Act (FSA) involving an alleged misrepresentation in the firm's prospectus used in its IPO must be brought in federal court, unless the company agreed in writing to suit in state court. The FSA provides that federal and state courts have concurrent jurisdiction in such suits. The court held that the Sections 102(b)(1) and 109(b) of the Delaware statute do not authorize charter or bylaw provisions to regulate external relationships, such as the purchase of stock. The court held that the statute only reaches matters and relationships internal to the corporation.

Query, could a board adopt a bylaw that requires a certain number of shares to be owned to initiate a derivative suit? How about a bylaw that conditioned the plaintiff initiating any kind of shareholder suit to post a bond to secure the defendant's litigation costs?

———

CHAPTER 14

CORPORATE COMBINATIONS, TENDER OFFERS AND DEFENDING CONTROL

1. CORPORATE COMBINATIONS

A. SALE OF SUBSTANTIALLY ALL ASSETS

———

DEL. GEN. CORP. LAW § 271

[See Statutory Supplement]

———

MODEL BUS. CORP. ACT §§ 12.01, 12.02, 13.02(3)

[See Statutory Supplement]

———

Hollinger, Inc. v. Hollinger International, Inc.

Court of Chancery of Delaware, 2004.
858 A.2d 342.

Opinion

■ STRINE, VICE CHANCELLOR. . . .

Hollinger Inc. (or "Inc.") seeks a preliminary injunction preventing Hollinger International, Inc. (or "International") from selling the *Telegraph* Group Ltd. (England) to Press Holdings International, an entity controlled by Frederick and David Barclay (hereinafter, the "Barclays"). The *Telegraph* Group is an indirect, wholly owned subsidiary of International and publishes the *Telegraph* newspaper and the *Spectator* magazine. The *Telegraph* newspaper is a leading one in the United Kingdom, both in terms of its circulation and its journalistic reputation.

The key question addressed in this decision is whether Inc. and the other International stockholders must be provided with the opportunity to vote on the sale of the *Telegraph* Group because that sale involves "substantially all" the assets of International within the meaning of 8 Del. C. § 271. The sale of the *Telegraph* followed a lengthy auction process whereby International and all of Hollinger's operating assets were widely shopped to potential bidders. As a practical matter, Inc.'s vote would be the only one that matters because although it now owns only 18% of International's total equity, it, through high-vote Class B shares, controls 68% of the voting power. . . .

. . . Does § 271 Apply to a Sale of Assets By an Indirect, Wholly Owned Subsidiary?

International [first] argues that the sale of the *Telegraph* Group simply does not implicate § 271 at all. The reason is that the operating assets that the Barclays are buying and that comprise the *Telegraph* Group are actually held by a 6th tier U.K. subsidiary and not by International.

It is undisputed that the chain of subsidiaries through which International controlled the *Telegraph* Group maintained the corporate formalities necessary for it to comply with U.K. and U.S. regulatory requirements. It is also undisputed that these subsidiaries are long-standing parts of the International structure and were formed because they had valuable tax, financial, and liability-insulating purposes. There is no indication that any third parties dealing with the subsidiaries in the ordinary course of business or any tort plaintiff allegedly injured by one of the subsidiaries would have been entitled to pierce their corporate veil and seek recourse directly against International.

On the other hand, the chain of subsidiaries is wholly owned by International. The Strategic Process that resulted in the proposal to sell the *Telegraph* Group was, as a matter of obvious reality, conducted entirely at the International level. . . .

Notably, the contract for sale of the *Telegraph* Group does not run simply between the Barclays and the U.K. subsidiary that directly own the *Telegraph* Group. Instead, International is a direct signatory to that agreement and its lawyers negotiated its terms. . . .

In essence, it is clear to me that the *Telegraph* sale was directed and controlled by International and that its wholly owned subsidiaries did what wholly owned subsidiaries do—the bidding of their sole owner. It is no disrespect to the employees who populated the subsidiary boards to recognize this obvious reality.

From this, to my view, clear factual picture, the parties draw starkly different legal conclusions. For its part, International contends that it is plain that § 271 does not contemplate ignoring the separate existence of subsidiary corporations unless the stringent test for veil piercing is met. . . .

If International's argument is accepted, § 271's vote requirement will be rendered largely hortatory—reduced to an easily side-stepped gesture, but little more, towards the idea that transactions that dispose of substantially all of a corporation's economic value need stockholders' assent to become effective. An example tied to this case points out this implication. Assume that the [board, acting through its Corporate

Review Committee] decided to sell all four of International's operating groups. Further assume that each is held by subsidiaries that would not be subject to veil piercing but that it is equally clear that International dictated the sale of the assets and was a signatory to and guarantor of the sales contracts. Under International's view, even that sale would not constitute a sale of substantially all of its assets. This would be the case even though the sales would, taken together, result in a de facto liquidation of the firm's operating assets into a pool of cash, a result akin to a sale of the entire company for cash or a liquidation. . . .

In drawing lines under § 271 itself, moreover, the facts of this case suggest a possible demarcation point. When an asset sale by the wholly owned subsidiary is to be consummated by a contract in which the parent entirely guarantees the performance of the selling subsidiary that is disposing of all of its assets and in which the parent is liable for any breach of warranty by the subsidiary, the direct act of the parent's board can, without any appreciable stretch, be viewed as selling assets of the parent itself. By its direct contractual action, the parent board is promising to dispose of all of the underlying assets of the subsidiaries by having the parent cause its wholly owned subsidiaries to sell, by promising to bear all the economic risks of the asset sale itself, and by therefore essentially eliminating the subsidiary's purpose and existence and monetizing for itself as parent the value of the assets held by that subsidiary. To find that § 271's vote requirement were implicated by such a contract if it involved the sale of assets that would, if owned directly by the parent, comprise substantially all of the parent's assets would not, despite International's well-stated arguments to the contrary, be an irrational implementation of the legislative intent expressed in that section of our corporation code.

I need not reach that conclusion, or a contrary one, in this case, however. This motion can be resolved without rendering any definitive pronouncement on this area of our law and, given the limited time for reflection on the question presented, prudential considerations counsel in favor of leaving the question to be answered in another case, or at later stage of this one, if that becomes necessary.

> *. . . As a Matter of Economic Substance, Does the Telegraph*
> *Group Comprise Substantially All of International's Assets?*

I now discuss the major question presented by this motion: whether the *Telegraph* Group comprises "substantially all" of International's assets, such that its sale requires a vote under § 271.

> 1. *The Legal Standards to Measure Whether the Telegraph*
> *Group Comprises Substantially All of International's Assets*

Section 271 of the Delaware General Corporation Law authorizes a board of directors of a Delaware corporation to sell "all or substantially all of its property and assets, including goodwill and corporate franchises" only with the approval of a stockholder vote. . . .

Therefore, I begin my articulation of the applicable legal principles with the words of the statute itself. . . . A fair and succinct equivalent to the term "substantially all" would . . . be "essentially everything."

In our jurisprudence, however, words of this kind arguably long ago passed from the sight of our judicial rear view mirrors, to be replaced by an inquiry more focused on the judicial gloss put on the statute than on the words of the statute itself.

> The Supreme Court has long held that a determination of whether there is a sale of substantially all assets so as to trigger section 271 depends upon the particular qualitative and quantitative characteristics of the transaction at issue. Thus, the transaction must be viewed in terms of its overall effect on the corporation, and there is no necessary qualifying percentage.[51]

In other words,

> Our jurisprudence eschewed a definitional approach to § 271 focusing on the interpretation of the words "substantially all," in favor of a contextual approach focusing upon whether a transaction involves the sale "of assets quantitatively vital to the operation of the corporation and is out of the ordinary and substantially affects the existence and purpose of the corporation." *Gimbel v. Signal Cos., Inc.*, Del.Ch., 316 A.2d 599, 606, *aff'd*, Del.Supr., 316 A.2d 619 (1974). . . . [52]

. . . *Gimbel* set forth a quantitative and qualitative test designed to help determine whether a particular sale of assets involved substantially all the corporation's assets. That test has been adopted by our Supreme Court as a good metric for determining whether an asset sale triggers the vote requirement of § 271. . . . [55]

The test that *Gimbel* articulated—requiring a stockholder vote if the assets to be sold "are quantitatively vital to the operation of the corporation' and 'substantially affect[ ] the existence and purpose of the corporation"—must . . . be read as an attempt to give practical life to the words "substantially all." It is for that reason that *Gimbel* emphasized that a vote would never be required for a transaction in the ordinary course of business and that the mere fact that an asset sale was out of the ordinary had little bearing on whether a vote was required.

Indeed, *Gimbel* stressed that "the statute does not speak of a requirement of shareholder approval simply because an independent, important branch of a corporate business is being sold." In that case, the court expressly rejected the argument that Delaware law ought to follow

---

[51]   *Winston v. Mandor*, 710 A.2d 835, 843 (Del.Ch.1997) (footnotes omitted).

[52]   *In re General Motors Class H S'holders Litig.*, 734 A.2d 611, 623 (Del.Ch.1999).

[55]   *Oberly v. Kirby*, 592 A.2d 445, 464 (Del.1991); *see also Thorpe v. CERBCO, Inc.*, 676 A.2d 436, 444 (Del.1996).

the law of other states that subjected all such major sales to stockholder approval. . . .

To underscore the point that the test it was articulating was tied directly to the statute, *Gimbel* noted that its examination of the quantitative and qualitative importance of the transaction at issue was intended to determine whether the transaction implicated the statute because it struck "at the heart of the corporate existence and purpose," in the sense that it involved the " 'destruction of the means to accomplish the purposes or objects for which the corporation was incorporated and actually performs.' " It was in that sense, Gimbel said, that the "statute's applicability was to be determined."

And it is in that sense that I apply the *Gimbel* test in this case.

2.   Is the Telegraph Group Quantitatively Vital to the Operations of International?

The first question under the *Gimbel* test is whether the *Telegraph* Group is quantitatively vital to the operations of International. The short answer to that question is no, it is not quantitatively vital within the meaning of *Gimbel*.

Why?

Because it is clear that International will retain economic vitality even after a sale of the *Telegraph* because it is retaining other significant assets, one of which, the Chicago Group [which owned, among other things, the Chicago *Sun-Times* and Jerusalem *Post* newspapers], has a strong record of past profitability and expectations of healthy profit growth.

Now, it is of course clear that the *Telegraph* Group is a major quantitative part of International's economic value and an important contributor to its profits. I am even prepared to decide this motion on the assumption that the *Telegraph* Group is the single most valuable asset that International possesses, even more valuable than the Chicago Group.

If one were to use the actual high bids received for each of the *Telegraph* and Chicago Groups as a result of the Strategic [Auction] Process and assume that those were the only assets of International— which is not an accurate assumption—the *Telegraph* Group accounts for 56–57% of International's asset value, while the Chicago Group accounts for only 43–44% of the value. Recognizing that quantitative vitality must be defined in light of the statutory language "substantially all," this breakdown does little to support Inc.'s position. It is less than 60% and the remaining asset is itself a quantitatively vital economic asset. . . .

Let's consider the relative contribution to International's revenues of the *Telegraph* Group and the Chicago Group. . . .

Put simply, the *Telegraph* Group has accounted for less than half of International's revenues during the last three years and the Chicago Group's contribution has been in the same ballpark. . . .

In book value terms, neither the *Telegraph* Group nor the Chicago Group approach 50% of International's asset value because the company's other operating groups and non-operating assets have value. . . .

In terms of vitality, however, a more important measure is EBITDA [Earnings Before Interest, Taxes, Depreciation, and Amortization] contribution, as that factor focuses on the free cash flow that assets generate for the firm, a key component of economic value. . . .

The [EBITDA] picture that emerges is one of rough equality between the two Groups—with any edge tilting in the Chicago Group's direction. . . .

Importantly, the record evidence regarding the future of both Groups also suggests that their cash flow-generating potential and sale value are not greatly disparate. . . .

The evidence therefore reveals that neither the *Telegraph* Group nor the Chicago Group is quantitatively vital in the sense used in the *Gimbel* test. Although both Groups are profitable, valuable economic assets and although the *Telegraph* Group is somewhat more valuable than the Chicago Group, International can continue as a profitable entity without either one of them. . . .

[A] sale of either Group leaves International as a profitable entity, even if it chooses to distribute a good deal of the cash it receives from the *Telegraph* sale to its stockholders through a dividend or share repurchase.

3. *Does the Telegraph Sale "Substantially Affect the Existence and Purpose of" International?*

The relationship of the qualitative element of the *Gimbel* test to the quantitative element is more than a tad unclear. If the assets to be sold are not quantitatively vital to the corporation's life, it is not altogether apparent how they can "substantially affect the existence and purpose of" the corporation within the meaning of *Gimbel*, suggesting either that the two elements of the test are actually not distinct or that they are redundant. In other words, if quantitative vitality takes into account factors such as the cash-flow generating value of assets and not merely book value, then it necessarily captures qualitative considerations as well. . . . Rather than endeavor to explore the relationship between these factors, however, I will just dive into my analysis of the qualitative importance of the *Telegraph* Group to International.

Inc.'s demand for a vote places great weight on the qualitative element of *Gimbel*. In its papers, Inc. stresses the journalistic superiority of the *Telegraph* over the *Sun-Times* and the social cachet the *Telegraph* has. . . .

The argument . . . misconceives the qualitative element of *Gimbel*. That element is not satisfied if the court merely believes that the economic assets being sold are aesthetically superior to those being retained; rather, the qualitative element of *Gimbel* focuses on economic quality and, at most, on whether the transaction leaves the stockholders with an investment that in economic terms is qualitatively different than the one that they now possess. Even with that focus, it must be remembered that the qualitative element is a gloss on the statutory language "substantially all" and not an attempt to identify qualitatively important transactions but ones that "strike at the heart of the corporate existence."

The *Telegraph* sale does not strike at International's heart or soul, if that corporation can be thought to have either one. . . .

. . . Whatever the social importance of the *Telegraph* in Great Britain, the economic value of that importance to International as an entity is what matters for the *Gimbel* test, not how cool it would be to be the *Telegraph's* publisher. The expected cash flows from the *Telegraph* Group take that into account, as do the bids that were received for the *Telegraph* Group. . . .

After the *Telegraph* Sale, International's stockholders will remain investors in a publication company with profitable operating assets, a well-regarded tabloid newspaper of good reputation and large circulation, a prestigious newspaper in Israel, and other valuable assets. While important, the sale of the *Telegraph* does not strike a blow to International's heart.

4.   *Summary of § 271 Analysis*

When considered quantitatively and qualitatively, the *Telegraph* sale does not amount to a sale of substantially all of International's assets. This conclusion is consistent with the bulk of our case law under § 271. Although by no means wholly consistent, that case law has, by and large, refused to find that a disposition involved substantially all the assets of a corporation when the assets that would remain after the sale were, in themselves, substantial and profitable. As *Gimbel* noted, § 271 permits a board to sell "one business . . . without shareholder approval when other substantial businesses are retained." In the cases when asset sales were deemed to involve substantially all of a corporation's assets, the record always revealed great doubt about the viability of the business that would remain, primarily because the remaining operating assets were not profitable.[77] But, "if the portion of the business not sold

---

[77]   *E.g., Winston v. Mandor*, 710 A.2d 835, 843 (Del.Ch.1997) (assets comprising 60% of net asset value might be substantially all assets for pleading purposes in situation when they allegedly constituted the only "income-generating assets"); *Thorpe v. CERBCO, Inc.*, 1995 WL 478954, at *9–*10 (Del.Ch. Aug.9, 1995) (assets that were held likely to constitute substantially all the assets comprised at least 68% of corporation's assets and were the corporation's "primary

constitutes a substantial, viable, ongoing component of the corporation, the sale is not subject to Section 271."[78]

To conclude that the sale of the *Telegraph* Group was a sale of substantially all of International's assets would involve a determination that International possesses two operating assets, the sale of either of which would trigger a stockholder vote under § 271. That is, because there is no significant distinction between the economic importance of the Chicago and *Telegraph* Groups to International, a conclusion that the *Telegraph* Group was substantially all of International's assets would (impliedly but undeniably) supplant the plain language and intended meaning of the General Assembly with an "approximately half" test.[79] I decline Inc.'s invitation for me to depart so markedly from our legislature's mandate. By any reasonable interpretation, the *Telegraph* sale does not involve substantially all of International's assets as

---

income-generating asset[s]"), *rev'd in part, aff'd in relevant part*, 676 A.2d 436 (Del.1996); *Katz v. Bregman*, 431 A.2d 1274, 1275 (Del.Ch.1981) (only case finding assets worth less than 60% of a company's value to be "substantially all" the company's assets, and doing so when sale at issue came on heels of other substantial asset sales and where the assets to be sold had been the company's only income-producing facility during the previous four years).

[78] 1 R. Franklin Balotti & Jesse A. Finkelstein, DELAWARE LAW OF CORPORATIONS & BUSINESS ORGANIZATIONS § 10.2, at 10–7 (3d ed. Supp. 2004).

[79] As International points out, the MBCA now includes a safe harbor provision that is intended to provide a "greater measure of certainty than is provided by interpretations of the current case law." MODEL BUS. CORP. ACT § 12.02 cmt. 1 (2002). The safe harbor is an objective test involving two factors:

If a corporation retains a business activity that represented at least 25 percent of total assets at the end of the most recently completed fiscal year, and 25 percent of either income from continuing operations before taxes or revenues from continuing operations for that fiscal year, in each case of the corporation and its subsidiaries on a consolidated basis, the corporation will conclusively be deemed to have retained a significant continuing business activity.

Id. § 12.02(a).

Moreover, both the MBCA and the ALI Principles of Corporate Governance usefully turn the "substantially all" inquiry on its head by focusing, as *Gimbel* does in a more oblique way, on what remains after a sale. *See* MODEL BUS. CORP. ACT § 12.02 cmt. 1 (2002) (stockholder vote required if asset sale would "leave the corporation without a significant continuing business activity"); PRINCIPLES OF CORP. GOVERNANCE §§ 1.38(a)(2), 6.01(b) (text requiring stockholder approval when asset sale "would leave the corporation without a significant continuing business"); *id.* § 1.38 cmt. 3 (commentary indicating that if a company has two principal operating divisions and one will remain following the asset sale, "there should normally be no doubt concerning the significance of the remaining division, even if the division to be sold represented a majority of the corporation's operating assets"). The MBCA, in particular, recognizes that while the "significant continuing business activity" test differs verbally from the "substantially all" language employed in many state corporation statutes, adoption of the MBCA provision would not entail a substantive change from existing law, because "[i]n practice, . . . courts interpreting these statutes [using the phrase 'substantially all'] have commonly employed a test comparable to that embodied in 12.02(a)." MODEL BUS. CORP. ACT § 12.02 cmt. 1 (2002). The commentary specifically cites several Delaware judicial decisions as examples of cases employing such a test. *Id.* These approaches support the conclusion I reach.

Although not binding on me, these interpretative approaches provide a valuable perspective on § 271 because they are rooted, as is *Gimbel*, in the intent behind the statute (and statutes like it in other jurisdictions). Indeed, taken together, a reading of § 271 that: 1) required a stockholder vote for any sales contract to which a parent was a party that involved a sale by a wholly owned subsidiary that, in economic substance, amounted to a disposition of substantially all the parent's assets; combined with 2) a strict adherence to the words "substantially all" (a la the MBCA), could be viewed as the most faithful way to give life to the General Assembly's intended use of § 271. That is, § 271 would have substantive force but only with regard to transactions that genuinely involved substantially all of the corporation's assets. . . .

substantial operating (and non-operating) assets will be retained, and International will remain a profitable publishing concern.

. . . Conclusion

Inc.'s motion for a preliminary injunction is DENIED. . . .

———

B. THE APPRAISAL REMEDY

———

DEL. GEN. CORP. LAW § 262

[See Statutory Supplement]

———

MODEL BUS. CORP. ACT §§ 13.01–13.03, 13.20–13.26, 13.30–13.31

[See Statutory Supplement]

———

ALI, PRINCIPLES OF CORPORATE GOVERNANCE §§ 7.21–7.23

[See Statutory Supplement]

———

CAL. CORP. CODE §§ 1300, 1311

[See Statutory Supplement]

———

NOTES ON THE APPRAISAL REMEDY

1. Background. Prior to the mid-19th Century, any change in the rights of shareholders, whether by amendment of the articles of incorporation, merger or sale of all the corporation's assets, required the approval of all stockholders. The then prevailing view was that shareholders had a vested right protected by the Constitution's Contract Clause so that relaxation of the unanimity requirement presented serious constitutional issues. As commerce expanded, conditioning corporate transactions that change the rights of stockholders on unanimous stockholder approval impeded the growth of firms and, more generally, retarded industrial development. Responding to a challenge to a merger that the state had authorized to occur by less than all the stockholders, *see* Lauman v. Lebanon Valley Railroad, 30 Pa. 42 (1858), Pennsylvania amended its statute to provide dissenters the right to receive cash for their shares, i.e., compensation for any constitutionally protected "taking." This was the first appraisal statute and the corporate landscape has not been the same since. Today, all state corporation statutes provide appraisal remedy for various types of corporate transactions. However, states vary widely how they identify the types of transactions for which appraisal is available.

States that are more solicitous of shareholders provide appraisal (subject to certain exceptions that apply to their appraisal statute generally) for amendments to the articles of incorporation that adversely affect the rights of stockholders, the sale of all or substantially all the firm's assets, and mergers and consolidations. *See e.g.,* Cal. Corp. Code §§ 181, 1200 et seq., 1300; N.Y. Bus. Corp. L. § 910. In contrast, Delaware limits its appraisal statute to mergers and consolidations. *See* Del. Code Ann., tit. 8 § 262(b). The Model Business Corporation Act follows a course between these two extremes, providing appraisal for sales of assets, mergers and consolidations. *See* MBCA § 13.02(a).

Appraisal statutes provide a process for shareholders meeting the statute's conditions to obtain fair value for their shares. The Model Act provides the most extensive description of "fair value" identifying that such value is to be determined "immediately before the effectuation of the corporate action" triggering the appraisal right as determined "using customary and current valuation concepts" and "without discounting for lack of marketability or minority status." Delaware's statute excludes from the fair value determination "any element of value arising from the accomplishment or expectation of the merger or consolidation," and invites an array of valuation methods by providing that "the Court shall take into account all relevant factors."

2. *Purposeful Process.* The appraisal remedy is commonly referred to as "dissenters" rights. In most states this is a misnomer because appraisal is not conditioned on the shareholder voting against the acquisition but rather not voting in favor of the transaction triggering the right of appraisal. *See* Del. Code. Ann., tit. 8 § 262(a), MBCA § 13.21(a)(2). There are, however, several procedural steps the shareholder must take to perfect the right of appraisal. For example, Delaware provides that before the vote on the merger or consolidation the shareholder must make a written demand for appraisal and provides a rather short period of time, 120 days after completion of the merger or consolidation, in which the appraisal proceeding is to be commenced. Del. Code Ann., tit. 8 § 262(d)(e). The Model Act also requires before the vote of the shareholders is taken that notice of the intent to seek appraisal must be given by the shareholder, sets forth other steps that must be taken after the vote approving the transaction has occurred, and the appraisal proceeding does not begin until the shareholder has rejected in writing the corporation's estimate of the share's fair value. MBCA §§ 13.21–13.26. In Delaware the costs of the appraisal proceeding are assigned as the court deems "equitable in the circumstances" Del. Code Ann., tit. 8 § 262(j), whereas in the Model Act the proceeding's costs are borne by the corporation unless otherwise assigned by the court. MBCA § 13.31(a). Even though pursuant to the "American Rule" litigants customarily bear the costs of their representatives and experts and not those of their opponents,

in limited instances the Model Act permits such costs to be assigned to the corporation. *Id.* § 13.31(b)(c). In sum, appraisal is a proceeding that one does not easily fall into but rather a process the shareholder must pursue with a close eye to the procedural steps set forth in the governing appraisal statute and with a healthy awareness of extraordinary remedy's costs.

     3.   *Appraisal Arbitrage.* Beginning in 2007, the practice of "appraisal arbitrage" stimulated an increase in Delaware appraisal proceedings. Two legal developments likely contributed to this rise. *In re Transkaryotic Therapies, Inc.*, 2007 Del. Ch. LEXIS 57 (Del. Ch. May 2, 2007), held that a hedge fund could pursue appraisal for shares purchased after the transaction's record date without having to establish the shares were not earlier voted in favor of the acquisition (provided the shares for which appraisal is sought held by a depository trust, e.g., Cede and Co., is not greater than the number of shares that did not vote in favor of the of the acquisition). Also in 2007, the Delaware legislature confirmed that prejudgment interest on any sum recovered in appraisal would be the federal discount rate *plus 5 percent*. In an era of very low interest rates, the prejudgment rate was something of honey pot that attracted hedge fund bears. To be noted here is that the Delaware statute did not then authorize, as does the Model Act, the company to reduce the amount of such pre-judgment interest by paying to the petitioner the amount offered pursuant to the merger's terms so that interest would be due only for any amount the stockholder gains above that amount via appraisal. *See* MBCA §§ 1324(a) & 1326(a). *See* Wm. Carney & Keith Sharfman, The Death of Appraisal Arbitrage: Ending Windfalls for Deal Dissenters, 43 Del. J. Corp. L. 61 (2018).

     4.   *Delaware Tightens Scope of Remedy.* In response to the above, in 2015 the Delaware appraisal provision was amended in several important ways. First, Section 262(h) was amended to mirror the Model Act's provision allowing the company to reduce the amount of the statutory pre-judgement interest by tendering some or all of the merger consideration to the appraisal petitioner. Second, Section 262(g) now requires a petitioner to hold a minimum of $1 million or 1 percent of the company's stock. An exception to this standing requirement exists for short-form mergers.

———

NOTES ON DETERMINING APPRAISED VALUE

1.   What to Consider in Determining Value. By far the most popular method for determining fair value in appraisal proceedings is the "Delaware Block" method which assigns a weight to each of several values: asset value, market value, earnings value and sometimes dividend value. The weight assigned to each of these not only turns on the unique characteristics of the firm but also reflects to some extent the trustworthiness of the figure in the overall valuation process. Thus, in a leading case, a low weight (10 percent) was assigned to the firm's market value (determined by its trading price) because the shares were thinly traded due to ninety percent of the shares being held by the firm's controlling stockholder whereas the firm's earnings value (present value of estimated future earnings) and net asset value (presumed piecemeal liquidation value of the firm) were weighted 40% and 50%, respectively. *See* Piemonte v. New Boston Garden Corp., 377 Mass. 719, 387 N.E.2d 1145 (Mass. 1979). Should any percentage greater than zero be assigned to a valuation factor if, as with *Piemonte*, that valuation factor is deemed either untrustworthy (market value) or an unlikely means (liquidation) by which value will for that entity be achieved?

2.   *Relevance of Market Price and Deal Price.* In an appraisal proceeding, how much weight, if any, should the court give to the price set in the merger negotiations if those negotiations are at arms-length? An earlier Delaware Supreme Court reasoned that according such deference would "inappropriately shift the responsibility to determine fair value from the court to the private parties." *Golden Telecom, Inc. v. Global GT, LP*, 11 A.3d 214, 218 (Del. 2010).

The Delaware Supreme Court in *Dell, Inc. v. Magnetar Global Event Driven Master Fund Ltd.*, 177 A.3d 1 (2017), pointedly criticized the Court of Chancery for failing to give any weight whatever to the "deal price" in determining value in an appraisal proceeding. In its post-trial decision, the Court of Chancery determined, based solely on its own discounted cash flow analysis, that the fair value of Dell Inc., at the time of the going-private transaction, was $17.62 per share, or approximately 28% above the $13.75 per share deal price. The Delaware Supreme Court observed: "[W]e agree with the Company's core premise that, on this particular record, the trial court erred in not assigning any mathematical weight to the deal price. In fact, the record as distilled by the trial court suggests that the deal price deserved heavy, if not dispositive weight." *Id* at 42.

The Supreme Court concluded that the market-based indicators of value, including both stock price and deal price, had "substantial probative value." The Court also emphasized that Dell's sale process had "adopt[ed] many mechanisms designed to minimize conflict and ensure stockholders obtain the highest possible value," and noted that if a company's reward for adopting "best practices" in deal structuring is to be exposed to the risk of appraisal at a premium to deal price based on a discounted cash flow analysis, the incentives to adopt "best practices" would diminish.

The Delaware court has also strongly endorsed substantial weight being given to the firm's market price. *DFC Global Corp. v. Muirfield Value Partners, L.P.*, 172 A.3d 346, 372 (Del. 2017) ("When, as here, the company had no conflicts related to the transaction, a deep base of public shareholders, and highly active trading, the price at which its shares trade is informative of fair value, as that value reflects the judgments of many stockholders about the company's future prospects, based on public filings, industry information, and research conducted by equity analysts").

———

NOTES ON EXCLUSIVITY OF THE APPRAISAL REMEDY

1.   Statutory Treatment of Exclusivity. The question frequently arises whether the appraisal right is intended by the legislature as an exclusive remedy, so that the availability of appraisal precludes shareholders from seeking equitable relief such as injunction or rescission. This question does not always admit of a hard-and-fast answer.

In some cases the issue is specifically addressed by language in the appraisal statute itself. *See e.g.,* MBCA § 13.40(a)(b). In the absence of explicit statutory language, it is clear that the availability of appraisal rights normally does not preclude an attack based on any of the following grounds:

> (a) That the transaction is illegal under corporation law in that it is not authorized by the statute. See, e.g., Eisenberg v. Central Zone Property Corp., 306 N.Y. 58, 115 N.E.2d 652 (1953).

> (b) That the transaction is illegal under corporation law in that the procedural steps required to authorize the transaction were not properly taken. See, e.g., Shidler v. All Am. Life & Fin. Corp., 775 F.2d 917 (8th Cir. 1985) (required number of votes not validly cast); Johnson v. Spartanburg County Fair Ass'n, 210 S.C. 56, 41 S.E.2d 599 (1947) (same).

> (c) That shareholder approval of the transaction was improperly obtained, as through fraudulent misrepresentation or violation of the Proxy Rules. See, e.g., Nagy v. Bistricer, 770 A.2d 43 (Del. Ch. 2000); Victor Broadcasting Co. v. Mahurin, 236 Ark. 196, 365 S.W.2d 265 (1963).

2.   Impact of Appraisal Remedy on Fiduciary Duty Claims. Most jurisdictions also hold that that the availability of appraisal rights normally *precludes* a shareholder from seeking to recover on an allegation that the transaction, e.g., merger, does not provide fair compensation for the shares. See, e.g., *Osher v. Ridinger*, 589 S.E.2d 905 (N.C. App. Ct. 2004); *Adams v. United States Distributing Corp.*, 184 Va. 134, 34 S.E.2d 244 (1945).

However, there is much less clarity in the case law whether a shareholder can challenge the transaction on the basis it breaches the directors' or dominant stockholder's fiduciary duties. A few cases have suggested or implied that even in the absence of explicit statutory language, the availability of appraisal rights precludes an attack based on any ground other than illegality or *fraudulent misrepresentation*. The general rule, however, is that the mere availability of appraisal rights does not preclude shareholders from seeking injunctive relief or rescission for *fraud*, using that term in the broad sense to include unfair self-dealing by fiduciaries. This means that the availability of appraisal rights more regularly precludes a shareholder from attacking an *arm's-length* transaction on the ground of unfairness, but will usually not insulate *self-interested* transactions from an attack on that ground—although in the latter case it may lead the court to impose a somewhat less rigorous standard of fairness than would otherwise prevail. See Hideki Kanda & Saul Levmore, The Appraisal Remedy and the Goals of Corporate Law, 32 UCLA L. Rev. 429 (1985); Vorenberg,

Exclusiveness of the Dissenting Stockholder's Appraisal Right, 77 Harv.L.Rev. 1189, 1214–15 (1964).

––––––––

CAL. CORP. CODE § 1312

[See Statutory Supplement]

––––––––

MODEL BUS. CORP. ACT § 13.02(d)

[See Statutory Supplement]

––––––––

ALI, PRINCIPLES OF CORPORATE GOVERNANCE §§ 7.24, 7.25

[See Statutory Supplement]

––––––––

C. STATUTORY MERGERS

(1) CLASSICAL MERGERS

––––––––

DEL. GEN. CORP. LAW §§ 251(a)–(e), 259–261

[See Statutory Supplement]

––––––––

MODEL BUS. CORP. ACT §§ 11.01, 11.02, 11.04, 11.06, 11.07

[See Statutory Supplement]

––––––––

1. Statutory Mergers. Del.Gen.Corp.Law §§ 251(a)–(e), 259–61 and Model Bus.Corp.Act §§ 11.01, 11.03 authorize a type of transaction commonly referred to as a statutory merger. Although the term *merger* is often used by nonlawyers to describe any form of combination, to a lawyer a merger is a combination involving the fusion of two constituent corporations pursuant to a formal agreement executed with reference to specific statutory merger provisions under which one corporation (the survivor) succeeds to the assets and liabilities of the other corporation by operation of law.

While details vary from state to state, generally the first formal step in such a merger, after negotiations have been completed, is a preliminary agreement (often embodied in a "letter of intent") signed by representatives of the constituent corporations. If the merger is approved by the board and shareholders of each constituent corporation, then: (1) articles of merger are filed with the secretary of state; and (2) stock or other consideration issued by the surviving corporation is exchanged for the stock and other securities of the disappearing corporation, which is fused into the survivor and loses its identity. In general, no deeds, bills of sale, or other instruments of conveyance, are necessary to pass title from the "disappearing" or nonsurviving corporation to the survivor: By operation of law, the survivor acquires all the rights, privileges, franchises, and assets of the disappearing corporation, and assumes all of its liabilities.

2. *Consolidations.* A statutory *consolidation* is identical to a statutory merger, except for the fact that in a merger one constituent fuses into another, while in a consolidation two (or more) constituents fuse to form a new corporation. Because the consolidation technique is seldom employed, and when employed is treated almost identically to a merger, no separate attention will be given in this Chapter to statutory consolidations.

3. *Short-Form and Small-Scale Mergers.* At one time, virtually all statutory mergers required approval by a majority or two-thirds vote of the outstanding shares of each constituent, and also triggered appraisal rights for the shareholders of each constituent. Many statutes now carve out exceptions to these requirements in the case of "short-form" and "small-scale" mergers. These types of merger will be considered in the next two sections.

———

(2) SMALL-SCALE MERGERS

———

DEL. GEN. CORP. LAW § 251(f)

[See Statutory Supplement]

———

MODEL BUS. CORP. ACT § 11.04(g)

[See Statutory Supplement]

———

E. Welch, A. Turezyn II & R. Saunders, Folk on the Delaware General Corporation Law § 251.2.2.1

(5th ed. 2006).

(1) [The requirement of Del. § 251(f) that the survivor's certificate of incorporation not be amended] is designed to assure that the merger technique cannot be used to deprive stockholders of the voting rights that they would enjoy if the certificate were being amended under section 242. . . .

(2) The theory underlying the . . . 20 percent limitation on increasing the number of common shares—is that a merger that involves less than 20 percent of the survivor's shares is not such a major change as to require a stockholder vote, and is really no more than an enlargement of the business that could be achieved by other means without triggering voting rights. For instance, a corporation purchasing assets need not secure approval of its stockholders to issue already authorized shares to the seller. Nor would voting rights exist if a corporation offered its own authorized shares in exchange for the shares of another corporation and thereby gained control, or if the corporation were to sell its authorized shares for cash and then use the proceeds of the sale to purchase assets. When business needs demand that the acquisition take the form of a merger rather than a purchase of assets or shares, the premise of the statute is that the merger should not require a stockholder vote when other procedures with nearly identical economic consequences do not require a stockholder vote. Stated otherwise, . . . [§ 251(f)] puts mergers more on a parity with acquisition of assets or shares so far as the legal requirements are concerned.

DEL. GEN. CORP. LAW § 253

[See Statutory Supplement]

MODEL BUS. CORP. ACT § 11.05

[See Statutory Supplement]

---

(3) SHORT-FORM MERGERS

Corporate statutes include provisions authorizing the so-called short-form merger, under which certain parent-subsidiary mergers can be effected simply by vote of the parent's board—that is, without a vote of the parent's or the subsidiary's shareholders, without appraisal rights in the parent's shareholders, and frequently without a vote of the subsidiary's board. Most of the early short-form statutes were applicable only to mergers involving a parent and its 100%-owned subsidiary, and were probably conceived as procedural in nature, designed to simplify the mechanics of mergers. Today, however, the reach of short-form merger provisions has been substantively extended in two important ways. First, many such provisions are now applicable to mergers between parents and less-than-100%-owned subsidiaries: typically, although not invariably, the floor is set at 90 percent. Second, it has been held that the purpose of these statutes is to provide the parent corporation with a means of eliminating the minority shareholder's interest in the enterprise by issuing cash rather than stock to the minority. See e.g., Beloff v. Consolidated Edison Co., 300 N.Y. 11, 87 N.E.2d 561 (1949). To the extent this view is followed, these statutory provisions operate as *cash-out* rather than *merger* statutes. Furthermore, they are cash-out statutes that run in one direction only: the parent can force the minority to sell at any time, but the minority cannot force the parent to buy.

———

D. THE STOCK MODES AND THE DE FACTO MERGER THEORY

Having considered the traditional form of combination, mergers, we now pass to a consideration of two newer modes of corporate combination: stock-for-assets combinations and stock-for-stock combinations. In a *stock-for-assets* combination, Corporation A issues shares of its own stock to Corporation B in exchange for substantially all of B's assets. Often, in such a combination, A agrees to assume B's liabilities. In some cases, however, A may assume B's liabilities on only a selective basis. Indeed, one reason for using this mode in preference to a statutory merger may be A's desire to avoid assuming all of B's liabilities. Usually, B agrees that upon completion of the exchange it will dissolve and distribute its stock in A to its own shareholders. The major reason for this is that A does not want a large block of its stock concentrated in a single holder. Frequently, it is also agreed or understood that some or all of B's officers and directors will join A's management.

In a *stock-for-stock* combination, Corporation A issues shares of its own stock directly to the shareholders of Corporation B in exchange for an amount of B stock—normally at least a majority—sufficient to carry control. By virtue of such a combination the shareholder groups of the two corporations are combined to a substantial extent, and B becomes a subsidiary of A. Frequently B is then liquidated or merged into A, but whether or not this occurs, B's assets will be under A's control. Such a combination does not require approval by B's management, since corporate action by B is not required. Often, however, the terms of the exchange of stock are worked out beforehand by the managements of both corporations, and often too, it is agreed or understood that some or all of

B's management will stay on with B in its new role as a subsidiary, or will join Corporation A itself.

There has been a sharp division of opinion on the issue how to characterize such combinations. Take, for example, a stock-for-assets combination in which A acquires substantially all of the assets of B in exchange for A's common stock; A assumes all of B's liabilities; and B agrees to dissolve and to distribute to its shareholders the A common stock it receives.

One possible way to view such a combination is as a de facto merger. This is the position taken in *Farris v. Glen Alden Corp.* and *Rath v. Rath Packing Co., infra.* If the combination is viewed as a de facto merger, then in the normal case (that is, in the absence of some special exception) it requires a vote of both A's shareholders and B's shareholders, and triggers appraisal rights in both A's shareholders and B's shareholders.

Alternatively, the transaction could be characterized as a purchase by A and a sale of substantially all assets by B. That is the position taken in *Hariton v. Arco Electronics Corp.* and *Heilbrunn v. Sun Packing Co., infra.* Under traditional corporate statutes, a purchase does not require shareholder approval and does not trigger appraisal rights. Therefore, if the combination is treated as a purchase by A, it neither requires a vote of A's shareholders nor triggers appraisal rights for those shareholders— although it would have required a shareholder vote, and triggered appraisal rights, if it had been characterized as a merger.

Now turn to B's shareholders. Under the corporate statutes, a sale of substantially all assets, unlike a purchase, does require shareholder approval. Therefore, the combination will require the approval of B's shareholders. Furthermore, most statutes provide that if a corporation sells substantially all of its assets, the transaction triggers appraisal rights in the corporation's shareholders. Therefore, B's shareholders, unlike A's shareholders, will usually have appraisal rights. However, under some statutes, most notably the Delaware statute, a sale of substantially all assets does not trigger appraisal rights. Under such statutes, if a stock-for-assets combination is treated as a purchase by A and a sale by B, rather than as a merger of A and B, B's shareholders will not have appraisal rights, although they would have had appraisal rights if the transaction had been characterized as a merger.

———

Hariton v. Arco Electronics, Inc.

Supreme Court of Delaware, 1963.
41 Del.Ch. 74, 188 A.2d 123.

■ SOUTHERLAND, CHIEF JUSTICE: This case involves a sale of assets under § 271 of the corporation law, 8 Del.C. It presents for decision the question presented, but not decided, in Heilbrunn v. Sun Chemical Corporation, 38 Del.Ch. 321, 150 A.2d 755. It may be stated as follows:

A sale of assets is effected under § 271 in consideration of shares of stock of the purchasing corporation. The agreement of sale embodies also a plan to dissolve the selling corporation and distribute the shares so received to the stockholders of the seller, so as to accomplish the same result as would be accomplished by a merger of the seller into the purchaser. Is the sale legal?

The facts are these:

The defendant Arco and Loral Electronics Corporation, a New York corporation, are both engaged, in somewhat different forms, in the electronic equipment business. In the summer of 1961 they negotiated for an amalgamation of the companies. As of October 27, 1961, they entered into a "Reorganization Agreement and Plan." The provisions of this Plan pertinent here are in substance as follows:

1.   Arco agrees to sell all its assets to Loral in consideration (*inter alia*) of the issuance to it of 283,000 shares of Loral.

2.   Arco agrees to call a stockholders meeting for the purpose of approving the Plan and the voluntary dissolution.

3.   Arco agrees to distribute to its stockholders all the Loral shares received by it as a part of the complete liquidation of Arco.*

At the Arco meeting all the stockholders voting (about 80%) approved the Plan. It was thereafter consummated.

Plaintiff, a stockholder who did not vote at the meeting, sued to enjoin the consummation of the Plan on the grounds (1) that it was illegal, and (2) that it was unfair. The second ground was abandoned. Affidavits and documentary evidence were filed, and defendant moved for summary judgment and dismissal of the complaint. The Vice Chancellor granted the motion and plaintiff appeals.

The question before us we have stated above. Plaintiff's argument that the sale is illegal runs as follows:

The several steps taken here accomplish the same result as a merger of Arco into Loral. In a "true" sale of assets, the stockholder of the seller retains the right to elect whether the selling company shall continue as a holding company. Moreover, the stockholder of the selling company is forced to accept an investment in a new enterprise without the right of appraisal granted under the merger statute. § 271 cannot therefore be legally combined with a dissolution proceeding under § 275 and a consequent distribution of the purchaser's stock. Such a proceeding is a misuse of the power granted under § 271, and a *de facto* merger results.

---

*   According to the Vice Chancellor's opinion below, 40 Del.Ch. 326, 182 A.2d 22 (1962), the agreement also provided that Loral would assume and pay all of Arco's debts and liabilities, and that after the closing date Arco would not engage in any business or activity except as might be required to complete the liquidation and dissolution of Arco. (Footnote by ed.)

The foregoing is a brief summary of plaintiff's contention.

Plaintiff's contention that this sale has achieved the same result as a merger is plainly correct. The same contention was made to us in Heilbrunn v. Sun Chemical Corporation, 38 Del.Ch. 321, 150 A.2d 755. Accepting it as correct, we noted that this result is made possible by the overlapping scope of the merger statute and section 271, mentioned in Sterling v. Mayflower Hotel Corporation, 33 Del.Ch. 293, 93 A.2d 107, 38 A.L.R.2d 425. We also adverted to the increased use, in connection with corporate reorganization plans, of § 271 instead of the merger statute. Further, we observed that no Delaware case has held such procedure to be improper, and that two cases appear to assume its legality. Finch v. Warrior Cement Corporation, 16 Del.Ch. 44, 141 A. 54, and Argenbright v. Phoenix Finance Co., 21 Del.Ch. 288, 187 A. 124. But we were not required in the *Heilbrunn* case to decide the point.

We now hold that the reorganization here accomplished through § 271 and a mandatory plan of dissolution and distribution is legal. This is so because the sale-of-assets statute and the merger statute are independent of each other. They are, so to speak, of equal dignity, and the framers of a reorganization plan may resort to either type of corporate mechanics to achieve the desired end. This is not an anomalous result in our corporation law. As the Vice Chancellor pointed out, the elimination of accrued dividends, though forbidden under a charter amendment (Keller v. Wilson Co., 21 Del.Ch. 391, 190 A. 115) may be accomplished by a merger. Federal United Corporation v. Havender, 24 Del.Ch. 318, 11 A.2d 331.

In Langfelder v. Universal Laboratories, D.C., 68 F.Supp. 209, Judge Leahy commented upon "the general theory of the Delaware Corporation Law that action taken pursuant to the authority of the various sections of that law constitute acts of independent legal significance and their validity is not dependent on other sections of the Act." 68 F.Supp. 211, footnote.

In support of his contentions of a *de facto* merger plaintiff cites Finch v. Warrior Cement Corporation, 16 Del.Ch. 44, 141 A. 54, and Drug Inc. v. Hunt, 5 W.W.Harr. 339, 35 Del. 339, 168 A. 87. They are patently inapplicable. Each involved a disregard of the statutory provisions governing sales of assets. Here it is admitted that the provisions of the statute were fully complied with.

Plaintiff concedes, as we read his brief, that if the several steps taken in this case had been taken separately they would have been legal. That is, he concedes that a sale of assets, followed by a separate proceeding to dissolve and distribute, would be legal, even though the same result would follow. This concession exposes the weakness of his contention. To attempt to make any such distinction between sales under § 271 would be to create uncertainty in the law and invite litigation.

We are in accord with the Vice Chancellor's ruling, and the judgment below is affirmed.

———

Farris v. Glen Alden Corp.

Supreme Court of Pennsylvania, 1958.
393 Pa. 427, 143 A.2d 25.

■ COHEN, JUSTICE. We are required to determine on this appeal whether, as a result of a Reorganization Agreement executed by the officers of Glen Alden Corporation and List Industries Corporation, and approved by the shareholders of the former company, the rights and remedies of a dissenting shareholder accrue to the plaintiff.

Glen Alden is a Pennsylvania corporation engaged principally in the mining of anthracite coal and lately in the manufacture of air conditioning units and fire-fighting equipment. In recent years the company's operating revenue has declined substantially, and in fact, its coal operations have resulted in tax loss carryovers of approximately $14,000,000. In October 1957, List, a Delaware holding company owning interests in motion picture theaters, textile companies and real estate, and to a lesser extent, in oil and gas operations, warehouses and aluminum piston manufacturing, purchased through a wholly owned subsidiary 38.5% of Glen Alden's outstanding stock.[1] This acquisition enabled List to place three of its directors on the Glen Alden board.

On March 20, 1958, the two corporations entered into a reorganization agreement, subject to stockholder approval, which contemplated the following actions:

1.   Glen Alden is to acquire all of the assets of List, excepting a small amount of cash reserved for the payment of List's expenses in connection with the transaction. These assets include over $8,000,000 in cash held chiefly in the treasuries of List's wholly owned subsidiaries.

2.   In consideration of the transfer, Glen Alden is to issue 3,621,703 shares of stock to List. List in turn is to distribute the stock to its shareholders at a ratio of five shares of Glen Alden stock for each six shares of List stock. In order to accomplish the necessary distribution, Glen Alden is to increase the authorized number of its shares of capital stock from 2,500,000 shares to 7,500,000 shares without according preemptive rights to the present shareholders upon the issuance of any such shares.

3.   Further, Glen Alden is to assume all of List's liabilities including a $5,000,000 note incurred by List in order to purchase Glen Alden stock in 1957, outstanding stock options, incentive stock options plans, and pension obligations.

---

[1]   Of the purchase price of $8,719,109, $5,000,000 was borrowed.

4. Glen Alden is to change its corporate name from Glen Alden Corporation to List Alden Corporation.

5. The present directors of both corporations are to become directors of List Alden.

6. List is to be dissolved and List Alden is to then carry on the operations of both former corporations.

Two days after the agreement was executed notice of the annual meeting of Glen Alden to be held on April 11, 1958, was mailed to the shareholders together with a proxy statement analyzing the reorganization agreement and recommending its approval as well as approval of certain amendments to Glen Alden's articles of incorporation and bylaws necessary to implement the agreement. At this meeting the holders of a majority of the outstanding shares (not including those owned by List), voted in favor of a resolution approving the reorganization agreement.

On the day of the shareholders' meeting, plaintiff, a shareholder of Glen Alden, filed a complaint in equity against the corporation and its officers seeking to enjoin them temporarily until final hearing, and perpetually thereafter, from executing and carrying out the agreement.

The gravamen of the complaint was that the notice of the annual shareholders' meeting did not conform to the requirements of the Business Corporation Law, 15 P.S. § 2852–1 et seq., in three respects: (1) It did not give notice to the shareholders that the true intent and purpose of the meeting was to effect a merger or consolidation of Glen Alden and List; (2) It failed to give notice to the shareholders of their right to dissent to the plan of merger or consolidation and claim fair value for their shares, and (3) It did not contain copies of the text of certain sections of the Business Corporation Law as required.[3]

By reason of these omissions, plaintiff contended that the approval of the reorganization agreement by the shareholders at the annual meeting was invalid and unless the carrying out of the plan were enjoined, he would suffer irreparable loss by being deprived of substantial property rights.

The defendants answered admitting the material allegations of fact in the complaint but denying that they gave rise to a cause of action because the transaction complained of was a purchase of corporate assets as to which shareholders had no rights of dissent or appraisal. For these reasons the defendants then moved for judgment on the pleadings.[4]

---

[3] The proxy statement included the following declaration: Appraisal Rights.

"In the opinion of counsel, the shareholders of neither Glen Alden nor List Industries will have any rights of appraisal or similar rights of dissenters with respect to any matter to be acted upon at their respective meetings."

[4] Counsel for the defendants concedes that if the corporation is required to pay the dissenting shareholders the appraised fair value of their shares, the resultant drain of cash would prevent Glen Alden from carrying out the agreement. On the other hand, plaintiff contends that if the shareholders had been told of their rights as dissenters, rather than

The court below concluded that the reorganization agreement entered into between the two corporations was a plan for a *de facto* merger, and that therefore the failure of the notice of the annual meeting to conform to the pertinent requirements of the merger provisions of the Business Corporation Law rendered the notice defective and all proceedings in furtherance of the agreement void. Wherefore, the court entered a final decree denying defendants' motion for judgment on the pleadings, entering judgment upon plaintiff's complaint and granting the injunctive relief therein sought. This appeal followed.

When use of the corporate form of business organization first became widespread, it was relatively easy for courts to define a "merger" or a "sale of assets" and to label a particular transaction as one or the other. See, e.g., 15 Fletcher, Corporations §§ 7040–7045 (rev. vol. 1938); In re Buist's Estate, 1929, 297 Pa. 537, 541, 147 A. 606; Koehler v. St. Mary's Brewing Co., 1910, 228 Pa. 648, 653–654, 77 A. 1016. But prompted by the desire to avoid the impact of adverse, and to obtain the benefits of favorable, government regulations, particularly federal tax laws, new accounting and legal techniques were developed by lawyers and accountants which interwove the elements characteristic of each, thereby creating hybrid forms of corporate amalgamation. Thus, it is no longer helpful to consider an individual transaction in the abstract and solely by reference to the various elements therein determine whether it is a "merger" or a "sale". Instead, to determine properly the nature of a corporate transaction, we must refer not only to all the provisions of the agreement, but also to the consequences of the transaction and to the purposes of the provisions of the corporation law said to be applicable. We shall apply this principle to the instant case.

Section 908, subd. A of the Pennsylvania Business Corporation Law provides: "If any shareholder of a domestic corporation which becomes a party to a plan of merger or consolidation shall object to such plan of merger or consolidation . . . such shareholder shall be entitled to . . . [the fair value of his shares upon surrender of the share certificate or certificates representing his shares]." Act of May 5, 1933, P.L. 364, as amended, 15 P.S. §§ 2852–908, subd. A.[5]

This provision had its origin in the early decision of this Court in Lauman v. Lebanon Valley R.R. Co., 1858, 30 Pa. 42. There a shareholder who objected to the consolidation of his company with another was held to have a right in the absence of statute to treat the consolidation as a

---

specifically advised that they had no such rights, the resolution approving the reorganization agreement would have been defeated.

  [5] Furthermore, section 902, subd. B provides that notice of the proposed merger and of the right to dissent thereto must be given the shareholders. "There shall be included in, or enclosed with . . . notice [of meeting of shareholders to vote on plan of merger] a copy or a summary of the plan of merger or plan of consolidation, as the case may be, and . . . a copy of subsection A of section 908 and of subsections B, C and D of section 515 of this act." Act of May 5, 1933, P.L. 364, § 902, subd. B, as amended, 15 §§ P.S. 2852–902, subd. B.

dissolution of his company and to receive the value of his shares upon their surrender.

The rationale of the Lauman case, and of the present section of the Business Corporation Law based thereon, is that when a corporation combines with another so as to lose its essential nature and alter the original fundamental relationships of the shareholders among themselves and to the corporation, a shareholder who does not wish to continue his membership therein may treat his membership in the original corporation as terminated and have the value of his shares paid to him. See Lauman v. Lebanon Valley R.R. Co., supra, 30 Pa. at pages 46–47. See also Bloch v. Baldwin Locomotive Works, C.P., Del.1950, 75 Pa.Dist. Co.R. 24, 35–38.

Does the combination outlined in the present "reorganization" agreement so fundamentally change the corporate character of Glen Alden and the interest of the plaintiff as a shareholder therein, that to refuse him the rights and remedies of a dissenting shareholder would in reality force him to give up his stock in one corporation and against his will accept shares in another? If so, the combination is a merger within the meaning of section 908, subd. A of the corporation law. See Bloch v. Baldwin Locomotive Works, supra. Cf. Marks v. Autocar Co., D.C.E.D.Pa.1954, 153 F.Supp. 768. See also Troupiansky v. Henry Disston & Sons, D.C.E.D.Pa.1957, 151 F.Supp. 609.

If the reorganization agreement were consummated plaintiff would find that the "List Alden" resulting from the amalgamation would be quite a different corporation than the "Glen Alden" in which he is now a shareholder. Instead of continuing primarily as a coal mining company, Glen Alden would be transformed, after amendment of its articles of incorporation, into a diversified holding company whose interests would range from motion picture theaters to textile companies. Plaintiff would find himself a member of a company with assets of $169,000,000 and a long-term debt of $38,000,000 in lieu of a company one-half that size and with but one-seventh the long-term debt.

While the administration of the operations, and properties of Glen Alden as well as List would be in the hands of management common to both companies, since all executives of List would be retained in List Alden, the control of Glen Alden would pass to the directors of List; for List would hold eleven of the seventeen directorships on the new board of directors.

As an aftermath of the transaction plaintiff's proportionate interest in Glen Alden would have been reduced to only two-fifths of what it presently is because of the issuance of an additional 3,621,703 shares to List which would not be subject to pre-emptive rights. In fact, ownership of Glen Alden would pass to the stockholders of List who would hold 76.5% of the outstanding shares as compared with but 23.5% retained by the present Glen Alden shareholders.

Perhaps the most important consequence to the plaintiff, if he were denied the right to have his shares redeemed at their fair value, would be the serious financial loss suffered upon consummation of the agreement. While the present book value of his stock is $38 a share after combination it would be worth only $21 a share. In contrast, the shareholders of List who presently hold stock with a total book value of $33,000,000 or $7.50 a share, would receive stock with a book value of $76,000,000 or $21 a share.

Under these circumstances it may well be said that if the proposed combination is allowed to take place without right of dissent, plaintiff would have his stock in Glen Alden taken away from him and the stock of a new company thrust upon him in its place. He would be projected against his will into a new enterprise under terms not of his own choosing. It was to protect dissident shareholders against just such a result that this Court one hundred years ago in the Lauman case, and the legislature thereafter in section 908, subd. A, granted the right of dissent. And it is to accord that protection to the plaintiff that we conclude that the combination proposed in the case at hand is a merger within the intendment of section 908, subd. A.

Nevertheless, defendants contend that the 1957 amendments to sections 311 and 908 of the corporation law preclude us from reaching this result and require the entry of judgment in their favor. Subsection F of section 311 dealing with the voluntary transfer of corporate assets provides: "The shareholders of a business corporation which acquires by sale, lease or exchange all or substantially all of the property of another corporation by the issuance of stock, securities or otherwise shall not be entitled to the rights and remedies of dissenting shareholders. . . . " Act of July 11, 1957, P.L. 711, § 1, 15 P.S. §§ 2852–311, subd. F.

And the amendment to section 908 reads as follows: "The right of dissenting shareholders . . . shall not apply to the purchase by a corporation of assets whether or not the consideration therefore be money or property, real or personal, including shares of bonds or other evidences of indebtedness of such corporation. The shareholders of such corporation shall have no right to dissent from any such purchase." Act of July 11, 1957, P.L. 711, § 1, 15 P.S. §§ 2852–908, subd. C.

Defendants view these amendments as abridging the right of shareholders to dissent to a transaction between two corporations which involves a transfer of assets for a consideration even though the transfer has all the legal incidents of a merger. They claim that only if the merger is accomplished in accordance with the prescribed statutory procedure does the right of dissent accrue. In support of this position they cite to us the comment on the amendments by the Committee on Corporation Law of the Pennsylvania Bar Association, the committee which originally drafted these provisions. The comment states that the provisions were intended to overrule cases which granted shareholders the right to dissent to a sale of assets when accompanied by the legal incidents of a

merger. See 61 Ann.Rep.Pa.Bar Ass'n. 277, 284 (1957). Whatever may
have been the intent of the *committee,* there is no evidence to indicate
that the *legislature* intended the 1957 amendments to have the effect
contended for. But furthermore, the language of these two provisions
does not support the opinion of the committee and is inept to achieve any
such purpose. The amendments of 1957 do not provide that a transaction
between two corporations which has the effect of a merger but which
includes a transfer of assets for consideration is to be exempt from the
protective provisions of sections 908, subd. A and 515. They provide only
that the shareholders of a corporation which acquires the property or
purchases the assets of another corporation, *without more,* are not
entitled to the right to dissent from the transaction. So, as in the present
case, when as part of a transaction between two corporations, one
corporation dissolves, its liabilities are assumed by the survivor, its
executives and directors take over the management and control of the
survivor, and, as consideration for the transfer, its stockholders acquire
a majority of the shares of stock of the survivor, then the transaction is
no longer simply a purchase of assets or acquisition of property to which
sections 311, subd. F and 908, subd. C apply, but a merger governed by
section 908, subd. A of the corporation law. To divest shareholders of
their right of dissent under such circumstances would require express
language which is absent from the 1957 amendments.

Even were we to assume that the combination provided for in the
reorganization agreement is a "sale of assets" to which section 908, subd.
A does not apply, it would avail the defendants nothing; we will not blind
our eyes to the realities of the transaction. Despite the designation of the
parties and the form employed, Glen Alden does not in fact acquire List,
rather, List acquires Glen Alden, cf. Metropolitan Edison Co. v.
Commissioner, 3 Cir., 1938, 98 F.2d 807, affirmed sub nom., Helvering v.
Metropolitan Edison Co., 1939, 306 U.S. 522, 59 S.Ct. 634, 83 L.Ed. 957,
and under section 311, subd. D[8] the right of dissent would remain with
the shareholders of Glen Alden.

We hold that the combination contemplated by the reorganization
agreement, although consummated by contract rather than in
accordance with the statutory procedure, is a merger within the
protective purview of sections 908, subd. A and 515 of the corporation
law. The shareholders of Glen Alden should have been notified
accordingly and advised of their statutory rights of dissent and appraisal.
The failure of the corporate officers to take these steps renders the
stockholder approval of the agreement at the 1958 shareholders' meeting

---

[8] "If any shareholder of a business corporation which sells, leases or exchanges all or
substantially all of its property and assets otherwise than (1) in the usual and regular course of
its business, (2) for the purpose of relocating its business, or (3) in connection with its dissolution
and liquidation, shall object to such sale, lease or exchange and comply with the provisions of
section 515 of this act, such shareholder shall be entitled to the rights and remedies of dissenting
shareholders as therein provided." . . .

invalid. The lower court did not err in enjoining the officers and directors of Glen Alden from carrying out this agreement.

Decree affirmed at appellants' costs.

————

NOTES ON FARRIS

1. Reasons for the Form in Which the Transaction Was Cast. It is clear that a major reason for structuring the transaction in *Farris* as a stock-for-assets combination, rather than as a statutory merger, was to avoid conferring appraisal rights on the Glen Alden shareholders. But given that reason for using the stock-for-assets mode, why did the parties also use an upside-down format, in which the smaller corporation nominally purchased the larger corporation's assets? Why didn't the parties arrange the transaction in a more natural way, by having the larger corporation, List, issue shares for assets of the smaller corporation, Glen Alden?

Again, one reason had to do with appraisal rights. List was a Delaware corporation. Under Delaware law, in a purchase and sale of assets, neither the purchaser's shareholders nor the seller's shareholders had appraisal rights. Under Pennsylvania law, however, a seller's shareholders did have appraisal rights, while a purchaser's did not—or so counsel thought. Therefore, by making List, a Delaware corporation, the nominal seller and Glen Alden, a Pennsylvania corporation, the nominal purchaser, the parties hoped to avoid giving appraisal rights to the shareholders of either corporation.

A second reason for the upside-down format may have been a desire to keep alive Glen Alden's tax loss carryover. While the rules governing the survival of such carryovers were complex, in general survival was more likely if the entity of the carryover corporation was left intact.

A third reason is given in the Supplemental Brief for Appellee: "In answer to the question of Mr. Justice Bell as to why List did not purchase the assets of Glen Alden, Mr. Littleton answered that the one percent Pennsylvania realty tax on the transfer of [the huge coal-mining] holdings of Glen Alden would make such a sale prohibitive."

2. Post-Farris Developments. Following the decision in *Farris v. Glen Alden*, the two corporations were combined pursuant to a statutory merger. Probably for some of the reasons just given, Glen Alden was the surviving corporation. The List shareholders received one Glen Alden share for each List share, and the Glen Alden shareholders ended up with five Glen Alden shares for each four they had previously held. New York Times, March 7, 1959; Moody's Industrial Manual 954 (1972).

The Pennsylvania statute now expressly rejects the reasoning in *Farris* (and suggestion in note 7 in *Terry v. Penn Central Corporation, infra*) that dissenters rights arise in the acquiring company shareholders by virtue of the fact that the acquisition has been structured so that the "mouse swallows the lion." *See* 15 Pa. Consol. Statutes Ann. § 1571(b)(3), Amended Official Comment (West Supp. 2010).

NEW YORK STOCK EXCHANGE, LISTED
COMPANY MANUAL § 312.00

[See Statutory Supplement]

CAL. CORP. CODE §§ 152, 160, 168, 181, 187,
194.5, 1001, 1101, 1200, 1201, 1300

[See Statutory Supplement]

MODEL BUS. CORP. ACT § 6.21(f)

[See Statutory Supplement]

NOTES ON THE SURVIVOR'S LIABILITY TO THE TRANSFEROR'S CREDITORS

1. Traditional Corporate Law Orientation. Stock-for-assets transactions are often used in preference to a statutory merger or a stock-for-stock combination because of a desire to avoid assuming the acquired corporation's liabilities—particularly undisclosed or contingent liabilities. In a statutory merger, the surviving corporation becomes liable by operation of law for all of the transferor's obligations, including those that are contingent or undisclosed. In a stock-for-stock combination, the survivor does not become directly liable for the debts of the acquired corporation, although the acquired corporation is now a subsidiary of the survivor, and carries its obligations along.

In contrast, in a stock-for-assets combination, the survivor may remain free of those liabilities it does not expressly assume, on the theory that it merely engaged in a purchase. Frequently, however, this theory is not accepted by the courts. The following formulation, or one very much like it, is found in a great number of cases:

> The general rule is that "a mere sale of corporate property by one company to another does not make the purchaser liable for the liabilities of the seller not assumed by it. . . . " There are, however, certain exceptions to this rule. Liability for obligations of a selling corporation may be imposed on the purchasing corporation when (1) the purchaser expressly or impliedly agrees to assume such obligations; (2) the transaction amounts to a consolidation or merger of the selling corporation with or into the purchasing corporation; (3) the purchasing corporation is merely a continuation of the selling corporation; or (4) the transaction is entered into fraudulently to escape liability for such obligations.

See James D. Cox & Thomas L. Hazen, 4 Treatise On The Law Of Corporations § 22.8 (3rd Ed. 2010).

Where the second or third exceptions apply, many (though not all) cases make the survivor in a typical stock-for-assets transaction liable to the transferor's shareholders under a de facto merger theory.

2. *Successor Liability Through the Product Liability Lens.* When the claim against the successor corporation arises from a defective product, a significant number, albeit a minority, of the states reject the formal corporate standards for successor liability and instead are guided by the policies underlying product liability claims. The leading case for this approach involved Herbert Ray who was seriously injured by a defective ladder manufactured by Alad Corporation (Alad I); prior to Ray's injury, Alad I sold for cash its assets to the defendant, Alad II, who continued to manufacture the same line of ladders under the "Alad" name, using the same equipment, designs, and personnel, and soliciting Alad I's customers through the same sales representatives with no outward indication of any change in the ownership of the business.

> [The] insulation from its predecessor's liabilities of a corporation acquiring business assets has the undoubted advantage of promoting the free availability and transferability of capital. However, this advantage is outweighed under the narrow circumstances here presented by considerations favoring continued protection for injured users of defective products. . . . [T]hese considerations include (1) the nonavailability to plaintiff of any adequate remedy against Alad I as a result of Alad I's liquidation prior to plaintiff's injury, (2) the availability to Alad II of the knowledge necessary for gauging the risks of injury from previously manufactured ladders together with the opportunity to provide for meeting the cost arising from those risks by spreading it among current purchasers of the product line and (3) the fact that the good will transferred to and enjoyed by Alad II could not have been enjoyed by Alad I without the burden of liability for defects in ladders sold under its aegis. Accordingly we have concluded that the instant claim of strict tort liability presents an exception to the general rule against imposition upon a successor corporation of its predecessor's liabilities and that the summary judgment should be reversed.

Ray v. Alad Corp., 19 Cal.3d 22, 25, 560 P.2d 3, 5, 136 Cal.Rptr. 574, 576 (1977). See also, Lefever v. K.P. Hovnanian Enterprises, Inc., 160 N.J. 307, 734 A.2d 290 (1999) (imposing liability on cash purchaser in bankruptcy); Foster v. Cone-Blanchard Mach. Co., 597 N.W.2d 506 (Mich. 1999); Roper Elec. Co. v. Quality Castings, Inc., 60 S.W.3d 708 (Mo. Ct. App. 2001); Michael Carter, Successor Liability Under CERCLA: It's Time To Fully Embrace State Law, 156 U. Pa. L. Rev. 767 (2008); Wendy B. Davis, Defacto Merger, Federal Common Law and Erie: Constitutional Issues In Successor Liability, 2008 Colum. Bus. L. Rev. 529; Comment, Successor Liability, Mass Tort, and Mandatory-Litigation Class Action, 118 Harv. L. Rev. 2357 (2005).

———

E. TRIANGULAR MERGERS AND SHARE EXCHANGES

NOTES ON TRIANGULAR MERGERS, SHARE EXCHANGES, ENTITY CONVERSIONS

1. Triangular Mergers. A statutory merger is often preferable to either a stock-for-assets or a stock-for-stock combination. To begin with, the Internal Revenue Code provides greater liberality as to the type of consideration that can be given in an A reorganization (a statutory merger) than in a B reorganization (a stock-for-stock combination) or a C reorganization (a stock-for-assets combination). See Section 1D, supra. Furthermore, a stock-for-assets combination may involve sales taxes, while a statutory merger ordinarily will not. A stock-for-assets combination also ordinarily involves a great amount of paperwork, in the form of deeds and assignments of the transferor's property and (in some cases) notice to creditors in compliance with the applicable bulk sales law. In contrast, in a statutory merger the survivor succeeds to the transferor's assets by operation of law, so that neither individual documents of title nor compliance with the bulk sales law is ordinarily required.

On the other hand, in a statutory merger the surviving corporation assumes the disappearing corporation's liabilities by operation of law. Furthermore, a statutory merger normally triggers voting and appraisal rights in the shareholders of both constituents. In contrast, in a stock-for-stock or stock-for-assets combination the acquiring corporation does not necessarily assume the transferor corporation's liabilities. Moreover, these forms of combination may require a vote only by the shareholders of one constituent, and may not trigger appraisal rights. Accordingly, the management of a corporation that proposes to engage in a corporate combination may prefer to use the statutory-merger form except for the voting and appraisal rights entailed by that form. The triangular merger is a technique designed to give management the best of both possible worlds: the form of a merger, but without necessarily assuming the liabilities of the disappearing corporation and without voting or appraisal rights in the survivor's shareholders.

2. "Forward" Triangular Merger. A conventional (or "forward") triangular merger works this way: Assume that Corporations S and T want to engage in a merger in which S will be the survivor and T's shareholders will end up with 100,000 shares of S. In a normal merger this would be accomplished by having S issue 100,000 shares of its own stock to T's shareholders. In a conventional triangular merger, however, S instead begins by creating a new subsidiary, S/Sub, and then transfers 100,000 shares of its own stock to S/Sub in exchange for all of S/Sub's stock. S/Sub and T then engage in a statutory merger, but instead of issuing its *own* stock to T's shareholders, S/Sub issues its 100,000 shares of S stock. The net result is that T's business is now owned by S's wholly owned subsidiary (rather than by S itself, as in a normal merger), and T's shareholders now own

100,000 shares of S stock. By use of this technique, S may therefore achieve the advantages of a statutory merger while insulating itself from direct responsibility for T's liabilities.[2] The final step is S using the short-form merger provision to merge S/Sub into S so that the assets and liabilities formerly held by T are now among the assets and liabilities of S.

Such a transaction would probably not have been permissible under the traditional statutory merger provisions, because those provisions usually contemplated that the surviving corporation would issue its *own* shares or securities. However, the merger statutes of most or all jurisdictions have now been amended to permit the survivor to issue shares or securities of *any* corporation. (*See, e.g.,* Del. § 251(b)(4).) In tandem with this development, the Internal Revenue Code was amended by adding § 368(a)(2)(D), which permits a conventional triangular merger to qualify as a tax-free A reorganization, if (i) substantially all of T's properties are acquired by S/Sub; (ii) the merger would have qualified as an A reorganization if T had merged directly into S; and (iii) no stock of S/Sub is used in the transaction.

3.   *"Reverse" Triangular Merger.* A *reverse* triangular merger proceeds like a conventional triangular merger, except that instead of merging T into S/Sub, S/Sub is merged into T, i.e., T not S/Sub survives. The merger agreement provides that all previously outstanding T shares are automatically converted into the 100,000 shares of S held by S/Sub, and that all shares in S/Sub (which are held by S) are automatically converted into shares in T. When all the shooting is over, therefore, S/Sub will have disappeared, T will be a wholly owned subsidiary of S, and T's shareholders will own 100,000 shares of S stock. By use of this technique S may therefore achieve the advantages of a statutory merger while preserving T's legal status, which could be important where T has valuable but non-assignable rights under contracts, leases, licenses, or franchises. Under IRC § 368(a)(2)(E), a reverse triangular merger will qualify as a tax-free A reorganization, if (i) T ends up with substantially all of the properties of both S/Sub and T, and (ii) S voting stock is exchanged for at least 80% of T's voting and nonvoting stock. (The balance of T's stock can be acquired for other types of consideration.)

An important problem raised by triangular mergers is that they may allow subversion of shareholder voting and appraisal rights. To avoid this result, it can be argued that despite the form of such transactions, voting and appraisal rights on the survivor's side are vested not in S, as the sole shareholder of S/Sub, but pass through to S's shareholders. This argument was rejected in Terry v. Penn Central Corp., supra, but that case was at least partly controlled by the unusual Pennsylvania legislative history. Ideally, this problem should be dealt with by statute. For example, consider the role of MBCA § 6.21(f) requiring shareholder vote if shares are issued for other than cash and the number of shares so issued are more than 20 percent of the voting power prior to such issuance. The Model Acts provision parallels listing requirements of the New York Stock Exchange and NASDAQ. *See also* Cal. Corp. Code §§ 1200(d), 1201 (a merger reorganization must be

---

[2]   However, a court might impose these liabilities on S under the de facto merger doctrine, on the theory that in effect S itself is a constituent to the merger.

approved by the shareholders of a corporation which is "in control of any constituent . . . corporation . . . and whose equity securities are issued or transferred in the reorganization").

4. Share Exchanges. Another new mode of combination is known as a share exchange. In a share exchange, the shareholders of the acquired corporation vote on whether to exchange their shares for designated consideration from the acquiring corporation. If the proposed transaction is approved by a majority of that corporation's outstanding shares, all of the shares must be surrendered—including those of nonconsenting shareholders (unless they exercise appraisal rights).

5. Entity Conversions. As an entity grows, it usually is both practical and necessary to reorganize itself into a different entity. Thus, a business that began informally as a partnership may evolve into a limited liability partnership or LLC and from there convert into a corporation. It could, of course, skip any intermediate step to becoming a corporation and it is not unheard of for a corporation to become some form of unincorporated entity, e.g., a limited partnership. Modern statutes have made the process of entity conversion considerably more efficient. *See generally* Robert C. Art, Conversion and Merger of Disparate Business Entities, 76 Wash. L. Rev. 349 (2001) (discussing the earlier difficulties of reorganizing into a new entity before modern statutes authorized conversions).

All entity conversion statutes have three core requirements: 1) the plan for conversion, 2) approval of the plan, and 3) filing specified documents with the state. The plan (referred to in the statutes as either the plan of conversion or the certificate of conversion) is generally brief, including the date the conversion will occur, the name and type of entity to be converted, and the manner of converting interests in the former entity. Approvals are in accordance with the requirements that apply to the original entity, e.g., partners of the partnership and members of an LLC as provided in the operating agreement. The final step is filing with the secretary of state the plan of conversion/certificate of conversion as well as the document needed to form the new entity, e.g., the articles of organization for an LLC or articles of incorporation for a corporation.

Most states have some version of the Model Business Corporation Act §§ 9.50 and 9.51 that straightforwardly sets forth the above described steps for converting various unincorporated business forms into corporate form and vice versa. Even further simplification is provided by the recently promulgated Model Entity Transaction Act (META) that is now adopted in a handful of states. While Delaware follows the same overall approach as outlined above, it does so by providing separate statutes detailing the conversion process into the desired entity. Thus, in Delaware conversion into a limited partnership is guided by 6 Del. C. § 15–1001, into a limited liability company by 6 Del. C. § 18–200 et. seq., and into a corporation by 8 Del. C. § 265.

F. FREEZEOUTS

NOTES ON FREEZEOUT TECHNIQUES

A freezeout is a corporate transaction whose principal purpose is to reconstitute the corporation's ownership by eliminating the equity interest of minority shareholders. Freezeouts can take several forms.

1. Dissolution Freezeouts. Assume that S (who may be an individual, a group, or a corporation) owns 70% of C Corporation, and wishes to eliminate C's minority shareholders. In a dissolution freezeout, S causes C to dissolve under a plan of dissolution which provides that C's productive assets will be distributed to S (or to an entity S controls), while cash or notes will be distributed to C's minority shareholders. This technique has been held illegal in a number of cases, most of which stress that such a plan of dissolution violates a corporate norm of equal treatment among all shareholders of the same class. See e.g., In re San Joaquin Light & Power Corp., 52 Cal.App.2d 814, 127 P.2d 29 (1942).

2. Sale-of-Assets Freezeouts. In a sale-of-assets freezeout, C's controlling shareholder, S, organizes a new corporation, T, all of whose stock S owns. S then causes C to sell its assets to T for cash or notes. Result: S owns C's business through T, while the equity interest of C's minority shareholders in C's business is involuntarily terminated. (C is then normally dissolved, although a freezeout will be effected even without dissolution.) Such a procedure has been disapproved in several cases. See, e.g., Theis v. Spokane Falls Gaslight Co., 34 Wash. 23, 74 P. 1004 (1904).

3. Debt or Redeemable-Preferred Mergers. A debt or redeemable-preferred merger begins like a sale-of-assets freezeout, with the organization by S of a new corporation, T. However, instead of causing C to transfer its assets to T, S causes C to merge into T; and instead of issuing common stock in the merger, T issues either short-term debentures or redeemable preferred stock. Accordingly, the interest of C's minority shareholders in T either terminates automatically after a period of years (in the case of debentures) or is terminable at T's election (in the case of redeemable preferred).

4. Cashout Mergers. Modern freezeouts commonly employ still a fourth technique. Most states now allow the survivor in any type of merger to issue cash as well as, or instead of, stock or other securities. This opens the door to cash mergers, which resemble debt or redeemable-stock mergers, except that the survivor issues cash rather than stock or other securities. Under this technique, the freezeout possibilities of the short-form merger are extended to cases where the parent does not own the percentage of stock requisite for a short-form merger.

5. Reverse Stock Split. The traditional stock split involves dividing the shares held into a larger number, so that after a 2-for-1 split a holder of 500 shares will hold 1000 shares. A reverse split, as the name suggests, is just the opposite so that a shareholder emerges with fewer shares. Thus, a 1-for-25 split will result in a holder of 500 shares owning 20 shares. This can result in a freezeout if the resolution approving the split provides that the corporation has a right to purchase the shares of any holder of less than a "round lot," (100 shares). Thus, a corporation that wishes to rid itself of a large number of smaller stockholders can through a carefully designed reverse stock split empower its board to redeem the large number of odd lot holders.

––––––––

Weinberger v. UOP, Inc.

Supreme Court of Delaware, 1983.
457 A.2d 701.

■ MOORE, JUSTICE:

This post-trial appeal was reheard en banc from a decision of the Court of Chancery. It was brought by the class action plaintiff below, a former shareholder of UOP, Inc., who challenged the elimination of UOP's minority shareholders by a cash-out merger between UOP and its majority owner, The Signal Companies, Inc. [T]he defendants in this action are Signal, UOP, [and] certain officers and directors of those companies. . . . The present Chancellor held that the terms of the merger were fair to the plaintiff and the other minority shareholders of UOP. Accordingly, he entered judgment in favor of the defendants. . . .

In ruling for the defendants, the Chancellor re-stated his earlier conclusion that the plaintiff in a suit challenging a cash-out merger must allege specific acts of fraud, misrepresentation, or other items of misconduct to demonstrate the unfairness of the merger terms to the minority. We approve this rule and affirm it.

The Chancellor also held that even though the ultimate burden of proof is on the majority shareholder to show by a preponderance of the evidence that the transaction is fair, it is first the burden of the plaintiff attacking the merger to demonstrate some basis for invoking the fairness obligation. We agree with that principle. However, where corporate action has been approved by an informed vote of a majority of the minority shareholders, we conclude that the burden entirely shifts to the plaintiff to show that the transaction was unfair to the minority. See, e.g., Michelson v. Duncan, Del.Supr., 407 A.2d 211, 224 (1979). But in all this, the burden clearly remains on those relying on the vote to show that they completely disclosed all material facts relevant to the transaction.

Here, the record does not support a conclusion that the minority stockholder vote was an informed one. Material information, necessary to acquaint those shareholders with the bargaining positions of Signal and UOP, was withheld under circumstances amounting to a breach of fiduciary duty. We therefore conclude that this merger does not meet the test of fairness, at least as we address that concept, and no burden thus shifted to the plaintiff by reason of the minority shareholder vote. Accordingly, we reverse and remand for further proceedings consistent herewith.

In considering the nature of the remedy available under our law to minority shareholders in a cash-out merger, we believe that it is, and hereafter should be, an appraisal under 8 Del.C. § 262 as hereinafter construed. We therefore overrule Lynch v. Vickers Energy Corp., Del.Supr., 429 A.2d 497 (1981) (*Lynch II*) to the extent that it purports to limit a stockholder's monetary relief to a specific damage formula. See *Lynch II.* 429 A.2d at 507–08 (McNeilly Quillen, JJ., dissenting). But to give full effect to section 262 within the framework of the General Corporation Law we adopt a more liberal, less rigid and stylized, approach to the valuation process than has heretofore been permitted by our courts. While the present state of these proceedings does not admit the plaintiff to the appraisal remedy per se, the practical effect of the remedy we do grant him will be co-extensive with the liberalized valuation and appraisal methods we herein approve for cases coming after this decision.

Our treatment of these matters has necessarily led us to a reconsideration of the business purpose rule announced in the trilogy of Singer v. Magnavox Co., supra; Tanzer v. International General Industries, Inc., Del.Supr., 379 A.2d 1121 (1977); and Roland International Corp. v. Najjar, Del.Supr., 407 A.2d 1032 (1979). For the reasons hereafter set forth we consider that the business purpose requirement of these cases is no longer the law of Delaware.

I.

The facts found by the trial court, pertinent to the issues before us, are supported by the record, and we draw from them as set out in the Chancellor's opinion.

Signal is a diversified, technically based company operating through various subsidiaries. Its stock is publicly traded on the New York, Philadelphia and Pacific Stock Exchanges. UOP, formerly known as Universal Oil Products Company, was a diversified industrial company engaged in various lines of business, including petroleum and petro-chemical services and related products, construction, fabricated metal products, transportation equipment products, chemicals and plastics, and other products and services including land development, lumber products and waste disposal. Its stock was publicly held and listed on the New York Stock Exchange.

In 1974 Signal sold one of its wholly-owned subsidiaries for $420,000,000 in cash. See Gimbel v. Signal Companies, Inc., Del.Ch., 316 A.2d 599, aff'd, Del.Supr., 316 A.2d 619 (1974). While looking to invest this cash surplus, Signal became interested in UOP as a possible acquisition. Friendly negotiations ensued, and Signal proposed to acquire a controlling interest in UOP at a price of $19 per share. UOP's representatives sought $25 per share. In the arm's length bargaining that followed, an understanding was reached whereby Signal agreed to purchase from UOP 1,500,000 shares of UOP's authorized but unissued stock at $21 per share.

This purchase was contingent upon Signal making a successful cash tender offer for 4,300,000 publicly held shares of UOP, also at a price of $21 per share. This combined method of acquisition permitted Signal to acquire 5,800,000 shares of stock, representing 50.5% of UOP's outstanding shares. The UOP board of directors advised the company's shareholders that it had no objection to Signal's tender offer at that price. Immediately before the announcement of the tender offer, UOP's common stock had been trading on the New York Stock Exchange at a fraction under $14 per share.

The negotiations between Signal and UOP occurred during April 1975, and the resulting tender offer was greatly oversubscribed. However, Signal limited its total purchase of the tendered shares so that, when coupled with the stock bought from UOP, it had achieved its goal of becoming a 50.5% shareholder of UOP.

Although UOP's board consisted of thirteen directors, Signal nominated and elected only six. Of these, five were either directors or employees of Signal. The sixth, a partner in the banking firm of Lazard Freres & Co., had been one of Signal's representatives in the negotiations and bargaining with UOP concerning the tender offer and purchase price of the UOP shares.

However, the president and chief executive officer of UOP retired during 1975, and Signal caused him to be replaced by James V. Crawford, a long-time employee and senior executive vice president of one of Signal's wholly-owned subsidiaries. Crawford succeeded his predecessor on UOP's board of directors and also was made a director of Signal.

By the end of 1977 Signal basically was unsuccessful in finding other suitable investment candidates for its excess cash, and by February 1978 considered that it had no other realistic acquisitions available to it on a friendly basis. Once again its attention turned to UOP.

The trial court found that at the instigation of certain Signal management personnel, including William W. Walkup, its board chairman, and Forrest N. Shumway, its president, a feasibility study was made concerning the possible acquisition of the balance of UOP's outstanding shares. This study was performed by two Signal officers, Charles S. Arledge, vice president (director of planning), and Andrew J. Chitiea, senior vice president (chief financial officer). Messrs. Walkup, Shumway, Arledge and Chitiea were all directors of UOP in addition to their membership on the Signal board.

Arledge and Chitiea concluded that it would be a good investment for Signal to acquire the remaining 49.5% of UOP shares at any price up to $24 each. Their report was discussed between Walkup and Shumway who, along with Arledge, Chitiea and Brewster L. Arms, internal counsel for Signal, constituted Signal's senior management. In particular, they talked about the proper price to be paid if the acquisition was pursued, purportedly keeping in mind that as UOP's majority shareholder, Signal owed a fiduciary responsibility to both its own stockholders as well as to UOP's minority. It was ultimately agreed that a meeting of Signal's Executive Committee would be called to propose that Signal acquire the remaining outstanding stock of UOP through a cash-out merger in the range of $20 to $21 per share.

The Executive Committee meeting was set for February 28, 1978. As a courtesy, UOP's President, Crawford, was invited to attend, although he was not a member of Signal's executive committee. On his arrival, and prior to the meeting, Crawford was asked to meet privately with Walkup and Shumway. He was then told of Signal's plan to acquire full ownership of UOP and was asked for his reaction to the proposed price range of $20 to $21 per share. Crawford said he thought such a price would be "generous", and that it was certainly one which should be submitted to UOP's minority shareholders for their ultimate consideration. He stated, however, that Signal's 100% ownership could cause internal problems at UOP. He believed that employees would have to be given some assurance of their future place in a fully-owned Signal subsidiary. Otherwise, he feared the departure of essential personnel. Also, many of UOP's key employees had stock option incentive programs which would be wiped out by a merger. Crawford therefore urged that some adjustment would have to be made, such as providing a comparable incentive in Signals' shares, if after the merger he was to maintain his quality of personnel and efficiency at UOP.

Thus, Crawford voiced no objection to the $20 to $21 price range, nor did he suggest that Signal should consider paying more than $21 per share for the minority interests. Later, at the Executive Committee meeting the same factors were discussed, with Crawford repeating the position he earlier took with Walkup and Shumway. Also considered was the 1975 tender offer and the fact that it had been greatly oversubscribed at $21 per share. For many reasons, Signal's management concluded that the acquisition of UOP's minority shares provided the solution to a number of its business problems.

Thus, it was the consensus that a price of $20 to $21 per share would be fair to both Signal and the minority shareholders of UOP. Signal's executive committee authorized its management "to negotiate" with UOP "for a cash acquisition of the minority ownership in UOP, Inc., with the intention of presenting a proposal to [Signal's] board of directors . . . on March 6, 1978. Immediately after this February 28, 1978" meeting, Signal issued a press release stating:

> The Signal Companies, Inc. and UOP, Inc. are conducting negotiations for the acquisition for cash by Signal of the 49.5 per cent of UOP which it does not presently own, announced Forrest N. Shumway, president and chief executive officer of Signal, and James V. Crawford, UOP president.
>
> Price and other terms of the proposed transaction have not yet been finalized and would be subject to approval of the boards

of directors of Signal and UOP, scheduled to meet early next week, the stockholders of UOP and certain federal agencies.

The announcement also referred to the fact that the closing price of UOP's common stock on that day was $14.50 per share.

Two days later, on March 2, 1978, Signal issued a second press release stating that its management would recommend a price in the range of $20 to $21 per share for UOP's 49.5% minority interest. This announcement referred to Signal's earlier statement that "negotiations" were being conducted for the acquisition of the minority shares.

Between Tuesday, February 28, 1978 and Monday, March 6, 1978, a total of four business days, Crawford spoke by telephone with all of UOP's non-Signal, i.e., outside, directors. Also during that period, Crawford retained Lehman Brothers to render a fairness opinion as to the price offered the minority for its stock. He gave two reasons for this choice. First, the time schedule between the announcement and the board meetings was short (by then only three business days) and since Lehman Brothers had been acting as UOP's investment banker for many years, Crawford felt that it would be in the best position to respond on such brief notice. Second, James W. Glanville, a long-time director of UOP and a partner in Lehman Brothers, had acted as a financial advisor to UOP for many years. Crawford believed that Glanville's familiarity with UOP, as a member of its board, would also be of assistance in enabling Lehman Brothers to render a fairness opinion within the existing time constraints.

Crawford telephoned Glanville, who gave his assurance that Lehman Brothers had no conflicts that would prevent it from accepting the task. Glanville's immediate personal reaction was that a price of $20 to $21 would certainly be fair, since it represented almost a 50% premium over UOP's market price. Glanville sought a $250,000 fee for Lehman Brothers' services, but Crawford thought this too much. After further discussions Glanville finally agreed that Lehman Brothers would render its fairness opinion for $150,000.

During this period Crawford also had several telephone contacts with Signal officials. In only one of them, however, was the price of the shares discussed. In a conversation with Walkup, Crawford advised that as a result of his communications with UOP's non-Signal directors, it was his feeling that the price would have to be the top of the proposed range, or $21 per share, if the approval of UOP's outside directors was to be obtained. But again, he did not seek any price higher than $21.

Glanville assembled a three-man Lehman Brothers team to do the work on the fairness opinion. These persons examined relevant documents and information concerning UOP, including its annual reports and its Securities and Exchange Commission filings from 1973 through 1976, as well as its audited financial statements for 1977, its interim reports to shareholders, and its recent and historical market prices and trading volumes. In addition, on Friday, March 3, 1978, two members of the Lehman Brothers team flew to UOP's headquarters in Des Plaines, Illinois, to perform a "due diligence" visit, during the course of which they interviewed Crawford as well as UOP's general counsel, its chief financial officer, and other key executives and personnel.

As a result, the Lehman Brothers team concluded that "the price of either $20 or $21 would be a fair price for the remaining shares of UOP". They telephoned this impression to Glanville, who was spending the weekend in Vermont.

On Monday morning, March 6, 1978, Glanville and the senior member of the Lehman Brothers team flew to Des Plaines to attend the scheduled UOP directors meeting. Glanville looked over the assembled information during the flight. The two had with them the draft of a "fairness opinion letter" in which the price had been left blank. Either during or immediately prior to the directors' meeting, the two-page "fairness opinion letter" was typed in final form and the price of $21 per share was inserted.

On March 6, 1978, both the Signal and UOP boards were convened to consider the proposed merger. Telephone communications were maintained between the two meetings. Walkup, Signal's board chairman, and also a UOP director, attended UOP's meeting with Crawford in order to present Signal's position and answer any questions that UOP's non-Signal directors might have. Arledge and Chitiea, along with Signal's other designees on UOP's board, participated by conference telephone. All of UOP's outside directors attended the meeting either in person or by conference telephone.

First, Signal's board unanimously adopted a resolution authorizing Signal to proposed to UOP a cash merger of $21 per share as outlined in a certain merger agreement and other supporting documents. This proposal required that the merger be approved by a majority of UOP's outstanding minority shares voting at the stockholders meeting at which the merger would be considered, and that the minority shares voting in favor of the merger, when coupled with Signal's 50.5% interest would have to comprise at least two-thirds of all UOP shares. Otherwise the proposed merger would be deemed disapproved.

UOP's board then considered the proposal. Copies of the agreement were delivered to the directors in attendance, and other copies had been forwarded earlier to the directors participating by telephone. They also had before them UOP financial data for 1974–1977, UOP's most recent financial statements, market price information, and budget projections for 1978. In addition they had Lehman Brothers' hurriedly prepared fairness opinion letter finding the price of $21 to be fair. Glanville, the Lehman Brothers partner, and UOP director, commented on the information that had gone into preparation of the letter.

Signal also suggests that the Arledge-Chitiea feasibility study, indicating that a price of up to $24 per share would be a "good investment" for Signal, was discussed at the UOP directors' meeting. The Chancellor made no such finding, and our independent review of the record, detailed infra, satisfies us by a preponderance of the evidence that there was no discussion of this document at UOP's board meeting. Furthermore, it is clear beyond peradventure that nothing in that report was ever disclosed to UOP's minority shareholders prior to their approval of the merger.

After consideration of Signal's proposal, Walkup and Crawford left the meeting to permit a free and uninhibited exchange between UOP's non-Signal directors. Upon their return a resolution to accept Signal's offer was then proposed and adopted. While Signal's men on UOP's board participated in various aspects of the meeting they abstained from voting. However, the minutes show that each of them "if voting would have voted yes".

On March 7, 1978, UOP sent a letter to its shareholders advising them of the action taken by UOP's board with respect to Signal's offer. This document pointed out, among other things, that on February 28, 1978 "both companies had announced negotiations were being conducted."

Despite the swift board action of the two companies, the merger was not submitted to UOP's shareholders until their annual meeting on May 26, 1978. In the notice of that meeting and proxy statement sent to shareholders in May, UOP's management and board urged that the merger be approved. The proxy statement also advised:

> The price was determined after *discussions* between James V. Crawford, a director of Signal and Chief Executive Officer of UOP, and officers of Signal which took place during meetings on February 28, 1978, and in the course of several subsequent telephone conversations. (Emphasis added.)

In the original draft of the proxy statement the word "negotiations" had been used rather than "discussions". However, when the Securities and Exchange Commission sought details of the "negotiations" as part of its review of these materials, the term was deleted and the word "discussions" was substituted. The proxy statement indicated that the vote of UOP's board in approving the merger had been unanimous. It also advised the shareholders that Lehman Brothers had given its opinion that the merger price of $21 per share was fair to UOP's minority. However, it did not disclose the hurried method by which this conclusion was reached.

As of the record date for UOP's annual meeting, there were 11,488,302 shares of UOP common stock outstanding, 5,688,302 of which were owned by the minority. At the meeting only 56%, or 3,208,652, of the minority shares were voted. Of these, 2,953,812, or 51.9% of the total minority, voted for the merger, and 254,840 voted against it. When Signal's stock was added to the minority shares voting in favor, a total of 76.2% of UOP's outstanding shares approved the merger while only 2.2% opposed it.

By its terms the merger became effective on May 26, 1978, and each share of UOP's stock held by the minority was automatically converted into a right to receive $21 cash.

II.

A.

A primary issue mandating reversal is the preparation by two UOP directors, Arledge and Chitiea, of their feasibility study for the exclusive use and benefit of Signal. This document was of obvious significance to both Signal and UOP. Using UOP data, it described the advantages to Signal of ousting the minority at a price range of $21–$24 per share. Mr. Arledge, one of the authors, outlined the benefits to Signal:*

Purpose of the Merger

(1) Provides an outstanding investment opportunity for Signal—(Better than any recent acquisition we have seen.)

(2) Increases Signal's earnings.

(3) Facilitates the flow of resources between Signal and its subsidiaries—(Big factor—works both ways.)

(4) Provides cost savings potential for Signal and UOP.

(5) Improves the percentage of Signal's "operating earnings" as opposed to "holding company earnings".

(6) Simplifies the understanding of Signal.

(7) Facilitates technological exchange among Signal's subsidiaries.

(8) Eliminates potential conflicts of interest.

Having written those words, solely for the use of Signal, it is clear from the record that neither Arledge nor Chitiea shared this report with their fellow directors of UOP. We are satisfied that no one else did either. This conduct hardly meets the fiduciary standards applicable to such a transaction. While Mr. Walkup, Signal's chairman of the board and a UOP director, attended the March 6, 1978 UOP board meeting and testified at trial that he had discussed the Arledge-Chitiea report with the UOP directors at this meeting, the record does not support this assertion. Perhaps it is the result of some confusion on Mr. Walkup's part. In any event Mr. Shumway, Signal's president, testified that he made sure the Signal outside directors had this report prior to the March 6, 1978 Signal board meeting, but he did not testify that the Arledge-Chitiea report was also sent to UOP's outside directors.

---

*   The parentheses indicate certain handwritten comments of Mr. Arledge.

Mr. Crawford, UOP's president, could not recall that any documents, other than a draft of the merger agreement, were sent to UOP's directors before the March 6, 1978 UOP meeting. Mr. Chitiea, an author of the report, testified that it was made available to Signal's directors, but to his knowledge it was not circulated to the outside directors of UOP. He specifically testified that he "didn't share" that information with the outside directors of UOP with whom he served.

None of UOP's outside directors who testified stated that they had seen this document. The minutes of the UOP board meeting do not identify the Arledge-Chitiea report as having been delivered to UOP's outside directors. This is particularly significant since the minutes describe in considerable detail the materials that actually were distributed. While these minutes recite Mr. Walkup's presentation of the Signal offer, they do not mention the Arledge-Chitiea report or any disclosure that Signal considered a price of up to $24 to be a good investment. If Mr. Walkup had in fact provided such important information to UOP's outside directors, it is logical to assume that these carefully drafted minutes would disclose it. The post-trial briefs of Signal and UOP contain a thorough description of the documents purportedly available to their boards at the March 6, 1978, meetings. Although the Arledge-Chitiea report is specifically identified as being available to the Signal directors, there is no mention of it being among the documents submitted to the UOP board. Even when queried at a prior oral argument before this Court, counsel for Signal did not claim that the Arledge-Chitiea report had been disclosed to UOP's outside directors. Instead, he chose to belittle its contents. This was the same approach taken before us at the last oral argument.

Actually, it appears that a three-page summary of figures was given to all UOP directors. Its first page is identical to one page of the Arledge-Chitiea report, but this dealt with nothing more than a justification of the $21 price. Significantly, the contents of this three-page summary are what the minutes reflect Mr. Walkup told the UOP board. However, nothing contained in either the minutes or this three-page summary reflects Signal's study regarding the $24 price.

The Arledge-Chitiea report speaks for itself in supporting the Chancellor's finding that a price of up to $24 was a "good investment" for Signal. It shows that a return on the investment at $21 would be 15.7% versus 15.5% at $24 per share. This was a difference of only two-tenths of one percent, while it meant over $17,000,000 to the minority. Under such circumstances, paying UOP's minority shareholders $24 would have had relatively little long-term effect on Signal, and the Chancellor's findings concerning the benefit to Signal, even at a price of $24, were obviously correct. . . .

Certainly, this was a matter of material significance to UOP and its shareholders. Since the study was prepared by two UOP directors, using UOP information for the exclusive benefit of Signal, and nothing whatever was done to disclose it to the outside UOP directors or the minority shareholders, a question of breach of fiduciary duty arises. This problem occurs because there were common Signal-UOP directors participating, at least to some extent, in the UOP board's decision-making processes without full disclosure of the conflicts they faced.[7]

B.

In assessing this situation, the Court of Chancery was required to:

> examine what information defendants had and to measure it against what they gave to the minority stockholders, in a context in which "complete candor" is required. In other words, the limited function of the Court was to determine whether defendants had disclosed all information in their possession germane to the transaction in issue. And by "germane" we mean, for present purposes, information such as a reasonable shareholder would consider important in deciding whether to sell or retain stock.

* * *

> . . . Completeness, not adequacy, is both the norm and the mandate under present circumstances.

Lynch v. Vickers Energy Corp., Del.Supr., 383 A.2d 278, 281 (1977) (*Lynch I*). This is merely stating in another way the long-existing principle of Delaware law that these Signal designated directors on UOP's board still owed UOP and its shareholders an uncompromising duty of loyalty. The classic language of Guth v. Loft, Inc., Del.Supr., 5 A.2d 503, 510 (1939), requires no embellishment:

> A public policy, existing through the years, and derived from a profound knowledge of human characteristics and motives, has established a rule that demands of a corporate officer or director, peremptorily and inexorably, the most scrupulous observance of his duty, not only affirmatively to protect the interests of the corporation committed to his charge, but also to refrain from doing anything that would work injury to the corporation, or to deprive it of profit or advantage which his skill and ability might properly bring to it, or to enable it to make in the reasonable and lawful exercise of its powers. The rule that requires an undivided and unselfish loyalty to the corporation

---

[7]   Although perfection is not possible, or expected, the result here could have been entirely different if UOP had appointed an independent negotiating committee of its outside directors to deal with Signal at arm's length. See, e.g., Harriman v. E.I. du Pont De Nemours & Co., 411 F.Supp. 133 (D.Del.1975). Since fairness in this context can be equated to conduct by a theoretical, wholly independent, board of directors acting upon the matter before them, it is unfortunate that this course apparently was neither considered nor pursued. Johnston v. Greene, Del.Supr., 121 A.2d 919, 925 (1956). Particularly in a parent-subsidiary context, a showing that the action taken was as though each of the contending parties had in fact exerted its bargaining power against the other at arm's length is strong evidence that the transaction meets the test of fairness. Getty Oil Co. v. Skelly Oil Co., Del.Supr., 267 A.2d 883, 886 (1970); Puma v. Marriott, Del.Ch., 283 A.2d 693, 696 (1971).

demands that there shall be no conflict between duty and self-interest.

Given the absence of any attempt to structure this transaction on an arm's length basis, Signal cannot escape the effects of the conflicts it faced, particularly when its designees on UOP's board did not totally abstain from participation in the matter. There is no "safe harbor" for such divided loyalties in Delaware. When directors of a Delaware corporation are on both sides of a transaction, they are required to demonstrate their utmost good faith and the most scrupulous inherent fairness of the bargain. Gottlieb v. Heyden Chemical Corp., Del.Supr., 91 A.2d 57, 57–58 (1952). The requirement of fairness is unflinching in its demand that where one stands on both sides of a transaction, he has the burden of establishing its entire fairness, sufficient to pass the test of careful scrutiny by the courts. Sterling v. Mayflower Hotel Corp., Del.Supr., 93 A.2d 107, 110 (1952). . . .

There is no dilution of this obligation where one holds dual or multiple directorships, as in a parent-subsidiary context. Levien v. Sinclair Oil Corp., Del.Ch., 261 A.2d 911, 915 (1969). Thus, individuals who act in a dual capacity as directors of two corporations, one of whom is parent and the other subsidiary, owe the same duty of good management to both corporations, and in the absence of an independent negotiating structure (see note 7, supra), or the directors' total abstention from any participation in the matter, this duty is to be exercised in light of what is best for both companies. Warshaw v. Calhoun, Del.Supr., 221 A.2d 487, 492 (1966). The record demonstrates that Signal has not met this obligation.

C.

The concept of fairness has two basic aspects: fair dealing and fair price. The former embraces questions of when the transaction was timed, how it was initiated, structured, negotiated, disclosed to the directors, and how the approvals of the directors and the stockholders were obtained. The latter aspect of fairness relates to the economic and financial considerations of the proposed merger, including all relevant factors: assets, market value, earnings, future prospects, and any other elements that affect the intrinsic or inherent value of a company's stock. . . . However, the test for fairness is not a bifurcated one as between fair dealing and price. All aspects of the issue must be examined as a whole since the question is one of entire fairness. However, in a non-fraudulent transaction we recognize that price may be the preponderant consideration outweighing other features of the merger. Here, we address the two basic aspects of fairness separately because we find reversible error as to both.

D.

Part of fair dealing is the obvious duty of candor required by *Lynch I*, supra. Moreover, one possessing superior knowledge may not mislead any stockholder by use of corporate information to which the latter is not privy. Lank v. Steiner, Del.Supr., 224 A.2d 242, 244 (1966). Delaware has long imposed this duty even upon persons who are not corporate officers or directors, but who nonetheless are privy to matters of interest or significance to their company. Brophy v. Cities Service Co., Del.Ch., 70 A.2d 5, 7 (1949). With the well-established Delaware law on the subject, and the Court of Chancery's findings of fact here, it is inevitable that the obvious conflicts posed by Arledge and Chitiea's preparation of their "feasibility study", derived from UOP information, for the sole use and benefit of Signal, cannot pass muster.

The Arledge-Chitiea report is but one aspect of the element of fair dealing. How did this merger evolve? It is clear that it was entirely initiated by Signal. The serious time constraints under which the principals acted were all set by Signal. It had not found a suitable outlet for its excess cash and considered UOP a desirable investment, particularly since it was now in a position to acquire the whole company for itself. For whatever reasons, and they were only Signal's, the entire transaction was presented to and approved by UOP's board within four business days. Standing alone, this is not necessarily indicative of any lack of fairness by a majority shareholder. It was what occurred, or more properly, what did not occur, during this brief period that makes the time constraints imposed by Signal relevant to the issue of fairness.

The structure of the transaction, again, was Signal's doing. So far as negotiations were concerned, it is clear that they were modest at best. Crawford, Signal's man at UOP, never really talked price with Signal, except to accede to its management's statements on the subject, and to convey to Signal the UOP outside directors' view that as between the $20–$21 range under consideration, it would have to be $21. The latter is not a surprising outcome, but hardly arm's length negotiations. Only the protection of benefits for UOP's key employees and the issue of Lehman Brothers' fee approached any concept of bargaining.

As we have noted, the matter of disclosure to the UOP directors was wholly flawed by the conflicts of interest raised by the Arledge-Chitiea report. All of those conflicts were resolved by Signal in its own favor without divulging any aspect of them to UOP.

This cannot but undermine a conclusion that this merger meets any reasonable test of fairness. The outside UOP directors lacked one material piece of information generated by two of their colleagues, but shared only with Signal. True, the UOP board had the Lehman Brothers' fairness opinion, but that firm has been blamed by the plaintiff for the hurried task it performed, when more properly the responsibility for this lies with Signal. There was no disclosure of the circumstances surrounding the rather cursory preparation of the Lehman Brothers' fairness opinion. Instead, the impression was given UOP's minority that a careful study had been made, when in fact speed was the hallmark, and Mr. Glanville, Lehman's partner in charge of the matter, and also a UOP director, having spent the weekend in Vermont, brought a draft of the "fairness opinion letter" to the UOP directors' meeting on March 6, 1978 with the price left blank. We can only conclude from the record that the rush imposed on Lehman Brothers by Signal's timetable contributed to the difficulties under which this investment banking firm attempted to perform its responsibilities. Yet, none of this was disclosed to UOP's minority.

Finally, the minority stockholders were denied the critical information that Signal considered a price of $24 to be a good investment. Since this would have meant over $17,000,000 more to the minority, we cannot conclude that the shareholder vote was an informed one. Under the circumstances, an approval by a majority of the minority was meaningless. *Lynch I,* 383 A.2d at 279, 281; Cahall v. Lofland, Del.Ch., 114 A. 224 (1921).

Given these particulars and the Delaware law on the subject, the record does not establish that this transaction satisfies any reasonable concept of fair dealing, and the Chancellor's findings in that regard must be reversed.

E.

Turning to the matter of price, plaintiff also challenges its fairness. His evidence was that on the date the merger was approved the stock was worth at least $26 per share. In support, he offered the testimony of a chartered investment analyst who used two basic approaches to valuation: a comparative analysis of the premium paid over market in ten other tender offer-merger combinations, and a discounted cash flow analysis.

In this breach of fiduciary duty case, the Chancellor perceived that the approach to valuation was the same as that in an appraisal proceeding. Consistent with precedent, he rejected plaintiff's method of proof and accepted defendants' evidence of value as being in accord with practice under prior case law. This means that the so-called "Delaware block" or weighted average method was employed wherein the elements of value, i.e., assets, market price, earnings, etc., were assigned a particular weight and the resulting amounts added to determine the value per share. This procedure has been in use for decades. . . . However, to the extent it excludes other generally accepted techniques used in the financial community and the courts, it is not clearly outmoded. It is time we recognize this in appraisal and other stock valuation proceedings and bring our law current on the subject.

While the Chancellor rejected plaintiff's discounted cash flow method of valuing UOP's stock, as not corresponding with "either logic or the existing law," it is significant that this was essentially the focus, i.e., earnings potential of UOP, of Messrs. Arledge and Chitiea in their evaluation of the merger. Accordingly, the standard "Delaware block" or weighted average method of valuation . . . shall no longer exclusively control such proceedings. We believe that a more liberal approach must include proof of value by any technique or methods which are generally considered acceptable in the financial community and otherwise admissible in court, subject only to our interpretation of 8 Del. C. § 262(h). . . .

It is significant that section 262 now mandates the determination of "fair" value based upon "all relevant factors." Only the speculative elements of value that may arise from the "accomplishment or expectation" of the merger are excluded. We take this to be a very narrow exception to the appraisal process, designed to eliminate use of *pro forma* data and projections of a speculative variety relating to the completion of a merger. But elements of future value, including the nature of the enterprise, which are known and susceptible of proof as of the date of the merger and not the product of speculation, may be considered. . . .

Although the Chancellor received the plaintiff's evidence, his opinion indicates that the use of it was precluded because of past Delaware practice. While we do not suggest a monetary result one way or the other, we do think the plaintiff's evidence should be part of the factual mix and weighed as such. Until the $21 price is measured on remand by the valuation standards mandated by Delaware law, there can be no finding at the present stage of these proceedings that the price is fair. Given the lack of any candid disclosure of the material facts surrounding establishment of the $21 price, the majority of the minority vote, approving the merger, is meaningless.

The plaintiff has not sought an appraisal, but rescissory damages of the type contemplated by Lynch v. Vickers Energy Corp., Del.Supr., 429 A.2d 497, 505–06 (1981) (*Lynch II*). In view of the approach to valuation that we announce today, we see no basis in our law for *Lynch II*'s exclusive monetary formula for relief. On remand the plaintiff will be permitted to test the fairness of the $21 price by the standards we herein establish, in conformity with the principle applicable to an appraisal— that fair value be determined by taking into account all relevant factors [see 8 Del.C. § 262(h), supra]. In our view this includes the elements of rescissory damages if the Chancellor considers them susceptible of proof and a remedy appropriate to all the issues of fairness before him. To the extent that *Lynch II,* 429 A.2d at 505–06, purports to limit the Chancellor's discretion to a single remedial formula for monetary damages in a cash-out merger, it is overruled.

While a plaintiff's monetary remedy ordinarily should be confined to the more liberalized appraisal proceeding herein established, we do not intend any limitation on the historic powers of the Chancellor to grant such other relief as the facts of a particular case may dictate. The appraisal remedy we approve may not be adequate in certain cases, particularly where fraud, misrepresentation, self-dealing, deliberate waste of corporate assets, or gross and palpable overreaching are involved. Cole v. National Cash Credit Association, Del.Ch., 156 A. 183,

187 (1931). Under such circumstances, the Chancellor's powers are complete to fashion any form of equitable and monetary relief as may be appropriate, including rescissory damages. Since it is apparent that this long completed transaction is too involved to undo, and in view of the Chancellor's discretion, the award, if any, should be in the form of monetary damages based upon entire fairness standards, i.e., fair dealing and fair price. . . .

[The quasi-appraisal remedy provided in this decision applies to this case and other cases around the same time period as this case.] Thereafter, the provisions of 8 Del.C. § 262, as herein construed, respecting the scope of an appraisal and the means for perfecting the same, shall govern the financial remedy available to minority shareholders in a cash-out merger. Thus, we return to the well-established principles of Stauffer v. Standard Brands, Inc., Del.Supr., 187 A.2d 78 (1962) and David J. Greene & Co. v. Schenley Industries, Inc., Del.Ch., 281 A.2d 30 (1971), mandating a stockholder's recourse to the basic remedy of an appraisal.

III.

Finally, we address the matter of business purpose. . . . The plaintiff says that no valid purpose existed—the entire transaction was a mere subterfuge designed to eliminate the minority. . . .

The requirement of a business purpose is new to our law of mergers and was a departure from prior case law. See Stauffer v. Standard Brands, Inc., supra; David J. Greene & Co. v. Schenley Industries, Inc., supra.

In view of the fairness test which has long been applicable to parent-subsidiary mergers, Sterling v. Mayflower Hotel Corp., Del.Supr., 93 A.2d 107, 109–10 (1952), the expanded appraisal remedy now available to shareholders, and the broad discretion of the Chancellor to fashion such relief as the facts of a given case may dictate we do not believe that any additional meaningful protection is afforded minority shareholders by the business purpose requirement of the trilogy of *Singer, Tanzer,*[10] *Najjar,*[11] and their progeny. Accordingly, such requirement shall no longer be of any force or effect.

The judgment of the Court of Chancery, finding both the circumstances of the merger and the price paid the minority shareholders to be fair, is reversed. The matter is remanded for further proceedings consistent herewith. Upon remand the plaintiff's post-trial motion to enlarge the class should be granted.

* * *

Reversed and Remanded.

---

[10] Tanzer v. International General Industries, Inc., Del.Supr., 379 A.2d 1121, 1124–25 (1977).

[11] Roland International Corp. v. Najjar, Del.Supr., 407 A.2d 1032, 1036 (1979).

———

KAHN v. LYNCH COMMUNICATION SYSTEMS

[Chapter 10, Section 6, *supra*]

———

Kahn v. M & F Worldwide Corp.

Supreme Court of Delaware, 2014.
88 A.3d 635.

[Suit was initiated on behalf of MFW stockholders against MacAndrews & Forbes challenging the pending merger of both firms that would result in MacAndrews & Forbes acquiring at a substantial premium 57 percent of MFW that it did not own. MacAndrews & Forbes promised that it would not pursue the transaction without the approval of a MFW special committee which therefore had the power to "say no." MacAndrews & Forbes also stated it would not proceed without the approval by a majority of the stockholders not affiliated with MacAndrews & Forbes.]

This appeal presents a question of first impression: what should be the standard of review for a merger between a controlling stockholder and its subsidiary, where the merger is conditioned *ab initio* upon the approval of **both** an independent, adequately-empowered Special Committee that fulfills its duty of care, and the uncoerced, informed vote of a majority of the minority stockholders. The question has never been put directly to this Court. . . .

The Court of Chancery held that the consequence should be that the business judgment standard of review will govern going private mergers with a controlling stockholder that are conditioned *ab initio* upon (1) the approval of an independent and fully-empowered Special Committee that fulfills its duty of care and (2) the uncoerced, informed vote of the majority of the minority stockholders. . . .

Business Judgment Review Standard Adopted

We hold that business judgment is the standard of review that should govern mergers between a controlling stockholder and its corporate subsidiary, where the merger is conditioned *ab initio* upon both the approval of an independent, adequately-empowered Special Committee that fulfills its duty of care; and the uncoerced, informed vote of a majority of the minority stockholders. We so conclude for several reasons.

First, entire fairness is the highest standard of review in corporate law. It is applied in the controller merger context as a substitute for the dual statutory protections of disinterested board and stockholder approval, because both protections are potentially undermined by the influence of the controller. However, . . . where the controller irrevocably and publicly disables itself from using its control to dictate the outcome of the negotiations and the shareholder vote, the controlled merger then acquires the shareholder-protective characteristics of third-party, arm's-length mergers, which are reviewed under the business judgment standard.

Second, the dual procedural protection merger structure optimally protects the minority stockholders in controller buyouts. As the Court of Chancery explained:

> [W]hen these two protections are established up-front, a potent tool to extract good value for the minority is established. From inception, the controlling stockholder knows that it cannot bypass the special committee's ability to say no. And, the controlling stockholder knows it cannot dangle a majority-of-the-minority vote before the special committee late in the process as a deal-closer rather than having to make a price move.

Third, and as the Court of Chancery reasoned, applying the business judgment standard to the dual protection merger structure:

> . . . is consistent with the central tradition of Delaware law, which defers to the informed decisions of impartial directors, especially when those decisions have been approved by the disinterested stockholders on full information and without coercion. . . . [I]t will provide a strong incentive for controlling stockholders to accord minority investors the transactional structure that respected scholars believe will provide them the best protection, a structure where stockholders get the benefits of independent, empowered negotiating agents to **bargain for the best price and say no** if the agents believe the deal is not advisable for any proper reason, plus the critical ability to determine for themselves whether to accept any deal that their negotiating agents recommend to them. A transactional structure with both these protections is fundamentally different from one with only one protection.

Fourth, the underlying purposes of the dual protection merger structure utilized here and the entire fairness standard of review both converge and are fulfilled at the same critical point: **price**. Following *Weinberger v. UOP, Inc.*, this Court has consistently held that, although entire fairness review comprises the dual components of fair dealing and fair price, in a non-fraudulent transaction "price may be the preponderant consideration outweighing other features of the merger." The dual protection merger structure requires two price-related pretrial determinations: first, that a fair price was achieved by an empowered, independent committee that acted with care; and, second, that a fully-informed, uncoerced majority of the minority stockholders voted in favor of the price that was recommended by the independent committee.

The New Standard Summarized

To summarize our holding, in controller buyouts, the business judgment standard of review will be applied *if and only if*: (i) the controller conditions the procession of the transaction on the approval of both a Special Committee and a majority of the minority stockholders; (ii) the Special Committee is independent; (iii) the Special Committee is empowered to freely select its own advisors and to say no definitively; (iv) the Special Committee meets its duty of care in negotiating a fair price; (v) the vote of the minority is informed; and (vi) there is no coercion of the minority.[14]

If a plaintiff that can plead a reasonably conceivable set of facts showing that any or all of those enumerated conditions did not exist, that complaint would state a claim for relief that would entitle the plaintiff to proceed and conduct discovery. If, after discovery, triable issues of fact remain about whether either or both of the dual procedural protections were established, or if established were effective, the case will proceed to a trial in which the court will conduct an entire fairness review.

. . .

Dual Protection Inquiry

To reiterate, in this case, the controlling stockholder conditioned its offer upon the MFW Board agreeing, *ab initio*, to both procedural protections, *i.e.*, approval by a Special Committee and by a majority of the minority stockholders. For the combination of an effective committee process and majority-of-the-minority vote to qualify (jointly) for business judgment review, each of these protections must be effective singly to warrant a burden shift.

. . .

. . . As we have previously noted, deciding whether an independent committee was effective in negotiating a price is a process so fact-intensive and inextricably intertwined with the merits of an entire fairness review (fair dealing and fair price) that a pretrial determination of burden shifting is often impossible. Here, however, the Defendants have successfully established a record of independent committee effectiveness and process that warranted a grant of summary judgment entitling them to a burden shift prior to trial.

[The court reviewed the challenges to the special committee members' independence. Although each had some prior financial,

---

[14] The Verified Consolidated Class Action Complaint would have survived a motion to dismiss under this new standard. First, the complaint alleged that Perelman's offer "value[d] the company at just four times" MFW's profits per share and "five times 2010 pre-tax cash flow," and that these ratios were "well below" those calculated for recent similar transactions. Second, the complaint alleged that the final Merger price was two dollars per share *lower* than the trading price only about two months earlier. Third, the complaint alleged particularized facts indicating that MWF's share price was depressed at the times of Perelman's offer and the Merger announcement due to short-term factors such as MFW's acquisition of other entities and Standard & Poor's downgrading of the United States' creditworthiness. Fourth, the complaint alleged that commentators viewed both Perelman's initial $24 per share offer and the final $25 per share Merger price as being surprisingly low. These allegations about the sufficiency of the price call into question the adequacy of the Special Committee's negotiations, thereby necessitating discovery on all of the new prerequisites to the application of the business judgment rule.

professional and social connections with either MFW's dominant stockholder, Perelman, or Perlman-related entities, the various dealings and interactions were not to rise to the level of being material. The Court reasoned:

> A plaintiff seeking to show that a director was not independent must satisfy a materiality standard. The court must conclude that the director in question had ties to the person whose proposal or actions he or she is evaluating that are sufficiently substantial that he or she could not objectively discharge his or her fiduciary duties. Consistent with that predicate materiality requirement, the existence of some financial ties between the interested party and the director, without more, is not disqualifying. The inquiry must be whether, applying a subjective standard, those ties were *material*, in the sense that the alleged ties could have affected the impartiality of the individual director.

The plaintiffs introduced evidence of various business relationships the committee members had over the years with Perelman and his related businesses. The Court of Chancery's found that the earlier dealings between individual committee members and Perelman or entities related to him either did not involve amounts shown to be significant to a particular committee member or had occurred many years earlier so that materiality today was not established. The Supreme Court held that the Court of Chancery's holding that the special committee members were independent was supported by the record.

In holding that the committee was duly empowered, the court observed:

> The Court of Chancery also found that it was "undisputed that the [S]pecial [C]ommittee was empowered not simply to 'evaluate' the offer, like some special committees with weak mandates, but to negotiate with [M&F] over the terms of its offer to buy out the noncontrolling stockholders. This negotiating power was accompanied by the clear authority to say no definitively to [M&F]" and to "make that decision stick." MacAndrews & Forbes promised that it would not proceed with any going private proposal that did not have the support of the Special Committee. Therefore, the Court of Chancery concluded, "the MFW committee did not have to fear that if it bargained too hard, MacAndrews & Forbes could bypass the committee and make a tender offer directly to the minority stockholders."

The Supreme Court found further support for the committee being duly empower and independent it its rejection of the initially tendered price of $24 per share by demanding $30. However, once the committee learned of MFW's deteriorating financial position it ultimately supported a buyout price of $25. In doing so, the committee met eight times, was advised by its own counsel and investment banker. The Supreme Court viewed these efforts supporting the conclusion the committee exercised due care.

A finding that 65 percent of the minority shares approved the acquisition and that proxy materials fully disclosed all facts, including the earlier committee $30 counter offer as well as internal estimates available to the committee, supported a finding that the majority-of-the-minority vote was fully informed and uncoerced.]

Business Judgment Review Properly Applied

We have determined that the business judgment rule standard of review applies to this controlling stockholder buyout. . . . In this case, it cannot be credibly argued (let alone concluded) that no rational person would find the Merger favorable to MFW's minority stockholders.

Conclusion

For the above-stated reasons, the judgment of the Court of Chancery is affirmed.

NOTE ON THE PURPOSE TEST

While Delaware subjects the transactions to scrutiny under the entire fairness standard, some courts examine the purpose surrounding the cash-out merger. For example, *Coggins v. New England Patriots Football Club, Inc.*, 397 Mass. 525, 492 N.E.2d 1112 (1986), involved the freezeout of the non-voting common stockholders by Michael H. Sullivan, Jr. who had recently acquired all the voting common for the New England Patriots using money borrowed from two banks. The banks' loans required him to pledge the voting shares as collateral for the loan and use his best efforts to reorganize the Patriots so that its income could be devoted to repayment of Sullivan's personal loans.

> "Unlike the Delaware court . . . we believe that the 'business-purpose' test is an additional useful means under our statutes and case law for examining a transaction in which a controlling stockholder eliminates the minority interest in a corporation. . . .

> A controlling stockholder who is also a director standing on both sides of the transaction bears the burden of showing that the transaction does not violate fiduciary obligations. . . .

> "Judicial scrutiny should begin with recognition of the basic principle that the duty of a corporate director must be to further the legitimate goals of the corporation. . . .

> The plaintiffs here adequately alleged that the merger of the Old Patriots and New Patriots was a freeze-out merger undertaken for no legitimate purpose, but merely for the personal benefit of Sullivan. While we recognize the right to "selfish ownership" in a corporation, such a right must be balanced against the concept of the majority stockholder's fiduciary obligation to the minority stockholders. *Wilkes v. Springside Nursing Home, Inc.*, 370 Mass.

842, 851 (1976). Consequently, the defendants bear the burden of proving, first, that the merger was for a legitimate business purpose, and second, that, considering the totality of the circumstances, it was fair to the minority.

The decision of the Superior Court judge includes a finding that "the defendants have failed to demonstrate that the merger served any valid objective unrelated to the personal interests of the majority shareholders. It thus appears that the sole reason for the merger was to effectuate a restructuring of the Patriots that would enable the repayment of the [personal] indebtedness incurred by Sullivan.". . .

397 Mass. at 531, 533–535, 492 A.2d at 1117, 1118–1119. The court declared the merger freezeout invalid and remanded the case to award rescission damages to the objecting minority holders based on the then current value of the company.

New York similarly requires proof of a business purpose.

"In the context of a freeze-out merger, variant treatment of the minority shareholders—i.e., causing their removal will be justified when related to the advancement of a general corporate interest. The benefit need not be great, but it must be for the corporation. For example, if the sole purpose of the merger is reduction of the number of profit sharers—in contrast to increasing the corporation's capital or profits, or improving its management structure—there will exist no 'independent corporate interest' (see Schwartz v. Marien, 37 N.Y.2d 487, 492, 373 N.Y.S.2d 122, 335 N.E.2d 334, supra). All of these purposes ultimately seek to increase the individual wealth of the remaining shareholders. What distinguishes a proper corporate purpose from an improper one is that, with the former, removal of the minority shareholders furthers the objective of conferring some general gain upon the corporation. Only then will the fiduciary duty of good and prudent management of the corporation serve to override the concurrent duty to treat all shareholders fairly (see Klurfeld v. Equity Enterprises, 79 A.D.2d 124, 136, 436 N.Y.S.2d 303, supra). We further note that a finding that there was an independent corporate purpose for the action taken by the majority will not be defeated merely by the fact that the corporate objective could have been accomplished in another way, or by the fact that the action chosen was not the best way to achieve the bona fide business objective."

Alpert v. 28 Williams St. Corp., 63 N.Y.2d 557, 573, 483 N.Y.S.2d 667, 676, 473 N.E.2d 19, 28 (1984) (finding the requisite purpose was established by evidence that that additional capital needed to repair the company's property was not available so long as the minority interest was outstanding).

———

Glassman v. Unocal Exploration Corp.

Supreme Court of Delaware (en banc), 2001.
777 A.2d 242.

■ BERGER, JUSTICE.

In this appeal, we consider the fiduciary duties owed by a parent corporation to the subsidiary's minority stockholders in the context of a "short-form" merger. Specifically, we take this opportunity to reconcile a fiduciary's seemingly absolute duty to establish the entire fairness of any self-dealing transaction with the less demanding requirements of the short-form merger statute. The statute authorizes the elimination of minority stockholders by a summary process that does not involve the "fair dealing" component of entire fairness. Indeed, the statute does not contemplate any "dealing" at all. Thus, a parent corporation cannot satisfy the entire fairness standard if it follows the terms of the short-form merger statute without more.

Unocal Corporation addressed this dilemma by establishing a special negotiating committee and engaging in a process that it believed would pass muster under traditional entire fairness review. We find that such steps were unnecessary. . . .

I.   Factual and Procedural Background . . .

[Unocal Corporation owned approximately 96% of the stock of Unocal Exploration (UXC). In December 1991 the boards of each company appointed special committees to consider a possible merger. UXC's special committee retained financial and legal advisors, met four times, and agreed to a merger exchange ratio where .54 Unocal shares would be issued for each UXC share. They announced their agreement on February 24, 1992 and carried it out pursuant to Delaware's short-form merger provision, 8 Del. § 253, on May 2, 1992. The plaintiffs filed a class action on behalf of the UXC minority holders alleging the merger violated *Weinberger's* entire fairness requirement.]

II.   Discussion

The short-form merger statute, as enacted in 1937, authorized a parent corporation to merge with its wholly-owned subsidiary by filing and recording a certificate evidencing the parent's ownership and its merger resolution. In 1957, the statute was expanded to include parent/subsidiary mergers where the parent company owns at least 90% of the stock of the subsidiary. The 1957 amendment also made it possible, for the first time and only in a short-form merger, to pay the minority cash for their shares, thereby eliminating their ownership interest in the company. . . . [W]e must decide whether a minority stockholder may challenge a short-form merger by seeking equitable relief through an entire fairness claim. Under settled principles, a parent corporation and its directors undertaking a short-form merger are self-dealing fiduciaries who should be required to establish entire fairness, including fair dealing and fair price. The problem is that *§ 253* authorizes a summary procedure that is inconsistent with any reasonable notion of fair dealing. In a short-form merger, there is no agreement of merger negotiated by two companies; there is only a unilateral act—a decision by the parent company that its 90% owned subsidiary shall no longer exist as a separate entity. The minority stockholders receive no advance notice of the merger; their directors do not consider or approve it; and there is no vote. Those who object are given the right to obtain fair value for their shares through appraisal.

The equitable claim plainly conflicts with the statute. If a corporate fiduciary follows the truncated process authorized by *§ 253*, it will not be able to establish the fair dealing prong of entire fairness. If, instead, the corporate fiduciary sets up negotiating committees, hires independent financial and legal experts, etc., then it will have lost the very benefit provided by the statute—a simple, fast and inexpensive process for accomplishing a merger. We resolve this conflict by giving effect the intent of the General Assembly.[21] In order to serve its purpose, *§ 253* must be construed to obviate the requirement to establish entire fairness.

Thus, we . . . hold that, absent fraud or illegality, appraisal is the exclusive remedy available to a minority stockholder who objects to a short-form merger. In doing so, we also reaffirm *Weinberger's* statements about the scope of appraisal. The determination of fair value must be based on *all* relevant factors, including damages and elements of future value, where appropriate. So, for example, if the merger was timed to take advantage of a depressed market, or a low point in the company's cyclical earnings, or to precede an anticipated positive development, the appraised value may be adjusted to account for those factors. We recognize that these are the types of issues frequently raised in entire fairness claims, and we have held that claims for unfair dealing cannot be litigated in an appraisal.[22] But our prior holdings simply explained that equitable claims may not be engrafted onto a statutory appraisal proceeding; stockholders may not receive rescissionary relief in an appraisal. Those decisions should not be read to restrict the elements of value that properly may be considered in an appraisal.

Although fiduciaries are not required to establish entire fairness in a short-form merger, the duty of full disclosure remains, in the context of this request for stockholder action. Where the only choice for the minority stockholders is whether to accept the merger consideration or seek appraisal, they must be given all the factual information that is material to that decision. The Court of Chancery carefully considered plaintiffs' disclosure claims and applied settled law in rejecting them. We affirm this aspect of the appeal on the basis of the trial court's decision.

---

[21]   *Klotz v. Warner Communications, Inc.,* Del.Supr., 674 A.2d 878, 879 (1995).

[22]   *Alabama By-Products Corporation v. Neal,* Del.Supr., 588 A.2d 255, 257 (1991).

III. Conclusion

Based on the foregoing, we affirm the Court of Chancery and hold that plaintiffs' only remedy in connection with the short-form merger of UXC into Unocal was appraisal.

———

Solomon v. Pathe

Supreme Court of Delaware, 1996.
672 A.2d 35.

■ HARTNETT, JUSTICE. . . .

[Credit Lyonnais Banque Nederland NV (CLBN) pursuant to a loan agreement with Pathe Communications Corporation controlled 89.5 percent of Pathe's voting stock. In response to CLBN's offer to make a tender offer for Pathe shares, Pathe created a special committee and supported CLBN's tender offer to acquire 5.8 million Pathe shares at $1.50 per share. John Solomon instituted a class action on behalf of the Pathe minority holders, alleging the tender offer was unfair, coercive, was a breach of the CLBN's duty of loyalty as a controlling stockholder and that the Pathe board had acted improperly by failing to obtain independent advisors to assess the tender offer.]

[The complaint] attempts to assert a breach of the duty of fair dealing by the directors because they did not oppose the tender offer. The asserted unfairness of the tender offer is based on its allegedly inadequate price. The Chancellor's holding that none of the facts cited by Solomon "can be said to arouse as much as a fleeting doubt of the fairness of the [disclosure] or the $1.50 tender offer" price is correct as a matter of law.

In the case of totally voluntary tender offers, as here, courts do not impose any right of the shareholders to receive a particular price. . . . Delaware law recognizes that, as to allegedly voluntary tender offers (in contrast to cash-out mergers), the determinative factor as to voluntariness is whether coercion is present, or whether there is "materially false or misleading disclosures made to shareholders in connection with the offer." *Eisenberg v. Chicago Milwaukee Corp.*, Del.Ch., 537 A.2d 1051, 1056 (1987) (citations omitted). A transaction may be considered involuntary, despite being voluntary in appearance and form, if one of these factors is present. *Id.* There is no well-plead allegation of any coercion or false or misleading disclosures in the present case, however.

Moreover, in the absence of coercion or disclosure violations, the adequacy of the price in a voluntary tender offer cannot be an issue. *Weinberger*, 457 A.2d at 703. . . . Solomon has plead no facts from which there could be drawn a reasonable inference that there was coercion or lack of complete disclosure. The amended complaint focuses mainly on a conclusory allegation that coercion was present. The complaint, therefore, falls well short of the minimum notice requirements. "Conclusions . . . will not be accepted as true without specific allegations of fact to support them." . . .

For the foregoing reasons, the Court of Chancery's dismissal of Solomon's claim under Rule 12(b)(6) for failure to state a claim upon which relief can be granted is AFFIRMED.

In re Pure Resources, Inc. Shareholder Litigation
Delaware Chancery Court, 2002.
808 A.2d 421.

■ STRINE, VICE-CHANCELLOR

[Unocal, which owned 65% of Pure Resources, made a tender offer for the remaining 35%. The tender offer included a non-waivable condition under which the offer would be effective only if a majority of the shares not owned by Unocal were tendered. Unocal's bid stated it intended to carry out a short-form merger at the same price if a majority of the minority Pure Resources shareholders tendered their shares. Shareholders in Pure Resources sought to enjoin the tender offer on the ground that the entire fairness standard was applicable to the transaction and argued that the transaction did not satisfy that standard because the tender-offer price was inadequate. Unocal replied that the entire fairness standard was inapplicable, because it applied only to negotiated transactions between a controlling shareholder and a controlled corporation, and Unocal had made a tender offer, rather than entering into a negotiated transaction. Accordingly, Unocal argued, under Solomon v. Pathe Communications, supra, Unocal was free to make the offer at whatever price it chose, so long Unocal did not (i) "structurally coerce" the Pure Resources minority by suggesting explicitly or implicitly that injurious events would occur to those shareholders who failed to tender; or (ii) mislead the Pure Resources minority into tendering by concealing or misstating material facts.]

This case . . . involves an aspect of Delaware law fraught with doctrinal tension: what equitable standard of fiduciary conduct applies when a controlling shareholder seeks to acquire the rest of the company's shares? . . .

In building the common law, judges . . . cannot escape making normative choices, based on imperfect information about the world. This reality clearly pervades the area of corporate law implicated by this case. When a transaction to buy out the minority is proposed, is it more important to the development of strong capital markets to hold controlling stockholders and target boards to very strict (and litigation-intensive) standards of fiduciary conduct? Or is more stockholder wealth generated if less rigorous protections are adopted, which permit acquisitions to proceed so long as the majority has not misled or strong-armed the minority? Is such flexibility in fact beneficial to minority stockholders because it encourages liquidity-generating tender offers to them and provides incentives for acquirers to pay hefty premiums to buy control, knowing that control will be accompanied by legal rules that permit a later "going private" transaction to occur in a relatively non-litigious manner?

At present, the Delaware case law has two strands of authority that answer these questions differently. In one strand, which deals with situations in which controlling stockholders negotiate a merger agreement with the target board to buy out the minority, our decisional law emphasizes the protection of minority stockholders against unfairness. In the other strand, which deals with situations when a controlling stockholder seeks to acquire the rest of the company's shares through a tender offer followed by a short-form merger under 8 Del.C. § 253, Delaware case precedent facilitates the free flow of capital between willing buyers and willing sellers of shares, so long as the consent of the sellers is not procured by inadequate or misleading information or by wrongful compulsion.

These strands appear to treat economically similar transactions as categorically different simply because the method by which the controlling stockholder proceeds varies. This disparity in treatment persists even though the two basic methods (negotiated merger versus tender offer/short-form merger) pose similar threats to minority stockholders. Indeed, it can be argued that the distinction in approach subjects the transaction that is more protective of minority stockholders when implemented with appropriate protective devices—a merger negotiated by an independent committee with the power to say no and conditioned on a majority of the minority vote—to more stringent review than the more dangerous form of a going private deal—an unnegotiated tender offer made by a majority stockholder. The latter transaction is arguably less protective than a merger of the kind described, because the majority stockholder-offeror has access to inside information, and the offer requires disaggregated stockholders to decide whether to tender quickly, pressured by the risk of being squeezed out in a short-form merger at a different price later or being left as part of a much smaller public minority. This disparity creates a possible incoherence in our law. . . .

To illustrate this possible incoherence in our law, it is useful to sketch out these two strands. I begin with negotiated mergers. In *Kahn v. Lynch Communication Systems, Inc.*, the Delaware Supreme Court addressed the standard of review that applies when a controlling stockholder attempts to acquire the rest of the corporation's shares in a negotiated merger pursuant to 8 Del.C. § 251. The Court held that the stringent entire fairness form of review governed regardless of whether:

i) the target board was comprised of a majority of independent directors; ii) a special committee of the target's independent directors was empowered to negotiate and veto the merger; and iii) the merger was made subject to approval by a majority of the disinterested target stockholders. . . .

The second strand of cases involves tender offers made by controlling stockholders—i.e., the kind of transaction Unocal has proposed. The prototypical transaction addressed by this strand involves a tender offer by the controlling stockholder addressed to the minority stockholders. In that offer, the controlling stockholder promises to buy as many shares as the minority will sell but may subject its offer to certain conditions. For example, the controlling stockholder might condition the offer on receiving enough tenders for it to obtain 90% of the subsidiary's shares, thereby enabling the controlling stockholder to consummate a short-form merger under 8 Del.C. § 253 at either the same or a different price. . . .

Before *Glassman*, transactional planners had wondered whether the back-end of the tender offer/short-form merger transaction would subject the controlling stockholder to entire fairness review. *Glassman* seemed to answer that question favorably from the standpoint of controlling stockholders, and to therefore encourage the tender offer/short-form merger form of acquisition as presenting a materially less troublesome method of proceeding than a negotiated merger.

Why? Because the legal rules that governed the front end of the tender offer/short-form merger method of acquisition had already provided a more flexible, less litigious path to acquisition for controlling stockholders than the negotiated merger route. Tender offers are not addressed by the Delaware General Corporation Law ("DGCL"), a factor that has been of great importance in shaping the line of decisional law addressing tender offers by controlling stockholders—but not, as I will discuss, tender offers made by third parties.

Because no consent or involvement of the target board is statutorily mandated for tender offers, our courts have recognized that "[i]n the case of totally voluntary tender offers . . . courts do not impose any right of the shareholders to receive a particular price. Delaware law recognizes that, as to allegedly voluntary tender offers (in contrast to cash-out mergers), the determinative factors as to voluntariness are whether coercion is present, or whether there are materially false or misleading disclosures made to stockholders in connection with the offer.[28]" . . .

The differences between this approach, which I will identify with the *Solomon* line of cases, and that of *Lynch* are stark. To begin with, the controlling stockholder is said to have no duty to pay a fair price, irrespective of its power over the subsidiary. Even more striking is the different manner in which the coercion concept is deployed. In the tender

---

[28]   *Solomon v. Pathe Communications Corp.*, 672 A.2d 35, 39 (Del.1996) (citations and quotations omitted).

offer context addressed by *Solomon* and its progeny, coercion is defined in the more traditional sense as a wrongful threat that has the effect of forcing stockholders to tender at the wrong price to avoid an even worse fate later on, a type of coercion I will call structural coercion. The inherent coercion that *Lynch* found to exist when controlling stockholders seek to acquire the minority's stake is not even a cognizable concern for the common law of corporations if the tender offer method is employed.

This latter point is illustrated by those cases that squarely hold that a tender is not actionably coercive if the majority stockholder decides to: (i) condition the closing of the tender offer on support of a majority of the minority and (ii) promise that it would consummate a short-form merger on the same terms as the tender offer. In those circumstances, at least, these cases can be read to bar a claim against the majority stockholder even if the price offered is below what would be considered fair in an entire fairness hearing ("fair price") or an appraisal action ("fair value"). That is, in the tender offer context, our courts consider it sufficient protection against coercion to give effective veto power over the offer to a majority of the minority. Yet that very same protection is considered insufficient to displace fairness review in the negotiated merger context. . . .

The problem is that nothing about the tender offer method of corporate acquisition makes the 800 pound gorilla's retributive capabilities less daunting to minority stockholders. Indeed, many commentators would argue that the tender offer form is more coercive than a merger vote. In a merger vote, stockholders can vote no and still receive the transactional consideration if the merger prevails. In a tender offer, however, a non-tendering shareholder individually faces an uncertain fate. That stockholder could be one of the few who holds out, leaving herself in an even more thinly traded stock with little hope of liquidity and subject to a § 253 merger at a lower price or at the same price but at a later (and, given the time value of money, a less valuable) time. The 14D–9 warned Pure's minority stockholders of just this possibility. For these reasons, some view tender offers as creating a prisoner's dilemma—distorting choice and creating incentives for stockholders to tender into offers that they believe are inadequate in order to avoid a worse fate. But whether or not one views tender offers as more coercive of shareholder choice than negotiated mergers with controlling stockholders, it is difficult to argue that tender offers are materially freer and more reliable measures of stockholder sentiment. . . .

. . . [T]he preferable policy choice is to continue to adhere to the more flexible and less constraining *Solomon* approach, while giving some greater recognition to the inherent coercion and structural bias concerns that motivate the *Lynch* line of cases. Adherence to the *Solomon* rubric as a general matter, moreover, is advisable in view of the increased activism of institutional investors and the greater information flows available to them. Investors have demonstrated themselves capable of resisting tender offers made by controlling stockholders on occasion, and even the lead plaintiff here expresses no fear of retribution. This does not mean that controlling stockholder tender offers do not pose risks to minority stockholders; it is only to acknowledge that the corporate law should not be designed on the assumption that diversified investors are infirm but instead should give great deference to transactions approved by them voluntarily and knowledgeably. . . .

The potential for coercion and unfairness posed by controlling stockholders who seek to acquire the balance of the company's shares by acquisition requires some equitable reinforcement, in order to give proper effect to the concerns undergirding *Lynch*. In order to address the prisoner's dilemma problem, our law should consider an acquisition tender offer by a controlling stockholder non-coercive only when: 1) it is subject to a non-waivable majority of the minority tender condition; 2) the controlling stockholder promises to consummate a prompt § 253 merger at the same price if it obtains more than 90% of the shares; and 3) the controlling stockholder has made no retributive threats. Those protections . . . minimize the distorting influence of the tendering process on voluntary choice. They also recognize the adverse conditions that confront stockholders who find themselves owning what have become very thinly traded shares. These conditions also provide a partial cure to the disaggregation problem, by providing a realistic non-tendering goal the minority can achieve to prevent the offer from proceeding altogether.

The informational and timing advantages possessed by controlling stockholders also require some countervailing protection if the minority is to truly be afforded the opportunity to make an informed, voluntary tender decision. In this regard, the majority stockholder owes a duty to permit the independent directors on the target board both free rein and adequate time to react to the tender offer, by (at the very least) hiring their own advisors, providing the minority with a recommendation as to the advisability of the offer, and disclosing adequate information for the minority to make an informed judgment. For their part, the independent directors have a duty to undertake these tasks in good faith and diligently, and to pursue the best interests of the minority. . . .

Turning specifically to Unocal's Offer, I conclude that the application of these principles yields the following result. The Offer, in its present form, is coercive because it includes within the definition of the "minority" those stockholders who are affiliated with Unocal as directors and officers. It also includes the management of Pure, whose incentives are skewed by their employment, their severance agreements [which gave the managers the right to severance payments, up to three times their annual salaries and bonuses, upon successful completion of the tender offer], and their Put Agreements [which give the managers the right to sell their Pure shares to Unocal upon the occurrence of certain events, arguably including the successful completion of Unocal's tender offer, at an amount that could exceed the tender-offer price]. This is, of course, a problem that can be cured if Unocal amends the Offer to condition it on approval of a majority of Pure's unaffiliated stockholders. Requiring the minority to be defined exclusive of stockholders whose independence from the controlling stockholder is compromised is the better legal rule (and result). Too often, it will be the case that officers and directors of controlled subsidiaries have voting incentives that are not perfectly aligned with their economic interest in their stock and who are more than acceptably susceptible to influence from controlling stockholders. Aside, however, from this glitch in the majority of the minority condition, I conclude that Unocal's Offer satisfies the other requirements of "non-coerciveness." Its promise to consummate a prompt § 253 merger is sufficiently specific, and Unocal has made no retributive threats. . . .

For all these reasons, therefore, I find that the plaintiffs do not have a probability of success on the merits of their attack on the Offer, with the exception that the majority of the minority condition is flawed. . . .

DELAWARE'S STREAMLINED BACK-END MERGER PROCEDURE

Should the boards of Bidder and Target, who are independent of one another, be able to agree that they will combine without a formal shareholder vote by the Target shareholders, provided Bidder first undertakes a tender offer that results in the Bidder obtaining enough shares to assure approval of merger were a merger vote to occur? Such an arrangement is referred to as a 'back-end merger." In 2013, Delaware added Section 251(h), authorizing streamlined back-end mergers if certain conditions are met. The provision applies only to publicly held corporations (i.e., listed on a national exchange or that have 2,000 holders) and requires:

    i.   The merger agreement expressly state the merger is governed by Section 251(h);

    ii.   The acquiring company undertakes a tender or exchange offer for all the outstanding shares of the target firm that would otherwise be entitled to vote on the agreement;

    iii.   The acquiring company owns at least the required amount of stock necessary to approve the merger;

    iv.   The acquiring firm is not an interested stockholder per DGCL § 203 (e.g., owns15 percent or more of the target); and

    v.   The outstanding shares of the target are acquired through a merger for the same amount and kind of consideration paid in the earlier offer.

It is important to note that Section 251(h) does not relieve the target board of its fiduciary duties in considering the merger. Moreover, the provision permits the target board to set the approval level higher than the level that otherwise provided by the statute for approval of mergers.

In re Volcano Corp. Stockholder Litig.

Court of Chancery of Delaware, 2016.
143 A.3d 727 (Del. Ch. 2016), aff'd, 2017 Del. LEXIS 56 (Del., Feb. 9, 2017).

[With the assistance of Goldman, Sachs, Volcano approached five companies concerning whether they had an interest in acquiring Volcano. No offer was forthcoming, but a sixth company, Phillips Holdings, made a non-binding indication of interest to acquire Volcano at $24 per share, subject to an eight-week exclusivity provision to permit Phillips to carryout due diligence (Volcano shares were then trading at $16.18 per share). Volcano, while welcoming Phillips' interest, nonetheless refused to grant Phillips any exclusive arrangement and communicated through Goldman, Sachs that the price would have to be above $24. In the ensuing weeks, poor performance by Volcano caused its stock to decline to $12.56 and Phillips reduced its offer to $17.25. This offer was rejected by Volcano. Five days later, Phillips presented a $16 per share offer and Volcano's board stated it would not consider an offer below $18. A week later, Volcano reported greater than expected earnings, Phillips raised its offer to $18, and the Volcano board approved a two-step transaction pursuant to Section 251(h), recommending that Volcano's shareholders tender their shares into the first-step tender offer. On February 17, 2015, the tender offer closed with 89.1 percent of Volcano's outstanding shares being tendered. That same day, the second-step merger was consummated.

Quarrelsome Volcano stockholders' interest in challenging the transaction was piqued by several results flowing from the transaction. Before Volcano began to seek any strategic buyer it had engaged Goldman, Sachs as its underwriter for $460 million in convertible notes. Fearing that the notes' convertibility could harmfully dilute the ownership interest of its stockholders, Volcano and Goldman, Sachs entered into a series of derivative transactions that had the ultimate effect of raising substantially the price at which conversion of the notes would make financial sense. Not surprisingly, this had potential costs and benefits; Goldman, Sachs fee increased as a result of the so-called change of control provision that was part of the derivative transactions. As a consequence of the merger with Phillips, Goldman, Sachs would thereby receive $24.6 million payment from Volcano pursuant to the terms of the call/spread derivative transaction. Furthermore, Volcano's senior management received about $8.9 million as a result of the change of control accelerating options and restricted stock rights they had. And, the CEO obtained a range of severance benefits totaling $7.8 million. These items, however, were all sufficiently disclosed to Volcano's stockholders so the court believe full disclosure had occurred.

The plaintiff's argued that a merger carried out pursuant to Section 251(h) should not enjoy the business judgment rule presumption equal to that of the typical straight merger authorized by Section 251, because of differences between shareholders manifesting their approval by tendering their shares in the former and shareholders voting in the latter.]

Two concerns have been raised [by the plaintiff] to support the argument that stockholder acceptance of a tender offer and a stockholder vote differ in a manner that should preclude the cleansing effect articulated by the Supreme Court in *Corwin* from applying to tender offers. Section 251(h) addresses each of those concerns. The first concern suggests that tender offers may differ from statutorily required stockholder votes based on "the lack of any explicit role in the [DGCL] for a target board of directors responding to a tender offer." A target board's role in negotiating a two-step merger subject to a first-step tender offer under Section 251(h), however, is substantially similar to its role in a merger subject to a stockholder vote under Section 251(c) of the DGCL. Section 251(h) requires that the merging corporations enter into a merger agreement that expressly "[p]ermits or requires such merger be effected under [Section 251(h)]." Because Section 251(h) requires a merger agreement, Sections 251(a) and (b) of the DGCL subject that agreement to the same obligations as a merger or consolidation consummated under any other section of the DGCL. For example, the target corporation's board must "adopt a resolution approving" that agreement "and declaring its advisability," and the merger agreement must provide "[t]he terms and conditions of the merger." The first-step tender offer also must be made "on the terms provided" in the negotiated merger agreement. And, in recommending that its stockholders tender their shares in connection with a Section 251(h) merger, the target corporation's board has the same disclosure obligations as it would in any other communication with those stockholders. Taken together, therefore, Sections 251(a), (b), and (h) of the DGCL mandate that a target corporation's board negotiate, agree to, and declare the advisability of the terms of both the first-step tender offer and the second-step merger in a Section 251(h) merger, just as a target corporation's board must negotiate, agree to, and declare the advisability of a merger involving a stockholder vote under Section 251(c). The target board also is subject to the same common law fiduciary duties, regardless of the subsection under which the merger is consummated.

The second concern suggests that a first-step tender offer in a two-step merger arguably is more coercive than a stockholder vote in a one-step merger. Section 251(h), however, alleviates the coercion that stockholders might otherwise be subject to in a tender offer because (1) the first-step tender offer must be for all of the target company's outstanding stock, (2) the second-step merger must "be effected as soon as practicable following the consummation of the" first-step tender offer, (3) the consideration paid in the second-step merger must be of "the same amount and kind" as that paid in the first-step tender offer, and (4) appraisal rights are available in all Section 251(h) mergers, subject to the conditions and requirements of Section 262 of the DGCL. Thus, Section 251(h) appears to eliminate the policy bases on which a first-step tender offer in a two-step merger may be distinguished from a statutorily required stockholder vote, at least as it relates to the cleansing effect rendered therefrom. . . .

When a merger is consummated under Section 251(h), the first-step tender offer essentially replicates a statutorily required stockholder vote in favor of a merger in that both require approval—albeit pursuant to different corporate mechanisms—by stockholders representing at least a majority of a corporation's outstanding shares to effectuate the merger. A stockholder is no less exercising her "free and informed chance to decide on the economic merits of a transaction" simply by virtue of accepting a tender offer rather than casting a vote. And, judges are just as "poorly positioned to evaluate the wisdom of" stockholder-approved mergers under Section 251(h) as they are in the context of corporate transactions with statutorily required stockholder votes. . . .

I conclude that the acceptance of a first-step tender offer by fully informed, disinterested, uncoerced stockholders representing a majority of a corporation's outstanding shares in a two-step merger under Section 251(h) has the same cleansing effect . . . as a vote in favor of a merger by a fully informed, disinterested, uncoerced stockholder majority. . . .

143 A.3d at 741–47.

* * *

The outcome in *Volcano Corp.* was greatly influenced by *Corwin v. KKR Fin. Holdings LLC*, 125 A.3d 304 (Del. 2015), which appears later in this chapter.

———

NOTES ON "GOING DARK"

1.   Reporting Cost Concerns. Weinberger illustrates a "going private" transaction. In the close corporation setting the more pejorative expressions of "freeze out" and "squeeze out" are used to describe the same result as occurs in "going private" transactions, namely the dominant stockholder undertaking a transaction or series of transactions with the objective of eliminating the minority stockholders. A related but not identical objective is "going dark." This expression refers to a process through which a *public* company reduces the number of public stockholders below 300 so that it no longer is required to file periodic reports with the SEC, i.e., it ceases to be an Exchange Act reporting company. Exchange Act Rule 12g–3 lifts the periodic reporting requirements for any class of security that is held by less than 300 persons. Thus, in a going dark transaction the objective is not necessarily to eliminate all minority holders, but just enough of them to reduce the number of owners to below 300.

With the passage of the Sarbanes-Oxley Act of 2002 (SOX), there has been a good deal of interest in whether the Act's strengthening the financial reporting requirements for public companies is causally connected to a post-2002 upward trend in the number of firms going dark. SOX-imposed regulations significantly increased the costs of being a public company so that firms, reassessing the costs and benefits of being a public company, would in a post-SOX era face a very different calculus and could, therefore, find better to be a non-reporting company than a reporting one. *See* William Carney, The Costs of Being Public After Sarbanes-Oxley: The Irony of "Going Private," 55 Emory L.J. 141 (2006). Since reporting costs generally have high fixed cost components, meaning they dwindle in relative importance as a firm gets larger (in assets and revenues), reporting costs appear to be a major consideration in going dark for small firms rather than medium-or large-sized firms. Robert P. Bartlett III, Going Private but Staying Public: Reexamining the Effect of Sarbanes-Oxley on Firm's Going-private Decisions, 76 U. Chi. L. Rev. 7, 37–38 (2009); Ehud Kamar, Pinar Karaca-Mandic, & Eric Talley, Going-private Decisions and the Sarbanes-Oxley Act of 2002: A Cross-country Analysis, 25 J. L. Econ. & Org., 107, 130 (2009) ("exodus of small firms from the public capital market" due to SOX-related reporting costs may be socially desirable if those firms are more prone to engage in fraud). Moreover, firms are more likely to go dark if they have fewer growth opportunities, a larger percentage of their shares owned by managers, and significant free cash flows. Andras Marosi & Nadia Massoud, Why Do Firms Go Dark?, 42 J. Fin. & Quantitative Analysis 421, 440 (2007) (gathering data that supports conclusion that going dark enables insiders to exploit future information asymmetries to capture the benefits of the firm's future free cash flow). The empirical evidence is a bit more scattered on the question of whether SOX precipitated an increase in going private transactions. To be sure, there is evidence that size appears related to the likelihood of going private, thus supporting the thesis that higher reporting costs introduced by SOX drove companies into the shadows. *See* Ellen Engel, Rachel M. Hayes & Xue Wang, The Sarbanes-Oxley Act and Firms' Going-private Decisions, 44 J. Accounting & Econ. 116, 143 (2007) (frequency of going private increased after SOX and was more common for smaller firms with high insider ownership); Christian Leuz, Was the Sarbanes-Oxley Act Really this Costly? A Discussion of Evidence from Event Returns and Going-Private Decisions, 44 J. Accounting & Econ. 146, 159 (2007) (going private more common among smaller firms, with weaker performance and poorer internal governance). However, comparison with the size and frequency of companies going dark in the U.S. with the U.K. reflects similar trends in size and frequency of going private transactions on both sides of the Atlantic. Leuz, *supra*, at 162. Finally, it should be remembered that the post-SOX era was the heyday of the private equity firms that exploited the availability of historically low interest rates that enabled them to take companies private via leveraged buyouts. Thus, the decision to go dark or private is likely a complex one, but one that is initiated by the firm's managers.

2.   *Compliance with SEC Rule 13e–3.* Securities Exchange Act Rule 13e–3 imposes significant disclosure requirements for certain going dark/private transactions. In broad overview, Rule 13e–3 applies to transactions that are either with the issuer of the security or a person that controls the issuer which transaction causes a class of the issuer's stock to cease to be listed on an exchange or will reduce the numbers of holders of that class of stock below 300 (i.e., the firm goes dark). The transaction producing either of these effects can be via a purchase, merger, reverse stock dividend, tender offer or recapitalization. If this occurs, within 20 days of the shares' acquisition, extensive disclosures called for by Schedule 13E–3 must be provided. For example, Item 8 of the form not only requires the directors to express their opinion regarding the transaction's fairness, but calls for a detailed discussion of the "material factors upon which the belief" is based. Courts have recognized an implied right of action for misrepresentations committed in 13e–3 transactions. *See* Howing v. Nationwide Corp., 826 F.2d 1470 (6th Cir. 1987), *cert. denied*, 486 U.S. 1059, 108 S.Ct. 2830, 100 L.Ed.2d 930 (1988). Several exemptions to Rule 13e–3 exist, the most significant are: 1) the transaction is the second step of a preannounced two-step acquisition, provided the consideration is at least equal to that offered in the earlier tender offer, the second step occurs within one year of the tender offer, and the earlier tender offer fully disclosed the intent to undertake the second step acquisition; 2) the transaction provides that the issuer's security holders receive only an equity security that has substantially the same rights as the equity security given up and is registered under the Exchange Act; or 3) the security's redemption, call or other acquisition is pursuant to the rights set forth in the articles of incorporation or other instrument setting forth rights, privileges or preferences of the security.

SECURITIES EXCHANGE ACT RULE 13e–3
AND SCHEDULE 13E–3

[See Statutory Supplement]

---

2. HOSTILE TAKEOVERS AND DEFENDING CONTROL

SECURITIES EXCHANGE ACT §§ 13(d), (e), 14(d), (e)

[See Statutory Supplement]

SECURITIES EXCHANGE ACT RULES 13d–1, 13d–3, 13d–5, 13e–1, 13e–4, 14d1 to 14d–4, 14d–6 to 14d–10, 14e–1 to 14e–3, 14e–5

[See Statutory Supplement]

SCHEDULE TO

[See Statutory Supplement]

SCHEDULE [I4D–9]

[See Statutory Supplement]

HART-SCOTT-RODINO ACT

[See Statutory Supplement]

THE LEXICON OF THE BATTLE FOR CONTROL

The legal profession has developed a rich terminology in connection with tender offers. The terms are too numerous and change too quickly to permit a comprehensive glossary, and some of the terms are fairly well defined in the cases that follow. This Note defines a few of the more important terms that are not defined in those cases.

Raider. The term *raider* refers to a person (normally, although not necessarily, a corporation) that makes a tender offer. The term is invidious; a more accurate term is *bidder.*

Target. The corporation whose shares the raider or bidder seeks to acquire is referred to as the *target.*

White knight. Often the management of a target realizes that it will be taken over, but prefers a takeover by someone (sometimes, anyone) other than the original bidder. The management therefore solicits competing tender offers from other corporations. These more friendly corporations are known as *white knights.*

Lock-up. A *lock-up* is a device that is designed to protect one bidder (normally, a friendly bidder or white knight) against competition by other bidders (deemed less friendly). The favored bidder is given an option to acquire selected assets, or a given amount of shares, of the target at a favorable price under designated conditions. These conditions usually involve either defeat of the favored bidder's attempt to acquire the corporation, or the occurrence of events that would make that defeat likely.

Crown jewels. To defeat or discourage a takeover bid by a disfavored bidder, the target's management may sell or (more usually) give to a white knight a lock-up option that covers the target's most desirable business or, at least, the business most coveted by the disfavored bidder—its *crown jewels.*

Fair-price provisions. A *fair-price provision* requires that a supermajority (usually eighty percent) of the voting power of a corporation must approve any merger or similar combination with an acquiror who owns a specified interest in the corporation (usually twenty percent of the voting power). The supermajority vote is not required under certain conditions— most notably, if the transaction is approved by a majority of those directors who are not affiliated with the acquiror and who were directors at the time the acquiror reached the specified level of ownership of the company, or if certain minimum-price criteria and procedural requirements are satisfied. A fair-price provision discourages purchasers whose objective is to seek control of a corporation at a relatively cheap price, and discourages accumulations of large blocks, because it reduces the options that an acquiror has once it reaches the specified level of shares.

Management buyout. A *management buyout (MBO)* is an acquisition for cash or non-convertible senior securities of the business of a public corporation, by a newly organized corporation in which members of the former management of the public corporation will have a significant equity interest, pursuant to a merger or other form of combination. See Lowenstein, Management Buyouts, 85 Colum.L.Rev. 730, 732 (1985).

Leverage. *Leverage* involves the use of debt to increase the return on equity. The extent of leverage is measured by the ratio of debt to equity. The higher the ratio, the greater the leverage (or, to put it differently, the more highly leveraged the corporation is).

Leveraged buyout. A *leveraged buyout* (LBO) is a buyout that is highly leveraged—that is, in which the newly organized acquiring corporation has a very high amount of debt in relation to its equity. Characteristically, an LBO is arranged by a firm that specializes in such transactions; can find investors (or will itself invest) that frequently include the former senior management in the new firm's securities; and can arrange for (or help arrange for) placement of the massive amount of debt that the new corporation must issue to finance the acquisition of the old corporation's business.

Junk bonds. A *junk bond* is a bond that has an unusually high risk of default (and is therefore below investment grade), but correspondingly carries an unusually high yield. (The theory is that by diversification—that is, by holding a portfolio of junk bonds—investors in junk bonds can insulate themselves from catastrophic loss if any one bond issue goes under.) Because an LBO is so highly leveraged, much or most of the debt issued to finance an LBO usually consists of junk bonds.

No-shop clauses. A board of a corporation that enters into an agreement for a merger or other corporate combination (whether with a white knight or otherwise) may agree that it will recommend the combination to its shareholders, that it will not shop around for a more attractive deal, or both.

Standstill. A target may seek an accommodation with a shareholder who has acquired a significant amount of stock, under which the shareholder agrees to limit his stock purchases—hence, *standstill.* In the typical standstill agreement, the shareholder makes one or more commitments: (i) it will not increase its shareholdings above designated limits for a specified period of time; (ii) it will not sell its shares without giving the corporation a right of first refusal; (iii) it will not engage in a proxy contest; and (iv) it will vote its stock in a designated manner in the election of directors, and perhaps on other issues. In return, the corporation may agree to give the shareholder board representation, to register the shareholder's stock under the Securities Act on demand, and to not oppose the shareholder's acquisition of more stock up to the specified limit.

A. THE WILLIAMS ACT

Tender offers, and the initial or *toehold* share acquisitions by the bidder that often precede them, are regulated in a great number of respects by the Williams Act, which added sections 13(d) and (e), and 14(d), (e), and (f), to the Securities Exchange Act. Section 14(d), and Rule 14d thereunder, apply to tender offers for more than 5% of any class of equity security that is registered under Section 12 of the Act. In contrast, section 14(e), and Rule 14e thereunder, apply to any tender offer for any class of security. Accordingly, in theory section 14(e) and Rule 14e cover more tender offers than section 14(d) and Rule 14d. In practice, however, most tender offers will be covered by both sections and both rules. For ease of exposition, in the balance of this Note all references to tender offers will mean tender offers that are covered by the relevant sections and rules, unless otherwise stated.

NOTES ON THE WILLIAMS ACT PROVISIONS.

1. *Early Warning.* Under section 13(d) of the Securities Exchange Act, a person who has acquired beneficial ownership of more than 5% of any class of equity securities registered under section 12 of the Act must file a

Schedule 13D within 10 days of the acquisition. The Dodd-Frank Wall Street Reform and Consumer Protection Act of 2010 amended section 13(d) to authorizes the SEC to shorten the filing time. Schedule 13D requires extensive disclosure including the purchaser's identity and background; the amount and sources of the funds for the purchase; the purpose of the purchase; any plans with respect to extraordinary corporate transactions involving the corporation whose stock has been acquired; and any contracts, arrangements, or understandings with other persons regarding the corporation's securities. Under Rule 13d–2, any material changes in the information disclosed in a Schedule 13D must be promptly updated, and any further acquisitions of an additional 1% or more of the corporation's stock will be deemed a material change thereby obligating the filer to update an earlier report of its holdings. Even further acquisitions of less than 1% of the corporation's stock may be deemed material, depending on the circumstances. Rule 13d–1(b) provides a more abbreviated disclosure regime for so-called "passive" investors, defined as one who acquired the stock in the ordinary course of business without the intent to change or influence the control of the issuer and whose ownership does not exceed a 10 percent threshold. Such passive owners file annually on Schedule 13G; a passive owner who changes her intent to a "control purpose" must file a Schedule 13D and is precluded from acquiring more shares until ten days after such filing.

Furthermore, under section 13(d)(3) of the Securities Exchange Act, as implemented by Rule 13d–5(b), when two or more persons agree to act together for the purpose of acquiring, holding, voting, or disposing of an issuer's equity securities, the group formed by the agreement is deemed to have acquired ownership of all securities of that issuer owned by any member of the group, for purposes of section 13(d). Even acting in concert may create a group for these purposes.

There long have been calls to shorten the ten-day window within which to make the mandated Section 13(d) filing. Who would be the winners and losers if the window were shortened? *See generally* Lucian Bebchuk, Alon Brav, Robert J. Jackson, Jr. & Wei Jiang, Pre-Disclosure Accumulations by Activist Investors: Evidence and Policy, 39 J. Corp. L. 1 (2013) (activist investors account for about ten percent of any year's 13(d) filings).

Wholly aside from the Williams Act, the Hart-Scott-Rodino Antitrust Improvements Act of 1976 requires notification of acquisitions of stock in medium-size and large publicly held companies. There are essentially two tests, either of which can require notice of the acquisition to be given; the dollar levels for the tests are set annually by the Federal Trade Commission (the following were the levels established in January 2018). First, notice must be filed for any acquisition that results in the acquiring company holding assets or voting stock of the acquired company in excess of $337.6 million. If the acquisition is smaller than this level, then no filing is required, unless the acquisition exceeds both a "size-of-transaction threshold" and a "size-of-person" threshold. The size of transaction threshold is $84.4 million and the size of person threshold is met because either the acquiring or acquired firm has annual sales or total assets of at least $168.8 million *and* the other party has annual sales or total assets of $16.9 million. For many corporations that are likely to be made subject to a tender offer, the applicable thresholds will be substantially less than 5% of its stock. Thus Hart-Scott-Rodino effectively lowers the reporting threshold for many toehold acquisitions.

     2.   *What Constitutes a Tender Offer.* What constitutes a "tender offer" within the meaning of the Williams Act is not completely settled. To provide flexibility to reach unconventional tender offers and takeover measures, Congress did not provide a definition of this "gateway" concept. At one extreme, a public offer, made by a bidder to all shareholders, to purchase, at a fixed stated price, shares that are tendered into the offer during a stated period of time, will almost certainly be deemed a tender offer within the meaning of the Williams Act. At the other extreme, purchases that a buyer makes anonymously in the stock market will almost certainly not be deemed a tender offer within the meaning of the Act. Kennecott Copper Corp. v. Curtiss-Wright Corp., 584 F.2d 1195 (2d Cir.1978); Calumet Industries, Inc. v. MacClure, 464 F.Supp. 19 (N.D.Ill.1978). The problem concerns transactions that fall between these two extremes, such as a series of private offers made to a limited number of potential sellers. Some courts have adopted an eight-factor test to determine whether offers like this are tender offers under the Act. These factors are: (i) Whether the purchasers engage in active and widespread solicitation of public shareholders. (ii) Whether the solicitation is made for a substantial percentage of the corporation's stock. (iii) Whether the offer to purchase is made at a premium over the prevailing market price. (iv) Whether the terms of the offer are firm rather than negotiable. (v) Whether the offer is contingent on the tender of a fixed number of shares. (vi) Whether the offer is open only for a limited period of time. (vii) Whether the offerees are under pressure to sell their stock. (viii) Whether public announcements of a purchasing program preceded or accompanied a rapid accumulation of large amounts of the corporation's stock. Wellman v. Dickinson, 475 F.Supp. 783 (S.D.N.Y.1979), aff'd on other grounds 682 F.2d 355 (2d Cir.1982), cert. denied 460 U.S. 1069, 103 S.Ct. 1522, 75 L.Ed.2d 946 (1983); SEC v. Carter Hawley Hale Stores, Inc., 760 F.2d 945 (9th Cir.1985). More generally, in determining whether there is a tender offer courts tend to focus on the pressure an offer or conduct places on shareholders as well as the sophistication of the shareholders and, therefore, there susceptibility to pressure.

     In *Hanson Trust PLC v. SCM Corp.*, 774 F.2d 47 (2d Cir.1985), the Second Circuit rejected the eight-factor test, and held instead that whether an offer to buy stock constitutes a tender offer under the Williams Act turns on whether there appears to be a likelihood, that unless the Act's rules are followed, there will be a substantial risk that solicited shareholders will lack information needed to make a carefully considered appraisal of the offer. Applying that standard, the Second Circuit held in *Hanson* that the offer before it was not a tender offer. The target had 22,800 shareholders and offers were made to only six. At least five of the sellers were highly sophisticated professionals, knowledgeable in the market place and well aware of the essential facts needed to exercise their professional skills and to appraise the offer. The sellers were not pressured to sell their shares by any conduct that the Williams Act was designed to alleviate, but only by the forces of the marketplace. There was no active or widespread advance publicity or public solicitation. The price received by the six sellers was not at a premium over the then-market price. The purchases were not made contingent upon acquiring a fixed minimum number or percentage of the target's outstanding shares. There was no time limit within which the buyer would purchase the target's stock.

3. *Schedule TO*. Section 14(d) of the Securities Exchange Act requires a schedule TO to be filed by any person who makes a tender offer for a class of registered equity securities that would result in that person owning more than 5% of the class. The Schedule TO must contain extensive disclosure of such matters as the offer; the identity of the bidder; past dealings between the bidder and the target corporation; the bidder's source of funds; the bidder's purposes and plans concerning the target; the bidder's contracts and understandings or relationships with respect to securities of the target; financial statements of the bidder, if they are material and the bidder is not an individual; and arrangements between the bidder and persons holding important positions with the target.

4. *Regulation of the Terms of Tender Offers*. Section 14(d) of the Securities Exchange Act, and Rules 14d and 14e, regulate the terms of tender offers. These provisions impose the following requirements, among others:

a). Minimum Duration. Under Rule 14e–1, a tender offer must be held open for at least twenty business days.

b). All-Holders Rule. Rule 14d–10 provides that a bidder may not make a tender offer for a class of securities unless the offer is open, at the same price and on the same terms, to all holders of the class. This rule is called the "all holders rule." Under the Supremacy Clause, the all-holders rule displaces the outcome of the *Unocal* case, infra, which held that under Delaware law a corporation can make an exclusionary self-tender—that is, a tender offer that excludes certain shares of the class for which the offer is made.

c). Best-Price Rule. Rule 14d–10 also provides that the price paid to any security holder pursuant to a tender offer must equal the highest price that the bidder pays to any other security holder during the tender offer. See Epstein v. MCA, Inc., 54 F.3d 1422 (9th Cir. 1995), rev'd on other grounds sub nom. Matsushita Electrical Industrial Corp. v. Epstein, 516 U.S. 367, 116 S.Ct. 873, 134 L.Ed.2d 6 (1996), reaffirmed on remand, 126 F.3d 1235 (9th Cir. 1997). Under this rule, if, as frequently occurs, the bidder increases the bid price during a tender offer, the new, higher price must be made retroactively available to all holders who tendered before the increase. In addition, Rule 10b–13 provides that during the pendency of tender offer, the bidder cannot purchase securities that are subject to the tender offer except under the tender offer—that is, the bidder cannot make private purchases during the duration of the tender offer. Bidders sometimes become ensnared by Rule 14d–10 due to there being no definition of tender offer. In a leading case, *Field v. Trump*, 850 F.2d 938 (2d Cir. 1988), Trump announced a $22 bid for Pay'n Save, only to cancel the bid five days later to "facilitate negotiations" with two Pay'n Save directors who opposed the offers. That same night Trump struck a deal of $23.50/per share, plus $900,000 for "fees and expenses" (roughly equal to $1.50 on a per share basis) with the two recalcitrant directors. The next day Trump announced a $23.50 bid. The Second Circuit concluded that an offer announced on September 7, withdrawn on September 12, and reannounced a bid on September 13th) constituted the same tender offer and supported a claim under Rule 14d–10. *See also* Epstein v. MCA, Inc., 50 F.3d 644, 655 (9th Cir. 1995) (considering whether the various steps were an integral part of the tender offer), *rev'd on other grounds*, 516 U.S. 367, 116 S.Ct. 873, 134 L.Ed.2d 6 (1996). Other courts have preferred a bright-line approach focused on the formal announcement and discontinuance of the bid. *See* In re Digital Island Securities Litig., 357 F.3d 322, 334 (3d Cir. 2004); Lerro v. Quaker Oats Co., 84 F.3d 239, 244–45 (7th Cir. 1996) (compensation promised to target management for future consulting and non-competition agreements the day before announcing a bid not part of the tender offer). *Contra* Gerber v. Computer Associates Int'l Inc., 303 F.3d 126 (2d Cir. 2002) ($5 million payment to target CEO for 5-year covenant was within the tender offer period). To provide some clarity in this area of severance pay, covenants not to compete and the like, Rule 14d–10(d)(2) now provides a safe harbor for severance and other compensation arrangements if they are approved by a body of independent directors of the target or bidder when the compensation is not based on a per share calculation.

   d).   Withdrawal Rights. Under section 14(d)(5) of the Williams Act, a tendering shareholder can withdraw tendered but unaccepted shares at any time after sixty days from the date the tender offer was disseminated. Under Rule 14d–7, a tendering shareholder can withdraw tendered shares during the entire duration of the offer and any extension of the offer.

   e).   Proration. Under Rule 14d–8, if a bidder makes a partial tender offer—that is, an offer for less than 100% of the target's securities—and more securities are tendered during the duration of the tender offer than the bidder has offered to accept, the bidder must accept all tendered securities, up to the stated percentage, on a pro rata basis.

   f).   Rule 14e–5 prohibits the bidder from buying the target company's securities outside the tender offer. The prohibition "applies from the time of public announcement of the tender offer until the tender offer expires." Rule 14e–5(a). Consider whether the rule is violated if a controlling stockholder launches a tender offer to increase its ownership to ninety percent with the stated purpose of thereafter undertaking a short-form merger of the target into the bidder. Simultaneously the bidder files a proxy statement with the SEC for the straight-form merger of the bidder and the target if tender offer does not raise the bidder's ownership to the ninety percent level. Why might this be a regulatory concern? *See* Popular Two-Track M&A Structure Could Trigger '34 Act, SEC Official Says, 44 BNA Sec. Reg.& Law Rep.1760 (Sept. 24, 2012).

   5.   Obligations of the Target's Management. Rule 14e–2 requires that no later than ten business days from the date the tender offer is first published, the target corporation (really, the target's board) must notify shareholders that the target takes one of the following positions: (A) Recommends acceptance of the tender offer. (B) Recommends rejection of the tender offer. (C) Expresses no opinion and is remaining neutral toward the tender offer. (D) Is unable to take a position with respect to the tender offer. The statement must also describe the reasons for target's position. After making such a statement, the company must update the statement for any material change.

Under Rule 14d–9, any person who solicits or makes a recommendation to shareholders in respect of a tender offer (as opposed to making a tender offer) must file a Schedule 14D–9. This Schedule requires disclosure of the nature of, and the reasons for, the solicitation or recommendation; conflicts of interest of the person filing the statement; and any negotiation or transaction being undertaken that relates to either an extraordinary transaction (such as a merger) involving the target, a purchase or sale of a material amount of assets by the target, an acquisition of securities by the target, or a material change in the target's capitalization or in its dividend policy. Under Rule 14d–9(f), the statement that a target is required to make concerning its position on the tender offer is a solicitation or recommendation to shareholders within the meaning of Rule 14d–9. Accordingly, as a practical matter a target corporation must make the disclosures required by Schedule 14D–9.

6.   Tender Offers by Issuers. Under section 13(e) of the Securities Exchange Act and Rule 13e, corporations that tender for their own stock ("issuer" or "self" tenders) are subject to obligations similar to those imposed on outside bidders under rules 14d and 14e.

7.   Anti-Fraud Provision. Section 14(e) of the Securities Exchange Act prohibits material misstatements, misleading omissions, and fraudulent or manipulative acts, in connection with a tender offer, or any solicitation in favor of or in opposition to a tender offer. Section 14(e) is closely comparable to Rule 10b–5, except that it does not contain the limiting language, "in connection with the purchase or sale" of securities, found in Rule 10b–5. Other elements of the private action under section 14(e) parallel those of Rule 10b–5. For example, early decisions held that a plaintiff who brings suit for damages under section 14(e) must establish scienter. See Connecticut National Bank v. Fluor Corp., 808 F.2d 957 (2d Cir.1987). This question will likely soon be clarified in Emulex Corp. v. Varjabedian, ___ U.S. ___, 139 S.Ct. 782 (Jan. 4, 2019), granting review of Varjabedian v. Emulex Corp., 888 F.3d 399 (9th Cir. 2018), which held that negligence, not scienter, can establish recovery under Section 14(e). And, the fraud on the market approach to causation is similarly available in section 14(e) private suits. See Semerenko v. Cendant Corp., 223 F.3d 165, 178 (3d Cir. 2000). However, as might be expected, section 14(e) claims by investors who have neither purchased nor sold securities confront a skeptical court where close scrutiny of claims of causality occur. See e.g., Lewis v. McGraw, 619 F.2d 192, 195 (2d Cir. 1980); Salsitz v. Peltz, 227 F. Supp. 2d 222, 225 (S.D.N.Y. 2002); P. Schoenfeld Asset Management, LLC v. Cendant Corp., 47 F. Supp. 2d 546, 549 (D. N.J. 1999).

8. *Standing.* The target's shareholders have standing to sue for damages under sections 14(d)(6) (the pro rata requirement), 14(d)(7) (the equal-consideration requirement), and 14(e) (the anti-fraud requirement), and, in appropriate cases, may sue for injunctive relief, under the anti-fraud provision. However, on the theory that the purpose of the Act is to protect the target's shareholders, a bidder does not have standing to sue for damages under the Williams Act. *See* Piper v. Chris-Craft Industries, Inc., 430 U.S. 1, 97 S.Ct. 926, 51 L.Ed.2d 124 (1977). Nonetheless, both the bidder and the target corporation can sue for an injunction against the target and bidder, respectively, for violation of the anti-fraud provision of section 14(e), because such an injunction will protect the interests of the target's shareholders. Gearhart Industries, Inc. v. Smith International, Inc., 741 F.2d 707 (5th Cir.1984).

In general, the courts have also accorded standing to shareholders of a target corporation to seek injunctive relief against continuing violations of § 13(d) (the 5% reporting requirement), including violations caused by false or misleading filings. The target corporation also has a private right of action to seek injunctive relief against continuing violations of § 13(d). The courts are divided on whether a shareholder of the target has an implied private right of action for damages under § 13(d). Similarly, the majority rule is that corporations do not have standing to sue for damages under section 13(d). See Hallwood Realty Partners, L.P. v. Gotham Partners, L.P., 286 F.3d 613 (2d Cir. 2002).

Rival bidders cannot seek damages under the Williams Act against each other resulting from the lost opportunity to gain control, even when they own a nominal amount of shares in the target company. Piper v. Chris-Craft Ind., 430 U.S. 1, 35, 97 S.Ct. 926, 960, 51 L.Ed.2d 124, 158 (1977); Kalmanovitz v. G. Heileman Brewing Co., 595 F.Supp. 1385, 1393 (D. Del. 1984). However, courts have allowed a rival bidder to seek injunctive relief by concluding that an injunctive remedy would better protect the target's shareholders interests than providing damages to shareholders after the transaction is complete. Mobil Corp. v. Marathon Oil Co., 669 F.2d 366, 371–72 (6th Cir. 1981); Humana, Inc. v. American Medicorp, Inc., 445 F.Supp. 613, 614–15 (S.D.N.Y. 1977).

B. ASSESSING THE TARGET'S RESPONSE

Unocal Corp. v. Mesa Petroleum Co.
Supreme Court of Delaware, 1985.
493 A.2d 946.

■ MOORE, JUSTICE.

We confront an issue of first impression in Delaware—the validity of a corporation's self-tender for its own shares which excludes from participation a stockholder making a hostile tender offer for the company's stock. . . .

I.   . . .

On April 8, 1985, Mesa, the owner of approximately 13% of Unocal's stock, commenced a two-tier "front loaded" cash tender offer for 64 million shares, or approximately 37%, of Unocal's outstanding stock at a price of $54 per share. The "back-end" was designed to eliminate the remaining publicly held shares by an exchange of securities purportedly worth $54 per share. However, pursuant to an order entered by the United States District Court for the Central District of California on April 26, 1985, Mesa issued a supplemental proxy statement to Unocal's stockholders disclosing that the securities offered in the second-step merger would be highly subordinated, and that Unocal's capitalization would differ significantly from its present structure. Unocal has rather aptly termed such securities "junk bonds".[2]

Unocal's board consists of eight independent outside directors and six insiders. It met on April 13, 1985, to consider the Mesa tender offer. Thirteen directors were present, and the meeting lasted nine and one-half hours. The directors were given no agenda or written materials prior to the session. However, detailed presentations were made by legal counsel regarding the board's obligations under both Delaware corporate law and the federal securities laws. The board then received a presentation from Peter Sachs on behalf of Goldman Sachs Co. (Goldman Sachs) and Dillon, Read Co. (Dillon Read) discussing the bases for their opinions that the Mesa proposal was wholly inadequate. Mr. Sachs opined that the minimum cash value that could be expected from a sale or orderly liquidation for 100% of Unocal's stock was in excess of $60 per share. In making his presentation, Mr. Sachs showed slides outlining the valuation techniques used by the financial advisors, and others, depicting recent business combinations in the oil and gas industry. The Court of Chancery found that the Sachs presentation was designed to apprise the directors of the scope of the analyses performed rather than the facts and

---

[2]   Mesa's May 3, 1985 supplement to its proxy statement states:

(i) following the Offer, the Purchasers would seek to effect a merger of Unocal and Mesa Eastern or an affiliate of Mesa Eastern (the "Merger") in which the remaining Shares would be acquired for a combination of subordinated debt securities and preferred stock; (ii) the securities to be received by Unocal shareholders in the Merger would be subordinated to $2,400 million of debt securities of Mesa Eastern, indebtedness incurred to refinance up to $1,000 million of bank debt which was incurred by affiliates of Mesa Partners II to purchase Shares and to pay related interest and expenses and all then-existing debt of Unocal; (iii) the corporation surviving the Merger would be responsible for the payment of all securities of Mesa Eastern (including any such securities issued pursuant to the Merger) and the indebtedness referred to in item (ii) above, and such securities and indebtedness would be repaid out of funds generated by the operations of Unocal; (iv) the indebtedness incurred in the Offer and the Merger would result in Unocal being much more highly leveraged, and the capitalization of the corporation surviving the Merger would differ significantly from that of Unocal at present; and (v) in their analyses of cash flows provided by operations of Unocal which would be available to service and repay securities and other obligations of the corporation surviving the Merger, the Purchasers assumed that the capital expenditures and expenditures for exploration of such corporation would be significantly reduced.

numbers used in reaching the conclusion that Mesa's tender offer price was inadequate.

Mr. Sachs also presented various defensive strategies available to the board if it concluded that Mesa's two-step tender offer was inadequate and should be opposed. One of the devices outlined was a self-tender by Unocal for its own stock with a reasonable price range of $70 to $75 per share. The cost of such a proposal would cause the company to incur $6.1–6.5 billion of additional debt, and a presentation was made informing the board of Unocal's ability to handle it. The directors were told that the primary effect of this obligation would be to reduce exploratory drilling, but that the company would nonetheless remain a viable entity.

The eight outside directors, comprising a clear majority of the thirteen members present, then met separately with Unocal's financial advisors and attorneys. Thereafter, they unanimously agreed to advise the board that it should reject Mesa's tender offer as inadequate, and that Unocal should pursue a self-tender to provide the stockholders with a fairly priced alternative to the Mesa proposal. The board then reconvened and unanimously adopted a resolution rejecting as grossly inadequate Mesa's tender offer. Despite the nine and one-half hour length of the meeting, no formal decision was made on the proposed defensive self-tender.

On April 15, the board met again with four of the directors present by telephone and one member still absent. This session lasted two hours. Unocal's Vice President of Finance and its Assistant General Counsel made a detailed presentation of the proposed terms of the exchange offer. A price range between $70 and $80 per share was considered, and ultimately the directors agreed upon $72. The board was also advised about the debt securities that would be issued, and the necessity of placing restrictive covenants upon certain corporate activities until the obligations were paid. The board's decisions were made in reliance on the advice of its investment bankers, including the terms and conditions upon which the securities were to be issued. Based upon this advice, and the board's own deliberations, the directors unanimously approved the exchange offer. Their resolution provided that if Mesa acquired 64 million shares of Unocal stock through its own offer (the Mesa Purchase Condition), Unocal would buy the remaining 49% outstanding for an exchange of debt securities having an aggregate par value of $72 per share. The board resolution also stated that the offer would be subject to other conditions that had been described to the board at the meeting, or which were deemed necessary by Unocal's officers, including the exclusion of Mesa from the proposal (the Mesa exclusion). Any such conditions were required to be in accordance with the "purport and intent" of the offer.

Unocal's exchange offer was commenced on April 17, 1985, and Mesa promptly challenged it by filing this suit in the Court of Chancery. On

April 22, the Unocal board met again and was advised by Goldman Sachs and Dillon Read to waive the Mesa Purchase Condition as to 50 million shares. This recommendation was in response to a perceived concern of the shareholders that, if shares were tendered to Unocal, no shares would be purchased by either offeror. The directors were also advised that they should tender their own Unocal stock into the exchange offer as a mark of their confidence in it.

Another focus of the board was the Mesa exclusion. Legal counsel advised that under Delaware law Mesa could only be excluded for what the directors reasonably believed to be a valid corporate purpose. The directors' discussion centered on the objective of adequately compensating shareholders at the "back-end" of Mesa's proposal, which the latter would finance with "junk bonds". To include Mesa would defeat that goal, because under the proration aspect of the exchange offer (49%) every Mesa share accepted by Unocal would displace one held by another stockholder. Further, if Mesa were permitted to tender to Unocal, the latter would in effect be financing Mesa's own inadequate proposal.

On April 24, 1985 Unocal issued a supplement to the exchange offer describing the partial waiver of the Mesa Purchase Condition. On May 1, 1985, in another supplement, Unocal extended the withdrawal, proration and expiration dates of its exchange offer to May 17, 1985.

Meanwhile, on April 22, 1985, Mesa amended its complaint in this action to challenge the Mesa exclusion. . . .

. . . [T]he Vice Chancellor granted Mesa a preliminary injunction . . . [reasoning that a selective exchange offer that excluded Mesa was permitted].

On May 13, 1985 the Court of Chancery certified this interlocutory appeal . . . and we accepted it. . . . on an expedited basis.

II.

The issues we address involve these fundamental questions: Did the Unocal board have the power and duty to oppose a takeover threat it reasonably perceived to be harmful to the corporate enterprise, and if so, is its action here entitled to the protection of the business judgment rule?

Mesa contends that the discriminatory exchange offer violates the fiduciary duties Unocal owes it. Mesa argues that because of the Mesa exclusion the business judgment rule is inapplicable, because the directors by tendering their own shares will derive a financial benefit that is not available to *all* Unocal stockholders. Thus, it is Mesa's ultimate contention that Unocal cannot establish that the exchange offer is fair to *all* shareholders, and argues that the Court of Chancery was correct in concluding that Unocal was unable to meet this burden.

Unocal answers that it does not owe a duty of "fairness" to Mesa, given the facts here. Specifically, Unocal contends that its board of directors reasonably and in good faith concluded that Mesa's $54 two-tier tender offer was coercive and inadequate, and that Mesa sought selective treatment for itself. Furthermore, Unocal argues that the board's approval of the exchange offer was made in good faith, on an informed basis, and in the exercise of due care. Under these circumstances, Unocal contends that its directors properly employed this device to protect the company and its stockholders from Mesa's harmful tactics.

III.

We begin with the basic issue of the power of a board of directors of a Delaware corporation to adopt a defensive measure of this type. Absent such authority, all other questions are moot. Neither issues of fairness nor business judgment are pertinent without the basic underpinning of a board's legal power to act.

The board has a large reservoir of authority upon which to draw. Its duties and responsibilities proceed from the inherent powers conferred by 8 Del.C. § 141(a), respecting management of the corporation's "business and affairs". Additionally, the powers here being exercised derive from 8 Del.C. § 160(a), conferring broad authority upon a corporation to deal in its own stock. From this it is now well established that in the acquisition of its shares a Delaware corporation may deal selectively with its stockholders, provided the directors have not acted out of a sole or primary purpose to entrench themselves in office. Cheff v. Mathes, Del.Supr., 199 A.2d 548, 554 (1964); Bennett v. Propp, Del.Supr., 187 A.2d 405, 408 (1962) . . .

Finally, the board's power to act derives from its fundamental duty and obligation to protect the corporate enterprise, which includes stockholders, from harm reasonably perceived, irrespective of its source. See e.g. . . . Cheff v. Mathes, 199 A.2d at 556; Martin v. American Potash & Chemical Corp., 92 A.2d at 302; Kaplan v. Goldsamt, 380 A.2d at 568–69; Kors v. Carey, 158 A.2d at 141 . . . Thus, we are satisfied that in the broad context of corporate governance, including issues of fundamental corporate change, a board of directors is not a passive instrumentality.[8]

Given the foregoing principles, we turn to the standards by which director action is to be measured. In Pogostin v. Rice, Del.Supr., 480 A.2d 619 (1984), we held that the business judgment rule, including the standards by which director conduct is judged, is applicable in the context of a takeover. Id. at 627.

When a board addresses a pending takeover bid it has an obligation to determine whether the offer is in the best interests of the corporation and its shareholders. In that respect a board's duty is no different from any other responsibility it shoulders, and its decision should be no less entitled to the respect they otherwise would be accorded in the realm of

---

[8]   Even in the traditional areas of fundamental corporate change, i.e., charter amendments [8 Del.C. § 242(b)], mergers [8 Del.C. §§ 251(b), 252(c), 253(a), and 254(d)], sale of assets [8 Del.C. § 271(a)], and dissolution [8 Del.C. § 275(a)], director action is a prerequisite to the ultimate disposition of such matters. See also, Smith v. Van Gorkom, Del.Supr., 488 A.2d 858, 888 (1985).

business judgment. See also Johnson v. Trueblood, 629 F.2d 287, 292–293 (3d Cir.1980). There are, however, certain caveats to a proper exercise of this function. Because of the omnipresent specter that a board may be acting primarily in its own interests, rather than those of the corporation and its shareholders, there is an enhanced duty which calls for judicial examination at the threshold before the protections of the business judgment rule may be conferred.

This Court has long recognized that:

> We must bear in mind the inherent danger in the purchase of shares with corporate funds to remove a threat to corporate policy when a threat to control is involved. The directors are of necessity confronted with a conflict of interest, and an objective decision is difficult.

Bennett v. Propp, Del.Supr., 187 A.2d 405, 409 (1962). In the face of this inherent conflict directors must show that they had reasonable grounds for believing that a danger to corporate policy and effectiveness existed because of another person's stock ownership. Cheff v. Mathes, 199 A.2d at 554–55. However, they satisfy that burden "by showing good faith and reasonable investigation. . . . " Id. at 555. Furthermore, such proof is materially enhanced, as here, by the approval of a board comprised of a majority of outside independent directors who have acted in accordance with the foregoing standards. See Aronson v. Lewis, 473 A.2d at 812, 815; Puma v. Marriott, Del.Ch., 283 A.2d 693, 695 (1971); Panter v. Marshall Field Co., 646 F.2d 271, 295 (7th Cir.1981).

IV.

A.

In the board's exercise of corporate power to forestall a takeover bid our analysis begins with the basic principle that corporate directors have a fiduciary duty to act in the best interests of the corporation's stockholders. Guth v. Loft, Inc., Del.Supr., 5 A.2d 503, 510 (1939). As we have noted, their duty of care extends to protecting the corporation and its owners from perceived harm whether a threat originates from third parties or other shareholders. But such powers are not absolute. A corporation does not have unbridled discretion to defeat any perceived threat by any Draconian means available.

The restriction placed upon a selective stock repurchase is that the directors may not have acted solely or primarily out of a desire to perpetuate themselves in office. See Cheff v. Mathes, 199 A.2d at 556; Kors v. Carey, 158 A.2d at 140. Of course, to this is added the further caveat that inequitable action may not be taken under the guise of law. Schnell v. Chris-Craft Industries, Inc., Del.Supr. 285 A.2d 437, 439 (1971). The standard of proof established in Cheff v. Mathes . . . is designed to ensure that a defensive measure to thwart or impede a takeover is indeed motivated by a good faith concern for the welfare of the corporation and its stockholders, which in all circumstances must be free of any fraud or other misconduct. Cheff v. Mathes, 199 A.2d at 554–55. However, this does not end the inquiry.

B.

A further aspect is the element of balance. If a defensive measure is to come within the ambit of the business judgment rule, it must be reasonable in relation to the threat posed. This entails an analysis by the directors of the nature of the takeover bid and its effect on the corporate enterprise. Examples of such concerns may include: inadequacy of the price offered, nature and timing of the offer, questions of illegality, the impact on "constituencies" other than shareholders (i.e., creditors, customers, employees, and perhaps even the community generally), the risk of nonconsummation, and the quality of securities being offered in the exchange. See Lipton and Brownstein, Takeover Responses and Directors' Responsibilities: An Update, p. 7, ABA National Institute on the Dynamics of Corporate Control (December 8, 1983). While not a controlling factor, it also seems to us that a board may reasonably consider the basic stockholder interests at stake, including those of short term speculators, whose actions may have fueled the coercive aspect of the offer at the expense of the long term investor.[9] Here, the threat posed was viewed by the Unocal board as a grossly inadequate two-tier coercive tender offer coupled with the threat of greenmail.

Specifically, the Unocal directors had concluded that the value of Unocal was substantially above the $54 per share offered in cash at the front end. Furthermore, they determined that the subordinated securities to be exchanged in Mesa's announced squeeze out of the remaining shareholders in the "back-end" merger were "junk bonds" worth far less than $54. It is now well recognized that such offers are a classic coercive measure designed to stampede shareholders into tendering at the first tier, even if the price is inadequate, out of fear of what they will receive at the back end of the transaction. Wholly beyond the coercive aspect of an inadequate two-tier tender offer, the threat was posed by a corporate raider with a national reputation as a "greenmailer".[13]

---

[9]　There has been much debate respecting such stockholder interests. One rather impressive study indicates that the stock of over 50 percent of target companies, who resisted hostile takeovers, later traded at higher market prices than the rejected offer price, or were acquired after the tender offer was defeated by another company at a price higher than the offer price. See Lipton, supra 35 Bus.Law. at 106–109, 132–133. Moreover, an update by Kidder Peabody & Company of this study, involving the stock prices of target companies that have defeated hostile tender offers during the period from 1973 to 1982 demonstrates that in a majority of cases the target's shareholders benefited from the defeat. The stock of 81% of the targets studied has, since the tender offer, sold at prices higher than the tender offer price. When adjusted for the time value of money, the figure is 64%. See Lipton & Brownstein, supra ABA Institute at 10. The thesis being that this strongly supports application of the business judgment rule in response to takeover threats. There is, however, a rather vehement contrary view. See Easterbrook & Fischel, supra 36 Bus.Law. at 1739–1745.

[13]　The term "greenmail" refers to the practice of buying out a takeover bidder's stock at a premium that is not available to other shareholders in order to prevent the takeover. The Chancery Court noted that "Mesa has made tremendous profits from its takeover activities although in the past few years it has not been successful in acquiring any of the target

In adopting the selective exchange offer, the board stated that its objective was either to defeat the inadequate Mesa offer or, should the offer still succeed, provide the 49% of its stockholders, who would otherwise be forced to accept "junk bonds", with $72 worth of senior debt. We find that both purposes are valid.

However, such efforts would have been thwarted by Mesa's participation in the exchange offer. First, if Mesa could tender its shares, Unocal would effectively be subsidizing the former's continuing effort to buy Unocal stock at $54 per share. Second, Mesa could not, by definition, fit within the class of shareholders being protected from its own coercive and inadequate tender offer.

Thus, we are satisfied that the selective exchange offer is reasonably related to the threats posed. It is consistent with the principle that "the minority stockholder shall receive the substantial equivalent in value of what he had before." Sterling v. Mayflower Hotel Corp., Del.Supr., 93 A.2d 107, 114 (1952). See also Rosenblatt v. Getty Oil Co., Del.Supr., 493 A.2d 929, 940 (1985). This concept of fairness, while stated in the merger context, is also relevant in the area of tender offer law. Thus, the board's decision to offer what it determined to be the fair value of the corporation to the 49% of its shareholders, who would otherwise be forced to accept highly subordinated "junk bonds", is reasonable and consistent with the directors' duty to ensure that the minority stockholders receive equal value for their shares.

V.

Mesa contends that it is unlawful, and the trial court agreed, for a corporation to discriminate in this fashion against one shareholder. It argues correctly that no case has ever sanctioned a device that precludes a raider from sharing in a benefit available to all other stockholders. However, as we have noted earlier, the principle of selective stock repurchases by a Delaware corporation is neither unknown nor unauthorized. Cheff v. Mathes, 199 A.2d at 554; Bennett v. Propp, 187 A.2d at 408; Martin v. American Potash & Chemical Corporation, 92 A.2d at 302. . . . The only difference is that heretofore the approved transaction was the payment of "greenmail" to a raider or dissident posing a threat to the corporate enterprise. All other stockholders were denied such favored treatment, and given Mesa's past history of greenmail, its claims here are rather ironic.

However, our corporate law is not static. It must grow and develop in response to, indeed in anticipation of, evolving concepts and needs. Merely because the General Corporation Law is silent as to a specific matter does not mean that it is prohibited. See Providence & Worcester Co. v. Baker, Del.Supr., 378 A.2d 121, 123–124 (1977). In the days when

---

companies on an unfriendly basis." Moreover, the trial court specifically found that the actions of the Unocal board were taken in good faith to eliminate both the inadequacies of the tender offer and to forestall the payment of "greenmail".

Cheff, Bennett, [and] *Martin* were decided, the tender offer, while not an unknown device, was virtually unused, and little was known of such methods as two-tier "front-end" loaded offers with their coercive effects. Then, the favored attack of a raider was stock acquisition followed by a proxy contest. Various defensive tactics, which provided no benefit whatever to the raider, evolved. Thus, the use of corporate funds by management to counter a proxy battle was approved. Hall v. Trans-Lux Daylight Picture Screen Corp., Del.Ch., 171 A. 226 (1934); Hibbert v. Hollywood Park, Inc., Del.Supr., 457 A.2d 339 (1983). Litigation, supported by corporate funds, aimed at the raider has long been a popular device.

More recently, as the sophistication of both raiders and targets has developed, a host of other defensive measures to counter such ever mounting threats has evolved and received judicial sanction. These include defensive charter amendments and other devices bearing some rather exotic, but apt, names: Crown Jewel, White Knight, Pac Man, and Golden Parachute. Each has highly selective features, the object of which is to deter or defeat the raider.

Thus, while the exchange offer is a form of selective treatment, given the nature of the threat posed here the response is neither unlawful nor unreasonable. If the board of directors is disinterested, has acted in good faith and with due care, its decision in the absence of an abuse of discretion will be upheld as a proper exercise of business judgment.

To this Mesa responds that the board is not disinterested, because the directors are receiving a benefit from the tender of their own shares, which because of the Mesa exclusion, does not devolve upon *all* stockholders equally. See Aronson v. Lewis, Del.Supr., 473 A.2d 805, 812 (1984). However, Mesa concedes that if the exclusion is valid, then the directors and all other stockholders share the same benefit. The answer of course is that the exclusion is valid, and the directors' participation in the exchange offer does not rise to the level of a disqualifying interest. . . .

Nor does this become an "interested" director transaction merely because certain board members are large stockholders. As this Court has previously noted, that fact alone does not create a disqualifying "personal pecuniary interest" to defeat the operation of the business judgment rule. Cheff v. Mathes, 199 A.2d at 554.

Mesa also argues that the exclusion permits the directors to abdicate the fiduciary duties they owe it. However, that is not so. The board continues to owe Mesa the duties of due care and loyalty. But in the face of the destructive threat Mesa's tender offer was perceived to pose, the board had a supervening duty to protect the corporate enterprise, which includes the other shareholders, from threatened harm.

Mesa contends that the basis of this action is punitive, and solely in response to the exercise of its rights of corporate democracy. Nothing precludes Mesa, as a stockholder, from acting in its own self-interest. . . .

However, Mesa, while pursuing its own interests, has acted in a manner which a board consisting of a majority of independent directors has reasonably determined to be contrary to the best interests of Unocal and its other shareholders. In this situation, there is no support in Delaware law for the proposition that, when responding to a perceived harm, a corporation must guarantee a benefit to a stockholder who is deliberately provoking the danger being addressed. There is no obligation of self-sacrifice by a corporation and its shareholders in the face of such a challenge.

Here, the Court of Chancery specifically found that the "directors' decision [to oppose the Mesa tender offer] was made in the good faith belief that the Mesa tender offer is inadequate." Given our standard of review. . . .

VI.

In conclusion, there was directorial power to oppose the Mesa tender offer, and to undertake a selective stock exchange made in good faith and upon a reasonable investigation pursuant to a clear duty to protect the corporate enterprise. Further, the selective stock repurchase plan chosen by Unocal is reasonable in relation to the threat that the board rationally and reasonably believed was posed by Mesa's inadequate and coercive two-tier tender offer. Under those circumstances the board's action is entitled to be measured by the standards of the business judgment rule. Thus, unless it is shown by a preponderance of the evidence that the directors' decisions were primarily based on perpetuating themselves in office, or some other breach of fiduciary duty such as fraud, overreaching, lack of good faith, or being uninformed, a Court will not substitute its judgment for that of the board. . . .

With the Court of Chancery's findings that the exchange offer was based on the board's good faith belief that the Mesa offer was inadequate, that the board's action was informed and taken with due care, that Mesa's prior activities justify a reasonable inference that its principle objective was greenmail, and implicitly, that the substance of the offer itself was reasonable and fair to the corporation and its stockholders if Mesa were included, we cannot say that the Unocal directors have acted in such a manner as to have passed an "unintelligent and unadvised judgment". Mitchell v. Highland-Western Glass Co., Del.Ch., 167 A. 831, 833 (1933). The decision of the Court of Chancery is therefore REVERSED, and the preliminary injunction is VACATED.*

––––––––––

NOTE ON UNITRIN, INC. V. AMERICAN GENERAL CORP.

In *Unitrin, Inc. v. American General Corp.*, 651 A.2d 1361 (1995), American General Corporation announced a tender offer to purchase all of the stock of

––––––––––

*   Accord: Burcham v. Bunten, 276 Kan. 393, 77 P.3d 130 (2003).

Unitrin, Inc. at $50-³/₈ per share. Unitrin's board responded by taking several defensive measures, including the adoption of a poison pill and a program to repurchase up to 10 million of Unitrin's 51.8 million shares on the open market at $50-³/₈ per share. Unitrin's certificate of incorporation provided that a business combination with a more-than-15% shareholder had to be approved by a majority of continuing directors or by a 75% shareholder vote. Unitrin's directors collectively held 23% of Unitrin's stock prior to adoption of the repurchase program. The directors did not intend to sell their stock to Unitrin under the repurchase program.

American General brought an action in Delaware Chancery court to enjoin Unitrin from completing its repurchase program. The Chancery court issued a preliminary injunction against Unitrin, at a point when Unitrin had purchased nearly 5 million shares of its stock, partly on the ground that since the director-shareholders were not selling their stock, the effect of the repurchase program would be to increase their stock ownership from 23% to over 25%, thereby giving them a veto under the 75% supermajority voting provision. The Delaware Supreme Court reversed, and remanded for a decision by Chancery under the standards it set out. The Supreme Court's opinion provides an important gloss on *Unocal*:

> . . . [T]he Court of Chancery erred in applying the proportionality review *Unocal* requires by focusing upon whether the Repurchase Program was an "unnecessary" defensive response. The Court of Chancery should have directed its enhanced scrutiny: first, upon whether the Repurchase Program the Unitrin Board implemented was draconian, by being either preclusive or coercive and; second, if it was not draconian, upon whether it was within a range of reasonable responses to the threat American General's Offer posed. Consequently, the interlocutory preliminary injunctive judgment of the Court of Chancery is reversed. . . .

> The Court of Chancery and all parties agree that proxy contests do not generate 100% shareholder participation. The shareholder plaintiffs argue that 80–85% may be a usual turnout. Therefore, *without* the Repurchase Program, the director shareholders' absolute voting power of 23% would already constitute *actual voting power greater than* 25% in a proxy contest with normal shareholder participation below 100%. . . .

> The Unitrin Board did not have unlimited discretion to defeat the threat it perceived from the American General Offer by any draconian means available. *See Unocal*, 493 A.2d at 955. Pursuant to the *Unocal* proportionality test, the nature of the threat associated with a particular hostile offer sets the parameters for the range of permissible defensive tactics. Accordingly, the purpose of enhanced judicial scrutiny is to determine whether the Board acted reasonably in "relation . . . to the threat which a particular bid allegedly poses to stockholder interests." *Mills Acquisition Co. v. Macmillan, Inc.*, Del.Supr., 559 A.2d 1261, 1288 (1989).

. . . Courts, commentators and litigators have attempted to catalogue the threats posed by hostile tender offers. . . . Commentators have categorized three types of threats:

> (i) *opportunity loss* . . . [where] a hostile offer might deprive target shareholders of the opportunity to select a superior alternative offered by target management [or, we would add, offered by another bidder]; (ii) *structural coercion,* . . . the risk that disparate treatment of non-tendering shareholders might distort shareholders' tender decisions; and (iii) *substantive coercion,* . . . the risk that shareholders will mistakenly accept an underpriced offer because they disbelieve management's representations of intrinsic value. . . . *

The record reflects that the Unitrin Board perceived the threat from American General's Offer to be a form of substantive coercion. . . .

The record appears to support Unitrin's argument that the Board's justification for adopting the Repurchase Program was its reasonably perceived risk of substantive coercion, *i.e.,* that Unitrin's shareholders might accept American General's inadequate Offer because of "ignorance or mistaken belief" regarding the Board's assessment of the long-term value of Unitrin's stock. *See Shamrock Holdings, Inc. v. Polaroid Corp.,* Del.Ch., 559 A.2d 278, 290 (1989). . . . The adoption of the Repurchase Program also appears to be consistent with this Court's holding that economic inadequacy is not the only threat presented by an all cash for all shares hostile bid, because the threat of such a hostile bid could be exacerbated by shareholder "ignorance or . . . mistaken belief." *Paramount Communications, Inc. v. Time, Inc.,* 571 A.2d at 1153. . . .

An examination of the cases applying *Unocal* reveals a direct correlation between findings of proportionality or disproportionality and the judicial determination of whether a defensive response was draconian because it was either coercive or preclusive in character. . . .

. . . As common law applications of *Unocal's* proportionality standard have evolved, at least two characteristics of draconian defensive measures taken by a board of directors in responding to a threat have been brought into focus through enhanced judicial scrutiny. In the modern takeover lexicon, it is now clear that since *Unocal,* this Court has consistently recognized that defensive measures which are either preclusive or coercive are included within the common law definition of draconian.

If a defensive measure is not draconian, however, because it is not either coercive or preclusive, the *Unocal* proportionality test requires the focus of enhanced judicial scrutiny to shift to "the

---

*   See Paramount Communications, Inc. v. Time Inc., n. 17, pp. 1270–1271, supra. (Footnote by ed.)

range of reasonableness." *Paramount Communications, Inc. v. QVC Network, Inc.,* Del.Supr., 637 A.2d 34, 45–46 (1994). Proper and proportionate defensive responses are intended and permitted to thwart perceived threats. When a corporation is not for sale, the board of directors is the defender of the metaphorical medieval corporate bastion and the protector of the corporation's shareholders. The fact that a defensive action must not be coercive or preclusive does not prevent a board from responding defensively before a bidder is at the corporate bastion's gate. . . .

The Court of Chancery found that the Unitrin Board reasonably believed that American General's Offer was inadequate. . . . Upon remand, in applying the correct legal standard to the factual circumstances of this case, the Court of Chancery may conclude that the implementation of the limited Repurchase Program was also within a range of reasonable additional defensive responses available to the Unitrin Board. In considering whether the Repurchase Program was within a range of reasonableness the Court of Chancery should take into consideration whether: (1) it is a statutorily authorized form of business decision which a board of directors may routinely make in a non-takeover context; (2) as a defensive response to American General's Offer it was limited and corresponded in degree or magnitude to the degree or magnitude of the threat (*i.e.,* assuming the threat was relatively mild, was the response relatively "mild"?); (3) with the Repurchase Program, the Unitrin Board properly recognized that all shareholders are not alike, and provided immediate liquidity to those shareholders who wanted it. . . .

* * *

In re Gaylord Container Corp. Shareholder Litigation, 753 A.2d 462, 481(Del.Ch. 2000) (Ch. Leo Strine) observed, "A defensive measure is preclusive when its operation precludes an acquisition of the company. A defensive measure is coercive when it operates to force management's preferred alternative upon the stockholders."

———

NOTE ON UNOCAL

The specific outcome in *Unocal,* allowing an exclusionary (discriminatory) tender offer, has been superseded by the all-holders rule under the Williams Act, Securities Exchange Act Rule 14d–10, which ousts Delaware law under the Supremacy Clause of the Constitution. However, the basic standard of review of defensive tactics adopted in the *Unocal* decision has survived, with some glosses, as the central rule governing takeovers under Delaware law. *Unocal's* heightened scrutiny has a reasonable following outside of Delaware. *See e.g.,* International Ins. Co. v. Johns, 874 F.2d 1447 (11th Cir. 1989) (involving Florida incorporated target firm); In re Bear Stearns Litig., 870 N.Y.S.2d 709 (2008); and Crandon Capital Partners v. Shelk, 219 Or.App. 16, 181 P.3d 773 (Or. Ct. App. 2008). Some jurisdictions reject the heightened scrutiny called for by *Unocal*, and test the decision under the standard business judgment rule. Shenker v. Laureate Educ. Inc., 983 A.2d 408 (Md. 2009). This appears to be the approach recommended by the American Law Institute which places the burden of proof on the person challenging the defensive maneuver and states the "board may take into account all factors relevant to best interests of the corporation and its shareholders." ALI, Principles of Corporate Governance: Analysis and Recommendations § 6.02(a)–(c) (1994).

ALI, PRINCIPLES OF CORPORATE GOVERNANCE § 6.02

[See Statutory Supplement]

C. POISON PILLS

A *poison pill* (also known as a *Rights Plan* or a *Shareholder Rights Plan*) is a plan under which the board of directors of a corporation creates Rights that are distributed or distributable to shareholders. Under the Rights, upon the occurrence of certain events shareholders *other than a tender-offer bidder or prospective bidder* have the right to purchase stock in the corporation, or under certain circumstances in an acquiror, at a deep discount—normally, half-price. Because the potential exercise of the Rights would dramatically dilute the value of the target stock that the bidder proposes to acquire, the mere potential that the Rights will be exercised may serve as a deterrent to making a bid in the first place (although for reasons that will be explored in the materials that follow, a pill is usually not a complete show-stopper).

The actual mechanics of pills are highly complex, and have evolved over time. Here is a description of a fairly standard modern version of the pill, taken from Carmody v. Toll Brothers, Inc., 723 A.2d 1180 (Del.Ch. 1998). The corporation whose pill is described was named Toll Brothers:

> The Rights Plan would operate as follows: there would be a dividend distribution of one preferred stock purchase right (a "Right") for each outstanding share of common stock as of July 11, 1997. Initially the Rights would attach to the company's outstanding common shares, and each Right would initially entitle the holder to purchase one thousandth of a share of a newly registered series Junior A Preferred Stock for $100. The Rights would become exercisable, and would trade separately from the common shares, after the "Distribution Date," which is defined as the earlier of (a) ten business days following a public announcement that an acquiror has acquired, or obtained the right to acquire, beneficial ownership of 15% or more of the company's outstanding common shares (the "Stock Acquisition Date"), or (b) ten business days after the commencement of a

tender offer or exchange offer that would result in a person or group beneficially owning 15% or more of the company's outstanding common shares. Once exercisable, the Rights remain exercisable until their Final Expiration Date (June 12, 2007, ten years after the adoption of the Plan), unless the Rights are earlier redeemed by the company.

The dilutive mechanism of the Rights is "triggered" by certain defined events. One such event is the acquisition of 15% or more of Toll Brothers' stock by any person or group of affiliated or associated persons. Should that occur, each Rights holder (except the acquiror and its affiliates and associates) becomes entitled to buy two shares of Toll Brothers common stock or other securities at half price. That is, the value of the stock received when the Right is exercised is equal to two times the exercise price of the Right. In that manner, this so-called "flip in" feature of the Rights Plan would massively dilute the value of the holdings of the unwanted acquiror. . . .

The "flip-in" feature of a rights plan is triggered when the acquiror crosses the specified ownership threshold, regardless of the acquiror's intentions with respect to the use of the shares. At that point, rights vest in all shareholders other than the acquiror, and as a result, those holders become entitled to acquire additional shares of voting stock at a substantially discounted price, usually 50% of the market price. Commonly, rights plans also contain a "flip-over" feature entitling target company shareholders (again, other than the acquiror) to purchase shares of the acquiring company at a reduced price. That feature is activated when, after a "flip-in" triggering event, the acquiror initiates a triggering event, such as a merger, self-dealing transaction, or sale of assets. . . .

The Rights [in the case at bar] have a standard "flip over" feature, which is triggered if after the Stock Acquisition Date, the company is made a party to a merger in which Toll Brothers is not the surviving corporation, or in which it is the surviving corporation and its common stock is changed or exchanged. In either event, each Rights holder becomes entitled to purchase common stock of the acquiring company, again at half-price, thereby impairing the acquiror's capital structure and drastically diluting the interest of the acquiror's other stockholders.

Id. at 1183–84 n.5.

A flip-over pill is normally triggered only by a corporate combination between the bidder and the target following the initial tender offer. The effect of a flip-over pill may therefore be moderated where the bidder's business plan allows it to forgo such a merger. A flip-in pill is much more wide-ranging in its applicability, but usually the Rights issued under such a pill can be redeemed by the target's board for a nominal consideration at any time before a triggering event and, often, for a brief period thereafter. Among public companies, poison pills are ubiquitous. Should the validity of the pill turn on whether a company's board adopted a pill before there was a contest for control? *See e.g.,* Independence Fed. Sav. Bank. v. Bender, 326 F.Supp. 2d 36, 49–50 (D.D.C. 2004) (refusing to compel pill's redemption because it was adopted during a merger contest); Burcham v. Unison Bancorp, Inc., 276 Kan. 393, 409, 77 P.3d 130, 145 (2003) (denying summary judgment on question whether adoption of a poison pill in the heat of a takeover was itself a breach of the directors' fiduciary duty).

A case of national importance, *Moran v. Household International, Inc.,* 500 A.2d 1346 (Del. 1985), held that a corporation's board of directors could validly adopt a poison pill and do so unilaterally (i.e., without approval of the stockholders). In issuing the shareholder rights, Household's board invoked the authority it enjoyed under the so-called "blank stock" authorization, by which Delaware (*see* Del. Gen. Corp L. § 157) and most states permit the articles of incorporation to contain a provision that empowers the board of directors to issue shares, rights and options with such rights, privileges and preferences as the board may from time to time establish. To the complaint that the rights plan usurped the shareholders' rights to receive tender offers by changing Household's fundamental structure, the court observed:

> [T]he Rights Plan is not absolute. When the Household Board of Directors is faced with a tender offer and a request to redeem the Rights, they will not be able to arbitrarily reject the offer. They will be held to the same fiduciary standards any other board of directors would be held to in deciding to adopt a defensive mechanism, the same standard as they were held to in originally approving the Rights Plan. *See Unocal,* 493 A.2d at 954–55, 958. . . .

> There is little change in the governance structure as a result of the adoption of the Rights Plan. The Board does not now have unfettered discretion in refusing to redeem the Rights. The Board has no more discretion in refusing to redeem the Rights than it does in enacting any defensive mechanism.

Moran emphasized the redemption provision of the pill, seeing this as crucial to the pill's validity. What are the benefits of kicking the pill's validity down the road to when there is a contest and the bidder or target shareholder challenge the board's decision not to redeem the pill? Is there a down side of testing the pill's validity in the heat of a takeover contest?

In a few early decisions the court reviewing the non-redemption decision were disposed to order the target board to redeem the pill. *See* Southdown, Inc. v. Moore McCormack Resources, Inc., 686 F. Supp. 595, 605 (S.D. Tex. 1988) (concluding that entrenchment not the stockholders' interest motivated board's decision not to redeem the pill); A Copeland

Enterprises, Inc. v. Guste, 706 F. Supp. 1283, 1286 (W.D. Tex. 1989) (upholding the validity of the pill at the moment the hostile bid was commenced, but expressing an intent to order the pill's redemption when the bidder's tender offer closed if the pill was then still outstanding). As the pill became more prevalent, judicial decisions have been more deferential to the target board. *See e.g.,* Dynamics Corp. of Amer. v. WHX Corp., 967 F. Supp. 59, 65 (D. Conn. 1997); Moore Corp. v. Wallace Computer Services, 907 F. Supp. 1545, 1553 (D. Del. 1995) (refusing to order redemption where board alleged the hostile bid undervalued the firm even though seventy percent of the shareholders had tendered their shares in response to the bid). While legal skirmishes continue on a variety of issues posed by the pill, the courtroom is not the only antidote the frustrated bidder can seek. There is the avenue of the proxy fight, electing a new majority beholding to the bidder who can be expected to not just redeem the pill, but do the deal. Can setting a very low ownership percentage at which the flip-in or flip-over rights are triggered violate *Unocal-Unitrin* standards? *Versata Enterprises, Inc. v. Selectica, Inc.,* 5 A.3d 586, 604 (Del. 2010), holds that setting the pill level at 4.99 percent did not render the pill beyond the range of reasonableness.

Pills provide important protection against unwanted suitors and lawyers have been very innovative in their quest to make their client's pill bullet proof. The "dead hand" provision of a poison pill is one such innovation; it provides that the rights plan cannot be redeemed except by the incumbent directors who adopted the plan or were their designated successors. The dead hand provision seeks to reduce one obvious route for an unwanted suitor to ultimately overcome the pill: undertaking a successful proxy contest so its nominees make up the new majority of the target board and thus can redeem the pill and do the deal. In *Carmody v. Toll Brothers, Inc.,* 723 A.2d 1180 (Del. Ch. 1998), Vice-Chancellor Jacobs declared the dead-hand pill invalid under Delaware law, on several grounds:

> First, a dead hand pill violates the Delaware statute by impermissibly creating voting-power distinctions among directors without authorization in the articles of incorporation, and by interfering with the directors' statutory power to manage the business and affairs of the corporation.

> Second, a dead hand pill is unlawful under *Blasius* (See Chapter 4, supra), because it purposefully interferes with the shareholder voting franchise without a compelling justification.

> Third, a dead hand pill is a "disproportionate" defensive measure under *Unocal/Unitrin,* because it either precludes or materially abridges the shareholders' rights to receive tender offers and to wage a proxy contest to replace the board.

In contrast to *Carmody,* a dead hand pill was upheld by in a decision that relied heavily on the language of the pill validation statute of the corporation's domicile, Georgia. *Invacare Corp. v. Healthdyne Technologies, Inc.*, 968 F. Supp. 1578 (N.D. Ga. 1997).

Somewhat of a sequel to the dead-hand bill is the delayed redemption provision which provides that if a majority of the directors are replaced by stockholder action, the newly elected board cannot redeem the rights for six months if the purpose or effect of the redemption is to facilitate a transaction with an "interested person." *Quickturn Design Systems, Inc. v. Shapiro*, 721 A. 2d 1281 (Del. 1998), held the delayed redemption provision invalid under Delaware law.

> One of the most basic tenets of Delaware corporate law is that the board of directors has the ultimate responsibility for managing the business and affairs of a corporation.[36] Section 141(a) requires that any limitation on the board's authority be set out in the certificate of incorporation.[37] The Quickturn certificate of incorporation contains no provision purporting to limit the authority of the board in any way. The Delayed Redemption Provision, however, would prevent a newly elected board of directors from completely discharging its fundamental management duties to the corporation and its stockholders for six months. While the Delayed Redemption Provision limits the board of directors' authority in only one respect, the suspension of the Rights Plan, it nonetheless restricts the board's power in an area of fundamental importance to the shareholders negotiating a possible sale of the corporation. Therefore, we hold that the Delayed Redemption Provision is invalid under Section 141(a), which confers upon any newly elected board of directors full power to manage and direct the business and affairs of a Delaware corporation. . . .

> The Delayed Redemption Provision prevents a newly elected board of directors from completely discharging its fiduciary duties to protect fully the interests of Quickturn and its stockholders.[41] . . .

> The Delayed Redemption Provision "tends to limit in a substantial way the freedom of [newly elected] directors' decisions on matters of management policy."[44] Therefore, "it

---

[36] 8 Del.C. § 141(a). See Mills Acquisition Co. v. Macmillan, Inc., Del.Supr., 559 A.2d 1261, 1280 (1989).

[37] 8 Del.C. § 141(a) states: "The business and affairs of every corporation organized under this chapter shall be managed by or under the direction of a board of directors, except as may be otherwise provided in this chapter or in its certificate of incorporation. If any such provision is made in the certificate of incorporation, the powers and duties conferred or imposed upon the board of directors by this chapter shall be exercised or performed to such extent and by such person or persons as shall be provided in the certificate of incorporation."

[41] See Moran v. Household International, Inc., 500 A.2d at 1354.

[44] Abercrombie v. Davies, Del.Ch., 123 A.2d 893, 899 (1956), rev'd on other grounds, Del.Supr., 130 A.2d 338 (1957).

violates the duty of each [newly elected] director to exercise his own best judgment on matters coming before the board."[45] . . .

Conclusion

The Delayed Redemption Provision would prevent a new Quickturn board of directors from managing the corporation by redeeming the Rights Plan to facilitate a transaction that would serve the stockholders' best interests, even under circumstances where the board would be required to do so because of its fiduciary duty to the Quickturn stockholders. Because the Delayed Redemption Provision impermissibly circumscribes the board's statutory power under Section 141(a) and the directors' ability to fulfill their concomitant fiduciary duties, we hold that the Delayed Redemption Provision is invalid. On that alternative basis, the judgment of the Court of Chancery is AFFIRMED.

Contra. AMP, Inc. v. Allied Signal, Inc., 1998 WL 778348 (E.D. Pa. 1998) (relying on both the state's poison pill validation and constituency statutes, the court reasoned that a delayed redemption feature of a poison pill was valid being consistent with the state's public policy and because it interfered with the board's discretion for only for a finite period of time).

––––––––––

In the last few proxy seasons, shareholders have frequently proposed "declassifying" board of directors. Recall that corporations can provide that directors can serve staggered three-year terms so that only one-third of the board turns over each year. In reflecting on why activist shareholders are eager that their portfolio companies elect all their directors annually consider the following. During a five-year study period, Professors Bebchuk, Coates and Subramanian found that staggered boards increased the likelihood of a company remaining independent from 34% to 61% and that staggered boards reduce the likelihood of the first bidder being successful from 34% to 14%. Lucian Arye Bebchuk, John C. Coates IV & Guhan Subramanian, The Powerful Antitakeover Force of Staggered Boards: Theory, Evidence, and Policy, 54 Stan. L. Rev. 887, 930–31 (2002). Why should a staggered board make the pill more effective? Hint-consider the protection from removal that directors serving on a classified board enjoy in Delaware. *See* Del. Code Ann., tit. 8 § 141(k)(1).

––––––––––

––––––––––

[45] Id.

Air Products and Chemicals, Inc. v. Airgas, Inc.

Delaware Court of Chancery, 2011.
16 A.3d 48.

■ CHANDLER, CHANCELLOR.

[Air Products launched a hostile bid to acquire Air Gas. However, after a number of reversals in the Delaware courts, after the instant decision, it ultimately terminated its quest for Air Gas after having fought a sixteen month battle for Air Gas. The source of much of the skirmishing was due to Air Gas having both a poison pill and a classified board—nine directors serving three-year staggered terms. At the September 2010 annual meeting, three directors supported by Air Products were elected to Air Gas' board over the Air Gas nominees. Air Products' proxy materials supporting their election identified them as "independent" individuals who, "without any bias," would consider Air Product's offer and in doing so act in Air Gas stockholders' best interest. And independent they were; shortly after the three newly elected directors learned more about Air Gas from its various advisers, they joined the other directors in the unanimous view that Air Product's $70 per share offer was inadequate. Although Air Gas' charter allowed a 33 percent holder to call a special stockholders meeting and authorized the removal of the entire board by a vote of 67 percent of the outstanding shares, Air Products chose not to seek the entire board's removal. Instead it challenged the validity of the board's refusal to redeem the poison pill. After an exhaustive review of the Delaware jurisprudence surrounding defensive maneuvers, Chancellor Chandler provides the following insights on the efficacy of staggered boards and a board's refusal to redeem the pill in the face of a determined, but unwanted, suitor.]

1. Preclusive or Coercive

A defensive measure is coercive if it is "aimed at 'cramming down' on its shareholders a management-sponsored alternative." Airgas's defensive measures are certainly not coercive in this respect, as Airgas is specifically *not* trying to cram down a management sponsored alternative, but rather, simply wants to maintain the status quo and manage the company for the long term.

. . . Air Products and Shareholder Plaintiffs argue that Airgas's defensive measures are preclusive because they render the possibility of an effective proxy contest realistically unattainable. What the argument boils down to, though, is that Airgas's defensive measures make the possibility of Air Products obtaining control of the Airgas board and removing the pill realistically unattainable *in the very near future*, because Airgas has a staggered board in place. Thus, the real issue posed is whether defensive measures are "preclusive" if they make gaining control of the board realistically unattainable in the short term (but still realistically attainable sometime in the future), or if "preclusive" actually means "preclusive"—i.e. forever unattainable. . . .

This precise question was asked and answered four months ago in *Versata Enterprises, Inc. v. Selectica, Inc.,* [5 A.3d 586 (Del. 2010)]. There, Trilogy (the hostile acquiror) argued that in order for the target's defensive measures not to be preclusive: (1) a successful proxy contest must be realistically attainable, and (2) the successful proxy contest must result in gaining control of the board at the next election. The Delaware Supreme Court rejected this argument, stating that "[i]f that preclusivity argument is correct, then it would apply whenever a corporation has both a classified board and a Rights Plan. . . . *[W]e hold that the combination of a classified board and a Rights Plan do not constitute a preclusive defense.*"

The Supreme Court explained its reasoning as follows:

> Classified boards are authorized by statute and are adopted for a variety of business purposes. Any classified board also operates as an antitakeover defense by preventing an insurgent from obtaining control of the board in one election. More than a decade ago, in *Carmody* [*v. Toll Brothers, Inc.*], the Court of Chancery noted "because only one third of a classified board would stand for election each year, a classified board would *delay—but not prevent—a hostile acquiror from obtaining control of the board*, since a determined acquiror could wage a proxy contest and obtain control of two thirds of the target board over a two year period, as opposed to seizing control in a single election."

The Court concluded: "The fact that a combination of defensive measures makes it more difficult for an acquirer to obtain control of a board does not make such measures realistically unattainable, i.e., preclusive." . . .

I am thus bound by this clear precedent to proceed on the assumption that Airgas's defensive measures are not preclusive if they delay Air Products from obtaining control of the Airgas board (even if that delay is significant) so long as obtaining control at some point in the future is realistically attainable. I now examine whether the ability to obtain control of Airgas's board in the future is realistically attainable. . . .

a.   Call a Special Meeting to Remove the Airgas Board by a 67% Supermajority Vote

Airgas's charter allows for 33% of the outstanding shares to call a special meeting of the stockholders, and to remove the entire board without cause by a vote of 67% of the outstanding shares. . . . [W]hat matters is the "realistic attainability" of actually achieving a 67% vote of the outstanding Airgas shares in the context of Air Products' hostile tender offer (which equates to achieving approximately 85–86% of the unaffiliated voting shares), or whether, instead, Airgas's continued use of its defensive measures is preclusive because it is a near "impossible task."

The fact that something might be a theoretical possibility does not make it "realistically attainable." In other words, what the Supreme Court in *Unitrin* and *Selectica* meant by "realistically attainable" must be something more than a mere "mathematical possibility" or "hypothetically conceivable chance" of circumventing a poison pill. One would think a sensible understanding of the phrase would be that an insurgent has a reasonably meaningful or real world shot at securing the support of enough stockholders to change the target board's composition and remove the obstructing defenses. It does not mean that the insurgent has a right to win or that the insurgent must have a highly probable chance or even a 50–50 chance of prevailing. But it must be more than just a theoretical possibility, given the required vote, the timing issues, the shareholder profile, the issues presented by the insurgent and the surrounding circumstances.

. . . [The Chancellor then reviewed the extensive evidence produced by the parties at the supplemental evidentiary hearing, concluding in the end that it was "unhelpful and unconvincing" on the fundamental question whether a 67% vote was realistically attainable.] Both experts essentially admitted, moreover, that one cannot really know how an election will turn out until it is held and that, generally speaking, it is easier to obtain investor support for electing a minority insurgent slate than for a controlling slate of directors.

In the end, however, the most telling aspect of the expert testimony was the statement that Air Products could certainly achieve 67% of the vote if its offer was "sufficiently appealing." Harkins [Air Gas' proxy expert] explained that he was "not predicting that a $70 offer will result in a 67 percent vote to remove the board." He was simply predicting that, with an appealing enough offer or platform, a 67% vote is possible, but he was not providing his opinion (nor did he have one) on how appealing $70 is, or whether it would make victory at a special election attainable. The following final, tautological insight by the expert just about sums up the usefulness of this particular day in the life of a trial judge:

Q.   [So w]hat is a sufficiently appealing offer?

A.   An offer that will garner 67 percent of the vote, I suppose.

But what seems clear to me, quite honestly, is that a poison pill is assuredly preclusive in the everyday common sense meaning of the word; indeed, its *rasion d'etre* is preclusion—to stop a bid (or *this* bid) from progressing. That is what it is intended to do and that is what the Airgas pill has done successfully for over sixteen months. Whether it is realistic to believe that Air Products can, at some point in the future, achieve a 67% vote necessary to remove the entire Airgas board at a special meeting is (in my opinion) impossible to predict given the host of variables in this setting, but the sheer lack of historical examples where an insurgent has ever achieved such a percentage in a contested control election must mean something. . . . Nonetheless, while the special meeting may not be a realistically attainable mechanism for circumventing the Airgas defenses, that assessment does not end the analysis under existing precedent.

b.   Run Another Proxy Contest

Even if Air Products is unable to achieve the 67% supermajority vote of the outstanding shares necessary to remove the board in a special meeting, it would only need a simple majority of the voting stockholders to obtain control of the board at next year's annual meeting. Air Products has stated its unwillingness to wait around for another eight months until Airgas's 2011 annual meeting. There are legitimately articulated reasons for this—Air Products' stockholders, after all, have been carrying the burden of a depressed stock price since the announcement of the offer. But that is a business determination by the Air Products board. The reality is that obtaining a simple majority of the voting stock is significantly less burdensome than obtaining a supermajority vote of the outstanding shares, and considering the current composition of Airgas's stockholders (and the fact that, as a result of that shareholder composition, a majority of the voting shares today would likely tender into Air Products' $70 offer), if Air Products and those stockholders choose to stick around, an Air Products victory at the next annual meeting is very realistically attainable.

Air Products certainly realized this. It had actually intended to run an insurgent slate at Airgas's 2011 annual meeting—when everyone thought that meeting was going to be held in January. The Supreme Court has now held, however, that each annual meeting must take place "approximately" one year after the last annual meeting.[1] If Air Products is unwilling to wait another eight months to run another slate of nominees, that is a business decision of the Air Products board, but as the Supreme Court has held, waiting until the next annual meeting "delay[s]—but [does] not prevent—[Air Products] from obtaining control of the board." I thus am constrained to conclude that Airgas's defensive measures are not preclusive.

2.   Range of Reasonableness

"If a defensive measure is neither coercive nor preclusive, the *Unocal* proportionality test requires the focus of enhanced judicial scrutiny to shift to the range of reasonableness." The reasonableness of a board's

---

[1]   Ed. Note: Through its own proxy solicitation in connection with the September 2010 annual meeting, Air Products was successful in obtaining stockholder approval to set the annual meetings in January 2011. It thus sought to advance by many months the time when the next group of three directors would stand for reelection. The change was struck down in Airgas, Inc. v. Air Prods. and Chems., Inc., 8 A.3d 1182 (Del.Supr. 2010), holding that the discretion to fix an annual meeting date is not unfettered; it must pick a date that is "approximately" one year after its last annual meeting.

response is evaluated in the context of the specific threat identified—the "specific nature of the threat sets the parameters for the range of permissible defensive tactics' at any given time."

Here, the record demonstrates that Airgas's board, composed of a majority of outside, independent directors, acting in good faith and with numerous outside advisors concluded that Air Products' offer clearly undervalues Airgas in a sale transaction. The board believes in good faith that the offer price is inadequate by no small margin. Thus, the board is responding to a legitimately articulated threat.

This conclusion is bolstered by the fact that the three Air Products Nominees on the Airgas board have now wholeheartedly joined in the board's determination—what is more, they believe it is their fiduciary duty to keep Airgas's defenses in place. . . .

Certainly what occurred here is not what Air Products expected to happen. Air Products ran its slate on the promise that its nominees would "consider without any bias [the Air Products] Offer," and that they would "be willing to be outspoken in the boardroom about their views on these issues." Air Products *got what it wanted*. Its three nominees got elected to the Airgas board and then questioned the directors about their assumptions. (They got answers.) They looked at the numbers themselves. (They were impressed.) They requested outside legal counsel. (They got it.) They requested a third outside financial advisor. (They got it.) And in the end, they *joined in the board's view* that Air Products' offer was inadequate. . . .

Based on all of the foregoing factual findings, I cannot conclude that there is "clearly no basis" for the Airgas board's belief in the sustainability of its long-term plan.

On the contrary, the maintenance of the board's defensive measures must fall within a range of reasonableness here. The board is not "cramming down" a management-sponsored alternative—or *any* company-changing alternative. Instead, the board is simply maintaining the status quo, running the company for the long-term, and consistently showing improved financial results each passing quarter. The board's actions do not *forever* preclude Air Products, or any bidder, from acquiring Airgas or from getting around Airgas's defensive measures if the price is right. In the meantime, the board is preventing a change of control from occurring at an inadequate price. This course of action has been clearly recognized under Delaware law . . .

The contours of the debate [over the poison pill] have morphed over the years, but the fundamental questions have remained. Can a board "just say no"? If so, when? How should the enhanced judicial standard of review be applied? What are the pill's limits. And the ultimate question: Can a board "just say never"? . . .

[I]n this case, the Airgas board has continued to say "no" even after one proxy fight. . . . Vice Chancellor Strine recently posed . . . [a]

hypothetical in *Yucaipa Am. Alliance Fund II, L.P. v. Riggio,* 1 A.3d 310, 351 n. 229 (Del. Ch. 2010) raising the limits of the board in the face of an effective staggered board (ESB)]:

> [T]here is a plausible argument that a rights plan could be considered preclusive, based on an examination of real world market considerations, when a bidder who makes an all shares, structurally non-coercive offer has: (1) won a proxy contest for a third of the seats of a classified board; (2) is not able to proceed with its tender offer for another year because the *incumbent board majority* will not redeem the rights as to the offer; and (3) is required to take all the various economic risks that would come with maintaining the bid for another year.

At that point, it is argued, it may be appropriate for a Court to order redemption of a poison pill. That hypothetical, however, is not exactly the case here for two main reasons. First, Air Products did not run a proxy slate running on a "let the shareholders decide" platform. Instead, they ran a slate committed to taking an independent look and deciding for themselves afresh whether to accept the bid. . . . This situation is different from the one posited by Vice Chancellor Strine. . . .

Second, Airgas does not have a true "ESB". . . . Airgas's charter allows for 33% of the stockholders to call a special meeting and remove the board by a 67% vote of the outstanding shares. . . . This factual distinction also further differentiates this case from the *Yucaipa* hypothetical.

CONCLUSION . . .

There is no question that poison pills act as potent anti-takeover drugs with the potential to be abused. Counsel for plaintiffs (both Air Products and Shareholder Plaintiffs) make compelling policy arguments in favor of redeeming the pill in this case—to do otherwise, they say, would essentially make all companies with staggered boards and poison pills "takeover proof."[514] The argument is an excellent sound bite, but it is ultimately not the holding of this fact-specific case, although it does bring us one step closer to that result.

As this case demonstrates, in order to have any effectiveness, pills do not—and can not—have a set expiration date. To be clear, though, this case does not endorse "just say never." What it does endorse is Delaware's long-understood respect for reasonably exercised managerial discretion, so long as boards are found to be acting in good faith and in accordance with their fiduciary duties (after rigorous judicial fact-finding and enhanced scrutiny of their defensive actions). The Airgas board serves as a quintessential example.

Directors of a corporation still owe fiduciary duties to *all stockholders—this undoubtedly includes short-term as well as long-term holders.* . . . For the foregoing reasons, Air Products' and the Shareholder

Plaintiffs' requests for relief are denied, and all claims asserted against defendants are dismissed with prejudice. . . .

___

NOTE ON DEAD HAND PROXY PUTS

A defensive maneuver of fairly recent origin is the "Dead Hand Proxy Put" that causes a credit default that in turn calls for the company to immediately repay that corporate indebtedness. The event triggering the default occurs if a dissident captures a majority of the seats of the company's board. The unique toxicity of the put is that only the creditor holding the put can waive the provision. The prospect of repaying the company's debt is daunting and hence deters hedge fund activism. *See Pontiac General Employees Retirement System v. Ballantine,* 2015 Del. Ch. LEXIS 139 (May 8, 2015); *See* Sean J. Griffith & Natalia Reisel, Dead Hand Proxy Puts and Shareholder Value, 84 U. Chi. L. Rev. 1027 (2017) (examining effects of poison proxy puts in over 2,700 loan agreements and about 60 bond indentures from 1995 through 2014, finding that adoption of such a put is not associated with statistically significant decline in the adopting firm's market value). Delaware courts have greeted proxy puts skeptically and examined them under *Unocal. See e.g., Kallick v. Sandridge Energy, Inc.*, 68 A.3d 242, 259–60 (Del. Ch. 2013) (the directors failed to demonstrate a reasonable justification for their refusal to consider whether to approve the hedge fund's slate—so that the proxy put's trigger would not be activated—for purposes of the good faith standard of *Unocal*).

___

D. THE "REVLON MOMENT"

Revlon, Inc. v. MacAndrews & Forbes Holdings, Inc.
Supreme Court of Delaware, 1986.
506 A.2d 173.

In this battle for corporate control of Revlon, Inc. (Revlon), the Court of Chancery enjoined certain transactions designed to thwart the efforts of Pantry Pride, Inc. (Pantry Pride) to acquire Revlon. The defendants are Revlon, its board of directors, and Forstmann Little Co. and the latter's affiliated limited partnership (collectively, Forstmann). The injunction barred consummation of an option granted Forstmann to purchase certain Revlon assets (the lock-up option), a promise by Revlon to deal exclusively with Forstmann in the face of a takeover (the no-shop provision), and the payment of a $25 million cancellation fee to Forstmann if the transaction was aborted. The Court of Chancery found that the Revlon directors had breached their duty of care by entering into the foregoing transactions and effectively ending an active auction for the company. The trial court ruled that such arrangements are not illegal *per se* under Delaware law, but that their use under the circumstances here was impermissible. We agree. . . . Accordingly, we affirm.

I.

The somewhat complex maneuvers of the parties necessitate a rather detailed examination of the facts. The prelude to this controversy began in June 1985, when Ronald O. Perelman, chairman of the board and chief executive officer of Pantry Pride, met with his counterpart at Revlon, Michel C. Bergerac, to discuss a friendly acquisition of Revlon by Pantry Pride. Perelman suggested a price in the range of $40–50 per share, but the meeting ended with Bergerac dismissing those figures as considerably below Revlon's intrinsic value. All subsequent Pantry Pride overtures were rebuffed, perhaps in part based on Mr. Bergerac's strong personal antipathy to Mr. Perelman.

Thus, on August 14, Pantry Pride's board authorized Perelman to acquire Revlon, either through negotiation in the $42–$43 per share range, or by making a hostile tender offer at $45. Perelman then met with Bergerac and outlined Pantry Pride's alternate approaches. Bergerac remained adamantly opposed to such schemes and conditioned any further discussions of the matter on Pantry Pride executing a standstill agreement prohibiting it from acquiring Revlon without the latter's prior approval.

On August 19, the Revlon board met specially to consider the impending threat of a hostile bid by Pantry Pride.[3] At the meeting, Lazard Freres, Revlon's investment banker, advised the directors that $45 per share was a grossly inadequate price for the company. Felix Rohatyn and William Loomis of Lazard Freres explained to the board that Pantry Pride's financial strategy for acquiring Revlon would be through "junk bond" financing followed by a break-up of Revlon and the disposition of its assets. With proper timing, according to the experts, such transactions could produce a return to Pantry Pride of $60 to $70 per share, while a sale of the company as a whole would be in the "mid 50" dollar range. Martin Lipton, special counsel for Revlon, recommended two defensive measures: first, that the company repurchase up to 5 million of its nearly 30 million outstanding shares; and second, that it adopt a Note Purchase Rights Plan. Under this plan, each Revlon shareholder would receive as a dividend one Note Purchase Right (the Rights) for each share of common stock, with the Rights entitling the holder to exchange one common share for a $65 principal Revlon note at 12% interest with a one-year maturity. The Rights would become effective whenever anyone acquired beneficial ownership of 20% or more of Revlon's shares, unless the purchaser acquired all the company's stock

---

[3]   There were 14 directors on the Revlon board. Six of them held senior management positions with the company, and two others held significant blocks of its stock. Four of the remaining six directors were associated at some point with entities that had various business relationships with Revlon. On the basis of this limited record, however, we cannot conclude that this board is entitled to certain presumptions that generally attach to the decisions of a board whose majority consists of truly outside independent directors. . . .

for cash at $65 or more per share. In addition, the Rights would not be available to the acquiror, and prior to the 20% triggering event the Revlon board could redeem the rights for 10 cents each. Both proposals were unanimously adopted.

Pantry Pride made its first hostile move on August 23, with a cash tender offer for any and all shares of Revlon at $47.50 per common share and $26.67 per preferred share, subject to (1) Pantry Pride's obtaining financing for the purchase, and (2) the Rights being redeemed, rescinded or voided.

The Revlon board met again on August 26. The directors advised the stockholders to reject the offer. Further defensive measures also were planned. On August 29, Revlon commenced its own offer for up to 10 million shares, exchanging for each share of common stock tendered one Senior Subordinated Note (the Notes) of $47.50 principal at 11.75% interest, due 1995, and one-tenth of a share of $9.00 Cumulative Convertible Exchangeable Preferred Stock valued at $100 per share. Lazard Freres opined that the notes would trade at their face value on a fully distributed basis. Revlon stockholders tendered 87 percent of the outstanding shares (approximately 33 million), and the company accepted the full 10 million shares on a pro rata basis. The new Notes contained covenants which limited Revlon's ability to incur additional debt, sell assets, or pay dividends unless otherwise approved by the independent (non-management) members of the board.

At this point, both the Rights and the Note covenants stymied Pantry Pride's attempted takeover. The next move came on September 16, when Pantry Pride announced a new tender offer at $42 per share, conditioned upon receiving at least 90% of the outstanding stock. Pantry Pride also indicated that it would consider buying less than 90%, and at an increased price, if Revlon removed the impeding Rights. While this offer was lower on its face than the earlier $47.50 proposal, Revlon's investment banker, Lazard Freres, described the two bids as essentially equal in view of the completed exchange offer.

The Revlon board held a regularly scheduled meeting on September 24. The directors rejected the latest Pantry Pride offer and authorized management to negotiate with other parties interested in acquiring Revlon. Pantry Pride remained determined in its efforts and continued to make cash bids for the company, offering $50 per share on September 27, and raising its bid to $53 on October 1, and then to $56.25 on October 7.

In the meantime, Revlon's negotiations with Forstmann and the investment group Adler & Shaykin had produced results. The Revlon directors met on October 3, to consider Pantry Pride's $53 bid and to examine possible alternatives to the offer. Both Forstmann and Adler & Shaykin made certain proposals to the board. As a result, the directors unanimously agreed to a leveraged buyout by Forstmann. The terms of this accord were as follows: each stockholder would get $56 cash per share; management would purchase stock in the new company by the exercise of their Revlon "golden parachutes";[4] Forstmann would assume Revlon's $475 million debt incurred by the issuance of the Notes; and Revlon would redeem the Rights and waive the Notes covenants for Forstmann or in connection with any other offer superior to Forstmann's. The board did not actually remove the covenants at the October 3, meeting, because Forstmann then lacked a firm commitment on its financing, but accepted the Forstmann capital structure, and indicated that the outside directors would waive the covenants in due course. Part of Forstmann's plan was to sell Revlon's Norcliff Thayer and Reheis divisions to American Home Products for $335 million. Before the merger, Revlon was to sell its cosmetics and fragrance division to Adler Shaykin for $905 million. These transactions would facilitate the purchase by Forstmann or any other acquiror of Revlon.

When the merger, and thus the waiver of the Notes covenants, was announced, the market value of these securities began to fall. The Notes, which originally traded near par, around 100, dropped to 87.50 by October 8. One director later reported (at the October 12 meeting) a "deluge" of telephone calls from irate noteholders, and on October 10 the Wall Street Journal reported threats of litigation by these creditors.

Pantry Pride countered with a new proposal on October 7, raising its $53 offer to $56.25, subject to nullification of the Rights, a waiver of the Notes covenants, and the election of three Pantry Pride directors to the Revlon board. On October 9, representatives of Pantry Pride, Forstmann and Revlon conferred in an attempt to negotiate the fate of Revlon, but could not reach agreement. At this meeting Pantry Pride announced that it would engage in fractional bidding and top any Forstmann offer by a slightly higher one. It is also significant that Forstmann, to Pantry Pride's exclusion, had been made privy to certain Revlon financial data. Thus, the parties were not negotiating on equal terms.

Again privately armed with Revlon data, Forstmann met on October 11 with Revlon's special counsel and investment banker. On October 12, Forstmann made a new $57.25 per share offer, based on several conditions.[5] The principal demand was a lock-up option to purchase Revlon's Vision Care and National Health Laboratories divisions for $525 million, some $100–$175 million below the value ascribed to them by Lazard Freres, if another acquiror got 40% of Revlon's shares. Revlon also was required to accept a no-shop provision. The Rights and Notes covenants had to be removed as in the October 3 agreement. There would

---

[4]　In the takeover context "golden parachutes" generally are understood to be termination agreements providing substantial bonuses and other benefits for managers and certain directors upon a change in control of a company.

[5]　Forstmann's $57.25 offer ostensibly is worth $1 more than Pantry Pride's $56.25 bid. However, the Pantry Pride offer was immediate, while the Forstmann proposal must be discounted for the time value of money because of the delay in approving the merger and consummating the transaction. The exact difference between the two bids was an unsettled point of contention even at oral argument.

be a $25 million cancellation fee to be placed in escrow, and released to Forstmann if the new agreement terminated or if another acquiror got more than 19.9% of Revlon's stock. Finally, there would be no participation by Revlon management in the merger. In return, Forstmann agreed to support the par value of the Notes, which had faltered in the market, by an exchange of new notes. Forstmann also demanded immediate acceptance of its offer, or it would be withdrawn. The board unanimously approved Forstmann's proposal because: (1) it was for a higher price than the Pantry Pride bid, (2) it protected the noteholders, and (3) Forstmann's financing was firmly in place.[6] The board further agreed to redeem the rights and waive the covenants on the preferred stock in response to any offer above $57 cash per share. The covenants were waived, contingent upon receipt of an investment banking opinion that the Notes would trade near par value once the offer was consummated.

Pantry Pride, which had initially sought injunctive relief from the Rights plan on August 22, filed an amended complaint on October 14 challenging the lock-up, the cancellation fee, and the exercise of the Rights and the Notes covenants. Pantry Pride also sought a temporary restraining order to prevent Revlon from placing any assets in escrow or transferring them to Forstmann. Moreover, on October 22, Pantry Pride again raised its bid, with a cash offer of $58 per share conditioned upon nullification of the Rights, waiver of the covenants, and an injunction of the Forstmann lock-up.

On October 15, the Court of Chancery prohibited the further transfer of assets, and eight days later enjoined the lock-up, no-shop, and cancellation fee provisions of the agreement. The trial court concluded that the Revlon directors had breached their duty of loyalty by making concessions to Forstmann, out of concern for their liability to the noteholders, rather than maximizing the sale price of the company for the stockholders' benefit. MacAndrews & Forbes Holdings, Inc. v. Revlon, Inc., 501 A.2d at 1249–50.

II.

To obtain a preliminary injunction, a plaintiff must demonstrate both a reasonable probability of success on the merits and some irreparable harm which will occur absent the injunction. Gimbel v. Signal Companies, Del.Ch., 316 A.2d 599, 602 (1974), aff'd, Del.Supr., 316 A.2d 619 (1974). Additionally, the Court shall balance the conveniences of and possible injuries to the parties. Id.

---

6   Actually, at this time about $400 million of Forstmann's funding was still subject to two investment banks using their "best effort" to organize a syndicate to provide the balance. Pantry Pride's entire financing was not firmly committed at this point either, although Pantry Pride represented in an October 11 letter to Lazard Freres that its investment banker, Drexel Burnham Lambert, was highly confident of its ability to raise the balance of $350 million. Drexel Burnham had a firm commitment for this sum by October 18.

A.

We turn first to Pantry Pride's probability of success on the merits. The ultimate responsibility for managing the business and affairs of a corporation falls on its board of directors. 8 Del.C. § 141(a). In discharging this function the directors owe fiduciary duties of care and loyalty to the corporation and its shareholders. Guth v. Loft, Inc., 23 Del.Supr. 255, 5 A.2d 503, 510 (1939); Aronson v. Lewis, Del.Supr., 473 A.2d 805, 811 (1984). These principles apply with equal force when a board approves a corporate merger pursuant to 8 Del.C. § 251(b);[9] Smith v. Van Gorkom, Del.Supr., 488 A.2d 858, 873 (1985); and of course they are the bedrock of our law regarding corporate takeover issues. . . .

If the business judgment rule applies, there is a "presumption that in making a business decision the directors of a corporation acted on an informed basis, in good faith and in the honest belief that the action taken was in the best interests of the company." Aronson v. Lewis, 473 A.2d at 812. However, when a board implements antitakeover measures there arises "the omnipresent specter that a board may be acting primarily in its own interests, rather than those of the corporation and its shareholders . . . " Unocal Corp. v. Mesa Petroleum Co., 493 A.2d at 954. This potential for conflict places upon the directors the burden of proving that they had reasonable grounds for believing there was a danger to corporate policy and effectiveness, a burden satisfied by a showing of good faith and reasonable investigation. Id. at 955. In addition, the directors must analyze the nature of the takeover and its effect on the corporation in order to ensure balance—that the responsive action taken is reasonable in relation to the threat posed. Id.

B.

The first relevant defensive measure adopted by the Revlon board was the Rights Plan, which would be considered a "poison pill" in the current language of corporate takeovers—a plan by which shareholders receive the right to be bought out by the corporation at a substantial premium on the occurrence of a stated triggering event. See generally Moran v. Household International, Inc., Del.Supr., 500 A.2d 1346 (1985). By 8 Del.C. §§ 141 and 157,[10] the board clearly had the power to adopt the measure. Moran v. Household International, Inc., 500 A.2d at 1351. Thus, the focus becomes one of reasonableness and purpose.

---

[9]   The statute provides in pertinent part:

(b) The board of directors of each corporation which desires to merge or consolidate shall adopt a resolution approving an agreement of merger or consolidation. 8 Del.C. § 251(b).

[10]   The relevant provision of Section 122 is:

Every corporation created under this chapter shall have power to:

(13) Make contracts, including contracts of guaranty and suretyship, incur liabilities, borrow money at such rates of interest as the corporation may determine, issue its notes, bonds and other obligations, and secure any of its obligations by mortgage, pledge or other encumbrance of all or any of its property, franchises and income,. . . . 8 Del.C. § 122(13). . . .

The Revlon board approved the Rights Plan in the face of an impending hostile takeover bid by Pantry Pride at $45 per share, a price which Revlon reasonably concluded was grossly inadequate. Lazard Freres had so advised the directors, and had also informed them that Pantry Pride was a small, highly leveraged company bent on a "bust-up" takeover by using "junk bond" financing to buy Revlon cheaply, sell the acquired assets to pay the debts incurred, and retain the profit for itself.[11] In adopting the Plan, the board protected the shareholders from a hostile takeover at a price below the company's intrinsic value, while retaining sufficient flexibility to address any proposal deemed to be in the stockholders' best interests.

To that extent the board acted in good faith and upon reasonable investigation. Under the circumstances it cannot be said that the Rights Plan as employed was unreasonable, considering the threat posed. Indeed, the Plan was a factor in causing Pantry Pride to raise its bids from a low of $42 to an eventual high of $58. At the time of its adoption the Rights Plan afforded a measure of protection consistent with the directors' fiduciary duty in facing a takeover threat perceived as detrimental to corporate interests. *Unocal,* 493 A.2d at 954–55. Far from being a "show-stopper," as the plaintiffs had contended in *Moran,* the measure spurred the bidding to new heights, a proper result of its implementation. See *Moran,* 500 A.2d at 1354, 1356–67.

Although we consider adoption of the Plan to have been valid under the circumstances, its continued usefulness was rendered moot by the directors' actions on October 3 and October 12. At the October 3 meeting the board redeemed the Rights conditioned upon consummation of a merger with Forstmann, but further acknowledged that they would also be redeemed to facilitate any more favorable offer. On October 12, the board unanimously passed a resolution redeeming the Rights in connection with any cash proposal of $57.25 or more per share. Because all the pertinent offers eventually equaled or surpassed that amount, the Rights clearly were no longer any impediment in the contest for Revlon. This mooted any question of their propriety under *Moran* or *Unocal.*

C.

The second defensive measure adopted by Revlon to thwart a Pantry Pride takeover was the company's own exchange offer for 10 million of its shares. The directors' general broad powers to manage the business and affairs of the corporation are augmented by the specific authority conferred under 8 Del.C. § 160(a), permitting the company to deal in its own stock. *Unocal,* 493 A.2d at 953–54; Cheff v. Mathes, 41 Del.Supr. 494, 199 A.2d 548, 554 (1964); Kors v. Carey, 39 Del.Ch. 47, 158 A.2d 136, 140 (1960). However, when exercising that power in an effort to forestall a hostile takeover, the board's actions are strictly held to the

---

[11] As we noted in *Moran,* a "bust-up" takeover generally refers to a situation in which one seeks to finance an acquisition by selling off pieces of the acquired company, presumably at a substantial profit. See *Moran,* 500 A.2d at 1349, n. 4.

fiduciary standards outlined in *Unocal*. These standards require the directors to determine the best interests of the corporation and its stockholders, and impose an enhanced duty to abjure any action that is motivated by considerations other than a good faith concern for such interests. *Unocal*, 493 A.2d at 954–55; see Bennett v. Propp, 41 Del.Supr. 14, 187 A.2d 405, 409 (1962).

The Revlon directors concluded that Pantry Pride's $47.50 offer was grossly inadequate. In that regard the board acted in good faith, and on an informed basis, with reasonable grounds to believe that there existed a harmful threat to the corporate enterprise. The adoption of a defensive measure, reasonable in relation to the threat posed, was proper and fully accorded with the powers, duties, and responsibilities conferred upon directors under our law. *Unocal*, 493 A.2d at 954; Pogostin v. Rice, 480 A.2d at 627.

D.

However, when Pantry Pride increased its offer to $50 per share, and then to $53, it became apparent to all that the break-up of the company was inevitable. The Revlon board's authorization permitting management to negotiate a merger or buyout with a third party was a recognition that the company was for sale. The duty of the board had thus changed from the preservation of Revlon as a corporate entity to the maximization of the company's value at a sale for the stockholders' benefit. This significantly altered the board's responsibilities under the *Unocal* standards. It no longer faced threats to corporate policy and effectiveness, or to the stockholders' interests, from a grossly inadequate bid. The whole question of defensive measures became moot. The directors' role changed from defenders of the corporate bastion to auctioneers charged with getting the best price for the stockholders at a sale of the company.

III.

This brings us to the lock-up with Forstmann and its emphasis on shoring up the sagging market value of the Notes in the face of threatened litigation by their holders. Such a focus was inconsistent with the changed concept of the directors' responsibilities at this stage of the developments. The impending waiver of the Notes covenants had caused the value of the Notes to fall, and the board was aware of the noteholders' ire as well as their subsequent threats of suit. The directors thus made support of the Notes an integral part of the company's dealings with Forstmann, even though their primary responsibility at this stage was to the equity owners.

The original threat posed by Pantry Pride—the break-up of the company—had become a reality which even the directors embraced. Selective dealing to fend off a hostile but determined bidder was no longer a proper objective. Instead, obtaining the highest price for the benefit of the stockholders should have been the central theme guiding director action. Thus, the Revlon board could not make the requisite showing of good faith by preferring the noteholders and ignoring its duty of loyalty to the shareholders. The rights of the former already were fixed by contract. Wolfensohn v. Madison Fund, Inc., Del.Supr., 253 A.2d 72, 75 (1969); Harff v. Kerkorian, Del.Ch., 324 A.2d 215 (1974). The noteholders required no further protection, and when the Revlon board entered into an auction-ending lock-up agreement with Forstmann on the basis of impermissible considerations at the expense of the shareholders, the directors breached their primary duty of loyalty.

The Revlon board argued that it acted in good faith in protecting the noteholders because *Unocal* permits consideration of other corporate constituencies. Although such considerations may be permissible, there are fundamental limitations upon that prerogative. A board may have regard for various constituencies in discharging its responsibilities, provided there are rationally related benefits accruing to the stockholders. *Unocal,* 493 A.2d at 955. However, such concern for non-stockholder interests is inappropriate when an auction among active bidders is in progress, and the object no longer is to protect or maintain the corporate enterprise but to sell it to the highest bidder.

Revlon also contended that by Gilbert v. El Paso Co., Del.Ch., 490 A.2d 1050, 1054–55 (1984), it had contractual and good faith obligations to consider the noteholders. However, any such duties are limited to the principle that one may not interfere with contractual relationships by improper actions. Here, the rights of the noteholders were fixed by agreement, and there is nothing of substance to suggest that any of those terms were violated. The Notes covenants specifically contemplated a waiver to permit sale of the company at a fair price. The Notes were accepted by the holders on that basis, including the risk of an adverse market effect stemming from a waiver. Thus, nothing remained for Revlon to legitimately protect, and no rationally related benefit thereby accrued to the stockholders. Under such circumstances we must conclude that the merger agreement with Forstmann was unreasonable in relation to the threat posed.

A lock-up is not *per se* illegal under Delaware law. Its use has been approved in an earlier case. Thompson v. Enstar Corp., Del.Ch. (1984). Such options can entice other bidders to enter a contest for control of the corporation, creating an auction for the company and maximizing shareholder profit. Current economic conditions in the takeover market are such that a "white knight" like Forstmann might only enter the bidding for the target company if it receives some form of compensation to cover the risks and costs involved. Note, Corporations—Mergers— "Lock-up" Enjoined Under Section 14(e) of Securities Exchange Act— Mobil Corp. v. Marathon Oil Co., 669 F.2d 366 (6th Cir.1981),12 Seton Hall L.Rev. 881, 892 (1982). However, while those lock-ups which draw bidders into the battle benefit shareholders, similar measures which end an active auction and foreclose further bidding operate to the shareholders' detriment. Note, Lock-up Options: Toward a State Law Standard, 96 Harv.L.Rev. 1068, 1081 (1983). . . .

The Forstmann option had a . . . destructive effect on the auction process. Forstmann had already been drawn into the contest on a preferred basis, so the result of the lock-up was not to foster bidding, but to destroy it. The board's stated reasons for approving the transaction were: (1) better financing, (2) noteholder protection, and (3) higher price. As the Court of Chancery found, and we agree, any distinctions between the rival bidders' methods of financing the proposal were nominal at best, and such a consideration has little or no significance in a cash offer for any and all shares. The principal object, contrary to the board's duty of care, appears to have been protection of the noteholders over the shareholders' interests.

While Forstmann's $57.25 offer was objectively higher than Pantry Pride's $56.25 bid, the margin of superiority is less when the Forstmann price is adjusted for the time value of money. In reality, the Revlon board ended the auction in return for very little actual improvement in the final bid. The principal benefit went to the directors, who avoided personal liability to a class of creditors to whom the board owed no further duty under the circumstances. Thus, when a board ends an intense bidding contest on an insubstantial basis, and where a significant by-product of that action is to protect the directors against a perceived threat of personal liability for consequences stemming from the adoption of previous defensive measures, the action cannot withstand the enhanced scrutiny which *Unocal* requires of director conduct. See *Unocal,* 493 A.2d at 954–55.

In addition to the lock-up option, the Court of Chancery enjoined the no-shop provision as part of the attempt to foreclose further bidding by Pantry Pride. MacAndrews & Forbes Holdings, Inc. v. Revlon, Inc., 501 A.2d at 1251. The no-shop provision, like the lock-up option, while not *per se* illegal, is impermissible under the *Unocal* standards when a board's primary duty becomes that of an auctioneer responsible for selling the company to the highest bidder. The agreement to negotiate only with Forstmann ended rather than intensified the board's involvement in the bidding contest.

It is ironic that the parties even considered a no-shop agreement when Revlon had dealt preferentially, and almost exclusively, with Forstmann throughout the contest. After the directors authorized management to negotiate with other parties, Forstmann was given every negotiating advantage that Pantry Pride had been denied: cooperation from management, access to financial data, and the exclusive opportunity to present merger proposals directly to the board of directors. Favoritism for a white knight to the total exclusion of a hostile bidder might be justifiable when the latter's offer adversely affects shareholder interests, but when bidders make relatively similar offers, or dissolution of the company becomes inevitable, the directors cannot fulfill their enhanced *Unocal* duties by playing favorites with the contending factions. Market forces must be allowed to operate freely to bring the target's shareholders the best price available for their equity.[14] Thus, as the trial court ruled, the shareholders' interests necessitated that the board remain free to negotiate in the fulfillment of that duty.

The court below similarly enjoined the payment of the cancellation fee, pending a resolution of the merits, because the fee was part of the overall plan to thwart Pantry Pride's efforts. We find no abuse of discretion in that ruling.

IV.

Having concluded that Pantry Pride has shown a reasonable probability of success on the merits, we address the issue of irreparable harm. The Court of Chancery ruled that unless the lock-up and other aspects of the agreement were enjoined, Pantry Pride's opportunity to bid for Revlon was lost. The court also held that the need for both bidders to compete in the marketplace outweighed any injury to Forstmann. Given the complexity of the proposed transaction between Revlon and Forstmann, the obstacles to Pantry Pride obtaining a meaningful legal remedy are immense. We are satisfied that the plaintiff has shown the need for an injunction to protect it from irreparable harm, which need outweighs any harm to the defendants.

V.

In conclusion, the Revlon board was confronted with a situation not uncommon in the current wave of corporate takeovers. A hostile and determined bidder sought the company at a price the board was convinced was inadequate. The initial defensive tactics worked to the benefit of the shareholders, and thus the board was able to sustain its *Unocal* burdens in justifying those measures. However, in granting an asset option lock-up to Forstmann, we must conclude that under all the circumstances the directors allowed considerations other than the maximization of shareholder profit to affect their judgment, and followed a course that ended the auction for Revlon, absent court intervention, to the ultimate detriment of its shareholders. No such defensive measure can be sustained when it represents a breach of the directors' fundamental duty of care. See Smith v. Van Gorkom, Del.Supr., 488 A.2d 858, 874 (1985). In that context the board's action is not entitled to the deference accorded it by the business judgment rule. The measures were properly enjoined. The decision of the Court of Chancery, therefore, is

AFFIRMED.

---

[14]   By this we do not embrace the passivity thesis rejected in *Unocal*. See 493 A.2d at 954–55, nn. 8–10. The directors' role remains an active one, changed only in the respect that they are charged with the duty of selling the company at the highest price attainable for the stockholders' benefit.

Paramount Communications, Inc. v. Time Inc.

Supreme Court of Delaware, 1989.
571 A.2d 1140.

■ HORSEY, JUSTICE:

Paramount Communications, Inc. ("Paramount") and two other groups of plaintiffs ("Shareholder Plaintiffs"), shareholders of Time Incorporated ("Time"), a Delaware corporation, separately filed suits in the Delaware Court of Chancery seeking a preliminary injunction to halt Time's tender offer for 51% of Warner Communication, Inc.'s ("Warner") outstanding shares at $70 cash per share. The court below consolidated the cases and, following the development of an extensive record, after discovery and an evidentiary hearing . . . , the Chancellor refused to enjoin Time's consummation of its tender offer. . . .

[Plaintiffs filed an interlocutory appeal.]

I

Time is a Delaware corporation with its principal offices in New York City. Time's traditional business is publication of magazines and books; however, Time also provides pay television programming through its Home Box Office, Inc. and Cinemax subsidiaries. In addition, Time owns and operates cable television franchises through its subsidiary, American Television and Communication Corporation. During the relevant time period, Time's board consisted of sixteen directors. Twelve of the directors were "outside," nonemployee directors. Four of the directors were also officers of the company. . . .

As early as 1983 and 1984, Time's executive board began considering expanding Time's operations into the entertainment industry. In 1987, Time established a special committee of executives to consider and propose corporate strategies for the 1990s. The consensus of the committee was that Time should move ahead in the area of ownership and creation of video programming. This expansion . . . was predicated upon two considerations: first, Time's desire to have greater control, in terms of quality and price, over the film products delivered by way of its cable network and franchises; and second, Time's concern over the increasing globalization of the world economy. Some of Time's outside directors, especially Luce and Temple, had opposed this move as a threat to the editorial integrity and journalistic focus of Time.[4] Despite this concern, the board saw the advantages of a vertically integrated video enterprise to complement Time's existing HBO and cable networks would enable it to compete on a global basis.

---

[4] The primary concern of Time's outside directors was the preservation of the "Time Culture." They believed that Time had become recognized in this country as an institution built upon a foundation of journalistic integrity. Time's management made a studious effort to refrain from involvement in Time's editorial policy. Several of Time's outside directors feared that a merger with an entertainment company would divert Time's focus from news journalism and threaten the Time Culture.

In late spring of 1987, a meeting took place between Steve Ross, CEO of Warner Brothers, and [N.J.] Nicholas [president and chief operating officer] of Time. Ross and Nicholas discussed the possibility of a joint venture between the two companies through the creation of a jointly-owned cable company. Time would contribute its cable system and HBO. Warner would contribute its cable system and provide access to Warner Brothers Studio. The resulting venture would be a larger, more efficient cable network, able to produce and distribute its own movies on a worldwide basis. Ultimately the parties abandoned this plan, determining that it was impractical for several reasons, chief among them being tax considerations.

On August 11, 1987, Gerald M. Levin, Time's vice chairman and chief strategist, wrote J. Richard Munro [Time's chairman and CEO] a confidential memorandum in which he strongly recommended a strategic consolidation with Warner. In June 1988, Nicholas and Munro sent to each outside director a copy of the "comprehensive long-term planning document" prepared by the committee of Time executives that had been examining strategies for the 1990s. The memo included reference to and a description of Warner as a potential acquisition candidate.

Thereafter, Munro and Nicholas held meetings with Time's outside directors to discuss, generally, long-term strategies for Time and, specifically, a combination with Warner. Nearly a year later, Time's board reached the point of serious discussion of the "nuts and bolts" of a consolidation with an entertainment company. On July 21, 1988, Time's board met . . . to consider Time's expansion into the entertainment industry on a global scale. . . .

Without any definitive decision on choice of a company, the board approved in principle a strategic plan for Time's expansion. The board gave management the "go-ahead" to continue discussions with Warner concerning the possibility of a merger. With the exception of Temple and Luce, most of the outside directors agreed that a merger involving expansion into the entertainment field promised great growth opportunity for Time. Temple and Luce remained unenthusiastic about Time's entry into the entertainment field. See supra note [3].

The board's consensus was that a merger of Time and Warner was feasible, but only if Time controlled the board of the resulting corporation and thereby preserved a management committed to Time's journalistic integrity. To accomplish this goal, the board stressed the importance of carefully defining in advance the corporate governance provisions that would control the resulting entity. Some board members expressed concern over whether such a business combination would place Time "*in play*." The board discussed the wisdom of adopting further defensive measures to lessen such a possibility.[5]

---

[5]   Time had in place a panoply of defensive devices, including a staggered board, a "poison pill" preferred stock rights plan triggered by an acquisition of 15% of the company, a fifty-day

Of a wide range of companies considered by Time's board as possible merger candidates, Warner Brothers, Paramount, Columbia, M.C.A., Fox, MGM, Disney, and Orion, the board, in July 1988, concluded that Warner was the superior candidate for a consolidation. Warner stood out on a number of counts. Warner had just acquired Lorimar and its film studios. Time-Warner could make movies and television shows for use on HBO. Warner had an international distribution system, which Time could use to sell films, videos, books and magazines. Warner was a giant in the music and recording business, an area into which Time wanted to expand. None of the other companies considered had the musical clout of Warner. Time and Warner's cable systems were compatible and could be easily integrated; none of the other companies considered presented such a compatible cable partner. Together, Time and Warner would control half of New York City's cable system; Warner had cable systems in Brooklyn and Queens; and Time controlled cable systems in Manhattan and Queens. Warner's publishing company would integrate well with Time's established publishing company. Time sells hardcover books and magazines, and Warner sells softcover books and comics.[6] Time-Warner could sell all of these publications and Warner's videos by using Time's direct mailing network and Warner's international distribution system. Time's network could be used to promote and merchandise Warner's movies.

In August 1988, Levin, Nicholas, and Munro, acting on instructions from Time's board, continued to explore a business combination with Warner. . . .

From the outset, Time's board favored an all-cash or cash and securities acquisition of Warner as the basis for consolidation. Bruce Wasserstein, Time's financial advisor, also favored an outright purchase of Warner. However, Steve Ross, Warner's CEO, was adamant that a business combination was only practicable on a stock-for-stock basis. Warner insisted on a stock swap in order to preserve its shareholders' equity in the resulting corporation. Time's officers, on the other hand, made it abundantly clear that Time would be the acquiring corporation and that Time would control the resulting board. Time refused to permit itself to be cast as the "acquired" company.

Eventually Time acquiesced in Warner's insistence on a stock-for-stock deal, but talks broke down over corporate governance issues. Time wanted Ross' position as a co-CEO to be temporary and wanted Ross to retire in five years. Ross, however, refused to set a time for his retirement and viewed Time's proposal as indicating a lack of confidence in his leadership. Warner considered it vital that their executives and creative

---

notice period for shareholder motions, and restrictions on shareholders' ability to call a meeting or act by consent.

    [6]   In contrast, Paramount's publishing endeavors were in the areas of professional volumes and text books. Time's board did not find Paramount's publishing as compatible as Warner's publishing efforts.

staff not perceive Warner as selling out to Time. Time's request of a guarantee that Time would dominate the CEO succession was objected to as inconsistent with the concept of a Time-Warner merger "of equals." Negotiations ended when the parties reached an impasse. Time's board refused to compromise on its position on corporate governance. Time, and particularly its outside directors, viewed the corporate governance provisions as critical for preserving the "Time Culture" through a pro-Time management at the top. . . .

Throughout the fall of 1988 Time pursued its plan of expansion into the entertainment field; Time held informal discussions with several companies, including Paramount. Capital Cities/ABC approached Time to propose a merger. Talks terminated, however, when Capital Cities/ABC suggested that it was interested in purchasing Time or in controlling the resulting board. Time steadfastly maintained it was not placing itself up for sale.

Warner and Time resumed negotiations in January 1989. The catalyst for the resumption of talks was a private dinner between Steve Ross and Time outside director, Michael Dingman. Dingman was able to convince Ross that the transitional nature of the proposed co-CEO arrangement did not reflect a lack of confidence in Ross. Ross agreed that this course was best for the company and a meeting between Ross and Munro resulted. Ross agreed to retire in five years and let Nicholas succeed him. Negotiations resumed and many of the details of the original stock-for-stock exchange agreement remained intact. . . .

Time insider directors Levin and Nicholas met with Warner's financial advisors to decide upon a stock exchange ratio. Time's board had recognized the potential need to pay a premium in the stock ratio in exchange for dictating the governing arrangement of the new Time-Warner. Levin and outside director Finkelstein were the primary proponents of paying a premium to protect the "Time Culture." The board discussed premium rates of 10%, 15% and 20%. Wasserstein also suggested paying a premium for Warner due to Warner's rapid growth rate. The market exchange ratio of Time stock for Warner stock was .38 in favor of Warner. Warner's financial advisors informed the board that any exchange rate over .400 was a fair deal and any exchange rate over .450 was "one hell of a deal." The parties ultimately agreed upon an exchange rate favoring Warner of .465. On that basis, Warner stockholders would own slightly over 62%[7] of the common stock of Time-Warner.

On March 3, 1989, Time's board, with all but one director in attendance, met and unanimously approved the stock-for-stock merger with Warner. Warner's board likewise approved the merger. The agreement called for Warner to be merged into a wholly-owned Time

---

[7]   As was noted in the briefs and at oral argument, this figure is somewhat misleading because it does not take into consideration the number of individuals who owned stock in both companies.

subsidiary with Warner becoming the surviving corporation. The common stock of Warner would then be converted into common stock of Time at the agreed upon ratio. Thereafter, the name of Time would be changed to Time-Warner, Inc.

The rules of the New York Stock Exchange required that Time's issuance of shares to effectuate the merger be approved by a vote of Time's stockholders. The Delaware General Corporation Law required approval of the merger by a majority of the Warner stockholders. Delaware law did not require any vote by Time stockholders. . . .

The resulting company would have a 24-member board, with 12 members representing each corporation. The company would have co-CEO's, at first Ross and Munro, then Ross and Nicholas, and finally, after Ross' retirement, . . . Nicholas alone. The board would create an editorial committee with a majority of members representing Time. A similar entertainment committee would be controlled by Warner board members. . . .

At its March 3, 1989 meeting, Time's board adopted several defensive tactics. Time entered an automatic share exchange agreement with Warner. Time would receive 17,292,747 shares of Warner's outstanding common stock (9.4%) and Warner would receive 7,080,016 shares of Time's outstanding common stock (11.1%). Either party could trigger the exchange. Time sought out and paid for "confidence" letters from various banks with which they did business. In these letters, the banks promised not to finance any third-party attempt to acquire Time. Time argues these agreements served only to preserve the confidential relationship between itself and the banks. The Chancellor found these agreements to be inconsequential and futile attempts to "dry up" money for a hostile takeover. Time also agreed to a "no-shop" clause, preventing Time from considering any other consolidation proposal, thus relinquishing its power to consider other proposals, regardless of their merits. Time did so at Warner's insistence. Warner did not want to be left "on the auction block" for an unfriendly suitor, if Time were to withdraw from the deal.

Time's board simultaneously established a special committee of outside directors, Finkelstein, Kearns, and Opel, to oversee the merger. The committee's assignment was to resolve any impediments that might arise in the course of working out the details of the merger and its consummation. . . .

Time representatives lauded the lack of debt to the United States Senate and to the President of the United States. Public reaction to the announcement of the merger was positive. Time-Warner would be a media colossus with international scope. The board scheduled the stockholder vote for June 23; and a May 1 record date was set. On May 24, 1989, Time sent out extensive proxy statements to the stockholders regarding the approval vote on the merger. In the meantime, with the merger proceeding without impediment, the special committee had concluded, shortly after its creation, that it was not necessary either to retain independent consultants, legal or financial, or even to meet. Time's board was unanimously in favor of the proposed merger with Warner; and, by the end of May, the Time-Warner merger appeared to be an accomplished fact.

On June 7, 1989, these wishful assumptions were shattered by Paramount's surprising announcement of its all-cash offer to purchase all outstanding shares of Time for $175 per share. The following day, June 8, the trading price of Time's stock rose from $126 to $170 per share. Paramount's offer was said to be "fully negotiable."[8]

Time found Paramount's "fully negotiable" offer to be in fact subject to at least three conditions. First, Time had to terminate its merger agreement and stock exchange agreement with Warner, and remove certain other of its defensive devices, including the redemption of Time's shareholder rights. Second, Paramount had to obtain the required cable franchise transfers from Time in a fashion acceptable to Paramount in its sole discretion. Finally, the offer depended upon a judicial determination that section 203 of the General Corporate Law of Delaware (The Delaware Anti-Takeover Statute) was inapplicable to any Time-Paramount merger. While Paramount's board had been privately advised that it could take months, perhaps over a year, to forge and consummate the deal, Paramount's board publicly proclaimed its ability to close the offer by July 5, 1989. Paramount executives later conceded that none of its directors believed that July 5th was a realistic date to close the transaction.

On June 8, 1989, Time formally responded to Paramount's offer. Time's chairman and CEO, J. Richard Munro, sent an aggressively worded letter to Paramount's CEO, Martin Davis. Munro's letter attacked Davis' personal integrity and called Paramount's offer "smoke and mirrors." Time's nonmanagement directors were not shown the letter before it was sent. However, at a board meeting that same day, all members endorsed management's response as well as the letter's content.

Over the following eight days, Time's board met three times to discuss Paramount's $175 offer. The board viewed Paramount's offer as inadequate and concluded that its proposed merger with Warner was the better course of action. Therefore, the board declined to open any negotiations with Paramount and held steady its course toward a merger with Warner.

In June, Time's board of directors met several times. During the course of their June meetings, Time's outside directors met frequently without management, officers or directors being present. At the request

---

[8]   Subsequently, it was established that Paramount's board had decided as early as March 1989 to move to acquire Time. However, Paramount management intentionally delayed publicizing its proposal until Time had mailed to its stockholders its Time-Warner merger proposal along with the required proxy statements.

of the outside directors, corporate counsel was present during the board meetings and, from time to time, the management directors were asked to leave the board sessions. During the course of these meetings, Time's financial advisors informed the board that, on an auction basis, Time's per share value was materially higher than Paramount's $175 per share offer. On this basis, the board concluded that Paramount's $175 offer was inadequate.

At these June meetings, certain Time directors expressed their concern that Time stockholders would not comprehend the long-term benefits of the Warner merger. Large quantities of Time shares were held by institutional investors. The board feared that even though there appeared to be wide support for the Warner transaction, Paramount's cash premium would be a tempting prospect to these investors. In mid-June, Time sought permission from the New York Stock Exchange to alter its rules and allow the Time-Warner merger to proceed without stockholder approval. Time did so at Warner's insistence. The New York Stock Exchange rejected Time's request on June 15; and on that day, the value of Time stock reached $182 per share.

The following day, June 16, Time's board met to take up Paramount's offer. The board's prevailing belief was that Paramount's bid presented a threat to Time's control of its own destiny and retention of the "Time Culture." Even after Time's financial advisors made another presentation of Paramount and its business attributes, Time's board maintained its position that a combination within Warner presented greater potential for Time. Warner presented Time with a much desired production capability and an established international marketing chain. Time's advisors presented the board with various options, including defensive measures. . . . Finally, Time's board formally rejected Paramount's offer.[11]

At the same meeting, Time's board decided to recast its consolidation with Warner into an outright cash and securities acquisition of Warner by Time; and Time so informed Warner. Time accordingly restructured its proposal to acquire Warner as follows: Time would make an immediate all-cash offer for 51% of Warner's outstanding stock at $70 per share. The remaining 49% would be purchased at some later date for a mixture of cash and securities worth $70 per share. To provide the funds required for its outright acquisition of Warner, Time would assume 7–10 billion dollars worth of debt, thus eliminating one of the principal transaction-related benefits of the original merger agreement. . . .

On June 23, 1989, Paramount raised its all-cash offer to buy Time's outstanding stock to $200 per share. Paramount still professed that all aspects of the offer were negotiable. Time's board met on June 26, 1989 and formally rejected Paramount's $200 per share second offer. The

---

[11] Meanwhile, Time had already begun erecting impediments to Paramount's offer. Time encouraged local cable franchises to sue Paramount to prevent it from easily obtaining the franchises.

board reiterated its belief that, despite the $25 increase, the offer was still inadequate. The Time board maintained that the Warner transaction offered a greater long-term value for the stockholders and, unlike Paramount, did not pose a threat to Time's survival and its "culture." Paramount then filed this action in the Court of Chancery.

II

The Shareholder Plaintiffs first assert a *Revlon* claim. They contend that the March 4 Time-Warner agreement effectively put Time up for sale, triggering *Revlon* duties, requiring Time's board to enhance short-term shareholder value and to treat all other interested acquirors on an equal basis. The Shareholder Plaintiffs base this argument on two facts: (i) the ultimate Time-Warner exchange ratio of .465 favoring Warner, resulting in Warner shareholders' receipt of 62% of the combined company; and (ii) the subjective intent of Time's directors as evidenced in their statements that the market might perceive the Time-Warner merger as putting Time up "for sale" and their adoption of various defensive measures.

The Shareholder Plaintiffs further contend that Time's directors, in structuring the original merger transaction to be "takeover-proof," triggered *Revlon* duties by foreclosing their shareholders from any prospect of obtaining a control premium. In short, plaintiffs argue that Time's board's decision to merge with Warner imposed a fiduciary duty to maximize immediate share value and not erect unreasonable barriers to further bids. . . .

Paramount asserts only a *Unocal* claim in which the shareholder plaintiffs join. Paramount contends that the Chancellor, in applying the first part of the *Unocal* test, erred in finding that Time's board had reasonable grounds to believe that Paramount posed both a legally cognizable threat to Time shareholders and a danger to Time's corporate policy and effectiveness. Paramount also contests the court's finding that Time's board made a reasonable and objective investigation of Paramount's offer so as to be informed before rejecting it. Paramount further claims that the court erred in applying *Unocal*'s second part in finding Time's response to be "reasonable." Paramount points primarily to the preclusive effect of the revised agreement which denied Time shareholders the opportunity both to vote on the agreement and to respond to Paramount's tender offer. Paramount argues that the underlying motivation of Time's board in adopting these defensive measures was management's desire to perpetuate itself in office.

The Court of Chancery posed the pivotal question presented by this case to be: Under what circumstances must a board of directors abandon an in-place plan of corporate development in order to provide its shareholders with the option to elect and realize an immediate control premium? As applied to this case, the question becomes: Did Time's board, having developed a strategic plan of global expansion to be launched through a business combination with Warner, come under a fiduciary duty to jettison its plan and put the corporation's future in the hands of its shareholders?

While we affirm the result reached by the Chancellor, we think it unwise to place undue emphasis upon long-term versus short-term corporate strategy. Two key predicates underpin our analysis. First, Delaware law imposes on a board of directors the duty to manage the business and affairs of the corporation. 8 Del.C. § 141(a). This broad mandate includes a conferred authority to set a corporate course of action, including time frame, designed to enhance corporate profitability. Thus, the question of "long-term" versus "short-term" values is largely irrelevant because directors, generally, are obliged to charter a course for a corporation which is in its best interests without regard to a fixed investment horizon. Second, absent a limited set of circumstances as defined under *Revlon*, a board of directors, while always required to act in an informed manner, is not under any *per se* duty to maximize shareholder value in the short term, even in the context of a takeover.[12] In our view, the pivotal question presented by this case is: "Did Time, by entering into the proposed merger with Warner, put itself up for sale?" A resolution of that issue through application of *Revlon* has a significant bearing upon the resolution of the derivative *Unocal* issue.

A.

We first take up plaintiffs' principal *Revlon* argument, summarized above. In rejecting this argument, the Chancellor found the original Time-Warner merger agreement not to constitute a "change of control" and concluded that the transaction did not trigger *Revlon* duties. The Chancellor's conclusion is premised on a finding that "[b]efore the merger agreement was signed, control of the corporation existed in a fluid aggregation of unaffiliated shareholders representing a voting majority—in other words, in the market." The Chancellor's findings of fact are supported by the record and his conclusion is correct as a matter of law. However, we premise our rejection of plaintiffs' *Revlon* claim on different grounds, namely, the absence of any substantial evidence to conclude that Time's board, in negotiating with Warner, made the dissolution or breakup of the corporate entity inevitable, as was the case in *Revlon*.

Under Delaware law there are, generally speaking and without excluding other possibilities, two circumstances which may implicate *Revlon* duties. The first, and clearer one, is when a corporation initiates an active bidding process seeking to sell itself or to effect a business reorganization involving a clear break-up of the company. See, e.g., Mills Acquisition Co. v. Macmillan, Inc., Del.Supr., 559 A.2d 1261 (1989). However, *Revlon* duties may also be triggered where, in response to a

---

[12] Thus, we endorse the Chancellor's conclusion that it is not a breach of faith for directors to determine that the present stock market price of shares is not representative of true value or that there may indeed be several market values for any corporation's stock. We have so held in another context. See *Van Gorkom*, 488 A.2d at 876.

bidder's offer, a target abandons its long-term strategy and seeks an alternative transaction also involving the breakup of the company. Thus, in *Revlon*, when the board responded to Pantry Pride's offer by contemplating a "bust-up" sale of assets in a leveraged acquisition, we imposed upon the board a duty to maximize immediate shareholder value and an obligation to auction the company fairly. If, however, the board's reaction to a hostile tender offer is found to constitute only a defensive response and not an abandonment of the corporation's continued existence, *Revlon* duties are not triggered, though *Unocal* duties attach.[14] See, e.g., Ivanhoe Partners v. Newmont Mining Corp., Del.Supr., 535 A.2d 1334, 1345 (1987).

The plaintiffs insist that even though the original Time-Warner agreement may not have worked "an objective change of control," the transaction made a "sale" of Time inevitable. Plaintiffs rely on the subjective intent of Time's board of directors and principally upon certain board members' expressions of concern that the Warner transaction *might* be viewed as effectively putting Time up for sale. Plaintiffs argue that the use of a lock-up agreement, a no-shop clause, and so-called "dry-up" agreements prevented shareholders from obtaining a control premium in the immediate future and thus violated *Revlon*.

We agree with the Chancellor that such evidence is entirely insufficient to invoke *Revlon* duties; and we decline to extend *Revlon's* application to corporate transactions simply because they might be construed as putting a corporation either "in play" or "up for sale." See Citron v. Fairchild Camera, Del.Supr., 569 A.2d 53 (1989); *Macmillan*, 559 A.2d at 1285 n. 35. The adoption of structural safety devices alone does not trigger *Revlon*. Rather, as the Chancellor stated, such devices are properly subject to a *Unocal* analysis.

Finally, we do not find in Time's recasting of its merger agreement with Warner from a share exchange to a share purchase a basis to conclude that Time had either abandoned its strategic plan or made a sale of Time inevitable. The Chancellor found that although the merged Time-Warner company would be large (with a value approaching approximately $30 billion), recent takeover cases have proven that acquisition of the combined company might nonetheless be possible. . . . The legal consequence is that *Unocal* alone applies to determine whether the business judgment rule attaches to the revised agreement. . . .

B.

We turn now to plaintiffs' *Unocal* claim. We begin by noting, as did the Chancellor, that our decision does not require us to pass on the

---

[14] Within the auction process, any action taken by the board must be reasonably related to the threat posed or reasonable in relation to the advantage sought, see Mills Acquisition Co. v. Macmillan, Inc., Del.Supr., 559 A.2d 1261, 1288 (1989). Thus, a *Unocal* analysis may be appropriate when a corporation is in a *Revlon* situation and *Revlon* duties may be triggered by a defensive action taken in response to a hostile offer. Since *Revlon*, we have stated that differing treatment of various bidders is not actionable when such action reasonably relates to achieving the best price available for the stockholders. *Macmillan*, 559 A.2d at 1286–87.

wisdom of the board's decision to enter into the original Time-Warner agreement. That is not a court's task. Our task is simply to review the record to determine whether there is sufficient evidence to support the Chancellor's conclusion that the initial Time-Warner agreement was the product of a proper exercise of business judgment. . . .

We have purposely detailed the evidence of the Time board's deliberative approach, beginning in 1983–84, to expand itself. Time's decision in 1988 to combine with Warner was made only after what could be fairly characterized as an exhaustive appraisal of Time's future as a corporation. After concluding in 1983–84 that the corporation must expand to survive, and beyond journalism into entertainment, the board combed the field of available entertainment companies. By 1987 Time had focused upon Warner; by late July 1988 Time's board was convinced that Warner would provide the best "fit" for Time to achieve its strategic objectives. The record attests to the zealousness of Time's executives, fully supported by their directors, in seeing to the preservation of Time's "culture," i.e., its perceived editorial integrity in journalism. We find ample evidence in the record to support the Chancellor's conclusion that the Time board's decision to expand the business of the company through its March 3 merger with Warner was entitled to the protection of the business judgment rule. . . .

The Chancellor reached a different conclusion in addressing the Time-Warner transaction as revised three months later. He found that the revised agreement was defense-motivated and designed to avoid the potentially disruptive effect that Paramount's offer would have had on consummation of the proposed merger were it put to a shareholder vote. Thus, the court declined to apply the traditional business judgment rule to the revised transaction and instead analyzed the Time board's June 16 decision under *Unocal*. The court ruled that *Unocal* applied to all director actions taken, following receipt of Paramount's hostile tender offer, that were reasonably determined to be defensive. Clearly that was a correct ruling and no party disputes that ruling.

In *Unocal*, we held that before the business judgment rule is applied to a board's adoption of a defensive measure, the burden will lie with the board to prove (a) reasonable grounds for believing that a danger to corporate policy and effectiveness existed; and (b) that the defensive measure adopted was reasonable in relation to the threat posed. *Unocal*, 493 A.2d 946. Directors satisfy the first part of the *Unocal* test by demonstrating good faith and reasonable investigation. . . .

Unocal involved a two-tier, highly coercive tender offer. In such a case, the threat is obvious: shareholders may be compelled to tender to avoid being treated adversely in the second stage of the transaction. . . . In subsequent cases, the Court of Chancery has suggested that an all-cash, all-shares offer, falling within a range of values that a shareholder might reasonably prefer, cannot constitute a legally recognized "threat" to shareholder interests sufficient to withstand a *Unocal* analysis. AC

Acquisitions Corp. v. Anderson, Clayton & Co., Del.Ch., 519 A.2d 103 (1986); see Grand Metropolitan, PLC v. Pillsbury Co., Del.Ch., 558 A.2d 1049 (1988); City Capital Associates v. Interco Inc., Del.Ch., 551 A.2d 787 (1988). In those cases, the Court of Chancery determined that whatever threat existed related only to the shareholders and only to price and not to the corporation.

From those decisions by our Court of Chancery, Paramount and the individual plaintiffs extrapolate a rule of law that an all-cash, all-shares offer with values reasonably in the range of acceptable price cannot pose any objective threat to a corporation or its shareholders. Thus, Paramount would have us hold that only if the value of Paramount's offer were determined to be clearly inferior to the value created by management's plan to merge with Warner could the offer be viewed— objectively—as a threat.

Implicit in the plaintiffs' argument is the view that a hostile tender offer can pose only two types of threats: the threat of coercion that results from a two-tier offer promising unequal treatment for nontendering shareholders, and the threat of inadequate value from an all-shares, all-cash offer at a price below what a target board in good faith deems to be the present value of its shares. See, e.g., *Interco*, 551 A.2d at 797; *see also* BNS, Inc. v. Koppers, D.Del., 683 F.Supp. 458 (1988). Since Paramount's offer was all-cash, the only conceivable "threat," plaintiffs argue, was inadequate value. We disapprove of such a narrow and rigid construction of *Unocal*, for the reasons which follow.

Plaintiffs' position represents a fundamental misconception of our standard of review under *Unocal* principally because it would involve the court in substituting its judgment for what is a "better" deal for that of a corporation's board of directors. To the extent that the Court of Chancery has recently done so in certain of its opinions, we hereby reject such approach as not in keeping with a proper *Unocal* analysis. See, e.g., *Interco*, 551 A.2d 787 . . .

The usefulness of *Unocal* as an analytical tool is precisely its flexibility in the face of a variety of fact scenarios. *Unocal* is not intended as an abstract standard; neither is it a structured and mechanistic procedure of appraisal. Thus, we have said that directors may consider, when evaluating the threat posed by a takeover bid, the "inadequacy of the price offered, nature and timing of the offer, questions of illegality, the impact on [constituencies] other than shareholders, the risk of nonconsummation and the quality of securities being offered in the exchange." 493 A.2d at 955. The open-ended analysis mandated by *Unocal* is not intended to lead to a simple mathematical exercise: that is, of comparing the discounted value of Time-Warner's expected trading price at some future date with Paramount's offer and determining which is the higher. Indeed, in our view, precepts underlying the business judgment rule mitigate against a court's engaging in the process of attempting to appraise and evaluate the relative merits of a long-term versus a short-term investment goal for shareholders. To engage in such an exercise is a distortion of the *Unocal* process and, in particular, the application of the second part of *Unocal's* test, discussed below.

In this case, the Time board reasonably determined that inadequate value was not the only legally cognizable threat that Paramount's all-cash, all-shares offer could present. Time's board concluded that Paramount's eleventh hour offer posed other threats. One concern was that Time shareholders might elect to tender into Paramount's cash offer in ignorance or a mistaken belief of the strategic benefit which a business combination with Warner might produce. Moreover, Time viewed the conditions attached to Paramount's offer as introducing a degree of uncertainty that skewed a comparative analysis. Further, the timing of Paramount's offer to follow issuance of Time's proxy notice was viewed as arguably designed to upset, if not confuse, the Time stockholders' vote. Given this record evidence, we cannot conclude that the Time board's decision of June 6 that Paramount's offer posed a threat to corporate policy and effectiveness was lacking in good faith or dominated by motives of either entrenchment or self-interest.

Paramount also contends that the Time board had not duly investigated Paramount's offer. Therefore, Paramount argues, Time was unable to make an informed decision that the offer posed a threat to Time's corporate policy. Although the Chancellor did not address this issue directly, his findings of fact do detail Time's exploration of the available entertainment companies, including Paramount, before determining that Warner provided the best strategic "fit." In addition, the court found that Time's board rejected Paramount's offer because Paramount did not serve Time's objectives or meet Time's needs. Thus, the record does, in our judgment, demonstrate that Time's board was adequately informed of the potential benefits of a transaction with Paramount. We agree with the Chancellor that the Time board's lengthy pre-June investigation of potential merger candidates, including Paramount, mooted any obligation on Time's part to halt its merger process with Warner to reconsider Paramount. Time's board was under no obligation to negotiate with Paramount. *Unocal*, 493 A.2d at 954–55; see also *Macmillan*, 559 A.2d at 1285 n. 35. Time's failure to negotiate cannot be fairly found to have been uninformed. The evidence supporting this finding is materially enhanced by the fact that twelve of Time's sixteen board members were outside independent directors. . . .

We turn to the second part of the *Unocal* analysis. The obvious requisite to determining the reasonableness of a defensive action is a clear identification of the nature of the threat. As the Chancellor correctly noted, this "requires an evaluation of the importance of the corporate objective threatened; alternative methods of protecting that objective; impacts of the 'defensive' action, and other relevant factors." . . . As applied to the facts of this case, the question is whether the record evidence supports the Court of Chancery's conclusion that the restructuring of the Time-Warner transaction, including the adoption of several preclusive defensive measures, was a *reasonable response* in relation to a perceived threat.

Paramount argues that, assuming its tender offer posed a threat, Time's response was unreasonable in precluding Time's shareholders from accepting the tender offer or receiving a control premium in the immediately foreseeable future. Once again, the contention stems, we believe, from a fundamental misunderstanding of where the power of corporate governance lies. Delaware law confers the management of the corporate enterprise to the stockholders' duly elected board representatives. 8 Del.C. § 141(a). The fiduciary duty to manage a corporate enterprise includes the selection of a time frame for achievement of corporate goals. That duty may not be delegated to the stockholders. . . . Directors are not obliged to abandon a deliberately conceived corporate plan for a short-term shareholder profit unless there is clearly no basis to sustain the corporate strategy. . . .

Although the Chancellor blurred somewhat the discrete analyses required under *Unocal*, he did conclude that Time's board reasonably perceived Paramount's offer to be a significant threat to the planned Time-Warner merger and that Time's response was not "overly broad." We have found that even in light of a valid threat, management actions that are coercive in nature or force upon shareholders a management-sponsored alternative to a hostile offer may be struck down as unreasonable and nonproportionate responses. *Macmillan*, 559 A.2d 1261; *AC Acquisitions Corp.*, 519 A.2d 103.

Here, on the record facts, the Chancellor found that Time's responsive action to Paramount's tender offer was not aimed at "cramming down" on its shareholders a management-sponsored alternative, but rather had as its goal the carrying forward of a pre-existing transaction in an altered form. Thus, the response was reasonably related to the threat. The Chancellor noted that the revised agreement and its accompanying safety devices did not preclude Paramount from making an offer for the combined Time-Warner company or from changing the conditions of its offer so as not to make the offer dependent upon the nullification of the Time-Warner agreement. Thus, the response was proportionate. We affirm the Chancellor's rulings as clearly supported by the record. Finally, we note that although Time was required, as a result of Paramount's hostile offer, to incur a heavy debt to finance its acquisition of Warner, that fact alone does not render the board's decision unreasonable so long as the directors could reasonably perceive the debt load not to be so injurious to the corporation as to jeopardize its well being.

C.

Conclusion

Applying the test for grant or denial of preliminary injunctive relief, we find plaintiffs failed to establish a reasonable likelihood of ultimate success on the merits. Therefore, we affirm.

————

NOTE ON WHEN *REVLON* APPLIES

Courts considering whether *Revlon* duties apply emphasize whether the transaction portends a "change in control." What does this mean and why should this type of transaction trigger the heightened fiduciary obligations illustrated by *Revlon* and its progeny? Emphasis in analyzing these questions is on the transaction's structure so that *Revlon* is triggered if the transaction is seen as the last opportunity for shareholders to participate in a control premium. Does such an occurrence necessarily occur if the transaction will ultimately lead to a breakup of the firm? Consider the following summary of when *Revlon* duties arise:

> [A] board sells "control" and thus triggers *Revlon* duties . . . when it agrees to exchange a controlling stake in the company, either for cash or non-voting securities, or for voting shares in an acquirer with a controlling shareholder but not when it exchanges 100% of its voting shares for voting shares in a widely held acquirer, most commonly through a stock-for-stock merger. . . .
>
> The exchange of all the target's voting shares of another widely held company is not a sale of control, and thus does not trigger *Revlon*, on the logic that control of the target company was before, and control of the combined company remains afterward, in a "fluid aggregation of unaffiliated stockholders."

Bernard Black & Rainier Kraakman, Delaware's Takeover Law: The Uncertain Search for Hidden Value, 96 Nw. U. L. Rev. 521, 534–35 (2002).

The classic example of a transaction falling within the third instance is *Paramount Communications Inc. v. QVC Network*, 637 A.2d 34 (1994). The Supreme Court elaborated on its emphasis on control being transferred in the Viacom-Paramount combination where Viacom's Chairman and CEO, Sumner M. Redstone, owned 85.2 percent of Viacom's voting stock and under the terms of the acquisition would own a majority of the combined companies voting stock, thereby prompting the court to apply *Revlon*:

> When a majority of a corporation's voting shares are acquired by a single person or entity, or by a cohesive group acting together, there is a significant diminution in the voting power of those who thereby become minority stockholders. Under the statutory framework of the General Corporation Law, many of the most fundamental corporate changes can be implemented only if they are approved by a majority vote of the stockholders. Such actions include elections of directors, amendments to the certificate of incorporation,

mergers, consolidations, sales of all or substantially all of the assets
of the corporation, and dissolution. 8 Del.C. §§ 211, 242, 251, 258,
263, 271, 275. Because of the overriding importance of voting
rights, this Court and the Court of Chancery have consistently
acted to protect stockholders from unwarranted interference with
such rights.

In the absence of devices protecting the minority stockholders,
stockholder votes are likely to become mere formalities where there
is a majority stockholder. For example, minority stockholders can
be deprived of a continuing equity interest in their corporation by
means of a cash-out merger. *Weinberger,* 457 A.2d at 703. Absent
effective protective provisions, minority stockholders must rely for
protection solely on the fiduciary duties owed to them by the
directors and the majority stockholder, since the minority
stockholders have lost the power to influence corporate direction
through the ballot. The acquisition of majority status and the
consequent privilege of exerting the powers of majority ownership
come at a price. That price is usually a control premium which
recognizes not only the value of a control block of shares, but also
compensates the minority stockholders for their resulting loss of
voting power.

In the case before us, the public stockholders (in the aggregate)
currently own a majority of Paramount's voting stock. Control of
the corporation is not vested in a single person, entity, or group,
but vested in the fluid aggregation of unaffiliated stockholders. In
the event the Paramount-Viacom transaction is consummated, the
public stockholders will receive cash and a minority equity voting
position in the surviving corporation. Following such
consummation, there will be a controlling stockholder who will
have the voting power to: (a) elect directors; (b) cause a break-up of
the corporation; (c) merge it with another company; (d) cash-out the
public stockholders; (e) amend the certificate of incorporation; (f)
sell all or substantially all of the corporate assets; or (g) otherwise
alter materially the nature of the corporation and the public
stockholders' interests. Irrespective of the present Paramount
Board's vision of a long-term strategic alliance with Viacom, the
proposed sale of control would provide the new controlling
stockholder with the power to alter that vision.

Because of the intended sale of control, the Paramount-Viacom
transaction has economic consequences of considerable significance
to the Paramount stockholders. Once control has shifted, the
current Paramount stockholders will have no leverage in the future
to demand another control premium. As a result, the Paramount
stockholders are entitled to receive, and should receive, a control
premium and/or protective devices of significant value. There being
no such protective provisions in the Viacom-Paramount
transaction, the Paramount directors had an obligation to take the

maximum advantage of the current opportunity to realize for the stockholders the best value reasonably available.

Id. at 42–43.

————

C&J Energy Servs. v. City of Miami Gen. Employees' & Sanitation Employees' Ret. Trust

Supreme Court of Delaware, 2014.
107 A.3d 1049.

■ STRINE, CHIEF JUSTICE:

I. INTRODUCTION

This is an expedited appeal from the Court of Chancery's imposition of an unusual preliminary injunction. City of Miami General Employees' and Sanitation Employees' Retirement Trust (the "plaintiffs") brought a class action on behalf of itself and other stockholders in C&J Energy Services, Inc. ("C&J") to enjoin a merger between C&J and a division of its competitor, Nabors Industries Ltd. ("Nabors"). The proposed transaction is itself unusual in that C&J, a U.S. corporation, will acquire a subsidiary of Nabors, which is domiciled in Bermuda, but Nabors will retain a majority of the equity in the surviving company. To obtain more favorable tax rates, the surviving entity, C&J Energy Services, Ltd. ("New C&J"), will be based in Bermuda, and thus subject to lower corporate tax rates than C&J currently pays.

To temper Nabors' majority voting control of the surviving company, C&J negotiated for certain protections, including a by-law guaranteeing that all stockholders would share *pro rata* in any future sale of New C&J, which can only be repealed by a unanimous stockholder vote. C&J also bargained for a "fiduciary out" if a superior proposal was to emerge during a lengthy passive market check, an unusual request for the buyer in a change of control transaction. And during that market check, a potential competing bidder faced only modest deal protection barriers.

Although the Court of Chancery found that the C&J board harbored no conflict of interest and was fully informed about its own company's value, the court determined there was a "plausible" violation of the board's *Revlon* duties because the board did not affirmatively shop the company either before or after signing. On that basis, the Court of Chancery enjoined the stockholder vote for 30 days, despite finding no reason to believe that C&J stockholders—who must vote to approve the transaction—would not have a fair opportunity to evaluate the deal for themselves on its economic merits.

The Court of Chancery's order also required C&J to shop itself in violation of the merger agreement between C&J and Nabors, which prohibited C&J from soliciting other bids. . . .

We assume for the sake of analysis that *Revlon* was invoked by the pending transaction because Nabors will acquire a majority of New C&J's voting shares. But we nonetheless conclude that the Court of Chancery's injunction cannot stand. A preliminary injunction must be supported by a finding by the Court of Chancery that the plaintiffs have demonstrated a reasonable probability of success on the merits. The Court of Chancery made no such finding here, and the analysis that it conducted rested on the erroneous proposition that a company selling itself in a change of control transaction is required to shop itself to fulfill its duty to seek the highest immediate value. But *Revlon* and its progeny do not set out a specific route that a board must follow when fulfilling its fiduciary duties, and an independent board is entitled to use its business judgment to decide to enter into a strategic transaction that promises great benefit, even when it creates certain risks.[7] When a board exercises its judgment in good faith, tests the transaction through a viable passive market check, and gives its stockholders a fully informed, uncoerced opportunity to vote to accept the deal, we cannot conclude that the board likely violated its *Revlon* duties. It is too often forgotten that *Revlon*, and later cases like *QVC*,[8] primarily involved board resistance to a competing bid after the board had agreed to a change of control, which threatened to impede the emergence of another higher-priced deal. No hint of such a defensive, entrenching motive emerges from this record.

. . . .

III. ANALYSIS . . .

B. The Plaintiffs Have Not Demonstrated A Reasonable Probability Of Success On The Merits

1. The Court of Chancery's Ruling Rested on an Erroneous Understanding of What Revlon Requires of a Board of Directors

. . . *Revlon* involved a decision by a board of directors to chill the emergence of a higher offer from a bidder because the board's CEO disliked the new bidder, after the target board had agreed to sell the company for cash. . . .

Revlon does not require a board to set aside its own view of what is best for the corporation's stockholders and run an auction whenever the board approves a change of control transaction. As this Court has made clear, "there is no single blueprint that a board must follow to fulfill its duties," and a court applying *Revlon*'s enhanced scrutiny must decide "whether the directors made a *reasonable* decision, not a *perfect* decision."

---

[7]   *See, e.g., Lyondell Chemical Co. v. Ryan*, 970 A.2d 235, 243 (Del. 2009); *Paramount Communications Inc. v. QVC Network Inc.*, 637 A.2d 34, 44 (Del. 1993) ("Delaware law recognizes that there is 'no single blueprint' that directors must follow."); *In Re Fort Howard Corp. S'holders Litig.*, 1988 Del. Ch. LEXIS 110, 1988 WL 83147 (Del. Ch. Aug. 8, 1988) (a pre-signing auction is not required where directors allowed for an effective post-signing market check).

[8]   *QVC*, 637 A.2d at 39.

In a series of decisions in the wake of *Revlon*, Chancellor Allen correctly read its holding as permitting a board to pursue the transaction it reasonably views as most valuable to stockholders, so long as the transaction is subject to an effective market check under circumstances in which any bidder interested in paying more has a reasonable opportunity to do so. Such a market check does not have to involve an active solicitation, so long as interested bidders have a fair opportunity to present a higher-value alternative, and the board has the flexibility to eschew the original transaction and accept the higher-value deal. The ability of the stockholders themselves to freely accept or reject the board's preferred course of action is also of great importance in this context.

Here, the Court of Chancery seems to have believed that *Revlon* required C&J's board to conduct a pre-signing active solicitation process in order to satisfy its contextual fiduciary duties. . . .

The Court of Chancery imposed a pre-signing solicitation requirement because of its perception that C&J's board did not have "an impeccable knowledge of the value of the company that it is selling." In so ruling, the Court of Chancery seemed to imply that *Revlon* required "impeccable knowledge," and that there was only one reasonable way to comply, *i.e.*, requiring a company to actively shop itself, which ignores the Court of Chancery's own well-reasoned precedent and that of this Court, including our recent decision in *Lyondell*. And the court's perception that the board was not adequately informed was in tension with its other findings, grounded in the record, that C&J's directors were well-informed as to Nabors CPS' value.

Nor does the record indicate that C&J's board was unaware of the implications of structuring the deal so that Nabors would have majority voting control over the surviving entity.[97] As the undisputed facts demonstrate, the C&J board was aware that Nabors would own a majority of the voting stock of New C&J, and indeed that such a shift in control was required to effect the tax-motivated re-domiciling that the board believed would be beneficial to C&J's stockholders. The board took steps to mitigate the effects of that change in control, including by providing that a two-thirds vote will be required to amend the corporate bye-laws, sell the company, or issue stock for a period of five years; and preventing Nabors from acquiring additional shares or selling its shares for the five year standstill period. Most important, the board negotiated for a by-law providing that all stockholders will receive *pro rata* consideration in any sale of the company or its assets, a by-law that cannot be repealed without unanimous stockholder approval.

Although we are reluctant in the context of this expedited appeal to conclude that these provisions were, in themselves, sufficient to take the transaction out of the reach of *Revlon*, they do constitute important

---

[97] *See, e.g.*, App. to Opening Br. at 1750, 2377, 2383, 2539.

efforts by the C&J directors to protect their stockholders and to ensure that the transaction was favorable to them.

It is also important to note that there were no material barriers that would have prevented a rival bidder from making a superior offer. As discussed, the C&J board negotiated for a broad "fiduciary out" that enabled the board to terminate the transaction with Nabors if a more favorable deal emerged. . . . Therefore, if a competing bidder emerged, it faced only the barrier of a $65 million termination fee.[100] Further, the transaction was announced on July 25, and was not expected to be consummated until near the end of 2014, a period of time more than sufficient for a serious bidder to express interest and to formulate a binding offer for the C&J board to accept. . . .

It is also contextually relevant that C&J's stockholders will have the chance to vote on whether to accept the benefits and risks that come with the transaction, or to reject the deal and have C&J continue to be run on a stand-alone basis.[104] Although the C&J board had to satisfy itself that the transaction was the best course of action for stockholders, the board could also take into account that its stockholders would have a fair chance to evaluate the board's decision for themselves. . . .

For these reasons, the Court of Chancery should not have issued any injunction at all.

———

Corwin v. KKR Fin. Holdings LLC

Delaware Supreme Court, 2015.
125 A.3d 304.

■ STRINE, CHIEF JUSTICE:

[The Delaware Supreme Court addressed the effect of shareholder approval on a claim that Financial Holdings' board breached its duty under *Revlon* in connection with KKR's acquisition of Financial Holdings. The acquisition was approved by both the independent directors of Financial Holding and the company's stockholders. Even though there were various contractual relations between KKR and Financial Holdings that limited Financial Holdings' discretion in some areas, the Chancellor concluded there was no evidence on which to conclude that KKR possessed power that would prevent Financial Holdings' board from exercising an independent judgment on the desirability of the merger or its terms. Hence both the Chancery Court and the Supreme Court concluded KKR was *not* a controlling stockholder so that the acquisition was not subject to review pursuant to the entire fairness standard. The

---

[100] In the event that C&J stockholders reject the merger, C&J is required to pay Nabors $17 million in "fees and expenses," regardless of whether C&J engages in another transaction thereafter. . . .

[104] *See* note 88 *supra.*

court therefore moved to consider whether *Revlon* provided relief to the plaintiffs.]

On appeal, the plaintiffs further contend that, even if the Chancellor was correct in determining that KKR was not a controlling stockholder, he was wrong to dismiss the complaint because they contend that if the entire fairness standard did not apply, *Revlon* did . . . .

The Chancellor agreed with that argument below, and adhered to precedent supporting the proposition that when a transaction not subject to the entire fairness standard is approved by a fully informed, uncoerced vote of the disinterested stockholders, the business judgment rule applies. Although the Chancellor took note of the possible conflict between his ruling and this Court's decision in *Gantler v. Stephens*, he reached the conclusion that *Gantler* did not alter the effect of legally required stockholder votes on the appropriate standard of review. Instead, the Chancellor read *Gantler* as a decision solely intended to clarify the meaning of the precise term "ratification." He had two primary reasons for so finding. First, he noted that any statement about the effect a statutorily required vote had on the appropriate standard of review would have been dictum because in *Gantler* the Court held that the disclosures regarding the vote in question—a vote on an amendment to the company's charter—were materially misleading.[18] Second, the Chancellor doubted that the Supreme Court would have "overrule[d] extensive Delaware precedent, including Justice Jacobs's own earlier decision in *Wheelabrator*, which involved a statutorily required stockholder vote to consummate a merger" without "expressly stat[ing] such an intention."

On appeal, the plaintiffs . . . argue that *Gantler* bound the Court of Chancery to give the informed stockholder vote no effect in determining the standard of review. They contend that the Chancellor's reading of *Gantler* as a decision focused on the precise term "ratification" and not a decision intended to overturn a deep strain of precedent it never bothered to cite, was incorrect. . . .

. . . No doubt *Gantler* can be read in more than one way, but we agree with the Chancellor's interpretation of that decision and do not accept the plaintiffs' contrary one. Had *Gantler* been intended to unsettle a long-standing body of case law, the decision would likely have said so. Moreover, as the Chancellor noted, the issue presented in this case was not even squarely before the Court in *Gantler* because it found the relevant proxy statement to be materially misleading. To erase any doubt on the part of practitioners, we embrace the Chancellor's well-reasoned decision and the precedent it cites to support an interpretation of *Gantler* as a narrow decision focused on defining a specific legal term,

---

[18]   *Id.* ("The Supreme Court in *Gantler* did not expressly address the legal effect of a fully informed stockholder vote when the vote is statutorily required. Having determined that the proxy disclosures were materially misleading, the Supreme Court did not need [**12] to reach that question."); *Gantler*, 965 A.2d at 710.

"ratification," and not on the question of what standard of review applies if a transaction not subject to the entire fairness standard is approved by an informed, voluntary vote of disinterested stockholders. This view is consistent with well-reasoned Delaware precedent.

Furthermore, although the plaintiffs argue that adhering to the proposition that a fully informed, uncoerced stockholder vote invokes the business judgment rule would impair the operation of *Unocal* and *Revlon*, or expose stockholders to unfair action by directors without protection, the plaintiffs ignore several factors. First, *Unocal* and *Revlon* are primarily designed to give stockholders and the Court of Chancery the tool of injunctive relief to address important M & A decisions in real time, before closing. They were not tools designed with post-closing money damages claims in mind, the standards they articulate do not match the gross negligence standard for director due care liability under *Van Gorkom*, and with the prevalence of exculpatory charter provisions, due care liability is rarely even available.

Second and most important, the doctrine applies only to fully informed, uncoerced stockholder votes, and if troubling facts regarding director behavior were not disclosed that would have been material to a voting stockholder, then the business judgment rule is not invoked. Here, however, all of the objective facts regarding the board's interests, KKR's interests, and the negotiation process, were fully disclosed.

Finally, when a transaction is not subject to the entire fairness standard, the long-standing policy of our law has been to avoid the uncertainties and costs of judicial second-guessing when the disinterested stockholders have had the free and informed chance to decide on the economic merits of a transaction for themselves. There are sound reasons for this policy. When the real parties in interest—the disinterested equity owners—can easily protect themselves at the ballot box by simply voting no, the utility of a litigation-intrusive standard of review promises more costs to stockholders in the form of litigation rents and inhibitions on risk-taking than it promises in terms of benefits to them. The reason for that is tied to the core rationale of the business judgment rule, which is that judges are poorly positioned to evaluate the wisdom of business decisions and there is little utility to having them second-guess the determination of impartial decision-makers with more information (in the case of directors) or an actual economic stake in the outcome (in the case of informed, disinterested stockholders). In circumstances, therefore, where the stockholders have had the voluntary choice to accept or reject a transaction, the business judgment rule standard of review is the presumptively correct one and best facilitates wealth creation through the corporate form.

For these reasons, therefore, we affirm the Court of Chancery's judgment on the basis of its well-reasoned decision.

———

Sciabacucchi v. Liberty Broadband Corp.[1]
Court of Chancery of Delaware, 2017.
2017 WL 2352152.

[As a step in acquiring Time Warner Cable and Bright House Networks, Charter Communications entered into two contracts—one involving the issuance of shares and another granting a proxy—to its largest stockholder, Liberty Broadband. Charter conditioned the two lucrative acquisitions on the disinterested shareholders approving the share issuance and proxy transactions. Following shareholder approval, Sciabacucchi initiated a shareholders' suit challenging the share issuance and proxy alleging they were unfair to Charter and the product of a breach of fiduciary duty by its director and largest stockholder. Charter moved to dismiss the complaint, arguing that because the share issuance and proxy transactions had been approved by a majority of the disinterested Charter stockholders they were presumptively valid. The court rejected the argument, stating that "ratification will not cleanse a transaction where the vote is *structurally* coercive." It defined this as occurring when "the directors have created a situation where a vote may be said to be in avoidance of a detriment created by the structure of the transaction the fiduciaries have created, rather than a free choice to accept or reject the proposition voted on."]

"Coercion" is a loaded term, but a vote so structured by the Defendants, to accept one (allegedly self-interested) transaction so as not to lose the benefit of another independent transaction, cannot to my mind be considered uncoerced. . . . The stockholders did not decide, necessarily, that the Liberty Share Issuances and the Voting Proxy Agreement were "in their best interests," they only decided that the Acquisitions *and* the Issuances and Voting Proxy Agreement were, on net beneficial. The facts are sufficient to an inference that the Liberty Share Issuances (and the Voting Proxy Agreement) were unnecessary to the Acquisitions. If so, and if such a vote were cleansing, then fiduciaries could attach self-dealing riders to any transaction under consideration, and avoid being held to account by a favorable stockholder vote. That is not equity; it would represent, not a cleanse, but a white-wash.

––––––––

NOTE ON DEFENSIVE MANEUVERS OUTSIDE OF DELAWARE

States are evenly divided whether they apply heightened *Unocal/Revlon* scrutiny to defensive maneuvers or instead examine defensive maneuvers through the lens of the business judgment rule so that plaintiff has the burden on issues of care and loyalty. State anti-takeover statutes, discussed later, play a very significant role in determining which of these two approaches is followed. *See* Michal Barzuza, The State Of State Antitakeover Law, 95 Va. L. Rev. 1973 (2009) (courts in states with relatively strong

––––––––

[1]   (Del. Ch. May 31, 2017).

antitakeover statutes generally invoke the protective statutes to support their holding that that directors are not under enhanced duties when defending control). Thus, a majority of the non-Delaware decisions address defensive maneuvers by according the directors' actions the presumptions of the business judgment rule. For example, in upholding the directors' issuance of a poison pill to all shareholders except the hostile bidder, the federal district court applying New York law concluded that under New York law "a board's decision . . . made on the basis of reasoned judgment and in the absence of self-dealing, conflict of interest, or bad faith" would be valid in the absence of a prima facie showing to the contrary. Dynamics Corp. v. WHX Corp., 967 F. Supp. 59, 64 (D. Conn. 1997) (further emphasizing that the New York poison pill validation statute expressly authorizes boards of directors to impose such conditions and limitations as the board believes in the corporation's and its shareholders' interests). Similarly, Seidman v. Central Bancorp, Inc., 16 Mass. L. Rptr. 383, 2003 WL 21528509 (Mass. Super. 2003), rejected engrafting Delaware's heightened review standards onto the Massachusetts' other-constituency statute that provided, in part:

> In determining what . . . [the director] reasonably believes to be in the best interests of the corporation, a director may consider the interests of the corporation's employees, suppliers, creditors and customers, the economy of the state, region and nation, community and societal considerations, and long-term and short-term interests of the corporation and its stockholders, including the possibility that these interests may be best served by the continued independence of the corporation.

The court noted the legislative history of the provision reflected the desire "to give protection to Massachusetts' corporations from abusive takeovers which challenge the long-term growth of the Commonwealth's economy, the creation of new jobs and the long-term interests of shareholders." 2003 WL 21528509 at 8.

> In responding to the arguments . . . that this Court should either import the proportionality doctrine in *Unocal* . . . or aspects of the Massachusetts common law relating to fiduciary duties of directors, as a gloss on the protective reach . . . [of the other constituency provision], the Court is reminded of Justice Cardozo's eloquent comments on the role of the judge, particularly at the trial level:
>
>> The judge, even when he is free, is still not wholly free. He is not to innovate at pleasure. He is not a knight-errant, roaming at will in pursuit of his own ideal of beauty or of goodness. He is to draw inspiration from consecrated principles. He is not to yield to spasmodic sentiment, to vague and unregulated benevolence. He is to exercise discretion informed by tradition, methodized by analogy, disciplined by system, and subordinated to "the primordial necessity of order in the social life." Cardozo, Nature of Judicial Process, 141 (1921)).

2003 WL 21528509 at 9–10 The Massachusetts and New York decisions are consistent with the approach embraced by the American Law Institute:

§ 602   Action of Directors That Has the Foreseeable Effect of Blocking Unsolicited Tender Offers

(a)   The board of directors may take an action that has the foreseeable effect of blocking an unsolicited tender offer . . . , if the action is a reasonable response to the offer.

(b)   In considering whether its action is a reasonable response to the offer:

(1)   The board may take into account all factors relevant to the best interests of the corporation and shareholders . . .

(2)   The board may, in addition to the analysis under § 6.02(b)(1), have regard for interests or groups (other than shareholders) with respect to which the corporation has a legitimate concern if to do so would not significantly disfavor the long-term interests of shareholders.

(c)   A person who challenges an action of the board on the ground that it fails to satisfy the standards of Subsection (a) has the burden of proof that the board's action is an unreasonable response to the offer. . . .

Comment:

a.   . . . Section 6.02 reflects the view that judicial review of directors' blocking actions against unsolicited tender offers should not be based on an analysis of the directors' motives. Such a review cannot effectively distinguish between cases in which directors favored themselves and cases in which directors properly looked to the interests of the shareholders. Equally important, a motivational standard of review gives no guidance to directors—particularly disinterested directors—as to what constitutes appropriate behavior. Accordingly, § 6.02 directs judicial inquiry initially to the question whether action taken by the directors has the foreseeable effect of blocking a tender offer, and thereby precluding holders of voting equity securities from having the opportunity to accept the tender offer. If the directors' action does have that effect, then the court must further inquire whether the directors' action was a reasonable response to the offer

There has been modest success in striking down anti-takeover measures even when the burden of proof is not placed on the directors to justify their defensive maneuvers or to prove they have acted as auctioneers. *See* First Union Corp. v. SunTrust Banks, Inc., 2001 WL 1885686 (N.C. Super. 2001) (rejecting *Unocal* and *Revlon* but nonetheless holding invalid a non-termination provision that was part of a bundle of deal protection items because its operation could coerce shareholders to support acquisition supported by the board of directors). Query, in assessing defensive maneuvers is the allocation of the burden of proof as significant as the substantive standard, such as proportionality, coercion and the reasonableness of the directors' behavior?

———

3. PROTECTING THE DEAL

Omnicare, Inc. v. NCS Healthcare, Inc.

Supreme Court of Delaware, 2003.
818 A.2d 914.

■ HOLLAND, JUSTICE, for the majority: . . .

NCS Healthcare, Inc. ("NCS"), a Delaware corporation, was the object of competing acquisition bids, one by Genesis Health Ventures, Inc. ("Genesis"), a Pennsylvania Corporation, and the other by Omnicare, Inc. ("Omnicare"), a Delaware corporation. . . .

NCS, is a Delaware corporation headquartered in Beachwood, Ohio. NCS is a leading independent provider of pharmacy services to long-term care institutions . . . . NCS common stock consists of Class A shares and Class B shares. The Class B shares are entitled to ten votes per share and the Class A shares are entitled to one vote per share. The shares are virtually identical in every other respect.

The defendant Jon H. Outcalt is Chairman of the NCS board of directors. Outcalt owns 202,063 shares of NCS Class A common stock and 3,476,086 shares of Class B common stock. The defendant Kevin B. Shaw is President, CEO and a director of NCS. At the time the merger agreement at issue in this dispute was executed with Genesis, Shaw owned 28,905 shares of NCS Class A common stock and 1,141,134 shares of Class B common stock. [In combination, Outcalt and Shaw hold a majority of the voting power.]

The NCS board has two other members, defendants Boake A. Sells and Richard L. Osborne. . . . The defendant Genesis is a Pennsylvania corporation with its principal place of business in Kennett Square, Pennsylvania. It is a leading provider of healthcare and support services to the elderly. . . .

The plaintiffs . . . represent a class consisting of all holders of Class A common stock. As of July 28, 2002, NCS had 18,461,599 Class A shares and 5,255,210 Class B shares outstanding.

Omnicare is a Delaware corporation with its principal place of business in Covington, Kentucky. Omnicare is in the institutional pharmacy business. . . .

FACTUAL BACKGROUND . . .

NCS Seeks Restructuring Alternatives

Beginning in late 1999, . . . [NCS began to experience operating and financial difficulties, causing its share price to tumble. The stock traded in a range of $0.09–$0.50 per share. It had also defaulted on $350 million in debt.]

NCS Financial Improvement

. . . In March 2002, NCS decided to form an independent committee of board members who were neither NCS employees nor major NCS stockholders (the "Independent Committee") [to consider transactions that would provide some value for NCS's stockholders]. The NCS board thought this was necessary because, due to NCS's precarious financial condition, it felt that fiduciary duties were owed to the enterprise as a whole rather than solely to NCS stockholders.

Sells and Osborne were selected as the members of the committee, and given authority to consider and negotiate possible transactions for NCS. The entire four member NCS board, however, retained authority to approve any transaction. The Independent Committee retained the same legal and financial counsel as the NCS board.

The Independent Committee met for the first time on May 14, 2002. At that meeting Pollack suggested that NCS seek a "stalking-horse merger partner" to obtain the highest possible value in any transaction. The Independent Committee agreed with the suggestion.

Genesis Initial Proposal

. . . [On June 26, Genesis's representatives, as a condition of further discussions regarding its acquisition of NCS, demanded that NCS enter into an "exclusivity agreement" with Genesis. As a prelude to considering whether to approve such an agreement, the Independent Committee received a summary of the terms Genesis proposed for the acquisition. NCS executed the exclusivity agreement on July 3rd.]

Omnicare Proposes Negotiations . . .

On the afternoon of July 26, 2002, Omnicare faxed to NCS a letter outlining a proposed acquisition. . . . Omnicare's proposal, however, was expressly conditioned on negotiating a merger agreement, obtaining certain third party consents, and completing its due diligence. . . .

Late in the afternoon of July 26, 2002, NCS representatives received voicemail messages from Omnicare asking to discuss the letter. The exclusivity agreement prevented NCS from returning those calls. In relevant part, that agreement precluded NCS from "engag[ing] or particpat[ing] in any discussions or negotiations with respect to a Competing Transaction or a proposal for one." The July 26 letter from Omnicare met the definition of a "Competing Transaction."

. . . Nevertheless, the Independent Committee [decided] to use Omnicare's letter to negotiate for improved terms with Genesis.

Genesis Merger Agreement and Voting Agreements

Genesis responded to the NCS request to improve its offer as a result of the Omnicare fax the next day. On July 27, Genesis proposed substantially improved terms. . . . In return for [its] concessions, Genesis stipulated that the transaction had to be approved by midnight the next day, July 28, or else Genesis would terminate discussions and withdraw its offer. . . .

. . . [The NCS board met on July 28.] After receiving similar reports and advice from its legal and financial advisors, the board concluded that "balancing the potential loss of the Genesis deal against the uncertainty of Omnicare's letter, results in the conclusion that the only reasonable alternative for the Board of Directors is to approve the Genesis transaction." The board first voted to authorize the voting agreements [described below] with Outcalt and Shaw, for purposes of Section 203 of the Delaware General Corporation Law ("DGCL"). The board was advised by its legal counsel that "under the terms of the merger agreement and because NCS shareholders representing in excess of 50% of the outstanding voting power would be required by Genesis to enter into stockholder voting agreements contemporaneously with the signing of the merger agreement, and would agree to vote their shares in favor of the merger agreement, shareholder approval of the merger would be assured even if the NCS Board were to withdraw or change its recommendation. *These facts would prevent NCS from engaging in any alternative or superior transaction in the future.*" (emphasis added).

After listening to a summary of the merger terms, the board then resolved that the merger agreement and the transactions contemplated thereby were advisable and fair and in the best interests of all the NCS stakeholders. The NCS board further resolved to recommend the transactions to the stockholders for their approval and adoption. A definitive merger agreement between NCS and Genesis and the stockholder voting agreements were executed later that day. . . .

NCS/Genesis Merger Agreement

Among other things, the NCS/Genesis merger agreement provided the following:

- NCS stockholders would receive 1 share of Genesis common stock in exchange for every 10 shares of NCS common stock held;

- NCS stockholders could exercise appraisal rights under 8 Del.C. § 262;

- NCS would redeem NCS's Notes in accordance with their terms;

- NCS would submit the merger agreement to NCS stockholders regardless of whether the NCS board continued to recommend the merger;

- NCS would not enter into discussions with third parties concerning an alternative acquisition of NCS, or provide non-public information to such parties, unless (1) the third party provided an unsolicited, bona fide written proposal documenting the terms of the acquisition; (2) the NCS board believed in good faith that the proposal was or was likely to result in an acquisition on terms superior to those contemplated by the NCS/Genesis merger agreement; and (3) before providing non-public information to that third party, the third party would execute a confidentiality agreement at least as restrictive as the one in place between NCS and Genesis; and

• If the merger agreement were to be terminated, under certain circumstances NCS would be required to pay Genesis a $6 million termination fee and/or Genesis's documented expenses, up to $5 million.

[The merger agreement did not include a fiduciary out. A fiduciary out clause is a provision in a merger agreement that provides that *another* provision (or covenant) in the agreement, which restricts in a certain way the discretion of the board of the corporation that is to be acquired, does not apply if the restriction would result in a breach of the board's fiduciary duties to the corporation and its shareholders. Among the kinds of provisions to which a fiduciary out may apply are no-talk clauses, which prohibit the Board from discussing a merger of the Corporation into a third party, and provisions, like the one in *Omnicare*, that require the Board to submit the merger to the shareholders for their approval.]

Voting Agreements

[Contemporaneously with, and as required by, the merger agreement,] Outcalt and Shaw, in their capacity as NCS stockholders, entered into voting agreements with Genesis. NCS was also required to be a party to the voting agreements by Genesis. Those agreements provided, among other things, that:

• Outcalt and Shaw were acting in their capacity as NCS stockholders in executing the agreements, not in their capacity as NCS directors or officers;

• Neither Outcalt nor Shaw would transfer their shares prior to the stockholder vote on the merger agreement;

• Outcalt and Shaw agreed to vote all of their shares in favor of the merger agreement; and

• Outcalt and Shaw granted to Genesis an irrevocable proxy to vote their shares in favor of the merger agreement.

• The voting agreement was specifically enforceable by Genesis.

The merger agreement further provided that if either Outcalt or Shaw breached the terms of the voting agreements, Genesis would be entitled to terminate the merger agreement and potentially receive a $6 million termination fee from NCS. Such a breach was impossible since Section 6 provided that the voting agreements were specifically enforceable by Genesis.

Omnicare's Superior Proposal . . .

On October 6, 2002, Omnicare irrevocably committed itself to a transaction with NCS. Pursuant to the terms of its proposal, Omnicare agreed to acquire all the outstanding NCS Class A and Class B shares [through a tender offer] at a price of $3.50 per share in cash. [The Omnicare bid offered the NCS stockholders cash equal to more than twice the then-current market value of the shares to be received in the Genesis merger. The transaction offered by Omnicare also treated NCS's other stakeholders on equal terms with the Genesis agreement.]

The merger agreement between Genesis and NCS contained a provision authorized by Section 251(c) of Delaware's corporation law.* It required that the Genesis agreement be placed before the corporation's stockholders for a vote, even if the NCS board of directors no longer recommended it. At the insistence of Genesis, the NCS board also agreed to omit any effective fiduciary clause from the merger agreement. In connection with the Genesis merger agreement, two stockholders of NCS, who held a majority of the voting power, agreed unconditionally to vote all of their shares in favor of the Genesis merger. Thus, the combined terms of the voting agreements and merger agreement guaranteed, ab initio, that the transaction proposed by Genesis would obtain NCS stockholder's approval. As a result of this irrevocable offer, on October 21, 2002, the NCS board withdrew its recommendation that the stockholders vote in favor of the NCS/Genesis merger agreement. NCS's financial advisor withdrew its fairness opinion of the NCS/Genesis merger agreement as well. . . .

LEGAL ANALYSIS . . .

Deal Protection Devices Require Enhanced Scrutiny

The dispositive issues in this appeal involve the defensive devices that protected the Genesis merger agreement. The Delaware corporation statute provides that the board's management decision to enter into and recommend a merger transaction can become final only when ownership action is taken by a vote of the stockholders. Thus, the Delaware corporation law expressly provides for a balance of power between boards and stockholders which makes merger transactions a shared enterprise and ownership decision. Consequently, a board of directors' decision to adopt defensive devices to protect a merger agreement may implicate the stockholders' right to effectively vote contrary to the initial recommendation of the board in favor of the transaction. . . .

There are inherent conflicts between a board's interest in protecting a merger transaction it has approved, the stockholders' statutory right to make the final decision to either approve or not approve a merger, and the board's continuing responsibility to effectively exercise its fiduciary

---

* [(Ed. note) DGCL § 251(c) then provided that the merger agreement can include a provision that the agreement for merger will be submitted to the stockholders even if the board of directors no longer recommend it.]

duties at all times after the merger agreement is executed. These competing considerations require a threshold determination that board-approved defensive devices protecting a merger transaction are within the limitations of its statutory authority and consistent with the directors' fiduciary duties. Accordingly, in *Paramount v. Time*, we held that the business judgment rule applied to the Time board's original decision to merge with Warner. We further held, however, that defensive devices adopted by the board to protect the original merger transaction must withstand enhanced judicial scrutiny under the *Unocal* standard of review, even when that merger transaction does not result in a change of control.

Enhanced Scrutiny Generally . . .

A board's decision to protect its decision to enter a merger agreement with defensive devices against uninvited competing transactions that may emerge is analogous to a board's decision to protect against dangers to corporate policy and effectiveness when it adopts defensive measures in a hostile takeover contest. . . .

Since *Unocal*, "this Court has consistently recognized that defensive measures which are either preclusive or coercive are included within the common law definition of draconian." . . .

Therefore, in applying enhanced judicial scrutiny to defensive devices designed to protect a merger agreement, a court must first determine that those measures are not preclusive or coercive *before* its focus shifts to the "range of reasonableness" in making a proportionality determination. . . .

Deal Protection Devices

Defensive devices, as that term is used in this opinion, is a synonym for what are frequently referred to as "deal protection devices." Both terms are used interchangeably to describe any measure or combination of measures that are intended to protect the consummation of a merger transaction. Defensive devices can be economic, structural, or both.

Deal protection devices need not all be in the merger agreement itself. In this case, for example, the Section 251(c) provision in the merger agreement was combined with the separate voting agreements to provide a structural defense for the Genesis merger agreement against any subsequent superior transaction. Genesis made the NCS board's defense of its transaction absolute by insisting on the omission of any effective fiduciary out clause in the NCS merger agreement. . . .

In this case, the stockholder voting agreements were inextricably intertwined with the defensive aspects of the Genesis merger agreement. In fact, the voting agreements with Shaw and Outcalt were the linchpin of Genesis' proposed tripartite defense. Therefore, Genesis made the execution of those voting agreements a non-negotiable condition precedent to its execution of the merger agreement. . . .

With the assurance that Outcalt and Shaw would irrevocably agree to exercise their majority voting power in favor of its transaction, Genesis insisted that the merger agreement reflect the other two aspects of its concerted defense, i.e., the inclusion of a Section 251(c) provision and the omission of any effective fiduciary out clause. Those dual aspects of the merger agreement would not have provided Genesis with a complete defense in the absence of the voting agreements with Shaw and Outcalt.

These Deal Protection Devices Unenforceable

In this case, the Court of Chancery correctly held that the NCS directors' decision to adopt defensive devices to completely "lock up" the Genesis merger mandated "special scrutiny" under the two-part test set forth in *Unocal.* . . .

Pursuant to the judicial scrutiny required under *Unocal*'s two-stage analysis, the NCS directors must first demonstrate "that they had reasonable grounds for believing that a danger to corporate policy and effectiveness existed. . . . " To satisfy that burden, the NCS directors are required to show they acted in good faith after conducting a reasonable investigation. The threat identified by the NCS board was the possibility of losing the Genesis offer and being left with no comparable alternative transaction.

The second stage of the *Unocal* test requires the NCS directors to demonstrate that their defensive response was "reasonable in relation to the threat posed." This inquiry involves a two-step analysis. The NCS directors must first establish that the merger deal protection devices adopted in response to the threat were not "coercive" or "preclusive," and then demonstrate that their response was within a "range of reasonable responses" to the threat perceived. In *Unitrin*, we stated:

- A response is "coercive" if it is aimed at forcing upon stockholders a management-sponsored alternative to a hostile offer.

- A response is "preclusive" if it deprives stockholders of the right to receive all tender offers or precludes a bidder from seeking control by fundamentally restricting proxy contests or otherwise.

This aspect of the *Unocal* standard provides for a disjunctive analysis. If defensive measures are either preclusive or coercive they are draconian and impermissible. In this case, the deal protection devices of the NCS board were both preclusive and coercive.

This Court enunciated the standard for determining stockholder coercion in the case of *Williams v. Geier*. A stockholder vote may be nullified by wrongful coercion "where the board or some other party takes actions which have the effect of causing the stockholders to vote in favor of the proposed transaction for some reason other than the merits of that transaction." . . .

[A]ny stockholder vote [in this case] would have been robbed of its effectiveness by the impermissible coercion that predetermined the outcome of the merger without regard to the merits of the Genesis transaction at the time the vote was scheduled to be taken. Deal protection devices that result in such coercion cannot withstand *Unocal*'s enhanced judicial scrutiny standard of review because they are not within the range of reasonableness.

Although the minority stockholders were not forced to vote for the Genesis merger, they were required to accept it because it was a fait accompli. The record reflects that the defensive devices employed by the NCS board are preclusive and coercive in the sense that they accomplished a fait accompli. In this case, despite the fact that the NCS board has withdrawn its recommendation for the Genesis transaction and recommended its rejection by the stockholders, the deal protection devices approved by the NCS board operated in concert to have a preclusive and coercive effect. Those tripartite defensive measures—the Section 251(c) provision, the voting agreements, and the absence of an effective fiduciary out clause—made it "mathematically impossible" and "realistically unattainable" for the Omnicare transaction or any other proposal to succeed, no matter how superior the proposal.

The deal protection devices adopted by the NCS board were designed to coerce the consummation of the Genesis merger and preclude the consideration of any superior transaction. The NCS directors' defensive devices are not within a reasonable range of responses to the perceived threat of losing the Genesis offer because they are preclusive and coercive. Accordingly, we hold that those deal protection devices are unenforceable.

Effective Fiduciary Out Required

The defensive measures that protected the merger transaction are unenforceable not only because they are preclusive and coercive but, alternatively, they are unenforceable because they are invalid as they operate in this case. . . .

Under the circumstances presented in this case, where a cohesive group of stockholders with majority voting power was irrevocably committed to the merger transaction, "[e]ffective representation of the financial interests of the minority shareholders imposed upon the [NCS board] an affirmative responsibility to protect those minority shareholders' interests." The NCS board could not abdicate its fiduciary duties to the minority by leaving it to the stockholders alone to approve or disapprove the merger agreement because two stockholders had already combined to establish a majority of the voting power that made the outcome of the stockholder vote a foregone conclusion. . . .

The directors of a Delaware corporation have a continuing obligation to discharge their fiduciary responsibilities, as future circumstances develop, after a merger agreement is announced. Genesis anticipated the likelihood of a superior offer after its merger agreement was announced and demanded defensive measures from the NCS board that completely protected its transaction.[117] Instead of agreeing to the absolute defense of the Genesis merger from a superior offer, however, the NCS board was required to negotiate a fiduciary out clause to protect the NCS stockholders if the Genesis transaction became an inferior offer. By acceding to Genesis' ultimatum for complete protection in futuro, the NCS board disabled itself from exercising its own fiduciary obligations at a time when the board's own judgment is most important, i.e. receipt of a subsequent superior offer.

Any board has authority to give the proponent of a recommended merger agreement reasonable structural and economic defenses, incentives, and fair compensation if the transaction is not completed. To the extent that defensive measures are economic and reasonable, they may become an increased cost to the proponent of any subsequent transaction. Just as defensive measures cannot be draconian, however, they cannot limit or circumscribe the directors' fiduciary duties. Notwithstanding the corporation's insolvent condition, the NCS board had no authority to execute a merger agreement that subsequently prevented it from effectively discharging its ongoing fiduciary responsibilities.

The stockholders of a Delaware corporation are entitled to rely upon the board to discharge its fiduciary duties at all times. The fiduciary duties of a director are unremitting and must be effectively discharged in the specific context of the actions that are required with regard to the corporation or its stockholders as circumstances change. The stockholders with majority voting power, Shaw and Outcalt, had an absolute right to sell or exchange their shares with a third party at any price. This right was not only known to the other directors of NCS, it became an integral part of the Genesis agreement. In its answering brief, Genesis candidly states that its offer "came with a condition—Genesis would not be a stalking horse and would not agree to a transaction to which NCS's controlling shareholders were not committed."

The NCS board was required to contract for an effective fiduciary out clause to exercise its continuing fiduciary responsibilities to the minority stockholders.[121] . . .

In the context of this preclusive and coercive lock up case, the protection of Genesis' contractual expectations must yield to the supervening responsibility of the directors to discharge their fiduciary

---

[117] The marked improvements in NCS's financial situation during the negotiations with Genesis strongly suggests that the NCS board should have been alert to the prospect of competing offers or, as eventually occurred, a bidding contest.

[121] See *Paramount Communications Inc. v. QVC Network Inc.*, 637 A.2d at 42–43. Merger agreements involve an ownership decision and, therefore, cannot become final without stockholder approval. Other contracts do not require a fiduciary out clause because they involve business judgments that are within the exclusive province of the board of directors' power to manage the affairs of the corporation. See *Grimes v. Donald*, 673 A.2d 1207, 1214–15 (Del.1996).

duties on a continuing basis. The merger agreement and voting agreements, as they were combined to operate in concert in this case, are inconsistent with the NCS directors' fiduciary duties. To that extent, we hold that they are invalid and unenforceable. . . .

■ VEASEY, CHIEF JUSTICE, with whom STEELE, JUSTICE, joins dissenting. . . .

Going into negotiations with Genesis, the NCS directors knew that, up until that time, NCS had found only one potential bidder, Omnicare. Omnicare had refused to buy NCS except at a fire sale price through an asset sale in bankruptcy. Omnicare's best proposal at that stage would not have paid off all creditors and would have provided nothing for stockholders. The Noteholders, represented by the Ad Hoc Committee, were willing to oblige Omnicare and force NCS into bankruptcy if Omnicare would pay in full the NCS debt. Through the NCS board's efforts, Genesis expressed interest that became increasingly attractive. Negotiations with Genesis led to an offer paying creditors off and conferring on NCS stockholders $24 million—an amount infinitely superior to the prior Omnicare proposals.

But there was, understandably, a sine qua non. In exchange for offering the NCS stockholders a return on their equity and creditor payment, Genesis demanded certainty that the merger would close. If the NCS board would not have acceded to the Section 251(c) provision, if Outcalt and Shaw had not agreed to the voting agreements and if NCS had insisted on a fiduciary out, there would have been no Genesis deal! Thus, the only value-enhancing transaction available would have disappeared. NCS knew that Omnicare had spoiled a Genesis acquisition in the past, and it is not disputed by the Majority that the NCS directors made a reasoned decision to accept as real the Genesis threat to walk away.

When Omnicare submitted its conditional eleventh-hour bid, the NCS board had to weigh the economic terms of the proposal against the uncertainty of completing a deal with Omnicare. Importantly, because Omnicare's bid was conditioned on its satisfactorily completing its due diligence review of NCS, the NCS board saw this as a crippling condition, as did the Ad Hoc Committee. As a matter of business judgment, the risk of negotiating with Omnicare and losing Genesis at that point outweighed the possible benefits. The lock-up was indisputably a sine qua non to any deal with Genesis.

A lock-up permits a target board and a bidder to "exchange certainties." Certainty itself has value. The acquirer may pay a higher price for the target if the acquirer is assured consummation of the transaction. The target company also benefits from the certainty of completing a transaction with a bidder because losing an acquirer creates the perception that a target is damaged goods, thus reducing its value. . . .

The very measures the Majority cites as "coercive" were approved by Shaw and Outcalt through the lens of their independent assessment of the merits of the transaction. The proper inquiry in this case is whether the NCS board had taken actions that "have the effect of causing the stockholders to vote in favor of the proposed transaction for some reason other than the merits of that transaction." . . .

Outcalt and Shaw were fully informed stockholders. As the NCS controlling stockholders, they made an informed choice to commit their voting power to the merger. The minority stockholders were deemed to know that when controlling stockholders have 65% of the vote they can approve a merger without the need for the minority votes. Moreover, to the extent a minority stockholder may have felt "coerced" to vote for the merger, which was already a fait accompli, it was a meaningless coercion—or no coercion at all—because the controlling votes, those of Outcalt and Shaw, were already "cast." . . .

In applying *Unocal* scrutiny, we believe the Majority incorrectly preempted the proportionality inquiry. In our view, the proportionality inquiry must account for the reality that the contractual measures protecting this merger agreement were necessary to obtain the Genesis deal. The Majority has not demonstrated that the director action was a disproportionate response to the threat posed. Indeed, it is clear to us that the board action to negotiate the best deal reasonably available with the only viable merger partner (Genesis) who could satisfy the creditors and benefit the stockholders, was reasonable in relation to the threat, by any practical yardstick.

An Absolute Lock-up is Not a Per Se Violation of Fiduciary Duty

We respectfully disagree with the Majority's conclusion that the NCS board breached its fiduciary duties to the Class A stockholders by failing to negotiate a "fiduciary out" in the Genesis merger agreement. What is the practical import of a "fiduciary out?" . . .

In this case, Genesis made it abundantly clear early on that it was willing to negotiate a deal with NCS but only on the condition that it would not be a "stalking horse." Thus, it wanted to be certain that a third party could not use its deal with NCS as a floor against which to begin a bidding war. As a result of this negotiating position, a "fiduciary out" was not acceptable to Genesis. The Majority Opinion holds that such a negotiating position, if implemented in the agreement, is invalid per se where there is an absolute lock-up. We know of no authority in our jurisprudence supporting this new rule, and we believe it is unwise and unwarranted. . . .

Conclusion

It is regrettable that the Court is split in this important case. One hopes that the Majority rule announced here—though clearly erroneous in our view—will be interpreted narrowly and will be seen as sui generis.

By deterring bidders from engaging in negotiations like those present here and requiring that there must always be a fiduciary out, the universe of potential bidders who could reasonably be expected to benefit stockholders could shrink or disappear. Nevertheless, if the holding is confined to these unique facts, negotiators may be able to navigate around this new hazard.

Accordingly, we respectfully dissent.

[The separate dissenting opinion of Justice Steele is omitted.]

NOTE ON FORCE-THE-VOTE PROVISIONS.

Delaware and the Model Act now authorize force-the-vote provisions. *See* Del. Gen. Corp. Law. § 146 and MBCA § 8.26. The typical provision requires the target to seek the approval of the acquisition transaction and prohibits the target board approving an acquisition by a third party until the original transaction has been voted on by the target shareholders. Why would the target board agree to such a provision? Does the authorization of a force-the-vote provision excuse directors of their fiduciary obligations when they approve a force the vote provision, e.g., must the provision itself include a fiduciary out?

----

4. STATE TAKEOVER STATUTES

Most states now have statutes regulating takeover bids. These statutes tend to fall into several patterns, although they are highly variable within those patterns. This Note will canvass the major patterns, generally by discussing one statute within each pattern. However, it should be borne in mind that even statutes that fall into a given pattern often diverge in material respects. Furthermore, because the statutes are highly complex, only their main features will be discussed.

State takeover statutes have evolved over time. Conventionally, they are categorized as first-, second-, and third-generation statutes.

1. First-Generation Statutes. The *first-generation* statutes tended to impose very stringent requirements on takeover bids, including fairness reviews by state agencies. Moreover, generally speaking the application of the statutes was not limited to corporations incorporated in the relevant state. In *Edgar v. MITE Corp.*, 457 U.S. 624, 102 S.Ct. 2629, 73 L.Ed.2d 269 (1982), the Supreme Court held one such statute, the Illinois Takeover Act, unconstitutional. Six justices addressed the merits of the case. All six justices held that the Illinois Act violated the Commerce Clause in two ways. First, the Act unconstitutionally regulated commerce taking place across state lines, because the Act applied to prevent an offeror from making an offer even to non-Illinois shareholders. Second, the Act imposed an excessive burden on interstate commerce, because the Act permitted the Illinois secretary of state to block a nationwide tender offer. Three of the justices also held that the Illinois statute was unconstitutional under the Supremacy Clause on the ground that a major objective of the Williams Act was to maintain a neutral balance between management and the bidder and the Illinois Act violated this balance.

2.   *Second-Generation Statutes.* After the decision in Edgar v. MITE Corp., a number of states adopted *second-generation* takeover statutes. These statutes fall into two major patterns: control-share-acquisition statutes and fair-price statutes.

a). *Control-Share-Acquisition Statutes. Control-share-acquisition statutes* provide that if an acquiring shareholder crosses a designated threshold of stock ownership, the shareholder is prohibited from voting the acquired shares unless he obtains approval to do so by vote of a majority of the corporation's disinterested shareholders, that is, shareholders other than the acquiror and the corporation's management.

In *CTS Corp. v. Dynamics Corp. of America*, 481 U.S. 69, 107 S.Ct. 1637, 95 L.Ed.2d 67 (1987), the Supreme Court upheld the constitutionality of Indiana's control-share-acquisition statute. That statute applied whenever a person acquired shares that, but for the operation of the statute, would bring the person's voting power in the corporation to or above 20%, 33 $1/3$%, or 50% of total voting power. An acquiror that crossed one of these thresholds could not vote the acquired stock unless voting rights were approved by a majority of all disinterested shareholders voting at the next regularly scheduled meeting of the shareholders or at a specially scheduled meeting. The statute was limited to target corporations incorporated in Indiana. The Court concluded that the Indiana statute did not violate the Commerce Clause, because it did not discriminate against interstate commerce, and did not subject activities to inconsistent regulation. The statute applied only to Indiana corporations, and a state has authority to regulate domestic corporations, including the authority to define the voting rights of shareholders.

The Court also held that the Indiana statute was not preempted by the Williams Act. In this regard, the Court contrasted the Indiana statute with the Illinois statute that was found unconstitutional in *MITE*.

First, the Illinois statute provided for a twenty-day precommencement period. During this time, management could disseminate its views on the upcoming tender offer to shareholders, but bidders could not publish their offers. This conflicted with the Williams Act, because Congress had deleted precommencement-notice provisions from the Williams Act. In contrast, the Indiana statute did not give either management or the would-be acquiror an advantage in communicating with shareholders about an impending tender offer.

Second, the Illinois statute provided for a review of the fairness of tender offers by the Illinois Secretary of State. This conflicted with the Williams Act, because Congress intended shareholders to be free to make their own decisions. In contrast, the Indiana statute did not allow the state government to interpose its views of fairness between willing buyers and sellers of shares of the target company. Rather, the statute allowed shareholders to collectively evaluate the fairness of the offer.

Third, the Illinois statute set no deadline for the state-agency hearing on a tender offer, so that management could indefinitely stymie a takeover. This conflicted with the Williams Act, because Congress anticipated that bidders would be free to go forward without unreasonable delay. In contrast, the Indiana statute did not impose an indefinite delay on tender offers. Nothing in the Indiana statute prohibited an offeror from consummating an offer on the twentieth business day, the earliest day permitted under federal law, and full voting rights would be vested or denied within fifty days after commencement of the tender offer.

b). Fair-Price Statutes. *Fair-price statutes* essentially require that if a winning bidder makes a two-tier tender offer, it must pay nontendering shareholders the highest price it has paid for target shares within a specified recent period (typically, two years) if, after having acquired control of the target, the bidder seeks to engage in a business combination, or one of certain other defined transactions, with the target. There is an exception if the transaction is approved by (typically) 80 percent of all shares and two-thirds of the shares not owned by the bidder.

3.   Third-Generation Statutes.

a). Waiting-Period (Business Combination) Statutes. Waiting-period or Business Combination statutes prohibit a corporation, B, who acquires more than a specific percentage of another corporation, T, from merging with T, or engaging in certain other transactions with T, for a designated waiting period, unless certain conditions are satisfied. The idea is that in many cases a prospective bidder (B) expects to finance a tender offer for the stock of the target (T) partly by using T's assets as collateral. If B cannot expect to merge with T shortly after the tender offer succeeds, that kind of financing will be difficult or impossible to obtain. In addition, B may have various business reasons for wanting to merge with T after a tender offer, rather than running T as a partly owned subsidiary. These purposes are also frustrated by waiting-period statutes.

The New York statute, N.Y. Bus.Corp.Law § 912, provides for a five-year delay in effecting specified transactions, even if the transaction is not self-interested, unless the transaction is approved by T's board of directors prior to B's acquisition of the designated percentage of T's stock. The less stringent Delaware statute, Del.G.C.L. § 203, prohibits business combinations and other designated transactions between B and T for a period of three years unless B acquires 85% of T's shares in the initial tender offer, or the transaction is approved by 85% of T's shares other than the shares held by B.

The potency of this variety of statute in discouraging hostile bids is reflected by the 94 percent decline in hostile bids being launched for Delaware corporations following the enactment of the Delaware business combination statute. Gregg A. Jarrell, A Trip Down Memory Lane: Reflections on Section 203 and Subramanian, Herscovici and Barbetta, 65 Bus. Law. 779, 786 (2010). Should the total disappearance of successful hostile bids for Delaware companies following the state's enactment of Section 203 invite reconsideration whether the statute imposes an unconstitutional burden on commerce? *See* Guhan Subramanian, Steven Herscovici & Brian Barbetta, Is Delaware's Antitakeover Statute Unconstitutional? Evidence from 1988–2008, 65 Bus. Law. 685 (2010).

b). Amanda. In *Amanda Acquisition Corp. v. Universal Foods Corp.,* 877 F.2d 496, cert. denied, 493 U.S. 955, 110 S.Ct. 367, 107 L.Ed.2d 353 (1989), the Seventh Circuit held that the Wisconsin waiting-period statute was constitutional:

> [Arguments against state anti-takeover statutes based on preemption have] not won easy acceptance among the Justices for several reasons. First there is § 28(a) of the '34 Act, 14 U.S.C. § 78bb(a), which provides that "[n]othing in this chapter shall affect the jurisdiction of the securities commission . . . of any State over any security or any person insofar as it does not conflict with the provisions of this chapter or the rules and regulations thereunder." . . . [T]he SEC has not drafted regulations concerning mergers with controlling shareholders, and the Act itself does not address the subject. . . .
>
> . . . [T]he best argument for preemption is the Williams Act's "neutrality" between bidder and management, a balance designed to leave investors free to choose. This is not a confident jumping-off point, though. . . .
>
> There is a big difference between what congress *enacts* and what it *supposes* will ensue. Expectations about the consequences of a law are not themselves law. To say that Congress wanted to be neutral between bidder and target . . . is not to say that it also forbade the states to favor one of these sides. . . .
>
> Any bidder complying with federal law is free to acquire shares of Wisconsin firms on schedule. Delay in completing a second-stage merger may make the target less attractive, and thus depress the price offered or even lead to an absence of bids; it does not, however, alter any of the procedures governed by federal regulation. . . .

. . . It is not attractive [under the statute] to put bids on the table for Wisconsin corporations, but because Wisconsin leaves the process alone once a bidder appears, its law may co-exist with the Williams Act. . . .

The Commerce Clause, Art. I, § 8 cl. 3 of the Constitution, grants Congress the power "[t]o regulate Commerce . . . among the several States". . . .

When state law discriminates against interstate commerce expressly—for example, when Wisconsin closes its border to butter from Minnesota—the [anti-discrimination aspect of the] Commerce Clause steps in. The law before us is not of this type; it is neutral between inter-state and intra-state commerce. Amanda therefore presses on us the broader, all-weather, be-reasonable vision of the Constitution. Wisconsin has passed a law that unreasonably injures investors, most of whom live outside of Wisconsin, and therefore it has to be unconstitutional, as Amanda sees things. . . . [However, the Supreme] Court has looked for discrimination rather than for baleful effects. . . .

. . . The Commerce clause does not demand that states leave bidders a "meaningful opportunity for success."

c). Other Third-Generation Statutes. Amanda, and perhaps other factors, emboldened some states to adopt other, extremely exotic, and in some cases draconian, third-generation statutes. For example, the Pennsylvania statute provides, among many other things, that persons who own, offer to acquire, or publicly announce an intention to acquire, 20% of the stock of a publicly traded Pennsylvania corporation must disgorge any profits they realize from the disposition of that corporation's stock within a defined period. 15 Pa. Cons. Stat. Ann. §§ 2571–75 (West 1995). Ohio has a similar "disgorgement" provision. Ohio Rev. Code Ann. § 1707.043 (Anderson 2001). The Massachusetts statute requires every public corporation to have a classified board. Mass.Ann. Laws ch. 156D § 8.06(b) (Law Co-op 2007).

d). Constituency Statutes. A number of states have also adopted *constituency statutes,* which allow a board to consider the interests of groups ("constituencies") other than shareholders in making decisions, including decisions to resist takeovers. These statutes give the board increased leeway to resist a takeover, because often these other constituencies—for example, labor and the local community—are opposed to takeovers.

e). Pill Validation Statutes. Approximately one-half the states have statutes that endorse the use of a poison pill.

Very few state anti-takeover statutes are opt-in statutes. That is, all firms incorporated in the state are subject to state's anti-takeover provision unless specifically prescribed steps to opt out of the provision are pursued. Why would the default rule favor application of the statutorily provided defense?

In an extensive analysis of state takeover statutes, Professor Subramanian provides strong evidence that state antitakeover statutes, particularly control share, waiting period and pill validation statutes, assume a significant role in the public company's corporate domicile. Moreover, his data reflects that companies migrate away from the draconian antitakeover provisions of Massachusetts, Ohio and Pennsylvania. Guhan Subramanian, The Influence Of Antitakeover Statutes On Incorporation Choice: Evidence On The "Race" Debate And Antitakeover Overreaching, 150 U. Pa. L. Rev. 1795, 1852 (2002) ("these results support the view that managers migrate to, and fail to migrate away from, typical antitakeover statutes that are generally acknowledged to reduce shareholder value (business combination statutes, control share acquisition statutes, and pill validation statutes)"). Another impact of state antitakeover statues is their existence greatly influences whether the state court rejects the heightened *Unocal/Revlon* scrutiny and instead accords defensive maneuvers the more deferential review under the business judgment rule. *See* Michal Barzuza, The State Of State Antitakeover Law, 95 Va. L. Rev. 1973, 2018 (2009) (finding *Unocal* duties were rejected in 11 states and followed in 11 while *Revlon* duties were rejected in 9 states and followed in 6):

> The direct implication of this study is that in some states there are no enhanced fiduciary duties in change-of-control situations.... The famous *Unocal* and *Revlon* duo taught in corporations courses and followed by academics simply does not apply to some firms. The BJR and other weakened duties replace them either explicitly in states' statutes or in states' case law. As a result, mangers in those firms have wide latitude to use defensive tactics and as long as they do not have a direct conflict of interest and are adequately informed, they will enjoy the protection of the BJR.

Id. at 2029. Since the results captured in Professor Barzuza's study are linked directly to the impact of the legislature's adoption of state antitakeover statutes, does the legislature's action necessarily support the court's conclusion that management initiated defensive maneuvers that are not covered by the state antitakeover statute should nonetheless similarly be removed from heightened scrutiny?

An interesting question is what impact does a state antitakeover statute have on managers? The empirical evidence focused on this question suggests some positive features of state antitakeover statutes. Firms incorporated in states providing "second generation" antitakeover statutes are less highly leveraged than firms without such protection from takeovers. Gerald T. Garvey & Gordon Hanka, Capital Structure and Corporate Control: The Effect of Antitakeover Statutes on Firm

Leverage, 54 J. Fin. 519 (1999). Such firms also engage in greater capital expenditures and research and development than firms not enjoying the protection of state antitakeover statutes. Wm. N. Pugh & John S. Jahera, Jr., 18 Managerial and Decision Economics 681 (1997), and pursue less aggressive accounting policies in reporting their performance, Yijang Zhao & Kung H. Chen, 28 J. Acct'g Policy 92 (2009). On the negative side, there is some evidence that pay is more poorly linked to performance when firms have both firm-specific antitakeover defenses (e.g., a poison pill) as well as a state antitakeover statute than when firms have only firm-specific antitakeover defenses. Scott W. Barnhart, Michael F. Spivey & John C. Alexander, 21 Managerial and Decision Economics 315 (2000).

———

CHAPTER 15

DISTRIBUTIONS TO SHAREHOLDERS

Corporations normally can distribute funds to shareholders in one of four ways:

> (1) As dividends, that is, by making pro rata distributions of cash, securities, or interests in other kinds of property.

> (2) By repurchasing shares.

> (3) By paying shareholder-employees inflated salaries. This technique is most commonly used in close corporations, for tax reasons: In calculating taxable income, a corporation can deduct salaries, but cannot deduct dividends.

> (4) On liquidation, by paying each shareholder her pro rata share of corporate assets remaining after the claim of creditors have been satisfied or provided for.

This Chapter will concern the first two kinds of distributions—dividends and stock repurchases. Inflated salaries are considered in Chapters 7 (Close Corporations) and 10 (Duty of Loyalty), supra. Distributions in liquidation only infrequently raise significant legal problems if creditors have been either paid or provided for.

The architecture of this Chapter is as follows: Dividend policy is considered in Section 1. Limitations on dividends under creditors' rights law are considered in Section 2. Limitations on dividends under traditional corporate statutes are considered in Section 3. Limitations on dividends under the modern dividend statutes are considered in Section 4 and contractual limitations on dividends are considered in Section 5. The liability of directors and shareholders for improper dividends is considered in Sections 6 and 7. The repurchase by a corporation of its own stock is considered in Section 8. An issue related to dividends, liability for watered stock, is considered in section 9.

––––––

1. DIVIDEND POLICY

Dividend policy raises two very different kinds of issues. The first issue is how a corporation should determine the level of dividends it should pay. The materials in Section 1.A address that issue. Although dividend policy is largely an issue of efficiency, it spills over into law when shareholders bring a suit to force a corporation to pay dividends or when creditors complain the distribution violated legal standards intended for their protection. That issue will be considered in Section 1.B.

―――――

A. THE ELEMENTS OF DIVIDEND POLICY

Richard A. Brealey & Stewart C. Myers & Franklin Allen, Principles of Corporate Finance

Eighth ed., 2006.

In the mid-1950s John Lintner conducted a classic series of interviews with corporate managers about their dividend policies. His conclusions can be summarized in four stylized facts:

1.   Firms have long-run target dividend payout ratios. Mature companies with stable earnings generally pay out a high proportion of earnings; growth companies have low payouts (if they pay any dividends at all).

2.   Managers focus more on dividend changes than on absolute levels. Thus, paying a $2.00 dividend is an important financial decision if last year's dividend was $1.00, but no big deal if last year's dividend was $2.00.

3.   Dividend changes follow shifts in long-run, sustainable earnings. Managers "smooth" dividends. Transitory earnings changes are unlikely to affect dividend payouts.

4.   Managers are reluctant to make dividend changes that might have to be reversed. They are particularly worried about having to rescind a dividend increase. . . .

When Lintner conducted his interviews, dividends were effectively the only means of distributing cash. More recent work on payout policy since the dramatic increase in repurchases suggests a fifth stylized fact.

5.   Firms repurchase stock when they have accumulated a large amount of unwanted cash or wish to change their capital structure by replacing equity with debt.

THE INFORMATION IN DIVIDENDS AND STOCK REPURCHASES

In some countries you cannot rely on the information that companies provide. Passion for secrecy and a tendency to construct multilayered corporate organizations produce asset and earnings figures that are next to meaningless. Some people say that, thanks to creative accounting, the situation is little better for some companies in the United States.

How does an investor in such a world separate marginally profitable firms from the real money makers? One clue is dividends. Investors can't read managers' minds, but they can learn from managers' actions. They know that a firm which reports good earnings and pays a generous dividend is putting its money where its mouth is. We can understand, therefore, why investors would value the information content of dividends and would refuse to believe a firm's reported earnings unless they were backed up by an appropriate dividend policy.

Of course, firms can cheat in the short run by overstating earnings and scraping up cash to pay a generous dividend. But it is hard to cheat in the long run, for a firm that is not making enough money will not have enough cash to pay out. If a firm chooses a high dividend payout without the cash flow to back it up, that firm will ultimately have to reduce its investment plans or turn to investors for additional debt or equity financing. All of these consequences are costly. Therefore, most managers don't increase dividends until they are confident that sufficient cash will flow in to pay them.

Researchers, who have attempted to measure the information in dividend changes, have come up with mixed evidence. Some have found that dividend changes have little or no ability to predict future earnings. However, Healey and Palepu, who focus on companies that paid a dividend for the first time, find that on average earnings jumped 43 percent in the year a dividend was paid. If managers thought that this was a temporary windfall, they might have been cautious about committing themselves to paying out cash. But it looks as if these managers had good reason to be confident about prospects, for earnings continued to rise in the following years.[1]

THE PAYOUT CONTROVERSY

We have seen that a change in payout may provide information about management's confidence in the future and so affect the stock price. But eventually this change in the stock price would happen anyway as information about future earnings seeps out through other channels. But does the payout policy *change* the value of the stock, rather than simply providing a signal of its value?

On this issue, economists fall into three groups. On the right, there is a conservative group which believes that an increase in the dividend payout increases firm value. On the left, there is a radical group which believes that a higher dividend payout reduces value. And in the center, there is a middle-of-the-road party which claims that payout policy makes no difference.

The middle-of-the-road party was founded in 1961 by Miller and Modigliani (always referred to as "MM" or "M and M"), when they published a theoretical paper showing the irrelevance of dividend policy in a world without taxes, transaction costs, or other market imperfections.[12] . . .

In their classic 1961 article MM argued as follows: Suppose your firm has settled on its investment program. You have worked out how much

---

[1]   See P. Healey and K. Palepu, "Earnings Information Conveyed by Dividend Initiations and Omissions," Journal of Financial Economics 21 (1988), pp. 149–175.

[12]   M.H. Miller and F. Modigliani: "Dividend Policy, Growth and the Valuation of Shares," *Journal of Business,* 34: 411–433 (October 1961).

of this program can be financed from borrowing, and you plan to meet the remaining funds requirement from retained earnings. Any surplus money is to be paid out as dividends.

Now think what happens if you want to increase the dividend payment without changing the investment and borrowing policy. The extra money must come from somewhere. If the firm fixes its borrowing, the only way it can finance the extra dividend is to print some more shares and sell them. The new stockholders are going to part with their money only if you can offer them shares that are worth as much as they cost. But how can the firm do this when its assets, earnings, investment opportunities and, therefore, market value are all unchanged? The answer is that there must be a *transfer of value* from the old to the new stockholders. The new ones get the newly printed shares, each one worth less than before the dividend change was announced, and the old ones suffer a capital loss on their shares. The capital loss borne by the old shareholders just offsets the extra cash dividend they receive. . . .

Does it make any difference to the old stockholders that they receive an extra dividend payment plus an offsetting capital loss? It might if that were the only way they could get their hands on cash. But as long as there are efficient capital markets, they can raise the cash by selling shares. Thus the old shareholders can "cash in" either by persuading the management to pay a higher dividend or by selling some of their shares. In either case there will be a transfer of value from old to new shareholders. The only difference is that in the former case this transfer is caused by a dilution in the value of each of the firm's shares, and in the latter case it is caused by a reduction in the number of shares held by the old shareholders. . . .

Because investors do not need dividends to get their hands on cash, they will not pay higher prices for the shares of firms with high payouts. Therefore firms ought not to worry about dividend policy. They can let dividends fluctuate as a by-product of their investment and financing decisions. [This conclusion is known as the MM dividend-irrelevance proposition.] . . .

[One reason that some or many corporations may pay high dividends in the real world is that there] is a natural clientele for high-payout stocks. Trusts and endowment funds may prefer high-dividend stocks because dividends are regarded as spendable "income," whereas capital gains are "additions to principal."

There is also a natural clientele of investors who look to their stock portfolios for a steady source of cash to live on. In principle this cash could be easily generated from stocks paying no dividends at all; the investor could just sell off a small fraction of his or her holdings from time to time. But it is simpler and cheaper for AT & T to send a quarterly check than for its stockholders to sell, say, one share every 3 months. AT & T's regular dividends relieve many of its shareholders of transaction costs and considerable inconvenience. . . .

There is another reason that shareholders often clamor for more generous payouts. Suppose a company has plenty of free cash flow but few profitable investment opportunities. Shareholders may not trust the managers to spend retained earnings wisely and may fear that the money will be plowed back into building a larger empire rather than a more profitable one. In such cases investors may clamor for higher dividends or a stock repurchase not because these are valuable in themselves, but because they encourage a more careful, value-oriented investment policy.

————

Professors Brav, Graham, Harvey and Michaely, Payout Policy in the 21st Century, 77 J. Fin. Econ. 483 (2005) in a survey of executives found that while 65 percent of those surveyed believed they would raise funds externally to maintain the firm's dividend, only 16 percent would do so to continue prior share repurchase practices. Less than half the executives opined that the existence of good investment projects for the firm was important factor affecting dividend decision it increased to 80 percent when asked if it would affect a share repurchase decision. Finally, 94 percent of those surveyed said they would try to avoid reducing dividends and 88 percent believed there would be negative consequences if dividends were reduced. *Id.* at 490 & 499.

————

B. Judicial Review of Dividend Policy

(1) Publicly Held Corporations with a Controlling Shareholder

Baron v. Allied Artists Pictures Corporation
Court of Chancery of Delaware. 1975.
337 A.2d 653.

■ Brown, Vice Chancellor. . . .

Plaintiff charges that the present board of directors of Allied has fraudulently perpetuated itself in office by refusing to pay the accumulated dividend arrearages on preferred stock issued by the corporation which, in turn, permits the preferred stockholders to elect a majority of the board of directors at each annual election so long as the dividend arrearage specified by Allied's certificate of incorporation exists. Defendants contend that the recent financial history and condition of the corporation has justified the nonpayment of the preferred dividend arrearages, at least to the present . . .

By way of background, Allied was originally started in the mid-1930s as Sterling Pictures Corporation and later changed its name to Monogram Films under which it gained recognition for many B-pictures and western films. In the early 1950's it changed its name to the present one. Around 1953, with the advent of television, it fell upon hard times. Being in need of capital, Allied's certificate of incorporation was amended in 1954 to permit the issuance of 150,000 shares of preferred stock at a par value of $10.00, with the dividends payable quarterly on a cumulative basis. The amended language of the certificate provides that the preferred shareholders are entitled to receive cash dividends "as and when declared by the Board of Directors, out of funds legally available for the purpose. . . . " The amended certificate further provides that

> ". . . in case at any time six or more quarterly dividends (whether or not consecutive) on the Preferred Stock shall be in default, in whole or in part, then until all dividends in default on the Preferred Stock shall have been paid or deposited in trust, and the dividend thereon for the current quarterly period shall have been declared and funds for the payment thereof set aside, the holders of the Preferred Stock, voting as a class, shall have the right, at any annual or other meeting for the election of directors, by plurality vote to elect a majority of the Directors of the Corporation." . . .

Thereafter, as to the preferred stock issued under the 1954 offering, regular quarterly dividends were paid through March 30, 1963. Subsequently, Allied suffered losses which ultimately impaired the capital represented by the preferred stock as a consequence of which the payment of dividends became prohibited by *8 Del.C. § 170*. Allied has paid no dividends as to the preferred shares since 1963. By September 1964 the corporation was in default on six quarterly dividends and thus the holders of the preferred stock became entitled to elect a majority of the board of directors. They have done so ever since.

As of December 11, 1973 election of directors, Kalvex, Inc. owned 52 per cent of the outstanding preferred stock while owning only 625 shares of Allied's 1,500,000 shares of common stock. Since the filing of the first action herein Kalvex has taken steps to acquire a substantial number of common shares or securities convertible into the same. Thus unquestionably Kalvex, through its control of the preferred shares, is in control of Allied, although its holdings are said to represent only 7 1/2 per cent of the corporation's equity.

Plaintiff points out that the defendant Emanual Wolf, as director, president and chief executive officer of Allied at an annual salary of $100,000, is also president and chief executive officer of Kalvex. Defendant Robert L. Ingis, a director, vice-president and chief financial officer of Allied, is the executive vice-president of Kalvex. Defendants Strauss and Prager, elected as directors by the preferred shareholders, are also vice-presidents of Allied. Of the four directors nominated by management to represent the common stockholders, and duly elected, two serve Allied at salaried positions and two serve as counsel for Allied receiving either directly or through their firm's substantial remuneration for their efforts. Plaintiff asserts that for fiscal 1973, the officers and directors of Allied, as a group, received $402,088 in compensation.

Returning briefly to the fortunes of the corporation, in 1964 Allied was assessed a tax deficiency of some $1,400,000 by the Internal Revenue Service. At the end of fiscal 1963, it had a cumulative deficit of over $5,000,000, a negative net worth of over $1,800,000 and in that year had lost more than $2,700,000. As a consequence Allied entered into an agreement with the Internal Revenue Service to pay off the tax deficiency over a period of years subject to the condition that until the deficiency was satisfied Allied would pay no dividends without the consent of Internal Revenue.

Thereafter Allied's fortunes vacillated with varying degrees of success and failure which, defendants say, is both a hazard and a way of life in the motion picture and theatrical industry. Prior to fiscal 1973 there were only two years, 1969 and 1970, when its preferred capital was not impaired. But plaintiff points out that in 1970 the preferred capital surplus was $1,300,000 at a time when the preferred dividend arrearages were only $146,500. And, while recognizing that Allied suffered net income loss of over $3,000,000 in the following year, 1971, plaintiff further points out that during several years between 1964 and 1973 the corporation had, on occasion, sufficient net income to contribute to the sinking fund or to pay the dividend arrearages. Defendants argue that when viewed overall it was not until the end of the fiscal year terminating June 30, 1973 that Allied had, for the first time, a capital surplus available for preferred dividends, and that this surplus was only $118,000, or less than half of the amount necessary to liquidate the preferred dividend arrearage. (If this constitutes a dispute of fact, I do not consider it to be material for the purpose of this decision.)

Starting with 1972, Allied's financial condition began to improve substantially. It acquired the rights to, produced and distributed the film "Cabaret," which won eight Academy Awards and became the largest grossing film in Allied's history up to that time. It thereafter took a large gamble and committed itself for $7,000,000 for the production and distribution of the film "Papillon." In his initial litigation plaintiff complained vigorously of this, but he has since abandoned his objection since "Papillon" proved to be even a greater financial success than "Cabaret." For fiscal 1973 Allied had net income in excess of $1,400,000 plus a $2,000,000 tax carry-over remaining from its 1971 losses. Presumably its financial situation did not worsen prior to the December 11, 1974 election of directors although unquestionably it has gone forward with financial commitments as to forthcoming film releases.

Throughout all of the foregoing, however, the Internal Revenue agreement, with its dividend restriction, persisted. Prior to the 1973 election the balance owed was some $249,000 and as of the 1974 election, one final payment was due, which presumably has now been made. Prior to the 1973 election, Allied was in default on forty-three quarterly preferred dividends totalling more than $270,000. By the time of the 1974 election, the arrearages exceeded $280,000.

Without attempting to set forth all of the yearly financial data relied upon by the plaintiff, his position is, quite simply, that for one or more years since the preferred shareholders have been in control of Allied the corporate financial statements show that there was either a net income for the preceding fiscal year or a capital surplus at the end of the preceding fiscal year in an amount larger than the accumulated preferred dividend arrearages, and that consequently the board of directors elected by the preferred shareholders, being only a caretaker board, had a duty to use such funds to pay the dividend arrearage, and also the balance due on the Internal Revenue agreement, if necessary, and to thereupon return control of the corporation to the common stockholders at the next annual election. Specifically, plaintiff charges that the corporation had both the legal and financial capability to pay off the Internal Revenue obligation and the dividend arrearage prior to both the 1973 and 1974 annual election of directors which, had it been done, would have prevented the preferred shareholders, as controlled by Kalvex, from reelecting a majority of the board. Thus, plaintiff seeks the Court to order a new election at which Allied's board of directors will be elected by the common stockholders.

Plaintiff stresses that he is not asking the Court to compel the payment of the dividend arrearages, but only that a new election be held because of the preferred board's allegedly wrongful refusal to do so. Since the certificate of incorporation gives preferred shareholders the contractual right to elect a majority of the directors as long as dividends are six quarters in arrears, plaintiff, in effect, is asking that this contractual right be voided because of the deliberate refusal of the preferred shareholders to see themselves paid as soon as funds became legally available for that purpose. . . .

While preferences attaching to stock are the exception and are to be strictly construed, . . . it is well established that the rights of preferred stockholders are contract rights. In *Petroleum Rights Corporation v. Midland Royalty Corp., 19 Del.Ch. 334, 167 A. 835 (1933)* a somewhat similar provision of the corporate charter extended to preferred shareholders the right to elect a majority of the board when six quarterly dividends became in arrears, which right continued "*so long as the surplus . . . applicable to the payment of dividends shall be insufficient to pay all accrued dividends.*" The Chancellor there held that as long as there was the prescribed default in dividends and the surplus remained insufficient, the preferred stockholders were entitled to elect a majority of the board. It was argued to him that this right of election and control was limited by the language "so long as the surplus . . . shall be insufficient" and that the accumulation of a surplus sufficient to pay all accrued dividends constituted a condition subsequent, the existence of which would forthwith defeat the right to elect control. This view was rejected, on the theory that if accepted it would mean that the sole purpose of such a scheme would be to put the preferred in control to force a payment of passed dividends once a dividend fund became available. The Chancellor concluded that a shift of control should not be made to turn on the personal interests of the preferred shareholders in dividends alone but, in addition, on the consideration that if surplus fell below unpaid dividends the time had arrived to try a new management. *167 A. 837.* He also stated as follows at *167 A. 836*:

> "... if the surplus does in fact exceed the six quarterly dividends in arrears and the preference stock should elect a majority of the board and the board should resolve not to pay the dividends, the right of the preference stock to continue to elect a majority of the board would undoubtedly terminate."

I interpret this to mean that the contractual right to elect a majority of the board continues until the dividends can be made current in keeping with proper corporate management, but that it must terminate once a fund becomes clearly available to satisfy the arrearages and the preference board refuses to do so. Plaintiff seeks to limit this requirement to a mere mathematical availability of funds, and indeed the charter language in *Petroleum Rights* may have intended such a result. Here, however, Allied's charter, and thus its contract with its preferred shareholders, does not limit the right merely until such time as a sufficient surplus exists, as it did in *Petroleum Rights*, but rather it entitles the preferred shareholders to their dividends only "as and when declared by the Board of Directors, out of funds legally available for the purpose." This obviously reposes a discretion in Allied's board to declare preferred dividends, whether it be a board elected by the common or by the preferred shareholders.

The general rule applicable to the right to receive corporate dividends was succinctly stated by Justice Holmes in *Wabash Ry. Co. v. Barclay, 280 U.S. 197, 203, 50 S. Ct. 106, 107, 74 L. Ed. 368 (1930)*:

> "When a man buys stock instead of bonds he takes a greater risk in the business. No one suggests that he has a right to dividends if there are no met earnings. But the investment presupposes that the business is to go on, and therefore even if there are net earnings, the holder of stock, preferred as well as common, is entitled to have a dividend declared only out of such part of them as can be applied to dividends *consistently with a wise administration of a going concern.*"

Although one purpose of allowing the preferred to elect a majority of the board may be to bring about a payment of the dividend delinquencies as soon as possible, that should not be the sole justification for the existence of a board of directors so elected. During the time that such a preference board is in control of the policies and business decisions of the corporation, it serves the corporation itself and the common shareholders as well as those by whom it was put in office. Corporate directors stand in a fiduciary relationship to their corporation and its shareholders and their primary duty is to deal fairly and justly with both. . . .

The determination as to when and in what amounts a corporation may prudently distribute its assets by way of dividends rests in the honest discretion of the directors in the performance of this fiduciary duty. *Eshleman v. Keenan, 22 Del.Ch. 82, 194 A. 40 (1937),* aff'd *23 Del.Ch. 234, 2 A.2d 904; Treves v. Menzies, 37 Del.Ch., 330, 142 A.2d 520 (1958).* Before a court will interfere with the judgment of a board of directors in refusing to declare dividends, fraud or gross abuse of discretion must be shown. *Moskowitz v. Bantrell, Del.Supr., 41 Del.Ch. 177, 190 A.2d 749 (1963).* And this is true even if a fund does exist from which dividends could legally be paid . . .

Plaintiff here appears to be asking that an exception be carved from these well-established principles where the nonpayment of dividends and arrearages results in continued control by the very board which determines not to pay them. As I understand his argument, he asks for a ruling that a board of directors elected by preferred shareholders whose dividends are in arrears has an absolute duty to pay off all preferred dividends due and to return control to the common shareholders as soon as funds become legally available for that purpose, regardless of anything else. Thus, in effect, he would have the court limit the discretion given the board by the certificate of incorporation, and make the decision to pay arrearages mandatory upon the emergence of a lawful financial source even though the corporate charter does not require it (as perhaps it did in *Petroleum Rights*). He has offered no precedent for such a proposition, and I decline to create one. . . .

When the yearly hit-and-miss financial history of Allied from 1964 through 1974 is considered along with the Internal Revenue obligation during the same time span, I cannot conclude, as a matter of law, that Allied's board has been guilty of perpetuating itself in office by wrongfully refusing to apply corporate funds to the liquidation of the preferred dividend arrearages and the accelerated payment of the Internal Revenue debt. Thus I find no basis on the record before me to set aside the 1974 annual election and to order a new one through a master appointed by the court. . . .

It is clear, however, that Allied's present board does have a fiduciary duty to see that the preferred dividends are brought up to date as soon as possible in keeping with prudent business management. *Petroleum Rights Corporation v. Midland Royalty Corp., supra; Eshleman v. Keenan, supra.* This is particularly true now that the Internal Revenue debt has been satisfied in full and business is prospering. It cannot be permitted indefinitely to plough back all profits in future commitments so as to avoid full satisfaction of the rights of the preferred to their dividends and the otherwise normal right of the common stockholders to elect corporate management. While previous limitations on net income and capital surplus may offer a justification for the past, continued limitations in a time of greatly increased cash flow could well create new issues in the area of business discretion for the future. . . .

Plaintiff's motion for summary judgment is denied. Defendants' motion for summary judgment is granted. . . .

———

See also Sinclair Oil Corp. v. Levien, Chapter 10, supra; Gabelli & Co. v. Liggett Group Inc., 479 A.2d 276 (Del.1984); Berwald v. Mission Development Co., 40 Del.Ch. 509, 185 A.2d 480 (Del. 1962).

———

(2) CLOSE CORPORATIONS

———

DODGE v. FORD MOTOR CO.

[See Chapter 3, supra]

———

SMITH v. ATLANTIC PROPERTIES, INC.

[See Chapter 7, supra]

———

2. LIMITATIONS ON DIVIDENDS UNDER CREDITORS' RIGHTS LAW

Traditionally, dividends have been regulated by two very different, overlapping, sets of legal rules. The first set of rules is located in creditor's rights (or fraudulent-conveyance) law. These rules center on, but are not limited to, the concept of insolvency, and emphasize the liability of *shareholders* for the *receipt* of improper dividends. The second set of rules is located in state corporation law. These rules emphasize the liability of *directors* for the *payment* of improper dividends. Limitations on dividends under the law of creditor's rights will be considered in this Section. Limitations on dividends under corporation law will be considered in Section 3.

———

N.Y. BUS. CORP. LAW §§ 102(a)(8), 510(a), (b)

[See Statutory Supplement]

———

UNIFORM FRAUDULENT TRANSFER ACT §§ 1, 2, 4, 5

[See Statutory Supplement]

BANKRUPTCY CODE §§ 101(32), 548(a)

[See Statutory Supplement]

NOTES ON THE LAW OF CREDITORS' RIGHTS

1. Definition. Creditors' rights law imposes several limitations on transfers of assets without adequate consideration. The most prominent limits turns on the concept of insolvency. Insolvency limits on transfers are based on the transferor's financial condition in terms of either (i) its inability to pay its debts as they become due, or (ii) whether its liabilities exceed its assets. Accordingly, there are two broad definitions of the term *insolvency*.

The first definition—inability to pay debts as they become due—is embodied in most corporate dividend statutes, such as N.Y.Bus.Corp.Law § 102(a)(8). This is known as the *equity meaning* of insolvency, because it was the test generally applied by the equity courts, which had jurisdiction over insolvent estates before the enactment of the federal bankruptcy statute.

The second definition of insolvency—liabilities in excess of assets—is embodied in the Bankruptcy Code and the Uniform Fraudulent Transfer Act ("UFTA"). This second definition is known as the *bankruptcy meaning* of insolvency.[1]

> The difference between these two conceptions can be very great. The equity insolvency test is concerned with current liquidity of the going enterprise; the emphasis of the bankruptcy sense of insolvency is upon liquidation of the enterprise. It is easily possible for an enterprise to be short of cash and other liquid means of payment while at the same time holding illiquid assets of great value; such an enterprise may well fail the equity insolvency test. It is also a quite possible occurrence for an enterprise to have a large current cash flow while steadily operating at a loss and suffering a continuing erosion of its asset base; in time, such an enterprise will fail to meet the bankruptcy test of insolvency.
>
> Those with any familiarity with accounting will recognizes that the equity insolvency test is concerned with the income and

---

[1] Under the Bankruptcy Code, the test for whether a debtor can be put into involuntary bankruptcy turns principally on whether the debtor is insolvent in the equity sense. See 11 U.S.C.A. § 303(h). However, once a debtor has been put into bankruptcy, the bankruptcy trustee's right to avoid a pre-bankruptcy transfer turns in large part on whether at the time of the transfer the debtor was insolvent in the bankruptcy sense. See 11 U.S.C.A. §§ 101(32), 548.

The bankruptcy meaning of insolvency is itself susceptible to different nuances, as may be seen by comparing 11 U.S.C.A. § 101(32) with UFTA § 2(a).

cash flow statements of the enterprise while the bankruptcy insolvency test is focused on the balance sheet of the enterprise. For this reason, the bankruptcy insolvency test is frequently referred to as the "balance sheet" or "net worth" test.

B. Manning & J. Hanks, Legal Capital 69 (4th ed. 2013).

2. *Application of Fraudulent Conveyance Laws to Dividends.* There is some academic controversy concerning whether fraudulent-conveyance laws are applicable to dividends. However, the cases, while few, uniformly hold that dividends are subject to those laws. See Barbara Black, Corporate Dividends and Stock Repurchases § 4.05[6][b] (1998).

3. *Unreasonably Small Capital.* Another important limitation on transfer under the UFTA and cognate Acts is that a transfer without adequate consideration is prohibited if it would leave the transferor with unreasonably small capital.

> After the promulgation of the [Uniform Fraudulent Conveyance Act,] section 5 [the predecessor of UFTA § 4] received little independent notice. The case law that did develop, however, did little to illuminate the basic question: what is the scope of the unreasonably small capital provision? . . . The main view, to the extent that one developed, focused on the transferor's ability to marshall sufficient cash, either from operations, equity infusions, new loans or some combination of these, to pay expected creditors. These cases took a forward looking view, comparing anticipated cash flow against anticipated debt incurrence.

Markell, Toward True and Plain Dealing: A Theory of Fraudulent Transfers Involving Unreasonably Small Capital, 21 Ind.L.Rev. 469, 487 (1988).

4. *Insolvency Under the Dividend Statutes.* Many corporate-law dividend statutes explicitly incorporate an insolvency limitation on the payment of dividends. See, e.g., N.Y.Bus.Corp.Law § 510. Others do not, although they may embody parallel concepts. The Official Comment to Model Act § 6.40 states that "[t]he Revised Model Business Corporation Act establishes the validity of distributions from the corporate law standpoint under section 6.40 and determines the potential liability of directors for improper distributions under sections 8.30 and 8.33. The federal Bankruptcy Act and state fraudulent conveyance statutes, on the other hand, are designed to enable the trustee or other representative to recapture for the benefit of creditors funds distributed to others in some circumstances. In light of these diverse purposes, it was not thought necessary to make the tests of section 6.40 identical to the tests for insolvency under these various statutes." Cal.Corp.Code § 506(d), which governs the liability of shareholders who have received improper dividends, provides that "[n]othing contained in this section affects any liability which any shareholder may have under [the Uniform Fraudulent Transfer Act]."

———

3. LIMITATIONS ON DIVIDENDS UNDER THE CORPORATE STATUTES

A. INTRODUCTION

1.   In General. In addition to limitations placed on dividends under the law of creditors' rights, corporate law also governs the power to declare and pay dividends. Cases like Dodge v. Ford, supra, concern the issue, when may a corporation be *compelled* to pay dividends. Most of the law of dividends, however, centers on *limitations* on a corporation's power to pay dividends. These limitations may be thought of as financial, in the narrow sense that they are not based on judicial determinations of sound dividend policy, but instead turn on quantified objective tests. Under traditional statutes, however, the limitations involve concepts that are typically of little or no relevance under modern financial theory.

2.   Who Does Corporate Dividend Law Protect? A preliminary issue raised by the corporate law of dividends is, who does this body of law protect? The class of persons protected by creditors' rights law is clear—creditors. The classes of persons protected by the corporate dividend statutes has not always been clear.

Obviously, one group of persons who could be protected by these statutes is creditors. As stated in D. Kehl, Corporate Dividends (1941), "With the liability of corporate stockholders . . . limited to the amount of capital subscribed . . . it soon became apparent that the original capital should be permanently devoted to the needs of the corporation as at least a partial substitute for the unlimited personal liability existing in individual enterprise." But then, "If the creation of a capital fund was not to defeat its purpose, safeguards against its withdrawal by repayment to shareholders in the guise of dividends, or otherwise, were indispensable. Historically, the principal objective of dividend law has therefore been the preservation of a minimum of assets as a safeguard in assuring the payment of creditors' claims."

In addition to creditors, some of the corporate dividend statutes are also designed to protect the preferences of preferred shareholders.

Finally, at one time it was thought that the corporate dividend statutes were intended to protect common shareholders, partly on the ground that excessive dividends might injure the corporate enterprise, and partly on the ground that dividends out of capital might mislead shareholders into thinking that the corporation was earning money when in fact it wasn't.

Today, the concept that the corporate dividend statutes protect common shareholders is not generally accepted. Furthermore, although the protection that the statutes give to preferred shareholders may sometimes be significant, many corporations have no preferred shareholders. That leaves the protection of creditors. As the following materials will show, however, in fact creditors get very little protection from the traditional dividend statutes.

3. Traditional and Modern Dividend Statutes. The dividend statutes can be divided into traditional and modern statutes. The traditional statutes, in turn, can be divided into two subcategories. Most of the traditional statutes center on a *capital-impairment test* (sometimes referred to as the *capital-and-surplus* or *balance-sheet test*). A few are centered on an *earned-surplus* (or *income-statement* test). The following sections will discuss the traditional capital-impairment statutes, the traditional earned-surplus statutes, and the modern statutes, respectively.

B. TRADITIONAL STATUTES—CAPITAL-IMPAIRMENT STATUTES

(1) THE CAPITAL-IMPAIRMENT TEST AND ITS MEANING

DEL. GEN. CORP. LAW §§ 141(e), 154, 170

[See Statutory Supplement]

N.Y. BUS. CORP. LAW §§ 102(a)(9), (12), (13), 506, 510

[See Statutory Supplement]

---

1. Legal Capital and Par Value. Most traditional statutes turn on the concept of *legal capital*. That concept, in turn, can only be understood against the background of a concept known as *par* or *par value*.

a). Par Value. Originally, the par value of a share was the price at which it was expected that the share would be issued (sold) by the corporation. Thus in the paradigm case, a share that carried a $100 par value would be issued for $100. Indeed, where par value continues, corporate statutes provide that the shares will be deemed fully paid and beyond any assessment only if the full par value of the shares was paid when initially issued. Eventually, a practice emerged under which the par value of stock was not the price at which the stock was to be issued, but a purely nominal amount. For example, stock that was to be issued at $100 might carry a par value of only $1, or even less. Such stock is known as *low-par value* stock. Still later, the statutes were amended to allow the issuance of *no-par value* stock—that is, stock that did not carry any par value at all.

b). Legal Capital. Legal capital is the sum of (i) the par value of all par-value stock, and (ii) such additional amounts as the board assigns to capital, either in connection with the issuance of low-par or no-par stock, or thereafter. Legal capital (or *stated capital*) is a legal construct, with little or no economic reality. *Economic capital* is the amount that the owners of an enterprise have invested in the enterprise, directly or indirectly. When stock was issued at its par value, the concepts of economic and legal capital were tied together. The advent of low-par and no-par stock severed that tie. Because the concept of legal capital is tied to par value, it has become artificial. Nevertheless, the concept still remains important under the traditional dividend statutes.

2.   *Structure of the Traditional Statutes.* Most traditional corporate dividend statutes begin with an insolvency test. There are three possible reasons why these statutes employ an insolvency test, which would be applicable in any event under creditors' rights law. First, it has not always been entirely clear whether creditors' rights law applies to dividends. Second, creditors' rights laws emphasize the liability of transferees (in the case of corporations, shareholders) for improper distributions. In contrast, the corporate dividend statutes emphasize the liability of directors. Third, the basic creditors' rights laws—the Bankruptcy Code and the Uniform Fraudulent Transfer Act, and cognate statutes—turn on the bankruptcy meaning of insolvency. In contrast, a dividend statute may employ either the equity meaning of insolvency or both the bankruptcy and the equity meanings.

After beginning with an insolvency test, the traditional dividend statutes add a second basic test, which is frequently subject to important exceptions. The most common second basic test is a capital-impairment test. The capital-impairment statutes center on whether after the dividend the corporation's assets exceed its liabilities plus its legal capital. Under this test, a dividend cannot be paid if, before or after payment of the dividend, the corporation's assets are or would be less than the sum of its liabilities plus its legal capital or, in some cases, the sum of liabilities, capital, and liquidation preferences. (In contrast, under the bankruptcy meaning of the insolvency test, a dividend may be paid as long as after the payment the corporation's assets will exceed its liabilities.) Capital-impairment statutes can be conceptualized in two, functionally identical ways: as prohibiting dividends out of legal capital, or as permitting dividends only out of surplus (the excess of the firm's assets over the combined amount of its liabilities and legal capital).

———

NOTE ON REVALUATION OF ASSETS AND KLANG V. SMITH'S FOOD & DRUG CENTERS, INC.

Corporate dividend statutes invariably contain accounting-based terms such as "assets" and "liabilities." Financial statements are prepared according to a host of conventions and principles; the bedrock of most of these principles is that in reporting a firm's financial position and performance accounting items such as an asset or a liability are based on its historical cost figure and do not reflect increases in an item since its acquisition. Thus, assets are recorded at cost, *reduced* by reasonable charges for amortization or depreciation to reflect that assets (with the exception of land) lose their usefulness due to obsolescence, wear and tear, and the like. Similarly, liabilities are recorded at the amount of the contractual obligation due the creditor, even if in the hands of the creditor the debt's market value is substantially below the face value of the debt because of uncertainty whether the debtor firm will be able to fully satisfy the debt when it comes due. Thus, the convention that assets and liabilities should be recorded at their cost is a pervasive convention under generally accepted accounting principles (GAAP). This statement, however, is qualified, in the case of assets for which, as mentioned earlier, are reduced by periodic amortization and depreciation as well as any material permanent impairment of the asset's value. Given the pervasiveness of the cost convention within GAAP, should similar conservatism carry over to interpreting dividend statutes use of accounting-based terms such as assets and liabilities?

Beginning in the 1940s, there was a long debate in the scholarly literature on whether a capital-impairment test permitted the payment of dividends up to the difference between the *actual value* of the corporation's assets and its liabilities and capital, or only up to the difference between the corporation's assets and its liabilities and capital *as shown on the corporation's balance sheet*. The debate was largely triggered by the leading case of *Randall v. Bailey,* 23 N.Y.S.2d 173 (Sup.Ct. 1940), aff'd, 288 N.Y. 280, 43 N.E.2d 43 (1942), in which the New York courts permitted the board of directors to premise declaration of a dividend on an *upward* valuation of the firm's assets, i.e., without the increase in the amount of assets the dividend would have impaired the firm's capital.

Similar to the result reached in *Randall*, the Delaware Supreme Court in *Klang v. Smith's Food & Drug Centers, Inc.,* 702 A.2d 150 (Del. 1997), held that a firm did not impair its capital and thereby violate section 160 of the Delaware General Corporation Law by repurchasing its shares when they relied on a consultant's (Houlihan's) report that the firm's assets were significantly above their level determined according to GAAP.

It is helpful to recall the purpose behind Section 160. The General Assembly enacted the statute to prevent boards from draining corporations of assets to the detriment of creditors and the long-term health of the corporation. That a corporation has not yet realized or reflected on its balance sheet the appreciation of assets is irrelevant to this concern. Regardless of what a balance sheet that has not been updated may show, an actual, though unrealized, appreciation reflects real economic value that the corporation may borrow against or that creditors may claim or levy upon. Allowing corporations to revalue assets and liabilities to reflect current realities complies with the statute and serves well the policies behind this statute. . . .

We believe that plaintiff reads too much into Section 154. The statute simply defines "net assets" in the course of defining "surplus." It does not mandate a "facts and figures balancing of assets and liabilities" to determine by what amount, if any, total assets exceeds total liabilities. The statute is merely definitional. It does not require any particular method of calculating surplus, but simply prescribes factors that any such calculation must include. . . .

We are satisfied that the Houlihan opinion adequately took into account all of SFD's assets and liabilities. . . .

The record contains, in the form of the Houlihan opinion, substantial evidence that the transactions complied with Section 160. Plaintiff has provided no reason to distrust Houlihan's analysis. In cases alleging impairment of capital under Section 160, the trial court may defer to the board's measurement of surplus unless a plaintiff can show that the directors "failed to fulfill their duty to evaluate the assets on the basis of acceptable data and by standards which they are entitled to believe reasonably reflect present values." In the absence of bad faith or fraud on the part of the board, courts will not "substitute [our] concepts of wisdom for that of the directors." Here, plaintiff does not argue that the SFD Board acted in bad faith. Nor has he met his burden of showing that the methods and data that underlay the board's analysis are unreliable or that its determination of surplus is so far off the mark as to constitute actual or constructive fraud.[12] Therefore, we defer to the board's determination of surplus, and hold that SFD's self-tender offer did not violate 8 *Del.C.* § 160.

702 A.2d at 154–156.

Are there good policy reasons to reject the outcomes reached in *Randall* and *Klang*? When a board relies on appraised value of the firm's assets that are higher than their historical cost, does this erode the protection of creditors (assuming the appraisal is a reliable one)? Assume the company is a wholesaler of copper and that the price for copper has increased world-wide by 20 percent and ninety percent of the firm's assets are its inventory of copper. Under the Delaware statute can this firm rely on this increase in the value of its inventory to declare a dividend to its stockholders? Repurchase shares? Does such a distribution pose a threat to creditors? The future of the firm?

---

[12] We interpret 8 *Del.C.* § 172 to entitle boards to rely on experts such as Houlihan to determine compliance with 8 *Del.C.* § 160. Plaintiff has not alleged that the SFD Board failed to exercise reasonable care in selecting Houlihan, nor that rendering a solvency opinion is outside Houlihan's realm of competence. Compare 8 *Del.C.* § 141(e) (providing that directors may rely in good faith on records, reports, experts, etc.).

(2) EXCEPTIONS TO THE BASIC CAPITAL-IMPAIRMENT TEST

(a) *Nimble Dividends*

―――――

DEL. GEN. CORP. LAW § 170

[See Statutory Supplement]

―――――

Under a few statutes, like that of Delaware, dividends can be paid out of current profits even if capital is or would be impaired. Such dividends are known as *nimble dividends*. The term "nimble" is used to describe such dividends because under the statutes the dividend can be paid only out of *current* profits, so that directors must be sufficiently nimble to declare the dividends before the close of the current period or within a short time thereafter.

One justification that has been put forward for permitting dividends out of current profits, even when capital is impaired, is that this technique allows the corporation to continue regular dividends on its preferred stock. Another is that a corporation that has suffered heavy losses may need to attract new capital to remain viable, and may be unable to attract new capital if it cannot pay dividends.

Both justifications are thin. Essentially, the ability to pay nimble dividends, in states that permit such dividends, seems to be an erosion— one of many—in the idea that capital should be preserved to protect creditors.

―――――

(b) *Wasting-Asset Corporations*

NOTE ON WASTING-ASSET CORPORATIONS

Normally, in determining profits—and therefore surplus—a corporation must subtract from its gross revenues an appropriate amount for depreciation or depletion. However, some statutes, like N.Y.Bus.Corp.Law § 510(b) and Del.Gen.Corp.Law § 170(b), provide that in the case of a wasting-asset corporation, profits can be calculated for dividend purposes without regard to depreciation or depletion, subject to certain limitations. A *wasting-asset* corporation is a corporation that is in the business of exploiting a non-replenishable asset, like a coal mine, an oil well, a rock quarry, or a patent.

The justification sometimes given for permitting dividends without regard to an allowance for depletion of a wasting asset is that all concerned parties expect that the corporation's lifetime will be limited to the lifetime of the wasting asset, so that there is no reason to preserve the corporation's capital beyond the lifetime of that asset. This justification, like the justification for nimble dividends, is thin, because many corporations with wasting assets either hold nonwasting assets as well, hold a portfolio of wasting assets that is continually refreshed, or both.

————

(c) Dividends out of Capital Surplus

————

N.Y. BUS. CORP. LAW §§ 102(a)(9), (13), (14), 510, 516, 520

[See Statutory Supplement]

————

DEL. GEN. CORP. LAW §§ 154, 170, 242(a)(3), 244

[See Statutory Supplement]

————

NOTE ON DIVIDENDS OUT OF CAPITAL SURPLUS

The capital-impairment statutes routinely permit dividends out of both paid-in surplus and reduction surplus, with no significant safeguards for creditors beyond those imposed by the insolvency test. The payment of dividends out of capital surplus seems anomalous under a capital-impairment statute, in which the emphasis is placed on preservation of capital. The power of the corporation to reduce capital, and pay dividends out of the resulting reduction surplus, creates a gaping breach in the purported wall set up by dividend law to protect the interests of creditors.

————

C. TRADITIONAL STATUTES—EARNED-SURPLUS STATUTES

NOTE ON THE EARNED-SURPLUS TEST

At one time, the Model Act employed a test for dividends that centered on whether a corporation had *earned surplus*. Earned surplus was defined as "the portion of . . . surplus . . . equal to the balance of . . . net profits, income, gains and losses from the date of incorporation . . . after deducting subsequent distributions to shareholders and transfers to stated capital and capital surplus made out of earned surplus." William Hackney commented as follows:

> In attempting to formulate statutory language limiting dividends to income, two distinct approaches were found possible.
>
> One is, like the capital-impairment restriction, a balance-sheet test. The surplus of net assets in excess of capital is obtained and then analyzed and any which is not paid-in or other capital surplus is deemed accumulated income.

> The second approach ... is to take the balance of all the corporate income statements to date and deduct dividends and other transfers therefrom, with the remainder being earned surplus.
>
> The [1969] Model Act definition, it seems, utilizes the aggregate-income-statement method of arriving at earned surplus. It does not use the balance sheet as a source of reference but directs one to take the balance of net profits, income, gains and losses over a period of time.[1]

Despite the focus on earned surplus, the prior version of the Model Act, and the statutes that continue to follow this earlier version of the Model Act also permit dividends out of capital surplus if so authorized by the articles of incorporation, or approved by the shareholders, and was identified as a distribution from capital; there were no accrued dividends on an issue of cumulative preferred stock; and the dividend did not impair the liquidation preference of preferred stock. In practice, therefore, the earned surplus test tended to converge with the capital-impairment test.

As Hackney pointed out, "The net result [of earned-surplus statutes based on the old Model Act] is an apparent limitation of the funds available for dividends to earned surplus, but actually, in so far as real protection to creditors or preferred stockholders is concerned, there is a complete eradication of the concept of common capital as a cushion protecting the senior interests." Hackney, The Financial Provisions of the Model Business Corporation Act, 70 Harv.L.Rev. 1357, 1389 (1957).

The current version of the Model Act has dropped the earned-surplus approach. That approach is now followed by only a few statutes.

4. THE MODERN DIVIDEND STATUTES FOR CORPORATIONS AND LLCS

———

CAL. CORP. CODE §§ 114, 166, 500–503, 507

[See Statutory Supplement]

———

MODEL BUS. CORP. ACT §§ 1.40(6), 6.40

[See Statutory Supplement]

———

DEL. L.L.C. ACT § 18–607(a)

[See Statutory Supplement]

---

[1] Hackney, The Financial Provisions of the Model Business Corporations Act, 70 Harv.L.Rev. 1357, 1365–66 (1957).

U.L.L.C. ACT § 405

[See Statutory Supplement]

California's corporate dividend provisions, enacted in 1977, marked a sweeping break with traditional dividend statutes. Until that time, the foundation of most statutes was a legal concept—stated capital. In contrast, the foundation of the California statute is a set of economic realities: retained earnings, asset-liability ratios, liquidation preferences, and an insolvency test. The Model Business Corporation Act followed suit in breaking with the traditional statutes, although it employed a much different approach than the California statute. Among other things, these statutes eliminate the concept of par value for all practical purposes.

Both Delaware and the Uniform Limited Liability Company Acts parallel the approach taken by California and the Model Business Corporation Act. Each proscribe distributions that reduce assets below liabilities and the Uniform act further restricts distributions that will render the company "not able to pay its debts as they become due in the ordinary course of the company's activities."

Kummert, State Statutory Restrictions on Financial Distributions by Corporations to Shareholders (Pt. II)

59 Wash.L.Rev. 185, 282–84 (1984)

"[The California and Model Business Corporation Act approaches] have some remarkable similarities. [Both] proceed from a common assessment of the inadequacies of the concept of legal capital to abolish not only the statutory underpinnings of the concept (the notion of par value and accounting rules for consideration received for shares), but also the series of exceptions (nimble dividends, depletion dividends, and special repurchases of shares) and fictions (treasury shares) erected because of the existence of the concept. [Both] subject transfers of cash or property, or incurrences of indebtedness, by a corporation without consideration to its shareholders to a single set of restrictions, regardless of the form in which the transfer, or incurrence, occurs. [Both] address applications of the restrictions to such transfers, or incurrences, where the transferor, or obligor, is either the parent, or the subsidiary, of another corporation. Finally, drafters of each of the systems based their efforts on the premise that statutory systems founded on legal capital were essentially misleading insofar as they led creditors and senior security holders to believe that such systems operated to protect their interests.

5. CONTRACTUAL RESTRICTIONS ON THE PAYMENT OF DIVIDENDS

Bayless Manning & James J. Hanks, Jr., Legal Capital 94–95

(4th ed. 2013).

The best argument suggesting that . . . [corporate statute's regulation of dividends and share repurchases] has some protective consequences for creditors is historical, cultural and psychological. For more than 150 years, it has been thought important that an enterprise have something called "capital." And the concept has acquired its own independent aura of respectability, whatever its actual significance to real creditors in real business situations. Bankers and other businesspeople occasionally view a "thin" stated capital with suspicion, and it is—in some sense—considered to be a mark of fiscal probity to have a substantial stated capital on the right side of the corporate balance sheet. Deep in the consciousness of the American businessperson, lawyer, accountant and banker is the general principle that distributions to shareholders are not supposed to be made "out of" capital. Everybody knows that ways are available to design around statutory restrictions; but the restrictions themselves are a reflection of that general principle. The statutory provisions on stated capital and distributions to equity investors are expressions of a general norm of behavior to which the businesspeople have accustomed themselves, if only because of the essential irrelevance of the statutes to anything the business community cares about. For this reason, among others, changes in the legal capital system have not originated with businesspeople.

Perhaps it may be argued that the statutes hang in just the right balance. They announce a general and salutary principle that commands wide assent; but they are so feebly constructed and loosely enforced that a corporation's financial managers, lawyers and accountants can move as they wish when it is necessary to do so, as everyone agrees they should be able to do. If this line of thought is valid, creditors do, in some general sense, benefit from the statutory scheme to the extent that the stated capital provisions contribute to an atmosphere in which corporate managements psychologically feel themselves inhibited from distributing assets to shareholders indiscriminately. In addition, the potential personal liability of directors who assent to an improper distribution is undoubtedly a strong incentive for compliance.

A second line of speculation, unprovable, is that the statutory provisions may have a degree of actual operating impact upon medium-sized corporations. Those in control of the incorporated small enterprise typically manage its, and their, economic lives with little or no awareness of or regard for the niceties of procedure spelled out in legal capital provisions. Large public enterprises on the other hand can draw on lawyers and other professionals who see to it that wide flexibility of corporate financial action and decisions is maintained while scrupulously observing the statutory mandates. But it may also be that the managers of a medium-sized incorporated enterprise may be sufficiently conscious of statutory and regulatory requirements to be affected in their behavior and yet not served with sufficient continuity of professional advice to enable them to control their own destinies in the legal capital thicket. And perhaps the medium-sized corporation is the one that offers the greatest problem for the creditor; there he has not the close personal contact that grounds his extension of credit to the incorporated barbershop nor has he the institutional protections that back up a credit to Microsoft.

But whatever may be argued at these general and abstract levels, one basic bit of evidence almost compels the conclusion that creditors do not gain very much from the system. That evidence is the almost total lack of interest that creditors show in this subject. Creditors' groups do not try to lobby changes into the corporation acts to tighten up the obvious loopholes. They do not clamor for participation in the procedures by which corporations shuffle about their capital accounts. Indeed, if legal capital had any real practical merit, creditors (and others) would be likely to have sought its adoption into the statutes authorizing the new forms of entity of the late twentieth and early twenty-first centuries—limited liability companies, limited partnerships and the like—and there has been no such pressures at all.

———

It should be obvious by now that the traditional dividend statutes provide little protection to creditors beyond that already afforded by the law of creditors' rights. These statutes are so liberal in allowing capital surplus to be created, either through the use of no-par or low-par capitalization when stock is originally issued, or thereafter through a reduction of capital, that corporations can usually make routine distributions out of economic (although not "legal") capital, even in the absence of retained earnings.

Involuntary creditors, trade creditors, and short-term lenders must normally take the protection of dividend law as they find it. Institutional lenders, however, who provide large amounts of money over a long period of time, have the power to impose contractual restrictions on dividends beyond the weak limits imposed by corporation law, and often do so. Similar restrictions are often extracted by underwriters in connection with bonds and preferred stock issued to the public. Indeed, as a practical matter, it may be said that much of the modern law of dividends is contractual rather than statutory. The practical question is usually not whether a dividend is prohibited by statute, but whether it is prohibited by arrangements with lending institutions or provisions agreed upon in connection with bond or preferred-stock financing.

_____

FORM OF BOND INDENTURE PROVISION RESTRICTING DIVIDENDS

[See Statutory Supplement]

_____

6. LIABILITY OF DIRECTORS, MANAGERS, SHAREHOLDERS AND MEMBERS FOR IMPROPER DISTRIBUTIONS

Liability for an improper dividend is governed by two bodies of law: corporation law, and the law of creditors' rights. Liability may be imposed on the directors who authorize the dividend, on the shareholders who receive it, or both. In general, corporation law tends to emphasize the liability of directors, while creditors' rights law tends to emphasize the liability of shareholders.

Subject to certain exceptions, liability for an improper repurchase of a corporation's own stock is treated the same way as liability for an improper dividend.

With respect to LLCs, it is interesting to contrast the approach taken in Delaware with that of most states and the Uniform Limited Liability Act. For example, the latter clearly sets forth the liability of those (i.e., members of a member-managed LLC or managers of a manager-managed LLC) who approve a distribution that is improper. U.L.L.C.A. § 406(a). In contrast, Delaware does not directly address the question; Delaware instead provides broadly that members and managers who rely in good faith on the professional competence of others or reports, etc. that the value or amount of assets will be sufficient to make distributions will be fully protected. Del. L. L. C. A. § 18.406. If the consenting manager or member does not act in good faith, who then may recover for an improper distribution? Neither Delaware nor the Uniform Act directly address, as do most corporate statutes, the rights of the manager or member to recover from members who received a distribution knowing it was improper.

_____

N.Y. BUS. CORP. LAW § 719

[See Statutory Supplement]

_____

MODEL BUS. CORP. ACT § 8.33

[See Statutory Supplement]

DEL. GEN. CORP. LAW §§ 172, 174

[See Statutory Supplement]

DEL. L. L. C. A § 18–406 & 18–607(b)

[See Statutory Supplement]

U.L.L.C.A. § 406

[See Statutory Supplement]

U. L. L. C. A. § 406(a) & (b)

[See Statutory Supplement]

7. REPURCHASE BY A CORPORATION OF ITS OWN STOCK

A repurchase by a corporation of its own stock may implicate a variety of legal rules. Some of the relevant legal rules are financial. These rules are the subject of Subsection A. Other rules are designed to deal with problems like unfairness and manipulation. Some of those rules will be briefly considered in Subsection B.

**Wm. A. Klein, John C. Coffee & Frank Partnoy,
Business Organization and Finance 398–99**

(10th ed. 2010).

Suppose . . . [a] corporation [eds. With 1000 outstanding shares] has reached the end of the year with earnings and spare cash of $12,000 and a total value of $112,000 (including the spare cash) or $112 per share. Suppose further that it has decided not to invest the $12,000. Instead of paying a dividend, it can use the cash to buy (redeem) its shares from those stockholders willing to sell. It might do this simply by buying shares on the market. With its $12,000 it should be able to buy 107 shares at the existing price of $112 per share. The total value of the corporation will then be $100,000 and the value of each of the remaining 893 shares will be $112. The corporation will be rid of the spare cash and each of original shareholders will have either cash of $112 per share or shares each of which is worth that amount. What is important is that the $12 gain is made available to the shareholders who hold on to their shares in the form of unrealized (and therefore untaxed) capital appreciation. For taxable shareholders other than taxable corporations this is clearly preferable to the same amount of gain the form of dividends. These shareholders will enjoy the substantial tax advantage of deferral of tax—equivalent to an interest-free loan from the government of the amount of the tax-until they decide to sell. Even if they decide to sell some of their shares in order to draw down their gain, they will have the advantage of paying tax only on the pro rata gain on the shares that they sell, rather than on the entire proceeds of the sale. For example, imagine a shareholder who bought 100 shares at $100 at the beginning of the year, for a total of $10,000. At the end of the year the shares are worth $112, a total of $11,200, and the shareholder sells 18 shares for $112, a total of $2,016. The amount subject to tax is only the $216 difference between the proceeds of the sale ($2,016) and the cost of the shares sold ($1,800). This obviously beats paying tax on the entire amount of any dividend that might be received. . . . Finally, capital gain can be offset by capital losses, if any; net capital losses offset ordinary income, such as dividends, only to a maximum of $3,000.

Nontaxable shareholders should be indifferent as to whether their gain is in the form of dividends or capital gain.

———

A. FINANCIAL LIMITATIONS ON STOCK REPURCHASES

———

N.Y. BUS. CORP. LAW §§ 513, 515

[See Statutory Supplement]

———

DEL. GEN. CORP. LAW § 160(a)

[See Statutory Supplement]

———

MODEL BUS. CORP. ACT §§ 1.40(6), 6.40

[See Statutory Supplement]

———

CAL. CORP. CODE § 510(a)

[See Statutory Supplement]

———

1. General Rule. When a corporation purchases shares of its own stock, corporate assets flow out to shareholders. Accordingly, from the perspective of creditors a repurchase of stock is economically indistinguishable from a dividend. Ideally, therefore, the financial limitations on repurchases should generally be the same as those for dividends. Thus the California statute and the Model Act treat repurchases and dividends together under the heading, "distributions." Most other statutes provide that, with specified exceptions, a corporation can expend funds to purchase its own stock only if it could pay a dividend in the same amount.

2. Exceptions. Despite the general parity in the treatment of dividends and repurchases, most of the traditional statutes permit a corporation to purchase its own stock out of capital for certain specified purposes. The most common such purposes are (i) eliminating fractional shares, (ii) collecting or compromising a shareholder's indebtedness to the corporation, (iii) paying dissenting shareholders for their shares pursuant to the exercise of appraisal rights, and (iv) redeeming or purchasing redeemable stock. See, e.g., Del.Gen.Corp.Law § 160(a)(1); N.Y.Bus.Corp.Law § 513(b), (c). The last of these exceptions, which is probably the most important, is usually supported on the grounds that redeemable stock is temporary by the terms of its creation, so that senior interests will not rely on the cushion provided by the capital such shares have contributed; that the exception facilitates refunding of higher-dividend-rate preferred with lower-dividend-rate preferred (redeemable stock is almost invariably preferred); and that abuse is unlikely because the board, which must make a decision to redeem, normally represents the interests of common, not preferred.

3. Installment Payments. Dividends are normally made payable shortly after being declared. In contrast, payment for repurchased stock is sometimes made in installments over a period of years. This raises the issue whether the permissibility of a repurchase under an installment contract should be determined: (i) at the time the original contract is made, based on the effect of paying the full amount of the contract price; (ii) at the time each installment is scheduled to be paid, based on the effect of paying the installment at that time; or (iii) both. "Most courts have held that [in the case of an installment contract to repurchase stock] the corporation must pass the equitable insolvency test, initially at the time of contract, with respect to the entire purchase price, and subsequently, at the time of each payment, with respect to the amount of the installment. . . . While there is less consensus on the proper application of the surplus test, currently the favored view is that the surplus limitation is applied only once, when the contract is entered into, with respect to the entire purchase price." Barbara Black, Corporate Dividends and Share Repurchases § 6:19 (2003).

4. "Funds Legally Available" ≠ Surplus. The holders of preferred stock sometimes are granted the right to require the corporation to redeem the shares. In SV Investment Partners, LLC. v. Thoughtworks, Inc., 37 A.3d 205 (Del. 2011), an investor in Thoughtworks had the right after five years to require the preferred shares in the startup to be redeemed at fair market value, provided Thoughtworks' had "funds legally available therefor." The investment was made during the dot.com bubble when it was expected that Thoughtworks would soon undertake an IPO and the preferred could then be redeemed. But the bubble burst, five years passed without redemption, and the holder of the preferred shares demanded redemption, arguing that "funds legally available therefor" was synonymous with "surplus" and that the company had sufficient surplus from which the redemption could be made. The board refused to redeem the shares, believing "that funds required to fund the working capital requirements of the company [were] an amount in excess of available cash . . . ." The Delaware Supreme Court held that "funds legally available" was not equivalent to "surplus" so that the board's determination should be deferred to unless the board (1) acted in bad faith, (2) relied on unreliable methods and data, or (3) made determinations so far off the mark as to constitute actual or constructive fraud." *Id.* 211.

———

INDEX

References are to Pages

SELF-INTERESTED TRANSACTIONS
See also Conflicts of Interest, this index
Approvals by disinterested directors, 640
Burden of proof of good faith, honesty and fairness, 638
Corporate Opportunity Doctrine, this index
Disclosures, 637
Disinterested director approvals, 622, 641
Fairness requirement, 638, 1025
Fairness review, 641
Fiduciary self-dealing, standard of review, 1037
Good faith approvals by disinterested directors, 641
Good faith duties, 1025
Limited liability companies, 463
Loyalty duties
Generally, 690 et seq.
See also Loyalty Duties, this index
Ratification by shareholders, 643
Shareholder ratification, 643
Shareholder suit demands on interested boards
Generally, 912, 719
Standard of review of fiduciary self-dealing, 1037
Statutory approaches to loyalty duties, 624 et seq.

SELF-REGULATING ORGANIZATIONS (SRO)
Director independence standards, 271

SELF-TENDERS
Takeovers, self-tender defenses, 1059

SEPARATE LEGAL ENTITY STATUS
See also Entity vs Aggregate Legal Status, this index
Corporations, 126

SHAREHOLDER SUITS
Generally, 883 et seq.
Arbitration, 980
Attorneys
Corporate counsel roles, 961
Fees. Plaintiff fee awards, below
Privilege issues, 965, 966
Beneficial owners, party status, 886
Bondholders, standing, 886
Business judgment rule applicability, demand on board, 934
Care duty and loyalty duty breaches distinguished, relative graveness, 963
Choice of law, 980
Close corporations, fiduciary standards, 899
Conflicts of interest
Corporate counsel roles, 961
Policy considerations, 964
Separate counsel requirements, 963
Settlement challenges, 961
Contemporaneous-ownership rule
Generally, 903

Continuing-wrong theory, 911
Exceptions, 911
Continuing-wrong theory, 911
Corporate counsel roles, 961
Corporation as indispensable party, 888
Corporation's role
Generally, 883
Demand on board, below
Counsel fees. Plaintiff fee awards, below
Creditors, standing, 886
Demand on board
Generally, 912 et seq.
Business judgment rule applicability, 934
Director compensation suits, 919
Excuse of demand, 912
Futility of
Generally, 913
Independent directors, consideration by, 929, 933
Interested director cases
Generally, 912, 919
Irreparable injury cases, 916
Rejected demands, 912
Special litigation committees to consider, 927
Universal demand proposals, 916
Wrongful refusal, 934
Demand on shareholders, 944
Direct and derivative actions distinguished, 895
Directors' and officers' liability insurance, 589
Directors as plaintiffs, 887
Discovery of shareholder list, 979
Entity vs aggregate legal status, 907
Excuse of demand on board, 912
Executive compensation, 913
Family corporations, 898
Fees. Plaintiff fee awards, below
Forum selection, 980
Futility of demand on board
Generally, 913
Implied Private Rights of Action, this index
Indemnification
Generally, 945
Good faith requirements, 947
Statutes, 960
Independent directors
Generally, 944
Demand on board matters, 929, 933
Individual recovery, 899
Irreparable injury cases, 916
Limited liability company derivative suits, 479
Loyalty duty and care duty breaches distinguished, relative graveness, 963
Nature of action, 888
New vs former shareholders, 909
Nuisance claims, 884
Officers as plaintiffs, 887
Party status
Generally, 885
Beneficial owners, 886